WORLD OF READING

·R E V I E W·

TRADE BOOK RENAISSANCE
Great children's literature captures students' hearts

LANGUAGE AND THE CHILD
Engaging activities connect listening, speaking, reading, and writing

CAN YOU CUSTOMIZE YOUR INSTRUCTIONAL PLAN? YOU BET!
Instructional choices help you meet each new challenge

PLUS:
Emergent Literacy
Home Ties
Strategic Reading
Vocabulary
Informal Assessment

MAKE·A·WISH

SILVER BURDETT & GINN
Sterling Edition

SILVER BURDETT & GINN
Sterling Edition

WORLD OF READING
AUTHORS SPEAK OUT ON:

SILVER BURDETT & GINN

We believe

We believe that reading is the freedom to explore the ideas of all people, everywhere, past and present. Freedom to participate fully in our society. Freedom to share more experiences and investigate more interests than a single lifetime could ever allow. Freedom, even, to enjoy the pleasures of a simple, well-turned phrase.

We believe that reading is a conversation between a reader and an author. Both reader and author have something to contribute, and the setting in which the conversation occurs adds its own murmur or roar. Reading is an active, ever-evolving process, from a child's first halting attempts at decoding to the wondrous ability to construct meaning.

We believe that the teaching of reading begins with the child—the child's language, the child's own experiences, the child's world. The art and science of a teacher's work is to provide experiences that allow each child to build upon an ever-expanding body of knowledge and ability, and to invite that child to question, to reflect, and to gain understanding. It is in so doing that each child builds a passion for reading and a vision of the future.

SILVER BURDETT & GINN

Welcome to WORLD OF READING

There's More to Our Story

At the core of any successful reading program are stories that touch children's hearts and speak to their own experience. In *World of Reading,* classic and contemporary literature was carefully selected for both its beauty and its power to inspire children to discover the lifelong rewards of reading.

But because the nourishment of young readers requires more than simply placing a good book in a child's hand, *World of Reading* offers a full, rich literary experience that goes beyond its selections. An optional reserve of literary support—always placed in the context of literature—makes the acquisition of reading and language arts tools a relevant and enjoyable process. Instructional lessons artfully weave together the selection with larger lessons in literature, language arts, and the rest of the curriculum.

In many ways *World of Reading* takes the best of children's literature and helps you harvest the most pleasure, meaning, and instruction from it. We invite you to explore our World and see for yourself how much more there is to our story.

WORLD
OF
READING

10 Ways to Recognize Great Children's Literature

Dr. Theodore Clymer
Author, World of Reading.

Great literature, everyone agrees, is the foundation of a successful reading program. But what makes a particular story or poem worthy of the label?

Great literature for young readers lends insight into their own lives, as well as those of others, and gives children a new way of looking at the world. The language is rich and fresh. It delights, informs, surprises. It instructs as it entertains. It helps a child find a secure place in a complex world.

As we selected literature for **World of Reading,** we established ten guidelines to ensure a standard of literary excellence throughout our program. As you choose children's literature for your own students, we hope you find these guidelines helpful.

1 Great literature captures the heart.

Reading involves thinking and feeling. The stories that are remembered long after they are read, the stories that are read over and over again, the stories that reveal something new with each reading—these are literature of merit. These are the stories that touch the heart and introduce children to a lifetime of reading.

2 It elicits high praise from adults and children.

Several important awards honor excellence in literature for children and young adults. These include the Newbery and Caldecott awards, the Pulitzer prize, the American Library Association notables, and the Children's Choice awards. We have chosen selections from the ranks of this honored literature, including, *Dear Mr. Henshaw* by Beverly Cleary, *Island of the Blue Dolphin* by Scott O'Dell, *Mrs. Frisby and the Rats of NIMH,* by Robert O'Brien,

Call It Courage, by Armstrong Sperry, and *The Hero and the Crown* by Robin McKinley.

We also have established our own literary honor—the Silver Burdett & Ginn Readers' Choice Award—based on the responses of hundreds of young readers in kindergarten through grade eight. These powerful, child-pleasing stories have passed the scrutiny of teachers, parents, and children. Look for them throughout the program.

3 It meets the reader's needs and growth level.

As children grow and mature, their needs clearly change. In the early primary levels, adjusting to school routine or learning to take turns might feel strange and new. At other levels, peer approval is a vital concern. As students change, literature selections should reflect the kinds of challenges they encounter.

At the end of every selection in this program, you'll find a useful feature, Reader's Response, that helps make the connection between the story and each child's life. It invites children to share personal reactions to the selections and form opinions based on their own experience.

4 It stimulates thought and imagination.

A great selection tends to raise more questions than it answers. In a non-fiction piece on Mars, for example, a reader will learn a great deal about that planet. This new knowledge will lead to questions about other planets and the solar system. If a character in a work of fiction solves a problem in a new or unusual way, the student discovers a new way of looking at the world. This literary quality helps develop readers who are active and independent.

5 It carries an important message.

Great literature has something important to say to a reader. It helps a reader discover how people think about and respond to life's everyday challenges. The message may be pointed, as in Aesop's fable "The Tortoise and the Hare," or subtle, as in Robert Frost's poem, "Nothing Gold Can Stay."

6 It acquaints a reader with many literary genres.

Folk tales, plays, realistic fiction, autobiography, poetry, and essay are just a few of the genres that a student should encounter in any reading program. Each style has its own characteristics and special way of telling a story. In this program, you'll find selections as varied as "The Bremen Town Musicians," "I Hear America Singing," "West with the Night," "Young Pelé, Soccer Player," Martin Luther King Jr.'s "I Have a Dream" speech and the play "The Diary of Anne Frank."

7 It adds to a reader's store of information.

Great literature should represent a world of knowledge and experience. We have organized each level of our program into four thematic units—Imagination, Expression, Environments, and People. Within each of those units, students are given the opportunity to explore such topics as "Friends Forever," "Animal Tales," or "The Challenge of the Sea." By thinking about what they already know about a topic and then examining it through the eyes of the characters in several different situations, students use their reading to build and expand their understanding of the world around them.

Looking For Great Literature? Follow These Signs

Medals designate Newbery, Caldecott, and Children's Choice award-winners and other highly honored literature. These outstanding stories by talented authors and illustrators will engage students and make them want to read more.

READERS' CHOICE AWARD

Children are the toughest critics. So no one is better suited to recommend a great story than another child. Readers' Choice stories received a stamp of approval from student reviewers nationwide.

WORLD OF READING Magazine *News About Reading*

Students gain insight into the importance of reading as they explore informative articles about how books are central to art, history, careers, science, and technology. The articles also direct students to print sources related to these fields.

This feature encourages students to spend time with outstanding trade books. Time Out for Books piques student interest in four trade books per grade with an intriguing quote from the book, a full-color photograph of the cover, and interesting facts about the book and author.

TIME OUT FOR BOOKS
ALA Notable Book
Newbery Award-winning Author

For students who love to read just for fun, the Reading Corner selection at the end of each unit is a perfect opportunity. Each of these independent reading selections exemplifies a literary element or genre in which students have received prior instruction.

READING CORNER

After seeing the eye-catching book covers that accompany this theme-related bibliography, children won't be able to resist checking these books out of the library.

BOOKS TO ENJOY

Twice in each Beginning Reader, a popular classic provides the chance for young children to "follow" printed lyrics as they sing.

Sing With Me

Read With Me

At the end of each Beginning Reader, a story by Bill Martin Jr. written especially for our program offers a whimsical treat.

FULL-LENGTH BOOK

This book-within-a-book at the end of each grade provides an opportunity for uninterrupted, sustained silent reading. At grades 7 and 8, these selections are novellas.

As they read through this feature, children are encouraged to find their own special times and places for reading, and to collect and cherish books.

BROWSING FOR BOOKS

(Don't miss Trade Book Renaissance, page M20.)

8 It introduces the reader to great authors.

Getting to know authors and understanding that they are people with issues and experiences similar to one's own helps readers to understand the world of writing. At each level, we include an interview with or profile of a renowned author, such as Isaac Bashevis Singer, Nathaniel Hawthorne, Gwendolyn Brooks, Beverly Cleary, Lawrence Yep, E.B. White, Carl Sandburg, and Rachel Field. You'll also find author biographies and photographs to acquaint children with the people behind the literature.

9 It contributes to a reader's cultural literacy.

In order for children to thrive in today's world, they need to encounter a range of experience that includes all of the areas of human activity and provides a basis for understanding our commonality. Our program seeks to broaden your students' experience with a variety of selections from stories like "Henny Penny" and "The Ugly Duckling" to "Daedalus and Icarus" and "Gift of the Magi."

10 It develops a life-long love of reading.

Great literature leads to more great literature. It follows that as children read stories and books they love they will want to read more. Many helpful program features provide opportunities for children to read beyond the text. Reading Corner, at the end of each unit, is an entertaining story children can read independently. Books to Enjoy, at the end of every unit, suggests additional titles on the same theme or by familiar authors that students can explore on their own. Browsing for Books reinforces the idea of reading as a lifelong activity. It talks to children about how to go about finding books. Our special *World of Reading Magazine* feature explores the art and history of the printed word.

Dr. Theodore Clymer is Director of the Institute for Reading Research, Carmel, California. He is founding editor of the Reading Research Quarterly and is an authority on children's literature.

WORLD OF READING

EVALUATION CHECKLIST
- ✓ Presents a variety of genres
- ✓ Includes award-winners
- ✓ Introduces notable authors
- ✓ Develops cultural literacy
- ✓ Creates active, independent readers
- ✓ Expands the reader's world

Literacy *in the* 1990s

An interview with authors Dale D. Johnson & David Pearson.

> **"One important reading research discovery is the importance of *prior knowledge.***"
>
> *David Pearson*
> *Author,* World of Reading

In their roles as teachers, researchers, and authors, Dale Johnson and David Pearson have looked at reading from every angle. In this interview they share insights into current reading theory and practice.

Question: Many teachers feel that fads come and go in education but that nothing important ever really changes. Is that true in reading?

Several things have changed the world of reading in the past decade. One is our discovery of the importance of *prior knowledge.* Another, related to it, is vocabulary, the rediscovery of words. We realize more than ever that for children to understand text, they have to know the words and the way they're used within that text.

Another change is the emphasis on inference as the heart of the reading process. These three issues, the importance of background knowledge, vocabulary as a key instructional activity, and the emphasis on inference, resolve into one major point: You understand new things in terms of what you already know.

Question: Many people would say that is obvious. What specific changes have these three ideas brought about in the way we think about reading instruction?

They've given us a new, more interactive, model of reading. Our earlier models said that children start by turning letters into sounds and bundling them together into words.

Then children use prior knowledge of the world and of language to understand the meaning of those words. In our new model, prior knowledge is fantastically more important. We start using it much earlier in the reading process.

We now see reading as a much more active process, not a passive act where the meaning is on the printed page and we just extract it. From the moment we pick up a page, we begin to construct meaning from the combination of the text and our own background knowledge.

Question: And the implications for teaching?

One lesson we've learned from research in the last fifteen years is that prior knowledge is the most important factor in determining how you understand something. If the teacher assumes children don't have sufficient prior knowledge, then something has to be done before they begin reading.

Question: How do you make sure children have the knowledge they need?

One way is to expand their knowledge through good, solid vocabulary instruction. Students' knowledge of key words in the text is a better predictor of comprehension than any other measure of reading ability or achievement. One of the procedures that we know works beautifully to expand knowledge prior to reading is *semantic mapping,* or *mapping* or *webbing* as some people call it. It's like brainstorming, and what it does is to start with what some children know about a topic and, through discussion, broaden that network of knowledge before students are asked to attack the printed page.

Question: Do teachers really use semantic mapping? Does it represent real change?

When I give speeches, I invariably ask teachers how many are familiar with semantic mapping. Today, 70 to 90 percent of the hands go up. When I ask how many use it, half the hands go up. It's an instructional strategy that has really spread over the past half-dozen years.

The thing I like about it is the way it deals with the dilemma of the teacher who must be sure that twenty-five children all have the prior knowledge they need for a selection or story. If I'm in the class and I don't know anything about a key concept in the story but Dale does, and shares it, then what becomes new knowledge for me is, for him, a reminder that he should bring that knowledge to bear.

Semantic mapping is really child-centered. The teacher is not the only one who holds the authority for new knowledge and experiences. It's a form of cooperative learning and a wonderful culminating activity too. One thing a lot of teachers do is to put "What We Knew Before" on the chalkboard in one color, and "What We Added After" in a second color. And you can literally help students watch their knowledge grow.

Question: Let's get back to inferences, which you said were the heart of reading.

I find this area incredibly exciting. You could always teach children to decode and get the words on the page right, but when it came to comprehension, especially inferential comprehension, we just sort of hoped they'd be able to do it. One of the great breakthroughs we've made is that now we're taking what is normally a covert process and making that kind of thinking public. Through modeling the process and then by engaging students and practicing it, we can help them become a lot better at drawing inferences, which is the way good readers read. As they're reading, they're constantly making inferences, using their background knowledge to make sense out of what is new in the text.

Question: Is our understanding of inferences changing teaching practices too?

Definitely. Around twenty years ago, 75 percent of the questions teachers asked required factual, on-the-page kinds of answers. A year ago, we found that almost 50 percent of the questions teachers asked in the second, fourth, and sixth grades required children to draw inferences.

Some people use the terms "making inferences" and "drawing conclusions" interchangeably. I do not. In my view, readers make inferences *while* they read. Inferences are understandings we form by combining evidence with experience. Making inferences, thus, is a continuous process. Drawing conclusions, on the other hand, involves reflection. It occurs *after* the reader finishes reading a segment of text. Conclusions are usually broader and more general than inferences which are specific. Conclusions occur at the end of a chain of reasoning.

Question: So children need to be consciously aware of what they do to understand text?

Exactly! We stop and look at what for many readers happens automatically. But we move it from the automatic to a conscious control mode and we sit and talk about this process we've gone through. The idea, of course, is that then children will put it into their repertoire so it will happen automatically but more effectively.

Then there are those times when you're reading and you say, "My goodness, I don't know what's going on here." That's when it's important to shift strategies in a conscious control mode. The good reader can say "Uh-oh, I have to stop here, now. I have to think through this problem very carefully because I'm not making sense out of this."

Question: Isn't that metacognition?

Yes, it is. In reading, metacognition has two components. One is monitoring. It's an awareness of whether things are clicking or not. The minute you discover that they're not, you do something about it.

So you go to the second component, a fixing-up strategy. There are still many things to learn about these strategies. But it's clearly the direction we need to take in the future.

> **"A procedure that works well to expand a child's prior knowledge is *semantic mapping,* or *webbing.*"**
>
> *Dale D. Johnson*
> *Author,* World of Reading

EMERGENT LITERACY and the BEGINNING READER

Dr. Elfrieda Hiebert, *Author,* World of Reading *is Associate Professor at the University of Colorado, Boulder. She is involved in research in emergent literacy and is an author of the influential report,* **Becoming a Nation of Readers.**

Mark decides on *Football Game* as the title for his painting, and his teacher writes the phrase on the picture. As she leafs through a book, Sara murmurs words from the story her teacher has read. Tanya describes highlights of her birthday party. These are just a few of the ways to get children ready to read and write.

Recent research in what is often called

emergent literacy and in whole language indicates that a range of activities—from listening to stories to learning about letter-sound correspondences—helps create readiness for literacy in children. These activities share two characteristics. They foster active involvement by children, because that is how young children learn best. They also develop the foundation for more formal instruction in reading and writing. Some children will learn to read by participating in the repeated reading of big, shared books, reading words on labels in their classrooms, and writing messages with invented spelling. Most children, though, will require guidance in acquiring the word identification strategies of independent reading. As children participate in beginning reading lessons, they talk, listen, write, and have experiences with books and print. Such experiences continue to be central to their development as readers, because children learn to read and write in an environment rich in language.

Oral Language

Learning to read and write is rooted in oral language. For children to understand stories —whether they are listening to an adult or reading themselves —they must have some background knowledge about the topics and the structure of stories. Both this "world" knowledge and "story" knowledge are aided by oral language activities. When teachers guide children in talk about common or unfamiliar experiences, the foundation is laid for children's comprehension development. As children share stories about events in their lives, and as teachers read stories aloud, children get a sense of the natural progression of stories from beginning to end. Learning to express oneself by summarizing experiences, asking questions, and predicting what will happen in a story allows children to apply orally the comprehension strategies they use in reading. Encouraging children to retell and reenact stories gives them other opportunities and reasons to explore oral language.

Oral language continues to be important as children learn to read on their own. Listening to the rhythms and patterns of language, manipulating the sounds that make up words and the words that make up sentences, and talking about stories all support and extend reading.

Experience With Books

Frequent and varied experiences with books are central in learning to read. Enlarged storybooks—like big shared books—have an especially important role in early-childhood programs. As the teacher reads aloud, children follow along and may track the print. After several readings, children will often be able to call the words as the teacher points to them. The big book permits everyone to participate, to see the pictures and the written message. Reading is shared, in much the same way parents and children share storybook reading at home.

Small, personal books also play a key role. They might be small versions of big shared books, or they might be wordless storybooks with pictures to illustrate key events. They might contain a simple phrase or two

repeated over and over. They may be books the children have created. Children can leaf through their own books as they wish, retelling the story to themselves, a classmate, or a family member. When children can write their names, add detail to a picture, or label a picture—perhaps with invented spelling—they express their ownership. Having a book of one's own brings a child closer to books and words and helps establish a pattern of reading.

Learning About Words

An abundance of words exists in the environment of young children. Children may be aware of some words (for example, *stop* on a traffic sign), but they may not associate these words with reading and writing. A goal of the beginning reading program is to focus children's attention on familiar words, such as *stop* or *exit,* and to use these words to develop children's understanding of the relationship between oral and written language.

There's special value in showing children the written words for people, objects, or events that are meaningful to them. These favorite words can be brought into daily conversations and placed around the class-room.

Writing

Providing many occasions for young children to express themselves in writing activities, which may initially take the form of drawing and simple labeling, comprises a critical component of an early childhood literacy program. These activities serve several functions. Naturally, one function is that young children take the first steps to becoming independent writers. The connections between writing and reading also mean that writing activities foster strategies basic to reading. Most specifically, writing affords children opportunities to apply the knowledge of letter-sound cor-respondences that is so fundamental to reading. Young children's avid interest in communicating their messages makes these activities central to the early-childhood literacy program.

Some children entering school will begin at the earliest stage of composing, which is drawing. Other children will be ready to write words as they label pictures or make up stories. In these efforts, children may be rather inventive in their spelling efforts but, with experience and guidance, they move from these invented spellings to more conventional ones.

In designing the early-childhood components of *World of Reading,* we have drawn upon knowledge of how children learn to read to develop materials and activities that will help children understand the relationship between oral language and print. The tools we provide will delight young readers. Big and Little Shared Books, *My Storybook* for every child, story characters for retelling and dramatic play, environmental print cards, concept cards, story sequence cards, a puppet, a game, and many more activities stimulate language and imagination.

LANGUAGE & the CHILD

Literature-based reading. Integrated language arts. Holistic approaches to language. You love the idea, but how can you make it happen?

It's an extraordinary time to be teaching reading. There's fresh understanding of the complexity and wonder of the reading process. There's real excitement about great children's literature and its catalytic power to develop language abilities. Wherever you turn, an educator is talking about *literature-based reading, integrated language arts,* and *holistic approaches to language.* These alluring phrases seem so full of promise for kids and teachers. The question is: How can you turn these concepts into responsible, manageable classroom applications?

You need a framework. It should be a sound framework that helps you help children learn to read, become strategic readers, and grow in experience with a wide range of literary styles and purposes. It should be a holistic framework that responds to your students' diversity and develops all language abilities. And it should be a professional framework that supports your need for real choices in planning instruction.

World of Reading provides this framework. It gives you fine children's literature, a wealth of trade-book opportunities, and unit and lesson structures rich with choices in sound strategies and engaging activities.

Let's take a closer look at how *World of Reading* embodies each of these notions: *literature-based reading, integrated language arts,* and *holistic approaches to language.*

Literature-based reading
The idea here, of course, is that great children's literature becomes the foundation for instructional activities. Among the benefits: Not only are students motivated and given access to valuable literature, but the specifics of reading instruction occur in a meaningful, fluid context that stimulates thinking and learning.

Anyone wanting to pursue literature-based reading needs—for starters—a carefully chosen collection of fine literature. Not only should each story be wonderful and appropriate in its own right, but it needs to fit into a mosaic of reading that acquaints children with many literary genres and broadens their horizons.

The framework in *World of Reading* supports these goals on several levels. First, the program's Student Text provides each reader with a thoughtfully selected collection of fine literature that includes stories, poems, myths, folk tales, songs, plays, biographies, science fiction, essays, speeches, informational articles, parodies, and interviews. (See "10 Ways to Recognize Great Children's Literature," page M6.) The program also makes many specific suggestions for further reading, and it offers two classroom collections of popular trade books, *Time Out for Books* and *World of Books Classroom Libraries.* (See "Trade Book Renaissance," page M20.) Equally important, *World of Reading* accommodates a number of pacing patterns for concentrated periods of trade-book reading. (See "Can You Customize Your Instructional Plan?" page M32.)

Literature-based reading also requires an instructional design that uses sound teaching methods to accomplish a number of goals and to meet the diverse needs of students.

Among the most valuable features in *World of Reading* is a lesson structure that introduces story vocabulary, builds background by drawing on what students already know, develops a purpose for reading, guides comprehension, promotes strategic reading, elicits personal responses, and provides a range of other opportunities for writing, speaking, listening, and extending learning. In each part of the lesson, teachers select approaches and activities according to students' needs and interests.

The phrase *literature-based reading* can also mean substantial independent reading. To achieve this for some students, teachers need only provide time, access to good books, and a means of drawing out the reader's response. But *World of Reading*

recognizes that other children may need a bit of coaxing. To provide that, the program includes just-for-fun Reading Corner stories in the Student Text, a Full-Length Book at each grade level, selection-related suggestions for further reading, tempting collections of well-known trade books, and ideas for shared-reading activities.

Integrated language arts
Interest in integrated language arts became widespread when cognitive research backed up what common sense suggested: that reading, writing, listening, and speaking are interrelated and interdependent. Research revealed close ties between listening comprehension and reading comprehension and between the thinking processes involved in reading and writing. It also told us that children tend to remember what they give voice to. Studies showed that growth in one area can enhance growth in the others, so it makes sense to plan language-arts experiences that are mutually supportive.

The quality of these experiences makes all the difference in how well an integrated language-arts approach works. Activities need kid-appeal, they need to promote learning, they need to be true to the spirit of the story, and they should range in type from whole-class to small-group to individual. Because *World of Reading* is literature-based *and* integrates language arts, it weaves writing, speaking, and listening activities around the literature children read. Take, for example, listening and speaking activities. Each selection prompts discussion before, during, and after reading. These discussions are enhanced when teachers choose among the many thought-provoking questions suggested in the Teacher Edition.

Teachers also choose among such lively suggestions for story-related speaking/listening activities as retelling, round-table discussions, choral readings, puppet shows, songs, impromptu interviews of students playing the roles of story characters, "newscasts" about story events, and more. (These suggestions are found in Language Arts

Connections after each selection.)

When teachers read aloud or play an audiocassette of a Listening Lesson selection, they help students appreciate the rhythms and rhymes of literature and focus on listening for a specific purpose.

What about integrated writing opportunities? They abound in **World of Reading.** Here are some examples:

♦ Young children experiment with writing by painting letter shapes, using invented spellings, labeling pictures and classroom objects, illustrating words, sending messages, and composing simple stories.

♦ Students might write in preparation for reading and listening experiences. For example, prior to reading, students might use new vocabulary words to write about a story-related topic.

♦ Reader's Response questions may be used to provide a writing experience that helps children put fleeting ideas into words, discover what they know, and become more aware of themselves as readers.

♦ Writing to Learn, a brief, impromptu activity following every story, improves comprehension by encouraging students to write in response to reading and to connect the story to their own experience. Writing to Learn activities also help students learn to see text as a collection of ideas for their evaluation.

♦ The Reader's Journal stimulates children's search for personal meaning in stories by encouraging them to think about and respond openly to reading.

♦ Language Arts Connections also suggest many engaging story-related writing activities, including writing a letter of reference for a character, rewriting events from a minor character's point of view, writing a postcard from the story site, and writing invitations, lost and found ads, letters, poems, and more.

♦ Writing About Reading, a five-step process-writing experience at the conclusion of each unit, leads students to generate a fully developed expression of their ideas. This writing emphasizes content, clarity, and accuracy as well as style and mechanics.

One final example of how **World of Reading** helps teachers integrate the language arts: Spelling Connection masters that use vocabulary words as spelling words, along with student-selected words and content-area words.

Holistic approaches to language

Whole language, it's been said, is about real kids using real language in ways that are meaningful to them. Or, to put it more abstractly, it's about instructional approaches that move from whole to part. But beyond these general notions, what *whole language* is—once you get it inside a classroom—changes according to who is doing the defining.

The vigorousness of the discussion, however, needn't get in the way of developing holistic approaches to language that make use of research findings and what teachers know about their students.

If you're interested in a holistic approach, you'll want to consider the same research that underlies integrated language arts: The fact that speaking, listening, reading, and writing are interrelated and mutually supportive. Your focus here is children's acquisition of language through meaningful contexts and situations—that is, meaningful from a child's point of view. How do you measure meaningfulness? By evaluating whether kids are actually using language for purposes that are personally rewarding, natural, functional, interactive, and varied.

How does **World of Reading** help you turn the holistic idea into a classroom reality? Consider, for example, how the thematic structure of units leads children to natural discoveries of ties among ideas in several stories and to expression of their discoveries. Or look at two Beginning Reader features, Sing With Me and Read With Me, which offer each child exciting, interactive experiences with natural language. Another example: Natural Language Storybooks,

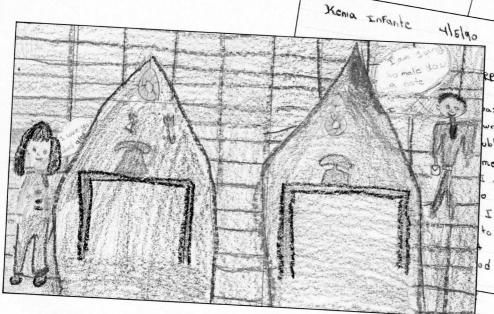

which offer first graders holistic language experiences.

Perhaps the most significant holistic aspect is the whole foundation of **World of Reading:** fine literature that piques curiosity, motivates thinking, and stimulates self-expression. When kids care about a story, it becomes more meaningful to them, so related reading, writing, speaking, and listening activities provide channels for children's authentic desire to communicate.

The personal involvement of each child in each story is heightened by prereading activities that tap prior knowledge and develop a purpose for reading. Students also have chances to apply self-questioning strategies during reading and to respond personally after reading each selection.

In addition, **World of Reading** offers teachers many choices in interactive experiences, including working in pairs and in cooperative groups. (See "A New Melody," page M15.)

The I◆T Kit (Interactive Teaching Kit) provides more shared adventures. This collection of story-related materials for multicultural and multisensory activities develops language, builds experience, and enhances learning in literature, fine arts, and the content areas. The kit includes videos, audiocassettes, posters, activity suggestions, and more.

Other **World of Reading** components that support interactive experiences include Big Books (kindergarten and first grade) and Big Shared Books (kindergarten through second grade), which offer unique contexts for instruction and enjoyment. They help teachers create a community of readers and provide positive experiences for all children. (See "Emergent Literacy and the Beginning Reader," page M10.)

Teachers may also choose among Curriculum Connections activities that help students relate what they learn in each reading lesson to their growing knowledge in science, social studies, math, health, physical education, and careers.

Holistic approaches require appropriate assessment tools and techniques. The holistic formal and informal assessment options found in **World of Reading** give teachers the information they need to design instruction that meets students' needs. (See "Assessment Comes of Age," page M26.)

Teacher choice

Something more is required to turn the grand ideas of reading instruction into reality—your knowledge, skill, and judgment. The framework in **World of Reading** pays much more than lip service to the notion that teachers possess unique and critical understanding of the changing needs of their students. The program supports a number of real choices teachers can make, both in overall emphasis of instruction and in specific lesson activities. (Many of these are highlighted with a Teacher Choice logo in the Teacher Edition. Also see "Can You Customize Your Instructional Plan?" page M30.)

Dr. Marian Davies Toth, *an author of* World of Reading *and* World of Language, *is an authority on writing and a consultant to schools nationwide.*

WORLD OF READING

EVALUATION CHECKLIST

✔ Weaves instruction around fine children's literature in a variety of genres

✔ Encourages students to read, think about, write about, discuss, and listen to others' ideas about the literature

✔ Integrates the language arts through a natural, language-rich environment

✔ Encourages both impromptu writing in response to reading and theme-related five-step process-writing experiences

✔ Provides holistic ways of assessing students

A New Melody

Creating classroom organizational patterns that add rhythm to reading

Imagine for a moment that your design for instruction has been put to music. What does it sound like? Listen to the rhythms and melodies of your teaching techniques and ways of organizing students. Do you hear interludes of solo effort, cooperative activity, and whole-group discussion? How do these interludes relate to one another? What does each contribute to the quality of the composition?

The analogy may be a bit thin, but it's true that a thoughtful mix of effective teaching techniques can make an astonishing difference in student learning. Here's a sampling of some interesting "tunes" to stimulate your thinking about your own instructional planning.

Whole class—with a difference

When this approach is used, the whole class is the framework for introduction to new strategies and selections in the reading program. Students next break into groups for reading and other activities, then return to whole-class discussion, then go into groups again. With this approach, the small groups change from lesson to lesson in a fluid pattern designed to avoid the problems of tracking.

Here's a more detailed example: You convene the class to introduce vocabulary and concepts and to elicit predictions about the story. (Corresponding **World of Reading** sections include Vocabulary Strategies, Building Background, and Developing a Purpose for Reading.)

Following the whole-group lesson, two smaller groups form. Student placement depends on interest in the selection, familiarity with the topic, complexity of the selection, and knowledge of vocabulary and concepts.

In the first group, students read the story silently, then pair up to discuss it and complete a task, such as mapping major events. Students then write responses to the story in individual journals.

While this group works independently, you lead the second group in a discussion to provide additional vocabulary practice prior to reading the story. Then you engage students in guided reading of the selection, and then students form pairs to reread the story aloud.

Next, the whole class reconvenes to discuss the story. (**World of Reading**

Selection Follow-Up ideas may be useful.)

Finally, the smaller groups work together again. This time, you work with the first group, giving students an opportunity to share the work they completed in pairs and guiding them to more expert responses. Meanwhile, the second group writes in response journals.

Cooperative learning

In this approach, students work in small, heterogeneous groups. Evidence suggests that cooperative learning strategies increase academic achievement, develop thinking and problem-solving skills, and boost long-term retention. Cooperative learning also builds group cohesion and promotes positive student-to-student interaction.

The essence of cooperative learning is the team spirit that motivates students to care how well others on the team are learning. Team members become responsible for one another's learning as well as for their own. Because team success depends on the individual learning of each person, members share ideas and reinterpret recent instruction to one another. In this setting, students convey to one another the idea that learning is valuable and fun.

With this approach, you act as a facilitator, setting academic and collaborative objectives, explaining options and tasks, providing materials, supporting and assessing group interaction, and guiding children in monitoring their individual progress. You also provide an opportunity for closure, which includes discussion by students of their group's performance.

Consider this example: After reading a selection, students are divided into heterogeneous groups of four or five. Each group chooses a specific task to complete, such as composing a character analysis, story summary, prelude, or sequel. In order to accomplish the group task, each member selects his or her own mini-topic (within the larger task) to explore. Students may reread for details. When the individual tasks are completed, the group joins to discuss, analyze, and reach conclusions. Students organize their ideas into a presentation, skit, debate, written report, or some other form they choose. Before these final events, you and the class collaborate to determine how the events will be evaluated. In a final assessment, students discuss how well they collaborated with each other.

World of Reading offers many other opportunities for cooperative learning, starting at the kindergarten level. At the end of every unit, for example, a Working Together section provides a small-group activity to extend the unit theme. Many Language Arts Connections sections in the Teacher Editions also suggest cooperative-learning projects, such as creating a skit retelling a story from different characters' points of view.

Reciprocal teaching

Reciprocal teaching is an active discussion technique that develops students' strategic reading skills. When it is used, students work in cooperative groups or pairs. It is especially appropriate with nonfiction and develops comprehension in children of all ages.

You begin by repeatedly modeling four strategies—questioning, summarizing, clarifying, and predicting—during the course of reading with small, hetero-geneous groups. Gradually, over a period of days, students are asked to "be the teacher" more and more often: The child-teacher might ask a question of others about what was just read, offer a summary, ask others if any clarifications are needed, and make predictions about what will come next. Your role shifts to coaching and prompting. You also help the group see that inadequate responses by children are valuable tipoffs to comprehension gaps that can then be addressed through discussion, like working out a puzzle.

With *questioning,* you'll want to guide the child-teacher to focus on the main idea of the passage just read. Other students respond to the questions to begin discussion. If the child-teacher's initial question centers on interesting details, acknowledge that the details are part of the passage and explain how they fit in with the main idea. Aim to "think aloud" and shape your responses into forms children can imitate.

Summarizing reinforces and follows up questioning and its responses. If this is too difficult for the child-teacher initially, ask him or her to identify the topic. Discussion continues. Strive to convey that every child is expected to participate.

Clarifying can be particularly useful in identifying what may be blocking compre-hension. "In essence, students are given per-mission to find the text confusing," notes one researcher. "Some react with genuine surprise to discover that even adults may find a passage unclear."

When students are initially reluctant to call attention to difficulties in under-standing, try asking them to identify sections that younger children might find confusing.

Predicting provides clues about stu-dents' prior knowledge and offers an oppor-tunity to talk about patterns and text structures. The goal here is not so much the accuracy of the prediction as helping children learn that they should make predictions as they read.

Peer tutoring

Studies indicate that peer tutoring sub-stantially boosts academic achievement and nurtures positive attitudes in both tutors and those tutored.

To organize peer tutoring, give close attention to a few key guidelines. First, describe to the class the instructional purpose and nature of peer tutoring, define students' roles, and explain your expecta-tions. Avoid creating pairs in which some students are always tutors and others are always tutored. Pairs or teams should be selected for tutoring potential and com-patibility.

To prepare tutors, model instructional strategies and clarify the kinds of support you'll provide. When tutors are comfortable with their roles, they explain to their partners what they will be learning and why. During tutoring, the teacher circulates and monitors each group's performance.

EVALUATION CHECKLIST

✔ Offers a variety of instruc-tional approaches that enable teachers to meet the needs of all students

✔ Supports a range of organiza-tional approaches, including whole class, small group, and individual.

✔ Provides many opportuni-ties for children to work cooperatively.

You might try these approaches:

◆ Create tutoring pairs for extra practice of essential skills. One effective approach is pairing students for writing tasks, so that each reads the other's work and makes suggestions.

◆ Create tutoring pairs for reading an occasional selection or book. The tutor could help three ways. One way is to first read the story aloud to his or her partner in preparation for individual silent rereading. A second way is to listen to the partner read and help with unknown words. In a third method, after individual silent reading, the partners take turns rereading aloud.

◆ Create cross-age buddies by pairing older students with children in lower grades. Schedule a time at least once each week when the buddies meet. Ask the older student to read to the younger student. It is important for tutors to first preview and rehearse reading the text.

With all approaches, it's a good idea to encourage informal discussion of the story by tutors and their partners.

Independent learning

Independent learning is a valuable element in your organizational composition. What's important here? Strive for rich, self-motivating activities that help students make connections with the rest of their reading experiences. Students need to know why they are doing something, how it relates to other things, and how to evaluate their own performance. Writing assignments, for example, need a clear purpose.

It's also worthwhile to plan frequent opportunities for students to make their own decisions—selecting what to read, which problem to solve, which resources to select, or what form a response will take.

World of Reading supports independent learning experiences through Reading Corner stories, Writing to Learn and Selection Follow-Up activities, Books to Enjoy listings, *Time Out for Books, World of Books Classroom Libraries,* and the Reader's Journal. (See "Trade Book Renaissance," page M20.)

Perhaps the most exciting thing about this new range of organizational options is that you can choose different approaches to fit different selections, to suit your students' changing needs, to give yourself a different diagnostic perspective, or to bring a fresh note into children's days.

Dr. Jeanne R. Paratore *is Consulting Author,* World of Reading; *Associate Professor, Boston University School of Education; and Director of the Center for the Assessment and Design of Learning.*

Rethinking Ability Grouping

Recent research—often combined with teachers' own observations—is prompting educators to take a close look at traditional methods of ability grouping and to search for practical alternatives.

Findings indicate that traditional methods generally have not offered students equity in content, in opportunities for interaction, or in amount of reading completed. Research also tells us that those very things are important to low-achieving students: Low-performers benefit from interesting, challenging content and student-to-student interaction as much as their higher-achieving peers. Further, time spent reading is one of the most important factors in reading achievement.

This evidence is at odds with some familiar practices. For example, researchers observe that, in a typical classroom, the good reader completes a page of oral reading, while the less-able reader is asked to read only a paragraph. Although well intentioned, this practice promotes a "rich get richer, poor get poorer" experience for students.

If you find it useful to group students by achievement levels, these suggestions can help you avoid many of the problems of traditional ability groups.

◆ Make groups flexible enough to permit frequent reassignment and change. Forming groups for instruction in specific skills promotes continual reassessment of each child's progress and, when appropriate, reassignment to other groups.

◆ Strive to vary the pace and level of instruction within groups, responding to the needs of the children within the group, rather than to preconceived notions of how that group will perform. (See "Helping Children At Risk," page M18.)

Helping Children at Risk

You need instructional approaches that engage every child.

What comes to mind when you hear the term *at risk?* It's most useful to think of students at risk as those who require special assistance in order to achieve literacy and other school-based knowledge and skills. In addition, students who read below grade level or who can read but dislike all reading may be considered among those at risk.

When the term is considered this way, it's clear that students at risk come from every cultural, economic, and social background. Students at risk may have difficulty for many reasons.

Q: How can I develop realistic expectations for students?

Teachers' expectations of students have often proved to be self-fulfilling prophecies. Research indicates that, when teachers believe students are capable, students tend to become more capable. And when you think about how much children grow and change, who can define the limits of a child's potential? We must assume all students can learn.

Of course, children come into your classroom with a variety of backgrounds and levels of prior achievement. Your professional challenge is to maintain high expectations of all students while making the most of their experience and matching teaching strategies to their needs.

Q: How can I help my at-risk students to achieve success?

With some students, you'll focus on developing confidence that they can overcome a history of frustration or marginal achievement. Until now, conventional wisdom has held that learners experiencing problems should be served with special programs. Recent research suggests, however, that changing the *approach to instruction,* rather than changing the program, may be more effective in helping every learner. The findings support what many teachers believe: Every child should have access to great literature and have the benefit of core teaching strategies. This notion, sometimes called *content equity,* is reflected in the program.

World of Reading enables you to tailor reading instruction to each child while keeping the class together. The program's strategies provide a lesson within the lesson for every learner, and they allow everyone to share in the pleasure of a good story. (See "Can You Customize Your Instructional Plan?" page M32.)

Individual conferences to develop personal goals can also help students feel good about learning and can identify appropriate challenges. By reminding children of their strengths and focusing on goals, you'll help them venture into self-directed learning with greater confidence.

Q: How can I accommodate student diversity and still have time to teach the whole class?

Exploring diverse backgrounds can enrich the dynamics of the entire class and help students learn from one another.

Consider, for example, one of the four core strategies in ***World of Reading:*** prereading activities that establish the purpose for reading and tap students' background knowledge to improve comprehension. One such activity engages children in contributing to a prediction list. When the whole class adds ideas, predictions are refined. Then you can discuss the value of sharing ideas among students with diverse backgrounds.

A second core strategy of ***World of Reading*** is to show relationships between known concepts and new vocabulary to promote better comprehension. Here again, as the whole class adds words and phrases to a chalkboard activity, students learn from one another's contributions and come to take pride in their own expertise.

A third core strategy involves students in rereading or retelling parts of a story to help them comprehend and retain more. Students at risk will gain some of the reinforcement they need without adding management chores to your lesson.

A fourth core strategy is to provide all students with self-monitoring techniques to make them aware of

WORLD OF READING

EVALUATION CHECKLIST

✔ Addresses needs of at risk students through core instruction, content equity, and teaching choices

✔ Offers a wide variety of experiences to meet individual needs

✔ Motivates with high-interest selections and activities

✔ Helps students monitor their own progress

effective reading strategies and help them develop their own comprehension tools. Research tells us that this instruction, in what is called *strategic reading*, is especially effective with at-risk learners. (See "Becoming a Strategic Reader," page M22.)

Q: How can I plan instructional strategies that accommodate my students' varied achievement levels?

Research indicates that instructional strategies beneficial to higher achievers also benefit learners of all levels. In fact, recent findings have confirmed what many teachers have known all along: All students thrive on intellectual challenge and a lively approach to learning.

World of Reading supports a full repertoire of instructional strategies that engage all students. For example, you'll find that cooperative-learning activities promote both social skills and real learning, especially in children at risk. (See "A New Melody," page M15.)

Intriguing writing activities, self-selected reading, multimedia experiences, and dozens of other approaches also motivate and increase learning among all

students. The *World of Reading* I◆T Kit (Interactive Teaching Kit), for example, provides videos, audios, posters, and other materials for multicultural and multisensory activities that complement selections and enhance learning in literature, fine arts, and content areas.

Of course, extra guidance is often needed. The design of *World of Reading* helps you pinpoint areas of individual need and provides research-supported Extra Help strategies with every lesson. Here's one example: Use a visual display of story events to help students focus when making predictions about what may occur next. This approach supports content equity by making both predicting and recalling ideas easier without providing simpler text.

Another strategy is reading a selection aloud just before students read it on their own. This gives readers a chance to become familiar with both the content and language of the story. When they read it themselves, they have the background that boosts word identification and comprehension. Here again, this strategy has the effect of making the task easier without changing the material. Paired reading and rereading provide more practice.

In addition, *World of Reading* supplementary materials are provided both in the Meeting Individual Needs and Resource Center sections of each lesson. Look for these special features:

◆ Achieving English Proficiency suggestions help nonnative speakers with concept and skill development.

◆ Challenge Activities provide independent opportunities for children to apply skills in thought-provoking ways.

◆ Skills Practice activities reinforce specific critical reading skills.

◆ Reteaching masters offer additional practice in tested skills. Worksheets are

sequenced from easiest to most difficult and include many graphic aids.

Q: How can I coordinate instruction with a reading specialist?

It's worthwhile to work with administrators and specialists to coordinate instruction, so that children at risk experience a consistent approach to reading.

Consider ways of coordinating instruction. For example, a specialist might introduce a selection or skill immediately before the classroom teacher introduces it, permitting the lowest-achieving students to preview upcoming material. Or support staff may review selections or skills immediately after the classroom teacher introduces them, providing students with extra practice prior to the next lesson. These approaches can speed acquisition of skills and strategies that enable more rapid pacing for the lowest-performing students.

Q: How can I help students build positive self concepts?

Giving all students challenging responsibilities—and offering support that reduces frustration—conveys the message that each student is capable, important, and worthy. Children of all ages thrive when they perceive others' belief in their abilities.

Another way to nurture self-esteem is to encourage students at risk to give recognition and recommendations to others. When students are asked to identify something of merit in another's work or behavior, the self-esteem of the student giving the compliment is enhanced. When students are asked to recommend possible books, they are often rewarded with feelings of confidence.

Finally, remember how crucial family support can be. Work with colleagues and administrators to develop ways to reach parents of children at risk. (See "Home Is Where the Help Is," page M28.)

Dr. Roselmina Indrisano (l) and *Dr. Jeanne R. Paratore (r)*
Dr. Indrisano, a World of Reading *Author, is Professor of Education and Chairman of Developmental Studies and Counseling Psychology at Boston University School of Education. Dr. Paratore, a* World of Reading *Consulting Author, is Associate Professor, Boston University School of Education. She is also Director of the Center for the Assessment and Design of Learning.*

Trade Book
RENAISSANCE

It's a new era abundant with ideas for integrating the riches of trade books into reading lessons

You've known for a long time that a great story can capture a child's heart and inspire learning. But now your affection for great children's literature, like that of hundreds of thousands of your colleagues, has coalesced into what might be called a trade-book renaissance in America's classrooms.

Fresh ideas are flourishing as teachers design approaches that offer students more of the sheer joy of reading fine trade books. Of course, great stories are their own reward, but they can be even more than that. Teachers are recognizing that reading trade books enhances the benefits of engaging students in discussion, developing strategic-reading abilities, and other activities arising from the reading program. Trade books give children more chances to apply what they've learned. When trade books relate to unit themes or selections, content is mutually supportive and can lead to whole-is-greater-than-the-parts discoveries for kids. With teachers coaching, children construct new meaning and grow as individuals.

This renaissance includes even young children. When they're not ready to read extensively on their own, wordless picture books can prompt them to create their own meaning. And *World of Reading* Big Books and Big Shared Books allow whole classes of primary students to discover the world of print and engage in enjoyable shared reading experiences. (See "Emergent Literacy," page M10, and "Language and the Child," page M12.)

Connections between the reading program and trade books are enhanced by the quality of *World of Reading* selections. Readers' interest may be piqued by an author, subject, or literary mode they first

encounter in the Student Text. It's natural to encourage students to follow their curiosity and seek out related library or trade books to read on their own. But that's just the beginning. You can also choose among several more structured ways to bring your students and trade books together.

Setting aside time for trade-book reading

First, students need time to read trade books. While we hope children will read at home, it's important to provide class time too. The flexible structure in *World of Reading* offers teachers more choices than ever in scheduling this time.

Consider for a moment the entire school-year period. You might spread *World of Reading* evenly across the year and simultaneously involve students in trade-book reading. To find extra time for such reading, many teachers regularly invite kids to read trade books while the teacher works with other students. Another favorite option is 15 minutes of daily sustained silent reading, with teachers modeling by reading silently themselves. Another choice is to devote four days to *World of Reading* and the fifth to trade books.

If you prefer more concentrated trade-

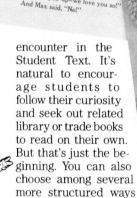

book reading, you might divide *World of Reading* into segments and alternate these with trade books. Several patterns are possible, depending on how much concentrated time you want for each period. You might, for example, devote two weeks to trade-book reading after each *World of Reading* unit (grades 4–8). Or you could plan two, month-long trade-book periods at the middle and end of the school year. (For more ideas, see "Can You Customize Your Instructional Plan?" page M32.)

Choosing books and organizing students

When students wish to pursue individual reading that relates to a specific story or unit theme, you'll find helpful suggestions

Dr. Marian Davies Toth, *an Author of* World of Reading *and* World of Language, *is an authority on writing and a reading-language arts consultant to schools nationwide.*

listed in Reading Every Day and Language Arts Connections in each selection, in Books to Enjoy in each unit, and in the Teacher Edition bibliography.

World of Reading offers two collections to broaden your options—*Time Out for Books* and *World of Books Classroom Libraries*.

Time Out for Books is a collection of four trade-book titles per grade level. Teachers may order multiple copies to provide each student with his or her own books. These paperbacks are related to unit themes and are featured in the Student Text. (See the separate Teacher Guide inside the front cover of each Teacher Edition.)

World of Books Classroom Libraries is a rich collection of award-winning children's trade books for grades K–8. Each grade-level library contains multiple copies of 12 titles and single copies of four titles for a total of 16 titles, 52 books in all. While this collection is ideal for free reading, multiple copies of a title also allow you to plan a variety of reading experiences for students. In addition to a Teacher Guide full of suggestions, each title comes with Bookshelf Activity Cards and Lit Box Cards that elicit personal responses to reading.

Once you've provided access to books, you'll want to consider ways of organizing students. Here are some ideas:

◆ *Partner reading,* in which two partners read the same title. At regular intervals, partners pause to exchange ideas about what they have read.

◆ *Small-group reading,* in which children form small groups based on their interest in a particular title. Each day, students read, write in a journal, and share their ideas.

◆ *Whole-class reading,* in which the class shares a trade book, perhaps through oral reading, by using multiple copies with staggered reading groups, or with each child reading his or her own paperback. Each day, students read or listen, write responses in journals, and discuss the story's progress.

Drawing out student response

When students are engaged in trade-book reading, encourage them to think about what they're reading:

◆ Ask students to relate the literature to individual experience through drawing or writing. If young children make sketches, you may want to ask them to explain the images.

◆ Invite students to write in a form or style that echoes what they're reading. Kids might experiment, for example, with writing a fable or myth modeled on one they're reading. Or they might try imitating a writer's style.

◆ Lure even reluctant readers with opportunities for interpretive reading and storytelling. Encourage children to bring favorite books to share with the class. Guide students in selecting and practicing to present interesting passages to the whole class. Or you could organize story-sharing groups, in which kids talk with peers about what they have been reading.

◆ Develop empathy with literary characters through dramatic play and role-playing.

◆ Ask students to make "I wonder" lists before, during, and after reading.

MING LO MOVES THE MOUNTAIN

ARNOLD LOBEL

◆ Encourage students to create additional adventures for a favorite character. You might also ask pairs or teams of students to co-author these episodes. Prepare kids by talking about maintaining reasonable consistency of character.

Inspiring kids to explore trade books

Time-honored teachers' techniques for encouraging reading are still effective: Create a cozy reading corner, maintain an intriguing classroom library, and continually offer suggestions for books students might enjoy.

Another good idea is to ask teams of students to take turns creating a "book of the week" or "favorite author" bulletin board highlighting a title or author they select.

These days, you also have the option of using video presentations to stimulate reading. You can use videos from the **World of Reading** I◆T Kit (Interactive Teaching Kit) to stimulate interest in authors and topic-related literature and to build background before reading. (See "Can You Customize…" page M32.) Also more than 200 children's books have been dramatized and many are available on video. Try showing some "teaser" segments, short but tempting enough to lead children to the book. Older students could even make their own story videos to share. Or use the same technique by reading brief passages from a trade book.

Another strategy is to enlist students in surveying schoolmates about their favorite titles. You might also ask your class to decide which 10 titles read this year should be recommended to children in the grade next year.

Families, of course, can be instrumental in encouraging trade-book reading. It's important to let them know how valuable you believe such reading to be. (See "Home Is Where the Help Is," page M28.)

Above all, enjoy yourselves! With great books to help, it won't be hard.

WORLD OF READING

EVALUATION CHECKLIST

✔ Conveys that trade-book reading is an important part of the curriculum

✔ Suggests practical strategies for weaving trade books into core instruction

✔ Makes a wide variety of well-known trade books easily accessible

Becoming a Strategic Reader

Good thinkers make good readers.

One student scans a book of records to learn about the world's shortest man. Another flips back in his mystery book to check the color of the stranger's hat. Their teacher glances at her plans before beginning the next phase of instruction.

All these people are strategic readers. Each has a clear purpose in mind and a plan for achieving that purpose. If they aren't achieving their purpose, they recognize the problem and draw upon a set of strategies to get themselves back on track.

Each of these three readers is also reading differently from the others. That's because strategic readers change the way they read according to their purpose for reading, the complexity of the text, and their familiarity with the topic. They size up the demands of the task in relation to their prior knowledge, decide how to approach the text, monitor their comprehension, and use fix-up strategies when they notice a problem in understanding.

Such fix-up strategies include keeping the problem "on hold" in the hope that it will be clarified later in the story, rereading parts of the selection, looking ahead, and seeking help from outside sources.

Struggling readers often do not control the way they read, perhaps because they don't see the point of reading or aren't aware enough of their own thinking.

How can we help struggling readers develop strategic reading skills? How can we help skilled readers strengthen their strategies?

Before reading

This is when strategic readers identify their purpose for reading, size up the demands of the task in relation to their prior knowledge, and decide how to approach the text. These behaviors help readers subsequently make inferences, understand causal relationships, and make predictions about what will happen.

In *World of Reading,* child-centered prereading activities tap students' prior knowledge of key concepts. These discussions and activities help students recall what they already know about the topic, learn critical vocabulary, and call up an internalized set of expectations about the writing at hand. (Look for Developing Concepts, Teaching Vocabulary, Building Background, and Developing a Purpose for Reading.)

Together, these prereading activities provide a rich backdrop against which the action of the story will unfold and acquire meaning. They also build toward an activity that helps children arrive at a clear purpose for reading.

During reading

Now the strategic reader builds a mental picture of the text: He or she checks story events against expectations and sees how each part fits the whole. The strategic reader then revises and creates new expectations by combining prior knowledge with new clues found in the text.

World of Reading Teacher Editions provide sets of questions that nurture these processes. Guided Reading questions involve students in key events of the story map by focusing on important relationships and characteristics, such as character, setting, plot structure, cause/effect, problem/solution, and other elements. Strategic Reading questions help children monitor their comprehension through visualizing, summarizing, predicting, and other actions. The overall goal of this set of questions is to help students "take stock" of their comprehension as it evolves. Highlighting Literature questions make students aware of the structure of the text and of the author's craft. Teachers choose among questions in these three instructional paths for each child or group of readers.

After reading

After reading, the strategic reader reflects and double checks to see whether the reading purpose has been achieved.

In *World of Reading,* teachers and students have several options that

WORLD OF READING

EVALUATION CHECKLIST

✔ Encourages students to monitor their own comprehension before, during, and after reading

✔ Applies thinking strategies to reading and writing

✔ Puts students in control of the reading process

✔ Builds competence in recalling, analyzing, inferring, synthesizing, and evaluating

encourage reflection, from questions that stimulate critical and creative thinking, to the more personal Reader's Response, to Language Arts Connections that help children reprocess the story through writing or speaking. These options help students think about whether their reading satisfied their purpose.

We know that students who learn how to read strategically are better able to comprehend new texts. They acquire skill and confidence in their own reading—and often develop a lifelong love for reading.

Thinking About Your Thinking

OK, so strategic readers blend prior knowledge with ideas from the text to construct a full mental picture of the story. Each new event is assimilated into the mental picture as reading continues. Let's stop the reader right here for a moment, and ask him or her to do a bit of self-monitoring, to consider the sort of the thinking that's going on.

Easier said than done, you say? Here's where **World of Reading** can help, through a comprehensive approach that weaves thinking strategies through units at every grade level. With help from **World of Reading,**

teachers nurture self-awareness in readers by modeling thought processes and by providing experience with specific thinking strategies, such as visualizing or rating understanding. Behaviors that occur constantly during reading—recalling, analyzing, inferring, synthesizing, and evaluating—get special attention. Students learn strategies directly through specific lessons in the

Student Text, and also indirectly, through the questions teachers ask during and after reading. Optional activities geared to unit themes focus on nurturing problem-solving, creative thinking, and critical thinking abilities.

These experiences help make the structures of thinking visible to children, which in turn helps them organize information. Readers then more easily recognize when they're not understanding a passage or when that mental picture breaks down.

Dr. P. David Pearson, is Dean, College of Education, University of Illinois in Urbana-Champaign, and researcher at the Center for the Study of Reading. A World of Reading Author, he is recognized for his research on reading comprehension and assessment.

VOCABULARY
THE KEY TO COMPREHENSION

❝Teaching new vocabulary is easier when you use *definition, context,* and *concept associations* to help children construct meaning.❞

Dr. Dale D. Johnson
Author, World of Reading

Ever notice how much fun some kids have when they learn a new word? They act as if they've found a new friend. They'll play with the word, spell it, yell it, invent new meanings, introduce it to parents until they know it well. **World of Reading** makes it possible for every child to build vocabulary, to enjoy word ownership, and to develop a love of language.

Building a strong vocabulary is a key factor for a child in developing a positive attitude toward reading. Research shows conclusively that knowing or not knowing word meanings makes all the difference in students' ability to comprehend text. Our own experience also confirms that simple fact. Think back to the last time you read something with an unfamiliar but key word you couldn't figure out from context. Not only did you lose the meaning, but frustration and impatience built quickly. It takes only a few unfamiliar words in a single selection before you're tempted to stop.

The implications for reading instruction are clear: An effective reading program is built on a strong foundation of sound vocabulary instruction. The first goal should be to ensure that students know *story critical words*—words so important that meaning will be lost without them—before

reading begins. A second must be to provide *engaging vocabulary activities* that develop a love of language. And a third must be to *connect students' prior knowledge* to new words and concepts. **World of Reading** offers teachers three alternatives to achieve these goals for successful vocabulary instruction:

1. *Definition*—explicitly teaching the meaning of a word.

2. *Context*—guiding students to the meaning of a word by examining it in context-rich sentences.

3. *Concept Associations*—helping children to associate the word with other words they already know through a variety of ac-

tivities, including classification and semantic mapping.

What does this mean for the way you teach? Suppose, for example, a story describes a typhoon. Teaching this word by *definition* would mean explaining to students that a typhoon is a big tropical storm characterized by strong winds and blinding rain. In **World of Reading** Teacher Editions, you'll find definitions of story-critical words right on the page where these new words are taught. In the Student Text Glossary, definitions and context sentences are provided for story-critical and support words.

Teaching *typhoon* through *context* involves presenting the word in a sentence full of clues to the words meaning: "When the typhoon overtook the fishing boat, the wild wind, drenching downpours, and massive waves nearly capsized it." You will find context sentences for each story-critical word in **World of Reading.**

Teaching *typhoon* by *concept associations* could involve any one of many strategies, such as semantic mapping, analogy, semantic feature analysis, or a variety of playful and stimulating classification activities based on synonyms, antonyms, connotations, and homophones. The vocabulary lesson for each selection in this program offers opportunities for using one or more of these strategies.

World of Reading delivers an instructional model that combines *definition, context,* and *concept associations* in every lesson. The lessons not only teach students new words and how to use those words to understand selections they read in the classroom, they also build a solid foundation for a lifetime of independent reading.

Dr. Dale D. Johnson, *Director, Instructional Research and Development Institute in Boston, is well known for his study of vocabulary development and his work on category inferences.*

WORLD OF READING

EVALUATION CHECKLIST

✓ Taps students' prior knowledge

✓ Teaches story critical words

✓ Uses definition, context, and concept associations

✓ Presents a variety of teaching strategies for vocabulary

BREAKING THE CODE

Phonics and Decoding Are Means to an End

Dr. Richard L. Venezky, Author, World of Reading, *is Unidel Professor of Educational Studies at the University of Delaware. He is widely known for his research on decoding and study skills and was a consultant to the Commission on Reading of the National Academy of Education.*

Decoding is about the frustration of trying to solve a puzzle—and the satisfaction of finding the key. For the beginner just unlocking meaning in those mysterious strings of letters and words, decoding provides the link from spoken language to the world of print. Decoding leads young readers to use phonics, supported by context, to gain control over the reading process.

It's important to keep in mind that decoding and phonics are means to an end—not ends in themselves. Decoding does not always produce the exact pronunciation of a word. It may provide clues that, supported by context, can lead a reader to word recognition.

Decoding has two ends: first, to develop the ability to recognize words in print, and second, to build confidence in one's own ability to extract meaning from unfamiliar texts.

Stage 1: The Early Years
Decoding in *World of Reading* progresses through three stages. In the first, phonics instruction gives the beginning reader a key to unlock the mysteries of letters and sounds. Letter shapes, names, and sounds are learned; then readers learn to blend the sounds to make words. Both vowel and consonant patterns are introduced, allowing quick access to printed words.

Phonics lessons are structured in a reliable, systematic pattern, so the reader moves from letter to sound to meaning. Six steps—*see, hear, say, practice, read, write*—move children through this process and provide help for every kind of learner. Direct instruction in blending unifies the phonetic process, while immediate application of the newly acquired skill reinforces learning and clarifies for children why they are doing what they are doing.

Stage 2: The Developing Reader
The second stage introduces the rest of the major phonetic patterns and some structural patterns. Because English often breaks rules of convention, emphasis is placed on developing strategies for diversity. Children are encouraged to make a good guess at an unknown word. If the first attempt fails, they learn to try again with an alternate pattern. By now the reader's whole-word recognition is developing rapidly, so decoding increasingly becomes just one strategy for accessing new words.

Stage 3: The Fluent Reader
The third stage emphasizes techniques for recognizing longer and less-frequent words. Structural analysis, long-word decoding, and—if all else fails—use of the dictionary are the main tools. Always supporting the decoding strand is instruction in context clues. This provides learners with both power and depth in their now rapidly expanding facility for word recognition and vocabulary growth.

By the time this three-stage process is complete, decoding is a natural and automatic process. Your students have been empowered to become active readers, fully involved with the meaning and the enjoyment of their reading.

WORLD OF READING

EVALUATION CHECKLIST

✔ Provides both phonics and structural skills

✔ Supports phonics instruction with context

✔ Completes all essential decoding and phonics skills by the end of second grade

ASSESSMENT
Comes of Age

Today's choices meet a range of evaluation needs

Not so long ago, most teachers had two sources of information about student learning: impressions gathered from daily teaching, and results of paper-and-pencil tests with short, clipped passages that measured isolated skills and bits of knowledge.

In recent years, both of these traditional sources have matured. Those impressions have developed into what we now call *informal assessment,* which tends to be diagnostic, individualized, and an integral part of daily teaching. Those paper-and-pencil tests have evolved into various types of *formal assessment,* which are administered in a prescribed manner, often to groups of students.

Dr. James F. Baumann *(l) and*
Dr. P. David Pearson *(r)*

Informal Assessment

Among the most exciting developments is the refinement of a set of informal assessment techniques that make use of teachers' knowledge, skill, and judgment to identify students' changing strengths and needs. These techniques become an integral part of everyday teaching and help teachers make more informed decisions.

In selecting techniques, teachers first consider what they want to find out, then they engage students in a learning activity that reveals this information. Insights are then recorded in a way that helps in planning future instruction.

Insights are also shared with learners, who begin to assume more responsibility for their own learning. Kids are asked such questions as "What is something new that you've learned to help you understand what you read?" or "What would you like to learn so that you will be a better reader?" This aspect of informal assessment emphasizes students' potential as well as their performance.

World of Reading Teacher Editions highlight many informal opportunities for assessing such student behaviors as self-monitoring, summarizing, generalizing, evaluating, synthesizing, visualizing, predicting, and more. In addition, ***World of Reading*** provides many tools to help teachers observe, record, and evaluate individual student progress. Teachers' informal-assessment choices include the following techniques:

Verbal student reports pinpoint specific needs as kids "think out loud." While engaged in reading, writing, listening, or speaking, learners tell what they are

thinking. The teacher discovers individual strengths and needs, as well as what part of the process needs to be modeled.

Anecdotal records made by the teacher provide an ongoing account of student learning behaviors. These dated observations are often kept for each reader in a folder.

Interviews, in which the teacher asks planned questions, produce insights into student thinking. For example, while assigning oral reports, students are interviewed to find out whether they understand how to form questions and gather information.

Conferences after a learning session are held for small groups of children. The teacher asks questions, offers assistance, and notes strengths, needs, and the teaching strategies that proved most helpful.

Portfolio assessment involves folders of individual student work samples, collected and dated systematically. Portfolios offer a particularly useful way to note progress and recurring needs, to share these insights with the student, and to develop student responsibility for self-assessment and motivation over time.

The *World of Reading* Teacher Resource Kit includes helpful suggestions for developing portfolios. A child's portfolio might include a reading log with titles, authors, dates, and general reactions, as well as periodic audiocassette recordings of the child reading a favorite passage aloud. It might also include writing samples, such as responses to reading, story summaries, or other writing activities. Evidence from a child's participation in group projects can also be included.

From time to time, the student and teacher evaluate the student's progress and consider new personal goals. This encourages students to take more responsibility for improvement. When these reflections are written and tucked into the portfolio, they set the stage for later self-evaluation.

As students become skilled at assessing their own progress, they can create and add to their portfolio a "personal best" folder made up of work they wish to showcase for the teacher and for family conferences.

Observational checklists help focus the teacher's attention on behaviors that signal a child's success or difficulty in learning. The Teacher Resource Kit includes checklists that provide a suggested list of student behaviors to look for during reading and writing. If these are dated and included in portfolios, progress can be reviewed by teachers, students, and parents.

Informal Reading Inventories are *World of Reading* materials that provide a context for observing specific student behaviors and for making placement decisions. A test, in the form of graded passages with questions, is administered individually to assess both comprehension and decoding skills. The student first reads the passage silently, then summarizes orally. If the teacher judges the student's summary to be inadequate, more information is gathered by asking the student comprehension questions. The student's responses help determine the best place in the program for that student to begin and clue the teacher in to strengths and needs.

Checkpoints in *World of Reading* aid in the development of students' ability to control their own learning. Students see their strengths and weaknesses even as the teacher does. These measures, which occur twice in each unit, also offer teachers a systematic approach to assessing the skills and strategies children are responsible for in each unit. In addition, each Checkpoint provides reteaching and practice ideas that allow students to continue to progress.

Formal Testing
As with informal assessment, formal testing has grown more responsive to educators' need for a range of tools to measure learning. Formal tests now help evaluate improvement in both specific skills and in more holistic reading processes. They are also useful in noting progress through a program and in providing an estimate of the achievement of one group of students in relation to another.

Formal assessment options in *World of Reading* include the following measures.

Placement Tests, help determine the most appropriate initial level for students in grades 1–8. These group tests employ a multiple-choice format and focus on comprehension. In difficult or ambiguous cases these tests are followed by Informal Reading Inventories.

Unit Process Tests (grades 1–8) take a holistic approach by assessing general reading comprehension ability through writing. Students read a whole passage, article, or story, then respond to open-ended questions.

Unit Skills Tests (grades 1–8), alternatives to Unit Process Tests, provide diagnostic information about how well students learned the most important objectives of the unit.

Mid-Book (grades 4–8) and **End-of-Book** (grades K–8) **Tests** are general survey instruments that help teachers decide how well students have achieved critical objectives. By examining cumulative learning midway through the year, Mid-Book Tests offer a timely means of identifying areas for instructional adjustment. Mid-Book and End-of-Book Tests may also be used diagnostically to identify strands in which students show particular strength or need.

Management Tools
World of Reading offers management tools to help you track student progress.

Reading Assessment Portfolios are sets of special folders for collecting samples of each student's work, keeping the student's notes about his or her improvement, and recording observations.

Student Score Sheets, Class Score Sheets, and the **Reading Progress Card** are optional forms that help you record and analyze individual or group test results.

School Curriculum Manager is school-based instructional management software for an IBM or IBM-compatible computer. It scores tests, maintains results, recommends activities to address needs, and generates reports at student, group, class, or school levels.

Dr. James Baumann is Professor and Head of the Department of Reading Education at the University of Georgia. He is a World of Reading *author and is editor of* The Reading Teacher. ***Dr. P. David Pearson,*** *Dean, College of Education, University of Illinois in Urbana-Champaign, and researcher at the Center for Reading is an author of* World of Reading.

WORLD OF READING

EVALUATION CHECKLIST

✔ Provides for informal assessment of student behaviors

✔ Provides both holistic and objective-based tests

✔ Offers practice with all test formats

✔ Provides a variety of management tools from portfolios to software

Home is where the help is

Gaining the support of families can be one of teaching's most challenging—and rewarding—responsibilities. These tips will help you reach out to parents and promote home reading.

Parents as partners

Even if research didn't emphasize the importance to kids of reading at home, lots of families would do it anyway. These print-loving parents are natural allies, needing just a few suggestions to fully support their child's growth in reading.

It's the other families who can be a mystery. Because it's common knowledge that home reading helps children succeed in school, we might conclude that students who don't read much have families who are indifferent. But research tells us we'd probably be mistaken.

Rather than lack of interest, it may be lack of specific information that limits family encouragement of home reading. Lots of families may not know how *vital* home reading is for all kids, regardless of age, or what to do or how often to do it. Some may doubt their ability to be of much help. Here's where you can make a profound difference.

Researchers report that when asked to help and when given specific suggestions, parents tend to cooperate with teachers. This makes it important to ask and expect every family to promote home reading.

First, you'll want to contact families to let them know you're joining them as partners in educating their child. Explain how important family help is to the child's success in school. Encourage parents and other caregivers to ask questions.

This initial contact builds good will and makes you aware of parents who have difficulty reading, who are not fluent in English, who are blind, or who have other conditions you'll want to consider.

When you've established a link, provide specific suggestions. One way is by sharing the videotape *Your Child and the World of Reading.* Or create and lend your own video, in which you model home-reading techniques. You could also conduct a workshop for family members who have primary responsibility for each child.

As the year progresses, keep families informed. You might ask students to help put together a lively newsletter that brings families up to date, commends student work, and suggests books and activities families can share.

World of Reading Home Connection Letters, in English and Spanish, help families understand unit themes and goals. Each letter also suggests theme-related activities and books kids might enjoy.

It's also worthwhile to send home brief, individual notes of praise about some academic accomplishment, so that parents may share your pleasure in a child's improvement. When parents' efforts have contributed to the child's accomplishment, be sure to let them know.

Reaching the hard-to-reach parent

Sometimes connecting with a family presents a special challenge. This is when you'll want to seek help from administrators and community agencies.

If, for example, a language barrier exists, ask ethnic organizations or other family members to translate. If a parent has difficulty reading your notes and reading with the child, make frequent phone calls and tactfully steer the family toward community-library and literacy programs. If the family has no phone, if you've asked—in vain—that the parent come to the school, or if a home visit isn't appropriate, you might arrange to meet in some neutral and secure spot where the parent will feel comfortable, perhaps a church hall or quiet corner of a shopping mall. Remember that some parents may feel alienated from school, be unsure of how to talk with you, or think they haven't the right to ask for anything special for their child.

It's important to be clear that home reading is really vital and that it can make a remarkable difference in a child's success at school. Research tells us that parents are more likely to become involved if they see how their involvement helps. If relatives share in the responsibility for the child, seek their support too. In some cases, you may want to discuss the child's need for a quiet place to retreat and work. Other times, you'll want to emphasize specific suggestions, such as asking a child to describe a character he or she is reading about.

It's natural to need not only logistical help but collegial support in these efforts, so don't hesitate to ask another teacher or administrator to help you maintain high expectations, good spirits, and a sense of partnership.

Homework that's homeplay

Sometimes families eager to help their children—but not aware of appropriate ways to do so—unfortunately end up conveying to kids that reading is a chore. Other families may assume it's sufficient if a child occasionally shows interest in print on his or her own. So it's important to let families know that nurturing the child's *desire* to read is one of your main goals. Share these four suggestions:

1. *Kids should read at home because they genuinely want to.* If the reading matter too often has no appeal to the child, he or she may go through the motions but lose interest in reading overall. To nurture the desire to read, parents should take the child to a library and provide plenty of time for making selections. It's important for children to choose what interests them.

2. *In reading together, parents should stay relaxed and ask questions that stimulate thinking.* If the book the child has selected is too difficult for him or her to read, the parent can read it aloud at a normal pace, and the child can ask questions when they occur to him or her. From time to time, the parent should stop and ask the child to retell what has happened up to this point, what the child thinks of the story, or what might happen next. Let families know that the goal here is not right/wrong questions and answers, but an informal discussion of ideas. Explain that reading aloud by parents—or older siblings—provides children with a model of fluency and opportunities to acquire knowledge, as well as experience in making predictions and summarizing.

If the child can read some text, the parent puts a finger under a line of print, reads along, and occasionally stops. The child reads as much as he or she can, then the parent continues. Here again, the adult invites the child to ask questions, make summaries and predictions, and give opinions.

If the child can read the text, the parent and child sit and read silently together. If the child gets stuck, he or she points to the word. The parent reads the word aloud and the child continues reading. Explain to families that it's better not to break the flow of the story, because fluency in home reading is more important than sound-it-out efforts. This reading too should include discussions.

3. *Reading is more likely to flourish when families provide time and a conducive environment.* At the very least, this means placing limits on TV viewing. Families might also establish regular times when everyone is engaged in quiet activities and distractions are kept to a minimum.

4. *Children benefit when families make a point of demonstrating how much they*

value reading and other language skills. Families can do this by making sure there are books and magazines in the home, by writing notes to kids and encouraging them to do the same, by inquiring about the child's reading in school, by writing letters together, and by discussing print they discover in daily life, such as mail, newspapers, grocery labels, and so on. Encourage parents of older students to continue library trips and discussions of family members' reading.

Summer send-home suggestions

1. Create a list of book and magazine titles for recommended summer reading. Include a "teaser" sentence or two with each title to pique student interest, and try to select a majority of titles available at your community library. Titles suggested in *World of Reading* Home Connection Letters make a good beginning.

2. Suggest that parent and child do a *Siskel and Ebert,* that is, that they take on the roles of critics and share their views of a TV show, video, movie, or book with each other.

3. Provide sources of penpals and encouragement to get started.

4. Dream up a dozen ideas for a suggested family-trip-of-the-week list. Include such destinations as a grocery store, the post office, a park, or a relative's workplace, as well as more unusual spots. Suggest a related ongoing reading or writing activity for kids to undertake. Two such examples: Write a series of chapters or stories about a wandering puppy who visits each place, or collect six "secret" words from each spot for later games of "hangman" with parents or siblings.

5. Encourage families with young children to create their own illustrated alphabet poster or picture dictionary by cutting out magazine photos and illustrations and making drawings.

6. Provide an outline for how to organize a treasure hunt and encourage families to conduct one. Emphasize that one clue should lead to another, and that clues should be written and slightly mysterious.

7. Alert families of middle-schoolers to such sources of hobby and career information as the *Encyclopedia of Associations* and the *Gale Directory of Publications,* both found at community library reference desks.

8. Encourage families to create new dialogue for recurring TV commercials. Each time the chosen commercial comes on, the sound is turned off and family members take the parts of each character. Each "actor's" spontaneous comments should respond in some way to those of the others.

9. Collect summer-activity schedules from your community library and other cultural and recreational institutions and highlight events you think your students might especially enjoy.

10. As a challenge to avid readers, propose that families try to track down kids' books popular long ago. After parents and kids read these books, they might discuss how they are different from stories written today.

11. Encourage families to play phone-book games, such as guessing names of imagined people or businesses, then checking to see if they are actually listed. Or just ask families to enlist children's help in looking up phone numbers.

12. Offer tips on how to make paper-bag masks, sock puppets, or paper dolls. Suggest that kids use them to dramatize stories.

13. Urge families to establish their own summer holiday reading-related tradition. For example, they might celebrate the Fourth of July by reading the Declaration of Independence together, searching out a new recipe to try, or enacting a skit or word game involving fireworks, barbecues, swimming, baseball, or whatever the family does on the day.

Dr. Carl A. Grant, *Consulting Author,* World of Reading, *is Professor of Curriculum and Instruction at the University of Wisconsin-Madison. His research in multicultural and teacher education has been widely published.*

WORLD OF READING
COMPONENTS DESCRIPTION

At the heart of every *World of Reading* component is literature. Our Student Texts are filled with the very finest literary classics and contemporary works; our Teacher Editions base all instruction directly on the literature students read. Literature is deeply rooted in every component so that the primary purpose of instruction is never obscured: to nurture a love of reading.

Student Texts
Student Texts inform and entertain with a collection of classic and contemporary literature. Thematic units include a variety of genres.

◆ **AWARD-WINNING SELECTIONS** Newbery, Caldecott, Pulitzer, and other prize winners.

◆ **READERS' CHOICE STORIES** Chosen as favorites by a Silver Burdett & Ginn panel of more than 2000 students nationwide.

◆ **TIME OUT FOR BOOKS** A hard-to-resist preview of well-known trade books that can be integrated with the program.

◆ **WORLD OF READING MAGAZINE** Articles that explore the role reading plays in our lives.

Teacher Editions
Designed for special flexibility and ease of use, the Teacher Edition highlights options to meet individual needs.

◆ **LISTENING LESSONS** Read-aloud / Think-aloud lessons that open each unit with a classic piece of literature. Lessons model thinking, too.

◆ **UNIT/LESSON ORGANIZERS** Helpful overviews to simplify your planning.

◆ **SKILL TRACE BAR** A graphic organizer signaling where you are in the instructional cycle of every skill.

◆ **THE BRIDGE** New skills taught in the context of the prior story for application in the new story.

Workbooks
Visually appealing and packed with selection-related activities, the Workbooks provide multiple support opportunities for every tested skill.

◆ **INTEREST INVENTORY** Help in identifying students' reading interests.

◆ **BOOK LOGS** Special pages for personal response to books.

◆ **CHECKPOINTS** Informal assessment at the middle and end of the unit.

Reader's Journal
For those interested in eliciting more open-ended personal responses to literature, the Reader's Journal offers an exciting alternative—or complement—to the Workbook. Its "magazine" look, with fine art and photography, promotes creativity and critical thinking.

◆ **"BEFORE READING" ACTIVITIES** Designed to activate prior knowledge and serve as a warm-up for students.

◆ **"AFTER READING" ACTIVITIES** Two types of activities for encouraging personal and creative response. The first requires a personal response to the selection; the second extends the story and serves as a springboard for learning in other content areas.

◆ **RELATED READINGS** Another piece of literature for response, related to the unit theme.

◆ **CRITIC'S CORNER** End-of-unit activities (called "What I Think" in Gr. 1–2) requiring students to assess their own work in the Journal.

◆ **END-OF-BOOK** Student-generated materials including:
  - New Words I've Learned
  - Words I Often Misspell ("Words to Learn to Spell" in Gr. 1–2)
  - Books I Have Read
  - Books I Want to Read

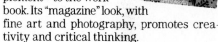

Interactive Teaching Kit

An imaginative collection of multicultural and multisensory experiences, the I◆T Kit opens students' minds to literature, fine arts, and other content areas.

◆ **VIDEOS** Mini-documentaries, drama, animation, author interviews, and more relating directly to Student Text literature and themes.

◆ **AUDIOS** Literature-related musical selections (classic and contemporary), movement activities, poetry, interviews, and more.

◆ **UNIT CARDS** Beautifully detailed cards featuring fine arts, nature photography, stories, poems, and more connect literature to the content areas.

◆ **POSTERS** Posters rich with art and photography for initiating activities and projects across the curriculum.

World of Books Classroom Libraries

Further reading adventures await your class with a "trunk" packed with outstanding trade books. Included at each grade:

◆ **52 PAPERBACKS** Four copies each of 12 different titles, plus a special Bonus Package of four additional titles per library.

◆ **BOOKSHELF ACTIVITY CARDS** Richly illustrated cards that complement each trade book and encourage creative responses to literature through writing, art, discussion, and dramatics.

◆ **LIT BOX** Thought-provoking game cards that invite students to share the reading experience through discussion, writing, and games.

◆ **TEACHER HANDBOOK** Practical suggestions for using each of the tradebooks in your classroom.

Time Out for Books Collection and Teacher Guide

Handy collections of trade books make it easy for students to "take time out" to read a well-known book. Every trade book explored in the Student Text feature, Time Out for Books, is available in multiple copies for whole-class or small-group enjoyment. Also, the Teacher Guide provides you with everything you need to integrate trade books into your curriculum.

Kindergarten

This unique early literacy program in *World of Reading* lets you choose from a variety of options to suit your classroom needs.

◆ **HICKORY DICKORY DOCK** The Pupil Book has plenty of opportunities for personal response to literature through echo reading, tracking print, retelling, and much more. Tucked in the back of the Pupil Book is a unique, 48-page wordless book for recalling and retelling read-aloud stories.

◆ **HICKORY DICKORY VILLAGE** A classroom kit filled with hands-on manipulatives plus Big and Little Shared Books, Cassettes, Read-Aloud Anthology, *A Treasury of Mother Goose,* Alphabetasaurus puppet, and much more.

◆ **HICKORY DICKORY STORYTIME** A smaller version of the *Village,* with all the literature components—Big and Little Shared Books, Cassettes, Fold-Out Books, and the Read-Aloud Anthology—but without the manipulatives.

Teacher Resource Kits

This exciting array of motivating activities, creative materials, and innovative instructional resources enrich and expand the reading experience. Just a few examples:

◆ **INTEGRATED CURRICULUM** A collection of Language Arts Connections, Curriculum Connections, and Writing activities to help you integrate the language arts.

◆ **LISTENING LESSON CASSETTES** Dramatic readings of the listening selections that open each unit.

◆ **MEETING INDIVIDUAL NEEDS** Provision for every need, from Reteaching to Challenge to Achieving English Proficiency to Informal Assessment suggestions and observation forms.

◆ **TEACHING POSTERS** Fine art reproductions from the Student Text, semantic and story maps, and an activity booklet.

Assessment

A comprehensive assessment program that accommodates a wide range of needs, from criterion-referenced testing to holistic assessment.

◆ **INFORMAL READING INVENTORY**
◆ **UNIT SKILLS TESTS**
◆ **UNIT PROCESS TESTS**
◆ **READING ASSESSMENT PORTFOLIO**

WORLD OF READING

Can You Customize Your Instructional Plan? *You Bet!*

World of Reading *offers you real choices in designing instruction that's right for your kids.*

The great thing about teaching is that it never stands still. A fresh batch of students presents new challenges, or you learn a new technique, or school curriculum goals change, or a child's needs evolve. To make the most of all these opportunities, you need plenty of choices and the flexibility to make decisions when new challenges present themselves.

World of Reading offers not only a flexible core structure to build on, but a full range of choices to support your decisions along the way.

As you work with **World of Reading** to meet your teaching goals, you'll want to consider long-range, medium-range, and short-range choices. For long-range decisions, think about how you prefer to organize time in an overall pattern for the school year. Medium-range decisions can be made for each unit, and short-range decisions can be made on a lesson-by-lesson basis. Here are just a few questions to stimulate your thinking.

LONG-RANGE PLANNING CHOICES

I'm interested in setting aside time for my students to read library books and trade books. How can I coordinate trade books with **World of Reading?**

You have many choices in patterns. In addition to responding to your curriculum goals, these choices allow instruction to vary and remain fresh year after year. Chart 1 shows average pacing of **World of Reading** over a 36-week school year. If you chose this pattern, you'll have time to include lots of **World of Reading** activities along with daily or weekly periods of trade-book reading.

To help students make thematic connections between trade books and literature in the Student Text, you'll find that the **World of Reading** *Time Out for Books* collection is a good choice. It includes such engaging titles as *Where the Wild Things Are, Charlotte's Web, In the Year of the Boar and Jackie Robinson, Zia, Johnny Tremain,* and many others. Chart 2 shows suggestions for patterns that integrate *Time Out for Books* at each grade level. Naturally, these books can also be used for free reading, along with titles from *World of Books Classroom Libraries.*

There are three teaching plans (Plan A, B, and C) provided for each *Time Out for Books* selection. For Plan A, simply review with students the *Time Out for Books* pages in the Student Text and invite children to read the featured book on their own as an alternative to the Reader's Corner selection.

Average Pacing Guidelines

| | 18 Weeks | 36 Weeks |

0   18 Weeks   36 Weeks

KINDERGARTEN

Orientation	Hickory Dickory Dock/Hickory Dickory Village	Early Reading*
4 Weeks	8 Units, 3 Weeks Each	8 Weeks

GRADE 1

Early Reading Review*	Beginning Readers	Primer	Reader
4 Weeks	3 Books, 4 Weeks Each	10 Weeks	10 Weeks

GRADES 2 AND 3

Book 1	Book 2
4 Units, 4.5 Weeks Each	4 Units, 4.5 Weeks Each

GRADES 4 TO 8

Student Text
4 Units, 9 Weeks Each

Chart 1. *This pattern, based on a 36-week school year, accommodates many* **World of Reading** *activities, as well as trade-book reading on a daily or weekly basis.*
Only one of these two programs—Buckle My Shoe or Clap Your Hands—is needed.

Getting to know *World of Reading*

What's it like to use **World of Reading**? We asked Judy Hjelseth, who teaches first and second grade in Beaverton, Oregon. Judy has worked with the program for a year, and here's what she has to say.

"I was so relieved when my district adopted **World of Reading,** because I felt it was something we could work with. I really like how **World of Reading** uses songs and familiar literature in the early grades—I think that's very helpful to all children.

"What I actually did to start was just pick up a child's book and look at it from the child's perspective. Then I went to the Teacher Edition. I use the Teacher Edition now mostly for ideas. I always use something in the Building Background section. Those ideas are really helpful! I like the guided reading questions too, but I find that the Teacher Edition thinks the same way I think, so I don't need to use it as much. I used it at first, and now I am more confident and don't rely on it as much.

"I also like the Reader's Response question and Writing to Learn. They're wonderful ideas. The kids get really involved in them. I love things like that, things that keep the kids going.

"The follow-ups and extensions—I pick up a lot of ideas there. The Language Arts Connections and Curriculum Connections are really helpful. In our district, we're trying to integrate the curriculum, so the ideas fit.

"How do I decide what strategies to use? A lot of it has to do with the children's interest and what fits with what I think they need. If the kids have shown that they know a particular skill, I just skip it. By

now, I've gotten so that I go through the Teacher Edition and skip around. Sometimes I skip a selection, and go back to it another time, if the kids are really excited about a story further along in the book. There are some lovely stories! I don't feel that I have to do things step by step.

"I want a variety of strategies and ways of organizing children, so that they learn a lot of ways to respond to books. I want children to feel secure, so I model a

Judy Hjelseth, first and second grade teacher, Beaverton, Oregon.

strategy for them, and they kind of build a repertoire. Eventually, it's nice for them to choose the way they want to respond. The Teacher Edition provides a lot of ideas, too—it kind of keeps you going and keeps the kids going.

"When I use trade books, I get ideas from the Teacher Edition or the Idea Factory, and make them my own. I also get ideas from the Workbook and just have the kids write about them. I pick and choose.

"I like to plan reading in interest-based groups. I get four or five copies each of four titles—such as those offered in the *World of Books Classroom Libraries.* It is a good way to mix the kids together in groups.

"Since this is the first year we're using **World of Reading,** the teachers are trying a lot of new things, finding some helpful new strategies. By next year, we'll be really comfortable just picking and choosing.

"What you do with **World of Reading** really depends on your philosophy of teaching. At the beginning, if you follow the Teacher Edition, and think about what is expected of your children and look

at your children, you can see what you need. It helps, when you're starting, to mix some strategies that are new with some you're already comfortable with. You begin to see all the ways you can teach the things you're accountable for. There's always something in the Teacher Edition you can use that's meaningful to kids. You use your own judgment. You know the children you have in your class. You know their needs and their interests. You know what they're going to learn the most from and get the most excited about. I have a lot of faith in kids. They really want to learn, and the ideas in **World of Reading** really help."

students are more likely to remember words connected to their own experience, *World of Reading* strategies build from the known to the new. (See "Vocabulary: The Key to Comprehension," page M24.)

You vary the length of instruction according to student need. For example, for the student who is weak in vocabulary, you might use all the strategies offered. Other kids may be generally quite skilled in vocabulary and likely to know the story-critical words. For these students, you might use only one vocabulary strategy.

Now let's consider comprehension. In each Reading and Responding section of the lesson, Building Background helps children use their own experiences to prepare for reading new material. Here again, you decide how many suggestions to use.

Three approaches to shared reading provide more opportunities to customize your instruction. The Guiding Reading questions lead students through key points of a story map. Strategic Reading questions develop students' ability to monitor their own comprehension. Highlighting Literature questions focus on the literary aspects of the story and emphasize the author's craft.

Writing to Learn suggestions after each selection enhance comprehension. Other follow-up questions and activities also develop comprehension and provide options for planning instruction that meets your goals and the needs of your students. When students become involved with Reader's Response and Selection Follow-Up questions, for example, you decide on a lesson-by-lesson basis whether they do so orally or in writing, individually or in groups. In a Teacher Edition section called More Ideas for Selection Follow-up, you'll find optional critical/creative thinking questions and an oral rereading activity. You also decide which Language Arts Connections—story related activities incorporating listening, speaking, writing, and thinking—to use.

The final part of the lesson, Selection Support, suggests instructional strategies for the occasional introduction of a skill, as well as for optional practice and maintenance of previously taught skills.

To help you keep track, the *World of Reading* Teacher Edition includes Skill Trace Bars with each specific skill. These tell you at a glance where the skill is taught, practiced, tested, and maintained. (See the annotated first lesson in the Teacher Edition for more information.)

I like to emphasize the reading-writing connection, so I want my students to keep a journal about their reading. Does **World of Reading** *support this approach?*

You'll find the *World of Reading* Reader's Journal particularly helpful. Of course, it provides readers with a place to write their thoughts and feelings about literature. What makes it especially valuable is the way it prompts entries before and after reading the Student Text selection. Intriguing story-related questions inspire writing and help cement the reading-writing connection. Many other story-related writing activities are suggested, both in the Student Text and the Teacher Edition. (See "Language and the Child," page 12.)

How can **World of Reading** *assist me in helping my students make connections between what they're reading and what they're learning in other subjects?*

The program reaches into the content areas in several ways. Selections themselves often overlap with what students are learning in other subjects. In addition, the Student Text includes special lessons addressing specific reading strategies for content-area textbooks. Teachers can also choose among Curriculum Connections activities suggested in the Teacher Edition after every selection. These help children connect story concepts, places, and events to math, social studies, science, health, careers, art, and more.

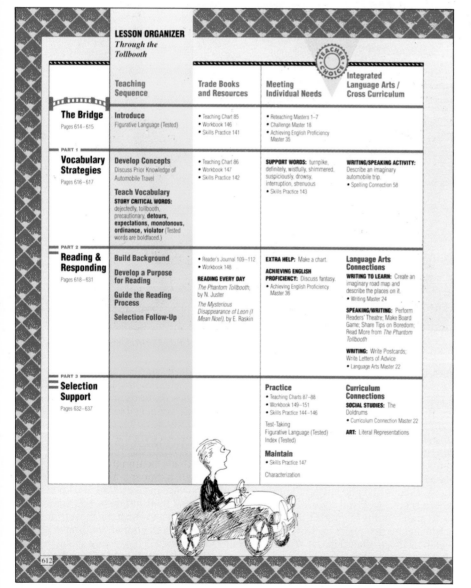

LESSON ORGANIZER *Through the Tollbooth*				
	Teaching Sequence	**Trade Books and Resources**	**Meeting Individual Needs**	**Integrated Language Arts / Cross Curriculum**
The Bridge Pages 614–615	Introduce Figurative Language (Tested)	• Teaching Chart 85 • Workbook 146 • Skills Practice 141	• Reteaching Masters 1–7 • Challenge Master 18 • Achieving English Proficiency Master 35	
PART 1 **Vocabulary Strategies** Pages 616–617	Develop Concepts Discuss Prior Knowledge of Automobile Travel **Teach Vocabulary** STORY CRITICAL WORDS: dejectedly, tollbooth, precautionary, **detours**, **expectations, monotonous, ordinance, violator** (Tested words are boldfaced.)	• Teaching Chart 86 • Workbook 147 • Skills Practice 142	SUPPORT WORDS: turnpike, definitely, wistfully, shimmered, suspiciously, drowsy, interruption, strenuous • Skills Practice 143	WRITING/SPEAKING ACTIVITY: Describe an imaginary automobile trip. • Spelling Connection 58
PART 2 **Reading & Responding** Pages 618–631	Build Background Develop a Purpose for Reading Guide the Reading Process Selection Follow-Up	• Reader's Journal 109–112 • Workbook 148 READING EVERY DAY *The Phantom Tollbooth,* by N. Juster *The Mysterious Disappearance of Leon (I Mean Noel),* by E. Raskin	EXTRA HELP: Make a chart. ACHIEVING ENGLISH PROFICIENCY: Discuss fantasy. • Achieving English Proficiency Master 36	**Language Arts Connections** WRITING TO LEARN: Create an imaginary road map and describe the places on it. • Writing Master 24 SPEAKING/WRITING: Perform Readers' Theatre; Make Board Game; Share Tips on Boredom; Read More from *The Phantom Tollbooth* WRITING: Write Postcards; Write Letters of Advice • Language Arts Master 22
PART 3 **Selection Support** Pages 632–637			Practice • Teaching Charts 87–88 • Workbook 149–151 • Skills Practice 144–146 Test-Taking Figurative Language (Tested) Index (Tested) Maintain • Skills Practice 147 Characterization	**Curriculum Connections** SOCIAL STUDIES: The Doldrums • Curriculum Connection Master 22 ART: Literal Representations

Chart 3. *This Lesson Organizer for "Through the Tollbooth," from* The Phantom Tollbooth, *is from Unit 3 of* Dream Chasers *(grade 5). The yellow stripe highlights core instruction, and the following columns present story-related strategies and activities you can choose from to support and extend learning. The Teacher Choice symbol in the yellow triangle appears throughout the Teacher Edition to help you quickly identify key teaching options.*

Time Out For Books Planning Suggestions

| | 18 Weeks | | 36 Weeks |

0 ————————————————————————— 18 Weeks ————————————————————————— 36 Weeks

GRADE 1

| Early Reading Review 4 Weeks | Beginning Readers 3 Books, 4 Weeks Each | Primer Unit 1 4 Weeks | Primer Unit 2 4 Weeks | Reader Unit 1 4 Weeks | Reader Unit 2 4 Weeks |

GRADES 2 AND 3

| Unit 1 4 Weeks | Units 2 and 3 8 Weeks | Unit 4 4 Weeks | Unit 1 4 Weeks | Units 2 and 3 8 Weeks | Unit 4 4 Weeks |

GRADES 4 TO 8

| Unit 1 7 Weeks | Unit 2 7 Weeks | Unit 3 7 Weeks | Unit 4 7 Weeks |

☐ = 1 Week Time Out For Books   ▨ = 2 Weeks Time Out For Books

Chart 2. *These suggestions for incorporating titles from the* Time Out for Books *collection are among many possible patterns for combining trade-book reading with* **World of Reading.** *Periods indicated here for* Time Out for Books *are often generous enough to accommodate additional trade-book reading of titles from* World of Books Classroom Libraries *or the library. Naturally, the time allotments are only suggestions. They can easily vary according to the needs and interests of your students.*

If you prefer to devote even more time to concentrated trade-book reading, think about what sort of pattern fits your needs. Say you teach students in grades 4–8. Many variations are possible. If you want the class to read a few full-length novels together, you could schedule two weeks after each unit, or you could plan two periods during the year of three or four weeks each, or you could create a different plan. You might choose one of the ideas found in this Teacher Edition (Plan B) to focus students' reading of the *Time Out for Books* selection. Ideas are provided for whole class, small group, and individual reading. Or, you might opt to follow Plan C and develop a full literature unit based on the trade book, using the *Time Out for Books* Guide tucked in the front cover of this Teacher Edition. A rough rule of thumb in grades 4–8 is seven to nine weeks to complete each unit, depending on the number of activities you choose. That provides you with as many as eight weeks for trade books.

In grades 2 and 3, which have eight units, you might, for example, set aside one week after each unit for concentrated reading of trade books. First grade teachers may use Big and Little Shared Books throughout the school year. Also first grade teachers might set aside time at the middle and end of both the Primer and the Reader for exploring other trade books.

If you're looking for multiple copies of several trade-book titles for small-group reading, *World of Books Classroom Libraries* can be especially useful.

MEDIUM-RANGE PLANNING CHOICES

What are the options in planning the pacing of a unit?

Naturally, the number of strategies you plan with each *selection* will affect how long you spend on the unit. But you have *unit*-level choices as well.

Consider, for example, Unit 3, Imagine a Place, in the grade 5 Student Text, *Dream Chasers*. The unit includes several theme-related lessons. Among them: a Thinking/Reading/Writing Lesson on making an expectation chart; Literature Link lessons on keeping track of characters and events, recognizing suspense in stories, and discovering hidden meanings; and a process-writing activity about exploring Mars.

You might choose to involve your students in all of these activities during your reading period. Or you might pick and choose among them, depending on the needs and interests of your students. The I◆T Kit (Interactive Teaching Kit) and titles from *Time Out for Books* and *World of Books Classroom Libraries* give you more options. These are just a few choices that can influence how much time you'll take for the unit.

What is in the I◆T Kit?

The I◆T Kit provides highly motivational materials for a range of multi-sensory activities to introduce and support each unit theme. For Unit 3, grade 5, I◆T Kit materials include a video and an audiocassette. The Kit also includes Unit Cards with intriguing images that prompt students to think and write, and a fascinating poster that leads kids to map out imaginary journeys of their own. An Activity Guide contains explanations, suggestions, and background information. Both flexible and fun, I◆T Kit activities easily adapt to your teaching style and agenda.

SHORT-RANGE PLANNING CHOICES

My students need focused instruction in vocabulary and comprehension skills. What choices does **World of Reading** *offer?*

Each selection lesson offers many paths to acquiring vocabulary skills and comprehension strategies all tied directly to a high-quality piece of literature. You'll find that your choices can be easily made. (See Chart 3.)

One such path is a feature called the Bridge. We all recognize the value of preteaching key skills that enhance kids' construction of meaning while reading. The Bridge supports this preteaching by focusing on a specific skill—such as predicting outcomes—by using the previous selection and kids' prior knowledge to prepare for the upcoming story.

Each lesson includes three other key parts: Vocabulary Strategies, Reading and Responding, and Selection Support. (See Chart 3.)

Let's first consider vocabulary, a critical variable affecting comprehension. Because

WORLD OF READING SCOPE AND SEQUENCE

Level	K	ER/ERR	1	2	3	4	5	6, 7	8, 9	10	11	12	13	14
Grade	K	K/1	BR1	BR2	BR3	P	Reader	2	3	4	5	6	7	8
EARLY LITERACY														
Shared Reading Experiences	◇	◇	◇	◇	◇	◇	◇	◇						
Oral Language Development	◇	◇	◇	◇	◇	◇	◇	◇						
Print Awareness	◇	◇	◇											
Letter Formation/Invented Spelling/Labeling	◇	◇	◇	◇	◇	◇	◇							
Auditory Discrimination	◇	◇	◇	◇	◇	◇	◇	◇						
Visual Discrimination	◇	◇	◇	◇	◇	◇	◇	◇						
Letter/Sound Correspondence (See Phonics Strand Below for Additional Instruction)	◆	◆	◆	◆	◆	◆	◆	◆						
Concept Development	◆	◆	◆	◆	◆	◆	◆	◆						
LANGUAGE ARTS														
Language Study														
Rhyming Words, Question Words	◇	◇	◇	◇	◇	◇	◇	◇	◇	◇	◇	◇	◇	◇
Punctuation, Mechanics	◇	◇	◇	◇	◇	◇	◇	◇	◇	◇	◇	◇	◇	◇
Word Play/Study, Etymology	◇	◇	◇	◇	◇	◇	◇	◇	◇	◇	◇	◇	◇	◇
Listening														
Appreciative	◇	◇	◇	◇	◇	◇	◇	◇	◇	◇	◇	◇	◇	◇
Informational	◇	◇	◇	◇	◇	◇	◇	◇	◇	◇	◇	◇	◇	◇
Attentive	◇	◇	◇	◇	◇	◇	◇	◇	◇	◇	◇	◇	◇	◇
Critical						◇	◇	◇	◇	◇	◇	◇	◇	◇
Speaking														
Choral Speaking/Reading, Reciting	◇	◇	◇	◇	◇	◇	◇	◇	◇	◇	◇			
Retelling the Story	◇	◇	◇	◇	◇	◇	◇	◇	◇	◇	◇	◇	◇	◇
Dramatization	◇	◇	◇	◇	◇	◇	◇	◇	◇	◇	◇	◇	◇	◇
Group Discussion	◇	◇	◇	◇	◇	◇	◇	◇	◇	◇	◇	◇	◇	◇
Oral Presentation	◇	◇	◇	◇	◇	◇	◇	◇	◇	◇	◇	◇	◇	◇
Oral Rereading														
Fluency			◇	◇	◇	◇	◇	◇	◇	◇	◇	◇	◇	◇
Specific Information			◇	◇	◇	◇	◇	◇	◇	◇	◇	◇	◇	◇
Enjoyment			◇	◇	◇	◇	◇	◇	◇	◇	◇	◇	◇	◇
Expression			◇	◇	◇	◇	◇	◇	◇	◇	◇	◇	◇	◇
Writing														
Creative Writing	◈	◈	◈	◈	◈	◈	◈	◈	◈	◈	◈	◈	◈	◈
Expository Writing	◈	◈	◈	◈	◈	◈	◈	◈	◈	◈	◈	◈	◈	◈
Functional/Personal Writing	◈	◈	◈	◈	◈	◈	◈	◈	◈	◈	◈	◈	◈	◈
Writing Rhymes, Poetry	◈	◈												
Writing to Learn			◈	◈	◈	◈	◈	◈	◈	◈	◈	◈	◈	◈
Process Writing			◈	◈	◈	◈	◈	◈	◈	◈	◈	◈	◈	◈
LITERATURE														
Responding to Literature/Relating Literature to Real Life	◇	◇	◇	◇	◇	◇	◇	◇	◇	◇	◇	◇	◇	◇
Drawing/Illustrating	◈	◈	◈	◈	◈	◈	◈	◈	◈	◈	◈	◈	◈	◈
Readers Response			◈	◈	◈	◈	◈	◈	◈	◈	◈	◈	◈	◈
Writing to Learn			◈	◈	◈	◈	◈	◈	◈	◈	◈	◈	◈	◈
Language Arts Connections			◈	◈	◈	◈	◈	◈	◈	◈	◈	◈	◈	◈
Curriculum Connections			◈	◈	◈	◈	◈	◈	◈	◈	◈	◈	◈	◈
Independent Reading	◇	◇	◇	◇	◇	◇	◇	◇	◇	◇	◇	◇	◇	◇
Read Aloud/Think Aloud	◇	◇	◇	◇	◇	◇	◇	◇	◇	◇	◇	◇	◇	◇
Story Structure														
Characterization	◇	◇	◇	◇	◇	◇	◆	◆	◆	◆	◆	◆	◆	◆

◇ Introduction, Instruction, and Application   ◈ Informal Assessment Opportunity   ◆ Assessment

Silver Burdett & Ginn

WORLD OF READING COMPONENTS

Components	Level	K	ER	ERR	1	2	3	4	5	6,7	8,9	10	11	12	13	14
	Grade	K	K/1	1	1	1	1	1	1	2	3	4	5	6	7	8
Student Text		◆	◆	◆	◆	◆	◆	◆	◆	◆	◆	◆	◆	◆	◆	◆
Teacher Edition		◆	◆	◆	◆	◆	◆	◆	◆	◆	◆	◆	◆	◆	◆	◆
Workbook					◆	◆	◆	◆	◆	◆	◆	◆	◆	◆	◆	◆
Workbook Teacher Edition					◆	◆	◆	◆	◆	◆	◆	◆	◆	◆	◆	◆
Reader's Journal					◆	◆	◆	◆	◆	◆	◆	◆	◆	◆		
Reader's Journal Teacher Edition					◆	◆	◆	◆	◆	◆	◆	◆	◆	◆		
Hickory Dickory Village		◆														
Hickory Dickory Storytime		◆														
Big Shared Books/Little Shared Books		◆	◆	◆	◆	◆	◆	◆	◆	◆						
Shared Book Cassettes		◆	◆	◆	◆	◆	◆	◆	◆	◆						
Big Books		◆	◆	◆	◆	◆	◆									
Time Out for Books Collection and Teacher Guide					◆	◆	◆	◆	◆		◆	◆	◆	◆	◆	◆
Natural Language Story Books					◆	◆	◆	◆								
Teacher Resource Kit					◆	◆	◆	◆	◆	◆	◆	◆	◆	◆	◆	◆
◆ Meeting Individual Needs:					◆	◆	◆	◆	◆	◆	◆	◆	◆	◆	◆	◆
–Reteaching					◆	◆	◆	◆	◆	◆	◆	◆	◆	◆	◆	◆
–Challenge					◆	◆	◆	◆	◆	◆	◆	◆	◆	◆	◆	◆
–Extra Help					◆	◆	◆	◆	◆	◆	◆	◆	◆	◆	◆	◆
–Achieving English Proficiency					◆	◆	◆	◆	◆	◆	◆	◆	◆	◆	◆	◆
–Checkpoints					◆	◆	◆	◆	◆	◆	◆	◆	◆	◆	◆	◆
–Informal Reading Inventory						◆	◆	◆	◆	◆	◆	◆	◆	◆	◆	◆
–Informal Assessment Checklists					◆	◆	◆	◆	◆	◆	◆	◆	◆	◆	◆	◆
◆ Integrated Curriculum:					◆	◆	◆	◆	◆	◆	◆	◆	◆	◆	◆	◆
–Language Arts Connections					◆	◆	◆	◆	◆							
–Writing								◆	◆	◆	◆	◆	◆	◆	◆	◆
–Curriculum Connections					◆	◆	◆	◆	◆	◆	◆	◆	◆	◆	◆	◆
◆ Listening Lesson Cassettes					◆	◆	◆	◆	◆	◆	◆	◆	◆	◆	◆	◆
◆ Teaching Posters with Activities					◆	◆	◆	◆	◆	◆	◆	◆	◆	◆	◆	◆
◆ Skills Practice					◆	◆	◆	◆	◆	◆	◆	◆	◆	◆	◆	◆
◆ Teaching Chart Masters					◆	◆	◆	◆	◆	◆	◆	◆	◆	◆	◆	◆
◆ Home Connection Letters					◆	◆	◆	◆	◆	◆	◆	◆	◆	◆	◆	◆
◆ Phonics Review					◆	◆	◆	◆	◆	◆						
Teaching Charts					◆	◆	◆	◆	◆	◆	◆	◆		◆		
Teaching Chart Transparencies												◆	◆		◆	◆
Idea Factory for Teachers		◆			◆	◆	◆	◆	◆	◆	◆	◆	◆	◆	◆	◆
Activity Cards		◆														
Word Cards					◆	◆	◆	◆	◆							
Assessment:																
◆ Reading Assessment Portfolio					◆	◆	◆		◆	◆	◆	◆	◆	◆	◆	◆
◆ Kindergarten ER, and ERR		◆	◆	◆												
◆ Placement Test						◆	◆	◆	◆	◆	◆	◆	◆	◆	◆	◆
◆ Unit Process Tests								◆	◆	◆	◆	◆	◆	◆	◆	◆
◆ Unit Skills Tests (Forms A & B)					◆	◆	◆			◆	◆	◆	◆	◆	◆	◆
◆ Mid-Book Tests												◆	◆	◆	◆	◆
◆ End-of-Book Tests					◆	◆	◆	◆	◆	◆	◆	◆	◆	◆	◆	◆
◆ Reading Progress Card		◆	◆	◆	◆	◆	◆	◆	◆	◆	◆	◆	◆	◆	◆	◆
◆ Computer Management Systems (Apple & IBM)					◆	◆	◆	◆	◆	◆	◆	◆	◆	◆	◆	◆
Strategies for Thinking					◆	◆	◆	◆	◆	◆	◆	◆	◆	◆	◆	◆
Spelling Connection						◆	◆	◆	◆	◆	◆	◆	◆	◆	◆	◆
Listening Program						◆	◆	◆	◆	◆	◆	◆	◆	◆	◆	◆
I•T Kits (Interactive Teaching Kits)					◆	◆	◆	◆	◆	◆	◆	◆	◆	◆	◆	◆
World of Reading Videos						◆	◆	◆	◆	◆	◆	◆	◆	◆	◆	◆
World of Books Classroom Libraries		◆	◆		◆	◆	◆	◆	◆	◆	◆	◆	◆	◆	◆	◆
World of Books Starter Libraries		◆	◆		◆	◆	◆	◆	◆	◆	◆	◆	◆	◆	◆	◆
Reading Skillsware											◆	◆	◆	◆	◆	◆

Silver Burdett & Ginn

Level	K	ER/ERR	1	2	3	4	5	6,7	8,9	10	11	12	13	14
Grade	K	K/1	BR1	BR2	BR3	P	Reader	2	3	4	5	6	7	8
Recall, Analyze, Infer, Synthesize, Evaluate	◈	◈	◈	◈	◈	◈	◈	◈	◈	◈	◈	◈	◈	◈
Metacognition														
Visualizing	◈		◈	◈	◈	◈	◈	◈	◈	◈	◈	◈	◈	◈
Summarizing and Predicting			◈	◈	◈	◈	◈	◈	◈	◈	◈	◈	◈	◈
Self-Monitoring, Self-Questioning				◈	◈	◈	◈	◈	◈	◈	◈	◈	◈	◈
Empathizing				◈	◈	◈	◈	◈	◈	◈	◈	◈	◈	◈
Rating Understanding									◈	◈	◈	◈	◈	◈
PHONICS, STRUCTURAL ANALYSIS, AND CONTEXT CLUES														
Phonics														
Consonants (Initial and Final)	◇	◇	◆	◆	◇	◆	◇	◆						
Phonemic Bases (Phonograms)		◆	◇	◇	◇									
Short Vowels, Long Vowels		◇	◆	◆	◆	◆	◆	◆	◇					
Consonant Clusters, Digraphs (Initial and Final)					◆	◆	◆	◆	◇					
Vowel Digraphs, Variant Vowels						◆	◆	◆	◇					
Structural Analysis														
Inflections (With Nouns, With Verbs, Possessives), Spelling Changes		◇	◆	◆	◆	◆	◆	◆	◇	◇				
Contractions						◆	◆	◇						
Compound Words, Long Word Decoding Strategies						◇	◆	◇	◆	◇				
Suffixes, Prefixes, Roots, Combining Forms							◇	◆	◆	◆	◆	◆	◆	◆
Context Clues	◇	◇	◇	◇	◇	◇	◇	◇	◆	◆	◆	◆	◆	◆
VOCABULARY														
Word Meaning/Selection Vocabulary	◇	◈	◈	◈	◈	◈	◈	◈	◈	◈	◈	◈	◈	◈
Classification	◆	◇	◇	◇	◇	◈	◈	◈	◈	◈	◈	◈	◈	◈
Synonyms/Antonyms	◇	◇	◇	◇	◇	◇	◈	◈	◆	◆	◆	◆	◇	◇
Semantic Mapping/Semantic Feature Analysis	◇	◇	◇	◇	◇	◇	◇	◇	◇	◇	◇	◇	◇	◇
Multiple Meanings, Homographs				◇	◇		◇	◇	◇	◈	◈	◈	◈	◈
Analogies					◇	◇	◇	◇	◇	◆	◆	◆	◆	◆
Homophones						◆	◆	◇	◇	◇	◇	◇	◇	◇
Connotation/Denotation									◇	◇	◈	◈	◈	◆
STUDY STRATEGIES														
Learning from Text														
Following Directions	◇	◇	◇	◇	◇	◇	◇	◇	◆	◇	◇	◇	◇	◇
Book Parts	◇	◇	◇	◇	◇	◇	◇	◇	◆	◇	◇	◇	◇	◇
Content Area Activities/Reading	◇	◇	◇	◇	◇	◇	◇	◇	◇	◇	◇	◇	◇	◇
Labels, Titles, Headings, Captions	◇	◇	◇	◇	◇	◇	◇	◇	◇	◇	◇	◇	◇	◇
Advertisements						◇		◇	◇	◇	◇	◇	◆	◆
Test-Taking									◇	◇	◇	◇	◇	◇
Note-Taking, Outlining, Skimming/Scanning, Reading Rate									◇	◇	◇	◇	◆	◇
Index									◇	◆	◇	◇	◇	◇
Learning from Graphic Organizers														
Maps, Diagrams, Symbols, Signs	◇	◇	◇	◇	◇	◇	◇	◇	◆	◇	◇	◆	◇	◆
Charts, Tables, Schedules, Forms	◇	◇	◇	◇	◇	◇	◇	◇	◇	◆	◆	◇	◇	◇
Graphs	◇	◇	◇	◇	◇	◇	◇	◇	◆	◇	◇	◆	◇	◇
Time Lines									◇	◇	◇	◇	◇	◇
Using Resources														
Dictionary, Glossary, Thesaurus		◇	◇	◇	◇	◇	◇	◇	◆	◆	◆	◆	◇	◇
Alphabetical Order				◇	◇	◆	◇	◆	◇	◇				
Encyclopedia, Atlas								◇	◇	◆	◆	◆	◇	◇
Newspaper, Telephone Directory									◇	◇	◇	◇	◇	◇
Choosing Among Resources									◇	◇	◇	◆	◆	◆
Card Catalog									◇	◆	◇	◇	◇	◇
Reader's Guide												◇	◇	◆

◇ Introduction, Instruction, and Application ◈ Informal Assessment Opportunity ◆ Assessment

Silver Burdett & Ginn

Level	K	ER/ERR	1	2	3	4	5	6,7	8,9	10	11	12	13	14
Grade	K	K/1	BR1	BR2	BR3	P	Reader	2	3	4	5	6	7	8
Story Elements	◇	◇	◇	◇	◇	◇	◇	◇	◆	◆	◆	◆	◆	◆
Genre														
Fantasy	◇	◇	◇	◇	◇	◇	◇	◇	◇	◇	◇	◇	◇	◇
Poetry	◇	◇	◇	◇	◇	◇	◇	◇	◇	◇	◇	◇	◇	◇
Nonfiction/Article	◇	◇	◇	◇	◇	◇	◇	◇	◇	◇	◇	◇	◇	◇
Folklore (Folktale, Fable, Fairy Tale, Myth, Tall Tale, Legend, Folk Song)	◇	◇	◇	◇	◇	◇	◇	◇	◇	◇	◇	◇	◇	◇
Song	◇	◇	◇	◇	◇	◇	◇	◇	◇	◇	◇	◇	◇	◇
Realistic Fiction	◇	◇	◇	◇	◇	◇	◇	◇	◇	◇	◇	◇	◇	◇
Interview						◇	◇	◇	◇	◇	◇	◇	◇	◇
Play						◇		◇	◇	◇	◇	◇	◇	◇
Newspaper						◇	◇	◇	◇	◇	◇	◇	◇	◇
Journal, Diary								◇	◇	◇	◇	◇	◇	◇
Cartoons/Limerick/Parody								◇	◇	◇	◇	◇	◇	◇
Biography, Autobiography								◇	◇	◇	◇	◇	◇	◇
Historical Fiction								◇	◇	◇	◇	◇	◇	◇
Speech								◇	◇	◇	◇	◇	◇	◇
Science Fiction										◇	◇	◇	◇	◇
Short Story												◇	◇	◇
Essay												◇	◇	◇
Novella												◇	◇	◇
Author's Craft														
Reality/Fantasy	◇	◇	◇	◇	◇	◆	◇	◆	◇	◇	◇	◇	◇	◇
Repetition, Rhythm, Rhyme	◇	◇	◇	◇	◇	◇	◇	◇	◇	◇	◇	◇	◇	◇
Description	◇	◇	◇	◇	◇	◇	◇	◇	◇	◇	◇	◇	◇	◇
Exaggeration, Humor, Pun	◇	◇	◇	◇	◇	◇	◇	◇	◇	◇	◇	◇	◇	◇
Dialogue		◇	◇	◇	◇	◇	◇	◇	◇	◇	◇	◇	◇	◇
Narrative Point of View				◇	◇	◇	◇	◇	◇	◇	◇	◇	◇	◇
Figurative Language						◇	◇	◆	◆	◆	◆	◆	◆	◆
Mood, Tone							◇	◇	◇	◇	◇	◇	◇	◇
Alliteration, Onomatopoeia								◇	◇	◇	◇	◇	◇	◇
Formal/Informal Language								◇	◇	◇	◇	◇	◇	◇
Flashback, Foreshadowing								◇	◇	◇	◇	◇	◇	◇
Symbolism												◇	◇	◇
Irony													◇	◇
COMPREHENSION														
Getting Information From Text														
Picture Details	◆	◆	◇	◇	◇	◇	◇	◇	◇					
Sequence	◆	◆	◆	◇	◇	◆	◇	◆	◆	◆	◆	◆	◇	◇
Main Idea/Details	◇	◇	◇	◇	◆	◇	◆	◆	◆	◆	◆	◆	◆	◆
Word Referents							◇	◆	◆	◆	◇	◆	◇	◆
Constructing and Organizing Meaning														
Retelling the Story	◇	◇	◇	◇	◇	◇	◇	◇	◇	◇	◇	◇	◇	◇
Comparison	◇	◇	◇	◇	◇	◇	◇	◆	◆	◆	◆	◆	◆	◆
Drawing Conclusions	◆	◆	◇	◇	◇	◇	◇	◆	◆	◆	◆	◆	◆	◆
Predicting Outcomes	◇	◆	◇	◇	◇	◆	◇	◆	◆	◇	◇	◆	◆	◆
Cause/Effect	◆	◇	◇	◆	◇	◇	◆	◆	◆	◆	◆	◆	◆	◆
Story Mapping	◇	◇	◇	◇	◇	◇	◇	◇	◇	◇	◇	◇	◇	◇
Inference	◇	◇	◇	◇	◇	◇	◇	◆	◆	◆	◆	◆	◆	◆
Summarizing	◇	◇	◇	◇	◇	◇	◇	◇	◇	◇	◇	◇	◆	◆
Paraphrasing	◇	◇	◇	◇	◇	◇	◇	◇	◇	◇	◇	◇	◇	◇
Evaluating Text														
Evaluating			◉	◉	◉	◉	◉	◉	◉	◉	◉	◉	◉	◉
Generalizing			◉	◉	◉	◉	◉	◉	◉	◉	◉	◉	◆	◆
Fact/Opinion									◇	◆	◆	◆	◆	◆
Author's Purpose									◇	◇	◆	◇	◆	◇
Author's Viewpoint/Bias										◇	◇	◇	◆	◆
THINKING STRATEGIES														
Building Background, Prior Knowledge	◇	◇	◇	◇	◇	◇	◇	◇	◇	◇	◇	◇	◇	◇
Setting Purpose	◇	◇	◇	◇	◇	◇	◇	◇	◇	◇	◇	◇	◇	◇

WORLD
OF
READING

TEACHER EDITION

CASTLES OF SAND

P. David Pearson   Dale D. Johnson

Theodore Clymer   Roselmina Indrisano   Richard L. Venezky

James F. Baumann   Elfrieda Hiebert   Marian Toth

Consulting Authors

Carl Grant   Jeanne Paratore

SILVER BURDETT & GINN

NEEDHAM, MA · MORRISTOWN, NJ
ATLANTA, GA · CINCINNATI, OH · DALLAS, TX
MENLO PARK, CA · DEERFIELD, IL

CONTENTS

CONTENTS

UNIT
THREE

Previewing the Student Text

Allow time to browse through the Student Text.

Distribute *Castles of Sand* and ask students to look through their new books. You might have pairs of students explore the books together, looking for authors or stories they know, illustrations that appeal to them, or special features they think might be interesting. Allow time for students to share their reactions to the book and to point out to their classmates what they have discovered about *Castles of Sand.*

Discussing Parts of the Book

Discuss the title page.

Tell students that the title of their new book appears both on the cover and inside. Have them turn to the title page and read the book's title, *Castles of Sand.* Point out that the title page also lists the authors of the book and the company that produced it, Silver Burdett & Ginn.

Use the table of contents to discuss the selections.

Most students will be familiar with the function of the table of contents. Have them turn to those pages. Point out that the book is divided into four units, each about a different topic or theme. Ask volunteers to find and read the name of each unit. Continue by explaining that each unit contains stories, nonfiction articles, poems, and skill pages. Have students name some of the selections in each category.

Discuss the end-of-book features.

Finally, point out that the back of the book has special information for readers—a glossary where difficult words are defined; a biographical section that gives information about some of the authors of the stories and articles; and a listing of authors. Ask students why they think these pages were included. How might they as readers use the pages as they read the selections in *Castles of Sand?*

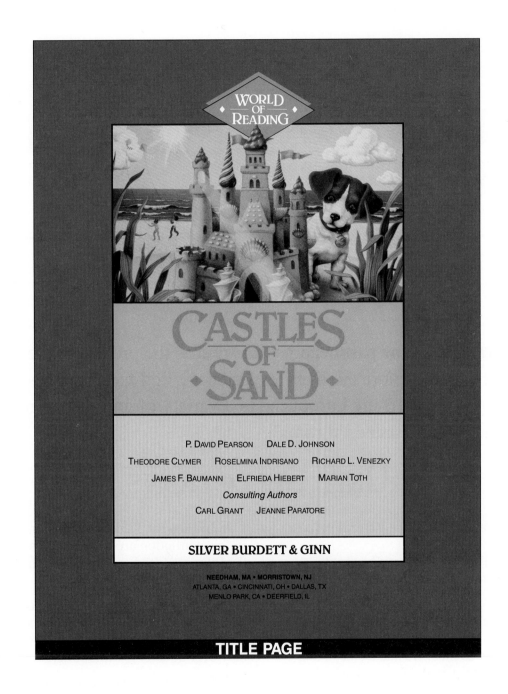

WORLD OF READING

CASTLES OF SAND

P. David Pearson   Dale D. Johnson

Theodore Clymer   Roselmina Indrisano   Richard L. Venezky

James F. Baumann   Elfrieda Hiebert   Marian Toth

Consulting Authors

Carl Grant   Jeanne Paratore

SILVER BURDETT & GINN

NEEDHAM, MA • MORRISTOWN, NJ
ATLANTA, GA • CINCINNATI, OH • DALLAS, TX
MENLO PARK, CA • DEERFIELD, IL

TITLE PAGE

UNIT
ONE
OVERVIEW

REMEMBER WHEN...

UNIT THEME   The past becomes as vivid as the present in these stories, which explore the lives, experiences, and feelings of people in the past. Readers are introduced to a variety of groups that include Quakers, pioneers, and Pilgrims.

UNIT SELECTIONS

Paul Bunyan Digs the St. Lawrence River, *by Dell J. McCormick*
For a million dollars, Paul Bunyan says he can dig a river between the United States and Canada. A read aloud/think aloud selection.

When I Was Nine, *by James Stevenson*
A well-known author/illustrator tells about a happy time in his life, the year he was nine. He had a bike, a dog named Jocko, a cowboy hat, and a family that had fun together. An **American Library Association Notable Book.**

Thy Friend, Obadiah, *by Brinton Turkle*
Obadiah, a young Quaker boy, becomes friends with a sea gull that follows him wherever he goes. A **Caldecott Honor** book.

Life In Pilgrim Times, *by Carlotta Dunn*
In this nonfiction article, readers learn of the hardships the Pilgrims faced and how they survived with the help of two English-speaking Indians.

Grandaddy's Place, *by Helen V. Griffith*
At first, Janetta is unhappy at Grandaddy's old house and afraid of the animals there. Soon she wonders how they ever got along without her.

The White Stallion, *by Elizabeth Shub*
A young girl is separated from her family's wagon train, but is protected by a wild stallion. An **American Library Association** award winner.

Mr. Peaceable Paints, *by Leonard Weisgard*
In this Reading Corner selection, Mr. Peaceable and Mr. Lion make a unique contribution to the town. Winner of the Silver Burdett & Ginn **Readers' Choice** award.

Title	Skills/Strategies	Integrated Language Arts	Cross-Curriculum
Listening Lesson: Paul Bunyan Digs the St. Lawrence River Pages 8–13	Story Mapping	**Active Listening**	
When I Was Nine Pages 14–35	★ Story Elements ★ Suffix: -ly	**Speaking:** Play Scenes **Writing:** Newspaper; Setting; Autobiography	**Social Studies:** Journals **Science:** Events in the Sky **Art:** Pictures by Western Artists
General Store (poem) Pages 36–37		**Listening:** Details Create Mood **Writing:** Description	
Thinking•Reading•Writing: Making a Comparison Chart Pages 38–39			
Thy Friend, Obadiah Pages 40–63	Characterization ★ Suffixes: -er, -or	**Speaking:** Historical Fiction **Writing:** Class Poster; Nursery Rhymes; Story Scene	**Art:** Dioramas **Social Studies:** Quakerism; Mills **Science:** Sea Gulls **Geography:** Relief Map of Nantucket
Life in Pilgrim Times Pages 64–87	★ Main Idea/Details Homographs	**Speaking:** Story Scene **Writing:** Nonfiction; Journal Entries; Pilgrim Histories; Sentences; Word Origins	**Social Studies:** Hornbooks **Art:** Dioramas **Geography:** Mapping
Understanding Maps: Reading Social Studies Pages 88–93			
Checkpoint INFORMAL ASSESSMENT Pages 94–95			
Grandaddy's Place Pages 96–119	Drawing Conclusions Forms	**Speaking:** Improvisation; Onomatopoeic Words **Writing:** Turning Point; A Tall Tale	**Science:** Owls and Animal Behavior; Stars or Constellations **Music:** Songs About Country Life
Over the River and Through the Wood (poem) Pages 120–121		**Listening:** Mood in Poetry **Speaking:** Reading Poems	
The White Stallion Pages 122–143	Sequence	**Speaking:** Dialogue; Interviews **Writing:** Historical Fiction; Story Rewrite	**Social Studies:** Westward Movement in America **Music:** Folk Songs of the Old West **Science:** Horse Charts; Plants and Animals of Guadalupe River Area, Texas **Geography:** Wagon Train Routes
Time Out for Books: *The Nightingale* Pages 144–145			
Reading Corner: Mr. Peaceable Paints Pages 146–150		**Writing:** Colonial Glossary	
Checkpoint INFORMAL ASSESSMENT Pages 152–153			

★ Tested skill in this unit

Reading Every Day

CREATE A CLASSROOM LIBRARY

The following books and magazines are referenced throughout the unit. You might gather them ahead of time to place in your classroom library.

Benchley, Nathaniel. **George, the Drummer Boy!**

Brenner, Barbara. **Wagon Wheels.**

Bulla, Clyde Robert. **A Grain of Wheat.**

Dalgliesh, Alice. **The Bears on Hemlock Mountain.**

Farley, Walter. **The Black Stallion.**

Fritz, Jean. **And Then What Happened, Paul Revere?**

Gleiter, Jan and Kathleen Thompson. **Paul Revere.**

Goble, Paul. **The Girl Who Loved Wild Horses.**

Hiser, Berniece T. **Charlie and His Wheat-Straw Hat.**

MacLachlan, Patricia. **Through Grandpa's Eyes.** 〰️

Sandin, Joan. **The Long Way to a New Land.** 〰️

Smith, E. Boyd. **The Farm Book.**

Sonberg, Lynn. **A Horse Named Paris.**

Stevenson, James. **Howard.**

————. **Will You Please Feed Our Cat?**

Streich, Corinne. **Grandparents' Houses.**

Szekers, Cyndy. **Long Ago.**

Turkle, Brinton. **Obadiah, the Bold.**

Weisgard, Leonard. **The Plymouth Thanksgiving.**

WORLD OF BOOKS Classroom Libraries

World of Books Classroom Libraries offer a wide selection of books that may be used for independent reading with this unit.

UNIT PROJECT CARDS **Project Cards 1–4,** in the *Idea Factory for Teachers,* give instructions for projects that can be done individually, in small groups or as cooperative learning projects. Projects include making a hornbook, making a covered wagon, and writing a story.

HOME CONNECTION LETTERS The Teacher Resource Kit includes letters, written in English and in Spanish, that explain what students have learned during this unit and suggest bibliographies and activities that support instruction.

The books listed on the "Reading Every Day" card in each lesson's Language Arts Connection may also be copied and sent home to encourage family involvement in independent reading.

BULLETIN BOARDS

Use the suggestions in the *Idea Factory for Teachers* to construct the unit bulletin boards.

Interactive Teaching Kit

The *Castles of Sand* I·T Kit offers materials and activities to motivate and enrich your students' reading experience. You may choose to use some or all of the unit activities to introduce Unit 1, "Remember When . . ." Later in the unit, you may choose to use some or all of the story-related activities. You will find complete teaching instructions in the I·T Kit Activity Guide.

The I·T Kit provides a menu of activities to introduce the unit theme.

VIDEO ◆ REMEMBER WHEN

What events from the past are worth remembering? The following video segments bring to life the unit theme, Remember When . . .

◆ Learn about life in Pilgrim times during a visit to Plimoth Plantation, a living history museum in Plymouth, Massachusetts.

◆ A docudrama introduces children to author Lydia Maria Child, who is remembered today through her popular poem, "Over the River and Through the Wood." Then enjoy several Currier and Ives prints and sing along to the musical version of the poem. (See Activity Guide.)   LITERATURE, CONTENT AREAS, CONTEMPORARY MUSIC

AUDIO ◆ "THIS LAND IS YOUR LAND"

From the rocky coast of Maine to the deserts of southern California stretches a land that has been the setting of many people's stories. Woody Guthrie's folk song paints a panorama of the American landscape in broad, joyous strokes. Students join in singing a tribute to the land Guthrie loved. (See Activity Guide.) CONTENT AREAS

UNIT CARDS ◆ THE GOOD OLD DAYS

Remember when children of all ages studied together in a one-room schoolhouse and when kids played marbles after school? Paintings such as William Bromley's *Playing at Marbles* allow the children to compare and contrast their world with the good old days. (See Activity Guide.)   CONTENT AREAS

POSTER ◆ "STOPPING BY WOODS ON A SNOWY EVENING"

The snowfall muffles the sounds of hooves and sleigh bells as a horse trots through the woods on a winter's day. As students read Robert Frost's classic poem, they will feel as though they are riding along in the old-fashioned sleigh. (See Activity Guide.) LITERATURE

The I·T Kit provides activities that may be used following these reading selections:

"When I Was Nine" (See TE page 27 and Activity Guide.)

"Life in Pilgrim Times" (See TE page 76 and Activity Guide.)

"Grandaddy's Place" (See TE page 111 and Activity Guide.)

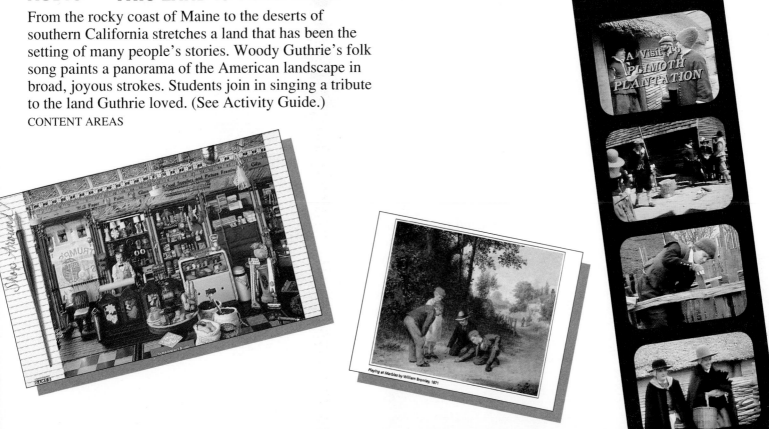

Playing at Marbles by William Bromley, 1871

Beginning the Unit

Appreciating Art

Provide background about the work of art.

Have students look at the painting by Winslow Homer on page 12 of the Student Text. A poster version of this illustration, found in the Teacher Resource Kit, may be displayed for the discussion. Explain that Homer (1836–1920) is one of the most famous American artists. He apprenticed as a lithographer, but became an illustrator for magazines. He is noted for the realistic style of his paintings of farm and country life and of the ocean.

Have students view the work of art and discuss the unit theme.

Ask students what details let them know that this picture is of an event that took place long ago. Point out the artist's use of light to create a mood, and ask students what mood they sense. Ask students whether they would like to be in the picture and how it makes them feel about the past. You may wish to encourage discussion of the use of realistic detail to make the viewer feel the grass can be touched and the heat of the sun felt. Have a student read aloud the question on page 13. Explain that the question is to encourage them to think about the past and why knowing about the past is valuable. Have students preview the unit, and encourage them to discuss any selection they feel will be particularly interesting or any by their favorite author(s).

Point out Time Out for Books.

Call attention to the feature on pages 82–83. Some students may wish to begin reading the book on their own. Additional suggestions for when and how this book might be used are provided in the *Time Out for Books Guide*.

Connecting the Known to the New

Encourage independent reading with the Interest Inventory and the Book Log.

Workbook page 5 is a questionnaire that asks students to identify unit-related topics that they might be interested in reading about. Workbook page 6 provides space for listing suggested titles from the Interest Inventory, as well as other titles students may wish to read. Workbook pages 163–176 provide space for students to record their personal responses to books.

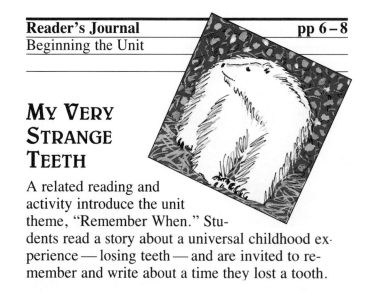

Reader's Journal   pp 6–8
Beginning the Unit

MY VERY STRANGE TEETH

A related reading and activity introduce the unit theme, "Remember When." Students read a story about a universal childhood experience — losing teeth — and are invited to remember and write about a time they lost a tooth.

UNIT ONE

REMEMBER WHEN...

*R*eading can help us learn about the past.

What events from the past are worth remembering?

detail of SNAP THE WHIP,
*oil on canvas by Winslow Homer,
American, 1872*

Workbook page 5

Workbook page 6

RESOURCE CENTER

UNIT ONE

Interest Inventory

Daily life in America's past was different from today in many ways. What part of that past interests you? Answer the questions below and use the chart to discover books that you may enjoy.

yes no
1. ▦ ▦ Would you like to read about the American Revolution?
2. ▦ ▦ Would you enjoy finding out about pioneer days?
3. ▦ ▦ Do you enjoy true stories about the past?
4. ▦ ▦ Does riding in a wagon sound like fun?
5. ▦ ▦ Do you enjoy stories about children from long ago?
6. ▦ ▦ Have you ever helped someone who was in trouble?
7. ▦ ▦ Would you like to read about living long ago?

Now find the numbers for the questions you checked YES. Follow the column down. When you see a star, move across the row to find the title. That's the book for you!

1	2	3	4	5	6	7	Title/Author
★		★			★		*Paul Revere* by Jan Gleiter and Kathleen Thompson
★		★		★		★	*George, the Drummer Boy* by Nathaniel Benchley
			★	★	★	★	*The Drinking Gourd* by F. N. Monjo
	★	★					*Johnny Appleseed* by Louis Sabin
	★	★	★		★		*The Long Way to a New Land* by Joan Sandin
★	★	★					*Long Ago* by Cyndy Szekers
			★	★	★		*The Adventure of Charlie & His Wheat-Straw Hat* recounted by Berniece T. Hiser

5

▶ **Workbook page 5** is a questionnaire that helps students identify topics and books of interest.

Workbook page 6 is a personal list of books students might read independently. ▶

UNIT ONE

Personal Book List

NAME _____

Title _____
Author _____

Title _____
Author _____

Title _____
Author _____

Title _____
Author _____

6

Listening Lesson

Each unit in Castles of Sand *opens with a Listening Lesson. These lessons introduce students to unit themes and foster a sense of enjoyment in literature. At the same time, they encourage the habit of listening and responding and establish a common background for all students.*

SELECTION SUMMARY

In this classic tall tale, Paul Bunyan demonstrates his physical prowess by digging the St. Lawrence River and creating both the Thousand Islands and the Green Mountains. He also shows his resourcefulness as he outwits Billy Pilgrim, who has bet Paul that he cannot dig the river in three weeks and then attempts to thwart him when Paul's victory becomes apparent. Students should enjoy this classic American tall tale with its exaggeration, simple conflict between good and "evil," and explanation of natural phenomena.

STRATEGIES FOR LISTENING

Explain the process of listening for enjoyment.

You may decide to read the selection aloud twice. During a first reading, students should relax and enjoy the selection. They should not worry if they do not understand the piece fully. Explain that when they listen to the selection they should try to picture what the characters look like, where they are, and what they are doing. Making pictures in their minds will help them follow the selection better and enjoy it more. Picturing the selection also will help them remember it and be able to share it with others. As an alternative to reading the selection aloud, you may choose to play the audio cassette that is available.

Set the purpose for a read aloud/think aloud.

When you finish the first reading, you may read the selection a second time. This time you will share your feelings and ideas about the characters, events, and places in the selection by thinking aloud. The annotations adjacent to the selection may serve as prompts for modeling your thinking. You may want to substitute your own or provide additional ones. Tell students that good readers always think as they read. Encourage them to be active thinkers during their own reading.

DISCUSSING THE SELECTION

Present discussion questions.

1. **When people read or hear "Paul Bunyan Digs the St. Lawrence River," they usually develop pictures in their minds of the two main characters, Paul and Billy. Were you able to picture these two characters? What did they look like?** (Students may share contrasting images of Paul and Billy, the biggest men along the Canadian-American border.)

2. **What did you think when you heard that Billy Pilgrim was digging a river and that Paul Bunyan said he could do it in only three weeks?** (Students might respond that they did not know anyone could dig a river, let alone dig one so quickly.)

3. **Paul Bunyan is an American folk *hero*. Besides digging the St. Lawrence River, what does Paul do that makes him a hero?** (He thinks of clever ways to do things; he is huge and strong; he outsmarts people who try to cheat him; he creates the Thousand Islands and the Green Mountains.)

Paul Bunyan Digs the St. Lawrence River[1]

By Dell J. McCormick

One summer Paul Bunyan decided to leave the North Woods and go back to Maine, where he was born, to visit his father and mother. When he arrived, they talked about old times, and Paul asked about Billy Pilgrim, the biggest man in that part of the country.

"What is this Billy Pilgrim doing?" asked Paul.

"He is digging the St. Lawrence River between the United States and Canada," said Paul's father. "There was nothing to separate the two countries. People never knew when they were in the United States and when they were in Canada."

Paul Bunyan went to see Billy. He found that Billy Pilgrim and his men had been digging for three years and had dug only a very small ditch. Paul laughed when he saw it.

"My men could dig the St. Lawrence River in three weeks," said Paul.

This made Billy angry for he thought no one could dig a large river in three weeks.

"I will give you a million dollars if you can dig the St. Lawrence River in three weeks!" said Billy Pilgrim. [2]

So Paul sent for Babe the Blue Ox, Ole the Big Swede, Brimstone Bill, and all his woodsmen.

1. Another tall tale about Paul Bunyan. I wonder if it will have Babe the Blue Ox and Paul's friend Ole. Tall tales are such fun to read because of the fantastic things the heroes do.

2. How could anyone be foolish enough to bet against Paul Bunyan? Billy must never have heard of Paul's reputation for being able to do anything. I cannot imagine how Paul will dig the river, but I know one way or another he will.

Paul told Ole to make a huge scoop shovel as large as a house. They fastened it to Babe with a long buckskin rope. He hauled many tons of dirt every day and emptied the scoop shovel in Vermont. You can see the large piles of dirt there to this day. They are called the Green Mountains.

Every night Johnnie Inkslinger, who did the arithmetic, would take his large pencil and mark one day off the calendar on the wall.

Billy Pilgrim was afraid they would finish digging the river on time. He did not want to pay Paul Bunyan the million dollars, for at heart he was a miser. So he thought of a plan to prevent Paul from finishing the work.

One night Billy called his men together and said, "When everybody has gone to bed we will go out and pour water on the buckskin rope so it will stretch, and Babe the Blue Ox will not be able to pull a single shovelful of dirt!"**3**

The next day, Babe started toward Vermont with the first load of dirt. When he arrived there, he looked around and the huge scoop shovel was nowhere to be seen. For miles and miles the buckskin rope had stretched through the forests and over the hills.

Babe didn't know what to do. He sat down and tried to think, but everyone knows an ox isn't very bright; so he just sat there.**4** After a while the sun came out and dried the buckskin and it started to shrink to normal size.

Babe planted his large hoofs between two mountains and waited. The buckskin rope kept shrinking and shrinking. Soon the scoop shovel came into view over the hills. Then Babe emptied it and started back after another load.

3. I never knew that leather stretched when it was wet. This is a very sneaky trick for Billy to play, but I am sure it will not work.

4. I can just picture Babe, this huge blue ox bigger than two mountains, sitting down to think. What a sight that would be.

In exactly three weeks the St. Lawrence River was all finished, but still Billy Pilgrim did not want to pay Paul the money.

"Very well," said Paul, "I will remove the water!" So he led Babe the Blue Ox down to the river, and Babe drank the St. Lawrence River dry.

Billy Pilgrim only chuckled to himself for he knew that the first rain would fill it again. Soon it began to rain, and the river became as large as ever.

So Paul picked up a large shovel.

"If you do not pay the money you owe me I will fill the river up again," said Paul. 5

He threw in a shovelful of dirt. He threw in another and another, but still Billy Pilgrim would not pay him the money.

"I will pay you half your money," said Billy.

Paul again picked up his shovel and tossed more dirt into the river.

"I will pay you two thirds of your money," said Billy.

Paul kept throwing more dirt into the river until he had thrown a thousand shovelfuls.

"Stop! I will pay you all your money!" cried Billy.

So Paul Bunyan was finally paid in full for digging the St. Lawrence River. The thousand shovelfuls of dirt are still there.

They are called the Thousand Islands. 6

5. I can hear Paul's voice so clearly, booming out at Billy as he said this. His voice must have been louder than the loudest thunder.

6. What a great story! I knew Paul would win. If I ever go to the Thousand Islands or see the St. Lawrence River or the Green Mountains, I will certainly think of Paul Bunyan and his bet. I am sure it will make seeing them more exciting.

Selection Support

COMPREHENSION

Story Mapping

OBJECTIVE   Using a story map to understand story structure.

1. WARM-UP

Explain the purpose of story mapping.

Tell students that when they follow a story from beginning to end, they are able to tell the important parts of the story in the correct order. Explain that using a story map will help them to organize these important parts of the story. Using a story map will help them to understand and remember a story better.

2. TEACH

Relate story mapping to the listening selection.

Tell students that they are going to make a story map of the story they listened to about Paul Bunyan.

Use the Teaching Chart to explain story mapping strategy.

Display the Teaching Chart. Direct students' attention to the first frame. Point out that "Characters" means the most important people or animals in the story. Ask a volunteer to name the main characters in the story about Paul Bunyan. *(Paul, Billy, Babe the Blue Ox)* Recall with students that the setting is where and when a story takes place. Ask volunteers to provide this information. *(North America, long ago)*

Model the story mapping strategy.

Point out to students the second frame of Teaching Chart 1. Ask them to think about the problem in the story. Then point out the numbered events. Tell students that the most important events in the story go on these lines in the order in which they happened. Ask students to name these events. Finally, point out the frame for the resolution. Explain that the resolution refers to what happens at the end of the story that solves the problem in the story.

1

TEACHING CHART 1: STORY MAPPING

The Setting:
   Characters: (Paul Bunyan, Billy Pilgrim, Babe the Blue Ox)
   Place: (North America)
   Time: (long ago)

The Problem: (Billy Pilgrim does not want to pay Paul Bunyan one million dollars for digging the St. Lawrence River in three weeks.)
      Event 1: (Billy stretches the buckskin ropes so Babe cannot dig the river.)
      Event 2: (Paul has Babe drink the river dry.)
      Event 3: (Paul throws many piles of dirt back into the river.)

The Resolution: (Billy finally pays Paul the million dollars; the piles of dirt become known as the Thousand Islands.)

3. GUIDED PRACTICE

Provide practice in using story maps.

Guide students in completing the story map. Ask volunteers to identify the problem, tell the most important events in the correct order, and describe how the problem was solved. Record their responses on the Teaching Chart.

4. WRAP-UP

Summarize instruction.

Review with students that when they make a story map, they should first name the characters, and then tell the setting, or when and where the story takes place. Students should then tell the problem in the story, and list the most important events in the correct order. Finally, they should tell how the problem was solved and how the story ended.

Review the importance of story mapping.

Remind students that using story maps will help them to understand and remember the stories they read or listen to.

Provide independent practice.

Options for independent practice are shown in the Resource Center below.

Workbook page 7

NAME _____

Story Mapping

COMPREHENSION

REMEMBER: The **beginning** of a story tells **who, when,** and **where.** The **middle** of a story tells about a **problem** the characters have. The **ending** of a story tells how the problem was **solved.**

A. Complete the story map. Write only the most important ideas in the story about Paul Bunyan.

1. BEGINNING

Who — Paul Bunyan, Babe the Blue Ox, Billy Pilgrim

When — long ago

Where — U.S.-Canadian border

2. MIDDLE

Problem — Paul digs the St. Lawrence River in three weeks for Billy, but Billy doesn't want to pay him the million dollars.

3. ENDING

Solution — When Paul begins to fill in the river, Billy agrees to pay.

B. On separate paper, write a different ending for the story. See Teacher Notes.

Story Mapping — Listening 7

RESOURCE CENTER

◀ **Workbook page 7** is intended for all students.

Skills Practice 1 may ▶ be assigned for additional practice.

Workbook reuse option: Have students circle the names of the main characters wherever they appear in the story map.

Skills Practice 1

NAME _____

SKILLS PRACTICE 1

Story Mapping

A **story map** shows the important parts of a story. It can help you understand and remember the story. The **beginning** tells *who* is in the story. It also tells *when* and *where* the story takes place. The **middle** tells about the *problem* the main character has. It tells how the character tries to solve the problem. The **ending** gives the *solution* to the problem.

Read the story. Then complete the story map. Don't try to write everything from the story. Write only the important ideas.

Helen put on her cape. She picked up the three empty water buckets and walked across the farmyard to the well. It was a long walk on a cold and rainy day. When the buckets were full, they would be heavy. Helen couldn't carry two at once. That meant three long and cold trips.

Helen passed the barn. Her brother Lew came out. She asked him if he would help. He said he would carry one back. He couldn't carry two either. "Two trips are better than three," Helen thought.

At the well Helen had an idea. Maybe they could each carry one bucket. And together they could carry the third. Lew liked the idea. And it worked.

Who: **Helen and Lew**
When: **a cold and rainy day**
Where: **a farm**

Problem: **Helen has three water buckets to fill at the well.**

Solution: **Helen asks Lew to help. They get the three water buckets filled and to the house.**

LEVEL 8   "Paul Bunyan Digs the St. Lawrence River"   1

TEACHER·CHOICE

	Teaching Sequence	Trade Books and Resources	Meeting Individual Needs	Integrated Language Arts / Cross Curriculum
The Bridge Pages 16–17	**Introduce** Story Elements—Setting (Tested)	• Teaching Chart 2 • Workbook 8 • Skills Practice 2	• Reteaching Masters 1–4 • Challenge Master 1 • Achieving English Proficiency Master 1	
PART 1 **Vocabulary Strategies** Pages 18–19	**Develop Concepts** Semantic Mapping **Teach Vocabulary** **STORY CRITICAL WORDS:** freight trains, icy, **neighborhood, radio,** television, **waterfall,** weekly (Tested words are boldfaced.)	• Teaching Chart 3 • Workbook 9 • Skills Practice 3	**SUPPORT WORDS:** bugle, mandolin, plunged, racketing, shimmering, touristy, tremendous • Skills Practice 4 **CHARACTER/SETTING WORDS:** August, Bill, Hudson River, Jocko, Missouri, New Mexico, Northern Lights, Tony	**WRITING/SPEAKING ACTIVITY:** Use new vocabulary to tell about "when I was six." • Spelling Connection 39
PART 2 **Reading & Responding** Pages 20–29	**Build Background** **Develop a Purpose for Reading** **Guide the Reading Process** **Selection Follow-Up**	• Reader's Journal 9–12 • Workbook 10 **I·T KIT** Discussing a Poster; Singing a Song **READING EVERY DAY** *Howard,* by J. Stevenson *Will You Please Feed Our Cat?,* by J. Stevenson	**EXTRA HELP:** Main Idea/Details Charts **ACHIEVING ENGLISH PROFICIENCY:** Discussing Newspapers • Achieving English Proficiency Master 2	**Language Arts Connections** **WRITING TO LEARN:** Write a story about a favorite memory. • Writing Master 1 **SPEAKING/LISTENING:** Acting Out Story Scenes; Planning a Class Newspaper **WRITING:** Writing Autobiographical Sketches; Creating a Story Setting • Language Arts Master 1
PART 3 **Selection Support** Pages 30–35	**Introduce** Suffix *-ly* (Tested)	• Teaching Chart 4 • Workbook 11 • Skills Practice 5	• Reteaching Masters 1–4 • Challenge Master 2 • Achieving English Proficiency Master 3 **Practice** • Teaching Chart 5 • Workbook 12 • Skills Practice 6 Story Elements—Setting (Tested) **Maintain** • Skills Practice 7–8 Cause/Effect Synonyms	**Curriculum Connections** **SCIENCE:** Researching Astronomical Events **SOCIAL STUDIES:** Studying and Writing Historical Journals • Curriculum Connection Master 1 **ART:** Discussing Western Paintings

When I Was Nine

written and illustrated by James Stevenson

SUMMARY   *In this first-person account, the author recalls the year he was nine. He had a bicycle, a dog named Jocko, a*

| AMERICAN |
| LIBRARY |
| ASSOCIATION |
| 1986 |

*father who played taps, and a slightly older brother. As a hobby, he printed a neighborhood newspaper. On a family trip to New Mexico, he visited caves, saw the Northern Lights, rode horses, and received a cowboy hat for his birthday. Everything seemed a little smaller when he returned home. James Stevenson has been honored with several **American Library Association Notable Children's Books** listings, including one for* When I Was Nine *in 1986.*

Each lesson opener summarizes and provides interesting information about the selection. The Lesson Organizer helps you make sound instructional decisions based on student need.

The Bridge teaches a priority skill for the new selection by using a previous selection or information students already know. The 5-step teaching sequence tells what the skill is, why it is important, and how it is used.

SKILL TRACE: STORY ELEMENTS							
Introduction	Practice	Test	Reteach	Maintain			
TE 16	32	138	157	159	206	294	326	558

Skill Trace shows the Teacher Edition page numbers for all lessons that develop this skill.

The Bridge

LITERATURE

Teaching Story Elements—Setting

OBJECTIVE Recognizing story setting.

1. WARM-UP

Use a passage to identify setting orally.

Tell students that in this unit they will read stories that tell how people lived at different times in America's past. Then say you will read a passage about a famous event in the past. Have them listen for clues that suggest the time and place described in the passage. *(November, 1621; the New World, or America)*

> **As the days grew shorter, the Pilgrims prepared for another winter. It seemed a lifetime, not a year, since that November day in 1620 when the good ship Mayflower had landed in the New World.**

Discuss story clues that suggest setting.

Reread the passage. Ask students what clues helped them figure out the time and place of the passage. *(year, November, 1620, New World)*

State the objective.

Tell students they will learn to use story clues to figure out the setting, or when and where a story takes place.

2. TEACH

Explain why understanding setting is important.

Understanding the time and place of a story gives readers a better understanding of what the story is about and what is happening in it.

Present a strategy for identifying setting.

Explain that there is a strategy students can use to help them recognize the setting of the story. Look for details that suggest where the story takes place, such as descriptions of scenery, kinds of animals, or weather. Also look for details that suggest when a story takes place, such as descriptions of what people are doing or of events in nature that happen only in certain seasons. Some kinds of clues, such as the way people travel and what they wear, can help in guessing both time and place.

Teaching Charts supply chalkboard materials. Full-size charts are available or you can prepare transparencies or photocopies from the black-line master in the Teacher Resource Kit.

> **TEACHING CHART 2: STORY SETTING** [2]
>
> Marishka had never seen so many tall buildings crowded close together. She had never seen a street filled with so many wagons, carriages, horses, and people. How exciting to begin the new year in a new country!
>
> **1.** When does this story take place? (in the past, in January)
> **2.** Where does the story take place? (in a city)
>
> The space ship landed smoothly at Luna Port. Robert had just returned to his home on the moon. "I'm sorry I could not stay longer in San Francisco. I will miss the sweet smell of trees now beginning to bloom there," he said.
>
> **3.** When does this story take place? (in the future; in spring)
> **4.** Where does the story take place? (on the moon)

Name _____

Marishka had never seen so many tall buildings crowded close together. She had never seen a street filled with so many wagons, carriages, horses, and people. How exciting to begin the new year in a new country!

1. When does this story take place?
2. Where does the story take place?

The spaceship landed smoothly at Luna Port. Robert had just returned to his home on the moon. "I'm sorry I could not stay longer in San Francisco. I will miss the sweet smell of trees now beginning to bloom there," he said.

3. When does this story take place?
4. Where does the story take place?

Model the strategy. Display the Teaching Chart. Read passage 1. Point out that the mention of horses and carriages shows that the story probably takes place in the past. The mention of starting the new year shows that the time of year is January.

3. GUIDED PRACTICE

Check for understanding. Before going on, have students explain how to figure out where and when a story takes place. *(Look for story clues that suggest time and place.)*

Guide students in using the strategy. Have students use the strategy to answer the second question about passage 1. Then have them read passage 2 and answer the questions. Discuss the story clues that helped them decide where and when each story is happening.

4. WRAP-UP

Summarize instruction. Review why readers need to know a story's setting and the kinds of clues they use to guess the setting.

Provide independent practice. Options for independent practice are shown in the Resource Center below.

5. APPLICATION

Students will recognize story setting as they read "When I Was Nine." The symbol ✔ marks specific questions and activities that apply this skill.

The "road map" in the narrow column helps you follow a lesson you are familiar with. The wide column gives specific lesson details.

Meeting Individual Needs

Reteaching, Challenge, and Achieving English Proficiency activities help you meet the needs of all students.

RETEACHING Use the activity on page 159 and Masters 1–4 in the Teacher Resource Kit.

CHALLENGE Use the activity on page 159 and Master 1 in the Teacher Resource Kit.

ACHIEVING ENGLISH PROFICIENCY Use the activity on page 159 and Master 1 in the Teacher Resource Kit.

Workbook page 8

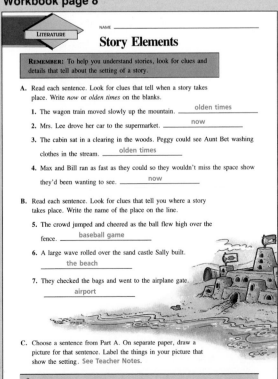

LITERATURE NAME _____

Story Elements

REMEMBER: To help you understand stories, look for clues and details that tell about the setting of a story.

A. Read each sentence. Look for clues that tell when a story takes place. Write *now* or *olden times* on the blanks.

1. The wagon train moved slowly up the mountain. _olden times_

2. Mrs. Lee drove her car to the supermarket. _now_

3. The cabin sat in a clearing in the woods. Peggy could see Aunt Bet washing clothes in the stream. _olden times_

4. Max and Bill ran as fast as they could so they wouldn't miss the space show they'd been wanting to see. _now_

B. Read each sentence. Look for clues that tell you where a story takes place. Write the name of the place on the line.

5. The crowd jumped and cheered as the ball flew high over the fence. _baseball game_

6. A large wave rolled over the sand castle Sally built. _the beach_

7. They checked the bags and went to the airplane gate. _airport_

C. Choose a sentence from Part A. On separate paper, draw a picture for that sentence. Label the things in your picture that show the setting. See Teacher Notes.

8 "When I Was Nine" Story Elements

RESOURCE CENTER

◀ **Workbook page 8** is intended for use by all students.

Skills Practice 2 may ▶ be assigned for additional practice.

The Resource Center provides a quick reference to practice materials. Suggestions for reuse options are found at the back of the Workbook Teacher Edition.

Workbook reuse option: Have students underline the words or phrases in the sentences in parts A and B that provide clues to the setting.

Skills Practice 2

NAME _____ SKILLS PRACTICE 2

Story Elements

Every story has a setting. The **setting** is *when* and *where* a story takes place. The words a writer uses to describe the setting help you picture the place and time in your mind. Look for clues that help you picture the story setting.

A. Read each sentence. Write **Yes** if it tells something about the setting. Write **No** if it does not.

1. Laura picked up the cat and held it tightly. _No_

2. Long ago in the land of Mum, a boy walked down a road. _Yes_

3. Isaac sat on the sand and watched the sea gulls. _Yes_

4. Bill was angry and kicked a stone. _No_

5. I sat at my desk and worried about the math test. _Yes_

6. The train slowed as it entered the station. _Yes_

7. Ata looked out the spaceship window at the earth far below. _Yes_

8. "I wish I could ride a bicycle," Clara thought. _No_

B. Read the paragraph. Answer the questions about the setting.

Sally and James walked along the path under a line of tall trees. They couldn't wait to get to the river and have their picnic lunch. But they had to walk slowly. Sally's long skirts caught on the bushes and small trees. Riding the horse would have been faster. But Pa needed the horse to work in the field that afternoon. Sally and James wouldn't be back in time.

9. What time of day does the story take place? _morning_

10. Where are Sally and James? _in the woods_
   at the river   in the woods   in a field

11. When does this story most likely take place? _in the past_
   in the past   now   in the future

12. Write clues from the story that help you know the setting. _path; picnic lunch; bushes and small trees catching on Sally's skirts; horse to work in the field_

2 LEVEL 8 "When I Was Nine"

Vocabulary Strategies

Developing Concepts

Build on prior knowledge of remembering the past with a semantic map.

Key concepts from the selection form the springboard for teaching vocabulary. Each word is presented using concept, context, and definition.

Make a semantic map about remembering the past as a starting point for teaching vocabulary. Ask students if older family members ever talk about "the way things used to be." Write *REMEMBERING* on the chalkboard and build a semantic map around the kinds of things students have heard. List responses under appropriate headings.

Where They Lived
(old neighborhood)
(neighborhood stores)
(sounds of things such as freight trains)
(parks or countryside)

REMEMBERING

What They Did
(listen to weekly radio shows)
(watch old television shows)
(games, movies)
(holiday celebrations)
(sitting and talking)

Teaching Vocabulary

Discuss meanings of Story Critical words.

Story Critical words are high frequency words that are key to story comprehension.

Read each context sentence on the Teaching Chart and identify the new word. Then use the questions below to help students understand each word. When necessary, provide a definition.

> **TEACHING CHART 3: VOCABULARY**   **3**
>
> 1. **neighborhood** (area or region near some place or person)
>   In the neighborhood where Dad grew up, everyone lived close by and knew one another.
> 2. **radio** (receiver that picks up sound waves from the air)
>   People got together to hear the news on *radio*.
> 3. **television** (sounds and images broadcast by electrical waves)
>   Neighbors watched *television* together because only one family on the block had a set.
> 4. **weekly** (happening once a week)
>   Every Tuesday they watched a *weekly* show.
> 5. **waterfall** (a steep fall of water)
>   Dad used to swim in the river and pretend he was taking a shower under the *waterfall*.
> 6. **icy** (very cold)
>   The *icy* water and cool wind made him shiver.
> 7. **freight trains** (trains that carry goods rather than passengers)
>   Freight trains used to carry goods to the city.

neighborhood **1. What is a neighbor?** (a person who lives near another) **What words in sentence 1 give a clue to the meaning of *neighborhood?*** (everyone lived close by)   STRATEGY: CONTEXT CLUES

radio **2. What do people listen to on the radio?** (possible answers: news, music, talk shows, commercials)   STRATEGY: PRIOR KNOWLEDGE

television **3. What main difference is there between radio and television?** (You can see pictures on television but not on radio.)   STRATEGY: PRIOR KNOWLEDGE

weekly

Different vocabulary strategies provide variety in teaching and help for every student.

4. What words in sentence 4 give a clue to the meaning of *weekly?* (every Tuesday) **What are some events that happen weekly?** (Possible answers: Certain magazines are published, certain radio or television shows are aired, some kinds of sports events take place.)   STRATEGY: CONTEXT CLUES

waterfall

5. What two shorter words do you see in the word *waterfall?* (*water* and *fall*)   STRATEGY: COMPOUND WORDS

icy

6. What does ice feel like? (It is very cold.) **What clue in sentence 6 made you think the water might be cold?** (the word *shiver*)   STRATEGY: CONTEXT CLUES

freight trains

7. What word in sentence 7 is a clue to the meaning of *freight trains?* (*goods*) **Why do you think there are fewer freight trains now than in the past?** (Possible answer: More goods are now shipped by truck or airplane.) STRATEGY: CONTEXT CLUES

Add new words to the map.

Challenge students to add any of the new words that have not been listed on the semantic map, adding new headings as needed. Have them explain how each added word fits.

Discuss Support words as needed.

The Glossary of the Student Text includes definitions of the Support words: *racketing, shimmering, bugle, mandolin, plunged, touristy, tremendous.*

Introduce Character/Setting words as needed.

Present and pronounce the following Character/Setting words before students read the selection: *Jocko, Bill, Tony, Hudson River, Missouri, Northern Lights, New Mexico, August.*

Provide independent practice.

Options for independent practice are shown in the Resource Center below.

Support and Character words enrich students' general reading vocabulary.

The Teacher Choice symbol highlights options that help you meet the needs of all students.

WRITING OR SPEAKING ACTIVITY *Have students use the new vocabulary in five sentences telling about the time "when I was six." Encourage them to get ideas from their semantic maps.*

Workbook page 9

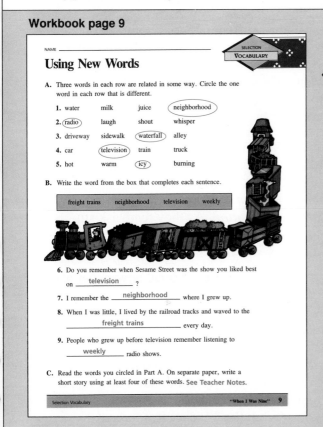

NAME _____

SELECTION
VOCABULARY

Using New Words

A. Three words in each row are related in some way. Circle the one word in each row that is different.

1. water   milk   juice   (neighborhood)
2. (radio)   laugh   shout   whisper
3. driveway   sidewalk (waterfall) alley
4. car   (television) train   truck
5. hot   warm   (icy)   burning

B. Write the word from the box that completes each sentence.

| freight trains | neighborhood | television | weekly |

6. Do you remember when Sesame Street was the show you liked best on ____television____ ?

7. I remember the ____neighborhood____ where I grew up.

8. When I was little, I lived by the railroad tracks and waved to the ____freight trains____ every day.

9. People who grew up before television remember listening to ____weekly____ radio shows.

C. Read the words you circled in Part A. On separate paper, write a short story using at least four of these words. See Teacher Notes.

Selection Vocabulary   "When I Was Nine"   **9**

RESOURCE CENTER

◀ **Workbook page 9** provides practice with Story Critical words.

Skills Practice 3 provides additional practice with Story Critical words.

Skills Practice 4 provides practice with Support words.

Spelling Connection Master 39 may be used for spelling instruction with the new vocabulary.

Workbook reuse option: Have students return to Part A and underline words that name things they can hear but not see. Have them check (√) words that describe things they can touch but not see.

Skills Practice 3

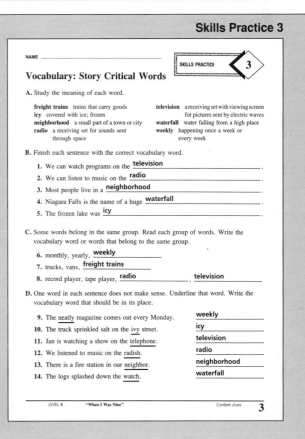

NAME _____

SKILLS PRACTICE
3

Vocabulary: Story Critical Words

A. Study the meaning of each word.

freight trains trains that carry goods
icy covered with ice; frozen
neighborhood a small part of a town or city
radio a receiving set for sounds sent through space
television a receiving set with viewing screen for pictures sent by electric waves
waterfall water falling from a high place
weekly happening once a week or every week

B. Finish each sentence with the correct vocabulary word.

1. We can watch programs on the ____television____
2. We can listen to music on the ____radio____
3. Most people live in a ____neighborhood____
4. Niagara Falls is the name of a huge ____waterfall____
5. The frozen lake was ____icy____

C. Some words belong in the same group. Read each group of words. Write the vocabulary word or words that belong to the same group.

6. monthly, yearly, ____weekly____
7. trucks, vans, ____freight trains____
8. record player, tape player, ____radio____   ____television____

D. One word in each sentence does not make sense. Underline that word. Write the vocabulary word that should be in its place.

9. The neatly magazine comes out every Monday.   ____weekly____
10. The truck sprinkled salt on the ivy street.   ____icy____
11. Jan is watching a show on the telephone.   ____television____
12. We listened to music on the radish.   ____radio____
13. There is a fire station in our neighbor.   ____neighborhood____
14. The logs splashed down the watch.   ____waterfall____

LEVEL B   "When I Was Nine"   Context clues   **3**

2

Reading & Responding

Building Background

Motivate discussion using the statements.

Building Background taps students' prior knowledge through poems, sayings, and other motivational activities.

Have students explain why they agree or disagree with the following statements. Then have them suggest other ways in which watching television makes today's children different from children of the past.

1. **Because they watch television so much, today's children know more about the world than their grandparents did.**

2. **Because they watch television so much, today's children do not talk with others or read as much as children used to.**

Build background about comparisons with the past.

Point out that people in the past did many of the same kinds of things people do today. The particular ways they did these things, however, were often different. Have students discuss ways in which they think their lives are like and different from the lives of children fifty or a hundred years ago.

Discuss autobiography.

Explain that an autobiography is a story that a person writes about his or her own life. Ask students why someone might choose to write an autobiography. Point out that the selection they are about to read, "When I Was Nine," is an example of autobiography.

Developing a Purpose for Reading

Option 1
Students set purpose.

ORAL "IF I WERE THE AUTHOR" LISTS Tell students that the author of this selection has written his memories of when he was nine. Have students imagine writing about their own lives. Have them begin their sentences with "If I were the author, I would write about. . . . " Record students' responses for later use. Ask them to read to see if the author wrote about the same things.

WRITING ACTIVITY Have students work individually or in pairs to create written "If I were the author" lists. Tell students to save their lists for later.

Option 2
Teacher sets purpose.

Ask students to read to find out what the author's life was like when he was nine, and how his life compares to their lives.

Meeting
Individual
Needs

These teaching suggestions provide practical story-specific activities that tailor the lesson to the needs of all students.

EXTRA HELP Explain that in the next story, the author remembers things that happened the year he was nine. Distribute two main idea/detail charts to each student, Form 10 in the Teacher Resource Kit. Have students write these headings on their forms: *The Author Remembers His Neighborhood* and *The Author Remembers His Summer Vacation*. As they read, ask students to list the memories that belong under each heading. After they read, have students share ideas about what they will remember about this year.

ACHIEVING ENGLISH PROFICIENCY Show students a local newspaper and point out such items as the weather, television and radio listings, local and international news. Ask students what other things they can find in a newspaper. Ask students if they receive a newspaper in their native language at home. If they do, ask them to bring copies to class and display them. Tell students that the boy they will read about in the next story writes a newspaper for his neighbors. Ask students what classroom news they could share with the rest of the school. List their ideas on the board. For additional help in story comprehension, use Master 2 in the Teacher Resource Kit.

When I Was Nine

written and illustrated by James Stevenson

The author of this story tells about a special time when he was about your age.

My own children are grown up now; that's how old I am. But sometimes I look back and I remember. . . .

When I was nine, we lived on a street with big trees.

I had a bicycle, and I knew where all the bumps were on the sidewalk.

We had a dog named Jocko.

Our telephone looked like this. Our number was 3348.

Reader's Journal   p 9
Preparing for Reading

REMEM-BERING

Students write about ideas they used to have that seem funny to them now.

The Reader's Journal provides opportunities for students to prepare for and respond to the selection in creative ways.

Guided Reading questions highlight the key events and concepts of the selection, helping students see the story structure.

Highlighting Literature helps make students aware of the literary aspects of the selection.

GUIDED READING

Page 15   How old do you think the author is? (at least forty; in fact, since he was born in 1929, he is about sixty)   SYNTHESIZE: DRAWING CONCLUSIONS

✔ **Page 15   When is this story happening?** (at least thirty years in the past) **How do you know?** (The author says he is grown up and has grown children but is remembering back to the time when he was nine.) **What other things are clues to the setting?** (the look of the telephone and the fact that the telephone number had only four digits)   RECALL: SETTING

HIGHLIGHTING LITERATURE

Page 15   Remind students that this selection is an autobiography. Point out that the author often uses pronouns such as *I, me,* and *my* to tell his own story. When this is done, it is called the first-person point of view. Ask students to tell why a biography would not be told from the first-person point of view. (The author is writing about someone else.)

Application of The Bridge skill is highlighted with a ✔.

✔ Skill from The Bridge applied through this question.

My father had boots and a bugle from when he was in the army in the First World War, and a mandolin from when he was in school. Sometimes when he came home from work, he would play taps for us.

At night our mother would read to us.

We lived near a railroad. Before I went to sleep, I listened to the steam locomotives. The freight trains and the express trains blew their whistles as they went racketing by in the dark.

In our backyard there was a beech tree. If you climbed high enough, you could see the Hudson River and smoke from the trains.

After school I listened to the radio and did homework. (There was no television.)

Bill, who lived next door, was my best friend. He was ten. Bill was pretty good fun, but only about half the time.

When my brother had a friend over, they wouldn't let me play. I learned to pitch by throwing a ball against the garage door.

I skated on a pond in the winter. The ice would crack with a tremendous booming noise. But everybody said not to worry.

I put out a weekly newspaper. I collected news from all the people on our block.

GUIDED READING

Page 16   What information about a bugle and a mandolin do you get from the illustrations? (The illustrations show what they look like. A bugle is something like a trumpet. A mandolin is something like a guitar.)   ANALYZE: PICTURE DETAILS

✔ **Page 17   What do you learn about the setting from the first two paragraphs on this page?** (Steam locomotives are another sign that the story is in the past. The beech tree in the back yard suggests a suburb or a small town. The town is near the Hudson River, which is in New York State.)   RECALL: SETTING

Page 17   What things in the author's life are mentioned on the rest of this page? (listening to the radio after school; doing homework; playing with his best friend Bill; learning to pitch by throwing a ball against the garage door; putting out a weekly newspaper.)   RECALL: DETAILS

✔ **Skill from The Bridge applied through this question.**

STRATEGIC READING

**Page 17   Have students imagine they are in the author's bedroom at night and have them describe in their own words what sounds they can hear. They should mention the rattling and whistling of the trains. They might also suggest the sound of wind in the beech tree leaves and the sounds of radios in neighbors' homes. If students have trouble imagining the sounds, have them look for clues in the first three paragraphs on this page.   METACOGNITION: VISUALIZING

Strategic Reading helps students become aware of how well they understand what they read. It provides self-monitoring and fix-up strategies students can use to improve their comprehension.

ANNOTATED LESSON PLAN

HOW I PRINTED THE NEIGHBORHOOD NEWS

① I TOOK A CAN OF HEKTOGRAPH AND OPENED IT. HEKTOGRAPH WAS LIKE A THICK JELLY SOUP.

② I DUMPED IT INTO A SAUCEPAN AND HEATED IT ON THE STOVE,

③ THEN POURED IT INTO A PAN AND LET IT COOL AND HARDEN.

④ MEANWHILE, I WROTE THE PAPER WITH A SPECIAL PURPLE PENCIL.

⑤ THEN I PUT THAT PAPER FACE-DOWN ON THE HARD JELLY AND RUBBED IT SMOOTH.

⑥ WHEN I PULLED OFF THE PAPER---

⑦ ---THE NEIGHBORHOOD NEWS WAS WRITTEN ON THE JELLY BACKWARDS!

⑧ THEN I PUT A CLEAN SHEET OF PAPER ON IT AND RUBBED, AND I GOT A COPY OF THE NEWS. I COULD MAKE LOTS OF COPIES.

Not everybody wanted one.

MR. FINERTY, WOULD YOU LIKE TO BUY A COPY OF THE NEIGHBORHOOD NEWS?

NOT RIGHT NOW.

GUIDED READING

Page 18　What did the author do with the copying fluid after he heated it? (He poured it into a pan and let it cool and harden.)　RECALL: SEQUENCE

Page 18　Why do you think the author includes step-by-step pictures of printing with the copying fluid? (Possible answers: to explain what he had to do because people today will not know the process; to give directions in case someone wants to try to print a paper in this way)　EVALUATE: AUTHOR'S PURPOSE

Page 19　How might printing a neighborhood newspaper today be different from the way the author printed one? (Possible answer: Today someone might type the paper and then have it photocopied, or the person might use a computer and a printer.)
SYNTHESIZE: COMPARISON

STRATEGIC READING

✔ **Page 19**　Have students summarize what they have learned about the author's life so far. (They have learned about the place where he lived, who was in his family, what he saw and heard each day, what he did for fun, and how he printed his newspaper.) Then ask students to predict what other memories the author might tell about. If some students have trouble summarizing, have them glance back at the illustrations for clues. If students have trouble predicting, have them think what other things might happen in a nine-year-old's life.　METACOGNITION: SUMMARIZING AND PREDICTING

Each Informal Assessment Opportunity indicated by a ✔ highlights a point at which you can evaluate a student's grasp of a concept or strategy.

✔ Informal Assessment Opportunity: SUMMARIZING

23

Most summers my brother and I went to visit our grandmother, who had a house near the beach. We went swimming every day.

Grandma was a lot of fun. We would crawl into her room in the morning and hide under her bed.

Then we would pretend to be a funny radio program; she always acted surprised and she always laughed.

But this summer was different. In July we packed up the car for a trip out west. A neighbor said he would take care of Jocko. Bill and Tony waved goodbye.

We drove for days and days. My brother and I argued a lot. When it got too bad, our father stopped the car and made us throw a football for a while. Then we got back in the car again.

At the end of each day we looked for a place to stay. "What do we think?" my father would say.

"Plenty good enough," my mother would say. And we would stop for the night.

My brother and I always wanted to stop and see something special. Our parents usually wanted to keep going. "Too touristy," they said. But in Missouri we visited a big cave.

Our parents woke us up one night to look at the sky. "What's happening?" I asked. The sky was shimmering.

"It's the Northern Lights," said my mother.

ANNOTATED LESSON PLAN

GUIDED READING

✔ **Page 20   If the author did not say his grandmother lived near the beach, how would you know anyway?** (The author and his brother went swimming every day when they visited her.)   SYNTHESIZE: SETTING

Page 20   Why does the author say one summer was different from others? (Instead of visiting their grandmother, the brothers went on a family trip out west.)   ANALYZE: MAIN IDEA/DETAILS

Page 21   Why do you think the author's father stopped the car and made the two brothers throw a football when they argued too much? (Possible answers: If the two boys played together, they would stop arguing; throwing the football would let them use up energy that they could not use up in the car.)   INFER: CAUSE/EFFECT

HIGHLIGHTING LITERATURE

Page 21   Point out that the author uses vivid details and descriptive words to make his memories seem real and interesting. For example, he includes the detail of throwing the football to make the car trip seem real and help readers feel how long and boring it was for him and his brother. He describes the Northern Lights by saying, "The sky was shimmering." Have students look back on other pages for vivid details and descriptive words.

✔ Skill from **The Bridge** applied through this question.

On my birthday we stopped in a small town and went into a store. My parents bought me exactly what I always wanted . . . a cowboy hat.

At last we came to New Mexico.

We stayed at a ranch and went on long, hot rides into the mountains.

One day we rode to a <u>waterfall</u>. While the horses rested, we slid down the waterfall and plunged into an <u>icy</u> pool. We did it again and again.

It was the most fun I'd ever had.

We drove back home in August. As we turned into our block, Jocko ran to greet us. It was great to get home.

Everything looked just the way it always had . . . except maybe a little smaller.

But I was probably a little bigger. I wasn't nine any more.

◆ LIBRARY LINK ◆

If you liked this story by James Stevenson, you might enjoy reading another of his books, Howard.

Reader's Response

Do you think you would have liked the trip to New Mexico as much as the author did? Why or why not?

See next page for suggested answers.

SELECTION FOLLOW-UP

When I Was Nine

 Thinking It Over

1. Why wasn't there a television set in the author's house?
2. How did the summer when the author was nine compare to other summers?
3. What were some of the sights the family saw on the way to New Mexico?
4. How can you tell that the author liked his grandmother?
5. Was the author happy when he was a boy? How do you know?

 Writing to Learn

THINK AND PREDICT Mr. Stevenson writes about a special year of his childhood. When you are grown up, what do you think you will remember about this year of your life? Read Mr. Stevenson's list. Then write your own list.

Things Mr. Stevenson Remembered	Things I Will Remember About This Year
• Dad had a bugle. • Mother read to us. • I put out a newspaper.	(Make your list.)

WRITE Read your list. Circle your favorite memory. Write sentences to tell what you will remember about this year when you grow up.

GUIDED READING

Page 22   Why do you think the author chose to write about the year he was nine? (Possible answer: That year, especially that vacation, was a special time for the author.) EVALUATE: AUTHOR'S PURPOSE

RETURNING TO THE READING PURPOSE

OPTION 1   If students set the purpose, return to the "If I were the author" lists they generated. Discuss whether their ideas were included in the memories the author wrote about. Ask students whether the author mentioned any memories that surprised them. (Printing the newspaper may have been surprising.)

OPTION 2   If you set the purpose, have students tell how the author's life when he was nine was the same and different from their lives today. (Similarities might include having a bicycle and dog, fighting with his brother, and taking family trips. Differences might include the lack of television, the telephone number with only four digits, and printing the newspaper.)

Returning to the Reading Purpose provides closure for the selection.

Reader's Journal   **p 10**
Responding to Reading

KEEPING IN TOUCH

Taking on the persona of James, students write letters to Grandma about their trip. Pictures and information provide inspiration.

SELECTION FOLLOW-UP

When I Was Nine

THINKING IT OVER

1. **Why wasn't there a television set in the author's house?** (There was no television in the author's house because it had not yet been invented when the author was a boy.) INFER: CAUSE/EFFECT

2. **How did the summer when the author was nine compare to other summers?** (The summer when the author was nine was different from other summers. Usually the author and his brother spent summers at the beach with their grandmother, but that summer the author's family took a trip out west.) ANALYZE: COMPARISON

3. **What were some of the sights the family saw on the way to New Mexico?** (They saw a cave, the Northern Lights, a waterfall.) RECALL: DETAILS

4. **How can you tell that the author liked his grandmother?** (The author says that his grandmother was a lot of fun. He appreciated her acting surprised even when she probably wasn't.) SYNTHESIZE: DRAWING CONCLUSIONS

5. **Was the author happy when he was a boy? How do you know?** (He seems to have been happy. He enjoys looking back on the things he did then; he writes of those days as if he enjoyed them. Encourage students to read portions of the text that support their conclusions.) INFER: FEELINGS/ATTITUDES; METACOGNITION

WRITING TO LEARN

THINK AND PREDICT   Mr. Stevenson writes about a special year of his childhood. When you are grown up, what do you think you will remember about this year of your life? Read Mr. Stevenson's list. Then write your own list. (Help students compile their lists to prepare for writing.)

Things Mr. Stevenson Remembered	Things I Will Remember About This Year
• Dad had a bugle. • Mother read to us. • I put out a newspaper.	(Make your list.)

WRITE   Read your list. Circle your favorite memory. Write sentences to tell what you will remember about this year when you are grown up. (Have students share their sentences.)

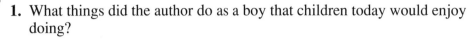
More Ideas for Selection Follow-Up

CRITICAL AND CREATIVE THINKING QUESTIONS

Encourage a variety of responses and points of view.

Use these open-ended questions to encourage critical and creative thinking about the selection.

✔ 1. What things did the author do as a boy that children today would enjoy doing?

These critical and creative thinking questions strengthen the reasoning abilities of all students.

2. In what ways have times changed since the author was a boy?

3. When James got back from vacation, everything in his neighborhood looked smaller to him. Why do you think this was so?

REREADING ORALLY

Have students reread for expression.

Have students reread the last two pages of the story, which describe the author's family trip to New Mexico. Remind them that this was a very exciting time for the author. Point out that he tells about it in narration, as a grown-up remembering a childhood experience, and also in dialogue, in which he speaks as a child and other family members also speak. Have some students read narration and others read the dialogue of the different family members. Have students vary their voices to show the excitement of the trip and also to help listeners understand who is talking, how old the person is, and how the person feels about his or her experience.

SELECTION COMPREHENSION

Provide comprehension check.

A Workbook page to check comprehension is shown in the Resource Center below. It may be used for informal assessment.

✔ **Informal Assessment Opportunity:** EVALUATING

Workbook page 10

RESOURCE CENTER

◀ **Workbook page 10** is intended for use by all students.

Writing Master 1 duplicates the Writing to Learn list.

I•T Kit Activities

Poster: "Shop Around!"
Teams of students take a closer look at Trump's General Store to identify over one hundred modern-day objects camouflaged in the shadow box construction. Students then list one hundred items that really might have filled the shelves in this store. (See Activity Guide.) CONTENT AREAS

Audio: "Daisy Bell"
While the narrator of "When I Was Nine" fondly recalled bicycle rides, the singer of this song anticipates the way his bride will look upon "a bicycle built for two." As students sing along, the music transports them back to the turn of the century, when bicycling was a popular new pastime. (See Activity Guide.)
CONTENT AREAS

ANNOTATED LESSON PLAN

LANGUAGE ARTS CONNECTIONS

Language Arts Connections *provide a variety of activities that integrate listening, speaking, reading, and writing.*

CREATIVE THINKING: ACTING OUT STORY SCENES

Discuss writing and acting in play scenes.

Tell students that the written form of a play is called a script. Remind them that in a script, the speaker's name and a colon appear before each speaker's words and quotation marks are not used. Directions to characters are written in parentheses. The setting is described at the beginning of the scene.

Have students write and act out scenes related to the story.

Divide the class into small groups. Have each group write a script for a scene that could appear in a play version of "When I Was Nine." Give groups time to rehearse their scenes and then present them to the class.   SHARED LEARNING: SPEAKING

PLANNING A CLASS NEWSPAPER

Discuss newspapers.

Have students bring newspapers to class and look through them to name the different kinds of stories. *(possible answers: national and local news stories, feature stories, sports stories, etc.)* Write their suggestions on the chalkboard. Point out that each story has a headline—a few words in large type that tell what the story is about. Discuss the placement of the stories.

Have students plan a class newspaper.

Have students list ideas for stories and other materials for a class newspaper and write a headline for each one. Then have them show the stories on a layout for a four-page paper. Explain that the layout shows where items will appear but does not show the text of the stories.   WHOLE CLASS ENRICHMENT

AUTOBIOGRAPHY AS A LITERARY GENRE

Review the features of an autobiography.

Remind students that "When I Was Nine" is an example of autobiography—the story of a person's life told by the person himself or herself, written from the first-person point of view. Ask students how they can tell that something is written from the first-person point of view. *(The story is told with pronouns such as* I, me, *and* mine.*)*

Have students write autobiographical sketches.

Have students imagine they are grown up and want to tell children what their lives were like. They may wish to use their lists from the Writing to Learn activity for ideas. Then have them write autobiographical sketches from the first-person point of view.   CHALLENGE: WRITING

CREATING A SETTING

Have students write and infer setting descriptions.

Remind students that authors do not tell exactly when and where a story is happening. Rather, they suggest the setting through details. Clues to setting may be found in what people wear, how they travel, what animals they see, what they do, what they eat, and what weather they experience.

Have each student write a descriptive paragraph that suggests but does not state the time and place in which a story happens. After the descriptions are finished, group students in pairs and have them take turns reading their descriptions aloud to their partners. Have each student try to guess the time and place of his or her partner's story from clues in the description. **Language Arts Master 1** can be used with this activity.   WRITING

READING EVERY DAY

Having become acquainted with author/illustrator James Stevenson in his story "When I Was Nine," students might enjoy meeting some of the story characters Stevenson has created, such as those featured in these two books.

Howard by James Stevenson. Greenwillow Books, © 1980. Howard, a young duck, misses the annual migration south and spends the winter in New York City, where he makes surprising discoveries and new friends.   EASIER TO READ

Will You Please Feed Our Cat? by James Stevenson. Greenwillow Books, © 1987. When Mary Ann and Louie tell Grandpa how hard it is to take care of their neighbor's dog for the weekend, Grandpa recalls the troubles and hilarious adventures he and his brother once had in a similar job involving *many* pets.

Reader's Journal   **pp 11, 12**
Extending Reading

THE LATEST MODEL

After seeing pictures of telephones and cars, old and new, students apply their creative skills to the task of designing a new telephone or car. They then read a poem about inventing and try to devise an entirely new object.

Selection Support

SKILL TRACE: SUFFIX				
Introduction	Practice	Test	Reteach	Maintain
TE 30	58	85	157	161	198

WORD STUDY

Suffix -ly

OBJECTIVE   Using structural analysis to determine word meaning.

1. WARM-UP

Use known sentences to identify a word ending in the suffix -ly.

Tell students they will listen to two sentences about "When I Was Nine," the selection they have just read. Explain that the two sentences have the same meaning. Have them decide how the sentences are different. (*The second sentence contains the word* weekly *in place of the words* every week.)

> **I put out a newspaper every week.**
> **I put out a newspaper weekly.**

Discuss the suffix -ly.

Selection Support provides options for instruction appropriate to the selection. Introductory lessons are intended for all students; practice and maintenance lessons provide options for tailoring instruction to individual needs.

Write the word *weekly* on the chalkboard and circle the letters *ly*. Remind students that a suffix is a letter or letters added to the end of a word. The word to which a suffix is added is called the base word. A suffix changes a base word's meaning and sometimes changes the way the word is used in a sentence. Words ending in *ly* usually tell how or how often something is done. Ask students what the base word is in *weekly. (week)* Then ask what *weekly* means. *(every week or once a week)*

State the objective.

Tell students they will learn to use the suffix *-ly* to help figure out meanings of words.

2. TEACH

Explain why identifying suffixes is important.

Being able to recognize suffixes helps readers figure out the meanings of unfamiliar words.

Present a strategy for identifying the meaning of words ending in ly.

Explain there is a strategy students can use to help them identify the meanings of words ending in the suffix *-ly*. First, identify the base word to which *-ly* has been added and think about the meaning of the base word. Then remember that words ending in *ly* usually tell how or how often something is done. Fit the base word in the phrase "in a _____ way" or "once a _____" to state the meaning of the word ending in *ly*.

> **TEACHING CHART 4: THE SUFFIX -LY**   **4**
>
> 1. James Stevenson   (lovingly)   remembered the year when he was nine.   sadly, quickly, lovingly
> 2. He rode his bicycle   (carefully)   because he knew there were bumps in the sidewalk.   carefully, sadly, wildly
> 3. His father played taps   (softly)   so he would not disturb the neighbors.   loudly, bravely, softly
> 4. When there was not much news, he printed his paper   (monthly)   instead of weekly.   daily, monthly, shortly
> 5. The boys liked to be with their grandmother because she laughed so   (easily) .   sadly, easily, shortly
> 6. They left   (happily)   on their trip west.   slowly, sadly, happily

Model the strategy. Read the first sentence on the Teaching Chart and the three words that follow it. Explain that the meaning of each of these words can be worked out by finding the base word and putting it in the phrase "in a _____ way." The word *lovingly* makes the most sense in the first sentence.

3. GUIDED PRACTICE

Check for understanding. Before going on, have students explain how to identify the meaning of a word ending in *ly*. *(find the base word and fit it in the phrase "in a _____ way" or "once a _____")*

Guide students in using the strategy. Have students use the strategy to choose the most appropriate word to fit in the blank in each of the sentences on the chart. Have students explain their choices.

4. WRAP-UP

Summarize instruction. Review why readers need to identify suffixes and how they can figure out the meanings of words ending in the suffix -*ly*. *(Identifying suffixes can help in figuring out the meanings of unfamiliar words; to figure out the meaning of a word ending in* ly, *find the base word and put it in the phrase "in a _____ way" or "once a _____.")*

Provide independent practice. Options for independent practice are shown in the Resource Center below.

Meeting Individual Needs

RETEACHING Use the activity on page 161 and Masters 1–4 in the Teacher Resource Kit.

CHALLENGE Use the activity on page 161 and Master 2 in the Teacher Resource Kit.

ACHIEVING ENGLISH PROFICIENCY Use the activity on page 161 and Master 3 in the Teacher Resource Kit.

Workbook page 11

RESOURCE CENTER

◄ **Workbook page 11** is intended for use by all students.

Skills Practice 5 may ► be assigned for additional practice.

Workbook reuse option: Have students circle each base word in Part B.

Skills Practice 5

Workbook page 11

NAME _____

WORD STUDY

Suffix -*ly*

REMEMBER: The suffix -*ly* tells how something is done.

A. Write the base word for each -*ly* word.

1. sadly __sad__   2. patiently __patient__
3. freely __free__   4. proudly __proud__
5. newly __new__   6. silently __silent__

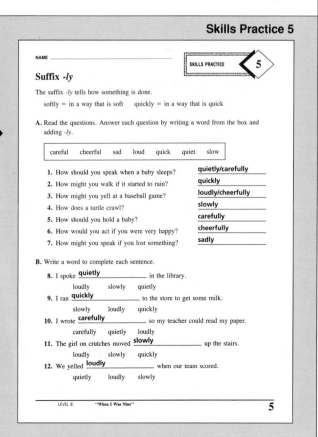

B. Read each sentence. Write the correct word in the blank.

7. Grandmother loved James and his brother __dearly__ . (dear, dearly)

8. When James rode his bicycle, he was __careful__ to go around the cracks in the sidewalk. (careful, carefully)

9. Their father got upset when James and his brother argued __loudly__ on the car trip. (loud, loudly)

10. When that happened, he __slowly__ stopped the car and got out the football. (slow, slowly)

11. The water from the waterfall felt __cold__ and refreshing. (cold, coldly)

12. After their long summer trip, James __quickly__ saw that everything looked smaller because he was bigger. (quick, quickly)

C. On separate paper, write three sentences telling something you remember doing during a vacation. Use an -*ly* word in each sentence. See Teacher Notes.

Suffix -*ly*   "When I Was Nine" **11**

Skills Practice 5

NAME _____

SKILLS PRACTICE 5

Suffix -*ly*

The suffix -*ly* tells how something is done.

softly = in a way that is soft   quickly = in a way that is quick

A. Read the questions. Answer each question by writing a word from the box and adding -*ly*.

| careful | cheerful | sad | loud | quick | quiet | slow |

1. How should you speak when a baby sleeps? __quietly/carefully__
2. How might you walk if it started to rain? __quickly__
3. How might you yell at a baseball game? __loudly/cheerfully__
4. How does a turtle crawl? __slowly__
5. How should you hold a baby? __carefully__
6. How would you act if you were very happy? __cheerfully__
7. How might you speak if you lost something? __sadly__

B. Write a word to complete each sentence.

8. I spoke __quietly__ in the library.
   loudly   slowly   quietly

9. I ran __quickly__ to the store to get some milk.
   slowly   loudly   quickly

10. I wrote __carefully__ so my teacher could read my paper.
    carefully   quietly   loudly

11. The girl on crutches moved __slowly__ up the stairs.
    loudly   slowly   quietly

12. We yelled __loudly__ when our team scored.
    quietly   loudly   slowly

LEVEL B   "When I Was Nine"   **5**

SKILL TRACE: STORY ELEMENTS							
Introduction	Practice	Test	Reteach	Maintain			
TE 16	32	138	157	159	206	294	326	558

LITERATURE

Story Elements—Setting

OBJECTIVE Recognizing story setting.

Review setting.

Remind students that the setting is the time and place of a story. Details that give clues about place can include descriptions of the land, animals, and weather. Details that give clues about time include how people travel, what people are doing, and seasonal changes.

Use Teaching Chart to review how to identify setting.

Display the Teaching Chart. Explain that these passages have setting clues. Have students identify the settings and explain their reasoning.

TEACHING CHART 5: SETTING

5

1. The author lived near a railroad. Before he went to sleep, he listened to the steam locomotives. (The place is near a railroad. The time is the past because steam trains are not used now.)

2. The author could see the Hudson River from a beech tree in his back yard. (The place is somewhere near the Hudson River, probably in New York State. It is probably a suburb or small town, since there is a tree in the back yard.)

3. After school the author listened to the radio and did homework. There was no television. (The time is the past before television.)

4. One summer the author's family went west for a vacation. They stayed at a ranch and went on long, hot rides into the mountains. (The place is west of where the family lived, hot in the summer, and has open land and mountains.)

Provide independent practice.

Options for independent practice are shown in the Resource Center below.

Workbook page 12

LITERATURE

NAME _____

Story Elements

REMEMBER: To help you understand stories, look for clues and details that tell about the setting of a story.

A. Some of these sentences about ''When I Was Nine'' tell *when* something took place. Some tell *where*. Some tell both *when and where*. Write the words *when, where,* or *when and where* at the end of each sentence.

1. We lived on a street with big trees. _____ where _____

2. My father played a bugle in the First World War. _____ when _____

3. We lived near a railroad. _____ where _____

4. At night we listened to radio programs because there was no television. _____ when _____

5. From the beech tree in our yard, you could see the Hudson River. _____ where _____

6. Our grandmother had a house near the beach. _____ where _____

7. In July we packed the car for a trip out West. _____ when and where _____

8. In Missouri we visited a big cave. _____ where _____

9. We stayed at a ranch in New Mexico. _____ where _____

10. We plunged into the icy pool under a waterfall. _____ where _____

B. On separate paper, write two sentences about a setting. In one sentence use words that tell *where*. In the other sentence use words that tell *when*. See Teacher Notes.

12 ''When I Was Nine''   Story Elements

RESOURCE CENTER

◂ **Workbook page 12** is intended for use by all students.

Skills Practice 6 may ▸ be assigned for additional practice.

Workbook reuse option: Have students underline the words or phrases in each sentence in Part A that provide information about when or where the story was set.

Skills Practice 6

NAME _____

SKILLS PRACTICE 6

Story Elements

The **setting** of a story is *when* and *where* the story takes place. Watch for clues about the setting. Writers don't always tell you everything about the setting in one sentence.

Read the beginning of the story.

Noah and May left their friends' house. It was almost dark. The wind was blowing hard around them. May fell down. The new snow and her long skirts made it hard for her to get up. She fell again. Then Noah fell.

''What are we going to do?'' Noah asked.

''Sit here and wait until spring,'' May said. They both laughed.

''Maybe Pa will bring the wagon,'' Noah said.

''No,'' May said. ''It couldn't get through the snow. Come on. Let's hold hands.''

They kept walking. After a while, they saw the light from candles in the cabin. They were almost home.

Now answer the questions.

1. What time of day is it? _____ late afternoon _____
   Underline the sentence in the story that gives you a clue.

2. When does the story take place? _____ long ago _____
   Write three things from the story that tell you that. _____ May's long skirts; the wagon; candles in the cabin _____

3. What was the weather like? _____ snowy and windy _____

4. How might the story be different if it had taken place today? _____ Answers will vary. _____

5. How might the story be different if it had taken place on a summer day? _____ Answers will vary. _____

6   LEVEL 8   ''When I Was Nine''

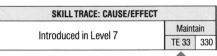

SKILL TRACE: CAUSE/EFFECT	
Introduced in Level 7	Maintain
	TE 33 │ 330

Maintenance of all tested skills, across levels, ensures learning.

COMPREHENSION

Cause/Effect

OBJECTIVE Recognizing stated and unstated cause-and-effect relationships.

Review causes and effects.

Remind students that some events make other events happen. An event that makes something else happen is a cause. An event that happens because of another event is an effect. Sometimes words such as *because, so,* and *therefore* signal a cause-and-effect relationship. If there are no signal words, students should look for clues in the story and think about what they already know to decide which story events are causes or effects of others.

Provide practice in identifying causes and effects.

You may wish to write the passages below on the chalkboard. Answers are printed in red. Have students read each passage and tell which event is a cause and which is an effect. Have students identify signal words that appear in the passages.

---

1. The author knew where all the bumps on the sidewalk were, so he never fell off his bike. (Cause: He knew where all the bumps were. Effect: He never fell off his bike. Signal word: *so*)

2. The author lived near a railroad. He could hear the trains go by at night. (Cause: The author lived near a railroad. Effect: He could hear the trains go by at night.)

3. Everything looked smaller when the author came home because he was probably a little bigger. (Cause: The author was probably a little bigger. Effect: Everything looked smaller when he came home. Signal word: *because*)

Provide independent practice.

An independent activity is shown in the Resource Center below.

RESOURCE CENTER

Skills Practice 7 may ▶ be assigned for additional practice.

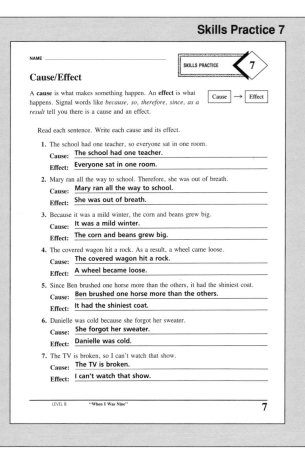

NAME _____

SKILLS PRACTICE ◁ 7

Cause/Effect

A **cause** is what makes something happen. An **effect** is what happens. Signal words like *because, so, therefore, since, as a result* tell you there is a cause and an effect.

Cause → Effect

Read each sentence. Write each cause and its effect.

1. The school had one teacher, so everyone sat in one room.
   Cause: The school had one teacher.
   Effect: Everyone sat in one room.

2. Mary ran all the way to school. Therefore, she was out of breath.
   Cause: Mary ran all the way to school.
   Effect: She was out of breath.

3. Because it was a mild winter, the corn and beans grew big.
   Cause: It was a mild winter.
   Effect: The corn and beans grew big.

4. The covered wagon hit a rock. As a result, a wheel came loose.
   Cause: The covered wagon hit a rock.
   Effect: A wheel became loose.

5. Since Ben brushed one horse more than the others, it had the shiniest coat.
   Cause: Ben brushed one horse more than the others.
   Effect: It had the shiniest coat.

6. Danielle was cold because she forgot her sweater.
   Cause: She forgot her sweater.
   Effect: Danielle was cold.

7. The TV is broken, so I can't watch that show.
   Cause: The TV is broken.
   Effect: I can't watch that show.

LEVEL 8   "When I Was Nine"   **7**

ANNOTATED LESSON PLAN

SKILL TRACE: SYNONYMS	
Introduced in Level 7	Maintain
	TE 34

VOCABULARY

Synonyms

OBJECTIVE   Recognizing and using words with similar meanings.

Review synonyms.

Remind students that synonyms are words that have the same or almost the same meaning. If they can tell from sentence context that a familiar and an unfamiliar word are likely to be synonyms, they can use the familiar word to help them guess the meaning of the unfamiliar word.

Provide practice in identifying synonyms.

You may wish to read aloud each pair of sentences below. Write the underlined word from the first sentence on the chalkboard. Ask students to identify which word in the second sentence is a synonym and gives a clue to the meaning of the underlined word from the first sentence. Answers are printed in red.

---

1. The author's father had boots and a <u>bugle</u> from when he was in the army. What a noise that horn made! (horn)

2. The trains went <u>racketing</u> by in the dark. The author could hear them rattling along all night. (rattling)

3. The author <u>collected</u> news from all the people on the block. When he had gathered enough news, he printed his paper. (gathered)

4. One summer the family made a <u>journey</u> out west. It was an exciting trip. (trip)

5. In New Mexico, the boys slid down a waterfall into a <u>frigid</u> pool. The icy water felt wonderful. (icy)

Provide independent practice.

An independent activity is shown in the Resource Center below.

RESOURCE CENTER

Skills Practice 8 may ▶ be assigned for additional practice.

Skills Practice 8

NAME _____

SKILLS PRACTICE ▷ 8

Synonyms

Synonyms are words that mean about the same thing. *Hat* and *bonnet* are synonyms.

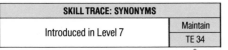
hat   bonnet

A. Read each sentence pair. Write the synonyms.

1. There is a large group of animals called insects.
   Sometimes we call them bugs.

   insects
   bugs

2. Some bugs are small.
   Others are really tiny.

   small
   tiny

3. Molly is fearless about catching bugs.
   Not too many others in her class are so brave.

   fearless
   brave

4. Some bugs are hard to catch.
   Molly keeps trying, even when it's difficult.

   hard
   difficult

5. Many insects can be found in fields.
   Molly looks in the meadows on her parents' farm.

   fields

   meadows

6. Some insects, like crickets, move by leaps.
   So when they do, Molly jumps too.

   leaps
   jumps

B. Write a sentence using each synonym.

7. quiet, silent
   Answers will vary.

8. finish, end

---

8   LEVEL 8   "When I Was Nine"

CURRICULUM CONNECTIONS

Curriculum Connections help you integrate Language Arts with other content areas.

DEAR DIARY SOCIAL STUDIES

Explain that a journal or diary is a book that a person writes in every day or almost every day to record events and feelings in his or her life. Point out that much can be learned about particular times and places in the past by reading the journals of people who lived in those times and places. Suggest that students look in the library for reprinted diaries and journals kept by people of other times. Then have them keep journals of their own for a week. Encourage them to include details that could help future readers learn about the time and place in which they live. **Curriculum Connection Master 1** can be used with this activity.

EVENTS IN THE SKY SCIENCE

Tell students that the Northern Lights are also known as the aurora borealis. The aurora borealis is not often seen in the United States, but it can be seen easily near the North Pole. Have students work in teams to prepare reports on the aurora borealis and other events in the sky. Tell them to use encyclopedias, nonfiction books, and science magazines such as *3-2-1 Contact* to prepare their reports. Have them show pictures with their reports if possible. The following are some topics they might report on and questions they might answer.

1. **Aurora Borealis:** What does the name *aurora borealis* mean? Where are the best places to see it? How often does it occur? What does it look like? What causes it? Are there also ''southern lights''?

2. **Comets:** What is a comet? What is it made of? What is a comet's tail made of? Does it always have a tail? How often do comets appear? How do they get their names?

3. **Eclipses:** What is an eclipse of the sun? What is an eclipse of the moon? How often do eclipses happen? Can an eclipse be seen from all over the world?

4. **Meteors:** What are meteors? Are they really ''falling stars''? How are meteors different from comets? Do meteors ever hit the earth?

VISIONS OF NEW MEXICO ART

Like the author of ''When I Was Nine,'' many American artists have been inspired by the landscapes and people of New Mexico and other southwestern states. If you wish, have students look in the library for reproductions of works by American artists that show the Southwest. Then have students do their own drawings or paintings of their impressions of New Mexico. They may wish to look at the work of the following artists:

Ansel Adams, photographer
Frederic Remington, painter and sculptor
Georgia O'Keeffe, painter
R. C. Gorman, painter

Reading the Poem

OBJECTIVE Understanding how a poet uses details to create a mood.

INTRODUCING THE POEM

Relate content of the poem to the unit theme.

Remind students that the selections in this unit are about the past. Point out that an important part of people's lives long ago was the general store. The general store carried food, cloth, tools, and many other things. It was also a place where people met and talked. Discuss the kinds of stores there are today and what they sell.

Relate content of the poem to students' experience.

Ask students if they have ever been in a general store or seen a picture of one. Have them relate the sights and smells they enjoyed there.

Set a listening purpose.

Tell students they are about to hear a poem about a general store. Ask them to think about how the poet's description of the place makes them feel.

READING THE POEM

Read the poem aloud.

Because poetry is a sound-based literary form, this part of the lesson is most important. Read the poem aloud to the students with Student Texts closed. Then have students open their books to page 24. Read the poem again or ask for volunteers to read it to the whole group. With this second reading, encourage students to picture themselves inside the general store that the poet is describing. Discuss any unfamiliar words as needed.

> **bolts of calico**   large rolls of cotton cloth with a figured pattern printed on it in color
> **crockery**   pots, plates, or jars made of hardened clay
> **sarsaparilla**   a soft drink flavored with the roots of a tropical plant

DISCUSSING THE POEM

Discuss students' responses to the poem.

Ask students what feelings the poem gave them. (*feelings of warmth, friendliness, the past*) Discuss why the girl in the poem might want to own a general store. (*perhaps she thinks it would be fun to have many kinds of things around her; she might enjoy being busy helping customers; because it has everything*) Then ask:

> **What details tell that a store is being described, even if the word *store* is not mentioned?** ("real glass cases"; "counters wide"; "the items themselves"; "fix the window/dust each shelf/take the money in all myself"; the question "What can I do for you to-day?")

> **What phrase does the poet use to describe how the drawers are full of things?** ("And drawers all spilly with things inside.")

Point out poetic techniques.

Explain to students that the short phrases naming the different items in the store help readers visualize the store and know just what the poet wants.

CLASS ENRICHMENT

Have students write descriptions of old-time stores.

Have students find pictures in magazines showing other kinds of stores that are not likely to be found today, such as hat shops, carriage shops, blacksmith shops, or shoeshine parlors. Then ask each student to write a short description of one of these stores, using details to convey the storekeeper's pride in the store. Tell students to keep in mind the reasons why someone might want to own such a place.

General Store

Some day I'm going to have a store
With a tinkly bell hung over the door,
With real glass cases and counters wide
And drawers all spilly with things inside.
There'll be a little of everything;
Bolts of calico; balls of string;
Jars of peppermint; tins of tea;
Pots and kettles and crockery;
Seeds in packets; scissors bright;
Kegs of sugar, brown and white;
Sarsaparilla for picnic lunches,
Bananas and rubber boots in bunches.
I'll fix the window and dust each shelf,
And take the money in all myself,
It will be my store and I will say:
"What can I do for you to-day?"

Rachel Field

Reader's Journal   p 13
Responding to Reading

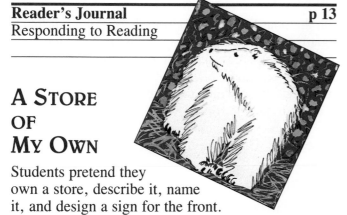

A STORE OF MY OWN

Students pretend they
own a store, describe it, name
it, and design a sign for the front.

Making a Comparison Chart

OBJECTIVE   Comparing our lives with the lives of story characters.

INTRODUCING AND READING THE LESSON

Read a paragraph that relates to the unit theme.

Remind students that the unit theme is "Remember When . . ." Then read the following paragraph aloud to them.

> Lucy and her brother Sam set out across the prairie early in the day. It was a long walk—over two miles—to their little one-room schoolhouse. They got to school just as the teacher was clanging the big bell that announced the beginning of the school day. Lucy sat in the long wooden bench in the back of the room with the older children. Sam was in front with the young ones. It was a dark day, and the teacher had lit four thick candles for light. The children took out their slates and began doing their sums.

Analyze the information in the passage.

Ask students if they think the author is writing about a boy and girl today. Encourage students to compare specific information in the paragraph with their own experiences. List student's comparisons on the board in a chart similar to the one below.

Lucy and Sam did this.	You do this.	You do not do this.
walked two miles to school		x
went to a one-room schoolhouse		x
did arithmetic	x	
used a slate		x

Explain strategy.

Tell students that the chart on the board is a *comparison chart*. Point out that a comparison chart helps organize what the author says about a character. Explain that it can also help them compare the character with themselves.

State the objective.

Tell students that this lesson will show how they can better understand a story character by making a comparison chart.

Refer students to their texts.

Have students read up to the heading "Using the Strategy."

DISCUSSING THE LESSON

Review the main points of the lesson.

Check students' understanding of the lesson with these questions.

Page 26   Why does an author tell you details about a character's life? (so that you will better understand the character)

Page 26   What is listed in a comparison chart? (details about a character)

Page 27   What things have you done that Karen did ? (Answers will probably include: bought candles and bought flour.)

Page 27   What are some things that Karen did that you have not done? (Answers will probably include: wore high-button shoes, went to the candle maker, went to the miller.)

Making a Comparison Chart

How can you better understand the characters you read about? One good way is to make a comparison chart.

Learning the Strategy

As you read, you learn some of the details of a character's life. You may learn what a character eats, and how he or she dresses and talks. The author uses these details to help you understand the world a character lives in. If you list details about the character's life, you can compare them with your own life. A comparison chart is one way to help you understand how a character's life and your life are the same and different.

Read the paragraph below and then look at the comparison chart that follows. Compare things that Karen has done with things you may have done.

Karen put on her shawl and walked to town. Her high-button shoes kept sinking in the mud. She went into the candle maker's shop and bought candles. Then she walked to the miller's. Her freshly ground bag of flour was waiting for her.

COMPARISON CHART

Where Karen went and what she did	I have done this.	I have not done this.
wore high-button shoes		✓
went to the candle maker		✓
bought candles	✓	
bought flour	✓	

A comparison chart may help you better understand how Karen's life and yours are the same and different.

Using the Strategy

Copy and fill out the chart below for "When I Was Nine." Then compare the things the author has done with the things you have done.

COMPARISON CHART

Where the boy went and what he did.	I have done this.	I have not done this.
traveled west		
listened to a radio		
learned to pitch		
saw the northern lights		

Applying the Strategy to the Next Story

As you read the next story, "Thy Friend, Obadiah," compare Obadiah's life with your life. Then you can make a comparison chart.

◆◆◆ The writing connection can be found on page 45.

Strategy for Thinking

Strategy for Thinking

WRAP-UP

Direct students to read the instructions under "Using the Strategy." Then have them copy the chart and fill it in.

Discuss answers for the independent practice activity.

When students have finished, make a composite chart of their responses. Write the items from the chart on the board. For each item, have students demonstrate by a show of hands whether they have or have not done what the boy did. Write the totals in the *have done* and *have not done* columns. Examine the results and discuss the comparisons. Which items show more similarities than differences? Which show more differences? In general, does the comparison chart show that the boy's life was fairly similar to the students' lives or very different from their lives?

Direct students to the next selection.

Tell students they will practice making a comparison chart in the next selection, "Thy Friend, Obadiah."

39

	Teaching Sequence	Trade Books and Resources	Meeting Individual Needs	Integrated Language Arts / Cross Curriculum
The Bridge Pages 42–43	**Maintain** Characterization	• Teaching Chart 6 • Workbook 13 • Skills Practice 9		
PART 1 **Vocabulary Strategies** Pages 44–45	**Develop Concepts** Semantic Mapping **Teach Vocabulary** **STORY CRITICAL WORDS: beak,** distress, fluttered, **perched,** thee, thy, **wharf** (Tested words are boldfaced.)	• Teaching Chart 7 • Workbook 14 • Skills Practice 10	**SUPPORT WORDS:** breeches, cobblestones, dangled, mainland, raw, wheeling • Skills Practice 11 **CHARACTER/SETTING WORDS:** Asa, Jacob Slade, Moses, Nantucket, Obadiah, Rachel, Rebecca, Starbuck	**WRITING/SPEAKING ACTIVITY:** Use new vocabulary to describe activities that take place around a wharf. • Spelling Connection 40
PART 2 **Reading & Responding** Pages 46–55	**Build Background** **Develop a Purpose for Reading** **Guide the Reading Process** **Selection Follow-Up**	• Reader's Journal 14–17 • Workbook 15 **READING EVERY DAY** *George, the Drummer Boy,* by N. Benchley *Obadiah, the Bold,* by B. Turkle	**EXTRA HELP:** Model Comparison Chart **ACHIEVING ENGLISH PROFICIENCY:** Discussing Historical Pronouns • Achieving English Proficiency Master 4	**Language Arts Connections** **WRITING TO LEARN:** Complete a thought link. • Writing Master 2 **SPEAKING/LISTENING:** Discussing Historical Fiction; Making a Friendship Poster; Creating Nursery Rhymes **WRITING:** Writing a Story Scene • Language Arts Master 2
PART 3 **Selection Support** Pages 56–63	**Introduce** Suffixes *-er, -or* (Tested)	• Teaching Chart 8 • Workbook 16 • Skills Practice 12	• Reteaching Masters 1–4 • Challenge Master 3 • Achieving English Proficiency Master 5 **Practice** • Teaching Chart 9 • Workbook 17–18 • Skills Practice 13 Suffix *-ly* (Tested) Strategy for Thinking **Maintain** • Skills Practice 14–15 Drawing Conclusions Prefixes *un-, re-*	**Curriculum Connections** **SCIENCE:** Studying Sea Gulls • Curriculum Connection Master 2 **SOCIAL STUDIES:** Researching Quakers; Researching Facts About Mills **GEOGRAPHY:** Creating Nantucket Relief Maps **ART:** Making Colonial Dioramas

Thy Friend, Obadiah

written and illustrated by Brinton Turkle

SUMMARY   *A young Quaker boy, Obadiah, has a friend—a sea gull who follows him everywhere, even to Meeting. Although*

Obadiah's entire family has noticed the friendly bird, he continues to ignore it. Then one day the sea gull is gone. Obadiah is relieved, but he soon spots the bird with a fishhook dangling from its beak. Feeling sorry for the sea gull, Obadiah removes the hook. Although the bird flies off, it soon returns to Obadiah's house. Obadiah finally admits the bird is his friend. Thy Friend, Obadiah *was named a* **Caldecott Honor** *book in 1970.*

The Bridge

SKILL TRACE: CHARACTERIZATION	
Introduced in Level 7. This skill is re-introduced in Unit 4 of this level.	Maintain
	TE 42 / 428

LITERATURE

Teaching Characterization

OBJECTIVE   Identifying character traits and emotions.

1. WARM-UP

Use a known passage to determine character traits and emotions.

Tell students they will listen to a passage from the preceding story, "When I Was Nine." Explain that an author may describe a character's traits, or what a character is like, by describing the actions, thoughts, and feelings of the character. Have students listen for clues that describe Grandma. (*playful, loving, caring, fun*)

> **Grandma was a lot of fun. We would crawl into her room in the morning and hide under her bed. Then we would pretend to be a funny radio program; she always acted surprised and she always laughed.**

Discuss story clues.

Reread the passage. Have students tell which words told them directly what kind of person Grandma was. (*a lot of fun*) Then ask which clues described Grandma's actions. (*she always acted surprised, she always laughed*) Explain that these words help readers decide what Grandma was like.

State the objective.

Tell students they will review how to use story clues to help them identify character traits and emotions.

2. TEACH

Explain why recognizing character traits is important.

Recognizing character traits helps readers understand a character's behavior and how that behavior affects the way the story ends.

Present a strategy for identifying character traits and emotions.

Explain that there is a strategy students can use to help them recognize character traits. First, look for direct descriptions of the character. Next, look for clues in words and actions that tell what a character thinks or feels. Finally, think about what these words and actions mean.

> **TEACHING CHART 6: CHARACTERIZATION**   6
>
> 1. My own children are grown up now; that's how old I am. But sometimes I look back and I remember. . . . (thoughtful)
> 2. I put out a weekly newspaper. I collected news from all the people on our block. (hardworking)
> 3. On my birthday we stopped in a small town and went into a store. My parents bought me exactly what I always wanted . . . a cowboy hat. (happy)

Model the strategy.

Read passage 1 and point out that the author gives clues to show what the character is like and how he feels. "My own children are grown up now" tells you that the character is a grown-up. "But sometimes I look back and I remember" tells you that the character likes to think about what his life used to be like.

3. GUIDED PRACTICE

Check for understanding.   Before going on, have students explain how to identify character traits and emotions. *(Look for descriptive words; look for clues in the character's thoughts, feelings, and actions.)*

Guide students in using the strategy.   Have students use the strategy to identify character traits and emotions in the remaining passages. Discuss the clues that helped students decide.

4. WRAP-UP

Summarize instruction.   Review with students why readers identify character traits and emotions and the kinds of clues that help them do so. *(to help them understand the way characters act in a story and how the story ends; descriptions, clues about the character's thoughts, feelings, and actions)*

Provide independent practice.   Options for independent practice are shown in the Resource Center below.

5. APPLICATION

Students will recognize character traits as they read "Thy Friend, Obadiah." The symbol ✔ marks specific questions and activities that apply this skill.

Workbook page 13

RESOURCE CENTER

Skills Practice 9

◀ **Workbook page 13** is intended for use by all students.

Skills Practice 9 may ▶ be assigned for additional practice.

Workbook reuse option: Have students compose the words the characters could have said to support their actions in Part A.

Workbook page 13

NAME _____

LITERATURE

Characterization

REMEMBER: To understand a character in a story, think about what the character says and does. Also think about how the character speaks and acts.

A. Write the words from the box that show what each character is like. Each question should have two answers.

put out a weekly newspaper	acted surprised to find them hiding
laughed at their radio shows	still liked to be read to
bought the right birthday present	shared the northern lights

1. What did James do that showed he liked words?
   put out a weekly newspaper

   still liked to be read to

2. What did James' parents do that showed they cared about their children?
   bought the right birthday present

   shared the northern lights

3. What did James' grandmother do that made her fun for her grandchildren?
   acted surprised to find them hiding

   laughed at their radio shows

B. On separate paper, write two or three sentences of your own about one of the characters in the story "When I Was Nine." See Teacher Notes.

Characterization   "Thy Friend, Obadiah"   **13**

Skills Practice 9

NAME _____

SKILLS PRACTICE 9

Characterization

Characters are people or animals in a story. Writers tell you how the characters look and what they are like. Think about what characters say and do. This will help you understand them.

Example: Bill studied hard and worked carefully.
         He felt proud when he did well on the test.

Read about the characters.

My name is Anna. I have a sister named Mary. We go to school in town. It is about two miles away. Sometimes Pa takes us in the wagon. Most days we walk. Mary is little and doesn't like school. The older children are noisy. And she thinks lessons are hard. I love the long walk. I love to watch the birds and little animals in the woods. I like school, too. I like to help the younger children. They are good at thinking up games to play. Everyone likes games, even Mary. We sometimes make up special games to play as we walk to school. That makes the long walk more fun for Mary.

Now write about the characters.

1. How does Mary feel about school?   She doesn't like it.
   Underline the sentence in the story that tells why.
2. What does Mary like?   games
3. Who likes school?   Anna
   What does she like to do at school?   help the younger children

4. What do the younger children do?   think up games
5. Who likes nature?   Anna
6. What word describes Anna?   kind
      brave   honest   kind
7. What things does she do that show she is kind?   helps younger children

LEVEL 8   "Thy Friend, Obadiah"   **9**

Vocabulary Strategies

Developing Concepts

Use a semantic map to tap prior knowledge of sea gulls.

Make a semantic map about sea gulls as a starting point for teaching vocabulary. Tell students they are going to read a story about a boy and a sea gull. Allow students several minutes to explain what they know about sea gulls. Guide the discussion by asking questions like the following: "Where are you likely to find sea gulls?" "What do they look like?" "What do they eat?" "How do they catch their food?" List responses on the map.

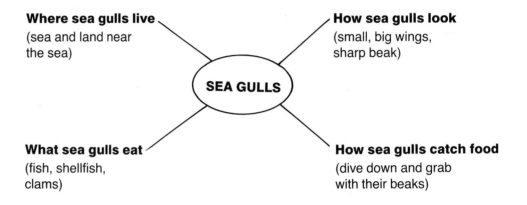

Where sea gulls live
(sea and land near the sea)

How sea gulls look
(small, big wings, sharp beak)

SEA GULLS

What sea gulls eat
(fish, shellfish, clams)

How sea gulls catch food
(dive down and grab with their beaks)

Teaching Vocabulary

Discuss meanings of Story Critical words.

Read each context sentence on the Teaching Chart and identify the new word. Then use the questions below to help students understand each word. When necessary, provide a definition.

> **TEACHING CHART 7: VOCABULARY**   `7`
>
> 1. **fluttered** (flapped the wings without flying)
>   A sea gull stood on the shore and *fluttered* its wings in the wind.
> 2. **beak** (a bird's bill)
>   It was carrying a small fish in its *beak*.
> 3. **perched** (alighted or rested)
>   Soon the sea gull flew up and *perched* on a high roof to rest.
> 4. **wharf** (pier; structure built along the water for ships to dock)
>   It could see the boats docked at the *wharf*.
> 5. **distress** (worry; upset)
>   Since it was safe and well fed, nothing could *distress* the bird.
> 6. **thy** (formerly used to mean "your")
>   "Fly down from *thy* perch," said the young boy to the sea gull.
> 7. **thee** (formerly used to mean "you")
>   "This clam is for *thee*."

fluttered   1. **What is another word for *fluttered*?** *(flapped)*   STRATEGY: SYNONYMS

beak   2. **What other word could you use in place of the word *beak*?** *(bill)*
Complete the following comparison: A *beak* is to a *bird* as a   (mouth)   is to a *person*.   STRATEGY: ANALOGIES

perched **3. What words in the sentence helped you figure out what** *perched* **means?** (high roof, rest)   STRATEGY: CONTEXT CLUES

wharf **4. What types of boats might be at a wharf?** (fishing boats, sailboats, motor boats)   STRATEGY: PRIOR KNOWLEDGE

distress **5. How was the sea gull feeling on the roof?** (safe, well fed) **What might distress it?** (something that went wrong; if it were not safe)   STRATEGY: CONTEXT CLUES

thy **6. What more familiar word could you use in place of the word** *thy*? (your)   STRATEGY: SYNONYMS

thee **7. What more familiar word could you use in place of the word** *thee*? (you)   STRATEGY: SYNONYMS

Add new words to the map.   Challenge students to add as many of the new words as they can to the semantic map, adding new headings as needed.

Discuss Support words as needed.   The Glossary of the Student Text includes definitions of the Support words: *dangled, wheeling, raw, mainland, breeches, cobblestones.* Explain the phrases *take a chill* ("*get sick*") and *burn a hole in the pocket* ("*get rid of quickly; spend*").

Present the Character/Setting words as needed.   Present and pronounce the Character and Setting words: *Nantucket, Obadiah, Asa, Rebecca, Rachel, Moses, Jacob Slade, Starbuck* before students read the selection.

Provide independent practice.   Options for independent practice are shown in the Resource Center below.

WRITING OR SPEAKING ACTIVITY   *Have students write a short paragraph about or discuss an activity that takes place around a wharf, such as fishing. Ask them to use as many new words as possible.*

Workbook page 14

SELECTION **VOCABULARY**   NAME _____

Using New Words

A. Write the word that goes with each group.

| beak | distress | thee | thy | wharf |

1. you	2. feathers	3. ships	4. thy	5. hurt
thee	wing	net	thou	pain
yours	tail	fisherman	you	upset

| thy | beak | wharf | thee | distress |

B. Read the paragraphs. Write the correct word in each blank.

| beak | distress | fluttered | perched | wharf |

Once I walked by the sea and saw sea gulls overhead. One gull flew until it saw a fish below. Then it dipped and caught the fish in its ___beak___ .

I came to a big ___wharf___ where fishing boats were tied up. More sea gulls were ___perched___ on the boats. Some ___fluttered___ around the boats, hoping to snatch a fish. It would ___distress___ the gulls if a hungry cat came to share the fish from the boats.

C. Picture yourself on a wharf. You are looking out to the ocean and back to the shore. On separate paper, draw a picture to show what you see. Then label each thing in your drawing. See Teacher Notes.

14   "Thy Friend, Obadiah"   Selection Vocabulary

RESOURCE CENTER

◄ **Workbook page 14** provides practice with Story Critical words.

Skills Practice 10 ► provides additional practice with Story Critical words.

Skills Practice 11 provides practice with Support words.

Spelling Connection Master 40 may be used for spelling instruction with the new vocabulary.

Workbook reuse option: Have students circle all the words in Parts A and B that have to do with the sea.

Skills Practice 10

NAME _____   SKILLS PRACTICE ◄10

Vocabulary: Story Critical Words

A. Study the meaning of each word.

beak a bird's bill
distress to worry; to upset
fluttered flapped the wings
perched rested on

thee an old-fashioned word meaning "you"
thy an old-fashioned word meaning "your"
wharf a place where ships can dock

B. Complete the word map. Use four of the vocabulary words. Then add words of your own. **Responses will vary.**

1. Parts of a Bird's Body	3. Things the Bird Did
beak	fluttered
	perched

Bird

| 2. Places That Birds Like | 4. Kinds of Birds |
| wharf | |

C. Each sentence tells about a vocabulary word. Write the word.

5. You can see boats here.   ___wharf___
6. It is not nice to do this to a person.   ___distress___
7. This means "you."   ___thee___
8. This word shows who owns something. ___thy___

D. Synonyms are words that have similar meanings. Write the vocabulary word for each underlined word.

9. The duckling has a yellow bill.   ___beak___
10. Playing loud music will upset neighbors.   ___distress___

10   LEVEL 8   "Thy Friend, Obadiah"   Classification

2 Reading & Responding

Building Background

Share the following quotation with students and paraphrase it as "Someone who is your friend when you need help is really your friend." Ask students what they think this means. *(that being a friend to someone who needs help is a test of friendship)* Then ask students whether they agree.

A friend in need is a friend indeed.

Build background about friendship.

Ask students to describe some ways in which people show friendship. Ask them what they do when they want to become friends with someone they have met. Have students discuss why people might not try to be friendly. (*not knowing someone well enough, shyness*) Tell students that this story is about a Quaker boy. The Quakers are a religious group, whose actual name is The Society of Friends. Their beliefs include friendship and respect for all living things.

Discuss historical fiction.

Tell students that the next story they will read, "Thy Friend, Obadiah," is historical fiction. Explain that the story takes place at a time in the past, and the characters behave like real people of that time. Mention that the author, Brinton Turkle, was careful to include true details about the time and place in both his words and his illustrations. Have students read the Brinton Turkle entry in the back of their texts.

Developing a Purpose for Reading

Have students apply the thinking strategy.

Remind children they can compare their lives with the lives of story characters by making a chart. Ask them what a comparison chart helps them to do. (*It helps them understand how a character's life is similar to, or different from, their own.*)

Have the children preview the story as you point out the questions with the diamond symbol (◆◆◆). Explain that these questions will ask them to think about details in the character's life. Direct students to have paper ready, but tell them they will only make mental comparisons as they read. Explain that they will make their charts *after* they finish reading.

Meeting

Individual

Needs

EXTRA HELP   Quickly draw a three-column chart on the board with the headings **Actions/Details, I have done this,** and **I have *not* done this.** Refer students to the first question with the diamond symbol on Student Text page 31. Discuss this detail about Obadiah's life and fill in the chart with their responses. Explain that they will make similar charts when they finish reading.

ACHIEVING ENGLISH PROFICIENCY   Write **thee, thy,** and **thyself** on the board. Tell students that the characters in the story use these pronouns instead of you, your, and yourself. Write **you, your,** and **yourself** next to the corresponding pronouns on the board. Explain that this way of speaking was common among people in New England in the 1600s. For additional help in story comprehension, use Master 4 in the Teacher Resource Kit.

If you had an unusual friend like Obadiah's, you might feel and act just the way he did!

Thy Friend, Obadiah

written and illustrated by Brinton Turkle

Wherever Obadiah went, a sea gull was following him. It followed him all the way to the candle maker's, and it was waiting for him when he came out of the shop.

When he was sent to the wharf for a fresh codfish, it hopped along behind him.

And at night when he went to bed, he could see it from his window. There it was, perched on the chimney of the shed, facing into the wind. Of all the sea gulls on Nantucket Island, why did this one go everywhere Obadiah went?

Reader's Journal   **p 14**
Preparing for Reading

BE A DETECTIVE

Students study a picture from the story and make predictions about the story.

GUIDED READING

Page 29   What does the sea gull do? (It follows Obadiah to the candle maker's, to the wharf, and home.)   RECALL: SEQUENCE

✔ **Page 29   What do the sea gull's actions seem to show?** (that it likes Obadiah)   INFER: FEELINGS/ATTITUDES

HIGHLIGHTING LITERATURE

Page 29   Point out to students that the author established the problem at the beginning of the story. Ask them to identify Obadiah's problem. (A sea gull followed him everywhere.) Ask them how Obadiah felt about this, and have them cite details to support their answers. (Possible responses: He did not like the sea gull, he was impatient about it. His impatience was conveyed by the sentence "Of all the sea gulls on Nantucket Island, why did this one go everywhere Obadiah went?")

✔ Skill from The Bridge applied through this question.

47

On First Day, everyone dressed up warmly and went to Meeting. The Starbuck family formed a little parade. First, Father and Mother. Then Moses and Asa and Rebecca and Obadiah and Rachel. Behind them came the sea gull, hopping along as if it were going to Meeting too.

"Go away!" said Obadiah. The bird <u>fluttered</u> off, but it soon came back.

"<u>Thee</u> has a friend, Obadiah," said Father as he turned in at the Meeting House gate.

"Obadiah has a friend!" said Moses.

"Obadiah has a friend!" said Rebecca.

"Ask <u>thy</u> friend to come into Meeting," said Asa.

Rachel didn't tease. She tried to take Obadiah's hand; but he didn't want to hold anybody's hand. He picked up a pebble and threw it at the bird. He missed. The sea gull flew out of sight, but when Meeting was over, there it was—waiting for him.

It got so that Obadiah didn't want to go out of his house.

At breakfast, Father said, "Obadiah, how is thy friend?"

"What friend?" asked Obadiah, his mouth full of muffin and plum jam.

"Thy very own sea gull!" said Asa.

Rebecca giggled.

"That bird is *not* my friend!" Obadiah shouted.

Mother raised a finger. "Don't distress thyself, Obadiah," she said. "I think it is very nice that one of God's creatures favors thee."

"Well, *I* don't like it," said Obadiah. "Sea gulls don't follow anyone else around!"

Soon after breakfast it began to snow. In the afternoon, Mother wrapped a woolen scarf around Obadiah and sent him to Jacob Slade's mill with some money and a sack for flour. ◄❖►

◄❖►
Have you ever gone to a mill to buy flour?

GUIDED READING

✔ **Page 30   Does Obadiah want the sea gull for a friend?** (no) **What story clues tell you this?** (Obadiah tells the bird to go away, he throws a pebble at it, and he does not want to leave his house.)   ANALYZE: CHARACTER

Pages 30–31   What actions by the rest of the family tell you how they feel about the sea gull? (The other children laugh and tease Obadiah, so they think it is funny. Father and Mother refer to the sea gull as Obadiah's friend, and Mother says that it is nice that one of God's creatures favors him, so they seem to feel that it is not so unusual or funny.)   SYNTHESIZE: DRAWING CONCLUSIONS

Page 31   Why do you think Obadiah is so upset by the sea gull? (Possible answers: He does not like the bird; he is afraid of it; he feels silly that a bird is following him since it follows no one else.)   INFER: CAUSE/EFFECT

✔ Skill from The Bridge applied through this question.

STRATEGIC READING   ◄❖►

Page 31   Refer students to the question with the diamond symbol. Discuss what might be nice about buying flour at a mill. (Possible responses: The flour would be freshly ground; it would be interesting to see the inside of a mill.) **Resume reading the story.** STRATEGY FOR THINKING

The bird was nowhere to be seen. "Maybe it doesn't like the snow," Obadiah told himself. "Maybe it flew away to the mainland." He was so glad it wasn't hopping along after him that he made duck tracks all the way up Jacob Slade's hill.

The miller filled the flour sack, and Obadiah gave him the money Mother had tucked in his mitten.

"Keep this, lad," Jacob Slade said, giving him a penny. "And don't let it burn a hole in thy pocket."

On the way home, Obadiah tried to slide on a patch of ice, but he skidded and fell head over heels. His hat went flying. Snow got in his ears and in his boots. His breeches got wet and so did the sack of flour. His knee hurt and the penny was gone forever in the snowbank. He was all alone on the hill. Shivering and sniffling, he picked himself up and limped home.

Sea gulls were perched on almost every housetop on Orange Street; but he couldn't find the special sea gull that had been following him. The birds were faced into the raw east wind and paid no attention to him at all.

Mother was very cross about the wet flour. She gave Obadiah a hot bath and dry clothes and right after supper she made him drink something hot that tasted awful. "Is thy knee still hurting thee?" she asked. ❖❖❖

"It's better." Obadiah wished he felt better about the lost penny.

"Then get into bed."

Obadiah said his prayers, and as soon as Mother was gone, he got out of bed and tiptoed to the window. The sea gull was not there. He got back into bed again and wondered what had happened.

The next day and the next day and the day after that, no bird followed Obadiah when he left his house. Every night he looked out of his window, but the sea gull didn't come back.

Then he saw it down at the wharf. It was with some other gulls where a little fishing boat was docked; but something was wrong. A large rusty fishhook dangled from its beak.

"That's what happens when thee steals from a fishing line. Serves thee right," Obadiah said and walked away.

THY FRIEND, OBADIAH

GUIDED READING

Page 32   Why is Obadiah happy when he goes on his errand to Jacob Slade's mill? (The sea gull is nowhere in sight.)   RECALL: DETAILS

Page 32   What words tell you that Obadiah is beginning to miss the sea gull? (". . . he couldn't find the special sea gull that had been following him"; and "he got out of bed and tiptoed to the window. The sea gull was not there.")   ANALYZE: CONTEXT

Page 33   Where is the bird and what happened to it? (at the wharf with a fish hook in its beak)   RECALL: DETAILS

✔ **Page 33   How would you describe Obadiah's character when he walks away from the sea gull?** (He is unkind, unhelpful, mean.)   ANALYZE: CHARACTER

STRATEGIC READING   ❖❖❖

Page 32   Read aloud the question with the diamond symbol, and discuss what students do when they arrive home wet and cold. (possible responses: take a hot bath, drink something warm, get into bed) Point out how Obadiah's mother fusses over him, and ask students if they think mothers have changed much since Obadiah's time. (Students will probably say that mothers have not changed at all.) Redirect children to the story.
STRATEGY FOR THINKING

✔ Skill from The Bridge applied through this question.

❖❖❖
What do you do when you come home wet and cold?

He was on the cobblestone street by the blacksmith's shop when he discovered that the sea gull was hopping along behind him.

Obadiah stopped. The bird stopped. The fishhook bobbed in the wind.

"If thee is quiet, I'll try to get that off thy beak."

The sea gull didn't move.

"I won't hurt thee," Obadiah said.

The bird allowed him to come nearer and nearer. In a moment, the fishhook was in Obadiah's hand, and the sea gull was wheeling into the sky making little mewing sounds. It flew out toward the lighthouse. Obadiah watched until he couldn't see it any longer; then he threw the rusty hook away and went home.

As soon as he opened the front door, Obadiah smelled bread baking. In the kitchen, Mother and Rachel were just taking it out of the oven. Mother cut him a slice of the fresh, warm bread and spread it with butter. He sat on a stool to eat it and between mouthfuls he told them what had happened. ◆◈◆

"Well," said Rachel, "thee won't see that silly old bird again."

"No," said Obadiah. "I expect I won't."

◆◈◆
Have you ever smelled freshly baked bread?

At bedtime, after she had tucked him in, Mother went to the window. "Obadiah," she said. "Look here."

He tumbled out of bed.

"Isn't that thy sea gull?"

There it was on the chimney, facing into the wind in the clear blue night!

"That's him!" said Obadiah. "He looks cold out there, Mother."

GUIDED READING

Page 34   What happens after Obadiah walks away from the wharf to the street by the blacksmith's shop? (Obadiah discovers that the sea gull has followed him.)   RECALL: SEQUENCE

✔ **Page 34   How would you now describe Obadiah, based on his actions and words?** (gentle, kind, caring, helpful)   SYNTHESIZE: CHARACTER

✔ **Page 34   How do you think Obadiah feels when the freed bird flies away?** (lonely, deserted, sorry)   INFER: FEELINGS/ATTITUDES

Page 35   Why do you think the sea gull returns? (Obadiah helped it, so it wants to be friends.)   SYNTHESIZE: DRAWING CONCLUSIONS

STRATEGIC READING ◆◈◆

**Page 34   Direct students' attention to the marginal question. Encourage volunteers to describe how freshly baked bread makes them feel. (Possible responses: They feel hungry; they feel curious about how the bread is baked.) Resume reading the story.   STRATEGY FOR THINKING

✔ Skill from The Bridge applied through this question.

"His feathers keep him warm. But thee doesn't have feathers, Obadiah. Get back into bed quickly before thee takes a chill."

Obadiah jumped into bed again and Mother kissed him good night.

The wind whistled around the corner of the house and Obadiah snuggled down into the quilts.

"Mother. . . ."

"Yes, Obadiah."

"That sea gull *is* my friend."

"I'm glad, Obadiah. Good night."

"And Mother. . . ."

Mother turned at the door. Her candle flickered and almost went out. "Yes, Obadiah," she said.

"Since I helped him, I'm *his* friend, too." ◆◆◆

◆ LIBRARY LINK ◆

If you enjoyed this story by Brinton Turkle, you might like to read his other books, such as Obadiah, the Bold *and* The Fiddler of High Lonesome.

 Reader's **Response**

Do you think an animal can really be your friend? Tell why.

◆◆◆
Make a comparison chart. List things Obadiah did. Check the things you have done. Check the things you have *not* done.

See next page for suggested answers.

SELECTION FOLLOW-UP

Thy Friend, Obadiah

◆ **T**hinking It Over

1. Why was Obadiah so annoyed at the beginning of the story?
2. Why did Obadiah try to send the bird away?
3. When did Obadiah first begin to miss the sea gull?
4. How did Obadiah feel about the bird before he helped it? How did he feel afterward?
5. Suppose Obadiah had not helped the bird. What might have happened? How did you decide on your answer?

◆ **W**riting to Learn

THINK AND CONNECT   Obadiah learns something about helping others. It is written in the "thought link" below.

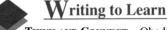

Because I helped the sea gull,   the sea gull is my friend.

Finish another "thought link."

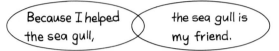

If I help someone,

WRITE   You discovered something about helping others when you finished your "thought link." Write some sentences to tell what may happen if you help someone.

GUIDED READING

Page 36   How has Obadiah shown that he will be the sea gull's friend? (by helping it, by welcoming its return)   SYNTHESIZE: DRAWING CONCLUSIONS

RETURNING TO THE READING PURPOSE

✔ **Page 36**   Read aloud the note with the diamond symbol. Allow students time to make their charts. Remind them there are three columns in the chart: the left column shows the details about the character's life; the middle column is labeled "I have done this"; the right column is labeled "I have *not* done this."

Use the marginal questions to review the details that students should list about Obadiah's life. (He went to the mill for flour, fell on ice and got wet, had a hot bath and some medicine, and smelled freshly baked bread.) Have students complete their charts. Finally, ask students if the charts helped them better understand how Obadiah's life was similar to, or different from, their own.

✔ Informal Assessment Opportunity: RESPONDING

Reader's Journal   pp 15, 16
Responding to Reading

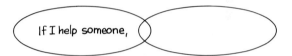

THE BIRD'S WORDS

Students pretend to be the sea gull and, responding to writing cues in the journal, write the story from the sea gull's perspective.

51

SELECTION FOLLOW-UP

Thy Friend, Obadiah

THINKING IT OVER

1. **Why was Obadiah so annoyed at the beginning of the story?**
   (Obadiah was annoyed because a sea gull kept following him.)   RECALL:
   CHARACTER

2. **Why did Obadiah try to send the bird away?** (Possible answers: It
   annoyed him; it embarrassed him; his sisters and brothers teased him
   about it.)   INFER: CAUSE/EFFECT

3. **When did Obadiah first begin to miss the sea gull?** (Obadiah began to
   miss the sea gull after he fell on the ice.)   ANALYZE: PLOT

4. **How did Obadiah feel about the bird before he helped it? How did
   he feel afterward?** (At first he did not like it and tried to make it go
   away. Then he began to miss it. After helping the sea gull, he cared
   about it. He felt that he and the sea gull were friends.)   ANALYZE:
   COMPARISON

5. **Suppose Obadiah had not helped the bird. What might have
   happened? How did you decide on your answer?** (Possible answers:
   The bird might have continued to follow him; the bird might have left
   forever; the bird might have died because of the fishhook; someone else
   might have helped the bird. Students may cite personal experiences and
   other stories they have read in support of their answers.)   SYNTHESIZE:
   PREDICTING OUTCOMES; METACOGNITION

WRITING TO LEARN

Use Writing Master 2, which duplicates this diagram.

THINK AND CONNECT   Obadiah learns something about helping others.
It is written in the "thought link" below. (Help students complete the
"thought link" to prepare for writing.)

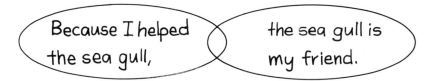

Because I helped the sea gull,   the sea gull is my friend.

Finish another "thought link."

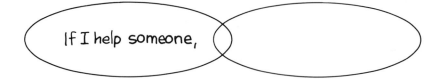

If I help someone,

Extend comprehension through writing.

WRITE   You discovered something about helping others when you
finished your "thought link." Write some sentences to tell what may
happen if you help someone. (Have students share their sentences.)

More Ideas for Selection Follow-Up

CRITICAL AND CREATIVE THINKING QUESTIONS

Encourage a variety of responses and points of view.

Use these open-ended questions to encourage critical and creative thinking about the selection.

✔ 1. When he first saw the fishhook in the sea gull's beak, Obadiah walked away. What do you think made him change his mind about helping the sea gull?

2. What ideas would you give the author, Brinton Turkle, for a story about the adventures shared by Obadiah and the sea gull?

REREADING ORALLY

Have students reread for pleasure.

Ask students to select and reread passages that they especially enjoyed and tell why they enjoyed them. Remind them that this story is set in a time long past. Since the language was spoken somewhat differently then, students should reread their chosen passages silently to become familiar with the different style of speech. Have students try to imagine themselves living in this period of time, dressed in Obadiah's clothing. This may help them with the unfamiliar speech. Remind students that oral reading is for others to listen to and enjoy, which requires careful pronunciation of words and changes in voice tone to sound like the different characters.

SELECTION COMPREHENSION

Provide comprehension check.

A Workbook page to check comprehension is shown in the Resource Center below. It may be used for informal assessment.

✔ Informal Assessment Opportunity: EMPATHIZING WITH STORY CHARACTERS

Workbook page 15

NAME _____

SELECTION COMPREHENSION

Thy Friend, Obadiah

A. Complete the summary of "Thy Friend, Obadiah."
Accept reasonable variations.
This story tells about ____Obadiah____ . Obadiah and his

family lived in early America near the ____ocean____ .

Obadiah was angry because ____a sea gull always followed him____ .
He didn't like the sea gull to follow him because his brothers and

sisters ____teased him about it____ .
One Sunday on the way to Meeting, Obadiah tried to get rid of the

sea gull by ____throwing a pebble at it____ .
He missed, but the gull flew out of sight. After Meeting, the gull

____was waiting for him again____ .
Finally the gull disappeared all by itself and Obadiah didn't know
what had happened to it. One day Obadiah saw the gull again. This time

a ____fishhook____ dangled from its beak. Obadiah helped the

gull by ____pulling out the fishhook____ .
Later that night as he was going to bed, he looked out his window and

saw the gull on a nearby ____chimney____ .
Obadiah was happy to see the gull. He didn't mind anymore that the

gull wanted to be his friend. He knew he was the gull's ____friend____
because he had helped the gull.

B. Think about how Obadiah and
the gull became friends. On
separate paper, list three people
you know and write something
you could do to be their friend.
See Teacher Notes.

Selection Comprehension   "Thy Friend, Obadiah"   **15**

RESOURCE CENTER

◄ **Workbook page 15** is intended for use by all students.

Writing Master 2 duplicates the Writing to Learn diagram.

LANGUAGE ARTS CONNECTIONS

CRITICAL THINKING: LEARNING FROM HISTORICAL FICTION

Discuss historical fiction.
Remind students that authors who write historical fiction about the past try to give true details about the time and place in which the story is set. These stories can teach readers facts about other times and places.

Have students determine facts from the story.
Have students make lists of the details in "Thy Friend, Obadiah" that tell about time and place. *(cobblestone streets, clothing, blacksmith shop, mill, candle maker)* Have students discuss what conclusions they can draw about the time and place from their lists of details. *(For example, if Obadiah's family needed candles, then they probably did not have electric lights; electricity had probably not yet been invented.)* SHARED LEARNING: SPEAKING

MAKING A CLASS POSTER

Discuss posters.
Tell students that posters often have both words and pictures. Ask students to describe posters they have seen.

Discuss the meaning of friendship and have students contribute to a class poster.
Have students think about and discuss friendship. Then give students a few minutes to complete the sentence: *A friend is* ——————. Make a list of students' completed sentences on the chalkboard. Then have students illustrate their own ideas. As a class activity, organize a class poster with the words *A friend is* in the center and the students' illustrations around the edges. Use students' written responses as captions to their illustrations. WHOLE CLASS ENRICHMENT

CREATING NURSERY RHYMES

Have students create rhymes about Obadiah and the sea gull.
Point out the rhythm in "Mary Had a Little Lamb" and have students name the words that rhyme. Then tell students that Obadiah's sea gull was a lot like Mary's lamb, following him everywhere. Have students work in pairs or small groups to write rhymes about Obadiah. The following is an example:

Obadiah had a friend	**One sad day the gull was**
Who hopped along behind him.	**gone;**
	Nowhere could he find him.

Have students recite their rhymes in unison, emphasizing rhythm and rhyming words. You might even have the class recite or sing one as a round. SHARED LEARNING: SPEAKING

WRITING A STORY SCENE

Have students write the next scene of the story.

Review the end of the story and ask students to imagine what Obadiah and the sea gull might do or say to each other when they meet the next day. Use the following questions to help students develop their story scenes:

What might Obadiah say about why he was unfriendly at first?

How would the gull explain why it wanted to be his friend?

How would each character explain why he liked the other?

How would each character show that he wanted to remain friends?

Encourage students to think about character traits and emotions as they write. Remind students to proofread and correct any errors. **Language Arts Master 2** can be used with this activity.   CHALLENGE: WRITING

READING EVERY DAY

In "Thy Friend, Obadiah" students meet a boy living in colonial times. To learn more about this period through the eyes or lives of children, students might enjoy reading the following books, including another about Obadiah.

George, the Drummer Boy! by Nathaniel Benchley. Harper & Row, © 1977. George, a British drummer boy, witnesses the events that occurred at the outset of the American Revolution in Lexington and Concord, Massachusetts.

Obadiah, the Bold by Brinton Turkle. Viking Press, © 1965. When Obadiah acquires a spy glass, he decides to become a pirate someday. Later however, after his ambition is dashed during a pirate game with his siblings, Obadiah gains new and even more exciting ideas about life at sea.   EASIER TO READ

Reader's Journal   p 17
Extending Reading

THINKING OF FRIENDS

To encourage thinking about the idea of friends, students learn about word maps and complete a word map for the word *friend*.

Selection Support

SKILL TRACE: SUFFIXES					
Introduction	Practice	Test	Reteach	Maintain	
TE 56	83	139	157	160	251

WORD STUDY

Suffixes -er, -or

OBJECTIVE Using structural analysis to determine word meaning.

1. WARM-UP

Define suffixes.

Remind students that a suffix is a letter or a group of letters added to the end of a word and that the suffix changes the meaning and sometimes the part of speech of the word.

Present a suffixed word in context.

Write the following sentence on the chalkboard:

> **The candle maker hung the newly dipped wax candles all around his shop.**

Ask students what a candle maker is. *(someone who makes candles)* Ask what clues in the sentence make this clear. *(The candles have just been made; the candle maker is hanging them around his shop.)* Point out that there is another clue in the sentence: the suffix *-er* means "one who." When added to the word *make*, the suffix changes the meaning of the word to "one who makes." Point out that the *-or* suffix does just what the *-er* suffix does.

State the objective.

Tell students they will learn to recognize and use the suffixes *-er* and *-or*.

2. TEACH

Explain why recognizing suffixes is important.

Learning to recognize these suffixes will help readers understand words and the way words are used in sentences.

Present a strategy for recognizing and using -er,-or.

Explain that there is a strategy students can use to help them recognize and use the suffixes *-er* and *-or*. First, figure out what the base word means. Then, remember that with the suffix, the new word means "one who does" whatever the base word means.

TEACHING CHART 8: SUFFIXES -ER, -OR　8

1. A sailor watched a sea gull search for fish.
2. A shell collector also watched the bird.
3. The sea gull was often a visitor to the wharf.
4. It was a very good fish catcher.
5. Sometimes it was a leader of many birds looking for fish.

Model the strategy. Read sentence 1 and point out the word containing the suffix *-or. (sailor)* Point out the base word *sail* and explain that since you know that sailing is traveling by boat, and the suffix *-or* means "one who," then *sailor* means "one who travels by boat."

3. GUIDED PRACTICE

Check for understanding. Before going on, have students explain how to define words that end in the suffixes *-er, -or. (Figure out what the base word means; change the meaning to "one who does" what the base word means.)*

Guide students in using the strategy. Have students use the strategy to define words ending in *-er* and *-or* in the remaining sentences. Discuss how the meaning of the base word and the meaning of the suffix helps them understand a new word.

4. WRAP-UP

Summarize instruction. Review the meaning of the suffixes *-er, -or*. Review how the suffixes change the meanings of base words. ("someone who does something")

Provide independent practice. Options for independent practice are shown in the Resource Center below.

Meeting Individual Needs

RETEACHING Use the activity on page 160 and Masters 1–4 in the Teacher Resource Kit.

CHALLENGE Use the activity on page 160 and Master 3 in the Teacher Resource Kit.

ACHIEVING ENGLISH PROFICIENCY Use the activity on page 160 and Master 5 in the Teacher Resource Kit.

Workbook page 16

RESOURCE CENTER

Skills Practice 12

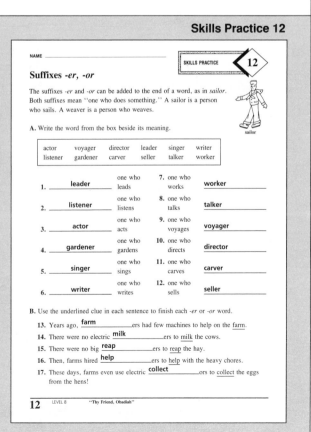

DECODING AND WORD STUDY	NAME _____

Suffixes *-er, -or*

REMEMBER: You can add the suffix *-er* or *-or* to an action word to make a new word. A word with *-er* or *-or* means "someone who does something."

A. Read the paragraph. Underline each word that ends with *-er* or *-or*. Then fill in the chart. The first one has been done for you.

Obadiah went to buy bread from the <u>baker</u>. On the way he heard someone singing. The <u>singer</u> was a <u>sailor</u>, working on the wharf. Nearby, a <u>worker</u> was cutting wood and a <u>sweeper</u> was cleaning up the dust from the saw. Obadiah even saw his <u>teacher</u> go down the street.

Base Word +	Suffix =	New Word	Meaning
bake	-er	baker	one who bakes
1. sing	-er	singer	one who sings
2. sail	-or	sailor	one who sails
3. work	-er	worker	one who works
4. sweep	-er	sweeper	one who sweeps
5. teach	-er	teacher	one who teaches

B. On separate paper, write three sentences about your town. Use three words that end in *-er* or *-or*. See Teacher Notes.

16 "Thy Friend, Obadiah" Suffixes *-er, -or*

◀ **Workbook page 16** is intended for use by all students.

Skills Practice 12 ▶ may be assigned for additional practice.

Workbook reuse option: Have students think of five more *-er* or *-or* words (e.g. farmer, shopper) and write these in the margins beside the chart.

NAME _____	SKILLS PRACTICE 12

Suffixes *-er, -or*

The suffixes *-er* and *-or* can be added to the end of a word, as in *sailor*. Both suffixes mean "one who does something." A sailor is a person who sails. A weaver is a person who weaves.

A. Write the word from the box beside its meaning.

actor	voyager	director	leader	singer	writer
listener	gardener	carver	seller	talker	worker

1. __leader__ one who leads
2. __listener__ one who listens
3. __actor__ one who acts
4. __gardener__ one who gardens
5. __singer__ one who sings
6. __writer__ one who writes

7. one who works __worker__
8. one who talks __talker__
9. one who voyages __voyager__
10. one who directs __director__
11. one who carves __carver__
12. one who sells __seller__

B. Use the underlined clue in each sentence to finish each *-er* or *-or* word.

13. Years ago, __farm__ers had few machines to help on the <u>farm</u>.
14. There were no electric __milk__ers to <u>milk</u> the cows.
15. There were no big __reap__ers to <u>reap</u> the hay.
16. Then, farms hired __help__ers to <u>help</u> with the heavy chores.
17. These days, farms even use electric __collect__ors to <u>collect</u> the eggs from the hens!

12 LEVEL 8 "Thy Friend, Obadiah"

SKILL TRACE: SUFFIX				
Introduction	Practice	Test	Reteach	Maintain
TE 30	58	85	157	161	198

WORD STUDY

Suffix -ly

OBJECTIVE   Using structural analysis to determine word meaning.

Review suffixes.

Remind students that a suffix is a letter or a group of letters added to the end of a word and that the suffix changes the meaning and sometimes the part of speech of the word. When the suffix *-ly* is added to a word, it tells how something is done.

Present suffixed words in context.

Display the Teaching Chart. Have students read each sentence and identify the suffixed word. Ask students to use the meaning of the base word, the meaning of the suffix, and the context of the sentence to replace the suffixed word with a synonym.

> **9**
>
> **TEACHING CHART 9: SUFFIX -LY**
>
> **1.** At first, Obadiah was mean to the sea gull and did not treat it kindly.
> (kindly — nicely)
> **2.** Slowly he began to like the sea gull.
> (slowly — gradually)
> **3.** Obadiah treated the bird gently when he saw it with a fishhook dangling from its beak. (gently — carefully)
> **4.** Obadiah greeted the sea gull happily when it returned to his window.
> (happily — cheerfully)

Provide independent practice.

Options for independent practice are shown in the Resource Center below.

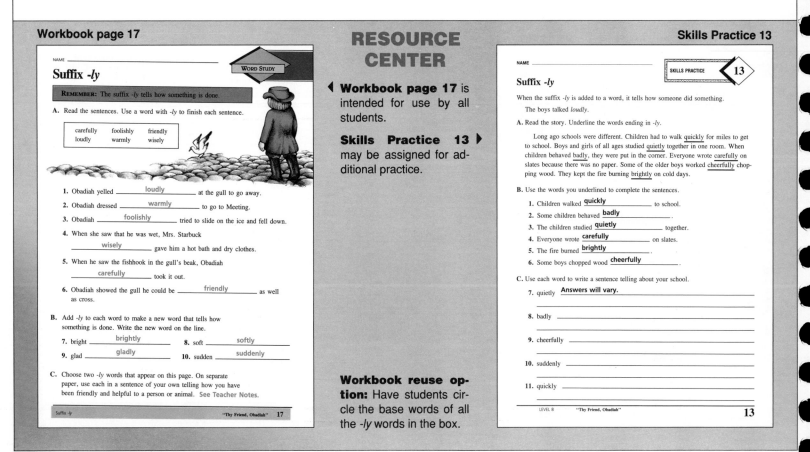

Workbook page 17

RESOURCE CENTER

Skills Practice 13

◀ **Workbook page 17** is intended for use by all students.

Skills Practice 13 ▶ may be assigned for additional practice.

Workbook reuse option: Have students circle the base words of all the *-ly* words in the box.

STRATEGY FOR THINKING
Making a Comparison Chart

OBJECTIVE   Comparing and analyzing our lives with the lives of story characters.

Review the story.

Review the story "Thy Friend, Obadiah." Help the students focus on the way Obadiah changes from the beginning to the end of the story by asking them how he felt about the sea gull at the beginning. *(He was upset and angry because the sea gull followed him around.)* Then have them recall how Obadiah felt at the end. *(He became friends with the sea gull.)* Ask students when his feelings about the gull changed. *(after he saw the gull with the fish hook in its beak)* Ask them why the fish hook might have made him feel sorry for a bird that he disliked so much at first. Help them recall Obadiah's trip to the mill and what happened. *(He slipped on the ice, hurt himself, lost his penny, and got scolded for getting the floor wet.)* Ask them if they can think of a connection between Obadiah's getting hurt and scolded and then feeling sorry for the sea gull. *(Because he had been hurt himself, Obadiah was able to feel sorry for another who was suffering.)*

Review the strategy.

Remind students that a comparison chart can help them better understand a story or article. Review students' comparison charts of Obadiah's and their lives. Focus on any comparisons they found beyond those suggested in the chart and on their conclusions about Obadiah's world and their own.

Provide independent practice.

An independent activity is shown in the Resource Center below.

Workbook page 18

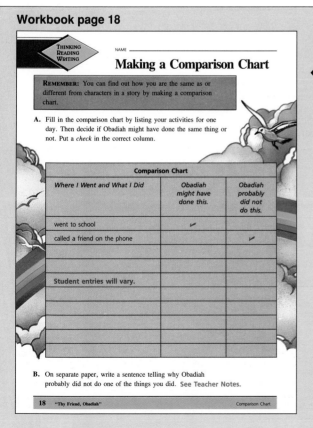

RESOURCE CENTER

◀ **Workbook page 18** is intended for use by all students.

Workbook reuse option: Have students add to the chart one more activity that Obadiah would probably *not* have done.

SKILL TRACE: DRAWING CONCLUSIONS		
Introduced in Level 7	Maintain	
	TE 60	98

COMPREHENSION

Drawing Conclusions

OBJECTIVE   Drawing conclusions from text.

Review steps for drawing conclusions.

Remind students that in order to draw conclusions about a passage they have read, they must follow these steps:

> **Look for clues in the passage about the event.**
> **Think about what you know about events like these. Things you know are called "what I know" clues.**
> **Use both kinds of clues to draw a conclusion that makes sense.**

Provide practice using the steps to draw a conclusion.

Write the following statement and questions on the chalkboard. Read the statement with students and have them answer the questions.

> **Obadiah drew the conclusion that the sea gull had stolen a fish from a fishing line.**

1. What was the clue Obadiah got from the event?
(He saw the fishhook dangling from the sea gull's beak.)

2. What clue did he get from his own knowledge?
(Since he probably knew that fish caught on fishing lines have hooks in their mouths, he may have thought that the sea gull tried to steal a hooked fish and got the hook caught in its beak.)

Have students discuss and decide whether Obadiah's conclusion made sense. Ask them to explain their decisions.

Provide independent practice.

An independent activity is shown in the Resource Center below.

RESOURCE CENTER

Skills Practice 14 ▶ may be assigned for additional practice.

Skills Practice 14

NAME _____

SKILLS PRACTICE   〈14〉

Drawing Conclusions

Drawing a **conclusion** means to figure out something that is not stated directly. Sometimes you use story clues plus what you already know to draw a conclusion. Sometimes you need to use only the facts that are given.

Story Clues

What I Know

Conclusion

Read the facts. Check the conclusion that goes with the facts. Then write it.

1. Facts: Audrey lowered the bucket to the bottom of the well. Then she pulled it back up. The bucket was empty.

_____ The well was deep.   _____ The bucket was too small.

✓ The well had no water.

Conclusion: The well had no water.

2. Facts: Mrs. Bradley packed enough food for five days. Everyone climbed into the wagon. Now the boys could really get to know each other.

_____ The boys were brothers.   ✓ The people in the wagon were taking a long trip.

_____ Mrs. Bradley packed what everyone liked.

Conclusion: The people in the wagon were taking a long trip.

_____

3. Facts: The wagon was moving very fast—too fast to be safe. Seth had trouble holding onto the reins. He called to his father for help.

✓ The horses were running wild.   _____ The wheel had fallen off.

_____ The horses pulling the wagon were lazy.

Conclusion: The horses were running wild.

_____

4. Facts: Sara closed the windows. She got out her umbrella and boots.

_____ It was evening and time to eat.   _____ Sara was cold and tired.

✓ Sara was going out in the rain.

Conclusion: Sara was going out in the rain.

14   LEVEL 8   "Thy Friend, Obadiah"

SKILL TRACE: PREFIXES	
Introduced in Level 7	Maintain
	TE 61

WORD STUDY

Prefixes un-, re-

OBJECTIVE Using structural analysis to determine word meaning.

Review prefixes.

Remind students that a prefix is a letter or a group of letters added to the beginning of a word and that the prefix changes the meaning of the word.

Present prefixes in context.

You may wish to read aloud the sentences below. Answers are underlined in red. Read each sentence and have students identify the prefixed word. Have students use the meaning of the base word, the meaning of the prefix, and the context of the sentence to write a definition of the prefixed word.

---

1. At the beginning of the story, Obadiah was unkind to the sea gull.
2. After he fell in the snow, his mother made him undress and go to bed.
3. He hoped that the sea gull would never return.
4. If he retraced his steps, maybe he would find his lost penny.
5. Do you recall when Obadiah began to be kind to the sea gull?
6. He decided to unhook the fishhook from its beak.
7. He knew that you can never replace a good friend.

Provide independent practice.

An independent activity is shown in the Resource Center below.

RESOURCE CENTER

Skills Practice 15 ▶ may be assigned for additional practice.

Skills Practice 15

NAME _____

SKILLS PRACTICE ◆ 15 ◆

Prefixes *re-, un-*

The prefix *un-* means "not." The box is *unpacked*.
The prefix *re-* means "again." I will *repack* the box.

A. Write the correct word to finish each sentence.

remake	reread	rewrap	undone	unmade	untrue
repaved	rewind	rewrite	uninteresting	unrolled	unwrapped

1. I read that book, but I will **reread** _____ it one more time.
2. She redid her shoe because it came **undone** _____.
3. When the road got bad, the workers **repaved** _____ it.
4. Something that is a lie is **untrue** _____.
5. I put the wrong name on the letter, so I will **rewrite** _____ it.
6. The book was **uninteresting** _____ so I stopped reading.
7. I opened the gift, but I will **rewrap** _____ it.
8. I saw the gift when someone **unwrapped** _____ it.
9. Since the ball of yarn is in knots, I will **rewind** _____ it.
10. I don't know how the ball of yarn **unrolled** _____.
11. The clay pot I made looks funny, so I will **remake** _____ it.
12. They never leave their beds **unmade** _____.

B. Answer each question with a complete sentence using the word in dark print.

13. Why did you **rewrite** your paper? **Answers will vary.**

14. How can you **reuse** a milk carton? _____

15. What's the best way to **unload** a wagon? _____

LEVEL 8   "Thy Friend, Obadiah"   **15**

CURRICULUM CONNECTIONS

COLONIAL DIORAMAS ART

Have students investigate the look of colonial New England, in both dress and architectural styles. They will need to look at picture books and paintings that illustrate the period and environment specifically. You might also ask them to recall the look and style of this period from television programs or movies they may have seen that were set in this time. When students have had sufficient opportunity to become familiar with these styles, have them plan and make dioramas that visually explain aspects of colonial life.

QUAKERS, PEOPLE OF PEACE SOCIAL STUDIES

Introduce the following information about the Quakers: the name of the group is actually The Society of Friends. Tell students that the Quaker faith was founded in 1650 by an Englishman, George Fox. Quakers try to be friendly and respect all living things. The Quaker Meeting contains long periods of silence for private thought. It occurs on *First Day,* Sunday, the day of rest.

Have students research Quakerism, especially Quaker dress, the way Quakers treat others, places in the country where Quakers settled, and Quaker contributions to American life. Students should work in groups. Each group should choose any one of the topics to research. Have groups write and illustrate booklets containing the information they have gathered. Ask groups to share their booklets with each other.

SEA GULL HABITS SCIENCE

Have students investigate the habits of sea gulls. Ask students to offer suggestions about habits they might like to learn more about (for example: nesting, breeding, food gathering, migrating, and the like). Remind students that the natural environment in which sea gulls are found will affect their patterns of behavior. Students may then write brief reports containing and explaining the information they have gathered. **Curriculum Connection Master 2** can be used with this activity.

NANTUCKET IN RELIEF GEOGRAPHY

Explain to students that the island of Nantucket is located in the Atlantic Ocean, approximately eighteen miles south of Cape Cod in Massachusetts. If possible, point out Nantucket on a map for students to see. Further explain that much of Nantucket's land is made up of beaches and moors.

Have students work in pairs to research the land area of Nantucket and make relief maps using papier mâché on boards or heavy cardboard. Encourage students to determine the size of the island and make drawings of the shape to transpose onto the hard surface. Have them investigate the types of growth they would find on the island to include on their maps. Ask any students who have visited a coastal area such as Nantucket to share what the land looked like and what kinds of grasses, wildflowers, and trees they saw. Discuss sand dunes—how they look and what function they serve. Have pairs of students display their relief maps and explain the features they have included.

MILL POWER SOCIAL STUDIES

Remind students that Obadiah was sent to the mill to buy flour for his mother. Have students research different types of grain mills. (Information is sometimes found by looking under the name of the grain, such as flour or corn.) Encourage students to find out how mills get their power, noting that Obadiah's mill probably used a windmill; why certain types of mills are located where they are; what kinds of work different mills do; and how modern technology has changed mills. Have students write several of the interesting facts they learned about mills on a large sheet of paper. They may want to include a drawing or photograph to illustrate one of their facts.

LESSON ORGANIZER
Life in Pilgrim Times

TEACHER CHOICE

	Teaching Sequence	Trade Books and Resources	Meeting Individual Needs	Integrated Language Arts / Cross Curriculum
The Bridge Pages 66–67	**Introduce** Main Idea/Details (Tested)	• Teaching Chart 10 • Workbook 19 • Skills Practice 16	• Reteaching Masters 1–8 • Challenge Master 4 • Achieving English Proficiency Master 6	
PART 1 **Vocabulary Strategies** Pages 68–69	**Develop Concepts** Listing Known Facts **Teach Vocabulary** STORY CRITICAL WORDS: **beliefs,** difficult, education, English, **Pilgrims, religious** (Tested words are boldfaced.)	• Teaching Chart 11 • Workbook 20 • Skills Practice 17	**SUPPORT WORDS:** ministers, provided, religion, weapons, worship • Skills Practice 18 **CHARACTER/SETTING WORDS:** Bible, God, Mayflower, Plymouth, Samoset, Squanto	**WRITING/SPEAKING ACTIVITY:** Use new vocabulary to describe life in a new country. • Spelling Connection 41
PART 2 **Reading & Responding** Pages 70–79	**Build Background** **Develop a Purpose for Reading** **Guide the Reading Process** **Selection Follow-Up**	• Reader's Journal 18–21 • Workbook 21 **I↔T KIT** Listening and Clapping to a Pawnee Song **READING EVERY DAY** *The Long Way to a New Land,* by J. Sandin *The Plymouth Thanksgiving,* by L. Weisgard	**EXTRA HELP:** Main Idea/Details Forms **ACHIEVING ENGLISH PROFICIENCY:** Discussing Settling in a New Country • Achieving English Proficiency Master 7	**Language Arts Connections** **WRITING TO LEARN:** Write a story comparing life in Pilgrim times to life today. • Writing Master 3 **SPEAKING/LISTENING:** Improvising Scenes **WRITING:** Writing Nonfiction Articles; Writing Journal Entries; Listing Word Origins; Creating a History of the Pilgrims; Writing Sentences About Pilgrim Life • Language Arts Master 3
PART 3 **Selection Support** Pages 80–87	**Introduce** Homographs	• Workbook 22 • Skills Practice 19	**Practice** • Teaching Charts 12–14 • Workbook 23–25 • Skills Practice 20–22 Main Idea/Details (Tested) Suffixes *-er, -or* (Tested) Suffix *-ly* (Tested) **Maintain** • Skills Practice 23 Sequence	**Curriculum Connections** **GEOGRAPHY:** Mapping the Mayflower's Voyage **SOCIAL STUDIES:** Making Hornbooks **ART:** Making Pilgrim Drawings and Dioramas • Curriculum Connection Master 3

Life in Pilgrim Times

by Carlotta Dunn

SUMMARY *Approximately 370 years ago, a group of people left England in search of religious freedom. Called Pilgrims, they landed in North America on November 9, 1620, and established the colony of Plymouth. This nonfiction article describes the difficulties the Pilgrims faced adjusting to their new home. However, with the help of two Indians, Samoset and Squanto, the Pilgrims learned how to farm, fish, and hunt. Their strong religious beliefs and their belief in education and the family also helped them to survive a most difficult year.*

The Bridge

SKILL TRACE: MAIN IDEA/DETAILS						
Introduction	Practice		Test	Reteach	Maintain	
TE 66	82	116	157	158	234	274	508

COMPREHENSION
Teaching Main Idea/Details

OBJECTIVE   Identifying stated and unstated main idea and supporting details.

1. WARM-UP

Use familiar content to present main idea and details.

Remind students of the sea gull in the selection they just read, "Thy Friend, Obadiah." Tell them they will listen to a paragraph that includes an important idea about sea gulls as well as details or small pieces of information. Write the following paragraph on the chalkboard and read it aloud.

> **Gulls eat different kinds of food. Gulls that live inland feast on insects. Other gulls feast on young sea turtles and hard-shelled clams or snails.**

Discuss main idea and details.

Ask students what all the sentences are about. (*gulls*) Have students find the author's important or main idea about gulls. (*Gulls eat different kinds of food.*) Point out that the kinds of food are named in the other sentences and these are the details. Tell students that sometimes the main idea is told in a paragraph and sometimes it is not. When it is not, readers can use the details to help them figure out the main idea.

State the objective.

Tell students they will learn how to recognize the main idea and details of a paragraph when the main idea is told in a paragraph and when it is not.

2. TEACH

Explain why recognizing the main idea and details is important.

Tell students that figuring out the main idea and details will help them to understand and remember important ideas in what they read.

Present a strategy for recognizing main idea and details.

Explain that there is a strategy students can use to help them find the main idea and details of a paragraph. First, read through the paragraph and decide what all or most of the sentences are about. This is the *topic*. Then read the sentences to decide what the author tells about the topic. Look for a sentence that tells the main idea. See how details in the other sentences explain or describe the main idea. If no sentence tells the main idea, create one.

TEACHING CHART 10: MAIN IDEA/DETAILS   `10`

1. Quakers believe strongly that there should be no war in the world. Quakers think students should learn about peace in school. They believe in solving problems by talking and not by fighting. (Unstated: Quakers believe in peace and friendship.)
2. Quakers made the things they needed in their daily lives. The candle maker made candles for light. The miller made flour for bread. (Stated: Quakers made the things they needed in their daily lives.)

Model the strategy. Read passage 1. Tell students that the topic is *What Quakers Believe.* Explain that each sentence tells something the Quakers believe, so these are details. No main idea is stated. You now know you will have to create a main idea sentence. Since most of what they believe has to do with peace and friendship, you can say *Quakers believe in peace and friendship.*

3. GUIDED PRACTICE

Guide students in using the strategy. Have students use the strategy to identify the topic, main idea, and details of the second passage. Have students explain how they knew the main idea.

4. WRAP-UP

Summarize instruction. Review why it is important to find main ideas. *(Knowing the main idea will help you remember important information.)*

Provide independent practice. Options for independent practice are shown in the Resource Center below.

5. APPLICATION

Students will identify main ideas as they read "Life in Pilgrim Times." The symbol ✔ marks specific questions and activities that apply this skill.

Meeting Individual Needs

RETEACHING Use the activity on page 158 and Masters 1–8 in the Teacher Resource Kit.

CHALLENGE Use the activity on page 158 and Master 4 in the Teacher Resource Kit.

ACHIEVING ENGLISH PROFICIENCY Use the activity on page 158 and Master 6 in the Teacher Resource Kit.

Workbook page 19

NAME _____

COMPREHENSION

Main Idea/Details

REMEMBER: A main idea tells the topic of the paragraph and what the paragraph says about the topic.

A. Read each paragraph. Copy the sentence that tells the main idea. Then copy two sentences that tell details about the main idea.

1. Obadiah's town contained many kinds of buildings. Most of them were houses, of course. In addition to those, there were several small stores, a church, a blacksmith's shop, and a school building. Many of these buildings contained only a single large room.

   Main Idea: Obadiah's town contained many kinds of buildings.

   Details: Accept any other sentences. _____

   _____

2. Sea gulls change color and markings as they grow older. Most very young gulls are gray or brown. After one year a gull's feathers become lighter, though they still look dull. An adult gull may be pure white or mostly white with black markings on its wings or tail.

   Main Idea: Sea gulls change color and markings as they grow older.

   Details: Accept any other sentences. _____

B. Read the paragraphs again. Think of another way to say the main ideas and write them in your own words on separate paper.
See Teacher Notes.

Main Idea/Details   "Life in Pilgrim Times" **19**

RESOURCE CENTER

◀ **Workbook page 19** is intended for use by all students.

Skills Practice 16 ▶ may be assigned for additional practice.

Workbook reuse option: Have students read each paragraph again. Then have them underline each detail that supports the main idea.

Skills Practice 16

NAME _____

SKILLS PRACTICE **16**

Main Idea/Details

A **main idea** tells what the whole paragraph is about. **Details** tell more about the main idea. Sometimes the main idea is stated in one sentence. Sometimes the main idea is **unstated.** An unstated main idea is not in one sentence. You must look at all the details and figure out the main idea from them.

A. Read each paragraph. Figure out the main idea by looking at all the sentences. Circle and write the main idea of each paragraph.

1. Little Maude Smith milked the cows. Young Willie Brown helped plow the fields. Jenny White helped with the cooking and baking. Carl Potts' boy worked in a factory.

   Children used to work on farms. [Children used to do hard jobs.]
   Children knew how to plow and bake.
   Children used to do hard jobs.

2. The things that went into the bread were fresh. The dough was squeezed and pounded and then popped into the oven. The smell of baking bread filled a house.

   Homemade bread had fresh things in it.   Homemade bread had a good smell.
   [Homemade bread was special.]
   Homemade bread was special.

3. Pilgrims grew their own food. They often made their own clothing. A Pilgrim family knew how to make up their own games.

   Pilgrims didn't have games. [Pilgrims did things for themselves]
   Pilgrims did things for themselves.

B. Choose one paragraph. Write a detail that would fit into it.
Details will vary.

16 LEVEL 8 "Life in Pilgrim Times"

PART 1

Vocabulary Strategies

Developing Concepts

Use a list to tap prior knowledge of Pilgrims.

Make a list about Pilgrims as a starting point for teaching vocabulary. Ask students what they know about who the Pilgrims were and what they did. List responses on the chalkboard.

Pilgrims

1. (Lived long ago.)

2. (Came from England in 1620.)

3. (Sailed on ships.)

4. (Lived in Massachusetts.)

5. (Were helped by the Indians to grow corn.)

6. (Had the first Thanksgiving.)

Teaching Vocabulary

Discuss meanings of Story Critical words.

Read each context sentence on the Teaching Chart and identify the new word. Then use the questions that follow to help students understand each word. When necessary, provide a definition.

TEACHING CHART 11: VOCABULARY `11`

1. Pilgrims (the people who came from England and settled in Massachusetts in 1620)
The *Pilgrims* left England in 1620 and crossed the Atlantic Ocean.
2. religious (showing a devotion to religion)
They were *religious* people who wanted to pray as they wished.
3. beliefs (ideas accepted as true)
The laws in England did not allow the Pilgrims to follow their religious *beliefs*.
4. difficult (hard)
It was winter when they got to Massachusetts, and life was very *difficult* for them because they had no warm clothes and little food.
5. education (formal schooling)
The Pilgrims built schools because they wanted their children to get a good *education*.
6. English (language of England)
The language the Pilgrims spoke was *English*.

Pilgrims

1. Do you think it took the Pilgrims a long time to cross the Atlantic Ocean? (Yes, because in 1620 they had to travel in sailing ships, which were slower than planes or today's ships.) STRATEGY: PRIOR KNOWLEDGE

religious

2. Where does a person who is religious sometimes go? (to church or synagogue) **Why?** (to pray or worship) STRATEGY: PRIOR KNOWLEDGE

beliefs

3. Ideas you believe to be true are called your beliefs. What happened to the Pilgrims because of their religious beliefs? (They left England and came to America.) STRATEGY: PRIOR KNOWLEDGE

difficult

4. What is a word that means the opposite of *difficult*? *(easy)* **What would have made things easier for the Pilgrims?** (to have warm clothes and plenty of food)   STRATEGY: ANTONYMS

education

5. What word in the sentence is a clue to the meaning of the word *education*? *(schools)*   STRATEGY: CONTEXT CLUES

English

6. What country does the English language come from? (England)
STRATEGY: PRIOR KNOWLEDGE

Discuss Support words as needed.

The Glossary of the Student Text includes definitions of the Support words: *religion, worship, ministers, provided, weapons.*

Discuss Character/Setting words as needed.

Present these words before students read the selection: *Samoset, Bible, Mayflower, Plymouth, Squanto, God.*

Provide independent practice.

Options for independent practice are shown in the Resource Center below.

WRITING OR SPEAKING ACTIVITY   *Have students make up sentences that might have been spoken or written by Pilgrims describing their lives in their new country. Ask them to use new vocabulary wherever possible.*

Teacher Choice

Workbook page 20

SELECTION VOCABULARY

NAME _____

Using New Words

A. Use the words in the box to complete the story.

| beliefs | difficult | education |
| English | Pilgrims | religious |

The children in our classroom are different from one another in many ways. We have different ___beliefs___, or ideas, about God and life, and our families belong to different ___religious___ groups. Therefore, we go to different churches and temples. Our classes are taught in the ___English___ language, but some children come from families who speak other languages, too. For some of us, learning to read or write English is ___difficult___. Though we children are all different from one another, we are getting a similar ___education___ in our school. If ___Pilgrims___ from long ago could see our school, they would be glad that people who are different can work together here.

B. Imagine that you are a Pilgrim. Write a letter to a friend in England. Use at least three words from the box in your letter. See Teacher Notes.

20   "Life in Pilgrim Times"   Selection Vocabulary

RESOURCE CENTER

◀ **Workbook page 20** provides practice with Story Critical words.

Skills Practice 17 ▶ provides additional practice with Story Critical words.

Skills Practice 18 provides practice with Support words.

Spelling Connection Master 41 may be used for spelling instruction with the new vocabulary.

Workbook reuse option: Have students underline the words and phrases in each sentence that helped them choose each correct response.

Skills Practice 17

NAME _____

SKILLS PRACTICE 17

Vocabulary: Story Critical Words

A. Study the meaning of each word.

beliefs ideas accepted as being true
difficult hard to do
education what you learn in school
English people or language from England
Pilgrims English people who settled in Massachusetts in 1620
religious showing belief in God

B. Use the clues to complete the puzzle.

Across
2. Students get this by going to school.
4. This is spoken in the United States.
5. A person who prays could be this.
6. These are things you believe in.

Down
1. These people came to America on a ship.
3. This means the opposite of *easy*.

(crossword puzzle: education, English, religious, beliefs, with Pilgrims, difficult)

LEVEL 8   "Life in Pilgrim Times"   Definition clues   17

2 Reading & Responding

Building Background

Motivate discussion using the paraphrased excerpt from a speech.

Share the paraphrase of part of a speech with students and ask them what they think it takes for people to be able to do these things.

> **It was a cold, harsh, and unfamiliar country the Pilgrims landed in. It took all the strength and intelligence of the men and women to find food and build shelter so they could live. To do that they worked very, very hard and wasted no food, time or effort in completing their necessary tasks. This is why the Pilgrims are great.**
>
> *— Paraphrase of excerpt from a speech by Ulysses S. Grant at New England Society dinner, Dec. 22, 1880*

Build background about moving and adjusting to a new place.

Invite students who have moved to new neighborhoods, towns, or countries to share some of the difficulties they faced in their moves. (*getting used to the language, different customs, new school, making new friends*)

Discuss nonfiction.

Tell students they will read a nonfiction selection about the Pilgrims. Point out that nonfiction does not tell a story or have characters speaking. It gives information about a subject, in the form of paragraphs with main ideas and details. The paragraphs are in sections with headings.

Developing a Purpose for Reading

Option 1
Students set purpose.

ORAL "QUESTION" LISTS   Ask students to think of questions they would like to have answered about the Pilgrims. Have students preview the selection by reading the headings and looking at the illustrations before forming their questions. Record students' questions for later use.

WRITING ACTIVITY   Have students work individually or in pairs to create written "Question" lists. Tell students to save their lists for use later.

Option 2
Teacher sets purpose.

Have students read the selection to find out who helped the Pilgrims after they arrived and in what ways these people were helpful.

Meeting
Individual
Needs

EXTRA HELP   Distribute the form for main ideas and details, Form 10 in the Teacher Resource Kit. Write these main ideas on the chalkboard: *The Pilgrims Work to Build a New Life, The Pilgrims Get Help from New Friends, The Pilgrims Believe in God and Education,* and *Pilgrim Families Work Together*. Have students copy these on their forms. Point out that these main ideas are the headings from the next selection about the Pilgrims. Suggest that as they read, students write details that support each main idea.

ACHIEVING ENGLISH PROFICIENCY   Tell students they are going to read about the Pilgrims who left their homes in England and came to America almost four hundred years ago. Help students trace their journey to America on a map. Explain to students that the Pilgrims learned many things about their new home from the Indians, who were the first people to live in this country. Ask students what new things they had to learn when they moved to America and who helped them learn. For additional help in story comprehension, use Master 7 in the Teacher Resource Kit.

Imagine leaving your home and moving to a new land across the ocean. A group of brave people made such a trip more than three hundred years ago.

Life in Pilgrim Times

by Carlotta Dunn

About 370 years ago, a group of people left their homes in England to come to a place they had never seen before. For two long months their ship, the *Mayflower,* sailed across the wide and stormy Atlantic Ocean. Finally, on November 9, 1620, they landed on the rocky shores of North America and settled in a place they called Plymouth, named after the city in England from which they had sailed.

Who were these brave people, and why did they leave their homes in England? This small group of brave families were the Pilgrims. A pilgrim is a person who makes a journey for religious reasons. These people were called Pilgrims because they left their homes to find a place where they would be free to follow their religious beliefs.

In 1620, the Pilgrims arrived on the *Mayflower.*

The Pilgrims Work to Build a New Life

After the Pilgrims arrived in North America, they had only the things they brought with them on the ship. They had clothes, weapons, some tools and books, and a few pieces of furniture. Their food was almost gone, so they had to hunt or fish. Luckily, the forests of North America were full of animals, nuts, and berries, and the ocean was rich in fish.

Reader's Journal   **p 18**
Preparing for Reading

A NEW TOWN IN A NEW LAND

As town planners for a group of settlers, students take on the job of designing a town and making a map of it.

GUIDED READING

Page 38   What do you think these "rocky shores" of North America were like 370 years ago? (Students may suggest wilderness with huge forests and many wild animals.)   SYNTHESIZE: DRAWING CONCLUSIONS

✔ **Page 39   What words on the page tell you what kind of information will be given next?** (the heading "The Pilgrims Work to Build a New Life") **What details about a new life are given in the paragraph?** (how the Pilgrims found food)   ANALYZE: MAIN IDEA/DETAILS

HIGHLIGHTING LITERATURE

Page 39   Ask students if this selection tells a story or gives information. (It gives information.) Explain that articles that give facts, or information, are called nonfiction. Point out that nonfiction is sometimes divided into sections with a heading at the beginning of each section. Ask someone to read the heading on this page. ("The Pilgrims Work to Build a New Life")

✔ Skill from The Bridge applied through this question.

The Pilgrims had to clear the land to build homes.

Still, life was very <u>difficult</u> for the Pilgrims. They had to chop down trees to get wood to build homes. The first houses the Pilgrims built were small and simple. The roofs were made of grasses mixed with mud, and the walls were made of wood. Most houses had only one large room with a large fireplace that provided the only heat for the family in the winter. The family cooked, ate, played, worked, and read together in that room.

After the Pilgrims built homes, they cut down trees to clear the land for farms. Most of the Pilgrims had come from cities in England, so they knew little about farming. If they were to survive, they would need help.

The Pilgrims Get Help from New Friends

Luckily for the Pilgrims, help came to them about four months after they landed in North America. One day, an Indian named Samoset walked into Plymouth, and to the surprise of the Pilgrims, Samoset spoke <u>English</u>. He had learned the language from English sailors who had come to fish in North America. The Pilgrims didn't know it at the time, but Samoset would help them build a new life in their new land.

Indians watch as the Pilgrims land at Plymouth.

GUIDED READING

✔ **Page 40   What is the main idea of the first paragraph on this page?** (Life was very difficult for the Pilgrims.) **What details explain this main idea?** (had to chop down trees to get wood to build homes; made roofs out of grass and mud; houses had one room; fireplaces gave the only heat in winter; family lived together in same room)   ANALYZE: MAIN IDEA/DETAILS

✔ **Page 41   How has the author presented a new topic for this page?** (in the heading: "The Pilgrims Get Help from New Friends")   ANALYZE: MAIN IDEA/ DETAILS

Page 41   Why do you think it was especially lucky for the Pilgrims that Samoset found them? (He could speak English, so they could communicate.)   INFER: CAUSE/EFFECT

STRATEGIC READING

✔ **Page 41**   Have students tell the most important information they have read so far about the Pilgrims. (They arrived in North America 370 years ago from England. They came so they could freely follow their religious beliefs. Life was very difficult; they had to build homes and learn farming. They made a new friend named Samoset.) **Ask students to predict how Samoset might help the Pilgrims build a new life.** (Students may predict that Samoset will show the Pilgrims how to farm.) Point out that when readers can remember the main ideas, they can be pretty sure that they are understanding the selection. If they have trouble summarizing or predicting, they should reread and look for main ideas.   METACOGNITION: SUMMARIZING AND PREDICTING

✔ Skill from The Bridge applied through this question.
✔ Informal Assessment Opportunity: GETTING INFORMATION FROM TEXT

Samoset brought an Indian named Squanto to Plymouth. Squanto spoke even better English than Samoset. Together, Squanto and Samoset taught the Pilgrims many things that helped them during their first year in North America. The Indians taught the Pilgrims how to farm and gave them corn to plant. Corn was new to the Pilgrims, for the people in England knew nothing about this crop. The Indians showed the Pilgrims where the best places to fish and hunt were. They took the Pilgrims into the forests and showed them which fruits and berries were safe to eat, and which ones would hurt them. The Pilgrims thanked God for their good fortune in finding such wonderful friends.

The Pilgrims share the harvest with their Indian friends.

The Pilgrims learned to read using horn books like this one.

The Pilgrims Believe in God and Education

God was never far from the minds and hearts of the Pilgrims. After all, they had come to North America so they could worship God in their own way. As soon as they were able to, the Pilgrims built a meetinghouse where they came together on Sunday to pray. Everyone in Plymouth attended services at the meetinghouse, and everyone followed the rules set down by the ministers, their religious leaders. It was the Pilgrims' strong beliefs that gave them the strength to build a new life.

The second most important part of Pilgrim life was education. The Pilgrims wanted their children to learn to read so that they would be able to read the Bible. They built the first English schools in North America.

GUIDED READING

Page 42   Compare Obadiah's friendship with the sea gull in the previous story to the friendship described in this selection. What is different about the start of the friendships? (Obadiah felt he was a friend of the gull only after he helped him. The Indians and Pilgrims become friends right away.)   ANALYZE: COMPARISON

Page 42   Can you describe what is happening in the picture on this page? (Squanto and Samoset are having a meal with the Pilgrims. The Pilgrims are cooking food, gathering food and water; maybe this is the first Thanksgiving.)   ANALYZE: PICTURE DETAILS

✔ **Page 43   What purpose does the heading on this page serve?** (It tells the important idea of the page, the two things that were important to the Pilgrims. It lets the reader know what the paragraphs will be about.)
ANALYZE: MAIN IDEA/DETAILS

✔ Skill from The Bridge applied through this question.

HIGHLIGHTING LITERATURE

✔ **Page 43   Explain that headings help an author** organize information and also help readers know what will be discussed. Point out that some headings name a topic, but some actually tell the main idea, as the headings do in this selection. Tell students that even with main ideas in headings, paragraphs also have individual main ideas. Have students find the main idea of each paragraph on this page. (first paragraph — stated in the last sentence; second paragraph — stated in the first sentence)

Pilgrim Families Work Together

Religion and education were not the only important parts of Pilgrim life. The family was also very important. Fathers taught their sons how to hunt, farm, fish, build tools and toys, and many other things. Mothers taught their daughters how to cook, sew, farm, and to care for younger children in the family. There was plenty of work for everyone, and the family had to work together to make sure that they had all the things they needed.

Everyone in the family was loved and cared for. Mothers and fathers liked to watch their children play games, and they liked to read to them and tell them stories from the Bible. Life may have been hard for the Pilgrims, but the love they shared and their strong religious beliefs more than made up for the hard times.

◆ LIBRARY LINK ◆

If you would like to learn more about the pilgrims, you might enjoy The Plymouth Thanksgiving *by Leonard Weisgard.*

Reader's Response

What is it about the Pilgrims that you most admire?

Life in Pilgrim Times

Thinking It Over

1. How do you think the Pilgrims felt when they landed in North America?
2. What were some of the ways in which the Indians showed their friendship?
3. Why did the Pilgrims know so little about living off the land? How do you know?
4. Do you think the Pilgrims would have survived without the help of the Indians? Why or why not?
5. Name three of the Pilgrims' strongest beliefs.

Writing to Learn

THINK AND COMPARE   Have you ever done any of the things the Pilgrims did? Compare your life with theirs. Complete the comparison chart below. Add more things the Pilgrims did. Then check the things you have done and the things you have never done.

What the Pilgrims did	I have done	I have not done
ate corn	✓	
ate fish		
built houses		

WRITE   Write a paragraph to explain how your life is like the Pilgrims' lives or how it is different.

GUIDED READING

Page 44   How do you think love and religion made up for the hard times the Pilgrims lived through?
(Love and religion gave the Pilgrims hope and made them feel better.)   SYNTHESIZE: DRAWING CONCLUSIONS

RETURNING TO THE READING PURPOSE

OPTION 1   If students set the purpose, return to the questions generated about the Pilgrims. Discuss whether these questions were answered in the selection. Ask students if they would like to have been a Pilgrim and to explain why or why not.

OPTION 2   If you set the purpose, ask students to explain who helped the Pilgrims and the importance of their help. (Samoset and his friend Squanto helped the Pilgrims to survive. If they had not taught the Pilgrims how to grow corn and farm, how to hunt and fish, and which foods in nature were unsafe, the Pilgrims most likely would not have survived.)

Reader's Journal   **p 19**
Responding to Reading

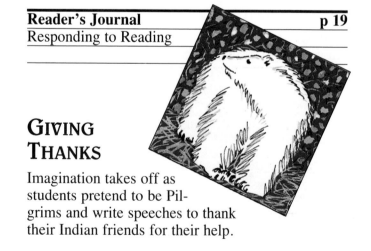

GIVING THANKS

Imagination takes off as students pretend to be Pilgrims and write speeches to thank their Indian friends for their help.

SELECTION FOLLOW-UP

Life in Pilgrim Times

THINKING IT OVER

1. **How do you think the Pilgrims felt when they landed in North America?** (Possible answers: The Pilgrims were happy that their long, difficult trip across the ocean was over; they may also have been afraid because they did not know what to expect in their new land; some may have looked forward to their new freedom and to making a new life for themselves and their families.) INFER: FEELINGS/ATTITUDES

2. **What were some of the ways in which the Indians showed their friendship?** (The Indians gave the Pilgrims corn and taught them how to farm. They also showed the Pilgrims where to hunt and fish, and taught them which foods in the forest were safe to eat.) ANALYZE: MAIN IDEA/DETAILS

3. **Why did the Pilgrims know so little about living off the land? How do you know?** (Most of the Pilgrims had lived in cities in England, not on farms. To back up their conclusion, students will probably cite the sentence "Most of the Pilgrims had come from cities in England, so they knew little of farming.") RECALL: CAUSE/EFFECT

4. **Do you think the Pilgrims would have survived without the help of the Indians? Why or why not?** (Possible answers: The Pilgrims were very hard working and would have learned through trial and error; fewer Pilgrims would have survived without the help of the Indians; they may have died out after the first or second year. Accept reasonable conclusions that students can support with examples from personal experience or books and stories they have read.) SYNTHESIZE: DRAWING CONCLUSIONS; METACOGNITION

5. **Name three of the Pilgrims' strongest beliefs.** (The Pilgrims believed in religion, education, and the importance of the family.) SYNTHESIZE: MAIN IDEA/DETAILS

WRITING TO LEARN ❖❖❖

Use Writing Master 3, which duplicates this chart.

THINK AND COMPARE   Have you ever done any of the things the Pilgrims did? Compare your life with theirs. Complete the comparison chart below. Add more things the Pilgrims did. Then check the things you have done and the things you have never done. (To prepare students for writing, encourage them to discuss the chart.)

What the Pilgrims did	I have done	I have not done
ate corn	✓	
ate fish		
built houses		

Extend comprehension through writing.

WRITE   Write a paragraph to explain how your life is like the Pilgrims' lives or how it is different. (Encourage students to share their writing with partners.)

More Ideas for Selection Follow-Up

CRITICAL AND CREATIVE THINKING QUESTIONS

Encourage a variety of responses and points of view.

Use these open-ended questions to encourage critical and creative thinking about the selection.

1. If you had lived during Pilgrim times, what do you think would have been the most difficult part of your life? What would have been the best part?

2. The American Indians shared many gifts with the Pilgrims. Why do you think the gift of corn was so important?

3. How do you think a Pilgrim child's day in school might be like your day in school? How might it be different?

REREADING ORALLY

✔ *Have students read for specific information.*

Ask each student to choose a part of the story he or she thinks describes the most important idea about the Pilgrims. Have each student tell why he or she thinks the idea is most important. Tell students to practice reading their parts. Ask students why paying attention to punctuation is important when reading aloud. (*Punctuation tells the reader when to pause, ask a question, and stop at the end of a sentence. This helps listeners to understand the information.*)

SELECTION COMPREHENSION

Provide comprehension check.

A Workbook page to check comprehension is shown in the Resource Center below. It may be used for informal assessment.

✔ Informal Assessment Opportunity: SELF-MONITORING

Workbook page 21

NAME _____

Life in Pilgrim Times

SELECTION
COMPREHENSION

A. Complete the summary of the selection "Life in Pilgrim Times."
Accept reasonable variations.
    This is an article that tells how the ___Pilgrims___ came to America. They landed in a special place. They named it ___Plymouth___ after a city in England.
    The Pilgrims had left England because ___they wanted___ ___religious freedom___.
They set to work to build a new life in America. The Indians helped the Pilgrims make a new life by showing which plants were ___safe to eat___, showing them how to ___hunt and fish___, and giving them ___corn___ to plant.

    One of the first things the Pilgrims did was to build a ___meeting house___. All the Pilgrims went to church on Sunday. Besides religion, ___education___ was very important to the Pilgrims because they wanted their children to be able to read the Bible.
    The Pilgrims felt family life was very important, too. Life was hard for the Pilgrims in the new world, but their loving ___families___ and strong ___religious beliefs___ made up for the hard times.

B. Pretend you are an American Indian. On separate paper, write five sentences telling about how you helped the Pilgrims make a new life in America. See Teacher Notes.

Selection Comprehension   "Life in Pilgrim Times"   **21**

RESOURCE CENTER

◄ **Workbook page 21** is intended for use by all students.

Writing Master 3 duplicates the Writing to Learn chart.

I•T **Kit Activity**

Audio: "H'Atira"
Students learn this Pawnee song about corn, which the Pawnees called "atira." The sound "h" meant "breath of life." Students listen to the tune and clap the steady beat. (See Activity Guide.)
MULTICULTURALISM

LANGUAGE ARTS CONNECTIONS

CREATIVE THINKING: IMPROVISING SCENES

Discuss improvising.

Tell students that *improvising* means doing something without a lot of planning. Point out that actors sometimes improvise a scene. Ask students to explain what they think this means. *(The actors have an idea of what they are going to do and say but they do not memorize any lines or actions. They listen to each other and make up what they say as they go along.)*

Have students improvise scenes from the story.

Have students work in pairs or small groups to improvise scenes of Pilgrim life. Students may choose to do a scene between Samoset and the first Pilgrim he met, with Samoset and Squanto showing the Pilgrims how to grow corn, or a family scene in a one-room home.   SHARED LEARNING: SPEAKING

NONFICTION AS A LITERARY GENRE

Review the features of nonfiction.

Review with students the kinds of information that readers expect to find in nonfiction. *(facts, information that includes dates, names of real people and places)* Remind students that "Life in Pilgrim Times" is nonfiction containing all of these features.

Have students write articles about aspects of Pilgrim life.

Tell students to choose a topic about Pilgrim life such as what Pilgrim children learned in school, or what Pilgrim families did after supper, or what games Pilgrim children played. Have students research their chosen topics and write articles about them. Students could work individually or in pairs.   WHOLE CLASS
ENRICHMENT

LEARNING MORE ABOUT WORDS

Discuss word origins.

Tell students that many words have interesting histories and uses. The more a person knows about words, the more a person can enjoy language and the better she or he can use it.

Have each student select three words to research.

Have each student choose three words from the selection and find out more about them. Tell students to write the words down and tell why they chose these words. Suggest that students use the dictionary and books about words. Students should record any information found. Students can share their findings in a round-table discussion.   WRITING

CREATING A HISTORY OF THE PILGRIMS

Discuss cooperative learning.

Explain to students that when a group works together *cooperatively*, the success of the project depends on the contributions of each member. Each member has to take responsibility for his or her share of the work.

Have students work cooperatively to create histories of the Pilgrims.

Divide students into groups of five. One member of each group will be responsible for a short article about the Pilgrims' clothing; a second will write about relationships between the Pilgrims and Indians; a third, about the Pilgrims' workday; a fourth, about the Pilgrims' religion. The fifth member will act as editor, and collect the articles into a short book, adding a cover, illustrations, and a table of contents.   COOPERATIVE LEARNING: WRITING

WRITING SENTENCES

Discuss sentences.

Review with students that a sentence expresses a complete thought. Point out that sentences give information. Sentences can also give descriptions that help the reader create a picture in his or her mind.

Have students write sentences about Pilgrim life.

Have each student write six sentences about Pilgrim life. In three of the sentences students should present facts about Pilgrims. In the three remaining sentences students should write descriptions. Point out two descriptive phrases from the selection: *the wide and stormy ocean* and *rich in fish*. Suggest that students use similar language in their descriptions. **Language Arts Master 3** can be used with this activity.   WRITING

WRITING JOURNAL ENTRIES

Discuss journals.

Explain that journals are like diaries. In both, people write about their thoughts and feelings and about what happens each day or over several days. The entries are dated. Point out that while journals are usually written for pleasure, they can also serve as a historical record of an important time.

Have students write journal entries.

Have students imagine they are Pilgrim children struggling through their first winter in a new land. Tell them to write entries in their "journals." In their writing, they should describe their feelings about leaving England, their feelings after they met the Indians, and their hopes for the future.   CHALLENGE: WRITING

READING EVERY DAY

"Life in Pilgrim Times" gives students a picture of how a group of people settled in North America. Here are two other stories about immigrants—another about the Pilgrims and one about a family that arrived in the 1800s.

The Long Way to a New Land by Joan Sandin. Harper & Row, © 1981. The year 1868 holds many hardships for Carl Erik's family in Sweden, so they pack their belongings and journey to a new land.

The Plymouth Thanksgiving by Leonard Weisgard. Doubleday, © 1967. After a long, hard journey to the New World, the Pilgrims settle, make friends with the Indians, farm the land, and have a bountiful Thanksgiving.

A **World of Books** Classroom Libraries selection

Reader's Journal   pp 20, 21
Extending Reading

LIFE IN OUR TIMES

Visited by a Pilgrim child who has traveled to the twentieth century by time machine, students plan how to explain their life and times.

Selection Support

VOCABULARY

Homographs

OBJECTIVE   Understanding words with the same spellings but different meanings and pronunciations.

1. WARM-UP

Use sentences to present the skill orally.

Read the following sentences aloud to students. As you read the word *bow* in each sentence, write it on the chalkboard.

  1. **Samoset was carrying a <u>bow</u> and arrows.**

  2. **The Pilgrims would <u>bow</u> their heads to pray.**

Point to each word as you reread each sentence. Ask students what they notice about these words. *(They are spelled alike but they are pronounced differently.)* Tell students that many words in the English language are spelled the same but have different pronunciations and different meanings. These words are called *homographs.*

State the objective.

Explain that students will learn how to figure out the meaning and pronunciation of a homograph in a sentence.

2. TEACH

Explain why it is important to learn about homographs. Tell students that knowing how to figure out the meanings and pronunciations of words that are spelled alike will help them to understand what they are reading.

Present a strategy for figuring out the meaning of a homograph.

Explain that there is a strategy students can use to help them understand homographs. First, expect to find homographs when you read. When you come across a homograph, think about the different meanings it can have and the different ways it can be pronounced. Look at the other words in the sentence to help you know which is the correct meaning of the word.

Model the strategy.

You may wish to write the sentences below on the chalkboard. Underline the homographs. Answers are printed in red. Read the first sentence aloud and point to the word *lead.* Explain that this word can be pronounced *lĕd* meaning "a heavy metal," or *lēd*, meaning "to show or guide." Tell students that you can figure out which meaning and pronunciation fit the sentence here from the other words in the sentence. Note that the words *I, you, to, grounds* tell you the word is *lēd* meaning "to show or guide."

  1. "I will <u>lead</u> you to better fishing grounds," said Samoset to the Pilgrims. ("to show or guide")
  2. The Indians brought the Pilgrims a <u>present</u> of corn and fish. ("gift")
  3. <u>Tears</u> ran down the Pilgrims' cheeks when they finally landed. ("water from the eyes")
  4. A strong <u>wind</u> blew during cold winter nights. ("rush of air")

3. GUIDED PRACTICE

Check for understanding. Before going on, ask students to explain the steps they should take to figure out meanings and pronunciations of homographs. *(Identify the word, think about the possible meanings and pronunciations of the word, use context clues to decide which meaning and pronunciation fit the sentence.)*

Guide students in using the strategy. Have students use the strategy to figure out which meanings and pronunciations of *present, tears,* and *wind* fit the rest of the sentences. Discuss context clues that helped students decide.

4. WRAP-UP

Summarize instruction. Review why it is important to know how to figure out the pronunciation and meaning of a homograph in a sentence. *(to understand what you are reading and to become independent readers)*

Provide independent practice. Options for independent practice are shown in the Resource Center below.

Workbook page 22

VOCABULARY

NAME _____

Homographs

REMEMBER: Homographs are words that have the same spelling but different meanings and pronunciations. Use context to decide the correct meaning and pronunciation of a homograph.

A. Write the homographs next to their meanings.

bow	lead	wound

1. a tied ribbon ___bow___
2. an injury ___wound___
3. a heavy metal ___lead___
4. wrapped around ___wound___
5. be in front ___lead___
6. bend from the waist ___bow___

B. Write the homograph from the box that completes each sentence.

7. Sarah happily tied her bonnet with a ___bow___ under her chin.
8. She was going to ___lead___ the walk to the Thanksgiving feast.
9. Her friend Seth arrived with a bandage ___wound___ around his knee.
10. He had suffered a slight ___wound___ when he fell during a race.
11. They admired the new plates and mugs of pewter, which were made with tin and ___lead___ .
12. They all applauded the cooks, and then each one took a ___bow___ .

C. Choose one of the words in the box. Show it as two homographs by writing a sentence for each meaning. See Teacher Notes.

22 "Life in Pilgrim Times"   Homographs

RESOURCE CENTER

◀ **Workbook page 22** is intended for use by all students.

Skills Practice 19 ▶ may be assigned for additional practice.

Workbook reuse option: Have students write the number of the homograph from Part A next to the sentence in which they have used it in Part B.

Skills Practice 19

NAME _____

SKILLS PRACTICE 19

Homographs

Homographs are words that have the same spelling but different meanings and pronunciations. Use context to decide the correct meaning and pronunciation.

Read each pair of sentences. Write the meaning of each underlined word.

1. The <u>dove</u> made a cooing sound.   a bird
   a bird

   Jessie <u>dove</u> into the lake.   jumped in
   jumped in

2. Bob's apron had a <u>tear</u> in it.   a drop of water
   a rip

   A <u>tear</u> ran down the boy's cheek.   a rip
   a drop of water

3. We <u>live</u> in a sod house.   to stay at each day
   to stay at each day

   A <u>live</u> rabbit is in the barn.   having life
   having life

4. Please <u>wind</u> the yarn into a ball.   a strong breeze
   to turn round and round

   The <u>wind</u> will dry the clothes.   to turn round and round
   a strong breeze

5. The <u>content</u> of the box was toys.   satisfied
   all things inside

   Nora was <u>content</u> with her new book.   all things inside
   satisfied

LEVEL 8   "Life in Pilgrim Times"   **19**

SKILL TRACE: MAIN IDEA/DETAILS						
Introduction	Practice	Test	Reteach	Maintain		
TE 66	82	116	157	158	234	274	508

COMPREHENSION

Main Idea/Details

OBJECTIVE   Identifying stated and unstated main idea and supporting details.

Review main idea/details.

Remind students that paragraphs are organized around a topic. Ask students to explain what the main idea of a paragraph is *(the most important idea about the topic)* and what details are *(less important ideas that tell about the main idea)*. Elicit that the main idea may be stated in a sentence in the paragraph. Other times it may not be stated.

Use Teaching Chart to present main idea and details.

Have students read the paragraphs and underline the main ideas.

TEACHING CHART 12: MAIN IDEA / DETAILS   12

1. Samoset and Squanto taught the Pilgrims how to farm and gave them corn to plant. The Indians showed the Pilgrims where the best places to fish and hunt were. They took the Pilgrims into the forest and showed them which fruits and berries were safe to eat, and which ones would hurt them.
   a.   The Pilgrims learned about corn.
   b.   The Indians were a great help to the Pilgrims.
2. Everyone in the Pilgrim family was loved and cared for. Mothers and fathers read to their children. They watched them play games.
   a.   Mothers and fathers read to their children.
   b.   Everyone in the Pilgrim family was cared for.

Provide independent practice.

Options for independent practice are shown in the Resource Center below.

Workbook page 23

NAME _____

Main Idea/Details   COMPREHENSION

REMEMBER: A **main idea** tells the topic of the paragraph and what the paragraph says about the topic.

A. Read each paragraph. Then underline the sentence below the paragraph that states the main idea.

 1. Pilgrims wanted their children to know how to read. They built the first English schools in North America. They also made sure their children had time to study.

 a. Education was important to the Pilgrims.

 b. Pilgrim children liked reading.

 c. Pilgrims worked hard to build schools.

 2. The roofs of the Pilgrim houses were made of grasses mixed with mud. The walls were made of wood. Most houses had only one room with a fireplace for heat.

 a. Pilgrim houses were difficult to build.

 b. Pilgrim houses were small and simple.

 c. It was very warm in Pilgrim houses.

B. Reread each paragraph and the main idea sentence you underlined. Think about details that would tell more about each main idea. On separate paper, write a new detail sentence for each paragraph. See Teacher Notes.

Main Idea/Details   "Life in Pilgrim Times"   **23**

RESOURCE CENTER

◀ **Workbook page 23** is intended for use by all students.

Skills Practice 20 ▶ may be assigned for additional practice.

Workbook reuse option: Above each paragraph in Part A, have students write an appropriate title.

Skills Practice 20

NAME _____

Main Idea/Details   SKILLS PRACTICE   20

A **main idea** tells what the whole paragraph is about. **Details** tell more about the main idea.

Read each paragraph. Underline the sentence that tells the main idea for the paragraph. Then write the main idea.

 1. Horses used to pull plows on farms. In cities, they pulled wagons carrying milk. They also pulled carriages.
   People used horses for different jobs.
   People use horses more now than before.
   Milk used to be delivered by horse and wagon.
   People used horses for different jobs.

 2. Long ago, a family might sit around a table after supper. On the table was a candle. The father or mother might read to everyone from an old book.
   Long ago, there were no electric lights.
   Long ago, families sometimes spent evenings at home together.
   All Americans read old books at night.
   Long ago, families sometimes spent evenings at home together.

 3. The brontosaurus spent most of its time in the water. It had a large, long neck so it could search under the water for food. On the top of its head were its nostrils for breathing. This made it possible for the brontosaurus to stay under the water.
   The brontosaurus spent most of its time in the water.
   The brontosaurus could swim under the water.
   The brontosaurus searched beneath the water for food.
   The brontosaurus spent most of its time in the water.

20   LEVEL 8   "Life in Pilgrim Times"

SKILL TRACE: SUFFIXES				
Introduction	Practice	Test	Reteach	Maintain
TE 56	83	139	157	160	251

WORD STUDY

Suffixes -er, -or

OBJECTIVE Using structural analysis to determine word meaning.

Present suffixed words in context.

Display the following sentences and have students read them aloud. Ask students which word in each sentence tells about someone who does something. *(sailor, hunters)*

1. **The sailor repaired the Mayflower's sail.**

2. **Hunters went out to find food for the first Thanksgiving meal.**

Review suffixes -er, -or.

Remind students that some words are formed by adding a suffix, a letter or group of letters, to the end of a word. Ask students to name the base words and suffixes in *sailor* and *hunters*. Review that the base words *sail* and *hunt* are verbs. When *-er* or *-or* is added to a verb it changes it to a noun meaning "one who does" something. Have students tell the meanings of *sailor* and *hunters*.

State the objective.

Tell students they are going to review how to use the suffixes *-er* and *-or* to understand the meanings of words.

Explain why learning about suffixes -er, -or is important.

Readers can use the meanings of suffixes to help them understand unfamiliar words and to form new words to make their writing more interesting.

Present a strategy for using suffixes -er, -or to determine word meaning.

Explain that there is a strategy students can use to help them use suffixes to understand word meaning. Look for the base word and think about what it means. Put the meaning of the base word together with the meaning of the suffix *-er* or *-or* — "one who does" — to figure out the meaning of the whole word. Use other words in the sentence as well to help understand the word's meaning.

TEACHING CHART 13: SUFFIXES -ER, -OR 13

1. The Pilgrims became builders in the new land. ("people who build things")
2. They were hard workers. ("people who work")
3. Pilgrims followed the rules set down by their religious leaders. ("people who lead or guide")
4. Parents became teachers of their children. ("people who teach")

Model the strategy.

Read the first sentence and tell students that you see the word *builders* is made up of *build* and the suffix *-er*. You know what build means and that *-er* means "one who," so *builders* are people who build or make things.

Check for understanding.

Before going on, have students explain how to use a suffix to help them discover the meaning of a word. *(Think about the meaning of the base word and put it together with the meaning of the suffix. Use other words in the sentence also.)*

Guide students in using the strategy.

Have students use the strategy to locate words with suffixes *-er, -or* and tell what they mean. Ask students to explain how they arrived at a word's meaning.

Summarize instruction.

Review the suffixes *-er, -or* and how students can use these suffixes to help them in their reading. *(The suffixes mean "one who does." Using the meaning of these suffixes can help them understand the meaning of unfamiliar words.)*

Provide independent practice.

Options for independent practice are shown in the Resource Center below.

Workbook page 24

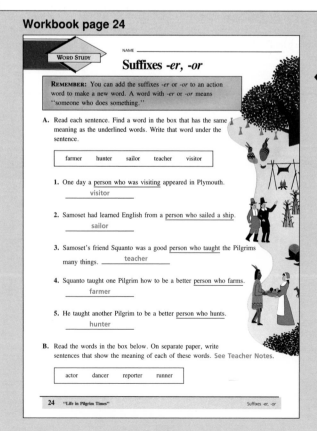

WORD STUDY

NAME _____

Suffixes *-er, -or*

REMEMBER: You can add the suffixes *-er* or *-or* to an action word to make a new word. A word with *-er* or *-or* means "someone who does something."

A. Read each sentence. Find a word in the box that has the same meaning as the underlined words. Write that word under the sentence.

| farmer | hunter | sailor | teacher | visitor |

1. One day a person who was visiting appeared in Plymouth.
   visitor

2. Samoset had learned English from a person who sailed a ship.
   sailor

3. Samoset's friend Squanto was a good person who taught the Pilgrims many things.
   teacher

4. Squanto taught one Pilgrim how to be a better person who farms.
   farmer

5. He taught another Pilgrim to be a better person who hunts.
   hunter

B. Read the words in the box below. On separate paper, write sentences that show the meaning of each of these words. See Teacher Notes.

| actor | dancer | reporter | runner |

24   "Life in Pilgrim Times"   Suffixes *-er, -or*

RESOURCE CENTER

◀ **Workbook page 24** is intended for use by all students.

Skills Practice 21 ▶ may be assigned for additional practice.

Workbook reuse option: Have students circle the suffix and underline the base word in each of their answers in Part A.

Skills Practice 21

NAME _____

SKILLS PRACTICE 21

Suffixes *-er, -or*

The suffixes *-er* and *-or* mean "one who does something."

A. Underline each word with a suffix. Then write the suffix and the root word.

	Suffix	Root Word
1. Jed Farley is a sign painter.	er	paint
2. He works with Caleb Jenkins, a wood worker.	er	work
3. These two sign fixers are the best in the county.	er	fix
4. Caleb says he needs Jed, because he is not a very good speller.	er	spell
5. He jokes that he might spell actor with a *k* instead of a *c*!	or	act
6. He might spell leader without an *a*.	er	lead

B. Now write the meanings of these words.

7. actor	a person who acts
8. leader	a person who leads
9. fixer	a person who fixes
10. painter	a person who paints
11. speller	a person who spells
12. director	a person who directs
13. teacher	a person who teaches
14. laborer	a person who labors
15. writer	a person who writes
16. helper	a person who helps
17. singer	a person who sings

LEVEL 8   "Life in Pilgrim Times"   **21**

SKILL TRACE: SUFFIX				
Introduction	Practice	Test	Reteach	Maintain
TE 30	58	85	157	161	198

WORD STUDY

Suffix -ly

OBJECTIVE   Using structural analysis to determine word meaning.

Review suffixes.

Remind students that a suffix is a letter or a group of letters added to the end of a word and that the suffix changes the meaning and sometimes the part of speech of the word. Review that the suffix -*ly* tells how something is done, so *quickly* means moving in a quick way.

Present suffixed words in context.

Display the Teaching Chart. Have students read each sentence and identify the suffixed word. Tell students to use the meaning of the base word, the suffix, and the context of the sentence to help them figure out the meaning of the word. Note that words ending in *y* change the *y* to *i* before -*ly* is added.

TEACHING CHART 14: SUFFIX -LY

14

1. The Pilgrims sang happily after coming to North America. ("in a happy way")
2. Luckily, the forests of North America were full of animals, nuts, and berries, and the ocean was rich in fish. ("in a lucky way ")
3. The Pilgrims felt strongly about their religion. ("in a strong way")

Provide independent practice.

Options for independent practice are shown in the Resource Center below.

Workbook page 25

NAME _____

Suffix -*ly*

WORD STUDY

REMEMBER: The suffix -*ly* tells how something is done.

A. Circle the word that completes each sentence. Then write the answer to each question.

1. The Pilgrims (brave, bravely) crossed the ocean. Which word tells how the Pilgrims crossed the ocean? _____ bravely

2. The Pilgrims' first houses in North America were built (simple, simply). Which word tells how the Pilgrims' first houses were built? _____ simply

3. Mothers taught their daughters to care (gentle, gently) for younger children. Which word tells how mothers taught their daughters to care for children? _____ gently

4. Most of their houses had one large (chill, chilly) room. Which word tells how their one room felt? _____ chilly

5. Grass mixed with mud was spread (smooth, smoothly) on the roofs. Which word tells how the mud was spread on the roof? _____ smoothly

6. The Pilgrims believed (strong, strongly) in their religion. Which word tells how the Pilgrims believed in their religion? _____ strongly

B. On separate paper, write three sentences. Tell how you would feel if you were a pilgrim arriving in a new land. Use three -*ly* words in your work. See Teacher Notes.

Suffix -*ly*   "Life in Pilgrim Times"   **25**

RESOURCE CENTER

◀ **Workbook page 25** is intended for use by all students.

Skills Practice 22 ▶ may be assigned for additional practice.

Workbook reuse option: Next to each word they wrote in Part A, have students write its base word.

Skills Practice 22

NAME _____

SKILLS PRACTICE   22

Suffix -*ly*

Suffixes change the meaning of words. The suffix -*ly* tells how something is done.

walked *quickly*   ate *hungrily*

A. Add the suffix -*ly* to the underlined word to tell how someone did something.

1. walked in a quick way   quickly
2. acted in a sudden way   suddenly
3. behaved in a bad way   badly
4. acted in a wise way   wisely
5. hummed in a quiet way   quietly
6. fixed in a neat way   neatly
7. talked in an honest way   honestly

B. Write one of the words you wrote to complete each sentence.

8. They were in a hurry, and so they walked quickly _____.
9. He spoke honestly _____ and did not try to fool me.
10. Our puppy is behaving badly _____ and chewing on everything.
11. She made her bed neatly _____ because she wanted her room to look nice.
12. The crowd was suddenly _____ quiet when the president came in.
13. Ann got an award for acting wisely _____ in an emergency.
14. They whispered and played quietly _____ while Mom slept.

C. Describe two people and how they did something. Use these words.

15. carefully Answers will vary. _____

16. quietly _____

22   LEVEL 8   "Life in Pilgrim Times"

SKILL TRACE: SEQUENCE		
Introduced in Level 7	Maintain	
	TE 86	124

COMPREHENSION

Sequence

OBJECTIVE   Understanding the sequence of events in text.

Review sequence.

Remind students that sequence is the order of events in a selection. Writers may give clues that help the reader figure out when things happened.

Refer students to the text to construct sequence charts.

Have students skim the selection to look for words that give clues to sequence. *(For two long months; November 9, 1620; about four months after they landed)* Have students work with partners and use these and other clues to construct sequence charts showing when events took place. Students' charts might resemble the following:

September 9, 1620   The Pilgrims leave England.
                                    They spend two months on the ocean

November 9, 1620   The Pilgrims land in North America.
                                    They name Plymouth settlement.
                                    The Pilgrims hunt and fish for food.
                                    They begin to build houses and farms.

March 9, 1621   The Pilgrims meet Samoset and Squanto.
                                    They learn how to farm from the Indians.
                                    The Pilgrims build churches and schools.

Have students refer to the chart to answer questions.

Check students' understanding by asking them to name events that happened before or after other events.

Provide independent practice.

An independent activity is shown in the Resource Center below.

RESOURCE CENTER

Skills Practice   23 ▶
may be assigned.

Skills Practice 23

NAME _____

SKILLS PRACTICE   23

Sequence

Events in stories happen in a certain order. This order is called **sequence.** Knowing sequence will help you picture events as they happen.

Event 1
↓
Event 2
↓
Event 3

To figure out the sequence:
1. Look for story clues.
2. Look for signal words like **next, after, before, then.**
3. Ask yourself: "Does this sequence make sense?"

Read each story. Try to understand the correct sequence. Answer each question.

Amos Forbes was the captain of a whaling ship. One day, he was leaving for a whaling trip. He had a big breakfast. He put on warm clothing and boots. Then he picked up his bag and said goodbye to his family. Off he went to his ship.

1. What was the first thing Amos Forbes did?
He had a big breakfast.

2. What was the second thing Amos Forbes did?
He put on warm clothing and boots.

3. What was the last thing he did?
He went off to his ship.

Pioneer women often made quilts together. Before they began, the women planned each quilt. Then they cut and sewed pieces of cloth together. When they were finished, they admired their work. Making a quilt took time and patience.

4. What was the first thing the women did?
They planned each quilt.

5. What did the women do after they planned the quilt?
They cut and sewed pieces of cloth together.

6. What was the last thing they did?
They admired their work.

LEVEL 8   "Life in Pilgrim Times"   23

CURRICULUM CONNECTIONS

HORNBOOKS GALORE SOCIAL STUDIES

Direct students' attention to the illustration on page 43. Point out that this is called a *hornbook*. Tell students that Pilgrim parents made their children hornbooks to study from. Hornbooks were made from wood in the shape of a paddle with a handle. A piece of paper with a poem, the alphabet, or a Bible verse was tacked on the hornbook and covered with a transparent layer of cow horn to protect the paper. Point out that hornbooks were the first school books and that paper was very scarce.

Have students make their own hornbooks. Cut thick cardboard in the shape of a rectangular paddle with a handle. Help students attach copies of stories or poems they have written about the Pilgrims on the pieces of cardboard. They might cover their hornbooks with plastic wrap.

MAPPING THE MAYFLOWER GEOGRAPHY

Have students locate England and Massachusetts on a map of the world. Tell each student to make a map that shows the path of the *Mayflower* from Plymouth, England, to Plymouth, Massachusetts.

PILGRIMS AND INDIANS ART

Tell students to think about scenes that illustrate the relationship between the Pilgrims and Indians. For example, students might think about Samoset and Squanto showing the Pilgrims how to fish or plant corn. Ask students to illustrate this scene or others they choose in dioramas or drawings. Tell students to write sentences to describe what is happening in the scenes. **Curriculum Connection Master 3** can be used with this activity.

Reading Social Studies

OBJECTIVE   Using a special strategy to read maps in social studies textbooks.

INTRODUCING THE STRATEGY

Point out the importance of maps in social studies books.

Ask students to tell about any maps they have come across in the fiction books they read for enjoyment. *(Some students might tell about treasure maps or maps giving directions to a specific place.)* Point out to students that social studies books contain many maps. Explain that the maps help readers understand new information. Tell students that the pages they will be reading today are from a social studies book and that they contain maps.

Discuss the usefulness of maps in daily life.

Discuss with students the different kinds of maps they have seen or used with their families. List these kinds of maps on the chalkboard. *(Lists may include any of the following: road maps, subway or bus maps, city maps, maps of states or groups of states, maps found in an atlas.)* Encourage students to talk about how the maps they have used have been helpful to them. Elicit or explain that maps contain different kinds of information and can be used for different purposes.

Ask students if they have ever seen or used a map located at the entrance to a zoo or an amusement park. Explain that this kind of map can be helpful by showing visitors where certain exhibits are located and where they can find restaurants, telephones, or first aid. Tell students that the maps they will study in this lesson also show where places are and how to get from one place to another.

If possible, display a map of your city or town for students to look at. Ask students to locate landmarks and street names. Point out that people use city maps to find out how to get from one place to another.

State the objective.

Tell students that in this lesson they will review how to read a map.

Review instructional vocabulary.

Special map vocabulary is defined in the bulleted items on page 46. Review the terms *map key, scale,* and *compass rose* with students. These terms will be discussed in more detail in the section "How to Read a Map."

Refer students to their texts.

Have students read up to the heading "Reading a Map Key."

READING ABOUT THE STRATEGY

Check students' understanding of the strategy with these questions.

Review the main points of the strategy.

Page 46   When do people read maps? (People read maps when they travel, when they want to see where other people live, and when they study people and places.)

Page 46   What does a map key explain? (the colors and symbols that are used in a map)

Reading Social Studies

You have been reading about daily life in America's past. Maps from long ago can also tell you about the past. An old map can show what your community was like one hundred years ago.

Today, maps are an important part of everyday life. We read maps when we travel or when we want to see where someone lives. We also read them when we study about people and places.

To read maps you need some special skills. These special skills include:

♦ Using a *map key*. A map key explains the colors and symbols that are used in a map.

♦ Using a *scale*. A scale is a numbered line that helps you find the distance between places.

♦ Using a *compass rose*. A compass rose is a drawing that shows where north, south, east, and west are on a map.

Learning how to use the map key, the scale, and the compass rose will help you read and understand maps.

How to Read a Map

You can use this map of California to practice using the map key, scale, and the compass rose.

Continue discussing the strategy.

Page 46   What does the scale on a map help you figure out? (the distance between places)

Page 46   What does a compass rose show? (where north, south, east, and west are on a map)

Reading a Map Key

First, learn what information a map can tell by looking at the map key. Map keys use symbols and colors to stand for real places. On the map of California, the key is in the bottom left corner. This map key has two symbols. One symbol shows the state capital. The other symbol shows other communities.

Use the map key to find the state capital of California. What community is closest to the state capital? Use the map key to name two other communities.

Reading a Scale

Next, look for the scale. You can use the scale on a map to find how far one place is from another. The scale is usually part of the map key. Where is the scale on the California map?

By using your ruler and the map scale, you can find the distance between any two places. Look at the line on the scale for the map of California. The line equals 150 miles of real distance. Measure the line with your ruler. You will find that the length of that line is 1¼ inches. So, you know that every 1¼ inches on the map is equal to 150 miles.

Now place your ruler on the map between the cities of Fresno and Sacramento. You can see on the ruler that the distance between these two cities is a little more than 1¼ inches. Therefore, the real distance between the two cities is a little more than 150 miles.

Look again at the scale. Notice that it gives distances in miles and kilometers. Map scales often show distance in both miles and kilometers.

Reading a Compass Rose

A compass rose is a special drawing that shows directions on the map. Now look for the compass rose on the map of California. You will find it in the top right corner.

The words *north*, *south*, *east*, and *west* name directions. The letters *N*, *S*, *E*, and *W* on the compass rose stand for these words. The line on the compass rose labeled *N* points in the direction of the earth's North Pole. The line labeled *S* points in the direction of the South Pole. The line labeled *E* is on the right of the rose, and the line labeled *W* is on the left. The in-between directions are northeast, southeast, southwest, and northwest. These are shown on the compass rose by the letters *NE, SE, SW,* and *NW.*

The compass rose helps you find places on maps. Look again at the map of California. Suppose someone asked you which direction to travel to go from San Jose to Bakersfield. You could answer by using the map and compass rose. Lay a ruler on a line from San Jose to Bakersfield. Notice that the ruler lies in the same direction as the line in the compass rose labeled *SE*. So, the person would need to travel southeast to go from San Jose to Bakersfield.

As You Read   Read the following pages from a social studies book. Then answer the questions on page 55.

Continue discussing the strategy.

Refer students to their texts.

Page 48   What do the symbols on the map of California show? (One shows the state capital. The other shows other communities.)

Have students read up to the heading "As You Read."

Page 49   In your own words, explain how you would find the distance between any two places on a map. (Possible response: Put your ruler next to the scale on the map to find out how many inches on the map equal the given number of miles or kilometers. Then put the ruler on the map and measure the number of inches between the two places. Then figure out how many miles there are between the two places.)

Page 49   What direction on the compass rose is between west and north? (northwest)

3 Studying One Community

Learning Through Maps

How do maps help you learn about your community?

VOCABULARY
port   county

Let's Learn About Our Community   We all live in communities. Each of us may think that our community is the most important one. The truth is that every community is important. Every community has its own special people and places.

We cannot learn about all of our communities. Instead we will visit a class in one community. The students in this class will tell us how they learned about their community. We can use many of these same ways to study our own community.

We will visit a class of girls and boys who go to Forest Hills Elementary School. The school is in Wilmington, North Carolina.

The city of Wilmington, North Carolina, is located on the Cape Fear River. Wilmington was settled in 1732.
■ Why, do you think, was this location for a city a good one?

Direct students to the content-area reading sample.

Have students read the paragraph under "As You Read" and the content sample "Studying One Community." Encourage them to focus on the maps as they read. Tell students they will answer the questions on page 55 about the reading. For students who need more direction, use the questions that appear under the reduced Student Text pages. These focus on the selection and call on students to apply the strategy they have learned.

DISCUSSING AND APPLYING THE STRATEGY

Check students' understanding of the lesson with these questions.

Page 50   Read the caption under the picture on this page. On a map of the United States, in what state would you find the city of Wilmington?
(North Carolina)

A Good Way to Begin The students told their teacher, Mrs. Reddrick, that they wanted to learn more about their community. Mrs. Reddrick asked them what they already knew about Wilmington. The students discovered that they really knew a lot. They knew that Wilmington is a **port** city. A port is a place where ships can be safe from the big waves and strong winds of stormy seas. The boys and girls knew that many ships come to their city's port every year.

Mrs. Reddrick then asked the students to tell her what they wanted to study. This helped her to group the class so that students with the same interests could work together.

Now we will look at each group to see how they studied their community and what they learned.

Learning from Maps Antonio, Tonya, Ben, and Kelsey had moved to Wilmington during the summer. They wanted to make maps. These maps would help them find places in their new community. They decided to make four maps. Mrs. Reddrick gave them some maps to

(Left) Mrs. Reddrick helps her class learn about their city and state. (Right) Kelsey, a student in Mrs. Reddrick's class, points to the location of Wilmington.
■ What tells you that this class is studying about North Carolina?

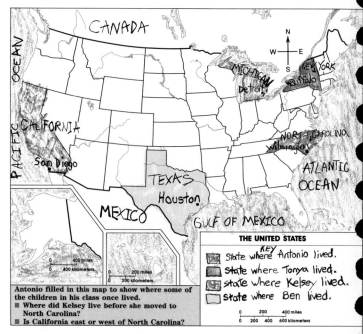

Antonio filled in this map to show where some of the children in his class once lived.
■ Where did Kelsey live before she moved to North Carolina?
■ Is California east or west of North Carolina?

use. These maps showed the outlines of certain places. The maps also showed a compass rose and a scale of miles. The girls and boys filled in the maps and made map keys.

Antonio filled in a map of the United States. He colored North Carolina red and put a black dot where Wilmington is located. Antonio also colored the states where he, Tonya, Ben, and Kelsey used to live. He put black dots where their old communities are located. Then he filled in the names of all these places. Look at Antonio's map above? Where did he live before moving to Wilmington?

Continue applying the strategy.

Page 53 **What feature of the map on page 53 helps you see that Wilmington is in southeastern North Carolina?** (the compass rose)

Page 53 **What part of the map tells you the state where each child lived before moving to North Carolina?** (the map key)

Page 53 **What part of the map could help you figure out how many miles Ben moved?** (the map scale)

Page 53 **What part of the map could help you figure out in what direction Tonya moved?** (the compass rose)

Page 53 **What two measures of distance are used on the scale of the map?** (miles and kilometers)

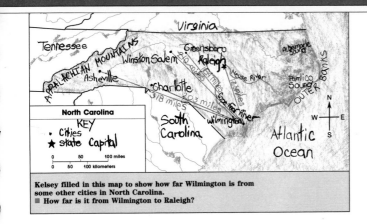

North Carolina

KEY
- Cities
★ state Capital

0   50   100 miles
0   50   100 kilometers

Kelsey filled in this map to show how far Wilmington is from some other cities in North Carolina.
■ **How far is it from Wilmington to Raleigh?**

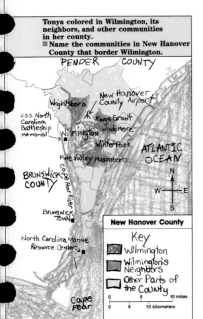

Tonya colored in Wilmington, its neighbors, and other communities in her county.
■ **Name the communities in New Hanover County that border Wilmington.**

New Hanover County

Key
- Wilmington
- Wilmington's Neighbors
- Other Parts of the County

0   5   10 miles
0   5   10 kilometers

Kelsey wanted to make a map of North Carolina. She located Wilmington on her map. She also showed other cities in the state and how far they are from Wilmington. Kelsey drew in the Appalachian Mountains, the Cape Fear River, the Neuse River, Albemarle Sound, Pamlico Sound, and the Outer Banks.

Tonya's map shows the **county** named New Hanover County. A county is a political division. Most of our states are divided into counties. Besides showing the shape of New Hanover County, Tonya's map shows some of the communities in the county.

Using What You Have Learned

Read the map on page 53 to answer the following questions.

1. What state did Ben live in before moving to Wilmington?

2. About how far apart are San Diego and Wilmington?

3. In what direction would you travel if you wanted to go from the state of New York to North Carolina?

Read the maps on page 54 to answer the following questions. In your answers, tell if you used the map key, the scale, or the compass rose to answer the question.

4. What color is used to show Wilmington on the New Hanover County map?

5. In New Hanover County, how far is Brunswick Town from Wilmington?

6. Look at the map of North Carolina. In what direction would you travel to go from Wilmington to Raleigh?

7. Which map would you use to find the state capital of North Carolina? Why would you use this map?

8. What city shown on the map of North Carolina is the farthest from Wilmington?

Examples and excerpts are from *Our Country's Communities, Silver Burdett & Ginn Social Studies,* © 1988.

Continue applying the strategy.

Page 54   How would you answer the question under the map at the top of the page? (by using the distance lines drawn on the map)

Page 54   What is the answer to the question above the map of New Hanover County? (Wrightsboro, Kings Grant, Windemere, Winter Park, Pine Valley, and Masonboro) **What part of the map helped you answer the question?** (the map key)

WRAP-UP

Discuss answers to "Using What You Have Learned."

Direct students to answer the questions on a separate sheet of paper.

1. *(Texas)*

2. *(about 2,000 miles or 3,180 kilometers)*

3. *(south)*

4. *(purple)*

5. *(about fifteen miles or eighteen kilometers)*

6. *(north; some students may answer NW.)*

7. *(The map of North Carolina; the map key gives a symbol for the capital.)*

8. *(Asheville)*

Checkpoint

USING THE CHECKPOINT PAGES

Use Checkpoints for informal evaluation.

Checkpoints are designed to help students and teachers monitor and improve student progress. For students, the Checkpoints serve as another step in the development of their ability to control their own learning. They see their own strengths and weaknesses even as the teacher does. For the teacher, the Checkpoints offer a systematic approach to informal assessment. Each Checkpoint helps identify areas of strength and weakness and then offers ideas for reteaching and extra practice before the formal assessment that comes at the end of the unit.

The extra help ideas in Checkpoint lessons give additional practice to those students having difficulty with the targeted skill while allowing them to remain with the regular reading group. Extra help ideas can also be used effectively with individual students or in small groups.

Informally diagnose strengths and weaknesses.

Checkpoints are in the same format as the Unit Skills Tests; you might review the directions before assigning the pages. Direct students to complete the pages shown in the Resource Center. Then have students work together to correct their papers, and encourage them to explain the thinking behind their answers. This affords you an opportunity to observe not only how students arrived at their answers, but also to identify and explain any item types that are causing difficulty. Note that in the Resource Center, questions are labeled by skill so that you can quickly assess areas in which a particular student needs additional help.

The following skills are included in this Checkpoint.

   main idea and supporting details
   suffixes *-er* and *-or*

For your information, the Checkpoint pages at the end of this unit include the skills listed below.

   story elements
   suffix *-ly*
   vocabulary — Story Critical words

PROVIDING EXTRA HELP

Provide extra help with main ideas and supporting details.

Strengthen reading comprehension by linking reading and writing. Draw on unit selections and Workbook pages for examples of passages having clear main ideas and supporting details. After students have studied these, have them use one as a model for writing a paragraph containing a clear main idea. Students might then work in pairs or small groups to exchange papers and identify main ideas, discussing whether these are supported by sufficient details and — if a main idea is not adequately supported — what kinds of details might be added to that paragraph to improve it.

Provide extra help with suffixes -er and -or.

OPTION 1 Develop better reading comprehension by linking reading, vocabulary development, and writing. Give students five minutes to list as many words as they can think of that end in the letters *-er* or *-or*. Then write words on the chalkboard as volunteers read them to you. As words are suggested distinguish when necessary between those that end in *-er* or *-or* (*laser, otter, motor, monster*) and those in which the letters are actually suffixes. Have students write five sentences, each containing one of the words from the list. Completed sentences might be read aloud to the group or sentences could be written on the chalkboard.

OPTION 2 Strengthen reading comprehension by linking reading, vocabulary development, and listening. Have students recognize and use in sentences words containing the suffixes *-er* and *-or*. First put these words on the chalkboard: *singer, painter, actor, thinker, inventor*. Have a student underline the suffix in each. Then discuss the meaning of each root. Finally have students write a brief paragraph or story using all five of the words. Completed stories could be read aloud as the group listens.

Workbook page 26

NAME _____

Checkpoint

Read the paragraphs. Then fill in the circle beside the correct answer.

    Imagine life long ago. It was different from today. Most people were farmers who grew their own food. Almost everything they needed they made for themselves. Sailors and fishermen used wooden boats that were powered by wind and oars, not motors.

    Schools were different then, too. Children of all ages learned together in the same room. They shared books and slates. They carried their lunches to school in pails. In warm weather they often went home after school to help with the farming.

    After doing their chores, children listened to stories. They did not have computers or televisions. It was not easy to visit friends. Cars were unknown. People on horseback galloped across the fields when they wanted to visit other families.

    Dinner was a happy family time. Hunters enjoyed rabbit stew after a day's work. Some people had biscuits, if they had baked them at home. None of the food on the table came from a supermarket. After dinner people went to bed. Work days began earlier and ended earlier than they do today.

26   Checkpoint

RESOURCE CENTER

◀ These pages provide informal assessment in the format of the Unit Skills Tests. ▶

Workbook page 27

NAME _____

main idea/details
1. What is the main idea of the selection?
   a) Long ago, life was hard.
   b) Pioneers had to be rugged.
   c) Life long ago was different from life today.
   d) You can go back in time.

main idea/details
2. What sentence helped you tell the main idea?
   a) It was different from today.
   b) Most people were farmers.
   c) Cars were unknown.
   d) Dinner was a happy family time.

main idea/details
3. What did children do after their chores?
   a) watched television
   b) drove wagons
   c) hunted bears
   d) listened to stories

main idea/details
4. Which paragraph helped you find out what children did?
   a) first paragraph
   b) second paragraph
   c) third paragraph
   d) fourth paragraph

suffixes *-er, -or*
5. Which word names one who farms?
   a) sailor
   b) farmer
   c) computer
   d) hunter

suffixes *-er, -or*
6. Which suffixes were added to words to name someone who does something?
   a) *-ing* and *-ed*
   b) *-er* and *-or*
   c) *-able* and *-ible*
   d) *-ment* and *-ness*

suffixes *-er, -or*
7. Which word group shows the meaning of the suffixes *-er* and *-or*?
   a) for, dinner, computer, earlier,
   b) other, power, higher, weather
   c) farmer, sailor, hunter, driver
   d) after, better, shower, nor

Checkpoint   27

TEACHER CHOICE

	Teaching Sequence	Trade Books and Resources	Meeting Individual Needs	Integrated Language Arts / Cross Curriculum
The Bridge Pages 98–99	**Maintain** Drawing Conclusions	• Teaching Chart 15 • Workbook 28 • Skills Practice 24		
PART 1 **Vocabulary Strategies** Pages 100–101	**Develop Concepts** Semantic Mapping **Teach Vocabulary** STORY CRITICAL WORDS: **chickens,** hoot owl, **mule,** purred, **wasps,** yowl (Tested words are boldfaced.)	• Teaching Chart 16 • Workbook 29 • Skills Practice 25	**SUPPORT WORDS:** mostly, planet, thump, worst • Skills Practice 26 **CHARACTER/SETTING WORDS:** Earth, Grandaddy, Janetta, Momma, Star, United States of America	**WRITING/SPEAKING ACTIVITY:** Use new vocabulary to describe country living. • Spelling Connection 42
PART 2 **Reading & Responding** Pages 102–113	**Build Background** **Develop a Purpose for Reading** **Guide the Reading Process** **Selection Follow-Up**	• Reader's Journal 22–25 • Workbook 30 **I▸T KIT** Singing a Song **READING EVERY DAY** *Grandparents' Houses,* by C. Streich *Through Grandpa's Eyes,* by P. MacLachlan	**EXTRA HELP:** Thinking About Character's Feelings **ACHIEVING ENGLISH PROFICIENCY:** Identifying Animals and Personal Reactions • Achieving English Proficiency Master 8	**Language Arts Connections** **WRITING TO LEARN:** Write words in speech balloons. • Writing Master 4 **SPEAKING/LISTENING:** Improvising Scenes **WRITING:** Listing and Illustrating Onomatopoeic Words; Writing About the Turning Point; Writing Tall Tales • Language Arts Master 4
PART 3 **Selection Support** Pages 114–119	**Introduce** Forms	• Teaching Chart 17 • Workbook 31 • Skills Practice 27	**Practice** • Teaching Chart 18 • Workbook 32 • Skills Practice 28 Main Idea/Details (Tested) **Maintain** • Skills Practice 29–30 Predicting Outcomes Final Consonant Clusters -*ld,* -*lk, -mb, -mn*	**Curriculum Connections** **SCIENCE:** Researching Owls/Animal Behavior; Reporting on Constellations • Curriculum Connection Master 4 **MUSIC:** Discussing and Singing Country Songs

Grandaddy's Place

written by Helen V. Griffith
illustrated by James Stevenson

SUMMARY *Janetta accompanies Momma on a visit to Grandaddy. His house is old and run-down, and the animals on the land seem mean and unfriendly. But Grandaddy is patient and understanding, and he jokes with Janetta. Soon she begins to feel more comfortable. The animals are not so mean after all, and Janetta decides to give them all names. As she comes to like Grandaddy's place, she wonders how all the animals got along without her for so long.*

The Bridge

SKILL TRACE: DRAWING CONCLUSIONS

Introduced in Level 7	Maintain
	TE 60	98

COMPREHENSION

Teaching Drawing Conclusions

OBJECTIVE   Drawing conclusions from text.

1. WARM-UP

Use a known passage to draw a conclusion.

Tell the students they will listen to a passage from the previous selection, "Life in Pilgrim Times." Read the passage aloud and ask the questions that follow. Help students put this information together to understand what the author is saying about the Pilgrims. *(The Pilgrims were willing to leave much of their lives behind in order to come to North America.)*

> **After the Pilgrims arrived in North America, they had only the things they could bring with them on the ship. They had clothes, weapons, some tools and books, and a few pieces of furniture.**

1. **Why did the Pilgrims have only the things they could bring with them on the ship?** *(The things did not take up much room and would help them begin a new life.)*

2. **Why did the Pilgrims bring the things they did?** *(The things they brought would help them build a new life.)*

Discuss story and knowledge clues.

Point out to students that they first thought about information given in the story — the ship and the things the Pilgrims brought with them. Explain that students used those story clues, what they already knew, and their own reasoning power to make a judgment about the Pilgrims.

State the objective.

Tell students they will learn to use story clues and their own knowledge to draw conclusions, or make judgments about given information.

2. TEACH

Explain why drawing conclusions is important.

Drawing conclusions helps readers better understand a story and know more about what an author is trying to say.

Present a strategy for drawing conclusions.

Explain to students that there is a strategy they can use to draw conclusions. First, read the passage and think about the information given. Next, think about what you already know about events such as this. Then use the story clues and what you already know to draw a conclusion about the passage.

TEACHING CHART 15: DRAWING CONCLUSIONS | 15

Story Clues
1. (The Pilgrims came by ship.)
2. (They brought weapons, tools, books, some furniture.)

"What I Know" Clues
1. (There is no room on a ship to bring a lot of things.)
2. (The things they brought would help the Pilgrims build a new life.)

Conclusion
(The Pilgrims were willing to leave much behind and were sensible about what they brought with them.)

Model the strategy. Explain that you can write down the steps used to draw the conclusion about the Pilgrims in the paragraph that you and the students discussed. Tell students that the first story clue was that the Pilgrims came by ship. Write this on the chart under the heading *story clues*. Ask students for the other story clue (*the things they brought with them*) and have this clue written on the chart.

3. GUIDED PRACTICE

Check for understanding. Before going on, have students explain how readers draw conclusions. (*Use clues from the story. Think about what you already know.*)

Guide students in using the strategy. Have the students tell what they already know about ships and about the kinds of things the Pilgrims brought. Fill in these clues on the chart. Discuss how these clues and the story clues lead to the conclusion. Complete the chart.

4. WRAP-UP

Summarize instruction. Review how readers draw conclusions and why drawing conclusions is helpful. (*Use story clues and your own knowledge. Drawing conclusions helps readers better understand what they are reading.*)

Provide independent practice. Options for independent practice are shown in the Resource Center below.

5. APPLICATION

Students will draw conclusions as they read "Grandaddy's Place." The symbol ✔ marks specific questions and activities that apply this skill.

Workbook page 28

COMPREHENSION   NAME _____
Drawing Conclusions

REMEMBER: When you draw a conclusion, you figure out things that are not explained in a story. Use story clues and what you already know to draw a conclusion.

A. Read the paragraphs. Think about story clues and what you already know to answer the questions.

1. The Pilgrims left their homes in England to come to America. They wanted to find a place where they would be free to follow their religious beliefs.

   What kind of freedom did America offer the Pilgrims?
   People were free to follow their religious beliefs.
   _____

2. The first houses the Pilgrims built were small. The roofs were made of grass and mud, and the walls were made of wood. Most houses had only one large room with a large fireplace that was used for cooking and for heating.

   How comfortable were the Pilgrims in their new homes?
   They must have been cold, crowded, and uncomfortable.
   _____

3. The Indians gave the Pilgrims corn to plant. They showed them the best places to fish and hunt. They showed them which fruits and berries were safe to eat in the forest.

   What kinds of food did the Indians eat?
   They ate corn, game, fish, fruit, and berries.
   _____

B. On separate paper, write one story clue from each paragraph in Part A that helped you draw a conclusion. See Teacher Notes.

28 "Grandaddy's Place"   Drawing Conclusions

RESOURCE CENTER

◀ **Workbook page 28** is intended for use by all students.

Skills Practice 24 ▶ may be assigned for additional practice.

Workbook reuse option: Have students underline the words and phrases in the sentences in Part A that provided clues to the conclusions they drew.

Skills Practice 24

NAME _____   SKILLS PRACTICE ⟨24⟩

Drawing Conclusions

When you draw a conclusion, you figure out things that are not explained in a story. Use story clues and what you already know to draw a conclusion.

| Story clues |
| What I know |
+ | Conclusion |

Read each story. Use the facts to draw the correct conclusion. Circle and write the best answer choice.

The postmaster stopped at the Brown's farm. He waved at Janie. She ran up to him and took what he gave her. Janie sat under the apple tree, where she could be alone. As she read, Janie wondered. Was Cousin Louise asking her to visit or only telling her the news? When she finished reading, Janie couldn't help smiling. What fun she and Louise would have together!

1. Why did the postmaster wave to Janie?
   He liked her.   He had a book for her.   [He had a letter for her.]
   He had a letter for her.

2. Why did Janie smile?
   Louise told a joke.   Janie heard something.   [Louise invited her to visit.]
   Louise invited her to visit.

Everyone who got off the ship had to go through the big building. Mr. Wang waited there now. The ship should come any minute. Mr. Wang could hardly wait. He hadn't seen Mrs. Wang in three years. Lo Ping had been a baby. Mr. Wang had worked hard during the past three years. Now, he had a good job and a nice apartment. He hoped his family would feel the way he did about their new home.

3. Why was Mr. Wang waiting in the building?
   He needed help.   [His family was arriving.]   He couldn't find a job.
   His family was arriving.

4. How do you think Mr. Wang was feeling?
   scared   [excited]   annoyed
   excited

24   LEVEL 8   "Grandaddy's Place"

Vocabulary Strategies

Developing Concepts

Tap prior knowledge about country life with a semantic map.

Make a semantic map about the concept of country life as a starting point for teaching vocabulary. Encourage students to discuss their thoughts about country life. What sights and sounds are associated with the country? What animals can often be seen? List responses, building a map around sights, sounds, and animals.

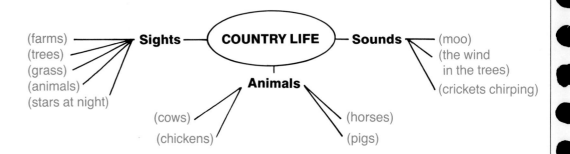

Teaching Vocabulary

Discuss meanings of Story Critical words.

Read each context sentence on the Teaching Chart and identify the new word. Then use the questions below to help students understand each word. When necessary, provide a definition.

TEACHING CHART 16: VOCABULARY 16

1. **chickens** (common farm fowl raised for eggs or food)
   In the country, we ate the eggs that the *chickens* laid.
2. **wasps** (flying stinging insects with slender bodies)
   We saw *wasps* flying around their nest, but we did not get too close because they sting.
3. **mule** (the offspring of a donkey and a horse)
   The *mule* sounded like a donkey but looked more like a horse.
4. **hoot owl** (a large night bird that makes a long, low sound)
   At night we heard the lonely call of the *hoot owl* and saw it in the tree.
5. **purred** (made a low, soft, rumbling sound)
   The cat sat in my lap and *purred* like a running car motor.
6. **yowl** (to make a loud cry, as a cat does)
   We sometimes woke up if the cats began to fight and *yowl*.

chickens

1. **What clues in the sentence helped you figure out what a chicken is?** (*eggs* and *laid* are clues that it is an animal that lays eggs) **Is this word on the map of COUNTRY LIFE and if not, where should it go?** (yes, under *Animals*) STRATEGY: CONTEXT CLUES

wasps

2. **What things that fly can also sting like wasps?** (bees, hornets) **What are wasps, bees, and hornets called?** (insects) **Where would you put wasps on the map?** (under *Animals*) **What sound that wasps make would you put on the map?** (buzz) STRATEGY: PRIOR KNOWLEDGE

mule
3. What clues in the sentence helped you figure out what a mule is? (the words *horse* and *donkey*) **What sounds do mules make?** (hee-haw, or bray) STRATEGY: CONTEXT CLUES

hoot owl
4. When are owls usually awake? (at night) **What sounds have you heard different birds make?** (chirp, chatter, caw, cheep) Point out that the vowel sound in *hoot* is the same sound as in the word *boot*. STRATEGY: PRIOR KNOWLEDGE

purred
5. What clue in the sentence helped you figure out what a cat that purred sounded like? (running car motor) **What other sounds do cats make?** (meow, hiss, yowl) STRATEGY: CONTEXT CLUES

yowl
6. Does *yowl* describe something you see or hear? (hear) **When might a cat yowl?** (when it is fighting, angry, or hungry, or possibly lonely) STRATEGY: PRIOR KNOWLEDGE

Discuss Support words as needed.
The Glossary of the Student Text includes definitions of the Support words: *thump, mostly, planet, worst.*

Present Character/Setting words.
Present and then pronounce Character and Setting words in the story: *Momma, Janetta, Grandaddy, United States of America, Earth, Star.*

Provide independent practice.
Options for independent practice are shown in the Resource Center below.

WRITING OR SPEAKING ACTIVITY *If students live in a city, ask them to tell how they would like to spend a day in the country. If they live in the country, ask them to describe some things they see and do. Encourage students to use new vocabulary when possible.*

RESOURCE CENTER

Workbook page 29

◄ **Workbook page 29** provides practice with Story Critical words.

Skills Practice 25 ► provides additional practice with Story Critical words.

Skills Practice 26 provides practice with Support words.

Spelling Connection Master 42 may be used for spelling instruction with the new vocabulary.

Workbook reuse option: Have students circle all the words on the page that indicate sounds.

NAME _____

Using New Words

A. Three words in each example belong together. One word does not. Cross out the word that doesn't belong. Then write a word from the box that does belong.

| chickens | hoot owl | mule | purred | wasps | yowl |

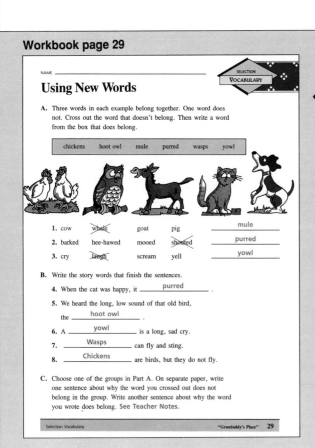

1. cow ~~whale~~ goat pig _____ mule
2. barked hee-hawed mooed ~~shouted~~ _____ purred
3. cry ~~laugh~~ scream yell _____ yowl

B. Write the story words that finish the sentences.

4. When the cat was happy, it _____ purred
5. We heard the long, low sound of that old bird, the _____ hoot owl .
6. A _____ yowl is a long, sad cry.
7. _____ Wasps can fly and sting.
8. _____ Chickens are birds, but they do not fly.

C. Choose one of the groups in Part A. On separate paper, write one sentence about why the word you crossed out does not belong in the group. Write another sentence about why the word you wrote does belong. See Teacher Notes.

Selection Vocabulary "Grandaddy's Place" **29**

Skills Practice 25

NAME _____

Vocabulary: Story Critical Words

A. Study the meaning of each word.

chickens farm birds
hoot owl a bird that makes a long, low sound
mule an animal with a donkey and a horse for parents

purred made a soft, happy sound
wasps flying insects with thin bodies
yowl to make a long, loud, unhappy cry

B. Write the vocabulary word that answers each question.

1. Which two words name kinds of birds?
_____ chickens and _____ hoot owl
2. Which animal has two different parents? _____ mule
3. What animals fly but are not birds? _____ wasps
4. What did the happy kitten do? _____ purred
5. What might a hungry dog do? _____ yowl

C. Read each group of words. Draw a line under the word that does not belong to the group. Write the vocabulary word that does belong.

6. bees, flowers, hornets _____ wasps 8. howl, giggle, yell _____ yowl
7. donkey, horse, rabbit _____ mule 9. ducks, geese, crows _____ chickens

D. Complete each sentence with the correct vocabulary word.

10. The _____ chickens laid lots of eggs.
11. Do not get stung by the _____ wasps buzzing over there.
12. Jack let out a _____ yowl when the horseshoe fell on his toe.
13. The small wagon was drawn by a _____ mule .
14. David's cat never _____ purred for strangers.
15. When Ted opened the barn door, a _____ hoot owl let out a long, low hoot.

LEVEL 8 "Grandaddy's Place" Definition clues **25**

101

Reading & Responding

Building Background

Motivate discussion using the poems.

Share the following poems with students. Tell students that the poems were written by children, and that each poem has to do with a feeling about being in a new situation. Discuss the feeling talked about in each poem.

Revving-Up

I was so excited
I felt like a car
with my engine going
round and round.
— *Danny Prohonas*

Lonely

Sometimes you feel
Lonely like
You are the only one
In the world.
— *Brian Smith*
From If a Poem Bothers You.

Build background about changes in feelings.

Remind students that the feelings we have when we face new situations often change as time passes. Have students tell about times in their lives when they faced something new, such as going to school for the first time, and how they felt. Ask students to tell how and why their feelings changed. (*nervous, uncomfortable; felt better when they knew what to expect*)

Discuss realistic fiction.

Tell students that in this story a girl must face *two* new situations. Point out that this story did not really happen but it could happen. It is realistic fiction. Explain that in such fiction, characters think and act like real people.

Developing a Purpose for Reading

Option 1
Students set purpose.

ORAL "I WONDER" LISTS   Have students preview the selection by reading the title and introduction. Ask them to suggest "I wonder" statements about how Janetta might feel and what might happen at her grandaddy's place. Record the students' statements for later use.

WRITING ACTIVITY   Have students work individually or in pairs to create written "I wonder" lists. Be sure that students save their lists for later use.

Option 2
Teacher sets purpose.

Have students read the story to find out how Janetta's feelings about Grandaddy and his place change during the story.

Meeting
Individual
Needs

EXTRA HELP   Explain that the poems you read told about feelings of excitement and loneliness, and that in the next story Janetta experiences these feelings. Have students predict what might cause Janetta's feelings of excitement and loneliness. Write their suggestions on the board. After they read, have students return to the lists and compare their predictions with what they read.

ACHIEVING ENGLISH PROFICIENCY   Write the following words on the board: *cat, wasp, chicken, bug, snake, mule,* and *hoot owl.* Have pictures of each of the animals. Show students a picture of each of the animals as you say the name of the animal. Have them repeat the name after you. Ask students which animals they have seen and if they were afraid of them when they saw them. Ask students if there are other things they are afraid of now or things they were afraid of when they were little. For additional help in story comprehension, use Master 8 in the Teacher Resource Kit.

Going to Grandaddy's place made Momma happy. But that's not the way Janetta felt.

Grandaddy's Place

written by Helen V. Griffith
illustrated by James Stevenson

※※ CHAPTER ONE ※※

One day Momma said to Janetta, "It's time you knew your grandaddy." Momma and Janetta went to the railroad station and got on a train. Janetta had never ridden on a train before. It was a long ride, but she liked it. She liked hearing about Momma's growing-up days as they rode along. She didn't even mind sitting up all night.

But when they got to Grandaddy's place, Janetta didn't like it at all.

The house was old and small. The yard was mostly bare red dirt. There was a broken-down shed and a broken-down fence.

"I don't want to stay here," said Janetta.
Momma said, "This is where I grew up."
An old man came out onto the porch.
"Say hello to your grandaddy," Momma said.
Janetta was too shy to say hello.
"You hear me, Janetta?" Momma asked.
"Let her be," said Grandaddy.
So Momma just said, "Stay out here and play while I visit with your grandaddy."

Reader's Journal   **p 22**
Preparing for Reading

STOP! LOOK! LISTEN!

To prepare for reading the next selection, students imagine that two city kids are visiting the country for the first time. The text directs them to visualize and describe various aspects of country life.

GUIDED READING

✔ **Page 56** **Where do you think Grandaddy's house is?** (in the country) **What makes you think so?** (Country homes often have dirt yards, sheds, and fences.) SYNTHESIZE: DRAWING CONCLUSIONS

✔ **Page 57** **What kind of house do you think Janetta lives in?** (new and large, probably in a city or suburb) **What helped you draw this conclusion?** (People often do not like what they are not used to. Janetta does not like her grandaddy's place and thinks it is old and small.) SYNTHESIZE: DRAWING CONCLUSIONS

HIGHLIGHTING LITERATURE

Pages 56–57 Remind students that because the events and characters seem real, this story is realistic fiction. Have students explain what seems real about the events. (Janetta and Momma's train ride; their words to each other; Janetta's feelings) Also point out that the description of Grandaddy's place helps the reader to imagine what Janetta sees.

✔ Skill from The Bridge applied through this question.

103

They left Janetta standing on the porch. She didn't know what to do. She had never been in the country before. She thought she might sit on the porch, but there was a mean-looking cat on the only chair. She thought she might sit on the steps, but there was a wasps' nest up under the roof. The <u>wasps</u> looked meaner than the cat. Some <u>chickens</u> were taking a dust-bath in the yard. When Janetta came near, they made mean sounds at her.

Janetta walked away. She watched the ground for bugs and snakes. All at once a giant animal came out of the broken-down shed. It came straight toward Janetta, and it was moving fast. Janetta turned and ran. She ran past the chickens and the wasps' nest and the mean-looking cat.

She ran into the house.

"There's a giant animal out there," she said.

Grandaddy looked surprised. "First I knew of it," he said.

"It has long legs and long ears and a real long nose," said Janetta.

Momma laughed. "Sounds like the <u>mule</u>," she said.

"Could be," said Grandaddy. "That mule's a tall mule."

"It chased me," said Janetta.

"It won't hurt you," Momma said. "Go back outside and make friends." But Janetta wouldn't go back outside.

"Nothing out there likes me," she said.

CHAPTER TWO

After dark Momma and Grandaddy and Janetta sat out on the steps. The mean-looking cat wasn't anywhere around. Janetta hoped the wasps were asleep. She was beginning to feel sleepy herself. Then a terrible sound from the woods brought her wide awake.

"Was that the mule?" she asked.

"That was just an old <u>hoot owl</u> singing his song," said Grandaddy.

"It didn't sound like singing to me," said Janetta.

GUIDED READING

Page 58   What word does the writer repeat to suggest that Janetta is frightened by the animals and thinks they do not like her? (*Mean* — every animal either looks mean or sounds mean to Janetta)   INFER: FEELINGS/ATTITUDES

Page 59   How do you think Janetta feels on the porch when her mother and Grandaddy are with her? (She probably is more relaxed because she begins to feel sleepy.)   INFER: FEELINGS/ATTITUDES

✔ **Pages 58–59   Use clues from the story and "what I know" clues to answer this question: "Do you think Janetta has any pets at home?"** (Students may present the following evidence: Each animal she meets scares her or acts "mean" to her.[story] People who are used to being around animals are usually not frightened of them.["what I know"] Conclusion: Janetta probably has no pets, or if she does, they are small and quiet.) SYNTHESIZE: DRAWING CONCLUSIONS

✔ Skill from The Bridge applied through this question.
✔ Informal Assessment Opportunity: VISUALIZING

STRATEGIC READING

✔ **Page 59   Have students close their eyes and picture Janetta as she tries to fall asleep. Have them remember how she acted and felt during the day. Ask these questions to help them form a mental picture: What does the bedroom look like? How is Janetta lying in the bed? What sounds does she hear? Does she see shadows, and what does she think they are? Does she sleep well? Tell children that if they cannot picture Janetta, then this is a signal that they may not be understanding the story. Ask them to reread parts of it and pay close attention to descriptive words.** METACOGNITION: VISUALIZING

"If you were an owl, you'd be tapping your feet," said Grandaddy.

They sat and listened to the owl, and then Grandaddy said, "It was just this kind of night when the star fell into the yard."

"What star?" asked Janetta.

"Now, Daddy," said Momma.

"It's a fact," said Grandaddy. "It landed with a thump, and it looked all around, and it said, 'Where am I?'"

"You mean stars speak English?" asked Janetta.

"I guess they do," said Grandaddy, "because English is all I know, and I understood that star just fine."

"What did you say to the star?" asked Janetta.

Grandaddy said, "I told that star, 'You're in the United States of America,' and the star said, 'No, I mean what planet is this?' and I said, 'This is the planet Earth.'"

"Stop talking foolishness to that child," Momma said.

"What did the star say?" asked Janetta.

"The star said it didn't want to be on the planet Earth," said Grandaddy. "It said it wanted to get back up in the sky where it came from."

"So what did you do, Grandaddy?" Janetta asked.

"Nothing," said Grandaddy, "because just then the star saw my old mule."

"Was the star scared?" Janetta asked.

"Not a bit," said Grandaddy. "The star said, 'Can that mule jump?' and I said, 'Fair, for a mule,' and the star said, 'Good enough.' Then the star hopped up on the mule's back and said, 'Jump.'"

Momma said, "Now, you just stop that talk."

"Don't stop, Grandaddy," said Janetta.

"Well," Grandaddy said, "the mule jumped, and when they were high enough up, the star hopped off and the mule came back down again."

GUIDED READING

Page 61   **Janetta asks Grandaddy if the star was afraid of the mule. What does this tell you about Janetta?** (That even though she is interested in the story she is still frightened by the mule.)   ANALYZE: CHARACTER

Page 61   **What kind of story does Grandaddy tell?** (make-believe/fantasy) **How do you know?** (The star and the mule talk and the star can hop. These things cannot happen in real life.)   EVALUATE: REALITY OR FANTASY

Page 61   **Momma keeps telling Grandaddy to stop telling Janetta the story about the star and the mule. Why do you think Grandaddy does not stop?** (He knows that Momma does not really mind and that the story is making Janetta feel better.)   INFER: FEELINGS/ATTITUDES

HIGHLIGHTING LITERATURE

Page 61   Point out to students that the writer of this story has created a very realistic character in Janetta. She lets the reader know everything that Janetta sees, thinks, and feels. She lets the reader see most things through Janetta's eyes. Knowing so much about Janetta makes her seem very real, like some person we might know in our own lives.

"Was the mule all right?" asked Janetta.

"It was thoughtful for a few days, that's all," said Grandaddy.

Janetta stared up at the sky. "Which star was it, Grandaddy?" she asked.

"Now, Janetta," Momma said, "you know that's a made-up story."

Grandaddy looked up at the stars. "I used to know," he said, "but I'm not sure anymore."

"I bet the mule remembers," Janetta said.

"It very likely does," said Grandaddy.

From somewhere in the bushes some cats began to yowl. "That's just the worst sound I know," Momma said. "Janetta, chase those cats."

"They're just singing their songs," said Grandaddy.

"That's right, Momma," said Janetta. "If you were a cat, you'd be tapping your feet."

Momma laughed and shook her head. "One of you is as bad as the other," she said.

⟫⟫⟫ CHAPTER THREE ⟪⟪⟪

The next day Grandaddy and Janetta went fishing. Janetta had never been fishing before. She didn't like it when Grandaddy put a worm on the hook.

"Doesn't that hurt him?" she asked.

"I'll ask him," said Grandaddy. He held the worm up in front of his face. "Worm, how do you feel about this hook?" he asked. He held the worm up to his ear and listened. Then he said to Janetta, "It's all right. That worm says there's nothing he'd rather do than fish."

"I want to hear him say that," Janetta said. She took the worm and held it up to her ear. "He's not saying anything," she said.

"That worm is shy," said Grandaddy. "But I know he just can't wait to go fishing."

GUIDED READING

Page 62   Do you think Janetta feels more comfortable about being with Grandaddy at the end of Chapter Two than she did at first? Why or why not? (Students may suggest that she makes a joke about the cat sounds and she has not made jokes before. Her feelings may be changing.)   ANALYZE: CHARACTER

Page 62   What do Momma's words and reactions on this page tell you about her? (She is a no-nonsense person, but she is understanding and accepting of other people's lightheartedness.)   SYNTHESIZE: CHARACTER

Page 62   What does Janetta's question about the worm tell you about Janetta? (She is concerned that the hook will hurt the worm.)   INFER: FEELINGS/ ATTITUDES

Page 63   Grandaddy talks to the worm and pretends that the worm talks back. What does this show you about Grandaddy? (He has a sense of humor.)   ANALYZE: CHARACTER

HIGHLIGHTING LITERATURE

**Pages 62–63   **Point out that this story is divided into chapters. Explain that authors sometimes divide stories into chapters to help readers understand that some time has passed or that the characters are in a new place. Have students tell what changes from the end of Chapter Two to the beginning of Chapter Three. (It is the next day. Grandaddy and Janetta are fishing.)

Grandaddy threw the line into the water. It wasn't long before he caught a fish. Then he gave Janetta the pole so that she could try. She threw the line in, and before long she had a fish, too. It was just a little fish. Janetta looked at it lying on the bank. It was moving its fins and opening and closing its mouth.

"I think it's trying to talk," Janetta said.

"It may be, at that," said Grandaddy. He held the fish up to his ear. "It says, 'Cook me with plenty of cornmeal,'" said Grandaddy.

"I want to hear it say that," said Janetta.

"Can you understand fish-talk?" asked Grandaddy.

"I don't know," said Janetta.

"Well, all that fish can talk is fish-talk," said Grandaddy.

Janetta held the fish up to her ear and listened. "It says, 'Throw me back,'" Janetta said.

Grandaddy looked surprised. "Is that a fact?" he asked.

"Clear as anything," said Janetta.

"Well, then I guess you'd better throw it back," said Grandaddy.

Janetta dropped the little fish into the water and watched it swim away. Grandaddy threw the line back in and began to fish again. "I never saw anybody learn fish-talk so fast," he said.

"I'm going to learn worm-talk next," said Janetta.

CHAPTER FOUR

When they had enough fish for supper, Janetta and Grandaddy walked on home. The mean-looking cat came running to meet them. He purred loud purrs and rubbed against their legs.

"I didn't know that cat was friendly," Janetta said.

"He's friendly when you've been fishing," said Grandaddy.

65

GUIDED READING

Page 64   What is the fish really doing when Grandaddy and Janetta say it is trying to talk? (It is trying to breathe. Fish cannot breathe out of water.) INFER: ACTIONS

✔ **Page 65   Even though you know that Grandaddy and Janetta have enough fish for supper, do you think Janetta caught any more or that Grandaddy caught them all? Why?** (Students may suggest that based on Janetta's behavior after she caught her first fish, she probably just sat there in the boat while Grandaddy caught fish.) SYNTHESIZE: DRAWING CONCLUSIONS

Page 65   What does Grandaddy mean when he tells Janetta that the cat is friendly "when you've been fishing"? (The cat likes to eat fish, so he acts friendly hoping that he will be given some.) INFER: CAUSE/EFFECT

HIGHLIGHTING LITERATURE

Page 65   Remind students that the words inside the quotation marks are the exact words the character spoke. Point out that a character's words and actions often give clues about how a character is feeling. Ask students what Janetta is revealing about her feelings when she holds the fish up to her ear and says, "It says, 'Throw me back.'" (She is feeling comfortable being with Grandaddy and she is able to joke with him. Also, she may know what it feels like to be sick and she feels sorry for the fish.)

✔ **Skill from The Bridge applied through this question.**

107

The mule came out of the shed and walked toward them with its ears straight up. Janetta didn't know whether to run or not. The mule walked up to her and pushed her with its nose. Janetta was sorry she hadn't run.

"What do you know," Grandaddy said. "That old mule likes you."

"How can you tell?" Janetta asked.

"It only pushes you that way if it likes you," said Grandaddy.

"Really?" asked Janetta.

"It's a fact," said Grandaddy. "Up until now that mule has only pushed me and the cat and one of the chickens." Janetta was glad she hadn't run. She reached out her hand and touched the mule's nose.

"Grandaddy," she said, "What's the mule's name?"

"Never needed one," said Grandaddy. "It's the only mule around."

"Can I name it?" asked Janetta.

"You surely can," said Grandaddy.

Janetta thought. "I could call it Nosey," she said.

"That would suit that mule fine," said Grandaddy.

Janetta thought some more. "Maybe I'll call it Beauty," she said.

"That's a name I never would have thought of," said Grandaddy.

The mule gave Janetta another push. "This mule really likes me," Janetta said. "It must know I'm going to give it a name."

"You don't have to give it anything," said Grandaddy. "That mule just likes you for your own self."

⟫⟫⟫ CHAPTER FIVE ⟪⟪⟪

After supper Grandaddy and Momma and Janetta sat out on the steps and watched the night come on. The stars began to show themselves, one by one.

"Now I know what I'll name that mule," Janetta said. "I'll call it Star."

GUIDED READING

Page 66   What is the difference between Janetta's reaction and Grandaddy's reaction when the mule walks up and pushes Janetta? (Janetta thinks the mule does not like her. Grandaddy says the mule only pushes people it likes.)   ANALYZE: COMPARISON

Page 67   Why do you think Janetta wants to name the mule? (She is beginning to feel more friendly toward the mule. People name animals they like or that are important to them.)   ANALYZE: CHARACTER

Page 67   Why does Grandaddy say that the name Nosey would suit the mule fine but that he never would have thought to name the mule Beauty? (The mule has a long nose and pushes people with it; most people do not consider mules beautiful.)   EVALUATE: CONNOTATIONS

STRATEGIC READING

Page 67   Have students recall what has happened so far in the story and predict how Janetta will feel about Grandaddy and his place by the end of the story. (Students may recall that Janetta dislikes everything. She does not like the house or the yard, is shy in front of Grandaddy, and is scared of the animals. But by the end of Chapter Four she has made jokes, gone fishing, and tried to name the mule. Students may predict that by the end of the story Janetta will realize that she likes Grandaddy and where he lives.) **Tell students that if they cannot recall what has happened so far in the story or make predictions then they should reread any parts that confused them.**   METACOGNITION: SUMMARIZING AND PREDICTING

"Should have thought of that myself," said Grandaddy.

"Tomorrow I'll give the cat a name," said Janetta.

"Only fair, now the mule has one," said Grandaddy.

"After I get to know the chickens, I'll name them, too," said Janetta. "Then you'll be able to call them when you want them."

"That'll be handy," said Grandaddy.

"You'll be naming the hoot owl next," Momma said.

"I've been thinking about it," said Janetta.

Momma laughed, and Grandaddy did, too.

"Now, how did we get along around here before you came?" he asked.

"I've been wondering that, too, Grandaddy," said Janetta.

◆ Reader's Response

Do you think you would like it at Grandaddy's place? Tell why or why not.

See next page for suggested answers.

SELECTION FOLLOW-UP

Grandaddy's Place

 ## Thinking It Over

1. Why didn't Janetta like her grandaddy's place at first?
2. When did Janetta begin to like being there? How do you know?
3. How did Janetta's grandaddy make her feel less afraid?
4. Why did Janetta name the mule "Star"?
5. Suppose Janetta had stayed indoors because she was afraid. What might have happened?

 ## Writing to Learn

THINK AND PREDICT When Janetta arrived at her grandaddy's place, she said, "Nothing out there likes me." What will she say when she leaves the farm? Draw a speech balloon.

Janetta

WRITE Fill the speech balloon with Janetta's words. Write what she might say when she leaves the farm.

GUIDED READING

Page 68 How do you know that Janetta is much happier now than she was when she first came to Grandaddy's place? (She is naming all of the animals and she wonders how they all got along before she came to visit.) ANALYZE: COMPARISON

RETURNING TO THE READING PURPOSE

OPTION 1 If students set the purpose, return to their "I wonder" statements about what happens to Janetta at Grandaddy's place. Ask students if they were surprised by anything that happened in the story.

OPTION 2 If you set the purpose, have students tell how Janetta's feelings changed during the story and why they changed. (Janetta is much happier and feels comfortable both with her Grandaddy and his place. Her feelings changed because she got to know him and understood him. She also got to know the animals and learned that there was no reason to be afraid of them.) Return to the semantic map created in Developing Concepts and have students add new information to it.

Reader's Journal   **p 23**
Responding to Reading

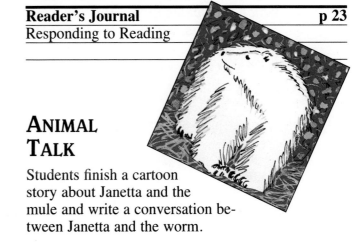

ANIMAL TALK

Students finish a cartoon story about Janetta and the mule and write a conversation between Janetta and the worm.

109

SELECTION FOLLOW-UP

Grandaddy's Place

THINKING IT OVER

1. **Why didn't Janetta like her grandaddy's place at first?** (Possible answers: It was old and run-down and the animals scared her; she was not used to life in the country and she was afraid of all the unfamiliar things; she felt that nothing on the farm liked her.)   RECALL: DETAILS

2. **When did Janetta begin to like being there? How do you know?** (She began to like being there when her grandaddy told the story about the mule and the star. She started to be interested in the things around her. Encourage students to read portions of the text that show both Janetta's interest in the story and her growing interest in her grandaddy's place.)
ANALYZE: PLOT; METACOGNITION

3. **How did Janetta's grandaddy make her feel less afraid?** (Possible answers: Grandaddy made her understand that the animal sounds were not unfriendly; he took her fishing and told her stories; he made her feel welcome and important.)   SYNTHESIZE: DRAWING CONCLUSIONS

4. **Why did Janetta name the mule "Star"?** (She liked the story in which the mule put the star back in the sky.)   ANALYZE: CHARACTER

✔ 5. **Suppose Janetta had stayed indoors because she was afraid. What might have happened?** (Possible answers: She would not have met the animals; she may have continued to be afraid; she may not have become so close to her grandaddy. Accept all reasonable responses.)
SYNTHESIZE: PREDICTING OUTCOMES

WRITING TO LEARN

Use Writing Master 4, which duplicates this illustration.

THINK AND PREDICT   When Janetta arrived at her grandaddy's place, she said, "Nothing out here likes me." What will she say when she leaves the farm? Draw a speech balloon. (Help students work with their speech balloons to prepare for writing. A possible answer is shown.)

Extend comprehension through writing.

WRITE   Fill in the speech balloon with Janetta's words. Write what she might say when she leaves the farm. (Have students share their balloons.)

✔ Informal Assessment Opportunity: PREDICTING

110

More Ideas for Selection Follow-Up

CRITICAL AND CREATIVE THINKING QUESTIONS

Encourage a variety of responses and points of view.

Use these open-ended questions to encourage critical and creative thinking about the selection.

1. The theme of this unit is "Remember When." When she grows up, what do you think Janetta will remember about her visit with Grandaddy?

2. Grandaddy helped Janetta learn about and enjoy a new place by using her imagination. How has using your imagination helped you feel better or more comfortable?

3. Imagine Janetta had a sister who was going to visit Grandaddy's place for the first time. What advice might Janetta give her?

REREADING ORALLY

Have students reread for pleasure.

Ask students to reread parts of "Grandaddy's Place" that they particularly liked. Have students tell why they liked the parts they chose. Did they smile or laugh? Were they reminded of an experience or feeling they had? Or did they simply enjoy the characters' words and actions? Tell students to vary the tones of their voices and the speeds at which they read. Remind students that punctuation marks help them know how to read some of a story.

SELECTION COMPREHENSION

Provide comprehension check.

A Workbook page to check comprehension is shown in the Resource Center below. It may be used for informal assessment.

Workbook page 30

SELECTION COMPREHENSION

NAME _____

Grandaddy's Place

A. Complete the summary of "Grandaddy's Place."
Accept reasonable variations.

_____ Janetta _____ and her Momma visited Grandaddy.
Grandaddy lived on a ____ farm ____ .
When they got to Grandaddy's place, Janetta didn't like it because
she was afraid of ____ the animals ____ . Some animals
Janetta met at Grandaddy's were wasps, chickens, a cat, and a mule.
Grandaddy made Janetta feel better about the mule by telling a story
about how the mule helped a falling star ____ get back in the sky ____
Then they heard the cat yowl and Momma said it was the worst sound
she knew. Janetta didn't agree. She said, "If you were a cat, you'd be
____ tapping your feet ____ ."
The next day Grandaddy took Janetta fishing. She threw her fish
back. She said it asked her to. Grandaddy told Janetta she learned
____ fish-talk ____ faster than anyone he knew. Then the cat
rubbed Janetta's leg and the mule ____ pushed her ____
with its nose.
Janetta decided to name the ____ mule ____ Star. Then she decided
to ____ name ____ the cat and the chickens.
Grandaddy wondered how he and the animals ever
got along ____ without Janetta ____ .

B. Pretend you are Janetta.
On separate paper, make up and write
five good names for the cat
and five good names for the chickens. See Teacher Notes.

30 "Grandaddy's Place"   Selection Comprehension

RESOURCE CENTER

◀ **Workbook page 30** is intended for use by all students.

Writing Master 4 duplicates the Writing to Learn illustration.

I•T Kit Activity

Audio: "Grandma's Farm"
The mischievous menagerie on Grandma's Farm would give even Grandaddy's lively animals a run for their money. Students listen to this song and make up their own add-on verses to the simple tune. (See Activity Guide.)

CONTENT AREAS

LANGUAGE ARTS CONNECTIONS

CREATIVE THINKING: IMPROVISING SCENES

Have students improvise interviews with the story characters.

Review that *improvising* means doing something without planning ahead of time. Explain that when actors improvise a scene together, the actors listen to one another so that they can respond in a way that makes sense.

Have students work in groups of four to play Grandaddy, Momma, Janetta, and a reporter from a local newspaper who is collecting news of social events. The reporter will ask questions of the three characters in the story. The student playing Grandaddy will respond with facts about his life with the animals on his place, the student playing Momma will respond with memories she has about growing up at Grandaddy's place, and Janetta will talk about how she first felt about Grandaddy's place and how she feels now.   SHARED LEARNING: SPEAKING/LISTENING

SELECTING AND ILLUSTRATING ONOMATOPOEIC WORDS

Discuss onomatopoeic words.

Have students recall some of the words in the story that imitate the sounds they name, such as *purr*, *hoot*, and *yowl*. Explain that these words and others help readers "hear" sounds and can make a story or poem seem more alive.

Have students select and illustrate onomatopoeic words.

Have students look through the story and list the words that sound like the sounds they name. Students can also add other onomatopoeic words that are suggested by the story. *(examples: thump, tap, buzz, hee haw, meow, hiss, cluck-cluck)* Ask students to illustrate five of the words by drawing the animals that make each of the sounds. Display the words and illustrations.   WHOLE CLASS ENRICHMENT

WRITING ABOUT THE TURNING POINT

Discuss turning point.

Remind students that the setting of a story or the situation of a particular character often affects the way the character feels. At some point in the story, there is a turning point where the character's feelings begin to change.

Have students write paragraphs identifying the turning point.

Have students make lists of words that describe Janetta's feelings at the beginning of the story. *(possible answers: shy, unhappy, scared)* Then have them look through the story to find the point where some of Janetta's feelings begin to change. *(when Grandaddy tells Janetta the story about the star and the mule)* Ask students to write paragraphs identifying the turning point and to include supporting details.   CHALLENGE: WRITING

WRITING TALL TALES

Discuss features of a tall tale.

Remind students of the story that Grandaddy tells Janetta about the star and the mule. Point out this story is a kind of tall tale. Explain that tall tales are mostly exaggerations of people, animals, or things from real life. The exaggerations may be about size, shape, or abilities.

Have students write tall tales.

Have students write their own tall tales about a mule and a star or about any subjects they wish. Remind students to give their subjects unusual traits or abilities. Have students illustrate their tall tales and read them aloud. **Language Arts Master 4** can be used with this activity.   WRITING

READING EVERY DAY

Like Janetta in "Grandaddy's Place," children often develop special feelings for their grandparents' homes as well as for grandparents themselves. The following books share this theme and will undoubtedly appeal to your students.

Grandparents' Houses. Poems about grandparents selected by Corinne Streich. Illustrated by Lillian Hoban. Greenwillow Books, © 1984. These poems about grandfathers and grandmothers represent such cultures as American, Chinese, German, Hebrew, Hispanic, Japanese, and Zuni.

Through Grandpa's Eyes by Patricia MacLachlan. Harper & Row, © 1980. With the help of his blind grandfather, young John sees, smells, hears, and experiences things in and around Grandpa's house in new and meaningful ways.   EASIER TO READ

A **World of Books** Classroom Libraries selection

Reader's Journal   pp 24, 25
Extending Reading

AMAZING TALES

After reading a tall tale similar to the one Grandaddy tells about his mule, students begin creating their own tall tales.

PART 3

Selection Support

SKILL TRACE: FORMS
This skill is untested at this level.

STUDY SKILLS

Forms

OBJECTIVE Reading and completing forms.

1. WARM-UP

Use prior knowledge to discuss forms.

Ask students if they have ever used a form to order a book or a magazine or filled out a form for a library card. Ask what kind of information they had to write down. (*name, address, telephone number; sometimes their grade)* Have them tell what forms are. *(papers that ask for information)* Have students tell what would happen if Grandaddy in "Grandaddy's Place" ordered a magazine and did not fill out the order form correctly. (*He probably would not get the magazine.*)

State the objective.

Tell students they will learn about reading and completing forms.

2. TEACH

Explain the purpose of forms and the importance of filling them out correctly.

Explain that forms are used to order such things as books, clothing, toys, and records. A form must also be filled out to receive a library card. The print on forms tells what is being offered. The form has spaces for information about *who*, *where*, *what*, and sometimes *how much*. Point out that if forms are filled out properly, the person to whom the form is sent can take care of it quickly, easily, and correctly.

Present a strategy for completing a form.

Tell students that there are steps they can follow that will help them complete a form properly. Then summarize the following steps. First look over the form to find out what information is needed. Look for words that tell how to write the answers. Then fill in the information that is asked for. Fit each answer in the right space, writing as neatly as possible and spelling everything correctly. After you make sure all the information is complete and correct, sign your name.

17

TEACHING CHART 17: FORMS

Country Life Book Club
Join now! Every month you will receive a catalogue. You can choose the book or books you want. Choose one book free just for joining.

Name ______________________________
(Please print)

Address ______________________________
(Street)

____
(City) (State) (ZIP)

Free Book—Please check [✔] one.

__ *My Mule, Star* __ *Grandaddy's Place*

__ *Country Kitchen*

Sign here ______________________________

Model the strategy. Tell students you see that the form is for joining Country Life Book Club. Point out the words that tell what information to fill in and how. (*Name, Please print, Address, Street, City, State, ZIP, Please check [✔] one*) Call on a volunteer or fill in the *Name* line. Ask how the name should appear. (*printed*)

3. GUIDED PRACTICE

Check for understanding. Before going on, ask students to explain the purpose of forms and why it is important to fill them in properly. (*to order something or to join something; so that the person receiving the form can take care of things quickly and easily, and the person who filled out the form will get what he or she wants*)

Guide students in using the strategy. Have students use the steps for completing a form by filling in the rest of the information.

4. WRAP-UP

Summarizing instruction. Review the steps for filling out a form. (*Look over the form to find out what information is asked for; look for words that tell how to provide the information; fill in the form neatly and correctly; review the form to make sure all the information is included and is correct; sign your name.*)

Provide independent practice. Options for independent practice are shown in the Resource Center below.

Workbook page 31

NAME _____

STUDY SKILLS

Forms

REMEMBER: Forms ask for specific information. Read the words on forms carefully to be sure you write in all the information needed.

A. Fill out the forms. First check to see what information is asked for. Then write neatly and fit the information in the space given. Finally check your spelling.

1.

CHILDREN'S CORNER

Please send me a full year of *Children's Corner*, 12 issues, at the money saving rate of $12.50.

Name Responses will vary. _____

Address _____

City _____ State _____ Zip _____

2.

Library Book Request Form

Name Responses will vary. ___ Grade ___ Teacher ___

Name of Book _____ Date ___

Signature _____

B. On separate paper, make up your own form for joining a book club. Then fill it in correctly. See Teacher Notes.

Forms "Grandaddy's Place" **31**

RESOURCE CENTER

◀ **Workbook page 31** is intended for use by all students.

Skills Practice 27 ▶ may be assigned for additional practice.

Workbook reuse option: Have students underline all the words that ask for specific responses. Then have them re-read their answers and mark a [✔] when they are satisfied they have filled in the space correctly.

Skills Practice 27

NAME _____

SKILLS PRACTICE 27

Forms

When you order something, you usually have to fill out an **order form**. Read the form carefully to see what information is needed. Write all the information that is asked for. Print neatly and keep your answers short. After you have finished, read over the form to make sure you have given the right information.

A. Read this magazine order form.

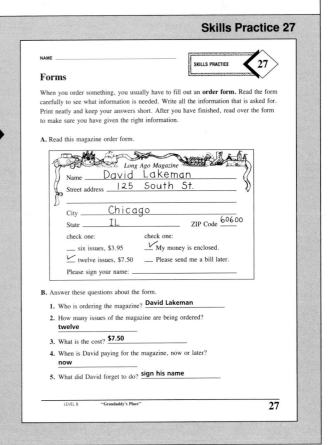

Long Ago Magazine

Name David Lakeman

Street address 125 South St.

_____

City Chicago

State IL ZIP Code 60600

check one: check one:

___ six issues, $3.95   ✔ My money is enclosed.

✔ twelve issues, $7.50   ___ Please send me a bill later.

Please sign your name: _____

B. Answer these questions about the form.

1. Who is ordering the magazine? David Lakeman

2. How many issues of the magazine are being ordered? twelve

3. What is the cost? $7.50

4. When is David paying for the magazine, now or later? now

5. What did David forget to do? sign his name

LEVEL 8   "Grandaddy's Place"   **27**

SKILL TRACE: MAIN IDEA/DETAILS						
Introduction	Practice		Test	Reteach	Maintain	
TE 66	82	116	157	158	234	274	508

COMPREHENSION

Main Idea/Details

OBJECTIVE Identifying stated and unstated main idea and supporting details.

Review stated and unstated main idea and details.

Remind students that paragraphs are organized in such a way that all or almost all of the sentences tell about one particular topic. Sometimes one sentence in the paragraph tells the most important idea about the topic and the other sentences tell the details — small pieces of information that explain the main idea. Sometimes the main idea is not told in one sentence. Then the reader must figure out the main idea.

Use Teaching Chart to review how to identify main idea and details.

Read and discuss each paragraph with students. Guide students to first name the topic of the paragraph. Then have them tell whether or not the main idea is stated. If it is stated, ask them to draw a line under it. If the main idea is not stated, ask them to name it. Ask them to name the details in each paragraph.

18

TEACHING CHART 18: MAIN IDEA/DETAILS

1. The country is a good place to live. The air is fresh. There is plenty of grass and trees. You can see the stars at night. (Topic: the country; children should underline the first sentence as the main idea.)

2. A mule has long ears like a donkey. A mule has the face of a horse. The rest of the mule's body is part donkey, part horse. (Topic: a mule; the main idea may be stated as "A mule is part donkey and part horse.")

Provide independent practice.

Options for independent practice are shown in the Resource Center below.

Workbook page 32

COMPREHENSION

NAME _____

Main Idea/Details

REMEMBER: A **main idea** tells the topic of the paragraph and what the paragraph says about the topic.

A. Read each of the following paragraphs. Underline the sentence that tells the main idea. Then write two sentences that tell details about the main idea. Be careful. Some of the ideas don't belong in the paragraphs.

1. Janetta liked the long train ride to Grandaddy's place. She liked to look out of the window. She liked to watch other people on the train. Momma always told her about growing up on a farm.

  a. _She liked to watch other people on the train._

  b. _She liked looking out the window._

2. Janetta didn't like Grandaddy's place at all. The house was old, and the yard was bare red dirt. The shed and fence were broken down. Grandaddy was a farmer.

  a. _The house was old and the yard was bare red dirt._

  b. _The shed and fence were broken down._

3. There were some scary things at Grandaddy's place. There was a mean-looking cat. There was a wasps' nest under the roof. Grandaddy said the mule put the star back in the sky.

  a. _There was a mean-looking cat._

  b. _There was a wasps' nest under the roof._

B. On separate paper, write what you would and would not have liked about Grandaddy's place if you had gone for a visit. See Teacher Notes.

32 "Grandaddy's Place" — Main Idea/Details

RESOURCE CENTER

◀ **Workbook page 32** is intended for use by all students.

Skills Practice 28 ▶ may be assigned for additional practice.

Workbook reuse option: Have students cross out the detail in each paragraph in Part A that does not belong with the main idea.

Skills Practice 28

NAME _____

SKILLS PRACTICE **28**

Main Idea/Details

A main idea tells what the whole paragraph is about. Details tell more about the main idea. When a paragraph has no main idea sentence, think about the details and figure out the main idea from them.

Read each group of details. Write a main idea sentence that tells about all the details in each group. **Answers will vary.**

1. Detail 1: American cities used to be smaller.
 Detail 2: Buildings weren't made of glass and steel.
 Detail 3: Many city streets were paved with cobblestones.
 Main Idea: **American cities have changed.**

2. Detail 1: Children used to play hide-and-seek and other games that children play today.
 Detail 2: They went ice skating in the winter.
 Detail 3: They swam in summer just as they do now.
 Main Idea: **Children used to do some of the same things children do now.**

3. Detail 1: The Pilgrims came here from England.
 Detail 2: Many early New Yorkers were Dutch.
 Detail 3: Some other groups that settled here were French, Polish, Chinese, German, and Spanish.
 Main Idea: **People came here from many other places.**

4. Detail 1: Puritans gave children names like *Cotton* and *Prudence*.
 Detail 2: Later, names like *James* and *Mary* were popular.
 Detail 3: Today, you may have friends named *Amy* and *Mike*.
 Main Idea: **People like different names at different times.**

28 LEVEL 8 "Grandaddy's Place"

Introduced in Level 7	Maintain
	TE 117	602

COMPREHENSION
Predicting Outcomes

OBJECTIVE   Using text and prior knowledge to predict logical outcomes.

Review predicting outcomes.

Remind students that predicting an outcome is making a guess about what will happen next. Point out that to predict what will happen next in a story, readers use story clues and their own knowledge and common sense.

Model how to predict an outcome.

You may wish to write the passages below on the chalkboard. Answers are shown in red. To model predicting outcomes, read the first passage. Note the story clues. Predict an outcome that makes sense — Janetta will turn and run.

1. A giant animal came out of the shed. It came straight toward Janetta, and it was moving fast. Janetta was frightened. (Story Clues: giant animal, heading for Janetta; Knowledge: People usually run away from something frightening; Prediction: Janetta will run.)

2. Grandaddy and Janetta began to talk and do things together, such as go fishing. Janetta got to know the animals and like them. (Story Clues: talking and going fishing together, knowing and liking the animals; Knowledge: Doing things together and becoming familiar with surroundings usually makes a person feel more comfortable and happy; Prediction: Janetta will be happy at Grandaddy's place.)

Have students predict an outcome.

Have volunteers identify the clues and suggest an outcome for the second passage. Ask students to explain their reasoning.

Provide independent practice.

An independent activity is shown in the Resource Center below.

RESOURCE CENTER

Skills Practice 29 ▶ may be assigned for additional practice.

Skills Practice 29

NAME _____

Predicting Outcomes

SKILLS PRACTICE 29

Have you ever made a guess about what was going to happen next in a story? If you have, you made a **prediction.** Use story clues and what you know to make a good prediction.

| Story clues |
| + What I know |
| Prediction |

Read the story about a pioneer family. Write what you think might happen as the story goes along. Do not look ahead. Then see if your predictions are correct.

Late in the fall, the Evans family traveled across country by wagon. They brought enough food for the winter. They also carried bags of vegetable seeds. The Evans family was looking for a good place to settle. The land was very rocky until they came to a valley with grass, trees, and a stream.

1. Predict what the Evans family did.   Answers will vary.

"We'll stay here," said Mr. Evans. The whole family pitched in to build a strong cabin and shelter for the horses.

2. What did the Evans family actually do?   They stayed there. They built a cabin and a shelter for the horses.

3. Now predict how the Evans family spent the winter.   Answers will vary.

That winter, the family kept snug and warm in their cabin. They lived on the food they brought and only went out when they had to.

4. How did the Evans family actually spend the winter?   They lived in their cabin and only went out when they had to. They ate the food they brought.

5. Were your predictions correct?   YES ☐   NO ☐
Why? or Why not? _____

LEVEL 8   "Grandaddy's Place"   29

117

SKILL TRACE: CONSONANT CLUSTERS ld, lk, mb, mn

Introduced in Level 7	Maintain
	TE 118

WORD STUDY

Final Consonant Clusters ld, lk, mb, mn

OBJECTIVE Reading words with final consonant clusters *ld, lk, mb,* and *mn.*

Review final consonant clusters ld, lk, mb, mn.

Remind students that in the final consonant clusters *ld,* as in *should,* and *lk,* as in *talk,* the *l* is not pronounced; the letter does not stand for any sound. In the final consonant clusters *mb,* as in *lamb,* and *mn,* as in *column,* the *b* and the *n* are not pronounced.

Present final consonant clusters in context.

You may wish to write the sentences below on the chalkboard. Have students read each sentence and identify the words with the final consonant clusters *ld, lk, mb,* and *mn.* Answers are printed in red.

---

1. Janetta asked if she could name the mule "Star."
2. She liked to walk with Star.
3. One day, Grandaddy lifted Janetta into a tree where she could sit on a limb.
4. Later she was able to climb down from the tree by herself.
5. Janetta wanted to stay at her grandaddy's place until autumn.

Provide independent practice.

An independent activity is shown in the Resource Center below.

RESOURCE CENTER

Skills Practice 30 ▶ may be assigned for additional practice.

Skills Practice 30

NAME _____

SKILLS PRACTICE 30

Words with *ld, lk, mb, mn*

Sometimes when a word ends with two consonants one of the letters is not pronounced.

would   talk   comb   column

A. Read the words. Look at the last two consonants in each word. Draw a line through the letter that does not stand for a sound.

chalk	could	lamb	should	thumb
column	crumb	limb	solemn	walk
comb	hymn	numb	talk	would

B. Write one of the words from the box to match each clue.

1. A tiny piece of something	crumb
2. Something you do with your feet	walk
3. Something you do with your mouth	talk
4. Something used for writing on the board	chalk
5. Something used for making your hair neat	comb
6. Part of your hand	thumb
7. A word that can mean a row	column
8. A word that means you must do something	should
9. Rhymes with *trim* and means "a song"	hymn
10. Rhymes with *column* and means "serious"	solemn

C. Write a word from the box to complete each sentence. **Possible answers:**

11. A branch of a tree can be called a tree limb _____.
12. I could _____ have solved that puzzle, with your help.
13. Ken's fingers were numb _____ from the cold.
14. The little lamb _____ was looking for its mother.

30 LEVEL 8 "Grandaddy's Place"

CURRICULUM CONNECTIONS

WHO'S HOO, AND OTHER ANIMAL FACTS SCIENCE

Have students do some research related to owls. Where do they live, what do they eat, and how are they important to the environment? Have students include lists of different owls and their habitats. Which owl, because of its voice, is most likely to be nicknamed a hoot owl? *(the great horned owl)* Have students collect or draw pictures of different kinds of owls and put them into a book along with other information about the different species.

Other students may wish to find out some things about animal behavior. Remind the class that Janetta was frightened by much of the animal behavior at Grandaddy's place. She saw the behavior of the animals as mean and threatening. Ask students if it is possible that the behavior was simply normal for each animal. Another possibility might be that the animals were frightened of Janetta. Have students do research to find out what behavior is typical of mules, chickens, wasps, and cats. What does a mule mean when he pushes his head into people? What do chickens mean to communicate with their short, sharp clucks as they scratch the dirt? Have each student find one example of an interesting behavior for each animal he or she researches and tell what it is supposed to mean or what he or she thinks it means.

STAR STORIES SCIENCE

Remind students of the story that Grandaddy told about the mule and the star. Have each student prepare a report about stars or about a particular constellation such as the Big Dipper or Little Dipper. Have students illustrate their reports. **Curriculum Connection Master 4** can be used with this activity.

BOTTLED FRESH AIR MUSIC

There are many songs and pieces of music that tell about country life or give the listener a feeling of country life. Some examples are the music of Aaron Copland, such as ''Appalachian Spring'' or ''Billy the Kid''; a banjo piece called ''Dueling Banjos''; and any number of country/western songs. Play a recording of one of these pieces. Ask students to discuss it and describe how it makes them feel. If students know a song about the country, encourage them to sing it.

Reading the Poem

OBJECTIVE Understanding and appreciating mood in poetry.

INTRODUCING THE POEM

Relate content of the poem to students' experience.

Ask students how their family members and friends get together to celebrate a holiday. Elicit the feelings they have in visiting or being visited by relatives or friends on a holiday. Discuss why it often seems that the time it takes to travel to a place is longer than the time it takes to return. Then ask students to tell how it might feel to ride in a sleigh through snow-covered woods. Encourage them to think about a horse's pulling the sleigh, eliciting sensations (*wind on cheeks*) and sounds (*hooves, bells*).

Set a listening purpose.

Tell students they are going to hear a poem about a sleigh ride through the woods on Thanksgiving Day. Ask them to think about how they feel as they hear the description of the trip through the woods.

READING THE POEM

Read the poem aloud.

Because poetry is a sound-based literary form, this part of the lesson is most important. Read the poem aloud to the students with Student Texts closed. Then have students open their books to page 70. Read the poem again or ask for volunteers to read it to the whole group. With this second reading, encourage students to tap their feet to the rhythm of the poem as they picture themselves on the sleigh ride that the poet is describing. Discuss any unfamiliar words as needed.

> **drifted snow** snow piled up by the wind
> **jingling** the noise that small bells make

DISCUSSING THE POEM

Discuss students' responses.

Ask students to describe how the poem made them feel. Then ask:

> **What phrase does the poet repeat to make you feel like you are traveling?** ("Over the river and through the wood")

> **How does the poet make the wind seem like an animal?** ("It stings the toes/And bites the nose")

CLASS ENRICHMENT

Have students share poems that repeat parts.

Have students find other examples of poems that have rhythms that are created by the repeating of words or sentences. Some students may enjoy reading these poems aloud as other students move to the rhythms. If a particular poem has a refrain, the whole group can join in and say the line.

Over the River and Through the Wood

Over the river, and through the wood,
To grandfather's house we go;
The horse knows the way
To carry the sleigh,
Through the white and drifted snow.

Over the river, and through the wood,
To grandfather's house away!
We would not stop
For doll or top,
For 'tis Thanksgiving Day.

Over the river, and through the wood—
Oh, how the wind does blow!
It stings the toes,
And bites the nose,
As over the ground we go.

Over the river, and through the wood,
With a clear blue winter sky,
The dogs do bark,
And children hark,
As we go jingling by.

Over the river, and through the wood—
When grandmother sees us come,
She will say, "Oh, dear,
The children are here,
Bring a pie for every one."

Over the river, and through the wood—
Now grandmother's cap I spy!
Hurrah for the fun!
Is the pudding done?
Hurrah for the pumpkin-pie!

Lydia Maria Child

A FROSTY RIDE

Inspired by a painting reminiscent of the poem, students imagine they are on a sleigh ride and write about their trip.

TEACHER CHOICE

	Teaching Sequence	Trade Books and Resources	Meeting Individual Needs	Integrated Language Arts / Cross Curriculum
The Bridge Pages 124–125	**Maintain** Sequence	• Teaching Chart 19 • Workbook 33 • Skills Practice 31		
PART 1 **Vocabulary Strategies** Pages 126–127	**Develop Concepts** Semantic Mapping **Teach Vocabulary** **STORY CRITICAL WORDS:** ambled, **distance**, mustangs, **nuzzled**, **stallion**, **whinnied** (Tested words are boldfaced.)	• Teaching Chart 20 • Workbook 34 • Skills Practice 32	**SUPPORT WORDS:** axle, clambered, drawn, lulled, mesquite, scolded • Skills Practice 33 **CHARACTER/SETTING WORDS:** Anna, Conestoga, Gretchen, Guadalupe	**WRITING/SPEAKING ACTIVITY:** Use new vocabulary to describe a herd of wild horses. • Spelling Connection 43
PART 2 **Reading & Responding** Pages 128–137	**Build Background** **Develop a Purpose for Reading** **Guide the Reading Process** **Selection Follow-Up**	• Reader's Journal 27–30 • Workbook 35 **READING EVERY DAY** *The Black Stallion,* by W. Farley *A Horse Named Paris,* by L. Sonberg	**EXTRA HELP:** Discussing/Predicting the Experience of Being Lost **ACHIEVING ENGLISH PROFICIENCY:** Creating Word Webs • Achieving English Proficiency Master 9	**Language Arts Connections** **WRITING TO LEARN:** Complete an experience chart. • Writing Master 5 **SPEAKING/LISTENING:** Imagining Dialogue; Interviewing Characters **WRITING:** Writing Historical Fiction; Summarizing the Story • Language Arts Master 5
PART 3 **Selection Support** Pages 138–143			**Practice** • Teaching Charts 21–22 • Workbook 36–37 • Skills Practice 34–36 Story Elements: Setting (Tested) Suffixes *-er, -or* (Tested) Vowel Digraph *ei* after *c* **Maintain** • Skills Practice 37 Spelling Changes *f* to *ve*	**Curriculum Connections** **SCIENCE:** Making a Chart of Horse Facts **SOCIAL STUDIES:** Settling the American West; Studying Plants and Animals of the Guadalupe River Region • Curriculum Connection Master 5 **GEOGRAPHY:** Tracing Settlers' Paths **MUSIC:** Listening to and Writing Lyrics for Folk Songs

The White Stallion

written by Elizabeth Shub
illustrated by Rachel Isadora

SUMMARY *Traveling westward with her family in 1845, Gretchen falls asleep while riding the family mare. The mare strays away from the wagon train, and Gretchen wakes up to encounter a group of wild horses.*

A white stallion appears, and lifts Gretchen to the ground. Gretchen spends a frightening night in the wilderness. The stallion appears the next day to lift her again onto the mare's back. The stallion then nudges the mare to take Gretchen back to her family. The White Stallion *appeared in the **American Library Association Notable Children's Books** listing in 1982.*

AMERICAN LIBRARY ASSOCIATION 1982

The Bridge

COMPREHENSION

Teaching Sequence

OBJECTIVE   Understanding the sequence of events in text.

1. WARM-UP

Use a known passage to present sequence of events.

List these events on the chalkboard:

(3)   **Janetta sat up all night.**
(1)   **Momma and Janetta went to the railroad station.**
(4)   **They got to Grandaddy's place.**
(2)   **They got on a train.**

Tell students they will listen to a passage from the previous selection, "Grandaddy's Place." Explain that the author has told the events of the passage in a particular order that makes sense. Have them listen for the correct order of the events you have listed on the chalkboard while you read the following passage.

> **One day Momma said to Janetta, "It's time you knew your grandaddy." Momma and Janetta went to the railroad station and got on a train. It was a long ride, but Janetta liked it. She didn't even mind sitting up all night. But when they got to Grandaddy's place, Janetta didn't like it at all.**

Have students number each event listed on the chalkboard in the correct order and explain why they numbered the events as they did.

State the objective.

Tell students they will learn to recognize and understand the sequence of events as they read.

2. TEACH

Explain why sequence is important.

Tell students that knowing the order in which events happen in a story helps readers understand and appreciate what they read.

Use Teaching Chart to review sequence.

Display the Teaching Chart. Have students read the sentences that describe events that occur in the story "Grandaddy's Place." Point out that the events described are out of order.

TEACHING CHART 19: SEQUENCE   **19**

(2)   The next day a mule pushed Janetta with its long nose.
(5)   She called him Star.
(3)   After that push, Grandaddy told her that the mule must like her.
(1)   When Janetta first arrived, she didn't like Grandaddy's place.
(4)   She decided to name the mule.

Model a strategy for understanding sequence.

Explain that there is a strategy students can use to help them understand the sequence, or order, of events in a story. Look for signal words in the sentences on the Teaching Chart. Which sentence should be labeled 1 and how do you know? (*The sentence includes the word* first.)

Review the role of signal words in understanding sequence.

Remind students that writers may use signal words to help the reader know the sequence of events in a story. Point out that such words as *first, last, before, next, after,* and *finally* can help them determine the order in which events happen. Add that when no signal words are used, students must use other clues within the text, knowledge about the way events happen, and their own good sense to know the correct sequence.

3. GUIDED PRACTICE

Check for understanding.

Before going on, have students explain how to recognize and understand the sequence of events in a story. *(Look for signal words and other word clues, think about what you already know, and think about what makes sense.)*

Guide students in using the strategy.

Have students use the strategy to order the other events on the chart. Have them explain why they completed the chart as they did. Discuss word and experience clues that helped them.

4. WRAP-UP

Summarize instruction.

Review why readers need to understand the sequence of events and the kinds of clues they can use to recognize the order in which things happen in a story.

Provide independent practice.

Options for independent practice are shown in the Resource Center below.

5. APPLICATION

Students will follow the sequence of events as they read "The White Stallion." The symbol ✔ marks specific questions and activities that apply this skill.

Workbook page 33

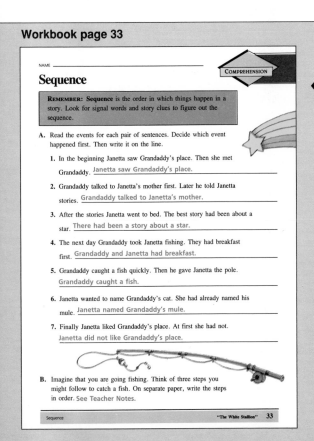

NAME _____

COMPREHENSION

Sequence

REMEMBER: **Sequence** is the order in which things happen in a story. Look for signal words and story clues to figure out the sequence.

A. Read the events for each pair of sentences. Decide which event happened first. Then write it on the line.

1. In the beginning Janetta saw Grandaddy's place. Then she met Grandaddy. Janetta saw Grandaddy's place.

2. Grandaddy talked to Janetta's mother first. Later he told Janetta stories. Grandaddy talked to Janetta's mother.

3. After the stories Janetta went to bed. The best story had been about a star. There had been a story about a star.

4. The next day Grandaddy took Janetta fishing. They had breakfast first. Grandaddy and Janetta had breakfast.

5. Grandaddy caught a fish quickly. Then he gave Janetta the pole. Grandaddy caught a fish.

6. Janetta wanted to name Grandaddy's cat. She had already named his mule. Janetta named Grandaddy's mule.

7. Finally Janetta liked Grandaddy's place. At first she had not. Janetta did not like Grandaddy's place.

B. Imagine that you are going fishing. Think of three steps you might follow to catch a fish. On separate paper, write the steps in order. See Teacher Notes.

Sequence   "The White Stallion" 33

RESOURCE CENTER

◀ **Workbook page 33** is intended for use by all students.

Skills Practice 31 ▶ may be assigned for additional practice.

Workbook reuse option: Have students read the sentences in Part A again and circle the signal words that helped them determine the sequence for each item.

Skills Practice 31

NAME _____

SKILLS PRACTICE 31

Sequence

Sequence is the order in which things happen in a story. Look for signal words and story clues to figure out the sequence.

Event 1
↓
Event 2
↓
Event 3

A. Read the story. Think about the sequence.

It was a sunny March day. It was time to get sap from the sugar maple trees. First, Mr. Smith drilled a hole in each tree. Prissy helped him put a hollow tube, or spigot, into each hole. Tom hung a pail over the spigots to catch the sap. By then, the children were cold, so they went home for a hot drink.

The next day, Prissy and Tom went back to the trees. The pails were full. They took them to the sugar house. Mrs. Smith poured the sap into a pan. She boiled it until it was syrup. The last thing she did was pour the syrup into a jar.

B. Write the sentences in the order in which they happened in the story.

Prissy and Tom took the full pails to the sugar house.
Mrs. Smith poured the syrup into a jar.
Mr. Smith drilled a hole in each tree.
Tom hung pails to catch the sap.
Mrs. Smith boiled the sap.
Prissy helped put spigots into the holes.

1. Mr. Smith drilled a hole in each tree.
2. Prissy helped put spigots into the holes.
3. Tom hung pails to catch the sap.
4. Prissy and Tom took the full pails to the sugar house.
5. Mrs. Smith boiled the sap.
6. Mrs. Smith poured the syrup into a jar.

C. Ask yourself: "Does this sequence make sense?"

LEVEL 8   "The White Stallion"   31

PART 1

Vocabulary Strategies

Developing Concepts

Use a semantic map to tap prior knowledge of horses.

Tell students they are about to read a story in which the behavior of horses plays an important part. Use a picture of horses to begin a discussion. Ask students what they know about horses. Ask students who have ridden horses to talk about their experiences. Build a semantic map about horses, allowing students to suggest appropriate categories.

Kinds of Horses
(mare, stallion, colt)

What Horses Do
(walk, gallop, trot, canter)

HORSES

Where Horses Are Found
(prairie, horse farm, circus)

How Horses Look
(graceful, strong, muscular)

Teaching Vocabulary

Discuss meanings of Story Critical words.

Display the Teaching Chart. Read each context sentence and identify the new word. Then use the sentences below to help students understand each word. When necessary, provide a definition.

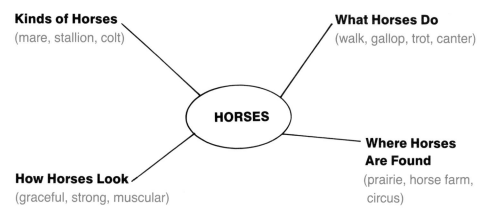

TEACHING CHART 20: VOCABULARY `20`

1. **mustangs** (wild horses; descendants of Spanish horses)
   The hooves of the *mustangs* made a sound like thunder as they galloped by.
2. **stallion** (a male horse)
   The leader of the herd, a white *stallion*, stood on his hind legs and pawed the air.
3. **ambled** (walked with an easy gait)
   Some mares with their young colts *ambled* from place to place as they nibbled grass.
4. **nuzzled** (rubbed with the nose; nudged)
   One horse *nuzzled* another's neck with her nose.
5. **whinnied** (made a low neighing sound)
   Suddenly the stallion *whinnied*, sounding a warning to the herd.
6. **distance** (the space between two points; a place far away)
   It would take the wagon train two weeks to travel the *distance* to the next town.

mustangs 1. **What do you think mustangs are?** (horses) **What clues helped you to know?** (hooves; galloped)   STRATEGY: CONTEXT CLUES

stallion 2. **Is a stallion a male or a female horse?** (male) **How do you know?** (his) **What is a female horse called?** (mare)   STRATEGY: PRIOR KNOWLEDGE

ambled

3. Do you think that the horses were running as they nibbled grass? (no)
Why not? (They would not be able to nibble grass if they were running.)
How do you think the horses were moving? (slowly, unhurriedly)
STRATEGY: CONTEXT CLUES

nuzzled

4. What was the horse doing as it nuzzled the other? (rubbing its nose on or nudging the other)   STRATEGY: CONTEXT CLUES

whinnied

5. What kind of sound does a horse make? (a neighing sound) Define whinny as a low, neighing sound.   STRATEGY: PRIOR KNOWLEDGE

distance

6. Was the next town close or far away? (far away)   STRATEGY: CONTEXT CLUES

Add new words to the map.

Challenge students to add as many of the new words as they can to the semantic map, adding new headings as needed. Have them explain how each added word fits.

Discuss Support words as needed.

The Glossary of the Student Text includes definitions of the Support words: *drawn, clambered, scolded, lulled, axle, mesquite.* Have students discuss which words can be added to the map.

Discuss Character/Setting words as needed.

Pronounce these Character/Setting words before students read the selection: *Conestoga, Gretchen, Anna, Guadalupe.* (gwä' de loop')

Provide independent practice.

Options for independent practice are shown in the Resource Center below.

WRITING OR SPEAKING ACTIVITY   *Have each student write or say one or two sentences describing a herd of wild horses. Encourage them to use as many new vocabulary words as possible.*

RESOURCE CENTER

Workbook page 34

NAME _____

Using New Words

A. Read the paragraph. On each number line under the story, write the word from the box that means the same as the underlined words in the story.

| ambled | distance | mustangs |
| nuzzled | stallion | whinnied |

We were passing through Texas on the train. Father was telling us a story. It was about (1) <u>wild horses</u> that used to run free in the West. The train suddenly stopped. It was then that Father noticed a mare and a (2) <u>male horse</u> in a nearby field. When the horses saw us, they (3) <u>walked slowly</u> toward the fence beside the tracks. The mare (4) <u>nudged with her nose</u> the stallion's neck and (5) <u>made a low neighing sound</u>. Just then the train whistle blew. The two horses ran away. We watched them until they were small dots in the (6) <u>place far away</u>. After the train began to roll again, my father went on with his story.

1. _____mustangs_____   2. _____stallion_____
3. _____ambled_____   4. _____nuzzled_____
5. _____whinnied_____   6. _____distance_____

B. Pretend that you have a horse. On separate paper, write four sentences about a day in your horse's life. Use at least four words from the box in your sentences. See Teacher Notes.

34 "The White Stallion"   Selection Vocabulary

◀ **Workbook page 34** provides practice with Story Critical words.

Skills Practice 32 ▶ provides additional practice with Story Critical words.

Skills Practice 33 provides practice with Support words.

Spelling Connection Master 43 may be used for spelling instruction with the new vocabulary.

Workbook reuse option: Have students circle the words in the box that are action words.

Skills Practice 32

NAME _____

SKILLS PRACTICE 32

Vocabulary: Story Critical Words

A. Study the meaning of each word.

ambled walked in a slow easy way   **nuzzled** rubbed with the nose
distance the space between two points   **stallion** a male horse
mustangs wild horses   **whinnied** made a low neighing sound

B. Write the vocabulary word that answers each question.

1. Which two words name kinds of horses?
   _____mustangs_____ and _____stallion_____

2. Which word tells how a horse moved when it was not in a hurry to get to a place?
   _____ambled_____

3. Which word tells what sound a horse made to its master?
   _____whinnied_____

4. Which word tells how a horse rubbed its nose against another horse?
   _____nuzzled_____

C. One word in each sentence does not make sense. Underline that word. Write the vocabulary word that belongs in its place.

5. It is a short <u>instance</u> from the beach to the water's edge.   _____distance_____

6. The horse <u>puzzled</u> her new baby.   _____nuzzled_____

7. The herd of <u>ducks</u> galloped up the hill.   _____mustangs_____

8. The shiny black <u>gallon</u> flicked his tail as he walked around the field.   _____stallion_____

D. Complete each sentence with the correct vocabulary word.

9. Eric whistled as he _____ambled_____ to the playground.

10. Ann's horse _____whinnied_____ after hearing a barking dog.

11. Carol's house is a short _____distance_____ from the park.

32   LEVEL 8   "The White Stallion"   Definition clues

Reading & Responding

Building Background

Motivate discussion with the quotation.

Share the following quotation with students and ask them what they think it means. Explain that in the last century, people were encouraged to travel west and settle the land. Ask students what they remember about the West from stories they have read or from movies and television programs they have seen. Discuss cowboys and horses.

> **Go West, young man!**
> — *Horace Greeley*

Build background about learning from others.

Explain that when people traveled to settle the land, they usually traveled in covered wagons pulled by horses or oxen. Together the wagons moved in a line like cars of a train, so they became known as wagon trains. Discuss the reasons why families traveled in groups. Lead students to see that the settlers needed one another's help to survive on their journey in the wilderness.

Discuss historical fiction.

Tell students they will read a story about a little girl who traveled west with a wagon train almost 150 years ago. Explain that the story is historical fiction. It is not true, but it gives many true details about life in a wagon train. Tell students that the author of this story pretends that the events really happened and that the story was passed down in a family from grandmother to granddaughter and then retold to her granddaughter, the great-great granddaughter of the person whom the story is about.

Developing a Purpose for Reading

Option 1
Students set purpose.

ORAL "PREDICTION" LISTS   Have students read the story introduction. Ask them to predict what might have happened to the little girl.

WRITING ACTIVITY   Have students work alone or in pairs to create written "Prediction" lists. Tell students to save their lists for later use.

Option 2
Teacher sets purpose.

Tell students this story is about a girl who becomes lost from a wagon train on its way west. Have them read to find out what happens to her.

Meeting
Individual
Needs

EXTRA HELP   Ask students if they have been told what to do if they get lost. Explain that the next story is about a young girl who gets separated from her family's wagon train. Ask students to predict what might happen to the girl. Have them read and find out what happens in the story.

ACHIEVING ENGLISH PROFICIENCY   Write the following groups of words in webs on the chalkboard: *Names for horses — mustang, stallion, mare; Ways horses move — gallop, trot, stray; Sounds horses make — neigh, nicker, whinny; What horses do with their mouths — nuzzle, nip, lap.* As you say the words and have students repeat them with you, pantomime or explain the meanings to help students further understand. After you have repeated the words again, erase the words (leaving the categories). Then say the words again in random order and have the group repeat each word and tell you which category it belongs in. If students wish, allow them to pantomime the motions and mimic the sounds. For additional help in story comprehension, use Master 9 in the Teacher Resource Kit.

The White Stallion

written by Elizabeth Shub
illustrated by Rachel Isadora

Imagine going on a trip with your family and meeting wild animals. This is what happens to Gretchen.

This is a true story, Gretchen. My grandmother Gretchen, your great-great-grandmother, told it to me. She was as young as you are when it happened. She was as old as I am when I heard it from her.

It was 1845. Three families were on their way West. They planned to settle there. They traveled in covered wagons. Each wagon was drawn by four horses. Conestoga wagons they were called.

Gretchen and her family were in the last wagon. Mother and Father sat on the driver's seat. The children were inside with the household goods.

Bedding, blankets, pots and pans, a table, chairs, a dresser took up most of the space. There was not much room left for Trudy, John, Billy, and Gretchen. Gretchen was the youngest.

Reader's Journal   p 27
Preparing for Reading

IF I WERE A HORSE . . .

What would it be like to be a horse? Students stretch their imaginations in this creative activity.

GUIDED READING

Page 73   Two people in this story have the same name — Gretchen. Who are they and how are they related? (One is a little girl listening to a story; the other is the little girl in the story; the little Gretchen in the story is the great-great-grandmother of the Gretchen who is listening.)   INFER: PEOPLE

HIGHLIGHTING LITERATURE

Page 73   Tell students to close their eyes and picture the setting of this story. Allow them to describe the pictures in their minds or ask them what they see, hear, smell and feel as they think about the setting. (four covered wagons; each pulled by four horses; a man and a woman sitting on the driver's seat of the last wagon; the smell of horses; the creaking of the wagon; the clanking of pots and pans; bumps as the wagon moves across uneven ground) Remind students that authors choose words to help readers picture where characters are so that readers can better understand what happens to the character and why.

Behind the wagon walked Anna, their old mare. She was not tied to the wagon but followed faithfully. She carried two sacks of corn meal on her back.

It was hot in the noonday sun. The children were cranky and bored. The wagon cover shaded them, but little air came in through the openings at front and back.

John kicked Billy. Billy pushed him, and he bumped Gretchen. Trudy, the oldest, who was trying to read, scolded them.

Their quarrel was interrupted by Father's voice. ''Quick, everybody, look out! There's a herd of mustangs.'' The children clambered to the back of the wagon.

In the distance they could see the wild horses. The horses galloped swiftly and in minutes were out of sight.

''Look at Anna,'' John said. The old mare stood rigid. She had turned her head toward the mustangs. Her usually floppy ears were lifted high. The wagon had moved some distance before Anna trotted after it.

It was hotter than ever inside.

''Father,'' Gretchen called, ''may I ride Anna for a while?''

Father stopped the wagon and came to the back. He lifted Gretchen onto the mare. The meal sacks made a comfortable seat. He tied her securely so that she would not fall off.

As they moved on, Gretchen fell asleep, lulled by the warmth of the sun. They were following a trail in Texas along the Guadalupe (gwäd ä lōō' pe) River. The rear wheel of the first wagon hit a boulder, and the axle broke. The whole train stopped. Anna strayed away, with Gretchen sleeping on her back. No one noticed.

The travelers made camp. Children were sent for firewood and for water from the river. The women prepared food.

GUIDED READING

Page 74 Why do you think the mare, Anna, is not tied to the wagon? (The family trusts her; she follows faithfully.) SYNTHESIZE: DRAWING CONCLUSIONS

Page 74 How do the children feel? Why? (They are cranky and bored; it is hot, airless, and crowded; they have been traveling for a long time.) INFER: CAUSE/EFFECT

✔ **Page 74 What sequence of events leads to the scolding by Trudy?** (John bumps Billy; Billy pushes John; John bumps Gretchen; Trudy scolds them; Father interrupts them to show them a herd of wild horses.) ANALYZE: SEQUENCE

Page 75 What does Anna do that is unusual for a trusted mare? (She strays from the wagon train.) ANALYZE: CHARACTER

Page 75 Why does the wagon train stop? (The rear wheel of the first wagon hits a boulder, and the axle breaks.) INFER: CAUSE/EFFECT

✔ Skill from The Bridge applied through this question.

STRATEGIC READING

Page 75 Have students close their eyes and visualize what happened as the wagon train stopped to make camp. Allow students to describe their mental pictures. (They may visualize children gathering firewood and bringing water; horses grazing; the men fixing the wheel; the women preparing a meal; Anna, with Gretchen asleep on her back, drifting further away. They might describe smells, such as food cooking, and sounds, such as water sloshing, horses neighing, the cranking of the wheel.) Suggest that students who are having difficulty visualizing reread the last two paragraphs on the page and try to picture each thing described. They can then close their eyes and try to see the whole scene. METACOGNITION: VISUALIZING

It was not until the axle had been fixed and they were ready to eat that Gretchen and Anna were missed.

The men tried to follow the mare's tracks but soon lost them. It was getting dark. There was nothing to do but remain where they were. They would search again at the first sign of light.

Faithful Anna, they thought, would return. She probably had discovered a rich patch of mesquite grass. She would come back when she had eaten all she wanted.

Gretchen awoke to the sound of lapping. Anna was drinking noisily from a stream. A short distance away stood a herd of ten or twelve wild horses. They were brownish in color. Some had darker stripes down their backs. Others had dark markings on their legs. They were mares.

After Anna had finished drinking, she moved toward them. And they walked forward as if to greet her. When they came close, they neighed and nickered.

They crossed necks with Anna, nuzzled her and rubbed against her. They were so friendly that Gretchen was not afraid. And she did not realize that Anna had wandered far from the wagon train.

Suddenly the horses began to nibble at the sacks on Anna's back. They had smelled the corn meal. In their eagerness they nipped Gretchen's legs. Gretchen screamed. She tried to move out of the way. She tried to loosen the ropes that tied her. But she could not reach the knots. Terrified, Gretchen screamed and screamed.

Out of nowhere a great white stallion appeared. He pranced and whinnied. He swished his long white tail. He stood on his hind legs, his white mane flying.

The mares moved quickly out of his way. The white stallion came up to Anna. He carefully bit through the ropes that tied Gretchen. Then, gently, he took hold of the back of her dress with his teeth. He lifted her to the ground.

GUIDED READING

✔ **Page 76   How do you think the family feels when they notice that Gretchen and Anna are missing?** (They are probably worried, but hopeful that Anna will come back.)   INFER: FEELINGS/ATTITUDES

Page 76   Why can the men not search longer for Gretchen and Anna? (It is getting dark; they cannot see the mare's tracks.)   INFER: CAUSE/EFFECT

✔ **Page 77   What happens to Gretchen from the time the wild horses smell the corn meal until the white stallion rescues her? List the events in the correct sequence.** (The horses nibble at the sack of corn meal; the horses nip at Gretchen's legs; she screams; the white stallion appears; he shoos off the horses, bites through the ropes, lifts her off the mare, and puts her on the ground.)   ANALYZE: SEQUENCE

✔ Skill from The Bridge applied through this question.
✔ Informal Assessment Opportunity: GENERALIZING

STRATEGIC READING

Page 77   Ask students to summarize what has happened to Gretchen from the beginning of the story to this point. (She was hot and bored in the wagon. She rode Anna and fell asleep. She woke up to see the wild mustangs, who nipped at her. The white stallion helped her free herself.) **Then have them predict whether** Gretchen will return to the wagon train. Point out that summarizing and predicting can help readers understand what they read. Suggest that students who have trouble reread any confusing parts. At the end of the story, have them check their predictions.
METACOGNITION: SUMMARIZING AND PREDICTING

He seemed to motion to the mares with his head, and then he galloped away. The mares followed at once. Anna followed them. Gretchen was left alone.

She did not know what to do. "Father will find me soon," she said out loud to comfort herself. She was hungry, but there was nothing to eat. She walked to the stream and drank some water. Then she sat down on a rock to wait.

She waited and waited, but there was no sign of Father. And no sign of Anna. Shadows began to fall. The sun went down. The dark came. "Anna!" Gretchen called. "Anna! Anna! Anna!"

There was no answering sound. She heard a coyote howl. She heard the rustling of leaves and the call of redbirds. Gretchen began to cry.

She made a place for herself on some dry leaves near a tree trunk. She curled up against it, and cried and cried until she fell asleep.

Morning light woke Gretchen. The stream sparkled in the sunlight. Gretchen washed her face and drank the clear water.

She looked for Anna. She called her name, but Anna did not come. Gretchen was so hungry she chewed some sweet grass. But it had a nasty taste, and she spat it out.

She sat on her rock near the stream. She looked at the red bite marks on her legs and began to cry again.

A squirrel came by. It looked at her in such a funny way that she stopped crying.

She walked along the stream. She knew she must not go far. "If you are lost," Mother had warned, "stay where you are. That will make it easier to find you." Gretchen walked back to her rock.

It was afternoon when she heard the sound of hooves. A moment later Anna <u>ambled</u> up to the stream. The sacks of meal were gone. The old mare drank greedily. Gretchen hugged and kissed her. She patted her back. Anna would find her way back to the wagon train.

GUIDED READING

Page 78   **Gretchen is lost and alone. Is she scared? Why or why not?** (Yes, she is alone in the dark; she could be hurt.)   INFER: FEELINGS/ATTITUDES

Page 78   **In what ways does Gretchen comfort herself?** (She talks to herself out loud; she cries; she curls up and goes to sleep.)   INFER: PROBLEM/SOLUTION

Page 79   **What had Gretchen's mother told her to do if she were ever lost? Why?** ("If you are lost, stay where you are. That will make it easier to find you.") **How is what Gretchen's mother tells her the same as or different from what your parents tell you?** SYNTHESIZE: COMPARISON

HIGHLIGHTING LITERATURE

Page 78   Point out how the author creates a scary mood by the way she describes what happens around Gretchen as the sun goes down. First there are shadows and then darkness. A coyote howls, birds cry, and Gretchen hears the rustling of leaves. Have one student read aloud the section starting with "She waited and waited . . ." to ". . . until she fell asleep." Ask the other students to close their eyes and picture what they would see, hear, feel, and smell if they were Gretchen. Allow them to describe the pictures in their minds and tell what they think would be most scary.

She tried to climb on Anna's back, but even without the sacks the mare was too high. There was a fallen tree not far away. Gretchen wanted to use it as a step. She tugged at Anna, but Anna would not move. Gretchen pulled and shoved. She begged and pleaded. Anna stood firm.

Now again the white stallion appeared. Again he lifted Gretchen by the back of her dress. He sat her on Anna's back. He nuzzled and pushed the old mare. Anna began to walk. The white stallion walked close behind her for a few paces. Then, as if to say goodbye, he stood on his hind legs, <u>whinnied</u>, and galloped away.

Gretchen always believed the white stallion had told Anna to take her back to the wagon train. For that is what Anna did.

Your great-great grandmother Gretchen bore the scars of the wild mare bites for the rest of her life. I know because when she told me the story, she pulled down her stockings. And I saw them.

◆ LIBRARY LINK ◆

If you enjoyed this story, you might want to read The Girl Who Loved Wild Horses *by Paul Goble.*

Reader's Response

Gretchen was in danger when she became separated from her family. Do you think she acted wisely? Tell why or why not.

See next page for suggested answers.

SELECTION FOLLOW-UP

The White Stallion

Thinking It Over

1. Who is telling the story?
2. Where does the story take place?
3. Why do you think Gretchen asked to ride Anna?
4. How did Gretchen get back to her family?
5. Why did many of the pioneers travel together in wagon trains? What makes you think that?
6. Do you think this is a true story? Tell why or why not.

Writing to Learn

THINK AND RECALL Gretchen got lost as her family traveled to a new place. Can you remember an adventure you have had? Have you ever gotten lost, gone to a new place, or had some other interesting experience? When it happened, how did you feel? Copy and complete the chart below.

What Happened to Gretchen	How Gretchen Felt
Gretchen got lost.	Gretchen felt scared.
What Happened to Me	How I Felt
I _____.	I felt _____.

WRITE Write some sentences about an adventure you have had. Tell what happened and how you felt about it.

THE WHITE STALLION

GUIDED READING

Page 80 Why do you think that the author wrote that she had seen the scars on her grandmother's legs? (She wanted to strengthen the impression that this is a true story, and that it was originally told in the past by a real person.) EVALUATE: AUTHOR'S PURPOSE

RETURNING TO THE READING PURPOSE

OPTION 1 If students set the purpose, return to their predictions and compare them with the actual events in the story. Students may wish to discuss any surprises they felt.

OPTION 2 If you set the purpose for reading, have students tell what happened to Gretchen. Encourage students to list the events of the story in correct sequence.

Reader's Journal   p 28
Responding to Reading

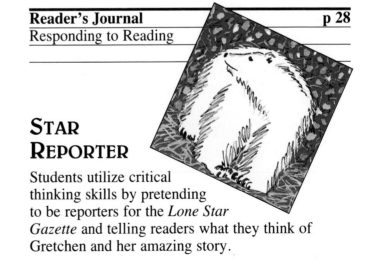

STAR REPORTER

Students utilize critical thinking skills by pretending to be reporters for the *Lone Star Gazette* and telling readers what they think of Gretchen and her amazing story.

SELECTION FOLLOW UP

⇸ The White Stallion ⇷

THINKING IT OVER

1. **Who is telling the story?** (The woman telling the story is the pioneer Gretchen's granddaughter and the modern-day Gretchen's grandmother.) SYNTHESIZE: DRAWING CONCLUSIONS

2. **Where does the story take place?** (The story takes place in Texas near the Guadalupe River.) ANALYZE: CHARACTER

3. **Why do you think Gretchen asked to ride Anna?** (The children were bored and cranky. They had begun to argue. Also, it was very hot and cramped inside the wagon.) ANALYZE: CHARACTER

4. **How did Gretchen get back to her family?** (The white stallion put Gretchen on Anna's back and pushed the horse in the direction of the wagon train.) RECALL: DETAILS

5. **Why did many of the pioneers travel together in wagon trains? What makes you think that?** (Possible answers: The pioneers traveled in wagon trains for safety; people could help each other if there was an accident, such as when the axle broke and when Gretchen was lost; jobs could be divided up; families could share supplies and materials; sharing dangers and hardships probably made the pioneers feel better. Students will probably cite instances in their own lives as well as other stories and books in support of their conclusions.) SYNTHESIZE: DRAWING CONCLUSIONS; METACOGNITION

6. **Do you think this is a true story? Tell why or why not.** (Some students will point out that the opening line says that the story is true. Others may feel that the author is trying to make the story sound true, but that no horse could really do what the white stallion did. Accept all reasonable answers that students can support.) EVALUATE: POINT OF VIEW

WRITING TO LEARN

Use Writing Master 5, which duplicates this chart.

THINK AND RECALL Gretchen got lost as her family traveled to a new place. Can you remember an adventure you have had? Have you ever gotten lost, gone to a new place, or had some other interesting experience? When it happened, how did you feel? Copy and complete the chart below. (Help students work with the chart to prepare for writing.)

What Happened to Gretchen	How Gretchen Felt
Gretchen got lost.	Gretchen felt scared.
What Happened to Me	How I Felt
I _____.	I felt _____.

Extend comprehension through writing.

WRITE Write some sentences about an adventure you have had. Tell what happened and how you felt about it. (Have students share their sentences.)

More Ideas for Selection Follow-Up

CRITICAL AND CREATIVE THINKING QUESTIONS

Encourage a variety of responses and points of view.

Use these open-ended questions to encourage critical and creative thinking about the selection.

1. Gretchen believed that the white stallion told Anna to take her back to the wagon train. Do you agree? Tell why or why not.

✔ 2. Do you think that this story belongs in a unit called "Remember When"? Why or why not?

REREADING ORALLY

Have students reread for expression.

There are several places in "The White Stallion" where the mood changes suddenly. For example: The children are bored, cranky, and quarrelsome, then they are excited by the appearance of a herd of wild horses. Point out to students that when there is a sudden change of mood in the story, the reader's voice should also change. For example, the reader's voice should become more lively when reading, "Quick, everybody, look out!"

Have students select a passage that shows a change of mood and practice it to read aloud to the class. Other examples are (a) the mood is friendly when Gretchen and Anna meet the wild horses, but it changes when the horses nip at her legs; (b) Gretchen screams in terror before the stallion carefully and gently rescues her; (c) Gretchen rather calmly waits for her father to come before the sun sets, then she is scared with the onset of darkness.

SELECTION COMPREHENSION

Provide comprehension check.

A Workbook page to check comprehension is shown in the Resource Center below. It may be used for informal assessment.

✔ **Informal Assessment Opportunity:** SYNTHESIZING ACROSS SELECTIONS

Workbook page 35

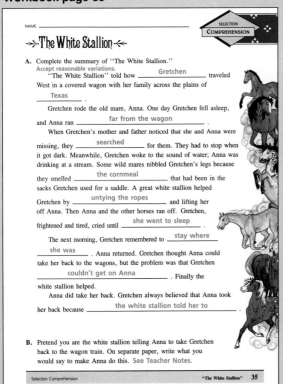

Workbook page 35

→ The White Stallion ←

SELECTION COMPREHENSION

NAME _____

A. Complete the summary of "The White Stallion."
Accept reasonable variations.
"The White Stallion" told how ____Gretchen____ traveled West in a covered wagon with her family across the plains of ____Texas____ .

Gretchen rode the old mare, Anna. One day Gretchen fell asleep, and Anna ran ____far from the wagon____ .

When Gretchen's mother and father noticed that she and Anna were missing, they ____searched____ for them. They had to stop when it got dark. Meanwhile, Gretchen woke to the sound of water; Anna was drinking at a stream. Some wild mares nibbled Gretchen's legs because they smelled ____the cornmeal____ that had been in the sacks Gretchen used for a saddle. A great white stallion helped Gretchen by ____untying the ropes____ and lifting her off Anna. Then Anna and the other horses ran off. Gretchen, frightened and tired, cried until ____she went to sleep____ .

The next morning, Gretchen remembered to ____stay where she was____ . Anna returned. Gretchen thought Anna could take her back to the wagons, but the problem was that Gretchen ____couldn't get on Anna____ . Finally the white stallion helped.

Anna did take her back. Gretchen always believed that Anna took her back because ____the white stallion told her to____ .

B. Pretend you are the white stallion telling Anna to take Gretchen back to the wagon train. On separate paper, write what you would say to make Anna do this. See Teacher Notes.

Selection Comprehension   "The White Stallion"   **35**

RESOURCE CENTER

◄ **Workbook page 35** is intended for use by all students.

Writing Master 5 duplicates the Writing to Learn chart.

LANGUAGE ARTS CONNECTIONS

CREATIVE THINKING: IMAGINING DIALOGUE

Discuss dialogue.

Remind students that dialogue is speech in a story—the words that one character says to another. Written dialogue includes only the words inside sets of quotation marks.

Have students imagine and speak their own dialogue.

Ask students to imagine what the horses might say to each other at two major
points in the story: when the white stallion rescues Gretchen from the wild
mares and when the stallion returns and nudges Anna to take the girl back.
Have students work in pairs to create dialogue for these two passages. Remind
them to think about how the horses might feel. SHARED LEARNING: SPEAKING

CONDUCTING INTERVIEWS

Have students interview characters from the story.

Have students share their knowledge of interviews. Then have them work in
pairs to conduct interviews with the characters from the story. Allow students
to choose among Gretchen, her brothers and sister, and her mother and father.
Have one student in each pair pretend to be a character while his or her partner
asks the questions. They should work together preparing their interviews
before presenting them orally for the class. The interviewer's questions should
touch upon the character's memory of the events in the story, how he or she
felt about them, what he or she did after Gretchen left the wagon train, and his
or her ideas about the future journey. After one interview is presented, have
the partners switch roles and do a second interview with another character.
WHOLE CLASS ENRICHMENT

HISTORICAL FICTION AS A LITERARY GENRE

Have students write historical fiction.

Review with students what kind of story would be called historical fiction. *(A
story—like* "The White Stallion"—*that is based on real events and/or real people
of the past, but has parts that are made up.)* Have students interview their mothers, fathers, grandparents, or other significant adults in their lives about an
event that happened when these people were children. Tell the students to find
out details about sights, smells, and sounds so they can really picture what it
was like then and how it was different from today. Tell them to use their imaginations to write stories that are historical fiction. They should call their main
characters by their first names and think of them as children even though they
may be writing about their parents, grandparents, or other adults.

CHALLENGE: WRITING

REWRITING THE STORY

Have students rewrite the story in their own words.

Review with students the three parts (beginning, middle, and end) of "The White Stallion." Have them list information using the following format.

Beginning	**Middle:**
Setting (time and place):	Problem to solve:
Characters:	Events leading to resolution of the problem:
	End:
	Resolution:

Then tell students to write a summary of the story using the information on the story map. **Language Arts Master 5** can be used with this activity.

WRITING

READING EVERY DAY

Among the best-loved children's stories are those about horses. Like "The White Stallion," each of the following stories—the first, fiction, and the second, nonfiction—depicts a young person's special friendship with a horse.

The Black Stallion by Walter Farley. Random House, © 1941. Having survived a shipwreck, Alec Ramsay and the wild black stallion he has tamed are rescued. They make their way to Alec's home in New York, where new adventures are in store for them as the horse is trained for championship racing.

A Horse Named Paris by Lynn Sonberg. Photographs by Ken Robbins. Bradbury Press, © 1986. Paris, a spirited dapple-gray horse, is cared for, exercised, ridden, and enjoyed by his owner and friend, eleven-year-old Amanda Kraus.

Reader's Journal   pp 29, 30
Extending Reading

GET READY TO GO

Pretending they are going on a long trip with their family, students plan how they will pass the time and how they would like to travel. They draw pictures or maps of their journey.

Selection Support

SKILL TRACE: STORY ELEMENTS							
Introduction	Practice		Test	Reteach	Maintain		
TE 16	32	138	157	159	206	294	326	558

LITERATURE

Story Elements: Setting

OBJECTIVE Recognizing story settings.

Review setting.

Remind students that the setting tells where and when a story takes place. Point out that understanding the setting helps readers picture events in a story more clearly and understand why they take place. Ask students where and when "The White Stallion" takes place. *(in 1845, on the way west, or in Texas before it was settled)* Then ask how the story would change if it were set in a different time and place, for example, in 2045, on the moon. Allow students several minutes to discuss what changes would occur in the story.

Provide practice in creating the setting.

Display the Teaching Chart. Ask students to decide which events from the story would change and how they would change if the setting were different. Suggest that the story be set in the winter of 1994 in a New England town.

TEACHING CHART 21: SETTING

21

1. They traveled in covered wagons.
2. Children were sent for firewood and for water from the river.
3. The women prepared food.
4. Gretchen heard a coyote howl.

Provide independent practice.

Options for independent practice are shown in the Resource Center below.

Workbook page 36

RESOURCE CENTER

Skills Practice 34

LITERATURE

NAME _____

Story Elements

REMEMBER: To help you understand stories, look for clues and details that tell about the setting of a story.

A. Read the paragraphs and think about the setting. Underline the best ending for each statement.

1. It was 1845. Three families were crossing a grassy plain on their way west. They were planning to build new homes in a place called California, but it would be months before they reached there. They traveled in covered wagons drawn by horses.

a. The time of this story is **(1)** very recent.
   (2) when your parents were young.
   (3) more than a hundred years ago.

b. The place of this story is **(1)** hot and sandy.
   (2) flat and grassy.
   (3) full of valleys and mountains.

2. Salty spray stung Abba's face as she sailed across the Massachusetts Bay. She squinted at the beach. If no Indian or wild animal stopped her, she might reach the Pilgrim settlement by nightfall. She shivered, prayed for luck, and turned her small boat toward shore.

a. This story takes place **(1)** before Columbus discovered America.
   (2) more than two hundred years ago.
   (3) in modern times.

b. This story takes place **(1)** on a quiet stream.
   (2) far out on an ocean.
   (3) near an ocean coastline.

B. Think about "The White Stallion." On separate paper, write how the story would change if Gretchen's family lived in a cold climate. See Teacher Notes.

36 "The White Stallion"   Story Elements

◄ **Workbook page 36** is intended for use by all students.

Skills Practice 34 ► may be assigned for additional practice.

Workbook reuse option: Have students read the paragraphs in Part A again, then circle the words that describe the setting of each.

NAME _____

SKILLS PRACTICE **34**

Story Elements

As you read, look for clues about the setting of the story. Picture when and where the story takes place.

Read each paragraph. Then answer the questions that follow it.

Far off in front of the wagons were the mountains. Behind them was just the prairie grass. Only a faint trail left by the wagon wheels could be seen. On either side was just more yellow grass. Overhead the sun was high and there was not a cloud in the sky.

1. Does the paragraph tell what is happening or where something is happening?
   where something is happening

2. What do you picture in your mind? **Answers may vary slightly.**
   a wagon train going across an open prairie; mountains in the far distance; a clear sky

3. What time of day is it?
   afternoon

Another gust of wind shook the little house. Matt picked up a rag. He stuffed it in a crack between two logs along one wall. Then he walked across the one room to the fireplace. Usually the fire warmed this room that the family lived in. Tonight it didn't. His sisters were already asleep in their bed in one corner. Matt didn't want to crawl into his cold cot next to their bed. He wanted to stay in front of the fire with his parents.

4. What do you picture in your mind? **a one-room log cabin with a bed in one corner; a cot next to the bed; a fireplace with a man and a woman sitting in front of it**

5. When does the story most likely take place? **in the past**
   in the past   now   in the future

6. Write the clues from the story that help you know the setting. _____
   log house; fireplace; one room house

34 LEVEL 8   "The White Stallion"

SKILL TRACE: SUFFIXES				
Introduction	Practice	Test	Reteach	Maintain
TE 56	83 | 139	157	160	251

WORD STUDY

Suffixes -er, -or

OBJECTIVE   Using structural analysis to determine word meaning.

Review suffixes -er, -or.

Write the following sentences on the chalkboard:

1. **Gretchen loves to <u>paint</u>. She wants to become a <u>painter</u>.**
2. **Her brother hopes to be a <u>sailor</u> and <u>sail</u> around the world.**

Remind students that when the suffix *-er* or *-or* is added to a word, it changes the meaning of the word. Point out that in the first sentence, the word *paint* describes an activity and the word *painter* means "someone who paints." Have students tell what the words *sailor* and *sail* describe. *(a person who sails; an activity in a boat with sails)*

Provide practice using suffixes -er, -or.

Display the Teaching Chart. Have students complete the sentences on the chart using the base word with the suffix *-er* or *-or*.

> **22**
>
> **TEACHING CHART 22: SUFFIXES -ER, -OR**
>
> teach   visit   act   drive
>
> 1. Every child in the class could be an (actor) in our play.
> 2. The (teacher) told us what parts we could have.
> 3. One boy played the (driver) of the wagon train.
> 4. A (visitor) to the class helped us create a make-believe covered wagon.

Provide independent practice.

Options for independent practice are shown in the Resource Center below.

Workbook page 37

NAME _____

Suffixes -er, -or   WORD STUDY

> **REMEMBER:** You can add the suffix *-er* or *-or* to an action word to make a new word. A word with *-er* or *-or* means "someone who does something."

A. Use the words in the box to complete each sentence. Each word is used only once.

| fighter | follower | leader | rider | runner |

1. The other horses followed the white stallion because he was their _____leader_____ .
2. No horse had ever beaten the stallion because he was a great _____fighter_____ .
3. Gretchen did not have to be a good ____rider____ because she was tied onto Anna's back.
4. Anna was not a fast ____runner____ because she was old.
5. One mare was a ____follower____ who always stayed behind the other horses.

B. Write what each word means.

6. helper _____one who helps_____
7. inventor _____one who invents_____
8. actor _____one who acts_____

C. Choose four other *-er* and *-or* words that name people who do something. On separate paper, use the words to write sentences. See Teacher Notes.

Suffixes *-er, -or*   "The White Stallion" **37**

RESOURCE CENTER

◀ **Workbook page 37** is intended for use by all students.

Skills Practice 35 ▶ may be assigned for additional practice.

Workbook reuse option: Have students circle the base words from which each *-er* or *-or* word on the page has been formed.

Skills Practice 35

NAME _____

SKILLS PRACTICE **35**

Suffixes -er, -or

Suffixes, like words, have meanings. The suffixes *-er* and *-or* mean "one who."

Put the people back into this Ghost Town. Read the clues. Write the words from the box in the puzzle.

conductor	sheepherders	store owner
jailer	stagecoach driver	tracker
rancher		

1. He takes travelers out of town.
2. This fellow follows tracks.
3. They shear sheep.
4. She sells soap and saddles.
5. He keeps cattle in the corral.
6. He works on trains.
7. He puts people who break the law behind bars.

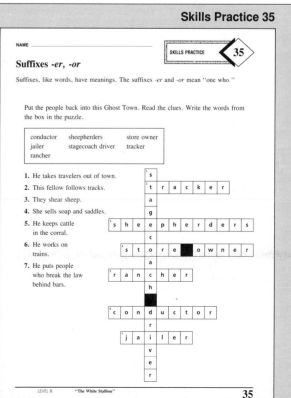

LEVEL 8   "The White Stallion"   **35**

SKILL TRACE: VOWEL DIGRAPH ei
This skill is untested at this level.

WORD STUDY
Vowel Digraph *-ei* after *c*

OBJECTIVE   Reading words with vowel digraph *-ei*.

Explain the use of -ei *following* c.

Tell students that the vowel digraph *-ei* has the sound of long *e* and that they will find this vowel group following the letter *c*. Write *receive* on the chalkboard. Ask students to pronounce the word and to notice the vowel digraph *-ei* following the *c*.

Provide practice recognizing the vowel digraph -ei.

Write the following words on the chalkboard. Have students pronounce the word *ceiling*. Then explain that the *p* in *receipt* is silent, and have students pronounce the word. Have a volunteer explain what a receipt is.

ceiling, receipt

Provide practice reading words in context.

Write the following sentences on the chalkboard.

1. **Did you _____ the gift I sent you?** (receive)

2. **The _____ in this room has two lights hanging from it.** (ceiling)

3. **When I paid for my new bike, the clerk gave me a _____ .** (receipt)

Have volunteers read each sentence and complete it with the word *receive, ceiling,* or *receipt.*

Provide independent practice.

An independent activity is shown in the Resource Center below.

RESOURCE CENTER

Skills Practice 36 ▶ may be assigned for additional practice.

Skills Practice 36

NAME _____

SKILLS PRACTICE ◀ 36 ▶

Words with *ei*

Sometimes two letters stand for one sound. The letters *ei* can stand for the long **e** vowel sound in *see*. This vowel sound sometimes follows the letter *c*.

A. Read the words and the meanings. Write the number of the meaning next to each word.

_3_ receive	**1.**	not one or the other of two things
_4_ ceiling	**2.**	to take hold of something with force
_1_ neither	**3.**	to get something given or sent
_2_ seize	**4.**	the inside top covering of a room
_6_ receiver	**5.**	one or the other of two things
_5_ either	**6.**	one who gets something given or sent

B. Write one of the words from the list in each sentence.

7. The reading room in the library has a large light hanging from the **ceiling** _____.

8. If you are the **receiver** _____ of a gift, you should thank the giver.

9. Our teacher said that we could choose **either** _____ of these two books to write a report on.

10. The police captain used twenty police officers to **seize** _____ the stolen painting from the robber.

11. The runner and the ball arrived at home plate so close together that **neither** _____ of the coaches could decide what to do.

12. Did you **receive** _____ a letter or a package from Grandpa last week?

13. The new owners painted the **ceiling** _____ white to add light to the room.

36   LEVEL 8   "The White Stallion"

Spelling Changes *f* to *ve*

OBJECTIVE Reading words with *f* changed to *ve* before an ending.

Review change in spelling for words ending in f or fe.

Remind students to change the *f* to *ve* when forming the plurals of words ending with *f* or *fe*. Write the following sentence on the chalkboard.

Gretchen sat down on some dry (leaf).

Ask students what word would complete the sentence. *(leaves)* Have them pronounce the word clearly to hear the change in spelling.

Provide practice forming plurals by changing f to ve.

Write the following words on the chalkboard. Have students form the plural of each word and then create a sentence using the plural form.

self, wolf, life, knife, scarf
(selves, wolves, lives, knives, scarves)

Provide independent practice.

An independent activity is shown in the Resource Center below.

RESOURCE CENTER

Skills Practice 37 ▶ may be assigned for additional practice.

Skills Practice 37

NAME _____

SKILLS PRACTICE 37

Spelling Changes

When a word ends in *f* or *fe*, change the *f* to *v* before adding *s* or *es*.

elf   elves

A. Change the *f* to *v*. Add *-s* or *-es* to mean more than one.

add es:
1. calf   **calves**
2. elf   **elves**
3. half   **halves**

add s:
4. knife **knives**
5. life   **lives**
6. wife   **wives**

B. Change the *f* to *v*. Add *s* or *es* to the word and write it in the sentence.

7. Long ago people used **knives** _____ to make things.
   knife

8. The fur from **wolves** _____ was used to make caps.
   wolf

9. Food buckets for **calves** _____ were carved from wood.
   calf

10. The **lives** _____ of people were different.
    life

11. The **wives** _____ made most of the family's clothes.
    wife

12. They made coats and **scarves** _____ for the family.
    scarf

13. The few things they had were kept on **shelves** _____.
    shelf

14. They burned **leaves** _____ and wood to cook.
    leaf

C. Choose three words that end in *f* or *fe* from this page. On separate paper, write a sentence for each word.

LEVEL 8   "The White Stallion"   **37**

CURRICULUM CONNECTIONS

PIONEERING PATHS GEOGRAPHY

Display a map of the United States. Comment on the enormous size of the United States and the number of miles between your home and other points on the map. Note the areas that early settlers came from and traveled to. Note the state of Texas where the story, "The White Stallion," takes place. Point out that the westward travelers had many adventures on their journeys. Ask students about adventures they have read about or imagined that might have happened on one of these trips by covered wagon.

Tell each student to choose a starting point in the East and a final destination in the West. Tell him or her to plan a trip by wagon train from one place to the other. Have the students make a list of the states he or she will travel through. More able students may want to figure out the number of miles to be covered and to estimate the number of days they will have to travel to get from one place to another.

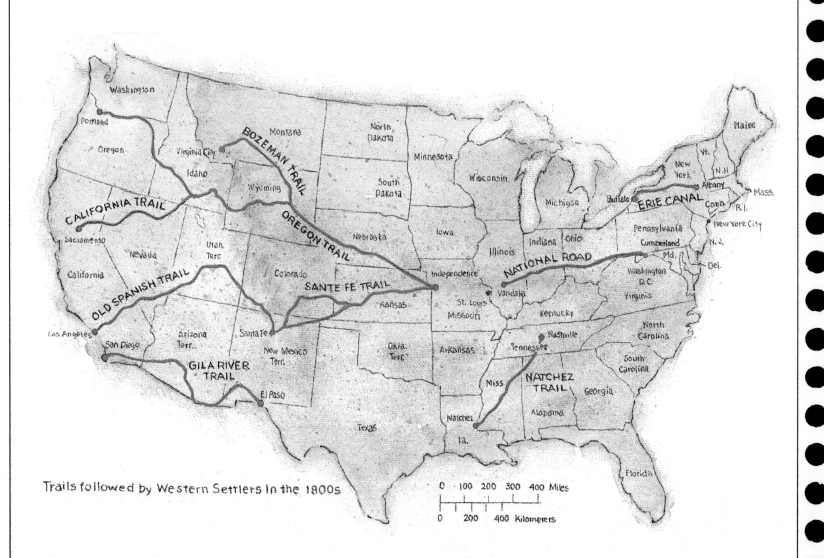

Trails followed by Western Settlers in the 1800s

WESTWARD, HO! SOCIAL STUDIES

Have each student research one part of the westward movement in the United States. Students may be interested in learning about the people who traveled west to settle the land, about where they settled, or more about the Conestoga wagons. Also have students suggest their own topics of interest. After each student has chosen a topic, have him or her collect five facts about it. Students could put together a book for classroom use on the subject "Settling the American West."

COWBOY FOLK SONGS MUSIC

Have students investigate and listen to some of the folk songs written and sung by cowboys and settlers of the Old West. Many traditional folk songs were created at this time. Students might enjoy learning some of these songs. You might have them describe the sound and flavor of the music. Then have students discuss how the songs tell about that time of history. Have students compare this earlier music with the music of their own time.

Students might enjoy writing lyrics of their own for folk songs about Gretchen and her experiences with the white stallion. Allow them to work in pairs or in small groups to create their lyrics. Provide time for them to share their results with the class.

HORSING AROUND SCIENCE

Have students collect information about different breeds of horses. Once they have selected particular breeds to investigate, they should find out the following information: common physical characteristics, places of origin, wild or domesticated, uses or abilities for work. Then have students organize the information on a chart. The chart could be a class record compiling all their research.

Breed of Horse	Wild or Domesticated	Place of Origin	Abilities for Work	Physical Characteristics
Mustang	wild	Spanish explorers brought them to North America.	Cowboys trained them for work with cattle and for transportation.	small sturdy

THE GUADALUPE RIVER SOCIAL STUDIES

There were many different plants and animals mentioned in the story in the area where Gretchen was lost around the Guadalupe River in Texas. The sounds of some of the animals scared her. She tried eating some plants when she got hungry. Have students go back to the story and make a list of all the plants and animals mentioned in the story that live in a natural, wild form near the Guadalupe River in Texas. Then have students research that area in encyclopedias, in books on plants and animals, or in books about Texas. Have them look for more native plants and animals to add to their lists. Have students pay particular attention to information about which plants can be eaten and which cannot. **Curriculum Connection Master 5** can be used with this activity.

Hans Christian Andersen's
THE NIGHTINGALE

TRANSLATED BY *Eva Le Gallienne*

ILLUSTRATED BY NANCY EKHOLM BURKERT

***S**uddenly, through the window, came the sound of an exquisite song. It was the little, living Nightingale, perched on a branch outside.* from *The Nightingale* by Hans Christian Andersen

Connecting to the Unit Theme: This classic fairy tale tells a story of a time long ago when a plain little bird could bring tears to a Chinese Emperor's eyes.

CHOOSE A PLAN THAT BEST FITS YOUR CLASSROOM

PLAN A Independent Reading

As an alternative to the Reading Corner, read Student Text page 83 (below) with the class and invite them to choose this book for independent reading.

Hans Christian Andersen was born almost two hundred years ago, but many of his stories are still favorites today. Some people think that "The Ugly Duckling," "The Emperor's New Clothes," and "The Princess and the Pea" are his best. These stories are so popular that you may have already read them, or maybe someone read them to you when you were younger.

When Mr. Andersen was a little boy, his father read to him a lot. His father also made Hans a toy theater so that Hans could write and act out his own plays and stories.

When Hans Christian Andersen grew up, he continued to write. He traveled and heard many tales and stories. Many of these stories he wrote down in his own words. He also wrote original stories like "The Little Mermaid," that he made up by himself. You can read *The Nightingale* to find out for yourself why Mr. Andersen and his stories are loved by readers even today.

PLAN B Mini-Teaching Plan

Choose one of the ideas below to present the book to your students. Use the "Response Activity" as a follow-up.

Whole Class Reading   Gather students in a special reading corner and read *The Nightingale*. Read dramatically and share the illustrations to engage them in the story.

Small Group Reading   Tell the story of *The Nightingale* to a small group of students. Then have them take turns reading the book.

Individual Reading   Have students listen to a tape of *The Nightingale*. Invite them to enjoy the story on their own as they follow along with the text and illustrations.

RESPONSE ACTIVITY   *Which Nightingale?*

Help the class to create a chart that lists the pros and cons of the real nightingale and the mechanical one, and discuss the reasons why the Emperor would want to own both kinds of bird. Then ask students to choose which bird they would rather have, and to write about why they chose it.

PLAN C Literature Unit

To develop a literature unit with this trade book, use the teaching ideas in the *Time Out for Books Guide*, found in the front of your Teacher Edition.

See order form in *Time Out for Books Guide* to purchase copies of this trade book.

written and illustrated
by Leonard Weisgard

SUMMARY

Long ago, in the town of Eagle's Landing, tradesmen used to hang outside their shops pictures that showed the kind of work they did. People used pictures because not everyone in the town could read. At the time of the story, many of the signs are made by Mr. Peaceable, the town artist and sign painter. One exception is Mr. George Lion's sign, which was made by a traveling painter. The sign contains his favorite poem and hangs upside down in front of his inn, since he cannot read. When the sign disappears, the innkeeper rushes to Mr. Peaceable's for help. There he finds, in addition to his sign, a new painting of a smiling lion. The men join the lion and poem together to make a new sign — the sign of the Peaceable Lion.

Members of Silver Burdett & Ginn's student panel chose *Mr. Peaceable Paints* for the **Reader's Choice** award.

INTRODUCING THE STORY

Review the key features of historical fiction.

Tell students that the story they are going to read, "Mr. Peaceable Paints," is historical fiction. Remind them that historical fiction contains factual details about the past, even though the characters or events are made up.

Develop the concept of picture signs as symbols.

Remind students that the stories and poems they have read in this unit have mostly been about events that happened in the past. Explain that long ago, picture signs were often used on people's shops instead of words and numbers because many people could not read. The picture signs let people know what was being sold or offered. Ask students what kind of picture or symbol they think a shopkeeper might have had on a fish store, a meat shop, a clock shop. Build a chart of picture signs.

Present vocabulary.

The following words appear in the story and may be new to students. Encourage students to use their knowledge of decoding long words, as well as the context, to help pronounce and understand unfamiliar words.

> **landing** a place where a ship can land
> **lodging** a place to live for a short time
> **dispatched** given quickly
> **trundled** moved along
> **lashed** tied with a rope
> **casks** barrels for holding liquids

READING THE STORY

Assign the reading.

Be sure students understand that *Mr. Peaceable Paints* is a book that can be found in the library. Reading this selection offers students the chance to practice uninterrupted, sustained silent reading. It allows them to read at their own rate, for their own enjoyment, and explore new books.

This story may be assigned for students to read at home. Another option is to have students choose a classmate with whom they would like to read this selection.

If people can't read, how can they find their way around? Long ago in Eagle's Landing, Mr. Peaceable had the answer.

Mr. Peaceable PAINTS

written and illustrated
by Leonard Weisgard

Once, long ago, there was a little town growing up on a hill beside the sea. A town called Eagle's Landing. And when the wind blew in from the water, there was the smell of salt and fish. And when the wind blew from the west across the hill, there was the smell of farms and of wood smoke rising from the chimneys.

In Eagle's Landing, long, long ago, there were little lanes that led around the town and down to the sea, but there were no street signs, since some of the people didn't know how to read. And the houses were not numbered. But the townspeople always knew where they were, or where they wanted to be, by the pictures hanging above the tradesmen's shops.

And in those long ago times, there was always a night watchman. Mr. Dunstable was the night watchman in Eagle's Landing. All night long he marched up and down the little streets, with his lantern and his bell. It was his job to keep watch, to see that all was well.

Down a lane he walked, past the Sign of the Lamb. All was well at Mr. Pettibone's meat shop.

He walked across to the Sign of the Fish. All was well at Mr. Goodspeed's fish market.

And under the big maple tree, at the Sign of the Boot, all was well at the cobbler's, Mr. Adams.

Mr. Dunstable turned right at the Sign of the Clock. All seemed well at Mr. Peabody's clock and furniture shop.

At the Sign of the Cracker Barrel, Mr. Goodey Gates waved to Mr. Dunstable from inside his general store.

And at the sign with the shapes of the sun and the moon and stars, all was always well. For this was the shop of the painter and decorator of coaches and carriages. All the signboards in Eagle's Landing—all but one—were made here by Mr. Peaceable, the artist and sign painter.

"Six o'clock! And from the watch I am free. And now everyone may his own watchman be!" At sunrise every morning, when the steeple bells struck six, Mr. Dunstable bellowed this. Then his watch was over. He blew out his lantern, hung it from his staff, and, shouldering his stick, he marched on. His night's work was done.

Mr. Dunstable climbed up on the hill, past the little schoolhouse and crossed the village green towards home. When he came up to Mr. George Lion's Inn, all was not well there. Something was wrong! The Inn sign was gone! This was the only sign in town that wasn't a picture. It had lettering on it and everyone agreed it wasn't pretty—especially since it was hung upside down!

MR. PEACEABLE PAINTS

The innkeeper in Eagle's Landing was Mr. George Lion. He was the jolliest man, and certainly the roundest, but everyone in town agreed he was also the stubbornest. George Lion liked to say he was a poet. He enjoyed words and loved to use them. So he made up rhymes. Once a traveling painter had stopped at the Inn. In exchange for food and lodging he had lettered George Lion's favorite poem on a signboard for the Inn.

But as Mr. George Lion could neither read nor write he had, by mistake, hung the sign upside down. Then who could possibly read it? But he stubbornly refused to put it right side up, so everyone, especially the children, called his tavern "Topsy Turvy Inn."

Just as Mr. George Lion was tying his apron around his middle, Mr. Dunstable came along.

"Ah, good morning to you, good Watchman Dunstable, what can I do for you?"

"A very good morning to you, Mr. Lion. I was just finishing off the watch, and on my way home. As a matter of fact, I was reciting your poem, which I know by heart:

Good cheer, good muffins and good tea
Dispatched with neatness and great dignity.
Coil up your ropes and anchor here
Till better weather does appear.
I've made my sign a little wider
To let you know I sell good cider!

"Well, I was thinking of a good cup of tea, when I looked up and saw your signboard gone! All could not be well, I thought."

"Heaven's to Betsy! MY SIGNBOARD GONE!" roared Mr. George Lion. "Six ships are sailing into the harbor this very morning. How will anybody ever know where to find my Inn? Where is my topsy turvy sign?"

Mr. George Lion rushed out, not even removing his apron, to search for his sign. Mr. Dunstable was just left standing there.

As the sun peered over the steeple that morning, six sailing vessels dropped anchor in the harbor of Eagle's Landing. The church bells began to ring.

Everyone came running. Farmers coming down from their farms to market, walked their sheep and cattle through the toll gate. They hurried through the little town to see the ships sail in. The children and their teacher declared that day a holiday. Even the tradesmen, excited as children, closed their shops. They all trundled down to see the ships come in. Sea captains' wives and sailors' families marched down to greet their men home from the seas. Everyone waved, everyone shouted and everyone watched.

The sailors tied the ships fast to the docks. The sails were folded and lashed safe to the masts. Then the sailors unloaded the ships, each with its cargo from some far-off land.

There was whale oil in the hold. There were barrels and boxes and chests and casks. Coffee beans in sacks. Sugar and tea and spices and rice. Silks and fans and ivory from the Orient. There were cats from Persia. Sleigh bells and iron work from Russia. Animal hides and gold dust from Africa.

And all this time Mr. George Lion was still searching everywhere for his topsy turvy sign.

Of course by now the little town was empty. Even the dogs and cats were down beside the sea, watching the boats unload. Everyone was there but Mr. Lion—and Mr. Peaceable.

Now anyone in Eagle's Landing could tell you right away who Mr. Peaceable was. He was a most happy man. Not just because he smiled and grinned a lot, and his eyes twinkled brightly. Not just because he sang or whistled while he worked. No, and not just because Mrs. Peaceable was very proud of him.

For from Mondays through Sundays, Mr. Peaceable, the artist and sign painter, did what he liked and liked what he did. He always said, "I like painting anything and everything under the sun and the moon and the stars!" And so if ever you were looking for Mr. Peaceable, at any time of the day or night, you could always find him painting in his shop.

Suddenly, without knocking, Mr. George Lion stormed through the sign painter's doorway.

"Mr. Peaceable! My signboard is gone!" raged Mr. Lion, "and the new stagecoach bringing in the mail is due any moment. The ships are already unloading in the harbor. Without my sign how will anybody ever be able to find my Inn? I can't letter a new one in time. It took a long time to make up the old sign. Heaven's to Betsy, but I am sunk!" And George Lion sank back into a chair. And just then he caught a glimpse of a painting that Mr. Peaceable was finishing.

"Mr. Peaceable, you do paint everything under the sun and the moon and the stars! What a handsome picture of a lion! He is not a wild lion, not an angry lion, not at all fearsome. He's almost a smiling lion! And Heaven's to Betsy! That lion does seem to resemble me!" Now Mr. George Lion began to look more like his old self.

"Good Mr. Peaceable, I would like to buy that lion! I will pay you well! Maybe with your picture of the lion they'll stop calling my tavern 'Topsy Turvy Inn'."

"The painting has already been sold, Mr. George Lion!" and Mr. Peaceable's eyes twinkled. "Your wife ordered this picture for you. Your sign is there in the corner. It fell down during the night. I was going to clean it up and bring them both over to you this very morning."

"Mr. Peaceable, I have an idea! Let's put your lion and my poem together!" suggested George Lion.

"What a wonderful signboard that will be!" agreed Mr. Peaceable. And, before you could say Eagle's Landing, the two men set the painting and the sign together.

Together they secured an iron hinge to hold it. Together they left the shop and hurried across the village green to the Inn. And together they hung the new signboard. But this time the letters—not topsy turvy—were right side up.

And just in time too! For now the sailors and the townspeople climbed up the hill to the village green. And just at that very moment the new mail coach rolled to a stop before the crowd of people.

"Shiver my timbers!" shouted a sailor. "The topsy turvy sign's gone!"

"Great guns!" said the coach driver. "A new sign!"

Mr. Pettibone the butcher said, "Hen's teeth and cow's horns, if that lion isn't the image of George Lion! And such a peaceful lion!"

"A Peaceable Lion!" corrected Mr. Goodspeed, who always knew Mr. Peaceable's work when he saw it.

Everyone was very pleased.

But that was long ago. And yet today if ever you should happen to find yourself in Eagle's Landing you may know it at once. There are some new signs but some of the old ones still remain. And if you climb up the hill from the sea and cross the village green you may still see an old Inn with a signboard swinging out front—an Inn which is known for miles around as the Inn of the Peaceable Lion.

 Reader's Response

Did you think Mr. Peaceable had a good idea for George Lion's sign? Why? What kind of sign might you have painted for the Inn?

DISCUSSING THE STORY

Summarize the story events.

Ask students to summarize the story. They should include why Mr. George Lion was so upset about his sign disappearing at the time that it did and what happened to it. *(It disappeared when many people were arriving on six ships; they would not be able to find Mr. Lion's inn. The poem sign had fallen down and had been brought to Mr. Peaceable. He was going to return it to Mr. Lion along with a new sign he had painted at the request of Mrs. Lion. Mr. Peaceable and Mr. Lion put the signs together and hung them up.)*

Discuss Mr. Peaceable's character.

Discuss Mr. Peaceable's character traits and why his name suits him. How does the reader know Mr. Peaceable was artistic? happy? hard-working? *(He smiled a lot, sang, and worked all the time painting pictures.)* What kind of lion did Mr. Peaceable paint and what effect did it have on Mr. George Lion? *(Mr. Peaceable's peaceful lion calmed Mr. George Lion.)*

Compare the setting of "Mr. Peaceable Paints" with the present-day world.

Remind students that the story takes place long ago in a busy seaport. Have students identify some similarities between the sights and sounds of Eagle's Landing and seaports today. *(similarities: smell of salt air, fish, the wind, perhaps some picture signs on shops; differences: more letter signs, more people, people with their own pleasure boats rather than big sailing ships arriving with goods, cars, perhaps engine-driven ships)*

CLASS ENRICHMENT

Have students make a mural of Eagle's Landing.

Have students create a mural of the town of Eagle's Landing. Help them list the elements they will include: houses, church with steeple, schoolhouse, village green, harbor with six ships, farms, shops. Be sure they name the different kinds of shops. After students have planned, drawn, and colored their mural, have them draw small paper signs for the shops. Encourage them to design a sign for Mr. Peaceable's shop. Attach the signs above the shops.
SHARED LEARNING: ART

Have students create a Glossary of Colonial Terms.

Encourage students to look back in the story for words and phrases that relate to the time of the story. Have students make a Glossary of Colonial Terms by writing the words and phrases in alphabetical order and defining them. Some possible terms are *night watchman, lantern, cobbler, general store, coach, carriage, stagecoach, traveling painter, tavern, signboard, staff, "shiver my timbers."* Some words may be illustrated. SHARED LEARNING: VOCABULARY

TEACHER NOTES

Checkpoint

USING THE CHECKPOINT AND VOCABULARY REVIEW

Use the Checkpoint for informal evaluation.

This Checkpoint provides another opportunity for informal evaluation before the formal end-of-unit assessment. If students have difficulty with the Checkpoint, you might use the extra-help activities suggested here or the Reteaching activities at the end of the unit before you give the test.

Like the mid-unit Checkpoints, these pages are in the format of the Unit Skills Tests. They might also be used to review and practice test-taking strategies. Direct students to complete the pages shown in the Resource Center. Then have students work together to correct their papers, and encourage them to explain the thinking behind their answers. This affords you an opportunity to observe not only how students arrived at their answers, but also to identify and explain any item types that are causing difficulty.

Use the Vocabulary Review.

These two pages review selected Story Critical words from the unit in the format of the Unit Skills Tests. If students' responses indicate that they have not mastered the vocabulary, you might use the extra-help activity suggested here before testing.

PROVIDING EXTRA HELP

Provide extra help with story elements.

Provide extra practice in determining story elements using story maps. Put the form for a story map on the chalkboard, or use Form 1 in the Teacher Resource Kit. Review "The White Stallion" with students, filling in the story map as each element is discussed. If necessary, repeat the activity with other stories from the unit.

Workbook page 38

RESOURCE CENTER

◄ These pages provide informal assessment in the format of the Unit Skills Tests. ►

Workbook page 39

NAME _____

Checkpoint

Read the paragraphs. Then fill in the circle beside the correct answer.

Once upon a time, long ago, there lived an old tortoise. He made his home on a small island. He moved slowly, but he easily found the food he wanted.

Yet the tortoise was unhappy. He looked at the strong eagles who flew overhead. How he wished he could fly.

One day an eagle chanced to stop by. The tortoise spoke shyly. "Can you teach me to fly?"

"You cannot fly," answered the eagle. "I fly gracefully. I have strong wings."

"I can promise you the treasures of my island," the tortoise insisted eagerly. "I could easily learn to fly. You would be a wise and good teacher."

The eagle was moved.

"I will do the best I can for you," he said. "I will carry you up into the sky. When you feel the air around you, you will know all that I can teach."

The eagle picked up the tortoise. They soared high in the sky.

"If you are ready," said the eagle, "I will release you now."

So saying, the eagle let the tortoise go. The poor tortoise fell straight down. Never again did the tortoise think he could fly with the eagles.

38   Checkpoint

NAME _____

story elements
1. When does the story take place?
   (a) today
   (b) long ago ●
   (c) five years ago
   (d) yesterday

story elements
2. Which sentence helped you tell when the story took place?
   (a) Once upon a time, long ago, there lived an old tortoise. ●
   (b) Yet the tortoise was unhappy.
   (c) "I have strong wings."
   (d) The eagle was moved.

story elements
3. Where did the tortoise live?
   (a) in a marsh
   (b) on an island ●
   (c) in the sea
   (d) in the mountains

story elements
4. Which sentence told you where he lived?
   (a) He made his home on a small island. ●
   (b) Yet the tortoise was unhappy.
   (c) "I will carry you up into the sky."
   (d) How he wished he could fly.

suffix -ly
5. The word slowly tells how the tortoise _____ .
   (a) ate
   (b) flew
   (c) spoke
   (d) moved ●

suffix -ly
6. The suffix -ly means _____ .
   (a) in a way or manner ●
   (b) one who
   (c) not having
   (d) full of

suffix -ly
7. What is the base word in the word slowly?
   (a) -ly
   (b) moved
   (c) slow ●
   (d) fast

Checkpoint   **39**

Provide extra help with the suffix -ly.

Strengthen reading comprehension by linking reading, vocabulary development, and writing. Have students recognize and use in sentences words containing the suffix *-ly*. First, put these words on the chalkboard: **carefully, beautifully, truthfully, calmly, yearly.** Have students come to the chalkboard and underline the suffixes in each. Make sure students understand that the first three words contain two suffixes. Then discuss the meaning of each root. Finally, have students write a paragraph containing all five words. Completed paragraphs might be read aloud to the class.

Provide extra help with Story Critical Words.

OPTION 1 Give additional practice with unit vocabulary by reusing semantic maps from earlier lessons in the unit. For example, the semantic map about flowers might be reused by focusing on one area of it such as the colors of flowers or places where flowers can be found. Students could then write paragraphs that describe either the various colors or a place where flowers grow, using in the description as many vocabulary words as possible.

OPTION 2 Strengthen reading comprehension by linking reading and vocabulary development. Make use of the semantic map about flowers by having students write synonyms and antonyms for as many words on the map as possible. Share and discuss results with the group.

Use Informal Assessment Checklist for observation.

An Informal Assessment Checklist is included in the Teacher Resource Kit. (See the Meeting Individual Needs booklet.) The Checklist will assist you in observing each student's performance in the following categories: Self-monitoring, Getting Information from Text, Summarizing, Generalizing, Evaluating, Synthesizing across Selections, Visualizing, Responding, Empathizing with Story Characters, and Predicting.

Workbook page 40

RESOURCE CENTER

◄ These pages review ► selected Story Critical words.

Workbook page 41

NAME _____

Vocabulary Review

Fill in the circle beside the word that best fits in the sentence.

1. I like to watch fishing boats unload at a busy _____ .
   - (a) waterfall
   - (b) wharf
   - (c) hotel
   - (d) hospital

2. I like to lie on my bed and listen to songs on my _____ .
   - (a) hoot owl
   - (b) radio
   - (c) television
   - (d) waterfall

3. Some children go to a temple or church for _____ instruction.
   - (a) distance
   - (b) radio
   - (c) religious
   - (d) icy

4. Sometimes we scatter seed on the ground to feed the _____ .
   - (a) chickens
   - (b) mustangs
   - (c) wasps
   - (d) mules

5. Before flying to the woods, the crow _____ on a branch in our yard.
   - (a) nuzzled
   - (b) whinnied
   - (c) perched
   - (d) purred

6. When the horse heard his trainer open the stable door, he _____ loudly.
   - (a) nuzzled
   - (b) perched
   - (c) whinnied
   - (d) purred

7. There are many different shops and restaurants in our _____ .
   - (a) wharf
   - (b) neighborhood
   - (c) distance
   - (d) waterfall

40   Vocabulary Review

NAME _____

8. The boy who poked that nest ended up being stung by several _____ .
   - (a) mustangs
   - (b) chickens
   - (c) wasps
   - (d) English

9. A baby bird breaks out of its shell by pecking with its _____ .
   - (a) wharf
   - (b) beak
   - (c) mule
   - (d) hoot owl

10. The river water moved much faster as it drew nearer to the steep drop of the _____ .
   - (a) waterfall
   - (b) neighborhood
   - (c) distance
   - (d) freight trains

11. As if to say "thanks" for the sugar cube, the pony gently _____ my sleeve.
   - (a) fluttered
   - (b) nuzzled
   - (c) perched
   - (d) ambled

12. The first Thanksgiving was a feast shared by Indians and _____ .
   - (a) chickens
   - (b) mustangs
   - (c) loggers
   - (d) Pilgrims

13. From our hiding place on the mountain, we could see the towers of the enemy castle far in the _____ .
   - (a) television
   - (b) education
   - (c) distance
   - (d) neighborhood

14. The wobbly colt, watching the herd of wild horses, tried to tell which _____ was its father.
   - (a) mule
   - (b) stallion
   - (c) hoot owl
   - (d) ox

15. In our country, people hold many different _____ about religion.
   - (a) beliefs
   - (b) loggers
   - (c) characters
   - (d) wasps

Vocabulary Review   41

Concluding Unit 1

Unit Wrap-Up

Discuss the unit theme.

The following questions may be used to guide a general discussion of the unit. The questions help students relate the selections and understand the development of the unit theme. As an option, have students respond in writing on Workbook page 42.

1. Both Gretchen in "The White Stallion" and James in "When I Was Nine" traveled west. How were their trips different?

2. In the story "Grandaddy's Place," why do you think Janetta's feelings towards her grandfather and his home changed after she spent some time with him there?

3. What did "Life in Pilgrim Times" and "Thy Friend, Obadiah" tell you about the kinds of people who were early settlers of the United States?

Writing About Reading: The Writing Process

OBJECTIVE Writing to express feelings.

Begin the writing activity.

In this activity, students will practice the writing process as they express their feelings about a past event. Thinking about stories they share with friends and families will help students prepare for writing.

Have students read the introductory paragraph in the Student Text. Discuss events students have already read about. Then use the following suggestions to guide them through the writing process.

Guide the writing process.

PREWRITING After students have completed their charts, discuss the order in which events are usually told. Ask what words they could use to help show that order. *(first, next, then, at last)* Suggest that they look at their finished charts and decide the order in which they will tell what happened and how they felt about it.

WRITING If students need help getting started, suggest they start by telling what happened and when it happened. Encourage them to focus on getting their ideas on paper, since they will have the opportunity to correct any mistakes in spelling, grammar, and punctuation later.

REVISING Have students make sure their first drafts answered the important questions from their charts. Before they read their paragraphs aloud, have them ask themselves if they have given all the important information. Then remind them that titles should be short and interesting.

PROOFREADING Have students check the capitalization of words in their titles and at the beginning of each sentence. Then remind them to check the capitalization of names of people and places. Tell students to reread what they wrote to make sure it makes sense before they make clean copies of their work.

PUBLISHING Have students make illustrations that show something about the characters or locations they wrote about. Then help students assemble the class magazine.

WRITING ABOUT READING

Writing About Something that Happened to You

The stories in this unit tell about events that people like to remember. For example, "When I Was Nine" describes a family trip to New Mexico. What exciting or fun things have happened to you? Think of an event to write about in a paragraph.

Prewriting

Think of a time that you like to remember. Copy the chart below onto your paper. Fill it in with information about the event.

The Time I _____	
What Happened?	
Who Was There?	
When?	
How Did I Feel?	

◆ *The Writing Process* ─────────────

Writing

Use the information in your chart to write a paragraph about the personal experience you chose. Put in enough information so that your readers know exactly what you are writing about. Tell the events in the order in which they happened.

Revising

Have someone else listen while you read your paragraph. Ask, "What part of my story do you want to know more about?" Add details that answer your partner's questions. Think of a title for your paragraph.

Proofreading

Check to see if you indented the first word in your paragraph. Make sure you put a period or a question mark at the end of each sentence.

Publishing

Make a magazine of everyone's stories. You might call the magazine *Remember When*.

───────────── *The Writing Process* ◆

Workbook page 42

UNIT ONE

Unit Wrap-Up

NAME _____

Read each question. Write your answer, using complete sentences.

1. Both Gretchen in "The White Stallion" and James in "When I Was Nine" traveled west. How were their trips different? Possible response: Gretchen went west to settle in a new home. She traveled by horse and wagon when there were no roads. It was a very long and tiring trip. James went on a vacation. He traveled quickly by car.

2. In the story "Grandaddy's Place," why do you think Janetta's feelings towards her grandfather and his home changed after she spent some time with him there? Possible response: When she got to know him, she found out that he was fun to be with. When she learned about the animals and the country, she was no longer afraid.

3. What did "Life in Pilgrim Times" and "Thy Friend, Obadiah" tell you about the kinds of people who were early settlers of the United States? Possible response: There were different kinds of people. They helped one another, lived simply, and worked hard. Like people today, they also liked to have fun.

42   Unit Wrap-Up

RESOURCE CENTER

Writing Master 6 duplicates the Writing About Reading chart.

Working Together: A Cooperative Learning Project

Plan for time and materials.

In this project, students will work in small groups to discuss life in the past and to compare and contrast it with life today. The project is designed to last about half an hour, but adapt this guideline to meet the needs of your class.

Present the project.

After students read page 98 in the Student Text, have them explain the group goal and how they should proceed in order to reach it. Ask students how a group project differs from an individual project. *(People share the work; more ideas are presented; not every idea may be used.)*

Define roles and responsibilities.

Identify groups. Ask students to tell how they might decide on one setting and one conclusion. Then have students name the individual tasks and decide who will be responsible for each task.

Observe the groups.

Observe the group discussions. If necessary, help students create additional questions about the past, such as, How would you get to school? How would you stay warm in the winter? What would you do for fun? Model how people disagree in a nice way by using a sentence such as, "That's a good idea, but I think another setting would give us more to talk about."

Have students present the project and evaluate their performance.

Have one student from each group present the group's setting and conclusions while others explain the reasons for those conclusions. Have students take turns explaining how working in a group affected this project. Was the project more or less enjoyable than if they had worked alone? Have them suggest ways to improve the workings of the group.

Books to Enjoy

Encourage independent reading.

Discuss with students the books described on the Student Text page. Encourage those who have read any of the suggested books to share them with the group. You might also suggest that students copy titles of interest onto their Workbook Book List and look for them in the library.

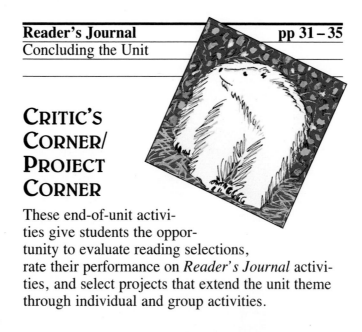

Reader's Journal   pp 31 – 35
Concluding the Unit

CRITIC'S
CORNER/
PROJECT
CORNER

These end-of-unit activities give students the opportunity to evaluate reading selections, rate their performance on *Reader's Journal* activities, and select projects that extend the unit theme through individual and group activities.

WORKING TOGETHER

Talking About the Past

In this unit you read about people who lived in America at different times and in different places. Now your group will "Remember When," and discuss what it might have been like to live in one of the story settings.

Here are some jobs you can do as you work together.

♦ Help others recall the stories in the unit.
♦ Ask questions to get people talking.

♦ Encourage others to share ideas.
♦ Agree or disagree in a nice way.

Begin by remembering some of the stories in this unit. Talk about where and when they took place. Agree on one setting to talk about.

As a group, think about what it might have been like to live in that place and time. Talk about questions such as: "What would your day be like?" "What would you like best about living then?" "What would be hard?" You might want to write a few words on paper to help the group remember all the ideas.

As a group, agree on one thing that would be the most different from life today and one thing that would be the same.

♦ *Cooperative Learning*

BOOKS TO ENJOY

And Then What Happened, Paul Revere? by Jean Fritz *(Putnam, 1973)* This is a funny account of Paul Revere's famous ride to alert the Americans that the British were coming.

The Bears on Hemlock Mountain by Alice Dalgliesh *(Scribner, 1952)* Jonathan believes bears *really* live on Hemlock Mountain. Then his mother sends him to borrow a kettle from an aunt who lives on the other side of the mountain!

The Farm Book by E. Boyd Smith *(Houghton Mifflin, 1982)* Two children visit their uncle's farm in the year 1910. Plowing, harvesting, and playing in the attic are among the children's activities.

Wagon Wheels by Barbara Brenner *(Harper & Row, 1984)* This story is based upon the true account of the Muldies, a black family who left the South after the Civil War to settle in the West.

Testing

Select the most appropriate test.

Unit Process Test is a holistic test that assesses overall comprehension. Students compose written responses to test questions.

Unit Skills Test is a criterion-referenced test that assesses how well a student has learned the specific skill objectives in the unit. The two forms, A and B, can be used to pretest and post-test or to test, reteach, and retest, depending on your preference.

Score and evaluate test results.

Keys and Record Sheets assist in scoring both kinds of tests, interpreting the results, and identifying students who need additional help. Students who perform well may proceed directly to the next unit. Those who do not will benefit from Reteaching activities on the pages that follow, Practice and Reteaching worksheets in the Teacher Resource Kit, and additional guided and independent reading.

Meeting Individual Needs

SKILL TRACE: MAIN IDEA/DETAILS					
Introduction	Practice	Test	Reteach	Maintain	
TE 66	82	116	157	158	234	274	508

COMPREHENSION

Main Idea/Details

OBJECTIVE Identifying stated and unstated main idea and supporting details.

RETEACHING

Reteach main idea and details.

Write this paragraph on the chalkboard:

> **Wherever Obadiah went, a seagull followed. It followed him to the candle maker's, and it was waiting for him outside the shop. When he was sent to the wharf, it hopped along behind him.**

Read the paragraph aloud and ask students who and what the paragraph is about. (*Obadiah and a seagull*) Then underline the first sentence. Tell students that this sentence tells the main idea. The other sentences tell more about it.

Explain that being able to identify the main idea and supporting details in what they read will help students better understand what they read.

Write the following strategy on the board for students to copy and answer.

1. **What is the whole paragraph about? Topic:** (Obadiah and sea gull)

2. **What is the most important idea? Main idea:** (sea gull follows him)

3. **Details that tell more about the main idea:** (all other sentences)

Provide independent practice.

Reteaching Masters 1–8 for main idea/details may be assigned.

ACHIEVING ENGLISH PROFICIENCY

Have students draw pictures of supporting details.

Distribute drawing paper to students. Write the following sentence on the chalkboard: **Spring is a time of change.** Read the sentence aloud and have students copy it onto their papers. Then invite students to draw pictures of changes that take place in spring. Have volunteers display their drawings and tell what they show. Record the answers on the chalkboard in sentence form. Then explain that the sentences, like the pictures, give us details that help us understand what *Spring is a time of change* means. Tell students they should watch for details such as those as they read.

Provide independent practice.

Achieving English Proficiency Master 6 may be assigned.

CHALLENGE

Have students write paragraphs about their favorite activities.

Tell students they will each write a paragraph about something they like to do. Then they will each be given someone else's paragraph to read and to do the following activity: Circle the topic, draw a box around the sentence that tells the main or most important idea or write a sentence that gives the main idea if no one sentence states it, and draw a line under each detail that tells more about the main idea. Have students write paragraphs of four or five sentences about their favorite activities. Then have them proofread their writing for content and spelling. Collect their work and redistribute the paragraphs so that each student has someone else's work.

Provide independent practice.

Challenge Master 4 may be assigned.

SKILL TRACE: STORY ELEMENTS							
Introduction	Practice	Test	Reteach	Maintain			
TE 16	32	138	157	159	206	294	326	558

Story Elements: Setting

OBJECTIVE   Recognizing story setting.

RETEACHING

Reteach recognizing story setting.

Write this paragraph on the chalkboard:

> **In 1845 Gretchen's family traveled West in a covered wagon. They followed a trail along the river. Tall grass, trees and hills could be seen, but not one town or farm. Suddenly a herd of wild mustangs galloped by in the distance.**

Explain that the writer has given information about the setting, or the time and place of the story. Tell students that dates, kinds of transportation, and other details are clues to the setting. Ask students if the time is today or long ago and how they know. *(long ago; date; details)*

Explain that knowing the place and time of a story will give the reader a better understanding of what the story is about and why characters and events and problems happen.

Have students answer these questions about the paragraph on the board:

1. **Does this story take place in the country or city?** (country)

2. **What clues tell about the place?** (trail, river, no towns or farms, wild horses)

Provide independent practice.

Reteaching Masters 1–4 for story elements may be assigned.

ACHIEVING ENGLISH PROFICIENCY

Review the concept of time and place.

Ask students to name some of the stories they have read. Write the names of the stories on the chalkboard. Help students to identify where and when the stories took place. Write this information on the board under the story title. Tell students that where and when a story takes place is the story's *setting*. Make up two sets of cards; one with places (on the moon, in a faraway country, in my neighborhood) and one with times (200 years from now, last year, when dinosaurs were alive). Turn the cards face down and have students pick a card from each pile. Have students draw a picture based on the information in the cards. When they have finished, have them tell a brief story based on the picture.

Provide independent practice.

Achieving English Proficiency Master 1 may be assigned.

CHALLENGE

Have students write paragraphs set in the present and in the past.

Tell each student to write a paragraph about a trip he or she has taken. Remind them that details about surroundings will help the reader understand the place and that details about transportation will help readers understand the time. Then have students rewrite the same paragraphs changing the setting so that their trips take place 100 years ago. Do not have them write titles for these paragraphs. Have students read one of their paragraphs aloud and ask other students to identify the setting and then name the clues that tell about the time and place.

Provide independent practice.

Challenge Master 1 may be assigned.

SKILL TRACE: SUFFIXES				
Introduction	Practice	Test	Reteach	Maintain
TE 56	83	139	157	160	251

Suffixes -er, -or

OBJECTIVE   Using structural analysis to determine word meaning.

RETEACHING

Reteach suffixes -er and -or.

Write on the chalkboard: **traveler, reader, sailor, actor.** Underline the *-er, -or* suffixes. Explain that these endings, called suffixes, mean "a person who." A traveler is a person who travels. Call on volunteers to define the remaining words on the board. Tell students that the suffixes *-er* and *-or* change a verb into a noun. Ask children to use the words in sentences.

Explain that knowing what suffixes mean will help students to read and understand new words.

Write the following sentences on the board. Have students read them and write the words with the suffixes *-er* and *-or*.

1. I learned to be a pitcher by throwing a ball against the garage door.

2. The reporter wrote stories for the newspaper.

3. He was an actor before he became a director.

Have students tell what they have learned about suffixes *-er* and *-or*. (*These suffixes mean "a person who." They change a verb to a noun.*)

Provide independent practice.

Reteaching Masters 1–4 for suffixes *-er, -or* may be assigned.

ACHIEVING ENGLISH PROFICIENCY

Model for students how to read words with the suffix -er, -or.

Write the following words on the chalkboard: **teach, help, paint, edit, act, conduct.** Read each word and have students repeat it after you. Then review the meanings of the words, using pictures or pantomime if necessary. Explain that words that name people who do each of those things can be made by adding *-er* or *-or* to the end. Add the following words to the chalkboard: **helper, conductor, painter, teacher, actor, editor.** Call on volunteers to come to the chalkboard and point to the previously written word that each new word comes from. Help students to read the new words and to figure out their meanings. Then have them copy each new word on a separate sheet of paper and draw a picture to illustrate it.

Provide independent practice.

Achieving English Proficiency Master 5 may be assigned.

CHALLENGE

Have students add -er, -or to words that name activities they enjoy.

Tell students to make lists of activities they like to do. Then have them add *-er* or *-or* to each one. Remind students that sometimes the final consonant of a word must be doubled or the final *e* dropped before a suffix is added. Suggest that they use the dictionary to check which ending is correct. Then have students use these words in paragraphs or stories about what they would like to do when they grow up. (*Suggestions: dancer, writer, painter, skater, runner, shopper, singer, builder, designer, flier, inventor, catcher, teacher, director, farmer, gardener*) Have them include details that tell why they are interested in those particular careers. Ask students to circle each word in their stories that ends with the suffix *-er* or *-or*.

Provide independent practice.

Challenge Master 3 may be assigned.

SKILL TRACE: SUFFIX				
Introduction	Practice	Test	Reteach	Maintain
TE 30	58	85	161	198

WORD STUDY

Suffix -ly

OBJECTIVE Using structural analysis to determine word meaning.

RETEACHING

Reteach suffix -ly.

Write on the chalkboard: **bravely, slowly.** Underline the *-ly* suffix. Explain that this ending means "in a way." The suffix *-ly* changes a noun or adjective to form an adverb. Write these sentences on the board:

> **The police officer is brave.**
> **The police officer acted bravely.**

Point to *brave* and explain that it tells about the officer. Ask students what *bravely* describes (*how the officer acted*). Repeat these steps for the word *slowly* by using these sentences:

> **A turtle is a slow animal. The turtle moved slowly across the rock.**

Explain that knowing what suffixes mean will help students read and understand new words.

Write the following sentences on the board. Have students read them and write the words with the suffix *-ly*.

1. **They tip-toed lightly across the room.**

2. **She sang so softly and so sweetly that the baby fell asleep.**

3. **He laughed loudly when he heard the joke.**

Have students tell what they have learned about the suffix *-ly*. (*It means "in a way" and changes a noun or adjective to an adverb.*)

Provide independent practice.

Reteaching Masters 1–4 for suffix *-ly* may be assigned.

ACHIEVING ENGLISH PROFICIENCY

Provide practice reading words ending in -ly.

Write the following words on the chalk board: **quickly, slowly, carefully, sadly, gladly.** Have students come to the chalkboard and underline the suffix. Tell students that words that end with *-ly* tell how someone or something does something. Review the meaning of the words on the board with students. Now write the following sentence on the chalkboard:

> **The boy runs quickly.**

Have a volunteer pantomime the meaning of the sentence. Erase *quickly* and write in another of the *-ly* words. Have another volunteer act out that sentence. Follow this procedure for all the adverbs.

Provide independent practice.

Achieving English Proficiency Master 3 may be assigned.

CHALLENGE

Have students write adverbs ending in -ly that describe people they admire.

Tell each student to write the name of a person he or she admires, real-life or fictional. Have the student write three sentences about the person using as many words that end in *-ly* as possible. Then have students switch papers, read the sentences, and circle the words that have the suffix *-ly*. Have students tell what these words mean.

Provide independent practice.

Challenge Master 2 may be assigned.

UNIT
TWO

OVERVIEW

A WATERY WORLD

UNIT THEME   Come to "A Watery World," where the people and animals live on, in, or near water, particularly the sea. Fiction and nonfiction explore nature, technology, and the interdependence of all creatures, including humans.

UNIT SELECTIONS

Amos and Boris, *by William Steig*
Amos the mouse and Boris the whale become unlikely friends. A read aloud/think aloud selection.

Tim to the Rescue, *by Edward Ardizzone*
Tim is delighted to go to sea as a ship's boy. He proves he is brave when he manages to rescue Ginger, the ship's first boy.

The Sea of Gold, *by Yoshiko Uchida*
For feeding the sea's fish, the kindhearted cook Hikoichi is rewarded with a treasure from the sea — a bucket of gold.

The Wonderful Underwater Machine, *by Josephine Edgar*
Meet Jason Jr., or J J for short. J J is a machine, a scientific marvel that explores the ocean floor.

Seals on the Land and in the Water, *by Betsey Knafo*
How do baby seals survive in cold water? This and other questions are answered in this fascinating look at some seagoing mammals.

The Monkey and the Crocodile, *by Paul Galdone*
A quick-thinking monkey outsmarts a hungry crocodile in this humorous folk tale about the jungle. Winner of the Silver Burdett & Ginn **Readers' Choice** award.

The House on East 88th Street, *by Bernard Waber*
In this Reading Corner selection, the Primm family discovers a crocodile named Lyle in the bathtub of their new home. Their initial fright soon becomes delight.

Title	Skills/Strategies	Integrated Language Arts	Cross-Curriculum
Listening Lesson: Amos and Boris Pages 168–173	Reality/Fantasy	**Active Listening**	
Tim to the Rescue Pages 174–199	★ Comparison ★ Suffix: -ness Summarizing	**Speaking:** Story Scenes; Nautical Terms **Writing:** Character Clusters; Friendly Letter	**Physical Education:** Square Knots **Social Studies:** Maps and Routes **Art:** Boats and Ships
Until I Saw the Sea (poem) Pages 200–201		**Listening:** Word Pictures **Writing:** Poem or Music Illustrations	
Understanding What You Read: Literature Link Pages 202–203			
The Sea of Gold Pages 204–229	Story Elements: Setting ★ Suffixes: -able, -ible ★ Book Parts (title page, copyright page, table of contents)	**Writing:** Story Map; Character Charts; Story Setting; Ocean Floor Description **Speaking:** Fish Market Scene; Presenting a Collage	**Social Studies:** Map of Japan; Japanese Village Life **Science:** Chart — Nutritional Value of Fish **Art:** Collage **Humanities:** Folk Tales
Checkpoint INFORMAL ASSESSMENT Pages 230–231			
The Wonderful Underwater Machine Pages 232–253	Main Idea/Details	**Writing:** Poem; Informational Article; First-person Descriptive Account **Speaking:** Alliteration	**Art:** Dioramas of Underwater Scenes **Social Studies:** Oceanographic Research **Science:** Farming **Mathematics:** Sea Animals and Word Problems **Careers:** Sea-related
Using Headings in an Article: Literature Link Pages 254–255			
Seals on the Land and in the Water Pages 256–275	Context Clues Test Taking	**Writing:** Analogies; "Just So" Stories; Cooperative Magazine **Speaking:** Role-play Seals	**Art:** Seal Colony Mural **Health:** Cold-weather Health Care Posters **Science:** Life Cycles of Sea Mammals
The Monkey and the Crocodile Pages 276–295	Making Inferences	**Writing:** Advice for the Crocodile; Folk Tale; Monkey Idioms **Speaking:** Story Lessons; Onomatopoeic Word Pictures	**Art:** Comparison Pictures — Crocodiles and Alligators; Folk Tale Illustration **Social Studies:** Maps of India **Science:** Reptile Chart **Mathematics:** Jungle Animal Bar Graph
How Doth the Little Crocodile (poem) Pages 296–297		**Listening:** Humor in Poetry **Writing:** Animal Poem	
World of Reading Magazine: Sea Shanties Pages 298–299			
Reading Corner: The House on East 88th Street Pages 300–305		**Speaking:** New Adventures for Lyle (Story Sequels) **Writing:** Fantasy from Story Map	
Checkpoint INFORMAL ASSESSMENT Pages 306–307			

★ Tested skill in this unit

Reading Every Day

CREATE A CLASSROOM LIBRARY

The following books and magazines are referenced throughout the unit. You might gather them ahead of time to place in your classroom library.

Aardema, Verna. **Rabbit Makes a Monkey of Lion.**

Anderson, Lena. **Stina.**

Ardizzone, Edward. **Little Tim and the Brave Sea Captain.**

Arnold, Caroline. **Bodies of Water: Fun, Facts and Activities.**

Aschenbrenner, Gerald. **Jack, the Seal, and the Sea.**

Bender, Lionel. **Crocodiles and Alligators.**

De Armond, Dale. **Berry Woman's Children.**

Freeman, Don. **Penguins, of All People.**

Grimm, Brothers. **The Water of Life.** Retold by Barbara Rogasky.

Kipling, Rudyard. **How the Rhinoceros Got His Skin.**

Laurin, Anne. **Perfect Crane.** 〰

Livingston, Myra Cohn. **Sea Songs.**

Marzollo, Jean. **Amy Goes Fishing.**

McGovern, Ann. **Little Whale.**

Moore, Lilian. **I Feel the Same Way.**

Patent, Dorothy Hinshaw. **All About Whales.**

Phleger, Fred. **The Whales Go By.**

Selsam, Millicent E. **Animals of the Sea.**

——— and Joyce Hunt. **A First Look at Seashells.**

Seuss, Dr. **McElligot's Pool.**

Shaw, Evelyn. **Sea Otters.**

Simon, Seymour. **How to Be an Ocean Scientist in Your Own Home.**

Steig, William. **Amos & Boris.**

Stephen, R.J. **Undersea Machines.**

Uchida, Yashiko. **The Best Bad Thing.**

———. **The Sea of Gold and Other Tales from Japan.**

———. **Sumi's Special Happening.**

Waber, Bernard. **An Anteater Named Arthur.**

———. **I Was All Thumbs.**

———. **The Snake, A Very Long Story.**

White, E.B. **Stuart Little.** 〰

〰 A **World of Books** Classroom Libraries selection

WORLD OF BOOKS Classroom Libraries

World of Books Classroom Libraries offer a wide selection of books that may be used for independent reading with this unit.

UNIT PROJECT CARDS   **Project Cards 5–8** in the *Idea Factory for Teachers* give instructions for projects designed for individual or small group work. Projects include making floating animals and creating a mural and a picture of the water cycle.

HOME CONNECTION LETTERS   The Teacher Resource Kit includes letters, written in English and in Spanish, that explain what students have learned during this unit and suggest bibliographies and activities that support instruction.

The books listed on the "Reading Every Day" card in each lesson's Language Arts Connection may also be copied and sent home to encourage family involvement in independent reading.

BULLETIN BOARDS

Use the suggestions in the *Idea Factory for Teachers* to construct the unit bulletin boards.

Interactive Teaching Kit

The *Castles of Sand* I·T Kit offers materials and activities to motivate and enrich your students' reading experience. You may choose to use some or all of the unit activities to introduce Unit 2, "A Watery World." Later in the unit, you may choose to use some or all of the story-related activities. You will find complete teaching instructions in the I·T Kit Activity Guide.

The I·T Kit provides a menu of activities to introduce the unit theme.

VIDEO ✦ A WATERY WORLD

What adventures await us in the tales of watery worlds? This video helps students answer the question as it brings literature to life with background experiences for the unit theme and stories. "A Watery World" leads students into literature by motivating them to read the story selections in the unit.

✦ Author Edward Ardizzone discusses the characters in his popular Tim series and tells why he likes to write stories that take place at sea.

✦ Find out what happened to the unsinkable *Titanic*, and how the search for the ship led scientists to the bottom of the ocean.

✦ Learn about the habits of these inhabitants of a watery world in this humorous rap about crocodiles. (See Activity Guide.)   LITERATURE, CONTENT AREAS, CONTEMPORARY MUSIC

AUDIO ✦ "YELLOW SUBMARINE"

The Beatles' yellow submarine carries students on a fantasy voyage beneath the waves. Students sing along and then discuss what it would be like to travel in a yellow submarine. (See Activity Guide.)
CONTEMPORARY MUSIC

UNIT CARDS ✦ WATER, WATER EVERYWHERE

Erupting geysers, a rainbow hovering over a meadow, and a sea where you can float on your back reading a book demonstrate some of the amazing forms that water takes in our world. Students discuss the photographs and do some scientific sleuthing in the library to explain in simple terms how each one occurs. (See Activity Guide.)   CONTENT AREAS

POSTER ✦ *A GOOD POOL, SAGUENAY RIVER* BY WINSLOW HOMER

The fisherman in *A Good Pool, Saguenay River* displays a fish worth bragging about. Is this painting just another fish story? Children must draw conclusions about the artist's message by analyzing elements of color and design. (See Activity Guide.)   FINE ARTS

The I·T Kit provides activities that may be used following these reading selections:

"The Sea of Gold" (See TE page 218 and Activity Guide.)

"The Wonderful Underwater Machine" (See TE page 245 and Activity Guide.)

"The Monkey and the Crocodile" (See TE page 289 and Activity Guide.)

WINSLOW HOMER'S "A GOOD POOL, SAGUENAY RIVER"

Beginning the Unit

Appreciating Art

Provide background about the work of art.

Have students look at the Chinese watercolor on page 100 of the Student Text. A poster version of this illustration, found in the Teacher Resource Kit, may be displayed for the discussion. Explain that Chinese watercolors are known for their delicate use of color and the fineness of detail. You may wish to point out that this contemporary watercolor is painted on silk, a traditional medium used to enhance the delicacy of the painting.

Have students view the work of art and discuss the unit theme.

Ask students if they have seen fishes like these before. Guide a discussion of what the fishes' lives are like under water and how life on or in water is different from life on land. Ask students to describe what it is like to be near water, including such considerations as what colors are seen and how water sounds, smells, and feels. Ask students how these sensations will be different in response to different bodies of water, for example, river, ocean, and pond. Have a student read aloud the question on page 101. Point out that this question is to help them think about the kinds of things that could happen in and around water. Have students preview the unit, and encourage them to discuss any selection they feel will be particularly interesting or any by their favorite author(s).

Connecting the Known to the New

Encourage independent reading with the Interest Inventory and the Book Log.

Workbook page 43 is a questionnaire that asks students to identify unit-related topics that they might be interested in reading about. Workbook page 44 provides space for listing suggested titles from the Interest Inventory, as well as other titles students may wish to read. Workbook pages 163–176 provide space for students to record their personal responses to books.

Reader's Journal   pp 36–38
Beginning the Unit

A VISIT
FROM
MISTER
SEA

A related reading introduces the unit theme, "A Watery World." Students read a folk tale that introduces the sea and its denizens. They use analytical skills to infer the moral of the tale and give their opinion of the story.

UNIT TWO

A WATERY WORLD

*M*any tales have been told about the seven seas.

What adventures await us in these watery worlds?

FISH IN WATER,
Contemporary Chinese Watercolor
On Silk

Workbook page 43

RESOURCE CENTER

Workbook page 44

UNIT TWO

Interest Inventory

The watery world is important in the lives of people, animals, and other living things. What interests you about water? Answer the questions below and use the chart to find a book that you may like.

	yes	no	
1.	☐	☐	Would you like to read about whales?
2.	☐	☐	Do you enjoy finding out about fantastic fish?
3.	☐	☐	Do you like to read tales about underwater animals?
4.	☐	☐	Would you like to know more about lakes and rivers?
5.	☐	☐	Are there things people can learn from animals?
6.	☐	☐	Would you like to find out about sea animals?
7.	☐	☐	Would it be fun to learn more about water?

Now find the numbers for the questions you checked YES. Follow the column down. When you see a star, move across the row to find the book title. That's the book for you!

1	2	3	4	5	6	7	Title/Author
							Bodies of Water by Caroline Arnold
							The Whales Go By by Fred Phleger
							Animals of the Sea by Millicent E. Selsam
							McElligot's Pool by Dr. Seuss
							Berry Woman's Children by Dale DeArmond
							Amos and Boris by William Steig
							Penguins of All People! by Don Freeman

43

◄ **Workbook page 43** is a questionnaire that helps students identify topics and books of interest.

Workbook page 44 is ► a personal list of books students might read independently.

UNIT TWO

Personal Book List

NAME _____

Title _____

Author _____

Title _____

Author _____

Title _____

Author _____

Title _____

Author _____

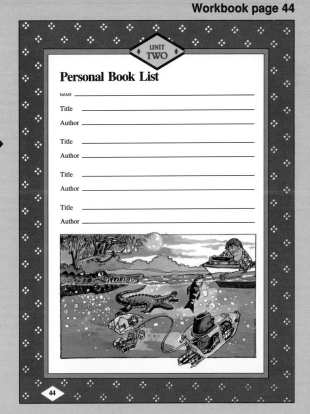

44

Listening Lesson

SELECTION SUMMARY

In this fantasy, Amos, an adventuresome mouse, takes to sea in a homemade sailboat to explore the world. He almost drowns when he rolls off the boat's deck, but a friendly whale named Boris saves him. Boris returns Amos to his home, and during conversations on the way, the two become fast friends. However, the two have to part. Years later a tidal wave washes Boris ashore on Amos's beach. Amos discovers Boris lying helplessly on land and devises a way to get him back into the sea.

STRATEGIES FOR LISTENING

Explain the process of listening for enjoyment.

You may elect to read the selection aloud twice. During a first reading, students should relax and enjoy the selection. They should not be concerned if there is something they do not understand. Explain that as they listen to the selection, however, they should be attentive to information about the characters. Listening carefully for such information will help them learn new things and increase their appreciation of the characters' actions. As an alternative to reading the selection, you may elect to play the audio cassette that is available.

Set the purpose for a read aloud/think aloud.

When you finish the first reading, you may read the selection a second time. As you read, you will share some of your thoughts and feelings about the characters, events, places, and information in the selection by thinking aloud. The annotations accompanying the selection may serve as prompts for modeling your thinking. You may choose to substitute your own or offer additional ones. Tell students that you will model the way good readers think as they read. Encourage them to be active thinkers during their own reading.

DISCUSSING THE SELECTION

Present discussion questions.

1. **Sometimes stories have information about characters, events, and places that we do not understand. What information does this story give that you were not sure of or did not understand?** (Students may mention information about mammals, soundings, and tidal waves or places such as the Ivory Coast.)

2. **Whenever we meet someone new, we always form a "first impression" of that person. What was your first impression of Amos? How did it change as you learned more about him?** (Students may mention that at the beginning of the story they thought Amos was adventurous because he wanted to go to sea and clever because he built a boat. They may also mention that they came to see Amos as brave for staying in the water alone and thoughtful for caring for Boris.)

3. **As we read stories, we often have many different feelings about the characters and the events that happen. We may feel happy, sad, worried, or relieved. What feelings did you have as you listened to this story?** (Students may mention feelings such as their concern that Amos would drown, relief when he was saved, and joy over Boris's rescue.)

AMOS & BORIS

By William Steig

Amos, a mouse, lived by the ocean. He loved the ocean. He loved the smell of sea air. He loved to hear the surf sounds—the bursting breakers, the backwashes with rolling pebbles.

He thought a lot about the ocean, and he wondered about the faraway places on the other side of the water. One day he started building a boat on the beach. He worked on it in the daytime, while at night he studied navigation.[1]

When the boat was finished, he loaded it with cheese, biscuits, acorns, honey, wheat germ, two barrels of fresh water, a compass, a sextant, a telescope, a saw, a hammer and nails and some wood in case repairs should be necessary, a needle and thread for the mending of torn sails, and various other necessities such as bandages and iodine, a yo-yo and playing cards.

On the sixth of September, with a very calm sea, he waited till the high tide had almost reached his boat; then, using his most savage strength, he just managed to push the boat into the water, climb on board, and set sail.

The *Rodent*, for that was the boat's name, proved to be very well made and very well suited to the sea. And Amos, after one miserable day of seasickness, proved to be a natural sailor, very well suited to the ship.

1. A mouse who loves the sea? I thought mice did not like water at all. Amos sounds like a very unusual mouse, and so clever, too. It should be interesting to find out what happens to him.

He was enjoying his trip immensely. It was beautiful weather. Day and night he moved up and down, up and down, on waves as big as mountains, and he was full of wonder, full of enterprise, and full of love for life.

One night, in a phosphorescent sea, he marveled at the sight of some whales spouting luminous water; and later, lying on the deck of his boat gazing at the immense, starry sky, the tiny mouse Amos, a little speck of a living thing in the vast living universe, felt thoroughly akin to it all. Overwhelmed by the beauty and mystery of everything, he rolled over and over and right off the deck of his boat and into the sea.

"Help!" he squeaked as he grabbed desperately at the *Rodent*. But it evaded his grasp and went bowling along under full sail, and he never saw it again.

And there he was! Where? In the middle of the immense ocean, a thousand miles from the nearest shore, with no one else in sight as far as the eye could see and not even so much as a stick of driftwood to hold on to. "Should I try to swim home?" Amos wondered. "Or should I just try to stay afloat?" He might swim a mile, but never a thousand. He decided to just keep afloat, treading water and hoping that something—who knows what?— would turn up to save him. But what if a shark, or some big fish, a horse mackerel, turned up? What was he supposed to do to protect himself? He didn't know.

Morning came, as it always does. He was getting terribly tired. He was a very small, very cold, very wet and

worried mouse. There was still nothing in sight but the empty sea. Then, as if things weren't bad enough, it began to rain.

At last the rain stopped and the noonday sun gave him a bit of cheer and warmth in the vast loneliness; but his strength was giving out. He began to wonder what it would be like to drown. Would it take very long? Would it feel just awful? Would his soul go to heaven? Would there be other mice there? **2**

As he was asking himself these dreadful questions, a huge head burst through the surface of the water and loomed up over him. It was a whale. "What sort of fish are you?" the whale asked. "You must be one of a kind!"

"I'm not a fish," said Amos. "I'm a mouse, which is a mammal, the highest form of life. I live on land."

"Holy clam and cuttlefish!" said the whale. "I'm a mammal myself, though I live in the sea. Call me Boris," he added.

Amos introduced himself and told Boris how he came to be there in the middle of the ocean. The whale said he would be happy to take Amos to the Ivory Coast of Africa, where he happened to be headed anyway, to attend a meeting of whales from all the seven seas. But Amos said he'd had enough adventure to last him a while. He wanted only to get back home and hoped the whale wouldn't mind going out of his way to take him there.

"Not only would I not mind," said Boris, "I would consider it a privilege. What other whale in all the world ever had the chance to get to know such a strange creature as you! Please climb aboard." And Amos got on Boris's back. **3**

"Are you sure you're a mammal?" Amos asked. "You smell more like a fish." Then Boris the whale went swimming along, with Amos the mouse on his back.

What a relief to be so safe, so secure again! Amos lay down in the sun, and being worn to a frazzle, he was soon asleep.

Then all of a sudden he was in the water again, wide awake, spluttering and splashing about! Boris had forgotten for a moment that he had a passenger on his back and had sounded. When he realized his mistake, he surfaced so quickly that Amos was sent somersaulting, tail over whiskers, high into the air.

Hitting the water hurt. Crazy with rage, Amos screamed and punched at Boris until he remembered he owed his life to the whale and quietly climbed on his back. **4** From then on, whenever Boris wanted to sound, he warned Amos in advance and got his okay, and whenever he sounded, Amos took a swim.

Swimming along, sometimes at great speed, sometimes slowly and leisurely, sometimes resting and exchanging ideas, sometimes stopping to sleep, it took them a week to reach Amos's home shore. During that time, they developed a deep admiration for one another. Boris admired the delicacy, the quivering daintiness, the light touch, the small voice, the gemlike radiance of the mouse. Amos admired the bulk, the grandeur, the power, the purpose, the rich voice, and the abounding friendliness of the whale.

They became the closest possible friends. They told each other about their lives, their ambitions. They shared their deepest secrets with each other. The whale was very curious about life on land and was sorry that he could never experience it. Amos was fascinated by the whale's

2. Poor Amos! I wonder how he will be saved. How could anyone in a ship ever see him to rescue him. He certainly is brave, though, and very strong to keep himself afloat all night.

3. I love stories where characters that are very different learn to like each other. It makes me wish more people were like Amos and Boris.

4. It surprises me that Amos would be so angry at his friend and start hitting him before he knew why his friend did what he did. His behavior reminds me of the saying, "Think before you act."

accounts of what went on deep under the sea. Amos sometimes enjoyed running up and down on the whale's back for exercise. When he was hungry, he ate plankton. The only thing he missed was fresh, unsalty water.

The time came to say good-bye. They were at the shore. "I wish we could be friends forever," said Boris. "We *will* be friends forever, but we can't be together. You must live on land and I must live at sea. I'll never forget you, though."

"And you can be sure I'll never forget *you*." said Amos. "I will always be grateful to you for saving my life and I want you to remember that if you ever need my help I'd be more than glad to give it!" How he could ever possibly help Boris, Amos didn't know, but he knew how willing he was. **5**

The whale couldn't take Amos all the way in to land. They said their last good-bye and Amos dived off Boris's back and swam to the sand.

From the top of a cliff he watched Boris spout twice and disappear.

Boris laughed to himself. "How could that little mouse ever help me? Little as he is, he's all heart. I love him, and I'll miss him terribly."

Boris went to the conference off the Ivory Coast of Africa and then went back to a life of whaling about, while Amos returned to his life of mousing around. And they were both happy.

Many years after the incidents just described, when Amos was no longer a very young mouse, and when Boris was no longer a very young whale, there occurred one of the worst storms of the century, Hurricane Yetta; and it just so happened that Boris the whale was flung ashore by a tidal wave and stranded on the very shore where Amos happened to make his home.

It also just so happened that when the storm had cleared up and Boris was lying high and dry on the sand, losing his moisture in the hot sun and needing desperately to be back in the water, Amos came down to the beach to see how much damage Hurricane Yetta had done. Of course Boris and Amos recognized each other at once. I

don't have to tell you how these old friends felt at meeting again in this desperate situation. Amos rushed toward Boris. Boris could only look at Amos.

"Amos, help me," said the mountain of a whale to the mote of a mouse. "I think I'll die if I don't get back in the water soon." Amos gazed at Boris in an agony of pity. He realized he had to do something very fast and had to think very fast about what it was he had to do. Suddenly he was gone.

"I'm afraid he won't be able to help me," said Boris to himself. "Much as he wants to do something, what can such a little fellow do?"

Just as Amos had once felt, all alone in the middle of the ocean, Boris felt now, lying alone on the shore. He was sure he would die. And just as he was preparing to die, Amos came racing back with two of the biggest elephants he could find.

Without wasting time, these two good-hearted elephants got to pushing with all their might at Boris's huge body until he began turning over, breaded with sand, and rolling down toward the sea. Amos, standing on the head of one of the elephants, yelled instructions, but no one heard him. **6**

In a few minutes Boris was already in water, with waves washing at him, and he was feeling the wonderful wetness. "You have to be *out* of the sea really to know how good it is to be *in* it," he thought. "That is, if you're a whale." Soon he was able to wiggle and wriggle into deeper water.

He looked back at Amos on the elephant's head. Tears were rolling down the great whale's cheeks. The tiny mouse had tears in his eyes too. "Good-bye, dear friend," squeaked Amos. "Good-bye, dear friend," rumbled Boris, and he disappeared in the waves. They knew they might never meet again. They knew they would never forget each other. **7**

6. So there is a way for a mouse to save a whale. I would never have predicted it. What a sight—those two elephants rolling Boris down the sand and Amos telling them what to do. I really can see and hear them as they try the rescue.

5. Is it possible that a mouse could ever do something to help a whale? It almost seems Amos will have to for the story to come out right. But what could it possibly be?

7. What a sad and happy ending. It is sad that Amos and Boris will probably never see each other again. Still, they will always have their friendship to remember, and that is happy.

Selection Support

LITERATURE

Reality/Fantasy

OBJECTIVE Recognizing elements of reality and fantasy in stories.

1. WARM-UP

Use a known passage to illustrate elements of reality and fantasy.

Tell students they will listen to a passage from "Amos & Boris." Explain that although the story does tell some information about a whale and a mouse, many things happen in the story that could not happen in real life. Remind students that a story with things that could not happen in real life is called a fantasy. Have students listen for the details in the passage that make it a fantasy. *(A whale and a mouse are talking and crying; a whale and a mouse are friends.)*

> **[Boris] looked back at Amos on the elephant's head. Tears were rolling down the great whale's cheeks. The tiny mouse had tears in his eyes too. "Good-bye, dear friend," squeaked Amos. "Good-bye, dear friend," rumbled Boris, and he disappeared in the waves.**

Discuss word and experience clues.

Reread the passage. Have students explain which word clues helped them know that this story is a fantasy. *(tears rolling down cheeks; animals talking to each other)* Ask students why these things make the passage a fantasy. *(Nothing like this could happen in the real world.)* Point out to students that they are using their own knowledge and experience to help them tell the difference between reality and fantasy.

State the objective.

Tell students they will learn to use word and experience clues to recognize elements of reality and fantasy in stories.

2. TEACH

Explain why recognizing reality and fantasy is important.

Recognizing elements of reality and fantasy helps readers better understand and appreciate what they listen to or read.

Present a strategy for recognizing reality and fantasy.

Explain that there is a strategy students can use to help them recognize elements of reality and fantasy. Tell students to ask themselves, "Do the characters act as they might in real life?" "What things could happen in real life?" "What things could not happen?"

TEACHING CHART 23: REALITY AND FANTASY   23

1. The whale spouted water.   (reality)
2. "Help!" squeaked Amos as he grabbed desperately to hold on to the whale.   (fantasy)
3. "What sort of fish are you?" the whale asked.   (fantasy)
4. When he was hungry, the whale ate plankton.   (reality)
5. Amos screamed and punched Boris until he remembered he owed his life to the whale.   (fantasy)

Model the strategy. Read sentence 1 and point out you know that whales do spout water in real life, so this sentence describes reality.

3. GUIDED PRACTICE

Check for understanding. Before going on, have students explain how to recognize elements of reality and fantasy. *(Look for word clues and ask yourself: "Could these things happen in real life?" Give reasons for your answers.)*

Guide students in using the strategy. Have students use the strategy to recognize descriptions of reality and fantasy in the remaining sentences. Discuss word and experience clues that helped them recognize each kind of element.

4. WRAP-UP

Summarize instruction. Review why readers look for elements of reality and fantasy and the kinds of clues they use to recognize such elements. *(Looking for elements of reality and fantasy will help them better understand what happens in a story; they use word and experience clues.)*

Provide independent practice. Options for independent practice are shown in the Resource Center below.

Workbook page 45

NAME _____

Reality/Fantasy

LITERATURE

REMEMBER: A **realistic** story tells about things that could really happen. A **fantasy** tells about things that could not happen in real life.

A. Read the list of events. Write *reality* if the event could happen in real life. Write *fantasy* if the event could happen only in fantasy.

1. Amos the mouse pushed the boat into the water and set sail. _____ fantasy _____

2. There was nothing in sight but the empty sea. ___ reality ___

3. Amos lay on the deck and counted stars. ___ fantasy ___

4. "What sort of fish are you?" a whale asked. ___ fantasy ___

5. Boris sounded and then came to the surface again. _____ reality _____

6. Amos and Boris became the closest possible friends. ___ fantasy ___

7. Amos warmed his fur in the sun. ___ reality ___

8. The whale spouted twice and disappeared. ___ reality ___

9. The whale was flung ashore by a tidal wave. ___ reality ___

10. Amos got two elephants to push Boris back into the sea. _____ fantasy _____

B. On separate paper, write two sentences about events in the story. Tell one realistic event and one fantastic event. See Teacher Notes.

Reality/Fantasy | Listening **45**

RESOURCE CENTER

◄ **Workbook page 45** is intended for use by all students.

Skills Practice 38 ► may be assigned for additional practice.

Workbook reuse option: Have students underline the unrealistic details they found in the fantasy sentences.

Skills Practice 38

NAME _____

SKILLS PRACTICE **38**

Reality/Fantasy

A **realistic story** tells about things that could happen.
A **fantasy** tells about things that could not really happen.

A. Read the story. Decide if it is real or if it is a fantasy.

Gregory was having a bad day. He spilled his milk at breakfast. His favorite shirt was dirty. He forgot to do his math homework. Now he wanted to walk along the beach. It was beginning to rain. He decided to go anyway.

An orange shell caught Gregory's eye. He picked it up. Since he didn't know what it was, he put it in his pocket. He'd ask his mother later.

"Help! Let me go!" Gregory looked around. Where did the voice come from? Who needed help? He didn't see anyone. Then he heard the voice again. It was coming from his pocket!

Gregory took the shell out. A tiny mermaid wiggled out of the shell. She sat on Gregory's hand.

"Maybe it has been a bad day for you," she laughed. "Do you have to make it bad for me, too?"

1. Write some things from the story that could happen. **Spilling milk, dirty shirt, walking along the beach, picking up shells**

2. Write some things from the story that could not really happen. **A voice coming out of Gregory's pocket; a mermaid in the shell**

3. Is the story realistic or is it a fantasy? **a fantasy**

B. On separate paper, write a paragraph continuing the story of Gregory and the mermaid. Include some real things and some things that could not happen.

38 LEVEL 8 "Amos and Boris"

LESSON ORGANIZER
Tim to the Rescue

	Teaching Sequence	Trade Books and Resources	Meeting Individual Needs	Integrated Language Arts / Cross Curriculum
The Bridge Pages 176–177	**Introduce** Comparison (Tested)	• Teaching Chart 24 • Workbook 46 • Skills Practice 39	• Reteaching Masters 1–7 • Challenge Master 5 • Achieving English Proficiency Master 10	
PART 1 **Vocabulary Strategies** Pages 178–179	**Develop Concepts** Using Synonyms and Antonyms **Teach Vocabulary** STORY CRITICAL WORDS: **adventure, courage, deck,** galley, hurricane, medal, scholar, **tremendous** (Tested words are boldfaced.)	• Teaching Chart 25 • Workbook 47 • Skills Practice 40	**SUPPORT WORDS:** disobey, managed, mischief, mixture, neglected, persuade, popular • Skills Practice 41 **CHARACTER/SETTING WORDS:** Alaska Pete, Captain McFee, Fireman Jones, Ginger, Old Joe, Seaman Bloggs, Tim	**WRITING/SPEAKING ACTIVITY:** Use new vocabulary to describe being at sea in a hurricane. • Spelling Connection 44
PART 2 **Reading & Responding** Pages 180–191	**Build Background** **Develop a Purpose for Reading** **Guide the Reading Process** **Selection Follow-Up**	• Reader's Journal 39–42 • Workbook 48 **READING EVERY DAY** *Little Tim and the Brave Sea Captain,* by E. Ardizzone *Stuart Little,* by E.B. White	**EXTRA HELP:** Finding Examples of Kind Deeds **ACHIEVING ENGLISH PROFICIENCY:** Discussing Nautical Terms • Achieving English Proficiency Master 11	**Language Arts Connections** **WRITING TO LEARN:** Write about an exciting part of the story. • Writing Master 7 **SPEAKING/LISTENING:** Acting Out Story Scenes; Developing Character Clusters; Creating a Chart of Nautical Terms **WRITING:** Writing Friendly Letters • Language Arts Master 6
PART 3 **Selection Support** Pages 192–199	**Introduce** Suffix *-ness* (Tested) Summarizing	• Teaching Chart 26 • Workbook 49–50 • Skills Practice 42–43	• Reteaching Masters 1–4 • Challenge Master 6 • Achieving English Proficiency Master 12 **Practice** • Teaching Chart 27 • Workbook 51 • Skills Practice 44 Comparison (Tested) **Maintain** • Skills Practice 45 Suffix *-ly*	**Curriculum Connections** **PHYSICAL EDUCATION:** Tying Knots **SOCIAL STUDIES:** Mapping Ocean Trade Routes • Curriculum Connection Master 6 **ART:** Drawing Ships

Tim
to the Rescue

written and illustrated by Edward Ardizzone

SUMMARY *Tim's fondest wish is granted—Captain McFee takes him on as second ship's boy. While on board, Tim faithfully continues his studies as he has promised his parents. Tim meets the crew, which includes Ginger, the ship's first boy, who is rather mean and mischievous. Ginger's personality provides a sharp contrast to the mild-mannered yet brave Tim. Ginger's mishaps and ultimate rescue by Tim secure their friendship and help Ginger become a more popular, clever boy.*

The Bridge

SKILL TRACE: COMPARISON						
Introduction	Practice	Test	Reteach	Maintain		
TE 176	196	292	311	312	349	578	619

COMPREHENSION

Teaching Comparison

OBJECTIVE   Understanding likenesses and differences in longer texts.

1. WARM-UP

Use a passage about the unit to introduce comparison.

Explain to students that water is important in all the selections in this unit. Tell students they will read a passage about the unit. The passage tells how some things in the selections are alike and how they are different. Display the following passage on the Teaching Chart.

> **TEACHING CHART 24: COMPARISON**
>
> As the stories in this unit show, both people and animals can travel on and under water. People cannot stay underwater for long; they also cannot move far in water under their own power. So they must use ships or submarines to travel on or under water. Animals such as seals and crocodiles, however, are able to swim for long periods of time because their bodies are especially made for living in water.

24

Discuss likenesses and differences.

Reread the passage. Ask students what is being compared. *(people and animals in the selections)* Have students tell in what way the people and animals are alike. *(They both travel on and under water.)* Then ask in what way the people are different from the animals. *(The people must use ships or submarines to travel in water.)*

Discuss signal words that show a comparison is being made.

Review the passage. Point out the words *both* and *however*. Point out that *both* signals that the information to follow is going to tell about what things are alike. Ask students what they think *however* signals. *(The information that follows is going to tell how things are different.)*

State the objective.

Tell students they will learn to recognize and make comparisons of people, places, and things in what they read and to use signal words and story clues to help them.

2. TEACH

Explain why being able to make comparisons is important.

Being able to identify and make comparisons helps readers to organize and remember information and to understand an author's ideas.

Present a strategy for making comparisons.

Explain that there is a strategy students can use to help them make comparisons. First, read the selection and ask yourself whether two or more things, persons, events, ideas, or stories are being compared. Next, look for comparison word clues. Then think about how the things are alike and how they are different. Finally, consider making lists or charts to show the comparisons.

Model the strategy.

Tell students that the comparison of people and animals talked about in the passage can be organized on a chart. List the following headings in a vertical column: *People, Seal, Crocodile.* Next to *People,* write *ride on a ship,* which the passage mentions as one way people travel in water.

3. GUIDED PRACTICE

Check for understanding. Ask students what steps they would follow to complete the chart. *(Read the passage. Ask what is being compared. Look for comparison words. Think how the things being compared are alike and how they are different.)*

Guide students in using the strategy. Have students use the strategy to make comparisons and complete the chart.

4. WRAP-UP

Summarize instruction. Review why readers make comparisons and the kinds of clues they use. *(to understand an author's ideas and to organize information; word clues)*

Provide independent practice. Options for independent practice are shown in the Resource Center below.

5. APPLICATION

Students will make comparisons as they read "Tim to the Rescue." The symbol ✔ marks specific questions and activities that apply this skill.

Meeting Individual Needs

RETEACHING Use the activity on page 312 and Masters 1–7 in the Teacher Resource Kit.

CHALLENGE Use the activity on page 312 and Master 5 in the Teacher Resource Kit.

ACHIEVING ENGLISH PROFICIENCY Use the activity on page 312 and Master 10 in the Teacher Resource Kit.

Workbook page 46

COMPREHENSION   NAME _____

Comparison

REMEMBER: Comparisons tell how things, people, or events are alike and different. Signal words and story clues help you understand comparisons.

A. Read the paragraph. Complete the sentences.

Frogs and toads are very much alike. They both spend part of their lives on land and part of their lives in the water. Both frogs and toads have strong back legs. Frogs and toads are also very good jumpers. Toads, however, have wider, flatter bodies than frogs do. Also, toads have skin that is covered with bumps, but frogs have smooth skin.

1. Frogs and toads both spend part of their lives on land and part of their lives ___in the water___ .

2. Frogs and toads both have strong ___back legs___ .

3. Frogs and toads are both good ___jumpers___ .

4. Toads' bodies are ___wider and flatter___ than frogs' bodies.

5. A toad's skin is ___covered with bumps___ , but a frog's skin is ___smooth___ .

B. On separate paper, make a chart to show how frogs and toads are alike and how they are different. Write *alike* at the top of one side of the paper. Write *different* at the top of the other side. Use the facts on this page to help you. See Teacher Notes.

46   "Tim to the Rescue"   Comparison

RESOURCE CENTER

◄ **Workbook page 46** is intended for use by all students.

Skills Practice 39 ► may be assigned for additional practice.

Workbook reuse option: Have students underline the words in the paragraph in Part A that helped them identify similarities and differences.

Skills Practice 39

NAME _____   SKILLS PRACTICE ◄ 39

Comparison

Comparisons tell how the people, places, or things in a story are alike or different. Signal words like *both, unlike,* and *however,* may help you find comparisons. Story clues can help too.

A. Read the paragraph about three kinds of whales. Compare the whales.

The narwhal, the sperm whale, and the killer whale all have teeth. (Not all whales have teeth.) However, narwhals, sperm whales, and killer whales have different numbers of teeth. The narwhal has only two teeth. The killer whale has about twenty-eight teeth. The sperm whale has forty to sixty teeth!

1. How are the three whales alike? ___They all have teeth.___

2. How are the whales different? ___Answers may vary.___
___They each have a different number of teeth.___

B. Read the paragraph about lakes and oceans.

Lakes and oceans are both bodies of water. There are thousands of lakes. But there are only five oceans. Most lakes have fresh water that is fairly still. Oceans, however, have salty water that is never still. Some lakes are shallow and some are deep. But oceans are very, very deep. You can swim, fish, and sail on many lakes. You can do these things in safe parts of the ocean, too.

3. In what two ways are lakes and oceans alike? ___They are both___
___bodies of water. You can swim, fish, and sail___
___in them.___

4. Give two examples of how they are different. ___Answers may vary. There___
___are thousands of lakes and only five oceans. Lakes___
___have fresh water that is fairly still. Oceans have salty___
___water that is never still. All oceans are deep.___

LEVEL 8   "Tim to the Rescue"   **39**

Vocabulary Strategies

Developing Concepts

Write the word *bravery* on the chalkboard as a starting point for teaching vocabulary. Ask students to define the word and suggest words that have a similar meaning. (*to face danger; not to be afraid; courage, daring, heroism*) Then have students suggest words that have an opposite meaning. (*cowardice, fear*)

Tell students that bravery does not necessarily mean big, showy deeds that make the evening news, such as saving lives. Explain that bravery and acts of courage can be small, personal things that no one else sees. As an example, ask volunteers to share how they overcame fears such as fear of the dark, of storms, of strange noises, and so on. Praise their efforts, using the words *brave, bravery,* and *courage.*

Teaching Vocabulary

Discuss meanings of Story Critical words.

Read each context sentence on the Teaching Chart and identify the new word. Then use the questions below to help students understand each word. When necessary, provide a definition.

TEACHING CHART 25: VOCABULARY　　　25

1. **adventure** (exciting, sometimes dangerous happening)
   Traveling on the ocean can be an *adventure.*
2. **courage** (control of fear when in danger)
   It takes *courage* to sail a ship through a storm.
3. **hurricane** (very strong windstorm)
   A *hurricane* has damaging winds and heavy rains.
4. **deck** (a floor of a ship)
   The captain walked the ship's *deck* checking on his crew.
5. **galley** (a ship's kitchen)
   The cook was not in the ship's small *galley.*
6. **tremendous** (very large)
   The cabin boy rescued the cook from the *tremendous* waves.
7. **medal** (small, flat piece of metal given as an award)
   The rescuer got a *medal* to honor his deed.
8. **scholar** (person who studies a great deal)
   A *scholar* might study past rescues at sea.

---

adventure　　**1. What adventure stories have you read? Which one did you like best and why? What would be your idea of an exciting adventure?**
STRATEGY: PRIOR KNOWLEDGE

courage　　**2. What sort of work do you think requires a lot of courage?** (Possible answers: police officer, fire fighter, sailor, nurse, pilot, doctor)　STRATEGY: CLASSIFICATION

hurricane　　**3. How are hurricanes different from rainstorms?** (higher winds) **Do you think that people caught in a hurricane need courage?** (yes) **Why?** (Hurricanes are dangerous.)　STRATEGY: PRIOR KNOWLEDGE

deck   **4. How are a deck and a ceiling alike?** (Both are smooth, flat surfaces and are parts of a room or structure.) **How are they different?** (They are opposites: one is above, one is below; you can walk on one but not on the other.)   STRATEGY: COMPARISON

galley   **5. The kitchen on an airplane is also called a galley. Can you think why?** (Possible answers: It is small like a ship's galley; an airplane is like a ship that sails through the air.)   STRATEGY: COMPARISON

tremendous   **6. What are some words that mean almost the same as *tremendous*?** (gigantic, huge, extra large) **Name some things that might be described as tremendous.** (Possible answers: large trucks, mountains, the ocean) STRATEGY: SYNONYMS

medal   **7. What is a medal?** (A piece of metal given as an award) **What words in the sentence helped you to know?** (honor, deed)   STRATEGY: CONTEXT CLUES

scholar   **8. In what subject would you like to become a scholar? Think of something you would enjoy studying.**   STRATEGY: PRIOR KNOWLEDGE

Discuss Support words as needed.   The Glossary of the Student Text includes definitions of the Support words: *persuade, neglected, disobey, mischief, popular, mixture, managed.*

Introduce Character words.   The selection contains the following Character words: *Alaska Pete, Seaman Bloggs, Ginger, Old Joe, Fireman Jones, Captain McFee, Tim.*

Provide independent practice.   Options for independent practice are shown in the Resource Center below.

WRITING OR SPEAKING ACTIVITY   *Have students speak or write paragraphs about what they think it would feel like to be on a ship at sea during a hurricane, using the vocabulary words when possible.*

Workbook page 47

Using New Words

SELECTION VOCABULARY

| adventure | courage | deck | galley |
| hurricane | medal | scholar | tremendous |

A. Write a word from the box beside each definition.

1. control of one's fear when in danger   **courage**

2. a very strong windstorm   **hurricane**

3. an exciting or dangerous happening   **adventure**

B. Write the word from the box that completes each blank in the paragraph.

The storm was almost as strong as a **hurricane**. The wind blew hard and the waves were **tremendous**. It took great **courage** to remain calm. No one dared to stand on the top **deck**, so all the sailors found jobs to do down below. The cook carefully closed all the drawers in the **galley**. A sailor who was quite a **scholar** read his book on his bed. Another sailor wrote in his diary about the great **adventure** of being in a storm at sea. After the storm was over, the captain received a **medal** for his bravery.

C. Pretend you are on a boat in a storm. On separate paper, write three sentences about what happens. Use three story words. See Teacher Notes.

Selection Vocabulary   "Tim to the Rescue"   **47**

RESOURCE CENTER

◄ **Workbook page 47** provides practice with Story Critical words.

Skills Practice 40 ► provides practice with Story Critical words.

Skills Practice 41 provides practice with Support words.

Spelling Connection Master 44 may be used for spelling instruction with the new vocabulary.

Workbook reuse option: Have students label the vocabulary words in the box with the letters TP (names of people or things), I (names of ideas), or D (describing words).

Skills Practice 40

SKILLS PRACTICE **40**

Vocabulary: Story Critical Words

A. Study the meaning of each word.

adventure   exciting or dangerous happening
courage   strength of mind to overcome fear
deck   the floor of a ship
galley   a ship's kitchen
hurricane   a very strong windstorm
medal   a flat piece of metal given as a prize
scholar   a person who studies a lot
tremendous   very large

B. Complete this word map. Use at least three of the vocabulary words. Then add words of your own. **Responses will vary.**

1. Parts of a Ship   **deck**   **galley**
   Ships
2. Why People Sail   **for adventure**

C. Some words belong together. Read each group of words. Write the vocabulary word that belongs to the same group.

3. prize, award, **medal**
4. enormous, huge, **tremendous**
5. tornado, storm, **hurricane**
6. strength, bravery, **courage**

D. Complete each sentence with the correct vocabulary word.

7. The fireworks made a **tremendous** bang in the sky.
8. The careful **scholar** spent many hours reading books.
9. Our trip to the mountains was an exciting **adventure**.
10. The ship's cook worked in the **galley**.
11. The winner of the contest won a **medal**.
12. Dee took a walk on the ship's **deck**.

40   LEVEL 8   "Tim to the Rescue"   Classification

Reading & Responding

Building Background

Motivate discussion using an imaginary situation.

Share the following situation with students and ask for their responses. Discuss why they responded as they did.

> **A friend of your family has a sailing ship and is planning to sail around the world. The trip will take over a year. He asks if you would like to go along as a working member of the crew. Your parents say yes, as long as you keep up with your studies. Will you go or not?**

Build background about the time the selection takes place.

Discuss what it might be like to live on a ship for a year. Also discuss what kind of work a child might be able to do. *(help repair ropes, nets, and sails; help in the kitchen; do some cleaning or painting)* Point out that at the time the next story takes place, young children like themselves often went to work instead of going to school. There were no laws that said children must go to school.

Review British spellings.

In this story, the following British spellings are used: *realise* and *colour*. Write these words on the board with their American spellings next to them. Have students identify how the American and British spellings differ.

Developing a Purpose for Reading

Option 1
Students set purpose.

ORAL "PREDICTION" LISTS Ask students to read the introduction to the story and predict what kinds of adventures a young boy will have at sea. Record their responses for use later.

WRITING ACTIVITY Have students work individually or in pairs to create written "I predict" statements. Have students save their statements for later use.

Option 2
Teacher sets purpose.

Have students read to discover what adventures Tim finds at sea. ✓

Meeting
Individual
Needs

EXTRA HELP Write the following headings on the chalkboard: *Courageous Deeds, Kind Deeds,* and *Mischievous Deeds*. Explain to students that there are examples of each of these kinds of deeds in the story they are about to read. Have the students write the topics on a sheet of paper with space below each to take notes. Then suggest that as they read, they list examples of each kind of deed under the appropriate heading. After reading, have them share their notes about the story.

ACHIEVING ENGLISH PROFICIENCY Write *sailing ship* on the board. Show students a model of or pictures of a sailing ship and point out to them the location of the *deck, rigging, hatches,* and *galley*. Write these words on the board and have students repeat them with you. Then say the word and have students point to the appropriate spot. Tell students that people who work on a ship are called *hands* and that the *captain* is the leader or boss on a ship. Write the following expressions on the board and explain their meaning: *All hands on deck. Batten down the hatches. Keep below*. For additional help in story comprehension, use Master 11 in the Teacher Resource Kit.

Tim had always wanted to be a sailor. One happy day, he got his wish. He found that life at sea was full of adventure and exciting challenges.

Tim to the Rescue

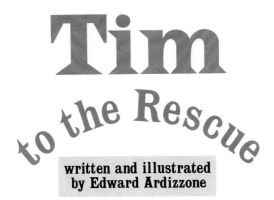

written and illustrated by Edward Ardizzone

Little Tim was in his house by the sea. It was stormy weather, and Tim was looking out the window and wishing that he were on some ship tossing about among the waves. But Tim had promised his parents to stay at home and work hard, and a promise like this has to be kept.

"Oh, dear," said Tim to himself. "I am bored with my sums, but I suppose I must learn them if I am to become a real sailor."

Suddenly there was a knock at the door. It was Tim's good friend Captain McFee, the old sea captain. Tim longed to go to sea with the captain, and he begged his mother and father to let him go.

SEA VIEW

At last, as he had been a good boy and had worked hard at his lessons, they agreed, but said that he must promise to work at his books in his spare time. Captain McFee was pleased. He would take Tim as second ship's boy.

The first person Tim met on board was a tall, red-haired boy called Ginger. When Tim told Ginger that he was the new second ship's boy, Ginger said meanly, "Well, I am first ship's boy, so you will have to do what I tell you." However, as Tim did not seem afraid, Ginger became quite nice.

Once at sea, Tim was kept busy doing odd jobs. But when the weather was good and he had no work to do, he would sit on <u>deck</u> in some sunny spot and study hard. Soon he had the reputation of being a <u>scholar</u>.

Reader's Journal	p 39
Preparing for Reading	

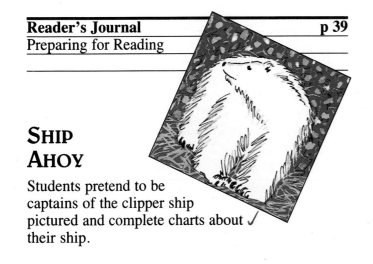

SHIP AHOY

Students pretend to be captains of the clipper ship pictured and complete charts about their ship. ✓

GUIDED READING

Page 102   Why does Tim have to learn to do his sums if he is to become a real sailor? (Possible answer: Tim will need to know math as a sailor in order to be able to measure rope or to figure out a course of travel at sea.)   SYNTHESIZE: DRAWING CONCLUSIONS

Page 103   Why does Ginger become nice when Tim does not seem afraid of Ginger's meanness? (He sees that being mean does not give him any control over Tim.)   INFER: CHARACTER

HIGHLIGHTING LITERATURE

Page 103   Tell students that in England, addition is called "sums." Also mention that Ginger is one of many nicknames given to people with red hair. Explain that a ship's boy is a cabin boy who waits on passengers, if any, and officers. He also may do odd jobs. Ginger, as first ship's boy, is ahead of Tim.

He gave lessons in—READING AND WRITING to Ginger, who had had little schooling. ARITHMETIC to Fireman Jones, who wanted to become an engineer. HISTORY to Alaska Pete, who had a passion for King Charles I and wanted to know all about him. In the evening Tim wrote letters for Old Joe, the cook, who could not read or write at all.

Ginger I am sorry to say, was a lazy and mischievous boy. Instead of working he would hide in some corner and look at comics. When he was hungry he would steal the seamen's marmalade, and when he wished to amuse himself he teased the ship's cat which made Tim very cross because he liked cats. Now Ginger's worst mischief was to have the most terrible results for him.

The third mate was very bald. In his cabin he had many bottles filled with different-coloured hair growers. One day Ginger went to the third mate's cabin. Finding that he was out, Ginger could not resist trying all the bottles. The last bottle that Ginger tried had a very odd shape and was full of a strange-smelling green liquid. When he put it on his head, it gave him a lovely tingly feeling. Poor Ginger! Little did he know what was happening. His hair was growing and growing and GROWING.

"Bosun," roared Captain McFee when he saw Ginger, "get that boy's hair cut!"

In one hour it was like this.

In two hours it was like this.

From now on, everybody who saw Ginger shouted, "Go and get your hair cut!" until the boy was almost in tears.

Alaska Pete and Joe the cook spent so much time making mixtures to stop Ginger's hair from growing (the mixtures never did) that they neglected the cooking, which made the crew very cross. In fact, the ship was going to the dogs.

Ginger became so unhappy that he took to hiding in the boats. His only friends were Tim and the ship's cat.

And so things went from bad to worse.

GUIDED READING

Page 104   What does Tim do in his spare time? (He studies and gives lessons to Ginger, Fireman Jones, and Alaska Pete. He writes letters for the cook.)   RECALL: DETAILS

✔ **Page 104   How is the way Ginger spends his time different from the way Tim spends his?** (Ginger is mischievous and gets into trouble; Tim is hardworking and helps others.)   ANALYZE: COMPARISON

Page 105   Why is the ship "going to the dogs"? (The efforts of the crew to stop Ginger's hair from growing cause them to neglect their jobs.)   INFER: CAUSE/EFFECT

HIGHLIGHTING LITERATURE

**Page 105   Explain to students that the phrase "going to the dogs" is an idiom, or an expression whose meaning cannot be understood from the usual meanings of the ordinary words in it. Point out that "going to the dogs" does not mean that the ship was actually traveling toward real dogs. Ask students to suggest meanings for the phrase. Then explain it means that everything was becoming a real mess.

✔ **Skill from The Bridge applied through this question.**

182

One day the sky became cloudy and the seas began to rise. The crew grumbled about the food. The bosun was worried, and the new mixture that Pete and Joe were making smelled horrible. Tim heard Captain McFee say to the mate, "There's a hurricane blowing up or I'll eat my hat! Order all hands on deck to batten down hatches, and see that the ship's boys keep below!"

Soon the wind was blowing great guns and the waves were getting bigger and bigger, sometimes dashing over the side and wetting the crew with spray. But Ginger would not leave his hiding place.

In the meantime, Tim was sitting in the galley with Old Joe. He was terribly worried, thinking how cold and hungry Ginger must be up there in the great gale.

GUIDED READING

Page 106   In what ways do things one day go from bad to worse? (The sky becomes cloudy; the seas rise; the crew grumbles about the food; Pete and Joe's new mixture smells horrible.)   RECALL: DETAILS

✔ **Page 107   Why do you think Ginger will not leave his hiding place? How do you think you would feel if you were in his place? Does Ginger's behavior make sense to you?** (Possible answers: He is scared of being swept overboard; he is too ashamed to come out even for a storm. Accept all reasonable answers.)
SYNTHESIZE: DRAWING CONCLUSIONS

HIGHLIGHTING LITERATURE

**Page 107   Point out to students two additional idioms on this page. Explain that the expression "I'll eat my hat" is a way of saying that "I am so sure that I am right, I will promise to do something I am sure I will never have to do." The wind blowing "great guns" means that the wind was extremely strong and powerful.

✔ Informal Assessment Opportunity: EMPATHIZING WITH STORY CHARACTERS

Finally, orders or no orders, he decided to try once more to persuade Ginger to come down.

Tim crept up the stairs and with great difficulty pushed open the door onto the deck. What he saw there made him very frightened. The sky was black with flying clouds, and great waves towered up on every side as if at any moment they would swamp the ship.

Tim dashed across the deck and just managed to reach the boat. Inside the boat was Ginger. He was cold, wet, and frightened and was holding the ship's cat in his arms.

"Come below with me," shouted Tim.

"No!" Ginger cried. "I can't, I'm too frightened!" Nothing that Tim could do or say would make him move, so Tim started back to ask the crew to help.

He had only gone a short way when a tremendous wave rushed down upon him. He leaped for the rigging and then looked around. There was no boat, no Ginger, and no cat.

Tim was horrified. "Poor Ginger, poor cat," he thought. Then in the backwash of the wave he saw the half-drowned cat floating in the water. Quickly he pulled it out and put it in the rigging.

GUIDED READING

Page 108   Do you think that Tim is brave or foolish to go out in the storm to try to get Ginger? (Some students may think he is foolish to risk his own life. Others may think he is brave because he cares enough about Ginger to risk his life.)   EVALUATE: CHARACTER

Page 109   Was your conclusion about why Ginger will not leave the boat correct? What part of your conclusion did you have to change? (Those who said he stays because he is ashamed will have to change their conclusion. He is too frightened to leave the boat.)   EVALUATE: DRAWING CONCLUSIONS

✔ **Pages 108–109   How are Tim's and Ginger's reactions to the storm similar and different?** (The storm frightens them both. Tim, however, is willing to brave going out in it to get Ginger, whereas Ginger will not move from the boat.)   ANALYZE: COMPARISON

✔ Skill from The Bridge applied through this question.

STRATEGIC READING

Page 109   Have students stop reading at the end of the second paragraph. Ask volunteers to summarize the main points of what Tim has done up to this point in the story. Then ask them to predict whether or not Ginger and the cat will be saved and what role Tim might play in their rescue. Point out to students that summarizing and predicting is one way for them to check on how well they understand the story. Suggest to students who have trouble summarizing and predicting that they reread any parts of the story they do not understand or do not remember.   METACOGNITION: SUMMARIZING AND PREDICTING

184

Next he saw a great red mop of hair floating by. It was Ginger's. He grabbed it and hung on. He thought his arm would break, so hard did the rushing water try to tug Ginger away.

Captain McFee had seen them. "All hands to the rescue!" he shouted.

Alaska Pete and Old Joe tied themselves to ropes and with tremendous <u>courage</u> dashed across the deck and soon carried all three of them to safety.

The captain seemed furious. "How dare you disobey my orders and go on deck?" he said to Tim and Ginger. "Go below at once! Bosun," he roared, "get that boy's HAIR CUT!"

However, as they left to go, Tim saw the captain brush a tear from his eye and heard him say, "Bless those boys, Mr. Mate. Wouldn't lose them for the world. Fine boy, Tim. Fine boy."

GUIDED READING

Page 110 How is Ginger rescued? (Tim grabs his hair and calls for help, and Alaska Pete and Old Joe carry them to safety.) RECALL: DETAILS

Page 111 Why is the captain angry? (The boys have disobeyed orders and gone up on deck.) INFER: CAUSE/EFFECT

✔ **Page 111 What is the difference between what the captain says to Tim and Ginger and what he says to Mr. Mate?** (He is angry when he speaks to the boys. He expresses his relief and happiness in their safety and how much he cares for them when talking to Mr. Mate.) ANALYZE: COMPARISON

STRATEGIC READING

**Pages 110 **Have students visualize, or make a mental picture, as you read aloud the section in which Ginger is rescued. Allow students to describe their mental pictures. Then encourage them to visualize as they read the rest of the story. Visualizing is one way readers keep track of how well they are understanding the story. Remind students that when they are unable to visualize while reading, they might reread that section paying particular attention to descriptive words.
METACOGNITION: VISUALIZING

✔ Skill from The Bridge applied through this question.

185

Once the boys were below, Seaman Bloggs cut Ginger's hair. Then Pete and Joe wrapped Tim and Ginger in blankets and put them to bed. Soon they were fast asleep.

Tim woke up feeling very well. He looked at Ginger and had a great surprise. Ginger's hair had not grown at all.

"Crikey, Ginger! Look at yourself in the mirror," Tim said. You can just imagine how pleased and surprised Ginger was to see his nice short hair. Now from this time on, Ginger's hair grew in the ordinary slow way.

In a few days the sun came out, the sea was calm, and the weather became warm and fine. Tim and Ginger were back at their usual jobs and the crew were busy hanging out their clothes to dry when the captain ordered all hands to the forward well deck. There he made a speech.

"Men," he said, "during the storm the two ship's boys disobeyed my orders and nearly drowned. However, now that I have heard the full story I realise that ship's boy Tim only went on deck to rescue his friend Ginger. It was a very brave action, and I am going to ask the Royal Humane Society to give him a gold <u>medal</u>." (Cheers from the crew.) "Alaska Pete and Old Joe," the captain went on, "were very brave to face the raging sea and rescue the two boys and the cat. I will give them each £5." (Loud cheers.) "But I hope that in the future they will both give up making nasty-smelling mixtures and get on with the cooking." (Very loud and long cheers.)

As you can imagine, after this Tim was very popular with everyone. Ginger began to work hard, and he became quite popular, too.

From now on, the bosun took a special interest in Tim and spent much time teaching him many things that a sailor should know. Tim repeated the lessons to Ginger, who became quite clever.

But with all this you must not think that Tim neglected his lessons, because he did not.

GUIDED READING

Page 112   Why do you think Ginger's hair stops growing so fast? (Students may suggest that his terrible experience in the ocean stopped his hair growth or that the hair-grower was washed out.) INFER: CAUSE/EFFECT

Page 113   What is the captain's speech about? (He praises Tim's bravery and announces that he will receive a medal; he rewards the crew that helped rescue the boys and the cat.) RECALL: DETAILS

Page 113   Why does the bosun now take a special interest in Tim and teach him what a sailor should know? (Possible answers: The bosun now knows that Tim has the courage and intelligence to become a sailor; he wants to be sure that Tim knows as much as possible to be prepared for any new emergency; he admires what Tim did.) INFER: CAUSE/EFFECT

HIGHLIGHTING LITERATURE

Pages 112–113   Explain to students that *crikey* is a British exclamation of surprise, something like *yipes*. Then point out that the Royal Humane Society is a British organization that honors heroes. Finally, write the symbol £ on the board and explain that it stands for a form of British money called a *pound,* just as our dollar sign ($) stands for money. Point out that nowadays a pound is worth about $2.00.

After a long and happy voyage, the ship went back to port. Tim's mother and father were on the dock to meet him. They invited Ginger to stay with them, which he was very pleased to do as he had no home of his own.

Tim went back to school and Ginger went with him. Tim was first in Reading, Writing, Arithmetic, History, and Geography, which just goes to show how hard he had worked at his books. Ginger was second in Geography, which shows that he had worked hard, too.

But Tim's proudest moment came when there arrived by post a beautiful gold medal and a roll of fine paper on which was written the story of his brave <u>adventure</u>. Tim's father had the roll framed and hung it in the drawing room.

◆ LIBRARY LINK ◆

If you liked this story by Edward Ardizzone, you might enjoy reading some of his other books, such as Little Tim and the Brave Sea Captain *and* Tim and Charlotte.

◢ Reader's Response

Imagine that you could step into this story. Where would you enter? What would you do? When would you leave?

See next page for suggested answers.

SELECTION FOLLOW-UP

Tim
to the Rescue

◆ Thinking It Over

1. How did Ginger cause trouble for himself?
2. Why did Ginger hide in the boats?
3. What kind of boy was Tim?
4. Why did Tim disobey the captain?
5. What might have happened to Ginger if Tim had not gone on deck?
6. How did Ginger change after he had his frightening experience? What clues told you this?

◆ Writing to Learn

THINK AND DECIDE   Measure how you felt about each of the four parts of the story. Copy the chart and fill it in. The first part has been marked for you. Change it if you like.

Score	Tim goes to sea.	Ginger's hair grows wildly.	Tim saves Ginger.	Tim gets a medal.
very exciting				
a little exciting	✗			
not exciting				

WRITE   Use the chart to help you choose the most exciting part of the story. Write some sentences to tell what happened in the part you chose.

GUIDED READING

Page 114   What happens to the boys when the ship returns to port? (Tim goes home; Ginger goes with him. They go to school and do very well. Tim receives a beautiful gold medal and a roll of paper on which is written the story of his adventure.)   RECALL: DETAILS

RETURNING TO THE READING PURPOSE

OPTION 1   If students set the purpose, return to their "I predict" statements and discuss whether any of their predictions came true. Have them predict whether or not Tim will ever go to sea again and discuss why or why not.

OPTION 2   Have the students recall the adventures Tim had at sea. Discuss whether Tim could have had the same adventures on land. (Possible answers: He could have met a boy like Ginger, and could have experienced a hurricane on land. He saw much more of Ginger on the ship than he might have on land, and the hurricane was more dangerous on shipboard. He probably wouldn't have had the chance to teach adults on shore.)

Reader's Journal   **p 40**
Responding to Reading

TWO TALES

Students utilize what they have read by pretending to be Tim or Ginger and writing first-person accounts of one event in the story.

SELECTION FOLLOW-UP

Tim
to the Rescue

THINKING IT OVER

1. How did Ginger cause trouble for himself? (Ginger was very mischievous. He could not resist trying all the hair growers. This was the deed that started all the trouble for him.) RECALL: DETAILS

2. Why did Ginger hide in the boats? (Ginger's hair kept growing. Everyone kept shouting that it should be cut. Also, Alaska Pete and Joe neglected the cooking, which made the crew angry. Everyone blamed Ginger. Ginger was embarrassed and miserable.) RECALL: CHARACTER

3. What kind of boy was Tim? (Possible answers: Tim was hard-working, helpful, honest, loyal, spunky, and brave.) SYNTHESIZE: CHARACTER

4. Why did Tim disobey the captain? (Tim was worried about Ginger. Ginger was in a boat on deck during the storm; Tim thought he might be able to convince Ginger to come below.) RECALL: CHARACTER

5. What might have happened to Ginger if Tim had not gone on deck? (Possible answers: No one might have seen that the boat he was in had washed away; Ginger might have drowned; the captain or a crew member might have seen the danger; the captain might have insisted that Ginger go below.) SYNTHESIZE: PREDICTING OUTCOMES

6. How did Ginger change after he had his frightening experience? What clues told you this? (Possible answers: Ginger's hair stopped growing so fast; he acted as if he had learned his lesson; he began to work hard and was popular with the crew; he studied with Tim. Encourage students to read aloud portions of the text that support their conclusions.) ANALYZE: COMPARISON; METACOGNITION

WRITING TO LEARN

✔ *Use Writing Master 7, which duplicates this chart.*

THINK AND DECIDE Measure how you felt about each of the four parts of the story. Copy the chart and fill it in. The first part has been marked for you. Change it if you like. (Help students work with the chart to prepare for writing.)

	Tim goes to sea.	Ginger's hair grows wildly.	Tim saves Ginger.	Tim gets a medal.
very exciting				
a little exciting	X			
not exciting				

Extend comprehension through writing.

WRITE Use the chart to help you choose the most exciting part of the story. Write some sentences to tell what happened in the part you chose. (Have students read their sentences to partners.)

✔ Informal Assessment Opportunity: RESPONDING

More Ideas for Selection Follow-Up

CRITICAL AND CREATIVE THINKING QUESTIONS

Encourage a variety of responses and points of view.

Use these open-ended questions to encourage critical and creative thinking about the selection.

1. Tim followed his parents' advice and studied hard. How did this help him change the lives of the people around him?

2. Do you think that Tim would ever get into trouble the way Ginger did? Why or why not?

3. In what ways is Tim's life different from yours? In what ways is it the same?

REREADING ORALLY

Have students reread for pleasure.

Discuss with students which parts of the story they liked best and why. Then have students select favorite passages to read aloud. Point out the importance of reading with expression. Encourage them to read their passages silently first and look for punctuation and word clues that will help them read with expression. Then allow students time to prepare for their reading by going over their passages several times for fluency. Some students will need to work with partners if their passages involve dialogue. Students who have elected to read by themselves should practice reading aloud with other students who also plan to read alone. Then give each student an opportunity to read his/her favorite section aloud. Before they begin, have readers tell what they like about the selected passages.

SELECTION COMPREHENSION

Provide comprehension check.

A Workbook page to check comprehension is shown in the Resource Center below. It may be used for informal assessment.

Workbook page 48

SELECTION COMPREHENSION

NAME _____

Tim to the Rescue

A. Complete the summary of "Tim to the Rescue."
Accept reasonable variations.
   This story told how ___Tim___ and Ginger became friends. Most of the story took place while Ginger was first ship's boy and Tim was second ship's boy ___Captain McFee's ship___.

   While they were on the ship, a terrible storm came up. Captain McFee told the boys to stay below deck, but Ginger stayed in a boat on deck with the ship's cat. Tim decided he must ___rescue Ginger___

   Tim tried to get Ginger to ___go below___, but Ginger refused because he was too frightened to move. Just then Ginger and the cat were washed over the side by a huge wave.

   Tim grabbed the cat and put it ___in the rigging___.

   He grabbed Ginger's long hair and held on until ___Alaska Pete and Old Joe___ came to help. Ginger was saved, but the captain seemed furious because the boys had ___disobeyed orders to stay below___

   The next day the captain praised Tim for ___his bravery___ and said he deserved a medal. As the voyage continued, Tim and Ginger learned many things. When they were back in port, Ginger moved in with Tim's family and the boys ___went to school together___.

   Tim was very proud of ___his gold medal___, which his father hung on the drawing room wall.

B. Pretend you are Alaska Pete or Old Joe, the cook. On separate paper, write a recipe for a mixture to make Ginger's hair stop growing so fast. See Teacher Notes.

48   "Tim to the Rescue"   Selection Comprehension

RESOURCE CENTER

◀ **Workbook page 48** is intended for use by all students.

Writing Master 7 duplicates the Writing to Learn chart.

189

LANGUAGE ARTS CONNECTIONS

CREATIVE THINKING: ACTING OUT THE STORY

Have students present scenes from the story.

Explain that when actors perform extemporaneously they know what they will say in general, but they do not memorize a script. Have students work in small groups to develop extemporaneous scenes from the story. Each group should decide who plays what roles and then develop a general plan of what the characters will say to each other if the dialogue is not provided in the story. Also have the groups discuss the emotions the characters will be portraying. You might suggest these passages for possible scenes: Captain McFee's arriving at Tim's house on pages 102–103, Ginger's putting on the hair tonic and the reactions of the crew to his growing hair on pages 104–105, the hurricane and Ginger's rescue on pages 107–111, or the captain's speech on page 113. SHARED LEARNING: SPEAKING

DEVELOPING CHARACTER CLUSTERS

Guide students in making character clusters.

Remind students of how to make character clusters by writing a character's name in the middle of a piece of paper and circling it. After looking at what a character does, says, and feels in a story, have them think of words that describe the character's qualities such as *friendly* or *mischievous*. Tell students to draw lines out from the circle and write their words on them.

Divide the class into two groups. One group will make clusters for Tim and Ginger at the beginning of the story on pages 102–107. The other group will make clusters for each boy at the story's end. Direct one half of each group to write about Tim and one half to write about Ginger. Next, regroup students to compare how each boy did or did not change during the story. Have a volunteer from each group report its findings to the class. WHOLE CLASS ENRICHMENT

CATEGORIZING AND DEFINING NAUTICAL TERMS

Have students create charts and speak in nautical terms.

Have students look for nautical, or sailing, terms in the story about Tim. Tell students that they will be grouping the terms they find and creating charts for them. Write the following headings on the chalkboard for students to copy and use in grouping: *Parts of a Ship; People Who Work on a Ship; Directions to Follow.* Under these write sample terms such as *rigging, cabin, captain,* and *bosun.* Include a sample direction such as, *"All hands on deck."* Have students work in small groups to review the story and complete the chart. Have them use dictionaries and encyclopedias to find meanings and add to the chart. Students may enjoy trying to give directions in nautical terms for everyday activities, such as sitting in assigned seats ("all hands to your stations") or writing ("haul on your pencils"). SHARED LEARNING: SPEAKING

WRITING FRIENDLY LETTERS

Review the parts of a letter.

Ask students to name different kinds of letters and their purposes. *(business—to ask for information or order something; notes—to invite people to a party or to announce an event; friendly—to tell personal news)* A letter includes a heading; the greeting; the body; and the closing.

Have students write friendly letters.

Ask each student to pick a person from the story and imagine what that person might say in a letter to a friend or family member. Suggest that the letter could be about life at sea or any other topic the story suggests. Have students write their letters. Then, display letters on a bulletin board. **Language Arts Master 6** can be used with this activity.   WRITING

READING EVERY DAY

Following "Tim to the Rescue," invite students along on another exciting adventure at sea with Tim and on some surprising adventures with one of the world's best-loved mice, whose travels take him into watery worlds, too.

Little Tim and the Brave Sea Captain by Edward Ardizzone. Henry Z. Walck, © 1955. When Tim accidentally becomes a stowaway on a steamer, he discovers what a sailor's life is like and just how brave a ship's captain can be.   EASIER TO READ

Stuart Little by E. B. White. Illustrated by Garth Williams. Harper & Row, © 1973. A tiny but very humanlike mouse, Stuart ventures forth from the Little home at age seven in search of his dear friend Margolo, a bird, and finds himself facing some challenging and even harrowing situations.

A **World of Books** *Classroom Libraries selection*

Reader's Journal   **pp 41, 42**
Extending Reading

CROAKING FROGS AND RED MOONS

After looking at examples of different weather signs in nature, students look for weather signs in a picture, write a weather forecast for the next day, and invent some weather signs of their own.

Selection Support

SKILL TRACE: SUFFIX				
Introduction	Practice	Test	Reteach	Maintain
TE 192	226	272	311	313	396

Suffix -ness

OBJECTIVE Using structural analysis to determine word meaning.

1. WARM-UP

Discuss ways to form new words.

Remind students they have been learning to form new words by adding a letter or a group of letters to the ends of base words. Review that a word part added to a base word changes the word's meaning and part of speech. Tell students word parts added to the end of base words are called *suffixes.*

State the objective.

Tell students they will learn how to use the suffix *-ness* to figure out the meanings of words and to form new words they can use in their own writing.

2. TEACH

Explain why understanding the meanings of suffixes is important.

Knowing what suffixes mean and how they change the way a base word is used in a sentence helps readers figure out word meanings and form new words.

Present words ending with the suffix -ness.

Write the following pairs of words on the chalkboard: *mean — meanness, lazy — laziness.* Tell students that these words tell about the character Ginger in the story "Tim to the Rescue." Explain that the first word in each pair is the base word; the second word is the new word formed by adding the suffix *-ness.* Have students read the words aloud. Then explain that the suffix *-ness* means "state of being." Using this definition, the meanings of the words on the board could be given as "being mean" and "being lazy."

Discuss spelling changes with some base words.

Point out to students that sometimes the suffix *-ness* is added to the end of a word and no changes are made in the base word's spelling, as in *mean* and *meanness.* For words ending in *y,* such as *lazy,* the *y* is changed to *i* before the suffix *-ness* is added. Have students look at both pairs of words as examples to clarify the statements you have just made. Tell students that when the suffix *-ness* is added to a base word, it changes the way the base word is used in a sentence.

TEACHING CHART 26: SUFFIX *-NESS*

26

1. At first Ginger was *mean* to Tim.
   Ginger's (meanness) did not scare Tim.
2. Ginger was also *lazy.*
   Ginger's (laziness) gave him time to get into mischief.
3. Ginger was *foolish* to use the bottle of green liquid.
   Ginger's (foolishness) brought terrible results for him.
4. That boy was very *unhappy* because his hair grew and grew.
   Ginger's (unhappiness) led him to hide in the boat.
5. Tim talked in a *gentle* way to Ginger.
   Not even Tim's (gentleness) could make Ginger come out.

Model adding suffixes to form new words.

Read the first sentence aloud. Tell students that *mean* describes how Ginger first spoke to Tim. Explain that you can add the suffix *-ness* to *mean* and use it in the second sentence to name what Ginger showed, which was "being mean." Complete the second sentence by writing *meanness*. Review that in the first sentence *mean* describes Ginger, so *mean* is an adjective. In the second sentence *meanness* names something about Ginger, so *meanness* is a noun. Repeat this procedure with the second set of sentences. Have students point out the spelling change.

3. GUIDED PRACTICE

Check for understanding.

Before going on, have students review what happens when the suffix -*ness* is added to the end of a base word and what the suffix means. *(It changes the way the base word is used; it means "state of being.")*

Have students complete Teaching Chart activity.

Have the sentences read aloud and guide students to complete the second sentence in each pair by adding the suffix -*ness* to the highlighted word in the first sentence and writing the new word in the blank. Review any words with spelling changes. Then have students define the new words.

4. WRAP-UP

Summarize instruction.

Review why it is important to understand the meanings of suffixes and how they change base words. *(Readers can figure out word meanings and form new words; the base word changes its part of speech.)*

Provide independent practice.

Options for independent practice are shown in the Resource Center below.

Meeting Individual Needs

RETEACHING Use the activity on page 313 and Masters 1–4 in the Teacher Resource Kit.

CHALLENGE Use the activity on page 313 and Master 6 in the Teacher Resource Kit.

ACHIEVING ENGLISH PROFICIENCY Use the activity on page 313 and Master 12 in the Teacher Resource Kit.

Workbook page 49

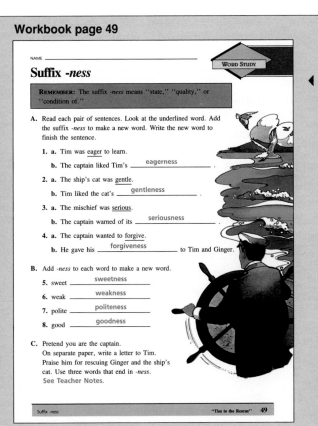

NAME _____

WORD STUDY

Suffix -*ness*

REMEMBER: The suffix -*ness* means "state," "quality," or "condition of."

A. Read each pair of sentences. Look at the underlined word. Add the suffix -*ness* to make a new word. Write the new word to finish the sentence.

1. a. Tim was eager to learn.
   b. The captain liked Tim's __eagerness__ .

2. a. The ship's cat was gentle.
   b. Tim liked the cat's __gentleness__ .

3. a. The mischief was serious.
   b. The captain warned of its __seriousness__ .

4. a. The captain wanted to forgive.
   b. He gave his __forgiveness__ to Tim and Ginger.

B. Add -*ness* to each word to make a new word.

5. sweet __sweetness__
6. weak __weakness__
7. polite __politeness__
8. good __goodness__

C. Pretend you are the captain.
On separate paper, write a letter to Tim. Praise him for rescuing Ginger and the ship's cat. Use three words that end in -*ness*.
See Teacher Notes.

Suffix -*ness*   "Tim to the Rescue"   **49**

RESOURCE CENTER

◀ **Workbook page 49** is intended for use by all students.

Skills Practice 42 ▶ may be assigned for additional practice.

Workbook reuse option: Have students number the -*ness* words in Part B to show alphabetical order. Have them write the numbers next to the words.

Skills Practice 42

NAME _____

SKILLS PRACTICE ◀ **42**

Suffix -*ness*

Sometimes the suffix -*ness* can be added to the end of a word, as in *sickness*. The suffix -*ness* means "state, quality, or condition of." For example, *sickness* means "the state of being sick."

A. Read each sentence and find each -*ness* word. Underline it, and write what it means.

1. Mom felt the dampness of my swimsuit.
   the state of being damp

2. Carmen feels a tightness in her legs if she swims a long time.
   the state of being tight

3. Because of Kim's kindness, we can use her rowboat.
   the state of being kind

4. I admire Carrie's quickness in diving.
   the state of being quick

5. We giggle at Dad's slowness when he swims.
   the state of being slow

6. All I can see is darkness at the bottom of the lake.
   the state of being dark

7. For Dave, happiness is going fishing.
   the state of being happy

8. We like the quietness of the lake.
   the state of being quiet

B. Now write a -*ness* word to match each meaning.

9. the state of being full __fullness__
10. the state of being cold __coldness__
11. the state of being sore __soreness__
12. the state of being flat __flatness__

42 LEVEL 8   "Tim to the Rescue"

COMPREHENSION

Summarizing

OBJECTIVE Summarizing the important points of a passage.

1. WARM-UP

Explain summarizing.

Explain to students that summarizing a story means to retell briefly the most important information in the story in their own words. Point out that a summary of a story is short and that it tells about a character's problem and how it was solved. As an example of important information in a story, have students turn to the first page of "Tim to the Rescue." Ask them what they think is the most important idea on this page. *(Tim is a boy who wants to be a sailor.)* Point out that his goal is to be a sailor and his problem is that he has to stay home and study. His problem is solved when his parents allow him to become a ship's boy for Captain McFee if he promises to continue his studies.

State the objective.

Tell students they will learn to summarize a story in a few sentences, giving only the most important ideas.

2. TEACH

Explain why summarizing is important.

Summarizing helps readers decide what is important in a story and gives them a way to review and remember important ideas.

Use a story map to identify the story's most important ideas.

Write the following form on the chalkboard and explain to students that it is a story map that will help them write a summary of "Tim to the Rescue." Point out that a story map helps in organizing the most important ideas of a story.

Setting _____
Characters _____
Problems _____
Goals _____
Events _____
Resolution _____

Model how to complete a summary using a story map.

Tell students that each line of the story map is to be filled in with a few words. Point to the first line and tell students that here you would write when and where the important parts of the story take place. Explain that you know the story takes place long ago and that the important parts take place on a ship at sea. The words *long ago* and *at sea* can be written on the first line. Point to *characters* on the map and ask students who were the most important characters in the story. *(Tim, Ginger, Captain McFee)* Write their names on the line. For *problems* ask students which was the first problem: Ginger's hair growing or his being washed overboard. *(Ginger's hair growing)* Ask students how this led to the most important problem of being washed overboard. *(Ginger was so upset that he hid on deck during a storm.)* For *goals* refer students to the problem. *(rescue Ginger and the cat)* For *events* ask which was more important: Ginger hiding in the boat because he was unhappy, or Ginger and the cat being washed away in the boat by the storm. *(being washed away)* Point to *resolution* and say that this means how the problem was solved. *(Tim rescues the cat and helps rescue Ginger.)*

3. GUIDED PRACTICE

Check for understanding.

Before going on, have students explain what summarizing a story means. *(to retell briefly a story in your own words, giving only the most important information)*

Guide students in writing summaries of "Tim to the Rescue."

Have students use the information on the completed story map to write summaries of "Tim to the Rescue." Encourage students to use no more than three sentences to summarize the main points. *(Suggestion: Long ago on a ship at sea, Ginger, the first ship's boy, hides in a boat on deck. He and the ship's cat are washed overboard during a storm. Tim, the second ship's boy, rescues the cat and helps the crew rescue Ginger.)*

4. WRAP-UP

Summarize instruction.

Review why it is important to be able to summarize a story. *(Summarizing helps you decide what is important in the story. It is a way of reviewing and remembering important ideas.)*

Provide independent practice.

Options for independent practice are shown in the Resource Center below.

Workbook page 50

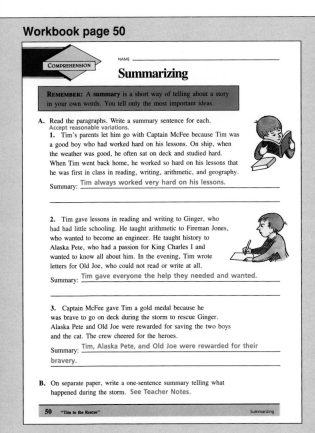

RESOURCE CENTER

◀ **Workbook page 50** is intended for use by all students.

Skills Practice 43 ▶ may be assigned for additional practice.

Workbook reuse option: Have students underline the most important facts in each paragraph in Part A.

Skills Practice 43

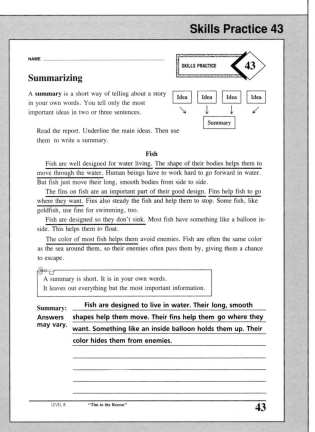

SKILL TRACE: COMPARISON						
Introduction	Practice		Test	Reteach	Maintain	
TE 176	196	292	311	312	349	578	619

COMPREHENSION

Comparison

OBJECTIVE   Understanding likenesses and differences in longer texts.

Review what comparisons are.

Remind students that comparisons are descriptions of how two or more things, people, events, or places are alike and how they are different.

Review why being able to make comparisons is important.

Ask students to explain why it is important to be able to make comparisons. *(to organize information and remember it; to understand an author's ideas)*

Present a strategy for making comparisons.

Review that there is a strategy students can use to help them make comparisons. First, read the selection and ask yourself whether two or more things, persons, events, ideas, or stories are being compared. Next, look for signal words. Then think about how the things are alike and how they are different. Finally, consider making lists or charts to show the comparisons.

> **TEACHING CHART 27: COMPARISON** 27
>
> Tim gave lessons in — *READING AND WRITING* to Ginger, who had little schooling. *ARITHMETIC* to Fireman Jones, who wanted to become an engineer. *HISTORY* to Alaska Pete, who had a passion for King Charles I and wanted to know all about him. In the evening Tim wrote letters for Old Joe, the cook, who could not read or write at all.

Use Teaching Chart to provide practice in making comparisons.

Display the Teaching Chart and have students read it aloud. Point out to students that a number of people are mentioned in this passage. Point out that the passage has no signal words such as *the same as, like, however,* and *different,* but you can still figure out that the author is comparing what Tim does for Ginger, Fireman Jones, Alaska Pete, and Old Joe the cook. Ask students how the things are alike and different. *(They are alike for three of the people, since Tim gives lessons to them. They are different in that the lessons are in different subjects. The other difference is that Tim gives lessons to Ginger, Fireman Jones, and Alaska Pete while Tim writes letters for Old Joe the cook.)*

Create a chart that reflects the likenesses and differences.

Create a chart with students to show the comparisons just made with you. List the people's names in a vertical column and write the headings *Same* and *Different.* Have students fill in the information under the appropriate headings.

Create a chart to compare Tim and Ginger.

Tell students they can make a chart to compare Tim and Ginger. Write the heading *Kind of Person* on the chalkboard. Next to it, write *Tim* and *Ginger*. Then ask students to think about what kinds of people Tim and Ginger were in the story. Have students suggest words that could be used to describe Tim's or Ginger's personality. If students completed the character clusters activity in the Language Arts Connections, ask them to name words they used in their clusters. List, or have volunteers list, these words under the heading *Kind of Person*. Complete the chart by asking students which boy each word describes. Have volunteers put a checkmark under the boy's name next to the character trait. Then discuss how the boys were alike and how they were different.

Discuss character changes.

In some cases, especially for Ginger, students may find they have listed opposite qualities for a character, such as mean and nice. Discuss how people may have both good and bad qualities that they show at different times depending on the situation. Also point out that a character might change during a story. Discuss the differences between Tim and Ginger at the beginning of the story and how they were much more alike at the end of the story.

Provide independent practice.

Options for independent practice are shown in the Resource Center below.

Workbook page 51

NAME _____

COMPREHENSION

Comparison

REMEMBER: **Comparisons** tell how things, people, or events are alike and different. Signal words and story clues help you understand comparisons.

A. Read the paragraphs. Then complete the sentences.

1. Tim and Ginger both worked for Captain McFee. Both boys wanted to be sailors. Tim was hard-working and studious. Ginger, however, was lazy and mischievous. Tim was second ship's boy, but Ginger was first ship's boy.

    a. Tim and Ginger were alike in two ways. Tell how they were alike.

    Both boys worked _____ for Captain McFee _____ .

    Both boys wanted _____ to be sailors _____ .

    b. Tell how Tim and Ginger were different.

    _____ Tim _____ was hard-working and studious.

    _____ Ginger _____ was lazy and mischievous. Tim was second

    ship's boy, but Ginger was _____ first ship's boy _____ .

2. Tim had a reputation for being a scholar. Ginger had had little schooling. Tim became Ginger's teacher. Later, they discovered that they both enjoyed geography.

    a. Tim and Ginger were different because Tim was a _____ scholar _____

    but _____ Ginger _____ was not.

    b. They both enjoyed _____ geography _____ .

B. On separate paper, make a chart with two headings: *alike* and *different*. Under *alike* write the ways Tim and Ginger were alike. Under *different* write the ways they were different. See Teacher Notes.

Comparison   "Tim to the Rescue"   **51**

RESOURCE CENTER

◀ **Workbook page 51** is intended for use by all students.

Skills Practice 44 ▶ may be assigned for additional practice.

Workbook reuse option: Have students underline all the words that signal differences and circle all the words that signal similarities in the paragraphs in Parts A and B.

Skills Practice 44

NAME _____

SKILLS PRACTICE ◆ **44**

Comparison

Comparisons tell how things, people, or events are alike and different. Signal words and story clues help you understand comparisons.

A. Read the paragraph. Underline the ways mussels, barnacles, and snails are alike. Circle the ways they are different. Draw boxes around comparison words.

    Mussels, barnacles, and snails are all shellfish. Their shells protect them. Each of the three open their shells to get food. However, their ways of getting food are different. Mussels let the food float in. Barnacles kick the food into their shell with their feet. Unlike the other two, the snail comes out of its shell for food.

B. Read the next paragraph. Answer the questions.

    People ride on waves both with and without surfboards. With a surfboard, the rider lies on the board and paddles out to where the waves start. Then the person stands on the board and rides a big wave to shore. A person without a board swims out to where the waves start. When a big wave comes, the person swims to the top. Then the person lies stiff and rides the wave to shore. Both kinds of surfing are fun. It is also important to swim well to do either kind of surfing.

    1. What is being compared? _____ riding on waves with a surfboard and riding on waves without a surfboard _____

    2. In what two ways are the two sports different? _____ One uses a surfboard and the other doesn't. One stands on the board and the other lies stiff and rides the wave. _____

    3. In what ways are they alike? _____ You ride an ocean wave to shore. _____ You have fun. _____ You need to swim well. _____

44   LEVEL 8   "Tim to the Rescue"

SKILL TRACE: SUFFIX				
Introduction	Practice	Test	Reteach	Maintain
TE 30	58	85	157	161	198

WORD STUDY

Suffix -ly

OBJECTIVE Using structural analysis to determine word meaning.

Review suffix -ly.

Explain that the suffix *-ly* means "in a way" or "like." When it is added to a base word, it may change an adjective to an adverb or a noun to an adjective. When the suffix *-ly* is added to some base words, the spelling of the base word changes.

Use sentences to review the suffix -ly.

You may wish to read aloud the pairs of sentences below. Answers are printed in red. Read the first pair, explaining that the second sentence can be completed by adding *-ly* to the word *terrible* after dropping the *e*. The new word can be defined as "in a terrible way." Call on students to complete the remaining sentences. Point out the spelling change in *tingly*. Then ask them to define the new words that use the suffix *-ly*.

---

1. Tim felt *terrible* when he thought of Ginger in the storm.
Tim was (terribly) worried about Ginger in the storm.
2. When Ginger put on the hair tonic, he felt a *tingle*.
The hair tonic gave Ginger a (tingly) feeling.
3. With a *quick* movement, Tim grabbed the cat from the water.
Tim (quickly) pulled the cat out of the water.
4. Tim was a *brave* boy to rescue the cat.
Tim acted (bravely) when he rescued the cat.

Provide independent practice.

An independent activity is shown in the Resource Center below.

RESOURCE CENTER

Skills Practice 45 ▶ may be assigned for additional practice.

Skills Practice 45

NAME _____

SKILLS PRACTICE ◆ **45**

Suffix -ly

When *-ly* is added to a word, it tells how something is done. It means "in a way" or "like."

A. Add *-ly* to each numbered word. If the word ends in *y*, change the *y* to *i* before you add *-ly*.

1. quick **quickly**
2. quiet **quietly**
3. loud **loudly**
4. soft **softly**
5. fearful **fearfully**
6. sad **sadly**
7. joyful **joyfully**
8. calm **calmly**
9. slow **slowly**
10. honest **honestly**
11. bright **brightly**
12. nice **nicely**
13. sudden **suddenly**
14. neat **neatly**

B. Use a word from 1–14. Complete each sentence.
Answers will vary.
15. The children ran **quickly/joyfully** up the trail to get to the campsite.
16. "I am afraid," someone said **sadly/softly**.
17. "You don't have to be afraid," someone whispered **quietly/nicely**.
18. "Here is the campsite," the leader called **suddenly/loudly**.
19. The children felt good and worked **quickly/joyfully** to set up camp.
20. They yelled to each other **loudly/joyfully**.
21. After that, the children rested **quietly/calmly**.

C. Answer the question with a sentence containing the underlined word.
22. When might someone whisper <u>quietly</u>? **Answers will vary.**

LEVEL 8   "Tim to the Rescue"   **45**

CURRICULUM CONNECTIONS

KNOTTING TO IT! PHYSICAL EDUCATION

Tell students that a square knot ties down the part of the sail on a ship that is not being used. Point out that it is a useful knot for holding things together because it will not come undone by pulling on one end. Explain that this is useful for rope climbing or any sport in which two things need to be tied together. Give each student a piece of twine, string, or rope approximately twelve inches long. Guide students in making a square knot:

1. Take the right end of the rope, put it over the left end, and make the first loop as you would for an ordinary knot.

2. Next, take what is now the left end, put it over the right end, and make the knot loop. Your finished square knot should look like this:

For more knots and ties, *The Book of Rope and Knots* by Bill Severn (New York: David McKay Company, 1960) is recommended.

TRADE ROUTES SOCIAL STUDIES

Explain to students that the story about Tim probably takes place in the late 1800s when sailing ships were the most important method of travel on the oceans. Point out that Tim's ship would have started from Liverpool or London in England and may have sailed to South Africa or India. Help students find England on a world map or globe and then follow a possible ocean route to South Africa or India. Explain that long ago there was no Suez Canal for ships to travel through so that any ship that wanted to go to India had to travel around the Cape of Good Hope at the bottom of Africa. Then ask students for suggestions about the purpose of the ship's voyage (*suggestions: delivering supplies, picking up goods such as cotton, wool, or silk to take back to England*) Have students write paragraphs telling where Tim's ship may have gone and the cargo it may have carried. **Curriculum Connection Master 6** can be used with this activity.

SILENT SHIPS ART

Have students use encyclopedias or nonfiction books about boats and ships to locate and study pictures of old sailing ships similar to the one on which Tim traveled. Have each student select a ship and draw or trace it on a piece of paper. Have each student label his or her picture with the name of the ship and write two or three sentences telling about the ship.

When students are finished, display the pictures on the bulletin board. Or suggest that students collect the pictures into a class book about sailing ships. Have students decide if they want to arrange the ships alphabetically by name, size, or by use. Later, you might want to add a title page, copyright page, and table of contents.

AWARD
WINNING
AUTHOR

Reading the Poem

OBJECTIVE   Understanding how a poet creates pictures in the minds of readers.

INTRODUCING THE POEM

Relate subject of the poem to the previous selection.

Remind students that the story "Tim to the Rescue" takes place at sea and tells about a boy named Tim who worked on a ship. Recall for students some of the author's descriptions of the sea. (*"sky was black with flying clouds"*, *"great waves towered up on every side."*) Point out that the author's choice of words helps readers to picture what the sea was like.

Relate content of the poem to students' experience.

Discuss with students their first experiences of the ocean or another large body of water. Ask them to recall the sights, sounds, smells, and feelings they experienced. Have volunteers share how they felt and name some words they would use to describe their feelings.

Set a listening purpose.

Tell students they are about to hear a poem about the sea. Ask them to think about the words that describe the sea and what pictures come to mind.

READING THE POEM

Read the poem aloud.

Because poetry is a sound-based literary form, this part of the lesson is most important. Read the poem aloud to the students with the Student Texts closed. Then have students open their books to page 117. Read the poem again or ask for volunteers to read it to the whole group. With this second reading, encourage students to visualize the wind on the water and the waves upon the shore. Clarify these words as needed:

> **wrinkle**   make something not smooth, with folds or ridges
> **splinter**   split or break sharply

DISCUSSING THE POEM

Discuss students' responses to the poem.

Ask students if they think the poet likes the sea and appreciates it or dislikes it and is afraid of it. Have students tell why they feel as they do. If necessary, help students realize that the poet likes the sea and is expressing her feelings about its beauty. Then ask:

> **What picture of the sea do you get in your mind by the poet's use of the word *wrinkle?*** (little waves; the sea is not smooth and calm)

> **What do you see as you think of the sun as it *splinters* the sea?** (the sun's rays cutting into the sea, breaking it into little pieces)

> **What words in the poem make you think of the sea as a person?** ("breathes in and out")

Point out poetic techniques.

Review with students that the poet's use of the words *wrinkle* and *splinter* and the phrase "breathes in and out upon the shore" makes the sea come alive for readers. Point out that these words help readers picture the sea.

CLASS ENRICHMENT

Have students illustrate the poem or music.

Have students illustrate one of the verses in the poem. Or, if possible, play part of Handel's "Water Music Suite." Invite students to draw pictures as they listen to a portion of the music. Later, encourage students to talk about their pictures and their reactions to the music.

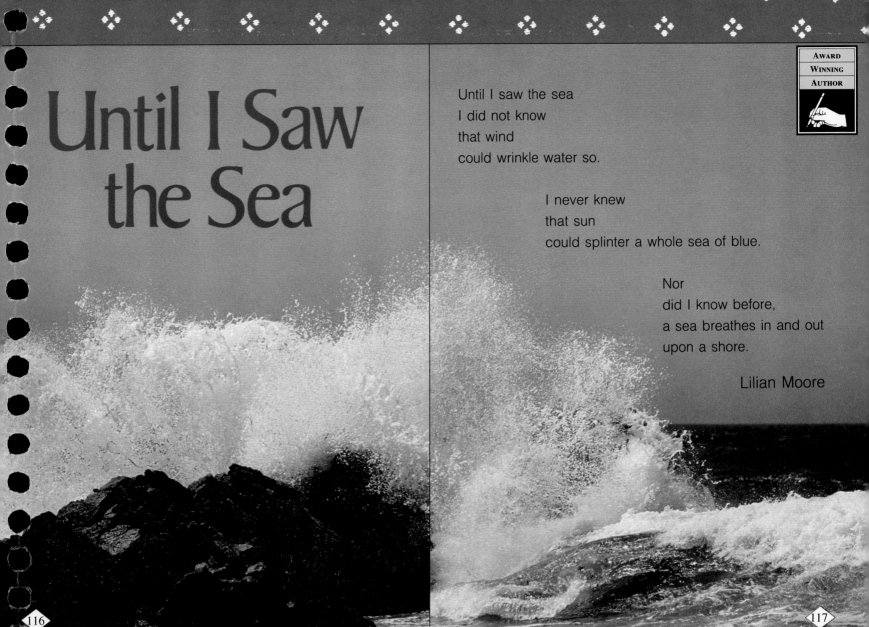

Until I Saw the Sea

Until I saw the sea
I did not know
that wind
could wrinkle water so.

I never knew
that sun
could splinter a whole sea of blue.

Nor
did I know before,
a sea breathes in and out
upon a shore.

Lilian Moore

Reader's Journal   **p 43**
Responding to Reading

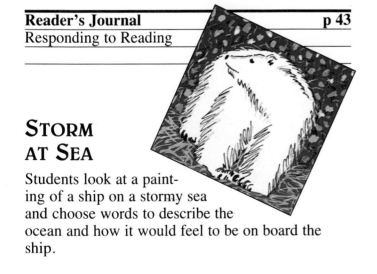

STORM AT SEA

Students look at a painting of a ship on a stormy sea and choose words to describe the ocean and how it would feel to be on board the ship.

LITERATURE LINK

OBJECTIVE Recognizing real and make-believe story events.

INTRODUCING AND READING THE LESSON

*Tap students'
prior knowledge.*

Ask a volunteer to retell the details of a recent event, such as a field trip or class activity. For example, a realistic description might be: "On Tuesday, we went to the Media Center to hear *St. George and the Dragon* by Margaret Hodges. On the way, we passed two bulletin boards showing book reports by our class. After we heard the story of St. George, we came up with ideas for stories of our own."

Next, have a different volunteer retell the same event, adding make-believe details that would make the story more interesting but less realistic. For example: "On Tuesday, we went to the Media Center to hear a story. On the way, we passed two bulletin boards with book reports pasted on them. An amazing thing happened! The characters described in the book reports joined our class and marched down the hall with us to the Media Center. There was Winnie-the-Pooh, Fern, Charlotte, Paul Bunyan, St. George, and the dragon. When we got to the Media Center, St. George and the dragon kept interrupting the story to tell their own version. When the story was finished, the characters offered to help us come up with ideas for stories of our own."

Point out that even though the second version contained some make-believe parts, it was fun to follow along and believe them for a while. Explain to students that authors will sometimes mix real and imaginary events to make a story more fun, more interesting, and more enjoyable.

*Explain the usefulness
of understanding what you read.*

Explain to students that they will understand and enjoy stories more if they recognize which parts are real and which are make-believe, and then believe the make-believe parts while they read the story.

State the objective.

Tell students that this lesson will help them recognize real and make-believe events in stories.

Refer students to their texts.

Have students turn to pages 118–119 in their books and read the lesson.

LITERATURE LINK

How can you understand what you read?

In "Tim to the Rescue," Ginger's hair grew very fast. In two hours it grew to his waist.

Were you confused when that happened? You probably knew it was make-believe, but went along with the author—at least for the time being.

Mixing Real and Make-Believe

When a story is *all* real or *all* make-believe, it's easy to understand. But sometimes in a story that seems real, suddenly something strange happens. You're confused.

What can you do? Stop and ask yourself if the author is mixing up real and make-believe events. By doing this, the author may hope to make you laugh, give you a happy surprise, or make you notice something special. So, try believing the make-believe while you're reading. You'll understand and enjoy the story more.

Strategy for Reading

How about looking at an example? Do you remember how Tim rescued Ginger? Notice how the author mixes up real and make-believe things.

> Next he saw a great red mop of hair floating by. It was Ginger's. He grabbed it and hung on. He thought his arm would break, so hard did the rushing water try to tug Ginger away.

Could a small boy really rescue someone from the huge waves by the hair? You know he couldn't. But Tim's unbelievable act makes him a bigger hero and makes the story more fun.

As you read "The Sea of Gold," you may be confused by a strange event. If you are, don't be alarmed. Just try using the following tips:

- Stop and ask yourself: Is the author mixing up real and make-believe?
- Believe the make-believe while you read, and enjoy the story!

Understanding What You Read

DISCUSSING THE LESSON

Review the main points of the lesson.

Check students' understanding of the strategy with these questions.

Page 118   Why might an author mix real and make-believe events in the same story? (possible responses: to make a story more interesting, to make you laugh, to make you notice something special)

Page 119   What two things can you do when you become confused while reading a story? (You can stop and think if the author is mixing real and make-believe events. Then believe the make-believe parts of the story while you read.)

WRAP-UP

Direct students to the next selection.

Explain to students that the author of the next selection, "The Sea of Gold," weaves real and make-believe events into her story about the adventures of a man named Hikoichi (hē ko′ē chē). Remind students to use what they learned in this lesson to help them if they become confused or surprised by events in the story.

TEACHER CHOICE

	Teaching Sequence	Trade Books and Resources	Meeting Individual Needs	Integrated Language Arts / Cross Curriculum
The Bridge Pages 206–207	**Maintain** Story Elements: Setting	• Teaching Chart 28 • Workbook 52 • Skills Practice 46		
PART 1 **Vocabulary Strategies** Pages 208–209	**Develop Concepts** Semantic Mapping **Teach Vocabulary** STORY CRITICAL WORDS: **aboard,** anchor, bunk, **fisherman,** prepare, **reward** (Tested words are boldfaced.)	• Teaching Chart 29 • Workbook 53 • Skills Practice 47	**SUPPORT WORDS:** deserve, echo, familiar, glitter, kindness, laden, morsel, sparkle • Skills Practice 48 **CHARACTER/SETTING WORD:** Hikoichi	**WRITING/SPEAKING ACTIVITY:** Use new vocabulary to tell about a day aboard a fishing boat. • Spelling Connection 45
PART 2 **Reading & Responding** Pages 210–221	**Build Background** **Develop a Purpose for Reading** **Guide the Reading Process** **Selection Follow-Up**	• Reader's Journal 44–47 • Workbook 54 **I↔T KIT** Singing a French Folk Song **READING EVERY DAY** *Perfect Crane,* by A. Laurin *Stina,* by L. Anderson *Sumi's Special Happening,* by Y. Uchida	**EXTRA HELP:** Using a Story Map to Summarize **ACHIEVING ENGLISH PROFICIENCY:** Recognizing Story Language • Achieving English Proficiency Master 13	**Language Arts Connections** **WRITING TO LEARN:** Write thought links. • Writing Master 8 **SPEAKING/LISTENING:** Role-playing Scenes at a Fish Market; Creating Collages **WRITING:** Making a Story Map; Creating Character Charts; Describing a Story Setting; Writing About the Ocean Floor • Language Arts Master 7
PART 3 **Selection Support** Pages 222–229	**Introduce** Suffixes *-able, -ible* (Tested) Title Page, Copyright Page, Table of Contents (Tested)	• Teaching Charts 30–31 • Workbook 55–56 • Skills Practice 49–50	• Reteaching Masters 1–4 (Suffixes) • Reteaching Masters 1–4 (Book Parts) • Challenge Master 7–8 • Achieving English Proficiency Master 14 **Practice** • Teaching Chart 32 • Workbook 57 • Skills Practice 51 Suffix *-ness* (Tested) **Maintain** • Skills Practice 52 Inference	**Curriculum Connections** **SCIENCE:** Researching Nutritional Value of Fish **SOCIAL STUDIES:** Researching Japanese Fishing Villages • Curriculum Connection Master 7 **HUMANITIES:** Telling Folk Tales **ART:** Creating a Fishing Boat Collage

The Sea of Gold

adapted by Yoshiko Uchida

SUMMARY *Hikoichi is a gentle young man who lives on a small island where everyone is a fisherman. However, because he is slow, Hikoichi takes a job as a cook on a fishing boat instead of becoming a fisherman. For many years, Hikoichi works on the boat, calling to the fish each evening, inviting them to eat. The crew members laugh at his actions. Hikoichi's kindness to the fish is finally rewarded when he unexpectedly receives a treasure from the sea—a bucket of "sand" that really is gold. Although he becomes rich and stops working, Hikoichi continues to feed the fish.*

The Bridge

SKILL TRACE: STORY ELEMENTS							
Introduction	Practice	Test	Reteach	Maintain			
TE 16	32	138	157	159	206	294	326	558

LITERATURE

Teaching Story Elements: Setting

OBJECTIVE   Recognizing story setting.

1. WARM-UP

Use a known passage to discuss a story's setting orally.

Tell students they will listen to a passage from the previous story, "Tim to the Rescue." Have them listen and think about what words are clues to where and when the story takes place.

> **Tim longed to go to sea with the captain, and he begged his mother and father to let him go. . . . They agreed, but said that he must promise to work at his books in his spare time. Captain McFee was pleased. He would take Tim as second ship's boy.**

Discuss identifying a story's setting.

Reread the passage. Have students tell where the story takes place. *(at sea)* Then ask them what clues in the passage helped them to decide. *(Tim wanted to go to sea with the captain. Captain McFee took Tim as second ship's boy.)* Then have students tell what clues in the passage might help them decide when the story takes place. *(A young boy leaving to work on a ship at sea suggests the story took place long ago when children did such things.)*

State the objective.

Tell students they will review how to identify the setting of a story using clues in the story and in the pictures.

2. TEACH

Explain why identifying the setting of a story is important.

Understanding the setting of a story helps readers to picture in their minds a time and place. It also helps them know more about what is happening to the characters and why.

Present a strategy for identifying the setting of a story.

Explain that there is a strategy students can use to help them figure out the setting of a story. Look for clues in the story to see how the people talk, what words are used to describe a place, and if any dates or seasons are mentioned. Point out that a story may be set in a real place or in a make-believe land. A story may also happen in the present [today], in the past [long ago], or in the future.

TEACHING CHART 28: STORY ELEMENTS

1. Tim was sitting in the galley with Old Joe. He was terribly worried, thinking how cold and hungry Ginger must be up there in the great gale. (below deck)
2. In a few days the sun came out, the sea was calm, and the weather became warm and fine. Tim and Ginger were back at their usual jobs and the crew were busy hanging out their clothes to dry. (on deck)
3. After a long and happy voyage, the ship went back to port. Tim's mother and father were on the dock to meet him. (on land)

Model the strategy.   Read the first passage on the Teaching Chart and identify clues to the setting of this part of the story. *(The words* galley *and* up there *show that Tim is below deck in the ship's kitchen.)*

3. GUIDED PRACTICE

Check for understanding.   Before going on, have students explain what the setting of a story is and how to identify it. *(the time and place; look for clues to where the characters are, what they are wearing and doing, and what time period and season it is)*

Guide students in using the strategy.   Have students use the strategy to determine the settings of the remaining paragraphs on the chart.

4. WRAP-UP

Summarize instruction.   Review why it is important to identify the setting of a story. *(Knowing the setting of a story makes it easier to picture where and when the story takes place and to understand the characters and what happens to them.)*

Provide independent practice.   Options for independent practice are shown in the Resource Center below.

5. APPLICATION

Students will recognize elements of a story as they read "The Sea of Gold." The symbol ✔ marks specific questions and activities that apply this skill.

Workbook page 52

LITERATURE

NAME _____

Story Elements

REMEMBER: To help you understand stories, look for clues and details that tell about the setting of a story.

A. Read the sentences from "Tim to the Rescue" and answer the questions.

1. It was stormy weather, and Tim was looking out the window and wishing that he were on some ship tossing about among the waves.

   a. Where does this part of the story take place? <u>Tim's house by the sea</u>

   b. What words help you form a picture in your mind? <u>stormy weather, window, ship tossing, waves</u>

2. But when the weather was good and he had no work to do, he would sit on deck in some sunny spot and study hard.

   a. When does this part of the story take place? <u>during a sunny day</u>

   b. What words help you form a picture in your mind? <u>on deck, weather was good, sunny spot</u>

3. In a few days the sun came out, the sea was calm, and the weather became warm and fine. Tim and Ginger were back at their usual jobs and the crew was busy hanging out their clothes to dry.

   a. Where does this part of the story take place? <u>on the ship</u>

   b. What words help you form a picture in your mind? <u>sun came out, sea calm, weather warm and fine, crew hanging clothes</u>

B. On separate paper, use your own words to tell about the setting in the first example in Part A. See Teacher Notes.

52 "The Sea of Gold"   Story Elements

RESOURCE CENTER

◀ **Workbook page 52** is intended for use by all students.

Skills Practice 46 ▶ may be assigned for additional practice.

Workbook reuse option: Have students underline all the words in the sentences from "Tim to the Rescue" in Part A that tell where that part of the story took place.

Skills Practice 46

NAME _____

   SKILLS PRACTICE   46

Story Elements

The **setting** tells you *when* and *where* a story takes place. Look for clues that help you understand the setting. Picture the setting as you read. You'll understand and enjoy the story more if you do.

Read each paragraph and answer the questions about the setting.

Kay stopped walking and looked around. She only saw hills of sand. She called out but heard only the sound of the wind. She listened carefully. She thought she heard the waves crashing on the shore, but she wasn't sure. It was hard to tell which direction the sound came from. The sun was right overhead. It was the hottest part of the day. Kay was lost and worried. The space taxi would come soon. Kay didn't want to miss it.

1. Does the story take place in the early morning, in the middle of the day, or late in the afternoon? <u>in the middle of the day</u>

2. Write the clues from the story that help you know the setting. <u>hills of sand; waves crashing; sun overhead</u>

3. What do you picture in your mind? <u>Answers may vary. A girl surrounded by sand dunes. The sun is overhead. She looks worried and/or confused.</u>

Otis sat on the dock looking at the ships in the harbor. He counted five large sailing ships. There were lots of small boats, too. His father's ship was due in today. Otis couldn't wait to see him. He had sailed to China and had been gone a long time. In three hours it would be getting dark. Otis hoped to see the sails of his father's ship before then.

4. What time of day does the story take place? <u>afternoon</u>

5. Write the clues from the story that help you know the setting. <u>dock; ships in harbor; dark in three hours</u>

46   LEVEL 8   "The Sea of Gold"

Vocabulary Strategies

Developing Concepts

Build on prior knowledge of fishing boats with a semantic map.

Make a semantic map about things to see and do on a fishing boat as a starting point for teaching vocabulary. Tell students they are going to read a story that takes place on a fishing boat. Point out that fishing boats are often at sea for days or weeks and that everyone on board has a job to do. Then ask students to name things they might see at sea, jobs they might do, places they might be, and things they might use while on a fishing boat. List responses under the appropriate headings. Point out that the cook has an important job.

Things at Sea
(fish)
(boats)
(sea birds)

Jobs to Do
(cook food)
(catch/clean fish)
(repair engine/sail)

FISHING BOAT

Places to Be
(galley)
(on deck)
(cabin)

Things to Use
(fishing nets)
(pots and pans)
(ropes)

Teaching Vocabulary

Discuss meanings of Story Critical words.

Read each context sentence on the Teaching Chart and identify the new word. Then use the questions below to help students understand each word.

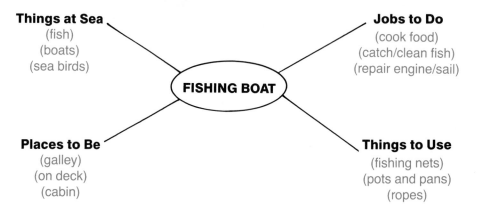

29

TEACHING CHART 29: VOCABULARY

1. **fishermen** (men who fish)
   Fishermen catch fish to earn their living.
2. **anchor** (a heavy object that keeps a boat from drifting)
   We throw the *anchor* into the water to keep the boat from drifting away.
3. **bunk** (a narrow bed)
   The fisherman likes to rest in his *bunk* after fishing.
4. **aboard** (on a boat or ship)
   With a cook *aboard*, the fishermen will not go hungry.
5. **prepare** (to make ready)
   The cook gets up early to *prepare* breakfast.
6. **reward** (something given in return for a good deed)
   A good meal after a hard day's work is a fine *reward*.

fishermen

1. **How can you tell what the word** *fishermen* **means by looking at it?** (The words *fish* and *men* give the idea of people who catch fish.) **Under what heading on the map could the word** *fishermen* **be placed?** *(Jobs to Do)* STRATEGY: COMPOUND WORDS

anchor

2. **For what is an anchor used?** (to keep a boat from drifting too far from one spot in the water) **When a boat is at anchor, it is not being used for work. At what time of day would a fisherman's boat usually be at anchor?** (probably at the end of the work day) STRATEGY: PRIOR KNOWLEDGE

bunk

3. Bunk beds are stacked to save space. Why would it be important to save space on a fishing boat? (Boats are small; room is needed for fishing equipment and for fish.) STRATEGY: DRAWING CONCLUSIONS

aboard

4. The word *aboard* means "on." Besides a boat, what other kinds of transportation can a person be aboard? (plane, bus, subway) STRATEGY: CLASSIFICATION

prepare

5. Which new vocabulary word tells what a cook does to food? (*prepare*) **What might a cook do to prepare food?** (possible answers: clean meat, chop vegetables, mix things, bake, roast or fry foods) STRATEGY: PRIOR KNOWLEDGE

reward

6. A reward is "something given in return for a good deed." How do people usually feel when they do a good deed? (They feel good about what they did.) **Is being kind to someone a good deed?** (Yes, being nice to someone or doing something for someone is a kind thing to do.) STRATEGY: PRIOR KNOWLEDGE

Discuss Support words as needed.

The Glossary of the Student Text includes definitions of the Support words: *familiar, laden, morsel, echo, deserve, glitter, sparkle, kindness.* Be sure to explain the phrase *put out to sea.* (to leave land and travel on the sea)

Introduce Character word as needed.

The selection contains the following Character word: *Hikoichi* (hē-ko´-ē-chē). Pronounce the name for students before they read the selection.

Provide independent practice.

Options for independent practice are shown in the Resource Center below.

WRITING OR SPEAKING ACTIVITY *Remind students of their discussion of fishing boats. Have them use the semantic map to write or speak about a day aboard a fishing boat, using the new vocabulary words.*

Workbook page 53

NAME _____

SELECTION VOCABULARY

Using New Words

A. Read each sentence. Write the word that completes the sentence. Use the clue in parentheses.

| aboard | anchor | bunk |

1. Everyone was ___aboard___ (on the boat) by noon.

2. The sailors had to drop ___anchor___ (a weight that holds the ship in place) before they went ashore.

3. Later the cabin boy went to his ___bunk___ (bed on a ship) to sleep.

B. Write the word that completes each question.

| aboard | fishermen | prepare | reward |

4. Who will ___prepare___ the captain's dinner?

5. Which sailor deserves a ___reward___ ?

6. Are they the ___fishermen___ who caught the giant fish?

7. Are all the sailors ___aboard___ yet?

C. On separate paper, write three orders a captain might give. Use at least two names for the parts of a ship. See Teacher Notes.

Selection Vocabulary   "The Sea of Gold" **53**

RESOURCE CENTER

◀ **Workbook page 53** provides practice with Story Critical words.

Skills Practice 47 ▶ provides additional practice with Story Critical words.

Skills Practice 48 provides practice with Support words.

Spelling Connection Master 45 may be used for spelling instruction with the new vocabulary.

Workbook reuse option: Have students add a question to Part B, using a word from Part A.

Skills Practice 47

NAME _____

SKILLS PRACTICE ◀ 47

Vocabulary: Story Critical Words

A. Study the meaning of each word.

aboard on a boat or ship
anchor a heavy object that keeps a boat from drifting
bunk a narrow hanging bed on a ship
fishermen men who fish
prepare to make ready
reward something given in return for a good deed

B. Draw a line from each phrase to the word that completes it.

1. went _____ the ship — bunk
2. sleep in the _____ — anchor
3. drop the ship's _____ — aboard
4. _____ the meal — reward
5. receive a _____ — prepare

C. Complete the story with the correct vocabulary words.

Captain McTavish had a good crew on his boat. They were salmon
(6.) ___fishermen___. He owned a big boat that he sailed near
Alaska. One bright morning he woke up, stretched, and hopped out of his
(7.) ___bunk___. He was very happy because today the boat
was going into port. After his usual hearty breakfast, he was going to
(8.) ___prepare___ for the trip home. The first thing he and his
crew did was haul the fish nets (9.) ___aboard___. Then they
raised the (10.) ___anchor___ and set sail.

D. One word in each sentence does not make sense. Underline that word. Write the vocabulary word that belongs in its place.

11. Luis received a punishment for finding and returning the man's wallet. ___reward___

12. The coast guard went broad the lost ship. ___aboard___

LEVEL 8   "The Sea of Gold"   Context clues **47**

Reading & Responding

Building Background

Motivate discussion using the poem.

Share the following poem with students and ask them what they think it means. Discuss whether students agree that kindness and love make people happy. Then have students suggest what "little deeds of kindness" might be.

> **Little deeds of kindness, little words of love, Help to make earth happy, like the heaven above.**
> — *From the poem "Little Things" by Julia Carney*

Build background about kindness.

Have students discuss what *kindness* means. Ask them to describe ways they show kindness to friends or family members. Point out that kindness can be shown to animals, too, such as feeding a pet or leaving out food for wild birds. Have volunteers share how they have shown kindness to animals. Then have students discuss rewards for kindness and give examples.

Discuss folk tales.

Tell students that "The Sea of Gold" is a folk tale. Explain that a folk tale is a story that has been passed down through the years by a particular group of people. Anything can happen in a folk tale and good is often rewarded in the end. Tell students that Yoshiko Uchida, the author, often writes folk tales. Have students find and read the Yoshiko Uchida entry in the About the Author section at the back of their texts.

Developing a Purpose for Reading

Option 1
Students set purpose.

ORAL "I EXPECT" STATEMENTS   Remind students of their discussion about kindness. Explain that in the next story a man named Hikoichi is kind to the ocean fish. Have students read the story introduction and look at the illustrations. Then have them suggest how they expect Hikoichi is kind and how they expect his kindness is rewarded.

WRITING ACTIVITY   Have students work individually or in pairs to create written "I expect" sentences. Have students save their lists for later use.

Option 2
Teacher sets purpose.

Have students read the selection to find out how Hikoichi is kind and what he receives as a reward.

Meeting
Individual
Needs

EXTRA HELP   Explain to students that in the next story, a man shows kindness to the fish of the sea and, after many years, his kindness is rewarded. Have students read to find out how the man shows his kindness and how he is rewarded. After reading, have students summarize the major events by completing a story map, Form 1 in the Teacher Resource Kit. Then have them use the completed maps to retell the story in their own words.

ACHIEVING ENGLISH PROFICIENCY   Write on the chalkboard the sentences *There once lived a young man named Hikoichi* and *He lived a long and happy life.* Say the sentences and have the group repeat them with you. Tell students that sentences like those are often used at the beginning and end of make-believe stories. Ask students to share similar expressions from their own language or English, such as *Once upon a time.* Point out that when a story begins with such a phrase, students can expect that it will be a make-believe story. For additional help in story comprehension, use Master 13 in the Teacher Resource Kit.

In this folk tale, everyone laughs at Hikoichi for being kind to the fish in the sea.

The Sea of Gold

adapted by Yoshiko Uchida

On a small island, where almost everyone was a fisherman, there once lived a young man named Hikoichi (hē kō′ ē chē). He was gentle and kind, but he was slow, and there was no one on the whole island who was willing to teach him how to become a fisherman.

"How could we ever make a fisherman out of you?" people would say to him. "You are much too slow to learn anything!"

But Hikoichi wanted very badly to go to work, and he tried hard to find a job. He looked and looked for many months until finally he found work as a cook on one of the fishing boats. He got the job, however, only because no one else wanted it, but Hikoichi didn't mind. He was happy to have any kind of job at last.

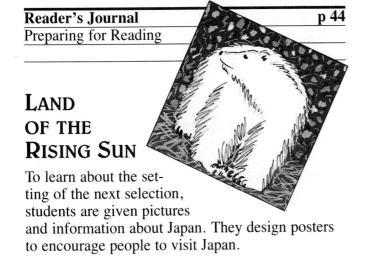

Reader's Journal   **p 44**
Preparing for Reading

LAND OF THE RISING SUN

To learn about the setting of the next selection, students are given pictures and information about Japan. They design posters to encourage people to visit Japan.

GUIDED READING

Page 120 Why might a person's slowness be a reason for not wanting to teach that person how to do something? (Some people do not like to wait for a slow person to study and learn something.) INFER: FEELINGS/ATTITUDES

✔ **Pages 120–121 Besides the word *island*, what other clues tell you that the story takes place near water?** (Almost everyone is a fisherman; there are boats in the picture.) INFER: LOCATION

HIGHLIGHTING LITERATURE

Page 120 Tell students that folk tales are stories that were told aloud long before anyone wrote them down in books. Have students imagine how the first part of this story would sound if told aloud by a storyteller. Ask them to think about how the storyteller's voice would rise and fall and what words he or she would say with more expression. Have students read the first two paragraphs aloud to show the use of expression.

✔ Skill from The Bridge applied through this question.

211

Hikoichi was very careful with the food he cooked, and he tried not to waste even a single grain of rice. In fact, he hated to throw away any of the leftovers, and he stored them carefully in the galley. On the small, crowded fishing boat, however, there was no room for keeping useless things. Every bit of extra space was needed to store the catch, for the more fish they took back to the island, the more money they would all make. When the men discovered that Hikoichi was saving the leftovers, they spoke to him harshly.

"Don't use our galley space for storing garbage!" they shouted. "Throw it into the sea!"

"What a terrible waste of good food," Hikoichi thought, but he had to do as he was told. He gathered up all the leftovers he had stored and took them up on deck.

"If I must throw this into the sea," he said to himself, "I will make sure the fish have a good feast. After all, if it were not for the fish, we wouldn't be able to make a living." And so, as he threw the leftovers into the water, he called out, "Here, fish, here, good fish, have yourselves a splendid dinner!"

From that day, Hikoichi always called to the fish before he threw his leftovers into the sea. "Come along," he would call. "Enjoy some rice from my galley!" And he continued talking to them until they had eaten every morsel he tossed overboard.

The fishermen laughed when they heard him. They said, "Maybe someday the fish will answer you and tell you how much they enjoyed your dinner."

But Hikoichi didn't pay any attention to the fishermen. He silently gathered all the scraps from the table and continued to toss them out to the fish at the end of the day. Each time he did, he called to the fish as though they were his best friends, and his gentle voice echoed far out over the dancing waves of the sea.

GUIDED READING

Page 122   Why are the fishermen angry at Hikoichi for storing the leftovers? (The leftovers take up too much room. They need the space to store the fish they catch.) RECALL: CAUSE/EFFECT

Page 122   How does Hikoichi make himself feel better about throwing the leftovers into the sea? (He comes up with the idea that instead of wasting the leftovers he will be feeding the fish.) RECALL: CHARACTER

Page 123   Why do the fishermen think Hikoichi's talking to the fish is funny? (They probably think that a man talking to animals that do not understand is silly.) SYNTHESIZE: DRAWING CONCLUSIONS

Page 123   What do Hikoichi's actions after the fishermen laugh tell you about him? (He does not let the fishermen's teasing bother him. He wants to do the right thing even though the fishermen laugh.) INFER: CHARACTER

✔ **Informal Assessment Opportunity:** SELF-MONITORING

STRATEGIC READING

✔ **Page 123**   Have students stop reading at the end of the page and summarize what has happened up to this point. Discuss why Hikoichi is kind to the fish. (to not waste food; because he is a kind and gentle person; because "if it were not for the fish, we wouldn't be able to make a living") Ask students in what way Hikoichi's kindness may have been rewarded. (in the happiness he gets from feeding the fish) Then have students predict whether there will be another reward and what it might be. Point out to students that summarizing and predicting is one way for them to check on how well they understand the story. Suggest to students who have trouble summarizing that they reread any parts of the story they do not understand or do not remember.
METACOGNITION: SUMMARIZING AND PREDICTING

Many years went by until Hikoichi was no longer a young man. He continued to cook for the men on his fishing boat, however, and he still fed and talked to the fish every evening.

One day, the fishing boat put far out to sea to find bigger fish. It sailed for three days and three nights, going farther and farther away from the small island. On the third night, they were still far out at sea when they dropped <u>anchor</u>. It was a quiet star-filled night with a full moon glowing high in the sky. The men were tired from the day's work and not long after dinner, they were all sound asleep.

Hikoichi, however, still had much to do. He scrubbed the pots, cleaned up the galley and washed the rice for breakfast. When he had finished, he gathered all the leftovers in a basket and went up on deck.

"Gather around, good fish," he called as always. "Enjoy your dinner."

He emptied his basket and stayed to watch the fish eat up his food. Then, he went to his <u>bunk</u> to <u>prepare</u> for bed, but somehow the boat felt very strange. It had stopped rolling. In fact, it was not moving at all and felt as though it were standing on dry land.

"That's odd," Hikoichi thought, and he ran up on deck to see what had happened. He leaned over the railing and looked out.

"What!" he shouted. "The ocean is gone!"

And indeed it had disappeared. There was not a single drop of water anywhere. As far as Hikoichi could see, there was nothing but miles and miles of sand. It was as though the boat were standing in the middle of a huge desert of shimmering sand.

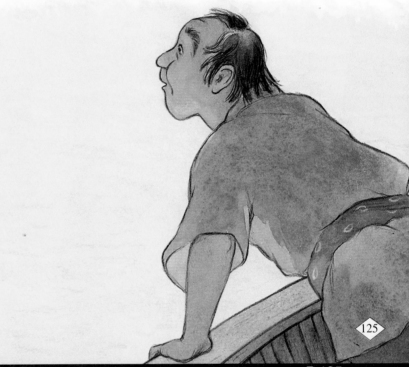

GUIDED READING

✔ **Page 124   How much time has passed in the story?** (many years) **How do you know?** (from the words "many years went by")   INFER: TIME

Page 124   Why does the fishing boat go far out to sea? (to find bigger fish)   RECALL: CAUSE/EFFECT

Page 124   Why is Hikoichi the last person still awake on the ship? (The fishermen are tired and go to sleep after dinner. Hikoichi stays up to clean the galley, prepare the rice for breakfast, and feed the fish.) RECALL: CAUSE/EFFECT

Page 124   How does Hikoichi know that something strange has happened to the boat? (He feels that it has stopped rolling.)   RECALL: CAUSE/EFFECT

Page 125   What do you think has happened when Hikoichi shouts that the ocean is gone? (Possible answers: Hikoichi is dreaming; Hikoichi thinks he sees something that is not happening; something magical has happened.)   SYNTHESIZE: DRAWING CONCLUSIONS

✔ Skill from The Bridge applied through this question.

STRATEGIC READING

Page 125   Have students read to the end of the page. Invite them to describe Hikoichi's strange experience. (The ocean disappears and the ship is standing in a huge desert.) Ask students to tell whether or not this surprised them. (Some students may have been surprised since the story was very realistic up to this point.) Remind students that authors sometimes choose to mix real and make-believe events to make a story more interesting. Believing the make-believe while they read the story can help students understand the story.   APPLICATION: STRATEGY FOR READING

Hikoichi could not believe his eyes. He simply had to get off the boat to see if they really were standing on dry land. Slowly, he lowered himself down a rope ladder and reached the sand below. Carefully, he took a step and felt his foot crunch on something. No, it wasn't water. It really was sand after all. Hikoichi blinked as he looked around, for under the light of the moon, the sand glittered and sparkled like a beach of gold. He scooped up a handful and watched it glisten as it slid through his fingers.

"Why, this is beautiful," Hikoichi thought, and his heart sang with joy at the sight. "I must save some of this sand so I can remember this wonderful night forever." He hurried back onto the boat for a bucket, filled it with sparkling sand and then carried it <u>aboard</u> and hid it carefully beneath his bunk. He looked around at the other men, but they were all sound asleep. Not one seemed to have noticed that the boat was standing still. Hikoichi slipped quietly into his bunk, and soon he too was sound asleep.

The next morning Hikoichi was the first to wake up. He remembered the amazing happening of the night before, and he leaped out of bed, ready to call the other men to see the strange sight. But as he got dressed, he felt the familiar rocking of the boat. He hurried up on deck and he saw that once again they were out in the middle of the ocean with waves all about them. Hikoichi shook his head, but now he could no longer keep it all to himself. As soon as the other men came up on deck, he told his story.

"It's true," he cried as he saw wide grins appear on the men's faces. "The ocean was gone and for miles and miles there was nothing but sand. It glittered and sparkled under the full moon and it was as though we were sailing on a sea of golden sand!"

GUIDED READING

✔ **Page 126 From what you see in the picture and read in the story, where is Hikoichi?** (He is off the boat and kneeling on the sand at the bottom of the ocean.) RECALL: SETTING

Page 126 From looking at Hikoichi's face and reading the description of what he is doing and seeing, what do you think Hikoichi has in his hands? (gold that is as fine as sand) INFER: THINGS

Page 127 Why does Hikoichi fill a bucket with the sand? (He thinks the sight is so beautiful he wants to remember it forever.) RECALL: CAUSE/EFFECT

Page 127 Do you think the fishermen will believe Hikoichi's story? Why or why not? (No; the boat is now sailing normally; no one else saw what Hikoichi did; the fishermen have laughed at Hikoichi in the past.) SYNTHESIZE: DRAWING CONCLUSIONS

HIGHLIGHTING LITERATURE

Pages 123, 127 In this selection, the author's use of figurative language helps the reader feel and experience the story. For example, on page 123, the author describes "the dancing waves of the sea." Ask students to close their eyes and picture "dancing waves." Then have them look through the selection and discover other examples of figurative language, paying particular attention to the ones that highlight the story setting. You might write some suggestions on the chalkboard. ("His heart sang for joy"; "as though we were sailing on a sea of golden sand"; "quiet, star-filled night")

✔ Skill from **The Bridge** applied through this question.

214

The men roared with laughter. "Hikoichi, you were surely dreaming," they said. "Now put away your daydreams and fix us some breakfast."

"No, no, I wasn't dreaming," Hikoichi cried. "I climbed down the ladder and I walked on the sand. I picked it up and felt it slip through my fingers. It wasn't a dream. It really wasn't."

It was then that Hikoichi remembered his bucket. "Wait! Come with me and I can prove it," he said, and he led the men down to his bunk. Then, getting down on his hands and knees, he carefully pulled out his bucket of sand. "There," he said proudly, "I scooped this up when I went down and walked on the sand. Now do you believe me?"

The men suddenly stopped laughing. "This isn't sand," they said, reaching out to feel it. "It's gold! It's a bucket full of pure gold!"

"Why didn't you get more?" one of the men shouted.

"You've got to give some of it to us," another added.

"We share our fish with you. You must share your gold with us," said still another.

Soon all the men were yelling and shouting and pushing to get their hands on Hikoichi's bucket of gold.

Then the oldest of the fishermen spoke up. "Stop it! Stop it!" he called out. "This gold doesn't belong to any of you. It belongs to Hikoichi."

He reminded the men how Hikoichi had fed the fish of the sea for so many years as though they were his own children.

"Now the King of the Sea has given Hikoichi a reward for his kindness to the fish," he explained. And turning to Hikoichi, he added, "You are gentle and kind and good. This gift from the Kingdom of the Sea is your reward. Take all the gold and keep it, for it belongs only to you."

GUIDED READING

Page 128   Do the fishermen believe Hikoichi's story? What do they do? (No; they roar with laughter.)   INFER: FEELINGS/ATTITUDES

Page 128   How do the fishermen's reactions to Hikoichi's story change after they see what is in the bucket? (When they see that the sand is really gold, they stop laughing. They become greedy and want the gold.)   INFER: FEELINGS/ATTITUDES

Page 129   Why does the oldest fisherman say it is the King of the Sea that gave the gold to Hikoichi? (Possible answers: the gold has come to Hikoichi in a magical way; Hikoichi has always been kind to the fish, which are a part of the Kingdom of the Sea: the fishermen believe in the King of the Sea.)   SYNTHESIZE: DRAWING CONCLUSIONS

Page 129   Why does Hikoichi deserve his reward? (He is gentle, kind, and good, especially to the fish he has been feeding for years.)   RECALL: CAUSE/EFFECT

STRATEGIC READING

Page 128   Have students tell whether a bucket of sand really could turn to gold. (not in real life, only in make-believe) Help students understand that the author wanted to use a magical event to thank Hikoichi for his goodness. The make-believe sets Hikoichi apart from the other characters, so that they, and we learn to appreciate him. Make-believe is often used in folk tales to give a "message." Encourage students to tell whether the make-believe makes the story more enjoyable or fun to read. (Students may suggest that unexpected or unusual events make stories more interesting.)
APPLICATION: STRATEGY FOR READING

215

The shouting, pushing fishermen suddenly became silent and thoughtful, for they knew the old fisherman was right. They were ashamed of having laughed at Hikoichi year after year, and they knew that he truly deserved this fine reward.

Without another word the men went back to work. They completed their catch that day and the heavily laden boat returned once more to the little island.

The next time the boat put out to sea, Hikoichi was no longer aboard, for now he had enough gold to leave his job forever. He built himself a beautiful new house, and he even had a small boat of his own so he could still sail out to sea and feed the fish. He used his treasure from the sea wisely and well, and he lived a long and happy life.

◆ LIBRARY LINK ◆

If you enjoyed this story by Yoshiko Uchida, you might enjoy reading other books written by the author. A few titles are The Best Bad Thing *and* Sumi's Special Happening.

Reader's Response

What did you think of Hikoichi? Would you like him to be your friend? Why?

See next page for suggested answers.

SELECTION FOLLOW-UP

The Sea of Gold

 ## Thinking It Over

1. Why did Hikoichi feed the fish?
2. What unusual event took place one night?
3. What made Hikoichi so happy on that special night?
4. Why do you think the King of the Sea waited until late at night to do his magic? How did you get your answer?
5. How did the reward affect Hikoichi's life? What was the same? What was different?

Writing to Learn

THINK AND CONNECT In Hikoichi's story, one thing leads to another. Read the first "thought link" below. Then copy and finish the second "thought link."

Because he fed the fish,   he found sand of pure gold.

Because he had gold,

WRITE Make up your own "thought link" about a happy day you remember. In the first link write "Because ___," and in the second link write "I had a happy day." Finish the first link with your own words.

GUIDED READING

Page 130 How does the reward change Hikoichi? How does he stay the same? (Hikoichi is able to leave the boat and build a beautiful new house. He is still kind and gentle, and he still feeds the fish.) ANALYZE: CHARACTER

RETURNING TO THE READING PURPOSE

OPTION 1 If students set the purpose, return to the "I expect" sentences they generated about Hikoichi. Discuss whether their expectations were fulfilled. Talk about how Hikoichi's kindness was rewarded. Be sure students understand that Hikoichi's enjoyment in helping the fish was an important reward.

OPTION 2 If you set the purpose for reading, ask students why Hikoichi was kind to the fish. (They help the fishermen make a living; he is gentle and kind; the fish are hungry.) As students what Hikoichi's reward was besides gold. ("Kindness is its own reward"; he got happiness from helping the fish.)

Reader's Journal   **p 45**
Responding to Reading

THAT'S HIKOICHI!

Students write how they think the fishermen would have described Hikoichi at the beginning of the story and then at the end.

216

SELECTION FOLLOW-UP

The Sea of Gold

THINKING IT OVER

1. **Why did Hikoichi feed the fish?** (Possible answers: Hikoichi did not want to waste the leftover food; it was Hikoichi's way of thanking the fish for giving the fishermen a living.)   RECALL: CAUSE/EFFECT

2. **What unusual event took place one night?** (One night the ocean disappeared. There were miles of sand all around the boat.)   RECALL: DETAILS

✔ 3. **What made Hikoichi so happy on that special night?** (Hikoichi was so happy because the sand sparkling in the moonlight was beautiful; the fact that the ocean had disappeared and the scene was so beautiful seemed magical — he would always remember it. Students should understand that Hikoichi's happiness was not due to the fact that the sand was gold, for he did not realize that this was so.)   INFER: FEELINGS/ATTITUDES

4. **Why do you think the King of the Sea waited until late at night to do his magic? How did you get your answer?** (Students will probably say that the King of the Sea meant the reward to be for Hikoichi alone; so he waited until all the fishermen were asleep to change the ocean into a beach of gold. They will reach their answer by reviewing story events.) INFER: DRAWING CONCLUSIONS; METACOGNITION

5. **How did the reward affect Hikoichi's life? What was the same? What was different?** (What was different was that Hikoichi left his job as a cook; he built himself a house and bought a boat. What was the same was that Hikoichi continued to feed the fish.) COMPARISON

WRITING TO LEARN

Use Writing Master 8, which duplicates this diagram.

THINK AND CONNECT   In Hikoichi's story, one thing leads to another. **Read the first "thought link" below. Then copy and finish the second "thought link."** (Help students complete the "thought link." Possible answers are shown below.)

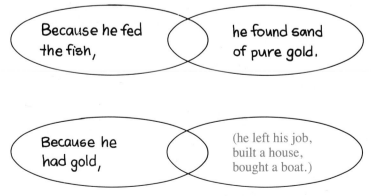

Because he fed the fish,   he found sand of pure gold.

Because he had gold,   (he left his job, built a house, bought a boat.)

Extend comprehension through writing.

WRITE   **Make up your own "thought link" about a happy day you remember. In the first link write "Because," and in the second link write "I had a happy day." Finish the first link with your own words.** (Have students share their "thought links.")

✔ Informal Assessment Opportunity: GENERALIZING

More Ideas for Selection Follow-Up

CRITICAL AND CREATIVE THINKING QUESTIONS

Encourage a variety of responses and points of view.

Use these open-ended questions to encourage critical and creative thinking about the selection.

1. Do you think Hikoichi would have continued to be good and kind even if the King of the Sea had not rewarded him for being kind to the fish?

2. What about this story lets you know that it is a folk tale?

3. If you received a treasure as a reward for your kind deeds, what would you do with it?

REREADING ORALLY

Have students reread for a specific purpose.

Remind students that one of the reasons Hikoichi fed the fish was because he enjoyed helping them. Have students choose, then reread aloud, the parts of the story that show that Hikoichi was rewarded for feeding the fish by the pleasure it gave him. Provide students time to rehearse the section silently before reading aloud. *(page 123: "... he continued talking to them ...";* *" ... he called to the fish as though they were his best friends, and his gentle voice ..."; page 124: "He emptied his basket and stayed to watch the fish eat up his food.")* Remind students to use expression in their voices to make their reading more interesting.

SELECTION COMPREHENSION

Provide comprehension check.

A Workbook page to check comprehension is shown in the Resource Center below. It may be used for informal assessment.

Workbook page 54

The Sea of Gold

A. Complete the summary of "The Sea of Gold."
Accept reasonable variations.

The hero of this story was ___Hikoichi___, who was a kind and gentle man. Hikoichi lived on a small island in Japan, and most of the story took place on the ___boat___ where Hikoichi worked.

Hikoichi was a cook on a fishing boat. When the men on the boat told him not to save the leftover food, he began to ___throw it in the water to feed the fish___.

Whenever he did this he called to the fish and spoke gently to them.

One night Hikoichi was the only one awake. The boat felt as though ___it was on dry land___. Hikoichi found that the ocean was gone. In order to remember the wonderful sight of the glittering sand, Hikoichi ___took a bucket back to the boat___.

The next morning when Hikoichi told his story to the other men, none of them believed him until he showed them ___the bucket of sand___. Hikoichi's sand was really ___gold___. All the fishermen began to fight over the gold. Finally the oldest fisherman said the gold was a reward for Hikoichi from the King of the Sea because he had been ___so kind to the fish___. The men realized the old fisherman was right.

Hikoichi used his treasure ___wisely and well___. Though he didn't work on the fishing boat anymore, he still continued to ___feed the fish___.

B. On separate paper, write three sentences of your own telling how you could be kind and gentle to animals, as Hikoichi was to the fish. See Teacher Notes.

54 "The Sea of Gold"   Selection Comprehension

RESOURCE CENTER

◀ **Workbook page 54** is intended for use by all students.

Writing Master 8 duplicates the Writing to Learn diagram.

I•T Kit Activity

Audio: "A Little Ship"

When their rations run dry, the sailors in this humorous French folk song prepare to navigate their way through a hungry morning. A hundred thousand flying fish jump on board, providing a tasty *petit déjeuner,* or breakfast. Students sing along. (See Activity Guide.)

CONTEMPORARY MUSIC

LANGUAGE ARTS CONNECTIONS

CRITICAL THINKING: MAPPING A STORY

Have students create story maps of "The Sea of Gold."
Remind students that all stories have a beginning, a middle, and an end. On the chalkboard write the following story map headings:

Title:	Author:	
Beginning	**Middle**	**End**
Setting:	Problem:	Resolution:
Characters:	Event 1:	
	Event 2:	
	Event 3:	
	Event 4:	

   Have students copy the story map on paper and fill in each part for "The Sea of Gold." After students have finished, ask them to share their maps.   WRITING

ACTING OUT A FISH MARKET SCENE

Have students role-play people in a fish market.
Tell students that fishermen often sell their fish to the owner of a fish market, who in turn sells it to customers. Divide the class into four groups: fishermen, fish market owners, fish salespeople, customers. Have two or three members from each group take turns acting out their parts together. Present students with the following ideas to help them: The fishermen try to sell different kinds of fish—tuna, salmon, sole, cod, lobster, crabs, and shark—for the best price, explaining why their fish is the freshest. The market owners tell the fishermen what kind of fish they will buy and why. The salespeople tell customers why they should buy the fish. Customers explain what they are looking for. Have each group prepare a short presentation. Afterwards, have the class vote on which fish to buy and tell why.   WHOLE CLASS ENRICHMENT

CREATING CHARACTER CHARTS

Explain the uses of a character chart.

Point out to students that a character chart is a way to look more closely at a character. Explain that knowing a character will help them better understand the character and what happens in a story.

Guide students in making character charts.

Have students draw pictures of Hikoichi or write his name on paper and circle it. Have them list, in one column, words that describe Hikoichi's character. *(gentle, kind, friendly, generous, slow)* In a second column, have students write details from the story that illustrate a particular character trait. Allow students to review the story in their texts if they wish. When students have finished, display the charts and have students compare them. WRITING

DESCRIBING A STORY SETTING

Discuss setting words.

Point out to students that in order to appreciate this selection fully they need to know as much as possible about the story setting: a fishing boat out on the open sea. Have students look through the selection and pick out the words they feel are most important for fully appreciating the setting and atmosphere on board a fishing boat in the ocean. *(possible words: galley, bunk, anchor, deck, crowded, rolling, ocean)* List these words on the chalkboard.

Have students write paragraphs about Hikoichi's fishing boat.

Review with students the meaning of each of the words listed on the board. Then tell students to write paragraphs describing the fishing boat. Tell students to use the words listed on the board in their paragraphs. WRITING

CREATING COLLAGES

Discuss collages.

Explain that a collage is a visual display of words and pictures to show an idea or feeling. The words and pictures are usually cut out and pasted together, sometimes overlapping, to make a larger picture.

Have students create collages about the sea.

Have students work in pairs to create collages about the sea. Students can cut out pictures and words from old magazines or draw some and cut them out. Encourage students to find pictures that suggest feeling, color, and the idea that the sea can be calm or rough—it can be a friend or enemy. When students show their collages, encourage viewers to ask questions about the words and pictures. SHARED LEARNING: SPEAKING

WRITING ABOUT THE OCEAN FLOOR

Have students write descriptions of the ocean floor.

Explain to students that authors help readers visualize scenes by using words that appeal to their senses of sight, sound, smell, taste, and touch. Remind them of the description of Hikoichi on the ocean floor. (". . . the sand glittered and sparkled like a beach of gold.") Have students suggest other words that would help readers "see" the ocean floor.

Tell students to write four sentences describing what Hikoichi saw. Suggest that before writing they list words that will help others visualize the ocean floor. Invite students to read their sentences aloud and discuss which ones more clearly help them picture the scene. **Language Arts Master 7** can be used with this activity.   CHALLENGE: WRITING

READING EVERY DAY

Like Hikoichi in "The Sea of Gold," a character in each of the following stories unexpectedly receives an unusual and treasured gift.

Perfect Crane by Anne Laurin. Harper & Row, © 1981. The perfect crane that Gami creates from folded paper and magically brings to life gives him the gift of joy and friendship and allays his loneliness. 〰

Stina by Lena Anderson. Greenwillow Books, © 1989. On a stormy night, the sea presents Stina with a gift that she uses creatively.   EASIER TO READ

Sumi's Special Happening by Yoshiko Uchida. Scribner's, © 1966. The gift Sumi gives to Ojii Chan for his ninety-ninth birthday brings joy to them both.
〰 **A World of Books** Classroom Libraries selection

Reader's Journal   **pp 46, 47**
Extending Reading

LESS IS MORE

Students read a haiku poem and an explanation about writing haiku. They try their hand at writing a haiku poem in response to provided art.

Selection Support

WORD STUDY

Suffixes -able, -ible

OBJECTIVE   Using structural analysis to determine word meaning.

1. WARM-UP

Use familiar content to present suffixes.

Write the following sentences on the chalkboard and have them read aloud.

1. A boat is a <u>movable</u> object.

2. Being a cook on a boat was a <u>sensible</u> job for Hikoichi.

Ask students what the underlined word in each sentence means. (movable — *"able to be moved"*; sensible — *"made sense"*) Write the base words *move* and *sense* and point out the spelling change when *-able* or *-ible* is added to some words.

Discuss suffixes -able, -ible.

Explain to students that the suffixes *-able* and *-ible* change the meaning of the base word. The suffixes *-able* and *-ible* both mean "able to" or "can be." These suffixes help words describe. By using the meaning of the base word plus the meaning of *-able* or *-ible,* readers can figure out new words.

State the objective.

Tell students they will learn about the suffixes *-able* and *-ible* and how to use these suffixes to help them figure out the meanings of words.

2. TEACH

Explain why understanding the meanings of suffixes is important.

Knowing the meanings of suffixes and how they change the uses of base words in sentences helps readers figure out the meanings of words and form new words to use in their own writing.

Present a strategy for using suffixes to determine word meanings.

Explain that there is a strategy students can use to help them figure out word meanings using the suffix *-able* or *-ible*. Look for the base word in the unfamiliar word. Use the meaning of the base word plus the meaning of *-able* or *-ible,* which is "able to" or "can be," to figure out the meaning of the whole word.

TEACHING CHART 30: SUFFIXES -ABLE, -IBLE   **30**

1. The fishermen think Hikoichi's feeding the fish is <u>laughable</u>.
2. Catching fish is the <u>sensible</u> thing to do, not feeding fish.
3. All extra <u>usable</u> space on the boat is for storing fish.
4. Hikoichi's story about a disappearing ocean is not <u>believable</u>.

Model the strategy.

Read the first sentence on the Teaching Chart. Underline the word *laughable* and explain to students that you can break the word into the base word *laugh* and the suffix *-able*. Tell students that by using the meanings of both the base word and the suffix, you know the word means "able to be laughed at."

3. GUIDED PRACTICE

Check for understanding.
Before going on, have students review what happens when the suffix *-able* or *-ible* is added to the end of a base word. (*It changes the meaning of the base word and the way it is used in a sentence.*) Then ask students to tell what the suffix means. (*"capable of being," "able to"*)

Guide students in using the strategy.
Have students read each remaining sentence, underline the suffixed word, and then explain how to use the meaning of the base word and the suffix to figure out the meaning of the whole word. Review spelling changes in *sensible, usable,* and *believable.*

4. WRAP-UP

Summarize instruction.
Review why it is important to understand the meanings of suffixes and to be able to add them to base words. (*Readers can use the meanings of suffixes to figure out new words; writers can make new words with suffixes.*)

Provide independent practice.
Options for independent practice are shown in the Resource Center below.

Meeting Individual Needs

RETEACHING Use the activity on page 314 and Masters 1–4 in the Teacher Resource Kit.

CHALLENGE Use the activity on page 314 and Master 8 in the Teacher Resource Kit.

ACHIEVING ENGLISH PROFICIENCY Use the activity on page 314 and Master 14 in the Teacher Resource Kit.

Workbook page 55

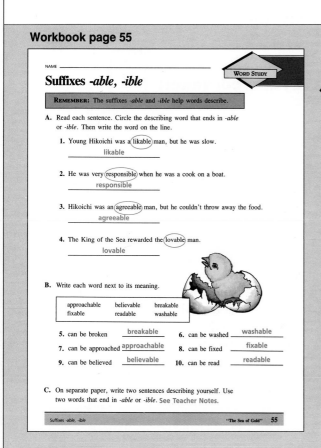

RESOURCE CENTER

◀ **Workbook page 55** is intended for use by all students.

Skills Practice 49 ▶ may be assigned for additional practice.

Workbook reuse option: Have students think of someone or something they know that could be described by each of the *-able* and *-ible* words in Part A. Have them write their answers beside each word on the line.

Skills Practice 49

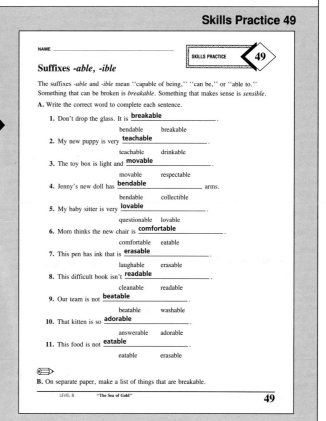

SKILL TRACE: TABLE OF CONTENTS				
Introduction	Practice	Test	Reteach	Maintain
TE 224	249	273	311	315	445

STUDY SKILLS

Title Page, Copyright Page, Table of Contents

OBJECTIVE   Using the title and copyright pages and the table of contents.

1. WARM-UP

Use the Student Text to define title, author, publisher, and table of contents.

Tell students they can find out something about a book by looking at the first few pages. Have students open their texts to the title page. Point out the name of the book, author(s), publisher, and the city where the publisher is located. Explain that the name of a book is its *title*, the person who writes the book is the *author*, and the company that prints the book is the *publisher*. Turn to the first page of the table of contents and explain that it is a list of all the stories and poems in the book. Have students find "The Sea of Gold" in the table of contents and tell on which page it begins.

State the objective.

Tell students they will learn to use the title and copyright pages and the table of contents to help them find out what a book is about and to locate information in it.

2. TEACH

Explain why using book parts is important.

Knowing how to use the title and copyright pages and the table of contents in a book helps readers choose books and find information easily.

Explain how to use book parts.

Remind students the title page, copyright page, and table of contents are located in the front of a book. The title page contains the name of the book and the author or authors, as well as the name and the place of the publisher. This information is helpful if a reader wants to write to the publisher with a question or to order a copy of the book. Point out that the copyright date indicates whether the information in a book is recent or possibly out of date. The table of contents tells the reader what selections are included in the book and where they are located.

TEACHING CHART 31: TITLE PAGE, COPYRIGHT PAGE, TABLE OF CONTENTS   `31`

JAPANESE FOLK TALES	Contents	
by Leslie Ido	The Boy on the Boat	5
	The Paper Bird	14
Paper Press, Barton Publishing	The Tiniest Fish	22
New York, N.Y.	Over the Mountain	26
© Copyright 1988	The Plum Tree	35

Model using the book parts.

Read the material on the Teaching Chart with students. Explain that you want to know the title and author, so you look at the title page. Read the title and author's name aloud. Also tell students you can see on the table of contents that the book has the story "The Tiniest Fish." You see that it begins on page 22.

3. GUIDED PRACTICE

Check for understanding.

Before going on, have students explain what information the title and copyright pages and the table of contents give about a book. *(The title page tells the name of the book, the author, and the publisher; the copyright page tells in what year the book was published and more information about the publisher; the table of contents lists the stories or selections in the book.)*

Guide students in using the title page, copyright page, and table of contents.

Have students use the information on the title and copyright pages and table of contents to answer the following questions.

1. What is the name of the book? (Japanese Folk Tales)

2. Who is the author? (Leslie Ido)

3. Who is the publisher? (Paper Press, a division of Barton Publishing)

4. In what year was the book published? (1988)

5. How many stories are in the book? (five)

6. On what page does "The Plum Tree" start? (page 35)

4. WRAP-UP

Summarize instruction.

Review why it is important to look at the title and copyright pages and the table of contents before reading a book. *(to make sure the book is what you want; to find out what is in the book; to find out where selections begin)*

Provide independent practice.

Options for independent practice are shown in the Resource Center below.

Meeting Individual Needs

RETEACHING   Use the activity on page 315 and Masters 1–4 in the Teacher Resource Kit.

CHALLENGE   Use the activity on page 315 and Master 7 in the Teacher Resource Kit.

Workbook page 56

RESOURCE CENTER

Skills Practice 50

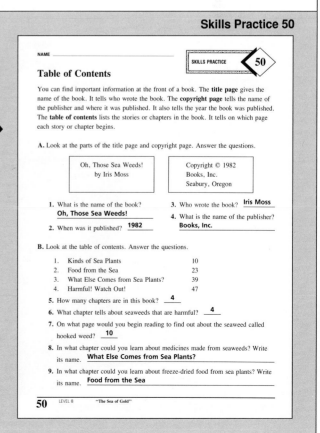

◀ **Workbook page 56** is intended for use by all students.

Skills Practice 50 ▶ may be assigned for additional practice.

Workbook reuse option: Have students circle the number of the page on which each story begins. Have them add a folk tale and a page number to the table of contents.

SKILL TRACE: SUFFIX				
Introduction	Practice	Test	Reteach	Maintain
TE 192	226	272	311	313	396

WORD STUDY

Suffixes -ness

OBJECTIVE Using structural analysis to determine word meaning.

Review suffix -ness.

Explain that the suffix *-ness* means "state, quality, or condition of." When it is added to a base word, it may change a word that describes something to a word that names something, or an adjective to a noun. The spelling of some base words changes when the suffix *-ness* is added.

> **TEACHING CHART 32: SUFFIX -NESS**
>
> 32
>
> | kind | kindness |
> |---|---|
> | happy | happiness |
> | hopeful | hopefulness |
>
> Hikoichi was *kind* to the fish.
> His *kindness* was rewarded.

Display the Teaching Chart. Use the sentences at the bottom of the chart to point out how the suffix *-ness* changes an adjective to a noun. Point out that the word *kindness* can be defined as "a quality of being kind."

Have students write sentences about "The Sea of Gold."

Using the pairs of words on the chart, have students write sentences about the story. Students should model their sentences on the ones at the bottom of the chart. Each student should write one sentence for the first word, then add the suffix to form a new word and write a sentence that includes the new word. Have students read their sentences aloud and give definitions for the words with *-ness*, using the meaning of the suffix.

Provide independent practice.

Options for independent practice are shown in the Resource Center below.

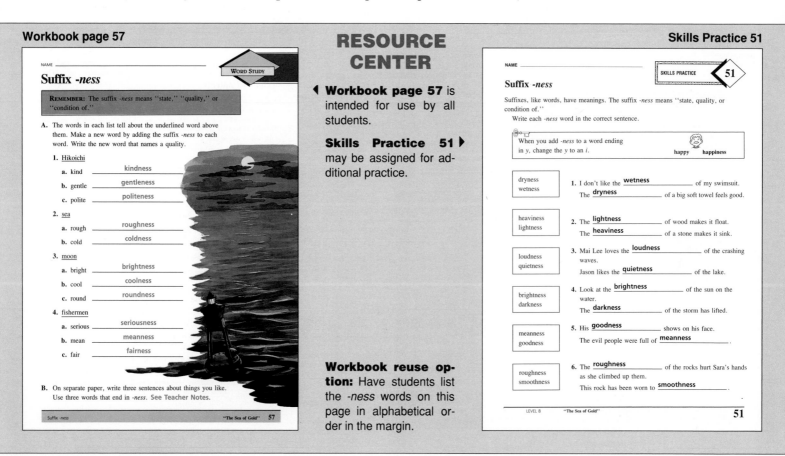

Workbook page 57

NAME _____

Suffix *-ness*

REMEMBER: The suffix *-ness* means "state," "quality," or "condition of."

A. The words in each list tell about the underlined word above them. Make a new word by adding the suffix *-ness* to each word. Write the new word that names a quality.

1. <u>Hikoichi</u>
   a. kind — kindness
   b. gentle — gentleness
   c. polite — politeness

2. <u>sea</u>
   a. rough — roughness
   b. cold — coldness

3. <u>moon</u>
   a. bright — brightness
   b. cool — coolness
   c. round — roundness

4. <u>fishermen</u>
   a. serious — seriousness
   b. mean — meanness
   c. fair — fairness

B. On separate paper, write three sentences about things you like. Use three words that end in *-ness*. See Teacher Notes.

Suffix *-ness*   "The Sea of Gold"   **57**

RESOURCE CENTER

◀ **Workbook page 57** is intended for use by all students.

Skills Practice 51 ▶ may be assigned for additional practice.

Workbook reuse option: Have students list the *-ness* words on this page in alphabetical order in the margin.

Skills Practice 51

NAME _____

SKILLS PRACTICE 51

Suffix *-ness*

Suffixes, like words, have meanings. The suffix *-ness* means "state, quality, or condition of."

Write each *-ness* word in the correct sentence.

> When you add *-ness* to a word ending in *y*, change the *y* to an *i*.
> happy   happiness

dryness wetness	1. I don't like the **wetness** _____ of my swimsuit. The **dryness** _____ of a big soft towel feels good.
heaviness lightness	2. The **lightness** _____ of wood makes it float. The **heaviness** _____ of a stone makes it sink.
loudness quietness	3. Mai Lee loves the **loudness** _____ of the crashing waves. Jason likes the **quietness** _____ of the lake.
brightness darkness	4. Look at the **brightness** _____ of the sun on the water. The **darkness** _____ of the storm has lifted.
meanness goodness	5. His **goodness** _____ shows on his face. The evil people were full of **meanness** _____.
roughness smoothness	6. The **roughness** _____ of the rocks hurt Sara's hands as she climbed up them. This rock has been worn to **smoothness** _____.

LEVEL 8   "The Sea of Gold"   **51**

SKILL TRACE: INFERENCES	
Introduced in Level 6. This skill is re-introduced in Unit 3 of this level.	Maintain
	TE 227 / 278

COMPREHENSION

Inference

OBJECTIVE Making inferences about feelings and attitudes.

Review making inferences.

Explain to students that when they make an inference about something they have read, they fill in ideas or information the author has left out of the story. They do this by looking at clues from the story itself along with "what I know" clues, or things they already know about the world.

Use selection passages to review how to make inferences.

You may wish to read aloud the three passages below from the story "The Sea of Gold." Tell students that each passage is followed by a short question that asks for an inference. For each passage, have a different student lead the rest of the group through making an inference by writing text clues and "what I know" clues on the board.

> **1.** The fishermen laughed when they heard him. They said, "Maybe someday the fish will answer you and tell you how much they enjoyed your dinner." How did the fishermen feel about Hikoichi talking to the fish?
>
> **2.** "There," he said proudly, "I scooped this up when I went down and walked on the sand." What did Hikoichi think was in the bucket?
>
> **3.** "Why, this is beautiful," Hikoichi thought, and his heart sang with joy at the sight. How did Hikoichi feel when he saw the sea of shimmering sand?

Provide independent practice.

An optional independent practice is shown in the Resource Center below.

RESOURCE CENTER

Skills Practice 52 ▶ may be assigned for additional practice.

Skills Practice 52

NAME _____

SKILLS PRACTICE 52

Inference

Sometimes you can figure out things about a story even if they are not stated in the story. This is called making **inferences.**

Story clues
+ What I know
Inference

> The diver swam over to the treasure chest. It was from a ship that had sunk years before. The chest was covered with seaweed.

We know that the treasure chest is at the bottom of the ocean, even though the writer doesn't state that.

Read the stories. Think about what all the sentences really mean. Answer each question. **Answers may vary.**

1. The sailor rowed the boat to the tiny island. Lois was waiting on the beach. She was thrilled to see him. She would never go out alone in a leaky rowboat again! What happened to Lois? **She went out in a leaky boat and couldn't get back home.**

2. Sea cucumbers break in two when they are scared. This mixes up other animals that may be after them. Then the two parts can escape. Later, each part grows back its missing part. What could a sea cucumber be? **an animal that looks like a cucumber**

3. A sea lion dived deep into the ocean. A diver followed. The diver went as far as he could safely go. Then he came back up. Why didn't the sea lion come back up then, too? **The sea lion could dive deeper than the diver.**

4. It was a windy day. The water was very rough. Gale and Margaret spent the day building a large sand castle on the beach. Why didn't the girls go in the water? **The water was too rough for swimming.**

52   LEVEL 8   "The Sea of Gold"

227

CURRICULUM CONNECTIONS

JAPAN, LIFE ON AN ISLAND SOCIAL STUDIES

Using a map or globe, show students where Japan is located. Point out that Japan is a country made up of islands, like the island where Hikoichi grew up, and that many people on the smaller islands still rely on fishing for their income. Then have students copy or trace the outline of the Japanese islands from a social studies book or atlas. Direct them to label each island with its correct name by copying the information from a map.

Have students read about Japanese culture and fishing villages in an encyclopedia, social studies book, or library book. Then have them work in small groups to paint and draw large pictures that show what life in a small Japanese fishing village might be like. The pictures can be done on long strips of paper and should include features such as the harbor, with fishing boats; fishermen going to sea; houses and stores; people in the streets, walking or riding bicycles; and fishermen mending their nets. Display the completed pictures and have each group present its picture. Have the group members describe how they did their research and why they included specific elements. **Curriculum Connection Master 7** can be used with this activity.

FISHY FACTS SCIENCE

Have students research why fish is considered a healthy food to eat. Students might use encyclopedias, science texts, and other nonfiction books. Cookbooks are also a possible resource. Tell students to take notes and then list the facts on a chart. Students can illustrate their charts with a drawing or cutout of one or several fish. Display the charts and discuss students' findings.

COLLAGE—A PICTURE THROUGH PIECES ART

Review that a collage is a picture made by pasting onto a background such things as parts of pictures and newspapers, cloth, and string. Have students work in pairs to create collages that illustrate one aspect of life on Hikoichi's fishing boat. Possibilities include: Hikoichi preparing a meal in the crowded galley; the fishermen hauling in their nets or asleep in their bunks at night. Provide large, stiff sheets of paper, glue, scissors, and stacks of old magazines. Encourage students to pick out pictures that suggest the feeling and the color of the scene, as well as the actual details it includes. Students can add to their collages with drawings of characters and other setting elements if they wish. When each pair presents its finished collage, have students discuss the ways the picture helps convey the look and feeling of life on board a fishing boat.

TELLING TALES HUMANITIES

Have each student find a short folk tale from Japan or from another culture that tells about a sea kingdom. Ask students to read their tales several times so that they can easily read them aloud or tell them from memory. Then have students tell their tales to the class as storytellers told folk tales long ago before they were written down. Remind students that to make their stories sound more interesting, they should change the speed of their reading, saying some sentences or phrases more slowly and softly and some more quickly and loudly, depending on what is happening in their stories. Also tell students that punctuation marks in the stories will help them know how to use their voices.

Checkpoint

USING THE CHECKPOINT PAGES

Use Checkpoints for informal evaluation.

Checkpoints are designed to help students and teachers monitor and improve student progress. For students, the Checkpoints serve as another step in the development of their ability to control their own learning. They see their own strengths and weaknesses even as the teacher does. For the teacher, the Checkpoints offer a systematic approach to informal assessment. Each Checkpoint helps identify areas of strength and weakness and then offers ideas for reteaching and extra practice before the formal assessment that comes at the end of the unit.

The extra-help ideas in Checkpoint lessons give additional practice to those students having difficulty with the targeted skill while allowing them to remain with the regular reading group. Extra-help ideas can also be used effectively with individual students or in small groups.

Informally diagnose strengths and weaknesses.

Checkpoints are in the same format as the Unit Skills Tests; you might review the directions before assigning the pages. Direct students to complete the pages shown in the Resource Center. Then have students work together to correct their papers, and encourage them to explain the thinking behind their answers. This affords you an opportunity to observe not only how students arrived at their answers but also to identify and explain any item types that are causing difficulty. Note that in the Resource Center, questions are labeled by skill so that you can quickly assess areas in which a particular student needs additional help.

The following skills are included in this Checkpoint.

comparison/contrast
suffix *-ness*

For your information, the Checkpoint pages at the end of this unit include the skills listed below.

suffixes *-able, -ible*
parts of a book
vocabulary — Story Critical words

PROVIDING EXTRA HELP

Provide extra help with comparison and contrast.

Strengthen reading comprehension by linking reading and listening. Have students listen as you read them a short passage about two cats. Tell them to listen for ways in which the cats are alike and different.

> **Furface was huge and orange, with long fluffy hair that often became matted. Button had silvery gray, medium-length fur and was — at best — medium sized. Both cats were friendly, but Button was the friendlier of the two. Button was pretty sure that everyone loved her, so she'd climb immediately into the laps of all guests, while Furface sat — calm and dignified — and waited for an invitation.**

Put a Venn diagram on the chalkboard, or use Form 4 from the Teacher's Resource Kit. Fill in the diagram as students offer suggestions from the passage they just heard.

FURFACE		**BUTTON**
orange, big, long silky hair		silvery gray, medium sized
friendly, but waits for	cat	more friendly, is "pretty
people to come to her	friendly	sure everyone loves her"

Provide extra help with the suffix -ness.

Have the students make a chalkboard display of words that end in -*ness*. First write that suffix in the center of the chalkboard and draw a circle around it. Then have students take turns coming to the board and writing a word that ends in -*ness* until the area all around the circled suffix is filled. Discuss meanings as necessary.

Workbook page 58

NAME _____

Checkpoint

Read the paragraphs. Then fill in the circle beside the correct answer.

All types of boats are popular today. To find out what kind of boat is best for you, compare sailboats and motorboats. Both are enjoyed by sailors. Both can be used in either oceans or lakes. They both offer a chance to explore new places.

Some people prefer sailboats. These people like the look of a sailboat's bright sails. They like the quietness of a sailboat, too. Because sailboats work with the wind, they don't need noisy engines. They can ride all day around a beautiful lake. Sailboat lovers like the peacefulness of a sail on a quiet lake.

Other people prefer motorboats because motorboats go faster. Because they have engines, they can be used even on calm and quiet days when there is no wind. Motorboats offer speed, noise, and excitement. You may decide that motorboats are for you.

58   Checkpoint

RESOURCE CENTER

◀ These pages provide informal assessment in the format of the Unit Skills Tests. ▶

Workbook page 59

NAME _____

comparison
1. What does the selection compare?
   - (a) lakes and rivers
   - (b) boating and swimming
   - (c) sailboats and motorboats ●
   - (d) swimming and skiing

comparison
2. Which words or sentences helped you tell what was compared?
   - (a) All types of boats are popular today.
   - (b) Some people prefer sailboats.
   - (c) compare sailboats and motorboats ●
   - (d) motorboats go faster

comparison
3. In which way are sailboats and motorboats similar?
   - (a) They are both fast.
   - (b) They are both slow.
   - (c) They are both fun. ●
   - (d) They are both noisy.

comparison
4. Which sentence told how they are alike?
   - (a) All types of boating are popular today.
   - (b) Both are enjoyed by sailors. ●
   - (c) Some people prefer sailboats.
   - (d) Motorboats offer speed, noise, and excitement.

comparison
5. How are the boats different?
   - (a) Motorboats are slower.
   - (b) Motorboats are faster. ●
   - (c) Motorboats hold more people.
   - (d) Motorboats tip more easily.

comparison
6. Which words or sentences named a difference?
   - (a) They both offer a chance to explore new places.
   - (b) motorboats go faster ●
   - (c) All types of boats are popular today.
   - (d) compare sailboats and motorboats

suffix -ness
7. What is the meaning of quietness?
   - (a) not quiet
   - (b) able to be quiet
   - (c) state of being quiet ●
   - (d) one who is quiet

suffix -ness
8. Which suffix is used to name a quality?
   - (a) -ment
   - (b) -est
   - (c) -or
   - (d) -ness ●

Checkpoint   59

231

	Teaching Sequence	Trade Books and Resources	Meeting Individual Needs	Integrated Language Arts / Cross Curriculum
The Bridge Pages 234–235	**Maintain** Main Idea/Details	• Teaching Chart 33 • Workbook 60 • Skills Practice 53		
PART 1 **Vocabulary Strategies** Pages 236–237	**Develop Concepts** Using a Graphic Organizer **Teach Vocabulary** **STORY CRITICAL WORDS:** cable, **engineers**, pilot, **scientists**, shipwreck, **submarine** (Tested words are boldfaced.)	• Teaching Chart 34 • Workbook 61 • Skills Practice 54	**SUPPORT WORDS:** eager, fiberglass, future, iceberg, millions, sonar, survive • Skills Practice 55 **CHARACTER/SETTING WORDS:** Alvin, Atlantis II, Jason, Jr., Titanic, Woods Hole Oceanographic Institution	**WRITING/SPEAKING ACTIVITY:** Use new vocabulary to describe a submarine. • Spelling Connection 46
PART 2 **Reading & Responding** Pages 238–247	**Build Background** **Develop a Purpose for Reading** **Guide the Reading Process** **Selection Follow-Up**	• Reader's Journal 48–51 • Workbook 62 **I→T KIT** Discussing a Sea Poster; Listening to an Interview with a Deep-sea Diver **READING EVERY DAY** *How to Be an Ocean Scientist in Your Own Home,* by S. Simon *Undersea Machines,* by R.J. Stephen	**EXTRA HELP:** Charting Information About Underwater Equipment **ACHIEVING ENGLISH PROFICIENCY:** Discussing Marine Life • Achieving English Proficiency Master 15	**Language Arts Connections** **WRITING TO LEARN:** Write about an imaginary sea creature. • Writing Master 9 **SPEAKING/LISTENING:** Creating Sea Poems; Creating Alliteration • Language Arts Master 8 **WRITING:** Writing Informational Articles; Writing First-person Accounts
PART 3 **Selection Support** Pages 248–253			**Practice** • Teaching Charts 35–36 • Workbook 63–64 • Skills Practice 56–57 Suffixes *-able, -ible* (Tested) Title Page, Copyright Page, Table of Contents (Tested) **Maintain** • Skills Practice 58–59 Spelling Changes: *f* to *ve* Suffixes *-er, -or*	**Curriculum Connections** **SCIENCE:** Researching Underwater Farming **SCIENCE/MATHEMATICS:** Researching Sea Animals and Ocean Depth Measurements • Curriculum Connection Master 8 **SOCIAL STUDIES:** Discussing the Woods Hole Oceanographic Institution **CAREERS:** Researching Undersea Jobs **ART:** Creating Underwater Dioramas

The
Wonderful
Underwater Machine

by Josephine Edgar

SUMMARY   *Jason Jr., "JJ" for short, is the name of a machine scientists developed to explore the ocean floor. Equipped with lights, television, and still cameras, JJ photographs rocks, fish, and shipwrecks in the deepest parts of the ocean. Scientists used JJ to see inside the wreck of the* Titanic.

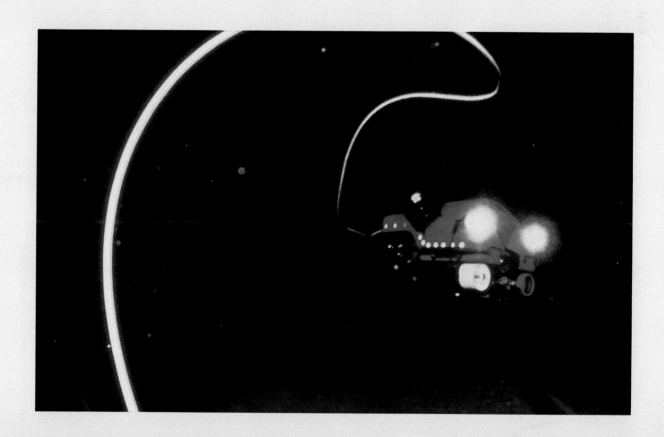

The Bridge

SKILL TRACE: MAIN IDEA/DETAILS						
Introduction	Practice		Test	Reteach	Maintain	
TE 66	82	116	157	158	234	274	508

COMPREHENSION

Teaching Main Idea/Details

OBJECTIVE   Identifying stated or unstated main idea and supporting details.

1. WARM-UP

Use a known passage to discuss the main idea and supporting details.

Remind students that in the previous selection, "The Sea of Gold," Hikoichi received a wonderful gift from the King of the Sea. Tell students they will listen to a passage about the sea. Have them identify the main idea and the supporting details.

> **The sea is a source of food. It is filled with animals and plants. Fish and plants are food for other fish and sea animals. Fish and sea animals are food for people.**

Discuss the main idea and supporting details of the paragraph.

Reread the passage. Ask students why the first sentence in the paragraph is the main idea and not the other sentences. *(The first sentence tells the most important idea about the sea. The other sentences give details.)* Explain that the main idea in this paragraph is stated, but often a main idea is unstated. When this happens, readers must think about what the details have in common and then figure out the main idea.

State the objective.

Tell students they will review how to identify both stated and unstated main ideas and supporting details in paragraphs.

2. TEACH

Explain why identifying main idea and supporting details is important.

Understanding the main idea and supporting details helps readers understand the author's main points, which helps readers better remember what they have read.

Present a strategy for identifying main idea and supporting details.

Explain that there is a strategy students can use to help them identify the main idea and supporting details in a paragraph. First, look to see what all or most of the sentences are about. This will be the topic. Then decide which sentence tells the most important or main idea about the topic. If no sentence tells the main idea directly, create a sentence that includes the topic and the most important idea that the sentences in the paragraph talk about. This will be the main idea.

TEACHING CHART 33: MAIN IDEA/DETAILS

1. The swordfish has a long jawbone that looks like a sword. The leopard shark has the coloring and spots of a leopard. The seahorse has a head that looks something like a horse. (Main idea — sea animals are often named for body parts or coloring; Details — jawbone that looks like a sword; coloring and spots of a leopard, head that looks something like a horse)
2. People on a fishing boat have different jobs. Someone has to guide the boat. Another person cooks. The fishermen catch the fish. (Main idea — People on a fishing boat have different jobs. Details — guide the boat, cook, catch fish)

Model the strategy.

Read the first paragraph on the Teaching Chart. Tell students that you see that all the sentences are about sea animals. You notice that the supporting details are about the names of sea animals and their shapes or coloring. Since the main idea is not stated, you can create your own main idea sentence: Some sea animals are named for their body parts or coloring.

3. GUIDED PRACTICE

Check for understanding.

Before going on, have students explain how to identify the main idea of a paragraph. *(Figure out the topic, decide what is the most important idea, look for a sentence that states the main idea. If there is none, use the details in the paragraph to help you state the main idea in your own words.)*

Guide students in using the strategy.

Help students use the strategy to determine the main idea and supporting details of the second paragraph. Ask them to read the paragraph, decide what is the most important idea, look to see if there is a sentence that states the main idea, and underline the sentence. Then have students name the supporting details.

4. WRAP-UP

Summarize instruction.

Review why it is important to be able to identify the main idea and supporting details of a paragraph. *(Knowing the main idea and supporting details make it easier to understand and remember an author's main points.)*

Provide independent practice.

Options for independent practice are shown in the Resource Center below.

5. APPLICATION

Students will recognize main idea and supporting details as they read "The Wonderful Underwater Machine." The symbol ✔ marks specific questions and activities that apply this skill.

Workbook page 60

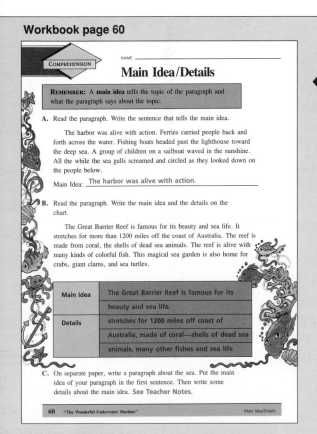

COMPREHENSION

NAME _____

Main Idea/Details

REMEMBER: A **main idea** tells the topic of the paragraph and what the paragraph says about the topic.

A. Read the paragraph. Write the sentence that tells the main idea.

The harbor was alive with action. Ferries carried people back and forth across the water. Fishing boats headed past the lighthouse toward the deep sea. A group of children on a sailboat waved in the sunshine. All the while the sea gulls screamed and circled as they looked down on the people below.

Main Idea: The harbor was alive with action.

B. Read the paragraph. Write the main idea and the details on the chart.

The Great Barrier Reef is famous for its beauty and sea life. It stretches for more than 1200 miles off the coast of Australia. The reef is made from coral, the shells of dead sea animals. The reef is alive with many kinds of colorful fish. This magical sea garden is also home for crabs, giant clams, and sea turtles.

Main Idea	The Great Barrier Reef is famous for its beauty and sea life.
Details	stretches for 1200 miles off coast of Australia, made of coral—shells of dead sea animals, many other fishes and sea life

C. On separate paper, write a paragraph about the sea. Put the main idea of your paragraph in the first sentence. Then write some details about the main idea. See Teacher Notes.

60 "The Wonderful Underwater Machine"   Main Idea/Details

RESOURCE CENTER

◀ **Workbook page 60** is intended for use by all students.

Skills Practice 53 ▶ may be assigned for additional practice.

Workbook reuse option: Have students circle the main idea and underline the details in Part A.

Skills Practice 53

NAME _____

SKILLS PRACTICE 53

Main Idea/Details

A **main idea** tells what a paragraph is all about. **Details** tell more about the main idea.

Read each paragraph. Write the main idea sentence that goes with each paragraph.

1. An iceberg is a large piece of floating ice. Some icebergs are more than 300 feet high. Only the top of the huge iceberg shows above water. The larger part is under water, so ships must keep a safe distance away from them.
   An iceberg is a large piece of floating ice.

2. Some fine ships' captains have been women. One woman took over a ship when her husband became ill. She brought the ship safely to port thousands of miles away. At the same time, she took care of her husband, and she cooked all the meals for the crew.
   Some fine ships' captains have been women.

3. Lighthouses are often on islands or on the coast to guide ships. The flashing light of a lighthouse can be seen from miles away. The light tells sailors where they are. It warns them that rocks are nearby and to steer into safer waters.
   Lighthouses are often on islands or on the coast to guide ships.

4. An animal's body size does not always match the size of its brain. Dinosaurs once lived on the earth. The Stegosaurus is famous for its small brain. This dinosaur was very large, weighing more than an elephant. However, its brain was only the size of a walnut.
   An animal's body size does not always match the size of its brain.

LEVEL 8   "The Wonderful Underwater Machine"   **53**

1

Vocabulary Strategies

Developing Concepts

Tap prior knowledge about underwater life and machines with a chart.

Make a chart about underwater life as a starting point for teaching vocabulary. Ask students to name some things that can be found underwater in the seas and oceans of the world. Also have students name things that help people go underwater. List students' responses in columns. As they suggest words, students will most likely mention the prefix *sub-*, meaning "under," and the base word *marine*, meaning "of the sea." Encourage students to mention the Story Critical words *submarine* and *shipwreck*.

Underwater Sights
(plants)
(fish)
(seaweed)
(rock, coral, wood)
(shipwreck)

Underwater Equipment/Machines
(mask)
(flippers)
(snorkel)
(cameras)
(submarine)

Teaching Vocabulary

Discuss meanings of Story Critical words.

Read each context sentence on the Teaching Chart and identify the new word. Then use the questions below to help students understand each word. When necessary, provide a definition.

34

TEACHING CHART 34: VOCABULARY

1. **scientists** (experts in science)
   Some *scientists* study the animals and plants that live in the sea.
2. **submarine** (a ship that operates underwater)
   People often work in a *submarine* as they explore the ocean floor.
3. **pilot** (a person who steers a ship)
   The *pilot* steers the submarine out of the harbor.
4. **engineers** (people skilled in planning and operating in some technical field)
   The *engineers* built a machine that could reach the bottom of the ocean.
5. **cable** (a bundle of insulated wires)
   The camera is hooked to the submarine by a strong *cable*.
6. **shipwreck** (the remains of a destroyed ship)
   The machine found a *shipwreck* of a boat that sank during a storm.

scientists

1. **What do you call the study of the earth and universe?** (science) **What do you call people who work in the field of science?** (scientists)
STRATEGY: PRIOR KNOWLEDGE

submarine

2. **Where does a submarine travel?** (underwater) **How far down in the water do you think some submarines can go?** (all the way to the bottom)
STRATEGY: PRIOR KNOWLEDGE

pilot **3. Does a pilot drive a ship or just ride in it?** (drives it) **How do you know from the sentence what a pilot does?** (from the word *steers*)
STRATEGY: CONTEXT CLUES

engineers **4. What clue in the sentence helps you understand the word *engineers*?** (built a machine) STRATEGY: CONTEXT CLUES

cable **5. Where might you see a cable?** (Students may suggest a telephone pole, on any television set, in a building, on a large machine.) **What are cables for?** (to hook up things; to carry electricity) STRATEGY: CLASSIFICATION

shipwreck **6. Where would you find a shipwreck?** (at the bottom of the ocean) **What might cause a ship to sink to the bottom of the ocean?** (a bad storm)
STRATEGY: PRIOR KNOWLEDGE

Add new words to the chart. Ask students to write *cable* under the correct heading on the chart. Then ask students to think of a new heading that could include the words *pilot*, *scientist*, and *engineer*. *(People Who Work Underwater)*

Discuss Support words as needed. The Glossary of the Student Text includes definitions of the Support words: *eager, iceberg, millions, future, survive, sonar, fiberglass.*

Present Character/Setting words. The selection contains the following Character/Setting words: *Alvin, Atlantis II, Jason, Jr., Titanic, Woods Hole Oceanographic Institution.*

Provide independent practice. Options for independent practice are shown in the Resource Center below.

WRITING OR SPEAKING ACTIVITY *Remind students of their discussion of a submarine. Have them describe a submarine, using as many of the new vocabulary words as possible. Some students might enjoy drawing a picture of an underwater scene that includes a shipwreck and a submarine.*

Workbook page 61

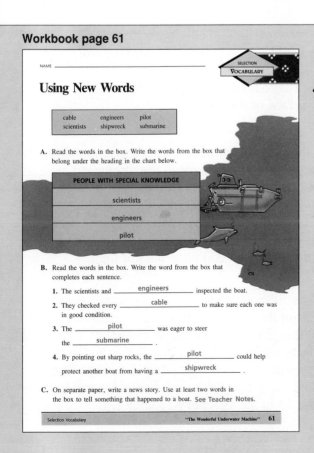

NAME _____

SELECTION VOCABULARY

Using New Words

| cable | engineers | pilot |
| scientists | shipwreck | submarine |

A. Read the words in the box. Write the words from the box that belong under the heading in the chart below.

PEOPLE WITH SPECIAL KNOWLEDGE
scientists
engineers
pilot

B. Read the words in the box. Write the word from the box that completes each sentence.
1. The scientists and _____engineers_____ inspected the boat.
2. They checked every _____cable_____ to make sure each one was in good condition.
3. The _____pilot_____ was eager to steer the _____submarine_____ .
4. By pointing out sharp rocks, the _____pilot_____ could help protect another boat from having a _____shipwreck_____ .

C. On separate paper, write a news story. Use at least two words in the box to tell something that happened to a boat. See Teacher Notes.

Selection Vocabulary   "The Wonderful Underwater Machine" **61**

RESOURCE CENTER

◄ **Workbook page 61** provides practice with Story Critical words.

Skills Practice 54 ► provides additional practice with Story Critical words.

Skills Practice 55 provides practice with Support words.

Spelling Connection Master 46 may be used for spelling instruction with the new vocabulary.

Workbook reuse option: Have students circle one word in the box and use it in a sentence. Tell them to write their sentences below the box.

Skills Practice 54

NAME _____

SKILLS PRACTICE **54**

Vocabulary: Story Critical Words

A. Study the meaning of each word.

cable strong rope made of wires	**scientists** experts in science
engineers people who plan and build things	**shipwreck** a destroyed ship
pilot a person who steers a ship	**submarine** a ship that travels under water

B. Read each row of words. Write the vocabulary word that tells what kind of people do the things in that row.
1. _scientists_
find out about plants
explore space
find out how the body works
2. _engineers_
design airplanes
plan bridges
design energy plants

C. Answer each question with the correct vocabulary word.
3. What does a ship need to guide it? _____pilot_____
4. What kind of ship can dive deep into the ocean? _____submarine_____
5. What does a ship become if it sinks? _____shipwreck_____

D. Complete each sentence with the correct vocabulary word.
6. A team of _____engineers_____ designed the new highway.
7. The _____scientists_____ wore white coats at work.
8. A telephone has a _____cable_____ coming out of it.
9. At low tide people could see the _____shipwreck_____ on the rocks.
10. Our ship's _____pilot_____ steered around the small island.
11. The crew of the _____submarine_____ travelled under water for weeks.
12. The _____cable_____ broke, and all the wires spilled out.

54 LEVEL 8 *"The Wonderful Underwater Machine"* Classification

Reading & Responding

Building Background

Motivate discussion using the quote.

Share the following quotation with students and explain that it is part of the opening scene of a popular television series about the exploration of outer space. Discuss whether the quote could also describe a show about underwater exploration.

> . . . to explore strange new worlds, to seek out new life forms, to boldly go where no one has gone before . . .

Build background about why scientists use submarines.

Ask students how the equipment scientists use to explore outer space is similar to what they use to explore the ocean. (*Students may note that both in outer space and underwater scientists use equipment to provide air for breathing and to measure and photograph what they see.*) Be sure that students understand that scientists use machines to explore places where humans cannot safely go.

Discuss nonfiction.

Write the word *nonfiction* on the chalkboard. Explain that nonfiction writing gives information and facts about things. Tell students that what they are about to read is a nonfiction article about a submarine. Ask students what facts they might expect to find. (*How the machine was built, what it does.*)

Developing a Purpose for Reading

Option 1
Students set purpose.

ORAL "I PREDICT" STATEMENTS   Have students read the title of the selection and the introduction and talk about what people in a submarine might see on the ocean floor. Ask students to make predictions about what the submarine would allow people to see. Record students' suggestions for later use.

WRITING ACTIVITY   Have students work individually or in pairs to create written "I predict" sentences. Have students save their lists for later use.

Option 2
Teacher sets purpose.

Have students read the selection to find out what an underwater machine named Jason, Jr. finds below the surface of the water.

Meeting
Individual
Needs

EXTRA HELP   Tell students that the next selection describes a machine that goes deep under the ocean's surface. Have students recall the discussion in Building Background. Then use a blank KWL chart, Form 8 in the Teacher's Resource Kit, to have the students tell what they know about underwater equipment and ask what they would like to know. As they read, have students fill in the chart with what they learn from the selection. After reading, volunteers may reread parts of the selection that answer their questions.

ACHIEVING ENGLISH PROFICIENCY   Show students pictures of the *ocean*. Point out *waves*. Write these words on the board and have students repeat them after you. Ask students what things they might find in the ocean. List their answers on the board. Introduce and explain *starfish* and *submarine* if students do not suggest them. Have students draw a picture of life under the ocean using some of the things from the list on the board. For additional help in story comprehension, use Master 15 in the Teacher Resource Kit.

*Who can dive into the deepest ocean and
see in the watery darkness? You and I can't,
but Alvin and Jason Jr. can!*

The Wonderful
Underwater Machine

by Josephine Edgar

A team of engineers and scientists at the
Woods Hole Oceanographic Institution in
Massachusetts wanted to study the deepest
parts of the ocean. They knew it was impossible
for people to survive outside a submarine in the
deepest parts of the ocean, so the team worked
together to build a machine called Jason Jr., or
"JJ" for short.

If you saw Jason Jr., swimming at the
bottom of the ocean, you might think you were
looking at a big, blue bug with two bright eyes.
But JJ is not a bug, and its bright eyes are really
two bright lights! JJ is a small machine, only
twenty-eight inches long, but it is capable of
swimming deep in the ocean.

Deep under the ocean, the weight of the
water pushes down very hard on anything found
on the ocean floor. Sometimes there are sharp
rocks and coral that can harm and even tear
apart a machine. So the engineers knew they
had to make JJ strong. The engineers could not
make all of JJ's parts out of metal though,
because a heavy metal machine would sink to
the bottom of the ocean. They solved this
problem by making a special skin for JJ.

The outside of JJ's skin is made of blue
fiberglass. The fiberglass covers millions of tiny
glass balls. These balls are smaller than grains
of sand, and each ball has air inside, like a tiny
bubble. The balls are glued together and help JJ
float in the water. The tiny glass balls are also
hard like marbles. When JJ bumps into
something sharp, the balls protect it.

**This is Jason Jr., also referred to as JJ. If you saw JJ in the
water, what would you think it was?**

Reader's Journal   **p 48**
Preparing for Reading

DIVE
RIGHT IN!

After reading about
three possible ways of seeing
what's under the sea, students
choose one and describe what they might find as
they explore.

GUIDED READING

✔ **Page 132   What is Jason, Jr.?** (a small underwater
machine)   RECALL: DETAILS

Page 132   Why did the team build JJ? (to study the
deepest parts of the ocean)   RECALL: CHARACTER

STRATEGIC READING

Pages 132–133   Have students read to the end of the
first paragraph on page 133. Ask them if they
understand why humans cannot go where JJ can. Have
volunteers read aloud the section they believe tells the
answer. (The weight of the ocean pushes down on
everything under it. The deeper you go, the heavier the
weight. Other underwater hazards include sharp coral
and rocks.) Explain that sometimes readers have to
reread parts of a selection before they understand it.
Have students predict what they will find out about JJ's
skin.   METACOGNITION: RATE UNDERSTANDING

✔ Skill from The Bridge applied through this question.

239

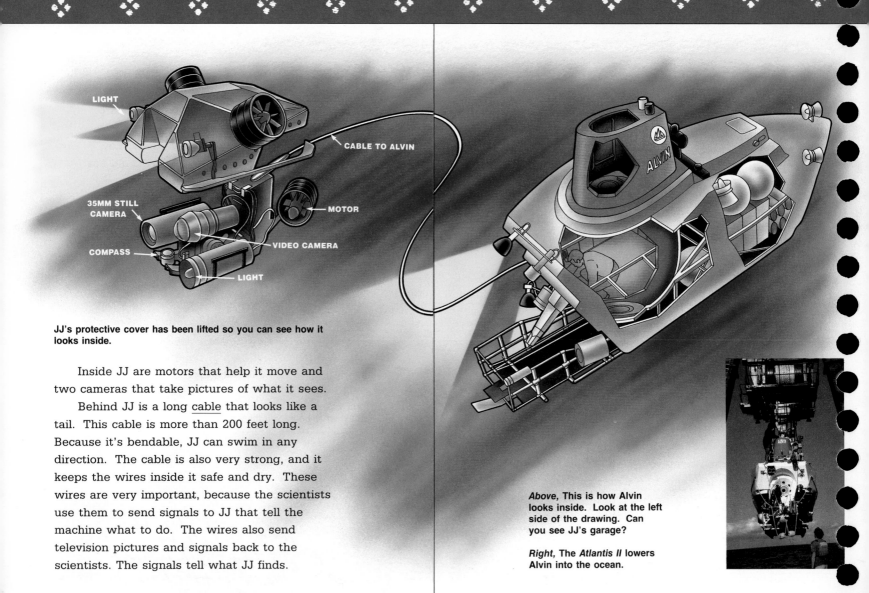

LIGHT

CABLE TO ALVIN

35MM STILL
CAMERA

MOTOR

COMPASS

VIDEO CAMERA

LIGHT

ALVIN

JJ's protective cover has been lifted so you can see how it looks inside.

Inside JJ are motors that help it move and two cameras that take pictures of what it sees.

Behind JJ is a long cable that looks like a tail. This cable is more than 200 feet long. Because it's bendable, JJ can swim in any direction. The cable is also very strong, and it keeps the wires inside it safe and dry. These wires are very important, because the scientists use them to send signals to JJ that tell the machine what to do. The wires also send television pictures and signals back to the scientists. The signals tell what JJ finds.

Above, This is how Alvin looks inside. Look at the left side of the drawing. Can you see JJ's garage?

Right, The *Atlantis II* lowers Alvin into the ocean.

GUIDED READING

Page 134   What kinds of cameras does JJ use? (35-mm still camera and a video camera)   ANALYZE:
ANALYZE: PICTURE DETAILS

Page 134   Can you think of reasons why scientists would want both kinds of cameras on board JJ? (Possible answers: Still pictures are useful for studying details like shapes or colors. Moving pictures are useful for studying how things move.)
SYNTHESIZE: DRAWING CONCLUSIONS

✔ **Page 134   The author says that the wires in JJ's cable are very important. What details support this idea?** (Through the wires scientists send signals to JJ that tell it what to do. Also, the pictures JJ takes are sent back to the scientists through the wires.)
ANALYZE: MAIN IDEA/DETAILS

Page 134   What might happen if the wires inside the cable became wet? (JJ might stop working.)
INFER: CAUSE/EFFECT

✔ Skill from *The Bridge* applied through this question.

HIGHLIGHTING LITERATURE

Pages 134–135   Point out to students that diagrams and pictures are often included in nonfiction selections to tell information about something. Ask students to study the diagram of JJ on page 134 and the picture on page 135. Then have them review the text on page 134 and discuss some of the facts about JJ.

Atlantis II stands by while Alvin takes JJ down to the ocean bottom to explore and to take pictures.

To get to the bottom of the ocean, Jason Jr., gets a ride from Alvin. Alvin is a submarine that can dive in very deep water. It carries JJ in a small garage, which is just under the front window. Inside Alvin there is room for two scientists and a <u>pilot</u> who drives the submarine.

The scientists use a big ship named *Atlantis II* to take Alvin and JJ out into the ocean. Then, *Atlantis II* lowers Alvin into the water, and the submarine starts to go down.

Alvin drops quickly because the scientists have put heavy steel weights on Alvin to make it sink. In one minute, Alvin can fall 100 feet. As Alvin goes down, the water gets darker and darker. First the ocean is blue. Then it is dark blue. In fifteen minutes, it is so dark that the scientists must turn on the lights inside Alvin to see. It is dark because sunlight can't reach the deepest parts of the ocean.

The scientists can't see the bottom, but they can tell when they are getting close to it by using Alvin's sonar. The sonar machine makes a noise and listens for the noise to bounce off the ocean floor. When the scientists hear the echo a short time after the noise is made, they know that the ocean floor is close.

Alvin's sonar tells scientists how close it is to the ocean bottom. This diagram shows how sonar works.

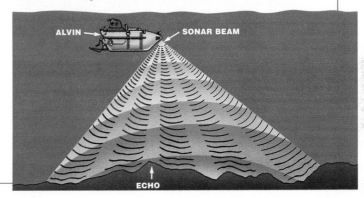

GUIDED READING

✔ **Page 136**   **How does JJ get to the ocean floor?** (A submarine takes it down.)   RECALL: DETAILS

Page 136   **Why do you think Alvin is able to dive in very deep water?** (It is probably made of strong materials like JJ is to keep it from being crushed by the water's weight.)   INFER: CAUSE/EFFECT

Page 137   **How deep is Alvin when the scientists need to turn on the lights? How do you know?** (Alvin is 1,500 feet under water. Alvin can dive 100 feet in one minute. After 15 minutes the scientists turn on the lights. Therefore, Alvin is 15 times 100 feet down, which is 1,500.) CONCLUSIONS

✔ **Page 137**   **How does sonar work?** (The sonar machine bounces a noise off the ocean floor, which makes an echo. The echo tells the location of the ocean floor.)   ANALYZE: MAIN IDEA/DETAILS

✔ Skill from The Bridge applied through this question.
✔ Informal Assessment Opportunity: VISUALIZING

STRATEGIC READING

✔ **Page 137**   As they read the passage about Alvin dropping deeper into the ocean have students visualize what it would be like to be inside Alvin. Then ask them to tell about what they imagined. Explain that trying to imagine the story helps them to understand it better.
METACOGNITION: VISUALIZING

241

When they are near to the bottom, the scientists drop one of Alvin's heavy weights. This makes Alvin slow down. Then, as they let go of more weights, Alvin settles down softly in the mud at the bottom. Using Alvin's lights, the scientists can see out of the small windows. Now, they are ready to use Jason Jr., to get a closer look.

Next, JJ swims out pulling its cable behind it. The scientists signal JJ where to look. It shines its lights on whatever the scientists are studying and takes pictures. JJ sends the pictures back to the scientists through the cable, which is also attached to Alvin.

The scientists are using JJ to look closely at rocks and mountains in the deepest parts of the ocean. They are learning where we can find important metals. They are also using JJ to study fish and other living things. JJ's pictures help the scientists understand how we can use the oceans to raise fish and other food.

After JJ has been on the ocean bottom for almost four hours, the scientists signal it to come back to Alvin. It is time to go home. Alvin comes back up to return to *Atlantis II.*

The next day the scientists will take Alvin and JJ down again. They are eager to find out more about what lies beneath the ocean.

In 1986 the scientists from the Woods Hole Oceanographic Institution used JJ to explore a famous ship that sank to the bottom of the ocean many years ago. In 1912 this large ship hit an iceberg and sank. The ship was the *Titanic.*

The scientists wanted to test JJ to find out how well it could swim inside the ship and take pictures. JJ did very well. It even swam down stairs and looked into rooms. The scientists sitting inside Alvin could see the pictures that JJ sent back. The pictures showed ceiling lamps and an old, rusty bathtub, but all the wooden furniture and stairs were gone. The scientists guessed that small shellfish had eaten anything wooden. The pictures also showed cups and bottles resting on the ocean bottom next to the shipwreck.

JJ approaches the sunken *Titanic.* Scientists were able to see the inside of the ship from the pictures JJ took.

GUIDED READING

✔ **Page 138   What are scientists using JJ for?** (to study rocks and mountains, to find metals, and study fish and other animals and plants that could be farmed for food.)   RECALL: DETAILS

✔ **Page 139   Why was JJ tested in 1986?** (to see how well it could swim inside the *Titanic* and to take pictures) **What details tell why the test was a success?** (JJ swam down stairs and into rooms. Its pictures showed ceiling lamps and an old rusty bathtub, and that the wooden furniture and stairs were gone.)
ANALYZE: MAIN IDEA/DETAILS

HIGHLIGHTING LITERATURE

Pages 138–139   Point out to students that on these pages they find out more details about what JJ sees and takes pictures of in the deepest parts of the ocean, in particular a famous shipwreck. Explain that these types of facts in a nonfiction selection help them to understand the topic better. In this selection, they can better understand what JJ was designed for if they know what it finds in the ocean.

✔ **Skill from The Bridge applied through this question.**

JJ took this photograph of the *Titanic's* deck. How can you tell the ship has been underwater for a long time?

Engineers at Woods Hole are now building newer and bigger machines like Jason Jr., and Alvin. Some of these machines will help them make better maps of the mountains and valleys on the ocean floor. Others will give us closer looks at shipwrecks. The underwater machines of the future will help scientists learn more about our oceans so that we can use them safely and wisely.

Reader's Response

What is it about undersea exploration that sounds exciting to you?

See next page for suggested answers.

The Wonderful Underwater Machine

 Thinking It Over

1. What problems did the engineers have to think about when they made Jason Jr.?
2. How does Alvin's sonar machine help scientists?
3. What would happen if JJ's cable were to break? How do you know?
4. Why is it important for scientists to learn about the ocean?
5. In what ways do you think scientists might use JJ to study the bottom of the ocean in the future?

 Writing to Learn

THINK AND IMAGINE Imagine you are in the submarine Alvin, using JJ to take pictures. Draw JJ, its long cable, and a sea creature it may be photographing.

WRITE Write sentences to describe your creature of the deep. What color is it? What shape? How big? Is its skin scaly or slippery?

GUIDED READING

Page 140   Why will underwater machines of the future be important? (because they will help scientists learn more about our oceans)   RECALL: CAUSE/EFFECT

RETURNING TO THE READING PURPOSE

OPTION 1   If students set the purpose, return to the sentences they wrote about the underwater machine. Discuss whether any of their predictions came true. Discuss what JJ saw in the deepest parts of the ocean. Then have them predict what machines like JJ might find in the ocean in the future.

OPTION 2   If you set the purpose, have students recall what JJ finds underneath the ocean. (rocks, mountains, fish, other animals, the wreck of the *Titanic* and such items in it as lamps, fans, cups, bottles, and a bathtub)

Reader's Journal   p 49
Responding to Reading

THERE'S GOLD DOWN THERE . . . SOMEWHERE

Students invent an underwater machine to help them locate underwater treasure.

243

SELECTION FOLLOW-UP

The Wonderful Underwater Machine

THINKING IT OVER

1. **What problems did the engineers have to think about when they made Jason, Jr.?** (Possible answers: The machine had to be strong enough to stand the weight of the water in the deepest part of the ocean; it had to be made out of something that would not sink to the bottom of the ocean; it had to be covered with something that would not be torn or broken down by coral and sharp rocks.)   RECALL: DETAILS

2. **How does Alvin's sonar machine help scientists?** (Since it is too dark to see the ocean floor, the scientists need sonar signals to tell them where it is.)   ANALYZE: MAIN IDEA/DETAILS

3. **What would happen if JJ's cable were to break? How do you know?** (The main idea here is that the cable is needed for all the work Alvin and JJ do together. Possible supporting details: the scientists could no longer tell what to do; JJ would stop sending television pictures and signals to the scientists; scientists might not be able to get JJ back. In support of their conclusions students may cite portions of the text that contain these details.)   SYNTHESIZE: MAIN IDEA/DETAILS; METACOGNITION

4. **Why is it important for scientists to learn about the ocean?** (Possible answers: They can learn how to use the ocean to grow fish and other food; they can find out more about how the earth and the oceans were formed; they can learn about underwater fish and plant life; they can find important metals and oil.)   SYNTHESIZE: DRAWING CONCLUSIONS

5. **In what ways do you think scientists might use JJ to study the bottom of the ocean in the future?** (Possible answers: JJ might help scientists study underwater volcanos and earthquakes; machines like JJ might be used to build underwater farms and even underwater cities.)
SYNTHESIZE: DRAWING CONCLUSIONS

WRITING TO LEARN

Use Writing Master 9, which provides guidelines.

THINK AND IMAGINE   Imagine you are in the submarine Alvin, using JJ to take pictures. **Draw JJ, its long cable, and a sea creature it may be photographing.** (Help students draw their pictures to prepare for writing.)

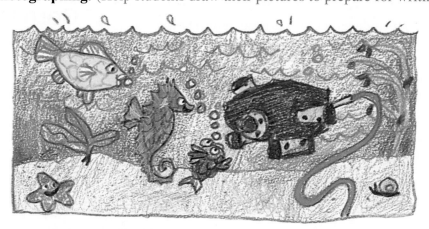

Extend comprehension through writing.

WRITE   Write sentences to describe your creature of the deep. What color is it? What shape? How big? Is its skin scaly or slippery? (Have students share their sentences and drawings.)

More Ideas for Selection Follow-Up

CRITICAL AND CREATIVE THINKING QUESTIONS

Encourage a variety of responses and points of view.

Use these open-ended questions to encourage critical and creative thinking about the selection.

1. Why is JJ called the wonderful underwater machine? In what ways do you think it is wonderful?

✔ 2. What did you learn about underwater exploration from this selection? What else would you like to learn?

3. What other kinds of machines take people places where they could not otherwise go?

REREADING ORALLY

Have students reread for specific information.

Explain to students that you are going to ask them to read aloud paragraphs in "The Wonderful Underwater Machine" containing specific information. Have students locate and read paragraphs that give the following information: what a person would think if he or she saw JJ swimming [page 132, paragraph 2, sentence 1], what is special about the cable that trails behind JJ [page134, paragraph 2, sentences 2–4], what Alvin is and what it does [page 136, paragraph 1], why scientists cannot see the bottom of the ocean [page 137, paragraph 1, sentence 7], how sonar works [page 137, paragraph 2, sentences 2–3]. Then ask students to reread a paragraph that tells about something new that they have learned.

SELECTION COMPREHENSION

Provide comprehension check.

A Workbook page to check comprehension is shown in the Resource Center below. It may be used for informal assessment.

✔ Informal Assessment Opportunity: GETTING INFORMATION FROM TEXT

Workbook page 62

SELECTION COMPREHENSION

NAME _____

The Wonderful Underwater Machine

A. Complete the summary of "The Wonderful Underwater Machine." Accept reasonable variations.

This article gives information about a machine which goes down to the deepest parts of the ocean. The machine is called ___Jason Jr. or JJ___ . JJ belongs to the Woods Hole Oceanographic Institution. Most of the events in the article take place ___under the water___ .

JJ gets to the bottom of the ocean with the help of ___a submarine named Alvin___ . The *Atlantis II* is a big ship that also helps by ___taking Alvin___ ___and JJ out to sea___ . By using sonar, Alvin can tell when they are ___nearing the bottom___ . When they near the bottom, they slow down.

The scientists on Alvin tell JJ where to go and what to do. JJ can ___shine a light___ on anything the scientists want to see better. For example, scientists once took a close look at the *Titanic*, a famous old shipwreck. JJ was good for this job because it was able to swim ___all around the inside of___ the *Titanic*.

More underwater machines like JJ and Alvin are being built. ___Scientists___ will use them to learn to use the oceans safely and well, to take a closer look at ___shipwrecks___ , and to make better maps of ___the ocean floor___ .

B. On separate paper, write three sentences telling about a wonderful machine you'd like to invent. See Teacher Notes.

62 "The Wonderful Underwater Machine" Selection Comprehension

---

RESOURCE CENTER

◀ **Workbook page 62** is intended for use by all students.

Writing Master 9 provides guidelines for the Writing to Learn activity.

I·T Kit Activities

Poster: "A Matter of Life and Depth"
Students meet a variety of sea creatures on the imaginary ocean dive suggested by this colorful poster. After identifying animals that live in surface, mid-, and deep water, students go fishing in books for an animal to add at each level. (See Activity Guide.) CONTENT AREAS

Audio: Interview with Martin Bowen, Robot Technician
Deep-sea diver and scientist Martin Bowen rides a tiny underwater craft miles below the ocean's surface to monitor Jason, Jr., the robot with a pair of video cameras for eyes. Students hear how Bowen and JJ have explored different underwater wonders. (See Activity Guide.) CAREERS

LANGUAGE ARTS CONNECTIONS

NONFICTION AS A LITERARY GENRE

Have students write informational articles.

Ask students what they would expect to find in a nonfiction selection. *(facts about a subject, photographs, diagrams)* Remind students that a nonfiction selection has paragraphs that contain main ideas and supporting details. Have students select and research topics about the sea and write informational articles. Some suggestions for topics are submarines, shipwrecks, sea animals such as dolphins or whales, and unusual fish or sea plants. Ask students where they might look to find information about their topics. *(encyclopedias, nonfiction books, newspapers, magazines)* Students may work in pairs or small groups and may include diagrams or illustrations. Combine the articles into a newsletter.

WHOLE CLASS ENRICHMENT

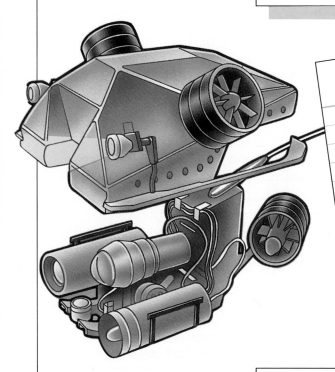

WRITING FIRST-PERSON DESCRIPTIVE ACCOUNTS

Discuss what a first-person descriptive account is.

Explain that when a writer describes a personal experience, he or she tells about the sights, sounds, and feelings as they happened, using pronouns such as *I, we, our.* The step-by-step telling makes a reader feel as if he or she were going through the experience right along with the writer.

Have students write first-person descriptive accounts.

Encourage students to write their own first-person descriptive accounts based on information from the selection. They might wish to imagine what they felt and saw as Alvin sank to the ocean bottom or as Jason Jr. explored the *Titanic.* Ask students to read the accounts aloud. CHALLENGE: WRITING

CREATIVE THINKING: WRITING POEMS

Have students write free verse about the sea.

Explain that free verse is a kind of poetry that uses words and rhythms to help a reader "see" and "hear" what the author is describing. Instead of rhyming words and a regular rhythm, a free verse poem about an ocean storm might use words like *crash* and *boom* and sharp, crashing rhythms to give the feeling of waves hitting a rocky shore. Words such as *floating* or *sleepy* and a slow, restful rhythm might be used instead to describe a calm sea. To help students understand how rhythms can change, recall the story of *The Little Engine That Could* and how the Engine says "I think I can" slowly when pulling a load uphill and quickly when going down. Have students work in pairs or small groups to create free verses about the sea and sea creatures seen from a submarine. Have students read their verses aloud. SHARED LEARNING: WRITING/SPEAKING

CREATING ALLITERATION

Discuss alliteration.

Point out to students that in "The Wonderful Underwater Machine," the author says, "You would think you were looking at a big blue bug with two bright eyes." Explain that the repeated sounds of the letter *b* make the sentence more fun and interesting.

Have students create phrases using repeated sounds.

Have each student select three words from the selection that begin with the same sound and create phrases or sentences using the repeated sounds. Students might also illustrate their choices. *(Some examples are: bubbles bouncing and bumping each other; sunlight softly shining)* **Language Arts Master 8** can be used with this activity.   SPEAKING

READING EVERY DAY

"The Wonderful Underwater Machine" showed students how JJ helps scientists explore the ocean's depths. The following books will provide students with an opportunity to become amateur ocean "explorers" and to learn about other underwater machines.

How to Be an Ocean Scientist in Your Own Home by Seymour Simon. Lippincott, © 1988. Twenty-four do-it-yourself experiments can help even the young landlubber investigate and unravel some of the ocean's many mysteries.

Undersea Machines by R. J. Stephen. Franklin Watts, © 1986. Colorful photographs and helpful diagrams accompany the information about manned and unmanned submersibles and the purposes for which they are used.

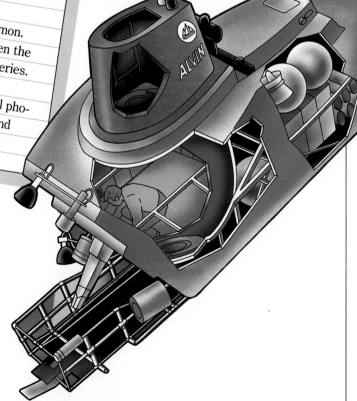

Reader's Journal   **pp 50, 51**
Extending Reading

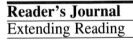

AN UNDERWATER WALK

Students read about and see pictures of colorful creatures that live deep in the ocean. They choose ones they would most and least like to meet, explaining why.

Selection Support

SKILL TRACE: SUFFIXES				
Introduction	Practice	Test	Reteach	Maintain
TE 222	248	293	311	314	424

WORD STUDY

Suffixes -able, -ible

OBJECTIVE Using structural analysis to determine word meaning.

Review suffixes -able, -ible.

Remind students that knowing the meanings of suffixes can help them figure out the meanings of unfamiliar words. Review the meanings of -*able* and -*ible* as "worthy of," "can be," "able to be." Point out that words with these suffixes are used to describe things.

Present suffixed words in context.

Display the Teaching Chart. Read the first sentence and identify the base word and suffix. (*collect, -ible*) Explain that the word means "can be collected."

TEACHING CHART 35: -ABLE, -IBLE

35

1. Jason, Jr. might be used to pick up collectible things from the ocean floor. (collect + -ible; "can be collected")
2. JJ has a bendable cable. (bend + -able; "can be bent")
3. Scientists learn important things about the sea with this valuable machine. (value + able; "worthy of value'

Have students identify the remaining examples.

Ask students to identify the remaining suffixed words, suggest a meaning for each word, and identify any context clues to the meaning.

Provide independent practice.

Options for independent practice are shown in the Resource Center below.

Workbook page 63

NAME _____

WORD STUDY

Suffixes -*able*, -*ible*

REMEMBER: The suffixes -*able* and -*ible* help words describe.

A. Read each pair of sentences. Use a word from the box to complete each pair. The underlined word is a clue.

breakable	floatable	horrible
movable	reliable	sensible

1. Tiny glass bubbles under JJ's fiberglass skin help the machine to <u>float</u> in water.
   JJ had to be _____ floatable _____ so it would not sink to the bottom of the ocean.
2. Motors helped JJ <u>move</u>.
   JJ was _____ movable _____.
3. It made <u>sense</u> for scientists to check JJ's motors every day.
   It was _____ sensible _____ to examine JJ before using it.
4. They would have felt <u>horror</u> if JJ had broken down underwater.
   It would have been _____ horrible _____ to lose JJ deep in the sea.
5. Luckily, JJ did not <u>break</u> often.
   JJ was not very _____ breakable _____.
6. The engineers had made a machine they could <u>rely</u> on.
   JJ was a _____ reliable _____ machine.

B. On separate paper, write about underwater machines. Use three words that end in -*able* or -*ible*. See Teacher Notes.

Suffixes -*able*, -*ible*   "The Wonderful Underwater Machine"   **63**

RESOURCE CENTER

◀ **Workbook page 63** is intended for use by all students.

Skills Practice 56 ▶ may be assigned for additional practice.

Workbook reuse option: Have students draw a slash through each word they have written to separate the suffix from its base word.

Skills Practice 56

NAME _____

SKILLS PRACTICE **56**

Suffixes -*able*, -*ible*

The suffixes -*able* and -*ible* mean "capable of being," "can be," or "able to." *Collectible* means that something can be collected. *Lovable* means that something can be loved.

I have collected many puppets. Puppets are *collectible*.
All my puppets are very cute and *lovable*.

Read each riddle and write the correct answer from the box.

beatable	collectible	fixable	sensible
believable	drinkable	lovable	sinkable
breakable	enjoyable	mentionable	washable

1. Glasses and some toys are like this.
   They can fall apart. _____ breakable _____
2. Puppies and babies are like this.
   It means something that can be liked a lot. _____ lovable _____
3. It means something that can go under water.
   It may be a boat with a hole. _____ sinkable _____
4. This is something you can understand.
   It makes sense. _____ sensible _____
5. This is what a team is when other teams beat it. _____ beatable _____
6. This is what baseball cards are when you gather them. _____ collectible _____
7. This is what clothes that can be cleaned are. _____ washable _____
8. You can put it back together again. _____ fixable _____
9. You can accept it as true. _____ believable _____
10. This is something that is pleasant. _____ enjoyable _____
11. This is something that can be talked about. _____ mentionable _____
12. Milk, juice, and water are this. _____ drinkable _____

56 LEVEL 8   "The Wonderful Underwater Machine"

SKILL TRACE: TABLE OF CONTENTS				
Introduction	Practice	Test	Reteach	Maintain
TE 224	249	273	311	315	445

STUDY SKILLS

Title Page, Copyright Page, Table of Contents

OBJECTIVE Using the title and copyright pages and the table of contents.

Review title page, copyright page, and table of contents.

Remind students that the title of a book is its name, the company that prints the pages was the publisher, and the copyright shows the year in which the book is published. The table of contents lists the chapters or units in the book and the page number on which each chapter or unit begins.

Provide practice in using the title and copyright pages and table of contents.

Display the Teaching Chart. Have students identify each example and answer the following questions: What is the title of the book? When was it published? How many chapters does the book have? (*4*) On what page does the chapter about underwater treasures begin?

TEACHING CHART 36: TITLE PAGE, COPYRIGHT PAGE, TABLE OF CONTENTS | 36

Under the Sea
by Nancy Jones

Bates Publishing, New York, NY
© Copyright 1985
by Nancy Jones

Contents

Creatures of the Sea	4
Submarines and Robots	12
Underwater Treasures	20
Into the Future	32

Provide independent practice.

Options for independent practice are shown in the Resource Center below.

Workbook page 64

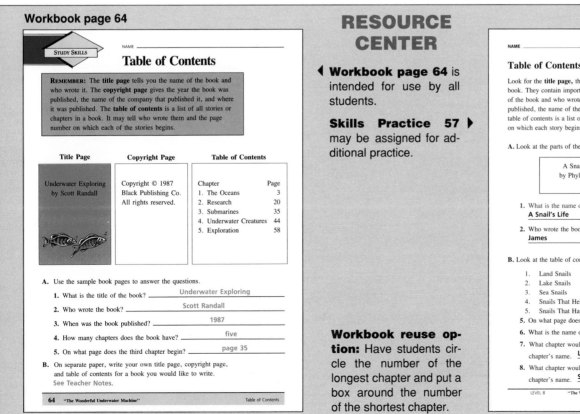

RESOURCE CENTER

◄ **Workbook page 64** is intended for use by all students.

Skills Practice 57 ► may be assigned for additional practice.

Workbook reuse option: Have students circle the number of the longest chapter and put a box around the number of the shortest chapter.

Skills Practice 57

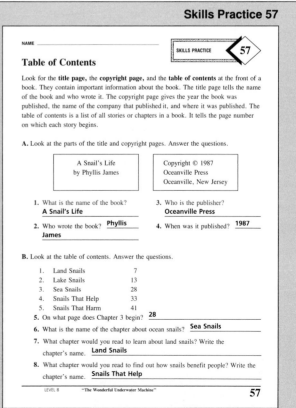

SKILL TRACE: SPELLING CHANGES	
Introduced in Level 7	Maintain
	TE 141 / 250

WORD STUDY

Spelling Changes: *f* to *ve*

OBJECTIVE   Reading words with *f* changed to *ve* before an ending.

Review changing f to ve.

Remind students that before adding *-s* to form the plural of some words that end in *f* or *fe*, the *f* or *fe* is changed to *ve*.

Provide practice in changing f to ve.

You may wish to write the sentences below on the chalkboard. Answers are printed in red. Read the first sentence. Point out that the word *leaf* needs to be plural to complete correctly the sentence so that it makes sense. Before adding *-s* to make *leaf* plural, the *f* must be changed to *ve*. The word that would be written on the blank would be *leaves* to complete the sentence.

---

1. We did not see any __(leaves)__ on the ocean floor.
       leaf

2. The kitchen in our submarine has four __(shelves)__ .
                                            shelf

3. One shelf holds our __(knives)__ .
                          knife

4. There are no __(thieves)__ on board this boat.
                    thief

Have students complete the remaining examples.

Ask students to copy the sentences on separate paper and complete them by writing the plural of the word below the answer line. Or have volunteers write the words on the chalkboard.

Provide independent practice.

An independent activity is shown in the Resource Center below.

RESOURCE CENTER

Skills Practice 58 ▶ may be assigned for additional practice.

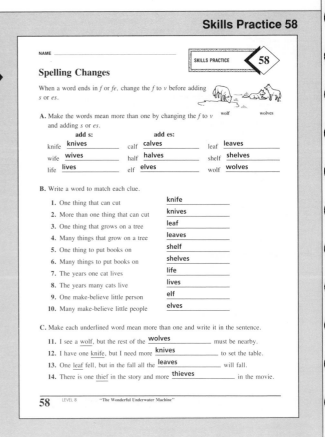

SKILL TRACE: SUFFIXES				
Introduction	Practice	Test	Reteach	Maintain
TE 56	83	139	157	160	251

WORD STUDY

Suffixes *-er, -or*

OBJECTIVE Using structural analysis to determine word meaning.

Review suffixes -er, -or.

Remind students that knowing the meanings of suffixes can help in figuring out the meanings of words. Review the meanings of the suffixes *-er* and *-or* as "one who" or "that which."

Review how to use suffixes to determine word meanings.

You may wish to write the sentences below on the chalkboard. Answers are printed in red. Read the first sentence and identify the base word and suffix. *(sail, -or)* The word can be defined as "one who sails." The word clues "travel the sea" also help define *sailor* as "one who travels on the sea."

---

1. The sailor loved to travel the sea.
(sail + -or; "one who sails")
2. My friend would like to be a teacher in our school.
(teach + -er; "one who teaches")
3. Mark is the best actor in the school play.
(act + -or; "one who acts")
4. The singer sang his favorite song.
(sing + -er; "one who sings")

Have students identify the remaining examples.

Call on students to identify the suffixed words in the remaining sentences, define the words, and identify any context clues that helped them decide on the definitions.

Provide independent practice.

An independent activity is shown in the Resource Center below.

RESOURCE CENTER

Skills Practice 59 ▶ may be assigned for additional practice.

Skills Practice 59

NAME _____

SKILLS PRACTICE 59

Suffixes *-er, -or*

Suffixes, like words, have meanings. The suffixes *-er* and *-or* mean "one who."

A. Write **over, on,** or **under** to show where you would find these sea things. Then write the meaning of each one.

Where Will You Find Me?		What Do I Mean?
1. diver **under** the sea		someone who dives
2. sailor **on** the sea		someone who sails
3. swimmer **on** the sea		someone who swims
4. floater **on** the sea		someone or something that floats
5. flier **over** the sea		someone or something that flies
6. sinker **under** the sea		something that sinks
7. rower **on** the sea		someone who rows

B. Write the word from the box that completes each sentence.

actor	collector	leader	survivor
cleaner	doctor	steamer	winner

8. The **survivor** of the shipwreck crawled up on the sand.
9. The woman steering the **steamer** blew the boat's whistle.
10. This **cleaner** doesn't work very well on the lighthouse windows.
11. Mr. Davis is a **collector** of all kinds of seashells.
12. The **leader** of the group showed everyone how to dive.
13. The **winner** of the fishing contest caught a ten-pound bluefish.
14. The **doctor** treated a person who had a cut from a fishhook.
15. The **actor** played the part of a steamship captain.

LEVEL 8   "The Wonderful Underwater Machine"   59

CURRICULUM CONNECTIONS

DEEPWATER DIORAMAS ART

Have students make dioramas of underwater scenes using shoe boxes. Students can make cutouts and hang them from string inside the shoe boxes so that the fish and plants can move. The fronts of the shoe boxes might be covered with blue cellophane to give an underwater effect.

WOODS HOLE, WATER, AND YOU! SOCIAL STUDIES

Explain that the research carried out at the Woods Hole Oceanographic Institution in Massachusetts may help scientists solve the problems that affect the future of water everywhere on earth. Discuss with students some of these problems, such as water pollution due to industrial waste, effects of acid rain on water supplies, and current problems in the fishing industry. Work with students to develop a list of questions related to these or other issues. Include the questions in letters students send to the Oceanographic Institution asking for information about the work being done there. Have students write: Public Information Office, Woods Hole Oceanographic Institution, Woods Hole, Massachusetts 02543.

UNDERWATER FARMING SCIENCE

Explain to students that scientists and researchers have developed means of growing edible plants and shellfish underwater. Have students research the topic of underwater farming to find out about the kinds of plants and fish being grown and the methods and techniques being used. Suggest that students work in groups to prepare a brief oral report. Tell them to use reference sources and other books in the library to get information. Encourage students to include illustrations, diagrams, maps, or other visual aids that will help explain their information.

DOWN TO THE DEPTHS SCIENCE/MATHEMATICS

Tell students there are many kinds of animals that live in the ocean at different depths. The depth of the ocean is often measured in nautical miles. Have students research sea animals such as sea snakes, seahorses, dolphins, and giant squid and find out the depths at which they live. Ask students to chart how many nautical miles below the surface of the water these animals live.

Explain that the depth of the ocean can also be measured in fathoms and that one fathom equals six feet. Have students create multiplication and division word problems that involve measurements with fathoms and feet. For example, ''How many feet equal two fathoms?'' *(12)* ''How many fathoms equal 24 feet?'' *(4)* **Curriculum Connection Master 8** can be used with this activity.

OCEANS OF OPPORTUNITIES CAREERS

Have students research different careers involved in the underwater world. Some suggestions are fishing, deep-sea diving, underwater searching or salvaging, and oceanography. Have students create charts to present their findings. Students might list the careers and then write sentences describing what each job involves. When students present their charts, they might tell if any of the careers interest them and why.

LITERATURE LINK

OBJECTIVE   Using the headings in an article to help organize and remember information.

INTRODUCING AND READING THE LESSON

Tap students' prior knowledge.

Hold up the front page of a newspaper for the class. Point out the headlines and ask students if they know what these are called. Ask students what they think the topics of the stories will be. Point out that headlines give important information about the stories. Discuss with students what they think it would be like to read a newspaper that just said "News" at the top of the page, with no headlines.

Have students come up with their own headlines.

Ask volunteers to think of possible headlines that might appear in a newspaper about their school. *(possible responses: "Third-Graders Visit Zoo," "School Lunch Menu to Change," "New Softball Field Almost Ready")* After each headline has been suggested, have students discuss what the story underneath that headline might be about. Guide students to the realization that the headlines in a newspaper help readers know what each news story is about. Tell students that other kinds of articles often include headings, which are similar to headlines in newspapers, since they help organize information.

Explain the usefulness of headings.

Explain that looking at the headings before reading an article can help readers learn what topics the article discusses.

State the objective.

Tell students that in this lesson they will learn how to use the headings in articles to learn and remember information.

Refer students to their texts.

Have students turn to pages 142–143 in their books and read the lesson.

LITERATURE LINK

How do headings help you read?

In "The Wonderful Underwater Machine," the author uses diagrams and pictures to show how Jason Jr. works. They help you learn new information.

Look quickly at the article below. Even before you read it, you can learn about whales from the picture. What else can help you learn about whales?

Whales Are Mammals

Breathing Air

Whales are mammals, so they must breathe air. They can dive under the water, but they must always return to the surface for air. A whale's nose is called a "blowhole." It is on top of the whale's head, so the whale can breathe without coming very far out of the water.

Staying Warm

Whales often swim in very cold water. To help them stay warm, they have a thick layer of fat around their bodies. This is called "blubber." It acts like an overcoat to keep heat inside the body from escaping.

—John Bonnett Wexo, *Whales*

Strategy for Reading

Headings Help

The article has phrases called headings at the beginning of each paragraph. Headings break the information into smaller parts. What can you learn just by reading the headings?

The headings in this article help you know that whales must breathe air and stay warm. And that is exactly what you will learn from reading this article. You've already learned a lot and you haven't read the whole article yet!

When you read an article with headings, try using these tips. They will help you organize your reading and learn new information.

- Read all the headings.
- Think about what you learn from them.
- Read the section under each heading.
- Stop after each section to sum up important details.

Try the tips for using headings as you read "Seals on the Land and in the Water." See if they help you learn and remember the information in the article.

Using Headings in an Article

DISCUSSING THE LESSON

Review the main points of the lesson.

Check students' understanding of the strategy with these questions.

Page 143   How are the headings in articles helpful to you? (Headings give you a quick overview of the topics that are covered.)

Page 143   What should you do when you see headings in an article? (Possible responses: Read the headings; think about what they tell you; read the section under each heading; sum up important details under each heading.)

WRAP-UP

Direct students to the next selection.

Ask students to look over the title and headings of the next selection, "Seals on the Land and in the Water." Encourage them to use the tips on page 143 of their books to help them organize and remember the information in the selection.

TEACHER · CHOICE

	Teaching Sequence	Trade Books and Resources	Meeting Individual Needs	Integrated Language Arts / Cross Curriculum
The Bridge Pages 258–259	**Introduce** Context Clues	• Teaching Chart 37 • Workbook 65 • Skills Practice 60		
PART 1 **Vocabulary Strategies** Pages 260–261	**Develop Concepts** Discussing Mammals **Teach Vocabulary** **STORY CRITICAL WORDS:** blubber, **climates, flippers,** lungs, mammals, **muscles,** seals, warm-blooded (Tested words are boldfaced.)	• Teaching Chart 38 • Workbook 66 • Skills Practice 61	**SUPPORT WORDS:** awkward, depending, dolphins, include, nature, surroundings • Skills Practice 62	**WRITING/SPEAKING ACTIVITY:** Use new vocabulary to discuss seals. • Spelling Connection 47
PART 2 **Reading & Responding** Pages 262–269	**Build Background** **Develop a Purpose for Reading** **Guide the Reading Process** **Selection Follow-Up**	• Reader's Journal 52–55 • Workbook 67 **READING EVERY DAY** *All About Whales,* by D.I. Patent *Jack, the Seal and the Sea,* by G. Aschenbrenner *Sea Otters,* by E. Shaw	**EXTRA HELP:** Making a Chart About Seals **ACHIEVING ENGLISH PROFICIENCY:** Discussing Animal Habitats • Achieving English Proficiency Master 16	**Language Arts Connections** **WRITING TO LEARN:** Write a comparison chart about seals. • Writing Master 10 **SPEAKING/LISTENING:** Completing Analogies; Role-playing Seals • Language Arts Master 9 **WRITING:** Writing Just-So Stories; Creating Magazines About Polar Life
PART 3 **Selection Support** Pages 270–275	**Introduce** Test-Taking	• Teaching Chart 39 • Workbook 68 • Skills Practice 63	**Practice** • Teaching Charts 40–41 • Workbook 69–70 • Skills Practice 64–65 Suffix *-ness* (Tested) Title Page, Copyright Page, Table of Contents (Tested) **Maintain** • Skills Practice 66 Main Idea/Details	**Curriculum Connections** **SCIENCE:** Researching and Writing About Mammals **ART:** Making a Mural of a Seal Community **HEALTH:** Creating Posters on Cold-weather Health Habits • Curriculum Connection Master 9

SEALS
On the Land and in the Water ≋

by Betsey Knafo

SUMMARY *Like cats, dogs, and people, seals are mammals: warm-blooded animals that breathe air with their lungs and usually have hair or fur on their bodies. Baby mammals are born, not hatched from eggs, and they drink milk from their mothers. Although most mammals live on land, seals live on the land and in the water. The blubber under the skin helps them survive in cold water, where they can stay for at least twenty minutes without breathing. Seals come out of the water to rest and to have their babies, which are called pups.*

The Bridge

SKILL TRACE: CONTEXT CLUES

This skill is untested at this level.

WORD STUDY

Teaching Context Clues

OBJECTIVE   Using context clues to determine word meaning.

1. WARM-UP

Use a known passage to discuss how to figure out the meaning of a new word.

Tell students they will listen to a passage from the previous selection, "The Wonderful Underwater Machine." Have them listen and think about what words are clues to the meaning of the word *sonar*. (*a machine that uses sound waves to locate objects or to measure the depth of water*)

The sonar makes a noise and listens for the noise to bounce off the ocean floor. When the scientists hear the echo a short time after the noise is made, they know that the ocean floor is close.

Discuss context clues.

Reread the passage. Have students explain what word clues helped them decide what sonar is. (*makes a noise, listens, bounce off the ocean floor, hear the echo*) Point out to students that the words in the sentence or paragraph in which they find an unfamiliar word can be used as clues to the word's meaning.

State the objective.

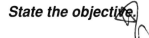

Tell students they will practice using the surrounding words, or context clues, to help them figure out the meaning of an unfamiliar word or the meaning of a familiar word used in a new way.

2. TEACH

Explain why being able to use context clues is important.

Using context clues helps readers to be more independent without having to stop and look up words in a dictionary.

Explain context clues of equivalence.

Remind students that there are different types of context clues. Explain that one type provides a definition of the unfamiliar word. The definition may include a specific explanation, a restatement of a thought in different words, a word or phrase set off by commas that defines the unfamiliar word, a word with similar meaning or a synonym, or information that makes the meaning of the unfamiliar word more clear. Point out that context clues can be found before or after the unfamiliar word, in the same sentence or within the paragraph.

TEACHING CHART 37: CONTEXT CLUES   37

1. Sometimes there are sharp rocks, or *coral*, that can harm and even tear apart a machine. (sharp rocks)
2. JJ's outer skin is *fiberglass*, which is a tough covering made of fine threads of woven glass. (a tough covering made of fine threads of woven glass)
3. JJ was made at an *institution* called Woods Hole. This place was built to bring scientists together to study the ocean. (place where scientists work)

Model how to use context clues.

Read the first sentence on the Teaching Chart. Explain that to find the meaning of the word *coral*, you could look at the rest of the words in the sentence for clues. Point out that because the word is set off by commas, you might try looking at what comes before the word. Here you find the context clue "sharp rocks," which gives a definition of *coral*.

3. GUIDED PRACTICE

Check for understanding.

Before going on, have students explain how to use context clues to figure out the meaning of an unfamiliar word or a new meaning for a known word. (*Read the words in the sentence or paragraph around the unfamiliar word and look for a definition, a restatement, a word or phrase set off by commas that defines the word, a synonym, or more information that makes the meaning clear.*)

Guide students in using context clues.

Have students use context clues to determine meanings of the words *fiberglass* and *institution*. Discuss how the clues helped them to figure out the meanings of the words.

4. WRAP-UP

Summarize instruction.

Review why it is important to be able to use context clues to figure out word meaning. (*Using context clues helps readers better understand what they read without having to stop and look up words in a dictionary.*)

Provide independent practice.

Options for independent practice are shown in the Resource Center below.

5. APPLICATION

Students will use context clues to determine the meaning of new vocabulary in Part 1. The symbol ✔ marks specific questions and activities that apply this skill.

Workbook page 65

NAME _____

WORD STUDY

Context Clues

REMEMBER: The words and sentences around an unknown word can help you figure out the meaning of that unknown word.

✔ **A.** Read the sentences. Look for clues that help you understand the underlined words. Then complete the statements.

oldword

1. Like any <u>submarine</u>, Alvin can dive in very deep water.
   A submarine is <u>a ship that dives in deep water</u>.

2. There are also two <u>cameras</u> inside JJ that take pictures of what it finds.
   A camera is an instrument that <u>takes pictures</u>.

3. Scientists can tell they are getting close to the bottom by turning on a <u>sonar machine</u>, which uses sounds to show how far away something is.
   A sonar machine uses <u>sounds</u> to show <u>the depth of the water in different locations and how far away something is</u>.

4. In 1912 a large ship hit an iceberg and sank. This ship, the <u>*Titanic*</u>, is now famous because of that disaster.
   The *Titanic* is <u>a famous ship that sank</u>.

B. Write a sentence that has a clue that explains the meaning of *anchor*. See Teacher Notes.

Context Clues   "Seals on the Land and in the Water" **65**

RESOURCE CENTER

◀ **Workbook page 65** is intended for use by all students.

Skills Practice 60 ▶ may be assigned for additional practice.

Workbook reuse option: Have students underline the context clues in each sentence of Part A that helped them understand the meaning of each word.

Skills Practice 60

NAME _____

SKILLS PRACTICE **60**

Context Clues

When you read, you may come to a word you don't know. The words and sentences around an unknown word can help you figure out the word's meaning.

> Make sure you look for clues both *before* and *after* the word you don't know.

A. Read the story.

A <u>beaver</u> is a small furry animal that builds its home in water. That is why this <u>creature</u> is known as the <u>engineer</u> or builder of the animal world. Its home is built in a wall called a <u>dam</u> that is built across a stream and causes the water to be blocked. The home <u>protrudes</u> or sticks up above the water. It is made of sticks and <u>twigs</u> held <u>securely</u> with mud. When the animal is inside its home, it stays in the <u>section</u> above the water. There is a front and back <u>entrance</u> where the animal goes in and out. Because of its hard work and <u>toil</u> the beaver earns the phrase, "busy as a beaver."

B. Use a word that is underlined in the story to answer each question.

1. What is someone called who builds things?   engineer
2. What is something built to hold back water?   dam
3. What is a place where you can go in?   entrance
4. Which word means "to stick up or out"?   protrude
5. Which words means "a part of something"?   section
6. Which is the name of an animal?   beaver
7. Which word means "firmly"?   securely
8. Which word means "hard work"?   toil
9. Which word means "sticks"?   twigs
10. Which word means "an animal"?   creature

60   LEVEL 8   "Seals on the Land and in the Water"

PART 1

Vocabulary Strategies

Developing Concepts

Motivate discussion with pictures of mammals.

Use the concept of mammals as a starting point for teaching vocabulary. Tell students they are going to read a selection about seals. Then explain that seals are mammals, like dogs, cats, horses, and people. Point out that mammals have certain things in common: they are warm-blooded, breathe air with their lungs, and give birth to living babies rather than hatch eggs. Most mammals have some kind of fur or hair on their bodies. Then show students pictures of different kinds of mammals, including people, seals, whales, dogs, and cats. Ask students whether each mammal lives on the land or in the water. Explain that even mammals that spend all of their time in the water, such as whales, must breathe air with their lungs.

Teaching Vocabulary

Discuss meanings of Story Critical words.

Read each context sentence on the Teaching Chart and identify the new word. Then use the questions below to help students understand each word. When necessary, provide a definition.

TEACHING CHART 38: VOCABULARY   **38**

1. **seals** (sea animals with four flippers)
   Seals are animals that live in the sea and on the land.
2. **mammals** (animals that feed their young with milk from the mother)
   Seals are *mammals*, which means that their babies feed on mother's milk.
3. **flippers** (broad, flat limbs for swimming)
   Seals use their flat *flippers* somewhat like hands to swim quickly through the water.
4. **warm-blooded** (having constant body temperature)
   Seals are *warm-blooded*, which means that their blood is always warm no matter how cold the water is.
5. **lungs** (organs for breathing)
   Even whales breathe air through their *lungs*.
6. **blubber** (the fat of a sea animal)
   Seals can spend a long time in icy water because a layer of *blubber*, or fat, keeps them warm.
7. **muscles** (organs that contract or expand to move parts of a body)
   Seals have strong *muscles* under their skin that make them good swimmers.
8. **climates** (usual year-round weather conditions of places)
   Seals have fur and blubber to protect them from the icy *climates* of the North and South Poles.

✔ seals

1. What context clues in the sentence help you know the meaning of *seals*? (animals, live, sea, land)   STRATEGY: CONTEXT CLUES

mammals

2. What do all mammals do according to the sentence? (feed their babies with milk from the mother) **Why are seals considered mammals?** (They give birth to living young, feed their young with mother's milk, breathe air, have fur.)   STRATEGY: PRIOR KNOWLEDGE

✔ *flippers*

3. What context clues in the sentence helped you to identify the meaning of *flippers*? (flat, like hands, swim)   STRATEGY: CONTEXT CLUES

warm-blooded

4. What do you feel when you put your hands in ice water? (cold) Explain that the water feels cold because humans are *warm-blooded*, which means that their body temperature remains the same no matter what the temperature around it. You feel the cold because your hand is still warm — a different temperature from the water.   STRATEGY: PRIOR KNOWLEDGE

✔ *lungs*

5. What word in the sentence is a clue to what the lungs do? (breathe) **What happens when you put your hand on your chest and take a deep breath?** (You can feel your chest rise.) **Why does this happen?** (The lungs are filling up with air.)   STRATEGY: CONTEXT CLUES

✔ *blubber*

6. What are the context clues that tell you the meaning of *blubber*? (layer, fat, warm) **What kind of context clue is the word *fat*?** (definition set off by commas)   STRATEGY: CONTEXT CLUES

✔ *muscles*

7. What are the context clues in the sentence? (strong, under their skin, swimmers) **What do muscles do in our bodies?** (move all of our body parts)   STRATEGY: CONTEXT CLUES

climates

8. What kinds of clothes do people wear in cold climates? (scarves, mittens, hats, sweaters, coats)   STRATEGY: PRIOR KNOWLEDGE

✓**Discuss Support words as needed.**

The Glossary of the Student Text includes definitions of the Support words: *depending, include, surroundings, dolphins, nature, awkward.*

Provide independent practice.

Options for independent practice are shown in the Resource Center below.

WRITING OR SPEAKING ACTIVITY *Have students use the new vocabulary and the sentences on the chart to create a few sentences telling what they have learned about seals so far.*

✔ Skill from **The Bridge** applied through this question.

Workbook page 66

SELECTION VOCABULARY
NAME _____

Using New Words

A. Use the words in the box to complete the sentences.

| blubber | climates | flippers | lungs |
| mammals | muscles | seals | warm-blooded |

Like dogs, people, and other ___mammals___ , seals are ___warm-blooded___ . They need lots of body fat to keep them warm in icy waters. A seal's fat is called ___blubber___ . Instead of arms, legs, or fins, seals have ___flippers___ to help them move around both in the water and on land.

B. Label each list with a word from the box.

1. ___mammals___   2. ___climates___
cow   hot and rainy
cat   cold and snowy

C. Write words from the box that belong in each group.
3. ___blood vessels___   4. ___whales___
   ___lungs___   ___porpoises___
   ___muscles___   ___seals___

D. On separate paper, write three sentences about parts of the human body. Use words from the box. See Teacher Notes.

66   "Seals on the Land and in the Water"   Selection Vocabulary

---

RESOURCE CENTER

◀ **Workbook page 66** provides practice with Story Critical words.

Skills Practice 61 ▶ provides additional practice with Story Critical words.

Skills Practice 62 provides practice with Support words.

Spelling Connection Master 47 may be used for spelling instruction with the new vocabulary.

Workbook reuse option: Have students add at least two words to each column in Part B to expand the lists.

Skills Practice 61

NAME _____   SKILLS PRACTICE 61

Vocabulary: Story Critical Words

A. Study the meaning of each word.

blubber the fat of a sea animal
climates the general weather conditions of a large area
flippers limbs for swimming
lungs organs for breathing
mammals milk-producing animals
muscles organs for moving parts of the body
seals sea mammals with four flippers
warm-blooded having constant body temperature

B. Analogies are pairs of words that are related to each other in the same way. Complete each analogy.

1. *Bees* are to *insects* as *seals* are to ___mammals___ .
2. *Hear* is to *ears* as *breathe* is to ___lungs___ .
3. *Reptiles* are to *cold-blooded* as *mammals* are to ___warm-blooded___ .
4. *Sweet and sour* are to *tastes* as *hot and cold* are to ___climates___ .
5. *People* are to *arms* as *seals* are to ___flippers___ .

C. Complete the word map. Use at least four of the vocabulary words. Then add words of your own. **Responses will vary.**

6. Parts of a Seal's Body   7. Words that Describe Seals
   blubber   warm-blooded
   flippers   Seal   mammals
   lungs   _____
   muscles   _____

D. One word in each sentence does not make sense. Underline the word. Then write the vocabulary word that belongs in its place.

8. Whales have sweaters to keep them warm.   ___blubber___
9. Different parts of the world have different kinds of close.   ___climates___
10. The steals were sunning on the rocks.   ___seals___

LEVEL 8   "Seals on the Land and in the Water"   Analogies   **61**

Reading & Responding

Building Background

Motivate discussion using a riddle.

Read this riddle to students. Ask them what they think the answer is. (*a seal*) Ask how the qualities mentioned may be clues to where seals live.

What barks like a dog but swims like a fish?

Build background about where animals live.

Ask students to suggest other animals besides fish that live only in the water. (*Possible answers: octopi, whales, dolphins, eels*) Have volunteers write the names of the animals on the board under the heading "in the water." Ask what animals live on land and make a similar list. Next, ask students if they can think of any animals that live both on land and in the water. Point out that most of these animals will live near the water's edge. Make a third list on the board. If students have a hard time naming animals that live both on land and in the water, suggest a few, such as turtles, penguins, seagulls, ducks, otters, and frogs. Explain that seals live on land and in the water. How they are able to do this will be explained in the next selection.

Discuss nonfiction.

Explain that the next selection is nonfiction. Review that nonfiction gives information and facts about things in the real world. Ask students what facts about seals they might expect to learn in the next selection. (*Possible answers: where they live, what they eat, what they look like*)

Developing a Purpose for Reading

Option 1
Students set purpose.

ORAL "I WONDER" LISTS   Using a map or globe, show students the North and South Poles. Explain that many seals live in cold places. Then write **"I wonder _____."** on the chalkboard.

Complete the statement with "how seals can live in such cold places." Ask students to suggest other ways to complete the sentence. For example, "I wonder how seals keep warm." For ideas, have students preview the selection illustrations. Record students' responses for later use.

WRITING ACTIVITY   Have students work individually or in pairs to create written "I wonder" statements. Have students save their lists for later use.

Option 2
Teacher sets purpose.

Have students read the selection to find out how seals are able to live in cold climates. Have them look for such facts as how seals stay warm.

Meeting
Individual
Needs

EXTRA HELP   Explain that the next selection tells about seals. Distribute a chart form, Form 8 in the Teacher Resource Kit. Ask students to fill in one column of the chart with what they know about seals and another column with what they would like to find out. As they read, have them complete the chart. After reading, have volunteers share what they learned.

ACHIEVING ENGLISH PROFICIENCY   Display pictures of the following animals: *cats, dogs, horses, whales, dolphins* and *seals*. Say the names of the animals. Have students repeat the names and describe the animals. Make three columns on the board, labelling them *on land, in the water* and *both*. Ask students where they think these animals live and list answers in the appropriate column. Suggest to students that as they read they look for reasons why animals live where they do. For additional help in story comprehension, use Master 16 in the Teacher Resource Kit.

Some animals live on land. Some live in the water. The amazing seal is at home in both places!

SEALS

On the Land and in the Water

by Betsey Knafo

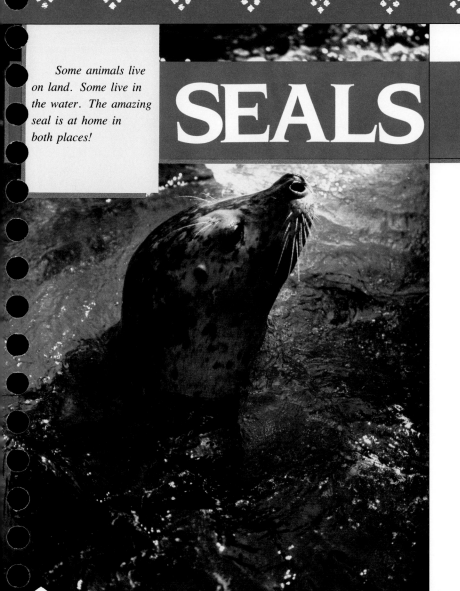

What do a seal and an elephant have in common? They are both <u>mammals</u>. Other mammals include cats, dogs, horses, people, whales, and dolphins. All mammals are alike in certain ways. They are <u>warm-blooded</u> and breathe air with their <u>lungs</u>. Their bodies are covered with hair or fur. Their babies are born, not hatched from eggs like birds and reptiles. Baby mammals also drink milk from their mothers.

Most mammals, like people, live on land. Some mammals, like whales and dolphins, live only in the water. Still other mammals, like <u>seals</u>, live both on land and in the water.

Seals in the Water 〰〰〰

The bodies of seals are filled with strong <u>muscles</u>. These strong muscles and the seals' flippers help them move through water swiftly and easily.

◀ This harbor seal enjoys the sun.
A fur seal takes time to rest. ▶

Reader's Journal   p 52
Preparing for Reading

SEAL

Students read a poem about a seal and write about it in response to questions.

GUIDED READING

✓ **Page 145   Are seals mammals, birds, or reptiles?** (mammals)   RECALL: DETAILS

✔ **Page 145   What context clues in the first paragraph help you understand what mammals are?** (warm-blooded, breathe air with lungs, bodies covered with hair or fur, born — not hatched from eggs, drink milk from their mothers; also other examples of mammals such as cats, dogs, horses)   ANALYZE: CONTEXT

HIGHLIGHTING LITERATURE

Page 145   Have students preview the article, looking at the title and headings. Ask them what they think the article will be about. (how seals are able to live on land and in water) Remind students that knowing what they will learn about sometimes makes it easier to read and keep track of information. Encourage students to check their predictions at the conclusion of the article.
APPLICATION: STRATEGY FOR READING

✔ Skill from The Bridge applied through this question.

Seals are shaped like long footballs. <u>Blubber</u>, or fat, under their skin gives them this odd shape. Blubber is important to help the seals survive. Most seals live in the icy, cold waters around the North and South Poles. Unlike fish who swim in the same cold waters, seals are warm-blooded. They need the blubber to keep them warm as they swim in the cold water or walk on the ice. Blubber also gives them extra energy.

Most seals can stay underwater for at least twenty minutes, and some can even stay under for almost an hour! Then they need to come up for air. How does a seal hold its breath so long? A seal's heartbeat slows down underwater, so it needs less air underwater than it does on land.

When swimming under ice, seals make breathing holes in the ice. They make these holes by chewing with their teeth and scratching with their claws or by using their warm breath to melt the ice.

Seals can even sleep underwater. If the water is not too deep, they sink to the bottom and rise to the top to get air when they need it. In deep water they sleep with just their noses above the water.

An elephant seal swims off the coast of California.

This mother harbor seal stays close to her pup.

Seals get their food from the water by diving deep under the water for fish and shellfish. Some seals have been known to dive so deep that they have brought up fish that most people have never seen before.

Seals on the Land 〰️

Seals have no feet or legs, so they must use their flippers to move around on land. They can move quickly on land, but they are faster and more graceful in water. The same flippers that help them glide through the water appear clumsy and awkward on rocks and ice.

One reason seals come out of the water is to rest. Depending on where they live, they can be found on rocks, sand, or ice. They choose spots to rest where they can easily get back into the water.

Another reason seals live on land is to have babies. These babies are called pups. Usually only one pup is born at a time.

GUIDED READING

Page 146   Why do seals need blubber to help them survive? (They live in cold climates and are warm-blooded. They need the blubber to keep them warm.) RECALL: CAUSE/EFFECT

Page 146   Some seals can hold their breath for an hour under water. Can seals hold their breath that long on land? Why or why not? (No; their heartbeats slow down underwater so they need less air than on land.)   SYNTHESIZE: DRAWING CONCLUSIONS

✔ **Page 147   In the first paragraph under "Seals on the Land," what is a synonym context clue and an antonym context clue for *awkward*?** (synonym — *clumsy*; antonym — *graceful*)   ANALYZE: CONTEXT

Page 147   If you were a seal, why would you choose resting spots near the water? (Possible answers: to be able to get back into the water; because it is hard to move very far on land)   INFER: CAUSE/EFFECT

✔ Skill from The Bridge applied through this question.
✔ Informal Assessment Opportunity: SUMMARIZING

STRATEGIC READING

✔ **Page 147   Have students stop reading just before the heading "Seals on the Land" on this page. Ask them to summarize what they have learned about seals up to this point. To check understanding, ask students why seals need blubber to keep them warm, but fish do not.** (Seals are warm-blooded.) Then ask if fish are warm-blooded. (No; fish are cold-blooded.) Then have students predict how seals will use their flippers on dry land. Point out that summarizing and predicting is one way to check on how well they understood the story. Suggest to students who have trouble summarizing that they reread any parts of the selection they do not understand or do not remember and look for important ideas.   METACOGNITION: SUMMARIZING AND PREDICTING

Nature helps protect the pups. The colors of their fur match the colors of their surroundings. In cold <u>climates</u>, the pups have white fur to match the ice around them. In warmer climates, the pups have dark fur to match the land and rocks. Most pups cannot swim for at least one month, so they must stay on land. The color of their coats helps protect baby seals from their enemies, because if the enemies cannot see the pups, they cannot harm them.

This is a baby harp seal.

Living in Two Worlds 〰

Water is where seals move with greatest ease, and water is where seals find their food. However, seals cannot survive by living in water alone. Seals need to be on land for resting and giving birth to baby seals. Seals are mammals that must survive in the two worlds of land and water.

◆ LIBRARY LINK ◆

If you would like to read about other sea animals, try Sea Otters *by Evelyn Shaw and* Little Whale *by Ann McGovern.*

◆ Reader's Response

What piece of information about seals did you find most interesting?

See next page for suggested answers.

SELECTION FOLLOW-UP

Seals
On the Land and in the Water

◆ Thinking It Over

1. Where are most seals found?
2. Which parts of a seal's body help it survive icy land and water?
3. Why do seals stay close to the water when they are on land? How did you find the answer?
4. The author says that seals are clumsy on land. Do you agree? Describe how they look.
5. What is the main idea in this article about seals?

◆ Writing to Learn

THINK AND RECALL Seals in the water behave differently from seals on land. Make a chart to show three differences. Copy and finish the chart below.

Seals

	In the Water	On the Land
How They Move	They move gracefully.	
How They Breathe		They breathe normally.
How They Sleep		They sleep well.

WRITE Write one paragraph about seals on land. Write another about seals in the water. Use the information in your chart to help you.

GUIDED READING

Page 148   Why do seals need to live in two worlds?
(Although they are more at home in the water, they need to be on land to rest and to give birth to baby seals.)   ANALYZE: MAIN IDEA/DETAILS

RETURNING TO THE READING PURPOSE

OPTION 1   If students set the purpose, return to their "I wonder" statements about seals. Discuss with students what they learned about seals, particularly about how seals live in cold climates. Have them check to see how many of their questions were answered in the selection. If they had questions that were not answered, ask them how they might find more information. (library, zoo, aquarium, encyclopedia)

OPTION 2   If you set the purpose for reading, ask students how seals are able to live in the cold climates of the North and South Poles. (Blubber protects seals from the cold; they can swim under the ice by making breathing holes.)

Reader's Journal   **p 53**
Responding to Reading

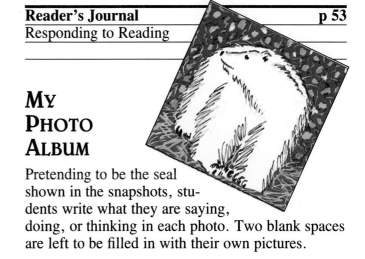

MY PHOTO ALBUM

Pretending to be the seal shown in the snapshots, students write what they are saying, doing, or thinking in each photo. Two blank spaces are left to be filled in with their own pictures.

265

SELECTION FOLLOW-UP

Seals On the Land and in the Water

THINKING IT OVER

1. **Where are most seals found?** (Most seals live near the North and South Poles.)   RECALL: DETAILS

2. **Which parts of a seal's body help it survive icy land and water?** (Possible answers: blubber keeps the seal warm; its claws and teeth enable it to make breathing holes in the ice; its warm breath can melt the ice.)   ANALYZE: MAIN IDEA/DETAILS

3. **Why do seals stay close to the water when they are on land? How did you find the answer?** (Possible answers: to be able to escape from their enemies quickly; to be close to their food supply. Students may cite information on the last two pages of the text to support their conclusions.)   INFER:CAUSE/EFFECT; METACOGNITION

✔ 4. **The author says that seals are clumsy on land. Do you agree? Describe how they look.** (Students may say the seals waddle or rock back and forth on their flippers. Accept all reasonable answers.) EVALUATE: FACT OR OPINION

5. **What is the main idea in this article about seals?** (The main idea is that seals need *both* land and water to survive.)   SYNTHESIZE: MAIN SYNTHESIZE: MAIN IDEA/DETAILS

WRITING TO LEARN

Use Writing Master 10, which duplicates this chart.

THINK AND RECALL   Seals in the water behave differently from seals on land. Make a chart to show three differences. Copy and finish the chart below. (Help students fill in the chart to prepare for writing.)

Seals

	In the Water	On the Land
How They Move	They move gracefully.	(They move clumsily.)
How They Breathe	(They hold their breath.)	They breathe normally.
How They Sleep	(They wake up often to get air.)	They sleep well.

Extend comprehension through writing.

WRITE   Write one paragraph about seals on land. Write another about seals in the water. Use the information in your chart to help you. (Have students share their paragraphs.)

✔ Informal Assessment Opportunity: EVALUATING

More Ideas for Selection Follow-Up

CRITICAL AND CREATIVE THINKING QUESTIONS

Encourage a variety of responses and points of view.

Use these open-ended questions to encourage critical and creative thinking about the selection.

1. The color of their fur helps protect seal pups from their enemies. Why do you think baby seals need this protection more than adult seals?

2. What did you learn about seals from this selection? What else would you like to know about them?

3. If you, like seals, could live in two places, what would they be? Why?

REREADING ORALLY

Have students reread for fluency.

Have students choose the part of the selection they found to be the most interesting to read aloud. Give students time to reread their parts several times silently to make sure they know where to stop or where to pause. Also have them identify any words they think would be difficult to pronounce. Then have students pair up with a reading partner to practice reading their parts. Encourage students to read with an expression that shows they are interested in what they are saying. Tell students that it may help to begin their reading with "Did you know that?" followed by the parts of the selection they have chosen. Model this procedure for students by selecting a paragraph from the selection and reading it aloud, beginning with "Did you know that?" Use expression in your voice and point out to students how the punctuation in the paragraph helps you to know where to stop or pause.

SELECTION COMPREHENSION

Provide comprehension check.

A Workbook page to check comprehension is shown in the Resource Center below. It may be used for informal assessment.

Workbook page 67

NAME _____

Seals on the Land and in the Water

SELECTION COMPREHENSION

A. Complete the summary of the selection "Seals on the Land and in the Water." Accept reasonable variations.

This article is about _____seals_____. The main point the article makes is that since seals are _____mammals_____, they must live near land even though they spend a lot of time in the water. Because seals are mammals, they are _____warm-blooded_____ and breathe _____with lungs_____.

Seals are comfortable in the water because they have flippers and strong muscles that help them swim easily. Their blubber helps them to _____survive_____ in very cold water. They can hold _____their breath_____ for a long time underwater because their hearts slow down under water and they need less air. They can even sleep underwater! Seals get most of their food from the water, too.

Seals also need the land. Because they cannot move as fast outside the water, seals always choose land that is near _____water_____. Some reasons seals need land are to rest and _____to have pups_____. Baby seals also need land because they can't _____swim_____ when they're born. To help them survive on land, the color of their fur matches their surroundings and helps them _____hide_____ from their enemies.

Seals are mammals that need both land and water to survive.

B. On separate paper, make a list of as many mammals as you can think of. Circle those that spend much of their time in the water. See Teacher Notes.

Selection Comprehension   "Seals on the Land and in the Water"   **67**

RESOURCE CENTER

◀ **Workbook page 67** is intended for use by all students.

Writing Master 10 duplicates the Writing to Learn chart.

LANGUAGE ARTS CONNECTIONS

CRITICAL THINKING: COMPLETING ANALOGIES

Have students complete analogies about seals.

Review comparisons with students. Point out that sometimes an unfamiliar idea or thing can be explained by comparing it to something that is already known. For example, an author might explain how a seal uses its flippers by comparing that motion to how people use their hands to swim. Present students with the following sentence pairs about seals. Have them copy the pairs and complete the comparisons. Model the first one for students.

A person has legs. A seal has _____(flippers)_____.
Dogs have puppies. Seals have _____(pups)_____.
People have fat. Seals have _____(blubber)_____.

Have students make up and share comparisons of their own.   WHOLE CLASS
ENRICHMENT

WRITING "JUST SO" STORIES

Have students write "Just So" stories about seals.

Explain to students that an author and poet named Rudyard Kipling wrote a book of stories about how some things came to be, such as "How the Leopard Got Its Spots," and in the story "The Elephant's Child," how the elephant got a long nose. Tell students these stories are in a book called *Just So Stories*. If possible, read a story from *Just So Stories* to students. Have students write their own "Just So" stories about seals. Suggest titles such as "How the Seal Got Its Flippers" or "How the Seal Got Its Blubber." Encourage students to use their imaginations but also to remember what seals are really like and where they live so that the stories make sense. Students might enjoy illustrating their stories. Collect the stories and make a new *Just So Stories*.

CHALLENGE: WRITING

CREATING MAGAZINES ABOUT POLAR LIFE

Have students work cooperatively to create magazines.

Explain to students that when a group works together *cooperatively* on a project, the success of the project depends on the contributions of each member of the group. Tell students they will be working cooperatively to create magazines about life at the North and South poles. Have students work in groups of five. One member of each group should be responsible for an article about the weather. A second member should write an article on the animal life. A third member should report on exploration and studies being done. A fourth member should act as editor-in-chief and collect the articles, create a cover, and a table of contents. The fifth member should act as designer and collect original drawings or photographs from old magazines for the articles.   COOPERATIVE
LEARNING: WRITING

ROLE-PLAYING SEALS

Have students create and act out conversations between seals.

Remind students that role-playing means to imagine you are a particular person or animal, talking and acting out what he or she might say and do. Explain that students can plan the dialogue by writing it in play form. Write a model on the board, showing that students can use numbers or made-up names.

SEAL 1: (words) **FLIPPER:** (words)

SEAL 2: (words) **WHISKERS:** (words)

Review with students the details of seals' lives and have them imagine what seals would say to each other. Encourage students to think about funny things the seals might say. **Language Arts Master 9** can be used with this activity. SHARED LEARNING: SPEAKING

READING EVERY DAY

You can support your students' awareness of the importance of learning about and protecting seals and other sea animals by recommending these titles.

All About Whales by Dorothy Hinshaw Patent. Holiday House, © 1987. A broad, informative view of different kinds of whales, the largest of all mammals.

Jack, the Seal, and the Sea by Gerald Aschenbrenner. English adaptation by Joanne Fink. Silver Burdett Press, © 1988. A seal pup and an inspirational message from the sea make Jack, a fisherman, determined to fight pollution.

Sea Otters by Evelyn Shaw. Harper & Row, © 1980. Susan, a scientist, closely studies some sea otters living in the Pacific Ocean. EASIER TO READ

Reader's Journal   **pp 54, 55**

Extending Reading

NAME THAT PINNIPED!

Students read about different members of the pinniped family. They choose one to write about and tell how they would spend the day together.

Selection Support

STUDY SKILLS

Test-Taking

OBJECTIVE   Identifying and practicing test-taking techniques.

1. WARM-UP

Display the following test examples. Tell students that these are examples from different kinds of tests. Have students explain what they should do with each example and then have volunteers perform the tasks. *(fill in; write* T *or* F*)*

 1. **Write the correct answer.**
     Seals have __(flippers)__ **instead of legs.**

 2. **Write** *T* **for true and** *F* **for false.**
     A seal is a mammal. __(T)__ .

Discuss kinds of tests and clues for how to take them.

Point out that taking tests can be made easier by knowing about the different kinds of tests and how to take them. Ask students how they knew what to do with each of the examples just discussed. (*They read the directions. They could also tell because of the form of the example.*) Explain that there is a name for each kind of test. Identify the first example as *completion*, the second as *true-false*. Stress that reading the directions carefully is the first and most important step in taking a test.

State the objective.

Tell students they will learn about and practice ways to take tests.

2. TEACH

Explain why it is important to be familiar with different kinds of tests and how to take them.

Being familiar with different kinds of tests and how to take them will help students feel more comfortable about taking tests and will help them successfully complete tests.

Present a strategy for taking tests.

Explain that there is a strategy students can use for taking tests. First, read the directions carefully. Make sure you know what is to be done and how many answers are asked for. If the directions are not clear, ask the teacher. Then read the items. Answer the ones you are sure of first. Then go back to any difficult ones. If there are answer choices, read them all before selecting an answer.

TEACHING CHART 39: TEST TAKING

39

A. Read each question. Circle the letter in front of the correct answer.
   1. What is a seal shaped like?
      a. baseball (b.) football c. tennis racket
   2. For how long can most seals stay underwater?
      a. three days b. five hours (c.) twenty minutes
B. Read the unfinished sentences. Write the correct answer or answers.
   1. Seals sleep in the water with their __(noses)__ just above the water.
   2. Seals come out of the water to __(rest)__ and to have __(babies)__ .

Model the strategy.

Tell students the first thing you will do is read the directions. Read them and explain that now you know what to do. Then you will read the first question and all the answer choices. Point out that the directions said to circle the letter in front of the correct answer, so you will circle the letter *b*. A seal is shaped like a *football*. Ask students why the answer might be marked wrong if you had circled the word *football* in addition to the letter *b*. (*The directions do not say to circle the answer itself.*)

3. GUIDED PRACTICE

Before going on, have students explain how to take a test. (*Read the directions; ask for help if necessary; answer all the questions you are sure of; read all the answer choices for a question before marking an answer; go back and answer the hardest questions.*)

Guide students in using the strategy.

Have students use the test-taking strategy to complete the second item in Part A. Then ask students what they will do before beginning Part B. (*Read the directions.*) Have students read the directions and tell what they will do. (*Fill in the correct answer for the first example. Fill in the two correct answers for the second example.*) Have students complete the "test."

4. WRAP-UP

Summarize instruction.

Review with students what they should do before taking a test and when they take a test. (*Read the directions and ask for help if necessary. Answer easy questions first, then go back to hard ones. Know what you have to answer and how many answers are needed.*)

Provide independent practice.

Options for independent practice are shown in the Resource Center below.

Workbook page 68

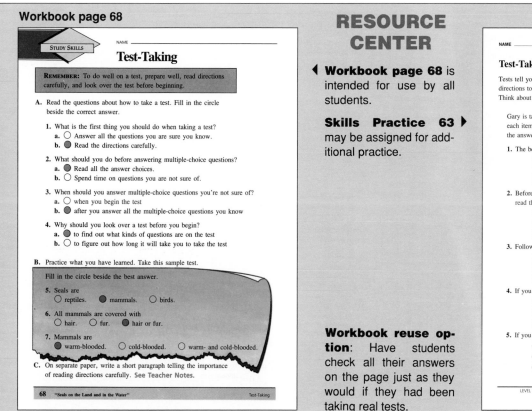

RESOURCE CENTER

◀ **Workbook page 68** is intended for use by all students.

Skills Practice 63 ▶ may be assigned for additional practice.

Workbook reuse option: Have students check all their answers on the page just as they would if they had been taking real tests.

Skills Practice 63

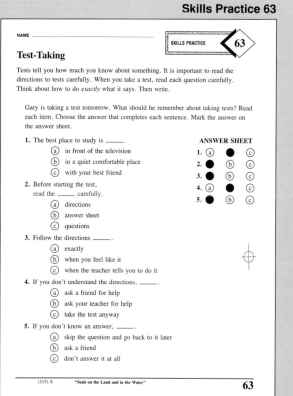

SKILL TRACE: SUFFIX				
Introduction	Practice	Test	Reteach	Maintain
TE 192	226	272	311	313	396

WORD STUDY

Suffix -ness

OBJECTIVE Using structural analysis to determine word meaning.

Review suffix -ness.

Review that when a suffix is added to a base word it changes the meaning of the word and often how it is used in a sentence. When the suffix -ness is added to an adjective, the word becomes a noun. Remind students that the spelling of a base word may change when a suffix is added. Also review the meaning of the suffix -ness. ("state, quality or condition of")

Use Teaching Chart to review the use of the suffix -ness.

Display the Teaching Chart. Have students add the suffix -ness to the word preceding the blank in each sentence. Ask for volunteers to write the new word on the chart or have students copy the sentences on separate paper. Then discuss what the new words mean, using the meaning of the suffix.

TEACHING CHART 40: SUFFIX -NESS

`40`

1. Seals are really water animals, so they move with awkward(ness) on land.
2. Seals' graceful(ness) in the water should be seen.
3. They use their strong muscles to swim with great swift(ness).
4. Seals do not feel the cold(ness) of the water because they have a layer of blubber.

Provide independent practice.

Options for independent practice are shown in the Resource Center below.

Workbook page 69

NAME _____

WORD STUDY

Suffix -ness

REMEMBER: The suffix -ness means "state," "quality," or "condition of."

A. Write a word that completes the second sentence in each pair. Form the word by adding -ness to a word in the box.

cold	dark	deep	eager	tired	white

1. Most seals live in very cold water.
   Because of the _____ coldness _____ they need blubber to keep them warm.
2. Seal pups in very cold climates have white fur.
   The _____ whiteness _____ of their fur matches the color of ice.
3. Seal pups in warmer climates may have dark fur.
   The _____ darkness _____ of their fur matches the color of rocks.
4. Most seals come out of the water when they are tired.
   The feeling of _____ tiredness _____ makes them think of a nap on land.
5. After a nap most seals are eager to return to water.
   Their _____ eagerness _____ may make them splash playfully.
6. No matter how deep the water is, young seals are confident swimmers.
   The _____ deepness _____ of the water is never a problem for seals.

B. On separate paper, write a paragraph about seals. Use three -ness words. See Teacher Notes.

Suffix -ness   "Seals on the Land and in the Water" **69**

RESOURCE CENTER

◀ **Workbook page 69** is intended for use by all students.

Skills Practice 64 ▶ may be assigned for additional practice.

Workbook reuse option: Have students think of a new -ness word that is either a synonym or an antonym of each -ness word they wrote in Part A. They should write these synonyms or antonyms in the margins.

Skills Practice 64

NAME _____

SKILLS PRACTICE `64`

Suffix -ness

Sometimes the suffix -ness can be added to the end of a word. The suffix -ness means the "state, quality, or condition of."

> Be sure to change y to i before adding -ness.

Read the sentences. Add -ness to the underlined word in the first sentence and write it to complete the second sentence.

1. Sand crabs are swift runners.
   This _____ swiftness _____ keeps sea gulls from catching them.
2. The painter collected bright, colored seashells.
   Their _____ brightness _____ made her paint many of them.
3. The sand was very hot.
   The _____ hotness _____ burned our feet.
4. Jellyfish are really clear.
   This _____ clearness _____ allows them to hide in the water.
5. The crashing waves were wild.
   Their _____ wildness _____ made me afraid to go in the water.
6. The seaweed was shiny and colorful.
   Its _____ colorfulness _____ made it look pretty.
7. The wet sand is rough.
   Its _____ roughness _____ feels funny on my toes.
8. The sea is very powerful.
   Its _____ powerfulness _____ is a danger to ships.
9. Seals are graceful in the water but awkward on land.
   Their _____ awkwardness _____ when they walk is fun to watch.
10. Rocks that have been tumbled by the sea are smooth.
    Their _____ smoothness _____ causes some people to collect them.

64   LEVEL 8   "Seals on the Land and in the Water"

SKILL TRACE: TABLE OF CONTENTS				
Introduction	Practice	Test	Reteach	Maintain
TE 224	249 273	311	315	445

STUDY SKILLS

Title Page, Copyright Page, Table of Contents

OBJECTIVE Using the title and copyright pages and the table of contents.

Review title page, copyright page, and table of contents.

Have students turn to the title page of their reading textbooks. Review with students what information the title page of a book contains. Repeat this procedure with the copyright page and the table of contents. Have students locate "Seals on the Land and in the Water" in the table of contents and tell on what page it begins.

Provide practice with title page, copyright page, and table of contents.

Display the Teaching Chart. Have students identify the title of the book, the author, the publisher, and the date of publication. For the table of contents, have students name different chapters as you call out their numbers.

TEACHING CHART 41: TITLE PAGE, COPYRIGHT PAGE, TABLE OF CONTENTS 41

The Seal Who Went South by Don Summer	**Contents**
Sea Books, Florida © 1987 by Don Summer	1 Cold Up North 5 2 Swimming South 13 3 Life on the Beach 17 4 Homesick 22

Provide independent practice.

Options for independent practice are shown in the Resource Center below.

RESOURCE CENTER

Workbook page 70

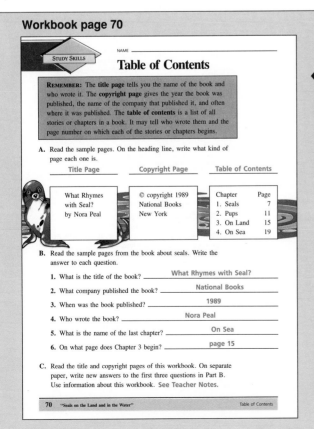

STUDY SKILLS   NAME _____

Table of Contents

REMEMBER: The **title page** tells you the name of the book and who wrote it. The **copyright page** gives the year the book was published, the name of the company that published it, and often where it was published. The **table of contents** is a list of all stories or chapters in a book. It may tell who wrote them and the page number on which each of the stories or chapters begins.

A. Read the sample pages. On the heading line, write what kind of page each one is.

Title Page	Copyright Page	Table of Contents
What Rhymes with Seal? by Nora Peal	© copyright 1989 National Books New York	Chapter Page 1. Seals 7 2. Pups 11 3. On Land 15 4. On Sea 19

B. Read the sample pages from the book about seals. Write the answer to each question.

1. What is the title of the book? _____ What Rhymes with Seal?
2. What company published the book? _____ National Books
3. When was the book published? _____ 1989
4. Who wrote the book? _____ Nora Peal
5. What is the name of the last chapter? _____ On Sea
6. On what page does Chapter 3 begin? _____ page 15

C. Read the title and copyright pages of this workbook. On separate paper, write new answers to the first three questions in Part B. Use information about this workbook. See Teacher Notes.

70 "Seals on the Land and in the Water"   Table of Contents

◀ **Workbook page 70** is intended for use by all students.

Skills Practice 65 ▶ may be assigned for additional practice.

Workbook reuse option: Have students put the letter *T* for title, *C* for copyright, or *TC* for table of contents next to each question in Part B to show where the answer was found.

Skills Practice 65

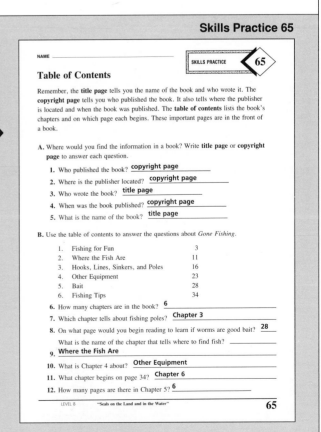

NAME _____   SKILLS PRACTICE 65

Table of Contents

Remember, the **title page** tells you the name of the book and who wrote it. The **copyright page** tells you who published the book. It also tells where the publisher is located and when the book was published. The **table of contents** lists the book's chapters and on which page each begins. These important pages are in the front of a book.

A. Where would you find the information in a book? Write **title page** or **copyright page** to answer each question.

1. Who published the book? _____ copyright page
2. Where is the publisher located? _____ copyright page
3. Who wrote the book? _____ title page
4. When was the book published? _____ copyright page
5. What is the name of the book? _____ title page

B. Use the table of contents to answer the questions about *Gone Fishing*.

1.	Fishing for Fun	3
2.	Where the Fish Are	11
3.	Hooks, Lines, Sinkers, and Poles	16
4.	Other Equipment	23
5.	Bait	28
6.	Fishing Tips	34

6. How many chapters are in the book? _____ 6
7. Which chapter tells about fishing poles? _____ Chapter 3
8. On what page would you begin reading to learn if worms are good bait? _____ 28
9. What is the name of the chapter that tells where to find fish? _____ Where the Fish Are
10. What is Chapter 4 about? _____ Other Equipment
11. What chapter begins on page 34? _____ Chapter 6
12. How many pages are there in Chapter 5? _____ 6

LEVEL 8   "Seals on the Land and in the Water"   **65**

SKILL TRACE: MAIN IDEA/DETAILS						
Introduction	Practice	Test	Reteach	Maintain		
TE 66	82	116	157	158	234	274	508

COMPREHENSION

Main Idea/Details

OBJECTIVE Identifying stated and unstated main idea and supporting details.

Review main idea and details.

Remind students that writers organize information in paragraphs around a main idea and provide details that support or explain the main idea. Point out that the main idea may or may not be stated in the paragraph.

Provide practice identifying the main idea and supporting details.

You may wish to read aloud the paragraphs below. Answers are printed in red. Have students identify the main idea and supporting details. Then have students relate the main idea in their own words.

> **1.** Seals come out of the water for two reasons. One reason is to rest. They choose spots to rest where they can easily get back into the water. Another reason is to have babies. (Main idea is stated in the first sentence. Details: to rest and have babies)
>
> **2.** Most seals stay underwater for at least twenty minutes. Some seals can stay underwater for almost an hour. Then they must come up for air. So seals are like fish in that they stay underwater, and like humans in that they need air. (Main idea is stated in the last sentence. Details: stay underwater twenty minutes, some almost an hour; need to come up for air.)

Provide independent practice.

An optional independent activity is shown in the Resource Center below.

RESOURCE CENTER

Skills Practice 66 ▶ may be assigned for additional practice.

Skills Practice 66

NAME _____

SKILLS PRACTICE ◁ 66

Main Idea/Details

A main idea tells what the paragraph is about. Details tell more about the main idea. Often the main idea of a paragraph is stated in a sentence. Sometimes it is not stated.

A. Find and circle the stated main idea in each paragraph.

> A main idea sentence almost always is at the beginning or the end of a paragraph.

1. Ocean liners are ships that are like floating hotels. They have places to eat, shops, and movies on board. They even have swimming pools.

2. Sandy brought her poodle onto the ship. There were five other dogs on board, too. One woman brought her goldfish, and a man brought a canary. There was no rule against pets on the big ship.

3. Ornitholestes was a small dinosaur, weighing a little more than a turkey. Because Ornitholestes was so lightly built it could move quickly, unlike the four-ton Stegosaurus who was slow moving. While some dinosaurs were giants, others were small in stature.

B. Read the following details. Decide what main idea they tell about. Then write the main idea. Choose from the sentences in the box.

Detail: Wind causes waves.
Detail: A ship moving through water causes waves.
Detail: An underwater earthquake causes waves.
Main Idea: **Waves are made by water that stops and starts.**

_____

> Waves can let you know that a ship has passed.
> Waves are made by water that stops and starts.
> Wind can be very strong.

66 LEVEL 8 "Seals on the Land and in the Water"

Curriculum Connections

Picturing Seals ART

Mention to students that seals live in groups called colonies. Encourage students to imagine what life might be like in a seal colony, either near the North or South Pole, or on the rocky northern California coastline. Have students use reference sources and the pictures in the selection, as well as any other available visual material, as ideas to help them create a mural that shows a panoramic view of a seal colony in one of these locations. Remind students to include such features as: seal families, birds, rocks and ice, seals both on the land and in the water along the shore. Students might also want to include an underwater scene, showing seals diving for fish under the water near the shore. One- or two-sentence captions can be added to the mural.

Being Weather-Wise HEALTH

Review with students how seals are able to live in very cold climates and stay healthy. *(Seals have a layer of blubber and fur to keep them warm; their fur sheds water easily.)* Then discuss what people must do to stay healthy during cold weather. Write students' suggestions on the board. *(Possible answers: Wear a warm coat, mittens or gloves, a hat, and scarf; do not stay out too long in cold temperatures; do not get wet and cold; eat properly to help avoid colds and flu; know how to treat frostbite.)* Encourage students to do research on cold-weather health care for more ideas. Then have students create posters illustrating different suggestions for taking care of oneself in cold weather. Students may wish to draw pictures or cut out pictures from magazines or newspapers to illustrate their suggestions. They should then write their recommendations under the pictures and create titles for their posters. Display finished posters in the classroom. If you live in an area where hot weather is more of a problem than cold weather, you may wish to give students a choice of which health-care problem they want to illustrate. **Curriculum Connection Master 9** can be used with this activity.

Meeting Mammals SCIENCE

Define *life cycle* as the different stages an animal goes through from birth to death. Point out that most mammals, such as people, horses, elephants, tigers, and dogs, spend their whole lives on land. A few mammals, such as dolphins and whales, spend their whole lives in the sea. Other mammals, such as sea lions, walruses, seals, and sea otters, spend part of their lives on the land and part in the sea. Have each student select a sea mammal that interests him or her. Direct the student to research the animal, looking for such facts as whether it is born on land or in the water, how long it stays on the land before it enters the water, what it eats, whether it lives in one general location all its life or moves from northern to southern waters and back again with the seasons. Suggest that students use encyclopedias and library books for their research. Some students may be interested in writing to a major aquarium to request information. Then have each student write a paragraph about one part of his or her animal's life cycle.

TEACHER CHOICE

	Teaching Sequence	Trade Books and Resources	Meeting Individual Needs	Integrated Language Arts / Cross Curriculum
The Bridge Pages 278–279	**Maintain** Inferences	• Teaching Chart 42 • Workbook 71 • Skills Practice 67		
PART 1 **Vocabulary Strategies** Pages 280–281	**Develop Concepts** Semantic Mapping **Teach Vocabulary** STORY CRITICAL WORDS: **crocodile,** cunning, determined, **dived, jungle,** shivered (Tested words are boldfaced.)	• Teaching Chart 43 • Workbook 72 • Skills Practice 68	**SUPPORT WORDS:** chattering, choked, mango, replied, sputtered, thrashed • Skills Practice 69	**WRITING/SPEAKING ACTIVITY:** Use new vocabulary to describe how a crocodile swims. • Spelling Connection 48
PART 2 **Reading & Responding** Pages 282–291	**Build Background** **Develop a Purpose for Reading** **Guide the Reading Process** **Selection Follow-Up**	• Reader's Journal 56–59 • Workbook 73 **I→T KIT** Singing a Song and Discussing Boat Safety Tips **READING EVERY DAY** *Crocodiles and Alligators,* by L. Bender *How the Rhinoceros Got His Skin,* by R. Kipling *Rabbit Makes a Monkey of Lion,* by V. Aardema	**EXTRA HELP:** Predicting Story Outcome **ACHIEVING ENGLISH PROFICIENCY:** Comparing Monkeys and Crocodiles • Achieving English Proficiency Master 17	**Language Arts Connections** **WRITING TO LEARN:** Write a new story ending. • Writing Master 11 **SPEAKING/LISTENING:** Creating Word Pictures **WRITING:** Giving Advice Through a Moral; Writing a Folk Tale; Writing a Booklet of Idioms • Language Arts Master 10
PART 3 **Selection Support** Pages 292–295			**Practice** • Teaching Charts 44–45 • Workbook 74–75 • Skills Practice 70–71 Comparison (Tested) Suffixes *-able, -ible* (Tested) **Maintain** • Skills Practice 72 Story Elements: Setting	**Curriculum Connections** **SCIENCE:** Researching Characteristics of Reptiles **SOCIAL STUDIES:** Mapping and Labeling India **MATHEMATICS:** Making a Jungle Bar Graph **ART:** Drawing and Labeling Crocodiles and Alligators; Illustrating Folk Tales • Curriculum Connection Master 10

The Monkey and the CROCODILE

written and illustrated by Paul Galdone

SUMMARY   *In this folk tale, a hungry crocodile persuades a monkey to jump down from a tree onto his back. When the crocodile tries to drown the monkey and eat him, the quick-thinking monkey fools the crocodile and escapes. The crocodile finally admits that the monkey is more cunning than he when the monkey outsmarts him a second time. Members of Silver Burdett & Ginn's student panel chose* The Monkey and the Crocodile *for the **Readers' Choice** award. Two books illustrated by Paul Galdone have been named **Caldecott Honor** books.*

The Bridge

SKILL TRACE: INFERENCES

Introduced in Level 6. This skill is re-introduced in Unit 3 of this level.	Maintain
	TE 227 | 278

COMPREHENSION
Teaching Inferences

OBJECTIVE Making inferences about time, location, people, animals, and feelings and attitudes.

1. WARM-UP

Use a known passage to review inferences.

Tell students they will listen to a passage from the previous selection, "Seals on the Land and in the Water." Explain that authors do not always tell all the facts about an animal, but readers can use the facts given and their own knowledge to figure out something new about the animal. Have students listen for clues to help them answer the question, Where do baby seals spend most of their time? *(on land)*

> **In cold climates, seal pups have white fur to match the ice around them. In warmer climates, the pups have dark fur to match the land and rocks.**

Discuss word and knowledge clues.

Reread the passage. Have students tell which word clues helped them to figure out that baby seals spend most of their time on land. (*white fur to match the ice, dark fur to match the land*) Ask them what they know about ice and rocks. (*Ice is white and is found on top of the water or on land. Rocks are dark in color and are also found on land.*) Point out that students used both clues in the passage and their own knowledge to figure out something about baby seals that the author did not state.

State the objective.

Tell students they will review how to make inferences, or figure out information not stated, by using facts in the story and their own knowledge.

2. TEACH

Making inferences is important.

Making inferences helps readers understand and enjoy what they read.

Present a strategy for making inferences.

Tell students there is a strategy they can use to make inferences. First, read and think about what the writer has written. Then think about information that is not in the selection. Next, look for word clues and think about what you already know to make an inference.

TEACHING CHART 42: INFERENCES `42`

1. Baby seals splash about together in shallow water near the shore. After a few months they are big enough to swim out to sea. How do baby seals learn to swim? (They might learn from one another. They practice in shallow water. Clues: splash about together in shallow water)
2. Harbor seals are quite small. They are most often seen on shore. How did harbor seals get their name? (Harbors are places where water meets land. These seals spend most of their time on shore. Clues: harbor, seen on shore)

Model the strategy.

Explain that the sentences on the Teaching Chart contain more information about seals. Read passage 1 aloud. Tell students that the passage does not state how seals learn to swim. Point out that the phrases *splash about together* and *in shallow water* are clues that tell what baby seals do before they are able to swim out to sea. Explain that these phrases as well as knowing that babies, both human and animal, learn from watching others helps to figure out that baby seals learn to swim from one another and by practicing in shallow water.

3. GUIDED PRACTICE

Check for understanding.

Before going on, have students tell how to make an inference. *(look for word clues and think about what they already know)*

Guide students in using the strategy.

Have students use the strategy to make an inference about the remaining passage. Discuss clues that helped them answer the question.

4. WRAP-UP

Summarize instruction.

Review why readers make inferences and the kinds of clues they use to make them. *(A writer does not always explain every detail in a story; readers use word and experience clues.)*

Provide independent practice.

Options for independent practice are shown in the Resource Center below.

5. APPLICATION

Students will make inferences as they read "The Monkey and the Crocodile." The symbol ✔ marks specific questions and activities that apply this skill.

Workbook page 71

NAME _____

Inference   COMPREHENSION

REMEMBER: Use story clues and what you already know to figure out things that the writer did not state.

A. Use what you read to make guesses. Complete each sentence with a word or words from the box.

| are safer | cold | different-colored coats | fur |
| land | need rest | slower heartbeats | warm |

1. A mammal is covered with hair or fur. Seals are mammals. Seals have _____ fur _____ .

2. Most seals live in the waters near the North and South Poles. The water there is very _____ cold _____ .

3. Seals are warm-blooded. Since the waters they swim in are cold, seals need something to keep them _____ warm _____ .

4. Seals choose a spot to rest where they can easily get back into the water. They need to be able to get in the water quickly because they _____ are safer _____ there.

5. Baby seals cannot swim, so seals must keep their babies on _____ land _____ .

6. When their hearts slow down, mammals do not have to breathe as often. Seals can stay underwater for a long time because of their _____ slower heartbeats _____ .

B. Pretend that you are a baby seal just learning to swim. On separate paper, write three or more sentences telling what the water is like and how your mother helps you. See Teacher Notes.

Inference   "The Monkey and the Crocodile"   **71**

RESOURCE CENTER

◀ **Workbook page 71** is intended for use by all students.

Skills Practice 67 ▶ may be assigned for additional practice.

Workbook reuse option: Have students draw a circle around each sentence about seals in Part A that also applies to people.

Skills Practice 67

NAME _____   SKILLS PRACTICE ◀67

Inference

When you make an **inference**, you use story clues and what you already know to figure out things that the writer did not state.

| Story clues |
| What I know |
| Inference |

A. Read the stories. Write an answer to each question.

Tillie and Tom heard the wind. It sounded like a shriek. They saw the palm trees bend. The water was getting rougher and the waves were rising. "Let's get inside fast," yelled Tillie.   **Answers may vary.**

1. What was happening?   A big storm was coming.
2. Why did the wind sound like a shriek?   because it was so loud
3. How do you think the children felt?   scared
4. Why did the palm trees bend?   because the wind was so strong

Jean waved good-by to her mother. Her mother seemed to be getting smaller and smaller. Then she was gone. That night, Jean didn't sleep very well. It wasn't just the waves crashing against her window or the loud horns. It was also the thought of not seeing her mother for a whole month.

5. Why did Jean wave goodbye to her mother?   because she was going away
6. Why did Jean's mother seem to be getting smaller?   Jean's ship was moving away from shore.
7. What is Jean travelling on?   a ship
8. How do you think Jean was feeling?   homesick

B. When you answer questions like those on this page you are _____. Check one.

_____ finding the main idea   _____ making a prediction

__✔__ making an inference

LEVEL 8   "The Monkey and the Crocodile"   **67**

Vocabulary Strategies

Developing Concepts

Build on prior knowledge of a jungle with a semantic map.

Make a semantic map about the jungle as a starting point for teaching vocabulary. Write the word *JUNGLE* on the chalkboard and read it aloud. Ask students what a jungle is. (*A jungle is an area of land that is covered with a thick growth of tropical trees and plants; many kinds of animals live in a jungle.*)

Then, write the headings from the map below and ask students to name words that fit under each one. List the responses. Encourage students to suggest as many of the Story Critical words as possible. Read the completed map aloud.

What Trees and Plants Grow There
(fruit trees, pines)

low plants

What Animals Live There
(lions, tigers, monkeys, crocodile)

JUNGLE

Where Animals Live
(trees, land, water)

What the Animals Are Like
(quick, hungry, cunning, determined) wild

Teaching Vocabulary

Discuss meanings of Story Critical words.

Read each context sentence on the Teaching Chart and identify the new word. Then use the questions below to help students understand each word. When necessary, provide a definition.

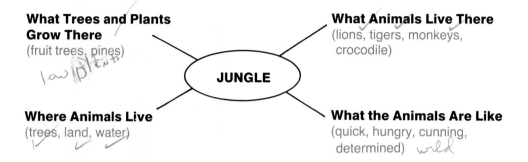

43

TEACHING CHART 43: VOCABULARY

1. **jungle** (land overgrown with trees and vegetation)
Tigers, lions, and other animals lived in the *jungle* of tropical trees.
2. **crocodile** (a large reptile that lives in tropical streams)
The *crocodile* flipped its long tail, opened its wide jaws, and snapped at other animals from the water.
3. **cunning** (clever, crafty)
The crocodile was as *cunning* as the smartest fox.
4. **shivered** (trembled in fear or from feeling cold)
Some animals *shivered* when they saw the crocodile, but others showed no fear.
5. **determined** (having one's mind set)
A monkey was *determined* to outsmart the crocodile and not get caught by it.
6. **dived** (plunged into the water)
One day the monkey *dived* headfirst into the water.

jungle **1. Name some animals you would find in a jungle.** (tigers, lions, crocodiles, monkeys) STRATEGY: PRIOR KNOWLEDGE

crocodile **2. Have you ever seen a real crocodile or a picture of one? What other animal does it look like?** (an alligator) STRATEGY: PRIOR KNOWLEDGE

cunning **3. What word in the sentence is a clue to the meaning of *cunning*?** (*smartest*) **What other words besides *cunning* might be used to describe someone who is clever and tries to outsmart others?** (*tricky, sly*) STRATEGY: SYNONYMS

shivered **4. Have you ever shivered in fear? For what other reason might a person shiver?** (with cold) STRATEGY: CONNOTATION

determined **5. How do people behave when they are determined to do something?** (they stick to their goal) STRATEGY: PRIOR KNOWLEDGE

dived **6. Have you ever dived into a swimming pool or lake? How did you do it?** (plunged headfirst into the water) STRATEGY: PRIOR KNOWLEDGE

Add new words to the map. Challenge students to add to the semantic map any of the new words that have not been listed yet, creating headings as needed. Have them explain how each added word fits.

Discuss Support words as needed. The Glossary of the Student Text includes definitions of the Support words: *choked, sputtered, thrashed, chattering, replied, mango.* Have students discuss which words can be added to the semantic map.

Provide independent practice. Options for independent practice are shown in the Resource Center below.

WRITING OR SPEAKING ACTIVITY *Have students use as many Story Critical and Support words as possible to describe how a crocodile might swim in a jungle stream or lake.*

TEACHER CHOICE

RESOURCE CENTER

Workbook page 72

SELECTION VOCABULARY NAME _____

Using New Words

A. Complete each sentence with a word from the box.

crocodile	cunning	determined
dived	jungle	shivered

1. Monkeys can get away from an enemy by being clever and ___cunning___

2. Many mammals live in the ___jungle___.

3. When the monkey heard the lion roar, it ___shivered___ in fear.

4. The ___crocodile___ rested in the sun, and then it ___dived___ under the water.

5. Animal lovers are ___determined___ to save mammals like the Indian elephant.

B. Choose an animal to answer each riddle. Write your answer on the line.

butterfly	crocodile

6. Who am I? I am often brightly colored. I fly through the hot, jungle air.
   I am a ___butterfly___.

7. Who am I? I am a reptile. I mostly live in the water. I have big, sharp teeth.
   I am a ___crocodile___.

C. On separate paper, make a chart of the animals you read about on this page. Use these two headings: Mammals, Other Kinds of Animals. See Teacher Notes.

72 "The Monkey and the Crocodile" Selection Vocabulary

RESOURCE CENTER

◀ **Workbook page 72** provides practice with Story Critical words.

Skills Practice 68 ▶ provides additional practice with Story Critical words.

Skills Practice 69 provides practice with Support words.

Spelling Connection Master 48 may be used for instruction with the new vocabulary.

Workbook reuse option: In Parts A and B, have students circle the names of animals that live on land, underline those that live in water, and put a star by those that live in both places.

Skills Practice 68

NAME _____ SKILLS PRACTICE 68

Vocabulary: Story Critical Words

A. Study the meaning of each word.

crocodile a very large reptile
cunning clever
determined having one's mind set
dived plunged headfirst into water
jungle an area with many trees and plants
shivered trembled in fear

B. Some words belong together. Read each row of words. Underline the word that does not belong in the group. Write the vocabulary word that should be in its place.

1. dog, snake, lizard, ___crocodile___
2. forest, woods, rabbit, ___jungle___
3. jumped, dropped, swam, ___dived___
4. crafty, sneaky, honest, ___cunning___

C. Complete the puzzle. Write the vocabulary word for each clue.

Across

2. A fox is called this by some people.
4. Someone who works hard to get a job done is this.
5. The frightened person did this.

Down

1. The swimmer did this to get into the pool.
2. This animal has a large mouth with many teeth.
3. This is a very green place.

68 LEVEL 8 "The Monkey and the Crocodile" Classification

281

Reading & Responding

Building Background

Motivate discussion with the verse. Share the following verse with students and have them guess what the law of the jungle might be. (*Animals must live together as well as hunt each other in order to survive*.)

> **Now this is the Law of the Jungle — as old and as true as the sky;**
> **And the Wolf that shall keep it may prosper, but the Wolf that**
> **shall break it must die.**
> From *The Law of the Jungle* by Rudyard Kipling

Build background about animals that hunt. Have students give examples of animals that hunt other animals. For example, cats hunt mice and hawks hunt squirrels. Have students look back at the semantic map about jungle animals and ask which animal might hunt other animals. Point out that crocodiles might hunt monkeys. Then ask students if they think it would be easy for a crocodile to catch a monkey. Guide a brief discussion about crocodiles and monkeys.

Discuss folk tales. Tell students that this folk tale from India explains what can happen when someone thinks it will be easy to outsmart someone else. Ask how the information in a folk tale is presented.(*Animals or people can often do things that real animals and people cannot do. Sometimes a lesson is learned*.) Mention that students will see the words "A Jataka [ja'-tu-ku] Tale from India." Jataka tales most likely came from northwestern India where a member of a certain group of people is known as a Jat.

Developing a Purpose for Reading

Option 1
Students set purpose. **ORAL "IF I WERE THE AUTHOR" STATEMENTS** Have students preview the selection by looking at the title and the pictures. Ask students to tell what they would write if they were the author of a folk tale about a monkey and a crocodile. Record students' statements for use later.

WRITING ACTIVITY Have students work individually or in pairs to create written "If I were the author" statements. Have students save their lists.

Option 2
Teacher sets purpose. Have students read to discover how the crocodile tried to catch the monkey and which animal actually outsmarted the other.

Meeting
Individual
Needs

EXTRA HELP Tell students the next story is about a crocodile who tries to catch a monkey. Ask whether a crocodile would find it easy or hard to catch a monkey, and why. Write students' responses on the chalkboard under the headings *Easy* and *Hard*. Then have students predict whether the crocodile will be able to catch the monkey. After they have read, have students return to their lists to discuss why the story had the outcome it did.

ACHIEVING ENGLISH PROFICIENCY Write the words *monkey* and *crocodile* on the board. Show students pictures of these animals and have them say the name of the animal with you. Ask students if they know where these animals live and what they eat. Ask students if a crocodile can go up a tree or if a monkey can swim. For additional help in story comprehension, use Master 17 in the Teacher Resource Kit.

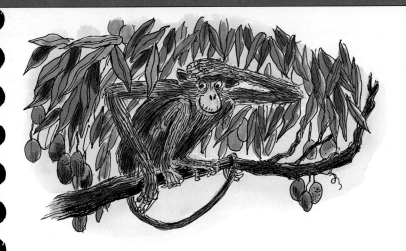

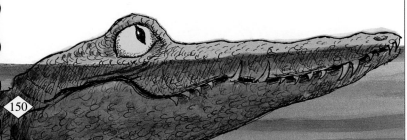

The Monkey and the CROCODILE

150

READERS' CHOICE AWARD

A Jataka Tale from India

written and illustrated by Paul Galdone

Watch out, monkey! Here comes crocodile!

Beside a river in the jungle stood a tall mango tree. In the tree lived many monkeys. They swung from branch to branch, eating fruit and chattering to each other.

Hungry crocodiles swam in the river and sunned themselves on the banks.

One young crocodile was hungrier than all the rest. He could never get enough to eat.

The young crocodile watched the monkeys for a long time. Then one day he said to a wise old crocodile: "I'd like to catch a monkey and eat him!"

"How would you ever catch a monkey?" asked the old crocodile. "You do not travel on land and monkeys do not go into the water. Besides, they are quicker than you are."

"They may be quicker," said the young crocodile, "but I am more cunning. You will see!"

For days the crocodile swam back and forth, studying the monkeys all the while.

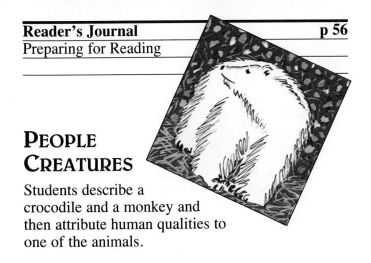

Reader's Journal   **p 56**
Preparing for Reading

PEOPLE CREATURES

Students describe a crocodile and a monkey and then attribute human qualities to one of the animals.

GUIDED READING

Page 151   **What does the old crocodile say about monkeys and crocodiles?** (Crocodiles do not travel on land; monkeys do not go into water, and they are quicker than crocodiles.)   RECALL: DETAILS

Page 151   **Why do you think the crocodile swims back and forth, studying the monkeys?** (The crocodile wants to find out about how monkeys behave so he can catch one and eat it.)   SYNTHESIZE: DRAWING CONCLUSIONS

HIGHLIGHTING LITERATURE

Page 151   Point out that this is a special kind of folk tale called a fable. A fable is a brief story that teaches a lesson. Fables can also show human behavior in a humorous way. The characters in a fable are usually animals who talk and act like people while keeping their animal qualities. Have students identify the crocodiles' human behavior, such as talking to one another, asking questions, and boasting.

283

Then he noticed one young monkey who was quicker than all the others. This monkey loved to jump to the highest branches of the tree and pick the ripe mangos at the very top.

"He's the one I want," the crocodile said to himself. "But how am I going to catch him?"

The crocodile thought and thought, and at last he had an idea.

"Monkey," he called, "wouldn't you like to come with me over to the island, where the fruit is so ripe?"

"Oh, yes," said the monkey. "But how can I go with you? I do not swim."

"I will take you on my back," said the crocodile, with a toothy smile.

The monkey was eager to get to the fruit, so he jumped down on the crocodile's back.

"Off we go!" said the crocodile, gliding through the water.

"This is a fine ride you are giving me," said the monkey.

"Do you think so? Well, how do you like this?" asked the crocodile. And suddenly he <u>dived</u> down into the water.

"Oh, please don't!" cried the monkey as he went under. He was afraid to let go and he did not know what to do.

When the crocodile came up, the monkey sputtered and choked. "Why did you take me under water, Crocodile?" he asked. "You know I can't swim!"

"Because I am going to drown you," replied the crocodile. "And then I am going to eat you."

The monkey <u>shivered</u> in fear. But he thought quickly and before the crocodile dived again, he said: "I wish you had told me you wanted to eat me. If I had known that, I would have brought my heart."

"Your heart?" asked the crocodile.

"Yes, it is the tastiest part of me. But I left it behind in the tree."

GUIDED READING

✔ **Page 152   What invitation does the crocodile give the monkey? Why?** (He invites the monkey to come with him over to the island where the fruit is ripe. The crocodile wants to get close to the monkey so he can eat him.)   INFER: CAUSE/EFFECT

Page 153   Why do you think the monkey tells the crocodile that he left his heart in the tree? (to gain time; to get the crocodile to take him back to the land) ANALYZE: CHARACTER

✔ **Page 153   What does the monkey think of the crocodile at first? What happens that changes his opinion of the crocodile?** (The monkey trusts the crocodile at first. When the crocodile tries to drown him and eat him, the monkey fears him and no longer trusts him.)   INFER: FEELINGS/ATTITUDES

STRATEGIC READING

✔ **Page 153**   Have students summarize how the crocodile has tried to catch the monkey so far. (The crocodile offers the monkey a ride on his back across the river to the island where the fruit is ripe. On the way the crocodile dives deep into the water, trying to drown the monkey.) Then have them predict what the crocodile will do next. (He will probably take the monkey back to the land to get his heart.) Point out that summarizing and predicting can help readers understand what they read. Suggest that when students have trouble summarizing, they reread those parts of the story that are confusing. When they finish reading the story, ask students to check their predictions. METACOGNITION: SUMMARIZING AND PREDICTING

✔ Skill from **The Bridge** applied through this question.
✔ Informal Assessment Opportunity: PREDICTING

284

"Then we must go back and get it," said the crocodile, turning around.

"But we are so near the island," said the monkey. "Please take me there first."

"No," said the crocodile. "First I am taking you straight to your tree. You will get your heart and bring it to me at once. Then we will see about going to the island."

"Very well," said the monkey.

And the crocodile headed back to the river bank.

No sooner did the monkey jump onto the bank than up he swung into the tree. From the highest branch he called down to the crocodile: "My heart is way up here. If you want it, come for it! Come for it!" And he laughed and laughed while the crocodile thrashed his tail in anger.

That night the monkey moved far down river from the mango tree. He wanted to get away from the crocodile so he could live in peace.

But the crocodile was still <u>determined</u> to catch him. He searched and searched and finally he found the monkey, living in another tree.

Here a large rock rose out of the water, halfway between the monkey's new home and the island. The crocodile watched the monkey jumping from the river bank to the rock, and then to the island where the fruit trees were.

"Monkey will stay on the island all day," the crocodile thought to himself. "And I'll catch him on his way home tonight."

The monkey had a fine feast, while the crocodile swam about, watching him all day. Toward night, the crocodile crawled out of the water and lay on the rock, perfectly still.

When it grew dark among the trees, the monkey started for home. He ran down to the river bank, and there he stopped.

"What is the matter with the rock?" the monkey wondered. "I never saw it so high before. Something must be lying on it."

The monkey went to the water's edge and called: "Hello, Rock!"

No answer.

He called again: "Hello, Rock!"

GUIDED READING

Page 154   Why do you think the monkey begs the crocodile to take him to the island? (The monkey knows that the crocodile will do just the opposite and take him back to the tree to get his heart, which is what the monkey really wants him to do.)   ANALYZE: CHARACTER

Page 154   Should the crocodile have believed the monkey's story about leaving his heart in a tree? Why or why not? (no, because a monkey cannot take out its heart)   EVALUATE: REALITY/FANTASY

Page 154   How is the monkey able to escape? (When the crocodile takes him back to his tree the monkey quickly swings up to the highest branches and tells the crocodile that if he wants the monkey and his heart he will have to come and get them.)   RECALL: SUMMARIZING

STRATEGIC READING

Page 154   Reread the description of the monkey's swinging into the tree and laughing at the crocodile. Encourage students to picture the way the crocodile looks as the monkey outsmarts him. Have them picture the way the monkey looks as he teases the crocodile. Allow students to describe their mental pictures. Remind them that when they are unable to visualize while reading, they might reread the section of the story that is confusing, paying particular attention to the descriptive words.   METACOGNITION: VISUALIZING

Still no answer.

Three times the monkey called, and then he said: "Why is it, friend Rock, that you do not answer me tonight?"

"Oh," said the crocodile to himself, "the rock must talk to the monkey at night. I'll have to answer for the rock this time."

So he answered: "Yes, Monkey! What is it?"

The monkey laughed and said: "Oh, it's you, Crocodile, is it?"

"Yes," said the crocodile. "I am waiting here for you. And I am going to eat you up!"

"You have certainly caught me this time," said the monkey, sounding afraid. "There is no other way for me to go home. Open your mouth wide so I can jump right into it."

GUIDED READING

✔ **Page 156   Why does the monkey call out to the rock?** (He thinks that the rock looks unusual and probably suspects that the crocodile might be trying to catch him.)   INFER: ACTIONS

Page 156   How do you know that the crocodile might be making a mistake by answering the monkey? (The monkey tricked the crocodile once before; the monkey is now trying to trick the crocodile into talking.)   SYNTHESIZE: DRAWING CONCLUSIONS

Page 157   Do you think the monkey is really afraid when he agrees with the crocodile that he is caught? Why or why not? (No, because he is too willing to jump into the crocodile's mouth; the monkey must have a plan to trick the crocodile.)   SYNTHESIZE: DRAWING CONCLUSIONS

Page 157   What do you think might happen next? (The crocodile will eat the monkey, or the monkey will escape again.)   SYNTHESIZE: PREDICTING OUTCOMES

✔ Skill from The Bridge applied through this question.

HIGHLIGHTING LITERATURE

Pages 156–157   Point out the way in which the author adds to the humorous human-like behavior of the characters by including descriptions of how they react when they speak, for example: "said the crocodile to himself"; "the monkey laughed"; "sounding afraid."

Now the monkey knew very well that when crocodiles open their mouths wide, they shut their eyes.

So while the crocodile lay on the rock with his mouth open and his eyes shut, the monkey jumped.

But not into his mouth!

He landed on the top of the crocodile's head, and then sprang quickly to the river bank.

Up he ran into his tree.

When the crocodile saw the trick the monkey had played on him, he said: "Monkey, I thought I was <u>cunning</u>, but you are much more cunning than I. And you know no fear. I will leave you alone after this."

"Thank you, Crocodile," said the monkey. "But I shall be on the watch for you just the same."

And so he was, and the crocodile never, never caught him.

Reader's Response

If you could be either the monkey or the crocodile, which would you choose? Why?

SELECTION FOLLOW-UP

The Monkey and the CROCODILE

Thinking It Over

1. Why was it so hard for a crocodile to catch a monkey?
2. How did the crocodile get the monkey to come to him?
3. Why did the crocodile think the monkey wouldn't see him on the rock?
4. List some of the ways the monkey proved he was clever. What clues did you use to make your list?
5. Do you think that the monkey should trust the crocodile to leave him alone?

Writing to Learn

THINK AND IMAGINE Do you think the crocodile will ever stop trying to catch the monkey? Do you think the monkey could catch the crocodile? Look at the picture below and imagine what might happen next time they meet.

WRITE Write a new ending for this story. Tell how the monkey catches the crocodile.

GUIDED READING

Page 158   What lessons do the crocodile and monkey learn? (The crocodile learns that the monkey is more cunning than he; the monkey, that he must be watchful of crocodiles.)   EVALUATE: MAIN IDEA/DETAILS

RETURNING TO THE READING PURPOSE

OPTION 1   Have students read their "If I were the author" statements and tell if any came close to what happened in the story. Ask students why the monkey escaped each time. (The monkey is used to being hunted by bigger animals. So it knows it has to be smart enough and quick enough to escape.)

OPTION 2   If you set the purpose for reading, ask students to explain why the crocodile was not able to outsmart the monkey. Help students conclude that because the crocodile was so eager to catch the monkey and so certain of outsmarting it, he did not notice when the monkey was trying to outsmart him.

Reader's Journal   **p 57**
Responding to Reading

SECOND THOUGHTS

Students speculate and write about what the two animals might be thinking at the end of the story.

SELECTION FOLLOW-UP

The Monkey and the CROCODILE

THINKING IT OVER

1. **Why was it so hard for a crocodile to catch a monkey?** (Crocodiles live in water and cannot travel far or quickly on land. Monkeys usually travel on land and are very quick.)   RECALL: CAUSE/EFFECT

2. **How did the crocodile get the monkey to come to him?** (The crocodile saw that the monkey loved ripe fruit. He tempted the monkey by telling him that there was ripe fruit on the island and that he would take the monkey there.)   RECALL: DETAILS

3. **Why did the crocodile think the monkey wouldn't see him on the rock?** (The crocodile's skin was very rough, and he thought he would look like the surface of the rock if he didn't move.)   SYNTHESIZE: DRAWING CONCLUSIONS

4. **List some of the ways the monkey proved he was clever. What clues did you use to make your list?** (Possible answers: He tricked the crocodile with his story about his heart; he moved down the river, away from the crocodile; he realized that the "rock" was the crocodile; he remembered that crocodiles close their eyes when they open their mouths wide. Encourage students to read sections of the story that support their conclusions.)   ANALYZE: CHARACTER: METACOGNITION

5. **Do you think that the monkey should trust the crocodile to leave him alone?** (Some children will think that the crocodile has had enough trouble trying to catch this particular monkey and that he has truly given up. Others will think that the crocodile will never give up because he is determined and enjoys trying to outwit the monkey.)   SYNTHESIZE: DRAWING CONCLUSIONS

WRITING TO LEARN

Use Writing Master 11, which duplicates this picture.

THINK AND IMAGINE   Do you think the crocodile will ever stop trying to catch the monkey? Do you think the monkey could catch the crocodile? **Look at the picture below and imagine what might happen next time they meet.** (Help students work with the drawing to prepare for writing.)

Extend comprehension through writing.

WRITE   Write a new ending for this story. Tell how the monkey catches the crocodile. (Have students read their endings aloud.)

More Ideas for Selection Follow-Up

CRITICAL AND CREATIVE THINKING QUESTIONS

Encourage a variety of responses and points of view.

Use these open-ended questions to encourage critical and creative thinking about the selection.

1. What about this story tells you that it is a folk tale?

2. At the beginning of the story, the old crocodile pointed out how difficult it would be to catch a monkey. If you were able to speak to the young crocodile, what advice would you give him?

✔ 3. This unit is titled "A Watery World." Which selection in it told you more about the differences between living on land and in the water? Explain your answer.

REREADING ORALLY

Have students reread for a specific purpose.

Have students reread the two main passages of the story that show that the crocodile was not as cunning as he thought he was. Help students locate the first passage in which the quick-thinking monkey talks the crocodile out of drowning and eating him. (*page 153: "I wish you had told me you wanted to eat me" to the middle of page 154: "My heart is way up here. If you want it, come for it! Come for it!"*) Have pairs of students take turns reading aloud the words spoken by the crocodile and the monkey while you read the narrative parts. Follow a similar procedure with the second passage beginning on page 156, in which the monkey gets the crocodile, who is pretending to be a rock, to speak.

SELECTION COMPREHENSION

Provide a comprehension check.

A Workbook page to check comprehension is shown in the Resource Center below. It may be used for informal assessment.

✔ **Informal Assessment Opportunity:** SYNTHESIZING ACROSS SELECTIONS

Workbook page 73

NAME _____

The Monkey and the **CROCODILE**

SELECTION COMPREHENSION

A. Complete the summary of "The Monkey and the Crocodile." Accept reasonable variations.

The ___monkey___ and the ___crocodile___ lived by a ___river___ in the Indian jungle. The crocodile wanted to eat the monkey. Since crocodiles don't travel as fast on land as monkeys, the crocodile decided he would have to get the monkey ___in the water___ to catch him.

The crocodile invited the monkey to go to an island. He said he'd carry the monkey ___on his back___ since the monkey couldn't swim. On the way to the island, the crocodile tried ___to drown___ the monkey so he could eat him. The monkey said he had left his heart behind and talked the crocodile into ___going back___. As soon as they reached the river bank, the monkey ran off.

Next the crocodile watched the monkey as he jumped to and from the island on rocks in the river. That night the crocodile lay flat on a rock, waiting. But the monkey saw him and tricked him into showing he was there by pretending to ___talk to the rock___. Then the monkey tricked him again by telling the crocodile to open his mouth so he could jump in. Instead of jumping into the crocodile's mouth, the monkey jumped ___on his head___ and then onto the river bank.

The crocodile did not get to eat the monkey, and he had to admit that the monkey was ___more cunning___ than he.

B. Pretend you are a person who catches animals for a zoo. On separate paper, write your plan for catching the monkey without hurting it. See Teacher Notes.

Selection Comprehension   "The Monkey and the Crocodile" **73**

RESOURCE CENTER

◀ **Workbook page 73** is intended for use by all students.

Writing Master 11 duplicates the Writing to Learn picture.

I•T Kit Activity

Audio: "Never Smile at a Crocodile"

This humorous song from the Disney movie *Peter Pan* gives sound advice about when it is safest to be silent. After students sing along, they discuss boating safety tips. (See Activity Guide.)   CONTEMPORARY MUSIC

LANGUAGE ARTS CONNECTIONS

CRITICAL THINKING: GIVING ADVICE

Discuss the moral of a fable.

Ask students what the *moral* of a story is. *(a lesson)* Then ask students what moral they think was taught in "The Monkey and the Crocodile." *(It is not wise to be overconfident because a person can be outsmarted.)*

Have students write advice.

Have students work in pairs to write short lessons, or morals, for Crocodile. Discuss how Crocodile was fooled by Monkey. Ask students what advice they would give Crocodile. If necessary, write a warning on the board to motivate them, such as *Do not use force when you can use your head!* Call on volunteers to suggest their own morals. Students may enjoy illustrating and sharing their work with one another. SHARED LEARNING: WRITING

CREATING WORD PICTURES

Have students illustrate words.

Explain to students that words can have meanings similar to the way they look. Have students engage in word play in which they draw the letters of words to illustrate the meanings. For example, students can draw the letters of the word *shivered* either horizontally or diagonally in quick, shaky strokes to show that the word means "trembled." Students should choose words to illustrate from the Story Critical and Support words. They may also select additional words from the story that lend themselves to this activity. The words *shivered, dived, choked, sputtered, thrashed,* and *chattering* provide excellent visual word play opportunities. When students have finished, display their word pictures around the classroom. WHOLE CLASS ENRICHMENT

THE FOLK TALE AS A LITERARY GENRE

Review the features of a folk tale.

Review with students the features of a folk tale. *(People or animals do things that they cannot do in real life; sometimes a lesson is learned.)* Remind students that "The Monkey and the Crocodile" is a folk tale that contains these features.

Have students write brief folk tales.

Have each student write a folk tale about two animal characters who have some kind of adventure together in which one animal learns a lesson. Tell students the adventure could be about one animal's trying to catch another or about anything else. CHALLENGE: WRITING

COLLECTING MONKEY IDIOMS

Have students make booklets of idioms.

Explain to students that words can be combined to create idioms—lively expressions that mean something different from the meaning of each individual word. Use *monkey business* as an example. Ask students what this expression means. *("fooling around"; something that involves trickery)* Have students brainstorm to create booklets of idioms containing the word *monkey*. Tell students to write an idiom at the top of the page and then use the rest of the page to illustrate it. Some idioms that might be included are: *monkey bars, monkey suit, monkey wrench, monkeyshines, more fun than a barrel of monkeys*. Have students share their booklets and compare their collections. **Language Arts Master 10** can be used with this activity.   WRITING

READING EVERY DAY

"The Monkey and the Crocodile" may inspire students to seek out other stories or information about jungle animals. Here are a few titles to share.

Crocodiles and Alligators by Lionel Bender. Gloucester Press, © 1988. An introduction to the different types of crocodiles and alligators that inhabit various parts of the world, with an identification chart for easy comparisons.

How the Rhinoceros Got His Skin by Rudyard Kipling. Philomel Books, © 1988. In this classic, an ill-mannered rhinoceros is taught a lesson.

Rabbit Makes a Monkey of Lion by Verna Aardema. Illustrated by Jerry Pinkney. Dial Books, © 1989. Rabbit and her clever pals outwit a feisty lion.   EASIER TO READ

Reader's Journal   pp 58, 59
Extending Reading

ANIMALS OF INDIA

Students view realistic drawings of four animals from India along with pictures of the same animals as they might appear in a folk tale. They write about how an animal might be presented in a factual article and in a folk tale.

Selection Support

COMPREHENSION

Comparison

OBJECTIVE Understanding likenesses and differences in longer texts.

Review comparison. Remind students that when making comparisons they should think about how things, persons, events, or stories are similar and different.

Use Teaching Chart to review comparisons. Display the Teaching Chart and read aloud the excerpt from "The Monkey and the Crocodile." Have students complete the chart by putting an X next to the details that are true for each character.

> **TEACHING CHART 44: COMPARISON**   **44**
>
> "How would you ever catch a monkey?" asked the old crocodile.
> "You do not travel on land and monkeys do not go into the water.
> Besides, they are quicker than you are."
>
> | Details | Monkey | Crocodile |
> |---|---|---|
> | lives in a jungle | X | X |
> | lives in trees | X | |
> | lives in a river | | X |
> | cannot swim | X | |
> | cannot climb | | X |

Provide independent practice. Options for independent practice are shown in the Resource Center below.

Workbook page 74

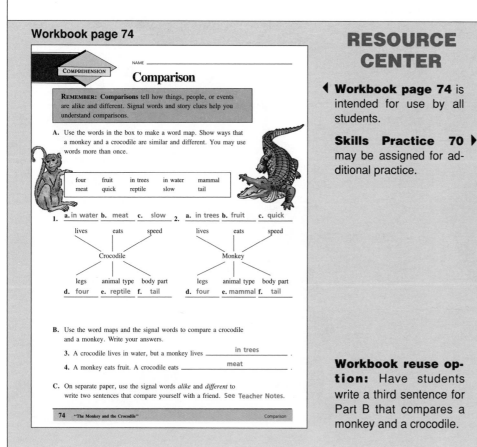

RESOURCE CENTER

◀ **Workbook page 74** is intended for use by all students.

Skills Practice 70 ▶ may be assigned for additional practice.

Workbook reuse option: Have students write a third sentence for Part B that compares a monkey and a crocodile.

Skills Practice 70

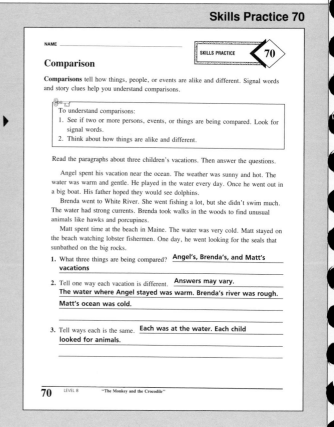

SKILL TRACE: SUFFIXES				
Introduction	Practice	Test	Reteach	Maintain
TE 222	248	293	311	314	424

WORD STUDY

Suffixes -able, -ible

OBJECTIVE Use structural analysis to determine word meaning.

Provide sentences to review known words with -able, -ible.

Display the following sets of sentences and read them aloud. Discuss the difference in meaning between the underlined words in each set. Remind students that the suffixes *-able* and *-ible* mean "can be" or "worthy of."

1. The monkey made us **laugh**.
   The crocodile's actions were **laughable**.

2. The crocodile showed that he had no **sense**.
   The monkey showed that he was **sensible**.

Use Teaching Chart to provide practice with -able, -ible.

Display the Teaching Chart. Have students combine the base words with the suffixes and then use the new words formed to complete the sentences.

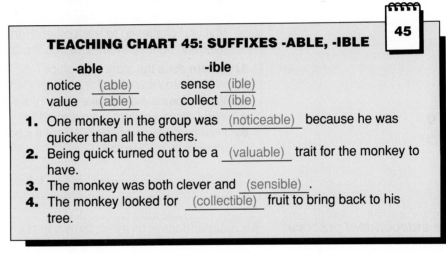

TEACHING CHART 45: SUFFIXES -ABLE, -IBLE   45

-able	**-ible**
notice (able)	sense (ible)
value (able)	collect (ible)

1. One monkey in the group was (noticeable) because he was quicker than all the others.
2. Being quick turned out to be a (valuable) trait for the monkey to have.
3. The monkey was both clever and (sensible) .
4. The monkey looked for (collectible) fruit to bring back to his tree.

Provide independent practice.

Options for independent practice are shown in Resource Center below.

Workbook page 75

NAME _____

WORD STUDY

Suffixes *-able, -ible*

REMEMBER: The suffixes *-able* and *-ible* help words describe.

A. Find the *-able* or *-ible* word in each sentence and write it on the blank. Then choose a base word from the box and write it next to the *-ible* or *-able* word formed from it.

comfort	notice	question	sense	work

1. The monkey was not comfortable in the water.
   comfortable , _comfort_

2. The monkey thought his idea about how to trick the crocodile was workable. _workable_ , _work_

3. Until an idea is carried out, it is always questionable.
   questionable , _question_

4. It was sensible of the monkey to move down the river to get away from the crocodile. _sensible_ , _sense_

5. The crocodile thought he was not noticeable as he lay on the rock waiting for the monkey. _noticeable_ , _notice_

B. Choose one of the base words on this page. On separate paper, use the word to write a sentence about the monkey or the crocodile. Then write a sentence in which you use the base word with *-ible* or *-able* added. **See Teacher Notes.**

Suffixes -able, -ible   "The Monkey and the Crocodile."   **75**

RESOURCE CENTER

◄ **Workbook page 75** is intended for use by all students.

Skills Practice 71 ► may be assigned for additional practice.

Workbook reuse option: Have students add the prefix *un-* to all the *-able* words to make the words into their opposites. Students can write the new words in the margins.

Skills Practice 71

NAME _____

SKILLS PRACTICE   71

Suffixes *-able, -ible*

The suffixes *-able* and *-ible* mean "capable of being," "can be," or "able to."

A. Read the words in the box. Circle each word that has a suffix. Then write a word you circled to complete each sentence.

beatable	candle	drinkable	handle	sensible
breakable	comfortable	fixable	movable	singable

1. This glass bowl is ____ .   _breakable_
2. The water in that bottle is ____ .   _drinkable_
3. That broken toy is ____ .   _fixable_
4. This chair is so ____ , I could sleep in it. _comfortable_
5. Everything you say is ____ .   _sensible_
6. This is so heavy that it is not ____ .   _movable_
7. No one else can win, because our team is not ____ .   _beatable_
8. The notes are too hard, so this song is not ____ .   _singable_

B. Answer each question in a sentence using the underlined word.

9. What kind of pet do you think is the most lovable?
   Answers will vary.

10. What is the most comfortable thing in your house?

11. Who is the most sensible person you know?

12. Which book do you think is the most readable?

LEVEL 8   "The Monkey and the Crocodile"   **71**

SKILL TRACE: STORY ELEMENTS							
Introduction	Practice	Test	Reteach	Maintain			
TE 16	32	138	157	159	206	294	326	558

LITERATURE

Story Elements: Setting

OBJECTIVE   Recognizing story setting.

Review setting.

Ask students what *setting* means. (*where and when a story takes place*) Explain that writers do not always tell both the place and the time. Then tell students they can often figure out the setting by carefully reading the details in the story.

Use a story passage to give practice in identifying setting.

You may wish to read aloud the passage and questions below. Have students listen for details in the story so that they can answer the questions that follow. Answers are printed in red.

Beside a river in the jungle stood a tall mango tree. In the tree lived many monkeys. They swung from branch to branch, eating fruit and chattering to each other. Hungry crocodiles swam in the river and sunned themselves on the banks.

1. Where does the story take place? (beside a river in a jungle)
2. What words are clues? (river, jungle)
3. When does the story take place? (not stated)
4. What do you picture in your mind?
5. How might the story be different if it had taken place in a zoo instead of in a jungle? (Possible answers: Monkeys and crocodiles are not in the same part of a zoo. The monkey would not have an opportunity to meet the crocodile.)

Provide independent practice.

An independent activity is shown in the Resource Center below.

RESOURCE CENTER

Skills Practice 72 ▶ may be assigned for additional practice.

Skills Practice 72

NAME _____

SKILLS PRACTICE 72

Story Elements

Every story has a **setting**, which tells *when* and *where* the story takes place. Pay attention to what the writer tells you about the setting. Picture the setting in your mind. You'll better understand what is happening in the story if you do.

A. Read each sentence. Write **Yes** if it tells something about the setting. Write **No** if it does not.

1. A flash of lightning lit up the dark sky. — Yes
2. Mario and Dina traded a pink shell for a starfish. — No
3. Dad turned on the radio. — No
4. I sat in the bow of the boat as Mom rowed across the bay. — Yes
5. Nan's family moved from the island to a house in the city. — Yes
6. Jeremy tossed the ball to Colleen. — No
7. I sat on the stone wall and looked at the river. — Yes
8. "Hello," Kate said into the telephone. — No

B. Read the paragraph. Then answer the questions about the setting.

Nick pushed his plate away from him. He looked across the table at his parents. "Last year when we moved here to the beach, you wanted me to learn to swim," he said. "I didn't want to then. After school today I saw some pictures at the library. They were taken underwater. They were beautiful. I'd like to learn to swim now. Someday I'd like to swim underwater."

9. Where does the story take place? **at the dinner table**
   on a beach   at the dinner table   at the library
10. Write the clues from the story that help you know the setting. **pushed his plate away; looked across the table; after school today**
11. What do you picture in your mind? **Answers may vary. A boy at dinner with his parents. He is talking to them.**

72   LEVEL 8   "The Monkey and the Crocodile"

CURRICULUM CONNECTIONS

CROCS AND GATORS ART

Have students use science books or encyclopedias to locate information about crocodiles and alligators. Students should report that both crocodiles and alligators have flattened bodies, short legs, and long, powerful tails. The crocodile has a long, narrow snout, while the alligator has a broad snout. The crocodile's fourth lower tooth is long and can be seen even when its jaw is shut. Encourage students to draw diagrams of crocodiles and alligators, labeling the features that differentiate them.

MAPPING INDIA SOCIAL STUDIES

Have students use social studies books, atlases, or encyclopedias to find information about the different kinds of land forms in India. Tell students to copy the shape of India onto a piece of paper and label the different kinds of topographical regions such as the Himalaya Mountains in the north, the fertile plain, and the peninsula in the south. Point out to students that the Ganges River flows through the center of the country.

REMARKABLE REPTILES SCIENCE

Have students locate information in science books or encyclopedias about reptiles, such as crocodiles, alligators, lizards, snakes, and turtles. Ask students to draw pictures of the different kinds of reptiles, or to cut out pictures of them from old newspapers or magazines. Have them label each kind of reptile and briefly note some of its characteristics. For example, reptiles typically have low-slung bodies, long tails, and four short legs (except for snakes). Display the students' reptile charts.

A JUNGLE BAR GRAPH MATHEMATICS

Tell students that in an imaginary jungle region there are seven lions, five tigers, nine monkeys, twelve crocodiles, ten birds, and three elephants. Then have students create bar graphs to show the numbers of animals in the jungle. Have them display their graphs around the classroom.

DRAWING TALES ART

Ask each student to choose a favorite part of the folk tale and illustrate it. Point out that facial expressions of the animals tell much about what is going on in their minds. Tell students to try to capture those expressions. **Curriculum Connection Master 10** can be used with this activity.

Reading the Poem

OBJECTIVE   Understanding and appreciating humor in poetry.

INTRODUCING THE POEM

Relate content of the poem to the preceding selection.

Remind students that a crocodile is one of the main characters in the last story they read. Point out that while a crocodile is a dangerous animal, it often appears in stories and poems. Ask students what they remember about the crocodile in "The Monkey and the Crocodile." (*It wanted to catch the monkey; it lived in the water; it had big jaws, sharp teeth, big eyes; it was not very smart; it could look like a rock in the water.*)

Set a listening purpose.

Tell students they are going to hear a poem about a crocodile. Ask them to think about how the poet's description makes them feel toward the crocodile.

READING THE POEM

Read the poem aloud.

Because poetry is a sound-based literary form, this part of the lesson is most important. Read the poem aloud to the students with Student Texts closed. Then have students open their books to page 161. Read the poem again or ask for volunteers to read it to the whole group. With this second reading, encourage students to picture the crocodile that the poet is describing. Discuss any unfamiliar words as needed.

doth   an old-fashioned form of the word *does*
scale   platelike part that forms the outer covering of a crocodile
Nile   a river in Africa

DISCUSSING THE POEM

Discuss students' responses to the poem.

Have students tell what kind of personality the crocodile in the poem seems to have. List key words on the board. (*cheerful, friendly, gentle*) Ask students how the poem makes them feel about this crocodile. Then ask:

What do you think makes the crocodile look golden? (the sun)

Does the poet really think the crocodile is a friendly animal, or is he trying to be funny? What makes you think that? (He is trying to be funny. The crocodile is eating the fish. The word little as applied to the crocodile means the opposite. A crocodile's jaws are not really gentle or smiling.)

Point out poetic technique.

Mention that the poet uses rhyming words. Ask students to name the words that rhyme. Help students identify where the rhyming pairs are located in each verse. (*end of first and third lines, second and fourth lines*) Point out that this is a rhyming pattern.

CLASS ENRICHMENT

Have students write friendly animal poems.

Have students find pictures or cartoons of other wild animals that are shown in funny ways. Advertisements are likely sources. Tell students to compare the animals' "picture personalities" to their real traits. Then ask each student to write a poem or at least two phrases that describe one of the wild animals in a way that makes it seem friendly.

How Doth the   Little Crocodile

How doth the little crocodile
  Improve his shining tail,
And pour the waters of the Nile
  On every golden scale!

How cheerfully he seems to grin,
  How neatly spreads his claws,
And welcomes little fishes in,
  With gently smiling jaws!

Lewis Carroll

Reader's Journal   **p 60**
Responding to Reading

FRIENDS?

Students write poems
about a crocodile. Sample
rhyming words are presented for
inspiration.

Magazine
News About Reading

Sea Shanties

OBJECTIVE   Connecting songs with the world of reading.

INTRODUCING AND READING THE ARTICLE

Relate the article to the unit theme.
Recall with students that the theme of the unit is "A Watery World." Remind students of the glimpses of life aboard ship in "Tim to the Rescue" and "The Sea of Gold." Have students tell what they know about the work of sailing a ship from these selections and other books they have read or movies they have seen. Students may also wish to share their own experience of sailing boats.

Discuss sailing on large ships.
Explain that the crew of a large sailing boat had to work together to sail the boat. Point out that all the work on boats used to have to be done by hand. Large boats had many sails, and changing the sails as the weather changed took a lot of work. Explain that it took many men pulling together on one rope to raise a heavy canvas sail or to pull it against a strong wind.

Discuss working in unison.
Ask students to name situations in which more than one person might need to pull on a rope and in which it would help to have a leader say, "1, 2, 3, pull" or "all together, pull!" (tug of war, pulling a heavy object)

State the objective.
Tell students that in this article they will learn about a type of song once sung by sailors that has been collected, written down, and recorded.

Refer students to their texts.
Have students read the article on their own.

DISCUSSING THE ARTICLE

Review the main points of the article.
Check students' understanding of the article with these questions.

Page 162 Why did sailors sing together?   (Singing together helped sailors to work as a team to pull ropes.)

Page 162 What are sailors' work songs called?   (shanties)

Magazine
News About Reading

Sea Shanties

Long ago, sailors sang songs as they worked on ships. Often they had to work for long hours, pulling heavy ropes. Singing helped them pull the ropes in time together.

A sailor's work song was called a *shanty*. (Sometimes the word is spelled *chanty* or *chantey*.) Each ship had a Shanty Man, or best singer, who helped keep the sailors together. The Shanty Man had a good sense of humor and an ability to make up verses to songs.

Sailors working on a ship in the 1890s

The Shanty Man would sing a verse. Then the sailors would chant, or sing back, in a lively chorus.

Here are some of the words to a famous, old sea shanty called "Blow the Man Down."

Blow the man down, bul-lies, blow the man down!
To me way - aye blow the man down.

SHANTY MAN: *Blow the man down, bullies, blow the man down!*

SAILORS: *To me way-aye blow the man down.*

SHANTY MAN: *Oh blow the man down, bullies, blow the man down.*

SAILORS: *Give me some time to blow the man down!*

"Blow the Man Down" has many verses that were sung over and over to help build cooperation and spirit during long voyages. Verses were added and changed over the years, but the familiar melody remains the same today.

If you are interested in learning the verses to this song, or other sea shanties, such as "Shenandoah" or "Rio Grande," look in the library for a songbook called *Fireside Book of Folk Songs*.

☞ *What if you want to learn the tune to a song but you cannot read musical notes? Ask your librarian to help you find songs on records or tapes.*

Page 163 How did the Shanty Man lead the singing? (The Shanty Man sang a verse and then the sailors sang back the chorus.)

Page 163 How might you use the library to learn the words and the tune of a shanty or a song? (Books of songs give the words and musical notes. You can hear the tune on records or tapes.)

CLASS ENRICHMENT

Have volunteers sing and pantomime a shanty.

Invite volunteers to sing and pantomime the shanty mentioned in the article. To expand students' knowledge of this type of song, have them research several shanties. Have them write down the chorus and one or two verses to share with the class.

READING CORNER

The House on East 88th Street

written and illustrated by Bernard Waber

SUMMARY

When the Primms move into their new house, they discover a crocodile named Lyle in the bathtub. Their initial fright turns to delight when Lyle performs his tricks. After Lyle has won the hearts of the Primms, his owner, Signor Valenti, returns to take him away on a performing tour. Lyle misses the Primms and instead of making his audiences laugh, he makes them cry. Signor Valenti realizes that Lyle's performances are not going to be profitable, so he sends Lyle back to the Primm family.

The Reading Teacher has honored several of Bernard Waber's books with the **Children's Choice** award.

INTRODUCING THE STORY

Review the key features of fantasy.

Remind students that fantasies tell about characters and events that could not happen in real life. Authors often begin fantasies with things that could really happen, but then the authors have a character or animal do something that could not possibly happen — such as a person flying through the air, or an animal talking. Ask students to name some stories or movies that are fantasies. "The House on East 88th Street" is a fantasy.

Develop the concept of missing someone.

Remind students that while the stories and poems in this unit all have to do with water, some selections also involve people and animals who show different feelings about one another. Mention that in "The House on East 88th Street," the Primms discover how much they miss a rather unusual friend. Ask students to explain the feelings a person might have when a best friend moves away or when a person has to give up a pet and why.

Present vocabulary.

The following words that appear in the story may be new to students. Encourage students to use their knowledge of long word decoding, as well as the context, to help them pronounce and understand unfamiliar words.

> **storage** a place where things are kept
> **trying** annoying
> **cordially** sincerely
> **caviar** fish eggs, thought by many people to be delicious, but very expensive
> **appreciatively** in a way that shows thankfulness
> **coax** to keep on asking for something in a gentle way

READING THE STORY

Assign the reading.

Be sure students understand that *The House on East 88th Street* is a book that can be found in the library. Reading this selection offers students the chance to practice uninterrupted sustained silent reading. It allows them to read at their own rate, for their own enjoyment, and encourages them to explore new books.

This story may be assigned for students to read at home. Another option is to have students choose a classmate with whom they would like to read this selection. When they have finished reading, direct partners to discuss favorite passages, chapters, or story outcomes.

Funny sounds come from the house on East 88th Street. . . . and that's strange because no one lives there!

The House on East 88th Street

written and illustrated by Bernard Waber

This is the house. The house on East 88th Street. It is empty now, but it won't be for long. Strange sounds come from the house. Can you hear them? Listen: SWISH, SWASH, SPLASH, SWOOSH . . .

It began one sunny morning when the Citywide Storage and Moving Company truck pulled up to the house on East 88th Street and unloaded the belongings of Mr. and Mrs. Joseph F. Primm and their young son Joshua. It was a trying day for everyone. Mrs. Primm just couldn't decide where to put the piano. And Mr. Primm's favorite hat was accidentally packed away in one of dozens of cartons lying about.

SWISH, SWASH, SPLASH, SWOOSH. Loudly and clearly the sounds now rumbled through the house. "It's only a little thunder," Mrs. Primm assured everyone. When a Citywide Storage and Moving man carried in their potted pistachio tree, everyone rejoiced; the truck was at last empty. The movers wished them well and hurried off to their next job for the day.

"Now, I'm going to prepare our lunch," announced Mrs. Primm. "But first I want to go upstairs and wash these grimy hands."

SWISH, SWASH, SPLASH, SWOOSH . . .

A puzzled Mrs. Primm stopped to listen. By and by her ears directed her to the bathroom door.

"What can it be?" she asked herself as she opened the door.

What she saw made her slam it quickly shut.

Mrs. Primm knew she was going to scream and just waited for it to happen. But she couldn't scream. She could scarcely even talk. The most Mrs. Primm was able to manage was the sharp hoarse whisper of a voice which she used to call Mr. Primm.

"Joseph," she said, "there's a crocodile in our bathtub."

Mr. Primm looked into the bathroom.

The next moment found them flying off in different directions.

"Help, help," Mrs. Primm cried out as she struggled with a window stuck with fresh paint.

"Operator, operator," Mr. Primm shouted into the telephone, and then he remembered that it was not yet connected.

Joshua, who had heard everything, raced to the front door, to be greeted there by an oddly dressed man who handed him a note. "This will explain everything about the crocodile," said the man, leaving quietly but swiftly.

Mr. Primm read the note:

> Please be kind to my crocodile. He is the most gentle of creatures and would not do harm to a flea. He must have tender, loving care, for he is an artist and can perform many good tricks. Perhaps he will perform some for you.
>
> I shall return.
>
> Cordially,
>
> *Hector P. Valenti*
>
> Hector P. Valenti
> Star of stage and screen
>
> P.S. He will eat only Turkish caviar.
> P.P.S. His name is Lyle.

"Turkish caviar indeed," exclaimed Mrs. Primm. "Oh, to think this could happen on East 88th Street. Whatever will we do with him?"

Suddenly, before anyone could think of a worthy answer, there was Lyle.

And just as suddenly he got hold of a ball that had been lying among Joshua's belongings and began to balance it on his nose . . . and roll it down the notches of his spine.

Now he was walking on his front feet . . . and taking flying leaps.

Now he was twirling Joshua's hoop, doing it so expertly that the Primms just had to clap their hands and laugh.

Lyle bowed appreciatively.

He had won his way into their hearts and into their new home.

"Every home should have a crocodile," said Mrs. Primm one day.

"Lyle is one of the family now. He loves helping out with chores."

"He won't allow anyone else to carry out old newspapers . . . or take in the milk."

"He folds towels, feeds the bird, and when he sets the table there is always a surprise."

"I had only to show him once how to make up a bed."

"People everywhere stop to talk with him. They say he is the nicest crocodile they ever met."

"Lyle likes to play in the park. He always goes once around in the pony cart."

"And now he has learned to eat something besides Turkish caviar."

"Lyle is a good sport. Everyone wants him to play on his side."

"He is wonderful company. We take him everywhere."

"Just give him his Turkish caviar and his bed of warm water and he is happy as a bird."

One day a brass band paraded past the house on East 88th Street.

The Primm family rushed to the window to watch. They called for Lyle, but there was no answer.

"Look," someone pointed out. "It's Lyle, he's in the parade."

There was Lyle doing his specialty of somersault, flying leaps, walking on front feet and taking bows just as he did the first day they laid eyes on him. The people watching cheered him on, while Lyle smiled back at them and blew kisses. A photographer was on hand to take pictures.

The next day Lyle was famous.

The telephone rang continually and bundles of mail were dropped by the door. One letter was from someone Lyle knew particularly well. Mr. Primm read it:

> Just a few words to say
> I shall return.
>
> Cordially,
>
> *Hector P. Valenti*
>
> Hector P. Valenti
> Star of stage and screen
>
> P.S. Very soon.
> P.P.S. To fetch my crocodile.

Several days later, Mrs. Primm and Lyle were in the kitchen shelling peas when they heard a knocking at the door.

It was Hector P. Valenti, star of stage and screen.

"I have come for Lyle," announced Signor Valenti.

"You can't have Lyle," cried Mrs. Primm, "he is very happy living here, and we love him dearly."

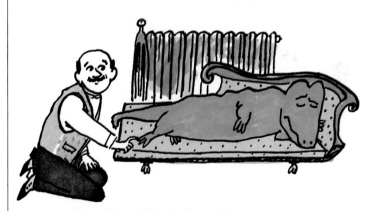

"Lyle must be returned to me," insisted Signor Valenti. "Was it not I who raised him from young crocodilehood? Was it not I who taught him his bag of tricks? We have appeared together on stages the world over."

"But why then did you leave him alone in a strange house?" asked Mrs. Primm.

"Because," answered Signor Valenti, "I could no longer afford to pay for his Turkish caviar. But now Lyle is famous and we shall be very rich." Mrs. Primm was saddened, but she knew Lyle properly belonged to Signor Valenti and she had to let him go.

It was a tearful parting for everyone.

Signor Valenti had big plans for Lyle. They were to travel far and wide . . . stay in many hotels . . . where sometimes the tubs were too big . . . and other times too small . . . or too crowded.

Signor Valenti did what he could to coax a smile from Lyle.

He tried making funny faces at him . . . he stood on his head. He tickled his toes and told him uproarious stories that in happier days would have had Lyle doubled over with laughter.

But Lyle could not laugh. Nor could he make people laugh. He made them cry instead . . . One night in Paris, he made an entire audience cry.

The theater manager was furious and ordered them off his stage.

Meanwhile at the house on East 88th Street, Mrs. Primm went about her work without her usual bright smile. And deep sighs could be heard coming from behind the newspaper Mr. Primm was reading.

Every morning Joshua anxiously awaited the arrival of the mailman in hope of receiving word from Lyle. One morning a letter did come. He knew the handwriting very well.

> Just a few words to say
> we shall return.
>
> Cordially,
>
>
>
> Hector P. Valenti
> Former star of stage and screen
>
> P.S. I am sick of crocodiles.
> P.P.S. And the tears of crocodiles.

Not too many days after, the Primms were delighted to find Hector P. Valenti and Lyle at their door.

"Here, take him back," said Signor Valenti. "He is no good. He will never make anyone laugh again."

But Signor Valenti was very much mistaken.

Everyone laughed . . . and laughed . . . and laughed.

And in the end so did Signor Valenti.

So now if you should happen to be walking past the house on East 88th Street and if you should happen to hear sounds that go: SWISH, SWASH, SPLASH, SWOOSH! don't be surprised. It's only Lyle. Lyle the crocodile.

◆ LIBRARY LINK ◆

If you like this story by Bernard Waber, you might enjoy reading some of his other books, such as I Was All Thumbs, The Snake, A Very Long Story, *and* An Anteater Named Arthur.

Reader's Response

How did you feel when Lyle left the Primms? Were you angry with Mr. Valenti? Tell why or why not.

DISCUSSING THE STORY

Summarize the story events.

Ask students to summarize the story. They should include who the story characters are, what the problem is, and what the outcome is. *(The Primms and their son, Joshua, move into a house on East 88th Street and discover a crocodile, who had been left by his owner, in their bathtub. The crocodile becomes their friend, companion, and part of the family. The owner returns to take Lyle the Crocodile on tour. The family and Lyle are very unhappy and miss one another. Lyle is so sad that he cannot perform, and Signor Valenti returns him to the Primms.)*

Discuss elements of fantasy in the story.

Ask students to tell what parts of the story could not happen in real life. *(a crocodile's living with a family, doing the tricks it does, and traveling with Signor Valenti)* Have students tell what happened at the beginning of the story that could happen in real life. *(the family's moving into a house and hearing sounds)*

Discuss Lyle's character and his relationship with the Primms.

Ask students to talk about what makes Lyle so likeable and how the Primms and Lyle feel about one another. Have students give some examples. *(Lyle is friendly and playful — does tricks, talks, and has surprises for the family. Lyle is also helpful, responsible, and a good sport — carries out old newspapers, takes in the milk, and sets the table. The Primms take Lyle everywhere and feel he is a part of the family.)* Have students describe the Primms's and Lyle's actions when they missed one another. *(Mrs. Primm did not smile, Mr. Primm sighed deep sighs, Joshua anxiously waited for a letter about Lyle. Signor Valenti could not make Lyle laugh and Lyle could not make his audiences laugh.)*

CLASS ENRICHMENT

Have students create new adventures for Lyle.

Now that Lyle is back with the Primms, he may have some new tricks to do. Have students make up new adventures. Students can work with partners to create the stories. Students can illustrate their stories and show the illustrations as they tell them.   SHARED LEARNING: SPEAKING

Have students write fantasies about unusual pets.

Have students write fantasies about unusual pets. Help students plan their writing by having them copy and complete the following sentences.

My pet is a _____.
My pet's name is _____.
My pet looks like _____.
My pet eats _____.
Things my pet and I like to do together are _____.

Encourage students to illustrate their stories. When they have finished, ask students to share their stories with their classmates.   WRITING

Checkpoint

USING THE CHECKPOINT AND VOCABULARY REVIEW

Use the Checkpoint for informal evaluation.

This Checkpoint provides another opportunity for informal evaluation before the formal end-of-unit assessment. If students have difficulty with the Checkpoint, you might use the extra-help activities suggested here or the Reteaching activities at the end of the unit before you give the test.

Like the midunit Checkpoints, these pages are in the format of the Unit Skills Tests. They might also be used to review and practice test-taking strategies. Direct students to complete the pages shown in the Resource Center. Then have students work together to correct their papers, and encourage them to explain the thinking behind their answers. This affords you an opportunity to observe not only how students arrived at their answers, but also to identify and explain any item types that are causing difficulty.

Use the Vocabulary Review.

These two pages review selected Story Critical words from the unit in the format of the Unit Skills Tests. If students' responses indicate that they have not mastered the vocabulary, you might use the extra-help activity suggested here before testing.

PROVIDING EXTRA HELP

Provide extra help with the suffixes -able and -ible.

Develop better reading comprehension by linking reading, vocabulary development, and writing. Give students five minutes to list as many words as they can think of that end in *-able* or *-ible*. When students are finished, give them time to check in the dictionary any spellings they are unsure of. Then write the words on the chalkboard as students read them to you. Have them write five sentences, each containing one of the words from the list. Completed sentences might be written on the chalkboard and read aloud to the group.

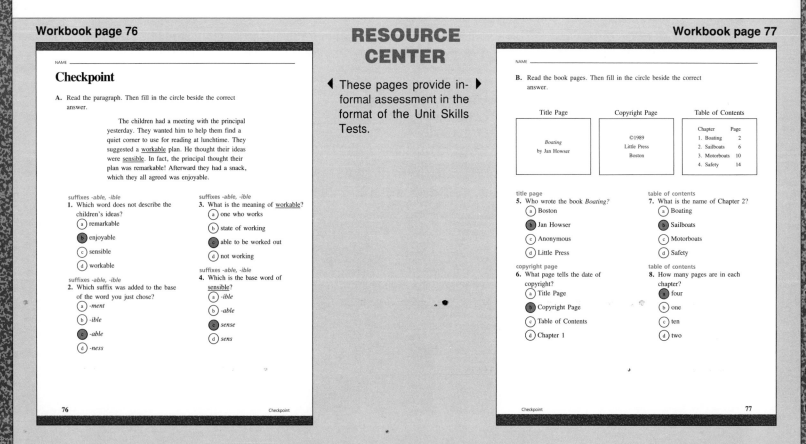

Workbook page 76

RESOURCE CENTER

◀ These pages provide informal assessment in the format of the Unit Skills Tests. ▶

Workbook page 77

NAME _____

Checkpoint

A. Read the paragraph. Then fill in the circle beside the correct answer.

> The children had a meeting with the principal yesterday. They wanted him to help them find a quiet corner to use for reading at lunchtime. They suggested a <u>workable</u> plan. He thought their ideas were <u>sensible</u>. In fact, the principal thought their plan was remarkable! Afterward they had a snack, which they all agreed was enjoyable.

suffixes -able, -ible
1. Which word does not describe the children's ideas?
  (a) remarkable
  (b) ● enjoyable
  (c) sensible
  (d) workable

suffixes -able, -ible
2. Which suffix was added to the base of the word you just chose?
  (a) -ment
  (b) -ible
  (c) ● -able
  (d) -ness

suffixes -able, -ible
3. What is the meaning of <u>workable</u>?
  (a) one who works
  (b) state of working
  (c) ● able to be worked out
  (d) not working

suffixes -able, -ible
4. Which is the base word of <u>sensible</u>?
  (a) -ible
  (b) -able
  (c) ● sense
  (d) sens

76   Checkpoint

NAME _____

B. Read the book pages. Then fill in the circle beside the correct answer.

Title Page	Copyright Page	Table of Contents
Boating by Jan Howser	©1989 Little Press Boston	Chapter Page 1. Boating 2 2. Sailboats 6 3. Motorboats 10 4. Safety 14

title page
5. Who wrote the book *Boating*?
  (a) Boston
  (b) ● Jan Howser
  (c) Anonymous
  (d) Little Press

copyright page
6. What page tells the date of copyright?
  (a) Title Page
  (b) ● Copyright Page
  (c) Table of Contents
  (d) Chapter 1

table of contents
7. What is the name of Chapter 2?
  (a) Boating
  (b) ● Sailboats
  (c) Motorboats
  (d) Safety

table of contents
8. How many pages are in each chapter?
  (a) ● four
  (b) one
  (c) ten
  (d) two

Checkpoint   77

Provide extra help with the parts of a book.

Use content-area textbooks, classroom reference books, and library books to provide extra practice with getting information from the pages at the front of a book. Have students work in pairs or small groups to choose and examine one of these books. Tell them to find the answers to these questions about the book they chose: **1.** What is the title? **2.** Who is the author? **3.** Who is the publisher? **4.** When was it printed? **5.** Does it have a table of contents? Then ask students questions that are more specific to the book they chose, such as how they can tell whether they would find information on an event that occurred during the past year *(by looking at the copyright page)* or how they can tell which chapter they might look at to find information on a particular topic. *(by looking at chapter titles in the table of contents)*

Provide extra help with Story Critical Words.

Use story rereadings to provide extra practice with unit vocabulary. Students will profit from several rereadings of a selection from the unit if you vary the purpose for each rereading. You might, for example, first have students reread for details that suggest setting. Following the rereading, ask them to write a description of the setting, using as many vocabulary words as possible. They might then read the selection again, this time looking for details of characterization. Following this reading, they might write a description of one character, including in it as many vocabulary words as possible.

Use Informal Assessment Checklist for observation.

An Informal Assessment Checklist is included in the Teacher Resource Kit. (See the Meeting Individual Needs booklet.) The Checklist will assist you in observing each student's performance in the following categories: Self-monitoring, Getting Information from Text, Summarizing, Generalizing, Evaluating, Synthesizing across Selections, Visualizing, Responding, Empathizing with Story Characters, and Predicting.

Workbook page 78

RESOURCE CENTER

◀ These pages review ▶ selected Story Critical words.

Workbook page 79

NAME _____

Vocabulary Review

Fill in the circle beside the word that best fits in the sentence.

1. To a tiny mouse even a small cat probably seems _____ .
- (a) tremendous ●
- (b) warm-blooded
- (c) religious
- (d) cunning

2. A seal swims by pushing through the water with its powerful _____ .
- (a) lungs
- (b) mammals
- (c) flippers ●
- (d) blubber

3. New discoveries about space are made every year by _____ .
- (a) engineers
- (b) Pilgrims
- (c) mammals
- (d) scientists ●

4. The girl who saved her dog from the fire showed great _____ .
- (a) adventure
- (b) reward
- (c) courage ●
- (d) medal

5. A young seal climbed to the highest rock and then _____ into the water.
- (a) shivered
- (b) dived ●
- (c) perched
- (d) nuzzled

6. The northern and southern parts of the world have different plant life because of their different _____ .
- (a) seals
- (b) climates ●
- (c) jungle
- (d) flippers

7. The boy who wanted to become a strong athlete worked hard to build up his _____ .
- (a) flippers
- (b) mammals
- (c) reward
- (d) muscles ●

78   Vocabulary Review

NAME _____

8. When we lost our pet, we offered a _____ for its safe return.
- (a) cable
- (b) galley
- (c) reward ●
- (d) deck

9. The only boat that can move freely underwater is a _____ .
- (a) crocodile
- (b) submarine ●
- (c) hurricane
- (d) shipwreck

10. We awoke before sunrise to set out on our _____ in the jungle.
- (a) courage
- (b) reward
- (c) submarine
- (d) adventure ●

11. The girls studied hard so they could become clever _____ and draw up plans for new kinds of ships.
- (a) loggers
- (b) climates
- (c) engineers ●
- (d) musicians

12. We were frightened when the long green body of a _____ moved toward us through the swamp.
- (a) fishermen
- (b) crocodile ●
- (c) pilot
- (d) cable

13. We always wear rubber-soled shoes so we won't slip on the _____ of the boat.
- (a) bunk
- (b) anchor
- (c) galley
- (d) deck ●

14. The largest fish were caught by some _____ on the wharf.
- (a) fishermen ●
- (b) pilot
- (c) scholar
- (d) waiter

15. Bright birds screech from the high branches of tropical trees in an African _____ .
- (a) galley
- (b) hurricane
- (c) jungle ●
- (d) submarine

Vocabulary Review   79

Concluding Unit 2

Unit Wrap-Up

Discuss the unit theme.

The following questions may be used to guide a general discussion of the unit. The questions help students relate the selections and understand the development of the unit theme. As an option, have students respond in writing on Workbook page 80.

1. Think about "Seals on the Land and in the Water" and "The Wonderful Underwater Machine." In what ways is Jason Jr. like a seal?

2. Think about Hikoichi in "The Sea of Gold" and Tim in "Tim to the Rescue." How do you think Tim would have treated Hikoichi, who was very slow, if they had been on the same boat?

3. At the end of the "The Monkey and the Crocodile," the crocodile said he would no longer bother the monkey. If you were the monkey, would you trust the crocodile to keep his word? Why or why not?

Writing About Reading: The Writing Process

OBJECTIVE Writing to narrate.

Begin the writing activity.

In this activity, students will practice the writing process as they narrate a dialogue between themselves and a unit character. Looking at written dialogue will help students prepare for writing.

Have the students read the introductory paragraph in the Student Text. Then use the following suggestions to guide them through the writing process.

Guide the writing process.

PREWRITING After students have completed their charts, review the capitalization and punctuation of dialogue. Show dialogue in which speaker tags both precede and follow the quotations. Then use the Student Text to point out placement of commas and end punctuation in dialogue. Discuss how dialogue differs from more formal writing. *(Dialogue may not always use complete sentences. It may contain slang.)*

WRITING Encourage students to use their charts to write dialogue that sounds natural, the way they actually speak. Have them "listen" to the conversation in their imaginations before they begin to write. Remind students not to worry about capitalization and punctuation while they write, since they will have the opportunity to make corrections later.

REVISING Have students listen as they read each other's dialogues. Encourage partners to make suggestions to each other. Have them continue this process until they are satisfied.

PROOFREADING Remind students to make sure all quotation marks and initial capital letters are correct. Then have them check for the commas that separate speaker tags from quotations. Help them with the punctuation of divided quotations. Finally, tell them to check other punctuation, spelling, and grammar and to make neat copies of their dialogues.

PUBLISHING Have students read their finished dialogues aloud to each other. Encourage natural expression.

WRITING ABOUT READING

Writing Dialogue

In the stories you have just read, characters talk to one another. What characters say to one another can help you understand how they feel. When you read what characters say to each other you are reading dialogue. Read this dialogue.

"How would you ever catch a monkey?" asked the old crocodile. "You do not travel on land and monkeys do not go into the water. Besides, they are quicker than you are."

"They may be quicker," said the young crocodile, "but I am more cunning. You will see!"

Think about a piece of dialogue you could write between two animals in the stories you have read.

Prewriting

Imagine a dialogue between two sharks, or other sea creatures, when they see Jason Jr., the wonderful underwater machine. Make a chart like the one on the next page, and use it to plan your dialogue.

◆ *The Writing Process* ───────────

A Dialogue Between Animals

First Shark Says	"Do you see what I see?"
Second Shark Says	
First Shark Says	
Second Shark Says	

Writing

Make up the rest of the dialogue between the two sharks. Start a new paragraph when there is a different speaker. Add more statements to finish the dialogue.

Revising

Read your dialogue again. Does it sound like a real conversation? Add more details if they are needed. Would using a synonym for one of the words make the dialogue sound more natural?

Proofreading

Check to make sure you used quotation marks at the beginning and end of each speaker's words. Make a neat copy.

Publishing

See if others in your class wrote dialogue about the same character you chose. If so, display them together.

─────────── *The Writing Process* ◆

Workbook page 80

UNIT TWO

Unit Wrap-Up

NAME _____

Read each question. Write your answer using complete sentences.

1. Think about "Seals on the Land and in the Water" and "The Wonderful Underwater Machine." In what ways is Jason Jr. like a seal? Possible response: Jason Jr. and a seal can both travel in the water. Like a seal, Jason Jr. can also dive deeper in the ocean than people can.

2. Think about Hikoichi in "The Sea of Gold" and Tim in "Tim to the Rescue." How do you think Tim would have treated Hikoichi, who was very slow, if they had been on the same boat? Possible response: Tim was a patient and kind boy. He liked to help people learn, so he probably would have taught Hikoichi all that he could.

3. At the end of "The Monkey and the Crocodile," the crocodile said he would no longer bother the monkey. If you were the monkey, would you trust the crocodile to keep his word? Why or why not? Possible response: Since the crocodile prided himself on his cunning and trickery, he probably could not be trusted.

80   Unit Wrap-Up

RESOURCE CENTER

Writing Master 12 supports the Writing About Reading activity.

Working Together: A Cooperative Learning Project

Plan for time and materials.

In this project, students will work cooperatively to make a collage. For each group, provide one large sheet of paper, several sheets of drawing paper, markers, scissors, and paste. The project is designed to last about one hour, but adapt this guideline to meet the needs of your class.

Present the project.

After students read page 180, review the material by having them explain what they will be creating and how. Then have them explain why the project will not be successful without everyone's efforts. *(The group can generate more ideas than one person. Also, a collage is made from many pieces.)*

Define roles and responsibilities.

Identify groups. Ask students which jobs must be done individually and which should be done by everyone. Then have students discuss different ways that roles might be assigned or chosen by group members. Remind students to keep the group goal in mind as they do their individual jobs.

Observe the groups.

Observe the groups. If necessary, help each group plan the time needed for every step. Model asking others to talk by using a question such as, "What do you think should go here, Jan?"

Have students present the project and evaluate their group's performance.

Invite each group to display its collage. Have each person tell what his or her drawing showed and what story it came from. Then have students discuss their group's strengths and weaknesses. You might suggest that they complete the following sentences: *The thing our group did best was . . . Our group had the most trouble . . .*

Books to Enjoy

Encourage independent reading.

Discuss with students the books described on the Student Text page. Encourage those who have read any of the suggested books to share them with the group. You might also suggest that students copy titles of interest onto their Workbook Book List and look for them in the library.

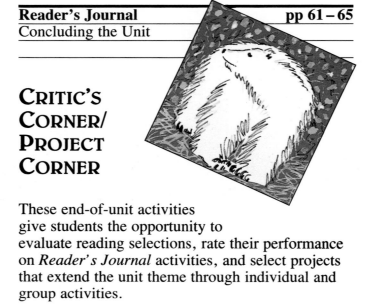

Reader's Journal pp 61–65
Concluding the Unit

CRITIC'S CORNER/ PROJECT CORNER

These end-of-unit activities give students the opportunity to evaluate reading selections, rate their performance on *Reader's Journal* activities, and select projects that extend the unit theme through individual and group activities.

Making a Watery World Collage

Stories in this unit told you many things about life in or near the water. You learned how seals live. You also read about an underwater vehicle named JJ. Your group will now make a collage that shows water scenes from this unit.

As you work together, do one or more of these jobs:

- ◆ Give your ideas to the group.
- ◆ Ask others to talk.
- ◆ Thank people for their ideas.
- ◆ Help the group finish on time.

Start by talking together about the stories in this unit. As a group, choose the stories you would like to show on your "Watery World" collage. Then, take turns giving ideas about animals, people, boats, or other vehicles from the stories that might go on your collage. Each of you should choose one thing to draw for the collage. When you have finished your drawing, cut it out. Take turns pasting the cut-out drawings on a large sheet of paper. Finally, add details like fish, rocks, or waves to finish your collage.

Will your friends know which stories you picked for your "Watery World" collage?

◆ *Cooperative Learning*

Amy Goes Fishing by Jean Marzollo *(Dial, 1980)* Amy is not at all sure that spending a Saturday fishing with her father is going to be very exciting, but a lunch and a "catch" change her view.

A First Look at Seashells by Millicent E. Selsam and Joyce Hunt *(Walker, 1983)* This book identifies the two main groups of shells, asks questions about them, and uses black-and-white drawings to help the reader answer the questions.

Little Whale by Ann McGovern *(Scholastic, 1979)* Follow a humpback whale from its birth to being full-grown. What whales eat, where they travel, and how humans have acted toward whales are also covered in this book.

Sea Songs by Myra Cohn Livingston *(Holiday, 1986)* This book has poems about sea life.

Testing

Select the most appropriate test.

Unit Process Test is a holistic test that assesses overall comprehension. Students compose written responses to test questions.

Unit Skills Test is a criterion-referenced test that assesses how well a student has learned the specific skill objectives in the unit. The two forms, A and B, can be used to pretest and post-test or to test, reteach, and retest, depending on your preference.

Score and evaluate test results.

Keys and Record Sheets assist in scoring both kinds of tests, interpreting the results, and identifying students who need additional help. Students who perform well may proceed directly to the next unit. Those who do not will benefit from Reteaching activities on the pages that follow, Practice and Reteaching worksheets in the Teacher Resource Kit, and additional guided and independent reading.

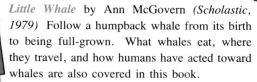

Meeting Individual Needs

SKILL TRACE: COMPARISON						
Introduction	Practice		Test	Reteach	Maintain	
TE 176	196	292	311	312	349	578	619

COMPREHENSION

Comparison

OBJECTIVE   Understanding likenesses and differences in longer texts.

RETEACHING

Reteach making comparisons.

Write the following passage on the chalkboard:

> **All mammals are warm-blooded and breathe air with their lungs. Baby mammals are born and not hatched from eggs like birds. Most mammals, like people, live on land. Some mammals, like whales, live only in the water. However, there are mammals, like seals, who live both on land and in the water.**

Tell students you will look for clue words such as *both, like,* and *all* to find ways animals are alike. Words such as *not, only,* and *however* point to differences. Have volunteers find and read sentences that describe likenesses and differences.

Explain that making comparisons helps the reader understand how things are alike and how they are different.

Have students read the passage above again and write the answers to the following questions: How are people and whales alike and how are they different? How are people and seals alike and how they are different?

Provide independent practice.   **Reteaching Masters 1–7** for making comparisons may be assigned.

ACHIEVING ENGLISH PROFICIENCY

Provide practice in identifying similarities and differences.

Write the headings **same** and **different** on the chalkboard. Hold up an apple and an orange and explain that they are the same in some ways — they are both types of fruit and are round. Write the words **fruit** and **round** under the heading *same.* Then ask students how an apple and an orange are different. List their responses under the heading *different.* Guide students in comparing and contrasting several objects, such as a pen, a pencil, a crayon, or a hat, an umbrella, and a scarf. Record students' responses in the appropriate columns. Then model for students statements about the objects, using the following comparison words: *alike, like, same, but, opposite, different.*

Provide independent practice.   **Achieving English Proficiency Master 10** may be assigned.

CHALLENGE

Have students make posters comparing two animals.

Have students brainstorm a list of animals. Write each animal on an index card and put the card in a bag. Then have each student grab two cards from the bag. These will be the animals he or she will use to make a comparison poster. Direct students to include at least two ways the animals are alike and two ways they are different. Students can use the encyclopedia and other books to find information. Encourage students to illustrate their posters. Display the posters under the title: *How Animals Are Alike . . . and Different.*

Provide independent practice   **Challenge Master 5** may be assigned.

SKILL TRACE: SUFFIX				
Introduction	Practice	Test	Reteach	Maintain
TE 192	226	272	313	396

WORD STUDY

Suffix -ness

OBJECTIVE   Using structural analysis to determine word meaning.

RETEACHING

Reteach suffix -ness.

Write on the chalkboard: **sadness, happiness.** Underline the *-ness* suffix Explain that this ending means "state of " or "being." Circle the base words *sad* and *happy* and the spelling change in *happy.* Write these sentences on the chalkboard:

> **We all felt sadness when school was over.**
> **We felt happiness about all we had learned this year.**

Ask students what each word with the suffix means. Point out that when *-ness* is added to a word, it changes the word to a noun.

Explain that knowing what suffixes mean will help students to read and understand new words.

Write the following sentences on the chalkboard. Have students read the sentences and then write and define the words with the suffix *-ness.*

1. **The dimness of the light made it difficult to see.**

2. **He smiled as he felt the softness of the kitten's fur.**

3. **Shyness can keep someone from meeting new people.**

Have students tell what they have learned about the suffix *-ness. (It means "state of " or "being.")*

Provide independent practice.

Reteaching Masters 1–4 for suffix *-ness* may be assigned.

ACHIEVING ENGLISH PROFICIENCY

Review words with the suffix -ness.

Write on the chalkboard:

> **The house was very dark. No one could see anything in the darkness.**

Read the sentences aloud, and pantomime the action of feeling where things are in the darkness. Ask students to find a word in the second sentence that is almost like a word in the first sentence *(darkness).* Have a student circle the letters that are different. Then write these sentences on the chalkboard:

1. **Farmers are very kind to animals. They treat animals with kindness.**
2. **Lana was very sad. Her sadness made her cry.**
3. **I heard a loud noise. Its loudness surprised me.**

Read each sentence pair aloud. Have a student circle the *-ness* suffix. Have students repeat the words with the *-ness* suffix after you.

Provide independent practice.

Achieving English Proficiency Master 12 may be assigned.

CHALLENGE

Have students write sentences with words ending in -ness and illustrate them.

Have students brainstorm a list of words ending in the suffix *-ness.* Remind them that the *-ness* ending means "state of " or "being." Have them think of words that describe how some things look, feel to the touch, taste, and how things make them feel. Write their *-ness* words on the chalkboard. Then have each student pick two words to use in sentences and then to illustrate. Suggested *-ness* words: *softness, hardness, darkness, lightness, gentleness.*

Provide independent practice.

Challenge Master 6 may be assigned.

SKILL TRACE: SUFFIXES				
Introduction	Practice	Test	Reteach	Maintain
TE 222	248	293	311	314	424

Suffix -able, -ible

OBJECTIVE   Using structural analysis to determine word meaning.

RETEACHING

Reteach suffix -ment.

Write on the chalkboard: **breakable, collectible.** Underline each suffix. Explain that these endings mean "can be" or "capable of being." Write these sentences on the board:

> **Glass is breakable.**
> **Stamps are collectible.**

Have students use the meaning of -*able* to define *breakable* and -*ible* to define *collectible.* *("able to break" or "can be broken"; "can be collected" or "capable of being collected")*
    Explain that knowing what suffixes mean will help students to read and understand new words.
    Write the following sentences on the board. Have students read them, write the words with the suffix -*able* or -*ible,* and tell their meanings.

1. **These marks on the wall are erasable.**

2. **It is sensible to eat right and get a lot of sleep.**

3. **Your new puppy is lovable.**

Have students tell what they have learned about the suffixes -*able,* -*ible.*

Provide independent practice.

Reteaching Masters 1–4 for suffix -*able,* -*ible* may be assigned.

ACHIEVING ENGLISH PROFICIENCY

Have students use words with -able and -ible in context.

Make word cards for the following: *break, read, collect, understand.* Show the cards to students and have them repeat the words after you. Explain words students do not know. Make up cards with the suffixes -*able* and -*ible.* Hold up a glass and ask students if it is possible to *break* it. Then say, "I can break the glass. It is *breakable.*" Hold up the word card *break* and the suffix card -*able.* Write the complete word on the board. Tell students the suffix -*able* means "can be." Tell students that sometimes -*able* as a suffix is spelled -*ible.* Hold up *collect* and -*ible.* Write out *collectible* on the board. Follow the same procedure for *read* and *understand.* Use the words in sentences.

Provide independent practice.

Achieving English Proficiency Master 14 may be assigned.

CHALLENGE

Have students write poems using -able, -ible words.

Have each student select one sport or activity such as bike riding or a hobby such as stamp collecting and list three words that describe it. The words should end with -*able* or -*ible.* Then have each student write three lines of a poem that end with his or her chosen -*able* and -*ible* words. Write the following example on the board so that students have a model.

> **A baseball is throwable.**
> **Then it is hittable.**
> **The bases are runnable.**
> **Unless the ball has been caught.**

Provide independent practice.

Challenge Master 8 may be assigned.

SKILL TRACE: TABLE OF CONTENTS				
Introduction	Practice	Test	Reteach	Maintain
TE 224	249	273	311	315

STUDY SKILLS

Title Page, Copyright Page, Table of Contents

OBJECTIVE   Using the title and copyright pages and table of contents.

RETEACHING

Reteach title and copyright pages and table of contents.

Write on the chalkboard the following: *All About the Sea by George Greer,* © *Copyright 1988,* and *Chapter 1, Sea Mammals; Chapter 2, How Waves Are Formed; Chapter 3, Fish.* Ask students which information on the board could be found on the title page of a book, the table of contents, and the copyright page. Explain that different kinds of information about a book are found in different parts of a book. Have students find those parts in their reading texts.

Explain that using the title and copyright pages and the table of contents will help students quickly and easily find important information about a book.

Write the following on the board and have students answer these questions: Who is the author? When and where was the book published? How many stories are in it? On which page does "Sailing Days" begin?

Sea Stories by Susan Brown	© 1988 New York, N.Y.	Sailing Days . . . . 3 Waves . . . . 10 The Beach . . . . 20 Sea Home 30

Have students tell what they have learned about the title and copyright pages and the table of contents. *(These pages help the reader find information about a book quickly and easily.)*

Provide independent practice.

Reteaching Masters 1–4 for title and copyright pages and table of contents may be assigned.

CHALLENGE

Have students create title pages and tables of contents for their own autobiographies.

Explain to students that an autobiography is the life story of someone written by that person. Tell students that they will create title pages and tables of contents for their own autobiographies. Have each student make up a title and name himself/herself as the author. For the table of contents, have the student list four different times in his or her life to tell about in a book. Suggest some possibilities such as learning to ride a bike, a special summer, and the first day of school. Display the title pages and table of contents. Encourage a discussion about the events listed. Some students may want to write their autobiographies of one of these events or all of them.

Provide independent practice.

Challenge Master 7 may be assigned.

UNIT THREE
OVERVIEW

ON YOUR OWN

UNIT THEME   Resourcefulness and strength help many of the characters in this unit meet the challenges they face. Everyone wins in the end, through personal growth, if not through success.

UNIT SELECTIONS

Slower Than the Rest, *by Cynthia Rylant*
Leo, a slow learner, finds happiness and appreciation through his turtle, Charlie. A read aloud/think aloud selection.

Jason Wants a Library, *by Margaret Tuley Patton*
When ten-year-old Jason grows tired of biking to the next town for books, he arranges to start his own library in the town hall basement.

The Recital, *by Johanna Hurwitz*
Maria is nervous before an important piano recital, but her soccer-playing sister offers her some good advice that helps her win a warm ovation.

Lee Bennett Hopkins Interviews Johanna Hurwitz
Learn how this prolific writer turned a passion for stories into two careers, one as a librarian and one as an author of children's books.

A Day When Frogs Wear Shoes, *by Ann Cameron*
In this excerpt from an **American Library Association** award winning book, three children and their father relax by the river on a hot summer day and discover the truth about frogs wearing shoes.

Phillis Wheatley, America's First Black Poet, *by Kacey Brown*
A young African girl, sold as a slave to a Boston family, becomes a poet and meets a famous fan — General George Washington.

Alexander and the Terrible, Horrible, No Good, Very Bad Day, *by Judith Viorst*
Everyone has bad days, but this one is so bad that Alexander wants to move to Australia. Read how Alexander's mother persuades him to stay, in this Reading Corner selection. A Silver Burdett & Ginn **Readers' Choice** award winner.

Title	Skills/Strategies	Integrated Language Arts	Cross-Curriculum
Listening Lesson: Slower Than the Rest Pages 322–327	Story Elements	**Active Listening**	
Jason Wants a Library Pages 328–351	Cause/Effect ★ Suffix: -ment ★ Symbols and Signs	**Speaking:** Problem Solving: Town Projects; Acting Out Scenes **Writing:** Nonfiction; Newspaper Articles	**Social Studies:** Mapping; Government Charts **Art:** Posters for National Library Week **Careers:** Librarians **Mathematics:** Library Word Problems **Humanities:** Book Recommendations **Library Science:** Library Diagram
	**Thinking·Reading·Writing: Making a Character Map** Pages 352–353		
The Recital Pages 354–377	Classification ★ Suffixes: -ion, -tion	**Writing:** Piano Tips for Soccer Players; Realistic Fiction; Feelings **Speaking:** Performance Situations Advice	**Music:** Keyboard Instruments **Social Studies:** Composer or Musician Reports **Music:** Lyrics **Careers:** Music Careers **Physical Education:** Soccer Report and Demonstration
Lee Bennett Hopkins Interviews Johanna Hurwitz Pages 378–397	★ Making Inferences ★ Homophones	**Speaking:** Author Reports; Musical Words for Instruments **Writing:** Interview; Journal Entries	**Art:** Self-Portrait **Careers:** Baseball Player/Ballet Dancer **Social Studies:** Well-known People **Mathematics:** Time Lines
	Checkpoint INFORMAL ASSESSMENT Pages 398–399		
	Looking at the Setting of a Story: Literature Link Pages 400–401		
A Day When Frogs Wear Shoes Pages 402–425	Figurative Language	**Speaking:** Figurative Language; Competing with Comparisons **Writing:** Realistic Fiction; Television Commercial; The Frog's Point of View; Car Words	**Science:** Frogs **Music:** Frog Songs **Art:** Wheeled Vehicle Designs
Phillis Wheatley, America's First Black Poet Pages 426–447	Characterization	**Writing:** Poem; Parts of a Story; Publishing a Poetry Journal; Biography **Speaking:** Poetry Reading	**Social Studies:** Time Line; George Washington Biography **Geography:** Map of Phillis's Travels **Humanities:** Past and Modern Poets **Art:** Scenes from Phillis's Life **Music:** Classical Music
Narcissa (poem) Pages 448–449		**Listening:** Mental Pictures of a Poem **Writing:** Description—Daydreams	
Time Out for Books: *Storm in the Night* Pages 450–451			
Reading Corner: Alexander and the Terrible, Horrible, No Good, Very Bad Day Pages 452–455		**Speaking:** Oral Reading; Dramatize the Story	
	Checkpoint INFORMAL ASSESSMENT Pages 456–457		

★ Tested Skill in this unit

Reading Every Day

CREATE A CLASSROOM LIBRARY

The following books and magazines are referenced throughout the unit. You might gather them ahead of time to place in your classroom library.

Barth, Edna. **The Day Luis Was Lost.**

Blair, Gwenda. **Laura Ingalls Wilder.**

Brooks, Gwendolyn. **Bronzeville Boys and Girls.**

Cameron, Ann. **More Stories Julian Tells.**

Collins, David. **To the Point: A Story About E. B. White**

Dalgliesh, Alice. **The Courage of Sarah Noble.**

Faulkner, Georgene, and John Becker. **Melindy's Medal.**

Flack, Marjorie and Kurt Wiese. **The Story About Ping.**

Gauch, Patricia Lee. **Aaron and the Green Mountain Boys.**

Hathorn, Elizabeth. **The Tram to Bondi Beach.**

Hurwitz, Johanna. **Aldo Applesauce.**

———. **Aldo Ice Cream.**

———. **Class Clown.**

———. **Yellow Blue Jay.**

Jukes, Mavis. **Like Jake and Me.**

Lasker, Joe. **Nick Joins In.**

Lord, Betty Bao. **In the Year of the Boar and Jackie Robinson.**

MacLachlan, Patricia. **Arthur, For the Very First Time.**

Martin, Charles. **Summer Business.**

McKissack, Patricia. **Flossie and the Fox.**

Monjo, F. N. **The Drinking Gourd.** 〰

Rowland, Florence Wightman. **Amish Boy.**

Sabin, Francene. **Harriet Tubman.**

Schlein, Miriam. **The Girl Who Would Rather Climb Trees.**

Steig, William. **Brave Irene.**

Stevens, Carla. **Anna, Grandpa, and the Big Storm.**

Wallace, Ian. **Chin Chiang and the Dragon's Dance.**

〰 A **World of Books** Classroom Libraries selection

WORLD OF BOOKS Classroom Libraries

World of Books Classroom Libraries offer a wide selection of books that may be used for independent reading with this unit.

UNIT PROJECT CARDS   Projects such as making a guitar, reviewing a film, and solving rebus puzzles extend and enrich the unit theme. Instructions for these and other projects are found on **Project Cards 9 –12** in the *Idea Factory for Teachers*. Project Cards are designed for students to use alone or in small groups.

HOME CONNECTION LETTERS   The Teacher Resource Kit includes letters, written in English and in Spanish, that explain what students have learned during this unit and suggest bibliographies and activities that support instruction.

The books listed on the "Reading Every Day" card in each lesson's Language Arts Connection may also be copied and sent home to encourage family involvement in independent reading.

BULLETIN BOARDS

Use the suggestions in the *Idea Factory for Teachers* to construct the unit bulletin boards.

Interactive Teaching Kit

The *Castles of Sand* I·T Kit offers materials and activities to motivate and enrich your students' reading experience. You may choose to use some or all of the unit activities to introduce Unit 3, "On Your Own." Later in the unit, you may choose to use some or all of the story-related activities. You will find complete teaching instructions in the I·T Kit Activity Guide.

The I·T Kit provides a menu of activities to introduce the unit theme.

VIDEO ✦ ON YOUR OWN

What makes some people so good at being on their own? This video helps students answer the question as it brings literature to life with background experiences for the unit theme and stories. "On Your Own" leads students into literature by motivating them to read the story selections in the unit.

◆ After practicing on their own for many hours, a group of young musicians presents a recital for family and friends.

◆ Meet award-winning author Gwendolyn Brooks, who talks about what writing means to her.

◆ Achieving something on your own is the theme of an inspiring music video set to the song "On Your Own." (See Activity Guide.)   LITERATURE, CONTENT AREAS, CONTEMPORARY MUSIC

AUDIO ✦ "IF AT FIRST YOU DON'T SUCCEED"

Even a really good plan can fail on the first try. Students sing a song that encourages persistence in reaching for goals. (See Activity Guide.)
CONTEMPORARY MUSIC

UNIT CARDS ✦ YOU'RE IN CHARGE

A cat is stuck in the branches of a tree. A wallet full of money lies in the middle of the sidewalk. As students take charge in the situation presented on each card, they will learn that there are many responsible ways to solve a problem. (See Activity Guide.)   CONTENT AREAS

POSTER ✦ "GOING TO SCHOOL"

Getting ready for school every day is quite a job, as the poem on this poster illustrates. Barbara Garrison's whimsical etchings show a child managing the process of getting out from under the bedcovers and in the school door before the bell rings. (See Activity Guide.)   LITERATURE

The I·T Kit provides activities that may be used following these reading selections:

"Jason Wants a Library" (See TE page 341 and Activity Guide.)

"A Day When Frogs Wear Shoes" (See TE page 416 and Activity Guide.)

"Phillis Wheatley, America's First Black Poet" (See TE page 438 and Activity Guide.)

Beginning the Unit

Appreciating Art

Provide background about the work of art.

Have students look at the picture of the juggler on page 182 of the Student Text. A poster version of this illustration, found in the Teacher Resource Kit, may be displayed for the discussion. Explain that this ink painting is by Katsushika Hokusai, one of Japan's greatest artists. He often painted landscapes, and he created a vast number of works — over 30,000 drawings and 500 illustrated books.

Have students view the work of art and discuss the unit theme.

Tell students that juggling is an ancient art popular all over the world. Ask if any of them has ever watched a juggler or ever themselves tried to juggle. Lead a discussion about what skills are necessary for juggling. Ask students how the juggler feels as he performs: Do they think he looks proud, or is he just concentrating? Where do they think he might be performing, and who might be watching him? Have a volunteer read aloud the question on page 183. Encourage discussion of why some people are more independent than others. Have students preview the unit, and encourage them to discuss any selection they feel will be particularly interesting or any by their favorite author(s).

Point out Time Out for Books.

Call attention to the feature on pages 236–237. Some students may wish to begin reading the book on their own. Additional suggestions for when and how this book might be used are provided in the *Time Out for Books Guide*.

Connecting the Known to the New

Encourage independent reading with the Interest Inventory and the Book Log.

Workbook page 81 is a questionnaire that asks students to identify unit-related topics that they might be interested in reading about. Workbook page 82 provides space for listing suggested titles from the Interest Inventory, as well as other titles students may wish to read. Workbook pages 163–176 provide space for students to record their personal responses to books.

Reader's Journal	pp 66 – 68
Beginning the Unit	

ARABELLE'S GARDEN

A related reading introduces the unit theme, "On Your Own." Students read a story about a girl who utilizes humor and ingenuity to meet a challenge. They then analyze the inner resources she draws upon to solve her problem.

UNIT THREE

ON YOUR OWN

*I*t can be fun to do things on your own.

What makes some people so good at being on their own?

BOY JUGGLING SHELLS,
*ink and color on paper by Katsushika Hokusai,
Japanese, (1760–1849)*

Workbook page 81

UNIT THREE

Interest Inventory

When you are on your own, you try to do things right even though it isn't always easy. Answer the questions below and use the chart to discover books that you may find especially interesting.

	yes	no	
1.	☐	☐	Would you like to read about clever animals?
2.	☐	☐	Do you like reading adventure stories?
3.	☐	☐	Do you like to try to do new things?
4.	☐	☐	Do you think it's fun to do things to surprise people?
5.	☐	☐	Do you sometimes enjoy doing things your own way?
6.	☐	☐	Do you sometimes need to be brave?
7.	☐	☐	Would you enjoy reading about a child's adventure?

Now find the numbers for the questions you checked YES. Follow the column down. When you see a star, move across the row to find the book title. That's the book for you!

1	2	3	4	5	6	7	Title/Author
							Chin Chang and the Dragon's Dance by Ian Wallace
	☆	☆					*Aaron and the Green Mountain Boys* by Patricia Lee Gauch
		☆	☆	☆			*The Girl Who Would Rather Climb Trees* by Miriam Schlein
☆							*The Story About Ping* by Marjorie Flack and Kurt Wiese
		☆			☆		*Brave Irene* by William Steig
☆			☆				*Flossie and the Fox* by Patricia C. McKissack
						☆	*Amish Boy* by Florence Wightman Rowland

81

RESOURCE CENTER

◀ **Workbook page 81** is a questionnaire that helps students identify topics and books of interest.

Workbook page 82 is ▶ a personal list of books students might read independently.

Workbook page 82

UNIT THREE

Personal Book List

NAME _____

Title _____

Author _____

Title _____

Author _____

Title _____

Author _____

Title _____

Author _____

82

Listening Lesson

SELECTION SUMMARY

Leo, the main character of this realistic story, is a ten year old with learning disabilities. Labeled even by his father as "slower than the rest," he is nearly friendless and very unhappy. In the car with his family one day, he spots a turtle by the side of the road and gets permission to retrieve it. "Charlie" soon becomes his constant companion and eventually accompanies him to school as his exhibit for Prevent Forest Fires week. Leo's impassioned explanation of how Charlie's slowness would make him especially vulnerable to forest fires and his moving description of his and Charlie's friendship win his classmates' admiration and an award for the best report. For the first time in his life, Leo feels proud and "fast."

STRATEGIES FOR LISTENING

Explain the process of listening for enjoyment.

You may choose to read the selection twice. During a first reading, students should relax and enjoy the selection. They should not worry about words or information they do not fully understand. They should listen carefully, however, for details that reveal qualities or traits of the main character in the selection. Knowing what the main character is like will make it easier to understand the character's behavior and predict his future actions. You may read the selection or use the audio tape which is available.

Set the purpose for a read aloud/think aloud.

If you choose, you may read the selection a second time. Tell students that as you read you will share some of your thoughts and feelings about the story's characters and events by thinking aloud. In this way you will model how good readers think as they read. The annotations adjacent to the selection may serve as prompts for modeling your thinking, but you may substitute your own or offer additional ones. Encourage students to be active thinkers during their own reading.

DISCUSSING THE SELECTION

Present discussion questions.

1. **Sometimes the characters in the stories we read or hear are very much like us. Other times they are very different. Almost always, though, we find ourselves saying, "I know how that character feels" or "I remember when I felt the way that character does." What are some feelings Leo had that you also have had?** (Students might mention the joy of getting a pet, the pleasure of making a pet their own, the pain of feeling different, and the joy and surprise of winning an unexpected award.)

2. **When we tell other people about stories we have read, we often use the words, "The best part is . . ." Imagine that you are telling someone about the story you just heard. How would you complete the line, "The best part of 'Slower Than the Rest' is . . ."? What would you say if the person asked why you chose that part?** (Students will give various responses as they recount episodes from the story and provide reasons for their choices.)

SLOWER *Than the Rest* [1]

By Cynthia Rylant

Leo was the first one to spot the turtle, so he was the one who got to keep it. They had all been in the car, driving up Tyler Mountain to church, when Leo shouted, "There's a turtle!" and everyone's head jerked with the stop.

Leo's father grumbled something about turtle soup, but Leo's mother was sympathetic toward turtles, so Leo was allowed to pick it up off the highway and bring it home. Both his little sisters squealed when the animal stuck its ugly head out to look at them, and they thought its claws horrifying, but Leo loved it from the start. He named it Charlie. [2]

The dogs at Leo's house had always belonged more to Leo's father than to anyone else, and the cat thought she belonged to no one but herself, so Leo was grateful for a pet of his own. He settled Charlie in a cardboard box, threw in some lettuce and radishes, and declared himself a happy boy.

Leo adored Charlie, and the turtle was hugged and kissed as if he were a baby. Leo liked to fit Charlie's shell on his shoulder under his left ear, just as one might carry a cat, and Charlie would poke his head into Leo's neck now and then to keep them both entertained.

Leo was ten years old the year he found Charlie. He hadn't many friends because he was slower than the rest. That was the way his father said it: "Slower than the rest. . . ." [3]

But Charlie took care of Leo's happiness, and he did it by being congenial. Charlie was the friendliest turtle anyone had ever seen. The turtle's head was always stretched out, moving left to right, trying to see what was in the world. His front and back legs moved as though he were swimming frantically in a deep sea to save himself, when all that was happening was that someone was holding him in midair. Put Charlie down and he would sniff at the air a moment, then take off as if no one had ever told him how slow he was supposed to be.

Every day, Leo came home from school, took Charlie to the backyard to let him explore and told him about the things that had happened in fifth grade. Leo wasn't sure how old Charlie was, and, though he guessed Charlie was probably a young turtle, the lines around Charlie's forehead and eyes and the clamp of his mouth made Leo think Charlie was wise the way old people are wise. So Leo talked to him privately every day.

Then one day Leo decided to take Charlie to school. [4]

It was Prevent Forest Fires week and the whole school was making posters, watching nature films, imitating Smokey the Bear. Each member of Leo's class was assigned to give a report on Friday dealing with forests. So Leo brought Charlie.

1. This title certainly makes me wonder who will be slower and who are the rest. I also wonder if the one who is slower will catch up with the others in the end.

2. I think I know now who will be slower. What could ever be slower than a turtle?

3. So Leo is slow, too? I was not expecting that. It sounds to me as if Leo is slow in learning how to do things. I hope having Charlie will help him.

4. Charlie has certainly become an important part of Leo's life. Now he is even going to school with him. I am beginning to think Leo will do better in school because Charlie will be there.

Leo was quiet about it on the bus to school. He held the covered box tightly on his lap, secretly relieved that turtles are quiet except for an occasional hiss. Charlie rarely hissed in the morning; he was a turtle who liked to sleep in.

Leo carried the box to his classroom and placed it on the wide windowsill near the radiator and beside the geraniums. His teacher called attendance and the day began.

In the middle of the morning, the forest reports began. One girl held up a poster board pasted with pictures of raccoons and squirrels, rabbits and deer, and she explained that animals died in forest fires. The pictures were too small for anyone to see from his desk. Leo was bored.

One boy stood up and mumbled something about burnt-up trees. Then another got up and said if there were no forests, then his dad couldn't go hunting, and Leo couldn't see the connection in that at all.

Finally it was his turn. He quietly walked over to the windowsill and picked up the box. He set it on the teacher's desk.

"When somebody throws a match into a forest," Leo began, "he is a murderer. He kills trees and birds and animals. Some animals, like deer, are fast runners and they might escape. But other animals"—he lifted the cover off the box—"have no hope. They are too slow. They will die." He lifted Charlie out of the box. "It isn't fair," he said, as the class gasped and giggled at what they saw. "It isn't fair for the slow ones."

Leo said much more. Mostly he talked about Charlie, explained what turtles were like, the things they enjoyed, what talents they possessed. He talked about Charlie the turtle and Charlie the friend, and what he said and how he said it made everyone in the class love turtles and hate forest fires. Leo's teacher had tears in her eyes. **5**

5. Leo knows he has something very important to say, and much of it is because of Charlie. What a terrific scene—Leo standing in front of the class giving his speech.

That afternoon, the whole school assembled in the gymnasium to bring the special week to a close. A ranger in uniform made a speech, then someone dressed up like Smokey the Bear danced with two others dressed up like squirrels. Leo sat with his box and wondered if he should laugh at the dancers with everyone else. He didn't feel like it.

Finally, the principal stood up and began a long talk. Leo's thoughts drifted off. He thought about being home, lying in his bed and drawing pictures, while Charlie hobbled all about the room.

He did not hear when someone whispered his name. Then he jumped when he heard, "Leo! It's you!" in his ear. The boy next to him was pushing him, making him get up.

"What?" Leo asked, looking around in confusion.

"You won!" they were all saying. "Go on!"

Leo was pushed onto the floor. He saw the principal smiling at him, beckoning to him across the room. Leo's legs moved like Charlie's— quickly and forward.

Leo carried the box tightly against his chest. He shook the principal's hand. He put down the box to accept the award plaque being handed to him. It was for his presentation with Charlie. Leo had won an award for the first time in his life, and as he shook the principal's hand and blushed and said his thank-you's, he thought his heart would explode with happiness.

That night, alone in his room, holding Charlie on his shoulder, Leo felt proud. And for the first time in a long time, Leo felt *fast*. **6**

6. This is one of the best endings I have ever read. No one should ever have to feel slow or different. Now Leo can feel both proud and fast.

Selection Support

LITERATURE

Story Elements: Setting

OBJECTIVE   Recognizing story setting.

1. WARM-UP

Use a known passage to discuss story setting.

Tell students they will listen to a passage from "Slower Than the Rest." Explain that the author tells where and when the story takes place. Have them listen for details that reveal the time and place of the story. *(in the classroom, in the morning)*

> **Leo carried the box to his classroom and placed it on the wide windowsill near the radiator and beside the geraniums. His teacher called attendance and the day began.**
> **In the middle of the morning, the forest reports began. One girl held up a poster board pasted with pictures of raccoons and squirrels, rabbits and deer, and she explained that animals died in forest fires.**

Discuss word and knowledge clues.

Reread the passage. Have students explain which word clues helped them figure out the setting. *(classroom, teacher, attendance, reports)* Then ask students whether they think the story itself, "Slower Than the Rest," takes place recently or long ago. How do they know? *(Leo takes the bus to school, and his family drives in their car, so the story could not have taken place before cars and school buses were in common use.)* Point out that students are using their own knowledge to help them understand the setting.

State the objective.

Tell students they will learn to use word clues and their own knowledge and experience to recognize the setting, or time and place, of a story.

2. TEACH

Explain why recognizing story setting is important.

Recognizing where and when a story takes place helps readers understand a character's situation and how the events affect the character's behavior.

Present a strategy for recognizing story setting.

Explain that there is a strategy students can use to help them recognize story setting. If the author does not name a *place,* look for details about familiar surroundings. If the author does not name a *time,* look for details about transportation, clothing, housing, and expressions of speech that reveal past, present, or future time. Think about how the setting affects what a character does.

Model the strategy.

Read passage 1 of the Teaching Chart. Tell students that this passage comes from another part of "Slower Than the Rest." Explain that the words *The pictures were too small for anyone to see from his desk* let you know that the event is taking place in Leo's classroom. These details help you to understanding Leo's situation.

TEACHING CHART 46: STORY SETTING

46

1. The pictures were too small for anyone to see from his desk. Leo was bored. *(Leo is in his classroom, probably not in the front row, while another student is showing pictures for a report.)*

2. That afternoon, the whole school assembled in the gymnasium to bring the special week to a close. A ranger in uniform made a speech, then someone dressed up like Smokey the Bear danced with two others dressed up like squirrels. Leo sat with his box and wondered if he should laugh at the dancers with everyone else. He didn't feel like it. *(Leo is at an assembly in the gymnasium during the afternoon.)*

3. GUIDED PRACTICE

Check for understanding.

Before going on, have students explain how to recognize story setting. *(Look for word clues and think about what is already known.)*

Guide students in using the strategy.

Have students use the strategy to tell where the event takes place in the second passage. Ask students what they already know about Leo that helps them understand why he feels the way he does. *(Leo does not find school exciting or a very happy place to be. He is happier at home with Charlie.)*

4. WRAP-UP

Summarize instruction.

Review the importance of recognizing story setting and the kinds of clues students use to understand the time and place of a story. *(Authors do not always tell both the time and place; details help people visualize a scene; students use both word and experience clues.)*

Provide independent practice.

Options for independent practice are shown in the Resource Center below.

Workbook page 83

RESOURCE CENTER

Skills Practice 73

NAME _____

LITERATURE

Story Elements

REMEMBER: To help you understand stories, look for clues and details that tell about the setting of a story.

A. Read each sentence. Look for clues that tell when a story takes place. Write *now* or *olden times* on the blanks.

1. We went to the video store and rented a movie. ___now___

2. He finished his letter, put his pen in the inkwell, and sealed the envelope with wax. ___olden times___

3. We knew many months would pass before our ship crossed the Atlantic. ___olden times___

4. The sleek, racing cars zoomed around the track. ___now___

B. Read each sentence about Leo. Think about where he is. Write the name of the place on the line.

5. Leo was looking out the window at the passing trees and hills when he spotted a turtle on the road. ___in a car___

6. Behind a pile of old boxes, Leo found a home for Charlie. ___Accept any answer that is a place for storing old boxes.___

7. Leo walked carefully down the long hallway filled with students. ___at school___

C. Pretend that you are Leo on the day that he gave his report and won the prize. Write a letter that he might have written to one of his grandparents telling what happened and how he felt about it.

Story Elements   Listening **83**

◀ **Workbook page 83** is intended for use by all students.

Skills Practice 73 ▶ may be assigned for additional practice.

NAME _____

SKILLS PRACTICE **73**

Story Elements

As you read, think about how the writer describes the **setting** of the story. Understanding the *place* and *time* of a story will help you know what the story is about.

Read each passage. Then answer the questions about the setting.

Emile's dog was lost. The leash had broken when they were walking. Emile was worried. The streets were filled with cars and trucks and buses. Would Emma be safe? Emile had walked around the neighborhood calling for her. He had talked to his friends in the park. No one had seen Emma.

Then Emile remembered how Emma always waited for him outside the food store. Emile ran to the store. There was Emma sitting out front, just like always.

1. Where does the story take place? ___in the city___

    at the beach   in the city   in the woods

2. What do you picture in your mind? ___Answer may vary. A boy looks for his dog in the city. He talks to many people. Finally he finds him.___

3. Write the clues from the story that help you know the setting. ___streets filled with cars, trucks, and buses; walked around neighborhood and park; food store___

Elan followed the dragon's tracks through the forest. The dragon left a wide trail. It was easy to follow. Elan's feet were wet. But that wasn't what worried him. He was worried about what he would do when he found the dragon. He didn't want to kill it. Could he ask the dragon not to destroy the castle? Would the dragon understand?

3. Underline the words that tell where the story takes place.

4. Is the story real or make-believe? ___make-believe___

5. How might the story be different if it took place in your town? ___Answers will vary.___

LEVEL 8   "Slower Than the Rest"   **73**

	Teaching Sequence	Trade Books and Resources	Meeting Individual Needs	Integrated Language Arts / Cross Curriculum
The Bridge Pages 330–331	**Maintain** Cause/Effect	• Teaching Chart 47 • Workbook 84 • Skills Practice 74		
PART 1 **Vocabulary Strategies** Pages 332–333	**Develop Concepts** Discussing Local Government **Teach Vocabulary** **STORY CRITICAL WORDS:** borrowed, business, **council**, **decision**, **hesitated**, library, literary, **mayor** (Tested words are boldfaced.)	• Teaching Chart 48 • Workbook 85 • Skills Practice 75	**SUPPORT WORDS:** embarrassed, favorite, oval, serious, suffer • Skills Practice 76 **CHARACTER/SETTING WORDS:** Dennis Jensen, Election Day, Elsinore, Jason Hardman, Johnny Carson, Monroe, President Ronald Reagan, *Ritchfield Reaper*, Utah	**WRITING/SPEAKING ACTIVITY:** Use new vocabulary to tell why to visit a library. • Spelling Connection 49
PART 2 **Reading & Responding** Pages 334–343	**Build Background** **Develop a Purpose for Reading** **Guide the Reading Process** **Selection Follow-Up**	• Reader's Journal 69–72 • Workbook 86 **I→T KIT** Listening to an Interview with Jason Hardman **READING EVERY DAY** *Summer Business,* by C. Martin *The Tram to Bondi Beach,* by E. Hathorn	**EXTRA HELP:** Taking Story Notes **ACHIEVING ENGLISH PROFICIENCY:** Borrowing Books from a Library • Achieving English Proficiency Master 18	**Language Arts Connections** **WRITING TO LEARN:** Write book recommendations. • Writing Master 13 **SPEAKING/LISTENING:** Discussing Solving Town Problems; Acting Out Scenes **WRITING:** Writing Nonfiction; Writing Newspaper Articles • Language Arts Master 11
PART 3 **Selection Support** Pages 344–351	**Introduce** Suffix *-ment* (Tested) Symbols and Signs (Tested)	• Teaching Charts 49–50 • Workbook 87–88 • Skills Practice 77–78	• Reteaching Masters 1–4 (Suffix *-ment*) • Reteaching Masters 1–4 (Symbols and Signs) • Challenge Masters 9–10 • Achieving English Proficiency Master 19 **Practice** • Skills Practice 79 Summarizing **Maintain** • Skills Practice 80 Comparison	**Curriculum Connections** **MATHEMATICS:** Creating Word Problems About Libraries **HUMANITIES:** Recommending and Listing Favorite Books **SOCIAL STUDIES:** Researching and Making Charts on Local Government Services; Writing Announcements and Drawing Maps • Curriculum Connection Master 11 **LIBRARY SCIENCE:** Diagraming a Library **CAREERS:** Discussing the Job of a Librarian **ART:** Designing Posters for National Library Week

Jason Wants a Library

by Margaret Tuley Patton

SUMMARY *Ten-year-old Jason Hardman lives in Elsinore, Utah, a town too small to have its own library. Jason gets tired of biking to the next town for books, so he asks Elsinore's mayor and town council for permisson to start a library in the town hall basement. They hesitate, but Jason persists. Finally they agree, and the delighted Jason opens his library. Spreading publicity brings many books for the library and praise for Jason from all over the country. Jason appears on television, addresses a congressional hearing, and even speaks with President Reagan.*

The Bridge

SKILL TRACE: CAUSE/EFFECT		
Introduced in Level 7	Maintain	
	TE 33	330

COMPREHENSION

Teaching Cause/Effect

OBJECTIVE Recognizing stated and unstated cause-and-effect relationships.

1. WARM-UP

Use a sentence to determine cause and effect orally.

Tell students they will listen to a sentence that describes a boy who is doing something on his own. Point out that all the stories students will read in this unit tell about people doing things on their own. Explain that in the sentence one event causes another event to happen. Have students decide which event is the cause and which event is the effect. (*The family's not having enough food for the party is the cause, and Mario's going to the market is the effect.*)

> **Mario's family did not have enough food for the party so Mario went to the market.**

Discuss signal words and experience clues.

Reread the sentence. Have students tell which word gives a signal that the sentence describes one event that causes another. (*so*) Ask them what they know about the described events that helped them decide which event caused the other event. (*They know that when people need food, they go to the store to buy what they need.*) Point out that sometimes signal words are used in cause-and-effect relationships and sometimes they are not used.

State the objective.

Tell students they will review how to recognize cause-and-effect relationships when signal words are included and when they are not included.

2. TEACH

Explain why understanding cause-and-effect is important.

Understanding which events cause other events helps readers to understand what is happening in a story and why.

Present a strategy for determining which events cause other events.

Explain that there is a strategy students can use to help them decide which events cause other events. Ask "What happened?" and "Why?" Then look for signal words and phrases such as *so*, *because*, and *as a result*, which link two events that have a cause-and-effect relationship. Think about what you already know from your own experience to help tell which events are likely to cause others.

> **47**
>
> **TEACHING CHART 47: CAUSE/EFFECT**
>
> **1.** Mario had to do the shopping because his mother was working late. (Cause — Mario's mother was working late; Effect — Mario had to do the shopping; Signal word — *because*)
> **2.** Many people came to the market. Mario had to stand in line a long time. (Cause — Many people came to the market; Effect — Mario had to stand in line a long time.)
> **3.** It started to rain on the way home, and Mario got wet. (Cause — It started to rain; Effect — Mario got wet.)

Model the strategy.

Read passage 1 on the Teaching Chart and point out that the sentence has a signal word, *because*. Explain that this word tells you the next event described will be the cause of an event described earlier. Also, your experience tells you that adults usually do the shopping, so a young person might have to do it if the adult cannot.

3. GUIDED PRACTICE

Check for understanding.

Before going on, have students explain how to decide which events cause other events. *(Look for signal words; look for story clues; think about what is already known.)*

Guide students in using the strategy.

Have students use the strategy to decide which event in each of the remaining passages is a cause and which is an effect. Discuss signal words, story clues, and experience clues that helped them decide which events were causes and which were effects.

4. WRAP-UP

Summarize instruction.

Review why readers need to decide which events cause other events and the kinds of clues they use to identify causes and effects. *(Deciding which events cause other events helps a reader make sense of a story; signal words, story clues, and experience clues help readers identify causes and effects.)*

Provide independent practice.

Options for independent practice are shown in the Resource Center below.

5. APPLICATION

Students will understand cause-and-effect relationships as they read "Jason Wants a Library." The symbol ✔ marks specific questions and activities that apply this skill.

Workbook page 84

COMPREHENSION   NAME _____

Cause/Effect

REMEMBER: Use signal words, story clues, and what you already know to figure out which events caused other events to happen.

A. Read the paragraph. Fill in the causes or effects.

The bright sun shining through the window woke Sue up. She looked at her clock. It said 8:15 A.M.! She must have forgotten to set her alarm. Quickly, Sue washed, dressed, ate breakfast, and grabbed her coat. She was in such a hurry on her way to the door that she bumped into her little brother and dropped her books all over the front hall. Before her brother could say a word, though, she was out the door, running as fast as she could down the block. "I'll sure remember to set my alarm from now on," she said to herself as her feet pounded on the sidewalk, "because I don't want to be the sort of person who's often late for school!"

1. Cause: The bright sun was shining through the window.
   Effect: Sue woke up.
2. Cause: Sue had forgotten to set her alarm.
   Effect: She overslept.
3. Cause: She was rushing and bumped into her brother.
   Effect: She dropped her books.
4. Cause: She didn't want to be late for school very often.
   Effect: She decided to be more careful about setting her alarm.

B. Imagine that you have arrived at school an hour late. On separate paper, describe three effects your lateness might have. See Teacher Notes.

84 "Jason Wants a Library"   Cause/Effect

RESOURCE CENTER

◀ **Workbook page 84** is intended for use by all students.

Skills Practice 74 ▶ may be assigned for additional practice.

Workbook reuse option: Have students re-read the paragraph in Part A and underline the signal words they find.

Skills Practice 74

NAME _____   SKILLS PRACTICE ◄74

Cause/Effect

Use signal words, story clues, and what you already know to figure out which events caused other events to happen. Words like *because, since, so, therefore,* and *as a result* signal or tell you that there is a **cause** and **effect**.

| Cause | → | Effect |

Read each story. Answer the questions that ask about cause and effect.

It was snowing hard after school. As a result, the school bus got stuck in a snow drift. The snowplow was busy with other cars and buses, so the children had to wait in the bus. Because one window didn't close all the way, it was chilly in the bus.

1. Why did the bus get stuck?
   It was snowing hard after school.

2. Why did the children have to wait after the bus got stuck?
   The snowplow was busy.

3. What happened because one window didn't close?
   It was chilly in the bus.

4. Write the words from the story that signal cause and effect.
   As a result, so, Because

Nick was shopping with his father. Because other people got in front of Nick, he didn't see his father. Nick's father thought Nick was right behind him, so he walked away too fast. Nick was a little worried, but he remembered where his father was going. As a result, Nick found his father quickly.

5. What happened when people got between Nick and his father?
   Nick didn't see where his father went.

6. Why did Nick's father walk away too fast?
   He thought Nick was right behind him.

7. Why did Nick find his father quickly?
   He remembered where his father was going.

8. Write the words from the story that signal cause and effect.
   Because, so, As a result

74 LEVEL 8   "Jason Wants a Library"

Vocabulary Strategies

Developing Concepts

Build on prior knowledge with questions about local government.

Ask students if they know what the head of the government of a city or town is called. (*a mayor*) Point out that a mayor usually is advised by a city or town council. Ask students how they think the mayor and town council are chosen. (*They are elected by the people of the city or town.*) Explain that not all cities and towns have this form of government, but many do. If yours does, ask if students know the name of the mayor of your city or town.

Teaching Vocabulary

Discuss meanings of Story Critical words.

Read each context sentence on the Teaching Chart and identify the new word. Then use the questions below to help students understand each word. When necessary, provide a definition.

> **TEACHING CHART 48: VOCABULARY** `48`
>
> 1. **mayor** (the head of government in a city or town)
>   Every four years the people of Danton pick a *mayor* to run the town.
> 2. **council** (a group that meets to make plans and decisions)
>   The town *council* helped the mayor decide what to do.
> 3. **decision** (the act of settling on something)
>   The mayor made a *decision* about each problem.
> 4. **business** (a matter or affair)
>   The mayor's *business* was taking care of the town.
> 5. **library** (a place where books are kept for reading or borrowing)
>   Danton needed a bigger *library* with more books.
> 6. **borrowed** (used something for a while and then returned it)
>   Many people *borrowed* books from the library.
> 7. **literary** (having to do with writing or reading)
>   The people of Danton used the library often because they had many *literary* interests.
> 8. **hesitated** (stopped or held back)
>   The council *hesitated* to build a new library because it would cost a lot of money.

mayor
1. **Which of the vocabulary words have to do with the job of mayor?** (council, decision, business)   STRATEGY: CLASSIFICATION

council
2. **What problems might a town council and mayor discuss?** (Possible answers: need for more taxes, how city money should be spent, whether to build or fix up a city building such as a school or library)   STRATEGY: PRIOR KNOWLEDGE

decision
3. **Imagine you are on a town council. What kinds of things would you like to know before making a decision about whether to build a public swimming pool for your town?** (Possible answers: how much building the pool would cost, how many people would use it, how many lifeguards and other workers would be needed)   STRATEGY: PRIOR KNOWLEDGE

business

4. What are some examples of businesses? (possible answers: grocery stores, department stores, printing newspapers, and so on) STRATEGY: CLASSIFICATION

library

5. What can people do in a library? (possible answers: read books, borrow books, look up information) **What other words in the vocabulary list might be used in talking about libraries?** (borrowed, literary) STRATEGY: PRIOR KNOWLEDGE

borrowed

6. What are some things that might be borrowed? (possible answers: tools, books, money, some articles of clothing, cars) **Why are books in a library borrowed?** (possible answers: so people can read them; so many different people can use the same book) STRATEGY: CLASSIFICATION

literary

7. What are some of your literary interests? (possible answers: reading magazines, reading fantasies, writing stories) STRATEGY: CLASSIFICATION

hesitated

8. When have you hesitated before making a decision? (possible answers: when there was not enough information to make the decision, when it was not clear what the right decision would be, when the decision would be hard to carry out) STRATEGY: PRIOR KNOWLEDGE

Discuss Support words as needed.

The Glossary of the Student Text includes definitions of the Support words: *favorite, embarrassed, serious, oval, suffer.*

Discuss Character/Setting words as needed.

Present and pronounce the Character/Setting words before students read the selection: *Jason Hardman, Monroe, Elsinore, Utah, Ritchfield Reaper, Dennis Jensen, Election Day, Johnny Carson, President Ronald Reagan.*

Provide independent practice.

Options for independent practice are shown in the Resource Center below.

WRITING OR SPEAKING ACTIVITY *Have students use the new vocabulary to tell why they might visit a library.*

Workbook page 85

Using New Words

SELECTION VOCABULARY

A. Read the paragraph. Write a word from the box to complete each sentence.

| borrowed | business | council | decision |
| hesitated | library | literary | mayor |

Last week I ____borrowed____ a book to read. While I was at the ____library____ , I saw that the paint was coming off the walls. I told my mother, who is the ____mayor____ of the town. She promised that she would tell the town ____council____ about the problem. At the next meeting, she brought up the ____business____ of the library paint. The members at first ____hesitated____ to spend money for painting. Then they listened to some people speak. One of them was the ____literary____ writer for the newspaper. Finally they reached a ____decision____ . The library will be painted this month.

B. Write a word from the box next to its meaning.

1. held back 1. ____hesitated____
2. used for a while 2. ____borrowed____
3. a matter 3. ____business____
4. place where books are kept 4. ____library____

C. On separate paper, write a letter to your mayor asking for a bike rack outside your library. Use four words from the box. See Teacher Notes.

Selection Vocabulary "Jason Wants a Library" **85**

RESOURCE CENTER

◄ **Workbook page 85** provides practice with Story Critical words.

Skills Practice 75 ► provides additional practice with Story Critical words.

Skills Practice 76 provides practice with Support words.

Spelling Connection Master 49 may be used for spelling instruction with the new vocabulary.

Workbook reuse option: Have students go back to Part A and underline the clues in each sentence that helped them choose the correct answer.

Skills Practice 75

Vocabulary: Story Critical Words

SKILLS PRACTICE 75

A. Study the meaning of each word.

borrowed used something that belongs to someone else after agreeing to return it
business work that one does to earn money
council a group that meets to make plans
decision the act of making up one's mind
hesitated stopped or held back for a moment
library a place where books are kept for reading and borrowing
literary having to do with writing and reading
mayor the head of government in a city or town

B. Complete each sentence with the correct vocabulary word.

1. The office of the ____mayor____ is in the town hall.
2. Marjory ____borrowed____ a quarter from her friend.
3. The horse ____hesitated____ before jumping over the fence.
4. Tony went to the ____library____ to return the books.
5. My mother runs a painting ____business____ out of our house.
6. The members of the ____council____ meet every Tuesday.
7. Mr. Anton made a firm ____decision____ to buy a new car.

C. Write the correct vocabulary word to answer each question.

8. Where can you go to borrow books? ____library____
9. What is made up of a number of people. ____council____
10. What might you call a person who likes to read? ____literary____
11. Who may be in charge of a city's government? ____mayor____
12. What must you make if you have choices? ____decision____

D. Draw a line from each phrase to the word that completes it.

13. ____ a dollar — mayor
14. elected a ____ — business
15. made a ____ — borrowed
16. started a new ____ — decision

LEVEL 8 "Jason Wants a Library" Context clues **75**

2

Guiding Comprehension

Building Background

Motivate discussion using the quote.

Share the following quotation with students. Explain that a frigate is a kind of ship. Then ask students why the author of the quote might think that a book is even better than a ship for helping people "travel." Have students tell whether they agree or disagree with the idea and why.

> **There is no frigate like a book to take us lands away.**
> — *Emily Dickinson*

Build background about libraries.

Ask students to name kinds of materials besides books that are found in a library. (*Possible answers: magazines, records, tapes, videocassettes*) Remind students of the locations of the closest libraries in your area. Encourage students to describe specific purposes for libraries or ways in which libraries are important.

Discuss nonfiction.

Tell students that the story they will read next is nonfiction. Explain that nonfiction is about things that really happened. Since this story is also about a real person, Jason, it is a kind of nonfiction called biography.

Developing a Purpose for Reading

Option 1
Students set purpose.

ORAL "I WONDER" LISTS   Have students preview the selection by reading the first paragraph and looking at the pictures. Then have students suggest a few statements they have about the story, such as, "I wonder why Jason wants to start a library," "I wonder who helps him," "I wonder how long it takes." Record students' statements for later use.

WRITING ACTIVITY   Have students work individually or in pairs to create written "I wonder" lists. Be sure that students save their lists for later use.

Option 2
Teacher sets purpose.

Have students read to find out why Jason wants to start a library and the steps he takes to start it.

Meeting
Individual
Needs

EXTRA HELP   The following story is about a ten-year-old boy named Jason who starts a library in his small hometown. Have students write the following headings on a sheet of paper: *People Who Helped Jason, How Jason Got Books,* and *How Jason Became Famous.* Then suggest that as they read, students take notes about each topic. After reading, have volunteers share their notes and thoughts about the story.

ACHIEVING ENGLISH PROFICIENCY   Write the word *borrow* on the board. Tell students that borrow means to use something for a while and then give it back. Demonstrate this by saying to students, "May I borrow your pencil for a minute?" Take the pencil and then give it back. Working in pairs and using the model sentence, have students borrow things from each other. Tell students that at a library people borrow books and agree to bring them back by a certain date. Visit the school library and show students how the librarian keeps track of the books that have been borrowed. For additional help in story comprehension, use Master 18 in the Teacher Resource Kit.

Jason has a dream. To make his dream come true, he will have to do something that even most grown-ups couldn't do.

Jason Wants a Library

by
Margaret Tuley Patton

Every time ten-year-old Jason Hardman wanted a book from a library, he borrowed his sister's bike and pedaled six miles to the next town, Monroe. Since Jason's favorite thing to do was to read books, he spent hours pedaling.

Jason's town of Elsinore, Utah, had only 650 people, too tiny for a library of its own. Elsinore was so small that the children even went to school in Monroe.

One night, Jason said to his parents, ''I want to start a library in Elsinore.'' They were pleased but told him that he would have to talk with the town council.

This is Jason, the boy who wants a library.

''What is a town council?'' Jason asked.

''It's a group of about eight elected members and the mayor. They run all the town's business,'' his mom said. ''Elsinore, like all towns, collects taxes from its citizens and uses the money for public services, such as fire and police protection,'' she explained.

''But the town can't afford a library,'' his dad added.

Reader's Journal   p 69
Preparing for Reading

DO DREAMS COME TRUE?

Students explore the notion of daydreaming by looking at pictures of dreams characters have had in other selections, and then write about their own dreams.

GUIDED READING

✔ **Page 184**   **Why does Jason ride to Monroe every time he wants a library book?** (His own town, Elsinore, is too small to have a library.)   INFER: CAUSE/EFFECT

✔ **Page 185**   **Why would Jason need to talk with the town council about starting a library in Elsinore?** (The town council makes decisions about matters that affect the town or would cost the town money, such as a library.)   INFER: CAUSE/EFFECT

STRATEGIC READING

Page 185   Have students show "thumbs up" if they understand how the town government of Elsinore works and "thumbs down" if they do not. Then have a volunteer read aloud the paragraph on this page that explains how the government works. Have other volunteers draw a diagram on the chalkboard that shows how the government and citizens affect each other.   METACOGNITION: RATING UNDERSTANDING

✔ Skill from The Bridge applied through this question.

335

"Maybe I can run it for the town," Jason said.

Talking to nine adults sounded scary, but Jason wanted to give it a try.

On the night of the next council meeting, he and his father went to the town hall. A two-storied stone building constructed in the 1890s, White Rock School was now the town hall. There in a large room he found the council members sitting around an oval table talking about town matters. They barely looked up when Jason came into the room. The council was talking about the new fire engine and how to fix the roads. The mayor, a thin, serious-looking man, sometimes looked over in Jason's direction. A council member, a gray-haired woman with large gold earrings, also watched him.

When it was Jason's time, *everyone* looked at him. At first he hesitated, then began to speak. "I want to start a library in Elsinore. It needs one very badly."

The council listened closely. Jason spent almost an hour talking with the council.

"We'll have to think about it," the mayor finally said to the brown-haired boy.

"At least they didn't say no," Jason told his parents after the meeting.

A week went by without any news from the town hall. Jason phoned the mayor at his home to ask if a decision had been made about the library. The mayor answered, "The council is still thinking about it."

Another week passed. Every day when Jason came off the school bus, he'd ask his mother: "Did the mayor phone?" Each day, the answer was, "No." Jason phoned the mayor every night for two weeks. Each night, the same answer was given: "The council is still thinking about it." Jason grew tired of waiting. Why can't I use the town hall basement for my library? he thought to himself.

During those weeks, Jason pedaled often to Monroe for library books. "I wonder if I will be biking these six miles forever for a book?" he asked himself sadly. He began to doubt that he would ever get a library for Elsinore.

At last it happened. When he phoned the mayor, Jason was invited to the council's next meeting. The mayor told him they might find space in the town hall basement. It was just too good to be true.

When Jason wanted library books, he pedaled six miles.

GUIDED READING

Page 186   What is the main idea of the paragraph that begins "On the night of the next council meeting . . ."? (The council members were talking about town matters and paid little attention to Jason.)
SYNTHESIZE: MAIN IDEA/DETAILS

Page 186   What might Jason and the council have discussed during the hour he spent with them? (Possible answers: where Jason planned to put the library; who would work there; where he would get books; what the library would cost)
DRAWING CONCLUSIONS

Page 187   How does Jason show that he is sticking to his goal? (He phones the mayor every night for two weeks.)   ANALYZE: CHARACTER

HIGHLIGHTING LITERATURE

Page 187   Point out that nonfiction stories or articles often have photographs showing real people and places. Ask students why photographs are helpful and what they can learn from them. (Writers do not always describe everything. Photographs show exactly what someone looks like and can help readers learn more about real places, such as Elsinore.)

When Jason entered the council room and saw them all sitting at the oval table, he suddenly felt terrible. He just knew that they had changed their minds. The mayor, with a stern face, turned toward Jason and asked him to come to the oval table. Jason sat down in the straight-back chair.

The council began asking him questions. Someone asked how many days the library would be open. "Tuesdays and Thursdays from 4 to 6 P.M.," Jason answered quietly.

At last, the mayor looked across the table and said in a firm voice, "After weeks of thinking, we have decided that you can use a room in the basement for a public library."

Jason was so shocked he could hardly speak. Now all the council members and the mayor smiled and wished him good luck. "We figure that you can run a library the right way, and we want to give you the chance," the mayor said. Jason almost danced out of the meeting.

In the next few weeks, Jason told every person he knew in Elsinore that he was opening a library in the town hall. He went to the Elsinore Literary Club asking for books. Then he began to phone people he didn't know throughout Sevier County. The *Ritchfield Reaper,* a weekly newspaper from the town of Ritchfield, wrote about Jason's plans for a library. Soon, the two daily papers in Salt Lake City wrote stories about Jason wanting books. One of the headlines read,

Young Librarian Opens Library — Needs Books!

Jason had to work hard to get his library books organized.

People mailed boxes of books to Jason's home. "Awesome! Where am I going to fit all these books?" Jason said, grinning. He knew that before long he would have enough books to open his library.

Jason, his older sister and brother, and his parents spent two months cleaning out the town hall basement and putting books on shelves. Jason arranged the books in a system so people could find what they wanted easily. His friends and their parents also came to help.

GUIDED READING

✔ **Page 188   Why does Jason feel terrible when he enters the council room?** (He is sure that the council has decided not to let him start the library after all.) INFER: CAUSE/EFFECT

Page 188   What is the main idea of the paragraph beginning "In the next few weeks . . ."? (Because of publicity, more and more people hear about Jason's library and his need for books.) **What details support this idea?** (Jason talks to the people he knows, goes to the Elsinore Literary Club, and phones other people to ask for books; two newspapers write stories about the library.) SYNTHESIZE: MAIN IDEA/DETAILS

Page 189   What system might Jason have used to arrange the books in his library? (Possible answers: He might have arranged the books alphabetically by title or author; he might have arranged them by subject.) INFER: PROBLEM/SOLUTION

✔ Skill from The Bridge applied through this question.
✔ Informal Assessment Opportunity: SELF-MONITORING

STRATEGIC READING

✔ **Page 188   Have students read to the sentence, "Jason sat down in the straight-back chair." Then have students summarize what has happened so far. Have them explain what Jason wants to do, why, and how he has gone about trying to get his wish. (Jason's town is too small to have its own library. Jason wants to start one because he is tired of having to bike to the next town every time he wants a library book. He has asked the town council for permission to start a library in the town hall basement and has repeatedly phoned the mayor to try to get a decision.) A review of the Guided Reading questions may help some students summarize the events. Ask students to predict what will happen next and whether the council will allow Jason to start his library. At completion of the story, ask students to check their predictions. METACOGNITION: SUMMARIZING AND PREDICTING

337

Jason's mother and friends helped, too.

The library opened on Election Day, November 4, 1980. Almost one hundred people came to see the new library. Jason was so tickled. His best friend Dennis Jensen helped Jason in the library after school. In the first year, Elsinore library had about one thousand books. It was a very busy place.

Soon worldwide newspapers wrote articles about Jason's new library. Jason appeared on various television shows, including *Good Morning, America*, *Fantasy*, *The Phil Donahue Show*, and even *The Tonight Show*. On *The Tonight Show*, Johnny Carson asked Jason if there were anything his parents didn't want him to say on television. Jason hesitated, then responded, "They told me not to ask for any more books." More bags full of books flooded Elsinore after the show.

At age eleven, Jason spoke at a joint congressional hearing in Washington, D.C., about the rural needs of America. "Why should I suffer because I live in Elsinore without a library? Salt Lake City has plenty of libraries. Why should my friends suffer?" he asked the joint panel.

Jason went to the White House two times to talk to President Ronald Reagan. *Reading Rainbow* filmed Jason in his library to encourage children to read books in the summer months. *Reader's Digest* wrote a story about Jason.

Jason meets President Ronald Reagan.

GUIDED READING

✔ **Page 190   What is the effect of Jason's opening the library?** (Many people in Elsinore use it.) **What does this suggest about whether Elsinore really needs a library?** (It suggests that the town does need a library.)   INFER: CAUSE/EFFECT

✔ **Pages 190–191   Why do you think people on major television shows and in the country's government want to talk to Jason?** (Possible answers: They think people all over the country will be interested in Jason's story. Jason's story shows how one young person can help a town. Jason knows something about the needs of small towns.)   INFER: CAUSE/EFFECT

Page 191   What might Jason have talked to President Reagan about? (possible answers: his library and why he started it; the needs of people in small towns; his ideas about other matters affecting the country)   INFER: ACTIONS

✔ Skill from The Bridge applied through this question.

HIGHLIGHTING LITERATURE

Page 190   Have students identify an *idiom*, or expression that does not really mean what it seems to say, that tells how Jason felt when so many people came to the library opening. (Jason was so tickled.) Point out that idioms are examples of figurative language. Have students discuss what this expression really means. Then have them give other examples of idioms that they know.

Here, Jason sits in his library enjoying a good book.

Jason is a bit embarrassed about all the fuss made over him. He just did what he thought was needed in Elsinore. His library today has sixteen thousand books and occupies two rooms in the town hall basement.

Jason, now eighteen years old, will soon go away to college. He and the council have discussed the future of the library. It will continue to stay open for others who want a library in Elsinore.

◆ LIBRARY LINK ◆

If you enjoyed this selection and would like to read something else about young people doing things on their own, read Summer Business *by Charles Martin.*

Reader's Response

What would you like very much to make happen that would help others?

See next page for suggested answers.

 SELECTION FOLLOW-UP
Jason
Wants a Library

 ## Thinking It Over

1. Why did Jason ride his bicycle six miles to another town?
2. How did Jason plan to run the library?
3. Why do you think the town council finally said yes to Jason's plan?
4. How did the other people in Elsinore feel about having their own library? Explain.
5. What kind of person was Jason? What leads you to describe him this way?
6. What might Jason have done if the town council had said no to his plan?

Writing to Learn

THINK AND DECIDE Jason loves to read good books. Think of three books that you would recommend to him. List the book titles on a sheet of paper.

WRITE Choose one book from your list. Write a letter to Jason telling why you think he would enjoy it.

JASON WANTS A LIBRARY

GUIDED READING

Page 192 Do you think Jason would be successful in politics if he chooses to follow that career after college? Why or why not? (Jason probably would be successful in politics. He knows people's needs, sticks to his goals, and has had experience in working with government.) EVALUATE: CHARACTER

RETURNING TO THE READING PURPOSE

OPTION 1 If students set the purpose, have them refer to their "I wonder" lists and tell whether their questions were answered and what those answers were.

OPTION 2 If you set the purpose, ask students to tell why Jason wants a library and describe the steps he takes to start a library for Elsinore. (Jason loves to read and is tired of going to another town to get books. He talks to the town council about Elsinore's need for a library. When they agree, he asks people he knows and people he does not know for books. He cleans the town hall basement and arranges the books.) You might have volunteers list on the chalkboard the steps Jason took.

Reader's Journal   p 70
Responding to Reading

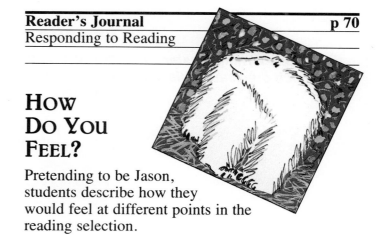

HOW DO YOU FEEL?

Pretending to be Jason, students describe how they would feel at different points in the reading selection.

SELECTION FOLLOW-UP

Jason
Wants a Library

THINKING IT OVER

1. **Why did Jason ride his bicycle six miles to another town?** (There was no library in Jason's town. Since he loved to read, he often bicycled six miles to the nearest library.)   RECALL: DETAILS

2. **How did Jason plan to run the library?** (Jason said that he would run the library himself. He planned to open the library two days after school and on Saturday mornings.)   RECALL: DETAILS

3. **Why do you think the town council finally said yes to Jason's plan?** (Possible answers: The council members knew that Jason was serious about his idea because he called the mayor every night; they, too, felt that the town needed its own library; the members realized that Jason was a capable, responsible boy and were impressed by his carefully thought-out plans.)   SYNTHESIZE: DRAWING CONCLUSIONS

4. **How did the other people in Elsinore feel about having their own library? Explain.** (The other people seemed to be happy and excited. People gave Jason boxes and boxes of books; one hundred people came to the library the day it opened.)   INFER: FEELINGS/ATTITUDES

5. **What kind of person was Jason? What leads you to describe him this way?** (Possible answers: Jason knew what he wanted and worked hard to get it; he was patient; he was a good organizer; he followed through; he was a leader.)   ANALYZE: CHARACTER; METACOGNITION

✔ 6. **What might Jason have done if the town council had said no to his plan?** (Possible answers: He might have tried to enlist the support of the community, written a letter to the editor of the newspaper, gotten signatures on a petition requesting another hearing with the town council.)   SYNTHESIZE: PREDICTING OUTCOMES

WRITING TO LEARN

Use Writing Master 13, which duplicates this list.

THINK AND DISCUSS   Jason loves to read good books. Think of three books that you would recommend to him. List the book titles on a sheet of paper. (Help students refine their lists to prepare for writing.)

Extend comprehension through writing.

WRITE   Choose one book from your list. Write a letter to Jason telling why you think he would enjoy it. (Have students share their letters.)

✔ Informal Assessment Opportunity: PREDICTING

More Ideas for Selection Follow-Up

CRITICAL AND CREATIVE THINKING QUESTIONS

Encourage a variety of responses and points of view.

Use these open-ended questions to encourage critical and creative thinking about the selection.

1. There's an old saying: "If at first you don't succeed, try, try again." In what ways did Jason follow this advice?

2. Jason's hard work added an important place, a library, to his community. What kind of place would you like to add to your community? Why?

REREADING ORALLY

Have students reread for pleasure.

Have students reread aloud to the class the parts of the story that were most surprising to them. Encourage students to practice their reading in advance and to read with expression. Remind them that when they read dialogue, they should use their voices to show how the characters feel. They should also use their voices to show why the parts of the story they chose are surprising, exciting, or interesting to them. Suggest that students who have chosen the same or similar parts of the story read together, each reading the dialogue of one character or part of the narration.

SELECTION COMPREHENSION

Provide comprehension check.

A Workbook page to check comprehension is shown in the Resource Center below. It may be used for informal assessment.

Workbook page 86

SELECTION COMPREHENSION

NAME _____

Jason Wants a Library

A. Complete the summary of "Jason Wants a Library."
Accept reasonable variations.
This selection is about a boy named _____Jason Hardman_____ ,
who lived in a town too small to have _____a library_____ .
Whenever he wanted to borrow a book, he had to ride his sister's
bike _____six miles to the next town_____ .

One night, Jason told his parents that he wanted to start a
_____library_____ in his town. His parents told him to
_____speak to the town council_____ .

Jason went to a meeting and told the mayor and the other members
about his plan. They listened to what he had to say. Then they told him
they needed time to _____think_____ . Jason waited for many weeks.
Finally the mayor said they had decided that Jason could _____use a_____
_____room in the town hall for a library_____ .

When people in the town learned of the council's decision, they
began giving Jason _____boxes of books_____ . It took months to
clean up the room and _____put the books on the shelves_____ .
Jason and his library received much publicity. Jason even went to the
_____White House_____ three times to see the President. In time
another room was added to the library.

B. Imagine that the council had not
given Jason a room for the library.
On separate paper, tell what he
might have done to change
their minds.
See Teacher Notes.

86 "Jason Wants a Library"   Selection Comprehension

RESOURCE CENTER

◀ **Workbook page 86** is intended for use by all students.

Writing Master 13 duplicates the Writing to Learn list.

I•T Kit Activity   I•T

Audio: **Interview with Jason Hardman**

The boy who started a library in Elsinore is today a young man who has stood in the national limelight. Jason talks about how it felt to be famous and what he is like as a person today. (See Activity Guide.) CAREERS

LANGUAGE ARTS CONNECTIONS

CRITICAL THINKING: PROBLEM-SOLVING

Have students suggest a town project.

Have students discuss changes that they would like in their town. These might include a new swimming pool, a new museum, a playing field, or a zoo. Write their ideas on the chalkboard. Have students choose one idea for discussion.

Have students list the effects of a project.

Explain to students that in order to persuade a person or group to do something, people usually describe its potential good effects. Have students develop a list of reasons to do their project. Then discuss to whom they might write a letter for help and what kinds of things would have to be considered. For example, is there land available? Is it a safe place? Have students list any problems.   WHOLE CLASS ENRICHMENT

NONFICTION AS A LITERARY GENRE

Have students write brief pieces of nonfiction.

Remind students that nonfiction is written to inform readers or convey facts. "Jason Wants a Library" is an example of nonfiction because it is about real people and events that actually happened. Point out that a good nonfiction writer should check reference works or talk to people involved to make sure that facts are accurate. Have students write a short account of an interesting event that happened recently in their school or town, such as an election, the opening of a new public building, or the coming of an important speaker or visitor. Give students time to do research to find out relevant facts if necessary.   CHALLENGE: WRITING

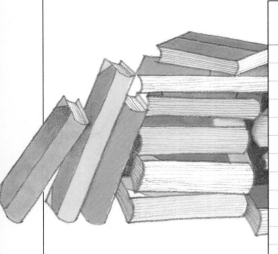

ACTING OUT SCENES

Discuss role-playing.

Explain to students that in acting out scenes from stories or plays, they are role-playing. They are speaking and thinking as the characters. When acting out a scene from the story, students can use the dialogue, or characters' exact words, and also make up some dialogue that they think is appropriate.

Have students role-play Jason and the council.

Have students work in small groups to role-play the meeting Jason has with the town council. One student in the group can be Jason and the other students can be the council members. Students should use dialogue from the story as well as dialogue they create. Have each group present its scene.   SHARED LEARNING: SPEAKING

WRITING NEWSPAPER ARTICLES

Have students plan and write newspaper articles.

Tell students that a newspaper article is nonfiction writing based on facts and not the feelings and opinions of the writer. Explain that the first or "lead" paragraph gives the important facts that tell *who, what, when, where,* and *why.* Divide the class into small groups and have each group choose a part of Jason's story and write a newspaper article about it. Possible events to report might be the opening day at the library or Jason's appearance on a television show. Before students start writing, have them discuss how they will tell who, what, when, where, and why in the first paragraph and what information the rest of their article will include. After finishing and revising their work, have students make up a short headline for their article. **Language Arts Master 11** can be used with this activity.   WRITING

READING EVERY DAY

Reading about young people who, like Jason, take the initiative to get things done on their own can serve as an inspiration to students. Here are two stories to recommend to your students that share this theme.

Summer Business by Charles Martin. Greenwillow Books, © 1984. The small summer business that Heather and her friends run on their island home earns them enough money for a trip to the mainland's Harvest Fair.   EASIER TO READ

The Tram to Bondi Beach by Elizabeth Hathorn. Kane/Miller, © 1989. Nine-year-old Kieran, who lives in a small town in Australia, figures out a way to fulfill his two dreams—being a paper boy and riding on the local tram.

Reader's Journal   **pp 71, 72**
Extending Reading

TACKLE A PROBLEM

To practice creative problem solving, students look at pictures of children presented with problems and write how they could solve them. Then they develop ideas of ways they could improve their school or community.

Selection Support

WORD STUDY

Suffix *-ment*

OBJECTIVE Using structural analysis to determine word meaning.

1. WARM-UP

Use familiar content to introduce the suffix -ment.

Tell students they will listen to two sentences about the story they have just read, "Jason Wants a Library." After reading aloud the sentences, write *agreement* and *announcement* on the chalkboard. Ask students what is the same in both words. (*The letters* ment *are at the ends of both words.*)

> **The town council members were in agreement that Elsinore should have a library.**
> **An announcement was made when the library was ready to open.**

Discuss the suffix -ment.

Explain that *-ment* is a suffix, a group of letters added to the end of a word that changes a word's meaning and its part of speech. The suffix *-ment* changes a word from a verb to a noun. Have volunteers circle the suffix in each word on the board. Then tell students that the suffix *-ment* means "action or process" or "state of." Students can use the meaning of the suffix along with the meaning of the base word to figure out the meaning of the whole word. Have students tell what each word on the chalkboard means. (*agreement* — "*the state of agreeing*," "*having the same feeling and understanding*"; *announcement* — "*the act of announcing*," "*making something known to people*") Tell students they will learn to use the suffix *-ment* to help them figure out the meanings of words.

2. TEACH

Explain why it is important to know how to recognize suffixes.

Recognizing suffixes helps readers figure out the meanings of unfamiliar words. Being able to add suffixes to familiar words is useful in writing.

Present a strategy for using the suffix -ment to figure out new words.

Explain that there is a strategy students can use to help them identify words ending in the suffix *-ment*. Use the meaning of the suffix along with the meaning of the base word to help figure out a word's meaning. Also use the sentence context to help with unfamiliar words.

TEACHING CHART 49: THE SUFFIX *-MENT*

49

enjoyment   arrangement
encouragement   placement

1. Jason's __(enjoyment)__ of books made him want to start a library in Elsinore. ("state of enjoying"; "feeling pleasure")
2. The __(placement)__ of the library worried the town council. ("act of placing"; "putting something in a particular spot")
3. Finally they worked out an __(arrangement)__ for Jason to use the town hall basement. ("act of arranging"; "putting something in order")
4. Jason received a lot of __(encouragement)__ from people who sent him many books. ("act of encouraging"; "giving support or help")

Model the strategy. Read the words at the top of the Teaching Chart and then read the first sentence. Explain that the word *enjoyment* best fits the sentence because *enjoyment* means "the state of enjoying" or "feeling pleasure."

3. GUIDED PRACTICE

Check for understanding. Before going on, have students explain how the meaning of the suffix *-ment* changes a word. (*adding* -ment *to the end changes the word's meaning to "the state or act of" the base word*)

Guide students in using the strategy. Have students select the word that fits each remaining sentence on the chart and read the sentence aloud. Then have students tell the meaning of the word.

4. WRAP-UP

Summarize instruction. Review why readers need to recognize suffixes and how adding the suffix *-ment* to a word changes the word. (*Recognizing suffixes helps readers understand the meanings of unfamiliar words; adding the suffix* -ment *to a verb changes the verb to a noun.*)

Provide independent practice. Options for independent practice are shown in the Resource Center below.

Meeting Individual Needs

RETEACHING Use the activity on page 465 and Masters 1–4 in the Teacher Resource Kit.

CHALLENGE Use the activity on page 465 and Master 9 in the Teacher Resource Kit.

Workbook page 87

NAME _____

WORD STUDY

Suffix -*ment*

REMEMBER: The suffix *-ment* forms a noun and means "result of."

A. Add the suffix *-ment* to each word. Write the new word on the line.

1. agree ___agreement___   2. improve ___improvement___
3. amaze ___amazement___   4. pay ___payment___
5. announce ___announcement___   6. puzzle ___puzzlement___
7. govern ___government___   8. treat ___treatment___

B. Complete each sentence with a word you wrote in Part A.

9. Jason spoke to the council, the elected members of the ___government___ of Elsinore.

10. It was a ___puzzlement___ to Jason that the council took more than five weeks to make a decision.

11. Maybe they did not think they had enough money to make a ___payment___ for a new library.

12. Jason made a deal, or an ___agreement___, with his friends to help in the new library.

13. Having a library was a big ___improvement___ for Elsinore.

14. To Jason's ___amazement___, many people sent books.

15. Jason got many books because of an ___announcement___ in the newspaper.

C. Choose three of the words ending with *-ment* on this page. On separate paper, write sentences of your own using these words. See Teacher Notes.

Suffix -ment   "Jason Wants a Library"   87

RESOURCE CENTER

◄ **Workbook page 87** is intended for use by all students.

Skills Practice 77 ► may be assigned for additional practice.

Workbook reuse option: Have students think of two more words that can add the suffix *-ment* and write each word and its new *-ment* word in the lists in Part A.

Skills Practice 77

NAME _____

SKILLS PRACTICE   77

Suffix -*ment*

The suffix *-ment* can be added to the end of a word. The ending *-ment* changes a verb to a noun. The suffix *-ment* means "the state or act of."

Write the correct word to answer each question.

amazement

Look at the root word for clues to each word's meaning.

1. What is the result when you get better at something? __improvement__
   improvement   movement

2. What is the result when people think the same thing? __agreement__
   agreement   arrangement

3. What is the result when you don't understand something?
   __puzzlement__
   enjoyment   puzzlement

4. What is the result when you put concrete on the ground?
   __pavement__
   pavement   statement

5. What might a doctor give you to make you feel better?
   __treatment__
   development   treatment

6. What is the result when you feel very good? __contentment__
   contentment   placement

7. What do you call something new that happens? __development__
   wonderment   development

8. What is the result when you say something? __statement__
   settlement   statement

9. What do you feel like when you win? __excitement__
   excitement   placement

LEVEL 8   "Jason Wants a Library"   77

SKILL TRACE: SYMBOLS/SIGNS				
Introduction	Practice	Test	Reteach	Maintain
TE 346	373	423	461	467	526

STUDY SKILLS

Symbols and Signs

OBJECTIVE   Understanding information from symbols and signs.

1. WARM-UP

Use prior knowledge to introduce the concept of symbols and signs.

Remind students that before he started the library in Elsinore, Jason had to ride his bike to the Monroe library to borrow books. Ask students how they think Jason knew how to get to Monroe and to the library. Ask how he knew what the library rules were and where in the library certain kinds of books were located. (*Signs probably told him these things.*)

Discuss symbols and signs.

Explain that symbols and signs are short, quick ways to tell people important messages or information. Symbols are things that stand for something else, such as a drawing that stands for a rule or idea. Symbols often appear on signs. Ask students to name some of the signs that Jason probably saw during a trip to the Monroe library. (*possible answers: mileage signs, street signs, signs posting library rules, signs naming different kinds of books or other library materials*) Ask students what other signs they see as they walk or ride around town. (*possible answers: store signs, traffic signs, advertising billboards*) Finally, ask them to name and give the meanings of symbols they have seen on signs. (*possible answers: green walking figure meaning "go" and red hand meaning "stop" at pedestrian crossings; diagonal slash over a drawing meaning "no" or "do not"*)

State the objective.

Tell students they will learn about the meanings of common symbols and signs.

2. TEACH

Explain why understanding symbols and signs is important.

Understanding symbols and signs helps people find out important information quickly.

Present a strategy for understanding symbols and signs.

Explain that there is a strategy students can use to help them understand symbols and signs. First, read all the words on a sign. If it has symbols, try to remember where you have seen the symbols before and what ideas the symbols stand for. If a symbol or word on a sign is not familiar, think about where the sign is and why it might be there, then use these facts and the familiar parts of the sign to guess the meaning of what you do not know.

TEACHING CHART 50: SYMBOLS AND SIGNS   50

Grocery Sign   No Dogs   Stop   Street Sign

No Left Turn   No Talking   Poison   One Way

Model the strategy. Point to the top sign on the Teaching Chart and read the words on it. Tell students you recognize that the dollar sign and dot, or decimal point, mean that the numbers on the sign refer to dollars and cents. You know that the abbreviation *lb.* means "pound." Thus, you know that this sign, which you might see in a supermarket, means "a pound of ground beef costs one dollar and forty-five cents."

3. GUIDED PRACTICE

Check for understanding. Have students explain how to understand symbols and signs. (*read the words on the sign, think about what the symbols mean, use what is known about the sign and where it is to help in figuring out what is not known*)

Guide students in using the strategy. Have students use the strategy to determine the meanings of the remaining symbols and signs. Discuss clues and experience that helped them.

4. WRAP-UP

Summarize instruction. Review why people need to understand symbols and signs and the kinds of clues they can use to understand them. (*Symbols and signs help people learn important information quickly; clues in the signs and experience.*)

Provide independent practice. Options for independent practice are shown in the Resource Center below.

Meeting Individual Needs

RETEACHING Use the activity on page 467 and Masters 1–4 in the Teacher Resource Kit.

CHALLENGE Use the activity on page 467 and Master 10 in the Teacher Resource Kit.

ACHIEVING ENGLISH PROFICIENCY Use the activity on page 467 and Master 19 in the Teacher Resource Kit.

Workbook page 88

RESOURCE CENTER

Skills Practice 78

STUDY SKILLS

Symbols and Signs

NAME

REMEMBER: Signs and **symbols** are short, quick ways to communicate important messages or information.

A. Use the words in the box to label each group of signs and symbols. Then write what each sign means.

| Library Signs | Street Signs |
| Signs for People Walking | Warning Signs |

1. Street Signs
ONE WAY / STOP / ℞
Cars can go in one direction only.
Cars must stop.
You cannot park here.

2. Warning Signs
DANGER / CAUTION
There is danger!
Be careful!
Poison or danger

3. Library Signs
CHILDREN'S ROOM / FOOD
Children's books are found here.
No food is allowed.

4. Signs for People Walking
RESTROOMS / WET FLOOR
Shows direction of restrooms.
The floor is wet.
Be careful.

B. On separate paper, design your own sign or symbol that gives information to people. Try to get your message across without using words. See Teacher Notes.

88 "Jason Wants a Library"   Symbols and Signs

◄ **Workbook page 88** is intended for use by all students.

Skills Practice Master 78 may be assigned for additional practice. ►

Workbook reuse option: Have students circle the symbols and signs from Part A that Jason might have seen on his way to the library. Tell students to draw in the margin signs they see on the way to school or the library.

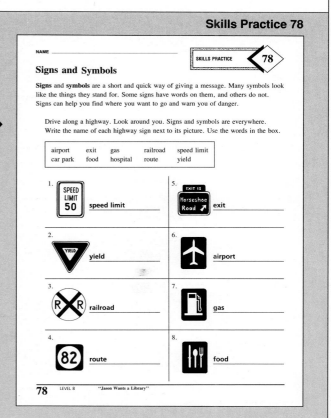

NAME

SKILLS PRACTICE ‹78›

Signs and Symbols

Signs and **symbols** are a short and quick way of giving a message. Many symbols look like the things they stand for. Some signs have words on them, and others do not. Signs can help you find where you want to go and warn you of danger.

Drive along a highway. Look around you. Signs and symbols are everywhere. Write the name of each highway sign next to its picture. Use the words in the box.

| airport | exit | gas | railroad | speed limit |
| car park | food | hospital | route | yield |

1. SPEED LIMIT 50 — speed limit
2. YIELD — yield
3. R×R — railroad
4. 82 — route
5. EXIT 13 Horseshoe Road — exit
6. ✈ — airport
7. ⛽ — gas
8. 🍴 — food

78   LEVEL 8   "Jason Wants a Library"

SKILL TRACE: SUMMARIZING
This skill is untested at this level.

COMPREHENSION

Summarizing

OBJECTIVE Summarizing the important points of a passage.

Review summarizing.

Remind students that a summary is a short way to tell what something is about. It contains only the most important information or main ideas of a passage or story. It should be written in the student's own words.

Provide practice in summarizing.

You may wish to read aloud the paragraphs below. The answer is shown in red. Have students tell which paragraph best summarizes "Jason Wants a Library." Have students explain their choices. Then ask students to write their own summaries of the selection.

> 1. Jason wanted to start a library in Elsinore. His parents were pleased but told him that he would have to talk with the town council.
> 2. The tiny town of Elsinore, Utah, did not have a library. Jason wanted to start one. He talked to the town council, which said he could have a library in the town hall basement. Stories about Jason spread all over the country and helped him get books for his library. (This is the best summary because it tells all the important points. It tells the main character's problem and how it was solved.)

Provide independent practice.

An independent activity is shown in the Resource Center below.

RESOURCE CENTER

Skills Practice 79 ▶ may be assigned for additional practice.

Skills Practice 79

NAME _____

SKILLS PRACTICE 79

Summarizing

A **summary** is a short statement in your own words. It gives the main points of what you have read. It tells only the main ideas.

Idea	Idea	Idea	Idea

Summary

A. Read the paragraphs. Underline the main ideas.

Rainy Days

There are all kinds of things you can do at home on a rainy day. One thing to do is to pick a book that looks good. Curl up in a chair, and enjoy yourself.

A rainy day can give you time for playing with your games and puzzles. Sometimes, boxes on the bottom of a pile have been forgotten. Dust them off, and see what's inside.

A rainy day can give you a chance to make something to show your family. For example, you might paint a picture, or model with clay. You could build something out of wood or cloth.

Maybe your favorite thing to do is to make believe. You could put on an adult's hat and be someone else. You might just tear up paper and make believe it's spaghetti. There are many ways to play make-believe.

B. Now write a summary of what you have read. **Answers will vary.**

Summary: There are many things to do at home when it rains.
You can read or play with your games and puzzles.
You can make things, or play make-believe.

LEVEL 8   "Jason Wants a Library"   **79**

SKILL TRACE: COMPARISON						
Introduction	Practice		Test	Reteach	Maintain	
TE 176	196	292	311	312	349	578	619

MAINTENANCE

COMPREHENSION

Comparison

OBJECTIVE Understanding likenesses and differences in longer texts.

Review comparison.

Remind students that when things are compared, they are described in terms that show how they are alike and how they are different. Comparing is often done with words that end in *-er* or *-est* or with words such as *more, most, less,* and *least.* Other words and phrases, such as *like, different, but,* and *however,* may also signal comparisons.

Provide practice in making comparisons.

You may wish to read aloud the paragraph below. Have students read the paragraph and then develop a chart that compares the towns of Elsinore and Monroe. Possible answers are shown in red.

Jason's town of Elsinore is so tiny that it has no library and no school, unlike the town of Monroe. However, Elsinore is like other towns in that it has a mayor and a town council. Like all towns, Elsinore collects taxes from its citizens and uses the money for public services. The town can afford fire and police protection, but it cannot afford a library.

Elsinore
no school
(no library)
(has mayor)
(has town council)
(collects taxes)

Monroe
has school
(has library)
(has mayor)
(has town council)
(collects taxes)

Provide independent practice.

An independent activity is shown in the Resource Center below.

RESOURCE CENTER

Skills Practice 80 ▶ may be assigned for additional practice.

Skills Practice 80

NAME _____

SKILLS PRACTICE **80**

Comparison

Knowing about **comparison** will help you understand how things, people, and events are alike and different.

Read the story. Look for ways things are alike and ways they are different.

Toby, Wayne, Sara, and Lee are at the zoo. Toby, Wayne, and Sara don't know where Lee is. The three children are in the zoo snack bar talking about what to do.

Toby's plan: Since Lee was last seen at the penguin house, everyone should go back there. If Lee isn't there, Toby, Wayne, and Sara should walk back to the snack bar the way they did before. Toby thinks they'll find Lee this way.

Wayne's plan: It makes sense to look for Lee at the Penguin house. It's also a good idea to follow their steps back to the snack bar, but only two people should go to look for Lee. One person should wait at the snack bar in case she comes there.

Sara's plan: Lee loves penguins, so she might still be looking at them. Someone should wait at the snack bar, because she might come there when they are gone. However, the two children who go to the penguin house shouldn't follow exactly the same path when they go back to the snack bar. Lee told Sara she wanted to see the seals. So they should go to the seal pool first.

Now complete the chart.

What is alike about all the plans?	They all say the children should go back to the penguin house. Children should go back to the snack bar.
How is Wayne's plan different from Toby's?	He says two children should go, not three. One should wait at the snack bar.
How is Sara's plan different from Wayne's?	She says the two children who go should look at the seal pool before they go back to the snack bar.

80 LEVEL 8 "Jason Wants a Library"

CURRICULUM CONNECTIONS

ANNOUNCEMENTS AND MAPS SOCIAL STUDIES

Have students write announcements telling that the library in Elsinore is now open. Then have them draw imaginary maps showing where the library is located. Have them label streets on the map and decorate the map with symbols and signs that might be seen in the town, such as traffic signs and store signs. **Curriculum Connection Master 11** may be used with this activity.

POSTERS FOR READING ART

Tell students that National Library Week, normally the third week in April, was established to encourage people to read books and use libraries. Libraries often have special displays or programs during that week. Then divide students into small groups. Tell the groups to brainstorm reasons why people should read books or use libraries; catchy slogans or phrases that might make people want to read or use their local library more often; or special programs that a library might have during National Library Week. They might wish to ask their local librarian what the library has done in the past. Have each group choose the idea or ideas they like best and use them as the basis for one or more posters for National Library Week. Each poster should include both words and illustrations (including graphic symbols, if possible) and should focus either on a reason for using books and libraries, a phrase or idea that will make people want to use books and libraries, or a program that a library is offering. Display the finished posters in the classroom or offer them to the local library for use during National Library Week.

CITY SERVICES SOCIAL STUDIES

Have students talk to their local librarian or write to their local government office to find out if someone in government might visit the class and explain how their town or city is governed. If a speaker is not possible, students could find out about public services in their city or town, such as police and fire protection, parks and recreation, local tax collection. Have students make charts that show the various services.

LISTENING TO A LIBRARIAN CAREERS

Invite your librarian to speak to the students about studying for and performing the job of a librarian. Students can prepare for the meeting by writing some questions they would like to have answered. Allow for more questions and answers at the close of the librarian's talk. Encourage students to tell what surprised them the most about a career as a librarian and why they might or might not like to become librarians.

PROBLEMS WITH LIBRARIES MATHEMATICS

Have each student create three word problems related to a library. The problems might involve the addition of books, miles to travel to a library, or hours spent at a library. Provide the following model for the students.

> **Jason pedals six miles to Monroe to go to the library. Then he pedals home. If Jason goes to the library two days in a row, how many miles will he have pedaled?**

BEST-EVER BOOKS HUMANITIES

Discuss with students some of their favorite books and why they like them. Have students write a recommendation for one of their favorite books. Tell students to include in their recommendations a brief summary of the book and the reasons why they think others might enjoy it. Allow students to read all the recommendations written by their classmates. A chart listing the recommended books might be created. After students have read one of the books, they might write brief comments on the chart, telling their feelings, such as ''I'm glad I read this book. It was as exciting as the recommendation promised it would be.''

DIAGRAMING A LIBRARY LIBRARY SCIENCE

Remind students that Jason arranged the books in his library in a system so that people could easily find what they wanted. Have students make a drawing that shows the different sections of their school or town library, or an imaginary library. Tell students to label the sections to show what different kinds of books and other reading materials are contained in each section. Display and discuss the diagrams and have students tell what they discovered about library systems from their experiences.

Making a Character Map

OBJECTIVE Inferring character traits and motives by making a character map.

INTRODUCING AND READING THE LESSON

Use a passage to introduce a character.

Tell students that you are going to read aloud a passage about a character named Judy. Have them listen for details that reveal what she is like.

> **"Oh tigers' tails," said Judy the clown. "I've got the biggest grin painted on my face, but a huge sadness in my heart."**
>
> **Every day at the circus, Judy made hundreds of people laugh with her zany clown act. But today she was sad because she had found out that one of the animals was missing. She had many friends — the giant, the dwarf, the lion tamer, and Madame Zola, the queen of the high wire. But no one could cheer her up.**

Show how to make a character map.

Have a volunteer draw on the chalkboard what he or she thinks Judy looks like. Near the picture make four or five lines for writing details about Judy. Reread the passage. Ask students what they know about Judy from the passage. *(Judy had a big grin on her face; she was sad; she made people laugh; she had many friends.)* Write the students' responses on the lines next to the student drawing.

Point out to the students that they have made a character map. Explain that in this map they have used what they learned in the passage to tell what Judy looks like, and they have organized information about her. Conclude by asking a volunteer to use what is said on the character map to describe Judy in one sentence. Write the sentence under the map.

Refer students to their texts.

Read up to the heading "Using the Strategy" with the students. Make sure the students understand the directions for making a character map.

DISCUSSING THE LESSON

Review the main points of the lesson.

Check students' understanding of the lesson with these questions.

Page 194 **How can you better understand a character in a story?** (by organizing information about the character in a character map)

Page 194 **What information in a story can help you find out about a character?** (the things a character says and does)

Page 194 **What is the final step in making a character map?** (writing a sentence that describes the character)

Making a Character Map

He kept calling the mayor.

He was a good talker.

He thought of using the basement.

He worked hard.

He was a good problem solver.

How can you understand the characters you meet in your reading? One good way is to make a character map.

Learning the Strategy

Here are the directions for making a character map.

1. Read the story.
2. Draw a simple picture of the character.
3. Near the picture make four or five lines for writing what the character does or says.
4. Make a long line beneath the picture for writing a sentence that tells what kind of person the character is.

Using the Strategy

Look at the character map for Jason Hardman, who started the library in Elsinore, Utah. The picture shows Jason. The sentences on the lines near his picture tell what he did. At the bottom of the map is the sentence that tells what kind of person Jason was.

Strategy for Thinking

Practice making a character map. On your own paper, copy this map about Jason. Add more things he did and said.

Does the sentence at the bottom tell what kind of person Jason was? You may change the sentence if you want to.

Applying the Strategy to the Next Story

The next story, "The Recital," is about two sisters. As you read, you can make a character map about one of the sisters.

◆◆◆ The writing connection can be found on page 233.

WRAP-UP

Have students read the paragraph under "Using the Strategy." Allow them a few minutes to look at the map on Student Text page 195. Have a volunteer give a characteristic of Jason that is not listed in the example. Direct students to write their sentences describing Jason on a separate sheet of paper.

Discuss answers for the independent practice activity.

Encourage volunteers to read their sentences aloud. (*Possible answer: Jason didn't give up.*) Ask them if the map helped them understand Jason better Have students explain their answers.

Direct students to the next selection.

Tell students they will make a character map for one of the characters in the next selection, "The Recital."

TEACHER CHOICE

	Teaching Sequence	Trade Books and Resources	Meeting Individual Needs	Integrated Language Arts / Cross Curriculum
The Bridge Pages 356–357	**Maintain** Classification	• Teaching Chart 51 • Workbook 89 • Skills Practice 81		
PART 1 **Vocabulary Strategies** Pages 358–359	**Develop Concepts** Semantic Mapping **Teach Vocabulary** **STORY CRITICAL WORDS:** **concentrate,** keyboard, notes, **piano, recital, relax, talent** (Tested words are boldfaced.)	• Teaching Chart 52 • Workbook 90 • Skills Practice 82	**SUPPORT WORDS:** announced, honor, hugging, mistake, movement, refrigerator, stage • Skills Practice 83 **CHARACTER/SETTING WORDS:** Maria, Mr. Torres, Mrs. Howard, Mrs. Torres, Sonia	**WRITING/SPEAKING ACTIVITY:** Use new vocabulary to describe a piano recital. • Spelling Connection 50
PART 2 **Reading & Responding** Pages 360–369	**Build Background** **Develop a Purpose for Reading** **Guide the Reading Process** **Selection Follow-Up**	• Reader's Journal 73–76 • Workbook 91 **READING EVERY DAY** *Aldo Ice Cream,* by J. Hurwitz *Class Clown,* by J. Hurwitz	**EXTRA HELP:** Model Character Map **ACHIEVING ENGLISH PROFICIENCY:** Understanding Idioms • Achieving English Proficiency Master 20	**Language Arts Connections** **WRITING TO LEARN:** Complete a chart about feelings. • Writing Master 14 **SPEAKING/LISTENING:** Brainstorming Advice About Overcoming Nervousness; Writing About Feelings • Language Arts Master 12 **WRITING:** Writing Piano Tips for a Soccer Player; Writing Realistic Fiction
PART 3 **Selection Support** Pages 370–377	**Introduce** Suffixes *-ion, -tion* (Tested)	• Teaching Chart 53 • Workbook 92 • Skills Practice 84	• Reteaching Masters 1–4 • Challenge Master 11 • Achieving English Proficiency Master 21 **Practice** • Teaching Charts 54–55 • Workbook 93–95 • Skills Practice 85–86 Suffix *-ment* (Tested) Symbols and Signs (Tested) Strategy for Thinking **Maintain** • Skills Practice 87 Antonyms	**Curriculum Connections** **MUSIC:** Reporting on Keyboard Instruments; Creating New Lyrics for Familiar Tunes **SOCIAL STUDIES:** Researching and Reporting on Famous Composers • Curriculum Connection Master 12 **CAREERS:** Talking with a Music Teacher **PHYSICAL EDUCATION:** Researching and Demonstrating Soccer

THE RECITAL

by Johanna Hurwitz

SUMMARY   *Maria Torres is a talented piano player. Her sister Sonia is equally skilled at soccer. When Maria is nervous about performing in an upcoming piano recital, Sonia helps her relax by running with her and passing on some advice from her soccer coach: concentrate and do not look back even if you make a mistake. Maria makes a mistake as she begins her recital piece and almost runs off the stage. But then she remembers Sonia's advice, starts the piece over, plays beautifully, and becomes the hit of the recital.*

The Bridge

SKILL TRACE: CLASSIFICATION	
Introduced in Level 6	Maintain
	TE 356 / 620

VOCABULARY

Teaching Classification

OBJECTIVE   Classifying words according to common characteristics.

1. WARM-UP

Use a known passage to classify words orally.

Tell students they will listen to a sentence from the preceding story, "Jason Wants a Library." Explain that the author names a group or category of things, *public services,* and then names two things that belong in that group. Have them listen to find the two things that fit in the group *public services. (fire and police protection)*

> **Elsinore, like all towns, collects taxes from its citizens and uses the money for public services, like fire and police protection.**

Discuss classifying into groups.

Remind students that things can be classified, or grouped, according to ways in which they are alike. Fire protection and police protection are alike in that both help all the people of a town and both are paid for with taxes. They fit in the group or category of public services. Words, too, can be classified into categories because of ways their meanings are alike.

State the objective.

Tell students they will learn to classify words according to the way they are alike.

2. TEACH

Explain why classifying words is important.

Classifying words helps readers organize information and therefore better understand and remember what they read. Classifying can also help readers guess the meanings of unfamiliar words.

Present a strategy for classifying words.

Explain that there is a strategy students can use to help them classify words into groups. First, look for words that are alike in some way. Then think about how the words' meanings are alike and try to think of a name for a group to which all the words could belong.

51

TEACHING CHART 51: CLASSIFICATION

told	tired	town hall
library	shocked	wrote
embarrassed	phoned	school

Words that (tell how people sent messages) :
    (told, wrote, phoned)
Words that (tell how people felt) :
    (embarrassed, tired, shocked)
Words that (name kinds of buildings) :
    (library, town hall, school)

Model the strategy.

Explain that all the words on the Teaching Chart are from "Jason Wants a Library." The words can be placed in three different groups according to the way their meanings are alike. Have volunteers read the nine words. Then explain that you can see the meaning of *told* has something in common with the meanings of *wrote* and *phoned,* so you will place these three words in the same group. Write the words on the chart under the first blank category. Have students help you think of a name for the group that shows how the meanings of the three words are alike and write the category name above the words.

3. GUIDED PRACTICE

Check for understanding.

Before going on, have students explain how to classify words. (*look for words whose meanings are alike in some way, then think of a group to which all the words could belong*)

Guide students in using the strategy.

Have students use the strategy to classify the remaining words and think of category names that show how the meanings of the words in each group are alike. Discuss what clues they used in deciding how to group the words.

4. WRAP-UP

Summarize instruction.

Review why readers classify words and how to classify words. (*to better understand what they read and guess the meanings of unfamiliar words; look for ways in which the meanings of words are alike*)

Provide independent practice.

Options for independent practice are shown in the Resource Center below.

5. APPLICATION

Students will classify new vocabulary in Part 1 of the lesson. The symbol ✔ marks specific questions and activities that apply this skill.

Workbook page 89

NAME _____

VOCABULARY

Classification

REMEMBER: To **classify** words, decide how they are alike and different in meaning.

A. Read each group of words about books. Write the word that does not belong in each group.

1. book	magazine	newspaper	building	building
2. pages	pictures	house	words	house
3. glasses	poetry	picture	story	glasses
4. dress	cover	glossary	page	dress
5. bookcase	library	yard	school	yard

B. Put each word from the box under the right heading.

| bed | bookcase | bus | chair | fable |
| math | mystery | shelf | table | tree |

BOOKS		
1. Kinds	**2.** Places to Keep	**3.** Places to Read
fable	bookcase	bed
math	shelf	bus
mystery	table	chair

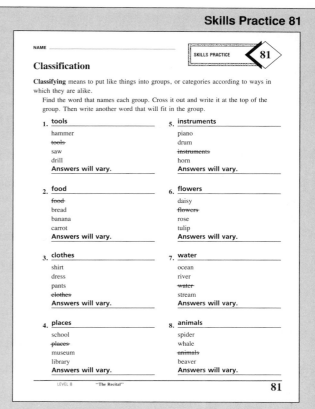

C. Choose three groups in Part A. On separate paper, explain why the word you chose does not belong in the group. See Teacher Notes.

Classification   "The Recital" **89**

RESOURCE CENTER

◀ **Workbook page 89** is intended for use by all students.

Skills Practice 81 ▶ may be assigned for additional practice.

Workbook reuse option: Have students give names to the groups in Part A. For example, the first group could be named "Printed Things to Read."

Skills Practice 81

NAME _____

SKILLS PRACTICE **81**

Classification

Classifying means to put like things into groups, or categories according to ways in which they are alike.

Find the word that names each group. Cross it out and write it at the top of the group. Then write another word that will fit in the group.

1. **tools**
   hammer
   ~~tools~~
   saw
   drill
   Answers will vary.

5. **instruments**
   piano
   drum
   ~~instruments~~
   horn
   Answers will vary.

2. **food**
   ~~food~~
   bread
   banana
   carrot
   Answers will vary.

6. **flowers**
   daisy
   ~~flowers~~
   rose
   tulip
   Answers will vary.

3. **clothes**
   shirt
   dress
   pants
   ~~clothes~~
   Answers will vary.

7. **water**
   ocean
   river
   ~~water~~
   stream
   Answers will vary.

4. **places**
   school
   ~~places~~
   museum
   library
   Answers will vary.

8. **animals**
   spider
   whale
   ~~animals~~
   beaver
   Answers will vary.

LEVEL 8   "The Recital"   **81**

Vocabulary Strategies

Developing Concepts

Tap prior knowledge about music with a semantic map.

Make a semantic map about music as a starting point for teaching vocabulary. Ask students to name and describe musical instruments they play or would like to play. Have students suggest words for each category on the map.

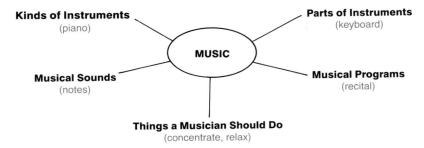

Kinds of Instruments
(piano)

Parts of Instruments
(keyboard)

MUSIC

Musical Sounds
(notes)

Musical Programs
(recital)

Things a Musician Should Do
(concentrate, relax)

Teaching Vocabulary

Discuss meanings of Story Critical words.

Read each context sentence on the Teaching Chart and identify the new word. Then use the questions below to help students understand each word. When necessary, provide a definition.

TEACHING CHART 52: VOCABULARY   52

1. **piano** (a large musical instrument with a keyboard)
   A *piano* makes different sounds because it has many keys.
2. **keyboard** (the row of keys on a piano)
   A piano *keyboard* has black and white keys.
3. **notes** (musical sounds or symbols for them)
   The *notes* on a sheet of music tell a piano player what keys to play.
4. **recital** (a musical program)
   During a *recital*, students show others how well they can play music.
5. **talent** (natural ability)
   Some students show great *talent* for music.
6. **concentrate** (to fix attention)
   Musicians must *concentrate* on their music if they want to play well.
7. **relax** (to rest from worry or work)
   Instead of worrying, they need to *relax.*

✔ *piano*   **1. Under what group on the map could *piano* be placed?** (Kinds of Instruments)   STRATEGY: CLASSIFICATION

✔ *keyboard*   **2. What does the sentence tell you about a keyboard?** (It has black and white keys.) **Under what group on the map could *keyboard* be placed?** (Parts of Instruments)   STRATEGY: CLASSIFICATION

✔ *notes*   **3. What meaning does *notes* have in sentence 3?** (symbols for musical tones) **Under what group on the map could *notes* be placed?** (Musical Sounds)   STRATEGY: CLASSIFICATION

✔ *recital*

4. How is playing in a recital like reciting? (You are performing something you already know.) **Under what group on the map could recital be placed?** (Musical Programs) STRATEGY: CLASSIFICATION

talent

5. What words mean about the same as *talent*? *(skill, ability, genius)* **What are some things besides music for which someone might have talent?** (sports, art, writing) STRATEGY: SYNONYMS

concentrate

6. What do you do when you concentrate? (You try to think about only one thing.) STRATEGY: PRIOR KNOWLEDGE

relax

7. What expressions mean about the same thing as *relax*? (take it easy, let go, ease up) **Why is it important for a musician to relax?** (Being able to relax keeps someone from becoming too tired or worried and makes the person less likely to make mistakes.) STRATEGY: SYNONYMS

Add new words to the map.

Challenge students to add the words to the appropriate categories on the map, creating new categories when necessary. Have them explain how the meaning of each added word is like the meanings of other words in its group.

Discuss Support words as needed.

The Glossary of the Student Text includes definitions of the Support words: *refrigerator, honor, announced, hugging, mistake, stage, movement.* Discuss which words can be added to the map.

Introduce Character words as needed.

Pronounce the Character names before students read the selection: *Mr. Torres (To'-res), Mrs. Torres, Mrs. Howard, Maria, Sonia (Sō'-nyu).*

Provide independent practice.

Options for independent practice are shown in the Resource Center below.

WRITING OR SPEAKING ACTIVITY *Have students use the new vocabulary to describe a piano recital.*

✔ Skill from The Bridge applied through this question.

RESOURCE CENTER

Workbook page 90

SELECTION VOCABULARY

NAME _____

Using New Words

| concentrate | keyboard | notes | piano |
| recital | relax | talent | |

A. On each line, write the word from the box that fits each meaning.

1. to rest from work or worry ___relax___
2. to fix attention ___concentrate___
3. natural ability ___talent___
4. a musical program ___recital___
5. symbols for musical tones ___notes___

B. Complete each sentence with a word from the box.

The band tuned up. June sat at the piano with her fingers on the ___keyboard___. The final ___recital___ of the year was about to begin. June played the first note on the ___piano___. The other players began to play their instruments, carefully reading the ___notes___ on the pages of music in front of them. They knew they must ___concentrate___ on the music and ___relax___ in front of the audience. Each player had musical ___talent___ and all of them had worked hard to get ready. The audience loved their show.

C. On separate paper, write a paragraph about your favorite kind of music. Use three words from the box. See Teacher Notes.

90 "The Recital" Selection Vocabulary

◀ **Workbook page 90** provides practice with Story Critical words.

Skills Practice 82 ▶ provides additional practice with Story Critical words.

Skills Practice 83 provides practice with Support words.

Spelling Connection Master 50 may be used for spelling instruction with the new vocabulary.

Workbook reuse option: Have students circle all the words on the page that have to do with music.

Skills Practice 82

NAME _____

SKILLS PRACTICE 82

Vocabulary: Story Critical Words

A. Study the meaning of each word.

concentrate to pay close attention
keyboard row of keys on a piano or organ
notes musical sounds or symbols for them
piano musical instrument with a keyboard
recital a musical program
relax to rest from worry or work
talent a natural ability

B. Write the correct vocabulary words to finish the story.

Ellen is learning how to play the ___piano___. She is taking lessons. Her teacher tells her she has to ___concentrate___ on the music. To get ready, Ellen places her hands above the ___keyboard___. She looks at her song book and reads the ___notes___ she must play. She then plays the right keys. Ellen's teacher told her she has a ___talent___ for playing well. Ellen hopes that she will play at her school's next music ___recital___.

C. Answer each question with the correct vocabulary word.

1. What do people do on their vacations? ___relax___
2. When might you hear musicians play? ___recital___
3. What do you have if you have musical ability? ___talent___
4. What must people do while driving? ___concentrate___
5. What part of a piano is played? ___keyboard___

D. Complete the word map. Use at least two of the vocabulary words. Then add words of your own. **Responses will vary.**

6. Kinds of Instruments
   piano
   _____
   _____

7. When People Play Music
   recital
   _____
   _____

Music

82 LEVEL 8 "The Recital" Context clues

Reading & Responding

Building Background

Motivate discussion using the quote.

Share the following quotation with students and ask them what they think it means. Discuss whether students agree with Roosevelt that fear can sometimes do more harm than the things that are feared.

> **"The only thing we have to fear is fear itself."**
> — *Franklin D. Roosevelt*

Build background about overcoming nervousness.

Point out that many people become nervous or afraid when called on to perform before an audience. Many famous actors, for example, suffer from stage fright all their lives. Then discuss these questions:

1. **Have you ever become nervous before a performance, such as giving an oral report?**

2. **What did you do to try to overcome your nervousness?**

3. **Did anyone give you advice about ways to overcome your nervousness? If so, what advice were you given?**

Have students discuss different techniques for overcoming nervousness about a performance, such as practicing before a friend or family member or pretending during the performance that the audience is not there. Have them decide which techniques are most effective and why.

Discuss realistic fiction.

Tell students they are about to read a realistic fiction story about a girl who overcomes her nervousness. Remind students that fiction means the events did not really happen. Realistic fiction, however, *could* happen. It usually has characters and settings that seem familiar.

Developing a Purpose for Reading

Have students apply the thinking strategy.

Remind students that a character map is one way to understand story characters better. Have the students preview the story as you point out the questions with the diamond symbol (◄◆►). Explain that these questions will ask them to add details about a character to a character map.

Tell students they will complete the map for a character named Maria. Draw a sample character map on the board: a stick figure with five short lines around it and one long line at the bottom. Explain that the long line is for a sentence they will write about Maria when they finish the story.

*Meeting
Individual
Needs*

EXTRA HELP   Model the strategy by referring students to the first paragraph with the diamond symbol on Student Text page 196. Discuss what the paragraph reveals about Maria. Elicit students' suggestions to fill in the first detail on the map. Use the Strategic Reading suggestions whenever the thinking strategy is applied.

ACHIEVING ENGLISH PROFICIENCY   Write the following idioms on the chalkboard: *clear the head, take a break, keep on going, look back on the past*. Help students understand the meanings of these expressions with context sentences such as "It's hard to keep on going when you are tired"; "I was tired and decided to take a break"; etc. After explaining the idioms, call on volunteers to give examples of the other idioms. For additional help in story comprehension, use Master 20 in the Teacher Resource Kit.

THE RECITAL

Maria and Sonia like to do different things—but they meet similar problems.

by Johanna Hurwitz

Anyone who saw Sonia and Maria Torres (tō′ res) together knew they were sisters. Both girls had long, dark hair and the same bright, brown eyes. When they smiled, they both had dimples in their cheeks.

Although the sisters looked alike, they were very different. Maria took piano lessons and loved making music. Sonia loved music, too, but she loved sports even more. Sonia was one of the best players on the girls' soccer team at school. ◆◆◆

One hot afternoon after soccer practice, Sonia carefully opened the front door to her house. She could hear Maria playing music, and she didn't want to bother her. Quietly, Sonia walked into the kitchen and opened the refrigerator to get a glass of orange juice.

◆◆◆
Make a character map for Maria. Add this information to the map.

197

Reader's Journal	p 73
Preparing for Reading	

MUSIC MAKERS

Students look at a painting of a musician and answer thought-provoking questions about being a musician and performing for an audience.

GUIDED READING

Page 196   How are Maria and Sonia alike? How are they different? (They look alike — long, dark hair, brown eyes, and dimples; they are sisters; they both love music. Music is more important to Maria, who takes piano lessons; and sports, especially soccer, are more important to Sonia.)   ANALYZE: COMPARISON

Page 196   What do Sonia's actions at home suggest about the kind of person she is? (She is a thoughtful, considerate person.)   EVALUATE: CHARACTER

STRATEGIC READING ◆◆◆

Page 196   Pause after reading the second paragraph. Direct students' attention to the note with the diamond symbol. Ask students what they know about Maria. (Possible responses: She takes piano lessons; she loves making music.) Write their suggestions on one line of the model and have students do the same on their character maps. Emphasize that they can write their answers in short phrases. Continue reading the story.
STRATEGY FOR THINKING

"Get a glass of juice for me, too," said Maria as she came into the kitchen.

"Did I make too much noise?" asked Sonia. "Sorry."

"You weren't noisy," said Maria. "I've been practicing all afternoon for Mrs. Howard's <u>recital</u>, and I was getting ready to take a break."

Sonia nodded her head. It was a real honor to be asked to play in Mrs. Howard's recital, and Maria had been taking lessons for only two years. Most of the students who would be playing had been studying with Mrs. Howard for four or five years. ◆◆◆

◆◆◆
Add this information to Maria's character map.

"I bet you're one of Mrs. Howard's best students," said Sonia.

"I know I play well when I'm at home," Maria said, "but I'm scared to go on stage. What if I make some awful mistakes?"

Sonia gave Maria a hug. "Don't be afraid," she said. "Just <u>relax</u> and pretend you're playing at home and that no one is listening but me."

"I'll try," Maria said.

Two weeks later the recital took place. That morning when she awoke, Maria said that her stomach hurt.

"You're probably just nervous," said Mrs. Torres.

"You should go running with me," said Sonia.

"Running?" said Maria. "You're the runner, not me."

"I know," laughed Sonia. "But if you run with me, it'll help you relax."

"It can't hurt," said Mrs. Torres.

The two sisters ran around the block three times. Sonia ran slowly so that her sister could keep up with her.

"Don't you feel better already?" Sonia asked. "Coach Reynolds says that lively movement, such as running, clears the head."

"What does she say about making mistakes at a recital?" asked Maria.

GUIDED READING

Page 198   Does Maria have much talent for piano playing? (yes) **How do you know?** (She has been asked to play in the recital, and she has been taking lessons for only two years.)   ANALYZE: CHARACTER

Page 198   How does Sonia feel about Maria? (She likes Maria and cares about her feelings.) **How do you know?** (She is quiet when Maria is practicing, and she reassures Maria and tries to help her overcome her nervousness.)   ANALYZE: CHARACTER

Page 198   What suggestions does Sonia make to help Maria overcome her nervousness? (She suggests that Maria pretend no one is listening but her and that Maria run with her before the recital.)   RECALL: DETAILS

✔ **Page 199   Do you agree with Sonia that running could help someone who is nervous? Why or why not?** (Possible answers: Yes, it could help someone relax; no, it would simply make the person tired.) EVALUATE: GENERALIZATION

✔ **Informal Assessment Opportunity:**   EVALUATING

STRATEGIC READING ◆◆◆

Page 198   Refer students to the paragraph with the diamond symbol. Read aloud the note that goes with it, and ask students what the paragraph tells them about Maria. (Possible responses: She is very good at the piano; she is talented.) Have students add this information to another line on their character maps. Then ask them to explain their answers. (Students will say that although Maria has not studied piano as long as other students, she has been asked to play in the recital.) Return to the reading as quickly as possible. STRATEGY FOR THINKING

"She says that if you make a mistake, you just <u>concentrate</u> harder and keep on going. Don't forget the terrible mistake I made in the first game my team played this year," Sonia said.

"What was that?" asked Maria. "I don't remember."

"I kicked the ball in the wrong direction and made a goal for the other team. I was so embarrassed. Imagine helping the other team score! It was awful."

"What did your coach say?" asked Maria.

"She said to concentrate on the next goal and not to look back on the past," Sonia answered. "You know, she was right. I concentrated on the game, and I didn't think about what had already happened. Before long, I scored a goal for our team."

The girls ran back to the house. Maria was out of breath from her run, but her stomach no longer hurt. They showered and dressed for the recital.

At the front of the recital hall there was a sign showing the way to the room for Mrs. Howard's recital. The room was large, and there seemed to be over a hundred chairs lined up for the audience.

Maria was beginning to look pale and frightened. Sonia squeezed her sister's hand. ◀◈▶

◀◈▶
Add this information to Maria's character map.

"Good luck," Sonia whispered to Maria.

Mrs. Howard got up in front of the audience and announced the name of the first student. He looked old enough to be in high school. Sonia watched as he walked stiffly toward the <u>piano.</u> He had black hair, and his face had turned bright red. He looked nervous, too.

The piece that the young man played was one that Sonia had heard Maria practicing at home a long time ago. He played it faster than Maria did. When he was finished, everyone clapped politely.

GUIDED READING

Page 200   What advice does Sonia's coach have about making mistakes? (concentrate; don't look back)   ANALYZE: PROBLEM/SOLUTION

Page 200   What effect did her coach's advice have on Sonia? (It helped her overcome her embarrassment after a mistake and go on to score a goal for her team.) INFER: CAUSE/EFFECT

Page 200   How might this same advice help Maria? (It might help her go on if she makes mistakes during the recital.)   SYNTHESIZE: PREDICTING OUTCOMES

Page 201   At the recital, how does the audience react to the first student's playing? (The people clap politely.) **What does this tell you?** (The audience was not very excited by the student's playing.)   INFER: FEELINGS/ATTITUDES

STRATEGIC READING ◀◈▶

Page 200   Have a volunteer read aloud the sentence with the diamond symbol. Ask students what they learn about Sonia at this point. (Possible responses: She is nice, because she tries to encourage Maria; she wishes her sister good luck.) **Then ask them to describe how Maria feels.** (Students will say she is frightened or scared about playing.) **Have them add this detail about Maria to another line on their maps. Continue reading the story.**   STRATEGY FOR THINKING

The next student was a grown woman. She played her piece very slowly, as if she were being extra careful not to make any mistakes. Again, the audience clapped when she finished playing.

Sonia took a deep breath. She listened as Mrs. Howard announced Maria's name and watched her sister as she slowly made her way towards the piano.

Maria sat down on the piano bench with her hands in her lap. Everyone waited for her to begin.

Maria played the opening <u>notes</u> of her piece, but then she made a mistake and stopped. For a moment it looked as if she were going to run off the stage. Sonia held her breath as she looked at her sister. Maria was sitting very stiffly. "You can do it. You can do it," Sonia whispered to herself, wishing that Maria could hear her. She knew how Maria was feeling. Then Maria took a deep breath. She bent toward the <u>keyboard</u> and started again from the beginning of her piece.

Sonia sat back in her chair to listen. The air was filled with the most wonderful sounds. If Maria was still nervous, you could not hear it in her music.

When the music ended, the audience clapped loudly. Everyone could tell that Maria had real <u>talent</u>. The other students had played the notes, but Maria had played music. ◄❖►

After the recital was over, Mrs. Howard shook hands with Mr. and Mrs. Torres. "Maria is my prize student," she said, hugging Maria. "I know you are proud of her."

◄❖►
Add this information to Maria's character map.

P 202   THE RECITAL   P 203

GUIDED READING

Page 202   What happens just after Maria begins playing? (She makes a mistake.)   RECALL: SEQUENCE

Page 202   How do you know that the coach's advice really helps Maria? (She takes a deep breath and starts again from the beginning.)
ANALYZE: PROBLEM/ SOLUTION

Page 203   How does the audience feel about Maria's playing? (The people like it better than the other students' playing.) **How do you know?** (They clap more loudly.)   INFER: FEELINGS/ATTITUDES

STRATEGIC READING   ◄❖►

Page 203   Ask a volunteer to read the paragraph with the diamond symbol. Discuss the meaning of the sentence "The other students had played the notes, but Maria had played music." Help students conclude that there is more to making music than playing notes. Then ask what the paragraph tells them about Maria. (Possible responses: She played with feeling; she was able to overcome her fear; her love for music helped her play well.) Have them add that information to their maps and continue reading.   STRATEGY FOR THINKING

Maria stood next to Sonia. "I couldn't have done it without your help," she whispered.

"What did I do?" asked Sonia.

"I was going to run off the stage after I made that first mistake, but then I remembered what you told me about soccer. You said that concentrating was the most important thing, and you said not to look back. So I started over, and if I made a little mistake, I just kept on going. I didn't let it upset me."

Sonia was amazed. "I can't believe that tips for playing soccer would be useful for playing the piano!" she laughed.

"Do you have any piano tips to help me play soccer?" Sonia asked Maria. It was something to look into.

 Write a sentence below the character map that describes Maria.

◆ LIBRARY LINK ◆

If you enjoyed this story by Johanna Hurwitz, you might enjoy reading her other books, such as Aldo Applesauce, Aldo Ice Cream, Class Clown, *and* Yellow Blue Jay.

 Reader's Response

Have you ever felt the way Maria did before the recital? If so, how did you deal with it?

See next page for suggested answers.

SELECTION FOLLOW-UP

THE RECITAL

 Thinking It Over

1. What was Maria worried about?
2. Why did Sonia take Maria running the morning of the recital?
3. In what way was Maria's recital like Sonia's first soccer game of the year?
4. Why did Sonia remember the mistake she made during the soccer game, while Maria did not remember it? How did you decide on your answer?
5. How did Sonia's advice help Maria?
6. If Maria had not talked to Sonia about her feelings, what might have happened during the recital?

Writing to Learn

THINK AND COMPARE Maria was worried about being in a recital. Copy the chart below. Finish it with words that tell how Maria felt after the recital was over.

Before	After
• anxious	
• worried	
• tense	
• nervous	
• afraid	

WRITE Use the words on your chart to help you write a paragraph. Tell how Maria felt after the recital.

GUIDED READING

Page 204 **How do you think both Sonia and Maria will handle mistakes in the future?** (Possible answer: Both of them will be able to perform well because they have learned how to overcome their nervousness and keep going.) SYNTHESIZE: PREDICTING OUTCOMES

RETURNING TO THE READING PURPOSE

Page 204 When the students finish the story, have them read the note with the diamond symbol. Ask them to read all the details on their maps and write a sentence at the bottom describing Maria. (Responses will vary depending on students' notes, but should generally conclude that Maria has learned to be a good performer.) Discuss students' answers. (Students might point out that Maria's love for music and her willingness to learn from others will help her become an even better piano player.)

Finally, ask students if they found this strategy helpful in understanding Maria. Discuss its helpfulness in understanding characters in other stories.

Reader's Journal   **p 74**
Responding to Reading

OVERCOMING STAGE FRIGHT

To explore the feelings involved in stage fright, students pretend they are doing one of the activities described. They write about feeling nervous and offer ideas about ways to relax.

365

SELECTION FOLLOW-UP

THE RECITAL

THINKING IT OVER

1. **What was Maria worried about?** (Maria was worried about making mistakes in her piano recital.) RECALL: CHARACTER

2. **Why did Sonia take Maria running the morning of the recital?** (Maria was very nervous. Sonia thought that running might help Maria to relax.) RECALL: CAUSE/EFFECT

3. **In what way was Maria's recital like Sonia's first soccer game of the year?** (Possible answers: The recital was very important to Maria, just as the soccer game had been to Sonia; both events were "firsts" for each girl, and they wanted to do well; they both had embarrassing experiences and learned from them.) ANALYZE: COMPARISON

4. **Why did Sonia remember the mistake she made during the soccer game, while Maria did not remember it? How did you decide on your answer?** (Sonia was very embarrassed by her mistake and could remember the feeling very well; Maria did not think Sonia's mistake was awful, so she did not remember it; Maria may have remembered the goal that Sonia scored for her own team rather than the mistake she made. Students may have come to their answers by drawing on personal experience, which they may wish to cite.) SYNTHESIZE: DRAWING CONCLUSIONS: METACOGNITION

5. **How did Sonia's advice help Maria?** (When Maria remembered Sonia's advice, she was able to concentrate and continue playing.) RECALL: DETAILS

6. **If Maria had not talked to Sonia about her feelings, what might have happened during the recital?** (Possible answers: Maria might have walked off the stage; Maria might not have been able to continue playing; Maria might have played poorly.) SYNTHESIZE: PREDICTING OUTCOMES

WRITING TO LEARN

Use Writing Master 14, which duplicates this chart.

THINK AND COMPARE **Maria was worried about being in a recital. Copy the chart below. Finish it with words that tell how Maria felt after the recital was over.** (Prepare students for writing by encouraging them to discuss the sense of relief and pride Maria must have felt when the recital was over and she realized how much people had liked her playing.)

Before	After
• anxious	
• worried	
• tense	
• nervous	
• afraid	

Extend comprehension through writing.

WRITE **Use the words on your chart to help you write a paragraph. Tell how Maria felt after the recital.** (Have students share their paragraphs.)

More Ideas for Selection Follow-Up

CRITICAL AND CREATIVE THINKING QUESTIONS

Encourage a variety of responses and points of view.

Use these open-ended questions to encourage critical and creative thinking about the selection.

1. The theme of this unit is "On Your Own." How did Sonia help Maria solve her problem "on her own"?

2. Suppose Jason Hardman and Sonia were to meet. What would they have in common? What would they say to each other?

3. Sonia and Maria were different in many ways, but they shared something special. In what ways do you think they might help each other as they grow up?

REREADING ORALLY

✔ *Have students reread for specific information.*

Tell students that when a reader looks back at a story to find certain information, the reader will reread the story differently from the way it was first read. The first sentence in each paragraph can be read and then the rest of the paragraph skimmed in order to see whether or not the paragraph contains the desired information. Have students locate and reread the parts of the story in which helpful advice is given to Maria or Sonia, including Sonia's advice to Maria. Remind students that Sonia gives several pieces of advice to Maria.

SELECTION COMPREHENSION

Provide comprehension check.

A Workbook page to check comprehension is shown in the Resource Center below. It may be used for informal assessment.

✔ **Informal Assessment Opportunity:** GETTING INFORMATION FROM TEXT

Workbook page 91

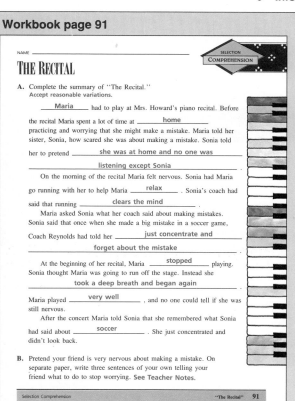

RESOURCE CENTER

◀ **Workbook page 91** is intended for use by all students.

Writing Master 14 duplicates the Writing to Learn chart.

LANGUAGE ARTS CONNECTIONS

CRITICAL THINKING: PIANO TIPS FOR SOCCER PLAYERS

Discuss using the same idea in different situations.

Point out that the same way of handling a problem can be used in several different situations. Review with students how the soccer tips from Sonia's coach helped Maria at her recital. Ask students in what other situations the soccer tips may help. *(speaking in front of a group, acting on stage, other sports)*

Have students write piano tips to help soccer players.

Remind students that at the end of the story Sonia asks Maria for piano tips that might help her play soccer. Have students work in pairs. Have them pretend they are Maria and write lists of suggestions for Sonia. Then have students decide which are the most valuable.   SHARED LEARNING: WRITING

DISCUSSING PERFORMANCE SITUATIONS

Have students brainstorm advice for performance situations.

Tell students that when groups get together to brainstorm ideas, each member of the group contributes several ideas as he or she thinks of them. Remind students that it is important to listen closely and not to try to evaluate or criticize each other's ideas. Have students work in groups to brainstorm situations in which someone might be nervous before a performance, such as giving an oral report, acting in a play, or taking part in a spelling bee. Then have them brainstorm advice that would help overcome nervousness in each situation. *(possible answers: using note cards during an oral report; rehearsing to prepare for a play; taking deep breaths and trying to relax so one is clear to concentrate on what has to be done)*   WHOLE CLASS ENRICHMENT

REALISTIC FICTION AS A LITERARY GENRE

Have students write short realistic fiction stories.

Review with students why "The Recital" is classified as realistic fiction. *(The story did not happen, but it contains events that could happen. The characters behave and have feelings very much like real people.)* Remind students that realistic fiction often, though not always, includes characters and settings that are familiar to most readers. Have each student imagine a situation in which a character overcomes nervousness before a performance of some kind, such as a sporting event or a speech contest. Have the student write a short realistic story showing how the character overcomes his or her nervousness. Remind students that their stories should not contain any events that could not happen, since they are realistic fiction.   CHALLENGE: WRITING

WRITING ABOUT FEELINGS

Have students write about scoring a goal for the wrong team.
Remind students that during a soccer game Sonia kicked the ball in the wrong direction and made a goal for the other team. Have students imagine they were on the other team, the one for which Sonia accidentally scored the goal. Have them discuss the feelings they might have had including surprise, amusement, pleasure, and perhaps feeling sorry for Sonia. Have students write their feelings based on the discussion. Students might choose to write a paragraph as a member of the team for which Sonia accidentally scored the goal or to write a letter to Sonia expressing their feelings. Have students read their paragraphs or letters aloud. **Language Arts Master 12** may be used with this activity.
WRITING/SPEAKING

READING EVERY DAY

Johanna Hurwitz, the author of "The Recital," has written many books featuring characters with whom children can readily identify. The following are among those your students won't want to miss.

Aldo Ice Cream by Johanna Hurwitz. William Morrow, © 1981. By helping his mother with her Meals-on-Wheels volunteer work, Aldo makes new friends among the town's elderly people and works out a way to earn some money.

Class Clown by Johanna Hurwitz. William Morrow, © 1987. When Lucas, a very rambunctious and mischievous third-grader, decides to turn over a new leaf, he discovers that good behavior and hard work can bring some unexpected rewards.

Reader's Journal   pp 75, 76
Extending Reading

A DIFFERENT KIND OF RECITAL

Students read a fable about a different kind of recital. They then draw and describe someone they know who has a special hobby and tell why that person enjoys it.

Selection Support

SKILL TRACE: SUFFIXES				
Introduction	Practice	Test	Reteach	Maintain
TE 370	395	422	461	466	502

WORD STUDY

Suffixes *-ion, -tion*

OBJECTIVE Using structural analysis to determine word meaning.

1. WARM-UP

Use familiar content to present words with suffixes -ion, -tion.

Display the following sentences. Tell students the sentences are about "The Recital." Read the sentences aloud and ask students what the underlined words mean. (direction — *"a way or path in which something moves"*; concentration — *"careful, close attention."*)

> **Sonia kicked the ball in the wrong <u>direction</u> by mistake.**
> **The coach told her to fix her <u>concentration</u> on the next goal.**

Discuss the suffixed words.

Have students reread the sentences. Explain that in each underlined word there is a base word and the suffix *-ion*. Have students identify each base word. (*direct, concentrate*) Point out that when the suffixes *-ion* and *-tion* are added to base words, the suffixes change the part of speech of the base words from a verb to a noun and also change their meanings.

State the objective.

Tell students they will learn to use the suffixes *-ion* and *-tion* to help them understand word meanings.

2. TEACH

Explain why it is important to use suffixes to determine word meanings.

Recognizing and using suffixes helps readers figure out the meanings of unfamiliar words. Being able to add suffixes to familiar words lets writers form additional words that can be useful in their writing.

Discuss understanding and using words with the suffixes -ion and -tion.

Remind students to use the meaning of the base word to figure out the meaning of a word ending in *-ion* or *-tion*. Then tell students that base words ending in *e* change their spelling slightly when the suffix *-ion* or *-tion* is added.

TEACHING CHART 53: SUFFIXES *-ION, -TION*   `53`

1. Maria's teacher wanted to __educate__ her about music.
2. Maria's musical __education__ began two years ago.
3. Maria tried to __act__ on her sister's advice.
4. The __action__ of running made her feel better.
5. Sonia meant to __direct__ the ball toward her team's net.
6. She kicked the ball in the wrong __direction__ .
7. Sonia has started to __collect__ soccer trophies.
8. Before long she will have quite a __collection__ .

Model using the suffixes -ion, -tion to read words.

Tell students they will be using words ending in the suffix *-ion* or *-tion* to complete sentences about "The Recital." Then read the first two sentences. Point out that the verb *educate* in sentence 1 is the base word of the noun *education* in sentence 2. Note that the final *e* in this verb is dropped when the *-ion* suffix is added.

3. GUIDED PRACTICE

Check for understanding.

Before going on, have students explain how to use the suffix *-ion* or *-tion* to help them understand words. (*use the meaning of the base word; remember that* -ion *and* -tion *change verbs to nouns.*)

Guide students in completing the sentences.

Have students fill in the incomplete sentences on the chart. Then have them read the underlined word that forms the base of each *-ion, -tion* word.

4. WRAP-UP

Summarize instruction.

Review why readers need to recognize suffixes and how adding the suffix *-ion* or *-tion* to a word changes the word. (*Recognizing suffixes helps readers understand the meanings of unfamiliar words; adding the suffix* -ion *or* -tion *to a verb changes the verb to a noun.*)

Provide independent practice.

Options for independent practice are shown in the Resource Center below.

Meeting Individual Needs

RETEACHING Use the activity on page 466 and Masters 1–4 in the Teacher Resource Kit.

CHALLENGE Use the activity on page 466 and Master 11 in the Teacher Resource Kit.

ACHIEVING ENGLISH PROFICIENCY Use the activity on page 466 and Master 21 in the Teacher Resource Kit.

Workbook page 92

RESOURCE CENTER

Skills Practice 84

◀ **Workbook page 92** is intended for use by all students.

Skills Practice 84 ▶ may be assigned for additional practice.

Workbook reuse option: Have students underline the base word of each *-ion, -tion* word in Part B. Have them circle the words that require a spelling change before the addition of the suffixes *-ion, -tion*.

WORD STUDY

Suffixes -ion, -tion

NAME _____

REMEMBER: The suffixes *-ion* and *-tion* are added to verbs to form nouns.

A. Add *-ion* to each word. Write the new word on the blank.

1. act — action
2. direct — direction
3. collect — collection
4. invent — invention
5. detect — detection
6. perfect — perfection

B. Write the word that correctly completes each sentence.

7. Mrs. Howard had a big (collect, collection) of music for her students to choose from. — collection

8. The piano recital was a chance for Mrs. Howard's students to (exhibit, exhibition) their skills. — exhibit

9. In her (imagine, imagination) Maria saw herself making a mistake at the recital. — imagination

10. Maria knew she needed good (concentrate, concentration) to play well. — concentration

11. She wanted everyone to enjoy the (perfect, perfection) of her playing. — perfection

12. Though Maria was nervous after she made a mistake, no one could (detect, detection) it in her music. — detect

C. Choose two of the word pairs in Part B. On separate paper, use each pair of words in sentences of your own. See Teacher Notes.

92 "The Recital" — Suffixes *-ion, -tion*

SKILLS PRACTICE 84

NAME _____

Suffixes -ion, -tion

Suffixes change a word's meaning. The suffixes *-ion* and *-tion* change a verb to a noun. Remember that a final *e* is dropped when this suffix is added. Look at the underlined words.

Ben will correct Jim's paper.
What Ben makes is a correction.

A. Write the word that completes each sentence.

1. She is trying to _____ a new dress.
   select   selection   section — select

2. She will wear her _____ to the party.
   select   selection   section — selection

3. He always makes a _____ when his brother speaks.
   correct   correction   creation — correction

4. Sometimes his brother will _____ him, too.
   correct   correction   creation — correct

5. My dad likes to _____ with other fathers.
   associate   association   application — associate

6. Together they are forming a Fathers' _____.
   associate   association   application — association

B. Write a sentence using each word. Use the sentences above as patterns.

7. select — Answers will vary.

8. selection —

9. association —

10. associate —

84 LEVEL 8 "The Recital"

371

SKILL TRACE: SUFFIX				
Introduction	Practice	Test	Reteach	Maintain
TE 344	372	421	461	465	574

WORD STUDY

Suffix -ment

OBJECTIVE   Using structural analysis to determine word meaning.

Review suffixes.

Remind students that a suffix is a letter or group of letters added to the end of a word and that some suffixes change the way a word is used in a sentence. Write the word *settle* on the chalkboard. Then add *ment* to the end of the word. Remind students that the suffix *-ment* can be added to some verbs to make them into nouns. One meaning of the verb *settle* is "to stay," so *settlement* can mean "a place where people have gone to stay."

Have students rewrite sentences using words that end in -ment.

Display the Teaching Chart. Have students read aloud the sentences about "The Recital." Then have them underline the words with the suffix *-ment* and tell what each word means.

TEACHING CHART 54: THE SUFFIX -*MENT*   `54`

1. Maria felt <u>excitement</u> about being in the recital.
2. Sonia's <u>encouragement</u> helped Maria get through the recital.
3. Sonia's face showed her <u>embarrassment</u> when she scored a goal for the wrong soccer team.
4. Mrs. Howard made an <u>announcement</u> before each student played.
5. The audience's <u>enjoyment</u> of Maria's playing was clear.

Provide independent practice.

Options for independent practice are shown in the Resource Center below.

Workbook page 93

NAME _____

Suffix -*ment*   WORD STUDY

REMEMBER: The suffix *-ment* forms a noun and means "result of."

A. On the lines write the base word and the suffix *-ment* for each word.

1. agreement =   2. shipment =
   __agree__ + __ment__   __ship__ + __ment__

3. puzzlement =   4. payment =
   __puzzle__ + __ment__   __pay__ + __ment__

B. Write the word that completes the sentence.

5. The piano recital gave the audience great ____enjoyment____ .
   (agreement, enjoyment)

6. At first each musician felt some understandable
   ____embarrassment____ in front of the audience.
   (embarrassment, argument)

7. A mouse that ran across the stage at one point caused
   brief ____excitement____ . (pavement, excitement)

8. Finally each musician who completed the recital felt relief, pride,
   and ____contentment____ . (contentment, puzzlement)

C. On separate paper, make a chart with two headings: *-ment* words that show feelings; other *-ment* words. Fill in your chart with words from the page. See Teacher Notes.

Suffix -ment   "The Recital"   93

RESOURCE CENTER

◄ **Workbook page 93** is intended for use by all students.

Skills Practice 85 ▶ may be assigned for additional practice.

Workbook reuse option: Have students locate all the words on the page with the suffix *-ment* and draw a vertical line between each base word and its suffix.

Skills Practice 85

NAME _____

SKILLS PRACTICE   `85`

Suffix -*ment*

Suffixes, like words, have meanings. The suffix *-ment* means "the state, or act of." The suffix *-ment* changes a verb to a noun.

A. Write the root word or the *-ment* word that finishes the sentence correctly.

1. Lee gets jobs baby-sitting when young families ____move____ into the neighborhood.
   move   movement

2. Lee is never ____content____ just to sit at home.
   content   contentment

3. He gets a lot of ____enjoyment____ from helping.
   enjoy   enjoyment

4. Lee always knows how to ____entertain____ children.
   entertain   entertainment

5. Kids look at Lee with ____amazement____
   amaze   amazement

6. The ____payment____ for baby-sitting is good.
   pay   payment

B. Add the suffix *-ment* to each word and write it in the sentence.

7. move   Shari saw some ____movement____ in the bushes.

8. puzzle   She looked at ____puzzlement____ .

9. develop   Then she said, "This is a scary ____development____ !"

10. agree   She will get only ____agreement____ from me!

11. announce   I made the ____announcement____ , "I'M GETTING OUT OF HERE!"

12. embarrass   When my baby brother crawled out of the bushes, my face showed my ____embarrassment____ .

LEVEL 8   "The Recital"   85

SKILL TRACE: SYMBOLS/SIGNS				
Introduction	Practice	Test	Reteach	Maintain
TE 346	373	423	461	467	526

STUDY SKILLS

Symbols and Signs

OBJECTIVE   Understanding information from symbols and signs.

Review symbols and signs.   Remind students that symbols and signs are visual ways of communicating important information. Symbols often appear on signs. A symbol is something that stands for something else. Certain simple drawings are used in special ways as symbols.

Provide practice with symbols and signs.   Display the Teaching Chart. Tell students that if they were traveling to a place where a recital is being given, they would probably see a lot of signs. Have students copy the signs and write the correct meaning next to each one.

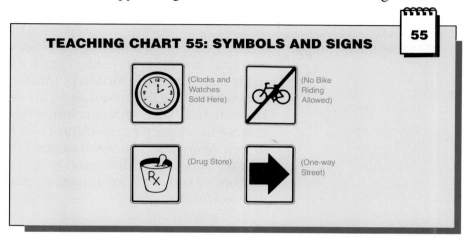

TEACHING CHART 55: SYMBOLS AND SIGNS

(Clocks and Watches Sold Here)

(No Bike Riding Allowed)

(Drug Store)

(One-way Street)

55

Provide independent practice.   Options for independent practice are shown in the Resource Center below.

Workbook page 94

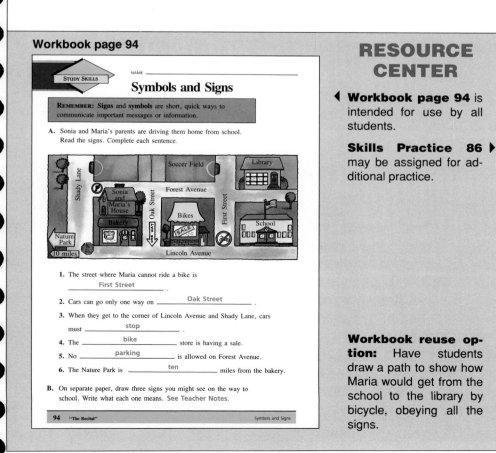

NAME _____

STUDY SKILLS

Symbols and Signs

REMEMBER: **Signs** and **symbols** are short, quick ways to communicate important messages or information.

A. Sonia and Maria's parents are driving them home from school. Read the signs. Complete each sentence.

1. The street where Maria cannot ride a bike is
   First Street
2. Cars can go only one way on ____ Oak Street ____
3. When they get to the corner of Lincoln Avenue and Shady Lane, cars must ____ stop ____ .
4. The ____ bike ____ store is having a sale.
5. No ____ parking ____ is allowed on Forest Avenue.
6. The Nature Park is ____ ten ____ miles from the bakery.

B. On separate paper, draw three signs you might see on the way to school. Write what each one means. See Teacher Notes.

94   "The Recital"   Symbols and Signs

RESOURCE CENTER

◀ **Workbook page 94** is intended for use by all students.

Skills Practice 86 ▶ may be assigned for additional practice.

Workbook reuse option: Have students draw a path to show how Maria would get from the school to the library by bicycle, obeying all the signs.

Skills Practice 86

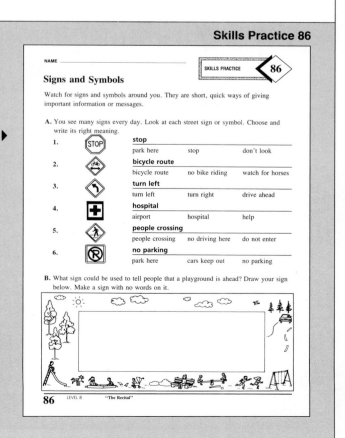

NAME _____

SKILLS PRACTICE 86

Signs and Symbols

Watch for signs and symbols around you. They are short, quick ways of giving important information or messages.

A. You see many signs every day. Look at each street sign or symbol. Choose and write its right meaning.

1. STOP — **stop**
   park here | stop | don't look
2. — **bicycle route**
   bicycle route | no bike riding | watch for horses
3. — **turn left**
   turn left | turn right | drive ahead
4. — **hospital**
   airport | hospital | help
5. — **people crossing**
   people crossing | no driving here | do not enter
6. — **no parking**
   park here | cars keep out | no parking

B. What sign could be used to tell people that a playground is ahead? Draw your sign below. Make a sign with no words on it.

86   LEVEL B   "The Recital"

STRATEGY FOR THINKING

Making a Character Map

OBJECTIVE   Inferring character traits and motives by making a character map.

Review the story.   Review the story "The Recital." Point out to students that both characters, Sonia and Maria, have the same wish at the beginning of the story: both girls hope Maria does well at her piano recital. Tell them that each girl's character is revealed by how she deals with Maria's nervousness about the recital. Review how the problem is resolved. *(Sonia discovers Maria practicing and hears about her nervousness; Sonia takes Maria running; Sonia tells Maria about her soccer mistake; Maria is fearful in the recital hall; Maria makes a mistake and recovers.)*

Review the strategy.   Remind students that making a character map is one way to understand a character in a story. Have them recall the details of what Maria said and did in the map they made for Maria. *(Maria loved music; she was talented; she was nervous and frightened about the recital; she played with real feeling.)* Have students state what conclusion they reached about her character by making the character map. *(Maria was brave, because she was able to play in spite of her fear.)* Now tell students that they can also make a character map for Sonia. Have them refer to the first page of the story and ask them to find one or two items for a character map for Sonia. *(She is good at soccer; nice to Maria.)*

Provide independent practice.   An independent activity is shown in the Resource Center below.

Workbook page 95

> NAME _____
>
> THINKING READING WRITING
>
> ### Making a Character Map
>
> **REMEMBER:** You can understand the characters in a story better by making character maps of them.
>
> **A.** Look at the picture of Maria Torres from "The Recital." Then, on the lines around the picture, write some things that Maria said or did in the story. Accept reasonable variations.
>
> She loved making | She played the
> music. | piano.
>
> She was scared of | She was friends
> making a mistake at | with her sister,
> the recital. | Sonia.
>
> She was Mrs. Howard's | She practiced the
> prize student | piano a lot.
>
> **B.** On separate paper, write a sentence that describes Maria Torres. See Teacher Notes.
>
> Character Map | "The Recital" 95

RESOURCE CENTER

◀ **Workbook page 95** is intended for use by all students.

Workbook reuse option: Have students put in order of importance the descriptions they wrote for the character map by numbering them from 1 (for most important) to 6 (for least important).

VOCABULARY

Antonyms

OBJECTIVE   Recognizing and using words with opposite meanings.

Review antonyms.

Remind students that antonyms are words with opposite meanings. Explain that *frowned* and *smiled* are antonyms. Have students show frowns and then smiles on their faces. Have students demonstrate some other antonyms that can be acted out. (stand — sit; left — right; high — low; open — close)

Provide practice in using antonyms in sentences.

You may wish to use the sentences below to practice antonyms. First write the word list on the chalkboard. Tell students that you are going to read several sentences about "The Recital," but they do not tell what really happened in the story. Have the students listen to the sentences and then choose an antonym from the word list that will make each sentence fit the story. Answers are shown in red.

---

loved	beginning	terrible
better	alike	well

1. Maria and Sonia looked <u>different</u>. (alike)
2. Maria <u>hated</u> music even more than Sonia did. (loved)
3. Maria was afraid of making <u>wonderful</u> mistakes at the piano recital. (terrible)
4. Maria felt <u>worse</u> after she ran with Sonia. (better)
5. Maria made a mistake near the <u>end</u> of her piece. (beginning)
6. Maria went on after her mistake and played very <u>badly</u>. (well)

Provide independent practice.

Options for independent practice are shown in the Resource Center below.

RESOURCE CENTER

Skills Practice 87 ▶ may be assigned for additional practice.

NAME _____

SKILLS PRACTICE 87

Antonyms

Antonyms are words that have opposite or nearly opposite meanings.

Write the antonym for the underlined word. Choose words from the box.

alike	public
continue	quiet
cool	relax
disagree	straight
fancy	walk
frowning	
later	
light	

1. Anna and Hannah are twins. Some twins are **alike** . But these twins are <u>different</u>.
2. Anna wears <u>plain</u>, simple clothes. But Hannah likes **fancy** , dresses with ribbon and bows.
3. Anna likes <u>warm</u> weather. Hannah prefers it **cool** .
4. If Hannah says "<u>sooner</u>," Anna says **"later"** .
5. If Anna wants to <u>exercise</u>, Hannah would rather **relax** .
6. Anna's hair is <u>curly</u> and wild. Hannah's is **straight** and neat.
7. If Anna is <u>grinning</u>, then Hannah is **frowning** .
8. Anna is quiet, <u>private</u>, and quite shy. Hannah gives **public** speeches and looks you in the eye.
9. If Anna wears a <u>heavy</u> coat, Hannah puts on a **light** jacket.
10. Hannah likes <u>noisy</u> parties. Anna would rather spend a **quiet** evening at home.
11. If Hannah says "**continue** ," Anna yells "<u>STOP!</u>"
12. When Hannah wants to **walk** , Anna is sure to <u>run</u>.
13. Only one thing they <u>agree</u> upon; to **disagree** is fun!

LEVEL 8   "The Recital"   **87**

CURRICULUM CONNECTIONS

ALL KEYED UP! MUSIC

Mention to students that the piano and other keyboard instruments such as the accordion, the organ, and the synthesizer can produce many different sounds. Have students report on the piano or one of the other keyboard instruments. Suggest that they include a photograph or drawing of the instrument and a diagram labeling its parts. Have students put their reports into booklets and create covers and title pages.

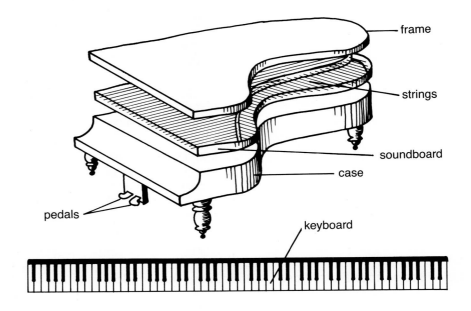

MUSIC MAKERS SOCIAL STUDIES

If possible, play some classical music. Then have students do library research to learn about the lives of famous composers. A student might research Bach, Beethoven, Mozart, Brahms, Vivaldi, Bernstein, Prokofiev, Stravinsky, or some other classical composer. Have students present their findings as oral reports. If you have access to appropriate equipment, encourage students to borrow recordings by their composers and play them for the class. For an alternative activity, have students research favorite contemporary musicians/composers such as Lionel Ritchie, Bruce Springsteen, Neil Diamond, Carly Simon, Barbra Streisand. **Curriculum Connection Master 12** can be used with this activity.

LYRICAL LICENSE MUSIC

Have students work in groups to write new words for a familiar tune. For example, students might change "Row, Row, Row Your Boat" to something like the following:

> Walk, walk, walk to school,
> This we do each day.
> Happily, happily, happily, happily,
> Now it's time to play.

Have each group sing its song for the rest of the class. Students who play portable musical instruments may wish to use these instruments to accompany the songs.

TEACHING MUSIC CAREERS

Invite a music teacher to talk with students about what he or she did to build a career in music. If the music teacher plays a portable instrument, he or she might demonstrate. Encourage students to ask questions. If any students in the class play musical instruments and take lessons, they might like to describe what goes on during a music lesson.

SOCCER FACTS AND PLAYERS PHYSICAL EDUCATION

Have students work in small groups to research the game of soccer and make a presentation, including a demonstration. Students should tell about the history of the game, how the game is played, and the names of the positions. A diagram of a team on the playing field would be helpful. Some students may want to report on a famous soccer player such as Pélé.

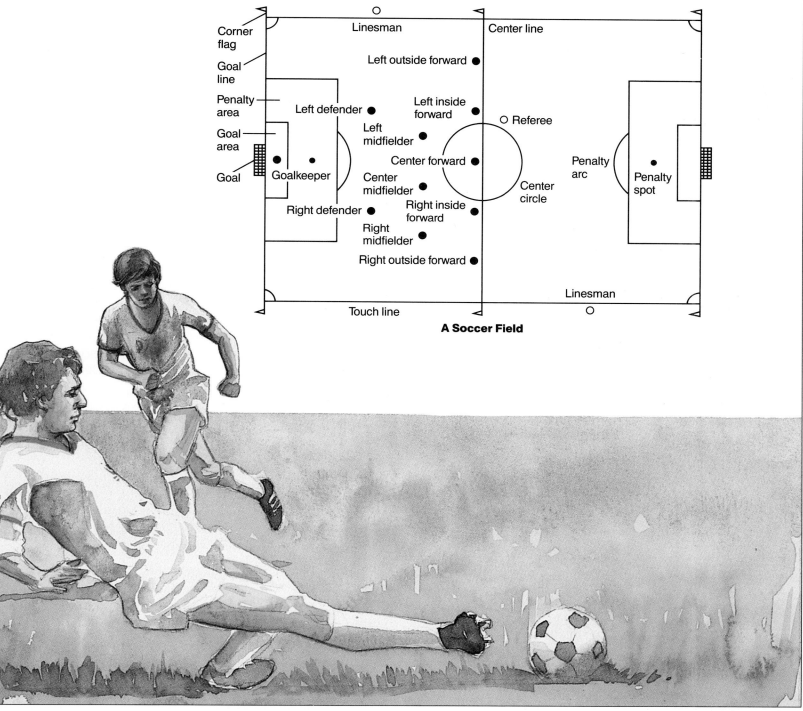

A Soccer Field

LESSON ORGANIZER
Lee Bennett Hopkins Interviews Johanna Hurwitz

TEACHER CHOICE

	Teaching Sequence	Trade Books and Resources	Meeting Individual Needs	Integrated Language Arts / Cross Curriculum
The Bridge Pages 380–381	**Introduce** Inferences (Tested)	• Teaching Chart 56 • Workbook 96 • Skills Practice 88	• Reteaching Masters 1–7 • Challenge Master 12	
PART 1 **Vocabulary Strategies** Pages 382–383	**Develop Concepts** Brainstorming Goals **Teach Vocabulary** **STORY CRITICAL WORDS:** advice, goal, **practice**, **published**, titled, **writer** (Tested words are boldfaced.)	• Teaching Chart 57 • Workbook 97 • Skills Practice 89	**SUPPORT WORDS:** ballet, magazines, marathon, memories, plugging, poem, schedule • Skills Practice 90 **CHARACTER/SETTING WORDS:** Aldo Applesauce, Aldo Ice Cream, Baseball Fever, Busybody Nora, Great Neck Library, Johanna Hurwitz, Maria, New York, Uri, Yankee Stadium	**WRITING/SPEAKING ACTIVITY:** Use new vocabulary to predict a character's goal. • Spelling Connection 51
PART 2 **Reading & Responding** Pages 384–391	**Build Background** **Develop a Purpose for Reading** **Guide the Reading Process** **Selection Follow-Up**	• Reader's Journal 77–79 • Workbook 98 **READING EVERY DAY** *Laura Ingalls Wilder,* by G. Blair *To the Point: A Story About E.B. White,* by D. Collins	**EXTRA HELP:** Main Idea/Details Form **ACHIEVING ENGLISH PROFICIENCY:** Role-playing an Interview with a Famous Person • Achieving English Proficiency Master 22	**Language Arts Connections** **WRITING TO LEARN:** Write advice to a younger child. • Writing Master 15 **SPEAKING/LISTENING:** Learning About Favorite Authors; Creating Musical Words for Instruments • Language Arts Master 13 **WRITING:** Writing Johanna's Journal; Writing an Interview
PART 3 **Selection Support** Pages 392–397	**Introduce** Homophones (Tested)	• Teaching Chart 58 • Workbook 99 • Skills Practice 91	• Reteaching Masters 1–4 • Challenge Master 13 • Achieving English Proficiency Master 23 **Practice** • Teaching Charts 59–60 • Workbook 100–101 • Skills Practice 92–93 Inferences (Tested) Suffixes *-ion, -tion* (Tested) **Maintain** • Skills Practice 94 Suffix *-ness*	**Curriculum Connections** **MATHEMATICS:** Making Time Lines for Favorite People • Curriculum Connection Master 13 **SOCIAL STUDIES:** Researching Famous People **CAREERS:** Researching Well-known Baseball Players or Ballet Dancers **ART:** Drawing Future Goals

Lee Bennett Hopkins
INTERVIEWS
Johanna Hurwitz

SUMMARY *Johanna Hurwitz always knew she would be a writer. At age eight or nine, she began to make up stories for her younger brother, and then she started writing them down. Her home was filled with books, and she was always delighted when her parents read to her. When she was a teenager, she worked in a library. Later on she became a full-time librarian. One of her jobs was reading and telling stories to children. After her own children were in school, she began writing down the stories she had been telling. Now she has written almost twenty books.*

The Bridge

SKILL TRACE: INFERENCES				
Introduction	Practice	Test	Reteach	Maintain
TE 380	394	442	461	462	596

COMPREHENSION

Teaching Inferences

OBJECTIVE Making inferences about time, things, and people.

1. WARM-UP

Use a known passage to make inferences.

Tell students they will listen to some sentences about the previous selection, "The Recital." Explain that the author, Johanna Hurwitz, has not told everything about the characters. Instead she has provided clues about them.

1. **"Did I make too much noise?" asked Sonia. "Sorry."** (concerned, considerate, thoughtful)

2. **That morning when she awoke, Maria said that her stomach hurt. But Maria was not sick.** (nervous, anxious, jittery)

Discuss word and "what I know" clues.

Reread each sentence. Have students explain which word clues helped them decide what the characters are like. *(sentence 1 — Sonia's question and the word* sorry*; sentence 2 — the words* stomach hurt, but not sick*)* Ask students what they know about people who say they are sorry. *(Often they are considerate and thoughtful.)* Then ask how their stomachs might feel if they had to perform in front of an audience. *(nervous, crampy)* Point out that these are "what I know" clues.

State the objective.

Tell students they will learn to use word and knowledge clues to make inferences, or figure out information that is not stated directly.

2. TEACH

Explain why inferences are important.

Making inferences helps readers better understand story characters and events. In this way, readers better understand and appreciate what they read.

Present a strategy for making inferences.

Point out that there is a strategy students can use to help them make inferences as they read. Use clues from the author's words and then think about what you know from your own personal experiences to make reasonable guesses about things not stated.

> **TEACHING CHART 56: INFERENCES** **56**
>
> 1. Maria chooses to practice the piano for many hours every day. How does Maria feel about music? (She loves music and is dedicated to it; chooses to practice, many hours every day.)
> 2. After Maria stopped playing, the audience cheered and clapped very loudly. How did Maria play? (very well; cheered, clapped very loudly)

Model the strategy.

Read sentence 1 on the Teaching Chart and point out that although the author does not say that Maria loves music and is dedicated to it, you have figured this out from the word clues *chooses to practice* and *many hours every day*. Tell students that you know that anyone who chooses to practice something every day most likely loves it. This is a "what I know" clue.

3. GUIDED PRACTICE

Check for understanding.

Before going on, have students explain how to make inferences. *(Look for word clues; relate story situations to what they know from their own experiences.)*

Guide students in using the strategy.

Have students use the strategy to make an inference about the remaining sentence. Have them discuss both the word and the experience clues that helped them make their inference.

4. WRAP-UP

Summarize instruction.

Go over with students the reasons why readers sometimes need to make inferences and the kinds of clues readers can use to figure out what an author has not stated. *(An author does not always give information about everything; readers can use word and experience clues.)*

Provide independent practice.

Options for independent practice are shown in the Resource Center below.

5. APPLICATION

Students will make inferences as they read "Lee Bennett Hopkins Interviews Johanna Hurwitz." The symbol ✔ marks specific questions and activities that apply this skill.

Meeting Individual Needs

RETEACHING Use the activity on page 462 and Masters 1–7 in the Teacher Resource Kit.

CHALLENGE Use the activity on page 463 and Master 12 in the Teacher Resource Kit.

Workbook page 96

COMPREHENSION

NAME _____

Inference

REMEMBER: Use story clues and what you already know to figure out things that the writer did not state.

A. Read the sentences. Write the answer to each question.

1. Maria was sitting very stiffly. For a moment it looked as if she was going to run offstage.

   How was Maria feeling? Maria was feeling nervous.

2. Maria bent over the keyboard and pressed the keys. The sounds of beautiful music filled the air.

   What was Maria doing? She was playing the piano.

3. Sonia held her breath as she watched Maria struggle to begin again after her mistake. "Come on!" she whispered, clutching the arm of her seat and leaning forward.

   What was Sonia feeling? Sonia was feeling anxious for her sister.

4. When Maria finished playing, the audience would not stop clapping.

   How did they feel about her playing? They liked her playing a lot.

5. After the recital was over, Mrs. Howard put her arms around Maria and hugged her. She had a big smile on her face.

   How did Mrs. Howard feel? Mrs. Howard felt pleased and proud.

B. Think about someone you know. On separate paper, describe how that person looks and behaves when he or she is angry. See Teacher Notes.

96   "Lee Bennett Hopkins Interviews Johanna Hurwitz"   Inference

---

RESOURCE CENTER

◀ **Workbook page 96** is intended for use by all students.

Skills Practice 88 ▶ may be assigned for additional practice.

Workbook reuse option: Have students underline the clues they used to make their inferences in Part A.

Skills Practice 88

NAME _____

SKILLS PRACTICE ◇ 88 ◇

Inference

An author does not always give information about everything. When you use story clues and what you already know to figure out information that is not directly stated, you are making **inferences**.

| Story clues |
| What I know |
| + |
| Inference |

To make an inference:
1. Look for clues in the story.
2. Think about what you know about events like those in the story.
3. Make an inference.
4. Ask yourself if your inference makes sense.

Jenny got her jacket from the dark coatroom. She rushed out to wait for the school bus. Later, the jacket felt tight. Jenny saw that it had pretty fasteners instead of plain buttons. "I made a mistake," she thought. "Tomorrow, I'll swap with . . . someone."

1. What was Jenny's mistake?
   She took someone else's jacket.

2. Why didn't she name the person whose jacket she took?
   She didn't know whose jacket she took.

3. Was the jacket the same or a different style?
   different

Kenny opened his door to get the newspaper. Slam! One turn of the knob and he knew he was in trouble. He might have to wait an hour or more! Then he remembered the open kitchen window.

4. What happened to Kenny?   He got locked out of his house.

5. Why did he think he might have to wait?   No one was home.

6. Why did Kenny start thinking about the kitchen window?   He thought he could get in that way.

88   LEVEL 8   "Lee Bennett Hopkins Interviews Johanna Hurwitz"

Vocabulary Strategies

Developing Concepts

Tap prior knowledge about goals.

As a starting point for teaching vocabulary, have students discuss goals and ambitions they have now and for the future — the things they would like to accomplish, the professions and careers they would like to pursue, and so on. List students' ideas on the chalkboard under the heading *Goals*. Then ask students to brainstorm ways they and other people might achieve their goals. Call on volunteers to write these ideas in a separate list with the heading *Ways to Reach Your Goals*. Elicit that in order to accomplish what you want in life, you can sometimes get advice from older, more knowledgeable people, and you should also be prepared to train or practice in order to become skilled.

Teaching Vocabulary

Discuss meanings of Story Critical words.

Read each context sentence on the Teaching Chart and identify the new word. Then use the questions below to help students understand each word. When necessary, provide a definition.

TEACHING CHART 57: VOCABULARY 57

1. **goal** (a purpose or aim)
   The young girl's *goal* was to work on a newspaper.
2. **writer** (a person who writes books, stories, and so forth)
   A *writer* shares information and ideas with people who read.
3. **practice** (to do something again and again to become skilled at it)
   To be a good writer, *practice* putting your ideas on paper many times.
4. **advice** (an opinion given about what to do)
   What *advice* might a professional writer give a young person who wants to become a writer?
5. **published** (prepared for sale as a book, magazine, or newspaper)
   The writer's goal was to have her book *published* and sold in stores.
6. **titled** (having a name or title)
   The last story you read in this book was *titled* "The Recital."

---

goal

1. What goal do you have for your life? Why do you have this goal? (It is important work. It will make me happy.)   STRATEGY: PRIOR KNOWLEDGE

writer

2. What does the suffix *-er* mean? (one who does something) **What does *write* mean?** (to put words on paper) **Define *writer*.** (one who writes)
STRATEGY: STRUCTURAL ANALYSIS

practice

3. What would you have to do in order to become good at something? (practice) **What kinds of professions or skills might people have to practice?** (dancing, singing, playing an instrument, sports, acting, writing) **Tell about when you have had to practice something.**   STRATEGY: PRIOR KNOWLEDGE

advice

4. What advice might a professional writer give to a young writer? (to practice writing; to read a lot) **Tell about good advice someone gave you and how it helped you.** STRATEGY: PRIOR KNOWLEDGE

published

5. What things do you know about that are published? (books, magazines, newspapers, articles, sheet music, photographs, pamphlets, newsletters, flyers) STRATEGY: CLASSIFICATION

titled

6. What are some synonyms for the word *titled*? (named, called) **From what noun does the word *titled* come?** (title) STRATEGY: SYNONYMS

Add new words to the lists.

Challenge students to add as many of the new words as they can to the lists on the chalkboard. If necessary, add new headings. Have students explain why each added word belongs.

Discuss Support words as needed.

The Glossary of the Student Text includes definitions of the Support words: *poem, magazines, plugging, marathon, schedule, memories, ballet.* Have students discuss which words can be added to the lists.

Introduce Character/Setting words.

Pronounce these Character/Setting words before students read the selection: *Johanna Hurwitz, Uri, Great Neck Library, Busybody Nora, Aldo Ice Cream, Aldo Applesauce, Baseball Fever, New York, Yankee Stadium, Maria.*

Provide independent practice.

Options for independent practice are shown in the Resource Center below.

WRITING OR SPEAKING ACTIVITY *Have students use as many of the new words as possible to tell what they think will be the goal of the person in the next selection.*

Workbook page 97

SELECTION VOCABULARY

NAME _____

Using New Words

A. Use the words in the box to complete the paragraph.

| advice | goal | practice | published | titled | writer |

One day in the school library, a famous ___writer___ came to talk about her books. She brought her latest book with her. It had just been ___published___ last year. The book was ___titled___ *How to Be a Writer.* In the book, she gave ___advice___ to young people about the things they should do to become writers. She told our class that young people must decide what they want to do and then try to reach that ___goal___ . She said to become good writers, we would have to ___practice___ again and again.

B. Write a word from the box next to its definition.

1. purpose ___goal___
2. named ___titled___
3. an opinion about what to do ___advice___
4. to do something over and over ___practice___

C. On separate paper, write a letter to a writer whose book you read and liked. Use at least three story words in your letter. See Teacher Notes.

Selection Vocabulary   "Lee Bennett Hopkins Interviews Johanna Hurwitz"   97

RESOURCE CENTER

◀ **Workbook page 97** provides practice with Story Critical words.

Skills Practice 89 ▶ provides additional practice with Story Critical words.

Skills Practice 90 provides practice with Support words.

Spelling Connection Master 51 may be used for spelling instruction with the new vocabulary.

Workbook reuse option: Have students write definitions for the two boxed words that are not defined in Part B.

Skills Practice 89

NAME _____

SKILLS PRACTICE ◇ **89**

Vocabulary: Story Critical Words

A. Study the meaning of each word.

advice an opinion given about what to do or how to do it
goal a purpose or aim
practice to do something over and over to become good at it
published planned and made a book or magazine for sale
titled having a title
writer a person who writes books, stories, etc.

B. Answer each riddle with the correct vocabulary word.

1. You can give or take this. It is meant to be helpful. What is it? ___advice___

2. I like to write. Some stories I tell are fact and others are fiction. Who am I? ___writer___

3. This is something you must do many times. It can help you do things better. What is it? ___practice___

4. This is something to set for yourself. You will feel good when you reach it. What is it? ___goal___

C. One word in each sentence does not make sense. Underline that word. Write the vocabulary word that should go in its place.

5. Todd was reading a new book misled, *Adventures on the Mississippi.* ___titled___

6. Joanna likes to praise playing her tuba. ___practice___

7. After saving his pennies, Seth reached his golf of $5.00. ___goal___

8. Wendell's aunt gave him some good address on his problems. ___advice___

9. A famous waiter presented our library with one of her books. ___writer___

10. This book was first punished in 1980. ___published___

LEVEL 8   "Lee Bennett Hopkins Interviews Johanna Hurwitz"   Definition clues   **89**

Reading & Responding

Building Background

Motivate students with a quotation.

Tell students that an author once made up what he called a recipe for writing a story. Share the following quotation and ask students what they think it means. *(A good story will include joy, sorrow, and interest in what will happen next.)*

> **A writer needs to "make readers laugh, make them cry, and make them wait."** *Paraphrase from a quotation by Charles Reade*

Have students discuss other ingredients they might add to the recipe. *(interesting and likeable characters, descriptive words, important ideas)*

Discuss the interview.

Tell students they will read an interview with Johanna Hurwitz, a well-known writer of children's books and stories, who wrote "The Recital," the previous story in this book. Have students explain what an interview is. *(a talk between a person who asks questions and another person who answers them)* Mention that the author of this interview, Lee Bennett Hopkins, often interviews well-know authors. Have students find and read the Lee Bennett Hopkins entry in the About the Author section at the back of their texts. Discuss what Hopkins enjoys about interviewing people.

Developing a Purpose for Reading

Option 1
Students set purpose.

ORAL "QUESTION" LISTS   Ask students to think of questions they would like to have answered about Johanna Hurwitz. Have students phrase the questions as if they were going to interview Mrs. Hurwitz. Tell students to read the title and the first page of the selection before formulating their questions. Record students' questions for later use.

WRITING ACTIVITY   Have students work individually or in pairs to create written "Question" lists. Be sure students save their lists for later use.

Option 2
Teacher sets purpose.

Have students read to find out what Johanna Hurwitz's goals were as a young person.

Meeting Individual Needs

EXTRA HELP   Distribute a form for main idea/details, Form 10 in the Teacher Resource Kit. Have students write these main idea headings on the form: *Mrs. Hurwitz explains where her ideas come from, Mrs. Hurwitz tells about her hobbies,* and *Mrs. Hurwitz gives advice to young writers.* Then suggest that as students read, they list the details they think belong under each main idea heading. After they have finished reading, have students use the lists to discuss and summarize the interview.

ACHIEVING ENGLISH PROFICIENCY   Write the word *interview* on the board. Tell students that in an *interview* someone is asked questions about his or her work, ideas, family and so on. Ask students what famous person they would like to interview. Then, as a group, have students come up with questions they would like to ask this person. To model the interview format role play the interview with you as the famous person and students asking their questions. Tell students that they are now going to read an interview with a writer, Johanna Hurwitz. For additional help in story comprehension, use Master 22 in the Teacher Resource Kit.

Lee Bennett Hopkins
INTERVIEWS

Johanna Hurwitz

Johanna Hurwitz always knew she would be a <u>writer</u>.

"When I was about eight or nine years old, I made up stories to tell to my younger brother," she says. "I started writing them down. I even sent some to children's magazines."

At the age of ten, she wrote and <u>published</u> her first poem, <u>titled</u> "Books." It was about what books meant to her. Mrs. Hurwitz was paid fifty cents for the poem. The fifty cents was sent to her by check!

Mrs. Hurwitz was born and raised in the Bronx, in New York City. "My home was filled with books," she says. "Some of my happiest early memories were when my father and mother read to me. I lived in a neighborhood that was filled with children. I could walk to the library, and I did so almost every day. The library was my other home. I loved it so much that I decided by the age of ten that someday I would become a librarian. I also knew then that I would one day write books."

In high school, Mrs. Hurwitz started working in a public library. After graduating from college, she became a full-time children's librarian.

She still finds time from her busy writing schedule to work part-time as a children's librarian at the Great Neck Library in Great Neck, New York. There she reads to children and tells them stories. "I'll never stop working in libraries," she says. "I love it so much."

Mrs. Hurwitz and her husband, Uri, a teacher and writer, have two grown children, Nomi and Beni. She made up stories to tell to her children when they were young. It was not until they were in school that she began to write the stories down.

Reader's Journal   **p 77**
Preparing for Reading

IF ONLY
I COULD
MEET
THEM

Imagining they could meet one of the people pictured, students make up questions they would ask that person.

GUIDED READING

✔ **Page 207   How do you think Johanna Hurwitz's children felt about books and reading when they were young?** (They most likely loved them because their mother's reading to them and telling them stories would have encouraged them.)   INFER: FEELINGS/ATTITUDES

HIGHLIGHTING LITERATURE

Page 207   Point out that the interview begins with a grown-up Johanna Hurwitz recalling her childhood. Ask students in what ways Johanna's childhood was similar to their own. Point out also that an interview includes answers to the interviewer's questions. The numerous quotations from Johanna Hurwitz that make up these answers make readers feel as if Johanna Hurwitz were speaking directly to them.

✔ Skill from The Bridge applied through this question.

Her first book, *Busybody Nora*, a story about a six-year-old girl who lives in an apartment in New York City, was published in 1976. Since then she has written almost twenty books.

"My ideas come from everywhere—from my own children, and from children I meet and work with when I visit schools and libraries," she says. "Sometimes, something that someone says, or something that I see on the street or on television will give me an idea.

"When I am not writing, I like to cook and listen to music. Both food and music have crept into several of my books. In *Busybody Nora*, the folk tales *Jack and the Beanstalk* and *Stone Soup* play an important part in the book." Food has also crept into some of the titles of her books, such as *Aldo Ice Cream* and *Aldo Applesauce*.

Another favorite hobby she enjoys is baseball. "I'm a baseball fanatic," she says. Her book *Baseball Fever* came about because of her love of the sport. "I grew up near New York's Yankee Stadium," she says. "I could hear the fans' screaming and cheering coming from the stadium every time a player hit a home run. Loving baseball as I do, it was natural for me to write *Baseball Fever*. I've got it!"

I asked Mrs. Hurwitz if she had any <u>advice</u> to give to young writers. "Yes," she said. "I would like boys and girls to know that writing does not come easily. If you want to be a good baseball player or a fine ballet dancer, you must <u>practice</u>, practice, practice. To become a fine writer, you must practice, also.

"Reading is very important, too. If you want to become a writer, read a lot. The more you read, the larger your vocabulary becomes. Also, the more you read, the more you become aware of how a story really works."

The story you have just read, "The Recital," was written by Mrs. Hurwitz especially for this book.

GUIDED READING

✔ **Page 208   What can you tell about the kinds of writing that Johanna Hurwitz does?** (She writes different kinds — folk tales, realistic fiction, and fantasy. Her subjects and settings are all different.) INFER: CATEGORY

Page 208   What kind of person is Johanna Hurwitz? Why do you think so? (She is smart and knows what is going on around her; she is full of life and energy; and she has many interests, including people.)   SYNTHESIZE: CHARACTER

Page 209   What details does Johanna Hurwitz give for why reading a lot is important for people who want to become writers? (It helps increase vocabulary. It helps you become more aware of how a story works.)   ANALYZE: MAIN IDEA/DETAILS

STRATEGIC READING

✔ **Page 209   Have students summarize what they have learned so far about Johanna Hurwitz. (From the time she was a young child, she knew she would be a writer; she began as a young girl telling and then writing stories, and she sent them to children's magazines. Her first poem was published when she was ten years old. Her love of books and reading influenced her to become a children's librarian. Her many interests and her enjoyment of children have given her ideas for books.) If students have trouble summarizing, suggest they reread those parts of the selection that are confusing. Ask students to predict whether or not they would enjoy reading stories written by Johanna Hurwitz. What information in the interview helped to interest them or not interest them in reading her stories?   METACOGNITION: SUMMARIZING AND PREDICTING**

✔ Skill from The Bridge applied through this question.
✔ Informal Assessment Opportunity: SUMMARIZING

See next page for suggested answers.

"Like most stories," she says, "it was made up. When I was a young girl, though, I did take piano lessons, and I did not like playing in front of people."

In "The Recital," Maria's sister tells her to concentrate on the next goal and not to look back at mistakes. "Writers should also remember not to look back at mistakes," she says. "If baseball players make mistakes in games and keep thinking about the mistakes, the rest of the game will not go as well for them. You should just think about the next thing you are going to do—as Maria did. You really have to forget past mistakes and keep going.

"Whatever you do in life, believe in yourself. Don't give up. Keep plugging away. Whether you are running in a marathon race, or creating a piece of artwork, or writing a poem, story, or a report, stay with it. Believe in it."

Reader's Response

How do you feel about Johanna Hurwitz's advice, "Believe in yourself. Don't give up"?

Johanna Hurwitz

Thinking It Over

1. How might Johanna Hurwitz's happy childhood have led her to become a writer? What makes you think this?
2. List the things Johanna Hurwitz does that show she still loves books.
3. What are some of Johanna Hurwitz's other interests?
4. Where does Johanna Hurwitz get her ideas for stories?
5. Explain what you think Mrs. Hurwitz meant when she said, "The more you read, the more you become aware of how a story really works." Do you agree?

Writing to Learn

THINK AND RECALL Mrs. Hurwitz says, "Whatever you do in life, believe in yourself. Don't give up. Keep plugging away." What advice would you give a younger child?

WRITE Share your ideas with a younger friend. Write a letter and give advice that you believe in.

GUIDED READING

Page 210   What advice does Johanna Hurwitz give to young writers? (practice writing a lot; read a lot; do not look back at mistakes, just keep going; believe in yourself)   SYNTHESIZE: SUMMARIZING

RETURNING TO THE READING PURPOSE

OPTION 1   Return to the students' lists of questions about Johanna Hurwitz. Discuss whether or not these questions were answered in the interview. Students may wish to discuss any information about her they had not anticipated learning. (Students may have been surprised that she has another job — that of a librarian — in addition to writing and that she loves baseball.)

OPTION 2   Review with students what Johanna Hurwitz's goals were when she was young. (She wanted to be a writer and a children's librarian.) Ask if she accomplished her goals. (Yes, she is both.) Have students tell if they have similar goals.

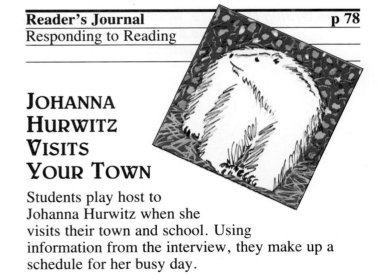

Reader's Journal   p 78
Responding to Reading

JOHANNA HURWITZ VISITS YOUR TOWN

Students play host to Johanna Hurwitz when she visits their town and school. Using information from the interview, they make up a schedule for her busy day.

SELECTION FOLLOW-UP

LEE BENNETT HOPKINS INTERVIEWS
Johanna Hurwitz

THINKING IT OVER

1. **How might Johanna Hurwitz's happy childhood have led her to become a writer? What makes you think this?** (Possible answers: There were books at home; Mrs. Hurwitz's parents often read to her; she visited the library every day; she liked telling stories to her brother; she had a poem published when she was ten. Encourage students to support their answers.)   INFER: CAUSE/EFFECT; METACOGNITION

2. **List the things Johanna Hurwitz does that show she still loves books.** (She works as a children's librarian; she reads to children and tells them stories; she writes for children.)   INFER: FEELINGS/ATTITUDES

3. **What are some of Johanna Hurwitz's other interests?** (She likes to cook and listen to music. She loves baseball.)   RECALL: DETAILS

4. **Where does Johanna Hurwitz get her ideas for stories?** (Possible answers: Her ideas come from experiences her own children or other children in schools and libraries have had; she may see something interesting on television; she listens to and watches what goes on around her. Accept all answers that reflect information in the interview.) SYNTHESIZE: MAIN IDEA/DETAILS

5. **Explain what you think Mrs. Hurwitz meant when she said "the more you read, the more you become aware of how a story really works." Do you agree?** (Students may say that the more you read, the more ideas you get. Reading may give a reader ideas on what makes a story interesting. Students who disagree may say that it takes more writing practice to make a good writer.)   EVALUATE: POINT OF VIEW

WRITING TO LEARN

Use Writing Master 15, which provides a form for letter writing.

THINK AND RECALL   Mrs. Hurwitz says, "Whatever you do in life, believe in yourself. Don't give up. Keep plugging away." What advice would you give a younger child? (Possible responses might include: Don't be afraid to ask for help; Just try it. It might be fun.)

✔ *Extend comprehension through writing.*

WRITE   Share your ideas with a younger friend. Write a letter and give advice that you believe in. (Have students share their letters.)

✔ Informal Assessment Opportunity: RESPONDING

More Ideas for Selection Follow-Up

CRITICAL AND CREATIVE THINKING QUESTIONS

Encourage a variety of responses and points of view

Use these open-ended questions to encourage critical and creative thinking about the selection.

1. Johanna Hurwitz always knew that she wanted to write books and become a librarian. Is there something you want to do or become? How will you achieve it?

2. In the past, Mrs. Hurwitz got some of her ideas for books and stories from her young children. Has anything happened to you that you think would be a good subject for a book or story?

REREADING ORALLY

Have students reread for fluency

Have students work in pairs to reread parts of the interview to each other. Tell half the students to reread the part in which Johanna Hurwitz gives advice to young writers. Have the rest of the students reread the parts that tell about Mrs. Hurwitz's early life. Before students begin, remind them that to write the selection an interviewer asked questions, and Johanna Hurwitz probably responded in a friendly, conversational tone. Tell students they should read those parts as if they were actually Johanna Hurwitz talking to someone.

SELECTION COMPREHENSION

Provide comprehension check.

A Workbook page to check comprehension is shown in the Resource Center below. It may be used for informal assessment.

Workbook page 98

SELECTION
COMPREHENSION

NAME _____

LEE BENNETT HOPKINS INTERVIEWS

Johanna Hurwitz

A. Complete the summary of the selection "Lee Bennett Hopkins Interviews Johanna Hurwitz." Accept reasonable variations.

In this interview, _____Johanna Hurwitz_____ tells about her life. She was born and raised in __the Bronx, New York__.

Her home was filled with ___books___ . Her other home was the ___library___ . She loved it there so much that she decided by the age of ten that she would someday be a librarian. She also knew that she would one day be a ___writer___ .

In high school, Mrs. Hurwitz began working in a public library. After college, she worked full-time as a ___children's librarian___ .

Mrs. Hurwitz became a writer when she began to write down the stories she had made up to tell ___her children___ when they were young. She gets her ideas for stories from ___everywhere___ . Because she likes to cook and listen to music, food and music have crept into some of her stories. Another favorite hobby she has written about is ___baseball___ .

When Mrs. Hurwitz was asked what advice she would give to young writers, she said they should ___read a lot___ and practice.

B. Think about a goal you have. On separate paper, write how you plan to reach this goal. See Teacher Notes.

98 "Lee Bennett Hopkins Interviews Johanna Hurwitz"   Selection Comprehension

RESOURCE CENTER

◀ **Workbook page 98** is intended for use by all students.

Writing Master 15 provides a form for letter writing.

LANGUAGE ARTS CONNECTIONS

CREATIVE THINKING: WRITING JOHANNA'S JOURNAL

Have students create a journal entry.

Tell students that a journal is a book in which a person writes what he or she feels and thinks about the important events of each day. Ask students to name another word for *journal (diary)*. Have students pretend to be Johanna Hurwitz as a ten-year-old girl. Explain that "Johanna" has just gotten news that her poem "Books" has been accepted for publication by a children's magazine and that she will be paid fifty cents for it. Ask students to write about this event from Johanna's point of view and to express her feelings about it. Remind them to date their entries. Suggest that students also mention Johanna's goal to continue writing so that she may have more of her work published. Display journal entries and collect them in a folder, or have students read their work aloud.   WRITING

LEARNING ABOUT AUTHORS

Have students research their favorite author's life.

Ask students to name types of books in which they might locate information about famous authors. *(encyclopedias, dictionaries, biographies, autobiographies)* Point out that librarians can help students locate and use special volumes of authors' biographies. Have students work in pairs or in small groups to find out about the childhood goals of their favorite authors. Tell students to use reference materials to discover what ambitions these authors had in their younger days and to find out whether or not these goals were realized. Have students share their findings with the rest of the class. Then invite comments about the similarities and differences students note among the different authors' goals. Have students tell if they share any goals in common with their favorite authors.   WHOLE CLASS ENRICHMENT

INTERVIEW AS A LITERARY GENRE

Review the features of a written interview.

Review with students what they might expect to learn about someone from reading an interview. *(facts about the person's childhood, education, hobbies, job, ambitions, family life)* Remind students that "Lee Bennett Hopkins Interviews Johanna Hurwitz" contains this kind of information.

Have students write a brief interview.

Have students interview friends, relatives, teachers, or community members and record the answers in a question-answer format or in a narrative form that contains direct quotes as in the selection. Remind students to be sure to quote their subjects' comments exactly and to include important events in their subjects' lives.   CHALLENGE: WRITING

CREATING MUSICAL WORDS FOR INSTRUMENTS

Discuss words that imitate sounds.

Have students name some words that imitate sounds; for example, *hiss* for a snake's sound and *buzz* for a bee's sound. Write *onomatopoeia* on the chalkboard; explain that it is the name for words that imitate sounds.

Have students list sound words to describe musical instruments.

Have each student think of five musical instruments and either recall or create sound words to describe the instruments. For example, "strum, strum, strum" could describe a guitar; "plink, plink, plink" could describe the sound of a piano. Have students list the words and read them aloud for others to guess what instruments are being described. **Language Arts Master 13** can be used with this activity.   SPEAKING/LISTENING

READING EVERY DAY

Meeting author Johanna Hurwitz might make students want to know about other authors of books they've enjoyed reading. The following biographies provide a glimpse of two authors' lives, "the story behind their stories."

Laura Ingalls Wilder by Gwenda Blair. Putnam, © 1981. The life of the author of the much-loved Little House books, this biography focuses on her early years and experiences living on the American frontier in the late 1800s.

To the Point: A Story About E. B. White by David Collins. Carolrhoda Books, © 1989. This popular author began writing as a child. Among the many literary honors E. B. White received was the Laura Ingalls Wilder Award.

Reader's Journal   **p 79**
Extending Reading

KEEP PLUGGING AWAY

To focus on the idea of believing in yourself, students recall a time when something was difficult for them and use this experience to create and write about a character who had the same problem and overcame it.

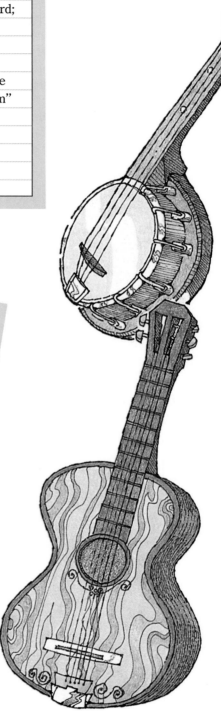

Selection Support

SKILL TRACE: HOMOPHONES				
Introduction	Practice	Test	Reteach	Maintain
TE 392	420	443	461	464	550

VOCABULARY

Homophones

OBJECTIVE   Understanding words that sound alike but have different meanings.

1. WARM-UP

Present familiar homophones in context.

Write the following sentences on the chalkboard and have them read aloud:

1. **We ate lunch together.** (had food)

2. **It is eight o'clock.** (number indicating time)

Point to the words *ate* and *eight* and repeat them. Ask students what they notice about these words. (*They sound alike but are spelled differently*.) Have students tell the meaning of each underlined word and what helped them to know its meaning. (*the other words in the sentence; the context*) Ask students to give some other examples of words that sound the same but are spelled differently, or provide some examples: *buy, by; road, rode; meet, meat*. Write these on the chalkboard.

State the objective.

Tell students they will learn about homophones, words that are pronounced the same but have different spellings and different meanings.

2. TEACH

Explain why knowing how to recognize homophones is important.

Recognizing homophones and knowing their meanings helps readers better understand what they are reading. Knowing the meanings of homophones will help students use the correct one when they write.

Present a strategy for identifying homophones.

Explain that there is a strategy students can use to help them understand homophones. Use the other words in the sentence to figure out the meaning of the homophone being used. Also look for spelling clues in the homophone itself. As examples, write the following homophone pairs on the board and explain the spelling clues:

meat — meet (The one meaning "food" has the word *eat* in it.)
heard — herd (The one to do with listening has the word *ear* in it.)

> **58**
>
> **TEACHING CHART 58: HOMOPHONES**
>
> **1.** Johanna Hurwitz always wanted (to, too) be a writer.
>   She thought about being a librarian, (to, too).
> **2.** She (red, read) many books at the library.
>   One book with a (red, read) cover caught her eye.
> **3.** Mrs. Hurwitz sometimes will (right, write) about things she learned from children.
>   She is (right, write) when she says that reading is fun.

Model the strategy. Read the first pair of sentences on the Teaching Chart. Explain that you know from the words *wanted* and *be a writer* that *to* is the correct homophone for the first sentence. The correct homophone for the second sentence is *too*, meaning "also," because Mrs. Hurwitz's career as a librarian was in addition to her career as a writer.

3. GUIDED PRACTICE

Check for understanding. Before continuing have students explain how to identify which of the words in a homophone pair fits in a sentence. (*Think of the spelling of each word and try each word in the sentence. Decide which meaning makes sense.*)

Guide students in using the strategy. Have students use the strategy to select which words correctly complete the remaining sentences. Have students explain the clues that helped them.

4. WRAP-UP

Summarize instruction. Review why it is important for readers to be able to tell the difference between homophones. (*so as not to get confused about what they are reading*) Have someone remind the other students how to decide which homophone to use in a sentence. (*See which meaning makes sense.*)

Provide independent practice. Options for independent practice are shown in the Resource Center below.

Meeting Individual Needs

RETEACHING Use the activity on page 464 and Masters 1–4 in the Teacher Resource Kit.

CHALLENGE Use the activity on page 464 and Master 13 in the Teacher Resource Kit.

ACHIEVING ENGLISH PROFICIENCY Use the activity on page 464 and Master 23 in the Teacher Resource Kit.

Workbook page 99

NAME _____

VOCABULARY

Homophones

REMEMBER: Homophones are words that sound the same but have different spellings and meanings. Use spelling and context to decide the correct meaning of homophones.

A. Read each sentence. Write the homophone that fits the sentence.

1. When Johanna Hurwitz was _____eight_____ years old, she told stories to her younger brother. (eight, ate)

2. She _____knew_____ that she would be a writer someday. (new, knew)

3. She began to _____write_____ down some of the stories she had made up. (right, write)

4. Johanna hoped that _____one_____ day some of her stories would be published. (one, won)

5. She thought it would be exciting to _____see_____ a book she had written in the library. (see, sea)

6. Johanna could not believe that people would really want to _____buy_____ a book she had written. (by, buy)

7. She knew she had reached her goal when she saw her book for _____sale_____ in a bookstore. (sail, sale)

B. Underline the word from each homophone pair that you did not use in the sentences on this page. On separate paper, write new sentences showing the correct use of these words. See Teacher Notes.

Homophones   "Lee Bennett Hopkins Interviews Johanna Hurwitz"   **99**

RESOURCE CENTER

◀ **Workbook page 99** is intended for use by all students.

Skills Practice 91 ▶ may be assigned for additional practice.

Workbook reuse option: Have students list as many pairs of homophones as they can. They can use the margins of the workbook page.

Skills Practice 91

NAME _____

SKILLS PRACTICE 91

Homophones

Homophones are words that sound the same but have different spellings and meanings. Use spelling and context clues to decide the correct meaning of homophones.

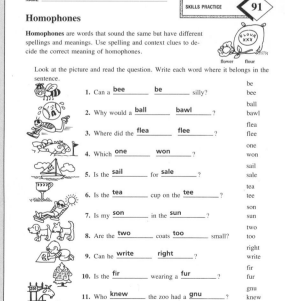

flower flour

Look at the picture and read the question. Write each word where it belongs in the sentence.

1. Can a **bee** _____be_____ silly?
2. Why would a **ball** _____bawl_____ ?
3. Where did the **flea** _____flee_____ ?
4. Which **one** _____won_____ ?
5. Is the **sail** for _____sale_____ ?
6. Is the **tea** cup on the _____tee_____ ?
7. Is my **son** in the _____sun_____ ?
8. Are the **two** coats _____too_____ small?
9. Can he **write** _____right_____ ?
10. Is the **fir** wearing a _____fur_____ ?
11. Who **knew** the zoo had a _____gnu_____ ?
12. Can the **sore** bird _____soar_____ ?

be
bee

ball
bawl

flea
flee

one
won

sail
sale

tea
tee

son
sun

two
too

right
write

fir
fur

gnu
knew

soar
sore

LEVEL 8   "Lee Bennett Hopkins Interviews Johanna Hurwitz"   **91**

SKILL TRACE: INFERENCES				
Introduction	Practice	Test	Reteach	Maintain
TE 380	394	442	461	462	596

COMPREHENSION

Inferences

OBJECTIVE   Making inferences about time, location, people, and feelings and attitudes.

Review inferences.

Remind students that to make an inference means to use clues to figure out information not stated by an author. Tell students that clues come from the words and phrases the author has written and from their own experience or prior knowledge — "what I know" clues.

Use Teaching Chart to practice making inferences.

Display the Teaching Chart. Have students read the sentences. Explain that they tell about Johanna's actions, but they do not say exactly how she feels.

> **TEACHING CHART 59: MAKING INFERENCES** **59**
>
> **1.** At the baseball game, Johanna screams, cheers, and jumps up and down. (Johanna feels excited, thrilled.)
> **2.** The music is slow and sad. As Johanna listens to it, her eyes fill with tears. (Johanna feels sad.)

Discuss word and "what I know" clues.

Ask how Johanna feels at the baseball game. (*excited, thrilled*) Ask which of the words give clues to how she feels. (*screams, cheers, jumps up and down*) Then ask how they know that screaming, cheering, and jumping up and down means that someone is excited and thrilled. (*They have done this themselves or they have seen others do it.*) Point out that students are using their own knowledge, or "what I know" clues, and experience. Discuss the second sentence in the same manner.

Provide independent practice.

Options for independent practice are shown in the Resource Center below.

Workbook page 100

COMPREHENSION   NAME _____

Inference

REMEMBER: Use story clues and what you already know to figure out things that the writer did not state.

A. Read each paragraph. Use clues to answer the questions.

1. Patricia looked around at all the books on the shelves. There were so many of them! Mrs. Jones finished filling out the card and gave it to Patricia. She said Patricia could take out two books. Patricia had a big smile on her face as she took the card. She could hardly wait to show her parents. She got her books and packed them in her schoolbag. She was sad to leave, but she had homework to do.

   a. Where was Patricia? Patricia was at the library.

   b. Who was Mrs. Jones? Mrs. Jones was the librarian.

   c. How did Patricia feel about her card? She felt proud and happy about it.

2. As she passed the schoolyard, she saw her little brother. His pants were torn at the knee, and he was crying. His baseball glove was on the ground nearby and several boys with gloves stood near him. Patricia wiped his tears. She saw that his knee was cut. Since the school nurse had already left for the day and the school was locked, she told her brother to walk home with her.

   a. Why was her brother crying? He was crying because he had hurt himself.

   b. What had he been playing? He had been playing baseball.

   c. About what time of day was it? It must have been late afternoon.

B. On separate paper, describe some clues that tell you a person is sad. See Teacher Notes.

100   "Lee Bennett Hopkins Interviews Johanna Hurwitz"   Inference

RESOURCE CENTER

◀ **Workbook page 100** is intended for use by all students.

Skills Practice 92 ▶ may be assigned for additional practice.

Workbook reuse option: Have students underline the clues they used to help them answer the questions.

Skills Practice 92

NAME _____   SKILLS PRACTICE **92**

Inference

When you make inferences, you think of ideas that are not stated in a story but are based on information in it. You also use what you know about events like those in the story to make an inference.

Story clues
What I know
Inference

A. Read each set of sentences. Make inferences. Circle each answer.

1. The girls saw the playing field with four bases. Where were the girls?
   swimming pool   ball park   zoo

2. The neighbors were waiting for the mail. Who were the neighbors waiting for?
   police officer   letter carrier   firefighter

3. Mom gave Dan some fruit. What did she give him?
   a carrot   a cookie   an apple

4. They sat in the yard looking at the stars. When were they in the yard?
   in the morning   at night   at noon

B. Read the story about Mario. Make inferences as you read each paragraph. Write your answers.

   Mrs. Bello was visiting Mario's family. She looked over in the corner. "What big leaves that has!" She said. "Where did you get it?"

5. What was Mrs. Bello looking at? a plant

   Mario smiled. "I grew it from a seed. Now I can't reach the top of it. I take care of it all by myself, too."

6. How did Mario feel? proud

   Mario was glad Mrs. Bello liked what he had done. After she left, he had an idea. Mario clipped a leafy stem and put it in some water. He got a pot and some earth ready. When it was time, he went to work. He would have a present for Mrs. Bello the next time she came.

7. What was Mario's idea? to start a new plant for Mrs. Bello

92   LEVEL 8   "Lee Bennett Hopkins Interviews Johanna Hurwitz"

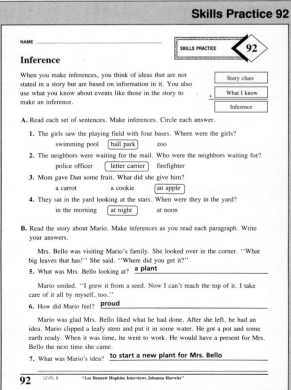

WORD STUDY
Suffixes -ion, -tion

OBJECTIVE Using structural analysis to determine word meaning.

Review definition of suffix and give examples.

Review with students that a suffix is a letter or group of letters added to the end of a base word. Point out that a suffix changes the meaning and sometimes the part of speech of the word to which it is added. As an example, write *protect + ion = protection* on the chalkboard and explain that when the suffix *-ion* is added to the word *protect*, it forms the new word *protection*. Adding the suffix changed *protect*, "to care for and keep safe," from a verb to a noun, "the state of being cared for and being kept safe."

Use Teaching Chart to present words with suffixes.

Display the Teaching Chart. Have students study the equations at the top. Ask students to form the new words by adding the suffix *-ion* to the base words. Then have students use the words to complete the sentences.

TEACHING CHART 60: SUFFIX *-ION, -TION* **60**

collect + ion =   concentrate + ion =
elect + ion =   educate + ion =

1. If you voted in an ___(election)___, which Johanna Hurwitz book would you pick as your favorite?
2. In Mrs. Hurwitz's story "The Recital," Maria gave all her ___(concentration)___ to her piano playing.
3. Johanna's ___(education)___ prepared her to be a librarian.
4. Johanna Hurwitz has created a ___(collection)___ of books for children.

Provide independent practice.

Options for independent practice are shown in the Resource Center below.

Workbook page 101

NAME _____

Suffixes *-ion*, *-tion* ◆ WORD STUDY

REMEMBER: The suffixes *-ion* and *-tion* are added to verbs to form nouns.

A. Write a word from the box next to the base word from which it was made.

| collection | direction | election | invention | perfection | protection |

1. invent _invention_
2. collect _collection_
3. elect _election_
4. perfect _perfection_
5. direct _direction_
6. protect _protection_

B. Write a word from the box to complete each sentence.

Some people want to be famous or rich. Others want to think up some exciting _invention_ or win an important _election_. But Johanna Hurwitz decided at an early age that her life would go in a different _direction_. She had always enjoyed getting books from the library. It had a large _collection_ of children's books. Whenever Johanna took a book, she carefully put it in a bag. This gave it some _protection_ in case of rain or snow. Because she loved books so much, she decided to be a librarian and a writer. As a writer today, she wants her stories to be just right. You might say that she hopes for _perfection_.

C. On separate paper, use words ending in *-ion* or *-tion* to write a pair of rhyming sentences. See Teacher Notes.

Suffixes -ion, -tion   "Lee Bennett Hopkins Interviews Johanna Hurwitz" **101**

RESOURCE CENTER

◄ **Workbook page 101** is intended for use by all students.

Skills Practice 93 ► may be assigned for additional practice.

Workbook reuse option: Have students draw a line to separate each base word from its suffix in each "*-ion*" word they have written.

Skills Practice 93

NAME _____

SKILLS PRACTICE **93**

Suffix *-ion*, *-tion*

The suffixes *-ion* and *-tion* change a verb to a noun. When a word ends in *e*, you must drop the *e* before adding the suffix.

Circle the word each phrase describes. Then write a sentence for each word. **Sentences will vary.**

1. what you do to help people meet   [introduce]   generation   introduction
2. something your teachers give you   collect   collection   [instruction]
3. something you make   create   institution   [creation]
4. to point something out   indication   investigation   [indicate]
5. a drawing of how to do something   [illustration]   correction   illustrate
6. to create a picture or model   illustration   collection   [illustrate]
7. what you show feelings with   [expression]   associate   express
8. a group that gets together   expression   associate   [association]

LEVEL 8   "Lee Bennett Hopkins Interviews Johanna Hurwitz"   **93**

SKILL TRACE: SUFFIX				
Introduction	Practice	Test	Reteach	Maintain
TE 192	226	272	311	313	396

WORD STUDY

Suffix -*ness*

OBJECTIVE Using structural analysis to determine word meaning.

Review suffix -ness.

Remind students they have already learned several suffixes and how to use the meanings of suffixes to help them figure out words in their reading and form new words in their writing. Remind students that -*ness* is a suffix they have learned. Ask for its definition. (*"being" or "state of being"*) Write examples on the chalkboard: *closeness, goodness, sadness.* Have students identify the base words, discuss what they mean, and explain how the meanings change with the addition of the suffix. (*changes adjectives to nouns*) Then have volunteers use the words in sentences.

Present suffixed words in context.

You may wish to write the sentences below on the chalkboard. Answers are shown in red. Have students read each sentence and identify the suffixed word. Have students use the meaning of the base word, the meaning of the suffix, and the context of the sentence to define the suffixed word.

> **1.** Johanna Hurwitz's kindness shows through in the way she speaks. (kindness — "being kind")
> **2.** Few things give her so much happiness as writing and being a librarian. (happiness — "being happy")
> **3.** The nearness of her home to the public library allowed her to visit it often. (nearness — "being near")

Provide independent practice.

An independent activity is shown in the Resource Center below.

RESOURCE CENTER

Skills Practice 94 ▶ may be assigned for additional practice.

Skills Practice 94

SKILLS PRACTICE 94

Suffix -*ness*

The suffix -*ness* means "state, quality, or condition of." Remember to change *y* to *i* before adding -*ness*.

A. Read the story. Complete the sentences. Use words from the box.

coldness	darkness	silliness
dampness	quickness	stickiness

sickness = the condition of being sick

Yipes! The lights are out and the door has slammed shut. Well, here I am, alone in the **darkness** in the cellar, where there are crawly things and **dampness** covering all the walls. But I know it is just plain **silliness** to be scared. The **stickiness** of the spider webs can't hurt me. There is no alligator to eat me up with such **quickness** that no one will know where I went. There is no monster to freeze me to death with **coldness** . So, am I scared of the dark? Oh, yes!

B. One word in each sentence should have -*ness* added to it. Circle that word. Then rewrite the sentence correctly.

1. (Lonely) can be a problem for sailors.
   Loneliness can be a problem for sailors.

2. It is hard to face the (empty) of the open sea for week after week.
   It is hard to face the emptiness of the open sea for week after week.

3. Sailors must learn to deal with their (sad).
   Sailors must learn to deal with their sadness.

94 LEVEL 8 "Lee Bennett Hopkins Interviews Johanna Hurwitz"

CURRICULUM CONNECTIONS

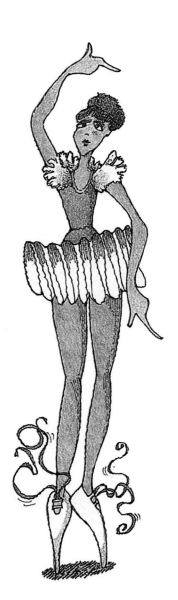

FUTURE FACES ART

Provide students with large sheets of paper. Have them draw portraits of themselves as they wish to appear in the future. They may depict themselves in a particular career or profession, or in a desired setting.

PRACTICE MAKES PERFECT! CAREERS

Remind students that according to Johanna Hurwitz, becoming a good writer takes practice, just as it does to become a good baseball player or fine ballet dancer. Have students research the steps it takes to become a professional baseball player or a ballet dancer and make an oral presentation. Students may include information about the sport of baseball or the steps a ballet dancer must learn. Students may also want to include photographs or drawings to show during their presentation.

GOALS TO GREATNESS SOCIAL STUDIES

Ask students to think about people they admire in a field—entertainment, literature, sports, science, politics, and so on. Have students work in pairs or in small groups. Have each group choose one person and use reference sources such as biographical dictionaries, junior encyclopedias, biographies, and autobiographies to discover what that person's goals were in early life. Have the group create a chart that compares the early goals with what that person is doing or has accomplished in his or her adult life.

TIME LINE TRIVIA MATHEMATICS

Have each student make a time line that charts the life of a favorite person from history; students may choose the same person whom they researched in the social studies activity described above. Tell students to begin with the subject's birthdate and mark off as many important events and particular stages in his or her life for which they can gather information. Encourage students to locate facts about the subject's childhood, early adulthood, middle years, and so on. Then have students figure out how old the person was at the various dates along the time line. **Curriculum Connection Master 13** can be used with this activity.

Checkpoint

USING THE CHECKPOINT PAGES

Use Checkpoints for informal evaluation.

Checkpoints are designed to help students and teachers monitor and improve student progress. For students, the Checkpoints serve as another step in the development of their ability to control their own learning. They see their own strengths and weaknesses even as the teacher does. For the teacher, the Checkpoints offer a systematic approach to informal assessment. Each Checkpoint helps identify areas of strength and weakness and then offers ideas for reteaching and extra practice before the formal assessment that comes at the end of the unit.

The extra-help ideas in Checkpoint lessons give additional practice to those students having difficulty with the targeted skill while allowing them to remain with the regular reading group. Extra-help ideas can also be used effectively with individual students or in small groups.

Informally diagnose strengths and weaknesses.

Checkpoints are in the same format as the Unit Skills Tests; you might review the directions before assigning the pages. Direct students to complete the pages shown in the Resource Center. Then have students work together to correct their papers, and encourage them to explain the thinking behind their answers. This affords you an opportunity to observe not only how students arrived at their answers, but also to identify and explain any item types that are causing difficulty. Note that in the Resource Center, questions are labeled by skill so that you can quickly assess areas in which a particular student needs additional help.

The following skills are included in this Checkpoint.

suffix -*ment*
signs and symbols

For your information, the Checkpoint pages at the end of this unit include the skills listed below.

suffixes -*ion*, -*tion*
inferences
homophones
vocabulary — Story Critical words

PROVIDING EXTRA HELP

Provide extra help with the suffix -ment.

Strengthen reading comprehension by linking reading, listening, and vocabulary development. Help students see how the suffix -*ment* changes the way a word is used in a sentence. Write on the board sentence pairs such as these and read them with students.

1. Five people govern our town. They form the town's government.

2. Fresh paint will improve the looks of that old bike. It will be an improvement.

3. I was embarrassed by that mistake. It was an embarrassment.

4. Herbert and Rosalie will entertain the guests with a song or two. They hope everyone likes this entertainment.

5. I will pay for the repairs. I'll put my payment in the mail tomorrow.

6. Carefully measure each ingredient for the muffins. If the measurements are not correct, the muffins may not taste good.

7. I truly enjoyed reading that book. I'll tell all my friends about my enjoyment.

8. I will advertise my old bike in the neighborhood newspaper. I hope lots of people read my advertisement.

Then provide word pairs from which students can create similar sentences, first orally and then in writing.

Provide extra help with signs and symbols.

Reinforce this study skill by making a bulletin board or display of common symbols and signs. Have students draw or cut from magazines symbols and signs that have special meanings, such as road signs, exit signs, and warning signs and symbols. Have them write a sentence or two for each symbol explaining what the symbol means and where it can be found. Post students' work on the bulletin board. Encourage students to continue to add new symbols and signs as they find them.

Workbook page 102

RESOURCE CENTER

◀ These pages provide informal assessment in the format of the Unit Skills Tests. ▶

Workbook page 103

NAME _____

Checkpoint

A. Read the paragraph. Then fill in the circle beside the correct answer.

Joey and Gail decided to sell lemonade. First they brought some lemons and squeezed them. Then they measured the right amounts of water and sugar. After completing this <u>measurement</u> and combining their ingredients, they set up a stand on the <u>pavement</u> by their house. Mr. Neil, their neighbor, bought the first glass. In his <u>judgment</u>, the lemonade was delicious. To the children's <u>amazement,</u> they earned seven dollars selling lemonade.

suffix *-ment*
1. Which suffix was added to the underlined words?
- (a) *-ness*
- (b) *-ment*
- (c) *-ing*
- (d) *-or*

suffix *-ment*
2. What is the meaning of <u>judgment</u>?
- (a) one who judges
- (b) result of judging
- (c) able to judge
- (d) opposite of judging

suffix *-ment*
3. What is the meaning of <u>amazement</u>?
- (a) state of being amazed
- (b) one who amazes
- (c) very amazed
- (d) not amazed

suffix *-ment*
4. Which base word changes its spelling when *-ment* is added?
- (a) measure
- (b) pave
- (c) judge
- (d) amaze

102   Checkpoint

NAME _____

B. Read the weather chart. Then fill in the circle beside the correct answer.

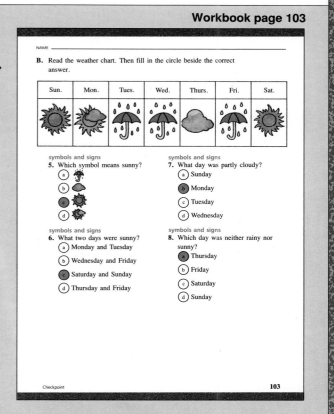

Sun.	Mon.	Tues.	Wed.	Thurs.	Fri.	Sat.

symbols and signs
5. Which symbol means sunny?
- (a)
- (b)
- (c)
- (d)

symbols and signs
6. What two days were sunny?
- (a) Monday and Tuesday
- (b) Wednesday and Friday
- (c) Saturday and Sunday
- (d) Thursday and Friday

symbols and signs
7. What day was partly cloudy?
- (a) Sunday
- (b) Monday
- (c) Tuesday
- (d) Wednesday

symbols and signs
8. Which day was neither rainy nor sunny?
- (a) Thursday
- (b) Friday
- (c) Saturday
- (d) Sunday

Checkpoint   103

LITERATURE LINK

OBJECTIVE Recognizing the elements of setting in a story.

INTRODUCING AND READING THE LESSON

Tap students' prior knowledge.

Have students describe where they are right now. Encourage them to give as many details about the place as they can. These should include details about location; the people around them; the colors, smells, shapes, sounds, and things in the room itself; and how they feel about where they are right now. Ask them which details let them know that they are in a classroom.

Discuss setting.

Explain that just as students used details to describe where they are, an author uses details to let you know where a story takes place. This description is called the setting. Tell students that authors use all kinds of details, including sounds, colors, smells, and textures to help you visualize where things in the story are taking place. Point out that another part of setting is time. Stories can be set in the past, in the present, or in the future. Even the season of the year or time of day can be important in a story.

Point out that sometimes the author does not say exactly where and when a story takes place. When this happens, students can guess the setting of the story. Suggest that students use clues such as pictures, actions of characters, and their own experiences to help them figure out the setting.

Explain the usefulness of knowing the setting.

Explain that knowing the setting of a story helps readers form a picture in their minds of where and when the story takes place. Point out that knowing the setting helps readers better visualize and enjoy the story.

State the objective.

Tell students that in this lesson they will learn how to recognize the setting of a story.

Refer students to their texts.

Have students turn to pages 212–213 in their books and read the lesson.

LITERATURE LINK

Why is the story setting important?

In "The Recital," you read about the place where Maria's recital was held.

> At the front of the recital hall there was a sign showing the way to the room for Mrs. Howard's recital. The room was large, and there seemed to be over a hundred chairs lined up for the audience.

Can you imagine how Maria felt as she waited to play the piano in front of so many people in such a large room? If so, you know why this setting is important to the story.

When and Where

The setting of a story is where and when the story takes place. Sometimes stories happen in places you know. Other times, they happen in faraway or make-believe lands. Stories can take place long ago, today, or many years from now.

Learning About Literature/Author's Craft

An author may use words alone or add pictures to help you see the setting in your mind. Picturing the setting can make you feel like you are there. You can understand, for example, why playing in a recital hall made Maria nervous.

You will enjoy the story more if you picture where and when it is happening. So, try keeping the setting in mind as you read.

As you read "A Day When Frogs Wear Shoes," ask yourself where and when the story takes place. Then put yourself in the story to make the time and place seem real.

Looking at the Setting of a Story

Review the main points of the lesson.

DISCUSSING THE LESSON

Check students' understanding of the lesson with these questions.

Page 212   What should you remember about story settings? (Possible responses: They help tell the story; they can be real or make-believe; they can take place in the past, present, or future.)

Page 213   How can knowing the setting of a story help you to understand the story better? (It helps you picture the story in your mind.)

WRAP-UP

Direct students to the next selection.

Suggest that students look at the pictures and look for clues that describe the setting of the next selection, "A Day When Frogs Wear Shoes." Encourage students to think about how the setting is important to the story.

	Teaching Sequence	Trade Books and Resources	Meeting Individual Needs	Integrated Language Arts / Cross Curriculum
The Bridge Pages 404–405	**Maintain** Figurative Language	• Teaching Chart 61 • Workbook 104 • Skills Practice 95		
PART 1 **Vocabulary Strategies** Pages 406–407	**Develop Concepts** Making Figurative Comparisons **Teach Vocabulary** **STORY CRITICAL WORDS:** **boring, customers,** fenders, **hike,** reminded (Tested words are boldfaced.)	• Teaching Chart 62 • Workbook 105 • Skills Practice 96	**SUPPORT WORDS:** absolutely, congressmen, especially, hood, introduces, minnows, webbed • Skills Practice 97 **CHARACTER/SETTING WORDS:** Gloria, Huey, Julian, Ralph	**WRITING/SPEAKING ACTIVITY:** Use new vocabulary in figurative language to describe a special car. • Spelling Connection 52
PART 2 **Reading & Responding** Pages 408–419	**Build Background** **Develop a Purpose for Reading** **Guide the Reading Process** **Selection Follow-Up**	• Reader's Journal 80–83 • Workbook 106 **I▸T KIT** Discussing Fact and Fiction Poster; Singing a Tongue-Twister Song **READING EVERY DAY** *More Stories Julian Tells,* by A. Cameron *Yellow Blue Jay,* by J. Hurwitz	**EXTRA HELP:** Making an Activity Chart for Story Characters **ACHIEVING ENGLISH PROFICIENCY:** Listing Boring Activities • Achieving English Proficiency Master 24	**Language Arts Connections** **WRITING TO LEARN:** Write character riddles. • Writing Master 16 **SPEAKING/LISTENING:** Using Figurative Language; Competing with Comparisons; Creating Television Commercials; Developing Lists of Words Related to Cars **WRITING:** Writing Realistic Fiction; Writing from the Frog's Point of View • Language Arts Master 14
PART 3 **Selection Support** Pages 420–425		**Practice** • Teaching Charts 63–65 • Workbook 107–110 • Skills Practice 98–101 Homophones (Tested) Suffix *-ment* (Tested) Suffixes *-ion, -tion* (Tested) Symbols and Signs (Tested) **Maintain** • Skills Practice 102 Suffixes *-able, -ible*		**Curriculum Connections** **SCIENCE:** Researching and Writing Facts About Frogs • Curriculum Connection Master 14 **MUSIC:** Listening to and Writing a Song About a Frog **ART:** Researching and Designing Wheeled Vehicles

A Day When Frogs Wear Shoes

written by Ann Cameron
illustrated by Ann Strugnell

SUMMARY *Julian, his brother, Huey, and their friend, Gloria, are bored on a hot summer day and decide to visit Julian and Huey's father at his car repair shop. Their father agrees that it is a very hot day—the sort of day when frogs wear shoes. Father and children go to the river. The children chase frogs to see whether they really do wear shoes on hot days. They do not—but when the children get back, every one of their shoes has a frog in it! Ann Cameron received an* **American Library Association Notable Children's Books** *listing in 1986 for* More Stories Julian Tells.

AMERICAN

LIBRARY

ASSOCIATION

1986

The Bridge

SKILL TRACE: FIGURATIVE LANGUAGE	
Introduced in Level 7	Maintain
	TE 404

LITERATURE

Teaching Figurative Language

OBJECTIVE Recognizing and interpreting figurative language.

1. WARM-UP

Use a known statement to demonstrate figurative language orally.

Tell students they will listen to two statements about Johanna Hurwitz, the subject of the previous selection. Explain that the statements have about the same meaning. Have them listen to decide how the statements are different. *(The second statement makes its point through an unusual comparison.)*

> **Johanna Hurwitz is excited about baseball.**
> **Johanna Hurwitz has baseball fever.**

Discuss figurative language.

Reread the sentences. Point out that the second statement shows how much Johanna Hurwitz likes baseball by comparing her excitement about the sport to something else. Ask what her excitement over baseball is compared to. *(an illness or fever)* Ask whether students think this excitement over baseball is really like an illness. *(no)* Explain that authors often use exaggerated comparisons to make their writing funny and lively or to make an idea clear and to create colorful word pictures in their readers' minds. Exaggerated comparisons are one kind of figurative language, or language that does not mean exactly what it says. Other kinds of figurative language appeal to readers' senses of sight, hearing, smell, touch, and taste.

State the objective.

Tell students they will review how to recognize and understand figurative language in their reading.

2. TEACH

Explain why understanding figurative language is important.

Being able to recognize and understand figurative language helps readers understand what they read, as well as see and write things in colorful ways.

Present a strategy for understanding figurative language.

Explain that there is a strategy students can use to help them recognize and understand figurative language. First, look for statements in which two very different things are being compared, such as excitement about a sport with a fever. [Sometimes, but not always, the word *like* or *as* shows the comparison.] Then, try to state in your own words what the author means by the comparison, looking for clues, if necessary, in nearby sentences. Last, ask yourselves what extra meaning the figurative language adds to the author's idea. Does it help you understand the idea or see it more clearly?

TEACHING CHART 61: FIGURATIVE LANGUAGE 61

1. Books fed Johanna Hurwitz's mind. (books and food; books helped Hurwitz's mind grow)
2. Johanna Hurwitz says good musicians practice until their fingers almost drop off. (fingers feeling tired and fingers dropping off; Johanna Hurwitz says good musicians practice a lot)
3. Because Johanna Hurwitz read a lot, her vocabulary grew as fast as a weed. (growing vocabulary and a weed; because Hurwitz read a lot, her vocabulary grew quickly)

Model the strategy.

Display the Teaching Chart and tell students that all the sentences on it use figurative language. Read the first sentence and explain that it compares books and food. People cannot eat books, of course, but books give the mind what it needs to grow, just as food gives the body what it needs to grow. The sentence means that books helped Johanna Hurwitz's mind grow.

3. GUIDED PRACTICE

Check for understanding.

Before going on, have students explain how to recognize and understand figurative language. *(Look for statements in which two very different things are being compared, state in your own words what the author means by the comparison, and ask what extra meaning it adds to the author's idea.)*

Guide students in using the strategy.

Have students use the strategy to tell what two things are being compared in each of the remaining sentences and what each sentence really means.

4. WRAP-UP

Summarize instruction.

Review why it is helpful for readers to understand figurative language and how figurative language can be recognized. *(Understanding figurative language helps in understanding what is read and seeing things in new, colorful ways; look for sentences that seem unusual and for things that are being compared in unusual ways.)*

Provide independent practice.

Options for independent practice are shown in the Resource Center below.

5. APPLICATION

Students will analyze figurative language as they read "A Day When Frogs Wear Shoes." The symbol ✔ marks specific questions and activities that apply this skill.

Workbook page 104

RESOURCE CENTER

Skills Practice 95

LITERATURE

NAME _____

Figurative Language

REMEMBER: **Figurative language** is a special use of words. Writers may compare things that are alike in one way but different in every other way. Figurative language can help you see things in a new and exciting way.

A. Read the sentences. Notice the special use of words. Write what the words really mean.

1. The cloud rolled like a large cotton ball across the sky.
   The cloud was moving. It was white and puffy.

2. The puppy's kiss felt like a wet rosebud against my cheek.
   The puppy's tongue felt wet and soft.

3. Baseball is my life!
   I enjoy baseball very much.

4. The morning sun is like a red, rubber ball.
   The rising sun looks large and red and round.

5. Mahalia is a bookworm.
   Mahalia loves to read.

6. Her house is overflowing with books.
   There are many, many books in her house.

B. Which special use of words did you like best? On separate paper, write a paragraph about something you enjoy. Use figurative language by making comparisons. See Teacher Notes.

104   "A Day When Frogs Wear Shoes"   Figurative Language

◀ **Workbook page 104** is intended for use by all students.

Skills Practice 95 ▶ may be assigned for additional practice.

Workbook reuse option: Have students underline all the words on the page that are used as figurative language.

NAME _____

SKILLS PRACTICE ◆ 95

Figurative Language

Writers often compare two things to make reading more interesting. Sometimes, but not always, the word *like* or *as* shows the comparison.

   The puppy was as active *as* a jumping bean.

   The river is a silver ribbon.

These two sentences show how writers compare things that are alike in some way or ways but different in other ways. Puppies and jumping beans are alike in being active. Rivers and silver ribbons are alike in that each looks long, curved, and shiny.

A. Read these sentences. Draw a line under the two things that are compared. Write how the two things are alike.

1. David is a computer of baseball facts.   Both David and a computer have a lot of facts.

2. My bad mood was a dark cloud around the day.   A bad mood and a dark cloud make a day seem less bright.

3. The breeze was like a gentle touch.   A breeze and a touch can feel soft.

4. That room is like an oven.   Both the room and an oven are very hot.

5. Joanna's hair is as black as night.   Both Joanna's hair and the night are dark.

B. Read the sentences. Notice the special use of words. Write what the underlined words really mean.

6. The butterfly is a flying rainbow.   brightly colored

7. Olivia is the class clown.   very funny

8. They are birds of a feather.   they are alike

LEVEL 8   "A Day When Frogs Wear Shoes"   95

Vocabulary Strategies

Developing Concepts

Have students use prior knowledge to make figurative statements about cars.

Have students make figurative statements about cars as a starting point for teaching vocabulary. Write the word *Cars* on the chalkboard and ask students to name as many parts of a car as they can. Write these on the board as well. Then remind students that they have learned that figurative language creates colorful word pictures. Ask them what figurative comparisons they can think of to describe how a car or its parts look, how a car sounds, or how it feels to ride in one. *(Possible answer: The car's headlights looked like bright yellow eyes.)*

Teaching Vocabulary

Discuss meanings of Story Critical words.

Read each context sentence on the Teaching Chart and identify the new word. Then use the questions below to help students understand each word. When necessary, provide a definition.

> **TEACHING CHART 62: VOCABULARY**
>
> **62**
>
> 1. **fenders** (metal frames over the wheels of a car)
>   The *fenders* on our old car were so dented that the wheels below them seemed to be pushed out.
> 2. **reminded** (caused to remember)
>   My dad almost forgot we were going to the car repair shop, but I *reminded* him.
> 3. **customers** (people who buy things or services from a store or business)
>   Other *customers* at the shop had brought in their cars to have them worked on.
> 4. **boring** (dull, uninteresting)
>   Waiting for our car to be fixed was so *boring* that my head as well as my feet went to sleep.
> 5. **hike** (a long walk)
>   While we waited Dad and I took a *hike* to the park, even though it was more than a mile from the shop.

fenders

1. Which words in sentence 1 give you clues about where on a car the fenders are? (*wheels below them*)   STRATEGY: CONTEXT CLUES

reminded

2. What clues in sentence 2 help you figure out the meaning of *reminded*? (forgot, but)   STRATEGY: CONTEXT CLUES

customers

3. What kinds of services might customers at a car repair shop need? (possible answers: flat tire fixed, fenders straightened, car body painted, parts replaced)   STRATEGY: PRIOR KNOWLEDGE

boring

4. What things do you see people do that you think are boring? (possible answers: household chores, waiting in line) **Do you think everyone finds the same things boring? Why not?** (Possible answer: No, because people like different things.)   STRATEGY: CLASSIFICATION

hike

5. What do you do on a hike? (walk a long way) **Would you say you had been on a hike if you walked a block?** (probably not) **Why not?** (because a block is not a very long distance)   STRATEGY: PRIOR KNOWLEDGE

Discuss Support words as needed.

The Glossary of the Student Text includes definitions of the Support words: *congressmen, webbed, absolutely, especially, hood, introduces, minnows.*

Present Character words.

Present and pronounce the Character words before students read the selection: *Ralph, Julian, Huey, Gloria.*

Provide independent practice.

Options for independent practice are shown in the Resource Center below.

WRITING OR SPEAKING ACTIVITY   *Have students use as many new words as possible to tell short stories about a special kind of car that keeps life from being boring. Encourage them to use figurative language to make the stories lively.*

Workbook page 105

NAME _____

SELECTION VOCABULARY

Using New Words

A. Write a word from the box next to its definition.

boring	customers	fenders	hike	reminded

1. a long walk _____ hike
2. people who buy things _____ customers
3. helped someone remember _____ reminded
4. not interesting or fun _____ boring
5. metal frames over wheels _____ fenders

B. Use the words in the box to complete the sentences.

My uncle sells parts for cars. At his shop, _____ customers _____ can buy things to fix their cars or make them nicer. If _____ fenders _____ are dented, my uncle has the tools to fix them. My uncle says the work he does with cars is never _____ boring _____ . He _____ reminded _____ me that someday we can take a _____ hike _____ to his shop to watch him work.

C. Imagine you want your car fixed. On separate paper, write a note that tells what needs to be done. Use at least two words from the box. See Teacher Notes.

Selection Vocabulary   "A Day When Frogs Wear Shoes"   **105**

RESOURCE CENTER

◄ **Workbook page 105** provides practice with Story Critical words.

Skills Practice 96 ► provides additional practice with Story Critical words.

Skills Practice 97 provides practice with Support words.

Spelling Connection Master 52 may be used for spelling instruction with the new vocabulary.

Workbook reuse option: Have students circle the words naming persons, places, or things and draw boxes around the action words in their answers.

Skills Practice 96

NAME _____

SKILLS PRACTICE **96**

Vocabulary: Story Critical Words

A. Study the meaning of each word.

boring not interesting	**hike** a long walk
customers people who buy things	**reminded** helped someone remember
fenders metal frames over the wheels of a car	something

B. Synonyms are words that have similar meanings. Write the vocabulary word that is a synonym for each underlined word.

1. The <u>people who shop</u> are buying apples. _____ customers
2. The movie was <u>not interesting</u>, so Ed left. _____ boring
3. Emma likes to <u>walk</u> in the woods. _____ hike

C. Write the correct vocabulary word to answer each question.

4. What does a car have over its wheels? _____ fenders
5. What does every store need? _____ customers
6. What can you do on a park trail? _____ hike
7. What is a book that isn't interesting? _____ boring

D. Finish each sentence with the correct vocabulary word.

8. A salesperson helps _____ customers _____ .
9. The _____ fenders _____ of a car help keep mud from the wheels.
10. Lorna and her mother took a long _____ hike _____ .
11. Betsy _____ reminded _____ her brother to buy some milk.
12. Sam went to sleep during the _____ boring _____ play.

E. Write the vocabulary word that rhymes with each word.

13. benders _____ fenders
14. storing _____ boring
15. bike _____ hike
16. blinded _____ reminded

96   LEVEL 8   "A Day When Frogs Wear Shoes"   Synonyms

Reading & Responding

Building Background

Motivate discussion using exaggerated statements.

Share the following statements with students and ask whether they think the statements are true. Then ask why an author might write sentences like these. (*possible answers: to make readers laugh, to make a point*)

> **It was so hot that you could fry eggs on the sidewalk.**
> **It was such a boring day that watching paint peel sounded exciting.**

Build background about summer days.

Ask students to think about the statements you read and tell how they feel and what they do during the summer. Have them describe how a very hot day makes them feel. Ask whether they ever get bored and, if so, what they do about it. Then have them express their feelings about summer by making up some exaggerated statements like those they have just read.

Discuss realistic fiction.

Tell students they are about to read a story that is fiction. Explain that fiction is made up by authors and never really happened. Point out that some fiction, called realistic fiction, tells about events that could happen in real life. Mention that the author of the story they will read next, Ann Cameron, often writes realistic fiction stories. Have students find and read the Ann Cameron entry in the About the Author section in the back of their books.

Developing a Purpose for Reading

Option 1
Students set purpose.

ORAL "PREDICTION" LISTS   Have students read the story title and introduction. Tell students to put together this information with the vocabulary discussion and the discussion about what they do about being bored to make some predictions about what will happen in this story. Record students' responses for later use.

WRITING ACTIVITY   Have students work individually or in pairs to create written "Prediction" lists. Tell students to save their lists for later use.

Option 2
Teacher sets purpose.

Have students read to find out what kind of day it is when frogs wear shoes.

Meeting
Individual
Needs

EXTRA HELP   Explain that the next selection is about what three children do on a boring, hot day. Distribute Form 5 in the Teacher Resource Kit, or a plain sheet of paper. As they read, ask students to record any four things the children did that day. After they have finished reading, have volunteers share their chart results and see how many different things were listed.

ACHIEVING ENGLISH PROFICIENCY   Write on the board: *We were watching the grass grow.* Read the sentence to the students. Ask students if they have ever watched grass grow and if they think it would be an interesting thing to do. Write the word *boring* on the board. Tell students that watching grass grow is *boring;* it makes you tired because it's not interesting. Ask students what other things are *boring.* Keep a list on the board. Write on the board: *I'm bored when I watch the grass grow.* Ask students when they are bored. Have them make sentences using the model *"I'm bored when _____ ."* For additional help in story comprehension, use Master 24 in the Teacher Resource Kit.

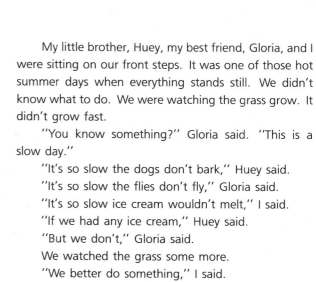

A Day When Frogs Wear Shoes

written by Ann Cameron
illustrated by Ann Strugnell

Frogs wearing shoes? This can't be an ordinary summer day!

My little brother, Huey, my best friend, Gloria, and I were sitting on our front steps. It was one of those hot summer days when everything stands still. We didn't know what to do. We were watching the grass grow. It didn't grow fast.

"You know something?" Gloria said. "This is a slow day."

"It's so slow the dogs don't bark," Huey said.

"It's so slow the flies don't fly," Gloria said.

"It's so slow ice cream wouldn't melt," I said.

"If we had any ice cream," Huey said.

"But we don't," Gloria said.

We watched the grass some more.

"We better do something," I said.

"Like what?" Gloria asked.

"We could go visit Dad," Huey said.

"That's a terrible idea," I said.

"Why?" Huey asked. "I like visiting Dad."

My father has a shop about a mile from our house, where he fixes cars. Usually it is fun to visit him. If he has <u>customers</u>, he always introduces us as if we were important guests. Sometimes he buys us treats.

"Huey," I said, "usually, visiting Dad is a good idea. Today, it's an especially dangerous idea."

"Why?" Gloria said.

"Because we're bored," I said. "My dad hates it when people are bored. He says the world is so interesting nobody should ever be bored."

Reader's Journal   p 80
Preparing for Reading

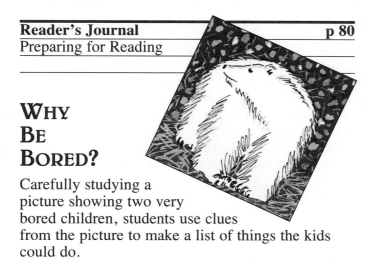

WHY BE BORED?

Carefully studying a picture showing two very bored children, students use clues from the picture to make a list of things the kids could do.

GUIDED READING

✔ **Page 215**   **In the first paragraph of the story what figurative language does the author use to show how slowly the time is passing?** ("everything stands still"; "We were watching the grass grow. It did not grow fast.")   ANALYZE: FIGURATIVE LANGUAGE

Page 215   **What is the relationship between the person telling the story and Huey? How do you know?** (They are brothers. They both talk about their dad.)   INFER: PEOPLE

HIGHLIGHTING LITERATURE

Page 215   Remind students that the setting of a story is where and when the story takes place, then ask them to describe the setting of this selection. (The story takes place on a hot summer day "when everything stands still." The children are sitting outside on their front steps.)   APPLICATION: LEARNING ABOUT LITERATURE/ AUTHOR'S CRAFT

✔ **Skill from The Bridge applied through this question.**

AMERICAN LIBRARY ASSOCIATION 1986

"I see," Gloria said, as if she didn't.

"So we'll go see him," Huey said, "and we just won't tell him we're bored. We're bored, but we won't tell him."

"Just so you remember that!" I said.

"Oh, I'll remember," Huey said.

Huey was wearing his angel look. When he has that look, you know he'll never remember anything.

Huey and I put on sweat bands. Gloria put on dark glasses. We started out.

The sun shined up at us from the sidewalks. Even the shadows on the street were hot as blankets.

Huey picked up a stick and scratched it along the sidewalk. "Oh, we're bored," he muttered. "Bored, bored, bored, bored, bored!"

"Huey!" I yelled. I wasn't bored anymore. I was nervous.

Finally we reached a sign that read, "Ralph's Car Hospital."

That's my dad's sign. My dad is Ralph.

The parking lot had three cars in it. Dad was inside the shop, lifting the hood of another car. He didn't have any customers with him, so we didn't get to shake hands and feel like visiting mayors or congressmen.

"Hi, Dad," I said.

RALPH'S CAR HOSPITAL
**Punctures
Rust
Dents & Bashes
Bad Brakes
Bad Breaks
Unusual Complaints**

"Hi!" my dad said.

"We're—" Huey said.

I didn't trust Huey. I stepped on his foot.

"We're on a hike," I said.

"Well, nice of you to stop by," my father said. "If you want, you can stay a while and help me."

"OK," we said.

So Huey sorted nuts and bolts. Gloria shined fenders with a rag. I held a new windshield wiper while my dad put it on a car window.

GUIDED READING

✔ **Page 216   How do you think the person telling the story feels when he sees Huey's "angel look"?** (Possible answers: worried, nervous) **Why do you think so?** (He has seen that look before and knows that it means Huey will not remember anything and probably will not do what he has been told to do.)
INFER: FEELINGS/ATTITUDES

✔ **Page 216   What two unlike things does the author compare in the middle of the page to show how hot it is?** (shadows and blankets)   ANALYZE: FIGURATIVE LANGUAGE

Page 216   Where do the children go to visit the boys' father? (to his car repair shop)   RECALL: SETTING

Page 217   How do the children help out? (sorting nuts and bolts; shining fenders; holding wipers)
RECALL: DETAILS

✔ **Skill from The Bridge applied through this question.**
✔ **Informal Assessment Opportunity:** GENERALIZING

HIGHLIGHTING LITERATURE

Page 217   Point out that this story is a good example of realistic fiction. The events in it could easily happen, and the characters and their feelings seem believable and familiar to most readers. In addition, the story is told by one of the characters, using such pronouns as *I*, *me*, and *we*. This way of telling a story, in which a character seems to be talking to the reader, can make the story and its characters seem more real.

410

"Nice work, Huey and Julian and Gloria!" my dad said when we were done.

And then he sent us to the store across the street to buy paper cups and ice cubes and a can of frozen lemonade.

We mixed the lemonade in the shop. Then we sat out under the one tree by the side of the driveway and drank all of it.

"Good lemonade!" my father said. "So what are you kids going to do now?"

"Oh, hike!" I <u>reminded</u> him.

"You know," my father answered, "I'm surprised at you kids picking a hot day like today for a hike. The ground is so hot. On a day like this, frogs wear shoes!"

"They do?" Huey said.

"Especially if they go hiking," my father said. "Of course, a lot of frogs, on a day like this, would stay home. So I wonder why you kids are hiking."

Sometimes my father notices too much. Then he gets yellow lights shining in his eyes, asking you to tell the whole truth. That's when I know to look at my feet.

"Oh," I said, "we like hiking."

But Gloria didn't know any better. She looked into my father's eyes. "Really," she said, "this wasn't a real hike. We came to see you."

"Oh, I see!" my father said, looking pleased.

"Because we were bored," Huey said.

GUIDED READING

Page 219   What is the name of the boy who is telling the story? (Julian) **How do you know?** (The father says, "Nice work, Huey and Julian and Gloria." The reader already knows who Huey and Gloria are, so the narrator must be Julian.)   INFER: PEOPLE

Page 219   Why would frogs wear shoes on a hot day? (to protect their feet from the hot ground) SYNTHESIZE: DRAWING CONCLUSIONS

✔ **Page 219   According to Julian, what happens when his father wants to know the truth?** (He gets yellow lights shining in his eyes.) **What do you think Julian really means?** (Possible answers: His father's eyes get very bright; his father stares very hard.)   ANALYZE: FIGURATIVE LANGUAGE

HIGHLIGHTING LITERATURE

Page 219   Encourage students to discuss the change in setting, noting how the author has taken the children from the front steps of their house to Ralph's Car Hospital to a tree outside. Invite students to visualize the children and the boys' father sitting around under the tree talking, then ask them to explain what the author has, or has not done, to make the setting seem realistic. (Students may note various details including the children sitting beneath a tree on a hot day sipping lemonade.)   APPLICATION: LEARNING ABOUT LITERATURE/AUTHOR'S CRAFT

✔ **Skill from The Bridge applied through this question.**

411

My father jumped up so fast he tipped over his lemonade cup. "BORED!" my father yelled. "You were BORED?"

He picked up his cup and waved it in the air. "And you think I don't get BORED?" my father roared, sprinkling out a few last drops of lemonade from his cup. "You think I don't get bored fixing cars when it's hot enough that frogs wear shoes?"

"'This is such an interesting world that nobody should ever be bored.' That's what you said," I reminded him.

"Last week," Huey added.

"Ummm," my father said. He got quiet.

He rubbed his hand over his mouth, the way he does when he's thinking.

"Why, of course," my father said, "I remember that. And it's the perfect, absolute truth. People absolutely SHOULD NOT get bored! However —" He paused. "It just happens that, sometimes, they do."

My father rubbed a line in the dirt with his shoe. He was thinking so hard I could see his thoughts standing by the tree and sitting on all the fenders of the cars.

"You know, if you three would kindly help me some more, I could leave a half hour early, and we could drive down by the river."

"We'll help," I said.

"Yes, and then we can look for frogs!" Huey said. So we stayed. We learned how to make a signal light blink. And afterward, on the way to the river, my dad bought us all ice cream cones. The ice cream did melt. Huey's melted all down the front of his shirt. It took him ten paper napkins and the river to clean up.

GUIDED READING

Page 220   Why does the boys' father act angry with the children when Huey says they are bored? (Possible answers: He thinks people should never be bored; he himself is bored but does not want to admit it.) SYNTHESIZE: DRAWING CONCLUSIONS

✔ **Page 220   What word picture does Julian use to describe his father's thinking very hard?** ("his thoughts standing by the tree and sitting on all the fenders of the cars") ANALYZE: FIGURATIVE LANGUAGE

Page 221   What did the children learn before they went down to the river? (They learned how to make a signal light blink.) RECALL: DETAILS

STRATEGIC READING

Page 221   Have students summarize what has happened to the characters so far. (They were feeling hot and bored on a summer day and decided to visit the boys' father at his car repair shop. They helped him fix cars and talked about whether people should ever be bored. The father said it was the kind of day frogs wear shoes. They went to the river. They bought and ate ice cream cones.) **Then have them predict what the children might do if they walk down the bank.** (They might try to catch some frogs to see whether the frogs are wearing shoes.) If students have trouble summarizing, have them review the part of the story they have already read. If they have trouble predicting, have them look for an exaggerated statement that the children might be curious about. METACOGNITION: SUMMARIZING AND PREDICTING

✔ Skill from The Bridge applied through this question.

After Huey's shirt was clean, we took our shoes and socks off and went wading. We looked for special rocks under the water—the ones that are beautiful until you take them out of the water, when they get dry and not so bright.

We found skipping stones and tried to see who could get the most skips from a stone.

We saw a school of minnows going as fast as they could to get away from us.

But we didn't see any frogs.

"If you want to see frogs," my father said, "you'll have to walk down the bank a ways and look hard."

So we decided to do that.

"Fine!" my father said. "But I'll stay here. I think I'm ready for a little nap."

"Naps are boring!" we said.

"Sometimes it's nice to be bored," my father said.

We left him with his eyes closed, sitting under a tree.

Huey saw the first frog. He almost stepped on it. It jumped into the water, and we ran after it.

Huey caught it and picked it up, and then I saw another one. I grabbed it.

It was slippery and strong and its body was cold, just like it wasn't the middle of summer.

Then Gloria caught one, too. The frogs wriggled in our hands, and we felt their hearts beating. Huey looked at their funny webbed feet.

"Their feet are good for swimming," he said, "but Dad is wrong. They don't wear shoes!"

"No way," Gloria said. "They sure don't wear shoes."

"Let's go tell him," I said.

We threw our frogs back into the river. They made little trails swimming away from us. And then we went back to my father. He was sitting under the tree with his eyes shut. It looked like he hadn't moved an inch.

"We found frogs," Huey said, "and we've got news for you. They don't wear shoes!"

My father's eyes opened. "They don't?" he said. "Well, I can't be right about everything. Dry your feet. Put your shoes on. It's time to go."

We all sat down to put on our shoes.

I pulled out a sock and put it on.

I stuck my foot into my shoe. My foot wouldn't go in. I picked up the shoe and looked inside.

"Oh no!" I yelled.

There were two little eyes inside my shoe, looking out at me. Huey and Gloria grabbed their socks. All our shoes had frogs in them, every one.

GUIDED READING

Page 222   What happens when they go to the river? (They look for special rocks, see some fish, and skip stones.)   RECALL: DETAILS

Page 222   Do you think the children are bored at the river? (no) **Why not?** (They are busy doing things.)   INFER: FEELINGS/ATTITUDES

Page 223   What happens after Julian tries to put his shoe on? (He finds a frog in it.)   ANALYZE: SEQUENCE

Page 223   What do you think the children will say to the boys' father about the frogs in the shoes? (Possible answer: Frogs do wear shoes.)   SYNTHESIZE: PREDICTING OUTCOMES

HIGHLIGHTING LITERATURE

Pages 222–223   Point out that many paragraphs on these pages contain only a single sentence. Sometimes this happens because a paragraph shows the words of a speaker, and the speaker says only one sentence. In other cases, however, the sentence tells something that happened or that the characters did. Have students find examples of these single-sentence descriptive paragraphs. Then discuss why the author might have decided to use such short paragraphs. (Possible answers: They help the story move faster; they show that a lot of actions happened quickly.)

413

"What did I tell you," my father said.

"You were right," we said. "It's a day when frogs wear shoes!"

◆ LIBRARY LINK ◆

This story was taken from the book More Stories Julian Tells *by Ann Cameron. You might enjoy reading the entire book to find out more about Julian, Gloria, and Huey.*

 Reader's Response

Do you think Julian's father was right in saying nobody should ever be bored? Explain your answer.

SELECTION FOLLOW-UP

A Day When Frogs Wear Shoes

◆ **Thinking It Over**

1. Why couldn't Julian, Huey, and Gloria find anything to do?
2. Why did the children visit Julian's dad in his shop?
3. Did Julian's dad understand how the children were feeling? How do you know?
4. Do you think the children believed they would find frogs wearing shoes? Tell why or why not.
5. How did the frogs get into the children's shoes?
6. What are some examples of figurative language in the story?

◆ **Writing to Learn**

THINK AND INVENT Riddles are fun. A character riddle gives clues about a person. Read the riddle below.

> **Character Riddle**
>
> I am always first to arrive at school.
> I work hard every day.
> I like children.
> Who am I?
>
> (Our teacher)

WRITE Make up a character riddle about someone you know. See if others can guess who your riddle is about.

GUIDED READING

Page 224   Why do you think the author does not tell how the frogs got in the children's shoes?
(Possible responses: She wants to leave readers wondering about how the frogs got there; she thinks it is more fun for readers to figure it out for themselves.)
EVALUATE: AUTHOR'S PURPOSE

RETURNING TO THE READING PURPOSE

OPTION 1 If students set the purpose, have them review the lists of predictions and see which ones are correct. Then have them discuss whether they have ever done anything like what the children did or whether they would want to.

OPTION 2 If you set the purpose, ask students whether the story told about what kind of a day it is when frogs wear shoes. (Yes, because it told about a hot day in which children found frogs in their shoes.)

Reader's Journal   **p 81**
Responding to Reading

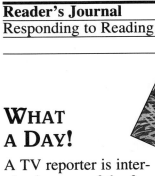

WHAT A DAY!

A TV reporter is interviewing one of the frogs in the story. Students imagine what the frog would say in response to the questions.

SELECTION FOLLOW-UP

A Day When Frogs Wear Shoes

THINKING IT OVER

1. **Why couldn't Julian, Huey, and Gloria find anything to do?** (It was a hot day and it seemed like everything was standing still. The children were bored.) INFER: PROBLEM/SOLUTION

2. **Why did the children visit Julian's dad in his shop?** (Possible answers: The children were bored; they thought there might be something interesting going on in the shop; they thought they might be introduced to customers and made to feel important; the children may have been hoping that Julian's dad would think of something they could do.) INFER: CAUSE/EFFECT

✔ 3. **Did Julian's dad understand how the children were feeling? How do you know?** (Possible answers: Julian's dad probably realized that the children were hot and had nothing to do, so he found jobs for them around the garage; he had them make lemonade. After they said they were bored, he found interesting things to teach them at the garage, and he thought of something that they could look forward to doing at the end of the day.) ANALYZE: CHARACTER; METACOGNITION

4. **Do you think the children believed they would find frogs wearing shoes? Tell why or why not.** (Some students will probably say yes, because the children actually caught frogs and looked to see if they were wearing shoes. Other students may think the children knew that such a thing was not possible.) SYNTHESIZE: DRAWING CONCLUSIONS

5. **How did the frogs get into the children's shoes?** (Dad put them there. He pretended to take a nap, but he really caught the frogs and put them in the shoes.) INFER: CAUSE/EFFECT

6. **What are some examples of figurative language in the story?** (possible answers: "It's so slow the dogs don't bark"; "so hot that frogs wear shoes") ANALYZE: FIGURATIVE LANGUAGE

WRITING TO LEARN

Use Writing Master 16, which duplicates this riddle.

THINK AND INVENT   Riddles are fun. A character riddle gives clues about a person. Read the riddle below. (Help students understand that the riddle describes their teacher.)

> ### Character Riddle
>
> I am always first to arrive at school.
> I work hard every day.
> I like children.
> Who am I?
>
> (Our teacher.)

Extend comprehension through writing.

WRITE   Make up a character riddle about someone you know. See if others can guess whom your riddle is about. (Have students share their riddles with the class.)

✔ **Informal Assessment Opportunity:**   EMPATHIZING WITH STORY CHARACTERS

415

More Ideas for Selection Follow-Up

CRITICAL AND CREATIVE THINKING QUESTIONS

Encourage a variety of responses and points of view.

Use these open-ended questions to encourage critical and creative thinking about the selection.

1. What did the children in the story do on their own to get over being bored? How did the father help?

2. What suggestions would you give the children the next time they are bored?

3. Do you think the father was teasing the children? When?

REREADING ORALLY

Have students reread for expression.

Have students reread two sections of the story: from the beginning to "I like visiting Dad'" [pages 214–215] and from " 'Good lemonade!' my father said" to " 'It just happens that, sometimes, they do.' " [pages 219–220] Have different students read the narration and the dialogue of the different characters. Encourage them to use their voices in exaggerated ways to show the characters' strong feelings. For example, in the first section, they might draw out the sounds of "so slow" to show how bored the children were. In the second section, they might give a different tone and emphasis to the word *bored* each time it is used. Model some of these tones of voice to show a character's feelings.

SELECTION COMPREHENSION

Provide comprehension check.

A Workbook page to check comprehension is shown in the Resource Center below. It may be used for informal assessment.

Workbook page 106

SELECTION COMPREHENSION

NAME _____

A Day When Frogs Wear Shoes

A. Complete the summary of the story "A Day When Frogs Wear Shoes." Accept reasonable variations.

One day three children named ___Julian, Huey, and Gloria___ were sitting outside. The day was very ___hot and slow___. The three children felt ___bored___. They were trying to think of something to do when Huey suggested that ___they go to his father's shop___. They agreed to do this, but Julian made them promise not to say that they were bored. Julian's dad thought the world was so ___interesting___ that no one should ever be bored.

At the shop, the boys' father said they could stay and help with some jobs. Then Huey told their father that they had really come because ___they were bored___. To their surprise, their father said that even he was bored on a day so hot that ___frogs wore shoes___. He offered to take the children to ___the river___ if they helped him until he closed the shop.

When they got to the river, the children found some frogs. They checked the frogs' feet to see if ___they really wore shoes___. They told the boys' father that the frogs were barefoot. When they put their own shoes back on, they found ___frogs inside___!

B. On separate paper, explain how you think the frogs got inside the children's shoes. See Teacher Notes.

106   "A Day When Frogs Wear Shoes"   Selection Comprehension

---

RESOURCE CENTER

◀ **Workbook page 106** is intended for use by all students.

Writing Master 16 duplicates the Writing to Learn riddle.

I•T Kit Activities

I•T

Poster: "That Will Be the Day!"
Frogs don't wear shoes but they do climb trees, as this humorous calendar shows. Students must determine which days display true facts about animals and which ones just tell fiction. (See Activity Guide.)   CONTENT AREAS

Audio: "Chickery Chick"
What can students do when they're tired of doing the same old thing, like on the kind of day when frogs wear shoes? Students sing along with the tongue-twister song and make up their own tongue-twister verses. (See Activity Guide.)   CONTEMPORARY MUSIC

LANGUAGE ARTS CONNECTIONS

CREATIVE THINKING: USING FIGURATIVE LANGUAGE

Have student groups brainstorm descriptive words.

Remind students that when they brainstorm, they should try to express as many different ideas as possible, listening to one another rather than criticizing or discussing. Divide the students into small groups. Have each group brainstorm words to describe the sounds they might hear in Ralph's Car Hospital and words to describe what the cars might look like. *(possible answers: hiss, sputter, shiny, rusty.)* Have one member of each group write down the words.

Have students write sentences with figurative language.

Have each group uses its lists to write at least five sentences that use figurative language to describe Ralph's Car Hospital. *(Possible response: The tires hissed like angry snakes.)* SHARED LEARNING: SPEAKING

COMPETING WITH COMPARISONS

Have students compete in making exaggerated statements.

Remind students that people sometimes enjoy trying to outdo each other in making figurative comparisons to describe something. They try to make each comparison funnier or more unusual than the one before. Have students agree on a topic for the contest, such as "The hottest day there ever was," or "The most boring time I ever spent." Then divide the class into groups. Tell each group to hold its own comparison contest, in which students either compete orally to make statements about the topic or write down statements and then read them aloud. After each group member has made at least one statement, have the group vote to decide on the statement it likes best. Then have each group read its best statement to the class and have the class vote to decide on an all-class winner. WHOLE CLASS ENRICHMENT

417

CREATING TELEVISION COMMERCIALS

Have students work cooperatively to present commercials.

Divide students into groups of four and tell each group that they will be working cooperatively to prepare a television commercial for Ralph's Car Hospital. Assign one student to be the poster artist who will create a colorful picture with a short slogan. Have a second student be the background writer and write about how Ralph learned about cars, how long he has worked on them, and the kinds of problems Ralph fixes. Assign the third and fourth students to be actors. The third will be a customer who asks about car problems. The fourth will be a sales manager who explains how Ralph can help the customer. Give the groups time to prepare and rehearse. Then, for each group, have the poster artist present the poster to the class, the background writer read about Ralph, and the actors present their dialogue. COOPERATIVE LEARNING

SELF-SELECTED VOCABULARY: CAR TALK

Have students research and speak about car words.

Recall with students words from the story that name automobile parts such as *hood, windshield, wiper, fender,* and *signal light.* Ask students where they might look to find out more about these and other car words. *(possible answers: a dictionary, an encyclopedia, and books and magazines about cars and car repair)* Have students research car words from the story and other car words that they are interested in. Have them prepare and give a short oral report on the meanings of several words and interesting facts about how they came to be used. Students may wish to include an illustrated diagram with names of the parts of an automobile. You may wish to provide students with the following books: *Cars and How They Go,* by Johanna Cole or *Car Care for Kids and Former Kids,* by Harvey Lord. SPEAKING

WRITING FROM THE FROGS' POINT OF VIEW

Have students rewrite the story from a frog's point of view.

Remind students that the story they just read was told from the point of view of Julian and written as if Julian himself were speaking. Have students discuss how the frogs in the last part of the story might have felt about what happened to them. How did they feel when three giants picked them up and held them? Were they scared? What did they think when they were put into the shoes? After students have discussed their ideas, have them rewrite the last part of the story from the point of view of one of the frogs. Tell them to describe what the frogs might see and feel. Have them use first-person pronouns such as *I, me,* and *we* to show that the frog is telling the story. **Language Arts Master 14** can be used with this activity. CHALLENGE: WRITING

REALISTIC FICTION AS A LITERARY GENRE

Have students write short realistic fiction stories.

Point out to students that the story they just read is an example of realistic fiction, which is a story that seems as if it could have happened. Discuss the story details that seemed especially "real" or familiar.

Remind students that "A Day When Frogs Wear Shoes" is about a very hot day. Then have them think of the coldest day they can remember and try to imagine an even colder day. Tell students that they are going to write short stories about what a group of children do and how they feel on a very cold day. First have them think of some comparisons to show how cold the day was. Then have students incorporate their comparisons into realistic fiction stories.   WRITING

READING EVERY DAY

Reading about children who use their ingenuity to create adventurous happenings is fun. Here are two titles to share with your students; the first is the book from which the story about Julian, Huey, and Gloria is taken.

More Stories Julian Tells by Ann Cameron. Knopf, © 1986. Among Julian's other stories are those in which Gloria seems able to move the sun indoors and Julian sends a message downstream in a bottle.

Yellow Blue Jay by Johanna Hurwitz. William Morrow, © 1986. Expecting his two-week vacation in Vermont to be boring, Jay, a city boy, is pleasantly surprised by the fun he has—and also by his newly acquired self-confidence.

Reader's Journal   **pp 82, 83**
Extending Reading

FROGS, FROGS, AND MORE FROGS!

Students read about unusual frogs and, choosing their favorite, make up an adventure they would have with it.

Selection Support

VOCABULARY

Homophones

OBJECTIVE   Understanding words that sound alike but have different meanings.

Review homophones.

Remind students that homophones are words that sound alike but have different meanings. Tell them they can use context clues to help them decide on the meaning of a homophone.

Use Teaching Chart to provide practice in identifying homophones.

Display the Teaching Chart. Have volunteers read the words at the top of the chart. Then read sentence 1 and point out that the word *one*, meaning "a single thing," makes more sense than *won*, or "came in first in a contest." Have students complete the remaining sentences and explain their choices.

63

TEACHING CHART 63: HOMOPHONES

won	by	board
one	buy	bored

1. It was (one) of those hot summer days when everything stands still.
2. Ralph sent the children to (buy) lemonade.
3. At the river, the children were too busy to be (bored) .

Provide independent practice.

Options for independent practice are shown in the Resource Center below.

Workbook page 107

VOCABULARY

Homophones

NAME

REMEMBER: Homophones are words that sound the same but have different spellings and meanings. Use spelling and context to decide the correct meaning of homophones.

A. Use the homophones in the box to complete the sentences from a conversation Huey, Gloria, and Julian could have had.

board	bored	buy	by	knew	new	weak	week

One hot summer day, Huey and Gloria and Huey's brother Julian were all ___bored___ from watching grass grow.

"Let's build a tree house," Gloria said. "I have one ___board___ we can use. Let's find another."

"I'm too ___weak___ from the heat," Huey said.

"Let's wait till next ___week___ when it's cooler."

"Well," said Julian, "maybe we could go ___buy___ some lemonade. I have some money."

"We could drink it down ___by___ the river," Huey added. "Maybe we'll catch some frogs while we're there."

"I ___knew___ you'd like my ___new___ idea," Julian said.

B. On separate paper, write another pair of homophones. Then write two sentences using the homophone pair. See Teacher Notes.

Homophones   "A Day When Frogs Wear Shoes"   **107**

RESOURCE CENTER

◀ **Workbook page 107** is intended for use by all students.

Skills Practice 98 ▶ may be assigned for additional practice.

Workbook reuse option: Have students circle the letters that are different in each pair of homophones in Part A.

Skills Practice 98

NAME _____

SKILLS PRACTICE **98**

Homophones

Homophones are words that sound the same but have different spellings and meanings. Use spelling and context clues to decide the correct meaning of homophones.

A. Read the question. Write the correct homophone.

1. Which can hop, a <u>hare</u> or a <u>hair</u>?	hare
2. Which is on a foot, a <u>heal</u> or a <u>heel</u>?	heel
3. Which is hello, <u>hi</u> or <u>high</u>?	hi
4. Which can you eat, <u>meat</u> or <u>meet</u>?	meat
5. Which can carry water, a <u>pail</u> or a <u>pale</u>?	pail
6. Which hurts, a <u>soar</u> or a <u>sore</u>?	sore
7. Which is a color, <u>blew</u> or <u>blue</u>?	blue
8. Which is something to eat, a <u>beat</u> or a <u>beet</u>?	beet
9. Which makes bread, <u>flour</u> or <u>flower</u>?	flour

a pair of pears

B. Read each sentence. If the homophones are used correctly, write **Yes**. If they are wrong, write **No**. Rewrite any sentence that is incorrect.

10. **No**   <u>Wear</u> are you going to <u>where</u> that hat?
Where are you going to wear that hat?

11. **Yes**   I can add <u>some</u> <u>sums</u>.

12. **No**   Plant the <u>rows</u> in one of those <u>rose</u>.
Plant the rose in one of those rows.

13. **Yes**   I <u>read</u> the book with the <u>red</u> cover.

14. **No**   Did it make <u>cents</u> to spend ten <u>sense</u>?
Did it make sense to spend ten cents?

98   LEVEL 8   "A Day When Frogs Wear Shoes"

SKILL TRACE: SUFFIX				
Introduction	Practice	Test	Reteach	Maintain
TE 344	372	421	461	465	574

WORD STUDY

Suffix -ment

OBJECTIVE   Using structural analysis to determine word meaning.

Review the suffix -ment.

Remind students that a suffix is a letter or letters added to the end of a word. A suffix changes the meaning of a word and sometimes also changes the way the word is used in a sentence. The suffix *-ment* changes a verb to a noun. The meaning of the base word is the best clue to the meaning of a word ending in *-ment*.

Use Teaching Chart to provide practice in using words with the suffix -ment.

Have volunteers read the words on the top of the Teaching Chart and find the base word in each. Then read the first sentence aloud. Ask students what word at the top makes most sense in the blank in the sentence. (*excitement*) Have students complete the remaining sentences and tell the meaning of each word they chose.

> **TEACHING CHART 64: THE SUFFIX -MENT**
>
> excitement   amazement   announcement
> **1.** It is hard to find any (excitement) on a hot, boring day.
> **2.** The boys' father made the surprising (announcement) that frogs wear shoes on hot days.
> **3.** The children's (amazement) was great when they found frogs in their shoes.

64

Provide independent practice.

Options for independent practice are shown in the Resource Center below.

Workbook page 108

WORD STUDY

NAME _____

Suffix -ment

REMEMBER: The suffix *-ment* forms a noun and means "result of."

A. Write the *-ment* word from the box next to its meaning.

agreement	amazement	enjoyment	pavement	payment

1. the result of being paved ___ pavement
2. the result of enjoying ___ enjoyment
3. the result of giving pay ___ payment
4. the result of agreeing ___ agreement
5. the result of being amazed ___ amazement

B. Complete each sentence with a *-ment* word from the box.

6. It was so hot you could fry an egg on the ___ pavement ___.
7. Julian and Huey can't reach an ___ agreement ___ about whether to go to their father's shop.
8. Someone in the shop is making a ___ payment ___ to their father.
9. Julian and Huey stare in ___ amazement ___ when their father says it's a day when frogs wear shoes.
10. He takes them to the river where they have much ___ enjoyment ___.

C. Choose two of the *-ment* words. On separate paper, write a sentence for each base word and a sentence for each *-ment* word. See Teacher Notes.

108   "A Day When Frogs Wear Shoes"   Suffix -ment

RESOURCE CENTER

◄ **Workbook page 108** is intended for use by all students.

Skills Practice 99 ► may be assigned for additional practice.

Workbook reuse option: Have students circle the base words of all the words with *-ment* as a suffix on the page.

Skills Practice 99

NAME _____

SKILLS PRACTICE   **99**

Suffix -ment

The suffix *-ment* means "the state or act of." The suffix *-ment* changes a verb to a noun.

A. Circle the word in each sentence that can have the suffix *-ment*. Then write your own sentence using the *-ment* word.

1. Two companies (employ) my mom.
   Sentence with *employment*
2. My mom gets her (pay) two times each month.
   Sentence with *payment*
3. My mom works to (arrange) flowers for special occasions.
   Sentence with *arrangement*
4. I knew my mom would (announce) I could not stay alone after school.
   Sentence with *announcement*
5. Mom said that she would (place) me in an after-school program.
   Sentence with *placement*
6. The teachers there (treat) me well.
   Sentence with *treatment*
7. I (enjoy) the projects we make after school.
   Sentence with *enjoyment*
8. Mom says things have worked out well, and I (agree).
   Sentence with *agreement*

B. Circle the word each phrase describes.

9. great surprise	amaze	amazement	pavement
10. to become better	agree	improve	improvement
11. a good feeling	announcement	content	contentment
12. the act of moving	development	move	movement

LEVEL 8   "A Day When Frogs Wear Shoes"   **99**

SKILL TRACE: SUFFIXES				
Introduction	Practice	Test	Reteach	Maintain
TE 370	395	422	461	466	502

WORD STUDY

Suffixes -ion, -tion

OBJECTIVE   Using structural analysis to determine word meaning.

Review the suffix - ion

Remind students that a suffix is a letter or letters added to the end of a word. A suffix changes the meaning of a word and sometimes also changes the way the word is used in a sentence. The suffix *-ion* or *-tion* changes a verb to a noun. Sometimes the spelling of the end of the base word is changed when this suffix is added. The meaning of the base word is the best clue to the meaning of a word ending in *-ion* or *-tion*.

Use Teaching Chart to provide practice in using words with the suffix - ion.

Have volunteers read the words on the top of the Teaching Chart and find the base word in each. Then read the first sentence aloud. Point out that *introduction*, which is made from the base word *introduce*, makes the most sense in the blank in this sentence. Have students complete the remaining sentences and tell the meanings of the words they chose.

> **TEACHING CHART 85: THE SUFFIXES -ION, -TION**
>
> 65
>
> action   introduction
> protection   direction
>
> 1. The boys' father gave them a grand _(introduction)_ to his customers.
> 2. He took _(action)_ when the children said they were bored.
> 3. Some of the frogs hopped in the wrong _(direction)_ .
> 4. Nothing gave any _(protection)_ from the hot day.

Provide independent practice.

Options for independent practice are shown in the Resource Center below.

Workbook page 109

Suffixes -ion, -tion

REMEMBER: The suffixes *-ion* and *-tion* are added to verbs to form nouns.

A. Write the nouns from the box next to the verbs from which they were made.

| action | collection | direction |
| election | pollution | |

1. direct _direction_   2. collect _collection_
3. pollute _pollution_   4. elect _election_
5. act _action_

B. Write a word from the box to complete each sentence.

6. The children were bored because there was no _action_
7. Huey's father had a _collection_ of old car parts.
8. Huey's father drove in the _direction_ of the river.
9. They passed a sign that reminded people to vote in the next _election_ .
10. The river was clear because there was no _pollution_ .

C. Have you collected cans and paper to help fight pollution? Can you think of other ways to help? On separate paper, list at least three ideas. See Teacher Notes.

Suffixes -ion, -tion   "A Day When Frogs Wear Shoes"   **109**

RESOURCE CENTER

◀ **Workbook page 109** is intended for use by all students.

Skills Practice 100 ▶ may be assigned for additional practice.

Workbook reuse option: Have students write the four base words in sentences 6, 7, 8, and 9 and write above each another suffix that could be added to the base word.

Skills Practice 100

Suffixes -ion, -tion

The suffix *-ion* and *-tion* change a verb to a noun.

A. Read the words in the box. Then write them to match the clues.

| collection | creation | directions | instructions | introduction |
| correction | illustration | association | investigation | indication |

1. these direct people how to do things — _directions_
2. a change made to make something right — _correction_
3. what you do when two people meet the first time — _introduction_
4. what teachers give in classes — _instructions_
5. similar things gathered together — _collection_
6. a sign of something — _indication_
7. a group of people who have something in common — _association_
8. how to look for the answer to a hard problem — _investigation_
9. a picture in a book — _illustration_
10. you get it when you create something — _creation_

B. Write a word from the box to complete each sentence.

11. If you don't understand what to do, look at the _instructions_ .
12. The president ordered an _investigation_ of the causes of dirty air.
13. Her smile is an _indication_ that she is happy.
14. Our school has an _association_ for parents and teachers.
15. I will give you _directions_ for getting to my house.
16. I call this costume my _creation_ because I made it myself.
17. I would like to have a _collection_ of stamps.

100 LEVEL 8   "A Day When Frogs Wear Shoes"

SKILL TRACE: SYMBOLS/SIGNS				
Introduction	Practice	Test	Reteach	Maintain
TE 346	373	423	461	467	526

STUDY SKILLS

Symbols and Signs

OBJECTIVE Understanding information from symbols and signs.

Review symbols and signs.

Remind students that symbols and signs are quick ways to communicate important messages or information. A symbol is an object or picture of an object that stands for something else. For example, a dove is a symbol for peace. Ask students to name symbols they have seen on signs and tell what they mean. (*possible answers: the diagonal slash through another symbol, meaning "no" or "do not;" the $ symbol, meaning "dollar;" the red hand symbol below a traffic light, meaning "pedestrians should not cross now"*)

Have students design and interpret signs.

Have students find the illustration that shows the sign for Ralph's Car Hospital. (*page 217*) Ask them what information the sign gives. (*the name of the shop and some of the kinds of things Ralph fixes*) Have them discuss what other information or pictures might be found on a sign for a store or business. (*possible answers: a picture of what is being sold or fixed; a price; the address of the business, the hours it is open: an advertising slogan*) Then have each student design a poster-size sign for a store or business, such as a gas station, a toy store, or a grocery store. When students have finished, have each student present his or her sign to the class and call on volunteers to tell what they learned about the business from reading the sign.

Provide independent practice.

Options for independent practice are shown in the Resource Center below.

Workbook page 110

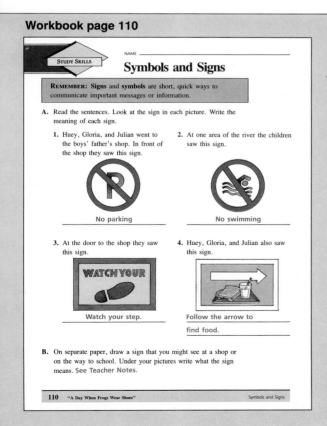

RESOURCE CENTER

◀ **Workbook page 110** is intended for use by all students.

Skills Practice 101 ▶ may be assigned for additional practice.

Workbook reuse option: In the bottom margin, have students draw and label a sign they might see at the zoo.

Skills Practice 101

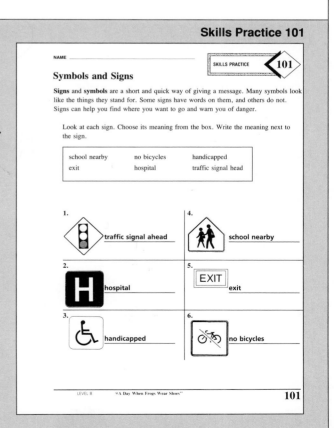

SKILL TRACE: SUFFIXES				
Introduction	Practice	Test	Reteach	Maintain
TE 222	248	293	311	314	424

WORD STUDY

Suffixes -able, -ible

OBJECTIVE   Using structural analysis to determine word meaning.

Review the suffixes -able, -ible.

Ask students if they remember what a suffix is. (*a letter or letters added to the end of a word*) Remind them that a suffix changes the meaning of a word and sometimes also changes the way the word is used in a sentence. The suffix *-able* or *-ible* changes a verb to an adjective. It adds the meaning "able to" or "can be" to the base word.

Provide practice in using words with the suffixes -able, -ible.

You may wish to write the word list and sentences below on the chalkboard. Answers are shown in red. Have volunteers read the words from the word list and find the base word in each. Then read the first sentence aloud. Ask students which word in the word list makes the most sense in the blank in this sentence. (fixable) Have students choose the word that makes the most sense in each of the remaining sentences and tell its meaning.

> comfortable   collectible
> movable   fixable
>
> 1. One car was in bad shape, but Julian's father thought it was (fixable).
> 2. The fender was so heavy it was not (movable).
> 3. The children found many (collectible) things at the river.
> 4. The children were more (comfortable) in the heat after putting their feet in cold water.

Provide independent practice.

An independent activity is shown in the Resource Center below.

RESOURCE CENTER

Skills Practice 102 ▶ may be assigned for additional practice.

Skills Practice 102

NAME _____

SKILLS PRACTICE 〈102〉

Suffixes -able, -ible

The suffixes *-able* and *-ible* mean "capable of being," "can be," or "able to."

A. Read the words in the box. Circle the suffix in each word. Then use the words to finish the sentences in the story.

accept(able)	break(able)	eat(able)	mov(able)	sens(ible)
agree(able)	comfort(able)	fix(able)	notice(able)	valu(able)

Do you remember Goldilocks? What she did in the Bear's house is hard to forget. She found porridge in bowls, and thought it was **eatable** _____. She sat in a chair that broke because it was **breakable** _____. The chair could not be fixed, because it was not **fixable** _____. Goldilocks got into a bed, and she felt **comfortable** _____. The Bears didn't notice Goldilocks at first, because she was not **noticeable**. Then they saw Goldilocks. They tried to move her, but she was not **movable** _____.

The Bears yelled, "It does not make any sense that you are here. It is not **sensible** _____."

Goldilocks was angry with herself. She knew that what she did was not **sensible** _____. But she learned a **valuable** _____ lesson. If you do not behave well, others will not find you **acceptable** _____.

B. Add a part to the story by writing sentences using these phrases.
Responses will vary.
lovable girl   considerable thought
_____
_____
_____

102   LEVEL 8   "A Day When Frogs Wear Shoes"

CURRICULUM CONNECTIONS

WHEELS OF TOMORROW ART

Have students do library research to learn more about cars and other wheeled vehicles, such as buses, trains, and bicycles. Have them find out what parts each vehicle has and how the parts work together to make the vehicle move. Then have each student design a wheeled vehicle he or she would like to own. Have the students either draw the design on paper or create a three-dimensional model of it. The vehicle may be an improved version of a kind that already exists, such as a super sports car, or it might be a new invention, such as a ''caroplane'' that can both run on roads and fly through the air. Students should provide labels or short written descriptions that explain the parts of their designs, how their vehicles work, and why they are ideal. Have students display their drawings and models under the sign ''Wheels of Tomorrow.''

ALL ABOUT FROGS SCIENCE

Remind students that they learned several scientific facts about frogs in the story they just read. For example, they learned that frogs can live in water, that they are slippery and cold, and that frogs are strong swimmers. Have them look in encyclopedias, science texts, or other reference sources to learn more about frogs. They might find out such things as the ''double life'' many frogs lead on land and in water, the changes that take place when a tadpole becomes a frog, how a frog catches insects, and how male frogs ''sing.'' Have them present what they have learned by writing poems or short prose descriptions about frogs. The writing should be from a frog's point of view and should use pronouns such as *I* and *me* to suggest that the frog is telling about its life. **Curriculum Connection Master 14** can be used with this activity.

FEELING FROGGY MUSIC

Most students will be familiar with *Sesame Street's* Kermit, perhaps the most famous of frogs. Play a recording of Kermit's song, ''It's Not Easy Being Green,'' and have students sing along. Have students discuss how Kermit feels about being a frog. Then encourage them to write other verses to the song. They might want to write about how Kermit would feel about wearing shoes.

TEACHER CHOICE

	Teaching Sequence	Trade Books and Resources	Meeting Individual Needs	Integrated Language Arts / Cross Curriculum
The Bridge Pages 428–429	**Maintain** Characterization	• Teaching Chart 66 • Workbook 111 • Skills Practice 103		
PART 1 **Vocabulary Strategies** Pages 430–431	**Develop Concepts** Discussing Fame **Teach Vocabulary** **STORY CRITICAL WORDS:** choice, fame, **poetry, popular, printed** (Tested words are boldfaced.)	• Teaching Chart 67 • Workbook 112 • Skills Practice 104	**SUPPORT WORDS:** charm, chores, popularity, recover, separated, servant, slave, valor • Skills Practice 105 **CHARACTER/SETTING WORDS:** Africa, America, Bible, Boston, Cambridge, Countess of Huntingdon, England, English, General George Washington, George Whitefield, John and Susannah Wheatley, Mary, Massachusetts, Nathaniel, Phillis Wheatley	**WRITING/SPEAKING ACTIVITY:** Use new vocabulary to describe a day in the life of a famous children's author. • Spelling Connection 53
PART 2 **Reading & Responding** Pages 432–441	**Build Background** **Develop a Purpose for Reading** **Guide the Reading Process** **Selection Follow-Up**	• Reader's Journal 84–87 • Workbook 113 **I-T KIT** Listening to an Interview with Lindamichellebaron **READING EVERY DAY** *The Drinking Gourd,* by F.N. Monjo *Harriet Tubman,* by F. Sabin	**EXTRA HELP:** Turning Nonfiction Titles and Headings into Questions **ACHIEVING ENGLISH PROFICIENCY:** Discussing Story Phrases • Achieving English Proficiency Master 25	**Language Arts Connections** **WRITING TO LEARN:** Complete a character map about Phillis Wheatley. • Writing Master 17 **SPEAKING/LISTENING:** Organizing a Poetry Reading **WRITING:** Writing Poems; Publishing Poetry Journals; Identifying Parts of a Story; Writing Biographies • Language Arts Master 15
PART 3 **Selection Support** Pages 442–447			**Practice** • Teaching Charts 68–70 • Workbook 114–115 • Skills Practice 106–108 Inferences (Tested) Homophones (Tested) Forms **Maintain** • Skills Practice 109 Title Page, Copyright Page, Table of Contents	**Curriculum Connections** **HUMANITIES:** Comparing Past and Present Poets **SOCIAL STUDIES:** Creating a Time Line for Phillis Wheatley; Researching George Washington **GEOGRAPHY:** Mapping Phillis's Travels • Curriculum Connection Master 15 **ART:** Drawing Pictures of Scenes from Phillis's Life **MUSIC:** Listening to Classical Music

Phillis Wheatley

America's First Black Poet

by Kacey Brown

SUMMARY *John Wheatley, a Boston tailor, and his wife, Susannah, buy a young African slave girl. They treat the young girl, whom they name Phillis, as part of the family. She learns to speak, read, and write English. At age seventeen she has her first poem published in a local newspaper. Soon her poetry becomes well known in Boston and in England. A poem she writes about General George Washington pleases him. Later on, the poet and her famous subject meet.*

The Bridge

SKILL TRACE: CHARACTERIZATION	
Introduced in Level 7. This skill is re-introduced in Unit 4 of this level.	Maintain
	TE 42 428

Teaching Characterization

OBJECTIVE   Identifying character traits and emotions.

1. WARM-UP

Use a known passage to discuss character traits.

Tell students they will listen to a passage from the previous selection, "A Day When Frogs Wear Shoes." Ask them to listen for clues the author has given about what Julian and Huey's father is like. *(hardworking, fun, caring)*

> **My father has a shop about a mile from our house, where he fixes cars. Usually it is fun to visit him. If he has customers, he always introduces us as if we were important guests. Sometimes he buys us treats.**

Discuss word clues.

Reread the passage. Have students explain which word clues helped them decide what Julian and Huey's father is like. *(fixed cars, fun to visit, introduces us as if we were important guests, buys us treats)* Point out that to help readers understand the father, the author has Julian tell what his father's job is and also how his father behaves with the children. Review that a character's actions can show a lot about what a character is like, just as real people's actions can show a lot about what they are like.

State the objective.

Tell students they will review how to use word clues in a story to determine what a character's traits are.

2. TEACH

Explain why identifying character traits is important.

Recognizing character traits helps readers understand why characters act the way they do and predict what characters may do.

Present a strategy for identifying character traits.

Explain that there is a strategy students can use to help them understand what kind of person a character is. First, look for words an author uses to describe a character. Next, look for word clues in what a character thinks or says. Finally, look for clues in actions and events in the story that directly show a character's traits.

TEACHING CHART 66: CHARACTERIZATION   **66**

helpful   active
upset   honest

1. My father jumped up so fast he tipped over his lemonade cup. "BORED!" my father yelled. "You were bored?" (upset)
2. "We'll help," I said. (helpful)
3. "Really," she said, "this wasn't a real hike. We came to see you." (honest)
4. We found skipping stones and tried to see who could get the most skips from a stone. (active)

Model the strategy.

Tell students that the sentences on the Teaching Chart are from "A Day When Frogs Wear Shoes." Read the first sentence and point out that Julian is telling about his father's actions and words. Point out that the words *jumped up so fast* and *tipped over his lemonade cup* are clues that something is wrong. The word *bored* in capital letters and the fact that Julian's father *yelled* along with the actions helps you decide that the word *upset* at the top of the chart best describes Julian's father.

3. GUIDED PRACTICE

Check for understanding.

Before going on, have students explain how to identify character traits in a story. (*Look for word clues in the author's description of a character, in what a character says and thinks, and in actions and events.*)

Guide students in using the strategy.

Have students use the strategy to match the character traits listed at the top of the chart with the remaining sentences. Discuss word clues that helped them identify the character traits suggested by the sentences.

4. WRAP-UP

Summarize instruction.

Review why it is important to understand a character's traits. (*Knowing what kind of person a character is makes it easier to understand the character's behavior, which helps the reader better understand and appreciate the story.*)

Provide independent practice.

Options for independent practice are shown in the Resource Center below.

5. APPLICATION

Students will recognize character traits as they read "Phillis Wheatley, America's First Black Poet." The symbol ✔ marks specific questions and activities that apply this skill.

Workbook page 111

NAME _____

Characterization

LITERATURE

REMEMBER: To understand a character in a story, think about what the character says and does. Also think about how the character speaks and acts.

A. Read about what each character says. Then use a word from the box to complete the sentence that describes the character. Use each word once.

| honest | surprised | tired | wise |

1. Julian suggested that they shouldn't visit Dad, because his father hated to hear that people were bored.

Julian was ___wise___ .

2. Dad wondered why the children were taking a hike on such a hot day.

Dad was ___surprised___ .

3. Gloria admitted truthfully that they weren't really taking a hike.

Gloria was ___honest___ .

4. Dad decided not to look for frogs. He said, "I'm ready for a little nap."

Dad was ___tired___ .

B. Write a statement that Julian, Gloria, or Dad might say. Write a describing word to show how the character is acting. See Teacher Notes.

Characterization   "Phillis Wheatley, America's First Black Poet"   **111**

RESOURCE CENTER

◀ **Workbook page 111** is intended for use by all students.

Skills Practice 103 ▶ may be assigned for additional practice.

Workbook reuse option: On each write-in line in Part A, have students write another word that describes each character.

Skills Practice 103

NAME _____

SKILLS PRACTICE ‹103›

Characterization

To understand a character in a story, think about what the character says and does.

Read what each character says. Write the word from the box that describes the person speaking. Four words in the box won't be used.

bossy	friendly	helpful	lazy
brave	frightened	honest	proud
careful	hard-working	merry	shy

1. "Don't be afraid, Lee," Missy said. "I'll hold onto the bicycle, and you won't fall."   **helpful** _____

2. "I don't know anyone in my new class," Scott said to his mother. "I don't have anyone to talk to."   **shy** _____

3. "Is this your wallet?" the librarian asked Mr. Adams. "I found it near where you were sitting."   **honest** _____

4. "But I've never ridden a horse before," Dan said. "What if it runs away with me!"   **frightened** _____

5. "Welcome," Paul said to his new neighbor. "Want to play ball?"   **friendly** _____

6. Susan looked at the old vase. "The glass vase might break easily," she thought. "I won't touch it."   **careful** _____

7. Melinda looked at the snowy sidewalk. "If I work quickly, I can get the sidewalks clear before lunch."   **hard-working** _____

8. "I don't think I want to do any work right now . . . or ever," he said.   **lazy** _____

9. "You have to do it the way I tell you to do it," she said.   **bossy** _____

LEVEL 8   "Phillis Wheatley, America's First Black Poet"   **103**

Vocabulary Strategies

Developing Concepts

Tap prior knowledge about the concept of fame.

Discuss fame as a starting point for teaching vocabulary. Ask students what fame is and whether they would like to be famous. Lead students to define *famous* as being well known and much talked about. Then discuss what students think would be good and bad about being famous. Ask if they think being famous solves a person's problems or whether it creates new ones. Have students think about what it means to be a famous writer. Ask them how they can tell a writer is famous and ask for examples of famous writers they know and whose work they may have read. (*possible suggestions: Beverly Cleary, Arnold Lobel, Donald Sobol, Peggy Parrish, Johanna Hurwitz*)

Teaching Vocabulary

Discuss meanings of Story Critical words.

Read each context sentence on the Teaching Chart and identify the new word. Then use the questions below to help students understand each word. When necessary, provide a definition.

TEACHING CHART 67: VOCABULARY   67

1. **poetry** (poems; the art of writing poems)
   Her *poetry* is fun to read because she can tell about something beautiful in only a few lines.
2. **fame** (the condition of being well known and much talked about)
   The author's sudden *fame* has brought her many more readers.
3. **printed** (published for sale)
   Having a book *printed* is an exciting event for any writer.
4. **popular** (very well liked)
   She is so *popular* that she is invited to speak in schools all over the United States.
5. **choice** (the act of choosing)
   If you had to make a *choice* between being rich or being happy from writing a book, which would you choose?

---

poetry **1. If poetry is the art of writing poems, what is a person who writes poems called?** (a poet) **Why would you write a poem?** (possible answer: to tell about a place, something that happens, or a person; to convey an emotion) STRATEGY: STRUCTURAL ANALYSIS

fame **2. How does someone find fame?** (He or she does something that gets other people's attention.) **What things might fame result in for a writer?** (possible answers: more books published and sold; a chance to go on television; invitations to more parties; more money; happiness) STRATEGY: PRIOR KNOWLEDGE

printed **3. What other word do you see in *printed?*** (print) **What does it mean to print a book?** (The manuscript is set into type, copies are made on a printing press, the book is sold.) **Why is it better to print a book than to write it by hand?** (You can make lots of copies; book printing is easier to read than handwriting.) STRATEGY: STRUCTURAL ANALYSIS *popular* **4. What does it mean when a book is popular?** (many people want to read it) **How do people become popular?** (by being nice to others; by being pleasant to be with) STRATEGY: PRIOR KNOWLEDGE

choice **5. What does it mean to have a choice?** (There are two or more things to do or have, and you can do or have only one.) **What kinds of things do you think about when you're trying to make a choice?** (possible answers: what is best for me, what will make me happiest, what will be nicest for someone else) STRATEGY: PRIOR KNOWLEDGE

Discuss Support words as needed. The Glossary of the Student Text includes definitions of the Support words: *charm, recover, popularity, valor, servant, slave, chores, separated.*

Present Character/ Setting words. The selection contains the following Character/Setting words: *Africa; Phillis Wheatley; Boston, Massachusetts; John and Susannah Wheatley; English; Mary; Nathaniel; Bible; George Whitefield; England; Countess of Huntingdon; General George Washington; America; Cambridge.*

Provide independent practice. Options for independent practice are shown in the Resource Center below.

WRITING OR SPEAKING ACTIVITY *Remind students of their discussion of fame. Have them describe a day in the life of a famous writer of children's books. Ask them to use new vocabulary if possible.*

Workbook page 112

NAME _____

Using New Words

A. Choose words from the box to complete each sentence.

| choice | fame | poetry | popular | printed |

1. Some poets gain ___fame___
(noun naming thing or idea)
when many people read their ___poetry___
(noun naming thing or idea)

2. Long ago, some poets ___printed___ their own poetry.
(verb naming action)

3. That poet is very ___popular___
(adjective that describes)
but my ___choice___ is another poet.
(noun naming a thing or idea)

B. Write the words from the box that belong in each group.

| choice | fame | poetry | popular | printed |

4. Nouns Naming Things or Ideas
___choice___
___fame___
___poetry___

5. Adjective that Describes
___popular___

6. Verb Naming Action
___printed___

C. On separate paper, write three sentences about a poem you read in school or choose a poem from your book. Use one or two words from the boxes in each sentence. See Teacher Notes.

112 "Phillis Wheatley, America's First Black Poet" Selection Vocabulary

---

RESOURCE CENTER

◀ **Workbook page 112** provides practice with Story Critical words.

Skills Practice 104 ▶ provides additional practice with Story Critical words.

Skills Practice 105 provides practice with Support words.

Spelling Connection Master 53 may be used for spelling instruction with the new vocabulary.

Workbook reuse option: Have students add another word to each grouping in Part B. The words do not have to come from the story.

Skills Practice 104

NAME _____

Vocabulary: Story Critical Words

SKILLS PRACTICE **104**

A. Study the meaning of each word.

choice the act of choosing
fame known by many people
poetry the art of writing poems
popular very well liked
printed published for sale

B. Write the vocabulary word that goes with each clue.

1. This was done to every book, magazine, or newspaper you see. ___printed___
2. A person with many friends is this. ___popular___
3. A well-known person has this. ___fame___
4. You have to decide before making this. ___choice___
5. This writing has rhythm and rhyme. ___poetry___

C. Complete each sentence with the correct vocabulary word.

6. Jack had to make a ___choice___ whether to see a movie or visit his friend.
7. Mrs. Glass teaches ___poetry___ in her English class.
8. Jeff is ___popular___ because he is always friendly to everyone.
9. The writer was happy when his story was ___printed___ in a magazine.

D. One word in each sentence does not make sense. Underline that word. Write the vocabulary word that belongs in its place.

10. The old book was pointed in 1879. ___printed___
11. Sandra is a very poplar person. ___popular___
12. Some famous people say that they do not enjoy their name. ___fame___
13. It is hard to write plainly and include rhyme. ___poetry___
14. You have a voice of a hot or cold drink. ___choice___

104 LEVEL 8 "Phillis Wheatley, America's First Black Poet" Definition clues

Reading & Responding

Building Background

Motivate discussion using the poem.

Share this poem with students. Ask whether they agree that poetry is a special way to describe things and how they think poetry is different from prose.

> **What is Poetry? Who knows?**
> **Not a rose, but the scent of the rose;**
> **Not the sky, but the light in the sky;**
> **Not the fly, but the gleam of the fly;**
> **Not the sea, but the sound of the sea;**
> **Not myself, but what makes me**
> **See, hear, and feel something that prose**
> **Cannot; and what it is, who knows?**
> by Eleanor Farjeon from *Eleanor Farjeon's Poems for Children*

Build background about poets.

Ask students the names of poets they know and what they like about those poets' poems. Discuss whether they think it is difficult to write poems and why. Point out that many people like to write poems to describe their feelings and experiences, but it is not easy for poets to get their poems published. Usually only the best poets get to see their poems in print.

Discuss biography.

Write the word *biography* on the chalkboard. Point out to students that the selection they are about to read is a biography, or true story of a person's life. Students will learn what happened in Phillis Wheatley's life to help make her a famous poet.

Developing a Purpose for Reading

Option 1
Students set purpose.

ORAL "QUESTION" LISTS   Have students read the introduction. Ask them to think of what questions they would like to have answered about Phillis Wheatley's life. Record students' questions for use later.

WRITING ACTIVITY   Have students work individually or in pairs to create written "Question" lists. Tell students to save their lists for later use.

Option 2
Teacher sets purpose.

Have students read the selection to find out how Phillis Wheatley became a famous poet and whether or not it was easy for her to become famous.

Meeting
Individual
Needs

EXTRA HELP   Explain to students that when reading nonfiction, one way the reader can help herself or himself understand the selection is by turning the title and headings into questions. Have volunteers read aloud the title and each heading and suggest questions for them.

ACHIEVING ENGLISH PROFICIENCY   Write the following sentences on the chalkboard, underlining words as shown:

1. **It was a rainy day, but the teacher made the best of it by letting us play games in the classroom.**

2. **I enjoyed staying at my pen pal's home in Italy because her parents treated me like one of the family.**

As you read the sentences aloud, call on students to figure out the meaning of the underlined words. Provide help as needed. For additional help with story comprehension, use Master 25 in the Teacher Resource Kit.

Phillis's Fame Grows

As more and more people in Boston read her poems, Phillis's <u>fame</u> grew. Her charm and pleasant company made her even more <u>popular</u>. When newspapers from Boston reached England, people there read her poems. The Countess of Huntingdon, an English woman who was related to the king of England, helped to make Phillis's poetry popular in England. The countess enjoyed reading Phillis's poem about George Whitefield so much that she had it <u>printed</u> in England. During this time, the countess and Phillis began writing letters to one another and a friendship between them grew.

Things were going well for Phillis. Then, in 1773, she became ill. The Wheatleys were very worried about her. Their family doctor thought that a sea voyage would help her recover. So Nathaniel took Phillis on a voyage to England. When the Countess of Huntingdon heard they were coming to England, she invited Phillis and Nathaniel to stay with her. While they were in England, the countess made arrangements to have Phillis's poems printed in a book. People in England began to talk about Phillis's poetry, and her popularity grew.

Phillis was only in England five weeks when she received a letter from Mr. Wheatley with the sad news that Mrs. Wheatley was very ill. Immediately Phillis made plans to return to Boston. She wanted to get back to Boston as soon as she could so that she could be with Mrs. Wheatley. Phillis did get back in time to see Mrs. Wheatley, who died a short time later. Mr. Wheatley died soon after. Even though these events caused great sadness for Phillis, she continued to write. Now she was writing not only for herself but also for the Wheatleys, who had helped her so much.

Phillis Meets George Washington

A few months after Phillis returned to Boston, America began its war against England. Americans wanted to be free from England's rule. To prepare for the war, General George Washington went to Cambridge, Massachusetts, as head of the American army. It was an exciting time for people in the Boston area! They were eager to meet the man who would lead them in their struggle for freedom. Phillis had heard about General Washington. She knew that he was a great man.

GUIDED READING

Page 230   What part did the Countess of Huntingdon play in Phillis's life? (The countess helped make Phillis's poetry popular in England by having her poems printed there. The countess and Phillis began writing letters and a friendship developed. When Phillis became ill, the countess had Phillis and Nathaniel visit with her in England to help Phillis recover.)   RECALL: DETAILS

✔ **Page 231   How did the death of the Wheatleys affect Phillis?** (It caused her great sadness, but it also made her more determined to continue writing. She felt she was writing not only for herself but also for the Wheatleys.)   RECALL: CHARACTER

Page 231   Phillis returned to Boston at a very exciting time in America. What was happening? (The war against England was beginning. General George Washington had come to Cambridge to talk and meet the people.)   RECALL: DETAILS

✔ Skill from The Bridge applied through this question.

STRATEGIC READING

Page 231 Have students summarize what had happened to Phillis since she came to Boston on the slave ship. (She had been bought by the Wheatleys, who had treated her well. They taught her to speak, read, and write English. She wrote many poems. Her poems were published in the United States and in England.) Discuss with students how the selection headings for each part of Phillis's life help readers. (Headings make it easy to find information and summarize it.) Ask students to predict what the last part of the selection will be about, based on the last heading on page 231 [Phillis Meets George Washington]. Then tell them to keep the headings in mind as they read the last part. Point out that summarizing and predicting is one way students can make sure they understand what they read. Suggest that students reread any parts of the selection that are confusing if they have trouble summarizing or predicting.   METACOGNITION: SUMMARIZING AND PREDICTING

The following year she wrote a letter to General Washington to wish him success. In her letter, she included a poem she had written about him. Part of the poem read:

Thee, first in peace and honours . . .
Fam'd for thy valour, for thy virtues
more. . . .

General Washington was so pleased with the poem that he sent Phillis a personal thank-you note and invited her to visit him in Cambridge, Massachusetts. Phillis was delighted.

Phillis Wheatley, the shy young girl who came to Boston as a slave in 1761, met and talked to the man who would become the first president of the United States. She had come to Boston unable to read or write and later went on to become a well-known poet. Phillis Wheatley's poetry is an example of what a young person can accomplish on her own.

 Reader's Response

If you could talk to Phillis Wheatley what questions would you ask her?

See next page for suggested answers.

SELECTION FOLLOW-UP
Phillis Wheatley
America's First Black Poet

 Thinking It Over

1. How did Phillis Wheatley come to America?
2. What was special about the way in which the Wheatleys treated Phillis?
3. How did learning to read and write change Phillis Wheatley's life?
4. Do you think Phillis Wheatley's life was unusual? What led you to your answer?

 Writing to Learn

THINK AND DESCRIBE Can you make a character map of Phillis Wheatley? Think about what she was like and the things she did. Then, on your paper, complete the character map of her.

Phillis had a will to learn.

_____

_____

_____

Phillis
Wheatley

WRITE Write sentences that tell what kind of person Phillis Wheatley was.

GUIDED READING

Page 232   Why is Phillis Wheatley's story important for people to read? (It is the story of a young woman who worked hard to accomplish something. It is also a part of our country's history.)
SYNTHESIZE: DRAWING CONCLUSIONS

RETURNING TO THE READING PURPOSE

OPTION 1 If students set the purpose, ask them to return to their questions about Phillis Wheatley. Discuss which questions were answered and how. Invite students to express reactions to Phillis's story.

OPTION 2 If you set the purpose, ask students how Phillis Wheatley became a famous poet. (She worked very hard to learn to read and write; the Wheatleys encouraged her; people in Boston and England read and liked her work; even George Washington liked her poetry.) Ask students if it was easy for Phillis to become a famous poet. (No; she was a slave and did not know how to speak English at first, let alone read and write; her patrons, the Wheatleys, died.)

Reader's Journal   p 85
Responding to Reading

A JOURNAL FOR PHILLIS

Pretending to be Phillis Wheatley, students write journal entries, imagining her feelings for each event described.

SELECTION FOLLOW-UP

Phillis Wheatley
America's First Black Poet

THINKING IT OVER

1. **How did Phillis Wheatley come to America?** (Phillis Wheatley made the voyage to America from Africa on a slave ship.)   RECALL: DETAILS

2. **What was special about the way in which the Wheatleys treated Phillis?** (Possible answers: she was treated as one of the family; she was taught to read and write; she was treated with respect and affection.)
SYNTHESIZE: DRAWING CONCLUSIONS

3. **How did learning to read and write change Phillis Wheatley's life?** (Learning to read and write helped Phillis to become a poet; being a poet helped her to meet new people and to travel to new places.)   INFER: CAUSE/EFFECT

4. **Do you think Phillis Wheatley's life was unusual? What led you to your answer?** (Students will most likely agree that Phillis Wheatley's life was highly unusual. She achieved a success that was extraordinary for a slave; she traveled and met famous people; she herself was famous; she was faced with terrible problems in her childhood and overcame them with intelligence, courage, and the help of a remarkable family.)
SYNTHESIZE: DRAWING CONCLUSIONS; METACOGNITION

WRITING TO LEARN ❖❖❖

Use Writing Master 17, which provides a character map.

THINK AND DESCRIBE   Can you make a character map of Phillis Wheatley? Think about what she was like and the things she did. Then, on your paper, complete the character map of her. (Possible answers are shown. This activity applies the Strategy for Thinking taught in this unit.)

Phillis had a will to learn.

(Phillis loved to write poetry.)

(Phillis was bright.)

(Phillis was gentle and caring.)

(Phillis enjoyed reading.)

(Phillis worked hard.)

Extend comprehension through writing.

WRITE   Write sentences that tell what kind of person Phillis Wheatley was. (Have students share their sentences.)

More Ideas for Selection Follow-Up

CRITICAL AND CREATIVE THINKING QUESTIONS

Encourage a variety of responses and points of view.

Use these open-ended questions to encourage critical and creative thinking about the selection.

1. Which events in Phillis's life do you think might have been the most exciting for her? Why?

✔ 2. Compare Phillis Wheatley with Jason Hardman and Johanna Hurwitz. How was her challenge like theirs? How was it different?

REREADING ORALLY

Have students reread for specific information.

Ask students to reread parts of the story that show how Phillis Wheatley became a famous poet. Ask them to tell why they chose the passage and then to read it orally. Students' selections should reflect an understanding of the events that led Phillis Wheatley to fame. Passages selected may tell Phillis's age when she wrote her first poem, page 229; how people first found out about her poetry, page 229; what made Phillis popular besides her poetry, page 230; how Phillis became known in England, page 230; and how Phillis was able to meet George Washington, page 232.

SELECTION COMPREHENSION

Provide comprehension check.

A Workbook page to check comprehension is shown in the Resource Center below. It may be used for informal assessment.

✔ **Informal Assessment Opportunity:** SYNTHESIZING ACROSS SELECTIONS

Workbook page 113

NAME _____

SELECTION COMPREHENSION

Phillis Wheatley
America's First Black Poet

A. Complete the summary of "Phillis Wheatley, America's First Black Poet." Accept reasonable variations.

This selection is about ____Phillis Wheatley____, who arrived in Boston, Massachusetts, in 1761. She had been taken from a village in ____Africa____ and put aboard a slave ship. A wealthy tailor named John Wheatley bought her as a servant for

____his wife____ . Phillis was treated like a member of the family. The Wheatleys' daughter, Mary, taught Phillis to speak English. Phillis also learned very quickly to ____read and write____

When Phillis was thirteen years old, she wrote her first ____poem____ . Later her poetry appeared in a ____newspaper____

The newspapers from Boston reached England, and people there also liked her poems. An English woman who liked them very much was ____the Countess of Huntington____

When Phillis became ill and went to England for a cure, the Countess had her poems ____printed in a book____

Phillis returned to Boston because ____Mrs. Wheatley____ was ill. Soon after that, war broke out between England and America. Phillis thought George Washington was a great man, so she ____wrote a poem____ about him and sent it to him. He liked it so much he invited Phillis to visit.

B. Pretend that you are Phillis Wheatley. On separate paper, write a letter to Mary Wheatley telling how you feel about meeting General George Washington. See Teacher Notes.

Selection Comprehension   "Phillis Wheatley, America's First Black Poet" **113**

RESOURCE CENTER

◄ **Workbook page 113** is intended for use by all students.

Writing Master 17 provides a character map.

I•T **Kit Activity**

I•T

***Audio:* Interview with Lindamichellebaron**

Both girls and boys can find something to relate to in the sensitive poems by this contemporary black poet. Lindamichellebaron reads a few of her poems and describes her writing process. Students discuss what the poems mean to them. (See Activity Guide.)   LITERATURE

LANGUAGE ARTS CONNECTIONS

CREATIVE THINKING: WRITING POEMS

Discuss writing poetry.

Ask students who have ever tried writing a poem to raise their hands. Have volunteers share their feelings about poetry writing with the group. Point out that writing a poem is a way to tell how they feel, what they see and imagine, and what they think of the world around them.

Have students write poems.

Have students write poems of their own about a topic related to Phillis Wheatley's story. An example is what it might be like to sail from the United States to England or what it might be like to meet George Washington. Remind students that a poem does not have to rhyme but that it should have some kind of flow or rhythm when read aloud.   WRITING

ORGANIZING A POETRY READING

Assist students in organizing a poetry reading.

Explain that poets often hold public readings of their poems. Provide books of poetry or have students check out library books by their favorite poets. Have students work individually or in pairs. Have each student select one or two poems to read aloud. Also encourage students to read poems of their own. Allow readers time to rehearse. Suggest that they first visualize what the poem describes and then practice reading it aloud with expression. Remind them to listen for rhythms and to look for punctuation that will tell them where to pause or stop. Caution students not to put too much stress on rhyming words. Have students plan the reading and invite other classes. Encourage those not reading to draw posters, write invitations, and advise readers about their clarity and loudness during rehearsals.   SHARED LEARNING: SPEAKING/LISTENING

IDENTIFYING PARTS OF A STORY

Have students identify the parts of Phillis's story.

Remind students that a biography, like a story, usually includes a beginning, a middle, and an end. The beginning often includes information about where a person was born. The middle tells about what happens as the person grows up and the problems that he or she might face. The end is usually about the person as an adult and how that person's problems are solved. You may want to write the sentences below on the chalkboard or reproduce and distribute them. Tell students that these sentences are events that really happened in Phillis Wheatley's life. As students copy the sentences on a separate piece of paper, have them arrange the events in the order in which they happened. Then have students label each sentence as belonging to the beginning, middle, or end of the biography.

IDENTIFYING PARTS OF A STORY (continued)

Phillis meets General George Washington.
As a young girl, Phillis is taken from an African village.
Phillis learns to read and write.
John Wheatley buys Phillis as a slave.
Phillis's poems are printed in England.
A Boston newspaper prints Phillis's poem about Mr. Whitefield.
The Countess of Huntingdon writes to Phillis.

Discuss why the author does not tell more about Phillis's early years in Africa. Then refer students to the end of the selection and ask them to tell what other information they might expect to be told as an end to Phillis's story. *(possible answers: details about Phillis's life after she met Washington, her death)*   WHOLE CLASS ENRICHMENT

BIOGRAPHY AS A LITERARY GENRE

Review the features of a biography.

Review with students that a biography is a true story about a person. Have students tell how they know the selection they read is a biography. *(The selection is about a person who really lived; dates and real people and places are mentioned.)* Have students summarize the selection by naming the people and places mentioned and some of the events in Phillis Wheatley's life.

Have students write brief biographies.

Have each student interview a friend, relative, or teacher in order to write a brief biography of that person. Tell students to be sure to include important events and dates as well as special people. **Language Arts Master 15** can be used with this activity.   CHALLENGE: WRITING

PUBLISHING POETRY JOURNALS

Have students create poetry journals.

Explain that poets sometimes publish poems in poetry journals, which are magazines that include poems and articles about poets and poetry. Tell students that they will be working cooperatively in groups of five. Fill each of the following positions: editor-in-chief, two poetry editors, an art director, and an artist. The editor-in-chief makes the final decision on which poems and art to include and checks to see that all the other jobs are going well. The two poetry editors select and neatly copy ten favorite poems from books or poems written by their classmates. The art director decides how to display the poems on pages and tells the artist what size picture is needed to go with each poem. The artist draws the illustrations. Distribute paper and art materials. Then have groups construct their journals.   COOPERATIVE LEARNING: WRITING

READING EVERY DAY

Students will profit from learning of individuals who, born into slavery, courageously achieve their own freedom.

The Drinking Gourd by F. N. Monjo. Harper & Row, © 1970. After discovering the family of slaves his father had hidden, Tommy finds out about the underground railroad and helps the family escape to Canada and to freedom.
EASIER TO READ

Harriet Tubman by Francene Sabin. Troll, © 1985. Having been born a slave in Maryland in about 1820, Harriet Tubman eventually escapes and helps countless other slaves escape to freedom through the underground railroad.
A World of Books Classroom Libraries selection

Reader's Journal	pp 86, 87
Extending Reading	

LIVING IN A COLONIAL VILLAGE

A description of shops during colonial times serves as a springboard for students to write about working and shopping in Phillis's time.

Selection Support

SKILL TRACE: INFERENCES				
Introduction	Practice	Test	Reteach	Maintain
TE 380	394 442	461	462	596

COMPREHENSION

Inferences

OBJECTIVE Making inferences about people, location, and feelings.

Review inferences.

Remind students that making inferences is using clues from a story and from what they already know to figure out information that is not stated.

Use Teaching Chart to review how to make inferences.

Read item 1 on the Teaching Chart and note that the author does not tell, but you can infer that Phillis spoke an African language. Call on students to make an inference for the second example.

TEACHING CHART 68: MAKING INFERENCES | 68 |

1. Phillis had been taken from a village in Africa. She could not speak English. The Wheatleys guessed that she was between seven and eight years old. Does Phillis speak any language? (African language; Story clues: Africa, between seven and eight years old)

2. Phillis received a letter with sad news about Mrs. Wheatley. Immediately, Phillis made plans to return to Boston. How worried was Phillis about Mrs. Wheatley? (very; story clues: sad news, returned immediately)

Provide independent practice.

Options for independent practice are shown in the Resource Center below.

Workbook page 114

RESOURCE CENTER

Skills Practice 106

Workbook page 114 is intended for use by all students.

Skills Practice 106 may be assigned for additional practice.

COMPREHENSION

NAME _____

Inference

REMEMBER: Use story clues and what you already know to figure out things that the writer did not state.

A. Read each statement. Place **X** next to the information you can figure out from clues in the statement.

1. She had been taken from a small village in Africa and put aboard a slave ship heading for Boston harbor.

   a. _X_ The girl was a slave.

   b. ____ The girl's father was a ship captain.

   c. ____ The girl was a sailor.

2. John Wheatley was a wealthy tailor.

   a. ____ The Wheatley family lived on a farm.

   b. ____ The Wheatley family was poor.

   c. _X_ The Wheatley family had plenty of money.

3. Phillis quickly learned to read and write.

   a. ____ Phillis was a slow learner.

   b. _X_ Phillis was a good student.

   c. ____ Phillis disliked study.

4. People from all over enjoyed reading her poetry.

   a. _X_ Phillis's poetry had been printed.

   b. ____ Phillis loved to read.

   c. ____ Phillis traveled to England.

B. On separate paper, write another guess you could make from the last statement in Part A. See Teacher Notes.

114 "Phillis Wheatley, America's First Black Poet" Inference

NAME _____

SKILLS PRACTICE 106

Inference

Sometimes you can figure out things about a story even if they are not stated in the story. This is called making inferences. Story clues and what you already know can help you to make inferences.

| Story clues |
| What I know |
+ | Inference |

Bob could only see out the side windows. Since he didn't bring any books, he made up games. Before long, they pulled up in front of Uncle Ted's house.

We can infer that Bob is riding in the back seat of a car even though the writer doesn't say so. The underlined words are the story clues.

A. Read the story. Answer the questions.

Lisa tried to keep Buster and Clyde apart as much as she could. When Buster saw Clyde, Buster curved his back. Clyde always hissed and backed away.

Lisa's mother didn't like what was going on. Neither did Lisa. She thought a lot about the problem. One day, she made up her mind. Lisa went to Eric's and rang the bell, and they talked. A few minutes later, Lisa was home. She put Clyde into a box with a window and a handle and went back outside again.

Lisa was happy with her plan. After all, she could still see Clyde as much as she wanted.

1. Who, or what, were Buster and Clyde? cats

2. Who owned Buster and Clyde? Lisa's family

3. What was the problem? Buster and Clyde didn't like each other.

4. About how far from Lisa did Eric live? close by

5. What was Lisa's plan? to give Clyde to Eric

B. Here are more statements about the story. Put an **X** before those that could be an inference made from the story.

6. _X_ Lisa makes decisions easily.   8. ____ Lisa was afraid of cats.

7. ____ Lisa's mother did not like cats.   9. _X_ Clyde was afraid of Buster.

106 LEVEL 8   "Phillis Wheatley, America's First Black Poet"

Workbook reuse option: Have students circle the words in the statements that helped them make inferences.

SKILL TRACE: HOMOPHONES				
Introduction	Practice	Test	Reteach	Maintain
TE 392	420 443	461	464	550

VOCABULARY
Homophones

OBJECTIVE Understanding words that sound alike but have different meanings.

Review homophones.

Remind students that homophones are words that are pronounced the same but have different spellings and different meanings. Point out that one way to figure out the correct meaning of a homophone is to use context clues.

Present homophones in context.

Display the Teaching Chart. Identify the homophone in each sentence and have students give a meaning for the homophone based on sentence context. Then have students think of the matching homophone and write a sentence using that homophone.

TEACHING CHART 69: HOMOPHONES

69

1. For Phillis, it was a long *sail* from Africa on the ship. (travel by water; sale)
2. Even George Washington *knew* who Phillis Wheatley was. (aware of; new)
3. Many people were eager to *meet* the young poet. (make the acquaintance of; meat)
4. In England, the Countess of Huntingdon *heard* about Phillis's poetry. (had word of; herd)

Provide independent practice.

Options for independent practice are shown in the Resource Center below.

Workbook page 115

NAME _____

Homophones

VOCABULARY

REMEMBER: Homophones are words that sound the same but have different spelling and meanings. Use spelling and context to decide the correct meaning of homophones.

A. Read each pair of homophones. Complete each sentence with the correct homophone.

1. by, buy
   a. John Wheatley went to ____buy____ a slave.
   b. Phillis was taught to speak English ____by____ Mary.

2. ate, eight
   a. Phillis ____ate____ her meals with the family.
   b. Phillis was seven or ____eight____ when she arrived

3. red, read
   a. Phillis ____read____ the Bible.
   b. The cover of the Bible was ____red____

4. right, write
   a. Phillis could read and ____write____ .
   b. The Wheatleys were ____right____ about Phillis.

5. see, sea
   a. Nathaniel and Phillis crossed the ____sea____ by boat.
   b. Phillis could ____see____ the Countess of Huntington.

B. On separate paper, write three sentences about the story. Use one of the homophones in each sentence. See Teacher Notes.

Homophones   "Phillis Wheatley, America's First Black Poet" **115**

RESOURCE CENTER

◄ **Workbook page 115** is intended for use by all students.

Skills Practice 107 ► may be assigned for additional practice.

Workbook reuse option: Have students write each homophone pair in alphabetical order in the margins.

Skills Practice 107

NAME _____

SKILLS PRACTICE ◄ 107

Homophones

Homophones are words that sound the same but have different spellings and meanings. Use spelling and context to decide the correct meaning of homophones.

beat   beet

A. Write the correct homophone from the box in each sentence.

tail	tide	toad	tow
tale	tied	toe	towed

1. The ____toad____ king is caught!
2. The frogs ____towed____ him to the beach.
3. They ____tied____ him to a stake.
4. Now the ____tide____ is coming up the sand.
5. An ant tickles the king's ____toe____ .
6. "I can ____tow____ you out of here," says the ant.
7. He tied the king to a whale's ____tail____ .
8. And that is how the ____tale____ ended. (Silly, wasn't it?)

B. Write your own sentences using these homophones. **Sentences will vary.**

9. throne _____
10. thrown _____
11. their _____
12. there _____
13. raise _____
14. rays _____
15. chews _____
16. choose _____

LEVEL 8   "Phillis Wheatley, America's First Black Poet"   **107**

SKILL TRACE: FORMS
This skill is untested at this level.

STUDY SKILLS

Forms

OBJECTIVE   Reading and completing forms.

Review forms.

Remind students that a form is a printed sheet of paper with spaces left blank for filling in requested information. Tell students that when filling out forms, they should provide all the information requested.

Present a form for practice.

Display the Teaching Chart. Have students review the form for any items they do not understand. Then have students copy the form onto paper and fill it out with their own names, addresses, and so on. Discuss which subscription is the better buy. Help students figure out how much money is spent per month for each subscription.

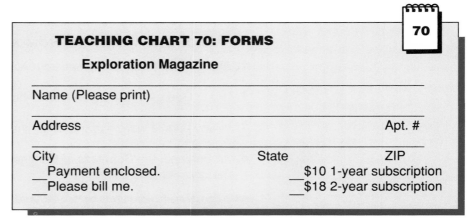

TEACHING CHART 70: FORMS

Exploration Magazine

Name (Please print)

Address   Apt. #

City   State   ZIP
___ Payment enclosed.   ___ $10 1-year subscription
___ Please bill me.   ___ $18 2-year subscription

70

Provide independent practice.

An independent activity is shown in the Resource Center below.

RESOURCE CENTER

Skills Practice 108 ▶ may be assigned for additional practice.

Skills Practice 108

NAME _____   SKILLS PRACTICE 108

Forms

You often have to fill out a form when you order something or when you want to do something. Read the form carefully. Write only the information that is asked for. Check the form after you have finished to make sure you have given the right information.

A. Fill out this form for Summer Kids' Adventures.

SUMMER KIDS' ADVENTURES

(please print) **Answers will vary.**

Name _____

Street address _____

City _____

State _____   ZIP code _____

Telephone number _____

Parents' names _____

School _____

Write three games you like to play _____

Write three arts or crafts you enjoy.

_____
_____
_____

Sign your name _____

B. On separate paper, make up a form you could use to order pencils.

108 LEVEL 8   "Phillis Wheatley, America's First Black Poet"

SKILL TRACE: TABLE OF CONTENTS				
Introduction	Practice	Test	Reteach	Maintain
TE 224	249	273	311	315	445

STUDY SKILLS

Title Page, Copyright Page, Table of Contents

OBJECTIVE   Using the title and copyright pages and the table of contents.

Review title page, copyright page, table of contents.

Remind students that the title page gives the title of the book, the author's name, and the name and place of the publisher. The copyright page tells the year the book was published. The table of contents lists all the stories, along with the page number where each story begins.

Provide practice with title page, copyright page, table of contents.

You may wish to write the material below on the chalkboard. Have students identify the book's title, author, and publisher, and when and where it was published. Have students use the table of contents to identify the first poem, what the poem on page 6 is about, and the longest of the four poems. You may also wish to provide students with the opportunity to examine the Title Page, Copyright Pages, and Table of Contents in various other books.

<table>
<tr><td>

The Boston Poems
by Phillis Wheatley

Cobble Books
London, England
© 1773
</td><td>

Contents

Poem	Page
"George Whitefield"	3
"Mary & Nathaniel"	5
"African Voyage"	6
"Starting Over"	9
</td></tr>
</table>

Provide independent practice.

An independent activity is shown in the Resource Center below.

RESOURCE CENTER

Skills Practice 109 ▶ may be assigned for additional practice.

Skills Practice 109

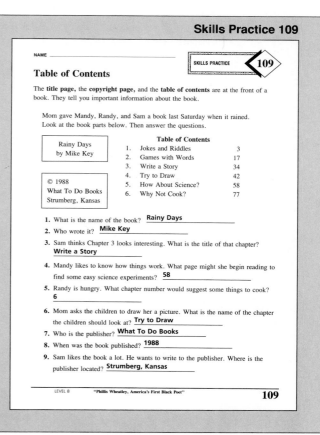

NAME _____

Table of Contents

The **title page,** the **copyright page,** and the **table of contents** are at the front of a book. They tell you important information about the book.

Mom gave Mandy, Randy, and Sam a book last Saturday when it rained. Look at the book parts below. Then answer the questions.

<table>
<tr><td>

Rainy Days
by Mike Key

© 1988
What To Do Books
Strumberg, Kansas
</td><td>

Table of Contents

1.	Jokes and Riddles	3
2.	Games with Words	17
3.	Write a Story	34
4.	Try to Draw	42
5.	How About Science?	58
6.	Why Not Cook?	77
</td></tr>
</table>

1. What is the name of the book?   **Rainy Days**

2. Who wrote it?   **Mike Key**

3. Sam thinks Chapter 3 looks interesting. What is the title of that chapter?
   Write a Story

4. Mandy likes to know how things work. What page might she begin reading to find some easy science experiments?   **58**

5. Randy is hungry. What chapter number would suggest some things to cook?
   6

6. Mom asks the children to draw her a picture. What is the name of the chapter the children should look at?   **Try to Draw**

7. Who is the publisher?   **What To Do Books**

8. When was the book published?   **1988**

9. Sam likes the book a lot. He wants to write to the publisher. Where is the publisher located?   **Strumberg, Kansas**

LEVEL 8   "Phillis Wheatley, America's First Black Poet"   **109**

CURRICULUM CONNECTIONS

TIME LINES AND MILESTONES SOCIAL STUDIES

Explain to students that the events that happen in a person's life and the years in which they happened can be shown on a drawing called a time line. Have students create a time line of events in Phillis's life. Display the following drawing to help students get started. Have students copy this information and then complete their own time lines. Point out that some years have been added based on time clues in the story.

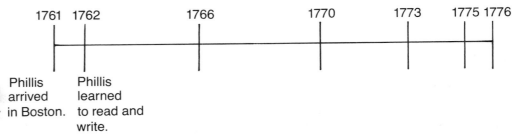

1761 | 1762 | 1766 | 1770 | 1773 | 1775 1776

Phillis arrived in Boston.

Phillis learned to read and write.

MAPPING PHILLIS'S TRAVELS GEOGRAPHY

Phillis Wheatley traveled a great deal in her life. She went from Africa to Boston, from Boston to England and back, and then to Cambridge to visit George Washington. Have students draw a map of Phillis's travels, using an atlas or globe as a guide. They can trace the continents from other maps, then fill in the names and places on their own. They should use different colors for different countries and continents. They also might wish to use different markings or symbols to indicate the way Phillis traveled: by slave ship from Africa; by ship to England; by carriage to Cambridge. Since we do not know exactly where in Africa Phillis came from, students should choose some place on the West African coast as her original home. Finally, have students use the mileage scales on the maps they consult to figure out, very roughly, about how many miles Phillis traveled during her lifetime. **Curriculum Connection Master 15** can be used with this activity.

WASHINGTON VS. WHEATLEY SOCIAL STUDIES

Phillis Wheatley started writing her poetry just before the Revolutionary War, when the American colonies rebelled against British rule so they could set up their own free government. When George Washington met Phillis Wheatley, he was just starting to lead the colonists' fight for freedom. He went on to become the first president of the United States. Have students read biographies or stories of Washington's life, concentrating on his early years and upbringing. They might want to illustrate a few events from his childhood. Point out the differences between Phillis Wheatley's and George Washington's upbringings. Discuss how two people from different backgrounds worked hard and became famous in their time.

PAST AND PRESENT POETS HUMANITIES

If possible, read aloud one or more poems by Phillis Wheatley or another American poet of her time, such as Anne Bradstreet, Edward Taylor, Philip Freneau, Joel Barlow, or Royall Tyler. Encourage students to try reading the poems themselves. Then read, or have students read, contemporary poets, such as Shel Silverstein, John Ciardi, or Eve Merriam. Ask students to compare poetry of long ago with that of today. Discuss ways in which the English language has changed in the way it is written. *(different expressions used; language less formal, more humorous, easier to understand)*

PICTURES OF A POET ART

Have students use encyclopedias, stories about George Washington or life in colonial America, and the illustrations in the selection to research the types of clothing people wore during the time Phillis Wheatley lived. Then have them select scenes from Phillis's life described in the selection and illustrate them. Possible scenes include the Wheatley children teaching Phillis to read and write, Phillis meeting Countess Huntingdon, and Phillis meeting George Washington. Direct students to write a sentence under their pictures telling what is happening. Display students' pictures on the bulletin board under the heading ''Phillis Wheatley, America's First Black Poet.''

SONGS OF NOW AND THEN MUSIC

Explain to students that when Phillis Wheatley visited Countess Huntingdon in England she may have heard music played that was popular at the time. Point out that the style of music that was popular between 1750 and 1820 is now known as *classical music*. Important composers were Haydn, Mozart, Beethoven, and Schubert. If available, play one or two recordings of selections by one or more of these composers. Ask students to compare the popular music of Phillis's time with what is popular in the present day.

Reading the Poem

OBJECTIVE   Understanding how a poet creates pictures in a reader's mind.

INTRODUCING THE POEM

Relate content of the poem to students' experience.

Remind students they have been reading about people being on their own and taking charge of their lives. Ask students if they ever imagined themselves as different persons or even as animals or things. Ask volunteers to tell who or what they imagined themselves to be. Discuss what would be special about being these persons, animals, or things. (*For example, as a bird, someone could fly; as the wind, someone could make weather.*)

Set a listening purpose.

Tell students they are going to hear a poem about a girl who daydreams about being other people, animals, and things. Ask them to think about what pictures of the girl and her daydreams come to their minds.

READING THE POEM

Read the poem aloud.

Because poetry is a sound-based literary form, this part of the lesson is most important. Read the poem aloud to the students with Student Texts closed. Then have students open their books to page 212. Read the poem again or ask for volunteers to read it to the whole group. With this second reading, encourage students to picture themselves in the girl's place as she daydreams. Discuss any unfamiliar words as needed.

> **tiger lilies**   tall plants with black-spotted flowers that curve up
> **ancient**   of time long past
> **nightingale**   a brownish bird of Europe or Asia that sings at night
> **pomp**   a showy or stately display

DISCUSSING THE POEM

Discuss students' responses to the poem.

Have students tell what they know about Narcissa and what her character is like. Point out her imagination and her sense of wonder. Then ask:

> **What do you see as you think of Narcissa's back yard?** (girls playing jacks and ball; tiger lilies; Narcissa sitting on a brick)

> **What picture of Narcissa do you get in your mind at the beginning of the poem?** (small; has pigtails; shaking head)

> **What words help you see Narcissa as a queen in her daydream?** (ancient; pomp; purple veil)

CLASS ENRICHMENT

Have students write sentences describing daydreams.

Have students think about different kinds of people, animals, or things they would want to be in their daydreams. Tell them to list their choices and then use the lists to write sentences describing their daydreams. Encourage them to use words that help readers get pictures of the dreams in their minds. Suggest they tell colors, sizes, shapes, and movements.

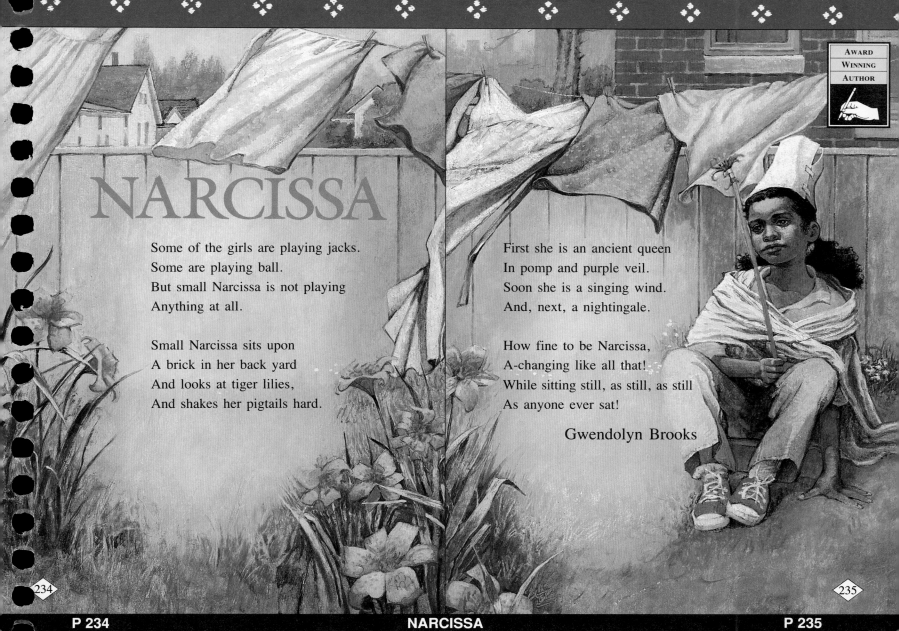

NARCISSA

Some of the girls are playing jacks.
Some are playing ball.
But small Narcissa is not playing
Anything at all.

Small Narcissa sits upon
A brick in her back yard
And looks at tiger lilies,
And shakes her pigtails hard.

First she is an ancient queen
In pomp and purple veil.
Soon she is a singing wind.
And, next, a nightingale.

How fine to be Narcissa,
A-changing like all that!
While sitting still, as still, as still
As anyone ever sat!

Gwendolyn Brooks

Reader's Journal   p 88
Responding to Reading

DAY-DREAMING

Students explore the
meaning of daydreaming by
answering thought-provoking
questions.

Student Text
pages 236–237

MARY STOLZ

Storm in the Night

illustrated by PAT CUMMINGS

Grandfather and Thomas sat on the swing, creaking back and forth, back and forth, as thunder boomed and lightning stabbed across the sky. from *Storm in the Night* by Mary Stolz

Connecting to the Unit Theme: In Storm in the Night, *Grandfather and Thomas share a story in the darkness. Thomas learns that being afraid is sometimes part of being on your own.*

CHOOSE A PLAN THAT BEST FITS YOUR CLASSROOM

PLAN A   Independent Reading

As an alternative to the Reading Corner, read Student Text page 237 (below) with the class and invite them to choose this book for independent reading.

❧

What would you do if the lights went out during a bad thunderstorm? Would you crawl under your bed and hide? You certainly wouldn't be able to watch television, and if the storm was at night, it would be too dark to read a book.

In *Storm in the Night*, Thomas and Grandfather plan to have a quiet evening, reading and watching television. But then a terrible thunderstorm hits, and the power goes out. It is dark and very stormy. Wind and rain toss the trees to and fro, thunder crashes loudly, and lightning splits the night sky. Even poor Ringo the cat shivers. There will be no television or books this night, and it is too early to go to bed.

If you read *Storm in the Night*, you will find out what Thomas and Grandfather do when the lights go out. Maybe you will get an idea of what *you* can do the next time a thunderstorm changes *your* plans.

❧

PLAN B   Mini-Teaching Plan

Choose one of the ideas below to present the book to your students. Use the "Response Activity" as a follow-up.

Whole Class Reading   Invite a guest reader (a grandparent, teacher, or older student) to visit the class and read *Storm in the Night* aloud.

Small Group Reading   Read *Storm in the Night* in a small group and guide students in acting out the parts of Grandfather and Thomas. Encourage them to use expression and to try different voices.

Individual Reading   Have students share experiences they have had during a storm before reading *Storm in the Night* on their own.

RESPONSE ACTIVITY   *Stormbound*

Ask students to imagine that they are confined to their home because a wild storm—which will last a few hours—is raging outside. The electricity is out, so like Grandfather and Thomas, they cannot watch television or read a book. Who would students like to be stormbound with, and what would they do during the storm? Invite students to write about their imaginary experiences.

PLAN C   Literature Unit

To develop a literature unit with this trade book, use the teaching ideas in the *Time Out for Books Guide*, found in the front of your Teacher Edition.

See order form in *Time Out for Books Guide* to purchase copies of this trade book.

READING CORNER

Alexander and the Terrible, Horrible, No Good, Very Bad Day

written by Judith Viorst
illustrated by Ray Cruz

SUMMARY

Alexander, the narrator of the story, is having the worst day of his life. He decides to move to Australia when everything goes wrong, starting with the lack of a prize in his box of breakfast cereal. The bad day continues when he is "scrunched" in the car on his way to school and when he makes mistakes during arithmetic. Life after school is no better. At the end of the story, his mother persuades Alexander that even if he moves to Australia, things could go wrong there.

Members of Silver Burdett & Ginn's student panel chose *Alexander and the Terrible, Horrible, No Good, Very Bad Day,* for the **Reader's Choice** award.

INTRODUCING THE STORY

Review the key features of realistic fiction.

Remind students that realistic fiction stories come from an author's imagination. These stories are about characters who are not real and events that have not actually happened. Many of these stories, however, *could happen* in real life.

Review author's use of repetition.

Remind students that authors sometimes repeat, or use the same word, phrase, or sentence again and again in certain places in stories. This is done to create a flow in a story, to let a reader know that an idea is important, and to add a feeling of humor, or sadness, or mystery.

Discuss the concept of being in a bad mood.

Remind students that the selections in the unit are about children who try to deal with their problems in their own ways. Have students tell how they feel when they are having a good day or a bad day. Mention that a little thing like spilling a glass of milk can put a person in a bad mood. Build a list with students of the things that happen that might put a person in bad mood.

Present vocabulary.

The following words that appear in the story may be new to the students. Encourage students to use their knowledge of long word decoding, as well as context clues, to help pronounce and understand unfamiliar words.

car pool a group of people who share a car
scrunched squashed
copying machine a machine that makes copies of papers

READING THE STORY

Assign the reading.

Be sure students understand that *Alexander and the Terrible, Horrible, No Good, Very Bad Day* is a book that can be found in the library. Reading this selection offers students the chance to practice uninterrupted sustained silent reading. It allows them to read at their own rate, for their own enjoyment, and encourages them to explore books outside their reading textbooks.

This story may be assigned for students to read at home. Another option is to have students choose a classmate with whom they would like to read this selection. When they have finished reading, direct partners to discuss favorite passages, characters, or story outcomes.

Alexander and the Terrible, Horrible, No Good, Very Bad Day

written by Judith Viorst
illustrated by Ray Cruz

We all have days when everything seems to go wrong. But wait until you hear what happens to Alexander!

I went to sleep with gum in my mouth and now there's gum in my hair and when I got out of bed this morning I tripped on the skateboard and by mistake I dropped my sweater in the sink while the water was running and I could tell it was going to be a terrible, horrible, no good, very bad day.

At breakfast Anthony found a Corvette Sting Ray car kit in his breakfast cereal box and Nick found a Junior Undercover Agent code ring in his breakfast cereal box but in my breakfast cereal box all I found was breakfast cereal.

I think I'll move to Australia.

In the car pool Mrs. Gibson let Becky have a seat by the window. Audrey and Elliott got seats by the window too. I said I was being scrunched. I said I was being smushed. I said, if I don't get a seat by the window I am going to be carsick. No one even answered.

I could tell it was going to be a terrible, horrible, no good, very bad day.

At school Mrs. Dickens liked Paul's picture of the sailboat better than my picture of the invisible castle.

At singing time she said I sang too loud. At counting time she said I left out sixteen. Who needs sixteen?

I could tell it was going to be a terrible, horrible, no good, very bad day.

I could tell because Paul said I wasn't his best friend anymore. He said that Philip Parker was his best friend and that Albert Moyo was his next best friend and that I was only his third best friend.

I hope you sit on a tack, I said to Paul. I hope the next time you get a double-decker strawberry ice-cream cone the ice cream part falls off the cone part and lands in Australia.

There were two cupcakes in Philip Parker's lunch bag and Albert got a Hershey bar with almonds and Paul's mother gave him a piece of jelly roll that had little coconut sprinkles on the top. Guess whose mother forgot to put in dessert?

It was a terrible, horrible, no good, very bad day.

That's what it was, because after school my mom took us all to the dentist and Dr. Fields found a cavity just in me. Come back next week and I'll fix it, said Dr. Fields.

Next week, I said, I'm going to Australia.

On the way downstairs the elevator door closed on my foot and while we were waiting for my mom to go get the car Anthony made me fall where it was muddy and then when I started crying because of the mud Nick said I was a crybaby and while I was punching Nick for saying crybaby my mom came back with the car and scolded me for being muddy and fighting.

I am having a terrible, horrible, no good, very bad day, I told everybody. No one even answered.

So then we went to the shoestore to buy some sneakers. Anthony chose white ones with blue stripes. Nick chose red ones with white stripes. I chose blue ones with red stripes but then the shoe man said, We're all sold out. They made me buy plain old white ones, but they can't make me wear them.

When we picked up my dad at his office he said I couldn't play with his copying machine, but I forgot. He also said to watch out for the books on his desk, and I was careful as could be except for my elbow. He also said don't fool around with his phone, but I think I called Australia. My dad said please don't pick him up anymore.

It was a terrible, horrible, no good, very bad day.

There were lima beans for dinner and I hate limas.

There was kissing on TV and I hate kissing.

My bath was too hot, I got soap in my eyes, my marble went down the drain, and I had to wear my railroad-train pajamas. I hate my railroad-train pajamas.

See next page for suggested answers.

When I went to bed Nick took back the pillow he said I could keep and the Mickey Mouse night light burned out and I bit my tongue.

The cat wants to sleep with Anthony, not with me.

It has been a terrible, horrible, no good, very bad day.

My mom says some days are like that.

Even in Australia.

◆ LIBRARY LINK ◆

If you enjoyed this story by Judith Viorst, you might enjoy reading some poems from her book, If I Were in Charge of the World and Other Worries.

 Reader's Response

Do you think that Alexander really wanted to move to Australia? Have you ever felt the way he did? Explain your answers.

DISCUSSING THE STORY

Summarize the story events.

Ask students to summarize the story. Students should mention that from the moment Alexander wakes up, the things that happen to him make him feel that it will be a bad day — and it is. Call on individuals to identify the things that happen to Alexander.

Have students compare Alexander's experiences to their own lives.

Ask students if similar things have happened to them. Invite students to tell which ones were similar and what happened. Have students discuss how they would have felt if they had been in Alexander's situation. Then ask them if they think that life is really so terrible for Alexander.

Discuss realistic elements in the story.

Ask students to tell what is realistic about this story. *(Students should note that Alexander is like a real boy; he goes to school, watches television, eats cereal, cries; his family does things that real families do such as go to the dentist and buy sneakers.)*

Discuss the use of repetition in the story and its effect.

Ask students what words or sentences are repeated in the story. *(I could tell it was going to be a terrible, horrible, no good, very bad day;* and *Australia)* Have students find all the places in the story where Alexander mentions Australia and read them aloud. *(pages 239, 241, 243, and 245)* Ask students why Alexander thinks about Australia. If students do not mention it, point out that Alexander uses Australia as a place to escape because it is very far away from the United States and his terrible, horrible day. Ask what is similar about each time Australia is mentioned and what is different. *(Each time Australia is mentioned, something "terrible" or "horrible" has just happened.)*

Ask students if they enjoyed reading a story of someone who experiences things just like they do.

Discuss point of view.

Point out that the story is told by Alexander. Ask students what words in the story let the reader know that he is telling it. *(the pronouns* I, we, my*)* Then ask students why the author has Alexander tell the story. *(so that the story is more personal; so that readers will have a better idea of how Alexander feels)* Point out that if someone else were telling the story, readers might not feel as close to him and know his thoughts.

CLASS ENRICHMENT

Have students read parts of the story orally.

Have small groups of students take turns reading parts of the story aloud. For the repetitive sentences and phrases, the whole group should join in.
SHARED LEARNING: SPEAKING

Have students dramatize parts of Alexander's day.

Have students work in small groups to act out parts of Alexander's day. Each group can choose one part and create dialogue. Students might enjoy doing the part of the story in the car, or in school, or at the shoe store. Provide time for students to practice and present their scenes.   SHARED LEARNING: SPEAKING

Checkpoint

USING THE CHECKPOINT AND VOCABULARY REVIEW

Use the Checkpoint for informal evaluation.

This Checkpoint provides another opportunity for informal evaluation before the formal end-of-unit assessment. If students have difficulty with the Checkpoint, you might use the extra-help activities suggested here or the Reteaching activities at the end of the unit before you give the test.

Like midunit Checkpoints, these pages are in the format of the Unit Skills Tests. They might also be used to review and practice test-taking strategies. Direct students to complete the pages shown in the Resource Center. Then have students work together to correct their papers, and encourage them to explain the thinking behind their answers. This affords you an opportunity to observe not only how students arrived at their answers, but also to identify and explain any item types that are causing difficulty.

Use the Vocabulary Review.

These two pages review selected Story Critical words from the unit in the format of the Unit Skills Tests. If responses indicate that students have not mastered the vocabulary, use the activity suggested here before testing.

PROVIDING EXTRA HELP

Provide extra help with the suffixes -ion and -tion.

Strengthen reading comprehension by linking reading, listening, and vocabulary development. Help students see how the suffixes *-ion* and *-tion* change the way a word is used in a sentence. Write on the chalkboard sentence pairs such as these and read them with students.

1. **The fire fighters *react* quickly to all alarms.
   Their quick *reaction* has saved many lives.**

2. **Mr. Yablonski *predicts* that we will all do well on the test.
   This *prediction* makes us relax a little.**

Workbook page 116

RESOURCE CENTER

◀ These pages provide informal assessment in the format of the Unit Skills Tests. ▶

Workbook page 117

NAME _____

Checkpoint

Read the paragraphs. Then fill in the circle beside the correct answer.

A fox sent an invitation to the stork for dinner. The stork thought this was a sign of friendliness. She tied a bow around her neck and went straight to the fox's den. When she arrived, the fox gave a grand bow and led her politely to the dinner table. Imagine her surprise when she saw that the table was set with two large flat saucers of soup and nothing else! The fox lapped his soup up with <u>satisfaction</u>. The stork, however, with her long bill, was unable to eat hers at all. The sly fox watched in amusement as the stork sat hungry.

Not long after, the stork invited the fox to dinner. The fox read his invitation with delight, and looked forward to a delicious meal. He arrived promptly. At dinner the stork put before him a tall pitcher with a long, narrow neck. It was easy for the stork to dip her bill into the pitcher, and she obviously enjoyed her dinner. The fox, however, was helpless. The neck of the pitcher was too narrow for his nose. He went home hungry—but wiser.

116   Checkpoint

---

suffixes *-ion, -tion*
1. What is the base word of the word <u>satisfaction</u>?
   (a) sat
   (b) satisfy
   (c) -tion
   (d) faction

suffixes *-ion, -tion*
2. What does the suffix *-tion* mean?
   (a) one who
   (b) able to be
   (c) state of being
   (d) not

inference
3. Why did the fox serve the stork soup in a saucer?
   (a) He didn't know better.
   (b) He didn't have bowls.
   (c) It was a mean trick.
   (d) It was polite.

inference
4. What did the fox do that helped you answer question 3?
   (a) watched in amusement
   (b) sent an invitation
   (c) went to the stork's for dinner
   (d) led her politely to the dinner table

inference
5. How did the stork feel when the fox served soup in a saucer?
   (a) annoyed
   (b) frightened
   (c) pleased
   (d) amused

inference
6. What event in the story showed you how the stork felt?
   (a) The stork spoke angrily.
   (b) The stork complained.
   (c) The stork got even.
   (d) The stork smiled.

homophones
7. Which is the correct word? I have _____ hands.
   (a) two
   (b) to
   (c) too
   (d) toe

homophones
8. How are homophones alike?
   (a) look alike
   (b) have similar meanings
   (c) sound alike
   (d) have opposite meanings

Checkpoint   117

456

**3. Gwen did not *interrupt* her father.
She knew he would not welcome an *interruption*.**

**Provide extra help
with making inferences.**

Strengthen reading comprehension by linking reading and listening. Use Form 11 from the Teacher Resource Kit or put a chart with the following labels on the chalkboard: **selection clues + experience clues = inference.** Have students listen as you read the following passage. As you discuss students' inferences, work with them to fill in the chart.

Pete and Teresa hid behind the sofa. Gretchen ducked behind the big chair, and Janey stood behind the door. On the dining room table was a cake with ten candles and a pile of presents. When Jenny opened the front door, the house was quiet. What can you infer about Jenny? *(She's being given a surprise birthday party.)*

**Provide extra help
with homophones.**

Have students work in pairs to write sentences using each of the following homophones: *bear, bare; bow, bough; sail, sale; die, dye.* Let them use dictionaries as necessary.

**Provide extra help with
Story Critical Words.**

Choose a selection from this unit in which a character solves a problem. Have students reread this selection and write a paragraph explaining what traits helped the character find a solution. In their paragraphs, students should use as many vocabulary words as possible.

**Use Informal Assessment
Checklist for observation.**

An Informal Assessment Checklist is included in the Teacher Resource Kit. (See the Meeting Individual Needs booklet.) The Checklist will assist you in observing each student's performance in the following categories: Self-monitoring, Getting Information from Text, Summarizing, Generalizing, Evaluating, Synthesizing across Selections, Visualizing, Responding, Empathizing with Story Characters, and Predicting.

Workbook page 118

NAME _____

Vocabulary Review

Fill in the circle beside the word that best fits in the sentence.

1. The boy who helped all his classmates was very _____ .
   - (a) titled
   - (b) literary
   - (c) boring
   - (d) popular

2. I like to make up stories, but my favorite thing to write is _____ .
   - (a) piano
   - (b) poetry
   - (c) printed
   - (d) council

3. Our town recently held an election to choose a new _____ .
   - (a) mayor
   - (b) business
   - (c) decision
   - (d) choice

4. Before jumping into the water, he _____ at the edge of the pool.
   - (a) hesitated
   - (b) reminded
   - (c) dived
   - (d) determined

5. Since it was a beautiful day, we went for a _____ through the countryside instead of driving.
   - (a) choice
   - (b) hike
   - (c) practice
   - (d) fame

6. We all told the teacher our favorite books so he could decide which _____ to invite to our library party.
   - (a) mayor
   - (b) engineers
   - (c) customers
   - (d) writer

7. Before a swimming meet, I try to _____ and stay calm so I'll have plenty of energy when my race begins.
   - (a) relax
   - (b) concentrate
   - (c) score
   - (d) hike

118

Vocabulary Review

RESOURCE CENTER

◄ These pages review ► selected Story Critical Words.

Workbook page 119

NAME _____

8. My favorite book, *Sylvester and the Magic Pebble*, was _____ before I was born.
   - (a) reminded
   - (b) published
   - (c) borrowed
   - (d) hesitated

9. She practiced playing the flute twice every day when she was preparing for her _____ .
   - (a) council
   - (b) keyboard
   - (c) recital
   - (d) poetry

10. Sometimes when you're faced with three choices, it's hard to make a _____ .
    - (a) goal
    - (b) decision
    - (c) business
    - (d) council

11. I almost fell asleep because that television show was so _____ .
    - (a) popular
    - (b) boring
    - (c) tremendous
    - (d) literary

12. Becoming a great athlete requires hard work and natural _____ .
    - (a) council
    - (b) decision
    - (c) talent
    - (d) advice

13. If you want to play the violin well, you have to _____ every day.
    - (a) hike
    - (b) promise
    - (c) practice
    - (d) relax

14. The store that sells the best toys the most cheaply will have the most _____ .
    - (a) notes
    - (b) advice
    - (c) customers
    - (d) adventure

15. She sat on the bench and arranged her fingers on the keys of the old _____ .
    - (a) radio
    - (b) recital
    - (c) talent
    - (d) piano

Vocabulary Review

119

Concluding Unit 3

Unit Wrap-Up

Discuss the unit theme.

The following questions may be used to guide a general discussion of the unit. The questions help students relate the selections and understand the development of the unit theme. As an option, have students respond in writing on Workbook page 120.

1. In "Phillis Wheatley: America's First Black Poet," what qualities did Phillis have that helped her overcome the problems she faced as a slave?

2. A family can be a big help when you have a problem to solve. How did the families of Jason in "Jason Wants a Library" and Maria in "The Recital" help these characters solve their problems?

3. Julian, Huey, and Gloria were all bored in "A Day When Frogs Wear Shoes." Think about Johanna Hurwitz in "Lee Bennett Hopkins Interviews Johanna Hurwitz." What advice do you think Johanna would give to someone who is bored?

Writing About Reading: The Writing Process

OBJECTIVE Writing to reason.

Begin the writing activity.

In this activity, students will practice the writing process as they use reasoning skills to write about a character's problem. Thinking about favorite characters from the unit will help students prepare for writing.

Have students read the introductory paragraph in the Student Text. Discuss problems that can have multiple solutions. Then use the following suggestions to guide students through the writing process.

Guide the writing process.

PREWRITING Review with students the form of a friendly note, including the greeting, the body, the closing, and the signature. Point out special capitalization and punctuation. Show examples of such a note. Then have students choose their characters and make diagrams like the one in the Student Text.

WRITING Stress to students that as they write they should focus on the ideas described in their diagrams. Encourage them to put their ideas on paper without worrying about correct form since they can make corrections later.

REVISING Have each student check her or his own note to be sure it contains a greeting, a statement about the problem, a suggested solution, and a reason why the writer thinks the solution is a good one. Then have students think about whether their notes sound friendly and helpful. Encourage them to make improvements.

PROOFREADING Have students make sure they have capitalized the word *I* and used the correct letter parts. Then have them check for the correct use of commas in the greeting and closing. Before they make clean copies, have students read the bodies of their notes and make other corrections in spelling, grammar, and punctuation.

PUBLISHING Help students assemble their newspaper column. Group the notes together according to the story character to whom each is written.

WRITING ABOUT READING

Writing a Helpful Note

Many of the characters that you read about in this unit had problems to solve. For example, Maria was nervous about her recital. Her sister found a way to help her.

Imagine that you are able to help a character from one of the stories in this unit. What could you do to help? You can write a note telling what you would do.

Prewriting

Choose a story character from this unit whose problem is interesting to you. Reread the story in which that character appears. Think about what you could do to help. This diagram may help you plan.

— Helping Hands —	
Name of Character	
Character's Problem	
What I Might Do To Help	

◆ *The Writing Process*

Writing

Begin your note with a greeting such as "Dear Julian." Explain to the character your view of the problem. Then write what you could do to help. Tell as clearly as you can *how* you would put your idea into action. Explain why you think you have a good idea.

Revising

Read your note to a partner. Ask your partner if you have explained your ideas clearly. Be sure that all the words tell exactly what you mean. If some words don't, think of other words that explain your ideas more clearly.

Proofreading

Use a dictionary to check your spelling. Make sure you have used periods and commas correctly. Then make a clean copy of your note.

Publishing

Use the notes to create a class newspaper column called "Helping Hands."

The Writing Process ◆

Workbook page 120

◆ UNIT THREE ◆

Unit Wrap-Up

NAME _____

Read each question. Write your answer, using complete sentences.

1. In "Phillis Wheatley, America's First Black Poet," what qualities did Phillis have that helped her overcome the problems she faced as a slave? Possible response: She was determined and willing to learn. She worked and studied hard. She also loved to read and was a talented writer.

2. A family can be a big help when you have a problem to solve. How did the families of Jason in "Jason Wants a Library" and Maria in "The Recital" help these characters solve their problems? Possible response: Jason's family told him to see the town council about his idea and later helped him set up the library. Maria's sister gave her advice about how to deal with mistakes.

3. Julian, Huey, and Gloria were all bored in "A Day When Frogs Wear Shoes." Think about what you learned about Johanna Hurwitz in Lee Bennett Hopkins's interview with her. What advice do you think Johanna would give to someone who was bored? Possible response: Johanna Hurwitz would have probably told them that they should read a book or practice doing something they liked to do.

120   Unit Wrap-Up

RESOURCE CENTER

Writing Master 18 duplicates the Writing About Reading diagram.

Working Together: A Cooperative Learning Project

Plan for time and materials.

In this project, students will work cooperatively to make a mobile. For each group, provide a thin stick or hanger, thread, colored paper, markers, and scissors. The project is designed to last about one hour, but adapt this guideline to meet the needs of your class.

Present the project.

After students read page 248 in the Student Text, review the material by having them tell what a mobile is and what procedure they will follow to make one. Ask students in what ways everyone's efforts are important. *(The work is shared; people will have different ideas.)*

Define roles and responsibilities.

Identify groups. Have students tell how they will assign tasks. Have them discuss which jobs are to be done individually and which are to be done by everyone. Encourage students to consider sharing the work in different ways.

Observe the groups.

Observe the discussion and the progress of the mobile. If necessary, help students resolve problems by asking open-ended questions. For example, you might ask: How else might this be done? Model showing appreciation with comments like, "Good idea, Sammy!"

Have students present the project and evaluate their group's performance.

Have a class display of mobiles. Encourage students to guess which story each mobile represents. Have students provide explanations for mobiles that are not guessed correctly. Have students discuss the advantages of working as a group. Encourage them to offer constructive criticism.

Books to Enjoy

Encourage independent reading.

Discuss with students the books described on the Student Text page. Encourage those who have read any of the suggested books to share them with the group. You might also suggest that students copy titles of interest onto their Workbook Book List and look for them in the library.

| Reader's Journal | pp 89 – 93 |
| Concluding the Unit | |

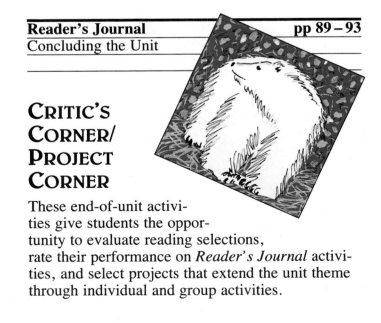

CRITIC'S CORNER/ PROJECT CORNER

These end-of-unit activities give students the opportunity to evaluate reading selections, rate their performance on *Reader's Journal* activities, and select projects that extend the unit theme through individual and group activities.

Making a Story Mobile

Lemonade, a hot sun, frogs, and shoes are all part of the story "A Day When Frogs Wear Shoes."

Today, you and your classmates will make a mobile about a story in this unit.

Before you begin, decide who will be responsible for one or more of these jobs:

◆ Encouraging everyone to share ideas

◆ Making sure everyone understands the directions

◆ Showing appreciation for people's ideas

◆ Recording everyone's ideas on a list

Start by asking someone in the group to gather the materials you will need. Then, together discuss the stories in this unit and choose one for your mobile. Take turns suggesting objects that are important in the story. Make a list of everyone's ideas. Next, each person will draw one of the objects and cut it out. Finally, everyone will help put the mobile together by hanging the pictures from a stick or hanger.

Ask your friends to guess which story your mobile is about.

◆ *Cooperative Learning*

The Courage of Sarah Noble by Alice Dalgliesh *(Scribner, 1952)* In 1707, a girl helps her father build a log house in the wilderness. When her father sets off to get the rest of the family, Sarah is left to deal with the wilderness alone.

Anna, Grandpa, and the Big Storm by Carla Stevens *(Houghton Mifflin, 1982)* During the great blizzard of 1888 in New York City, Anna is determined to go to the final round of the spelling bee. Grandpa offers to go with her.

Chin Chiang and the Dragon's Dance by Ian Wallace *(Atheneum, 1984)* A young boy is old enough to do the New Year's good luck dance. He is afraid he will be clumsy but finds the courage to try.

Testing

Select the most appropriate test.

Unit Process Test is a holistic test that assesses overall comprehension. Students compose written responses to test questions.

Unit Skills Test is a criterion-referenced test that assesses how well a student has learned the specific skill objectives in the unit. The two forms, A and B, can be used to pretest and post-test or to test, reteach, and retest, depending on your preference.

Score and evaluate test results.

Keys and Record Sheets assist in scoring both kinds of tests, interpreting the results, and identifying students who need additional help. Students who perform well may proceed directly to the next unit. Those who do not will benefit from Reteaching activities on the pages that follow, Practice and Reteaching worksheets in the Teacher Resource Kit, and additional guided and independent reading.

Meeting Individual Needs

SKILL TRACE: INFERENCES				
Introduction	Practice	Test	Reteach	Maintain
TE 380	394	442	461	462

Making Inferences

OBJECTIVE   Making inferences about time, location, cause and effect, and feelings and attitudes.

RETEACHING

Reteach making inferences about location and feelings.

Write the following passage on the chalkboard:

> **Jason loved to read. His favorite place was in the next town, six miles from home. Each room was filled with more books than he could count. Just walking in made him smile.**

Read aloud and encourage students to point out that the author describes a place and the way it makes Jason feel without naming either. Then tell them that to figure out what the writer did not say, they will use word clues and what they know from their own experience. Ask students to name a place they have been that is filled with books. (*library*) Then have them find the word clues that helped them know Jason's favorite place was the library. (*read, room filled with books*) Then ask them to find word clues about feelings and tell how Jason felt. (*Word clues:* loved, smile; *Jason felt happy.*)

Explain that making inferences helps the reader better understand what an author is describing and how characters feel.

Have students copy these sentences, circle word clues, and name the places and feelings. Point out that students should use what they know about the way other people and themselves have acted or felt in similar experiences.

1. **The tent was huge. There were wires and nets overhead and sawdust on the floor. You could hear animals roaring and people laughing.** (*circus; people are happy*)

2. **The last three minutes around the rink were the longest of Jan's life. Tears rolled down her cheeks and she smiled knowing she had skated her very best.** (*skating rink; Jan feels joy*)

Have students tell what they have learned about inferences. (*Word clues and your own experience can help you figure out what is not told by an author.*)

Provide independent practice.

Reteaching Masters 1–7 for making inferences may be assigned.

CHALLENGE

Have students create word puzzles about places or feelings.

Have each student create three word puzzles on three separate pieces of paper. The key word can either name a place or a feeling. On the top half of each sheet of paper, tell students to make boxes in which each letter of their key word will be written, as in a crossword puzzle. On the bottom half of the sheet students should write three clues. The clues can either be individual words or whole sentences. When the three word puzzles are done, have the students switch papers and try to figure out the key words. Present the following example for students to use as a model.

L	I	B	R	A	R	Y

1. **This place has many books.**

2. **Everyone is quiet here.**

3. **This place is found in schools, homes, and towns.**

Provide independent practice.

Challenge Master 12 may be assigned.

SKILL TRACE: HOMOPHONES				
Introduction	Practice	Test	Reteach	Maintain
TE 392	420	443	461	464	550

VOCABULARY

Homophones

OBJECTIVE Understanding words that sound alike but have different spellings and meanings.

RETEACHING

Reteach homophones.

Write on the chalkboard:

> **He ate his dinner.**
> **The alarm rang at eight o'clock.**

Underline the homophones. Point to the underlined words and explain that these words sound alike but have different spellings and meanings. Tell the students that to figure out the meaning of each word, you need to look at how the word is used in a sentence. Ask students to find a clue in the first sentence to help define *ate*. *(dinner)* Then ask them to use the word to explain what *ate* means. *("to have food")* Repeat for the second sentence. (Eight *is a number; o'clock means that* eight *tells a time*.)

Explain that understanding homophones will help students make sense of what they read.

Write the following sentences on the board. Have students copy the sentences, circle the homophones, and use context to define each one.

1. **He picked up the pen with his right hand. Then he sat down to write a letter.**

2. **She blew out the candles. The candles on the table were blue.**

Provide independent practice.

Reteaching Masters 1–4 for homophones may be assigned.

ACHIEVING ENGLISH PROFICIENCY

Reading homophone pairs in context.

Write on large cards sentences containing homophone pairs. Use the following sentences as models: *I can write the right answer! The sun shines on the farmer's son. We played for four hours. Last week we read the red book.* Show each card to the class and read the sentence aloud. Then divide the class into pairs of students and give each pair a sentence card. Ask students to underline the words in the sentence that sound the same but have different spellings and meanings. Then have pairs work together to illustrate their sentences and copy the two underlined words onto their drawings.

Provide independent practice.

Achieving English Proficiency Master 23 may be assigned.

CHALLENGE

Have students use homophone pairs in single sentences.

Have students write sentences using homophone pairs. Tell them to include context clues to the meanings of the homophones. Write this example on the board:

> **He rode a bike down the dirt road.**

Underline *rode* and *road*. Ask students to name the words that give clues to the meaning of *rode* and *road*. (*rode: bike, down; road: dirt*) Write these word pairs for them to choose from on the board: *meet-meat, flour-flower, hole-whole*.

Provide independent practice.

Challenge Master 13 may be assigned.

SKILL TRACE: SUFFIX				
Introduction	Practice	Test	Reteach	Maintain
TE 344	372	421	461	465	574

Suffix -ment

OBJECTIVE   Using structural analysis to determine word meaning.

RETEACHING

Reteach suffix -ment.

Write on the chalkboard: **arrangement, enjoyment.** Underline the *-ment* suffix. Explain that this ending means "act or state of." Write these sentences on the board:

> **The children argue about what movie to see.**
> **They solve the argument by voting.**

Read the sentences and then point to *argue*. Ask students what it means. (*to disagree*) Then point to *argument*. Ask students to use the meaning of *argue* and the meaning of the suffix, "the act of," to define *argument*. (*the act of disagreeing*). Repeat for *enjoyment* using these sentences:

> **We enjoy going to the movies.**
> **Popcorn makes our enjoyment even greater.**

Explain that knowing what suffixes mean will help students to read and understand new words.

Write the following sentences on the board. Have students write the words with the suffix *-ment* and define them.

1. The spinning movements of the dancers made us dizzy.

2. The treatment by the nurse made the pain go away.

3. Everyone had a different idea for the placement of the new table.

Have students tell what they have learned about the suffix *-ment*. (*It means "act or state of."*)

Provide independent practice.

Reteaching Masters 1–4 for suffix *-ment* may be assigned.

CHALLENGE

Have students find pictures from magazines to illustrate words.

Write these words on the board and discuss their meanings with students: **entertainment, employment, treatment, agreement, appointment, improvement, announcement.** Next have them look through and cut out pictures from old magazines and newspapers that illustrate these words. Have them tape these pictures to construction paper. Then have them write captions to go with each picture they selected. The caption should include the suffixed word. For example: a picture of the president and a foreign leader could have the caption: *The leaders of two countries made an agreement.*

Provide independent practice.

Challenge Master 9 may be assigned.

SKILL TRACE: SUFFIXES				
Introduction	Practice	Test	Reteach	Maintain
TE 370	395	422	461	466	502

Suffixes -ion, -tion

OBJECTIVE   Using structural analysis to determine word meaning.

RETEACHING

Reteach suffixes -ion, -tion.

Write on the chalkboard: **collection, direction.** Underline the *-ion* suffix. Explain that this ending means "act or outcome." Then write these sentences.

> **We collect stamps.**
> **Our stamp collection fills five books.**

Read the sentences and ask the students to define *collect*. (*gather*) Then point to *collection* and have students use the definition of *collect* and the meaning of the suffix to define it. (*the outcome of collecting*) Repeat for *direction* using these sentences:

> **The officer will direct traffic.**
> **The driver asked if he was going in the right direction.**

Explain that knowing what suffixes mean will help students read and understand new words.

Write the following sentences on the board. Have students read them and then write the words with the suffixes *-ion, -tion.*

1. Getting an education is hard work.

2. My reflection in the mirror is wavy.

Have students tell what they have learned about the suffixes *-ion, -tion.* (*These endings mean "act or outcome."*)

Provide independent practice.

Reteaching Masters 1–4 for suffixes *-ion, -tion* may be assigned.

ACHIEVING ENGLISH PROFICIENCY

Provide practice reading words ending in -ion and -tion.

Write on the chalkboard: **motion, lotion, vision, decision.** Then read aloud the following verse, pantomiming the actions described: *When I move my hand, I make a motion/When I'm at the beach, I rub in some lotion/When I look around, I use my vision/When I choose a book, I make a decision.* Have students repeat the verse with you. Point to each word as students say it. Circle the *-tion* endings of *motion* and *lotion* and the *-ion* endings of *vision* and *decision.* Invite students to suggest other words that end with the same sounds.

Provide independent practice.

Achieving English Proficiency Master 21 may be assigned.

CHALLENGE

Have students write question/answer reports about pollution and migration.

Write these words on the board and review their meanings: **pollution, migration.** Have students work in pairs. Tell them to select one topic and brainstorm a list of questions about it. Each pair should pick three questions to answer. Then have them write a Q-and-A report.

Provide independent practice.

Challenge Master 11 may be assigned.

SKILL TRACE: SYMBOLS/SIGNS				
Introduction	Practice	Test	Reteach	Maintain
TE 346	373	423	461	467	526

STUDY SKILLS

Symbols and Signs

OBJECTIVE   Understanding information from symbols and signs.

RETEACHING

Reteach symbols and signs.

Draw on the chalkboard simple outlines of the following: *a U.S. flag, a stop sign, an arrow pointing to the right.* Explain that picture signs use symbols to get their meanings across. Ask students to tell what each of the symbols on the board stands for. Have students tell what picture signs can do. *(give information in a quick, easy way)* Have students come to the board and draw signs they have seen. Have other students tell the meanings of the symbols on the signs.

Explain that knowing what different symbols and signs mean helps students understand the world around them.

Draw the following signs on the board. Ask students to tell their meanings and name where they might be seen.

(poison)

(road "s" curve)

Provide independent practice.

Reteaching Masters 1–4 for symbols and signs may be assigned.

ACHIEVING ENGLISH PROFICIENCY

Have students create their own international symbols.

Display several international symbols, such as those used to indicate parking for the handicapped and for a public telephone. Ask students to tell what the messages of those symbols are. Then draw a "prohibited" symbol — a circle with a diagonal line through it — on the chalkboard. Review with students the meaning of the symbol and ask them what it would mean if a drawing of a dog appeared inside the circle. *(no dogs allowed.)* Ask students to create their own "_____ prohibited" symbols. Tell them to make sure most people will be able to understand their message. Display students' symbols in the classroom and have volunteers "read" them aloud.

Provide independent practice.

Achieving English Proficiency Master 19 may be assigned.

CHALLENGE

Have students create charts of airport or highway symbols and signs.

Have students create charts of symbols and signs used at airports or on highways. Students can do research and also ask other students and adults for information. The charts should have pictures and words under the pictures that tell what the symbols and signs mean. Display the charts and have students compare their highway or airport charts. As an additional activity, have students create personal symbols. For example, a student who loves to run may choose a pair of running shoes as a symbol. Students can draw their symbols and tape them to their desks.

Provide independent practice.

Challenge Master 10 may be assigned.

UNIT
FOUR

OVERVIEW

GET THE
MESSAGE

UNIT THEME Verbal and nonverbal communication — and miscommunication — are explored in this unit that combines fiction, nonfiction, and photography.

UNIT SELECTIONS

Heidi, *by Johanna Spyri*
Young Heidi arrives in Frankfurt to study with twelve-year old Klara, who is confined to a wheelchair. A read aloud/think aloud selection.

Forecast, *by Malcolm Hall*
When Stan Groundhog retires, a new weather forecaster predicts snow in summer. Oscar Raccoon tries to help make the prediction come true. A Silver Burdett & Ginn **Readers' Choice** award winner.

Words in Our Hands, *by Ada B. Litchfield*
In his new town, Michael is embarrassed by his deaf parents' sign language. A performance by the National Theater of the Deaf helps him feel at home.

Sports Signals, *by Gary Apple*
The silent, and sometimes secret, language of sports signals is explained in this article. Readers will learn to recognize some of the signals used by coaches, players, and officials everywhere.

The Horse Who Lived Upstairs, *by Phyllis McGinley*
Joey's dream of carefree country living is soon tempered by the realities of life on a farm.

Mufaro's Beautiful Daughters, *by John Steptoe*
This African fairy tale explores goodness and greed. Winner of a **Boston Globe Award** and a **Caldecott Honor Award.**

The Boy Who Cried Wolf, *adapted by Genie Iverson*
This well-known Aesop fable about a shepherd boy illustrates why telling the truth is always best.

In Which Piglet Meets a Heffalump, *by A.A. Milne*
In this Reading Corner selection, an excerpt from *Winnie-the-Pooh,* readers will be introduced to Pooh, to his friend Piglet, and to the delightful illustrations of E.H. Shepard.

Title	Skills/Strategies	Integrated Language Arts	Cross-Curriculum
Listening Lessons: Heidi Pages 474–479	Homographs	**Active Listening**	
Forecast Pages 480–503	★ Characterization ★ Long Word Decoding	**Speaking:** Weather Information; Acting Out Story Scenes; Weather Broadcasts **Writing:** Word Collages; Weather Poems; Funny Weather Stories	**Science:** Weather Charts; Weather Instrument Book **Art:** Cloud Formation Pictures
Secret Talk (poem) Pages 504–505		**Listening:** A Poem's Message **Speaking:** Picture Comparisons	
Words in Our Hands Pages 506–527	Main Idea/Details Multiple Meanings	**Speaking:** Sign Language; Welcoming Committee Presentation; Finger Spelling	**Health and Safety:** Posters on Hearing Safety **Social Studies:** Famous People with Disabilities **Science:** Devices for the Deaf
World of Reading Magazine: Words and Other Codes Pages 528–529			
Sports Signals Pages 530–551	★ Word Referents ★ Prefixes: *de-, dis-*	**Speaking:** Television Sports Interviews; Reports on Sports Teams **Writing:** Illustrated Baseball Glossary; Comic Strips; Newspaper Article; Story Map	**Social Studies:** Research Names of Sports Teams **Science:** Pitching Speed Research **Geography:** Sports Teams' Locations **Careers:** Sports Stars
Checkpoint INFORMAL ASSESSMENT Pages 552–553			
Making Predictions: Literature Link Pages 554–555			
The Horse Who Lived Upstairs Pages 556–575	Story Elements	**Writing:** Travel Brochures; Post Cards; Fantasy **Speaking:** Improvisation **Listening:** Story Themes	**Social Studies:** Farm Crops of New York **Science:** Horses **Art:** Farms
Mufaro's Beautiful Daughters Pages 576–597	Comparison	**Speaking:** Folk Tale Improvisation; African Tales **Writing:** Modern Cinderella Story; Character Clusters	**Art:** African Masks **Social Studies:** Maps—African Countries **Mathematics:** Word Problems
Reading Plays: Literature Link Pages 598–599			
The Boy Who Cried Wolf Pages 600–621	Predicting Outcomes	**Speaking:** Story Mapping; Dramatization **Writing:** Character Clusters; Play Dialogue	**Art:** Story Character Puppets **Social Studies:** Sheep Farms; Wool Production **Music:** Songs for Story Characters
Reading Corner: In Which Piglet Meets a Heffalump Pages 622–628		**Writing:** Draw and Name Creatures; Illustrated Paragraph	
Checkpoint INFORMAL ASSESSMENT Pages 630–631			

★ Tested skill in this unit

Reading Every Day

CREATE A CLASSROOM LIBRARY

The following books and magazines are referenced throughout the unit. You might gather them ahead of time to place in your classroom library.

Aardema, Verna. **Why Mosquitos Buzz in People's Ears.**

Aliki. **Digging Up Dinosaurs.**

Arthur, Catherine. **My Sister's Silent World.**

Baylor, Byrd. **Hawk, I'm Your Brother.**

Brown, Marc. **Finger Rhymes.**

Charlip, Remy; and Ancona, George and Mary Beth. **Handtalk.**

Cole, William. **Poem Stew.** 〰

cummings, e.e. **Hist Whist and Other Poems for Children.**

Dang Manh Kha as told to Ann Nolan Clark. **In the Land of Small Dragon.**

Delton, Judy. **The Elephant in Duck's Garden.**

Fleischman, Sid. **By the Great Horn Spoon!**

Hegemen, Kathryn, editor. **Aesop's Fables.**

Galbraith, Clare K. **Victor.**

Galdone, Paul. **Three Aesop Fox Fables.**

Hall, Malcolm. **Headlines.**

Hunt, Bernice Kohn. **The Whatchamacallit Book.**

Hurwitz, Johanna. **Baseball Fever.**

McCloskey, Robert. **Burt Dow, Deep-Water Man.**

Merriam, Eve. **A Word or Two with You.**

Michel, Anna. **The Story of Nim: The Chimp Who Learned Language.**

Milne, A.A. **Winnie-the-Pooh.**

Mosel, Arlene. **Tikki, Tikki, Tembo.**

Parish, Peggy. **Thank You, Amelia Bedelia.** 〰

Patterson, Dr. Francine. **Koko's Story.**

Paxton, Tom. **Aesop's Fables.**

Pomerantz, Charlotte. **If I Had a Paka: Poems in Eleven Languages.**

Sattler, Helen Roney. **Train Whistles.**

Srivastava, Jane Jonas. **Computers.**

Stewig, John. **Sending Messages.**

Sullivan, Mary Beth and Bourke, Linda. **A Show of Hands: Say It in Sign Language.**

Winter, Milo, illustrator. **Aesop for Children.**

Yolen, Jane. **The Seeing Stick.**

〰 A **World of Books** Classroom Libraries selection

WORLD OF BOOKS Classroom Libraries

World of Books Classroom Libraries offer a wide selection of books that may be used for independent reading with this unit.

UNIT PROJECT CARDS   Projects such as making picture signs, completing similes, and learning Braille extend and enrich the unit theme. Instructions are on **Project Cards 9–12** in the *Idea Factory for Teachers.* Cards are designed for students to use alone or in small groups.

HOME CONNECTION LETTERS   The Teacher Resource Kit includes letters, written in English and in Spanish, that explain what students have learned during this unit and suggest bibliographies and activities that support instruction.

The books listed on the "Reading Every Day" card in each lesson's Language Arts Connection may also be copied and sent home to encourage family involvement in independent reading.

BULLETIN BOARDS

Use the suggestions in the *Idea Factory for Teachers* to construct the unit bulletin boards.

Interactive Teaching Kit

The *Castles of Sand* I•T Kit offers materials and activities to motivate and enrich your students' reading experience. You may choose to use some or all of the unit activities to introduce Unit 4, "Get the Message?" Later in the unit, you may choose to use some or all of the story-related activities. You will find complete teaching instructions in the I•T Kit Activity Guide.

The I•T Kit provides a menu of activities to introduce the unit theme.

VIDEO ✦ GET THE MESSAGE

Talking, writing, signaling, signing — why do people send their messages in different ways? These video segments bring to life the unit theme, "Get the Message?"

✦ Enjoy a special performance by the talented cast of the Little Theatre of the Deaf.

✦ Put on your Sherlock Holmes hat and see if you can solve the Case of the Secret Message.

✦ Take a look at some of the signs and signals people use every day. (See Activity Guide.)   LITERATURE, DRAMA, CONTENT AREAS

AUDIO ✦ "IT'S MORSE, OF COURSE!"

With a telegraph line, people can use Morse Code to communicate. This original song, performed on a synthesizer, familiarizes students with the dots and dashes that make up the Morse Code alphabet. With the help of the accompanying unit cards, students decode the names they hear in the dot-dash lyrics. (See Activity Guide.)   CONTEMPORARY MUSIC

UNIT CARDS ✦ LOOK AND LEARN

Students can explore and learn such languages as Morse Code and pictographs with the help of these unit reference cards. (See Activity Guide.)   CONTENT AREAS

POSTER ✦ 2 C-T J-S

Patterned after William Steig's book *CDB?* whose text appears completely in alphabet letters, the poster tells the story of two boys watching a pair of blue jays build a nest outside a city apartment window. Students work together to create their own rebus dictionary to use in writing a rebus story. (See Activity Guide.)   CONTENT AREAS

The I•T Kit provides activities that may be used following these reading selections:

"Words in Our Hands" (See TE page 519 and Activity Guide.)

"Sports Signals" (See TE page 542 and Activity Guide.)

"The Boy Who Cried Wolf" (See TE page 614 and Activity Guide.)

Beginning the Unit

Appreciating Art

Provide background about the work of art.

Have students look at the painting on page 250 of the Student Text. A poster version of this illustration, found in the Teacher Resource Kit, may be displayed for the discussion. Tell students that Mary Cassatt (1844–1926) is often called America's greatest woman painter. She spent much of her life in France as a leading member of the Impressionists, who were famous for their treatment of light and their disregard for realistic detail.

Have students view the work of art and discuss the unit theme.

Point out that the woman in the painting is at a writing desk. Ask students what they think she is doing and what clues in the picture help them to know that. Ask students to describe their own feelings about the painting. Point out that some details in this picture are not realistic; for example, no pen is shown, and the angle of the desk is wrong. Ask students why they think the picture was painted this way and how this affects the way they feel about the picture. Have a volunteer read aloud the question on page 251. Encourage discussion about the different reasons people have for sending messages and different ways of sending them. Have students preview the unit, and encourage them to discuss any selection they feel will be particularly interesting or any by their favorite author(s).

Connecting the Known to the New

Encourage independent reading with the Interest Inventory and the Book Log.

Workbook page 121 is a questionnaire that asks students to identify unit-related topics that they might be interested in reading about. Workbook page 122 provides space for listing suggested titles from the Interest Inventory, as well as other titles students may wish to read. Workbook pages 163–176 provide space for students to record their personal responses to books.

Reader's Journal   pp 94–96
Beginning the Unit

DON'T TELL WALLY

A related reading that involves readers in solving a riddle introduces the unit theme, "Get the Message." Students add riddles of their own to the collection presented in the reading.

UNIT FOUR

GET THE MESSAGE

Talking, writing, signaling, signing — why do people send their messages in different ways?

THE LETTER,
painting by Mary Cassatt, American, 1891

RESOURCE CENTER

Workbook page 121

UNIT FOUR

Interest Inventory

Messages are important in letting someone know what you think. What kinds of messages do you find fun? Answer the questions below and use the chart to discover books that you may find especially interesting.

yes no
1. ☐ ☐ Is it sometimes hard for you to say things the right way?
2. ☐ ☐ Are you interested in things that happened long ago?
3. ☐ ☐ Do you ever have trouble thinking of a word you need?
4. ☐ ☐ Would you enjoy learning new words?
5. ☐ ☐ Do you like to use your hands when you talk?
6. ☐ ☐ Do you like figuring out new ways to say things?
7. ☐ ☐ Would you like to know more about *how* people learn?

Now find the numbers for the questions you checked YES. Follow the column down. When you see a star, move across the row to find the title of a book in which you may read about your interests.

1	2	3	4	5	6	7	Title/Author
							My Sister's Silent World by Catherine Arthur
							Tikki Tikki Tembo retold by Arlene Mosel
							The Elephant in Duck's Garden by Judy Delton
							Digging Up Dinosaurs by Aliki
							The Watchamacallit Book by Bernice Kohn Hunt
							If I Had a Paka by Carlotte Pomerantz
							Sending Messages by John Stewig

121

◄ **Workbook page 121** is a questionnaire that helps students identify topics and books of interest.

Workbook page 122 ► is a personal list of books students might read independently.

Workbook page 122

UNIT FOUR

Personal Book List

NAME _____

Title _____

Author _____

Title _____

Author _____

Title _____

Author _____

Title _____

Author _____

122

Listening Lesson

SELECTION SUMMARY

In this excerpt from the realistic novel *Heidi,* young Heidi is taken to the house of Mr. Sesemann in Frankfurt, Germany, to keep his invalid daughter, Klara, company and to study with her. Miss Rottenmeier, the housekeeper, disapproves of Heidi because the child is not what she had expected: she is four years younger than Klara, has never been taught to read, and has very poor table manners. Klara, who is confined to a wheelchair and has become bored with her studies, seems intrigued by her new companion. Perhaps as a result, Miss Rottenmeier reluctantly accepts Heidi and the challenge of educating her.

STRATEGIES FOR LISTENING

Explain the process of listening for enjoyment.

You may wish to read the selection aloud twice. During a first reading, students should relax and enjoy the selection. They should not be concerned if there is something they do not understand. They should, however, listen carefully for important details about the characters and events in the piece. Remembering significant details helps a person better understand the characters' actions and feelings and therefore appreciate the story more. As an alternative to reading the selection aloud, you may choose to play the audio cassette that is available.

Set the purpose for a read aloud/think aloud.

When you finish the first reading, you may read the selection a second time. As you read, you will share some of your thoughts and feelings about the characters and events by thinking aloud. The annotations accompanying the selection may serve as prompts for modeling your thinking. You may substitute your own or offer additional ones. Tell students that you will model the way good readers think as they read. Encourage them to be active thinkers during their own reading.

DISCUSSING THE SELECTION

Present discussion questions.

1. **When reading or listening to a story, people often wonder how they would feel if they were in the same situation as the characters. Focus on Heidi, Klara, or Miss Rottenmeier. How would you feel if you were in her place?** (For Heidi, students might mention feeling overwhelmed, frightened, or abandoned; for Klara, disappointed, curious, or amused; for Miss Rottenmeier, angry, tricked, or ignored.)

2. **Story characters often do things which puzzle us — because we know we would not act as they had. Which characters in *Heidi* act in ways you did not understand?** (Students might mention Heidi's putting the roll in her pocket; the coachman's, butler's and maid's being so unpleasant; and Miss Rottenmeier's criticizing Heidi so sharply to her face.)

3. **Sometimes we use story details to make inferences about characters' lives before we first read or hear about them. Can you make an inference about either Heidi's or Klara's life before the story began? What details helped you make your inference?** (Students might mention that Heidi was poor and hungry because she took the dinner roll, or that Klara was bored and lonely because she was so glad to see Heidi.)

Heidi[1]

By Johanna Spyri

In the house of Mr. Sesemann, in Frankfurt, the little sick daughter, Klara, reclined in her comfortable wheelchair in the library.

Klara had a pale, thin face, out of which looked two gentle blue eyes, at this moment directed toward the large wall clock, which seemed to go unusually slow. Klara, who was hardly ever impatient, now said with some worry:

"Isn't it time yet, Miss Rottenmeier?"

While Klara, with signs of impatience, was for the second time asking Miss Rottenmeier whether it was not time for the expected guests to arrive, Dete, holding Heidi by the hand, was standing at the entrance door below, asking the coachman, Johann, who had just jumped down from the carriage, whether she might see Miss Rottenmeier at so late an hour.

"That is not my business," growled the coachman. "Ring for Sebastian, inside there in the corridor."

Dete did as he told her, and the butler, with big buttons on his coat and round eyes almost as big in his head, came down the stairs.

"I would like to ask whether I may see Miss Rottenmeier at this hour."

"That is not my business," answered the butler. "Ring the other bell for the maid, Tinette." And without giving further information Sebastian disappeared.

Dete rang again. This time the maid Tinette appeared on the stairs, with a little cap, dazzlingly white, on the top of her head, and a scornful expression on her face.

"What is it?" she asked from the stairs, without coming down. Dete repeated her request. Tinette disappeared, but soon came back again and called down the stairs:

"You are expected. Come this way."

Dete, with Heidi, went up the stairs and, following Tinette, entered the library.[2]

Miss Rottenmeier slowly rose from her seat and came nearer to examine the newly-arrived companion for the daughter of the house. Heidi's appearance did not seem to please her.

"What is your name?" asked Miss Rottenmeier, after having looked searchingly for some minutes at the child, who never took her eyes away from her.

"Heidi," she replied distinctly, in a ringing voice.

"What? What sort of name is that?"

"She was named Adelheid, like her mother, my late sister," said Dete.

"Well! That is a name that can be pronounced," observed Miss Rottenmeier. "But, Dete, I must say, she is a small child for her age. I told you that Miss Klara's companion must be of her own age, in order to follow the same studies with her and, especially, to share her occupations. Miss Klara is more than twelve years old; how old is this child?"

"I am eight now; Grandfather said so," explained Heidi. Her aunt Dete nudged her, but Heidi did not have the least idea why and was not at all bothered.

"What? Only eight years old!" exclaimed Miss Rottenmeier with some annoyance. "Four years too young! What have you learned? And what books have you studied?"

1. Heidi. I remember reading a whole book about Heidi when I was just about your age. I know I have forgotten many things about it, but I do remember that it was a favorite of mine and that it had some very sad parts.

2. So many names. I am getting a little confused so I had better stop and get them straightened out before I continue. Dete brought Heidi. She and Heidi are at Klara's house. Johann is the coachman at Klara's. Sebastian is the butler; Tinette is the maid.

"None," said Heidi.

"What? What? How did you learn to read then?" asked the lady again.

"I have never learned to read; neither has my friend Peter," stated Heidi.

"Good gracious! You cannot read! You really cannot read!" exclaimed Miss Rottenmeier with the greatest horror. "Is it possible that you are unable to read? What have you learned, then!"

"Nothing," said Heidi with exact truthfulness. **3**

"Dete," said Miss Rottenmeier, after she had calmed herself, "this is not according to the agreement. How could you bring me such a child?"

But Dete was not so easily upset; she answered eagerly:

"If you will allow me to explain, the child is exactly what I thought you wanted. You explained to me that she must be quite different and not at all like other children, and so I brought this little one; I thought she answered the description perfectly. But I must be going. My mistress is expecting me; if she will allow me, I will come again soon and see how Heidi is doing."

With a curtsy Dete went out the door and down the stairs as fast as she could go. Miss Rottenmeier stood still for a moment, then ran after Dete. It suddenly occurred to her that she would need to talk with the aunt about a number of things if the child were really going to stay. And here the child was, and, as Miss Rottenmeier saw, the aunt was determined to leave her.

Heidi was still in the spot by the door where she had stood from the beginning. Until then Klara had watched everything in silence from her chair. Now she beckoned to Heidi:

"Come here!"

Heidi went to the wheelchair.

"Would you rather be called Heidi or Adelheid?" asked Klara.

"My name is Heidi and nothing else," was Heidi's reply.

"Then that is what I will call you," said Klara. "I like the name for you; I have never heard it before, but I have never seen a child before that looks like you. Have you always had such short, curly hair?"

"Yes, I think so," answered Heidi.

"Did you want to come to Frankfurt?" asked Klara again.

"No; but tomorrow I am going back home," explained Heidi.

"You are a strange child!" said Klara. "They have

brought you to Frankfurt on purpose to stay with me and study with me, and you see now it will be very funny, because you don't know how to read at all, and there will be something entirely new in the study hours. It has often been so frightfully dull and has seemed as if the morning would never end. But now it will be more interesting, for I can listen while you learn to read." **4**

Heidi shook her head quite doubtfully when she heard about learning to read.

Just then Miss Rottenmeier came into the room. She went from the library to the dining room, and from there back again, and then immediately turned around and went to Sebastian, who passed his round eyes thoughtfully over the table, which was already set, to see if there were any fault to be found with his work.

"Think your great thoughts tomorrow, and today get ready for us to come to the table."

With these words Miss Rottenmeier passed by Sebastian and called Tinette in such an ungracious tone that she came with even shorter steps than usual, and stood before her with such a mocking face that Miss Rottenmeier herself did not dare to speak angrily to her; so her annoyance increased.

"The little visitor's room is to be put in order, Tinette," said the lady with forced calmness. "Everything is ready, but the furniture needs to be dusted."

"No doubt it is very important to do so," said Tinette sneeringly, and went out.

Meanwhile Sebastian had opened the double doors of the library with considerable noise; he then went quite calmly into the library to push out the wheelchair.

The chair came rolling along, and Sebastian placed Klara at the table.

Miss Rottenmeier sat next to Klara and beckoned to Heidi to take the place opposite. No one else came to the table, and as the three sat far apart there was plenty of room for Sebastian to serve his dishes. Next to Heidi's plate lay a lovely white roll; the child cast longing looks at it. Then she pointed to the roll and said:

"Can I have that?"

Sebastian nodded, and glanced at Miss Rottenmeier, for he wondered what impression the question would make on her. In a twinkling Heidi seized her roll and put it into her pocket. Sebastian made a face to keep from laughing, for he knew very well that this was not allowed. He remained standing silently by Heidi, for he did not dare to speak, and neither did he dare to move away until he was told to. Heidi looked at him for some time in amazement, and then asked:

3. I can just imagine how Heidi must feel standing in front of this unfriendly woman who has just criticized her for having a strange name, being too young, and not being able to read. I know I would be extremely upset. Heidi must be very brave.

4. I am not sure, but it certainly seems as if Klara and Heidi are about to become friends, even though Heidi is so much younger than Klara and they are very different. I think that at this point they both need a friend.

"Shall I eat some of that?"

Sebastian nodded again.

"Then give me some," she said, looking calmly at her plate.

Sebastian's face grew very thoughtful, to hide his amusement, and the tray in his hand began to tremble dangerously.

"You may put the tray on the table and come back later," said Miss Rottenmeier, looking severely at him.

Sebastian disappeared.

"As for you, Adelheid, I see that I must teach you some manners," continued Miss Rottenmeier with a deep sigh. "First, I will tell you how to behave at the table." And the lady explained clearly and exactly everything that Heidi had to do. "Then," she went on, "I must impress it upon you particularly that you are not to speak to Sebastian at the table, unless you have some order to give, or some necessary question to ask."**5**

5. Poor Heidi! It is clear that this will be a big change for her. It will not be easy to live in a house where there are so many rules, especially rules about whom she can talk to, since she seems like such a friendly girl. This is what I meant when I said that *Heidi* had some sad parts. But Heidi is brave, too, and I know that she will always make the best of every situation.

Then followed a long list of instructions about rising in the morning and going to bed, about coming in and going out, about shutting doors, and about orderliness in general. Meantime Heidi's eyes closed, for she had been up since five o'clock and had had a long journey. She leaned back in her chair and fell asleep. When Miss Rottenmeier finally came to the end of her speech, she said:

"Now think this all over! Have you understood everything?"

"Heidi has been asleep for a long time," said Klara, with a giggle. The supper hour had not passed so quickly in a long time.

"I never in all my life saw the like of this child!" exclaimed Miss Rottenmeier in great vexation, and she rang the bell so violently that Tinette and Sebastian both came rushing in together. In spite of all the noise, Heidi did not wake up, and they had the greatest difficulty in arousing her sufficiently to get her to her bedroom, which was now ready for the little girl. **6**

6. Heidi is worn out, and I certainly understand why. I am sure I would be tired, too, from meeting all those people in a strange place and having to listen to all those rules.

Selection Support

VOCABULARY

Homographs

OBJECTIVE Recognizing words with the same spelling but different meanings and pronunciations.

1. WARM-UP

Use familiar content to present homographs.

Write the following sentences on the chalkboard and tell students that the sentences are about Heidi and Klara from the story *Heidi*. Have the sentences read aloud and ask students to tell what they notice about the underlined words. *(They are spelled the same but are pronounced differently and have different meanings.)*

1. Heidi did not know how to <u>read</u> or write.

2. Klara had <u>read</u> many books.

Discuss context clues as aids to understanding homographs.

Ask students what helped them know the pronunciation and meaning of each underlined word. Elicit from students that other words in the sentence gave them the clues, and have students name the clues. *(in sentence 1, the words* how to *and* write; *in sentence 2, the word* had)

State the objective.

Tell students they will learn to use context clues to help them recognize and understand homographs, or words that have the same spellings but are pronounced differently and have different meanings.

2. TEACH

Explain why understanding homographs is important.

Many words in the English language have more than one meaning. The more that readers know about these words, the better they will be able to understand what they read and not be confused.

Present a strategy for understanding homographs.

Explain that there is a strategy students can use to help them understand homographs. Be alert for words that have more than one meaning. Use context clues to help pronounce the word and determine the meaning that fits. Look for word clues in the same sentence or in sentences before and after the homograph.

71

TEACHING CHART 71: HOMOGRAPHS

1. "Heidi has not met Klara yet," said Dete. "May I <u>present</u> Heidi to Klara?" she asked. (to introduce to another)
   "I wish I had a <u>present</u> to give Klara," thought Heidi. (a gift)
2. Klara had a pretty <u>bow</u> in her hair. (a knot with two or more loops, as made with a ribbon)
   Because the butler was holding dishes, he could not <u>bow</u> to Miss Rottenmeier. (bend the head and body in greeting)
3. "Heidi will <u>live</u> here with me," said Klara. (make a home with)
   "Here I am, <u>live</u> and in person!" shouted Heidi. (living; alive)

Model the strategy.

Read the first set of sentences. Explain that the words *has not met* and *may I* help you know to pronounce the underlined word *pre sent'* and that you also know that it means "to introduce to another." Point out that you also know from experience that if someone has not met another person, the proper thing to do is introduce them. Explain that the words *to give* help you know to pronounce the second underlined word *pres' ent* and that it means "a gift."

3. GUIDED PRACTICE

Check for understanding.

Before going on, have students explain how to recognize homographs. *(Think about the different meanings of homographs. Use context clues and think about what you know from your experience.)*

Guide students in using the strategy.

Have students use the strategy to figure out the meanings of the pairs of homographs in the remaining sentences. Discuss word and experience clues that helped them understand the homographs.

4. WRAP-UP

Summarize instruction.

Review why listeners need to understand homographs and the kinds of clues used to figure out the word meanings. *(Homographs have different meanings, so you need to know the right meaning in order to understand the sentence; word and experience clues are used.)*

Provide independent practice.

Options for independent practice are shown in the Resource Center below.

Workbook page 123

Homographs

REMEMBER: **Homographs** are words that have the same spelling but different meanings and pronunciations. Use context to decide the correct meaning and pronunciation of a homograph.

A. Read the pairs of homographs and their definitions. Choose the word with the correct definition for each sentence. Write the letter of the word on the line.

a. **wind** (wind) air in motion

b. **wind** (wīnd) wrap something around itself or something else

1. __a__ The strong wind is coming.
2. __b__ It will wind the flags around their poles.

a. **bow** (bou) bend the head

b. **bow** (bō) ribbon tied in a loop

3. __b__ It will blow the bow from Annie's hair.
4. __a__ I'll hold my hat and bow my head.

a. **read** (rēd) get the meaning of printed words

b. **read** (red) learned by reading

5. __a__ The wind is coming. You can read it in the paper.
6. __b__ The strong wind is coming. That's what I've read.

B. On separate paper, use two homographs from Part A to write a sentence about the weather. See Teacher Notes.

Homographs   Listening 123

RESOURCE CENTER

◀ **Workbook page 123** is intended for use by all students.

Skills Practice 110 ▶ may be assigned for additional practice.

Workbook reuse option: Have students write the respelling of each homograph next to the sentence where it belongs.

Skills Practice 110

Homographs

Homographs are words that are spelled the same but that have different meanings and pronunciations.

A. Read the sentence and the clue in parentheses. Write the correct homograph from the box to complete the sentence.

| bow | close | lead | present | record | sow |

1. Carl was the only boy __present__ at the party. (at a place)
2. There is banjo music on that __record__. (sound disk)
3. I think a skunk is __close__! (nearby)
4. Be sure to __close__ the door when you leave. (shut)
5. Lou will __present__ the award himself. (give)
6. The __sow__ gave a loud, "OINK!" (pig)
7. You can __record__ my voice on tape. (save)
8. The neighbors helped the farmer __sow__ his corn. (plant)
9. Ann put a big yellow __bow__ on the gift. (tied ribbon)
10. Under the sink was a __lead__ pipe. (heavy metal)
11. Please __lead__ the class in the salute to the flag. (be first)
12. Coretta sat in the __bow__ of the boat. (front part)

B. Write two sentences for each homograph. Use a different meaning in each sentence.

13. read __Sentences will vary.__

14. wind

110   LEVEL 8   "Heidi"

TEACHER · CHOICE

	Teaching Sequence	Trade Books and Resources	Meeting Individual Needs	Integrated Language Arts / Cross Curriculum
The Bridge Pages 482–483	**Introduce** Characterization (Tested)	• Teaching Chart 72 • Workbook 124 • Skills Practice 111	• Reteaching Masters 1–4 • Challenge Master 14	
PART 1 **Vocabulary Strategies** Pages 484–485	**Develop Concepts** Creating a Weather Chart **Teach Vocabulary** **STORY CRITICAL WORDS:** **considering,** editor, **flake,** **forecaster,** instruments, meteorology, prediction (Tested words are boldfaced.)	• Teaching Chart 73 • Workbook 125 • Skills Practice 112	**SUPPORT WORDS:** galoshes, gloomily, insist, official, presses, stubbornly, suspicious, yeowled • Skills Practice 113 **CHARACTER/SETTING WORDS:** Caroline Porcupine, *Claws and* *Paws*, Frank Beaver, Humphrey Snake, Oscar Raccoon, Stan Groundhog, Theodore Cat	**WRITING/SPEAKING ACTIVITY:** Use new vocabulary to make up a story about weather. • Spelling Connection 54
PART 2 **Reading & Responding** Pages 486–497	**Build Background** **Develop a Purpose for Reading** **Guide the Reading Process** **Selection Follow-Up**	• Reader's Journal 97–100 • Workbook 126 **READING EVERY DAY** *Headlines,* by M. Hall *Thank You, Amelia* *Bedelia*, by P. Parrish	**EXTRA HELP:** Predicting Story Outcome **ACHIEVING ENGLISH** **PROFICIENCY:** Discussing Weather Phrases and Making Weather Collages; Discussing Weather Lore • Achieving English Proficiency Master 26	**Language Arts** **Connections** **WRITING TO LEARN:** Prepare a weather map of your state and write about your state's weather. • Writing Master 19 **SPEAKING/LISTENING:** Comparing Weather Conditions; Creating Weather Collages; Acting Out Story Scenes; Producing Weather Broadcasts **WRITING:** Writing Weather Poems; Creating Funny Weather Stories • Language Arts Master 16
PART 3 **Selection Support** Pages 498–503	**Introduce** Long Word Decoding (Tested)	• Teaching Chart 74 • Workbook 127 • Skills Practice 114	• Reteaching Masters 1–4 • Challenge Master 15 • Achieving English Proficiency Master 27 **Practice** • Teaching Charts 75–76 • Workbook 128–129 • Skills Practice 115–116 Characterization (Tested) Test-Taking **Maintain** • Skills Practice 117 Suffixes *-ion, -tion*	**Curriculum** **Connections** **SCIENCE:** Making a Weather Chart; Creating a Weather Instrument Book • Curriculum Connection Master 16 **ART:** Creating a Picture About Cloud Formations

FORECAST

by Malcolm Hall

SUMMARY   *Stan Groundhog is retiring from his job as
weather forecaster, and his animal friends give a party in his
honor. Caroline Porcupine applies to be the new forecaster, and
starts making predictions, including one that states snow will
fall in five days—in midsummer! Oscar Raccoon decides to help
her get the job by releasing a pillow case of feathers so that it
appears that her prediction has come true. Then real flakes do
fall. Members of Silver Burdett & Ginn's student panel chose*
Forecast *for the **Readers' Choice** award.*

The Bridge

SKILL TRACE: CHARACTERIZATION				
Introduction	Practice	Test	Reteach	Maintain
TE 482	500	525	635	637	See Level 9.

LITERATURE

Teaching Characterization

OBJECTIVE   Identifying character traits and emotions.

1. WARM-UP

Use the unit theme to present character traits.

Remind students that the stories in this unit are about giving and getting different kinds of messages. Tell students they will listen to a passage about a secret message. Explain that the author has not told exactly what the characters are like, but the author has given clues. Have students listen for clues that help them know what the characters are like. *(friendly, curious)*

> **Jack Rabbit smiled and waved when he saw his pal Oliver Otter.
> "Look at this note," he called. "It's a secret message."
>   "Where did you find it? What do those letters mean? Do you
> think it's a code?" Oliver asked.**

Discuss clues to the characters' traits.

Reread the passage. Have students tell what Jack Rabbit is like and explain which word clues helped them decide. *(friendly; smiled, waved, pal)* Ask what Oliver Otter is like and what helped them to know. *(curious; he asks a lot of questions)* Explain that *friendly* and *curious* are character traits. The characters' actions, words they say, and the author's words about them are clues to what the characters are like.

State the objective.

Tell students they will learn to identify clues about character traits, or what a character is like. The clues include the way a character looks, feels, thinks, and behaves.

2. TEACH

Explain why identifying character traits is important.

The more readers know about characters' traits, the better they will understand the characters and appreciate what happens to them.

Present a strategy for identifying character traits.

Point out that students can use a strategy to help them understand character traits. Look for words that describe characters' feelings and thoughts. Then look for words spoken by characters that tell what they are feeling or thinking. Finally think about how characters behave to figure out what they are like.

72

TEACHING CHART 72: CHARACTERIZATION

1. Jack Rabbit showed the message to Wise Old Owl. Wise Old Owl put the note in front of a mirror and figured out the words. (clever; used mirror; *Wise, figured out*)
2. Jack read the message, "CLIMB MOUNTAIN. SWIM RIVER. CROSS DESERT." Then he exclaimed, "Let's do it! It will be exciting!" (adventurous, daring, brave; ready to climb, swim, cross; *exclaimed, exciting*)
3. The next day Oliver and Jack wrote a thank you letter to Wise Old Owl. (thoughtful; wrote a thank you letter)

Model the strategy. Read passage 1 and point out the author's words that describe Wise Old Owl: *Wise, put . . . in front of a mirror, figured out.* Explain that these descriptions and the fact that Jack Rabbit went to Wise Old Owl to get him to figure out the message help you to know that Wise Old Owl is clever.

3. GUIDED PRACTICE

Check for understanding. Before going on, ask students to explain what clues authors give to tell what a character is like. (*descriptions, characters' words, characters' actions*)

Guide students in using the strategy. Have students use the strategy to identify character traits in the remaining passages. Discuss whether the author's words or the character's words and behavior gave them clues to what the character is like.

4. WRAP-UP

Summarize instruction. Review why it is helpful to identify character traits while reading. (*A character is not always described in detail. Discovering how a character feels, thinks, and behaves will help the reader better understand a story.*)

Provide independent practice. Options for independent practice are shown in the Resource Center below.

5. APPLICATION

Students will identify character traits as they read "Forecast." The symbol ✔ marks specific questions and activities that apply this skill.

Meeting Individual Needs

RETEACHING Use the activity on page 637 and Masters 1–4 in the Teacher Resource Kit.

CHALLENGE Use the activity on page 637 and Master 14 in the Teacher Resource Kit.

Workbook page 124

LITERATURE

NAME _____

Characterization

REMEMBER: To understand a character in a story, think about what the character says and does. Also think about how the character speaks and acts.

A. In each sentence you learn something about a character. Write the word from the box that best describes the character.

bossy	curious	hopeful	kind

1. "Don't cry," said Adam. "I'll help you." _____kind_____

2. Bob made everyone play the game his way. _____bossy_____

3. "What is it?" asked Sara. "I can't wait to see." _____curious_____

4. George thought he could make it to the top, so he kept climbing. _____hopeful_____

B. Write the word from the box to describe the characters in each sentence.

brave	forgetful	shy

5. Joey opened the door even though he thought there was a monster inside. _____brave_____

6. "Hi," said Melissa in a soft voice. "May I sit here?" _____shy_____

7. "Where did I put my glasses this time?" said Phil. _____forgetful_____

C. Choose two sentences from Part A or B that showed what a character said. On separate paper, explain how each character's words showed you what the character was like. See Teacher Notes.

124 "Forecast"   Characterization

RESOURCE CENTER

◀ **Workbook page 124** is intended for use by all students.

Skills Practice 111 ▶ may be assigned for additional practice.

Workbook reuse option: Have students label each sentence "says" if it is the character's words or "does" if it is the character's actions that reveal what the character is like.

Skills Practice 111

NAME _____

| SKILLS PRACTICE | 111 |

Characterization

Traits are the special qualities of a story character. They can be seen in what a character says, does, and thinks.

A. Read the story. Then answer the questions about the characters.

It was Wednesday. That meant Wanda, Tess, and Lars had play practice after school. Tess was looking forward to it, Lars knew. Tess liked to do everything. Wanda wasn't happy about the school play. Play practice meant she had to stay inside. Wanda would rather be playing tag or soccer. Lars didn't know how he felt about the play. It was okay, he guessed.

The bell rang. Tess dashed out of the room. Wanda groaned. Lars grinned at her. "We need you, Wanda," Lars said. "And besides, today it's raining."

1. How does Wanda feel about the play? She wasn't happy about it.
   _____

2. Write the sentence in the story that tells how Tess feels about the play.
   Tess was looking forward to it, Lars knew.

3. What word describes Lars? kind
   daring   kind   musical

4. What word describes Tess? fun-loving
   bossy   fun-loving   patient

5. What word describes Wanda? athletic
   athletic   clever   honest

B. Go back in the story and underline clues to character traits.
Responses will vary. Accept any students can justify.

C. Which character would you like for a friend? Tell who and why.
Responses will vary.
_____
_____

LEVEL 8   "Forecast"   **111**

Vocabulary Strategies

Developing Concepts

Tap prior knowledge about weather with a chart.

Create a chart about weather as a starting point for teaching vocabulary. Ask students to name some kinds of weather and what part weather plays in their daily lives. (*It affects how they dress, what they can do outside, how they feel, how they might travel.*) Also ask what students know about the people who study weather and make predictions, and the instruments they use. An additional part of the discussion can center around weather story superstitions such as the ideas that birds roost before a storm, and if the groundhog sees its shadow, there will be six more weeks of winter. List responses, building a chart under the headings *Weather Facts* and *Weather Stories*.

Teaching Vocabulary

Discuss meanings of Story Critical words.

Read each context sentence on the Teaching Chart and identify the new word. Then use the questions that follow to help students understand each word. When necessary, provide a definition.

TEACHING CHART 73: VOCABULARY   73

1. **forecaster** (a person who tells how something will turn out)
   The weather *forecaster* said it would rain.
2. **prediction** (a declaration of what may happen in the future)
   His *prediction* was correct because it did rain.
3. **instruments** (devices used for scientific purposes)
   He looked at the dials on the *instruments*.
4. **meteorology** (the science of weather, climate, and the earth's atmosphere)
   Many instruments are used in *meteorology* to study the weather, climate, and the earth's air.
5. **flake** (a small, thin piece)
   One weather story says that a large *flake* means it will stop snowing soon.
6. **considering** (thinking about something in order to make up one's mind)
   You should be *considering* how to get to school during the storm.
7. **editor** (a person who decides what is printed in a newspaper)
   The newspaper *editor* put the story on page 5.

---

forecaster

1. **What does a forecaster have to do with the weather?** (A forecaster predicts what the weather will be either for the day or for many days ahead.) STRATEGY: PRIOR KNOWLEDGE

prediction

2. **What does it mean to predict?** (tell what will happen in the future) **What does the suffix -*ion* mean?** (result of) **If *predict* is a verb, what part of speech is *prediction*?** (noun) STRATEGY: STRUCTURAL ANALYSIS

instruments

3. **What clues in the sentence helped you figure out *instruments*?** (looked at, dials) **What are instruments?** (things that give information about weather, speed; things that measure conditions; and so on) CONTEXT CLUES

meteorology

4. According to the sentence, what things are associated with meteorology? (weather, climate, earth's air) Explain that *meteor* can be any object in the atmosphere, such as a stone or snow, and *-logy* means "study of." STRATEGY: PRIOR KNOWLEDGE

flake

5. What word in the sentence gives you a clue to the meaning of *flake*? (*snowing*) **Can you name one fact about a snowflake?** (Possible answers: It melts; no two are alike.) STRATEGY: PRIOR KNOWLEDGE

considering

6. What is the base word in *considering*? (consider) **What do you consider when you hear a weather report?** (what to wear, what to carry) STRATEGY: STRUCTURAL ANALYSIS

editor

7. Where would you find an editor working? (in a newspaper office, at a book publisher, on television or radio news) **What does a newspaper editor do?** (chooses story topics; makes sure copy is correct; decides where to put a story) STRATEGY: PRIOR KNOWLEDGE

Add new words to the chart. Have students add as many Story Critical words as they can to the chart. Have them explain how each new word fits.

Discuss Support words as needed. The Glossary of the Student Text includes definitions of the Support words: *suspicious, galoshes, yeowled, stubbornly, official, insist, gloomily, presses.*

Present Character/Setting words. Present and pronounce these words before students read the selection: *Theodore Cat, Stan Groundhog, Humphrey Snake, Oscar Raccoon, Frank Beaver, Caroline Porcupine,* Claws and Paws.

Provide independent practice. Options for independent practice are shown in the Resource Center below.

WRITING OR SPEAKING ACTIVITY *Have students make up stories about the weather. Ask them to use new vocabulary wherever possible.*

TEACHER CHOICE

Workbook page 125

NAME _____

SELECTION VOCABULARY

Using New Words

| considering | editor | flake | forecaster |
| instruments | meteorology | prediction | |

A. Write the word that completes each sentence.

George was ___considering___ being a weather forecaster.

He knew he would have to study ___meteorology___

He would have to learn to read weather ___instruments___

He thought he would like to work on a newspaper. He knew that the ___editor___ of a newspaper would want the forecaster to make a good ___prediction___ every day. Readers would want to know when even one ___flake___ of snow was going to fall.

B. Write a word from the box next to its meaning.

1. a person in charge of a newspaper ___editor___
2. a person who tells what something will be like in the future ___forecaster___
3. turning something over in your mind ___considering___
4. act of telling what may happen in the future ___prediction___
5. things scientists use to make measurements ___instruments___
6. the science that studies weather ___meteorology___

C. Choose three words to use in sentences of your own. On separate paper, use the words to make a prediction about what the weather will be next week. See Teacher Notes.

Selection Vocabulary   "Forecast" **125**

RESOURCE CENTER

◄ **Workbook page 125** provides practice with Story Critical Words.

Skills Practice 112 ► provides additional practice with Story Critical Words.

Skills Practice 113 provides practice with Support words.

Spelling Connection Master 54 may be used for spelling instruction with the new vocabulary.

Workbook reuse option: Have students circle all the words in Part A that have to do with forecasting weather.

Skills Practice 112

NAME _____

SKILLS PRACTICE **112**

Vocabulary: Story Critical Words

A. Study the meaning of each word.

considering thinking about in order to decide
editor a person who gets written material ready to be published
flake a small, thin piece
forecaster a person who tells how something will turnout

instruments tools for doing very exact work
meteorology the science that studies weather
prediction a statement telling what may happen in the future

B. Complete each sentence with the correct vocabulary word.

1. The ___editor___ selected the articles for the newspaper.
2. The weather ___forecaster___ said it would rain tomorrow.
3. Mrs. Black was ___considering___ what kind of car to buy.
4. A ___flake___ of snow fell on my nose.
5. Sam made a ___prediction___ that our school would win the game.
6. Scientists use many different kinds of ___instruments___.

C. One word in each sentence does not make sense. Underline that word. Write the vocabulary word that should go in its place.

7. A lake of paint came off the wall. ___flake___
8. Andy is consist what to give Dana for her birthday. ___considering___
9. Lana wants to study meters to learn about weather. ___meteorology___
10. She wants to become a weather taster. ___forecaster___
11. The jet corrected all the spelling mistakes. ___editor___
12. My mother made a present that I would be late. ___prediction___

112 LEVEL 8   "Forecast"   Context clues

2

Reading & Responding

Building Background

Share the following quotation with students and ask them what they think it means.

> **Self-trust is the first secret of success.**
> — *Ralph Waldo Emerson*

Build background about believing in yourself.

Ask students to think about a time when they were confident they could do something even though no one else thought they could. Perhaps it was riding a bike or getting up on a stage in front of a large audience. Ask what it was that gave them the confidence to take this risk. Had they practiced a lot? Had they seen someone else do it? Had they decided it was time to take a chance? Ask how they felt when they succeeded after taking a risk.

Discuss animal fantasy.

Tell students they will read a story where animals talk and act like people. Ask students why these animal stories are called fantasies. *(because animals cannot talk and act like people in real life)* In this fantasy, Caroline Porcupine wants a job on the *Claws and Paws* newspaper.

Developing a Purpose for Reading

Option 1
Students set purpose.

ORAL "QUESTION" LISTS   Ask students to think of questions they would like to have answered when they read the story. Have students read the title and the introduction before suggesting their questions. Record students' questions for use later.

WRITING ACTIVITY   Have students work individually or in pairs to create written "Question" lists. Have students save their lists for later use.

Option 2
Teacher sets purpose.

Have students read the selection to find out what challenge Caroline takes on and if she meets that challenge.

Meeting
Individual
Needs

EXTRA HELP   Tell students that the next story is about a porcupine who wants a job as a weather forecaster. Explain that after the porcupine predicts it will snow in the summer, her animal friends try to help her win a bet by making her forecast come true. Ask students to predict how her friends might make it "snow" in the summer. Then write their predictions on the chalkboard. Have students read the story to see how their predictions compare with the events in the story.

ACHIEVING ENGLISH PROFICIENCY   Write the following terms on the chalkboard: *warm and sunny, no chance of rain, crack of lightning, clear, windy and cold, rain, snow.* As you say the words, have students repeat them after you; then help students to tell what each kind of weather is like. Provide students with old magazines or art materials or both and ask them to make pictures or collages of different kinds of weather. Encourage them to label their pictures. Alternatively, write the weather terms on tagboard and place them on the bulletin board as captions for students to post their pictures under. Show students an illustration of a groundhog and tell them the legend of the *groundhog* and his shadow. For additional help with story comprehension, use Master 26 in the Teacher Resource Kit.

Some people think predicting the weather is a tough job. Others think it's a guessing game.

FORECAST

written by Malcolm Hall
illustrated by Bruce Degen

"Speech! Speech!" the animals chanted. Theodore Cat smiled and stood up.

"Well, if you insist," he said.

"We didn't mean *you,* Theodore," groaned the animals. "We want a speech from Stan!"

"Oh, *him,*" said Theodore.

Stan Groundhog stood up. He looked around shyly. The whole party was in his honor. After twenty years, Stan was retiring. He was leaving his job as weather <u>forecaster</u> for the *Claws and Paws* newspaper. "I can't think of anything to say," said Stan.

"Then make a forecast!" yelled Humphrey Snake from the back of the room.

"What a good idea," said Theodore, who was the <u>editor</u> of the paper and the boss of all the animals. "Stan, give us your last official weather prediction."

"Well—okay," said Stan. He went to the window and peeked outside; next he looked down at his shadow, then he sighed. "I predict it will be warm and sunny all afternoon. There is no chance of rain." The animals cheered. "Now I have to be going," said Stan. "Thanks for the party."

Stan put on a raincoat and galoshes. He opened an umbrella.

Reader's Journal   p 97
Preparing for Reading

WHAT ARE FRIENDS FOR?

Looking at pictures from other selections they have read encourages students to re-call a time they helped a friend or a friend helped them. They then write about what happened.

GUIDED READING

Page 253   What helps Stan Groundhog predict it will be sunny? Explain. (Seeing his shadow helps because the sun has to be shining to make shadows.)
SYNTHESIZE: DRAWING CONCLUSIONS

Page 253   Why do you think Stan puts on a raincoat and galoshes after predicting there is no chance of rain? (Possible answers: He does not trust his own forecast; he knows that weather can change very quickly; he does not want to take a chance.)
SYNTHESIZE: DRAWING CONCLUSIONS

HIGHLIGHTING LITERATURE

Page 253   Point out elements of an animal story. Explain that these stories are fantasies because the animals act like people. Have students point out how the animals behave like people. (asking Stan to give a speech; Stan's making a forecast; Stan's putting on his raincoat and galoshes)

"Wait a minute," said Oscar Raccoon. "Why are you going out dressed like that? I thought you said it wasn't going to rain."

"If I have learned one thing," said Stan, "it is never take chances."

And with that, a tremendous crack of lightning jumped across the sky! All the lights in the office went out. Rain began to pour down in bucketfuls. "Do you see what I mean?" said Stan. He waved good-bye and left.

The lights flickered a bit and finally came back on. Oscar looked around. "Is everybody okay?" One by one, the animals nodded. Except—where was Theodore? "Theodore!" shouted Oscar. "Where are you?"

"There he is!" shouted Frank Beaver. He pointed to the floor. "I see his tail!"

Theodore's face was red as he crawled out from under the desk. The animals grinned. "I wasn't hiding, if that's what you're all thinking," he snapped. "I was—uh—considering something—that's what I was doing."

"Oh? And what were you considering?" asked Oscar.

Theodore glared. "I was considering that we will need a new forecaster to take Stan's place. So there!" Theodore looked around the room. "Does anyone know a groundhog who needs a job?"

Caroline Porcupine raised her hand. "Does the forecaster *have* to be a groundhog?"

"Of course," said Theodore. "Everyone knows that groundhogs know *whether* or not spring is coming. That's why they make good *whethermen*." Theodore laughed at what he thought was a very good joke.

Most of the animals, however, moaned. Caroline went on. "Anyway, Theodore," she said, "I want the job, even if I am not a groundhog. I know a lot about the weather. Last year, I took a class in meteorology."

"Meteorology?" said Humphrey. "What's that mean?"

"Everyone knows that," said Theodore. "Meteorology is the science of meteors. You know, shooting stars."

"It is not!" snapped Caroline. "Meteorology is the science of weather!"

"Is that so?" said Theodore.

"Yes it is," said Caroline right back. "I can make real forecasts—not just guesses like Stan. If you give me a chance, I will prove it."

Page 254   What is Stan's real reason for putting on his raincoat and galoshes? (He says that he has learned never to take chances.)   RECALL: CHARACTER

✔ **Page 254   What does Oscar Raccoon do when the lights come back on?** (He looks around and asks if everybody is okay.) **What does this tell you about Oscar?** (that he is concerned, kind)
INFER: FEELINGS/ATTITUDES

✔ **Page 254   When Theodore Cat crawls out, the author says that his face is red. What does this tell you about Theodore?** (that he is embarrassed)
INFER: FEELINGS/ATTITUDES

✔ **Page 255   Do you think Caroline would make a better weather forecaster than Stan? Why or why not?** (Students might suggest that Caroline seems very determined; she is sure of herself; she took a course in meteorology; she does not make guesses like Stan.)
SYNTHESIZE: CHARACTER

✔ Skill from The Bridge applied through this question.

HIGHLIGHTING LITERATURE

Page 255   Point out the paragraph beginning with "Of course . . . ." Note the pun the characters are making with the homophone *whether*. The inferred pun is on the word *weather*. Explain that this is one way the author has created a mood of humor in the story.

[handwritten: group reader]

"Okay," grumbled Theodore. "Let's make a bet. You forecast the weather for all next week. If you are right five days in a row, I will *consider* you for the job. But if you are wrong once, I'll get a groundhog."

"Theodore, I'll take your bet," said Caroline.

The next day, Caroline brought in her weather <u>instruments</u>. All that morning, Caroline set them up. Soon wires and dials were everywhere.

By afternoon she was ready. She looked at the instruments, one after the other. On a pad of paper she wrote down how hot it was, how damp it was, how fast the wind was blowing, and everything else.

Then Caroline picked up the telephone. She called forecasters all over the country. They told her what the weather was like in their towns. Caroline wrote this down, too.

Finally, Caroline put all the numbers on a map. She connected the numbers with lines. Just then Theodore walked up. "Very good," he said. "I have never seen a better drawing of spaghetti!" He laughed and laughed at his own joke.

No one else did, however.

Caroline looked up. "I am ready to make my forecast. Today is Monday. It will be clear for the rest of the day. Tuesday, it will be sunny and warm. Wednesday, it will be windy and cold. Thursday, it will rain."

The animals looked at each other and smiled. So far, the forecast sounded good— maybe Caroline would be right!

Caroline went on. "And last, Friday. It will be cold in the morning, with snow in the afternoon."

Theodore yeowled with laughter. "Snow? Did you say *snow*? Caroline, look outside. It's the middle of summer!"

Caroline folded her arms stubbornly across her chest. "My instruments say it will snow on Friday. Anyway, every now and then it does snow in summer. In July of 1816, for example . . ."

GUIDED READING

[handwritten: Looked outside]

Page 256   What things does Caroline do before she makes her weather prediction? (She brings in her instruments and hooks them up; she records the information on the instruments; she calls other weather forecasters and compares the weather; she records her findings on maps and charts.)   RECALL: DETAILS

Page 257   What surprising prediction does Caroline make? (She says it will snow on Friday afternoon.)   RECALL: DETAILS

[handwritten: It was summer]

✔ **Page 257   How do you know Caroline is stubborn? Give two ways you know.** (from the words *folded her arms stubbornly*; from her behavior in defending her prediction)   ANALYZE: CHARACTER

[handwritten: Studied meteorology]
[handwritten: Believed in herself]

STRATEGIC READING

Page 257   Have students summarize what has happened so far in the story. (Stan Groundhog retires from his job as forecaster of the *Claws and Paws* newspaper and Caroline Porcupine applies for the job, even though it has always been held by a groundhog. Theodore Cat, who is the editor, says she can have the job if she predicts the weather correctly for five days. Caroline accepts the challenge.) **Ask students if they think it will in fact snow on Friday.** (Possible answers: It will snow because it is a fantasy; it will not snow, but Caroline gets the job anyway because of her scientific approach.) Point out that summarizing and predicting can help readers understand what they read. If any students have trouble summarizing, they should reread those parts of the story that they do not remember. At the completion of the story, ask students to check their predictions.   METACOGNITION: SUMMARIZING AND PREDICTING

✔ Skill from The Bridge applied through this question.

"Okay, okay," said Theodore. "If it snows on Friday, you get the job for sure. But meanwhile, I'm going to keep on looking for a groundhog!"

That afternoon was sunny. The day after that was warm and clear. Caroline had been right.

Wednesday was windy and cold. Caroline had been right again. Everyone clapped her on the back. Except Theodore. He stared gloomily out his window. "She has been right three days in a row," he thought. "That is better than Stan ever did."

Thursday started out rainy and stayed that way the whole day. Theodore tromped in, soaked, as mad and miserable as a wet cat. Again, he thought. "Four days in a row. Maybe I *should* give Caroline the job even if it doesn't snow on Friday."

But then—"Aaaaa—choooo!" Theodore sneezed. Papers flew everywhere.

"Now see what's happened," he snarled. "I have a cold. And it's all Caroline's fault! If she hadn't forecast this rain, it never would have happened!"

That night, Frank and Oscar walked home together. "It's too bad Caroline predicted snow," said Frank. "She really wants that job."

Oscar nodded. "It will never snow tomorrow. Poor Caroline." Then Oscar stopped. He winked at Frank. "Suppose we help the weather a bit? Even if it only snowed a little, Theodore would still have to give Caroline the job."

"What do you have in mind?" asked Frank.

"Come to my house for dinner," said Oscar, "and I will tell you."

Friday started out cold, just as Caroline had predicted. But by noon, there was still no sign of snow. Theodore sat in his office sniffling and looking out the window.

If Theodore had turned his head, he would have seen Frank and Oscar tiptoe past his door. Each one carried a large sack. They were headed for the ladder that went up to the roof.

GUIDED READING

✔ **Page 258   What does Theodore consider doing even if it does not snow on Friday?** (He might give Caroline the job anyway.) **What does this tell you about him?** (He is a fair editor; he can be a nice boss.) EVALUATE: CHARACTER

Page 259   What do you think Frank and Oscar are planning? (They will probably do something to make it seem like it is snowing.)   SYNTHESIZE: PREDICTING OUTCOMES

✔ **Page 259   What does this planning tell you about Frank's and Oscar's friendship with Caroline?** (They must be good friends if they want to help her out so much.)   EVALUATE: CHARACTER

STRATEGIC READING

✔ **Page 259**   Ask students to visualize the scene where Oscar and Frank sneak past Theodore's door. Ask them to describe what they see. (Oscar and Frank are tiptoeing; each one is carrying a large sack. Theodore is probably inside with his back turned.) Read aloud the last two paragraphs on this page while students visualize the scene. Explain that visualizing is one way readers keep track of how well they are understanding. If any students are unable to visualize, they should reread the paragraphs, paying particular attention to the actions of the characters.   METACOGNITION: VISUALIZING

✔ Skill from The Bridge applied through this question.
✔ Informal Assessment Opportunity: VISUALIZING

A few minutes later, Theodore gasped. A white <u>flake</u> had drifted down past his window! Then came another flake . . . and another . . . and another! He jumped up. "Snow! It's really snowing!"

Theodore ran out of his office. "Caroline! Congratulations! It's snowing! You are the greatest forecaster ever! I take back everything I said."

Theodore yelled to <u>Morris Squirrel</u>. "Stop the presses! I want a new headline for our new forecaster: 'CAROLINE EXPECTS SNOW!'"

Theodore was so excited, he nearly hugged Caroline. He remembered just in time that you *never* hug a porcupine.

So instead he dragged Caroline into his office. "See!" He pointed outside at the flakes.

Caroline squinted. "That doesn't look like snow to me," she said.

"Of course it is," said Theodore. He raised the window. Flakes started to drift in. One landed on Theodore's nose. "*Aaaa—choo*!!!" For a moment Theodore looked surprised. Then, he looked suspicious.

"Snow never tickled before. Let me see that 'snowflake.'" He grabbed the flake and held it up to the light. "I thought so. This is a *feather*!"

Theodore ran to the window. He poked his head outside and looked up at the roof. There was Oscar, holding a half-empty pillowcase in one hand and a handful of feathers in the other.

"Oh! Hello, Theodore. I was just—"

"Come down from there!" roared Theodore.

A few minutes later, Oscar and Caroline were standing side by side in Theodore's office. "So! You two thought you could trick me."

"Caroline had nothing to do with this," said Oscar. "It was all my idea."

GUIDED READING

✔ **Page 260   How does Theodore feel when he first sees the "snow" drifting past his window? How do you know?** (He is excited and happy for Caroline. He gasps and jumps up. He runs into Caroline's office to congratulate her.)   INFER: FEELINGS/ATTITUDES

Page 261   What happens that makes Theodore suspicious about the snowflakes? (The snowflakes tickle his nose and he sneezes, something that snow never has made him do before.)   INFER: CAUSE/EFFECT

✔ **Page 261   How does Theodore feel when he sees Oscar up on the roof?** (He is angry.)
INFER: FEELINGS/ATTITUDES

Page 261   What do you think Theodore will do next? What makes you think so? (Possible answers: Theodore will call off the bet; it is more likely that Theodore will think it is a big joke and laugh because up to now he has been nice to Caroline.)
SYNTHESIZE: PREDICTING OUTCOMES

✔ **Skill from The Bridge applied through this question.**

HIGHLIGHTING LITERATURE

Pages 260–261   Ask students to tell how the author keeps up the humorous tone of the story. (Oscar and Frank's scheme with the feathers is absurd and very funny; Theodore's sneezing with feathers drifting in is a funny scene; Caroline and Oscar with Theodore in his office is funny because Oscar did not mean to cause any trouble; he just wanted to be helpful.) Note that usually something makes us laugh if it is a total surprise or if it is so extreme it could not happen in real life. Point out that the idea of it snowing in the summer is funny because it is not something that happens in warm weather.

491

"Hah!" Theodore snorted. "I don't believe you, any more than I really believed it was snowing out there." He pointed out the window. Once more, flakes were drifting down.

"What? More feathers? That does it! I suppose Frank's up there, too."

Again Theodore poked his head out the window. But this time, it was *really* snowing. A large, powdery snowball whacked him between the eyes!

"*Whaaag!*" spat Theodore. Then he licked his whiskers. "That's *real* snow!"

"Of course it is," said Caroline. "I told you it would snow."

Just then, Frank came climbing down the ladder from the roof. His brown fur was covered with snow. "Theodore! Caroline! Oscar! Why are you still inside? Come on out!"

And they all did.

◆ LIBRARY LINK ◆

If you liked reading this story by Malcolm Hall, you might enjoy reading another of his books, Headlines.

Reader's Response

Would you try to help a friend the way Oscar and Frank did? Why or why not?

See next page for suggested answers.

SELECTION FOLLOW-UP

FORECAST

 Thinking It Over

1. Why were the animals having a party?
2. What did you learn about Theodore when you read he had crawled under his desk?
3. Why did Theodore think that a weather forecaster had to be a groundhog?
4. Why was Caroline confident she could do a good job?
5. Do you think the test Theodore gave Caroline was fair? Why? How did you decide on your answer?

Writing to Learn

THINK AND IMAGINE   Imagine that you are a weather forecaster. Draw a simple outline of the state where you live. Add symbols to show what the weather is like. Use snowflakes, raindrops, a sun, or clouds (with puffy cheeks for wind). Use numbers to show the temperature.

WRITE   Write sentences to describe the weather shown on your map. Is it sunny or cloudy? Is it going to rain or snow? Is it windy? What is the temperature?

GUIDED READING

✔ **Page 262   How do all the characters feel at the end of the story? Why?** (They are all excited, probably because it is snowing and because of their happiness for Caroline.)   INFER: FEELINGS/ATTITUDES

RETURNING TO THE READING PURPOSE

OPTION 1   If students set the purpose, return to their question lists about the story. Discuss whether these questions were answered. Students may wish to discuss surprises in the story. (snowing in the summertime)

OPTION 2   If you set the purpose, ask what challenge was given to Caroline and how she met the challenge. (If she could predict the weather correctly for five days in a row, she could have the job of weather forecaster. She uses many instruments and her predictions are correct for five days. It even snows as she said it would. Caroline gets the job of weather forecaster.)

✔ **Skill from The Bridge applied through this question.**

Reader's Journal   p 98
Responding to Reading

A NEW WEATHER FORECASTER

As reporters for the *Claws and Paws* newspaper, students plan articles evaluating how well Caroline Porcupine is doing her job. They write the opening lines.

SELECTION FOLLOW-UP

FORECAST

THINKING IT OVER

1. **Why were the animals having a party?** (The animals were having a party because Stan, the groundhog, was retiring after twenty years as a weather forecaster.) RECALL: DETAILS

2. **What did you learn about Theodore when you read he had crawled under his desk?** (Theodore's crawling under his desk probably meant that he was afraid of lightning and storms.) SYNTHESIZE: CHARACTER

3. **Why did Theodore think that a weather forecaster had to be a groundhog?** (Theodore was thinking of the old tradition of Groundhog Day, February 2, when groundhogs are supposed to come out of hibernation. If they come out and see their shadows, they supposedly go back underground for six more weeks of winter weather. If they do not see their shadows, it supposedly means that spring will come early. Make sure that students pick up on the play on words here — groundhogs make good *whethermen* because they know *whether* spring is coming — and that they connect it with the idea that forecasting by groundhogs is a guess, not a scientific process.) SYNTHESIZE: DRAWING CONCLUSIONS

4. **Why was Caroline confident she could do a good job?** (She had taken a course in meteorology where she learned how to make real forecasts, not just make guesses like Stan did.) ANALYZE: CHARACTER

5. **Do you think the test Theodore gave Caroline was fair? Why? How did you decide on your answer?** (In discussing their answers, students should consider how hard it would be for anyone, no matter how skilled, to make a perfect weather forecast for five days in a row. In support of their conclusions, students may cite personal experiences with mistaken weather predictions and with people who have fixed ideas about what they want and do not want.) SYNTHESIZE: DRAWING CONCLUSIONS: METACOGNITION

WRITING TO LEARN

Use Writing Master 19, which provides guidelines.

THINK AND IMAGINE   Imagine that you are a weather forecaster. Draw a simple outline of the state where you live. Add symbols to show what the weather is like. Use snowflakes, raindrops, a sun, or clouds (with puffy cheeks for wind). Use numbers to show the temperature. (Help students work with the maps to prepare for writing.)

Extend comprehension through writing.

WRITE   Write sentences to describe the weather shown on your map. Is it sunny or cloudy? Is it going to rain or snow? Is it windy? What is the temperature? (Have students share their sentences.)

More Ideas for Selection Follow-Up

CRITICAL AND CREATIVE THINKING QUESTIONS

Encourage a variety of responses and points of view.

Use these open-ended questions to encourage critical and creative thinking about the selection.

✔ 1. Did you expect Frank and Oscar's plan to help Caroline to work? Why or why not?

2. Caroline probably had mixed feelings when she discovered her friends' plan to help her. What do you think those feelings were?

3. The theme of this unit is "Get the Message." What is the message in "Forecast"? Who got the message?

REREADING ORALLY

Have students reread for specific information.

Have students read aloud passages in the selection that show that Caroline knew what she was doing, that she had confidence, and that she would not let anyone discourage her. Tell students to read paragraphs with dialogue as Caroline might have spoken the words. Remind students to pay attention to punctuation marks to help them know how to use their voices.

SELECTION COMPREHENSION

Provide comprehension check.

A Workbook page to check comprehension is shown in the Resource Center below. It may be used for informal assessment.

✔ **Informal Assessment Opportunity:** EVALUATING

Workbook page 126

SELECTION
COMPREHENSION

NAME _____

FORECAST

A. Complete the summary of the story "Forecast."
Accept reasonable variations.

This story tells how _____Caroline_____ Porcupine got Theodore Cat to let her be a weather forecaster. All the animals met in the *Claws and Paws* newspaper _____office_____ .

The newspaper needed a new forecaster because Stan Groundhog was _____retiring_____ . Theodore did not want to give Caroline the job. He wanted another _____groundhog_____ for the job. To get the job, Caroline bet Theodore that she could make the right forecast for _____five days_____ in a row.

If Caroline was wrong on any day's forecast, she would not get the job. The animals were surprised when they heard the forecast. Caroline said it would _____snow_____ on Friday even though it was _____the middle of summer_____ . For four days Caroline was right. On Friday Frank Beaver and Oscar Raccoon decided to help out. They climbed to the roof of the office and emptied _____feathers_____ from a pillow to look like snow. Theodore knew it was not real snow. He thought Caroline was trying to _____play a trick on him_____ .

Later when Theodore saw more flakes, he thought it was another trick. Then he leaned out the window and got hit with a _____real snowball_____ .

Caroline's forecast had been right for all the days so she got the job.

B. On separate paper, write three sentences explaining why forecasting the weather is important. See Teacher Notes.

126 "Forecast"   Selection Comprehension

RESOURCE CENTER

◀ **Workbook page 126** is intended for use by all students.

Writing Master 19 supports the Writing to Learn activity.

LANGUAGE ARTS CONNECTIONS

CRITICAL THINKING: COMPARING WEATHER DATA

Have students compare weather information.

Explain that weather conditions in cities and states are recorded and that these records include: temperature, precipitation (rain, snow), wind, and sunshine. Write these categories on the chalkboard. Point out that information is usually summarized for each month and for a year.

Have students work in small groups to compare the weather in their state to another state's weather. Tell each group to choose a month and a state for their comparison. Provide sources for research such as almanacs, encyclopedias, and science books. Have students record their findings on charts, using the headings on the board. Allow time for each group to present its weather data. As a class, discuss how this kind of weather information might be useful. SHARED LEARNING: SPEAKING

CREATIVE WEATHER COLLAGES

Discuss weather words.

Talk about weather words, eliciting categories such as weather conditions, instruments, people, and weather-related clothing. Ask students to give examples for each category. *(foggy; thermometer; meteorologist; galoshes)*

Have students create collages of weather words.

Provide old newspapers, especially sections with weather forecasts, and old magazines. Have students look through them for words about weather, cut out the words, and use them to create collages. Suggest to students that they use words of different sizes and colors to make their collages interesting. Point out that the words may be arranged on the paper in unusual ways, sometimes pasting parts on top of one another. WHOLE CLASS ENRICHMENT

ACTING OUT SCENES FROM THE STORY

Have students present scenes from the story.

Explain that when we speak we use expression to show the meaning and feeling behind the words we are saying. Point out that actors must practice saying their dialogue with expression to keep the interest of their audience.

Have students work in small groups to perform scenes from the story. Suggest the following scenes or have students decide their own scenes: Theodore at the party giving his last prediction; Caroline confronting Theodore about the job; Oscar and Frank devising their scheme to make snow; Theodore sneezing under a rain of feathers; the animals in Theodore's office reacting when it really begins to snow. Tell students to use dialogue from the story. Remind students to use expression in their voices to show how the characters are feeling.

SHARED LEARNING: SPEAKING

PRODUCING WEATHER BROADCASTS

Have students cooperatively produce a weather report.

Tell students that in a cooperative project, each person agrees to do a certain job or task, and that each job or task must be done fully and correctly in order for the whole project to be completed. Point out that in real life it takes many people to produce a weather forecast. Ask students to think about the jobs people must do to produce a weather forecast.

Have students work in groups of four to produce and present weather broadcasts for television. Assign one student the job of the meterologist who gathers the data; assign a second student to take the data and create a chart; assign a third student to write the weather forecast from the data; assign a fourth student to be the reporter and actually present the forecast. Allow time for each "station" to give its report.   COOPERATIVE LEARNING

CREATING FUNNY WEATHER STORIES

Have students write humorous weather stories.

Remind students of the humor in "Forecast"—the play on the word *weather* and the silliness of feathers flying around in place of snow. Point out that humor can be created both by having fun with words and by using things from real life in imaginative ways. If possible, get a copy of the book *Cloudy with a Chance of Meatballs* and read it to students. The weather that befalls a town is made up of different kinds of food.

Encourage students to create stories that involve feathers, soap bubbles, food, or other items to represent the weather. Students might work individually, in pairs, or in small groups. **Language Arts Master 16** can be used with this activity.   WRITING

WRITING WEATHER POEMS

Have students write their own weather poems.

Remind students that many people express their feelings about the weather in poems. Bring in poems that describe the weather and read them to the class. Possibilities are Carl Sandburg's "Fog," Rachel Field's "Snow in the City," and Robert Louis Stevenson's "Rain." Have students share any weather poems they know. Stress that not all poems have rhyming words. Tell students to listen for words that create pictures in their minds.

Then have students close their eyes and picture a certain kind of weather. It might be their favorite weather or their least favorite weather. Tell students to write what they see, hear, and feel. Students might like to illustrate their finished poems, which can then be bound into a book and placed in the classroom library.   CHALLENGE: WRITING

READING EVERY DAY

After reading "Forecast," students won't want to miss the following stories in which the main characters don't "get the message."

Headlines by Malcolm Hall. Illustrated by Wallace Tripp. Coward, McCann & Geoghegan, © 1973. Theodore Cat, a frustrated newspaper editor, refuses to listen when reporter Oscar Raccoon tries to give him a message that would unravel the mystery of some zany misspelled headlines.   EASIER TO READ

Thank You, Amelia Bedelia by Peggy Parrish. Harper & Row © 1964. In carrying out directions to the letter, Amelia Bedelia creates hilarious havoc in the Rogers household.

A **World of Books** Classroom Libraries selection

Reader's Journal   **pp 99, 100**
Extending Reading

HOW DO YOU LIKE THIS WEATHER?

After learning about unusual weather in four different parts of the world, students pretend to visit and write about one place.

Selection Support

Long Word Decoding

OBJECTIVE   Using the long word decoding strategy to read words.

SKILL TRACE: LONG WORD DECODING				
Introduction	Practice	Test	Reteach	Maintain
TE 498	524	595	635	640	See Level 9.

1. WARM-UP

Review listening for syllables.

Remind students that every syllable has a vowel sound. Say the following words from "Forecast" and have students identify the number of syllables they hear in each word: forecaster *(3)*, groundhog *(2)*, galoshes *(3)*, soaked *(1)*, congratulations *(5)*.

Review the known signals for recognizing syllables.

Review with students the steps for reading long words they have learned. Recall that they should first look for words and word-parts they know, then find syllables and vowel sounds. Review that vowels can have a long sound, a short sound, or have the sound of *a* in the word *about*. Students should then read the word, blending the syllables. If the word does not make sense, they should try different sounds for the vowels.

State the objective.

Tell students they are going to learn how to read long words by finding syllables and trying different vowel sounds.

2. TEACH

Explain why knowing how to decode long words is important.

Tell students that knowing how to read long words will help them better understand and enjoy what they read and help them to read more on their own.

Present and model the strategy for decoding long words.

Display the Teaching Chart. Use the word *raincoat* to model step 1. Ask a volunteer to read the word and tell what it means. Underline the words *rain* and *coat* and point out that these are both words students know. Repeat the procedure with the word *connected*. Underline the ending *-ed* and tell students this is a word-part they know. Underline the syllables *con* and *nect* and ask students to tell what vowel sounds they hear in each syllable. Then say the word *connected* slowly, stressing the second syllable.

TEACHING CHART 74: READING LONG WORDS   `74`

1.   Look for words and word-parts you know.
2.   Look for syllables and vowel sounds.
      a. Two consonants after the first vowel may signal a short sound.
      b. One consonant after the first vowel may signal a long sound.
      c. A consonant followed by *-le* forms its own syllable.
3.   Say the word, blending the syllables.
4.   If the word doesn't make sense, try different vowel sounds.

1.   raincoat   connected   prediction   powdery
2.   Caroline *carefully* predicted the weather conditions.
3.   She used charts and a *computer* to *determine* the storm's location.
4.   *Surprisingly*, a *blizzard arrived* in July.
5.   Caroline is *enjoying* her new *occupation*.

3. GUIDED PRACTICE

Check for understanding.

Have students read the remaining words on line 1. Then have them tell what steps helped them figure out the words.

Guide students in using the strategy.

Have students read sentences 2–5. Then ask volunteers to explain the steps they followed to read the italicized words.

4. WRAP-UP

Summarize instruction.

Ask students to tell what they should do when they come across long words in their reading. *(Look for words and word-parts they know, look for syllables and vowel sounds, try saying the word, using different vowel sounds until it makes sense.)*

Provide independent practice.

Options for independent practice are shown in the Resource Center below.

Meeting Individual Needs

RETEACHING Use the activity on page 640 and Masters 1–4 in the Teacher Resource Kit.

CHALLENGE Use the activity on page 640 and Master 15 in the Teacher Resource Kit.

ACHIEVING ENGLISH PROFICIENCY Use the activity on page 640 and Master 27 in the Teacher Resource Kit.

Workbook page 127

NAME _____

Long Word Decoding

DECODING

REMEMBER: When you try to read a long word, look for words and word parts you know.

A. Circle the words or word parts you know. Underline the vowel letters.

1. cartoon   2. emotions   3. fantastic   4. sunflower   5. unremarkable

B. Answer each question with a word from above.

6. Which word means the opposite of *ordinary*?
   fantastic

7. Which word means "a funny drawing"?
   cartoon

8. Which word means "feelings"?
   emotions

9. Which word means "ordinary" or "not worth talking about"?
   unremarkable

10. Which word names a kind of plant?
    sunflower

C. On another paper, use three of the words above to write a sentence. See Teacher Notes.

Long Word Decoding   "Forecast"   **127**

RESOURCE CENTER

◀ **Workbook page 127** is intended for use by all students.

Skills Practice 114 ▶ may be assigned for additional practice.

Workbook reuse option: Ask students to write above each word they wrote the number of syllables it contains.

Skills Practice 114

NAME _____

SKILLS PRACTICE ◀ **114**

Long Word Decoding

When you try to read a long word, look for words and word parts you know. Some word parts you know are *-ful, -less, -ly,* and *-y.*

A. Write the compound words from the box in the first list. Write words with suffixes in the second list.

bandstand	frostbite	lightly	restful	roadside
breathless	lifeboat	moonbeams	risky	toothless

Compound Words	**Words with Suffixes**
bandstand	breathless
frostbite	lightly
lifeboat	restful
moonbeams	risky
roadside	toothless

B. Write the word from the box that answers the question.

1. Which words have a vowel sound like the one in *cone*?
   roadside, lifeboat

2. Which words have a vowel sound like the one in *ruthless*?
   toothless, moonbeams

3. Which words have a vowel sound like the one in *fly*?
   frostbite, roadside, lightly, lifeboat

4. Which word has a vowel sound like the one in *cat*?
   bandstand

5. Which words have a suffix with a vowel sound like the one in *meet*?
   lightly, risky

114   LEVEL 8   "Forecast"

SKILL TRACE: CHARACTERIZATION					
Introduction	Practice		Test	Reteach	Maintain
TE 482	500	525	635	637	See Level 9.

LITERATURE
Characterization

OBJECTIVE   Identifying character traits and emotions.

Review character traits.

Remind students that character traits are what a character's personality and behavior are like. Knowing what a character is like helps the reader to understand a character and predict how he or she will behave. It also helps the reader better understand and enjoy the story. Words such as *brave, clever,* and *honest* are character traits. Students can identify a character's traits by words the character says and words that describe the character's feelings, thoughts, and actions.

Present passages for determining character traits.

Display the Teaching Chart. Have students read each passage and select the word that best describes the character.

> **75**
>
> **TEACHING CHART 75: CHARACTERIZATION**
>
> careful   embarrassed   confident
>
> 1. Theodore's face was red as he crawled out from under the desk. The animals grinned. "I wasn't hiding, if that's what you're thinking," he snapped. "I was — uh — considering something." (embarrassed)
> 2. "I predict it will be warm and sunny with no chance of rain. But I have learned never to take chances," Stan said as he put on a raincoat and galoshes. (careful)
> 3. "Meteorology is the science of weather," said Caroline. "I can make a real forecast — not just guesses like Stan. If you give me a chance, I will prove it." (confident)

Provide independent practice.

Options for independent practice are shown in the Resource Center below.

Workbook page 128

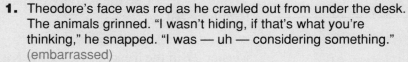

> LITERATURE
> ## Characterization
>
> **REMEMBER:** To understand a character in a story, think about what the character says and does. Also think about how the character speaks and acts.
>
> **A.** Read the sentences about some of the characters in "Forecast." Write the word that tells what the character is like. You may use some words more than once.
>
> | confident | joking | scared | shy |
>
> 1. When Stan Groundhog spoke, he said quietly, "I don't know what to say." _shy_
>
> 2. When a big storm put the lights out, Theodore hid. _scared_
>
> 3. Theodore said, "Everyone knows that groundhogs know *whether* or not spring is coming. That's why they make good *whethermen*." _joking_
>
> 4. Caroline said to Theodore, "I can make real forecasts—not just guesses. Give me a chance. I will prove it." _confident_
>
> 5. Caroline bet Theodore she could forecast the weather right five days in a row. _confident_
>
> **B.** A character's words help you understand the character. Caroline was confident. On separate paper, write a sentence Caroline might say that would show she is confident. See Teacher Notes.
>
> **128** "Forecast"   Characterization

RESOURCE CENTER

◀ **Workbook page 128** is intended for use by all students.

Skills Practice 115 ▶ may be assigned for additional practice.

Workbook reuse option: At the end of each sentence in Part A, have students write *says* if they learned about the character through the character's words and *does* if they learned about the character through the character's actions.

Skills Practice 115

> NAME _____
>
> SKILLS PRACTICE ◀ 115
>
> **Characterization**
>
> If you want to know why characters act the way they do, or predict how characters will behave, think about what they say, feel, and do. These are good clues.
>
> Read each paragraph. Answer the questions.
>
> Sonia is excited. Today is her first dancing lesson. She has been taking piano lessons for two years and plays well. She loves the piano. In fact, she loves everything about music. That's why she decided to take dancing lessons. She wants to learn to move with music, not just make music.
>
> 1. What word describes Sonia? _musical_
>
>   lazy   fun-loving   musical
>
> 2. What two things does she do that tell you that? _She takes piano lessons and dancing lessons._
>
> Fred hopped down from the chair and walked a few steps across the room. He stopped and stretched. His toy mouse was in the doorway. With a meow, Fred jumped. He threw it into the air. He batted it across the room. It slid under the couch. With his big green eyes, Fred peeked under the couch. The mouse was out of reach. Fred walked off.
>
> He washed his black and white face. Then he jumped onto Lisa's desk. He nosed under a pile of papers. He sniffed around the magazines. He peered at the can of pencils. One by one, he pulled the pencils out of the can with his mouth. He carried each to the edge of the desk and dropped it on the floor. Then he sat quietly in front of the window and waited for Lisa to come home.
>
> 3. Who is Fred and what does he look like? _a black and white cat with green eyes_
>
> 4. What did Fred do that showed he is curious? _He nosed under papers. He sniffed at magazines. He peered at the can of pencils._
>
> 5. Fred is also patient. Underline and write the sentence that tells you that. _Then he sat quietly in front of the window and waited for Lisa to come home._
>
> LEVEL 8   "Forecast"   **115**

STUDY SKILLS
Test Taking

OBJECTIVE   Identifying and practicing test-taking techniques.

Review types of tests.   Remind students that there are different types of tests. Three common types are completion, true-false, and multiple choice. They can tell what type of test they are taking by reading the directions and looking at the form of the example.

Use Teaching Chart to review each type of test.   Display the Teaching Chart. Have students read each example and tell what type of test it illustrates. Have students explain their answers.

> **TEACHING CHART 76: TEST-TAKING**   **76**
>
> **A.** Fill in the blank to complete the sentence.
> Caroline used a _____ to talk with other forecasters.
> (completion; it has a blank, and no answers are given)
> **B.** Write T if the sentence is true and F if it is false.
> Caroline got the job of forecaster. _____
> (true-false; the T and F stand for true and false)
> **C.** Circle the letter in front of the correct answer.
> Who was the editor of Claws and Paws?
> a. Stan   b. Theodore   c. Caroline
> (multiple choice; answer choices are given)

Provide independent practice.   Options for independent practice are shown in the Resource Center below.

Workbook page 129

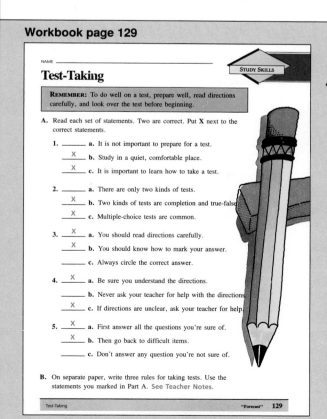

RESOURCE CENTER

◀ **Workbook page 129** is intended for use by all students.

Skills Practice 116 ▶ may be assigned for additional practice.

Workbook reuse option: Have students write a sentence beside each of three correct responses that tells why that study rule makes sense.

Skills Practice 116

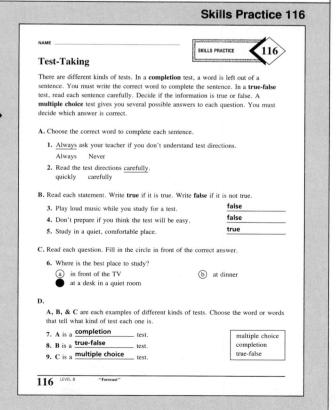

SKILL TRACE: SUFFIXES				
Introduction	Practice	Test	Reteach	Maintain
TE 370	395	422	461	466	502

WORD STUDY

Suffixes -ion, -tion

OBJECTIVE   Using structural analysis to determine word meaning.

Review suffixes.

Ask students to explain what a suffix is *(a letter or group of letters added to the end of a word)* and how it changes a word. *(It changes the meaning and sometimes the part of speech of the base word.)*

Present suffixed words in context.

You may wish to write the sentences below on the chalkboard. Possible answers are printed in red. Have students read the sentences and identify the suffixed word and the base word. Using the meaning of the base word, have students give the meaning of each suffixed word.

> **1.** Caroline made a correction on the chart. (correction; correct; a change made to fix an error)
> **2.** Her five-day prediction was correct. (prediction; predict; a statement of what would happen)
> **3.** "Congratulations! It's snowing!" (congratulations; congratulate; an expression of happiness or pleasure at another's good fortune or success.)

Provide independent practice.

An independent activity is shown in the Resource Center below.

RESOURCE CENTER

Skills Practice 117 ▶ may be assigned for additional practice.

Skills Practice 117

NAME _____

SKILLS PRACTICE ◁117▷

Suffixes *-ion, -tion*

The suffixes *-ion* and *-tion* change a verb to a noun.
   I will *invent* a tower math game. It will be my *invention*.

A. Read the words in the box. Then use them to answer the questions.

correction	directions	prevention	protection	situation
creation	prediction	production	selection	suggestion

1. What do we call keeping someone or something safe? — **protection**
2. What do we call a change to make something right? — **correction**
3. What is another word for the place someone is in? — **situation**
4. What do we call it when we keep something from happening? — **prevention**
5. What do we call making a choice? — **selection**
6. What do we make when we tell the future? — **prediction**
7. What do we call the process we use to make something? — **invention**
8. What can we call a story we make up? — **creation**
9. What is telling how to do something step by step? — **directions**
10. What do we call it when we give someone else an idea? — **suggestion**

✏️

B. On separate paper, write a question of your own. Answer it using one of the words in the box.

LEVEL 8   "Forecast"   **117**

CURRICULUM CONNECTIONS

WHETHER-OR-NOT CHARTS SCIENCE

Have students cut out the daily weather forecast each night from a newspaper or write down the television or radio weather forecast for the following day. Have them make charts each day showing whether or not the predictions were correct. The charts might resemble the following.

Date	Weather Forecast	Actual Weather	C	I

Students might wish to record whether the forecast was 100%, 75%, 50%, or 25% correct each day.

INSTRUMENTAL IN WEATHER SCIENCE

Tell students that some of the instruments Caroline brought into *Claws and Paws* were a barometer, a thermometer, a hygrometer, a weather vane, and an anemometer. Tell students to do research to find out the use of each of these instruments. Have students draw pictures of the instruments on separate pieces of paper and write descriptions under each one. Compile the papers into a book. **Curriculum Connection Master 16** can be used with this activity.

CLOUDING UP ART

Have students use resources on weather to learn cloud formations. Have each student choose one type of cloud and use cotton to show the formation at the top of a paper. Note that cirrus clouds, which are thin, white, and wispy, contain minute ice crystals. Stratus clouds are layered and sometimes cover the entire sky in a gray blanket before snow or rain. Cumulus clouds are piled high and fluffy. They are a sign of fair weather. Nimbus clouds are dark and rolling. They are a sign of heavy rain. Tell each student to draw a scene in his or her picture depicting an activity appropriate for the type of weather indicated by the cloud formation. Then have each student write a sentence to tell about the picture.

Reading the Poem

OBJECTIVE   Understanding and appreciating messages in poetry.

INTRODUCING THE POEM

Relate content of the poem to students' experience.

Ask students if they have ever spent time with a close friend but not talked for periods of time. Point out that good friends often do not have to speak a word to communicate because they know about each other and feel comfortable with each other.

Set a listening purpose.

Tell students they are going to hear a poem about two friends who meet and spend time together. Ask them to think about the poet's message.

READING THE POEM

Read the poem aloud.

Because poetry is a sound-based literary form, this part of the lesson is most important. Read the poem aloud to the students with Student Texts closed. Then have students open their books to page 264. Read the poem again or ask for volunteers to read it to the whole group. With this second reading, encourage students to think about how the friends feel as they share the day. Discuss any unfamiliar words as needed.

stalk   go after something in a quiet, sneaky way
blade   a thin, narrow leaf of grass
pungent   sharp or bitter to the sense of smell or taste
sifting   passing through as if through a mesh or a net

DISCUSSING THE POEM

Discuss students' responses to the poem.

Ask students if the poem gives them a feeling of excitement or a quiet feeling and why. *(quiet feeling because the friends do not speak and their activities are quiet)* Then ask:

By telling how the friends spend a day, what is the poet's message about friendship? (Friends know what each other enjoys doing, and they enjoy doing many of these things together.)

What do you think the poet's message is when she says, "When we say goodbye we just wave a hand and we understand"? (Friends do not need words to express how they enjoyed their day together.)

What message do you get from the poet's words "secret talk"? (Friends can "talk" without speaking, and what they "say" is a secret they share.)

CLASS ENRICHMENT

Have students write about friendly scenes.

Have students find pictures of children showing friendly feelings toward one another. *(children playing together, walking together, holding hands, hugging)* Some students may enjoy drawing their own pictures. Have them compare the various pictures and discuss why they think the children are friends. Then ask students to write what led up to the scenes in the pictures.

Secret Talk

I have a friend
and sometimes we meet
and greet each other
without a word.

We walk through a field
and stalk a bird
and chew a blade of
pungent grass.

We let time pass
for a golden hour
while we twirl a flower
of Queen Ann's lace

or find a lion's face
shaped in a cloud
that's drifting, sifting
across the sky.

There's no need to say,
"It's been a fine day"
when we say goodbye:
when we say goodbye
we just wave a hand
and we understand.

Eve Merriam

Reader's Journal   **p 101**

Responding to Reading

A SPECIAL DAY

Thinking about how they would enjoy spending a day with a friend, students plan and describe the day from start to finish.

	Teaching Sequence	Trade Books and Resources	Meeting Individual Needs	Integrated Language Arts / Cross Curriculum
The Bridge Pages 508–509	**Maintain** Main Idea/Details	• Teaching Chart 77 • Workbook 130 • Skills Practice 118		
PART 1 **Vocabulary Strategies** Pages 510–511	**Develop Concepts** Creating a Chart About Communicating **Teach Vocabulary** **STORY CRITICAL WORDS: alphabet, deaf, language, performers,** sign language, signs, throat (Tested words are boldfaced.)	• Teaching Chart 78 • Workbook 131 • Skills Practice 119	**SUPPORT WORDS:** actors, clerk, invitation, moustache, performance, sorts, wiggled • Skills Practice 120 **CHARACTER/SETTING WORDS:** Diane, Gina, Michael Turner, Pinocchio, Polly	**WRITING/SPEAKING ACTIVITY:** Use new vocabulary to describe how to communicate different feelings. • Spelling Connection 55
PART 2 **Reading & Responding** Pages 512–521	**Build Background** **Develop a Purpose for Reading** **Guide the Reading Process** **Selection Follow-Up**	• Reader's Journal 102–105 • Workbook 132 **I→T KIT** Listening to a Song and Singing with Hands **READING EVERY DAY** *Handtalk,* by R. Charlip *A Show of Hands: Say It in Sign Language*, by M.B. Sullivan and L. Bourke	**EXTRA HELP:** Discussing Problems of Moving to a New Town **ACHIEVING ENGLISH PROFICIENCY:** Discussing Sign Language • Achieving English Proficiency Master 28	**Language Arts Connections** **WRITING TO LEARN:** Tell what hand gestures say. • Writing Master 20 **SPEAKING/LISTENING:** Researching Sign Language; Communicating Through Finger Spelling • Language Arts Master 17 **WRITING:** Creating a Welcoming Committee
PART 3 **Selection Support** Pages 522–527	**Introduce** Multiple Meanings (Tested)	• Teaching Chart 79 • Workbook 133 • Skills Practice 121	• Reteaching Masters 1–4 • Challenge Master 16 • Achieving English Proficiency Master 29 **Practice** • Teaching Chart 80 • Workbook 134–135 • Skills Practice 122–123 Long Word Decoding (Tested) Characterization (Tested) **Maintain** • Teaching Chart 81 • Skills Practice 124 Symbols and Signs	**Curriculum Connections** **SCIENCE:** Researching Devices for the Deaf • Curriculum Connection Master 17 **SOCIAL STUDIES:** Researching Lives of People Who Overcame Disabilities **HEALTH AND SAFETY:** Creating Posters About Hearing Safety

Words In Our Hands

by Ada B. Litchfield

SUMMARY *Michael's parents were born deaf. They learned to speak, to read lips, and to communicate in sign language. When the family moves to a new town, people stare at Michael's parents as they sign and talk. Michael is embarrassed by his parents, and then ashamed of his feelings. When the National Theatre of the Deaf performs in his town, Michael learns that his family is not alone. Life in the new town turns out to be not so bad after all.*

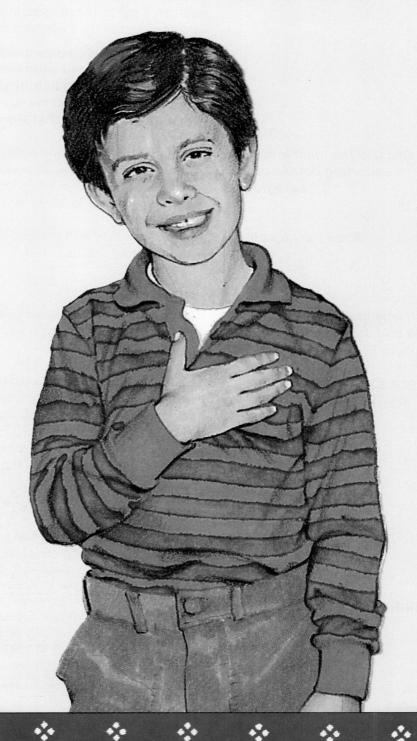

The Bridge

SKILL TRACE: MAIN IDEA/DETAILS						
Introduction	Practice		Test	Reteach	Maintain	
TE 66	82	116	157	158	234	274	508

COMPREHENSION
Teaching Main Idea/Details

OBJECTIVE Identifying stated and unstated main idea and supporting details.

1. WARM-UP

Use familiar content to review main idea and supporting details.

Remind students that "Forecast," the last story they read, was about predicting the weather. Tell students they will read a paragraph about the weather and look for the writer's main point as well as details about the weather. Display the paragraph and read it aloud with students. Have students identify the main idea and details.

> **Weather can change quickly in some parts of the United States. A day can start out sunny, warm, and clear, and by the afternoon there is thunder, lightning, and rain. A day can start out cloudy and cold and then become sunny and warm. Even a snowstorm can happen on a day that starts out sunny!**

Discuss the main idea and supporting details of the paragraph.

Ask students why the first sentence in the paragraph is the main idea. (*The first sentence tells the most important idea. The other sentences give details — the kinds of weather.*) Remind students that sometimes the main idea of a paragraph is stated in a sentence and sometimes it is not stated.

State the objective.

Tell students they will practice recognizing stated and unstated main ideas and supporting details.

2. TEACH

Explain why knowing about main idea and supporting details is important.

Knowing about the main idea and supporting details helps readers to understand and remember a writer's main points.

Present a strategy for identifying main idea and supporting details.

Tell students that there is a strategy for finding the main idea and details of a paragraph. First, read to see what all or most of the sentences are about — the topic. Then decide which sentence tells the most important or main idea about the topic. If no sentence tells the main idea, make up a sentence that includes the topic and what all or most of the sentences in the paragraph say about the topic. This will be the main idea.

TEACHING CHART 77: MAIN IDEA/DETAILS

77

1. Theodore Cat yowled with laughter. Frank looked confused. Oscar thought Caroline had made a mistake. Everyone knew it was the middle of summer. No one believed Caroline when she said it would snow on Friday.

2. Caroline brought in her weather instruments. She set up wires and dials everywhere. On a pad of paper she wrote down what the instruments told her. Then Caroline called forecasters all over the country. On a map she wrote all the information she had gathered.

Model the strategy.

Read paragraph 1 and tell students that the sentences have to do with Caroline's prediction of snow. The last sentence tells the main idea. Underline that sentence. Then explain that the other sentences tell how the animals reacted to Caroline's prediction, and so they are the details.

3. GUIDED PRACTICE

Check for understanding.

Before going on, have students tell how to recognize a main idea and supporting details. (*See what all or most of the sentences are about. Find the sentence that tells the main idea about the topic. See how the details explain the main idea. If the main idea is not stated, make up a sentence that tells what the sentences say about the topic.*)

Guide students in using the strategy.

Have students use the strategy to find the main idea of the second paragraph. Since the second paragraph has an unstated main idea, help students make up a main idea sentence after they conclude that each of the sentences gives a detail about all that Caroline did to make her weather forecast.

4. WRAP-UP

Summarize instruction.

Review that the main idea of a paragraph tells what the sentences are about. The details support or explain the main idea. A main idea can be stated at the beginning, middle, or end of a paragraph; or it may not be stated directly at all. Then a reader must make up a main idea sentence that tells what the other sentences in the paragraph are about.

Provide independent practice.

Options for independent practice are shown in the Resource Center below.

5. APPLICATION

Students will identify main ideas as they read "Words in Our Hands." The symbol ✔ marks specific questions and activities that apply this skill.

Workbook page 130

RESOURCE CENTER

Skills Practice 118

COMPREHENSION

NAME _____

Main Idea/Details

REMEMBER: A **main idea** tells the topic of the paragraph and what the paragraph says about the topic.

A. Read the paragraph and answer the questions.

Caroline set up her weather instruments. She worked all morning. Wires and dials were everywhere. She looked at the instruments to make sure they were set up correctly. She checked every dial.

1. What sentence tells you the topic? ___Caroline set up her weather___ ___instruments.___

2. What do the other sentences tell? ___details about Caroline setting___ ___up her equipment___

B. Each sentence below is the main idea of a paragraph. Read each sentence. Then answer the questions.

There are many different ways of forecasting weather.

3. What is the topic? ___forecasting weather___

4. What will the paragraph tell about the topic? ___different ways to forecast___ ___the weather___

Weather forecasting is more advanced now than it was in the past.

5. What is the topic? ___weather forecasting___

6. What will the paragraph tell about the topic? ___how weather forecasting___ ___has improved over the years___

C. On separate paper, write a paragraph about weather forecasting. Tell your topic in the first sentence. Then tell two or three details about your topic. See Teacher Notes.

130 "Words in Our Hands"   Main Idea/Details

◀ **Workbook page 130** is intended for use by all students.

Skills Practice 118 ▶ may be assigned for additional practice.

Workbook reuse option: Have students add another sentence to the paragraph in Part A that tells another detail about what Caroline might have done.

NAME _____

SKILLS PRACTICE ◆118◆

Main Idea/Details

Details support, or go with, **main ideas.** All details tell about the main idea. Read the example.

Example: Main Idea: Everyone in my family plays games.
Details: 1. My dad likes to play golf.
2. Mom loves tennis.
3. I think baseball is the best game.

A. Read the main idea sentence and the detail that tells more about it. Then write two detail sentences to go with each main idea.
Answers will vary. Sample answers are given.
1. Main Idea: Photographs of faces can show many feelings.
Detail: One picture can show someone having a good time.
Detail: **A picture can show a baby crying.**
Detail: **A photograph may show people smiling.**

2. Main Idea: You can use sign language to ask for things.
Detail: You can ask for a glass of milk.
Detail: **You can ask for someone to come to you.**
Detail: **You could ask for a pencil.**

B. Read the pairs of details. Think about the main idea they tell about. Write the main idea and another detail.
Answers will vary. Sample answers are given.
3. Detail: Shake your head and you mean "no."
Detail: Smile and you are saying that you feel good.
Detail: **Wink and you are saying that you are joking.**
Main Idea: **You can show what you mean without words.**

4. Detail: You can write more in a letter than in a telegram.
Detail: A letter costs less to send than a telegram.
Detail: **You can send pictures or drawings with a letter.**
Main Idea: **A letter can be better than a telegram.**

118 LEVEL 8   "Words in Our Hands"

Reading & Responding

Developing Concepts

Use a chart to tap prior knowledge about ways of communicating.

Build a chart about ways of communicating as a starting point for teaching vocabulary. Have students name ways of communicating that include the use of sound as well as no sound at all. List responses under each category.

Ways of Communicating	
Sound	**No Sound**
speaking	writing
singing	facial expressions
stamping feet	hand signals
clapping hands	body movements

Ask students what certain facial expressions show, such as a smile (*happiness*) or a frown (*sadness*). Discuss what hand signals mean, such as holding up a hand with a palm out (*stop*) or waving a hand inward toward the body (*come here*). Have students explain what body movements tell, such as wrapping arms around the body and shivering (*I'm cold*). Have students communicate without sound and guess each other's messages.

Teaching Vocabulary

Discuss meanings of Story Critical words.

Read each sentence on the Teaching Chart and identify the new word. Then use the questions that follow to help students understand each word.

TEACHING CHART 78: VOCABULARY 78

1. **language** (any means of communicating)
   In order for people to talk with one another, they must have a *language*.
2. **alphabet** (the letters of a language)
   Words are made up of letters of the *alphabet*.
3. **signs** (gestures that give information)
   A language can be made up of hand movements called *signs*.
4. **sign language** (language made up of hand movements)
   Hand signs can be used to talk in *sign language*.
5. **deaf** (unable to hear or unable to hear well)
   People who are *deaf* cannot hear sounds.
6. **throat** (the passage in the front part of the neck)
   When air passes through the vocal cords in the *throat*, sounds are made.
7. **performers** (people who do things for audiences)
   Sometimes *performers* on stage use sign language as well as speech.

language
1. **What phrase in the sentence is a clue to the meaning of *language*?** (talk with one another)   STRATEGY: CONTEXT CLUES

alphabet
2. **What makes up the English language alphabet?** (letters) **How many letters are there?** (26)   STRATEGY: PRIOR KNOWLEDGE

signs

3. How are *signs* explained in the sentence? (They are described as hand movements.)   STRATEGY: CONTEXT CLUES

sign language

4. How would you explain what sign language is to someone, based on the information in the sentence? (It is a language in which hand signs are used to communicate.)   STRATEGY: CONTEXT CLUES

deaf

5. What is the opposite of being *deaf?* (being able to hear most sounds well)   STRATEGY: ANTONYMS

throat

6. Where is the throat? (in the front part of the neck)   STRATEGY: PRIOR KNOWLEDGE

performers

7. What are the base word and suffix in *performers?* (*perform* and *-ers*) **What does the suffix mean?** (people who do something) **What clues in the sentence tell you about performers?** (*show, on stage*) **Using all of this information, what is the meaning of *performers?*** (people who do things for audiences)   STRATEGY: STRUCTURAL ANALYSIS

Discuss Support words as needed.

The Glossary of the Student Text includes definitions of the Support words: *moustache, clerk, performance, sorts, invitation, actors, wiggled.*

Present Character/Setting words.

Present the Character names before students read the selection: *Michael Turner, Gina, Diane, Polly, Pinocchio.*

Provide independent practice.

Options for independent practice are shown in the Resource Center below.

WRITING OR SPEAKING ACTIVITY *Have each student describe the signs he or she would use to communicate two different feelings: Feeling really happy with something a friend has done; feeling angry at something a friend has done. Encourage them to use as many vocabulary words as possible.*

Workbook page 131

NAME _____

Using New Words

| alphabet | deaf | language | performers |
| sign language | signs | throat | |

A. Write four vocabulary words that name things used for communication.

1. _____ language
2. _____ signs
3. _____ alphabet
4. _____ sign language

B. Write the word from the box that fits each blank in the paragraph.

The clowns were my favorite (5) _____ performers _____ at the circus. They said a lot without using spoken
(6) _____ language _____ . They communicated by using facial expressions and by making (7) _____ signs _____ with their hands. I saw one clown put a ball in his mouth. Then when he moved his neck, it looked as if there were a ball in his
(8) _____ throat _____ ! Another clown had the letters of the (9) _____ alphabet _____ all over his costume. He took off all the O's and juggled them. A (10) _____ deaf _____ person could have understood the clowns easily. They entertained us without making sounds.

C. On separate paper, write two sentences about a deaf person. Use three words from the box. **See Teacher Notes.**

Selection Vocabulary   "Words in Our Hands"   **131**

RESOURCE CENTER

◀ **Workbook page 131** provides practice with Story Critical words.

Skills Practice 119 ▶ provides practice with Story Critical words.

Skills Practice 120 provides practice with Support words.

Spelling Connection Master 55 may be used for spelling instruction with the new vocabulary.

Workbook reuse option: Have students label each vocabulary word with T (name of a thing), P (name of a person or people), or D (describing word).

Skills Practice 119

NAME _____

Vocabulary: Story Critical Words   SKILLS PRACTICE ◁119▷

A. Study the meaning of each word.

alphabet the letters of a language
deaf unable to hear or not able to hear well
language any means of communicating
performers people who entertain others

sign language a language using hand, finger, and arm movements
signs movements that mean something
throat the front of the neck

B. Complete the word map. Use at least three of the vocabulary words. Then add words of your own. **Responses will vary.**

Methods of Communication
1. language
   sign language
   signs

Why People Communicate
3. _____

Communication

Who Communicates
2. performers
   _____
   _____

Famous Communicators
4. _____

C. Finish each sentence with the correct vocabulary word.

5. A completely _____ deaf _____ person cannot hear any sounds.
6. We watched the _____ performers _____ sing and dance.
7. It is hard to talk when your _____ throat _____ is sore.
8. The English _____ alphabet _____ has 26 letters.

D. Write the correct vocabulary word for each clue.

9. The neck of your shirt goes around this.   throat
10. People have to learn this to write.   alphabet
11. You often see these people on a stage.   performers

LEVEL 8   "Words in Our Hands"   Classification **119**

Reading & Responding

Building Background

Motivate discussion with a listening activity.

Have students sit without talking for three minutes and make a list of all the sounds they hear. Make your own list to use in the discussion. Have students read aloud the lists of things they heard. Their lists might include the scraping of feet, the clock, a cough, other children in the hall, a horn, a sneeze, or the sound of a pencil on paper. Then ask them to imagine what it would be like if they could not hear those sounds. Ask students what other sounds they are capable of hearing, such as music, television, or the spoken word.

Build background about being deaf.

Ask students to think about some of the day-to-day problems deaf people may face. For example, how do they know when the doorbell rings? (*Houses may be equipped with lights for the telephone and doorbell. Some people have trained dogs to help them.*) How do deaf people communicate? (*They can read and write, read lips, use gestures, use sign language and many can speak.*) How do they watch television? (*Some shows have captions. Sometimes there is someone interpreting the show into sign language on television.*) If any students are hearing impaired, they may wish to answer their classmates' questions about their disability.

Discuss fiction that includes nonfiction information.

Tell students they will read a story told by a boy named Michael Turner, whose parents are deaf. Point out that although the story is not true, it includes facts about lip reading and sign language, and descriptions of living with deaf people. Have students find and read the Ada B. Litchfield entry in the About the Author section at the back of their texts.

Developing a Purpose for Reading

Option 1
Students set purpose.

ORAL "QUESTION" LISTS   Ask students to think of questions that might be answered in the selection about the ways deaf people communicate. Have students read the title and introduction and preview the illustrations before forming their questions. Record students' questions for later use.

WRITING ACTIVITY   Have students work individually or in pairs to create written "Question" lists. Tell students to save their lists for later use.

Option 2
Teacher sets purpose.

Have students read the selection to find out how Michael and his family communicate with one another.

Meeting

Individual

Needs

EXTRA HELP   Tell students that the next story is about a boy whose parents are deaf. The story tells about the problems the boy and his parents face when they move to a new town. Ask students if any of them have moved to a new town. Have them suggest the problems people face when they move, and list these ideas on the chalkboard. After students have read the story, refer to the list and have students compare their ideas to events in the story.

ACHIEVING ENGLISH PROFICIENCY   Tell students that the next story is about people who use a special language; they communicate with their hands. Show students samples of sign language and have them guess the meaning. Discuss the good points of being able to speak another language (able to talk to more people, having a language in which to share secrets, etc.). For additional help in story comprehension, use Master 28 in the Teacher Resource Kit.

Words In Our Hands

by Ada B. Litchfield

There are many ways to "talk" and to "listen."

My name is Michael Turner. I am nine years old. I have two sisters, Gina and Diane, a dog named Polly, and two parents who can't hear me when I talk.

They never have heard me. You see, my mom and dad were born <u>deaf.</u>

My parents never heard any sounds at all when they were babies. Some people think a person who can't hear can't learn to talk. That's not true.

My mom and dad went to a school for deaf kids when they were growing up. That's where they learned to talk. They learned by placing their fingers on their teacher's <u>throat</u> and feeling how words felt in her voice box as she said them. They learned how words looked by watching her face, especially her lips, as she spoke. It's hard to learn to say words that way. But my parents did.

They don't talk much now, but they can talk. Their voices are not like other peoples'. My parents have never heard other people talking or even their own voices, so they don't know how voices sound. It's not always easy to understand what they are saying, but Gina and Diane and I can.

Reader's Journal	p 102
Preparing for Reading	

SILENT SPEAKING

Students look at a picture of people "talking" without using their voices and write about what they might be saying.

GUIDED READING

Page 267   **What details in the first paragraph explain how Michael's parents learned to talk?** (They went to a school for the deaf. They learned by placing their fingers on their teacher's throat and feeling how words *felt* when she said them. They learned how words *looked* by watching her face.)

ANALYZE: MAIN IDEA/DETAILS

HIGHLIGHTING LITERATURE

Page 267   Point out that "Words in Our Hands" is a story told as though the person in the story were talking to the reader. Ask students what words let a reader know this. (*my, I*) Then ask students why they think the author has Michael tell the story. (It helps the reader feel closer to the main character. It makes the story seem very personal and believable. It lets the main character talk about his or her feelings.)

✔ Skill from The Bridge applied through this question.

Sometimes my mother and father can understand what people are saying by reading their lips. That's another thing my parents learned at their school—lip reading.

Reading lips is hard. Some people don't move their lips much when they talk, or they hide their mouths with their hands or with a moustache. Besides, many words look alike when you say them. Look in the mirror and say *pin* and *bin*, *hand* and *and*, *hill* and *ill*. See what I mean?

How we move our bodies and what our faces look like when we talk help our parents read our lips. But most of the time we talk to them with our hands as well as our mouths. Grandma Ellis says we have words in our hands.

One way to talk with your hands is to learn a special alphabet so you can spell words with your fingers. This is called finger spelling.

Look at this alphabet. Can you finger spell your name?

Another way to hand talk is to use sign language. Once you have learned sign language, it is easier and faster than finger spelling.

Everybody uses sign language. You can tell your friends to "go away" without using your voice. But sign language for the deaf is like French or Spanish. You have to learn many signs that other people understand before you can talk to anybody.

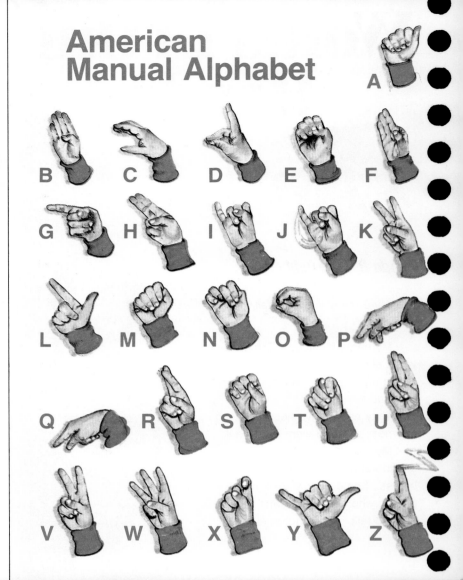

American Manual Alphabet

GUIDED READING

Page 268   If Michael's parents watch a person's lips while that person speaks, what might they be doing? (lip reading)   INFER: ACTIONS

✔ **Page 268   Reread the second paragraph on this page. What is the main idea?** (Reading lips is hard.) **What details support this?** (Some people do not move their lips much when they talk, or they hide their mouths with their hands or with a moustache. Many words look alike when you say them.)   ANALYZE: MAIN IDEA/DETAILS

Page 268   In what way is sign language like French or Spanish? (You have to learn it to be able to use it. You have to learn the signs that other people understand before you can talk to anyone.)   ANALYZE: COMPARISON

Page 269   Use the finger spelling alphabet to say, "Hello."   ANALYZE: PICTURE DETAILS

✔ **Skill from The Bridge applied through this question.**

HIGHLIGHTING LITERATURE

**Page 268   Point out that the title of this story is an example of figurative language. Use the following questions to guide students through a review of figurative language:

Why is the title of this story an example of figurative language? (No one can really hold a word in his or her hands.)

What does the author mean by "Words in Our Hands"? (The author is referring to sign language.) **How do you know that?** (You know it from the context. When Michael is explaining about sign language, he says that his grandmother used the expression, "words in our hands.")

Gina, Diane, and I are learning new signs all the time. My mother and father learned sign language when they were little. They taught us signs when we were babies, just as hearing parents teach their children words. Our grandparents, friends, and neighbors helped us learn to talk.

We are a happy family. At least we were until about six months ago. Then the publishing company where my father has always worked moved to a new town, one hundred miles away.

My father is the editor of a magazine about farming. Nobody in the family wanted to move. But my father loves his job so, of course, he wanted to go with his company.

We bought a new house with a big yard that everybody liked, but it took a long time to get used to our new town. Before, my mom had always done all the shopping and banking for our family. Now she felt a little strange going into a store or bank where the clerks didn't know her. Very often she wanted Gina or me to go with her.

In our old town, everybody knew our family. Nobody stared when they saw us talking with our hands. But in the new town, people did stare. Of course, they pretended they didn't see us, but I knew they were looking.

It was even worse when my mom and dad talked. It seemed as if everyone looked at us when they heard my parents' strange-sounding voices. Sometimes Gina and I felt embarrassed, especially when we had to tell someone what my mother or father had said.

Gina and I didn't want to feel that way. We knew how shy our parents felt. We knew mom missed her art classes. We knew they both missed their old friends. We knew they were as lonesome and homesick as we were!

One awful day I saw three kids making fun of my parents. They were standing behind Mom and Dad and pretending to talk with their hands. I was so upset I wanted to pretend something, too. Just for a minute, I wanted to pretend my mother and father were not my parents. I had never felt that way before.

I was really so ashamed of myself.

GUIDED READING

Page 270   How did Michael and his sisters learn sign language? (Their parents taught them, the same way hearing parents teach their children words.) RECALL: DETAILS

Page 270   Why did Michael's family move to a new town? (because his father's company moved there) RECALL: CAUSE/EFFECT

Page 270   Why does Michael's mother want Gina or Michael to go with her on errands? (so that they can talk for her)   SYNTHESIZE: DRAWING CONCLUSIONS

Page 270   Why do you think some people in the new town stare at Michael's family? (They are not used to seeing people talk with their hands.)   ANALYZE: CHARACTER

Page 271   How does Michael feel about himself when he wants to pretend that his mother and father are not his parents? (ashamed of himself)   INFER: FEELINGS/ATTITUDES

✔ **Informal Assessment Opportunity:** SUMMARIZING

STRATEGIC READING

✔ **Page 271   Have students read to the bottom of this page and summarize what they have learned about Michael's family so far in this story. (Although his parents are deaf, Michael and his sisters can communicate with them. They were a happy family until they moved to a new town. They feel strange in the new town. People who do not know them stare. Michael and Gina are sometimes embarrassed by the stares of strangers.)**

Then ask students to predict what might happen to help Michael's family be happy in their new town. (Students might predict that they will make some friends or meet other deaf people.) Point out that summarizing and predicting can help readers know if they understand what they have read. Suggest that when students have trouble summarizing, they reread those parts of the story that they do not remember clearly.
METACOGNITION: SUMMARIZING AND PREDICTING

That very same day Gina's favorite teacher gave her a note to take home. It was an invitation for our family to go to a performance of the National Theatre of the Deaf.

At first, I didn't want to give the invitation to my parents. I didn't want them to go. I didn't want people to make fun of them or feel sorry for Gina and me.

But Gina said they should go. She said that the play would be in sign language, and who would understand it better than our parents? I knew she was right. Besides, Mom and Dad needed to go out and meet new people.

Still, I was worried about what might happen. The night of the play, all sorts of questions were popping into my mind as I dragged up the steps into the hall. Then I saw those same three kids standing in the doorway. One of them grinned and wiggled his hands at me. That made me angry!

The big hall was filled with people. Just inside the door, my mother signed to me, "Where will we sit?"

To our surprise, a man stood up and said, "There are five seats over here."

We couldn't believe it. He was talking in sign language!

All around us, people were laughing and talking. Many of them were talking with their hands. They didn't seem to care who was watching.

Before the play started, we learned from our program that some of the actors were deaf and some could hear. The hearing actors and some of the deaf actors would speak in the play. All of the actors would sign, sometimes for themselves and sometimes for each other. Sometimes they would all sign together. Everyone in the audience would be able to understand what was going on.

The play we saw was called *The Wooden Boy*. It was about Pinocchio, a puppet who wanted to be a real boy. It was both funny and sad.

After the play, we went backstage to meet the actors. The deaf performers talked with people who knew sign language. The hearing performers helped the other people understand what was being said.

I was proud of my parents. They were smiling, and their fingers were flying as fast as anyone's. For the first time in many months, they seemed to feel at home.

GUIDED READING

Page 272   What happens that changes things for Michael and his family? (Gina's teacher gives them tickets to see a performance of the National Theatre of the Deaf.)   INFER: CAUSE/EFFECT

Page 272   What does Michael notice about the audience for the performance? (Many people are speaking with their hands and they do not seem to care who is watching.)   RECALL: DETAILS

✔ **Page 273   Where is the main idea stated in the first paragraph on this page?** (at the end of the paragraph) **What details explain this main idea? Read them aloud.**   ANALYZE: MAIN IDEA/DETAILS

Page 273   What is the difference between how Michael feels when he sees three kids making fun of his parents and how he feels watching his parents backstage after the performance? (He feels upset and ashamed when the kids make fun; backstage he feels proud and happy.)   ANALYZE: COMPARISON

✔ Skill from The Bridge applied through this question.

HIGHLIGHTING LITERATURE

**Page 273   Point out that the expression "fingers were flying" is another example of figurative language. Ask students what the expression means. (that their fingers were moving very quickly) Point out that when some birds fly, their wings move so quickly you cannot see the motion. When people are very good at signing, their hands move so quickly that you may not be able to see the individual signs.

Then we had another surprise. Gina's teacher came over to us. She talked very slowly and carefully so my mother could read her lips. Then she signed with her hands!

Gina was excited. Her favorite teacher, who wasn't deaf, had words in her hands, too. Gina was learning something she didn't know before. We all were. We were learning there were many friendly people in our new town who could talk with our parents. I decided this place wasn't going to be so bad, after all.

I think some hearing people around us were learning something, too—even those three kids, who were still following us around.

Maybe they never thought about it before, but being deaf doesn't mean you can't hear or talk. You can hear with your eyes and talk with your hands.

I'm glad that Gina and Diane and I know so many signs already. Why don't you learn a few yourself?

◆ LIBRARY LINK ◆

An interesting book about sign language is A Show of Hands *by Mary Beth Sullivan and Linda Bourke.*

Reader's Response

Who might have the hardest time getting used to the new town—Michael or his parents? Tell why.

See next page for suggested answers.

SELECTION FOLLOW-UP

Words In Our Hands

Thinking It Over

1. What were the different ways in which Michael's parents talked?
2. How did Michael's parents "hear" with their eyes?
3. Why did people in the new town stare at the family?
4. How did seeing *The Wooden Boy* make Michael feel? How do you know?
5. Why did Michael feel better about his family after seeing *The Wooden Boy*?

Writing to Learn

THINK AND DECIDE Do people "listen" with their eyes when they "talk" with their hands? Practice listening with your eyes. Tell what the children are saying with their gestures.

WRITE What did you learn about deafness? Tell one thing you will remember if you speak with a person who is hearing impaired.

WORDS IN OUR HANDS

GUIDED READING

Page 274   What do you think Michael learned from attending the theater performance? (There are friendly people in the new town. Other people who are not deaf, like Gina's teacher, know how to sign. He does not have to be ashamed of his parents. Michael realizes that perhaps hearing people just do not understand about deaf people and that they can learn at a theater performance like this.)
SYNTHESIZE: SUMMARIZE

RETURNING TO THE READING PURPOSE

OPTION 1   If students set the purpose, have them return to the questions they asked about the ways deaf people communicate. Discuss whether these ways are explained in the story. Have them compare the ways of communicating talked about in the story with the ways listed at the beginning of the lesson.

OPTION 2   If you set the purpose, have students tell how Michael and his family talk to one another. (They read lips. They read body movements. Mostly they use sign language.)

Reader's Journal   **p 103**
Responding to Reading

NEW KID ON THE BLOCK

Thought-provoking questions encourage students to write about going someplace for the first time and about welcoming new students to class.

517

SELECTION FOLLOW-UP

Words In Our Hands

THINKING IT OVER

1. **What were the different ways in which Michael's parents talked?** (Michael's parents could speak with their voices and "talk" with their hands by using finger spelling and sign language.)   RECALL: DETAILS

2. **How did Michael's parents "hear" with their eyes?** (by reading other people's lips, watching their expressions, and reading their sign language and finger spelling)   SYNTHESIZE: DRAWING CONCLUSIONS

3. **Why did people in the new town stare at the family?** (People stared because the family talked with their hands. They probably had never seen anyone using sign language and were curious. They also stared when they heard Michael's parents' voices.)   ANALYZE: CHARACTER

✔ 4. **How did seeing *The Wooden Boy* make Michael feel? How do you know?** (Possible answers: Michael felt better after seeing *The Wooden Boy* because he saw that his parents were happy and did not feel strange; he was proud of his parents; he saw that many people in town were interested in a play that had deaf actors who could speak and use sign language. Encourage students to read portions of the text that support their conclusions.)   INFER: FEELINGS/ATTITUDES; METACOGNITION

5. **Why did Michael feel better about his family after seeing *The Wooden Boy?*** (Michael felt better after seeing *The Wooden Boy* because his parents enjoyed talking with the performers after the play. He felt proud seeing how well his parents used sign language. Realizing that his sister's teacher also knew sign language made him feel less "different.")
SYNTHESIZE: DRAWING CONCLUSIONS

WRITING TO LEARN

Use Writing Master 20, which duplicates this illustration.

THINK AND DECIDE   Do people "listen" with their eyes when they "talk" with their hands? Practice listening with your eyes. Tell what the children are saying with their gestures. (Possible answers are shown below.)

(over there)   (love)   (stop)

Extend comprehension through writing.

WRITE   What did you learn about deafness? Tell one thing you will remember if you speak with a person who is hearing impaired. (Have students share their sentences.)

✔ Informal Assessment Opportunity: EMPATHIZING WITH STORY CHARACTERS

More Ideas for Selection Follow-Up

CRITICAL AND CREATIVE THINKING QUESTIONS

Encourage a variety of responses and points of view.

Use these open-ended questions to encourage critical and creative thinking about the selection.

1. What did you learn about deaf people from this story? What more would you like to know?

2. Other than including deaf parents, how would you describe Michael's family? Why?

REREADING ORALLY

Have students reread for information.

Have students reread orally the section on pages 268–270 where Michael talks about learning sign language. Discuss what they learn from this passage about how sign language is like other languages. (*It has an alphabet. It has a lot of words. It is complicated. Two people have to understand it to be able to use it. Deaf parents teach it to their children the same way hearing parents teach other languages.*)

SELECTION COMPREHENSION

Provide comprehension check.

A Workbook page to check comprehension is shown in the Resource Center below. It may be used for informal assessment.

Workbook page 132

SELECTION COMPREHENSION

NAME _____

Words In Our Hands

A. Complete the summary of the story "Words in Our Hands."
Accept reasonable variations.

This story was told by ___Michael Turner___, who lived with his two sisters, Gina and Diane, a dog, and his parents. His parents had never heard him speak because they were ___born deaf___. They had gone to a school where they learned to ___talk___ with their voices and hands. Everyone in the family knew how to use ___sign language___ to talk. They were happy together.

When the company Michael's father worked for moved to a new town, the whole family had to ___move to the new town, too___. They all felt lonely and homesick in the new town because people stared at them. When children made fun of his parents, Michael wanted to pretend that they ___weren't his parents___. He was ___ashamed___ to feel that way.

Then they were invited to a play for the deaf. They were surprised that many people in the audience talked by ___using sign language___.

After the play was over, Michael felt ___proud___ that his parents could talk easily with the deaf performers. When he saw that Gina's favorite teacher, who wasn't deaf, also signed, he decided that living in the new town wasn't going to be so ___bad after all___.

B. On separate paper, tell what you could do to go about learning sign language.
See Teacher Notes.

132 "Words in Our Hands"   Selection Comprehension

RESOURCE CENTER

◀ **Workbook page 132** is intended for use by all students.

Writing Master 20 duplicates the Writing to Learn illustration.

I•T Kit Activity

Audio: **"Say It with Your Hands"**
The children in "Words in Our Hands" could have used sign language to share with their parents the experience of music. Students listen to this original song and learn to sing with their hands. (See Activity Guide.) HUMANITIES

LANGUAGE ARTS CONNECTIONS

CREATING A WELCOMING COMMITTEE

Discuss cooperative learning.

Explain to students that *cooperation* means people working together in a group to accomplish a goal. Point out that each person in the group has a responsibility to complete his or her job, so that the goal can be achieved.

Discuss the difficulties of moving to a new town.

Point out that there are a lot of things a family will not know when they move to a new town, such as how to find their way around or where to shop or take their dry cleaning. They will not know where the library, movies, or grocery store is, or where activities take place or where clubs meet. Some towns have welcoming committees that try to think of ways to make newcomers feel welcome.

CREATING A WELCOMING COMMITTEE (continued)

Have students work cooperatively on welcoming committees.

Have students work cooperatively in groups of four. Say that the goal of each group will be to work as a welcoming committee to make Michael and his family feel at home in their town. One member of the group should write a welcoming letter that tells something about the town. Another member should list stores and services Michael's family will need and write a short description of each. A third member should research groups or clubs Michael's family might want to know about. The Chamber of Commerce can be a good source of information. The fourth member should prepare a list of ideas of how to make Michael feel at home in school. Together, students might decide on a welcoming gift. Have the groups present their welcoming committee letters, lists, and gifts, and have other students give their opinions about the plans. COOPERATIVE LEARNING

CRITICAL THINKING: RESEARCHING SIGN LANGUAGE

Have students research and use sign language.

Tell students that many hand movements in sign language represent words with movements that look very similar to what the words mean. For example the sign for "caterpillar" looks the way a caterpillar moves; one index finger pulls the hand along the opposite arm. The sign for "piano" looks like the movement of playing the piano.

Have students work in pairs to research sign language and learn the signs for several simple words, such as *ball, helicopter,* and *flame.* Encourage students to find out why the signs were chosen to represent these words, or to try to figure out by themselves why the signs were chosen and then check to see if they are correct. Ask students to practice their signs, then have each pair present the signs for other students to identify. WHOLE CLASS ENRICHMENT

COMMUNICATING THROUGH FINGER SPELLING

Discuss the hand alphabet.

Remind students that the hand alphabet appears on page 269 in the story. Ask students how they can use it to learn finger spelling. *(look at the position of the fingers and try to do it with their own fingers)*

Have students make finger-spelling introductions.

Have students use the alphabet presented in the story to introduce themselves to the class by finger spelling the following words:

Hello. My name is _____.

Tell students to practice their finger spelling before they make their introductions. **Language Arts Master 17** can be used with this activity.

CHALLENGE: SPEAKING

READING EVERY DAY

In "Words in Our Hands" students read about a family that uses sign language. To help students expand their understanding of sign language and try using it themselves, share the following titles with them.

Handtalk by Remy Charlip, Mary Beth and George Ancona. Four Winds Press, © 1974. A picture-book introduction to two forms of sign language—finger spelling and signing—from which readers can even create their own "secret codes."   EASIER TO READ

A Show of Hands: Say It in Sign Language by Mary Beth Sullivan and Linda Bourke. Addison-Wesley, © 1980. Lively cartoons and text show how deaf or hearing-impaired people communicate in sign language.

Reader's Journal   **pp 104, 105**
Extending Reading

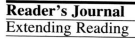

HELP FOR PEOPLE WITH HEARING LOSSES

After reading about ways to help people with hearing problems, students plan and describe new inventions to help people with hearing losses.

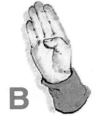

B

G

C

H

V

Selection Support

SKILL TRACE: MULTIPLE MEANINGS				
Introduction	Practice	Test	Reteach	Maintain
TE 522	549	573	635	638	See Level 9.

VOCABULARY

Multiple Meanings

OBJECTIVE   Choosing the most appropriate meaning of a multiple-meaning word.

1. WARM-UP

Use a known word to illustrate multiple meanings.

Tell students they will listen to two sentences that include the word *signs*, but the word has different meanings in the different sentences. Ask students to use the context to determine the correct definition of *signs* in each sentence.

1. **Michael followed the signs in the theater to go backstage.** (boards with writing on them that tell information)

2. **Michael's parents used hand signs to speak to the performers.** (gestures that give information)

Discuss context clues that help determine the meaning.

Reread the first sentence. Ask students what words helped them to know how *signs* is used in that sentence. (*followed, to go*) Read the second sentence again. Ask students what words in this sentence are clues. (*to speak*)

State the objective.

Tell students they will learn to look for multiple-meaning words and to use context clues to determine the correct meanings of those words in sentences.

2. TEACH

Explain the importance of recognizing multiple-meaning words.

Many words in the English language have more than one meaning. Knowing the correct meaning of a multiple-meaning word in a sentence will help readers understand information and not be confused. When readers come across homographs, which are also multiple-meaning words, sentence context will help them know the correct pronunciations and meanings.

Present a strategy for understanding multiple-meaning words.

Tell students that they can use a strategy to help them understand multiple-meaning words. Whenever you find multiple-meaning words, use context clues to decide in each case which meaning of the word is being used.

> **TEACHING CHART 79: MULTIPLE MEANINGS**   **79**
>
> 1. Michael's parents watched their teacher's **face**, mostly her lips, to learn how to talk. ("the front part of the head"; *lips* is the clue)
> 2. Michael was so ashamed of his bad feelings he couldn't **face** his parents. ("look at directly"; *ashamed* is the clue)
> 3. Reading lips is **hard** because some people hide their mouths with their hands. ("difficult"; *hide their mouths* is the clue)
> 4. Pinocchio felt **hard** to those who touched him because he was made of wood. ("very firm"; "not soft"; *made of wood* is the clue)

Model identifying multiple-meaning words.

Read the first two sentences aloud. Point out that in the first sentence, *face* means "the front part of the head" because it is something that can be watched and the word *lips* is a clue. In the second sentence, *face* is a verb because it is something that Michael does. The word *ashamed* is a clue.

3. GUIDED PRACTICE

Check for understanding.

Before going on, have students explain why it is important to know about multiple-meaning words *(because there are so many of them; in order not to be confused)* and how to determine the correct meaning of a multiple-meaning word *(look for context clues in the sentence)*.

Guide students in using the strategy.

Have students read the other two sentences on the Teaching Chart, name the multiple-meaning word, and use context clues to decide on its meaning.

4. WRAP-UP

Summarize instruction.

Review the main points of the lesson:

1. There are many multiple-meaning words in the English language.

2. Identifying the correct meaning of a multiple-meaning word is important for understanding.

3. Use context clues to determine the correct meaning of a multiple-meaning word.

4. Multiple-meaning words that are spelled the same but have different meanings and pronunciations are called homographs.

Provide independent practice.

Options for independent practice are shown in the Resource Center below.

Meeting Individual Needs

RETEACHING Use the activity on page 638 and Masters 1–4 in the Teacher Resource Kit.

CHALLENGE Use the activity on page 639 and Master 16 in the Teacher Resource Kit.

ACHIEVING ENGLISH PROFICIENCY Use the activity on page 639 and Master 29 in the Teacher Resource Kit.

Workbook page 133

Multiple Meanings

VOCABULARY

REMEMBER: Many words have more than one meaning. Use context to determine the meaning of a word in a sentence or story.

A. Read the meanings of each word. Then read each sentence. Decide which meaning fits the sentence. Write the correct letter on the line.

1. *feel*: (a) touch; (b) have a feeling

   __a__ Michael could feel his vocal cords move when he talked.

   __b__ Gina and Michael would sometimes feel ashamed.

2. *place*: (a) location of something; (b) to put in a spot

   __b__ Deaf children learn to place their fingers on a speaker's throat.

   __a__ Michael's family had moved to a new place.

3. *sound*: (a) something that can be heard; (b) healthy or free from problems; (c) a channel of water

   __a__ Michael's parents had never heard a sound.

   __b__ The new house Michael moved into was sound.

   __c__ That summer Michael's family went to swim in the sound.

4. *look*: (a) try to see; (b) seem; (c) expression on a face

   __b__ Michael was afraid his parents might look funny.

   __a__ People used to look at them when they signed.

   __c__ Michael gave a stern look to the mean boys.

B. On separate paper, write sentences containing *feel, place, sound,* and *look*. Label each with the meaning you have used. See Teacher Notes.

Multiple Meanings   "Words in Our Hands" **133**

RESOURCE CENTER

◀ **Workbook page 133** is intended for use by all students.

Skills Practice 121 ▶ may be assigned for additional practice.

Workbook reuse option: In Part A, have students circle each definition of an action, underline each definition of a place or thing, and mark D next to any definition of a describing word.

Skills Practice 121

SKILLS PRACTICE 121

Multiple Meanings

Many words have more than one meaning. Use context to determine the meaning of a word in a sentence or a story.

bats

Write the word that fits in all three sentences.

| back | left | open |

1. I go out the __back__ door of the bus.
2. Oh, my sore __back__!
3. I'll have to rest when I get __back__ home.

| block | pack | train |

4. I go to buy a wooden __block__ for my baby brother.
5. I run around the __block__ to the store.
6. Three trucks __block__ my path.

| park | fair | pick |

7. I want to go on the rides at the __fair__.
8. Mom says the sun is too hot on my __fair__ skin.
9. "I don't want to stay home," I say. "It's not __fair__!"

| felt | head | point |

10. Jeff is at the __head__ of the line.
11. Dad bought a __head__ of lettuce.
12. I patted the dog's __head__.

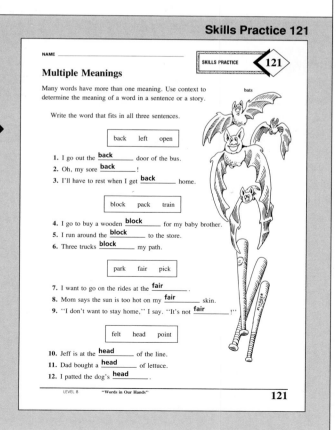

LEVEL 8   "Words in Our Hands"   **121**

SKILL TRACE: LONG WORD DECODING				
Introduction	Practice	Test	Reteach	Maintain
TE 498	524	595	635	640	See Level 9.

WORD STUDY

Long Word Decoding

OBJECTIVE   Using the long word decoding strategy to read words.

Review the long word decoding strategy.

Display the Teaching Chart. Review with students the steps they have learned for decoding long words. Then point out the word *performer* on line 1. Underline the word part *-er* and the syllables *per* and *form*. Say the word slowly, blending the syllables and adding the stress to the second syllable.

> **TEACHING CHART 80: READING LONG WORDS** 80
>
> 1. Look for words and word-parts you know.
> 2. Look for syllables and vowel sounds.
>   a. Two consonants after the first vowel may signal a short sound.
>   b. One consonant after the first vowel may signal a long sound.
>   c. A consonant followed by *-le* forms its own syllable.
> 3. Say the word, blending the syllables.
> 4. If the word does not make sense, try different vowel sounds and add stress to different syllables until the word makes sense.
>
> 1. performer   magazine   harshly   especially   invitation
> 2. Michael's father was a *successful* magazine editor.
> 3. He was surprised by his company's *announcement*.
> 4. His family's *happiness* was very important.

Provide practice in using the strategy.

Have students read the remaining words. Then have students read sentences 2–4. Ask for volunteers to tell how they figured out the words in italics and tell what they mean.

Provide independent practice.

Options for independent practice are shown in the Resource Center Below.

Workbook page 134

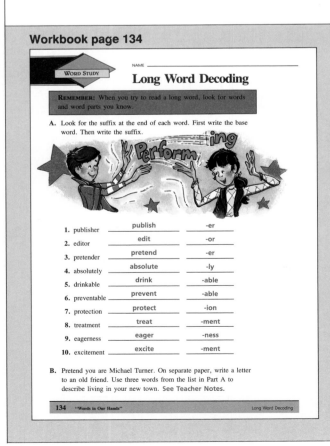

RESOURCE CENTER

◄ **Workbook page 134** is intended for use by all students.

Skills Practice 122 ► may be assigned for additional practice.

Workbook reuse option: Have students use slashes to divide each word in Part A into syllables. Remind them that each syllable contains one vowel sound.

Skills Practice 122

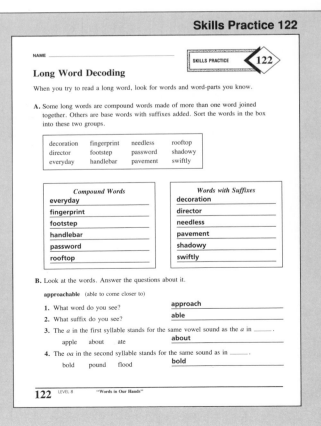

SKILL TRACE: CHARACTERIZATION				
Introduction	Practice	Test	Reteach	Maintain
TE 482	500	525	635	637	See Level 9.

LITERATURE
Characterization

OBJECTIVE Identifying character traits and emotions.

Review character traits.

Remind students that character traits tell what a character is like — the way a character looks, feels, and acts. Tell students that readers learn about a character's traits by descriptions of how a character looks and behaves, by a character's own words, and by what other characters say about a particular character.

Discuss Michael Turner's character.

Use the following questions to lead students in a discussion of what they know about Michael Turner's character from reading "Words in Our Hands."

1. **What are some facts the author has Michael tell us about himself?** (He is nine years old. He has two sisters and a dog. His parents are deaf.)

2. **How does Michael feel sometimes when his parents speak in public?** (embarrassed)

3. **How does Michael feel about himself when he wants to pretend that his mother and father are not his parents?** (He is ashamed of himself.)

4. **What does this tell you about Michael's character?** (He is concerned and he is honest. He sees that he is not always as brave as he would like to be.)

5. **Which four of these words would you say describes Michael's character: kind, bossy, lazy, thoughtful, concerned, daring, shy, proud, fearless?** (kind, thoughtful, concerned, proud)

Provide independent practice.

Options for independent practice are shown in the Resource Center below.

Workbook page 135

NAME _____

Characterization

LITERATURE

REMEMBER: To understand a character in a story, think about what the character says and does. Also think about how the character speaks and acts.

A. Read the sentences about the story. On each blank write a word from the box to complete the statements.

ashamed	excited	happy
helpful	sad	shy

1. Many friends in their old town had helped the children learn to talk.
   Everyone there was very ___helpful___ .

2. The children were unhappy about moving away from their friends.
   The children felt ___sad___ .

3. Mom felt strange going into a store where people didn't know her.
   Mom felt ___shy___ .

4. At first Michael wanted to pretend he didn't know his parents.
   He felt ___ashamed___ .

5. At the play the children were thrilled to see other people signing.
   The children felt ___excited___ .

6. Finally Michael felt glad about living in his new town.
   At last Michael felt ___happy___ .

B. Choose three words from the box. Write three new sentences about Michael's family using these words. See Teacher Notes.

Characterization   "Words in Our Hands" **135**

RESOURCE CENTER

◀ **Workbook page 135** is intended for use by all students.

Skills Practice 123 ▶ may be assigned for additional practice.

Workbook reuse option: Have students think of other describing words that could also fill the blanks in Part A. Have them write a new word beside each of their answers.

Skills Practice 123

NAME _____

SKILLS PRACTICE 123

Characterization

Writers tell you about the characters in a story. They often tell you what the character says and does and how the characters speak and act. We use this information to learn about character traits.

Read the letter Lauren wrote to her grandfather. Then answer the questions.

> Dear Grandpa,
> Guess what! The bad news is I fell off my bicycle last week. I have a broken foot. The good news is I can walk pretty well with the help of my trusty cane. Mom and Nora have been great. Mom painted my cane bright red. Nora pulls me to school in the wagon. I miss riding my bike. I don't like the broken foot.
> My friend Derek and I were riding in the woods. I hit a rock. Derek thinks I was riding too fast. He is worried that I might hurt myself again. What do you think?
> Love,
> Lauren

1. How does Lauren feel about having a broken foot? ___She doesn't like having a broken foot.___

2. What word describes how she feels about using her cane? ___proud___
   angry   proud   scared

3. What word describes Nora? ___helpful___
   bossy   forgetful   helpful
   What did she do that shows this? ___She pulls Lauren to school in the wagon.___

4. What word describes Derek? ___concerned___
   concerned   happy   brave

5. Underline the sentences in the letter that gave you clues to 2 and 4.

LEVEL 8   "Words in Our Hands"   **123**

SKILL TRACE: SYMBOLS/SIGNS				
Introduction	Practice	Test	Reteach	Maintain
TE 346	373	423	461	467	526

STUDY SKILLS

Symbols and Signs

OBJECTIVE Understanding information from symbols and signs.

Review symbols and signs.

Remind students that symbols and signs are short, quick, visual ways to communicate something important. Some signs have both words and pictures on them, and some signs have either words or pictures. Like other signs and symbols, sign language provides a short, quick way to communicate.

Use Teaching Chart to provide practice identifying symbols.

Display the Teaching Chart and have students identify what each symbol means. Have them guess what a symbol means if they do not know it.

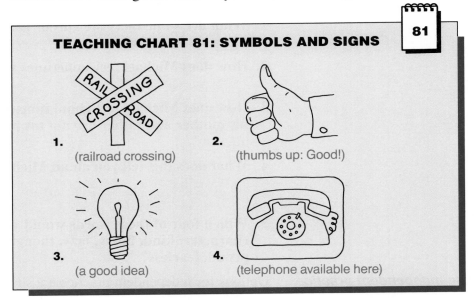

TEACHING CHART 81: SYMBOLS AND SIGNS 81

1. (railroad crossing)

2. (thumbs up: Good!)

3. (a good idea)

4. (telephone available here)

Provide independent practice.

An independent activity is shown in the Resource Center below.

RESOURCE CENTER

Skills Practice 124 ▶ may be assigned for additional practice.

Skills Practice 124

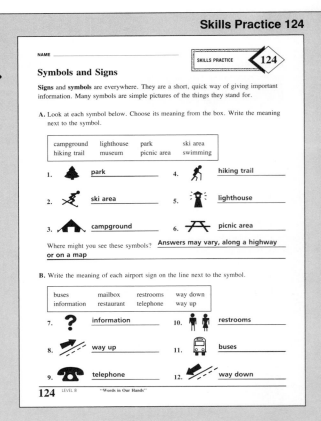

NAME _____

SKILLS PRACTICE 124

Symbols and Signs

Signs and **symbols** are everywhere. They are a short, quick way of giving important information. Many symbols are simple pictures of the things they stand for.

A. Look at each symbol below. Choose its meaning from the box. Write the meaning next to the symbol.

| campground | lighthouse | park | ski area |
| hiking trail | museum | picnic area | swimming |

1. park   4. hiking trail

2. ski area   5. lighthouse

3. campground   6. picnic area

Where might you see these symbols? Answers may vary, along a highway or on a map

B. Write the meaning of each airport sign on the line next to the symbol.

| buses | mailbox | restrooms | way down |
| information | restaurant | telephone | way up |

7. information   10. restrooms

8. way up   11. buses

9. telephone   12. way down

124 LEVEL 8 "Words in Our Hands"

526

CURRICULUM CONNECTIONS

SAFETY POSTERS HEALTH AND SAFETY

Michael's parents were born deaf, but people can lose their hearing through an accident or illness, or if they do not protect their ears from very loud noises over a long period of time. Point out that people who work in loud factories or with large drills generally wear ear plugs or some other kind of protection for their ears. Studies show that playing music too loudly, particularly with headphones, has resulted in damaged hearing for some people. Remind students of the saying that they should never put anything smaller than their elbows in their ears so that they will not damage their eardrums. Have students create safety posters about the ear and how to protect it and their hearing from damage.

ONLY A DUMB BUNNY PLAYS HIS HEADPHONES TOO LOUD!

PERSONAL TRIUMPHS SOCIAL STUDIES

People who have disabilities, such as deafness, may go on to accomplish a great deal in spite of their physical challenges. Have students use the encyclopedias or biographies to prepare short reports on people who are or were successful in spite of disabilities. Some possible subjects are Helen Keller, Ludwig van Beethoven, Franklin Delano Roosevelt, Ray Charles, and Stevie Wonder.

DEVICES FOR THE DEAF SCIENCE

Have students work in pairs to prepare presentations on devices for deaf people. The local telephone directory may list a school for the deaf or an organization that could provide information. Students may also write to:

> The National Information Center on Deafness
> Gallaudet University
> 800 Florida Avenue, N.E.
> Washington, D.C. 20002

Have students include charts and illustrations in their presentations. **Curriculum Connection Master 17** can be used with this activity.

Magazine
News About Reading

Words and Other Codes

OBJECTIVE   Connecting reading to other forms of communication.

INTRODUCING AND READING THE ARTICLE

Relate the topic to the unit theme.

Recall with students that the theme of this unit is "Get the message." Point out that sending and receiving coded information is one way to convey a message. Remind students of the previous selection about the deaf. Explain that sign language and finger spelling are special kinds of codes used by many hearing-impaired individuals and that Braille is a type of code which enables visually impaired people to read.

Ask students if they think they could "read" a message written in Braille, or a message given in sign language. *(Most will say no.)* Point out that students could learn what the signs mean, and what the Braille symbols represent. Then they would be able to send or receive these types of coded messages.

Discuss reasons for codes.

Discuss with students why people might want to use a code to communicate. Explain that some codes have to do with "secret intelligence," which is the information received from spies, others may be connected with a secret club, and still others may be used just for fun, such as a message sent to a friend. Ask students to tell about any codes that they have used or read about. Ask them to tell if they were able to learn how to use these codes and what kinds of messages they sent.

State the objective.

Tell the students that in this article they will learn about some simple codes, where some codes came from, and how they are used.

Refer students to their texts.

Have students read the article.

DISCUSSING THE ARTICLE

Review the main points of the article.

Check students' understanding of the article with these questions.

Page 276   How could you send a secret message to a friend? (by using a code that no one else will understand)

Page 277   What did Samuel Morse invent? (a new way to send messages by dots and dashes, called the Morse Code)

Page 277   Why was this invention important? (It allowed people to send messages over long distances.)

Magazine
News About Reading

Words and Other Codes

This person is reading a mirror-code message.

You want to tell your friend a secret. No one else must know what you're saying. So the way to do it is to use a code that only the two of you will understand.

MEE TME AFT ERS CHO OL

See if you can figure out this secret message. It is a simple "space code." Words are broken up by spacing after every third letter. Here is what the code means:

MEET ME AFTER SCHOOL

Now try to figure this one out. You can figure it out by holding it up to a mirror.

YM OT ƎMOƆ UOY NAƆ
ƨ YAƋЯUTAƨ NO ƎƨUOH

Samuel Morse made it possible to send messages over long distances instantly with his invention, the telegraph.

Not all codes are written. In the 1830s, Samuel Morse invented a new way to send messages by wire. His code uses dots and dashes to make letters and numbers. Dot-dot-dot means "S." Dash-dash-dash means "O." Dot-dot-dot again means "S." SOS means that a ship is in trouble.

What do codes have to do with reading? When you were first learning to read, all words looked like a code to you. By now you

have come a long way in breaking the reading code, a process that is sometimes called decoding. You will continue to read words that are new to you. If you think of them as codes to break, figuring out new words can be fun.

S●●●   O■■■   S●●●

In Morse code, dots and dashes stand for letters and numbers.

☞ *If you want to learn more about writing and talking in code, read the book* How to Keep a Secret *by Elizabeth James and Carol Barkin. You can get ideas for codes from magazines, too. See the "Adventures of the Puzzle Squad" in* U.S. Kids *and "Pencil Power" in* Kid City.

Page 277   How is learning to read like breaking a code? (When you are just starting to learn to read, the words look like a code. The more you read, the easier it is to "get the message.")

Page 277   What is the term for the process of breaking a code? (The term is *decoding*.)

CLASS ENRICHMENT

Have students research other forms of codes.

To expand the students' knowledge of codes, have volunteers research the use of different codes and report back to their classmates on these codes. Students might try to come up with new codes.

LESSON ORGANIZER
Sports Signals

	Teaching Sequence	Trade Books and Resources	Meeting Individual Needs	Integrated Language Arts / Cross Curriculum
The Bridge Pages 532–533	**Introduce** Word Referents (Tested)	• Teaching Chart 82 • Workbook 136 • Skills Practice 125	• Reteaching Masters 1–7 • Challenge Master 17 • Achieving English Proficiency Master 30	
PART 1 **Vocabulary Strategies** Pages 534–535	**Develop Concepts** Semantic Mapping **Teach Vocabulary** **STORY CRITICAL WORDS:** bunt, **communicate**, ignore, **official**, outfielders, **pitcher**, shortstop (Tested words are boldfaced.)	• Teaching Chart 83 • Workbook 137 • Skills Practice 126	**SUPPORT WORDS:** attention, inning, position, punt, suggest, suspicious • Skills Practice 127	**WRITING/SPEAKING ACTIVITY:** Use new vocabulary to describe one baseball player's turn at bat. • Spelling Connection 56
PART 2 **Reading & Responding** Pages 536–545	**Build Background** **Develop a Purpose for Reading** **Guide the Reading Process** **Selection Follow-Up**	• Reader's Journal 106–109 • Workbook 138 **I→T KIT** Singing a Sports Song and Describing Sports Signals **READING EVERY DAY** *Koko's Story,* by Dr. F. Patterson *The Story of Nim: The Chimp Who Learned Language,* by A. Michel	**EXTRA HELP:** Main Idea/Details Form **ACHIEVING ENGLISH PROFICIENCY:** Sharing Common Nonverbal Signals • Achieving English Proficiency Master 31	**Language Arts Connections** **WRITING TO LEARN:** Write a message in code. • Writing Master 21 **SPEAKING/LISTENING:** Acting Out Television Sports Interviews; Reporting on Sports Terms **WRITING:** Creating an Illustrated Baseball Glossary; Creating Comic Strips; Writing Sports Newspaper Articles; Developing Story Maps • Language Arts Master 18
PART 3 **Selection Support** Pages 546–551	**Introduce** Prefixes *de-, dis-* (Tested)	• Teaching Chart 84 • Workbook 139 • Skills Practice 128	• Reteaching Masters 1–4 • Challenge Master 18 • Achieving English Proficiency Master 32 **Practice** • Teaching Charts 85–86 • Workbook 140–141 • Skills Practice 129–130 Word Referents (Tested) Multiple Meanings (Tested) **Maintain** • Skills Practice 131 Homophones	**Curriculum Connections** **SCIENCE:** Researching Speed of Pitched Baseballs **SOCIAL STUDIES:** Creating a Chart About Names of Sports Teams **CAREERS:** Researching Sports Stars **GEOGRAPHY:** Locating Cities That Have a Professional Baseball Team • Curriculum Connection Master 18

SPORTS SIGNALS

by Gary Apple

SUMMARY *Many team sports have their own silent languages. Coaches, players, and officials all communicate with each other during play by using nonverbal signals. Some of these are understood by everyone, but others are secret, used when one team does not want the other team to know what is going on. Everyday movements such as scratching the chin, putting hands on knees, and dusting off a sleeve may be secret sports signals.*

The Bridge

SKILL TRACE: WORD REFERENTS				
Introduction	Practice	Test	Reteach	Maintain
TE 532	548	618	635	636	See Level 9.

COMPREHENSION

Teaching Word Referents

OBJECTIVE   Understanding relationships between substitute words and their referents.

1. WARM-UP

Use a known passage to find word substitutes orally.

Tell students they will listen to sentences from the previous selection, "Words in Our Hands." Explain that writers often use words that stand for, or substitute for, other words. Point out that the word substitutes can be pronouns that tell who and whose. Have students listen for the word substitutes. (*My, I*)

My name is Michael Turner. I am nine years old.

Discuss word referents.

Reread the sentences. Have students identify the words that *My* and *I* stand for. (*Michael Turner's, Michael Turner*) Explain that *Michael Turner's* and *Michael Turner* are word referents, the word or words in a sentence or paragraph that a word substitute stands for.

State the objective.

Tell students they will learn how to find the word referents for word substitutes that tell who, whose, when, and how many.

2. TEACH

Explain why understanding word referents is important.

Understanding word referents keeps readers from getting mixed up about what the pronouns and other types of word substitutes stand for.

Present a strategy for finding word referents.

Explain that there is a strategy students can use to help them find word referents. First, read and identify the word substitute. Next, look back in the sentence or paragraph for words it might stand for. Look for clues that answer the questions *Who? Whose? When?* or *How many?* Finally, read to see if the word referent makes sense in the sentence.

TEACHING CHART 82: WORD REFERENTS   `82`

Michael's parents are deaf. But both (Michael's parents) can read lips.
Michael's family moved to a new town. Before, his (Michael's) mom had always done the shopping for them (the family) . Now (After the family moved) , she felt a little strange about it (shopping) .
Michael dragged up the steps. He (Michael) saw the three kids standing in a doorway. One (One of the kids) grinned. The family saw the play and met the actors afterward (after the play ended) . Some of the actors were deaf and some could hear. All (all of the actors) could sign.

Model the strategy.

Read the first paragraph on the Teaching Chart. Explain that to find the word referent for *both*, you would look back in the paragraph for words that it might stand for and look for clues that tell who (*Michael's parents*) and how many (*both*). Fill in the blank on the chart.

3. GUIDED PRACTICE

Check for understanding.
Before going on, have students explain how to find word referents. (*Look for words the word substitute might stand for and ask the questions Who? Whose? When? or How many?*)

Guide students in using the strategy.
Have students use the strategy to fill in the word referents that are underlined in the remaining sentences. Discuss the questions they asked about *Who? Whose? When?* or *How many?*

4. WRAP-UP

Summarize instruction.
Review why readers identify word substitutes and the kinds of clues they use to find their word referents. (*to keep from getting mixed up about what they stand for; clues that answer the questions Who? Whose? When? or How many?*)

Provide independent practice.
Options for independent practice are shown in the Resource Center below.

5. APPLICATION

Students will recognize substitute words and their referents as they read "Sports Signals." The symbol ✔ marks specific questions and activities that apply this skill.

Meeting Individual Needs

RETEACHING   Use the activity found on page 636 and Masters 1–7 in the Teacher Resource Kit.

CHALLENGE   Use the activity on page 636 and Master 17 in the Teacher Resource Kit.

ACHIEVING ENGLISH PROFICIENCY   Use the activity on page 636 and Master 30 in the Teacher Resource Kit.

Workbook page 136

RESOURCE CENTER

Skills Practice 125

COMPREHENSION
NAME _____

Word Referents

REMEMBER: Some words can stand for the names of people, places, or things.

A. Read each sentence. The underlined word stands for another word or words in the sentence. Write the other word or words.

1. I am named Michael Turner.
   Michael Turner

2. My parents cannot hear me, but they can understand me.
   my parents

3. My parents read my lips, and both talk to me with their hands.
   my parents

4. They make hand signs, and these stand for different words.
   hand signs

5. My parents' fingers move quickly when they use them to sign.
   my parents' fingers

6. My father edits a farming magazine in his job.
   my father

7. My mother takes care of us and our new house with its big yard.
   house

B. On separate paper, write two sentences about Michael. In each sentence use a word to stand for another word. See Teacher Notes.

136   "Sports Signals"   Word Referents

◀ **Workbook page 136** is intended for use by all students.

Skills Practice 125 ▶ may be assigned for additional practice.

Workbook reuse option: Have students find three more examples of referents in the sentences in Part A, underline these, and draw arrows showing to what other word each refers.

NAME _____
SKILLS PRACTICE 〈125〉

Word Referents

Writers sometimes use words that stand for other words. **Referents** are the word or words a **word substitute** might stand for. Words like *then* and *now* are word substitutes that tell **when.** Words like *few, several, others, another,* and *three* are word substitutes that tell **how many.** Knowing words that stand for other words will help you to understand what you read.

> Example: We will be home at **three o'clock**. Call Sam **then.**
> Laura got ten **get-well cards,** and she answered **several.**

Read each sentence. The underlined words are word substitutes. Circle their referents. Draw an arrow from the word substitute to its referent. One is done for you.

1. I took dance lessons last summer. I practiced every day then.
2. The show is open today through Friday. I want to go now.
3. Gina asked in sign language, "How many pieces?" I said, "Three."
4. I wrote a letter to Larry. I wrote another to Ricky.
5. Some countries are easy to call. Others are harder.
6. Paintings can show how things really look. Few look as real as "Sailboats."
7. Sara had ten baseball cards. Lauren asked, "Could I have one?"
8. It is winter, and now I want to skate every Sunday.
9. Josh has twenty marbles, but I have none.
10. In art class, we made masks. Daniel made two and Jessica made three.
11. Ms. Wang asked students to help her. Several said they would.
12. I just ate an apple. I'd like another.
13. Our team won six games and lost four.
14. Today the library opens at noon, so I'll go then.
15. Ted's dog had five puppies. He gave one to me.

LEVEL 8   "Sports Signals"   **125**

Vocabulary Strategies

Developing Concepts

Build on prior knowledge of baseball with a semantic map.

If possible, display photos of a baseball game. Make a semantic map about baseball as a starting point for teaching vocabulary. Encourage students to discuss times they have played or watched others play baseball or softball. Talk about the baseball field, baseball team members, and positions. Encourage students to tell ways a batter may hit the ball. Write baseball terms that are mentioned under the appropriate headings.

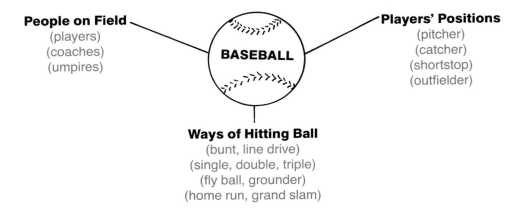

People on Field
(players)
(coaches)
(umpires)

BASEBALL

Players' Positions
(pitcher)
(catcher)
(shortstop)
(outfielder)

Ways of Hitting Ball
(bunt, line drive)
(single, double, triple)
(fly ball, grounder)
(home run, grand slam)

Teaching Vocabulary

Discuss meanings of Story Critical words.

Read each context sentence on the Teaching Chart and identify the new word. Then use the questions below to help students understand each word. When necessary, provide a definition.

83

TEACHING CHART 83: VOCABULARY

1. **shortstop** (a baseball infielder between second and third base)
   In the infield, the *shortstop* watches the catcher.
2. **outfielders** (people who play right, center, or left field in baseball)
   The *outfielders* are far away from the catcher.
3. **pitcher** (a person who throws the ball to the batter)
   The catcher signals the *pitcher* for a fastball.
4. **official** (a person who supervises athletic contests)
   An *official* watches and calls each pitch.
5. **bunt** (to bat the baseball so it stays in the infield)
   Sometimes a batter will *bunt*, hitting the ball in front of the infielders.
6. **communicate** (to pass along)
   The coach may use his hands to *communicate* directions to a batter.
7. **ignore** (to pay no attention to)
   A batter may *ignore* directions to bunt and hit a home run instead.

shortstop

1. What word clues in the sentence help you figure out the meaning of *shortstop?* (*infield, catcher*) **Where does the shortstop play?** (between second and third base) STRATEGY: CONTEXT CLUES

outfielders

2. What word is the opposite of *infielders?* (*outfielders*) **How many outfielders play on the field?** (three) STRATEGY: ANTONYMS

pitcher

3. How do you know from the sentence that *pitcher* **is a baseball word?** (Clues are *catcher* and *fastball*.) STRATEGY: CONTEXT CLUES

official

4. Have you ever seen the official in a baseball game who watches each pitch? What is this official called? (umpire) STRATEGY: PRIOR KNOWLEDGE

bunt

5. What clues in the sentence help you figure out the meaning of *bunt?* (hitting ball in front of infielders) STRATEGY: CONTEXT CLUES

communicate

6. How does a coach communicate with his hands? (by moving them, by making signs) STRATEGY: PRIOR KNOWLEDGE

ignore

7. When might a coach be both happy and unhappy about a batter's deciding to ignore directions to bunt? (happy if the batter hits a home run; unhappy because the batter paid no attention to directions) STRATEGY: PRIOR KNOWLEDGE

Add new words to the map.

Challenge students to add as many of the new words as they can to the semantic map, adding new headings as needed.

Discuss Support words as needed.

The Glossary of the Student Text includes definitions of the Support words: *punt, inning, suggest, attention, suspicious, position.*

Provide independent practice.

Options for independent practice are shown in the Resource Center below.

WRITING OR SPEAKING ACTIVITY *Have students use the new vocabulary to describe one baseball player's turn at bat.*

TEACHER CHOICE

Workbook page 137

NAME _____

SELECTION VOCABULARY

Using New Words

| bunt | communicate | ignore | official |
| outfielders | pitcher | shortstop | |

A. Write a word from the box beside each definition.

a person who enforces the rules at sports events _____ official

to pass along information _____ communicate

to pay no attention to _____ ignore

to bat a baseball so it stays in the infield _____ bunt

B. Write the word from the box that fits each blank in the paragraph.

The manager used signals to _____ communicate _____ with his players. As the _____ pitcher _____ wound up to throw the first ball, the manager told his first batter to _____ bunt _____ . When the pitch came, however, the batter decided to _____ ignore _____ the manager. He swung as hard as he could. The _____ shortstop _____ stood ready between second and third bases, but the ball sailed over his head. The _____ outfielders _____ moved back toward the wall, raising their gloves. The batter raced toward first, but when he got there the _____ official _____ said, "You're out!"

"Why didn't you bunt?" asked the manager when the batter returned.

C. On separate paper, list three jobs where people use signs or signals. Explain what the signals mean. See Teacher Notes.

Selection Vocabulary "Sports Signals" **137**

RESOURCE CENTER

◄ **Workbook page 137** provides practice with Story Critical words.

Skills Practice 126 ► provides additional practice with Story Critical words.

Skills Practice 127 provides practice with Support words.

Spelling Connection Master 56 may be used for spelling instruction with the new vocabulary.

Workbook reuse option: Have students circle each vocabulary word that names people and draw a box around each action word.

Skills Practice 126

NAME _____

SKILLS PRACTICE 126

Vocabulary: Story Critical Words

A. Study the meaning of each word.

bunt to bat a baseball softly
communicate to pass along information
ignore to pay no attention to
official a person who makes sure the rules are followed in sports

outfielders baseball players who play in right, center, or left field
pitcher the player who throws the ball to the batter
shortstop a baseball player who plays between second and third base

B. Complete the word map. Use at least four of the vocabulary words. Then add words of your own. **Responses will vary.**

1. Types of Players
outfielders
pitcher
shortstop

Baseball

2. Actions Players Perform
bunt

C. Complete each sentence with the correct vocabulary word.

3. Sam will _____ communicate _____ my message to Luis.

4. It is impossible to _____ ignore _____ loud sounds.

5. The _____ official _____ at the marathon told the runners to take their positions at the starting line.

6. The _____ pitcher _____ struck out the batter with her fastball.

7. The _____ outfielders _____ ran to catch the ball near the back wall.

8. Did you see the batter _____ bunt _____ the ball?

9. The _____ shortstop _____ took her place between second and third base.

126 LEVEL 8 "Sports Signals" Classification

Reading & Responding

Building Background

Motivate discussion with a code.

Write the following code on the chalkboard. Tell students that the dots and dashes are a message in Morse Code. Explain that the code is a set of signals sent over telegraph wires; each dot is a short sound, and each dash is a long sound. Write the following letters of the alphabet on the board and help students decode the message. (*HELLO*)

H ....   O---   E .   L .-..

Message: .... . .-.. .-.. ---

Build background about signals.

Establish that signals, letters, words, or gestures can have special meanings. Have students suggest different kinds of signals. (*sign language, flag codes, number codes, passwords, Braille, flashing lights*)

Discuss nonfiction.

Tell students that the selection they will read is nonfiction. It is an informational article about signals used in sports. Discuss what kinds of information students might expect to find in an informational article. (*facts that answer Who? What? Where? When? and Why?; drawings or photographs explaining things*)

Developing a Purpose for Reading

Option 1
Students set purpose.

ORAL "I WONDER" QUESTIONS   Have students preview the photographs and captions in the selection. Ask them to complete "I wonder" statements orally. For example, "I wonder who uses sports signals," or "I wonder what kinds of signals are used in baseball." Record their statements for later use.

WRITING ACTIVITY   Have students work individually or in pairs to create written "I wonder" statements. Have students save their statements for later.

Option 2
Teacher sets purpose.

Have students read the selection to find out how players and coaches in different sports communicate.

Meeting
Individual
Needs

EXTRA HELP   Remind students that knowing the main idea and supporting details helps us understand and remember what we read. Distribute blank main idea/detail forms, Form 10 from the Teacher Resource Kit. Have students write the statements *Sports signals are signs* and *Sports signals are important to players* on the forms. Explain that these are the main ideas of the selection they are about to read. Suggest that as students read, they list the details that support these main ideas. After reading, have students use the forms to summarize the selection.

ACHIEVING ENGLISH PROFICIENCY   Remind students that in the last story, they learned about people who speak with their hands. They also learned that we all use our hands to help us communicate. Have the group show common nonverbal signals such as pointing to show location, nodding or shaking the head, and so on. Tell students that in sports, coaches and players use hand signals to send messages to one another. Students who know about sports may be able to share some common signals. For additional help in story comprehension, use Master 31 in the Teacher Resource Kit.

SPORTS SIGNALS

by Gary Apple

In sports, messages to players often need to be kept secret from the other team. That's when sports signals become codes, and scratching an arm can mean something more than having an itch.

Can you tell which of these coaches is giving a signal?

Imagine that you are the coach of a football team. Your team is behind by one point, and there is time for only one more play. The other team expects you to throw a long pass, but you decide to surprise them and run with the ball.

How do you <u>communicate</u> your plan to your players? You can't shout, "Surprise them by running instead of passing!" Your players may not hear you, and if they do, the other team will hear you, too. The surprise will be lost.

Instead, you communicate by giving your team a secret signal using sign language. Before the game, you tell your team that if you put both hands on your head, it means to run with the ball. Your players read your signal and try to run with the ball. Success! Your team scores, and you win the game!

Sign language is used all the time in sports. Coaches signal players. Players signal other players. Officials signal players, and players signal officials. Everyone signals everybody!

Reader's Journal   p 106
Preparing for Reading

SIGNALS

Students view pictures of children demonstrating secret signals and invent meanings for the signals.

GUIDED READING

Page 278   **What was the problem you had to solve when you imagined yourself a football coach?** (how to communicate to the players on the field)
ANALYZE: PROBLEM/SOLUTION

Page 279   **Why did the author have you pretend to be a coach?** (so that you would understand the use of sign language in sports)   EVALUATE: AUTHOR'S PURPOSE

✔ **Page 279**   **In the last sentence, whom do the words *everyone* and *everybody* stand for?** (coaches, players, officials)   ANALYZE: WORD REFERENTS

HIGHLIGHTING LITERATURE

Page 279   Point out that this informational article gives facts about *who* uses sports signals — coaches, players, officials — and *what* the signals are — sign language. The article also answers *when* the signals are used — during a game — and *why* they are secret — so the other team does not know the plan.

✔ **Skill from The Bridge applied through this question.**

537

Of course, signals aren't used only for secret plays. In football, for example, before a player catches a punt, he can wave his hand to signal a *fair catch*. With this signal the player makes a deal with the other team. It means, "If you don't try to tackle me, I won't try to run with the ball when I catch it."

Another sports signal that everyone understands and uses is the "time-out" sign. This is done by making a letter "T" with the hands. It tells the official to stop the clock. Football and basketball are two of the sports that use this sign.

Fair Catch!   **Time Out!**   **Safe!**

How many secret signals can you find in this picture?

Secret signals are used when one team doesn't want the other team to know what's going on. If you have ever watched a football game, you may have noticed a coach on the sidelines making strange movements. What he is doing is giving secret directions to the players on the field.

Football coaches can be very tricky. Sometimes, two coaches on the same team give signals at the same time. One coach gives the real secret play while the other gives signals that the players ignore. This is done to confuse the other team, so they don't know which signal is the real signal.

Baseball is the sport in which secret signals are used the most. When you watch a baseball game, it might look like the players are just waiting around for the next pitch. If you look closer, however, you will see that secret communications are being sent all over the field. If you see a player scratch his chin or a coach push his cap back on his head, there is a good chance that you have just seen a secret signal.

GUIDED READING

Page 280   What are two ways to give sports signals? (secretly and not secretly)   INFER: CATEGORY

✔ **Page 281   In the sentence "One coach gives the real secret play while the other gives signals that the players ignore," what does the word *other* stand for?** (coach)   ANALYZE: WORD REFERENTS

Page 281   What may be the result when two coaches on the same team give signals at the same time? (The other team might be confused about which signal is the real signal.)   INFER: CAUSE/EFFECT

Page 281   Why do you think secret signals are used the most in baseball? (There is time to give signals before each pitch.)   INFER: CAUSE/EFFECT

STRATEGIC READING

**Page 280   Have students describe the sports signals that are not secret. (*fair catch; time out*) Then ask them to summarize what they have read so far and predict which players on a baseball team use secret signals. Tell students that if they have trouble summarizing or predicting, this is a clue they do not understand what they have read and they need to reread. If students have trouble summarizing, have them reread page 281. Review the last guided reading questions if they have difficulty predicting.   METACOGNITION: SUMMARIZING AND PREDICTING

✔ Skill from The Bridge applied through this question.

538

The catcher is about to signal for a certain type of pitch.

The pitcher and the catcher use sign language before every pitch. The catcher gives a sign to tell the pitcher the kind of pitch to throw. One finger may mean ''Throw a fastball.'' Two fingers may mean ''Pitch a curve ball.'' The catcher also uses a sign to tell the pitcher where to throw the pitch: inside, outside, high, or low. If the pitcher doesn't agree with the catcher, he will shake his head. The catcher will then secretly suggest another pitch.

Before every game, the catcher and the pitcher must talk about the sign language to be used. This way, there will be no mistakes. If a pitcher does not understand the signs, he might throw the wrong pitch, and the catcher may not be able to catch the ball.

The pitcher isn't the only one watching the catcher's secret signs. The second baseman and the shortstop also follow the sign language. If they know the kind of pitch to expect, they can guess where the ball will go if the batter hits it. The shortstop and second baseman have a set of secret signs of their own. They use them to tell the outfielders, who are far away and can't see the catcher, what kind of pitch is on the way. When a shortstop puts his hands on his knees, he might be telling the outfielders to expect a fastball.

The team that is up to bat also uses secret sign language. During a ballgame, coaches stand near first base and third base. Part of their job is to give secret directions to the batter. They also direct the runners who have reached a base. These coaches may seem to be just standing around, but don't be fooled. When they dust off their sleeve or hold their elbow, they may be telling the batter to bunt or the base runner to steal a base.

A base coach secretly signals batters and base runners.

GUIDED READING

✔ **Page 282   What is the main idea of this page?** (The pitcher and catcher communicate with sign language.)
SYNTHESIZE: MAIN IDEA/DETAILS

Page 282   If the pitcher does not understand the catcher's signals, he might throw the wrong pitch and the catcher might miss the ball. Can you think of other things that could happen if the pitcher does not understand the catcher's signals? (He may throw a pitch that gives the batter a hit, walk, or home run.)
SYNTHESIZE: PREDICTING OUTCOMES

Page 283   Why is sign language a good way to communicate in baseball? (It can be used across a long distance such as a baseball field. The shortstop can communicate with outfielders.)   EVALUATE: FACT OR OPINION

STRATEGIC READING

Page 282   Ask students to close their eyes and visualize as you read aloud the first paragraph. Students should be able to picture the finger signals the catcher makes and the pitcher shaking his head. Tell children that if they have trouble visualizing, this may be a signal that they do not understand the selection. If students have trouble, have them discuss the confusing section with a friend or study partner. Encourage students to continue visualizing as they read the rest of the selection.   METACOGNITION: VISUALIZING

✔ **Informal Assessment Opportunity:**   GETTING INFORMATION FROM TEXT

539

Teams are always trying to find out what the other team's signals are. To stop this from happening, teams often change their signals during a game. A sign that meant "steal the base" in one inning may mean "stay on base" in another. Coaches can get even trickier than that. For example, base runners might be told to ignore all signs unless the coach's feet are in a certain position.

The next time you're at the ballpark or stadium, pay attention to the movements of the team members. See if you can tell which are secret signals and which are everyday movements. Players and coaches can be tricky, so watch carefully; but don't be too suspicious. When a coach scratches his chin, he might just have an itch!

◆ LIBRARY LINK ◆

If you would like to learn more about signals, you might enjoy reading Train Whistles *by Helen Roney Settler.*

 ## Reader's Response

Do you think understanding sports signals will help you enjoy sports more? Why or why not?

See next page for suggested answers.

SPORTS SIGNALS

 ## Thinking It Over

1. Why are signals used in sports?
2. How are the signals for *fair catch* and *time out* different from the other signals described?
3. Who gives secret signals in baseball?
4. A team often changes its secret signals. Why is this helpful? How might it be a problem? How did you decide on your answers?
5. In which sports do you think secret signals would not be useful?

 ## Writing to Learn

THINK AND CREATE You, also, may create a secret language. If you want to send a message in code, put the first letter of each word at the end. Read the code chart below.

Real Word	Code Word
sports	portss
signal	ignals
message	essagem

WRITE Write a message to a friend. Write it in code. See if your friend can figure out the message.

GUIDED READING

Page 285 What was the author's purpose in including the last paragraph of this selection? (as a reminder not to think that every signal is secret; or that every movement is a signal) EVALUATE: AUTHOR'S PURPOSE

RETURNING TO THE READING PURPOSE

OPTION 1 If students set the purpose, ask them to return to their "I wonder" statements about sports signals. Discuss how they were answered in the article. Students may wish to discuss any surprises they encountered. (Two coaches on the same team give signals at the same time; teams change their signals very often.)

OPTION 2 If you set the purpose, ask how players and coaches communicate with each other. (with sign language, some secret signs) Encourage students to give examples of the kinds of signals used in football and baseball mentioned in the selection.

Reader's Journal   **p 107**
Responding to Reading

SECRET CIPHERS

Students learn what a cipher is and decode a secret message. They then make up codes of their own and see if partners can decipher them.

540

SELECTION FOLLOW-UP

SPORTS SIGNALS

THINKING IT OVER

1. **Why are signals used in sports?** (Most signals are used to tell players what to do. Sometimes signals are used to give information.) ANALYZE: MAIN IDEA/DETAILS

2. **How are the signals for *fair catch* and *time out* different from the other signals described?** (They are not secret signals; they are given openly for the information of both teams.) ANALYZE: COMPARISON

3. **Who gives secret signals in baseball?** (Many team members give secret signals in baseball. Among others, the pitcher and catcher signal each other, the infielders signal the outfielders, the coaches signal the batters and runners.) RECALL: DETAILS

4. **A team often changes its secret signals. Why is this helpful? How might it be a problem? How did you decide on your answers?** (A team changes its secret signals often so that the other team will not find out or guess what the signals are. However, this might be a problem if players on the same team get mixed up and do not remember the changes. Encourage students to draw from the text and from their own experience for their answers.) EVALUATE: FACT OR OPINION; METACOGNITION

5. **In which sports do you think secret signals would not be useful?** (Possible answers: Secret signals would not be useful in individual sports such as ice skating, skiing, swimming, and running.) SYNTHESIZE: DRAWING CONCLUSIONS

WRITING TO LEARN

Use Writing Master 21, which duplicates this chart.

THINK AND CREATE   You, also, may create a secret language. If you want to send a message in code, put the first letter of each word at the end. Read the code chart below. (Help students work with the chart to prepare for writing.)

Real Word	Code Word
sports	portss
signal	ignals
message	essagem

Extend comprehension through writing

WRITE   Write a message to a friend. Write it in code. See if your friend can figure out the message. (Have students exchange messages and decode them.)

More Ideas for Selection Follow-Up

CRITICAL AND CREATIVE THINKING QUESTIONS

Encourage a variety of responses and points of view.

Use these open-ended questions to encourage critical and creative thinking about the selection.

1. Do you think it is fair for sports teams to use secret signals? Why or why not?

✔ 2. How are sports signals like sign language? How are they different?

3. How can sports signals help players "get the message"? How do sports signals keep players from "getting the message"?

REREADING ORALLY

Have students reread for fluency.

Assign each member of the reading group a reading buddy, or let him or her choose one. Then assign pairs of students short passages in the selection that describe how sports signals are made and what the signals mean. Passages assigned may include the hand-on-head signal on page 279, fair catch on page 280, time out on page 280, or pitcher-catcher signs on page 282. Tell students they will read aloud to the group while volunteers demonstrate the signals. Explain that to prepare they should read their passages several times silently and then practice reading aloud with their partners.

SELECTION COMPREHENSION

Provide comprehension check.

A Workbook page to check comprehension is shown in the Resource Center below. It may be used for informal assessment.

✔ **Informal Assessment Opportunity:** SYNTHESIZING ACROSS SELECTIONS

Workbook page 138

SELECTION COMPREHENSION

NAME _____

SPORTS SIGNALS

A. Complete the summary of the selection "Sports Signals."
Accept reasonable variations.
This selection is about ____signals____ used in sports. The author says that almost everyone in sports uses signals to ____communicate____. Some of these signals are understood by everyone. But secret signals are used when a team doesn't want the other team ____to know what's being planned____.

In football, coaches can be very ____tricky____. Two coaches may give different signals at the same time to ____confuse____ the other team.

The sport in which secret signals are used the most is ____baseball____. The pitcher and catcher give signs before every pitch. The second baseman and shortstop also watch the signs so they can guess where ____the ball may go____ if the batter hits it. Then they use their own signs to pass this information to the outfielders.

The team at bat also uses secret signs. Coaches use signs to ____give directions____ to the batter and to the runners on base.

Teams are always trying to find out what other teams' ____secret signals____ are. Coaches try to stop this from happening. They ____change____ the signals often to confuse the other team.

B. On separate paper, explain why coaches and players must be careful about how they stand and move their arms during a game. See Teacher Notes.

138 "Sports Signals"   Selection Comprehension

RESOURCE CENTER

◀ **Workbook page 138** is intended for use by all students.

Writing Master 21 duplicates the Writing to Learn chart.

I•T Kit Activity

Audio: **"Take Me Out to the Ball Game"**
Reading the selection will put students in a sporting mood for singing along with this rousing song. After they sing, students can describe signals they may have noticed on the field at sports events. (See Activity Guide.)
CONTEMPORARY MUSIC

LANGUAGE ARTS CONNECTIONS

CREATIVE THINKING: ACTING OUT TELEVISION SPORTS INTERVIEWS

Have students present television sports interviews.

Explain that a cooperative activity is one in which the success of the group depends on the success of each individual person. Tell students that they will work cooperatively in groups of four to develop and act out television interviews with famous baseball players. One member of the group will be the interviewer and write questions to ask the baseball player. Another member will be the player and write answers to the questions. A third member will be the announcer for the show and write a short speech to introduce the player and interviewer. The fourth member will design and set up the television show's set. Have students present their interviews to the class. Afterward, ask the audience what they liked about the show. Discuss how well the groups worked together and what could be improved. COOPERATIVE LEARNING: SPEAKING

CREATING AN ILLUSTRATED BASEBALL GLOSSARY

Discuss illustrated glossaries.

Remind students that a glossary gives definitions of words. Explain that sometimes the definitions include context sentences showing the meanings. Point out that some glossaries also have pictures to help explain meanings.

Have students create a baseball glossary.

Have students create a glossary of baseball terms that can be illustrated. Help each student choose a baseball word. Ask each student to write a definition, write a context sentence, and draw an illustration for his or her word. Explain that each word will be one page of the glossary. Guide students in arranging their pages alphabetically, making letter dividers, and creating a cover with the title "Baseball Glossary." WHOLE CLASS ENRICHMENT

THE NEWSPAPER ARTICLE AS A LITERARY GENRE

Have students write sports articles.

Remind students that "Sports Signals" is an informational article. Explain that a newspaper article is a kind of informational article. Point out that a good newspaper article answers the questions *Who? What? Why? Where? When?* and *How?*

Encourage students to pretend that they are sports writers for a newspaper. Explain that they have just seen an exciting baseball game. Ask students to write short newspaper articles about the game, making up team names, players' names, and other details needed to answer the six news questions. Encourage students to mention some baseball plays that were signaled by coaches and players.   CHALLENGE: WRITING

REPORTING ON SPORTS TERMS

Discuss the languages of sports.

Remind students that some terms or words have special meanings related to sports. Have students name some terms in baseball. (*hit, strike, single, fly*) Point out that all sports have special terms.

Have students report on the language of sports.

Have students work in small groups. Have each group research and report on the terms used in a sport of its choice besides baseball and football. The group might choose tennis, basketball, soccer, golf, or any other sport. Tell students to use the encyclopedia and other nonfiction books to find information. Have students present oral reports and use charts and drawings they have made.   SHARED LEARNING: SPEAKING

DEVELOPING STORY MAPS

Have students complete story maps.

Review the parts of a story map by writing these headings on the chalkboard.

Title:	Author:	
The Setting:	**The Problem:**	**The Resolution:**
Place:	Decision 1:	
Time:	Decision 2:	
Characters:	Decision 3:	

Guide students in completing story maps of "Sports Signals." Students may have to infer the setting, and will need to identify characters by what they do rather than their names. To help students, ask them what coaches and players did to solve their communication problem and talk about signals as solutions.

Language Arts Master 18 may be used with this activity.   WRITING

CREATING COMIC STRIPS

Have students create comic strips about a character who breaks a code.

Have students tell what comic strips are. *(a series of pictures in frames that tell a story, with characters' words in speech bubbles)* Encourage students to name some of their favorite comic strips and tell why they like them.

Have students work in pairs. Have each pair create a comic strip about a character who breaks a code or a secret language. Students can use human or animal characters from comic strips they know or characters they make up. Codes or secret languages can be made up or ones they know already. Tell students to create five frames for their comic strips and put the words in speech bubbles. Display the comic strips on the bulletin board or collect them and put them in a booklet.   SHARED LEARNING: WRITING

READING EVERY DAY

After reading about how sign language is used in sports, students might enjoy reading about how sign language is used in another field—science—and about how animals are taught to communicate in sign with human beings.

Koko's Story by Dr. Francine Patterson. Photographs by Dr. Ronald H. Cohn. Scholastic, © 1987. Koko, a lovable gorilla, learns to communicate in sign, beginning with her first word, "food," and developing a vocabulary of more than 500 words that she uses in such phrases as "fine animal gorilla."

The Story of Nim: The Chimp Who Learned Language by Anna Michel. Knopf, © 1980. A close look at Project Nim, from Nim's infancy through the time when he "talks" with his teachers in sentences, using sign language.

Reader's Journal   pp 108, 109
Extending Reading

THE BABE HITS ONE

A story about an amazing baseball player serves as a springboard for students to pretend they are radio announcers giving play-by-play reports of Babe Ruth's home run.

Selection Support

Prefixes de-, dis-

OBJECTIVE Using structural analysis to determine word meaning.

SKILL TRACE: PREFIXES				
Introduction	Practice	Test	Reteach	Maintain
TE 546	572	594	635	641	See Level 9.

1. WARM-UP

Use familiar context to introduce prefixed words orally.

Tell students they will listen to sentences about information from "Sports Signals." Explain that there are words in the sentences that have the prefixes *de-* and *dis-*. Point out that these words have familiar base words. Have students listen for the words, identify them, and identify the base words. (*disagree, agree*; *debug, bug*)

> **If the pitcher does disagree with the catcher, he will shake his head. During the summer, sprays are used to debug the baseball field.**

Discuss meanings of prefixes.

Tell students that *dis-* means "not" and *de-* means "to do the opposite of" or "remove from." Reread the sentences. Help students determine the context meanings of *disagree (pitcher does not agree)* and *debug (bugs are removed from the baseball field).*

State the objective.

Tell students they will learn to use prefixes or word parts added to the beginnings of words and base words to determine word meanings.

2. TEACH

Explain why knowing about prefixes is important.

Knowing the meanings of prefixes and base words helps readers figure out the meanings of unknown words.

Present a strategy for determining word meanings.

Explain that there is a strategy students can use to help them determine a new word's meaning. First, identify the prefix and base word. Next, think about the meaning of the prefix. Then put this meaning with the base word to figure out the new word's meaning. Finally, see if the meaning makes sense in the sentence.

> **84**
>
> **TEACHING CHART 84: PREFIXES DE-, DIS-**
>
> 1. Members of the baseball team will deplane at gate 15. (deplane, get off a plane)
> 2. Fans of the team will detrain in St. Louis. (detrain, get off a train)
> 3. Sometimes a batter disobeys a coach's directions. (disobeys, does not obey)
> 4. Even if the player gets on base, the coach may be displeased. (displeased, not pleased)

Model the strategy. Read sentence 1 on the Teaching Chart, point out *deplane*, and identify the prefix *de-* and base word *plane*. Explain that *de-* may also mean "get off." Knowing this, you determine that *deplane* means "get off a plane."

3. GUIDED PRACTICE

Check for understanding. Before going on, have students explain how to use prefixes to determine word meanings. (*think about the meaning of the prefix and put it with the base word*)

Guide students in using the strategy. Have students use the strategy to figure out meanings of words with the prefixes *de-* and *dis-* in the remaining sentences. Discuss prefix meanings that helped them determine word meanings.

4. WRAP-UP

Summarize instruction. Review why prefixes are important to readers and how readers use them. (*to help figure out meanings of unknown words; to discover what a prefix means; to add prefix meanings to meanings of base words*)

Provide independent practice. Options for independent practice are shown in the Resource Center below.

Meeting Individual Needs

RETEACHING Use the activity on page 641 and Masters 1–4 in the Teacher Resource Kit.

CHALLENGE Use the activity on page 641 and Master 18 in the Teacher Resource Kit.

ACHIEVING ENGLISH PROFICIENCY Use the activity on page 641 and Master 32 in the Teacher Resource Kit.

Workbook page 139

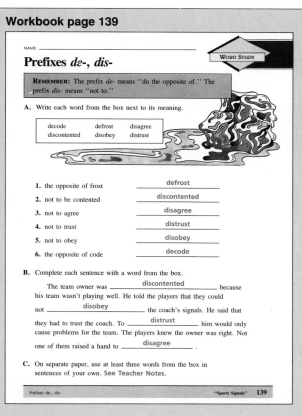

RESOURCE CENTER

◄ **Workbook page 139** is intended for use by all students.

Skills Practice 128 ► may be assigned for additional practice.

Workbook reuse option: Have students use vertical lines to separate each prefix from its base word in the box.

Skills Practice 128

NAME _____

SKILLS PRACTICE 128

Prefixes *de-*, *dis-*

The prefix *de-* means "to do the opposite of" or "to remove from."

I don't understand this because it is written in *code*. I will figure out what it says when I *decode* it.

The prefix *dis-* means "not."

I *like* codes that are made from letters. I *dislike* codes that are made from numbers.

Fill in the circle next to the word that finishes each sentence. Then write the word in the sentence.

1. Someone **disconnected** _____ the phone while I was talking.
   ○ derailed   ○ disallowed   ● disconnected

2. In winter, we have to **defrost** _____ the car windows.
   ○ decontrol   ● defrost   ○ deform

3. I felt **displeased** _____ when my friend was rude to me.
   ● displeased   ○ disconnect   ○ deforested

4. My brother **disapproves** _____ of people who cheat on tests.
   ○ deforms   ● disapproves   ○ discomforts

5. Sitting in one place all day can cause you some **discomfort** _____.
   ○ displeased   ○ disappear   ● discomfort

6. She knows how to **decode** _____ the secret message.
   ● decode   ○ defrost   ○ debug

7. Sometimes my mother **disagrees** _____ with what I say.
   ○ disowns   ● disagrees   ○ disadvantages

8. I like school, but I **dislike** _____ some subjects.
   ○ discomfort   ○ discontent   ● dislike

9. My papers were all **disarranged** _____ in my notebook.
   ○ displeased   ● disarranged   ○ disliked

128 LEVEL 8   "Sports Signals"

SKILL TRACE: WORD REFERENTS				
Introduction	Practice	Test	Reteach	Maintain
TE 532	548	618	635	636	See Level 9.

COMPREHENSION

Word Referents

OBJECTIVE Understanding relationships between substitute words and their referents.

Review word referents.

Remind students that a word referent is the word or words in the sentence or paragraph that a word substitute stands for. Review that word substitutes may tell who, whose, when, or how many.

Present sentences with word substitutes and referents.

Display the Teaching Chart. Point out that the underlined words are word substitutes. Have students find their referents by looking back in the sentence or sentences and asking the questions *Who? Whose? When?* or *How many?*

85

TEACHING CHART 85: WORD REFERENTS

1. A player who catches a punt can wave his (player's) hand to signal a catch.
2. What is a catcher doing when he (catcher) shows two fingers?
3. The catcher gives a sign. The pitcher will then (after catcher gives sign) throw the pitch.
4. Two coaches may signal at the same time. One (One of the coaches) gives the real play.
5. The second baseman and the shortstop follow sign language. Both (the second baseman and shortstop) signal the outfielders.
6. Pay attention to the field coach's movements. Some (some of the movements) may be secret signals.

Provide independent practice.

Options for independent practice are shown in the Resource Center below.

Workbook page 140

COMPREHENSION

Word Referents

NAME _____

REMEMBER: Some words can stand for the names of people, places, or things.

A. Read the sentences. On each line write the underlined word. Also write the word or words the underlined word refers to.

1. The coach gave a signal to her players.
   her - coach

2. With so many signals in a game, each player must know those to look for.
   those - signals

3. The catcher signaled the pitcher, but she shook her head "no."
   she - pitcher

4. The shortstop and second base player have their own signals.
   their - shortstop and second base player

5. Players should use the "time out" sign only when they really need it.
   it - "time out" sign

6. That team uses many secret signals, but our team uses only ten.
   ten - secret signals

B. Make up a secret signal for a baseball coach to use. Describe the signal and write its meaning on separate paper. Underline any words you use that stand for other words. See Teacher Notes.

140 "Sports Signals" Word Referents

RESOURCE CENTER

◄ **Workbook page 140** is intended for use by all students.

Skills Practice 129 ► may be assigned for additional practice.

Workbook reuse option: Have students underline two more examples of word referents in the sentences in Part A and draw arrows showing to what each refers.

Skills Practice 129

NAME _____

SKILLS PRACTICE ◄**129**►

Word Referents

Some words can stand for the names of people, places, and things. **Referents** are the word or words a **word substitute** might stand for. Words like *now, after,* and *then* are word substitutes that tell **when.** Words like *few, some, all, both, many,* and *one* are word substitutes that tell **how many.**

Examples: Jim ran on Monday. He ran two miles *then (Monday).*
Two weather reports said rain. Could *both (two weather reports)* be wrong?

Read the story. Each underlined word is a word substitute for other words in an earlier sentence. Decide who or what each underlined word stands for. Write the word or referent after each underlined word.

Nick had been to Pinewood State Park last summer. Then (last summer) he had gone hiking and camping there. He had spotted two moose on a trail. Both (two moose) had run into the woods.

Now Nick and his mother are on their way to the big state park. Both (Nick and his mother) are excited about the trip. After a while, they stop for lunch. Then they get back on the road.

It is afternoon. Now (afternoon) they are a half hour from the park. Nick tells his mother which way to go.

"Look for a diner called 'The Red Parrot,'" says Nick. "Turn right just before it (The Red Parrot)." They come to the diner and make a right turn.

Nick's mother says, "Where is that park? I can't wait to get there (the park)!"

"Just look for a sign about the park," says Nick. "Oh, here comes one (sign). It (the sign) says to take the second left turn. Not the first turn, but the next (turn)."

Five minutes later, Nick and his mother drive into Pinewood State Park.

LEVEL 8 "Sports Signals" **129**

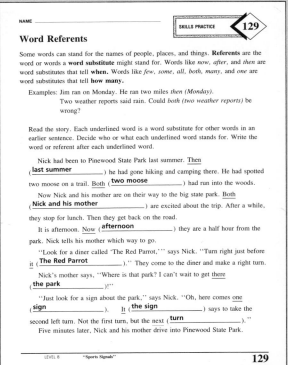

548

SKILL TRACE: MULTIPLE MEANINGS				
Introduction	Practice	Test	Reteach	Maintain
TE 522	549	573	635	638	See Level 9.

VOCABULARY
Multiple Meanings

OBJECTIVE Choosing the appropriate meaning of a multiple-meaning word.

Review multiple-meaning words.   Remind students that multiple-meaning words have more than one meaning.

Present multiple-meaning words in context.   Have students choose the appropriate meaning of each underlined word by using the context of the sentence.

TEACHING CHART 86: MULTIPLE MEANINGS   **86**

bat: to hit; an animal   **batter:** player at bat; dough
coach: a railroad car;   **pass:** a throw; a ball; a free
a team's trainer   ticket

1. During a ballgame, one <u>coach</u> stands near first base.
   Coach means   (a team's trainer) .
2. The player who is up to <u>bat</u> may get a signal from the coach.
   Bat means   (to hit) .
3. A shortstop can guess where the <u>batter</u> will hit a ball.
   Batter means   (player at bat) .
4. A football coach may signal a long <u>pass</u>.
   Pass means   (a throw of a ball) .

Provide independent practice.   Options for independent practice are shown in the Resource Center below.

Workbook page 141

RESOURCE CENTER

Skills Practice 130

◀ **Workbook page 141** is intended for use by all students.

Skills Practice 130 ▶ may be assigned for additional practice.

Workbook reuse option: Have students write a sentence for each underlined word in Part A, using a definition that is not shown in the sentences there.

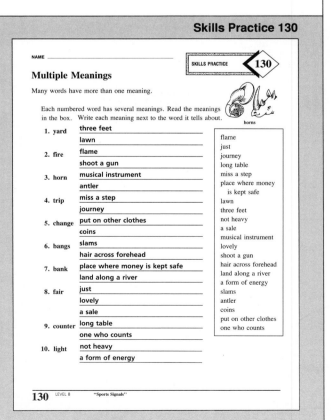

NAME _____

Multiple Meanings   VOCABULARY

REMEMBER: Many words have more than one meaning. Use context to determine the meaning of a word in a sentence or story.

A. Read each sentence. Write the letter of the definition that fits the underlined word.

   1. __c__ The football coach signaled his team to <u>pass</u>.
      (a) leave behind; (b) be successful in a test; (c) throw a ball from one player to another

   2. __a__ That long pass was the key <u>play</u> of the whole football season.
      (a) one particular action in a game; (b) to join in a game; (c) a story acted on a stage

   3. __c__ In our baseball game the batter swung at the first <u>pitch</u>.
      (a) thick substance made of tar; (b) the musical key of an instrument; (c) throw of a baseball to a batter

   4. __a__ The <u>bat</u> broke when it hit the fastball.
      (a) wooden stick used in a baseball game; (b) flying mammal; (c) wink of the eye

   5. __b__ The runner watched the <u>coach</u> for a signal.
      (a) large four-wheeled carriage; (b) person who teaches others to play a sport; (c) to train someone

   6. __c__ The coach signaled the runner to <u>steal</u> third base.
      (a) take dishonestly; (b) do secretly; (c) run to a base as the pitcher pitches to the batter

B. On separate paper, write an announcement for a sportscaster to read on television. Use three of the underlined words. See Teacher Notes.

Multiple Meanings   "Sports Signals" **141**

NAME _____

Multiple Meanings   SKILLS PRACTICE ◀**130**▶

Many words have more than one meaning.

Each numbered word has several meanings. Read the meanings in the box. Write each meaning next to the word it tells about.

horns

1. yard	three feet
	lawn
2. fire	flame
	shoot a gun
3. horn	musical instrument
	antler
4. trip	miss a step
	journey
5. change	put on other clothes
	coins
6. bangs	slams
	hair across forehead
7. bank	place where money is kept safe
	land along a river
8. fair	just
	lovely
	a sale
9. counter	long table
	one who counts
10. light	not heavy
	a form of energy

flame
just
journey
long table
miss a step
place where money
  is kept safe
lawn
three feet
not heavy
a sale
musical instrument
lovely
shoot a gun
hair across forehead
land along a river
a form of energy
slams
antler
coins
put on other clothes
one who counts

130 LEVEL 8   "Sports Signals"

SKILL TRACE: HOMOPHONES				
Introduction	Practice	Test	Reteach	Maintain
TE 392	420	443	461	464	550

VOCABULARY

Homophones

OBJECTIVE   Understanding words that sound alike but have different meanings.

Review homophones.

Remind students that homophones are words that are pronounced the same but have different spellings and different meanings. On the chalkboard, write the following sentence and have students make up a new sentence with a homophone of the underlined word.

"I counted eight books."

Present homophones in context.

You may wish to write the following pairs of homophones on the chalkboard: *know, no; to, two; rays, raise; steal, steel; Their, There.* Read aloud the sentences below. Answers are printed in red. Have students choose the correct homophone for each sentence.

---

1. Do you (know) what any sports signals mean?
2. A catcher may hold up (two) fingers.
3. A coach may (raise) both hands over his head.
4. Does this sign mean to (steal) the base?
5. (There) are many ways to hit a baseball.

Provide independent practice.

An independent activity is shown in the Resource Center below.

RESOURCE CENTER

Skills Practice 131 ▶ may be assigned for additional practice.

Skills Practice 131

NAME _____

SKILLS PRACTICE 〈131〉

Homophones

Words that sound the same but have different spellings and meanings are called **homophones.** Use spelling and context to figure out the correct meaning of homophones.

Choose the correct homophone to complete each sentence. Write it in the puzzle.

1. I am never _____ at a base-ball game. (board—bored)
2. There is robbery in base-ball! A runner can _____ a base. (steal—steel)
3. It takes good _____ to hit a fast ball. (sight—site)
4. The _____ of the pitcher is to throw the ball. (role—roll)
5. I hope we _____ the other team! (beat—beet)
6. Our runner just _____ third base! (passed—past)
7. The _____ is flying toward home plate! (ball—bawl)
8. Safe! I am so happy, I yell _____. (allowed—aloud)
9. The game is _____, 2 to 2. (tide—tied)
10. It is the _____ inning. (forth—fourth)
11. I love to watch the game for _____. (hours—ours)
12. Hurray! Our team _____! (one—won)

LEVEL 8   "Sports Signals"   **131**

CURRICULUM CONNECTIONS

TEACHER CHOICE

WHAT'S IN A NAME? SOCIAL STUDIES

Have students research and list baseball, football, and basketball teams with animal names along with the home cities of these teams. Have students try to find out the relationship between the city/state of each team and the animal name. Students can record their information on a chart and illustrate the chart with the animals.

Team	Animal	Reason
Baltimore Orioles		
Miami Dolphins		
Detroit Tigers		

THE SPEED KINGS SCIENCE

Assign a small group of students the task of finding out how fast different professional baseball pitchers can throw a baseball. Suggest they look in science books, baseball handbooks, books of facts, and world record books. Have students share their findings with the class. Interested students might like to compare the speed of a baseball to speeds of balls in other sports.

SPORTING CITIES GEOGRAPHY

Ask students to name and list the professional sports teams in baseball, football, and basketball. Have them work in small groups to find out the cities and states in which the teams are located. Provide a large map of the United States, and ask students to find the states, then the cities, of the sports teams they listed. Have them label each city with the appropriate team name. **Curriculum Connection Master 18** can be used with this activity.

SUPER STARS OF SPORTS CAREERS

Have each student choose a sports star to research. Tell students to use nonfiction books and magazines to discover how their heroes got started in their sports, what their special talents are, and any other interesting facts. Have students present their information orally and tell why they chose the people they did.

Checkpoint

USING THE CHECKPOINT PAGES

Use Checkpoints for informal evaluation.

Checkpoints are designed to help students and teachers monitor and improve student progress. For students, the Checkpoints serve as another step in the development of their ability to control their own learning. They see their own strengths and weaknesses even as the teacher does. For the teacher, the Checkpoints offer a systematic approach to informal assessment. Each Checkpoint helps identify areas of strength and weakness and then offers ideas for reteaching and extra practice before the formal assessment that comes at the end of the unit.

The extra-help ideas in Checkpoint lessons give additional practice to those students having difficulty with the targeted skill while allowing them to remain with the regular reading group. Extra-help ideas can also be used effectively with individual students or in small groups.

Informally diagnose strengths and weaknesses.

Checkpoints are in the same format as the Unit Skills Tests; you might review the directions before assigning the pages. Direct students to complete the pages shown in the Resource Center. Then have students work together to correct their papers, and encourage them to explain the thinking behind their answers. This affords you an opportunity to observe not only how students arrived at their answers, but also to identify and explain any item types that are causing difficulty. Note that in the Resource Center, questions are labeled by skill so that you can quickly assess areas in which a particular student needs additional help.

The following skills are included in this Checkpoint.

referents
characterization
multiple meanings

For your information, the Checkpoint pages at the end of this unit include the skills listed below.

long word decoding
prefixes *de-, dis-*
vocabulary — Story Critical words

PROVIDING EXTRA HELP

Provide extra help with referents.

Strengthen reading comprehension by linking reading and writing. Draw on selections already studied in this unit for sentences illustrating the use of referents. Rewrite these sentences on the chalkboard, repeating words rather than using word substitutes. Ask students to evaluate the writing style of these sentences *(they will be wordy and repetitious)* and how they might be improved *(by substituting other words for those words that are repeated).* Have students rewrite the sentences, making these substitutions. Improved sentences could be put on the chalkboard, with writers explaining what was replaced and why. Continue the activity throughout the unit by evaluating and rewriting sentences from students' reading or content textbooks.

Provide extra help with characterization.

Strengthen reading comprehension by linking reading and listening skills. Make use of material familiar to students by having them review "Forecast" for good examples of characterization. Remind students that we learn about characters from what they say, what they do, and what others say about them. Get students started by telling them to look for places in which they learned something about the character of Theodore, Caroline, or Stan. Have students read aloud their favorite pieces of characterization. As the group listens, they should note what they learn about these characters that they did not know before. Repeat the activity after the students have read "Mufaro's Beautiful Daughters" and "The Boy Who Cried Wolf."

Provide extra help with multiple meanings.

Strengthen reading comprehension by linking reading with speaking and listening. Divide students into pairs or small groups, and give each several words from the list that follows: *live, tear, read, creep, lead, right, course, glasses, left, heat, cover, iron, stick, judge, match.* For each word have students write two sentences, each illustrating a different one of the word's meanings. Tell students they may use dictionaries as they plan their sentences. As they work, move among them to give help with context as needed. Have completed sentences read aloud. During this activity, call attention to any words whose pronunciations change with context.

Workbook page 142

RESOURCE CENTER

◀ These pages provide informal assessment in the format of the Unit Skills Tests. ▶

Workbook page 143

NAME _____

Checkpoint

Read the paragraphs. Then fill in the circle beside the correct answer.

Once upon a time there was a curious girl named Pandora who received a gift from the gods. It was a box that held many harmful things. Pandora was warned never to open the box. She was so curious, however, that she wondered what the box might hold.

One day when she was home all alone, Pandora reached for the box. Carefully, she opened the lid. Out flew all the evils that the box had held. Sadness could now visit people all around the world.

Pandora was frightened to see the evil she had sent into the world. Quickly, she shut the lid. Only one thing stayed in the box. It was Hope. Pandora saved the one good thing the box had held. Even now people hold on to hope to help them through bad times.

142   Checkpoint

NAME _____

word referents
1. In the first paragraph, what word does *it* stand for?
   (a) gods
   (b) gift
   (c) girl
   (d) Pandora
word referents
2. Which statement does *not* help you see what *it* refers to?
   (a) It refers to a thing that has already been named.
   (b) It has to refer to a thing, not a person.
   (c) It is a two-letter pronoun.
   (d) It refers to one thing only, not to several.
characterization
3. What word describes Pandora?
   (a) friendly
   (b) lazy
   (c) curious
   (d) energetic
characterization
4. What sentence helped you describe Pandora who received a gift from the gods?
   (a) Once upon a time there was a curious girl named Pandora who recieved a gift from the gods.

   (b) It was a box that held many harmful things.
   (c) One day when she was home all alone, Pandora reached for the box.
   (d) Carefully, she opened the lid.
multiple meanings
5. What meaning for *box* is used in the story?
   (a) place where the batter stands in a baseball game
   (b) seat in a theater or stadium
   (c) container to put things in
   (d) space in a courtroom
multiple meanings
6. What sentence helped you find the meaning of *box*?
   (a) Once upon a time there was a curious girl named Pandora who received a gift from the gods.
   (b) It was a box that held many harmful things.
   (c) Sadness could now visit people all around the world.
   (d) It was Hope.

Checkpoint   143

LITERATURE LINK

OBJECTIVE   Using text and prior knowledge to make predictions.

INTRODUCING AND READING THE LESSON

Tap students' prior knowledge.

Share the following limerick with students. Ask them to listen carefully to fill in the missing word.

> **There was a hobbling young princess in Spain**
> **Who was frequently heard to complain**
> **"I'd run fast as a cat**
> **and I'd never go splat**
> **If my ankle I'd learn not to ____!"**

Have students try to figure out the missing word. *(sprain)* Ask students to identify the clues in the limerick that helped them predict the missing word. *(It's a word that rhymes with complain; it's a word that makes sense in the limerick.)* Point out that we frequently use clues and what we already know to predict something that is missing or what will happen next when we read. Lead students to see that this is exactly what they did when they found the missing word in the limerick.

Explain the usefulness of making predictions.

Explain to students that making predictions is a very important reading skill. It helps the reader get more involved in the story or article and therefore better understand and remember what he or she reads.

State the objective.

Tell students that in this lesson they will learn tips for making predictions as they read.

Refer students to their texts.

Have students turn to pages 286–287 in their books and read the lesson.

LITERATURE LINK

How can you make predictions when you read?

Charlie Brown guessed that Snoopy needed help. He soon found out that Snoopy can take care of himself!

When you read, do you guess what's going to happen next? That's called making predictions. Making predictions keeps you involved in the story. It keeps you thinking as you read. You may guess wrong, but that's not important. You can always change your mind. After all, who could have predicted what Snoopy would do?

Strategy for Reading

What's Next?

When you read this part of the story "Forecast," did you predict what would happen next?

> Theodore yeowled with laughter. "Snow? Did you say *snow*? Caroline, look outside. It's the middle of summer!"
>
> Caroline folded her arms stubbornly across her chest. "My instruments say it will snow on Friday. Anyway, every now and then it does snow in the summer. In July of 1816, for example…"

Theodore thought Caroline was wrong! Did you? What helped you decide? Did you change your mind as you read more of the story?

The tips below will help you make predictions when you read.

- Think about what is happening. Is it like anything you know about?
- Guess what might happen next.
- Read to find out if you are right.
- As you get more information, change your prediction if you need to.
- Keep thinking as you go.

As you read "The Horse Who Lived Upstairs," try to guess what will happen next. Use the tips above to stay involved in the story.

Making Predictions

Review the main points of the lesson.

DISCUSSING THE LESSON

Check students' understanding of the strategy with these questions.

Page 286   Why is it a good idea to make predictions as you read? (Possible responses: It gets you involved in the story; it keeps you thinking as you read.)

Page 286   What should you do if you make a prediction and it turns out to be wrong? (Make another prediction.)

WRAP-UP

Direct students to the next selection.

Encourage students to use the tips on page 287 to help them make predictions as they read the next selection, "The Horse Who Lived Upstairs."

	Teaching Sequence	**Trade Books and Resources**	**Meeting Individual Needs**	**Integrated Language Arts / Cross Curriculum**
The Bridge Pages 558–559	**Maintain** Story Elements: Setting	• Teaching Chart 87 • Workbook 144 • Skills Practice 132		
PART 1 **Vocabulary Strategies** Pages 560–561	**Develop Concepts** Semantic Mapping **Teach Vocabulary** **STORY CRITICAL WORDS: discontented, elevator,** picnicking, **plow,** pockets, policeman, stall (Tested words are boldfaced.)	• Teaching Chart 88 • Workbook 145 • Skills Practice 133	**SUPPORT WORDS:** babbling, horn, shafts, trough, weathervane • Skills Practice 134 **CHARACTER/SETTING WORDS:** Joey, Mr. Polaski, Percheron	**WRITING/SPEAKING ACTIVITY:** Use new vocabulary to write a brief story from a farm animal's point of view. • Spelling Connection 57
PART 2 **Reading & Responding** Pages 562–571	**Build Background** **Develop a Purpose for Reading** **Guide the Reading Process** **Selection Follow-Up**	• Reader's Journal 110–113 • Workbook 146 **READING EVERY DAY** *Burt Dow, Deep-Water Man,* by R. McCloskey *Poem Stew,* by W. Cole	**EXTRA HELP:** Main Idea/Details Form **ACHIEVING ENGLISH PROFICIENCY:** Adding the Prefix *dis-* to Words • Achieving English Proficiency Master 33	**Language Arts Connections** **WRITING TO LEARN:** Complete a chart about feelings. • Writing Master 22 **SPEAKING/LISTENING:** Improvising Story Scenes; Comparing Story Themes **WRITING:** Creating Travel Brochures; Writing Post Cards; Writing from a Point of View • Language Arts Master 19
PART 3 **Selection Support** Pages 572–575			**Practice** • Teaching Charts 89–90 • Workbook 147–148 • Skills Practice 135–136 Prefixes *de-, dis-* (Tested) Multiple Meanings (Tested) **Maintain** • Skills Practice 137 Suffix *-ment*	**Curriculum Connections** **SCIENCE:** Researching Horses **SOCIAL STUDIES:** Researching Farm Crops of New York State • Curriculum Connection Master 19 **ART:** Creating Farm Pictures, Maps, Diagrams, or Dioramas

The Horse Who Lived Upstairs

by Phyllis McGinley

SUMMARY   *A horse named Joey is comfortable living in the city, but he longs for the pleasures of the country. He wants to live in a red barn and frolic in a green meadow. One day Joey's owner gives him to a farmer. Will this be the answer to Joey's dream? Hardly, for Joey learns that barns are not all he imagined they were, and farm work leaves no time for kicking up his heels. When Joey's owner takes him back, Joey realizes that he is a city horse after all.*

The Bridge

SKILL TRACE: STORY ELEMENTS							
Introduction	Practice	Test	Reteach	Maintain			
TE 16	32	138	157	159	206	294	326	558

LITERATURE

Teaching Story Elements: Setting

OBJECTIVE   Recognizing story setting.

1. WARM-UP

Use familiar content to recognize a setting.

Tell students they will listen to a passage about a sport mentioned in the previous selection, "Sports Signals." Point out that the writer gives some clues about when and where the sport is taking place. Tell them to listen for the clues that tell when and where. (*early morning, a baseball field*)

> **The sun had just come up. The Little League team dressed and ran outside to warm up. Coach Brown grabbed some bats, balls, and gloves. "Let's play!" yelled the coach. The first batter stepped up to the plate.**

Discuss word and experience clues to the setting.

Reread the passage. Have students explain which word clues helped them know about the time and place. (*sun had just come up; Little League team; bats, balls, gloves*) Ask them how they knew that the sport is baseball. (*from having read about baseball, or seen a game, or played it themselves*)

State the objective.

Tell students they will review how to recognize the setting of a story, or where and when a story takes place.

2. TEACH

Explain why setting is important.

Understanding the time and place of a story gives readers a better understanding of what the story is about and why things happen as they do.

Present a strategy to recognize setting.

Explain that there is a strategy students can use to help them understand the setting. Look for word clues about time, such as time of day, weather, kinds of clothing, and kinds of transportation. Look for word clues about place, such as kinds of buildings, scenery, and special people or animals. Use what you know and your experience to help you understand the setting.

87

TEACHING CHART 87: SETTING

1. By the time Lee and his big brother, Ray, got to the school gym, the home team had already made two baskets. "I guess tonight's game started on time," said Ray. It was 8:15. (a school gym at a basketball game — school gym, team, baskets; at night — tonight's game, 8:15)

2. Although the afternoon air felt icy cold, not one person in the stands seemed to mind. The coach gave the signal, and the player ran with the ball. Then he passed it to another player who made the touchdown. The crowd stood up and cheered, "We won! We won!" (outside at a football stadium — air, stands, passed the ball, touchdown; late fall or winter afternoon — afternoon, icy cold)

Model the strategy.

Read passage 1 and point out that the sentences give clues to the place and time. Tell students that you see the words *school gym*, *team*, and *baskets*. You know that the words *team* and *baskets* mean a basketball game, so the place is in a school gym at a basketball game. The clues that it is nighttime are the words *tonight's game* and the time *8:15*.

3. GUIDED PRACTICE

Check for understanding.

Before going on, have students explain how to recognize the setting of a story. (*Look for word clues about where and when a story takes place. Think about what you already know from your own experience.*)

Guide students in using the strategy.

Have students use the strategy to understand the setting in the remaining passage. Discuss the word and experience clues that helped them to figure out the setting.

4. WRAP-UP

Summarize instruction.

Review why recognizing the place and time of a story is important, and the kinds of clues readers should look for. (*to better understand what a story is about and why things happen as they do; clues to time such as weather, time of day, clothing; clues to place such as kinds of buildings, scenery, and people or animals.*)

Provide independent practice.

Options for independent practice are shown in the Resource Center below.

5. APPLICATION

Students will recognize setting as they read "The Horse Who Lived Upstairs." The symbol ✔ marks specific questions and activities that apply this skill.

Workbook page 144

RESOURCE CENTER

◄ **Workbook page 144** is intended for use by all students.

Skills Practice 132 ► may be assigned for additional practice.

Workbook reuse option: Have students underline all the words that tell about *where* the story takes place and circle all the words that tell *when* the story takes place.

Skills Practice 132

Vocabulary Strategies

Developing Concepts

Use a semantic map to tap students' prior knowledge of farms.

As a starting point for teaching vocabulary, show students pictures of a farm. Discuss the objects and animals in the picture. Build a semantic map about a farm and have students suggest words that belong under each heading. List the responses on the map and have the map read aloud.

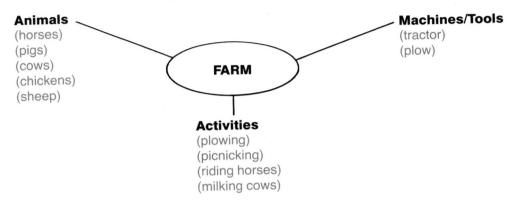

Animals
(horses)
(pigs)
(cows)
(chickens)
(sheep)

Machines/Tools
(tractor)
(plow)

FARM

Activities
(plowing)
(picnicking)
(riding horses)
(milking cows)

Teaching Vocabulary

Discuss meanings of Story Critical words.

Display the Teaching Chart. Read each sentence and identify the new word. Then use the questions below to help students understand each word. When necessary, provide a definition.

TEACHING CHART 88: VOCABULARY **88**

1. **discontented** (not happy; wanting things different)
   The horse was *discontented* in his new home at first, but soon he felt happy.
2. **elevator** (cage that carries people or things up or down in a building)
   He liked riding up and down in the *elevator*.
3. **stall** (a section for one animal in a stable)
   The *stall* he was given in the barn was stuffy and too small for him to move around in.
4. **picnicking** (having or going on a picnic)
   While some people were *picnicking*, the horse helped himself to some of their food!
5. **plow** (a tool used in farming to cut into the soil and turn it up)
   The horse pulled a *plow* through a field.
6. **policeman** (a member of the police department)
   The horse made friends with a *policeman*.
7. **pockets** (small pouches sewn into clothing)
   The policeman would put his hands in his *pockets* and take out treats.

---

discontented

1. What word in the sentence is the opposite of *discontented*? *(happy)*
When someone is discontented, how might they behave? (walk slowly, look sad, not want to do anything)   STRATEGY: ANTONYMS

elevator **2. Tell about times when you have ridden in an elevator. What did you like most about it?** STRATEGY: PRIOR EXPERIENCE

stall **3. What kinds of animals might stay in a stall in a barn?** (horses, cows, sheep, pigs) STRATEGY: CLASSIFICATION

picnicking **4. Tell about a time when you have gone picnicking. Under what heading on the map might *picnicking* be listed?** *(Activities)* STRATEGY: CLASSIFICATION

plow **5. What clues in sentence 5 helped you to know that a plow was a piece of farm equipment?** (horse pulled; through a field) STRATEGY: CONTEXT CLUES

policeman **6. Why is a policeman an important person in a neighborhood?** (He makes sure people obey the laws and helps keep people safe.) STRATEGY: PRIOR KNOWLEDGE

pockets **7. What kinds of things can you keep in your pockets?** (money, snacks, mittens, papers, pencils, toys) STRATEGY: CLASSIFICATION

Discuss Support words as needed. The Glossary of the Student Text includes definitions of the Support words: *trough, weathervane, shafts, babbling,* and *horn.*

Present Character words. Pronounce these Character words before students read the selection: *Joey, Mr. Polaski, Percheron.*

Provide independent practice. Options for independent practice are shown in the Resource Center below.

WRITING OR SPEAKING ACTIVITY *Have students tell or write brief stories from the points of view of farm animals. Ask them to use new vocabulary as much as possible.*

TEACHER CHOICE

Workbook page 145

Using New Words

SELECTION VOCABULARY

NAME _____

A. Complete the sentences with words from the box.

| discontented | elevator | picnicking | plow |
| pockets | policeman | stall | |

I know a farmer who will never get rich, and his

(1) _____pockets_____ are often empty. Yet he's almost

never (2) _____discontented_____ . In spring he uses a

(3) _____plow_____ in his fields. In summer he

sometimes takes a fine day off for (4) _____picnicking_____

He cleans out every animal (5) _____stall_____ all year

round. Life is quiet for the farmer, and he doesn't often need a

(6) _____policeman_____ . If he wants to see bright lights

and ride an (7) _____elevator_____ , he must visit the city.

B. Use a word from the box to write the answer to each riddle.

8. When can you see more ants than there are in an ant hill?
_____picnicking_____

9. What takes you up or down but may leave your stomach behind?
_____elevator_____

10. What can have change without changing? _____pockets_____

11. What may a car have in common with a horse? _____stall_____

C. On separate paper, write sentences of your own to describe what you might see on a farm. Use some of the story words. See Teacher Notes.

Selection Vocabulary "The Horse Who Lived Upstairs" **145**

RESOURCE CENTER

◄ **Workbook page 145** provides practice with Story Critical words.

Skills Practice 133 ▶ provides additional practice with Story Critical words.

Skills Practice 134 provides practice with Support words.

Spelling Connection Master 57 may be used for spelling instruction with the new vocabulary.

Workbook reuse option: Have students underline all the words on the page that name things usually found on farms.

Skills Practice 133

NAME _____

SKILLS PRACTICE 133

Vocabulary: Story Critical Words

A. Study the meaning of each word.

discontented not happy with how things are
elevator something that carries people and things between floors in a building
picnicking having or going on a picnic

plow a farm tool used to dig into and turn up earth
pockets small pouches sewn into clothing
policeman a member of the police force
stall a section in a stable for one animal

B. Use the clues to complete the puzzle.

Across

2. Farmers use this to get the earth ready for planting crops.
3. A happy person does not feel this way.
5. A horse or cow could sleep here.
6. You can put your hands in these.

Down

1. This person helps keep a neighborhood safe.
2. You could be doing this in a park.
4. Without this, you have to walk up stairs.

LEVEL 8 "The Horse Who Lived Upstairs" Definition clues **133**

561

Reading & Responding

Building Background

Motivate discussion with a challenge.

Give students the following challenge. Ask them to imagine where they might like to live, and the many ways in which their lives would be different if they lived elsewhere.

In the next three minutes, write down all the places you would like to live during your lifetime.

Build background about making changes.

Point out to students that while it is fun to imagine living in different places, it is often not easy to get used to living in another place. Ask students what might be fun and what might be difficult. (*A new place has new things to explore, new people to meet, new experiences that could be fun and exciting. A new place means getting used to new surroundings, missing old friends, missing favorite spots, having to get used to new things, not being able to do some of the same things.*)

Discuss fantasy.

Tell students they are going to read a fantasy about a horse who is not happy about his new home. Point out that in a fantasy, things happen that could never happen in real life. Ask students what kinds of things they could expect in a fantasy about a horse who lives in a city. (*Animals might act like people and talk to each other; the horse might live in a city building.*)

Developing a Purpose for Reading

Option 1
Students set purpose.

ORAL "PREDICTION" LISTS   Have students preview the title, the art, and the introduction to the story. Ask them to predict what changes the title character might make in his life. Record students' predictions for later use.

WRITING ACTIVITY   Have students work individually or in pairs to write their predictions. Instruct students to keep their papers for later use.

Option 2
Teacher sets purpose.

Have students read to find out what changes Joey wants in his life and what happens when he gets them.

Meeting
Individual
Needs

EXTRA HELP   Tell students that the next story is about a horse who moves from the city to the country. Distribute the form for main idea/details, Form 10 in the Teacher Resource Kit. Have students write these headings on the form: *The Horse Worked in the City* and *The Horse Worked in the Country*. Suggest that as students read, they write the details that belong under each heading. After reading, have students use the completed forms to summarize the story.

ACHIEVING ENGLISH PROFICIENCY   Write the word *discontented* on the chalkboard and have students repeat it after you. Tell them that *contented* means "happy." Point out that they already know the meaning of the prefix *dis-* ("not"); then call on a volunteer to tell the meaning of *discontented*. Write the following words on the chalkboard: *agree, approve, connect, honest, like*. Have students repeat the words with you and then discuss the meanings of the words. Finally, show how each can be made into a new word by adding *dis-* to the beginning. Have the group tell the meanings of the new words. For additional help in story comprehension use Master 33 in the Teacher Resource Kit.

The Horse Who Lived
Upstairs

by Phyllis McGinley

Joey was a city horse who wanted to live in the country. Then one day, Joey got his wish!

There was once a horse named Joey who was discontented. He was <u>discontented</u> because he didn't live in a red barn with a weathervane on top like this, and he didn't live in a green meadow where he could run about and kick up his heels like this. Instead, he lived upstairs in a big brick building in New York.

Joey worked for Mr. Polaski, who sold fruits and vegetables to city people. Joey pulled the vegetable wagon through the city streets. And in New York, there isn't room for barns or meadows.

Reader's Journal   **p 110**
Preparing for Reading

WHAT A LIFE

Looking at a painting of a farm scene, students pretend to be one of the animals and write about life on the farm.

GUIDED READING

✔ **Page 289   Where does the story take place?** (New York City)   RECALL: SETTING

✔ **Page 289   What kind of place would have the red barn and green meadow that Joey wants?** (a farm; the country)   INFER: LOCATION

STRATEGIC READING

Page 289   Have students think about story clues and use their own experiences to make a prediction about what Joey will do next. (run away to the country; feel more and more unhappy) Have students continue to read, encouraging them to change their predictions as necessary.   APPLICATION: STRATEGY FOR READING

✔ Skill from The Bridge applied through this question.

So every night when Joey came home, he stepped out from the shafts of the wagon and into an <u>elevator</u>, and up he went to his <u>stall</u> on the fourth floor of the big brick building. It was a fine stall and Joey was very comfortable there. He had plenty of oats to eat and plenty of fresh straw to lie on. He even had a window to look out of. But still Joey was discontented.

"How I long to sip fresh water from a babbling brook!" he often exclaimed. And then he would sniff discontentedly at the old bathtub near the elevator that served him as a watering trough.

It wasn't that he had to work hard. Mr. Polaski was kind to him and brought him home at five o'clock every day.

In the winter Joey had a blanket to wear on his back to keep him warm. And in the summertime Mr. Polaski got him a hat to wear on his head to keep him cool. And every day he had many interesting adventures. Sometimes he met a <u>policeman</u> who gave him sugar. Sometimes ladies patted him on the nose and fed him carrots. He was introduced to the high-bred horses who drew the hansom cabs along the plaza. He saw the children playing in the playgrounds and the parks. But it made no difference to Joey.

"This is no life for a horse," he used to say to the Percheron who lived in the next stall to him. "We city horses don't know what real living is. I want to move to the country and sleep in a red barn with a weathervane on top and kick up my heels in a green meadow."

So how happy he was when one day Mr. Polaski said to him, "Joey, I think I could sell more vegetables if I drove a truck. I will miss you, Joey, but you will like it on the farm where I am going to send you."

When Joey reached the country, sure enough, there was the barn with its weathervane, and there was the meadow.

GUIDED READING

Page 290   In what ways is Joey's life in the city a comfortable one? (He has a fine stall and plenty of food; he has a kind master; he has interesting adventures; people are kind to him.)   SYNTHESIZE; SUMMARIZING

Page 291   What kind of animal is a Percheron? What clues helped you to know? (Students should realize the Percheron is a horse because the story says it lives in a stall next to Joey; when Joey speaks to the Percheron, he says, "We horses.")   INFER: ANIMALS

✔ **Page 291   The author does not say when this story takes place. What do clues in the story and the pictures, and what you know yourself, tell you about the time?** (It is not the present. A horse pulling a vegetable wagon does not happen today. The pictures give a feeling of a different time.)   INFER: TIME

STRATEGIC READING

Page 291   Have students summarize what has happened so far in the story. (Joey, a horse who pulls a vegetable wagon in the city, longs for a life in the country. One day, Joey's owner decides to send him to a farm in the country.) Ask students to use story clues and their own experiences to predict how Joey's life will change when he moves to the farm. (Students may predict that Joey will be happy since this is what he has always wanted, or Joey will miss the old way of life in the city, Mr. Polaski, and his friends.) Remind students that no one can always guess correctly and that making predictions is useful even if the predictions are not always correct. Encourage students to continue making predictions as they read, changing and revising predictions as necessary. Have students check their predictions and decide if this strategy helped them at the end of the story.   APPLICATION: STRATEGY FOR READING

✔ Skill from **The Bridge** applied through this question.

"This is the life!" cried Joey to himself. But poor Joey! The barn was cold in winter and hot in summer. He didn't have a blanket and he didn't have a hat. And he had very little time to kick up his heels in the green meadow, for all day long he pulled a plow through the earth. A plow is harder to pull than a wagon, and besides, the farmer worked from sunrise to sundown instead of the eight hours Joey was used to. Sometimes they forgot to put fresh straw in his stall, and nobody thought to give him sugar or carrots. There were plenty of children but they climbed on his back and teased him when he wanted to eat. And instead of the Percheron, there was a cross old gray horse next to him, who looked down his nose at Joey because Joey knew so little about farm life.

One day, when he wasn't pulling a plow because it was Sunday, Joey saw several people picnicking in the meadow. He decided to join them, for they looked as if they came from the city, and he thought they might have a lump of sugar in one of their pockets.

When he reached the spot, they had gone for a walk, so he ate up their lunch. When they came back, they were very angry and Joey was shut up in his stall for the rest of the day. He didn't even have a window to look out of. He was lonely for his friends, the policeman and the ladies who patted him on the nose. He was lonely for the high-bred horses and all the interesting sights of the city.

"I don't think I belong in the country after all," sighed Joey. "I am now more discontented than ever."

Next day he heard the honk of a horn. He looked from the door of the barn, and whom should he see but Mr. Polaski, getting out of the truck!

"I have come for Joey," Mr. Polaski told the farmer. "I cannot get any more tires for my truck, so I think I will sell fruit and vegetables from my wagon again."

GUIDED READING

Page 292   What does Joey exclaim when he first arrives on the farm? ("This is the life!") **What is the first clue that suggests this may not be so?** (In the very next sentence, the author writes, "But poor Joey!")   ANALYZE: COMPARISON

Page 293   What does Joey realize? (that life in the country is not better; that he does not belong there) INFER: FEELINGS/ATTITUDES

Page 293   What happens to help Joey with his problem? (One day he hears a horn honk; it is Mr. Polaski who has come to take Joey back home to the city.)   RECALL: PLOT

STRATEGIC READING

✔ **Page 293   Call on individuals to summarize** what has happened since Joey moved to the country. (Joey thought he would be happy, but he was mistaken. He became more and more unhappy with country life.) **Then ask students to predict** what will happen to Joey and how he will feel if he returns to the city with Mr. Polaski. (Joey will probably be happy in his old stall with his old friends.) **Suggest** that when students have trouble summarizing, they reread those parts of the story that are confusing. At completion of the story, ask students to check their predictions.   METACOGNITION: SUMMARIZING AND PREDICTING

✔ Informal Assessment Opportunity: SELF-MONITORING

My goodness, but Joey was happy! He went back to the city with Mr. Polaski and got into the elevator, and up he went to the fourth floor of the big brick building. There was his stall, and there was the window for him to look out of. And there was the friendly Percheron.

"Welcome back, Joey," exclaimed the Percheron. "I have missed you. The policeman has missed you. The lady customers have missed you, and so have the children in the playgrounds and the parks. Tell me, how did you like the country?"

"The country is all right for country animals," Joey said, "but I guess I am just a city horse at heart."

And he was never discontented again.

 Reader's Response

What surprised you in this story?

See next page for suggested answe

SELECTION FOLLOW-UP

The Horse Who Lived
Upstairs

Thinking It Over

1. What did Joey wish for?
2. How did people show that they cared about Joey? Tell how you got your answer.
3. Compare Joey's life in the city with his life on the farm.
4. What made Joey finally realize that he belonged in the city?
5. Do you think Mr. Polaski took Joey back because he really couldn't get tires for his truck? Explain.

Writing to Learn

THINK AND ANALYZE   How did Joey feel about the country before he went there? How did he feel about it after he got there? Copy and finish the chart below.

How Joey Felt About the Country...	
Before He Went There	After He Went There
The country was nice.	

WRITE   Read what you wrote in the chart. Then write a sentence to tell how you think Joey might have felt when Mr. Polaski said, "I have come for Joey."

GUIDED READING

Page 294   Do you think it was good for Joey to have seen what farm life was really like? Why? (Students may say that it was good because he realized how happy he was with city life.)   EVALUATE: POINT OF VIEW

RETURNING TO READING PURPOSE

OPTION 1   If students set the purpose, have them return to their lists of predictions and read them aloud. Discuss how close their predictions were to what really happened. Students may wish to discuss any surprises they encountered. (A horse's *not* being happy in the country may have been surprising.)

OPTION 2   If you set the purpose, ask students what big changes take place in Joey's life and what he realizes about it. (Joey wants and gets to live in the country. However, he works harder, no longer has a comfortable home, does not have the companionship of friends or time to enjoy himself. He realizes that he belongs in the city.)

Reader's Journal   p 111
Responding to Reading

MAKE THIS HORSE FEEL AT HOME

Pretending to be Joey's country owner, students tell what they would do to make Joey feel more at home.

SELECTION FOLLOW-UP

The Horse Who Lived
Upstairs

THINKING IT OVER

1. **What did Joey wish for?** (Possible answers: Joey wished that he lived in the country on a farm; he wanted to live in a red barn with a weathervane on top, run in a meadow and kick up his heels, and drink water from a brook.) RECALL: CHARACTER

2. **How did people show that they cared about Joey? Tell how you got your answer.** (Possible answers: Mr. Polaski always had lots of oats and fresh straw for Joey; he gave Joey a blanket in winter and a hat in summer; he did not work Joey too hard.) SYNTHESIZE: DRAWING CONCLUSIONS; METACOGNITION

3. **Compare Joey's life in the city with his life on the farm.** (Possible answers: Joey was comfortable in the city; in the country he was cold in winter and hot in summer; people were kind to him in the city; in the country children teased him; in the city he pulled a fruit and vegetable wagon; in the country he pulled a plow; he had many friends in the city; in the country he had none.) ANALYZE: COMPARISON

4. **What made Joey finally realize that he belonged in the city?** (Joey began to miss his city friends.) RECALL: CAUSE/EFFECT

5. **Do you think Mr. Polaski took Joey back because he really couldn't get tires for his truck? Explain.** (Possible answers: possibly Mr. Polaski missed Joey and wanted him back; his customers may have missed Joey. Accept all reasonable answers.) ANALYZE: CAUSE/EFFECT

WRITING TO LEARN

✔ *Use Writing Master 22, which duplicates this chart.*

THINK AND ANALYZE How did Joey feel about the country before he went there? How did he feel about it after he got there? Copy and finish the chart below. (Have students discuss Joey's feelings.)

How Joey Felt About the Country...	
Before He Went There	After He Went There
The country was nice.	

Extend comprehension through writing.

WRITE Read what you wrote on the chart. Then write a sentence to tell how you think Joey might have felt when Mr. Polaski said, "I have come for Joey." (Have students display their charts.)

✔ Informal Assessment Opportunity: EMPATHIZING WITH STORY CHARACTERS

More Ideas for Selection Follow-Up

CRITICAL AND CREATIVE THINKING QUESTIONS

Encourage a variety of responses and points of view.

Use these open-ended questions to encourage critical and creative thinking about the selection.

1. How would the world be different if everyone learned the lesson Joey learned in this story?

2. What did you learn about taking care of animals from this story? Why is it important to take good care of them?

3. Have you ever wanted to visit or live in a different kind of place from the one you live in now? Has the story made you change your mind? Why or why not?

REREADING ORALLY

Have students reread for expression.

Before students begin, review with them the elements of good, expressive reading: reading the words as though they were being spoken, paying attention to end punctuation, reading loudly and clearly enough to be heard and understood. To foster good reading, model expressive reading for them. Encourage students to take turns reading expressively with a partner. Have them take turns rereading the parts of the story that tell why Joey wanted to live in the country and why he did not like it once he had finally gotten his wish.

SELECTION COMPREHENSION

Provide comprehension check.

A Workbook page to check comprehension is shown in the Resource Center below. It may be used for informal assessment.

Workbook page 146

SELECTION COMPREHENSION

NAME _____

The Horse Who Lived Upstairs

A. Complete the summary of the story "The Horse Who Lived Upstairs."
Accept reasonable variations.
    This story is about a ___horse___ named Joey. Joey lived upstairs in ___a big brick building in New York___.
He worked for ___Mr. Polaski___, who sold fruits and vegetables from a wagon. Joey had a blanket to keep him warm in the winter and a hat to keep him cool in the summer. People gave him ___sugar and carrots___. He did not work too hard, but he still thought city life was no life for a horse.
    One day, Mr. Polaski told Joey that he was getting a ___truck___ so he could sell more vegetables. Joey was happy that he would be going ___to a farm___. But he soon found out that a barn was ___cold in winter and hot in summer___. He also had to work hard pulling a ___plow___ for the farmer from sunrise to sunset.
    After Joey ate a family's picnic lunch, he was locked in his stall with no friends and no window to look out. He became lonely for ___his friends and the sights of the city___.
Then Mr. Polaski came to take him back to the city, and Joey was never ___discontented___ again.

B. Imagine that you could live anyplace you chose. On separate paper, describe that place and tell why it might be better than where you live now. See Teacher Notes.

146   "The Horse Who Lived Upstairs"   Selection Comprehension

---

RESOURCE CENTER

◀ **Workbook page 146** is intended for use by all students.

Writing Master 22 duplicates the Writing to Learn chart.

LANGUAGE ARTS CONNECTIONS

CREATIVE THINKING: MAKING TRAVEL BROCHURES

Have students create travel brochures.

Ask students to tell the purpose of travel brochures. *(possible answers: to give information about a place; to show how pretty it is and make people want to visit it; to give people a good idea of what they can expect to find or do at a place)*

Tell students they will be working in groups to create travel brochures that will advertise vacations on a farm or in a city. The groups can decide which. Have students brainstorm and list some words and phrases that will convince people to travel there. Have students list the kinds of pictures that would show nice things. Students may refer to their lists as they make their brochures. Students can draw pictures and write the "copy" for their illustrations. Suggest that one student in each group make the cover for the brochure.   SHARED LEARNING: WRITING

IMPROVISING STORY SCENES

Have students improvise scenes.

Review with students that *improvising* means making up dialogue as you go along. When improvising a scene, actors have an idea of what they will say and how they will act, but it is not planned. Actors listen to other actors carefully so they can respond with something that makes sense.

Have students work with partners to develop and act out scenes between Joey and one of the other characters. Suggest the following scenes for students to choose from: Joey telling Mr. Polaski why he is discontented and how the country will make him happier; Joey telling the farm horse about city life with the aim of convincing that animal to visit the city; Joey telling the Percheron why he is glad to be home again.   SHARED LEARNING: SPEAKING

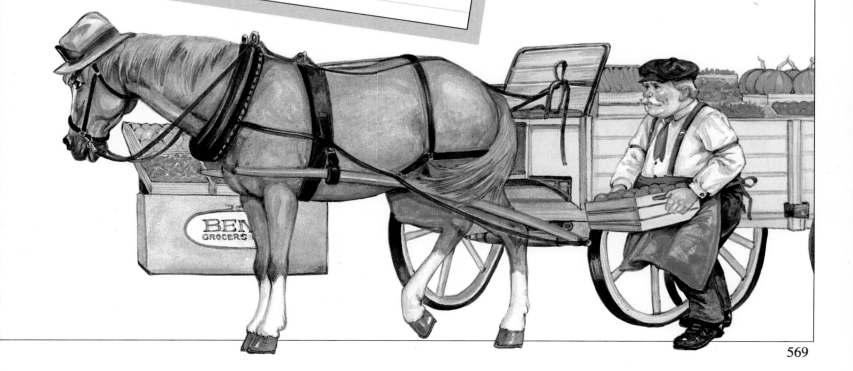

WRITING POST CARDS

Review the parts of a post card.

Review with students the purpose and parts of a post card. You may wish to reproduce or copy the diagram below on the chalkboard. Ask how a post card is different from a letter. *(It is shorter because there is less room to write. It has a space for the name and address.)*

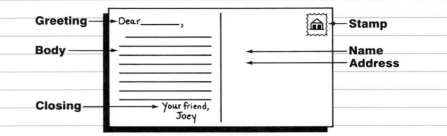

Greeting → Dear_____,

Body

Closing → Your friend,
Joey

Stamp

Name
Address

WRITING POST CARDS (continued)

Have students write post cards from Joey.

Have students pretend they are Joey and they live in the country. Tell them to write post cards as Joey to the Percheron in New York, describing what has happened to him on the farm. Remind students to cut out the post cards so they know the amount of space they have. Tell each student to draw a picture on one side and write a message and the Percheron's address on the other. Each student can make up a name and an address for the Percheron.   WRITING

POINT OF VIEW

Have students write stories from the point of view of a country horse.

Review with students that a story can be told from a particular point of view. Explain that "The Horse Who Lived Upstairs" is told from Joey's point of view—how he feels, what he wants to do, and what happens to him.

Tell students they will work in small groups to write stories from the point of view of a country horse who is discontented and wants to live in the city and what happens to him when he gets his wish. Remind students to include a beginning, a middle, and an end in their stories. Students may want to illustrate their stories and put the stories and drawings into a book for their classmates to read. **Language Arts Master 19** can be used with this activity.   CHALLENGE: WRITING

COMPARING STORY THEMES

Compare story themes.

Point out to students that in "The Horse Who Lived Upstairs" the author uses Joey's experience to give a message to readers. Ask students what it is that Joey learns. *(Something that one thinks is better somewhere else may not actually be better.)* Ask students if they know of any other stories with the same message. Mention the expression "the grass is always greener on the other side."

Read aloud the fable *Country Mouse, Town Mouse.* Discuss ways in which the stories are alike and different. Ask students how the lesson the country mouse learns is similar to the lesson Joey learns. *(When the country mouse moves to the city, he finds out that while there are more things in the city, it is safer and more peaceful in the country. The grass is not greener in the city.)* WHOLE CLASS ENRICHMENT

READING EVERY DAY

The fantasy "The Horse Who Lived Upstairs" might prompt students to want to read other humorous fantasies. Here are two titles to share with them.

Burt Dow, Deep Water Man by Robert McCloskey. Viking Press, © 1963. When Burt, an old Maine fisherman, doesn't heed the warning his pet gull may be trying to give him, he becomes embroiled in a fantastic adventure at sea— one that makes a *whale* of a story!

Poem Stew by William Cole. Harper & Row, © 1981. An amusing array of poems about food, with a generous dash of flavorful fantasy, including everything from a recipe rhyme for rhinoceros stew to a talking salami sub.

〰️ **A World of Books** Classroom Libraries selection 〰️

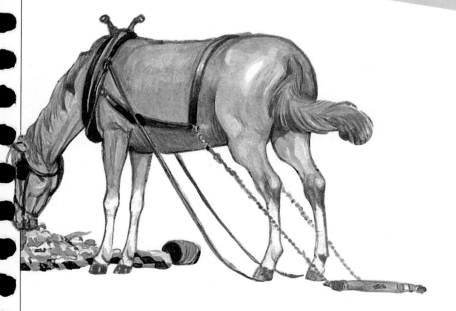

Reader's Journal	pp 112, 113
Extending Reading	

CLYDESDALE AND COMPANY

After looking at pictures of different types of horses, students decide which one they like best, explain their choice, and describe an adventure they might have together.

Selection Support

SKILL TRACE: PREFIXES				
Introduction	Practice	Test	Reteach	Maintain
TE 546	572	594	635	641	See Level 9.

WORD STUDY

Prefixes de-, dis-

OBJECTIVE Using structural analysis to determine word meaning.

Review prefixes de- and dis-.

Remind students that a prefix is a letter or group of letters added to the beginning of a word. The prefix *de-* means "remove from." The prefix *dis-* means "not."

Use Teaching Chart to review the use of prefixes de- and dis-.

Read sentence 1. Have students choose which of the two prefixes should be written in the blank to complete the word and the sentence correctly. Write the prefix and have students explain how it changes the meaning of the base word. Have students "think aloud" as they complete the remaining sentences.

TEACHING CHART 89: PREFIXES DE-, DIS-

89

1. Joey the horse was __(dis)__ pleased with his life in the city.
2. You might say he was __(dis)__ contented.
3. He was ready to __(de)__ camp and go home.
4. In the country the farmer __(dis)__ trusted Joey and locked him up.
5. Joey had felt like a king in the city, but he felt he had been __(de)__ throned in the country.

Provide independent practice.

Options for independent practice are shown in the Resource Center below.

Workbook page 147

RESOURCE CENTER

Skills Practice 135

NAME _____

WORD STUDY

Prefixes *de-, dis-*

REMEMBER: The prefix *de-* means "do the opposite of." The prefix *dis-* means "not to."

A. Complete the sentences with the words from the box.

debug	defrost	disappear
discontent	discover	displease

1. Did the sugar the policeman kept for Joey ___disappear___ quickly?
2. Joey wanted to move to the country because he felt such ___discontent___ .
3. Joey's country stall was so cold it needed to ___defrost___ .
4. Did Joey ___displease___ the people at the picnic?
5. They needed to ___debug___ the park because there were so many ants.
6. What did Joey ___discover___ in the stall?

B. Use the word you wrote in Part A to fill in the chart.

Prefix	Base Word		Prefix	Base Word
7. dis-	appear	8. dis-	content
9. de-	frost	10. dis-	please
11. de-	bug	12. dis-	cover

C. On separate paper, write a sentence of your own for each word in the chart in Part B. See Teacher Notes.

Prefixes *de-, dis-*　　　　"The Horse Who Lived Upstairs"　**147**

▸ **Workbook page 147** is intended for use by all students.

Skills Practice 135 ▸ may be assigned for additional practice.

Workbook reuse option: Have students draw a vertical line between the base word and the prefix of all the words in the box in Part A.

NAME _____

SKILLS PRACTICE 135

Prefixes *de-, dis-*

The prefix *de-* means "to do the opposite of" or "remove from."
The prefix *dis-* means "not."

deplane = remove from the plane
dislike = not like

A. Match the words to their definitions. Write the number of the correct definition next to each word.

1. not happy	defrost	4
2. to remove from sight	disappear	2
3. a feeling of pain or worry	deplane	6
4. to remove ice	displeased	1
5. not to agree	discomfort	3
6. to remove from the plane	distrust	8
7. to remove a code	disagree	5
8. not to have trust in something	decode	7

B. Use the words above to change the underlined word or phrase in each sentence. Write the word that has almost the same meaning.

9. He didn't want to remove himself from the plane. ___deplane___
10. The food in front of me will soon be gone . ___disappear___
11. They will remove the code from the message. ___decode___
12. He is not happy about what his sister did. ___displeased___
13. The man removes the ice from the car windows. ___defrosts___

C. Find an antonym for each of these words. Write a word with a *de-* or *dis-* prefix.

14. believe ___distrust___　17. agree ___disagree___
15. happy ___displeased___　18. be seen ___disappear___
16. comfort ___discomfort___　19. freeze ___defrost___

LEVEL 8　　"The Horse Who Lived Upstairs"　**135**

SKILL TRACE: MULTIPLE MEANINGS					
Introduction	Practice		Test	Reteach	Maintain
TE 522	549	573	635	638	See Level 9.

VOCABULARY SKILLS

Multiple Meanings

OBJECTIVE Choosing the appropriate meaning of a multiple-meaning word.

Review multiple meanings.

Remind students that many words have more than one meaning and readers have to watch for them so they will not be confused. As an example, read the following two sentences aloud and have students tell the meaning of *run*.

1. Joey wanted to live in a green meadow where he could *run* around. (move about quickly)

2. In the city, he had to push the elevator button to *run* it. (make something work; operate it)

Have students use multiple-meaning words in sentences.

Display the Chart. Read the sentences aloud. Tell students to write the letter of the correct meaning in the parentheses next to each underlined word.

TEACHING CHART 90: MULTIPLE MEANINGS **90**

1. Mr. Polaski made a living (a) with his horse Joey who enjoyed living (b) in the city.
  a. earned money in order to live   **b.** making a home in
2. For a long (a) time, Joey said, "How I long (b) to live in the country!"
  a. a great amount of   **b.** want very much; to have a great desire
3. Joey was through (b) pulling the wagon through (a) the city streets.
  a. in or to places   **b.** finished, done

Provide independent practice.

Options for independent practice are shown in the Resource Center below.

Workbook page 148

VOCABULARY

NAME _____

Multiple Meanings

REMEMBER: Many words have more than one meaning. Use context to determine the meaning of a word in a sentence or story.

A. Complete each sentence with a word from the box. Write each word twice, using a different meaning each time.

beat	block	fire	rings

1. When Joey hears the ___beat___ of a drum, he knows it means a parade is about to start.

2. Everyone on the ___block___ lines up on the street to watch.

3. At the head of the parade there is a ___fire___ engine.

4. Then comes a clown tossing ___rings___ in the air.

5. Other clowns ___fire___ toy guns.

6. The police are there to ___block___ cars from getting near the parade.

7. A bell around a horse's neck ___rings___ merrily.

8. When the parade is over, Joey tries to ___beat___ another horse back to his stall.

B. Choose one word from the box in Part A. On separate paper, write two meanings for the word. See Teacher Notes.

148 "The Horse Who Lived Upstairs" Multiple Meanings

RESOURCE CENTER

◀ **Workbook page 148** is intended for use by all students.

Skills Practice 136 ▶ may be assigned for additional practice.

Workbook reuse option: Have students write a sentence at the bottom of the page that shows a third meaning for one of the given words.

Skills Practice 136

NAME _____

SKILLS PRACTICE **136**

Multiple Meanings

Many words have more than one meaning. Use context clues to determine the meaning of a word in a sentence or a story.

A. In each sentence, write a word from the box that fits in both blanks.

back	kind	mean	park	running
can	left	meet	pet	train

1. Mom ___left___ her ___left___ shoe to be fixed at the shop.

2. Tim checked to make sure his watch was ___running___, and then went to buy some ___running___ shoes.

3. I ___can___ open the ___can___ of cat food.

4. Dad hurt his ___back___ at work, so he came ___back___ home.

5. Kim is ___kind___ to every ___kind___ of animal.

6. My baby brother likes to ___pet___ our ___pet___ pig.

7. I'll ___meet___ you at the track ___meet___.

8. Mr. Gale will ___park___ his car at the entrance of the ___park___.

9. What do you ___mean___ when you say I am a ___mean___ person?

10. We want to ___train___ our dog to sit in a cage so that we can take him on a ___train___ ride.

B. Circle the meaning of the underlined word in each sentence.

11. Meg got her glasses fixed today.
  things to drink from   [things to help you see]

12. Cleaning out the pen was Jake's least favorite job.
  [place to keep animals]   thing to write with

136 LEVEL 8   "The Horse Who Lived Upstairs"

SKILL TRACE: SUFFIX				
Introduction	Practice	Test	Reteach	Maintain
TE 344	372	421	461	465	574

WORD STUDY

Suffix -ment

OBJECTIVE Using structural analysis to determine word meaning.

Review suffix -ment.

Remind students that a suffix is a letter or a group of letters added to the end of a word. A suffix changes the meaning of a base word. Point out that the suffix *-ment* changes a verb to a noun.

Have students add the suffix -ment to base words.

You may wish to write the following base words on the chalkboard: *agree, enjoy, move, pave*, and *treat*. Read aloud or reproduce the sentences below. Have students add the suffix *-ment* to each base word and then use the resulting words to complete the sentences. Answers are printed in red.

> **1.** The (movement) of Joey's feet made a clacking sound.
> **2.** The high-bred horses stepped proudly along the (pavement) .
> **3.** Joey's (enjoyment) of the country ended very quickly.
> **4.** The farmer's (treatment) of Joey was not as good as Mr. Polaski's.
> **5.** Joey is in (agreement) with people who say the city is the best place to be.

Provide independent practice.

An independent activity is shown in the Resource Center below.

RESOURCE CENTER

Skills Practice 137 ▶ may be assigned for additional practice.

Skills Practice 137

NAME _____

SKILLS PRACTICE 137

Suffix *-ment*

The suffix *-ment* changes a verb to a noun. It means "the state or act of."

A. Read the story. Write each word from the box where it belongs.

| amazement | embarrassment | improvement |
| disagreements | entertainment | treatment |

Charlie and Diane always argue and get into **disagreements** _____.

If Charlie says "yes," Diane says "no." Being with them sometimes caused us **embarrassment** _____.

We thought their **treatment** _____ of each other was not very good. Imagine our **amazement** _____ when we saw Charlie and Diane laughing and playing together today. What an **improvement** _____! We asked what had happened. But Charlie and Diane laughed at us.

"We are friends," they said. "Don't you know a good argument can be great **entertainment** _____?"

B. Underline the root word in each word listed below. Then choose the meaning in the box that goes with each word, and write the meaning.

1. amazement   **state of being surprised**
2. agreement   **state of agreeing**
3. movement   **the act of moving**
4. amusement   **state of being entertained**

| the act of moving | state of being entertained |
| state of agreeing | state of being surprised |

LEVEL 8   "The Horse Who Lived Upstairs"   **137**

CURRICULUM CONNECTIONS

PICTURING FARMS ART

Have students make pictures, maps, diagrams, or dioramas of a farm, including its buildings, animals, and fields. Encourage students to use information from their personal experiences on farms, facts they have gathered from research, and what they imagine farms to be like after having read "The Horse Who Lived Upstairs."

CROPS IN NEW YORK STATE SOCIAL STUDIES

Students should use encyclopedias, product maps, and other reference sources to locate information about the products produced on farms in the state of New York. Instruct students to make lists of the main crops and where they are produced. Encourage students to copy or trace a map of New York on sheets of paper and to draw symbols on the map to represent the crops. Tell students also to locate facts about the products of their own state. **Curriculum Connection Master 19** can be used with this activity.

HORSE TRIVIA SCIENCE

Students may work with partners or in small groups to research horses. Have students locate information on these topics: what horses eat, breeds of horses, and which breeds are best suited for working, racing, riding, and so on. Some group members could prepare posters or large, labeled drawings showing different types of horses. The information may be gathered from encyclopedias and dictionaries that include pictures.

	Teaching Sequence	Trade Books and Resources	Meeting Individual Needs	Integrated Language Arts / Cross Curriculum
The Bridge Pages 578–579	**Maintain** Comparison	• Teaching Chart 91 • Workbook 149 • Skills Practice 138		
PART 1 **Vocabulary Strategies** Pages 580–581	**Develop Concepts** Brainstorming Feelings **Teach Vocabulary** **STORY CRITICAL WORDS:** complain, **dawn,** displeased, faults, **household,** messenger, temper, **worthy** (Tested words are boldfaced.)	• Teaching Chart 92 • Workbook 150 • Skills Practice 139	**SUPPORT WORDS:** chamber, destination, garments, interrupted, millet, preparations, relief • Skills Practice 140 **CHARACTER/SETTING WORDS:** Manyara, Mufaro, Nyasha, Nyoka	**WRITING/SPEAKING ACTIVITY:** Use new vocabulary to describe good and bad moods. • Spelling Connection 58
PART 2 **Reading & Responding** Pages 582–593	**Build Background** **Develop a Purpose for Reading** **Guide the Reading Process** **Selection Follow-Up**	• Reader's Journal 114–117 • Workbook 151 **READING EVERY DAY** *In the Land of Small Dragon,* told by D.M. Kha to A.N. Clark *Why Mosquitos Buzz in People's Ears,* by V. Aardema	**EXTRA HELP:** Classifying Story Events as Make-believe or Real **ACHIEVING ENGLISH PROFICIENCY:** Discussing Story Words and Phrases • Achieving English Proficiency Master 34	**Language Arts Connections** **WRITING TO LEARN:** Write character riddles. • Writing Master 23 **SPEAKING/LISTENING:** Improvising Story Scenes; Retelling African Tales **WRITING:** Composing Modern-Day Cinderella Stories; Making Character Clusters • Language Arts Master 20
PART 3 **Selection Support** Pages 594–597			**Practice** • Teaching Charts 93–94 • Workbook 152–153 • Skills Practice 141–142 Prefixes *de-, dis-* (Tested) Long Word Decoding (Tested) **Maintain** • Skills Practice 143 Inferences	**Curriculum Connections** **MATHEMATICS:** Creating and Solving Word Problems • Curriculum Connection Master 20 **SOCIAL STUDIES:** Making Maps of African Countries **ART:** Designing and Decorating African Masks

MUFARO'S *Beautiful* DAUGHTERS
AN AFRICAN TALE

written and illustrated by John Steptoe

SUMMARY *An African villager, Mufaro, has two beautiful daughters, Manyara and Nyasha. Manyara is as greedy and selfish as Nyasha is generous and kind. When the Great King decides to choose a wife, Mufaro sends both his daughters. During the journey Manyara and Nyasha face some "tests" by magical beings, and the true nature of each daughter is shown. The king chooses Nyasha, and Manyara becomes her servant. Mufaro's Beautiful Daughters was named a **Caldecott Honor** book in 1988, the second time John Steptoe received this award.*

CALDECOTT
MEDAL
1988

The Bridge

SKILL TRACE: COMPARISON					
Introduction	Practice	Test	Reteach	Maintain	
TE 176	196	292	311	312	349	578	619

COMPREHENSION

Teaching Comparison

OBJECTIVE Understanding likenesses and differences in longer texts.

1. WARM-UP

Use a known passage to make a comparison.

Tell students they will listen to a passage from the previous story, "The Horse Who Lived Upstairs." Point out that the author uses comparison to explain why Joey the horse was discontented. Have students listen for what things are being compared and for the word that signals a comparison is being made. *(where Joey didn't live — barn and meadow; where he did live — brick building; instead)*

> **There was once a horse named Joey who was discontented. He was discontented because he didn't live in a red barn with a weathervane on top . . . and he didn't live in a green meadow. . . . Instead, he lived upstairs in a big brick building in New York.**

Discuss words that signal comparisons.

Reread the passage. Ask students how they would know, even without the word *instead*, that a comparison is being made. *(The passage tells about different places to live.)* Ask students how these places are alike and how they are different. *(Alike: All are places to live. Different: Barn and meadow are in the country; brick building is in the city.)*

State the objective.

Tell students they will review how to recognize and understand comparisons, or how things are alike and different.

2. TEACH

Explain why knowing about comparisons is important.

Knowing about comparisons helps readers understand how things are alike and different. It also helps them better understand what they read.

Present a strategy for understanding comparisons.

Tell students there is a strategy they can use to help them understand comparisons. First, read and think about what things are being compared. See if any word signals the comparison. Then use word clues and your own experience to tell how the things are alike and different.

TEACHING CHART 91: COMPARISONS 91

Before there were many cars, people like Mr. Polaski sold things from horse-drawn wagons. People were able to buy only what the farmers nearby could grow. Today, high-speed trains, airplanes, and huge trucks carry food. They take food from where it is grown to big supermarkets.

Model the strategy.

Display the Teaching Chart and call on a volunteer to read the paragraph aloud. Explain to students that the writer is comparing how food was sold long ago with how it is sold today. Have students reread the paragraph to look for the comparison.

3. GUIDED PRACTICE

Before going on, have students explain how to recognize and understand comparisons. *(Look for what things are being compared and use word and experience clues to tell how the things are alike or different.)*

Guide students in using the strategy.

Call on a volunteer to name what is being compared. *(how food was sold in earlier times, how food is sold today)* Write these headings on the board. Have students list the points from the paragraph that belong under each heading. *(Long ago: carried and sold from horse-drawn wagons, sold what was grown locally; today: food carried by trains, planes, trucks; sold in supermarkets; sold all over country)* When students have finished, discuss the comparisons.

4. WRAP-UP

Summarize instruction.

Review why readers should know about comparisons and what kinds of clues they can use to understand them. *(to understand how things are alike and different; word and experience clues)*

Provide independent practice.

Options for independent practice are shown in the Resource Center below.

5. APPLICATION

Students will make comparisons as they read "Mufaro's Beautiful Daughters." The symbol ✔ marks specific questions and activities that apply this skill.

Workbook page 149

NAME _____

Comparison   COMPREHENSION

> **REMEMBER: Comparisons** tell how things, people, or events are alike and different. Signal words and story clues help you understand comparisons.

A. Write the word that completes each statement. Then write the answer to each question.

1. Tell how Joey got to his stall.
   a. In the city he took an ____elevator____ .
   b. In the country he just ____walked____ into his stall.
   c. Were the ways he got to his stall alike or different? ____different____

2. Tell about the kind of work Joey did.
   a. In the city he ____pulled____ things.
   b. In the country he ____pulled____ things.
   c. Were the kinds of work alike or different? ____alike____

3. Tell about Joey's friends.
   a. In the city he had ____many____ friends.
   b. In the country he had ____no____ friends.
   c. Were the places alike or different? ____different____

4. Tell about where Joey lived.
   a. In the city Joey lived in a big brick ____building____ .
   b. In the country he lived in a red ____barn____ .
   c. Were the places alike or different? ____different____

B. On separate paper, write two sentences. Tell one way you and a friend are alike. Tell one way you are different. See Teacher Notes.

Comparison   "Mufaro's Beautiful Daughters" **149**

RESOURCE CENTER

◀ **Workbook page 149** is intended for use by all students.

Skills Practice 138 ▶ may be assigned for additional practice.

Workbook reuse option: Have each student write one sentence at the bottom of the page telling what they think was the biggest difference between Joey's life in the city and his life in the country.

Skills Practice 138

NAME _____

SKILLS PRACTICE ◀**138**▶

Comparison

Comparisons tell how things, people, or events are alike and different. Signal words and story clues help you understand comparisons.

> 1. Read the story.
> 2. Look for what is being compared.
> 3. Think about how the things are alike and how they are different.

Read the two paragraphs about Helen Keller. Think about how she was *before* and *after* a teacher helped her.

> From the time that Helen Keller was very young, she couldn't see or hear. Helen seemed smart, but no one could be sure. Her family didn't know how to teach her anything, not even how to behave. So Helen did what she wanted. She grabbed food from plates. She acted wild. Sometimes Helen seemed angry, and sometimes she seemed sad. But no one really knew how Helen felt.
>
> Then Helen's family got a teacher for Helen. The teacher worked hard with Helen and had great success. Now Helen calmed down. Soon she learned how to behave well. Most important, Helen learned that there are words for people, things, and feelings. Helen learned to listen and speak through a sign language made by fingers moving in the palm of a hand. She also learned a way to read and write. Now Helen could tell people when she was angry or sad. Most of the time, she was happy, because she had become part of the world.

1. Tell how Helen Keller was when she was very young.
   She seemed smart. She acted wild. She did what she wanted.
   She grabbed food from plates. She was angry and sad.

2. Tell some ways that Helen was different later, after her teacher helped her.
   She knew what words were. She could use a sign language.
   She could read and write. She was happy.

3. How was Helen Keller the same before and after her teacher helped her?
   She still could not see or hear.

138 LEVEL 8   "Mufaro's Beautiful Daughters"

Vocabulary Strategies

Developing Concepts

Use brainstorming to tap prior knowledge about being in good moods and bad moods.

Discuss the expressions *good mood* and *bad mood* as a starting point for teaching vocabulary. Encourage students to describe how they feel and what they do when they are in good and bad moods. *(good mood: laugh, play, enjoy being with others; bad mood: do not feel like being with others, are sad or angry, seldom laugh)* Ask students to brainstorm words that describe someone in each mood. Then list their responses on the chalkboard.

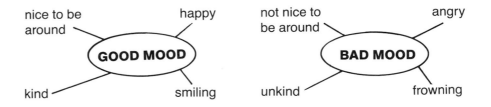

nice to be around   happy

GOOD MOOD

kind   smiling

not nice to be around   angry

BAD MOOD

unkind   frowning

Teaching Vocabulary

Discuss meanings of Story Critical words.

Read each context sentence on the Teaching Chart and identify the new word. Then use the questions below to help students understand each word. When necessary, provide a definition.

TEACHING CHART 92: VOCABULARY   92

1. **temper** (mood)
   The girl was in such a bad mood that she was sent to her room until she was in a better *temper*.
2. **complain** (to find fault)
   She would *complain* and find things wrong with everything.
3. **displeased** (failed to please)
   The girl *displeased* her father who was not at all happy about the way she acted.
4. **faults** (failings, imperfections)
   But he knew that some people act mean if they feel they are not perfect and have many *faults*.
5. **worthy** (having value)
   He told his daughter he felt she was a fine and *worthy* person.
6. **household** (all the persons who live in one house)
   The whole *household* thought he was wrong about his daughter.
7. **messenger** (a person who carries a communication)
   One night, a *messenger* brought news that a storm had destroyed a nearby village.
8. **dawn** (daybreak)
   At *dawn*, just as the sun was rising, the girl set out to help the villagers and prove her father was right.

---

temper   **1. What other words or phrases mean about the same as *temper*?**
(mood, state of mind, feeling)   STRATEGY: SYNONYMS

complain

2. What things might a person complain about? (Possible answers: doing homework, not feeling well) **Under which heading on the board would *complain* fit?** *(Bad Mood)* STRATEGY: PRIOR KNOWLEDGE

displeased

3. What is the prefix in *displeased* and what does it mean? *(dis-, "not")* **Under which heading would *displeased* fit?** *(Bad Mood)* STRATEGY: STRUCTURAL ANALYSIS

faults

4. What faults might someone have? (Possible answers: a bad temper, complaining, lying, being lazy) STRATEGY: PRIOR KNOWLEDGE

worthy

5. What character traits might make someone worthy of being liked or admired? (Accept all reasonable answers.) STRATEGY: PRIOR KNOWLEDGE

household

6. What people might live together in a household? (Possible answers: mother, father, brother, sister, grandparents) STRATEGY: CLASSIFICATION

messenger

7. What things might a messenger bring? (Possible answers: a letter, a telegram, a package) STRATEGY: CLASSIFICATION

dawn

8. What words and phrases mean about the same as dawn? (daybreak, sunrise, early morning) STRATEGY: SYNONYMS

Discuss Support words as needed.

The Glossary of the Student Text includes definitions of the Support words: *relief, destination, interrupted, preparations, chamber, millet, garments.*

Discuss Character words as needed.

Present and pronounce the character words: *Manyara* (män yä′ rə), *Nyoka* (nyo′ kä), *Nyasha* (nya′ shə), *Mufaro* (mə fä′ ro).

Provide independent practice.

Options for independent practice are shown in the Resource Center below.

WRITING OR SPEAKING ACTIVITY *Have students use some of the Story Critical and Support words to describe what they do when they are in good moods and what they do when they are in bad moods.*

Workbook page 150

SELECTION VOCABULARY

NAME _____

Using New Words

A. Complete each sentence with a word from the box.

| complain | displeased | faults | temper | worthy |

1. Manyara showed her bad mood by always being in a terrible __temper__ .

2. When she was in this mood, she would tease her sister and __complain__ about her.

3. At these times almost everything __displeased__ her.

4. She was not nice and had many other __faults__ as well.

5. Because of her faults, Manyara was not __worthy__ to be queen.

B. Write the center word of each word map. Choose a word from the box that relates to the other words in the map.

| dawn | household | messenger |

letter / travel / note / news / tell / carry — **3. messenger**

pink sky / sun / morning / early / wake / singing birds — **1. dawn**

sister / mother / father / aunt — **2. household**

C. On separate paper, make your own word map. Write a story word from Part A in the middle of the map. Then around it write other words that are related to it. See Teacher Notes.

150 "Mufaro's Beautiful Daughters" Selection Vocabulary

RESOURCE CENTER

◀ **Workbook page 150** provides practice with Story Critical words.

Skills Practice 139 ▶ provides practice with Story Critical words.

Skills Practice 140 provides practice with Support words.

Spelling Connection Master 58 may be used for spelling instruction with the new vocabulary.

Workbook reuse option: Have students add other words of their own choosing to the maps in Part B.

NAME _____

SKILLS PRACTICE 139

Vocabulary: Story Critical Words

A. Study the meaning of each word.

complain to find fault	**household** all the people who live in one house
dawn daybreak	**messenger** a person who carries a message
displeased failed to please	**temper** a mood
faults failings	**worthy** having value

B. Match a vocabulary word with each antonym given below.

1. sunset __dawn__
2. charmed __displeased__
3. cheap __worthy__

C. Write the vocabulary word that answers each riddle.

4. We keep things from being perfect. What are we? __faults__

5. I am made up of people who live together. What am I? __household__

6. I follow the night. What am I? __dawn__

7. I help people communicate with each other. Who am I? __messenger__

D. Complete each sentence with the correct vocabulary word.

8. The child was in a bad __temper__ because he was sick.

9. The food in the restaurant __displeased__ the man, so he did not eat there again.

10. It is no use to __complain__ about bad weather.

11. The __messenger__ carried all his messages in a big pouch.

12. Mother knows how to manage our __household__ .

13. At __dawn__ , the sun peeked up over the mountain.

14. Some people try to hide their __faults__ .

LEVEL 8 "Mufaro's Beautiful Daughters" Classification **139**

Reading & Responding

Building Background

Motivate discussion about folk tales using a phrase.

Write the phrase below on the chalkboard. Call on students to supply the titles of their favorite stories that begin with the words "Once upon a time. . . ." Then ask where students are most likely to see this phrase. *(at the beginning of folk or fairy tales)*

Once upon a time . . .

Build background about folk tales.

Explain to students that folk tales are stories that have been passed down through the years by a particular group of people. They often feature animals and sometimes have magical characters. The events in them are often things that could not happen in real life. Many folk tales have a moral or lesson, such as "Kind actions will be rewarded."

Discuss the Caldecott Medal and the author.

Tell students that the next story, "Mufaro's Beautiful Daughters," was a 1988 Caldecott Honor Book. Explain that this honor is given each year to certain books with outstanding illustrations. The author, John Steptoe, also illustrated the book. Have students find and read the John Steptoe entry in About the Authors at the back of their student texts. Discuss John Steptoe's feelings about writing.

Developing a Purpose for Reading

Option 1
Students set purpose.

ORAL "QUESTION" LISTS   Ask students to look at the title of the story and illustrations. Then have them read the story introduction. Have students form questions about what they think will happen to the sisters.

WRITING ACTIVITY   Have students work individually or in pairs to create written "Question" lists. Save them for later use.

Option 2
Teacher sets purpose.

Have students read to find out how the sisters Manyara and Nyasha are alike and different, and what the character of each sister has to do with what happens to her.

Meeting
Individual
Needs

EXTRA HELP   Remind students of the discussion about folk tales in Building Background. Tell students that many stories, such as the one they are about to read, combine make-believe things with events and people who could be real. Have students write two headings on a sheet of paper: *Make-believe* and *Real*. As they read, ask students to list the story events and characters they think belong under each heading. Later, have students share their lists and see how many elements were identified.

ACHIEVING ENGLISH PROFICIENCY   Assign the following words or phrases to small heterogeneous groups of students: *bad temper, servant, plentiful, to part from (someone), comfort*, and *celebration*. Tell each group that they are to find out the meaning of their word or phrase and then explain it to the rest of the class. Suggest that they begin by checking a dictionary for the meaning. Then, they should decide among themselves how to help their classmates understand the meaning. Tell students that they can use drawings, words, pantomime, or even short skits to convey the meanings. For additional help in story comprehension, use Master 34 in the Teacher Resource Kit.

A young woman expresses kindness to everyone she meets. Even the king learns of her goodness— in a most surprising way.

MUFARO'S *Beautiful* DAUGHTERS
AN AFRICAN TALE

written and illustrated by John Steptoe

CALDECOTT
HONOR
1988

A long time ago, in a certain place in Africa, a small village lay across a river and half a day's journey from a city where a great king lived. A man named Mufaro (əm fä′ rō) lived in this village with his two daughters, who were called Manyara (män yä′ rə) and Nyasha (nyä′ shə). Everyone agreed that Manyara and Nyasha were very beautiful.

Reader's Journal   **p 114**
Preparing for Reading

ANYTHING CAN HAPPEN!

Inspired by a fanciful picture, students list things that might happen if they were writing a folk tale to go with the picture.

GUIDED READING

Page 297   Where and when does the story take place? (a long time ago in a small village in Africa)
RECALL: SETTING

✔ **Page 297   How are Mufaro's two daughters alike?** (They are both beautiful.)   ANALYZE: COMPARISON

HIGHLIGHTING LITERATURE

Page 297   Point out to students that this folk tale comes from Africa and was told aloud long before it was written down. Read this first page aloud and have the students close their eyes and imagine the story being told by a storyteller around a fire.

✔ Skill from The Bridge applied through this question.

Manyara was almost always in a bad temper. She teased her sister whenever their father's back was turned, and she had been heard to say, "Someday, Nyasha, I will be a queen, and you will be a servant in my household."

"If that should come to pass," Nyasha responded, "I will be pleased to serve you. But why do you say such things? You are clever and strong and beautiful. Why are you so unhappy?"

"Because everyone talks about how kind *you* are, and they praise everything you do," Manyara replied. "I'm certain that Father loves you best. But when I am a queen, everyone will know that your silly kindness is only weakness."

Nyasha was sad that Manyara felt this way, but she ignored her sister's words and went about her chores. Nyasha kept a small plot of land, on which she grew millet, sunflowers, yams, and vegetables. She always sang as she worked, and some said it was her singing that made her crops more bountiful than anyone else's.

One day, Nyasha noticed a small garden snake resting beneath a yam vine. "Good day, little Nyoka (nyō' kä)," she called to him. "You are welcome here. You will keep away any creatures who might spoil my vegetables." She bent forward, gave the little snake a loving pat on the head, and then returned to her work.

P 298   MUFARO'S BEAUTIFUL DAUGHTERS   P 299

GUIDED READING

✔ **Page 298   What is the difference between Manyara's and Nyasha's personalities?** (Nyasha is humble and kind; Manyara is proud and cruel.)
ANALYZE: COMPARISON

Page 298   Why might Nyasha think that Manyara is unhappy? (Possible answer: Unhappy people often strike out at others.)   INFER: FEELINGS/ATTITUDES

Page 299   What does Nyasha's treatment of the garden snake show about the kind of person she is? (It shows she is trusting and kind to animals.)
INFER: FEELINGS/ATTITUDES

Page 299   How do you think Manyara would have treated Nyoka if he had appeared in her garden? Why do you think so? (Possible answer: She would have driven him away because she is an unkind person.)   INFER: PEOPLE

✔ **Skill from The Bridge applied through this question.**

HIGHLIGHTING LITERATURE

Page 298   Point out Manyara's statement, "Someday, Nyasha, I will be a queen and you will be a servant in my household." Explain that in folk tales, when "evil" or "nasty" characters predict something good will happen to them or something bad will happen to another character, it is often a clue that the opposite will happen.

From that day on, Nyoka was always at Nyasha's side when she tended her garden. It was said that she sang all the more sweetly when he was there.

Mufaro knew nothing of how Manyara treated Nyasha. Nyasha was too considerate of her father's feelings to <u>complain</u>, and Manyara was always careful to behave herself when Mufaro was around.

Early one morning, a <u>messenger</u> from the city arrived. The Great King wanted a wife. "The Most <u>Worthy</u> and Beautiful Daughters in the Land are invited to appear before the King, and he will choose one to become Queen!" the messenger proclaimed.

Mufaro called Manyara and Nyasha to him. "It would be a great honor to have one of you chosen," he said. "Prepare yourselves to journey to the city. I will call together all our friends to make a wedding party. We will leave tomorrow as the sun rises."

"But, my father," Manyara said sweetly, "it would be painful for either of us to leave you, even to be wife to the king. I know Nyasha would grieve to death if she were parted from you. I am strong. Send me to the city, and let poor Nyasha be happy here with you."

Mufaro beamed with pride. "The king has asked for the most worthy and the most beautiful. No, Manyara, I cannot send you alone. Only a king can choose between two such worthy daughters. Both of you must go!"

That night, when everyone was asleep, Manyara stole quietly out of the village. She had never been in the forest at night before, and she was frightened, but her greed to be the first to appear before the king drove her on. In her hurry, she almost stumbled over a small boy who suddenly appeared, standing in the path.

GUIDED READING

Page 300   Why doesn't Mufaro know how Manyara treats Nyasha? (Nyasha does not complain to her father. Manyara is careful to behave around her father.)   RECALL: CHARACTER

Page 301   Why does Manyara leave her village in the middle of the night? (She wants to reach the king before anyone else, hoping this will improve her chances of becoming queen.)   ANALYZE: CHARACTER

✔ **Page 301   Do you think Manyara will improve her chances of becoming queen? Why or why not?** (Possible answers: no, because the King will learn about her trick and find her unworthy; yes, because she will reach the King first and convince him to marry her.)   SYNTHESIZE: PREDICTING OUTCOMES

Page 301   Who do you think the little boy is that Manyara meets in the forest? (possible answers: just a lost little boy; a magical creature such as a fairy) SYNTHESIZE: PREDICTING OUTCOMES

✔ **Informal Assessment Opportunity:**   PREDICTING

STRATEGIC READING

**Page 301   Ask students to visualize Manyara's leaving the village. Encourage them to picture how Manyara looks as she steals quietly through the village and into the dark forest. Allow students to describe their mental pictures. Remind them that if they are unable to visualize while reading, they might reread the section of the story that is confusing, paying particular attention to the descriptive words.   METACOGNITION: VISUALIZING

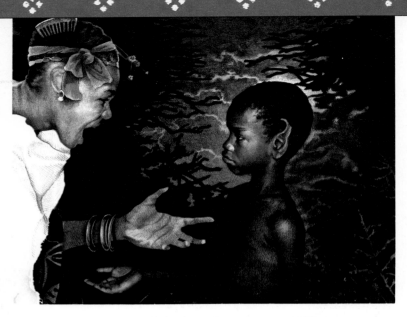

"Please," said the boy. "I am hungry. Will you give me something to eat?"

"I have brought only enough for myself," Manyara replied.

"But, please!" said the boy. "I am so *very* hungry."

"Out of my way, boy! Tomorrow I will become your queen. How dare you stand in my path?"

After traveling for what seemed to be a great distance, Manyara came to a small clearing. There, silhouetted against the moonlight, was an old woman seated on a large stone.

The old woman spoke. "I will give you some advice, Manyara. Soon after you pass the place where two paths cross, you will see a grove of trees. They will laugh at you. You must not laugh in return. Later, you will meet a man with his head under his arm. You must be polite to him."

"How do you know my name? How dare you advise your future queen? Stand aside, you ugly old woman!" Manyara scolded, and then rushed on her way without looking back.

Just as the old woman had foretold, Manyara came to a grove of trees, and they did indeed seem to be laughing at her.

"I must be calm," Manyara thought. "I will *not* be frightened." She looked up at the trees and laughed out loud. "I laugh at you, trees!" she shouted, and she hurried on.

It was not yet dawn when Manyara heard the sound of rushing water. "The river must be up ahead," she thought. "The great city is just on the other side."

But there, on the rise, she saw a man with his head tucked under his arm. Manyara ran past him without speaking. "A queen acknowledges only those who please her," she said to herself. "I will be queen. I will be queen," she chanted, as she hurried on toward the city.

GUIDED READING

Page 302   How does Manyara treat the little boy? (She is selfish and unkind. She refuses to give him anything to eat.)   RECALL: DETAILS

✔ **Page 303   How is Manyara's treatment of the old woman like her treatment of the little boy?** (She is rude and unkind to both, and she thinks being unkind is all right because she is their future queen.) ANALYZE: COMPARISON

Page 303   How is the old woman correct? (The trees seem to laugh at Manyara, and she meets a man with his head tucked under his arm.)   RECALL: DETAILS

Page 303   Who do you think this woman is? (possible answers: a fairy godmother, a magical queen)   INFER: PEOPLE

Page 303   Why does Manyara laugh at the trees and refuse to talk to the man? (to show that she is not frightened of them)   ANALYZE: CHARACTER

✔ Skill from The Bridge applied through this question.

HIGHLIGHTING LITERATURE

Pages 302–303   Tell students that things often happen in threes in folk tales. On these pages, for instance, Manyara meets three different beings: a small boy, an old woman, and a man with his head under his arm.

Nyasha woke at the first light of <u>dawn</u>. As she put on her finest garments, she thought how her life might be changed forever beyond this day. "I'd much prefer to live here," she admitted to herself. "I'd hate to leave this village and never see my father or sing to little Nyoka again."

Her thoughts were interrupted by loud shouts and a commotion from the wedding party assembled outside. Manyara was missing! Everyone bustled about, searching and calling for her. When they found her footprints on the path that led to the city, they decided to go on as planned.

As the wedding party moved through the forest, brightly plumed birds darted about in the cool green shadows beneath the trees. Though anxious about her sister, Nyasha was soon filled with excitement about all there was to see.

They were deep in the forest when she saw the small boy standing by the side of the path.

"You must be hungry," she said, and handed him a yam she had brought for her lunch. The boy smiled and disappeared as quietly as he had come.

Later, as they were approaching the place where the two paths crossed, the old woman appeared and silently pointed the way to the city. Nyasha thanked her and gave her a small pouch filled with sunflower seeds.

The sun was high in the sky when the party came to the grove of towering trees. Their uppermost branches seemed to bow down to Nyasha as she passed beneath them.

At last, someone announced that they were near their destination.

Nyasha ran ahead and topped the rise before the others could catch up with her. She stood transfixed at her first sight of the city. "Oh, my father," she called. "A great spirit must stand guard here! Just look at what lies before us. I never in all my life dreamed there could be anything so beautiful!"

Arm in arm, Nyasha and her father descended the hill, crossed the river, and approached the city gate. Just as they entered through the great doors, the air was rent by piercing cries, and Manyara ran wildly out of a chamber at the center of the enclosure. When she saw Nyasha, she fell upon her, sobbing.

GUIDED READING

Page 304   **Why does the wedding party decide to go on when they find Manyara's footprints on the path that leads to the city?** (Possible answers: They decide Manyara is safe; they guess what she has done and why.)   INFER: CAUSE/EFFECT

✔ **Page 304**   **How is Nyasha's treatment of the boy and the old woman different from Manyara's?** (Nyasha feeds the little boy, while Manyara let him go hungry; she is polite to the old woman and feeds her, while Manyara was rude to her.)   ANALYZE: COMPARISON

✔ **Page 305**   **How was Nyasha's journey different from Manyara's?** (Nyasha traveled in daylight, Manyara traveled at night; Nyasha traveled with her father and the wedding party, Manyara traveled alone; Nyasha did not meet laughing trees or a man with his head tucked under his arm as Manyara had.) SYNTHESIZE: COMPARISON

✔ **Skill from The Bridge applied through this question.**

STRATEGIC READING

Page 305   Have students summarize what has happened so far in the story and describe how Manyara and Nyasha are different. (The great king in the land where Manyara and Nyasha live wants to choose a wife. Mufaro wants both his daughters to go before the king. Manyara flees alone to get to the king before Nyasha. Nyasha travels with her father and the wedding party the following morning. Nyasha is good and kind to all she meets. Manyara is selfish and greedy.) Point out that summarizing and predicting can help readers understand what they read. Suggest that when students have trouble summarizing, they reread those parts of the story that are confusing. Then ask students to guess what they think caused Manyara to run screaming out of a chamber. Ask students to predict what will happen next. At the end of the story, ask students to check their predictions. METACOGNITION: SUMMARIZING AND PREDICTING

"Do not go to the king, my sister. Oh, please, Father, do not let her go!" she cried hysterically. "There's a great monster there, a snake with five heads! He said that he knew all my <u>faults</u> and that I <u>displeased</u> him. He would have swallowed me alive if I had not run. Oh, my sister, please do not go inside that place."

It frightened Nyasha to see her sister so upset. But, leaving her father to comfort Manyara, she bravely made her way to the chamber and opened the door.

On the seat of the great chief's stool lay the little garden snake. Nyasha laughed with relief and joy.

"My little friend," she exclaimed. "It's such a pleasure to see you, but why are you here?"

"I am the king," Nyoka replied.

And there, before Nyasha's eyes, the garden snake changed shape.

"I am the king. I am also the hungry boy with whom you shared a yam in the forest and the old woman to whom you made a gift of sunflower seeds. But you know me best as Nyoka. Because I have been all of these, I know you to be the Most Worthy and Most Beautiful Daughter in the Land. It would make me very happy if you would be my wife."

GUIDED READING

Page 306 How close was your prediction about why Manyara was screaming? Tell why it did or did not match what happened. (Allow students to discuss their predictions and evaluate them.)
EVALUATE: PREDICTING OUTCOMES

✔ **Page 306 How is Manyara's behavior different from the way she behaved toward Nyasha at the beginning of the story?** (Instead of being cruel to Nyasha, she tries to warn her away from danger.)
ANALYZE: COMPARISON

Page 306 Who had the king been before? (the garden snake, the hungry boy, and the old woman)
RECALL: DETAILS

HIGHLIGHTING LITERATURE

**Page 306 **Have students point out the events on this page that show it is a folk tale. (They will probably mention the king's ability to change shape by use of magic. They may also mention the idea of testing good and bad characters through disguises, a common theme in folk tales.) Encourage them to mention other folk tales in which good and bad characters are tested.

✔ Skill from **The Bridge** applied through this question.

And so it was that, a long time ago, Nyasha agreed to be married. The king's mother and sisters took Nyasha to their house, and the wedding preparations began. The best weavers in the land laid out their finest cloth for her wedding garments. Villagers from all around were invited to the celebration, and a great feast was held. Nyasha prepared the bread for the wedding feast from millet that had been brought from her village.

Mufaro declared to all who would hear him that he was the happiest father in all the land, for he was blessed with two beautiful and worthy daughters—Nyasha, the queen; and Manyara, a servant in the queen's household.

◆ LIBRARY LINK ◆

If you enjoyed reading this story by John Steptoe, you might like to read other books by this author, such as Train Ride.

Reader's Response

What pictures does this story create in your mind?

See next page for suggested answers.

SELECTION FOLLOW-UP

MUFARO'S BEAUTIFUL DAUGHTERS

Thinking It Over

1. How did Manyara feel toward her sister?
2. What was the real reason Manyara told her father that Nyasha should not leave home?
3. Why did the king appear to the sisters in so many different forms?
4. How did the king test Manyara and Nyasha? Tell some of the ways.
5. Do you think Manyara's behavior changed after what happened to her? How did you reach this conclusion?

Writing to Learn

THINK AND INVENT Many characters are in this story: Mufaro, Manyara, Nyasha, and the king who takes many shapes and forms. Read the character riddle below.

> **Character Riddle**
> I am a little creature.
> I stay by Nyasha's side.
> I like to hear her sing.
> Who am I?
>
> (Nyoka the snake)

WRITE Write a character riddle about one of the characters in the story. You may tell what the character says or does. See if others can guess your riddle.

GUIDED READING

Page 308 What do you think is the point or moral of this story? (Possible answers: Kind, humble people will be rewarded, and unkind, selfish people will not get what they want.) SYNTHESIZE: MAIN IDEA/DETAILS

RETURNING TO THE READING PURPOSE

OPTION 1 If students set the purpose, discuss the questions they generated. Then ask students to tell whether or not they think the outcome of the story was fair to both sisters. (Possible answer: Yes, because people who are good are rewarded.)

OPTION 2 If you set the purpose, ask students to compare Manyara and Nyasha. (Both are beautiful, but Nyasha is generous and kind while Manyara is greedy and selfish.) Have students explain how each sister's character had a lot to do with what finally happened to her. (Manyara treated the disguised king in a selfish and greedy way which kept her from being chosen as his wife. Nyasha treated him with kindness which caused him to choose her as his wife.)

Reader's Journal p 115
Responding to Reading

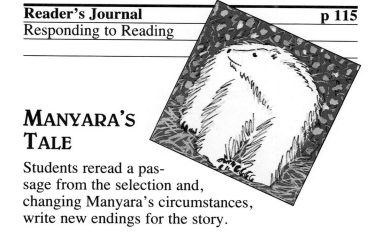

MANYARA'S TALE

Students reread a passage from the selection and, changing Manyara's circumstances, write new endings for the story.

SELECTION FOLLOW-UP

MUFARO'S BEAUTIFUL DAUGHTERS

THINKING IT OVER

1. **How did Manyara feel toward her sister?** (Manyara was jealous of Nyasha.)   INFER: FEELINGS/ATTITUDES

2. **What was the real reason Manyara told her father that Nyasha should not leave home?** (Manyara did not want the king to meet her sister; she was afraid the king would choose Nyasha as a wife.) ANALYZE: CHARACTER

3. **Why did the king appear to the sisters in so many different forms?** (Possible answers: The king wanted to find out what each sister was really like; the king was testing them; he had heard about their beauty and wanted to see what kind of people they were. Accept all reasonable responses.)   ANALYZE: CHARACTER

4. **How did the king test Manyara and Nyasha? Tell some of the ways.** (Possible answers: The king appeared in the forest as a hungry boy to see if the sisters were kind or selfish; he appeared as an old woman to see if they were respectful and if they followed advice; he appeared before Manyara as a man with his head under his arm to see if she could be polite to someone who did not please her.)   RECALL: DETAILS

5. **Do you think Manyara's behavior changed after what happened to her? How did you reach this conclusion?** (Students who say her behavior changed might suggest that Manyara had been so frightened by what happened that she became humble and offered to serve the king and queen. Students who say she did not change may suggest that she lived in the palace so that she would have a more comfortable life. Students may cite clues to Manyara's character in support of their conclusions; for example, her selfishness and acts of meanness toward her sister on the one hand and her desire to protect her sister from the snake with five heads on the other.)   SYNTHESIZE: PREDICTING OUTCOMES; METACOGNITION

WRITING TO LEARN

Use Writing Master 23, which duplicates this riddle.

THINK AND INVENT   Many characters are in this story: Mufaro, Manyara, Nyasha, and the king who takes many shapes and forms. Read the character riddle below. (Help students read the character riddle to prepare for writing.)

> **Character Riddle**
> I am a little creature.
> I stay by Nyasha's side.
> I like to hear her sing.
> Who am I?
>
> (Nyoka the snake.)

Extend comprehension through writing.

WRITE   Write a character riddle about one of the characters in the story. You may tell what the character says or does. See if others can guess your riddle. (Have students share their riddles.)

More Ideas for Selection Follow-Up

CRITICAL AND CREATIVE THINKING QUESTIONS

Encourage a variety of responses and points of view.

Use these open-ended questions to encourage critical and creative thinking about the selection.

1. Compare the way events turned out for Manyara with the way she had expected them to turn out.

✔ 2. The title of this unit is "Get the Message." What message do you think the author of this story wanted to share?

3. The illustrator of this story won the Caldecott Medal for his illustrations. Would you have chosen these illustrations for an award? Why or why not?

REREADING ORALLY

Have students reread for specific information.

Have students reread the parts of the story that remind them most strongly of the story of Cinderella. Examples might include the part where Manyara teases Nyasha on page 298 or the part where Manyara is unkind to the little boy and the old woman on pages 302–303, or the part where the king speaks to Nyasha on page 306. Encourage several students to work together to read the narration and dialogue. Suggest that they practice their reading together before performing for the class.

SELECTION COMPREHENSION

Provide comprehension check.

A Workbook page to check comprehension is shown in the Resource Center below. It may be used for informal assessment.

✔ Informal Assessment Opportunity: GENERALIZING

Workbook page 151

NAME _____

SELECTION COMPREHENSION

MUFARO'S BEAUTIFUL DAUGHTERS

A. Complete the summary of the story "Mufaro's Beautiful Daughters." Accept reasonable variations.

Mufaro and his daughters lived in ___a small village in Africa___

_____ . One daughter, ___Manyara___ , was greedy and bad-tempered. The other daughter, ___Nyasha___ , was kind and thoughtful. When Nyasha discovered a ___snake___ in her garden, she named it Nyoka and sang to it instead of chasing it away. She always tried her best to get along with her sister.

One day a king invited Mufaro to send his daughters to the city so that they could be considered when ___the king chose a wife___ .

Manyara left the village secretly at night so she could _____ ___be the first to see the king___ .

During her trip, she met a young boy who asked for food, an old woman who gave advice, and an old man. She did not ___help or listen to___ these people and hurried along.

Nyasha left for the city in the morning. When she met the boy and the old woman, she ___gave them food___ . At the city, she met her sister, who screamed a warning that the king was a terrible snake. Nyasha entered the city to find that the king was really ___Nyoka___ . He said that Nyasha was beautiful and worthy. He asked her to ___be his wife___ .

B. On separate paper, write what lesson you think Manyara learned from her experiences in the story. See Teacher Notes.

Selection Comprehension   "Mufaro's Beautiful Daughters"   **151**

RESOURCE CENTER

◄ **Workbook page 151** is intended for use by all students.

Writing Master 23 duplicates the Writing to Learn riddle.

LANGUAGE ARTS CONNECTIONS

CREATIVE THINKING: IMPROVISING SCENES

Have students present scenes from the story.

Have performers first decide on the scene they will act out; what the beginning, middle, and end of the scene should be; who the characters are; and what the setting is. Then, have students make up dialogue as the scene is being acted. The actors must listen carefully to one another so they will know how to respond in appropriate ways.

Have students work in small groups to improvise scenes from "Mufaro's Beautiful Daughters." Direct the groups to review the story and then choose scenes to improvise. As groups rehearse, remind them that each time they practice, the dialogue may be a little different. Then have the groups perform for the rest of the class.   SHARED LEARNING: SPEAKING

COMPOSING MODERN CINDERELLA STORIES

Have students compose modern versions of "Cinderella."

Discuss with students the plot of "Cinderella." Explain that this plot has been used time and again in folk tales, with just the location and characters changing. Remind them of the good and bad characters (Cinderella and her step sisters), the magical being who helps out (the fairy godmother), and the beings who change shape (mice into coach horses, coach into pumpkin).

Have students write modern-day versions of "Cinderella." Tell them to choose characters, decide if there will be magic in the story and which character will perform magic, decide if anything or anyone will change shape, decide if a lesson or moral will be included, and so on. Students may enjoy illustrating their stories. Call on several volunteers to share their work with the rest of the class.   CHALLENGE: WRITING

RETELLING AFRICAN TALES

Have students research African tales and retell one.

Remind students that "Mufaro's Beautiful Daughters" is an African tale. Tell students that they can find other African tales in collections of stories from around the world.

Have students research other African tales in the library. Then have each student select one that he or she particularly enjoys. Tell students to reread their selections several times to become thoroughly familiar with them. When students feel comfortable with the story lines of their tales, have them rehearse telling the story orally with partners. Then call on several volunteers to play "storyteller," and to retell their African tales to the rest of the group.   WHOLE CLASS ENRICHMENT

MAKING CHARACTER CLUSTERS

Have students create character clusters.

Explain to students that a character cluster is a diagram in which a character's name is written in the center and various traits the character has are written around it. In this way, a reader can better understand a story character's personality.

Have students discuss the character traits of each of the sisters in "Mufaro's Beautiful Daughters." Call on volunteers to name some of the events in the story that show what kind of person each of the sisters is. Then have students write the names Nyasha and Manyara on paper and add descriptive words around the characters' names. Have them use their character clusters to write short descriptive paragraphs about either Manyara or Nyasha. **Language Arts Master 20** can be used with this activity.   WRITING

READING EVERY DAY

Following their reading of "Mufaro's Beautiful Daughters," an African folk tale, students might enjoy reading other folk tales, such as the following.

In the Land of Small Dragon told by Dang Manh Kha to Ann Nolan Clark. Illustrated by Tony Chen. Viking Press, © 1979. In this Vietnamese version of the Cinderella story, a beautiful and obedient daughter whose stepmother treats her unfairly is finally rewarded for her kind deeds.

Why Mosquitos Buzz in People's Ears by Verna Aardema. Dial Press, © 1975. A retelling of a West African tale about a mosquito who tells an exaggerated story that sets off a chain of mishaps. In the end she realizes her mistake but takes up an even more disagreeable habit.   EASIER TO READ

Reader's Journal   pp 116, 117
Extending Reading

DIFFER-ENCES

Inspired by Nyasha and Manyara, students invent two main characters who share similarities but are also different in important ways. They write what could happen between these characters in a story.

Selection Support

WORD STUDY

Prefixes de-, dis-

OBJECTIVE   Using structural analysis to determine word meaning.

Review prefixes.

Remind students that a prefix is a letter or letters added to the beginning of a word and that a prefix changes the meaning of the word.

Use Teaching Chart to provide practice in building words with prefixes.

Display the Teaching Chart and read the prefixes and words at the top. Have students build and use the prefixed word that makes sense in each sentence. Then have them give the meaning of each prefixed word.

> **93**
>
> **TEACHING CHART 93: PREFIXES DE-, DIS-**
>
> de-   obeyed
> dis-   agreed
>   camped
>
> 1. Manyara often (disagreed) with Nyasha. (did not agree)
> 2. Manyara (disobeyed) her father and left the village before morning. (did not obey)
> 3. After the wedding, the wedding party (decamped) and went back to the village. (took apart their camp)

Provide independent practice.

Options for independent practice are shown in the Resource Center below.

Workbook page 152

RESOURCE CENTER

Skills Practice 141

NAME _____

WORD STUDY

Prefixes *de-, dis-*

REMEMBER: The prefix *de-* means "do the opposite of." The prefix *dis-* means "not to."

A. Add *dis-* to the base words. Write each new word and its meaning. Use the meaning of the base word to help you.

1. allow (let) ___disallow___ , ___not to let___
2. own (belong to) ___disown___ , ___not belong to___
3. band (to stay together) ___disband___ , not to stay together
4. prove (show something is true) ___disprove___ , show something is not true

B. Choose the word from the box that best completes each sentence.

decode	deflate	deplane	derail

5. The bicycle tires had been inflated with too much air, so the boys had to ___deflate___ them a little.
6. The engineer was afraid the train would ___derail___ , or go off the rails.
7. When the plane landed, Juan got ready to ___deplane___ .
8. Betsy and Brian had to ___decode___ the message written in code.

C. On separate paper, write four words that begin with the prefix *dis-* and four that begin with *de-*. Do not use words on this page. See Teacher Notes.

152 "Mufaro's Beautiful Daughters"   Prefixes *de-, dis-*

◄ **Workbook page 152** is intended for use by all students.

Skills Practice 141 ► may be assigned for additional practice.

Workbook reuse option: Have students circle the base word in each word they wrote in Parts A and B.

NAME _____

SKILLS PRACTICE ◄ **141**

Prefixes *de-, dis-*

The prefix *de-* means "to do the opposite of" or "to remove from."
The prefix *dis-* means "not."

> They were *disqualified* from the game because they couldn't *decode* the secret message.

A. Write the correct word to complete each sentence.

1. The sun came out, and the windows began to ___defrost___
   deform   defrost   detrain
2. The boys ___disagreed___ about how to play the game.
   distrust   disappeared   disagreed
3. In a magic trick, you can make something ___disappear___ .
   disappear   disagree   discomfort
4. Joe's cat jumped on his dresser and ___disarranged___ his things.
   disallow   disadvantage   disarranged
5. When we landed, the people began to ___deplane___ .
   dethrone   deplane   debug
6. You ___distrust___ people who do not tell the truth.
   displease   disagree   distrust
7. I was so ___displeased___ when I broke my bike.
   disliked   displeased   displaced
8. The small boy ___disconnected___ the wires in the TV.
   discontented   disconnected   disagreed

B. Answer each question using the word in dark print.

9. What food do you **dislike**? ___Sentences will vary.___

10. When were you **displeased** with a pet? _____

LEVEL B   "Mufaro's Beautiful Daughters"   **141**

SKILL TRACE: LONG WORD DECODING				
Introduction	Practice	Test	Reteach	Maintain
TE 498	524 595	635	640	See Level 9.

WORD STUDY
Long Word Decoding

OBJECTIVE Using the long word decoding strategy to read words.

Review the long word decoding strategy.

Recall with students the steps they have learned for figuring out long words when they read. Remind them to look first for words and word parts they know, then for syllables and vowel sounds. Next they should say the word, blending the syllables. If the word does not make sense, students should try different vowel sounds and add the stress to different syllables until the word makes sense.

Provide practice using the strategy.

Write the words *messenger, interrupted,* and *destination* on the chalkboard. Ask volunteers to read each word and tell what steps helped them. If necessary, guide students in using the strategy.

Have students read long words in context.

Display the Teaching Chart. Have students read the sentences and tell what steps helped them figure out the words in italics. Then have students tell the meanings of these words.

TEACHING CHART 94: READING LONG WORDS 94

1. Manyara was a *boastful* and *disagreeable* person.
2. She *willfully* betrayed her family.
3. Her *unpleasant* ways *troubled* the king.
4. The King *proclaimed* that the *splendid* Nyasha would be his queen.
5. Nyasha was *admired* for her *cheerful* and *generous* ways.

Provide independent practice.

Options for independent practice are shown in the Resource Center below.

Workbook page 153

NAME _____

DECODING

Long Word Decoding

REMEMBER: When you try to read a long word, look for words or word parts you know.

A. Circle the words or word parts you know. Underline the vowel letters.

1. brightness 2. gentle
3. cobra 4. basket
5. contentment 6. skateboard
7. battle 8. breakable

B. Use the words from Part A to complete each sentence.

9. A _____skateboard_____ is a board with wheels fixed to it.
10. People show their _____contentment_____ by smiling.
11. A _____cobra_____ is a kind of snake.
12. The _____brightness_____ of the sun is far greater than that of the moon.
13. Another word for a _____battle_____ is a fight.
14. The _____basket_____ was full of peaches.

C. On separate paper, use three of the words from Part A in sentences of your own. See Teacher Notes.

Long Word Decoding   "Mufaro's Beautiful Daughters" **153**

RESOURCE CENTER

◀ **Workbook page 153** is intended for use by all students.

Skills Practice 142 ▶ may be assigned for additional practice.

Workbook reuse option: Ask students to write above each word they wrote the number of syllables it contains.

Skills Practice 142

NAME _____

SKILLS PRACTICE 142

Long Word Decoding

To decode a long word:
1. Look for words or word parts.
2. Divide what is left into syllables.
3. Say each part slowly.
4. Try out different vowel sounds.

A. Here are some long words. Finish each sentence by circling the answer.

frostbite (damage to toes or other parts from cold)

1. The *o* in the first syllable sounds like the *o* in _____. tone [lost] torn
2. The second small word in this word rhymes with _____. dirt kit [kite]

accent (the special way people have of saying words)

3. The *a* in the first syllable sounds like the *a* in _____. train [avenue] able
4. The *e* in the second syllable sounds like the *e* in _____. tree steam [kept]

designate (to choose)

5. The second syllable rhymes with _____. age [pig] sigh
6. The third syllable rhymes with _____. [rate] flat cap
7. The first syllable has the same vowel sound you hear in _____. [less] least slipped

B. Write one of the three words from above to answer each question.

8. Which is a compound word?   frostbite
9. Which has three syllables in it?   designate

142 LEVEL 8   "Mufaro's Beautiful Daughters"

SKILL TRACE: INFERENCES				
Introduction	Practice	Test	Reteach	Maintain
TE 380	394	442	461	462	596

COMPREHENSION

Inferences

OBJECTIVE   Making inferences about feelings and attitudes.

Review inferences.

Remind students that making inferences is using clues to figure out information that is not stated.

Model making inferences.

You may wish to read aloud the passages below. Possible answers are shown in red. Each passage is followed by a question that asks students to make an inference. Read passage 1 and explain to students that the writer did not say how Nyasha feels about Nyoka. Since Nyasha sings more sweetly after Nyoka arrives, you can infer that she is happy to see Nyoka.

> **1.** Nyasha always sang as she worked. She sang all the more sweetly after Nyoka came to watch her. How do you think Nyasha feels about Nyoka? (happy to see him; story clues: *sang all the more sweetly*)
>
> **2.** After everyone was asleep, Manyara stole quietly out of the village. She had never been in the forest at night before. How do you think Manyara feels? (frightened; story clues; *never been in the forest at night before*)
>
> **3.** The air was filled with screaming. Manyara ran wildly out of a chamber. When she saw Nyasha, she fell upon her, sobbing. How do you think Manyara feels? (horrified, upset; story clues: *screaming, ran wildly, sobbing*)

Have students complete the remaining examples.

Call on students to make inferences for the remaining passages, giving the story clues they used.

Provide independent practice.

An optional independent activity is shown in the Resource Center below.

RESOURCE CENTER

Skills Practice 143 ▶
may be assigned for additional practice.

Skills Practice 143

NAME _____

SKILLS PRACTICE ◀143▶

Inference

When you make an **inference,** you use story clues and what you already know to figure out things that are not directly stated in the story.

Story clues
+ What I know
Inference

Read each story. Then read the sentence that follows each one. If it is an inference that can be made from the story, write **agree.** If it is not an inference that can be made from the story, write **disagree.** Then tell *why* you agree or disagree.

1. Mr. Harvey sat in the waiting room. He was meeting his sister's train. Mr. Harvey was a few minutes early. He was still waiting an hour later. Suddenly, there was a voice on the loudspeaker. Mr. Harvey smiled and jumped up.
   disagree _____ The train was going to be even later.
   Mr. Harvey seems happy. The train with his sister must be coming in.

2. Harold spends a lot of time in his garden. Each year he plans where to plant each vegetable. He prepares the ground and plants the seeds. He pulls the weeds and waters the young plants. When the vegetables are ready, he enjoys eating them. He also likes to share with friends.
   agree _____ Harold's garden is very important to him.
   He spends a lot of time in his garden.

3. Jodie woke up early Saturday. Her family was going on a picnic. Jodie's friend Max was invited. Jodie dialed Max's number. She let the phone ring two times and then hung up. Soon, Max arrived at Jodie's house.
   agree _____ Jodie told Max she would ring the phone twice when they were ready to leave.
   Max soon arrived at Jodie's house.

LEVEL 8   "Mufaro's Beautiful Daughters"   **143**

CURRICULUM CONNECTIONS

CEREMONIAL MASKS ART

Explain to students that masks are a traditional feature of many African ceremonies. If possible, show students pictures of African masks in encyclopedias and other reference books. Then provide each student with a large brown paper bag. Supply crayons and other crafts materials and have students design and decorate their own African masks.

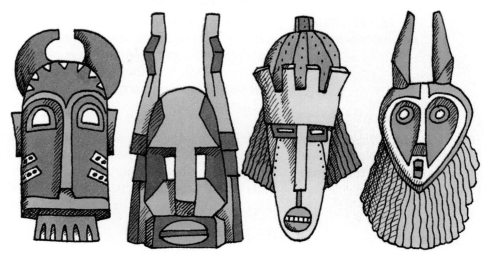

PROBLEMS TO PUZZLE MATHEMATICS

Tell students to imagine that although Nyasha's father returned to his village after the wedding, he often visited Nyasha and the king at the palace. Tell students that the distance between the village and the palace is ten miles. Tell them that Nyasha's father could walk two miles an hour. Then ask students to compute how long it would take Mufaro to walk from his village to the palace. *(five hours)* Have students make up and solve other word problems using the same information. Have them exchange papers and solve each other's word problems. **Curriculum Connection Master 20** can be used with this activity.

SHAPES OF AFRICA SOCIAL STUDIES

Show students a map of the continent of Africa. Point out the general shape of the continent and review the countries that are in Africa. Then have each student choose a country in Africa and make an outline map. Have him or her draw the general shape of the country and include the name of the capital city and other major cities. As an extension of this activity, you may wish to have students research the countries they have chosen.

LITERATURE LINK

OBJECTIVE   Recognizing and enjoying plays.

INTRODUCING AND READING THE LESSON

Tap students' prior knowledge.

Ask volunteers who have been in a play to tell the name of the play and the part they played. Then ask volunteers to tell how reading a play is different from reading a story. *(A play is a story that is acted out in front of an audience.)* Ask how they knew when to speak and what to say. *(Possible response: The characters' names are written next to the lines they are to say and act out.)*

Compare the structure of a play to the structure of a textbook.

Have students look at a social studies or science textbook. Ask them to name the parts of the book. *(possible responses: units, chapters, lessons)* Point out that like a textbook, a play is divided into parts, too. Plays are divided into parts called acts, and acts are sometimes divided into scenes. Explain that the lines the characters are to act out are included in each act and each scene.

Explain the usefulness of knowing how to recognize a play.

Explain to students that knowing the differences between plays and other kinds of writing will help them read plays more successfully, and therefore enable them to enjoy plays as they read or act them out.

State the objective.

Tell students that in this lesson they will learn how to recognize and enjoy plays.

Refer students to their texts.

Have students turn to pages 310–311 in their books and read the lesson.

LITERATURE LINK

Why are plays fun to read?

Picture yourself on a stage. You're in a costume. In front of you is an audience. You're in a play!

Looking Closely at a Play

A play is a story for people to act out. Sometimes, a writer will rewrite a story as a play. This lets the readers take part in the action. They can talk and act like the characters.

Here is a small part of the play "The Musicians of Bremen Town." You may have read the fairy tale as a story. Notice how the play looks different from the story.

Learning About Literature/Genre

NARRATOR: Now they were a very sad donkey, and cat, and dog, and rooster. *(All moan and cry.)* They didn't know what they could do. *(All shake their heads.)* They had to leave the farm. *(All nod.)* But where could they go, and what could they do to earn a living? *(All shrug.)* Then the donkey had an idea.
DONKEY: I have an idea!
CAT, DOG, and ROOSTER *(Excitedly)*: What? What?
DONKEY: Why don't we become famous singers? *(All look at him in surprise.)*

Here are some things you may have noticed. This play has a narrator who tells part of the story. The name of each character tells who is speaking. Often the speaking parts include directions that tell the characters what to do.

The following story, "The Boy Who Cried Wolf," is a famous fable rewritten as a play. Notice that the play is divided into acts. One of the acts is divided into scenes. Scenes let you know when there is a change in time or place.

Reading Plays

DISCUSSING THE LESSON

Review the main points of the lesson.

Check students' understanding of the lesson with these questions.

Page 311   How can you tell when a change in the time, place, or action occurs? (The scene changes.)

Page 311   How can you tell that you are reading a play rather than another kind of story? (Possible responses: Plays are written in acts and scenes; they often include directions that tell the characters what to do; the lines the characters are to act out are written next to the characters' names. Stories do not have acts and scenes, directions, or characters' lines written by their names.)

Page 311   If you were a character in a play, how would you know what to do and how to say your lines? (The writer includes directions for the characters.)

WRAP-UP

Direct students to the next selection.

Encourage students to use what they learned in this lesson to help them understand and enjoy the next selection, "The Boy Who Cried Wolf."

TEACHER CHOICE

	Teaching Sequence	Trade Books and Resources	Meeting Individual Needs	Integrated Language Arts / Cross Curriculum
The Bridge Pages 602–603	**Maintain** Predicting Outcomes	• Teaching Chart 95 • Workbook 154 • Skills Practice 144		
PART 1 Vocabulary Strategies Pages 604–605	**Develop Concepts** Creating a Concept Chart **Teach Vocabulary** **STORY CRITICAL WORDS:** exit, **flock, scene, sigh** (Tested words are boldfaced.)	• Teaching Chart 96 • Workbook 155 • Skills Practice 145	**SUPPORT WORDS:** empty, farmhands, nibble, pause • Skills Practice 146	**WRITING/SPEAKING ACTIVITY:** Use new vocabulary to write the first scene of a play about a shepherd boy. • Spelling Connection 59
PART 2 Reading & Responding Pages 606–617	**Build Background** **Develop a Purpose for Reading** **Guide the Reading Process** **Selection Follow-Up**	• Reader's Journal 118–121 • Workbook 156 **I→T KIT** Discussing and Creating a Fable; Listening to a Musical Story **READING EVERY DAY** *Aesop's Fables,* by T. Paxton *Three Aesop Fox Fables*, by P. Galdone	**EXTRA HELP:** Using Story Map Form **ACHIEVING ENGLISH PROFICIENCY:** Discussing Story Words • Achieving English Proficiency Master 35	**Language Arts Connections** **WRITING TO LEARN:** Write a journal entry for a shepherd boy. • Writing Master 24 **SPEAKING/LISTENING:** Developing a Story Map; Preparing to Dramatize a Play **WRITING:** Developing Character Clusters; Creating Dialogue for Minor Characters in a Play • Language Arts Master 21
PART 3 Selection Support Pages 618–621			**Practice** • Teaching Chart 97 • Workbook 157 • Skills Practice 147 Word Referents (Tested) **Maintain** • Skills Practice 148–149 Comparison Classification	**Curriculum Connections** **MUSIC:** Creating Songs for Story Characters • Curriculum Connection Master 21 **SOCIAL STUDIES:** Researching Sheep Farms; Researching Wool Production **ART:** Making Hand Puppets of Story Characters

The Boy Who Cried WOLF

an Aesop fable adapted by Genie Iverson

SUMMARY *Each day a shepherd boy must tend a herd of sheep alone, and he becomes lonely. On the first day, he sees an old woman and cries out that a wolf is after his sheep. The woman rushes to help, only to discover the boy has played a trick. On the next day, the boy plays the same trick on a farmer. A wolf really does appear on the third day, and when the boy cries, "Wolf!" to some passing farmhands, they ignore his cries for help. In the end, the boy realizes he should always tell the truth, saying to his father, ". . . because if I don't, people won't believe me when I do."*

The Bridge

SKILL TRACE: PREDICTING OUTCOMES	
Introduced in Level 7	Maintain
	TE 117 | 602

COMPREHENSION

Teaching Predicting Outcomes

OBJECTIVE   Using text and prior knowledge to predict logical outcomes.

1. WARM-UP

Use a known passage to make a prediction orally.

Tell students they will listen to a passage from the previous selection, "Mufaro's Beautiful Daughters." Explain that the author has not told exactly what will happen in the story, but he has given clues. Tell students that after you finish reading the passage, you are going to ask them to tell what they think will happen next. Have them listen for clues to make a guess about what will happen. *(Manyara will hurry on and not share her food.)*

> **Mufaro had two daughters. Nyasha was kind, and Manyara was selfish.**
>
> **"Please," the boy said to Manyara. "I am hungry. Will you give me something to eat?"**

Discuss story clues and "what I know" clues.

Reread the passage. Ask students whether they think Manyara will share her food. *(no)* Ask them why they think Manyara will not share. *(Manyara was selfish.)*

State the objective.

Tell students they will learn to use story clues and "what I know" clues to predict outcomes, or make guesses about what will happen in a story.

2. TEACH

Explain why predicting outcomes is important.

Predicting outcomes helps readers better understand and appreciate what they read.

Present a strategy for predicting outcomes.

Explain that there is a strategy students can use to help them predict outcomes. First, look for clues in the story that give you hints about what might happen. Next, think about what you know and make a prediction. Finally, read to see if your prediction was correct.

TEACHING CHART 95: PREDICTING OUTCOMES

95

1. Soon after Nyasha married the king, a small bird landed on her windowsill. "Oh, what a pretty little bird you are!" cried Nyasha. How will Nyasha treat the bird? (kindly; pretty little bird)
2. It was not long before Manyara became unhappy as a servant and jealous of her sister, the queen. One day a young kitchen maid came running to find Manyara. "Manyara, the cook wants you to tell her what Queen Nyasha's favorite dish is." What will Manyara do? (She will probably grumble; she may not know; Manyara is unhappy and jealous of Nyasha.)

Model the strategy.

Read passage 1 and point out the story clue—Nyasha's words "pretty little bird." Explain that since you know this clue indicates that Nyasha is good and kind, you can predict that she will treat the little bird kindly.

3. GUIDED PRACTICE

Check for understanding.

Before going on, have students explain how to predict outcomes. (*Look for story clues and think about what you know.*)

Guide students in using the strategy.

Have students use the strategy to predict outcomes for the second passage. Discuss story clues that helped them make predictions.

4. WRAP-UP

Summarize instruction.

Review why readers predict outcomes and the kinds of clues they use to make guesses about what will happen in a story. (*Exactly what will happen is not always explained in a story; readers use story clues and "what I know" clues.*)

Provide independent practice.

Options for independent practice are shown in the Resource Center below.

5. APPLICATION

Students will predict outcomes as they read "The Boy Who Cried Wolf." The symbol ✔ marks specific questions and activities that apply this skill.

Workbook page 154

COMPREHENSION
NAME _____
Predicting Outcomes

REMEMBER: When you **predict**, you make a guess about what will happen in a story. Use story clues and what you know to make a good prediction.

A. Find the story clues by answering the questions. Then use the clues to make each prediction.

1. a. What did Nyasha say when she found a snake in her garden? _____
She said, "You are welcome here."

b. What did people who knew Nyasha say about her? _____
They said she was kind and praised her.

c. Make a prediction about what kind of queen Nyasha will make. _____
She will be a kind and popular queen.

2. a. How did Manyara feel about Nyasha? _____
She was jealous.

b. What two dishonest things did she do to try and get the king to marry her? _____
She tried to have Nyasha stay home. She left early to get
to see the king first.

c. Make a prediction about how Manyara would act if she were queen. _____
She would still be jealous and do dishonest things.

B. On separate paper, write two or three sentences of your own to explain what helped you make the predictions you did. See Teacher Notes.

154   "The Boy Who Cried Wolf"   Predicting Outcomes

RESOURCE CENTER

◀ **Workbook page 154** is intended for use by all students.

Skills Practice 144 ▶ may be assigned for additional practice.

Workbook reuse option: Have students write sentences using figurative language to describe Manyara or Nyasha at the bottom of the page. Remind students that figurative language uses comparisons.

Skills Practice 144

NAME _____

SKILLS PRACTICE ◀144▶

Predicting Outcomes

When you read a story, think ahead and try to tell what will happen next. When you tell what you think will happen in a story, you are making a prediction. Use story clues and what you already know to make a good prediction.

| Story clues |
| What I know |
| Prediction |

Read the story about Cora's message. Write what you think might happen as the story goes along. Do not look ahead. Then see if your predictions are correct.

Cora called her friend Jill. Jill wasn't home. Jill's brother Freddy took the message. Cora said, "Tell Jill to come to my house Sunday at 1. Tell her to bring the white cat."

Freddy scribbled the message fast. His *t* in the word *cat* looked like an *r* and his *l* looked like a 7.

1. Predict the message Jill will read. _Answers will vary._

2. Underline the clues in the story that helped you make that prediction.
Jill read, "Go to Cora's house Sunday at 7. Bring the white car."
"What a funny message," said Jill. "Seven in the morning is too early, and seven at night is too late! Anyway, I don't have a white car!"

3. What message did Jill actually read? _Go to Cora's house Sunday at 7_
Bring the white car.

4. Now predict what Jill will do next. _Answers will vary._

5. What do you know from your own experience that helped you make that prediction? _Answers will vary._

Jill called Cora and read the message to her. Cora explained what she had said. "My brother Freddy needs to practice his handwriting," laughed Jill.

6. What did Jill actually do next? _She called Cora and asked her what_
she had said.

144   LEVEL 8   "The Boy Who Cried Wolf"

Vocabulary Strategies

Developing Concepts

Tap prior knowledge about shepherds with a concept chart.

Make a chart about the duties of a shepherd as a starting point for teaching vocabulary. Guide a discussion that includes ideas about a shepherd's responsibilities, what is enjoyable about a shepherd's job, and what is not enjoyable about it. Ask students for examples and list them on the chart under the following headings.

SHEPHERD'S JOB

Responsibilities	What Is Enjoyable	What Is Not Enjoyable
(watch over sheep, keep sheep from wandering off, protect sheep from wild animals)	(time to think, time to read, pleasant to work out of doors)	(no one to talk to, lonely, boring, have to stay out in all kinds of weather)

Teaching Vocabulary

Discuss meanings of Story Critical words.

Read each sentence on the Teaching Chart and identify the new word. Then use the questions that follow to help students understand each word. When necessary, provide a definition.

> **TEACHING CHART 96: VOCABULARY**   96
>
> 1. **flock** (a group of certain animals)
>   The play is about a shepherd boy who must watch his father's *flock* of sheep.
> 2. **scene** (part of a play)
>   In the first *scene* of the play the boy stands on a hillside talking to his father.
> 3. **sigh** (a long deep breath)
>   The shepherd gave a big *sigh* as he sat under a tree watching his sheep.
> 4. **exit** (leave)
>   After a farmer and his daughter speak to the boy, they walk away and then *exit* the stage.

flock   1. **What clue in sentence 1 helped you to know the meaning of *flock*?**
(of sheep)   STRATEGY: CONTEXT CLUES

scene

2. What clues in the sentence helped you figure out the meaning of *scene?* (first, play) **Where does this scene take place?** (on a hillside)
STRATEGY: CONTEXT CLUES

sigh

3. Have you ever let out a sigh? When do people sigh? (when they are tired, sad, bored, relieved) **Why might a shepherd boy let out a sigh?** (He might be tired, bored and lonely.)   STRATEGY: PRIOR KNOWLEDGE

exit

4. How do actors know when to exit the stage? (The director tells them; there are directions written in a play.) **Where in a play are the directions written that tell characters to exit?** (at the end of a character's lines, in parentheses, in the margin)   STRATEGY: PRIOR KNOWLEDGE

Discuss Support Words as needed.

The Glossary of the Student Text includes definitions of the Support words: *empty, nibble, pause, farmhands.* Have students discuss which words can be added to the chart.

Provide independent practice.

Options for independent practice are shown in the Resource Center below.

WRITING OR SPEAKING ACTIVITY   *Have students describe what might happen in the first scene of a play about a young shepherd boy. Encourage them to use as many of the new words as possible.*

Workbook page 155

NAME _____

SELECTION
VOCABULARY

Using New Words

A. Write a word from the box next to each meaning.

| exit | flock | scene | sigh |

1. ___exit___ to leave
2. ___sigh___ a long, deep breath
3. ___flock___ a group of certain animals
4. ___scene___ the place and time of a play

B. Write a word from the box to complete each sentence.

5. The air was so thin where the eagles flew, the mountain climber could only give a ___sigh___ .

6. First he lost his shoe, and then he lost his sock as he ran and chased the running ___flock___ .

7. The boy laughed at the end of the ___scene___ .

8. At the end of the play "The Boy Who Cried Wolf," all the characters ___exit___ .

C. Choose two words from the box. On separate paper, write your own two-line rhymes using these words. See Teacher Notes.

Selection Vocabulary   "The Boy Who Cried Wolf"   **155**

RESOURCE CENTER

◀ **Workbook page 155** provides practice with Story Critical words.

Skills Practice 145 ▶ provides additional practice with Story Critical words.

Skills Practice 146 provides practice with Support words.

Spelling Connection Master 59 may be used for spelling instruction with the new vocabulary.

Workbook reuse option: Have students use playwriting format to write one line that the boy in "The Boy Who Cried Wolf" might have said at the end of the play.

Skills Practice 145

NAME _____

SKILLS PRACTICE ◀**145**

Vocabulary: Story Critical Words

A. Study the meaning of each word.

| exit | to leave | scene | part of a play |
| flock | a group of animals | sigh | a long, deep breath |

B. Write the correct vocabulary word for each clue.

1. A tired person might make this.   ___sigh___
2. This means the opposite of *enter.*   ___exit___
3. This word rhymes with *block.*   ___flock___

C. Complete each pair of sentences with the correct vocabulary word.

4. The driver on the country road stopped his car.
A ___flock___ of sheep was crossing the road.

5. Jenny ran as fast as she could to catch the bus.
She breathed a ___sigh___ of relief when she got on it.

6. Our class performed a play about Old King Cole.
The first ___scene___ was set in Merry Old England.

7. The movie was over.
It was time to ___exit___ the theater.

D. One word in each sentence does not make sense. Underline that word. Then write the vocabulary word that belongs in its place.

8. The <u>dock</u> of birds flew high in the sky.   ___flock___

9. Abel looked for the nearest door in order to <u>excite</u> the building.   ___exit___

10. The second <u>seen</u> of the play about the gold miners was set in California.   ___scene___

11. Rob let out a <u>sly</u> when he thought about all the work he had to do.   ___sigh___

LEVEL 8   "The Boy Who Cried Wolf"   Definition clues **145**

Reading & Responding

Building Background

Motivate discussion with the quotation.

Share the following quotation with students. Remind them that it tells what Julian said about his father in "A Day When Frogs Wear Shoes." Help students to recall that in spite of that belief, Julian's father himself got bored from time to time. Discuss whether students agree with Julian's father and why or why not.

> **My dad hates it when people are bored. He says the world is so interesting nobody should ever be bored.**

Build background about boredom.

Ask students to think about times when they have been bored and what they did about it. On a section of the chalkboard, write the heading *WHAT TO DO WHEN BORED* and have students list their ideas. *(Students' responses might include read, draw a picture, visit a friend, make a puzzle, listen to music, take a bike ride.)*

Discuss a play.

Tell students the selection they are going to read is a play. Let them preview "The Boy Who Cried Wolf" by looking at titles, headings, labels, and words in parentheses. Then ask students to name five different features that make this selection a play. Write their responses on the board.

Developing a Purpose for Reading

**Option 1
Students set purpose.**

ORAL "IF I WERE" STATEMENTS   Ask students to think about different things they would do to keep from being bored if they were shepherds. For example, students might suggest, "If I were a shepherd, I would look for shapes in the clouds." Record students' statements for later use.

WRITING ACTIVITY   Have students work individually or in pairs to create written "If I were" statements. Be sure students save their lists for use later.

**Option 2
Teacher sets purpose.**

Have students read to find out what happens when a young shepherd boy becomes bored from being alone so much.

**Meeting
Individual
Needs**

EXTRA HELP   Using a story map, Form 1 in the Teacher Resource Kit, tell students that the setting for the selection is a lonely hillside and the young shepherd is faced with the problem of finding a way to stop his loneliness and boredom. Have students fill in information about the setting and problem on the form. Then have students read to discover how the shepherd tries to solve his loneliness and to discover the final outcome of the story. After reading, have students fill in the rest of the story map.

ACHIEVING ENGLISH PROFICIENCY   Write *sheep* and *shepherds* on the board. Show students pictures of sheep. As you show them the picture, say *sheep* and have them repeat it after you. Explain to students that *sheep* is the same in the singular and the plural. Tell pupils that a *shepherd* watches over or takes care of sheep. Tell students that to *drive* sheep is to make them move and to *herd* sheep means to take care of a large group of sheep. Have students role-play sheep and shepherds. Show students a picture of a *wolf*. Ask them if they think a wolf and sheep can be friends. For additional help in story comprehension, use Master 35 in the Teacher Resource Kit.

In this play, a young shepherd boy learns a lesson. . . . and so do we.

The Boy Who Cried
WOLF

from the fable by Aesop
adapted by Genie Iverson

Characters: Storyteller   Little Girl
             Shepherd Boy   First Farmhand
             Father   Second Farmhand
             Old Woman   Third Farmhand
             Farmer

ACT ONE

Storyteller: A shepherd boy and his father stand talking on a hillside. Their sheep move about them.

Father: Are you ready to look after these sheep by yourself, son? It's time for me to go back to the village.

Shepherd Boy: (*uncertain*) I think so, Papa.

Reader's Journal   p 118
Preparing for Reading

IS A SHEPHERD'S LIFE FOR YOU?

A pastoral painting serves as inspiration for students to pretend they are shepherds and to describe what their day would be like.

GUIDED READING

Page 313   Why does the author put the word *uncertain* in parentheses? (to tell the actor or reader that the character sounds uncertain when he speaks)
ANALYZE: PLAY

Page 313   What does the Storyteller do in this play? (The Storyteller acts as a narrator to tell the audience about the setting and to continue the action.)
ANALYZE: CHARACTER

HIGHLIGHTING LITERATURE

Pages 312–313   Remind students that this is a play, then ask them to name the features of a play. (Students may mention that a play is written to be acted out. It includes the words characters should say and sometimes tells how characters should act. Plays are usually divided into parts called acts. Acts may be divided into parts called scenes.)   APPLICATION: LEARNING ABOUT LITERATURE/GENRE

Father: I'll help you herd our sheep here each morning. And I'll come back at sunset to help you drive them home. But you must stay with them during the day.

Shepherd Boy: Yes, Papa. Only . . . (*looking around*) . . . I don't think I'll like being up here alone.

Father: Alone? Nonsense! Look down there at the road. People come and go all day.

Shepherd Boy: But they never stop.

Father: Maybe they don't stop. But they will come if you ever need help. Just call. (*handing boy the crook*) I have to go now. But I'll be back at sunset. (Father *leaves and the shepherd sits down to watch his sheep.*)

Storyteller: Slowly—very slowly the morning passes. The young shepherd boy feels more and more alone.

Shepherd Boy: I don't like staying here all day by myself. (*sighs*) It's lonely here.

Storyteller: Looking down the hill, the shepherd boy sees an old woman walking along the road. Pails of milk swing from a pole across her shoulders.

Shepherd Boy: I wish that old woman would stop and visit. I wish . . . (*pause*) . . . I know what I'll do! (*leaps up waving his crook*) Help! Help! A WOLF is after my sheep!

Storyteller: The old woman hurries up the hill to help. Milk splashes from her pails.

314   315

GUIDED READING

Page 314   Why do you think the boy is not sure that he will like his job? (He does not think he will like being on the hillside alone.)   RECALL: DETAILS

Page 314   What is the shepherd boy's problem? (He is lonely.)   ANALYZE: PROBLEM/SOLUTION

Page 315   Why do you think the boy makes up the trick about the wolf? (His father said people would stop if he needed help.)   INFER: CAUSE/EFFECT

✔ **Page 315   What is your opinion of what the shepherd boy did?** (It was wrong because he told a lie and made the woman spill her milk. It was understandable because he was lonely and wanted company.)   EVALUATE: CHARACTER

HIGHLIGHTING LITERATURE

**Page 315   Point out to students that the writer has included stage directions that tell how the characters are supposed to move and act. As an example, have students use the stage directions to explain how the boy should move when he cries "Help! Help! A wolf is after my sheep." (He should leap up waving his crook.) Encourage students to explain how knowing this might make the story come alive more. (Students may suggest that they are better able to take part in the action of the story.)   APPLICATION: LEARNING ABOUT LITERATURE/ GENRE

✔ Informal Assessment Opportunity: EVALUATING

608

Old Woman: (*winded*) Where? . . . Where is the wolf? We can chase him with my pole!

Shepherd Boy: (*looking down*) There is no wolf. I wanted you to stop and visit. So I played a trick on you.

Old Woman: No wolf! You mean you made me run up this hill for nothing? What is the matter with you, boy?

Shepherd Boy: I didn't mean any harm.

Old Woman: (*picking up her pails*) Hummf! Just look at these pails! Empty! All that good milk . . . spilled for nothing.

Shepherd Boy: I just wanted you to stop and visit. . . .

Old Woman: Tricking folks is a sorry business. I came to visit you today, but trouble may be your visitor tomorrow. Mark my words. (*walking away muttering*) He'll be sorry . . . sorry indeed. Just wait and see!

ACT TWO

Storyteller: It is the next morning. The unhappy shepherd boy sits on the hillside. As his sheep move about him, he thinks about the long, lonely day ahead.

Shepherd Boy: (*wearily*) Nibble . . . Nibble . . . Nibble!
Baaaa! . . . Baaaa! . . . Baaaa!
Nibble . . . Baaaa!
Baaaa! . . . Nibble! (*long sigh*)
All day long . . . that's all you old sheep ever do!

Storyteller: The shepherd boy hears the rumble of a cart.

Shepherd Boy: Listen! Someone's coming! (*stands and looks down the hill*)

Storyteller: A farmer and his little girl appear on the road, pulling a cart filled with turnips.

Shepherd Boy: Do I dare call out again that there is a wolf? If I do . . . maybe they'll stop. . . . (*pause*) . . . Help! Help! A wolf is after my sheep!

Storyteller: The farmer leaves his cart and runs up the hill to help. His little girl hurries along behind.

Farmer: Where? Where's the wolf?

Little Girl: (*afraid*) Is the wolf hiding behind that tree? Will he eat me?

GUIDED READING

Page 316 Based on the old woman's actions, how would you describe her? (concerned and helpful)
ANALYZE: CHARACTER

Page 316 What is the main idea of the old woman's last speech? (Tricking will cause the boy trouble.)
SYNTHESIZE: MAIN IDEA/DETAILS

Page 317 What does the boy mean when he says the words nibble . . . nibble and baaaa . . . baaaa? (He is mimicking the actions of the sheep, and he is bored by them.) ANALYZE: CONTEXT

✔ **Page 317 What do you think will happen next? What story and "what I know" clues give you hints?** (The farmer will become angry and warn the boy that playing tricks will cause trouble. Story clues: woman's angry reaction; "what I know" clues: people do not like being fooled about serious things.) SYNTHESIZE: PREDICTING OUTCOMES

✔ Skill from **The Bridge** applied through this question.

STRATEGIC READING

Page 317 Ask students to visualize the scene with the shepherd boy, the farmer, and the little girl. Encourage them to picture the hillside, the road, and the characters' actions and reactions. Allow students to describe their mental pictures. Remind them that when they are unable to visualize while reading, they might reread the section of the story that is confusing, paying particular attention to the descriptive words.
METACOGNITION: VISUALIZING

Farmer: I don't see any wolf. (*looking around*) There's no wolf here!

Shepherd Boy: It was just a trick.

Farmer: (*angrily*) You called for help when you didn't need it! Shame on you!

Shepherd Boy: Please don't be angry. I get lonely sitting here all day by myself.

Farmer: (*taking little girl by hand*) Come along, child. This boy has wasted enough of our time with his tricks. But someday he'll be sorry.

Little Girl: (*as they walk away*) Why will he be sorry, Papa?

Farmer: Because tricks bring trouble. Just wait and see. What that boy did today will be remembered tomorrow. (*They exit.*)

ACT THREE
(Scene One)

Storyteller: It is another bright, cool morning. The shepherd boy has watched his flock since sunrise. He is bored and lonely.

Shepherd Boy: Same old hillside! (*sigh*) Same old sheep! Same old grass! And the sun is not even overhead yet. It's still morning! (*long sigh*) Maybe I'll sit and watch the road. Somebody should be coming along soon.

Storyteller: The shepherd boy is about to sit when he hears a loud growl. He turns. A wolf is crouched near his flock.

Shepherd Boy: A WOLF! (*He crawls behind a rock and peeks out.*) A REAL wolf! What can I do!

Storyteller: As the wolf creeps nearer to the frightened sheep, singing is heard from the road below.

Farmhands: (*offstage*) Hey, ho! Hey, ho! It's to the fields we go, With hoe and rake, With rake and hoe, Hey, ho! Hey, ho!

Storyteller: Three farmhands come into view. The shepherd boy runs to the top of the hill shouting.

319

GUIDED READING

Page 318   Why is the farmer angry? (The boy has wasted his time with the trick.)   INFER: CAUSE/EFFECT

Page 318   How are the farmer's and the old woman's reactions to the boy alike? (Both are angry and warn him that he will be sorry he played tricks.) ANALYZE: COMPARISON

Page 319   What is the boy's problem at this point in the story? (A wolf really is after his sheep.)   INFER: PROBLEM/SOLUTION

STRATEGIC READING

Page 319   Have students summarize what the shepherd boy has done so far in the story because he is lonely. (He has made an old woman and then a farmer stop by calling out that a wolf is after his sheep.) Ask students to predict what will happen next. (He will cry "wolf" to the farmhands, and they will not stop.) Point out that summarizing and predicting can help readers understand what they read. Suggest that when students have trouble summarizing, they reread those parts of the story that are confusing. At the completion of the story, ask students to check their predictions. METACOGNITION: SUMMARIZING AND PREDICTING

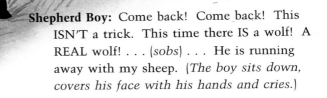

Shepherd Boy: *(waving his crook)* HELP! HELP! A WOLF is after my sheep!

First Farmhand: *(stopping)* Look. It's that shepherd boy! The one folks are talking about.

Second Farmhand: They say he cries "wolf" when there is no wolf.

Third Farmhand: *(nodding)* Foolish boy! You can't believe a word he says.

Shepherd Boy: *(calling as loudly as he can)* Hurry! Hurry! The wolf is taking my sheep!

First Farmhand: *(calling to shepherd)* We DON'T believe you!

Second Farmhand: That's right! We've heard about you and your tricks.

Third Farmhand: You can't fool us! We know there is no wolf! *(The farmhands walk away laughing.)*

320

Shepherd Boy: Come back! Come back! This ISN'T a trick. This time there IS a wolf! A REAL wolf! . . . *(sobs)* . . . He is running away with my sheep. *(The boy sits down, covers his face with his hands and cries.)*

(Scene Two)

Storyteller: It is sunset. The shepherd sits with his head in his hands. The wolf is gone. But so are some of the sheep. Father approaches.

Father: Are you ready to take the sheep home?

Shepherd Boy: Oh yes, Papa! But some of the sheep are gone! A wolf came—a great big wolf!

Father: A wolf! Did you call for help?

Shepherd Boy: Yes, Papa. Yes. There were men on the road. I called. But they wouldn't come. *(lowering his eyes)* They thought that I was playing a trick.

GUIDED READING

Page 320   Why do the farmhands not help the shepherd boy? (They do not believe him because they have heard about his trick of crying "wolf" when there is no wolf.)   INFER: CAUSE/EFFECT

Page 321   What happens to some of the sheep? (The wolf takes them.)   RECALL: DETAILS

Page 321   How does the shepherd boy feel when he tells his father about losing the sheep? How do you know? (He feels ashamed about what he has done. He lowers his eyes.)   INFER: FEELINGS/ATTITUDES

✔ **Page 321   How do you think the boy's father will react?** (He will be disappointed in the boy's behavior.)   SYNTHESIZE: PREDICTING OUTCOMES

HIGHLIGHTING LITERATURE

Page 321   Tell students that this play is based on a fable. Ask students what they know about fables. They may be able to identify that a fable is a story that teaches a lesson. Ask students to predict what lesson this play will teach.

✔ **Skill from The Bridge applied through this question.**

611

Father: (*puzzled*) A trick?

Shepherd Boy: (*hanging his head*) Before when I was lonely, I cried "wolf" so that people would stop and visit. Then . . . then there really was a wolf. And I called. But they didn't believe me.

Father: (*sitting down on a rock*) Well . . . have you learned something?

Shepherd Boy: (*sitting down beside his father*) Yes, Papa. I learned that I should always tell the truth . . . (*pause*) . . . because if I don't, people won't believe me when I do.

THE END

◆ LIBRARY LINK ◆

If you enjoyed this play based on a tale by Aesop, you might want to read Aesop's Fables, *edited by Anne White, or* Tales from Aesop, *edited by Harold Jones.*

 Reader's Response

How did you feel about the lesson in this play?

See next page for suggested answers.

SELECTION FOLLOW-UP

The Boy Who Cried WOLF

 Thinking It Over

1. Why did the boy call for help the first two times?
2. What did the farmer mean when he said that what the boy did today would be remembered tomorrow?
3. Was the farmer correct? Tell why or why not.
4. Why do you think that the boy's father didn't punish him?
5. What words would you use to describe the boy in this story? Why did you choose these words?

Writing to Learn

THINK AND IMAGINE The young shepherd boy learns many things about himself and his friends. Imagine what he might have written in his journal.

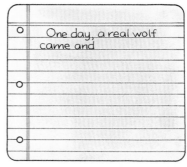

One day, a real wolf came and

WRITE Pretend you are the shepherd boy. On a page of your notebook, write about your frightening day. Tell how your adventure may have changed your life forever.

GUIDED READING

Page 322   What lesson do you think the author wants readers to learn? (If you do not always tell the truth, people will not believe you when you do.)
EVALUATE: AUTHOR'S PURPOSE

RETURNING TO THE READING PURPOSE

OPTION 1 If students set the purpose, return to the "If I were" statements they generated. Discuss their ideas for what to do to keep from being bored if they were shepherds.

OPTION 2 If you set the purpose, ask what happened when the young shepherd boy became bored from being alone so much. (He cried "wolf" to get people who were passing by to stop and visit. When he really needed help because of a wolf, no one believed him.)

Reader's Journal   **p 119**
Responding to Reading

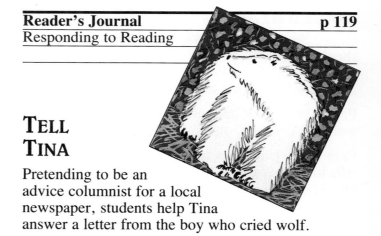

TELL TINA

Pretending to be an advice columnist for a local newspaper, students help Tina answer a letter from the boy who cried wolf.

612

SELECTION FOLLOW-UP

The Boy Who Cried
WOLF

THINKING IT OVER

1. **Why did the boy call for help the first two times?** (The first two times, the boy was lonely and bored. He called for help so that someone would come to keep him company.) ANALYZE: CHARACTER

2. **What did the farmer mean when he said that what the boy did today would be remembered tomorrow?** (The farmer meant that the things we say and do have lasting effects. The boy's trick would not be forgotten.) SYNTHESIZE: DRAWING CONCLUSIONS

3. **Was the farmer correct? Tell why or why not.** (The farmer was correct. The boy's tricks were well known to the people, so the farmhands did not take the boy seriously when he really needed help.) INFER: CAUSE/EFFECT

4. **Why do you think that the boy's father didn't punish him?** (Possible answers: The father saw that his son was upset and sorry; he realized that his son had learned his lesson; the frightening experience was punishment enough.) ANALYZE: CHARACTER

5. **What words would you use to describe the boy in this story? Why did you choose these words?** (Possible answers: *friendly, lonely, impatient, easily bored, selfish, willing to learn a lesson.* Students will probably cite the boy's actions as reasons for their conclusions — for example, his eagerness to talk to people as evidence of his friendliness.) SYNTHESIZE: CHARACTER; METACOGNITION

WRITING TO LEARN

✔ *Use Writing Master 24, which provides a journal form.*

THINK AND IMAGINE The young shepherd boy learned many things about himself and his friends. Imagine what he might have written in his journal. (Help list ideas to prepare for writing.)

Extend comprehension through writing.

WRITE Pretend you are the shepherd boy. On a page of your notebook, write about your frightening day. Tell how your adventure may have changed your life forever. (Have students share their journal entries.)

✔ Informal Assessment Opportunity: RESPONDING

613

More Ideas for Selection Follow-Up

CRITICAL AND CREATIVE THINKING QUESTIONS

Encourage a variety of responses and points of view.

Use these open-ended questions to encourage critical and creative thinking about the selection.

1. The shepherd boy learned a lesson about the importance of telling the truth. Why do you think this might be a lesson he never forgot?

2. What message do you think the shepherd boy was really giving when he cried "Wolf!"?

3. What ideas do you have for the shepherd boy on how he could pass his time while he's taking care of the sheep?

REREADING ORALLY

Have students reread for expression.

Guide students in selecting and rereading parts of the play that show how the young shepherd feels. Passages may include when the boy tells his father how he will feel about staying alone on the hillside on page 314, how the boy feels when he sees the old woman walking along the road on page 315, how he feels when the farmhands ignore him on pages 320–321, and how he feels when he has to tell his father about the missing sheep on pages 321–322. Encourage students to read the words with expression as if the characters were speaking. Point out that they should follow the directions in parentheses and emphasize the words in capital letters.

SELECTION COMPREHENSION

Provide comprehension check.

A Workbook page to check comprehension is shown in the Resource Center below. It may be used for informal assessment.

Workbook page 156

SELECTION COMPREHENSION

NAME _____

The Boy Who Cried WOLF

A. Complete the summary of the play "The Boy Who Cried Wolf." Accept reasonable variations.

A _____shepherd boy_____ was the main character of this play. His father told him that it was his job to stay on a hillside and watch _____the family's sheep_____ during the day. Pointing to the road, the father told the boy that if he ever needed help he should _____call out to people walking by_____ .

The boy told his father that he didn't think he would like _____being on the hill all alone_____

After his father left, the boy began to feel very _____lonely_____ . He saw an old woman carrying milk along the road and tricked her into coming to see him by yelling that _____a wolf was_____ _____after the sheep_____ . The old woman told him that he would be _____sorry_____ if he kept tricking people. But the next day, the foolish boy played the same trick on a farmer and his daughter.

One morning, a real _____wolf_____ began to take some of the sheep. The boy called for help, but no one came because _____everyone had heard of his tricks_____

Then the boy's father returned. The boy described the tricks he had played and told what had happened when the wolf really came. When his father asked him what he had learned, he said he had learned _____he should always tell the truth_____

B. Think about "The Boy Who Cried Wolf." On separate paper, tell what kind of person would be helped by hearing this story. See Teacher Notes.

156   "The Boy Who Cried Wolf"   Selection Comprehension

RESOURCE CENTER

◄ **Workbook page 156** is intended for use by all students.

Writing Master 24 provides a form for a Writing to Learn journal.

I•T Kit Activities

Poster: "Look Before You Leap"

After telling the story of the illustrated fable on this poster, students can discuss times in their own lives when they should have "looked before they leaped." Then students can write their own versions of this fable or create a new fable of their own. (See Activity Guide.) LITERATURE

Audio: Peter and the Wolf

When Peter wanders into the meadow, he encounters the very subject of his grandfather's warnings — the wolf. Students hear the story and its instrumental accompaniment from Prokofiev's *Peter and the Wolf*. Students listen for the different musical themes that represent characters in the drama. (See Activity Guide.)

CLASSICAL MUSIC

LANGUAGE ARTS CONNECTIONS

CRITICAL THINKING: DEVELOPING A STORY MAP

Discuss story mapping.

Explain that completing a story map helps readers to summarize a story, making it easier to remember the story. Ask students why they might want to remember this story. *(They enjoyed it; they learned something from it; they want to tell it to another person.)* Write the following story map headings on the chalkboard, pointing out the parts of a story map:

Title:	Author:	
The Setting	**The Problem:**	**The Resolution:**
Place:	Event 1:	
Time:	Event 2:	
Characters:	Event 3:	

CRITICAL THINKING: DEVELOPING A STORY MAP (continued)

Have students complete an oral story map for the play.

Call on students to tell the title and author of the play. To complete the story map, record students' responses to these questions: Who are the characters in the play? Where is the shepherd boy when his father leaves? Does the story take place in the past, present, or future? How does the boy feel? What would he like to do? What happens when he sees the farmer? What happens when he sees the old woman? What happens when he sees the farmhands? What lesson does the boy learn?   SPEAKING

615

DEVELOPING CHARACTER CLUSTERS

Review the parts of a character cluster.

Draw this graphic on the chalkboard for use in developing a character cluster. (Suggested answers are shown in red.) Ask students to copy it.

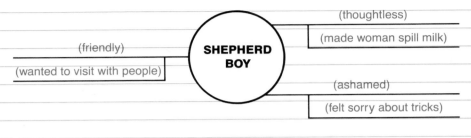

(thoughtless)

(made woman spill milk)

(friendly)

SHEPHERD BOY

(wanted to visit with people)

(ashamed)

(felt sorry about tricks)

DEVELOPING CHARACTER CLUSTERS (continued)

Have students write about the shepherd boy's character.

Tell each student to draw a circle in the center of a sheet of paper and write *Shepherd Boy* in it. Then have the student draw one line out for each character trait. Show how to connect supporting lines under each trait.

Help students complete the character clusters by thinking of traits and then writing examples from the story to support them. Have students use the information from the character clusters to write short paragraphs explaining why they would or would not want the shepherd boy for a friend. WRITING

DIALOGUE AS A FEATURE OF A PLAY

Have students write dialogue.

Present the following dialogue:

    Shepherd Boy: It was just a trick.

    Farmer: (angrily) You called for help when you didn't need it!

      Shame on you!

Discuss what helps the reader "feel" the farmer's anger. *(exclamations, stage direction, choice of words, such as* shame*)*

Have each student choose two characters who do not talk to each other, such as the old woman and the farmer. Tell students to make up conversations in which the characters react to an event. Have students write the dialogue as it would appear in a play. **Language Arts Master 21** can be used with this activity. CHALLENGE: WRITING

DRAMATIZING THE PLAY

Have students present a play.

Explain that there are a variety of tasks involved in presenting a play: making costumes, painting scenery, making or finding props, making and posting announcements, and making a program for the audience. The program lists the name of the play and the names of the people who are in the cast.

Have students work in small groups to discuss and complete one of the tasks. Point out that several of the groups may have to discuss things with each other. For example, the group making programs needs to know the names of the cast members; the group making props might have to meet with the actors to find out what props they will need. Have students perform the play for class-mates. They may also wish to invite other classes and/or parents to the perfor-mance.   WHOLE CLASS ENRICHMENT

READING EVERY DAY

"The Boy Who Cried Wolf" introduces students to Aesop's fables. Invite them to explore other treasured fables of Aesop by recommending these titles.

Aesop's Fables by Tom Paxton. Morrow Junior Books, © 1988. Ten of Aesop's classic tales retold in verse, including "The Goose That Laid the Golden Egg," "The Tortoise and the Hare," and another version of "The Boy Who Cried Wolf."

Three Aesop Fox Fables by Paul Galdone. The Seabury Press, © 1971. A lively picture-book collection of three of Aesop's best-loved fables featuring the Fox, that crafty fellow who thinks he's much cleverer than his friends but who is often outsmarted by them.   EASIER TO READ

Reader's Journal   pp 120, 121
Extending Reading

SPIN A FABLE

Using pictured charac-ters or inventing their own, students plan fables of their own, following step-by-step directions.

Selection Support

SKILL TRACE: WORD REFERENTS				
Introduction	Practice	Test	Reteach	Maintain
TE 532	548	618	635	636	See Level 9.

COMPREHENSION

Word Referents

OBJECTIVE Understanding relationships between substitute words and their referents.

Review word substitutes and word referents.

Remind students that writers often use words that stand for or substitute for other words and that word substitutes may stand for the names of people, places, or things.

Present sentences with word substitutes and word referents.

Display the Teaching Chart. Have students identify each underlined word substitute and ask the question *Who*?, *What*?, *Whose*?, *When*?, or *How many*? to figure out what word the substitute stands for. Then have students supply the word that the substitute stands for.

97

TEACHING CHART 97: WORD REFERENTS

1. Father helped the boy herd the sheep each morning and drive them home at sunset. (sheep)
2. The old woman walked with pails of milk swinging from a pole across her shoulders. (old woman)
3. The boy cried "Wolf!" The woman then hurried up the hill. (after the boy cried "Wolf!")

Provide independent practice.

Options for independent practice are shown in the Resource Center below.

Workbook page 157

NAME _____

COMPREHENSION

Word Referents

REMEMBER: Some words can stand for the names of people, places, or things.

A. Read the paragraph. Complete the chart by writing the word or words that each underlined word stands for.

The shepherd boy was supposed to watch the sheep, but <u>he</u> didn't like the job. He told <u>his</u> father that watching sheep was boring. Unhappily, he sat on the hill. He had been <u>there</u> for a little while when he saw an old woman. Quickly, the boy thought of a way to get <u>her</u> to visit him. She came running when he yelled, "Wolf!" The old woman told the boy that he would be sorry one day for tricking her, and she was right. Soon a real wolf came, and the boy yelled to some men. <u>None</u> would come. Later the boy's father returned and asked, "What happened to our sheep? <u>Three</u> are missing!" The boy felt ashamed.

Word	Referent
1. he	shepherd boy
2. his	boy
3. there	on the hill
4. her	old woman
5. none	men
6. three	sheep

B. Choose three of the sentences containing underlined words. On separate paper, write each sentence over but replace the underlined word with the word or words it stands for. See Teacher Notes.

Word Referents   "The Boy Who Cried Wolf"   **157**

RESOURCE CENTER

◀ **Workbook page 157** is intended for use by all students.

Skills Practice 147 ▶ may be assigned for additional practice.

Workbook reuse option: Have students find two other examples of one word standing for another in the paragraph in Part A. Tell them to draw arrows linking each replacement word they find with the word it stands for.

Skills Practice 147

NAME _____

SKILLS PRACTICE **147**

Word Referents

Remember that words can stand for the names of people, places, or things. **Referents** are the word or words a **word substitute** might stand for.

Read the story. Decide what each underlined word stands for. Write your answers next to the correct number after the story. Some answers may have more than one word.

She, her, and *hers* stand for girls. *He, him,* and *his* stand for boys.
You, we, they, them, your, and *ours* can stand for boys or girls.
This, that, these, and *those* tell which one or ones.
Here and *there* tell where someone or something is.

Mia and Sue wanted to earn some money. "<u>We</u> ¹ have to think of something to sell," said Mia.

"<u>I</u> ² know," said Sue. "Let's collect our old things. We can put <u>them</u> ³ on my lawn Saturday."

"Things I don't use?" asked Mia. "Good idea! I can think of <u>some</u>. ⁴"

Early Saturday, the girls brought things to Sue's yard. <u>They</u> ⁵ wrote price tags and leaned <u>them</u> ⁶ against each item. Three items were fifteen cents. <u>Five</u> ⁷ were ten cents. <u>Others</u> ⁸ were less.

Just before the first person came, the wind blew hard. The price tags flew in the air. <u>All</u> ⁹ were scattered.

"What should we do about the price tags?" asked Sue.

"You grab <u>some</u> ¹⁰ and so will I," said Mia. "Let's just write the prices on things. It will be okay."

Sue was right. Sue and Mia made three dollars from their sale.

1. Mia and Sue		6. price tags	
2. Sue		7. items	
3. old things		8. items	
4. things		9. the price tags	
5. the girls		10. the price tags	

LEVEL 8   "The Boy Who Cried Wolf"   **147**

SKILL TRACE: COMPARISON						
Introduction	Practice		Test	Reteach	Maintain	
TE 176	196	292	311	312	349	578	619

COMPREHENSION

Comparison

OBJECTIVE Understanding likenesses and differences in longer texts.

Review comparison.

Remind students that an author sometimes tells how things, people, or events are alike and different. Explain that signal words and story clues help readers to understand comparisons. Knowing about comparison will help them better understand what they read.

Practice comparing a character's feelings.

You may wish to write the phrases below on the chalkboard. Possible answers are given in red. Write the headings *Before* and *After* and have students tell how the shepherd boy probably felt before and how he might have felt after the wolf took some of his sheep.

		Before	**After**
1.	Staying alone on the hillside.	(unhappy, lonely)	(contented, occupied with something he brought with him to pass the time.)
2.	Crying "Wolf!" when there is no wolf.	(a good way to call for company)	(a foolish and selfish thing to do)
3.	Telling the truth.	(not important)	(very important)

Provide independent practice.

An independent activity is shown in the Resource Center below.

RESOURCE CENTER

Skills Practice 148 ▶ may be assigned for additional practice.

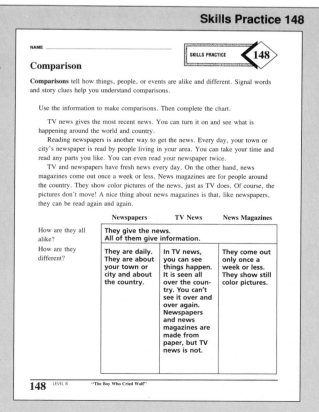

Comparison

Comparisons tell how things, people, or events are alike and different. Signal words and story clues help you understand comparisons.

Use the information to make comparisons. Then complete the chart.

TV news gives the most recent news. You can turn it on and see what is happening around the world and country.

Reading newspapers is another way to get the news. Every day, your town or city's newspaper is read by people living in your area. You can take your time and read any parts you like. You can even read your newspaper twice.

TV and newspapers have fresh news every day. On the other hand, news magazines come out once a week or less. News magazines are for people around the country. They show color pictures of the news, just as TV does. Of course, the pictures don't move! A nice thing about news magazines is that, like newspapers, they can be read again and again.

	Newspapers	TV News	News Magazines
How are they all alike?	They give the news. All of them give information.		
How are they different?	They are daily. They are about your town or city and about the country.	In TV news, you can see things happen. It is seen all over the country. You can't see it over and over again. Newspapers and news magazines are made from paper, but TV news is not.	They come out only once a week or less. They show still color pictures.

148 LEVEL 8   "The Boy Who Cried Wolf"

VOCABULARY SKILLS

Classification

OBJECTIVE   Classifying words according to common characteristics.

Review classification.

Remind students that words can be grouped together in ways that show how they are alike and different in meaning. Tell students that it is easier to remember new words if they see how they are related to known words. Ask students to tell you how the words *goat, cow,* and *horse* are alike *(they name farm animals)* and to name a word from the play that also names a farm animal. *(sheep)*

Provide a list of words to be classified.

You may wish to write the following words from "The Boy Who Cried Wolf" on the chalkboard: *cry, folks, sunrise, overhead,* and *crouch.* Read aloud the groups of words below. Answers appear in red. Then have students add one word from the chalkboard to each group.

1.	night	morning	sunset	day	(sunrise)
2.	sit	stand	crawl	leap	(crouch)
3.	yell	call	mutter	shout	(cry)
4.	women	people	men	farmhands	(folks)
5.	below	up	down	behind	(overhead)

Provide independent practice.

An independent activity is shown in the Resource Center below.

RESOURCE CENTER

Skills Practice 149 ▶ may be assigned for additional practice.

Skills Practice 149

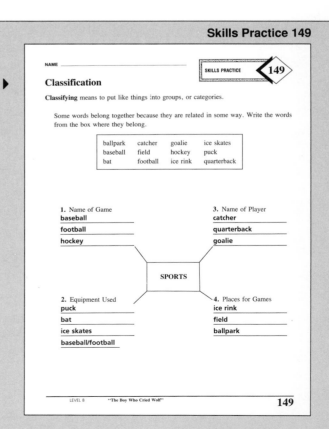

CURRICULUM CONNECTIONS

PUPPET PLAY ART

Have students make hand puppets of the story characters. Provide small paper bags, colored paper, scissors, and paste. Demonstrate how a student can put an arm/hand into a bag and work it as a puppet. Show students how to paste a character's head on the bottom of the bag, body/legs on the front, and arms on the sides. Let small groups of students put on scenes from the play with their puppets.

RAISING SHEEP SOCIAL STUDIES

Interested students might enjoy finding out about sheep and sheep farms. Suggest they look in encyclopedias, social studies books, and the card catalog in the library. Point out that sheep are raised for food and for wool. Let students share their findings with the class orally.

SINGING WITH CHARACTER MUSIC

Have students reread the song that the farmhands sing in "The Boy Who Cried Wolf." Encourage them to sing the song, making up a tune. Then have students work in small groups to create songs that other characters in the story might sing. Talk about what would be appropriate for different characters. For example, the old woman might sing about swinging pails of milk; the shepherd boy might sing of being lonely. Have a class singalong when songs are finished. **Curriculum Connection Master 21** can be used with this activity.

WOOLLY FACTS SOCIAL STUDIES

Review with students that sheep farming is an important industry and that many sheep are raised all over the world. Point out that different breeds of sheep live in different areas and that the kinds of wool produced are also different.

Divide students into small groups and work with each group to choose an aspect of the topic to research. Students may be curious about where different breeds of sheep are found, what varieties of wool different breeds produce, how wool is made, or how wool is dyed. Have students research their subtopic of wool production and write reports. When each group has completed its report, have it present the report orally to the other groups. Encourage each group to include visual aids in its presentation. Finally, display the work as a whole-group report on wool production.

READING CORNER

In Which Piglet Meets a Heffalump

from
Winnie-the-Pooh

written by A.A. Milne
illustrated by Ernest H. Shepard

SUMMARY

When Christopher Robin carelessly talks with his mouth full, Winnie-the-Pooh and his good friend Piglet mistakenly hear him say, "I saw a Heffalump today," instead of, "I saw an elephant today." Pooh and Piglet decide to catch a Heffalump. They have no idea exactly what this creature is, but they concoct a plan to trap it. The plan involves a Very Deep Pit and a jar of honey at the bottom of it. The only creature who gets caught, however, is Pooh, who gets hungry for the honey and gets his head stuck in the jar. When Piglet comes along and sees this creature with a jarlike head, he believes it to be a Heffalump and runs to Christopher Robin in terror. Christopher Robin laughs when he realizes what has happened, but poor Piglet goes home feeling very embarrassed.

A. A. Milne is an award-winning author.

INTRODUCING THE STORY

Review the key features of fantasy.

In fantasies, things happen that could never happen in real life. Animals talk, people fly through the air or disappear through walls — anything can happen. Tell students that the next story, "In Which Piglet Meets a Heffalump," is a fantasy.

Develop the concept of pretending to understand when you really do not.

Remind students that selections in this unit are about ways people communicate with each other and about understanding and misunderstanding messages. Ask students if they have ever overheard a conversation in which names, words, phrases, or expressions were used that they did not understand. Words often have more than one meaning and the speaker and listener could be thinking of different meanings. Then ask how not understanding things makes people feel. *(embarrassed, left out)* Point out that in the next story a misunderstanding of words leads to very funny adventures.

Present vocabulary.

The following words that appear in the story may be new to students. Encourage students to use their knowledge of long word decoding, as well as the context, to help them pronounce and understand unfamiliar words.

stumped walked in a heavy, clumsy way
heather a low plant with tiny purple flowers
cautiously carefully
larder a place in a home where food is kept
jigetting jumping around

READING THE STORY

Assign the reading.

Be sure students understand that this story is part of a book that can be found in the library. Reading this selection offers students the chance to practice uninterrupted, sustained silent reading. It allows them to read at their own rate, for their own enjoyment, and encourages them to explore new books.

This story may be assigned for students to read at home. Another option is to have students choose a classmate with whom they would like to read this selection. When they have finished reading, direct partners to discuss favorite passages, characters, or story outcomes.

Sometimes, as friends talk, the message gets all mixed up. This certainly is true for Piglet and Pooh.

In Which Piglet Meets a Heffalump

from
Winnie-the-Pooh

written by A. A. Milne
illustrated by Ernest H. Shepard

Piglet and Winnie-the-Pooh are two of Christopher Robin's stuffed animals. He brings them to life in his imagination, where they have many interesting and funny adventures.

One day, when Christopher Robin and Winnie-the-Pooh and Piglet were all talking together, Christopher Robin finished the mouthful he was eating and said carelessly: "I saw a Heffalump to-day, Piglet."

"What was it doing?" asked Piglet.

"Just lumping along," said Christopher Robin. "I don't think it saw *me*."

"I saw one once," said Piglet. "At least, I think I did," he said. "Only perhaps it wasn't."

"So did I," said Pooh, wondering what a Heffalump was like.

"You don't often see them," said Christopher Robin carelessly.

"Not now," said Piglet.

"Not at this time of year," said Pooh.

Then they all talked about something else, until it was time for Pooh and Piglet to go home together.

At first as they stumped along the path which edged the Hundred Acre Wood, they didn't say much to each other; but when they came to the stream and had helped each other across the stepping stones, and were able to walk side by side again over the heather, they began to talk in a friendly way about this and that, and Piglet said, "If you see what I mean, Pooh," and Pooh said, "It's just what I think myself, Piglet," and Piglet said, "But, on the other hand, Pooh, we must remember," and Pooh said, "Quite true, Piglet, although I had forgotten it for the moment." And then, just as they came to the Six Pine Trees, Pooh looked round to see that nobody else was listening, and said in a very solemn voice:

"Piglet, I have decided something."

"What have you decided, Pooh?"

"I have decided to catch a Heffalump."

Pooh nodded his head several times as he said this, and waited for Piglet to say "How?" or "Pooh, you couldn't!" or something helpful of that sort, but Piglet said nothing. The fact was Piglet was wishing that *he* had thought about it first.

"I shall do it," said Pooh, after waiting a little longer, "by means of a trap. And it must be a Cunning Trap, so you will have to help me, Piglet."

"Pooh," said Piglet, feeling quite happy again now, "I will." And then he said, "How shall we do it?" and Pooh said, "That's just it. How?" And then they sat down together to think it out.

Pooh's first idea was that they should dig a Very Deep Pit, and then the Heffalump would come along and fall into the Pit, and——

"Why?" said Piglet.

"Why what?" said Pooh.

"Why would he fall in?"

Pooh rubbed his nose with his paw, and said that the Heffalump might be walking along, humming a little song, and looking up at the sky, wondering if it would rain, and so he wouldn't see the Very Deep Pit until he was half-way down, when it would be too late.

Piglet said that this was a very good Trap, but supposing it were raining already?

Pooh rubbed his nose again, and said that he hadn't thought of that. And then he brightened up, and said that, if it were raining already, the Heffalump  would be looking at the sky wondering if it would *clear up,* and so he wouldn't see the Very Deep Pit until he was half-way down. . . . When it would be too late.

Piglet said that, now that this point had been explained, he thought it was a Cunning Trap.

Pooh was very proud when he heard this, and he felt that the Heffalump was as good as caught already, but there was just one other thing which had to be thought about, and it was this. *Where should they dig the Very Deep Pit?*

Piglet said that the best place would be somewhere where a Heffalump was, just before he fell into it, only about a foot farther on.

"But then he would see us digging it," said Pooh.

"Not if he was looking at the sky."

"He would Suspect," said Pooh, "if he happened to look down." He thought for a long time and then added sadly, "It isn't as easy as I thought. I suppose that's why Heffalumps hardly *ever* get caught."

"That must be it," said Piglet.

They sighed and got up; and when they had taken a few gorse prickles out of themselves they sat down again; and all the time Pooh was saying to himself, "If only I could *think* of something!" For he felt sure that a Very Clever Brain could catch a Heffalump if only he knew the right way to go about it.

"Suppose," he said to Piglet, "*you* wanted to catch *me*, how would you do it?"

"Well," said Piglet, "I should do it like this. I should make a Trap, and I should put a Jar of Honey in the Trap, and you would smell it, and you would go in after it, and——"

"And I would go in after it," said Pooh excitedly, "only very carefully so as not to hurt myself, and I would get to the Jar of Honey, and I should lick round the edges first of all, pretending that there wasn't any more, you know, and then I should walk away and think about it a little, and then I should come back and start licking in the middle of the jar, and then——"

"Yes, well never mind about that. There you would be, and there I should catch you. Now the first thing to think of is, What do Heffalumps like? I should think acorns, shouldn't you? We'll get a lot of—I say, wake up, Pooh!"

Pooh, who had gone into a happy dream, woke up with a start, and said that Honey was a much more trappy thing than Haycorns. Piglet didn't think so; and they were just going to argue about it, when Piglet remembered that, if they put acorns in the Trap, *he* would have to find the acorns, but if they put honey, then Pooh would have to give up some of his own honey, so he said, "All right, honey then," just as Pooh remembered it too, and was going to say, "All right, haycorns."

"Honey," said Piglet to himself in a thoughtful way, as if it were now settled. "*I'll* dig the pit, while *you* go and get the honey."

"Very well," said Pooh, and he stumped off.

As soon as he got home, he went to the larder; and he stood on a chair, and took down a very large  jar of honey from the top shelf. It had HUNNY written on it, but, just to make sure, he took off the paper cover and looked at it, and it *looked* just like honey. "But you never can tell," said Pooh. "I remember my uncle saying once that he had seen cheese just this colour." So he put his tongue in, and took a large lick. "Yes," he said, "it is. No doubt about that. And honey, I should say, right down to the bottom of the jar. Unless, of course," he said, "somebody put cheese in at the bottom just for a joke. Perhaps I had better go a *little* further . . . just in case . . . in case Heffalumps *don't* like cheese . . . same as me. . . . Ah!" And he gave a deep sigh. "I *was* right. It *is* honey, right the way down."

Having made certain of this, he took the jar back to Piglet, and Piglet looked up from the bottom of his Very Deep Pit, and said, "Got it?" and Pooh said, "Yes, but it isn't quite a full jar," and he threw it down to Piglet, and Piglet said, "No, it isn't! Is that all you've got left?" and Pooh said "Yes." Because it was. So Piglet put the jar at the bottom of the Pit, and climbed out, and they went off home together.

"Well, good night, Pooh," said Piglet, when they had got to Pooh's house. "And we meet at six o'clock tomorrow morning by the Pine Trees, and see how many Heffalumps we've got in our Trap."

"Six o'clock, Piglet. And have you got any string?"

"No. Why do you want string?"

"To lead them home with."

"Oh! . . . I *think* Heffalumps come if you whistle."

"Some do and some don't. You never can tell with Heffalumps. Well, good night!"

"Good night!"

And off Piglet trotted to his house TRESPASSERS W, while Pooh made his preparations for bed.

Some hours later, just as the night was beginning to steal away, Pooh woke up suddenly with a sinking feeling. He had had that sinking feeling before, and he knew what it meant. *He was hungry.* So he went to the larder, and he stood on a chair and reached up to the top shelf, and found—nothing.

"That's funny," he thought. "I know I had a jar of honey there. A full jar, full of honey right up to the top, and it had HUNNY written on it, so that I should know it was honey. That's very funny." And then he began to wander up and down, wondering where it was and murmuring a murmur to himself. Like this:

It's very, very funny,
'Cos I *know* I had some honey;
'Cos it had a label on,
    Saying HUNNY.

A goloptious full-up pot too,
And I don't know where it's got to,
No, I don't know where it's gone—
    Well, it's funny.

He had murmured this to himself three times in a singing sort of way, when suddenly he remembered. He had put it into the Cunning Trap to catch the Heffalump.

"Bother!" said Pooh. "It all comes of trying to be kind to Heffalumps." And he got back into bed.

But he couldn't sleep. The more he tried to sleep, the more he couldn't. He tried Counting Sheep, which is sometimes a good way of getting to sleep, and, as that was no good, he tried counting Heffalumps. And that was worse. Because every Heffalump that he counted was making straight for a pot of Pooh's honey, *and eating it all.* For some minutes he lay there miserably, but when the five hundred and eighty-seventh Heffalump was licking its jaws, and saying to itself, "Very good honey this, I don't know when I've tasted better," Pooh could bear it no longer. He jumped out of bed, he ran out of the house, and he ran straight to the Six Pine Trees.

The Sun was still in bed, but there was a lightness in the sky over the Hundred Acre Wood which seemed to show that it was waking up and would soon be kicking off the clothes. In the half-light the Pine Trees looked cold and lonely, and the Very Deep Pit seemed deeper than it was, and Pooh's jar of honey at the bottom was something mysterious, a shape and no more. But as he got nearer to it his nose told him that it was indeed honey, and his tongue came out and began to polish up his mouth, ready for it.

"Bother!" said Pooh, as he got his nose inside the jar. "A Heffalump has been eating it!" And then he thought a little and said, "Oh, no, *I* did. I forgot."

Indeed, he had eaten most of it. But there was a little left at the very bottom of the jar, and he pushed his head right in, and began to lick. . . .

By and by Piglet woke up. As soon as he woke he said to himself, "Oh!" Then he said bravely, "Yes," and then, still more bravely, "Quite so." But he didn't feel very brave, for the word which was really jiggeting about in his brain was "Heffalumps."

What was a Heffalump like?

Was it Fierce?

Did it come when you whistled? And *how* did it come?

Was it Fond of Pigs at all?

If it was Fond of Pigs, did it make any difference *what sort of Pig?*

Supposing it was Fierce with Pigs, would it make any difference *if the Pig had a grandfather called TRESPASSERS WILLIAM?*

He didn't know the answer to any of these questions . . . and he was going to see his first Heffalump in about an hour from now!

Of course Pooh would be with him, and it was much more Friendly with two. But suppose Heffalumps were Very Fierce with Pigs *and* Bears? Wouldn't it be better to pretend that he had a headache, and couldn't go up to the Six Pine Trees this morning? But then suppose that it was a very fine day, and there was no Heffalump in the trap, here he would be, in bed all the morning, simply wasting his time for nothing. What should he do?

And then he had a Clever Idea. He would go up very quietly to the Six Pine Trees now, peep very cautiously into the Trap, and see if there *was* a Heffalump there. And if there was, he would go back to bed, and if there wasn't, he wouldn't.

So off he went. At first he thought that there wouldn't be a Heffalump in the Trap, and then he thought that there would, and as he got nearer he was *sure* that there would, because he could hear it heffalumping about it like anything.

"Oh, dear, oh, dear, oh, dear!" said Piglet to himself. And he wanted to run away. But somehow, having got so near, he felt that he must just see what a Heffalump was like. So he crept to the side of the Trap and looked in. . . .

And all the time Winnie-the-Pooh had been trying to get the honey-jar off his head. The more he shook it, the more tightly it stuck. "Bother!" he said, inside the jar, and "Oh, help!" and, mostly "Ow!" And he tried bumping it against things, but as he couldn't see what he was bumping it against, it didn't help him; and he tried to climb out of the Trap, but as he could see nothing but jar, and not much of that, he couldn't find his way. So at last he lifted up his head, jar and all, and made a loud, roaring noise of Sadness and Despair . . . and it was at that moment that Piglet looked down.

"Help, help!" cried Piglet, "a Heffalump, a Horrible Heffalump!" and he scampered off as hard as he could, still crying out, "Help, help, a Herrible Hoffalump! Hoff, Hoff, a Hellible Horralump! Holl, Holl, a Hoffable Hellerump!" And he didn't stop crying and scampering until he got to Christopher Robin's house.

"Whatever's the matter, Piglet?" said Christopher Robin, who was just getting up.

"Heff," said Piglet, breathing so hard that he could hardly speak, "a Hell—a Heff—a Heffalump."

"Where?"

"Up there," said Piglet, waving his paw.

"What did it look like?"

"Like—like——It had the biggest head you ever saw, Christopher Robin. A great enormous thing, like—like nothing. A huge big—well, like a—I don't know—like an enormous big nothing. Like a jar."

"Well," said Christopher Robin, putting on his shoes, "I shall go and look at it. Come on."

Piglet wasn't afraid if he had Christopher Robin with him, so off they went. . . .

"I can hear it, can't you?" said Piglet anxiously, as they got near.

"I can hear *something*," said Christopher Robin.

It was Pooh bumping his head against a tree-root he had found.

"There!" said Piglet. "Isn't it *awful?*" And he held on tight to Christopher Robin's hand.

Suddenly Christopher Robin began to laugh . . . and he laughed . . . and he laughed . . . and he laughed. And while he was still laughing—*Crash* went the Heffalump's head against the tree-root, Smash went the jar, and out came Pooh's head again. . . .

Then Piglet saw what a Foolish Piglet he had been, and he was so ashamed of himself that he ran straight off home and went to bed with a headache. But Christopher Robin and Pooh went home to breakfast together.

"Oh, Bear!" said Christopher Robin. "How I do love you!"

"So do I," said Pooh.

◆ LIBRARY LINK ◆

This story was taken from the book Winnie-the-Pooh. *You might enjoy reading the entire book to learn more about Pooh and his friends and all the fun they have together.*

 Reader's Response

If you could talk with Piglet and Pooh, what questions would you ask them?

DISCUSSING THE STORY

Summarize the story events.

Ask students to summarize the story. Students should tell who the characters are, what they want to do, what problem they have, and the outcome.

Discuss what makes the story a classic.

Tell students the author A. A. Milne wrote the Winnie-the-Pooh stories in the late 1920s and they have been very popular with both children and adults since that time. Students will be interested to learn that Christopher Robin, the boy in the stories, was actually Milne's son, for whom the author wrote all the Pooh tales as well as the verse collections, *When We Were Very Young* and *Now We Are Six*. Ask students why they think the stories about Pooh and his friends have been loved through the years. Bring out that children like the stories because of their humor and because they can identify with the adventures and misadventures of the stories' characters. Adults enjoy them because they are well written, warm, funny, and remind them of the fun of their own childhood days.

Discuss the humor in the story.

Point out that part of the fun in this story comes from Pooh's and Piglet's pretending to understand what Christopher Robin said he had seen. Ask students why they think Piglet and Pooh did not admit that they did not understand what Christopher Robin had said. *(They most likely did not want to appear stupid. They wanted to feel important.)* Ask students if they knew what Christopher Robin was talking about and how they knew. *(Students might suggest that* Heffalump *sounds a little bit like* elephant, *and that the words* lumping along *were also a clue. The illustrations show an animal that looks very much like an elephant.)* Have students name other parts of the story that they found funny. *(Students most likely will mention Pooh's getting his head stuck in the jar; the funny poem about honey, spelled HUNNY; Piglet's dealings with the Heffalump; the removal of the jar from Pooh's head; and Piglet's discovery of how foolish he had been.)*

CLASS ENRICHMENT

Have students draw imaginary creatures.

Ask students if they had pictured in their minds what a Heffalump looked like before they knew that Christopher Robin was talking about an elephant. Have students tell what they imagined. Ask students to draw their creatures and give them names. Collect pictures in a booklet entitled "I Saw a _____ Today."   CREATIVE THINKING

Have students write paragraphs about how they would catch a Heffalump.

Have students tell what they would have done to catch a Heffalump. Ask them to write paragraphs about how they would catch a Heffalump. Suggest the following incomplete sentences as starters:

1. **I would catch a Heffalump by _____.**

2. **Catching a Heffalump is not easy, so you have to _____.**

Have students illustrate their paragraphs and then show the drawings as they read the paragraphs aloud.   WRITING

TEACHER NOTES

Checkpoint

USING THE CHECKPOINT AND VOCABULARY REVIEW

Use the Checkpoint for informal evaluation.

This Checkpoint provides another opportunity for informal evaluation before the formal end-of-unit assessment. If students have difficulty with the Checkpoint, you might use the extra-help activities suggested here or the Reteaching activities at the end of the unit before you give the test.

Like the midunit Checkpoints, these pages are in the format of the Unit Skills Tests. They might also be used to review and practice test-taking strategies. Direct students to complete the pages shown in the Resource Center. Then have students work together to correct their papers, and encourage them to explain the thinking behind their answers. This affords you an opportunity to observe not only how students arrived at their answers, but also to identify and explain any item types that are causing difficulty.

Use the Vocabulary Review.

These two pages review selected Story Critical words from the unit in the format of the Unit Skills Tests. If students' responses indicate that they have not mastered the vocabulary, you might use the extra-help activity suggested here before testing.

PROVIDING EXTRA HELP

Provide extra help with long word decoding.

Improve reading comprehension by linking reading and vocabulary development. Use a long and unfamiliar word such as *dishonorable* to provide additional practice in long word decoding. Model the steps in this process for students. First, put the word on the chalkboard and mark familiar parts. (*dishonorable*) Next, divide the word into syllables. (*dis hon or a ble*)

Workbook page 158

RESOURCE CENTER

◀ These pages provide informal assessment in the format of the Unit Skills Tests. ▶

Workbook page 159

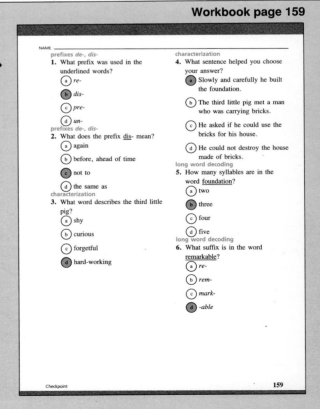

Then say the word parts slowly, using different vowel sounds until the word sounds familiar. (dis hon or a ble) Finally, place the main stress and say the word. *(dis än ər ə b'l)* Continue in the same manner with other long words until students are able to continue the activity on their own. At that time they might take turns coming to the chalkboard and demonstrating the process for the group.

Provide extra help with the prefixes de- and dis-.

Strengthen reading comprehension by linking reading and vocabulary development. Put each prefix at the top of the chalkboard. Tell students to determine which of the following root words can be combined with a prefix to form a new word and then to write that word in the correct column; *tour, agree, appoint, connect, plane.* Discuss the meaning of each new word formed.

Provide extra help with Story Critical words.

Strengthen comprehension of unit vocabulary by having students use Story Critical words in their writing. Give students three or four vocabulary words and have them write a paragraph using all of them. Choose related words such as *forecaster, meteorology, instruments* or *pitcher, outfielder, shortstop, bunt,* or make a more random selection such as *elevator, picnicking, temper* or *fault, complain, dawn, household.* When they have completed drafts of their paragraphs, students might work in pairs to discuss how to improve their writing before preparing final drafts to read to the group.

Use Informal Assessment Checklist for observation.

An Informal Assessment Checklist is included in the Teacher Resource Kit. (See the Meeting Individual Needs booklet.) The Checklist will assist you in observing each student's performance in the following categories: Self-monitoring, Getting Information from Text, Summarizing, Generalizing, Evaluating, Synthesizing across Selections, Visualizing, Responding, Empathizing with Story Characters, and Predicting.

Workbook page 160

RESOURCE CENTER

◀ These pages review ▶ selected Story Critical words.

Workbook page 161

NAME _____

Vocabulary Review

Fill in the circle beside the word that best fits in the sentence.

1. The _____ from the play was funny.
   - (a) prediction
   - (b) scene ●
   - (c) dawn
   - (d) household

2. Before planting seeds a farmer stirs up the soil with a _____.
   - (a) flock
   - (b) decision
   - (c) flake
   - (d) plow ●

3. I think the most important player on a baseball team is the _____.
   - (a) policeman
   - (b) flake
   - (c) pitcher ●
   - (d) forecaster

4. The shepherd was up on the mountain watching his _____.
   - (a) flake
   - (b) forecaster
   - (c) flock ●
   - (d) hike

5. The people in the theater clapped to show how much they had liked the _____.
   - (a) Pilgrims
   - (b) engineers
   - (c) outfielders
   - (d) performers ●

6. Every time my father does the food shopping, he buys more than enough for our _____.
   - (a) customers
   - (b) council
   - (c) household ●
   - (d) crocodile

7. A child who is _____ can learn sign language.
   - (a) worthy
   - (b) cunning
   - (c) popular
   - (d) deaf ●

160

Vocabulary Review

NAME _____

8. I think it will be sunny tomorrow even though rain was predicted by the _____.
   - (a) messenger
   - (b) official
   - (c) forecaster ●
   - (d) editor

9. After a busy day at work, my mom lets out a _____ of relief.
   - (a) sigh ●
   - (b) temper
   - (c) scene
   - (d) language

10. Because I worked hard, I feel _____ of the prize.
    - (a) worthy ●
    - (b) determined
    - (c) deaf
    - (d) displeased

11. There are days when we can't understand one another even though we speak the same _____.
    - (a) alphabet
    - (b) editor
    - (c) language ●
    - (d) meteorology

12. One of my favorite times of day is _____, when the morning is new.
    - (a) dawn ●
    - (b) official
    - (c) flake
    - (d) scene

13. It's impossible to read without first learning the _____.
    - (a) prediction
    - (b) instruments
    - (c) signs
    - (d) alphabet ●

14. The girl who hit that great home run is _____ whether to join our team.
    - (a) discontented
    - (b) considering ●
    - (c) dancing
    - (d) shaking

15. Sometimes, instead of talking, I like to _____ by using sign language.
    - (a) bunt
    - (b) concentrate
    - (c) complain
    - (d) communicate ●

Vocabulary Review

161

Concluding Unit 4

Unit Wrap-Up

Discuss the unit theme.

The following questions may be used to guide a general discussion of the unit. The questions help students relate the selections and understand the development of the unit theme. As an option, have students respond in writing on Workbook page 162.

1. Think about "Words in Our Hands" and "Sports Signals." How is the language used by deaf people similar to the signals used in sports? How is it different?

2. Think about the way people felt when the shepherd boy in "The Boy Who Cried Wolf" gave them false messages that caused them to waste their time. How do you think people felt about Stan when he gave them the wrong forecasts in "Forecast"? Why do you think they felt that way?

3. In "The Horse Who Lived Upstairs," Joey was discontented with life in the city until he learned a lesson. Think about "Mufaro's Beautiful Daughters." Do you think Manyara was discontented when she became a servant to her sister? Did Manyara learn a lesson also?

Writing About Reading: The Writing Process

OBJECTIVE   Writing to create.

Begin the writing activity.

In this activity, students will practice the writing process as they create a riddle about a story character. Recalling details about characters will help students prepare for writing.

Have students read the introductory paragraphs in the Student Text. Discuss the form of the riddle — several statements followed by a question. Then use the following suggestions to guide the students through the writing process.

Guide the writing process.

PREWRITING   Allow time for students to choose their characters. Then discuss with students the types of details about a character they might include; what the character said, did, or thought about something.

WRITING   If students have trouble deciding which details are most interesting, suggest they write a sentence about each detail and determine which sentences are most interesting. Encourage them to use clear and lively words as they write. Students can correct errors later.

REVISING   Have students check to be sure that the clues are in the same order as they are presented in the story. Have them make sure that their riddles end with a question. Then allow time for students to make changes.

PROOFREADING   Have students check their riddles to be sure that each sentence is clear and interesting. Then have them check the punctuation at the end of each sentence before they make neat copies of their riddles.

PUBLISHING   Have students put the answers to riddles on the backs of the index cards so they can easily check their answers. Students may also enjoy comparing different riddles about the same characters.

WRITING ABOUT READING

Writing a Character Riddle

This unit was about characters who sent and received messages in different ways. A character riddle is a message that asks you to guess who the story character is. The clues are from the story, and you can use those clues to guess the character. The clues are written in the order in which they come in the story.

Here is a character riddle. See if you can figure out who the character is.

◆ I want to run about and kick up my heels.

◆ I want to sleep in a red barn.

◆ I want to sip water from a bubbling brook.

◆ Who am I?

Did you get the message? Did you guess the horse in "The Horse Who Lived Upstairs"? Now you are going to write a character riddle, and your classmates are going to try to solve it.

Prewriting

Choose and draw a favorite character. Then draw five lines next to your character. On each line, write something the character does. This diagram will help you think of clues for your riddle.

◆ *The Writing Process* ───────────

Writing

Choose three interesting details from your diagram. Use the details to write a riddle about the character. Write the clues as if *you* are the character. Put the clues in the same order as they are in the story. End your riddle with the question "Who am I?"

Revising

Read your character riddle to a partner. Can your partner guess which character the riddle is about? If not, add more details to your clues.

Proofreading

Use a dictionary to check your spelling. Be sure you began the first word of each sentence with a capital letter. Make a neat copy of your riddle.

Publishing

Make a character-riddle game with index cards. You and your classmates can try to guess the answers to each other's riddles.

─────────────── *The Writing Process* ◆

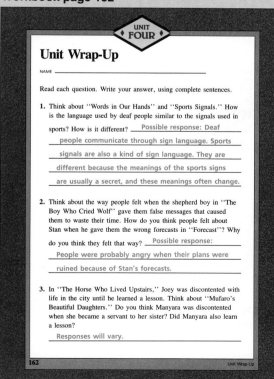

RESOURCE CENTER

Writing Master 25 supports the Writing About Reading activity.

Working Together: A Cooperative Learning Project

Plan for time and materials.

In this project, students will work in small groups to choose and send a nonverbal message. The project is designed to last about thirty minutes, but adapt this guideline to meet the needs of your class.

Present the project.

After students read page 344 in the Student Text, review the material by having them tell what they will be doing individually and as a group. Have them explain why each step is important. *(Looking at speakers helps them know if they have been understood; recording ideas ensures the ideas won't be forgotten; asking questions generates more ideas or information; making sure everyone understands helps ensure success.)*

Define roles and responsibilities.

Identify groups. Have students tell how they can encourage everyone's participation. Then discuss how they can handle disagreements. Direct attention to the first sentence in the last paragraph and have students tell how this might help them solve disagreements. *(They might see which message or delivery is easiest to understand.)* Encourage students to consider numerous messages before choosing one.

Observe the groups.

Observe the discussions among students, reminding them, if necessary, to record everyone's ideas and to ask questions. Encourage the participation of shy or less verbal students. Model the use of encouraging gestures.

Have students present the project and evaluate their performance.

Have groups send their messages to other groups and discuss how clear each message was. Have students discuss the role each played in the project and whether the person would choose that role again.

Books to Enjoy

Encourage independent reading.

Discuss with students the books described on the Student Text page. Encourage those who have read any of the suggested books to share their reactions with the group. You might also suggest that students copy titles of interest onto their Workbook Book List and look for them in the library.

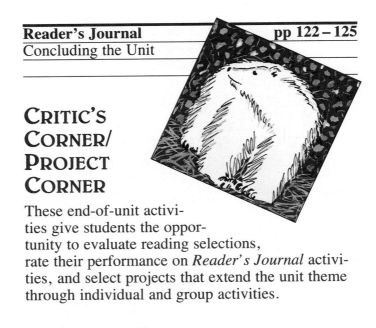

Reader's Journal	pp 122 – 125
Concluding the Unit	

CRITIC'S CORNER/ PROJECT CORNER

These end-of-unit activities give students the opportunity to evaluate reading selections, rate their performance on *Reader's Journal* activities, and select projects that extend the unit theme through individual and group activities.

WORKING TOGETHER

Sending a Message Without Words

In this unit you read how coaches send messages to their players without using words. Many people send messages without words. Have you ever seen a police officer directing traffic? Your group will practice sending a message without words.

Group members should do one or more of these tasks:

◆ Look at others when they talk.
◆ Record everyone's ideas on a list.
◆ Ask questions.
◆ Help group members understand what they should do.

Begin by talking about messages you might want to send. You might ask people to do something, go somewhere, or give you something, such as a pencil or a book. Take turns giving ideas for possible messages. Make a list of everyone's ideas. Together, choose one of them. Then discuss how a person could send the message without using words. Everyone should suggest ideas.

Try out the ideas on each other. If the message isn't easy to understand, think of ways to make it clearer. Then talk about when you might use this way of sending messages.

◆ *Cooperative Learning*

BOOKS TO ENJOY

Train Whistles by Helen Roney Sattler *(Lothrop, 1984)* The toots of a train whistle are a way for trains to signal to other trains, from one car of the train to another, and to people. Example: Two long toots, one short, and a long mean, ''Stop, cars and people! Wait until the train has passed!''

Computers by Jane Jonas Srivastava *(Harper & Row, 1972)* This book explains the basic units common to all computers and the kinds of tasks people program them to do.

The Seeing Stick by Jane Yolen *(Harper & Row, 1977)* This is the Chinese tale of an emperor who is sad because his daughter is blind. An old man says he can help her see with his ''seeing stick.''

Finger Rhymes by Marc Brown *(Dutton, 1980)* Fourteen familiar rhymes are presented.

Testing

Select the most appropriate test.

Unit Process Test is a holistic test that assesses overall comprehension. Students compose written responses to test questions.

Unit Skills Test is a criterion-referenced test that assesses how well a student has learned the specific skill objectives in the unit. The two forms, A and B, can be used to pretest and post-test or to test, reteach, and retest, depending on your preference.

End-of-Book Test is a general survey test to help determine how well a student has learned all the skills taught in the book. All skills tested on the End-of-Book Test are also tested on the individual Unit Skills Tests for each unit.

Score and evaluate test results.

Keys and Record Sheets assist in scoring the tests, interpreting the results, and identifying students who need additional help. Students who perform well may proceed directly to the next book. Those who do not will benefit from Reteaching activities on the pages that follow, Practice and Reteaching worksheets in the Teacher Resource Kit, and additional guided and independent reading.

Meeting Individual Needs

SKILL TRACE: WORD REFERENTS					
Introduction	Practice	Test	Reteach	Maintain	
TE 532	548	618	635	636	See Level 9.

COMPREHENSION

Word Referents

OBJECTIVE   Understanding relationships between substitute words and their referents.

RETEACHING

Reteach word referents.

Write on the chalkboard:

> **Ellen heard the telephone ring.**
> **Then she went to answer it.**

Explain that writers often use words that substitute or stand for other words. Word substitutes are used so that the same words, or referents, do not have to be repeated again and again. Point out that word substitutes can tell *who, what, when,* and *how many.* Circle *then* and explain that this word tells *when.* Ask students when Ellen went to answer the telephone. *(when she heard the telephone ring)* Have students circle the other word substitutes in the second sentence and tell what they refer to. *(she — Ellen; it — telephone)*
   Write on the board the following sentences. Have students copy them, circle the word substitutes, and draw arrows back to the referents.

1. **Stan bought string beans and carrots. Later, he cooked both.**

2. **Alex got on the bus. One seat was not taken, so he sat in it.**

Provide independent practice.

Reteaching Masters 1–7 for word referents may be assigned.

ACHIEVING ENGLISH PROFICIENCY

Provide practice identifying word substitutes and their referents.

Write the following sentences on the chalkboard: **Elena had fun in the park. She went there every day.**
   Read the sentences and have students repeat them after you . Circle the underlined words and draw arrows to their referents. Explain that *she* is Elena and *there* is in the park. Write the following sentence pairs and call on volunteers to draw arrows from the substitute words to their referents:

> **I will give two things to Kim. I will give her paper and a pen.**
> **Baseball is fun. It is my favorite sport.**
> **My aunt and uncle live in the city. They live in a tall building.**

Provide independent practice.

Achieving English Proficiency Master 30 may be assigned.

CHALLENGE

Have students write paragraphs with and without word substitutes.

Have each student write a paragraph using no word substitutes. Then have students exchange paragraphs and rewrite the paragraphs using word substitutes. Students can then return the paragraphs to the original writers for checking. Have students compare paragraph lengths and draw conclusions about the use of word substitutes. *(Using word substitutes shortens writing and makes it more interesting.)*

Provide independent practice.

Challenge Master 17 may be assigned.

SKILL TRACE: CHARACTERIZATION				
Introduction	Practice	Test	Reteach	Maintain
TE 482	500	525	635	637	See Level 9.

LITERATURE

Characterization

OBJECTIVE   Identifying character traits and emotions.

RETEACHING

Reteach characterization.

Write the following passage on the chalkboard:

> **Manyara was always in a bad mood. She teased her sister, Nyasha, when Father's back was turned. Nyasha ignored her sister's mean words and did not wish to complain to Father.**

Remind students that writers describe a character's personality by telling what they think and how they feel. These personality traits are clues to why characters behave as they do. Have students decide which of these words describe Manyara and which ones describe Nyasha: gentle *(N)*, mean *(M)*, kind *(N)*, nasty *(M)*, understanding *(N)*.

Explain that understanding a character's personality can help the reader understand why characters act and feel the way they do in stories.

Write the following sentences on the board. Have students copy them and identify the speaker as Manyara or Nyasha and name character traits for each.

1. **"How dare you stand in my way, old woman!"** *(Manyara, disrespectful, mean)*

2. **"You are welcome here."** *(Nyasha, kind, gentle)*

3. **"My little friend, what are you doing here?"** *(Nyasha, gentle, curious)*

Have students tell what they have learned about characterization. (*You can tell about characters' personalities from the way they act and what they say.*)

Provide independent practice.

Reteaching Masters 1–4 for characterization may be assigned.

CHALLENGE

Have students write character descriptions for a guessing game.

Have students brainstorm a list of story characters they all know well. *(Suggestions: Goldilocks, Clifford, Peter Rabbit, Ramona)* Write each name on an index card. Put the cards in a bag and have each student select one. Tell students to write character descriptions without naming the characters. Later, have students read their descriptions aloud and ask the others to guess the characters based on the personality traits described. Remind students that authors include physical descriptions, words that characters say, and descriptions of their actions.

Provide independent practice.

Challenge Master 14 may be assigned.

SKILL TRACE: MULTIPLE MEANINGS					
Introduction	Practice	Test	Reteach	Maintain	
TE 522	549	573	635	638	See Level 9.

VOCABULARY

Multiple Meanings

OBJECTIVE   Choosing the most appropriate meaning of a multiple-meaning word.

RETEACHING

Reteach multiple meanings.

Write the following passage on the chalkboard:

> **Joey and Mr. Polanski live in New York City. Imagine a live horse eating and sleeping in an apartment! This morning, Mr. Polanski read the newspaper. Joey, being a horse, does not read very much.**

Underline *live* and *read* in the sentences. Tell students that there are thousands of words in English that have more than one meaning. Some of those multiple-meaning words are also homographs. Define homographs as words that are spelled the same but have different pronunciations and meanings. Ask students to name any homographs they can think of. (Suggestions: *wind, lead, close*) Then add that to know which meaning of a word is being used and which pronunciation is correct, students must use context clues. Have students read the sentences and tell the meanings of the underlined words.

Explain that knowing about multiple-meaning words will help students be prepared to look carefully for context clues.

Write the following sentences on the board. Have students copy and define the underlined words.

1. **Joey had wanted more space on the farm than in his tiny apartment.**

2. **Have you ever thought about traveling through outer space?**

3. **There are eight steps leading up to the apartment building.**

4. **Some dance steps are easy to learn.**

5. **Joey liked the fine new stall in the red barn.**

6. **Mr Polanski paid a fine for parking his wagon at a bus stop.**

Have students tell what they have learned about multiple-meaning words. (*They must use the meanings of the other words in the sentence to figure out which meaning is correct.*)

Provide independent practice.

Reteaching Masters 1–4 for multiple meanings may be assigned.

ACHIEVING ENGLISH PROFICIENCY

Provide practice interpreting multiple-meaning words.

Write the following sentences on the chalkboard.

Lily has a ring on her finger.   They ring the bell at three o'clock.

Read the sentences aloud and ask students which word is spelled the same and pronounced the same in both sentences. Circle the word *ring*. Tell students that some words with the same spelling and the same pronunciation have meanings which are different. Follow a similar procedure for the following sentences.

1. **Sam can reach the table.   The can is full of water.**

2. **A hand has five fingers.   Please hand me the book.**

3. **The horse has a tough hide.   We hide in the grass.**

Help students understand any words which are new to them by using pictures or pantomiming actions.

Provide independent practice.

Achieving English Proficiency Master 29 may be assigned.

CHALLENGE

Have students write sentences for multiple-meaning words.

Write words with multiple meanings on the top line of index cards. Shuffle the cards and give one to each student. Have each student write a sentence using one meaning of the word on the first line of the index card. Then have them give the cards back to you. When all students have written sentences, reshuffle the cards and distribute them again. Have each student write a second sentence on the card using a second meaning of the word. Repeat several times. Suggest students use the dictionary to help them find additional meanings.

Provide independent practice.

Challenge Master 16 may be assigned.

SKILL TRACE: LONG WORD DECODING				
Introduction	Practice	Test	Reteach	Maintain
TE 498	524	595	635	640	See Level 9.

WORD STUDY

Long Word Decoding

OBJECTIVE   Using the long word decoding strategy to read words.

RETEACHING

Reteach decoding long words.

Write on the chalkboard: **discontented, unkindly.** Remind students that there are some steps they can follow to figure out long words. First find the familiar word parts such as prefixes and suffixes. Also look for known words in the long word. Then divide what is left into syllables. Try to say the parts, using different vowel sound combinations until the word makes sense. Direct students' attention to *discontented.* Have them find familiar word parts and known words. If necessary, underline the prefix *dis-* and the ending *-ed.* Have students say each syllable and then say the word normally. *(dis con tent′ ed)* Repeat the procedure with *unkindly. (un kind′ ly)* Ask volunteers to use the words in sentences.

Explain that knowing how to divide words into familiar parts will help students read and understand new words.

Write the following words on the board: **replacement, recognizable, invitation.** Have students use the decoding strategy to read the words. Then have students use each word in a sentence.

Have students tell what they have learned about long word decoding. *(Find familiar parts, say the syllables, try to say the whole word.)*

Provide independent practice.

Reteaching Masters 1–4 for long word decoding may be assigned.

ACHIEVING ENGLISH PROFICIENCY

Help students decode long words by breaking them down into known parts.

Print the word *respect* and the affixes *dis-* and *-ful* in large letters on separate cards. Have students repeat the word *respect* after you and then name people they respect. Call on a volunteer to hold the *respect* card in front of the class. Then have a second student hold the *-ful* card up at the end of *respect* and read the new word. Have students name ways in which they can be *respectful* of other people. Use the same procedure for adding the prefix *dis-.* Have students name ways in which some people are *disrespectful* of others. Clap out the syllables in *disrespectful* as students say the word aloud. Point out that when students come across a long word they don't know, they can look for the base word and word parts they already know.

Provide independent practice.

Achieving English Proficiency Master 27 may be assigned.

CHALLENGE

Have students find out about recycling.

Write the word **recycling** on the board and help students decode it. Discuss its meaning: "to treat something so that it can be used again." Have students tell what they know about why recycling is important and what sorts of things can be recycled. *(paper, cans, glass)* Then have students suggest questions about recycling to research. Record the questions on the board. Have students work with partners to pick questions to research. Students can use the encyclopedia or other references. Students can report their findings in a panel discussion on recycling.

Provide independent practice.

Challenge Master 15 may be assigned.

SKILL TRACE: PREFIXES				
Introduction	Practice	Test	Reteach	Maintain
TE 546	572	594	635	641	See Level 9.

WORD STUDY

Prefixes de-, dis-

OBJECTIVE Using structural analysis to determine word meaning.

RETEACHING

Reteach prefixes de-, dis-.

Write on the chalkboard: **debug, disobey.** Underline the *de-, dis-* prefixes. Explain that the prefix *de-* means "remove," "remove from," or "get off," and the prefix *dis-* means "refuse to," "fail to," or "not." Point to *debug* and ask students to use the meaning of *de-* and the base word *bug* to define the word. (*remove bugs*) Repeat for *disobey.* Ask volunteers to use each word in a sentence.

Explain that knowing what prefixes mean will help students read and understand new words.

Write the following sentences on the board. Have students read, write, and define the words with the prefixes *de-, dis-.*

1. **Wash the shirt until the stain disappears.**

2. **Discontented citizens often dethrone kings.**

3. **If you distrust the pilot, it is best to deplane before takeoff.**

Have students tell what they have learned about these prefixes. (De- *means "remove, remove from, get off"* ; dis- *means "refuse to, fail to, not"*)

Provide independent practice.

Reteaching Masters 1–4 for prefixes *de-, dis-* may be assigned.

ACHIEVING ENGLISH PROFICIENCY

Provide practice reading words with de- and dis-.

Write the words *like* and *dislike* on the chalkboard. Have pairs of students use the words to ask and answer questions. Use the following model: **Do you like cats? No, I dislike cats.** Then ask students what they think *dis-* means (*"not"*). Write on the chalkboard the following sentence pairs and have students repeat them after you:

> **There is too much frost on the windshield.   We must defrost it.**
> **This message is written in a secret code.   Can you decode it?**

Review the meaning of the underlined word pairs. Finally, help students to understand what *de-* means in the underlined words. (*"take out or away from" or "get off"*)

Provide independent practice.

Achieving English Proficiency Master 32 may be assigned.

CHALLENGE

Have students write reviews of movies or stories they dislike.

Have each student select a story or movie he or she dislikes and write a review of it explaining why. This paragraph should also include how the writer thinks the story or movie might be changed to improve it. Have the reviews read aloud.

Provide independent practice.

Challenge Master 18 may be assigned.

Full pronunciation key* The pronunciation of each word is shown just after the word, in this way: **abbreviate** (ə brē'vē āt).

The letters and signs used are pronounced as in the words below.

The mark ' is placed after a syllable with a primary or heavy accent as in the example above.

The mark ' after a syllable shows a secondary or lighter accent, as in **abbreviation** (ə brē'vē ā'shən).

SYMBOL	KEY WORDS	SYMBOL	KEY WORDS	SYMBOL	KEY WORDS
a	ask, fat	u	up, cut	r	red, dear
ā	ape, date	ur	fur, fern	s	sell, pass
ä	car, father			t	top, hat
		ə	a in ago	v	vat, have
e	elf, ten		e in agent	w	will, always
er	berry, care		e in father	y	yet, yard
ē	even, meet		i in unity	z	zebra, haze
			o in collect		
i	is, hit		u in focus	ch	chin, arch
ir	mirror, here			ng	ring, singer
ī	ice, fire	b	bed, dub	sh	she, dash
		d	did, had	th	thin, truth
o	lot, pond	f	fall, off	th	then, father
ō	open, go	g	get, dog	zh	s in pleasure
ô	law, horn	h	he, ahead		
oi	oil, point	j	joy, jump	'	as in (ā'b'l)
oo	look, pull	k	kill, bake		
oo	ooze, tool	l	let, ball		
yoo	unite, cure	m	met, trim		
yoo	cute, few	n	not, ton		
ou	out, crowd	p	put, tap		

*Pronunciation key and respellings adapted from *Webster's New World Dictionary, Basic School Edition,* Copyright © 1983 by Simon & Schuster, Inc. Reprinted by permission.

A

a·board (ə bôrd') *adverb.* on, in, or into a boat, train, airplane, or bus.

ab·so·lute·ly (ab'sə loot lē) *adverb.* completely; perfectly.

ac·tor (ak'tər) *noun.* a person, especially a boy or man, who performs in plays, in movies, or on television. **actors.**

ad·ven·ture (əd ven'chər) *noun.* **1.** a dangerous event. **2.** an unusual or exciting experience.

ad·vice (əd vīs') *noun.* an opinion given about what action to take or about how to do something.

al·pha·bet (al'fə bet) *noun.* **1.** the letters of a language placed in order. **2.** a system of symbols used in communicating, such as the Braille alphabet for the blind.

am·ble (am'b'l) *verb.* **1.** to walk in a slow, easy way. **2.** to move slowly and smoothly by raising both legs on one side, then both legs on the other side; used to describe the way a horse, donkey, etc., moves. **ambled.**

an·chor (ang'kər) *noun.* a heavy object that is lowered into the water on a rope or chain to keep a boat from drifting, usually a metal piece with hooks that dig into the ground under the water.

an·nounce (ə nouns') *verb.* **1.** to say or tell something to an audience. **2.** to make something known to others: He *announced* that the class would take a trip to the museum. **3.** to say or tell. **announced.**

at·ten·tion (ə ten'shən) *noun.* the ability to keep your mind or thoughts on something; notice.

awk·ward (ôk'wərd) *adjective.* **1.** not moving in a graceful way; clumsy. **2.** difficult to use or hold: It was *awkward* to carry so many packages.

ax·le (ak's'l) *noun.* a bar or rod on which the wheels at each end turn: When the *axle* broke on the wagon, one wheel rolled down the hill.

aboard

Alphabet is taken from two Greek words *alpha* and *beta.* These two words are the names of the first two letters in the Greek alphabet.

axle

B

Ballet is a French word that became part of the English language. Ballet started in France three hundred years ago. When it spread to England, people used the French word for the new style of dance.

breeches

bugle

bab·ble (bab''l) *verb.* **1.** to make sounds like talking that are not understood by others; baby talk. **2.** to chatter or talk fast. **3.** to speak foolishly. —**babbling** *adjective.* bubbling or gurgling sounds, like water running over stones: The deer drank water from the *babbling* brook.

bal·let (bal'ā *or* ba lā') *noun.* a dance that tells a story through a series of planned, graceful movements usually performed by dancers wearing costumes.

beak (bēk) *noun.* **1.** the bill of a bird, especially of an eagle, a hawk, or another bird of prey. **2.** anything that looks like a bird's beak.

be·lief (bə lēf') *noun.* **1.** a thought or feeling that something is true or real; faith. **2.** anything accepted as true. **beliefs.**

blub·ber (blub'ər) *noun.* fat under the skins of seals, whales, and other sea animals.

bore (bôr) *verb.* to tire by being dull or uninteresting. —**boring** *adjective.* dull, uninteresting.

bor·row (bor'ō *or* bôr'ō) *verb.* **1.** to use something that belongs to someone else after agreeing to return it. **2.** to use someone else's ideas, ways of doing things, etc., as your own. **borrowed.**

breech·es (brich'iz) *plural noun.* short pants that stop just below the knees.

bu·gle (byoo'g'l) *noun.* a type of small trumpet, usually without playing keys or valves.

bunk (bungk) *noun.* **1.** a built-in bed that hangs on a wall like a shelf. **2.** a narrow bed: The cowboy went to his *bunk* after a hard day's work.

bunt (bunt) *verb.* to bat a baseball lightly so that it does not go beyond the infield.

busi·ness (biz'nis) *noun.* **1.** work that someone does to earn money. **2.** a place where work is done or things are made or sold. **3.** a matter or affair: The girls met to make rules and talk about their club *business.*

C

ca·ble (kā'b'l) *noun.* **1.** a strong rope, usually made of covered wires or metal twisted together. **2.** a bundle of insulated wires that conduct electricity. **3.** a shorter word for *cablegram,* a telegraph message sent overseas.

cham·ber (chām'bər) *noun.* **1.** a room, usually a bedroom. **2.** a large room used for meetings, such as an assembly hall.

charm (chärm) *noun.* **1.** something believed to have magical powers, either good or evil. **2.** a small object on a bracelet or necklace. **3.** a physical feature or a personal characteristic that is pleasing, delightful, or attractive.

chat·ter (chat'ər) *verb.* **1.** to make short, quick noises that sound like talking: The birds were *chattering* outside the window. **2.** to talk fast and foolishly without stopping. **chattering.**

chick·en (chik'ən) *noun.* **1.** a young hen or rooster. **2.** the meat of a chicken. **chickens.**

choice (chois) *noun.* **1.** the act of choosing or picking. **2.** having the chance, power, or right to choose. **3.** someone or something chosen.

choke (chōk) *verb.* **1.** to try to breathe when something is stuck in the windpipe. **2.** to squeeze the throat to stop breathing. **3.** to have trouble breathing. **choked.**

chore (chôr) *noun.* **1.** the regular light work such as that done at home or on a farm: His *chores* on the farm include feeding the chickens. **2.** a task that is difficult or uninteresting. **chores.**

clam·ber (klam'bər) *verb.* to climb by trying hard, especially using both the hands and feet: The boy *clambered* up the tree. **clambered.**

clerk (klurk) *noun.* **1.** a person who sells in a store. **2.** an office worker who keeps records and types letters.

cli·mate (klī'mət) *noun.* the typical weather of a place, year after year: In some cold *climates* people wear coats all year long. **climates.**

cob·ble·stone (kob''l stōn) *noun.* a rounded stone that was used to pave the streets long ago. **cobblestones.**

a fat	oi oil	ch chin
ā ape	oo look	sh she
ä car, father	oo tool	th thin
e ten	ou out	th then
er care	u up	zh leisure
ē even	ur fur	ng ring
i hit		
ir here	ə = a in ago	
ī bite, fire	e in agent	
o lot	i in unity	
ō go	o in collect	
ô law, horn	u in focus	

chicken

Cobblestone is made up of *cobble* and *stone.* Cob is a very old word meaning "plump" or "round."

com·mu·ni·cate (kə myōō'nə kāt) *verb.* to make something known to others; to give or share information: Long ago, some Native Americans could *communicate* by sending smoke signals.

com·plain (kəm plān') *verb.* to tell about or show pain or unhappiness about something.

con·cen·trate (kon'sən trāt) *verb.* to focus all your attention on something: He will *concentrate* on learning how to play the piano.

con·gress·man (kăng' grəs mən) *noun.* an elected official who votes on laws in Congress. **congressmen.**

con·sid·er (kən sid'ər) *verb.* **1.** to think about something in order to make a decision. **2.** to keep something in mind while making a decision or in taking an action. **3.** to believe something about someone. **considering.**

coun·cil (koun's'l) *noun.* **1.** a group of people who meet to make plans or decisions. **2.** a group of people elected to make the laws for a town.

cour·age (kur'ij) *noun.* the ability to control fear in order to go through danger, pain, or trouble; bravery.

Consider comes from Greek. Its meaning was "to observe the stars." Perhaps the ancient Greeks also used their star-gazing hours to think. In time, *consider* came to mean "to think things over."

crocodile

dawn

croc·o·dile (krok'ə dīl) *noun.* a large tropical lizard like an alligator, with thick skin, a long tail, a long, narrow, triangular head with large jaws, and cone-shaped teeth.

cun·ning (kun'ing) *adjective.* clever; able to cheat or trick others: The *cunning* fox was able to fool the rabbit.

cus·to·mer (kus'tə mər) *noun.* a person who buys, often again and again, from the same place. **customers.**

D

dan·gle (dang'g'l) *verb.* to hang loosely so as to swing. **dangled.**

dawn (dôn) *verb.* **1.** to begin to be day; to grow light. **2.** to begin to happen. —*noun.* the first light of day.

deaf (def) *adjective.* **1.** not able to hear or not able to hear well. **2.** not wanting to hear or listen.

de·ci·sion (di sizh'ən) *noun.* the act of making up your mind about something, or the choice decided on: He made a *decision* about what to wear.

deck (dek) *noun.* **1.** the floor of a ship. **2.** a pack of 52 playing cards.

de·pend (di pend') *verb.* **1.** to trust someone to give help. **2.** to be determined by something or someone else: The amount of snowfall varies, *depending* on where you live. **depending.**

de·serve (di zurv') *verb.* to have the right to something: We worked hard and we *deserve* the prize.

des·ti·na·tion (des'tə nā'shən) *noun.* the place where someone is going.

de·ter·mined (di tur'mənd) *adjective.* **1.** having your mind made up. **2.** strong and sure.

dif·fi·cult (dif'i kəlt) *adjective.* **1.** hard to do or make; causing a lot of trouble, thought, time, or practice; hard to understand. **2.** hard to get along with.

dis·con·tent·ed (dis'kən tent'id) *adjective.* not satisfied; wanting something different.

dis·o·bey (dis ə bā') *verb.* to refuse to follow orders.

dis·please (dis plēz') *verb.* to anger or dissatisfy; to be bothered by: They were *displeased* by the long lines of people outside the store. **displeased.**

dis·tance (dis'təns) *noun.* **1.** the amount of space between two points. **2.** a place far away.

dis·tress (dis tres') *verb.* to cause worry, sorrow, or trouble. —*noun.* worry; pain; unhappiness.

dive (dīv) *verb.* **1.** to plunge headfirst into water. **2.** to go underwater to look for something. **3.** to move or drop suddenly. **dived.**

dol·phin (dol'fən) *noun.* a water animal belonging to the same family as the whale, but smaller than the whale. **dolphins.**

drawn (drôn) *verb.* to be pulled: The wagon was *drawn* by two horses.

deck

E

ea·ger (ē'gər) *adjective.* wanting very much to do or get something.

ech·o (ek'ō) *noun.* a sound heard again after it bounces off a surface. —*verb.* to repeat.

dolphin

a fat	oi oil	ch chin	
ā ape	oo look	sh she	
ä car, father	ōō tool	th thin	
e ten	ou out	th then	
er care	u up	zh leisure	
ē even	ur fur	ng ring	
i hit			
ir here	ə = a in ago		
ī bite, fire	e in agent		
o lot	i in unity		
ō go	o in collect		
ô law, horn	u in focus		

ed·i·tor (ed'ə tər) *noun.* a person in charge of putting together a newspaper or magazine.

ed·u·ca·tion (ej'ə kā'shən) *noun.* what you learn by being taught in school or by training.

el·e·va·tor (el'ə vāt'ər) *noun.* a platform or box that moves up and down in a shaft and that carries people and things between floors in buildings.

em·bar·rass (im ber'əs) *verb.* to make feel uncomfortable or uneasy. —**embarrassed** *adjective.* self-conscious; ashamed.

emp·ty (emp'tē) *adjective.* having nothing inside. —*verb.* to take everything out of a jar, bottle, etc.

en·gi·neer (en'jə nir') *noun.* a person who is trained to plan and build machines, roads, bridges, etc. **engineers.**

Eng·lish (ing'glish) *adjective.* of England, its language, or its people.

es·pe·cial·ly (ə spesh'əl ē) *adverb.* mostly; in particular: I like candy, *especially* chocolate.

ex·it (eg'zit *or* ek'sit) *noun.* a way out of a place, such as a door. —*verb.* to go out; to leave.

Elevator comes from a Latin word that means "to lighten" or "raise up."

engineer

Farmhand is a compound word made up of *farm* and *hand.* *Hand* in this case refers to a person who works with his or her hands.

F

fame (fām) *noun.* known by many people through books, television, newspapers, etc.

fa·mil·iar (fə mil'yər) *adjective.* **1.** close; friendly; knowing someone or something well. **2.** acting too friendly in a pushy way. **3.** ordinary or usual.

farm·hand (färm'hand) *noun.* a person who works on a farm to earn money. **farmhands.**

fault (fôlt) *noun.* **1.** a thing or problem that keeps something or someone from being perfect. He has many *faults,* but he is still my friend. **2.** a mistake. **3.** being the cause of something unwanted. **faults.**

fa·vor·ite (fā'vər it) *noun.* a person or thing that is liked better than others. —*adjective.* best liked; preferred.

fend·er (fen'dər) *noun.* a metal piece over each wheel of a car that protects the car from mud, stones, etc. **fenders.**

fib·er·glass (fī'bər glas') *noun.* material made of glass threads that is used to make cloth, insulation, boats, etc.

fish·er·man (fish'ər mən) *noun.* someone who catches or tries to catch fish for sport or for a living. **fishermen.**

flake (flāk) *noun.* a small, thin, usually flat piece of something.

flip·per (flip'ər) *noun.* **1.** the wide, flat body part on seals, whales, etc., used for swimming. **2.** a wide, flat rubber shoe that swimmers wear to help them move through water. **flippers.**

flock (flok) *noun.* a group of animals or birds that eat and travel together.

flut·ter (flut'ər) *verb.* **1.** to flap the wings quickly in a short flight or without flying. **2.** to move with quick motions. **fluttered.**

fore·cast·er (fôr'kast ər) *noun.* someone who tries to predict how events will turn out.

freight train (frāt trān) *noun.* a train that carries a load of goods. **freight trains.**

fu·ture (fyōō'chər) *noun.* a time that is to come: In the *future,* I will study more for tests.

G

gal·ley (gal'ē) *noun.* **1.** a long, low ship used long ago, moved by sails and oars. **2.** the kitchen of a boat or ship: The sailor went to the *galley* to start cooking.

ga·losh·es (gə losh'iz) *plural noun.* overshoes that come high above the ankles, worn in wet or snowy weather.

gar·ment (gär'mənt) *noun.* a piece of clothing, such as a skirt, a pair of pants, etc. **garments.**

glit·ter (glit'ər) *verb.* to shine with a sparkling light. **glittered.**

gloom·i·ly (glōōm'ə lē) *adverb.* very sadly; in a deeply unhappy way.

goal (gōl) *noun.* **1.** the destination at the end of a race or trip. **2.** a purpose toward which one's actions are aimed: Their *goal* was to finish cleaning the house before the guests arrived. **3.** a net, line, or pocket over or into which a ball must go for a team or player to score in certain games.

flock

Galoshes used to be a kind of high wooden sandal. These sandals were worn over shoes to keep a person's feet out of the mud. Today galoshes do the same thing, but they are made of rubber, not wood.

a fat	oi oil	ch chin	
ā ape	oo look	sh she	
ä car, father	ōō tool	th thin	
e ten	ou out	th then	
er care	u up	zh leisure	
ē even	ur fur	ng ring	
i hit			
ir here	ə = a in ago		
ī bite, fire	e in agent		
o lot	i in unity		
ō go	o in collect		
ô law, horn	u in focus		

H

hes·i·tate (hez′ə tāt) *verb.* **1.** to stop or hold back for a moment as if feeling unsure. **2.** to feel unwilling to do something. **hesitated.**

hike (hīk) *noun.* a long walk, especially through the woods or in the countryside.

hon·or (on′ər) *noun.* **1.** a sign of respect: It was an *honor* to be chosen for the advanced class. **2.** credit or glory, as in winning a prize. **3.** good name.

hood (hood) *noun.* **1.** a piece that covers the head and neck, often attached to a jacket or coat. **2.** a metal cover in the front of an automobile over the engine.

hoot owl (hoot oul) *noun.* a bird with a large head, large eyes, small hooked beak, and sharp claws. It makes a long, low sound.

horn (hôrn) *noun.* **1.** a musical instrument played by blowing. **2.** a device that makes a loud, warning noise.

house·hold (hous′hōld) *noun.* all the people who live in a house, especially a family.

hug (hug) *verb.* **1.** to put the arms around and hold close

in a loving way. **2.** to keep close. **hugging.**

hur·ri·cane (hur′ə kān) *noun.* a storm with strong winds blowing in a circle at 73 miles per hour or more, usually with heavy rains.

I

ice·berg (īs′burg) *noun.* a huge piece of ice, floating in the sea; most of an iceberg is under the water.

i·cy (ī′sē) *adjective.* **1.** covered with ice; frozen or slippery. **2.** feeling very cold like ice.

ig·nore (ig nôr′) *verb.* to act as if something is not happening: Try to *ignore* the noises from the street and just keep talking.

in·clude (in klood′) *verb.* to take something in as a part of a whole or group: Will you *include* this in the box?

in·ning (in′ ing) *noun.* a part of a baseball game in which both teams get a turn at bat; there are usually nine innings in a baseball game.

in·sist (in sist′) *verb.* **1.** to demand in a stubborn or strong way. **2.** to stick to an idea strongly.

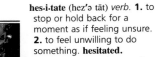
hood

hoot owl

Hoot is a good example of a word that is taken directly from a sound. The word *hoot* in *hoot owl* sounds like the call of an owl.

in·stru·ment (in′strə mənt) *noun.* **1.** a tool or machine used to do exact work: The doctor always washed his *instruments* after he used them. **2.** something on which music can be played, such as a drum, violin, flute, etc. **instruments.**

in·ter·rupt (in tə rupt′) *verb.* **1.** to make a break in something, as in someone talking: He *interrupted* the lesson when he came late to class. **2.** to keep something from going on; to cut off. **interrupted.**

in·tro·duce (in trə doos′ *or* in trə dyoos′) *verb.* to present or make known to others. **introduces.**

in·vi·ta·tion (in′və ta′shən) *noun.* **1.** the act of inviting a person to go somewhere or do something. **2.** the spoken or written way of inviting.

J

jun·gle (jung′gl) *noun.* land in warm, moist parts of the world, covered with trees, plants, and vines.

K

key·board (kē′bôrd) *noun.* **1.** the row or rows of black and white keys on a piano or organ. **2.** the lettered and numbered keys on a computer or typewriter.

kind·ness (kīnd′nis) *noun.* the habit or way of being friendly, good, generous, etc., to others.

L

lad·en (lād′n) *adjective.* having or carrying a heavy load: Mother left the department store *laden* with packages.

lan·guage (lang′gwij) *noun.* **1.** the speech or writing people use to understand each other. **2.** any way of communicating thoughts or feelings, such as the way sign language uses hand gestures to make words. **3.** the written or spoken words of a certain group of people: My pen pal speaks English as well as the Korean *language.*

a fat	oi oil	ch chin
ā ape	oo look	sh she
â car, father	oo tool	th thin
e ten	ou out	th then
er care	u up	zh leisure
ē even	ur fur	ng ring
i hit		
ī bite, fire	ə = a *in* ago	
o lot		e *in* agent
ō go		i *in* unity
ô law, horn		o *in* collect
		u *in* focus

keyboard

laden

li·brar·y (lī′brer′ē) *noun.* a place where a collection of books, magazines, records, or films is kept for reading or borrowing.

lit·er·ar·y (lit′ə rer′ē) *adjective.* **1.** having to do with the written work of a country, a time in history, etc., that people enjoy reading. **2.** having to do with writing.

lull (lul) *verb.* **1.** to make or become calm or quiet. **2.** to calm by using soft sounds or movements. **lulled.**

lung (lung) *noun.* one of the two organs in the chest used to breathe: The mountain climber took a deep breath and filled his *lungs* with fresh air. **lungs.**

mandolin

Marathon races are so named because of a messenger in Greece over two thousand years ago. This messenger ran 26 miles from a city named Marathon to the city of Athens. He delivered the message that the Greeks had defeated the Persians in battle. Modern marathons are the same distance that the ancient messenger ran.

M

mag·a·zine (mag ə zēn′ *or* mag′ə zēn) *noun.* a regular publication with stories, information, pictures, etc., usually coming out once each week or month. **magazines.**

main·land (mān′ land *or* mān′ lənd) *noun.* the greatest part of a country or continent; not an island.

mam·mal (mam′əl) *noun.* any of a group of animals where the females have special glands that produce milk to feed their young. **mammals.**

man·age (man′ij) *verb.* **1.** to be in charge of. **2.** to be sure that things get done in workplaces, homes, etc. **3.** to succeed in doing something: She *managed* to swim across the lake. **managed.**

man·do·lin (man′d'l in) *noun.* a musical instrument with eight or ten strings played with a pick.

man·go (mang′gō) *noun.* **1.** a tropical fruit with a yellowish-red thick skin and a hard stone inside. **2.** the tree on which this fruit grows.

mar·a·thon (mar′ə thon) *noun.* a race run on foot, about 26 miles long.

may·or (mā′ər *or* mer) *noun.* the person elected by the people of a city or town to be in charge of its government.

med·al (med′l) *noun.* a piece of metal with words or pictures on it, usually given as a prize to people who do something special.

medal

mem·o·ry (mem′ər ē) *noun.* **1.** the act of remembering things. **2.** anything that someone remembers: Her good *memories* of summer camp gave her pleasure all winter long. **3.** the part of a computer that stores information. **memories.**

mes·quite (mes kēt′ *or* mes′kēt) *noun.* a kind of tree or shrub with thorns and sugary, beanlike pods that are often used to feed animals.

mes·sen·ger (mes′'n jər) *noun.* a person who carries mail or things from one place to another: The *messenger* took the package and delivered it to the bank.

me·te·or·ol·o·gy (mēt′ē ə rol′ə jē) *noun.* the study or science of weather.

mil·let (mil′it) *noun.* **1.** a kind of grass grown for hay. **2.** the seeds of this grass, or grain, as used as food in some parts of the world.

mil·lion (mil′yən) *noun.* one thousand thousands (1,000,000). **millions.**

min·is·ter (min′is tər) *noun.* the head of a church, especially a Protestant church; a religious leader. **ministers.**

min·now (min′ ō) *noun.* a very small fish.

mis·chief (mis′chif) *noun.* **1.** harm, damage, or injury. **2.** an act that causes harm. **3.** a person, especially a child, who bothers people or things. **4.** playful tricks: He is always getting into *mischief* when his mother is busy.

mis·take (mi stāk′) *noun.* something done incorrectly or in error.

mix·ture (miks′chər) *noun.* something made by blending different things into a single, whole thing.

mor·sel (môr′ s'l) *noun.* a small bit of food.

most·ly (mōst′lē) *adverb.* for the greater part; mainly.

mous·tache (mə stash *or* mus′ tash) *noun.* the hair a man has let grow out on his upper lip.

move·ment (moov′mənt) *noun.* the act of moving or changing place.

mule (myool) *noun.* **1.** an animal whose parents are a horse and a donkey. **2.** a person who is stubborn. *used only in informal language.*

mus·cle (mus′l) *noun.* the tissue in the body that stretches and tightens to move the body. **muscles.**

a fat	oi oil	ch chin
ā ape	oo look	sh she
â car, father	oo tool	th thin
e ten	ou out	th then
er care	u up	zh leisure
ē even	ur fur	ng ring
i hit		
ir here	ə = a *in* ago	
ī bite, fire		e *in* agent
o lot		i *in* unity
ō go		o *in* collect
ô law, horn		u *in* focus

millet

mule

mustang

nuzzle

perch

mus·tang (mus′tang) *noun.* a small, wild horse that usually runs free in some parts of the southwestern United States. **mustangs.**

nuz·zle (nuz″l) *verb.* **1.** to rub with the nose: The dog *nuzzled* the puppy. **2.** to lie close and be comfortable. **nuzzled.**

N

na·ture (nā′chər) *noun.* **1.** the universe and everything in it that is not made by humans. **2.** the outdoors, including plants, animals, flowers, etc.

ne·glect (ni glekt′) *verb.* **1.** not to take care of as one should: He *neglected* to walk the dog yesterday. **2.** to take little notice of. **neglected.**

neigh·bor·hood (nā′bər hood) *noun.* **1.** a small part of a city, town, etc.: My school is in my *neighborhood.* **2.** people who live near each other.

nib·ble (nib″l) *verb.* **1.** to eat quickly in small bites. **2.** to bite carefully.

note (nōt) *noun.* **1.** a word or sentence written to help you remember something. **2.** a short letter. **3.** a musical tone or the symbol that stands for a musical tone as written on paper. **notes.**

O

of·fi·cial (ə fish′əl) *noun.* **1.** a person who holds office, usually in government. **2.** a person who makes sure that the rules are followed in sports. —*adjective.* coming from someone in authority.

out·field·er (out′fēl′dər) *noun.* a baseball player who stays in center, left, or right field. **outfielders.**

o·val (ō′v′l) *adjective.* having a shape like an egg.

P

pause (pôz) *noun.* to break for a moment when talking; stop for a moment.

perch (purch) *verb.* to rest, as on a place where a bird sits: The eagle *perched* on the rooftop. **perched.**

---

per·form·ance (pər fôr′məns) *noun.* the act of doing something before an audience.

per·for·mer (pər fôr′mər) *noun.* a person who acts, plays an instrument, or shows another skill before an audience. **performers.**

per·suade (pər swād′) *verb.* to get someone to act or think in a certain way by making it seem like a good thing.

pi·an·o (pē an′ō) *noun.* a large musical instrument with wire strings in a case and a keyboard.

pic·nic (pik′nik) *verb.* to go on an outing that includes eating a meal outdoors. **picnicking.**

pil·grim (pil′grəm) *noun.* **1.** a person who travels to places away from home for religious reasons. **2. Pilgrim.** one of the group of Puritans who left England and settled in Plymouth, Massachusetts, in 1620. **Pilgrims.**

pi·lot (pī′lət) *noun.* **1.** a person who steers a ship. **2.** a person who flies an airplane or helicopter.

pitch·er (pich′ər) *noun.* a baseball player who throws the ball so the batters can try to hit it.

plan·et (plan′it) *noun.* a large heavenly body that moves in an orbit or path around a star.

plow (plou) *noun.* a farm tool, pulled by an animal or a tractor, that breaks up the soil into rows to get it ready for planting.

plug (plug) *verb.* **1.** to close up a hole. **2.** to work hard and steadily at something: When we came home, the workers were still *plugging* away at digging the trench. **plugging.**

plunge (plunj) *verb.* **1.** to throw or push with great power. **2.** to dive. **plunged.**

pock·et (pok′it) *noun.* a small bag or pouch sewn into clothing and used to hold things. **pockets.**

po·em (pō′əm) *noun.* a written work that uses a pattern of sounds, tempo, and words that rhyme to show an idea or experience that is deeply felt by the writer.

po·et·ry (pō′ə trē) *noun.* **1.** the art of writing poems. **2.** poems.

po·lice·man (pə lēs′mən) *noun.* a member of the police department.

a fat	oi oil	ch chin
ā ape	oo look	sh she
ä car, father	ōō tool	th thin
e ten	ou out	th then
er care	u up	zh leisure
ē even	ur fur	ŋ ring
i hit		
ir here	ə = a in ago	
ī bite, fire		e in agent
o lot		i in unity
ō go		o in collect
ô law, horn		u in focus

piano

Piano comes from the Italian word, *pianoforte*, which means "soft" and "strong." The inventor of the piano chose this name because the new instrument could be played both softly and loudly.

practice

punt

pop·u·lar (pop′yə lər) *adjective.* **1.** being well liked by many people. **2.** something that is liked by a lot of people.

pop·u·lar·i·ty (pop′yə lar′ə tē) *noun.* the state of being well liked.

po·si·tion (pə zish′ən) *noun.* **1.** the way a person or thing is placed. **2.** the place where a person or thing is, especially how near or far from other things. **3.** a job that someone does.

prac·tice (prak′tis) *verb.* **1.** to make a habit of doing something regularly. **2.** to repeat an action in order to become skilled.

pre·dic·tion (pri dik′shən) *noun.* trying to tell what will happen in the future.

prep·a·ra·tion (prep′ə rā′shən) *noun.* **1.** getting or being ready for something. **2.** doing things to get ready. **preparations.**

pre·pare (pri par′) *verb.* **1.** to make or get ready: He can't go with us because he has to *prepare* for a test. **2.** to put something together.

press (pres) *noun.* **1.** a machine that prints pages from inked type, plates, or rolls: The newspaper was printed on a *press.* **2.** a machine that smooths or squeezes something. **3.** newspapers and magazines or the people who work for them. **presses.**

print (print) *verb.* **1.** to press letters or designs onto a surface. **2.** to produce writing to be sold. **3.** to write in letters similar to those in books. **printed.**

pro·vide (prə vīd′) *verb.* **1.** to give what is needed. **2.** to support. **3.** to get ready ahead of time. **provided.**

pub·lish (pub′lish) *verb.* to get a book, magazine, newspaper, etc., printed and brought to market for sale. **published.**

punt (punt) *noun.* the act of kicking a football after it is dropped from the hands but before it hits the ground.

purr (pur) *verb.* to make the soft sound a cat makes when it is happy. **purred.**

R

rack·et (rak′it) *verb.* to make a loud, clattering noise. **racketing.**

---

ra·di·o (rā′dē o′) *noun.* **1.** a way that sounds are sent from one place to another by changing them into electrical waves that travel through the air. **2.** a receiving set that picks up those waves and changes them back into sounds.

raw (rô) *adjective.* **1.** uncooked. **2.** in its natural state. **3.** uncomfortably cold and damp: The *raw* wind made us return home early.

re·ci·tal (ri sīt′l) *noun.* **1.** the act of telling every part of a story. **2.** a story told like this. **3.** a music or dance program where people perform on stage alone or in a small group.

re·cov·er (ri kuv′ər) *verb.* **1.** to get back something that was lost. **2.** to get well again after being sick: I am sure that she will *recover* soon from her bad cold.

re·frig·er·a·tor (ri frij′ə rāt′or) *noun.* a machine or room that keeps food, drinks, etc., cold and fresh.

re·lax (ri laks′) *verb.* **1.** to make something loose. **2.** to rest after working or doing something.

re·lief (ri lēf′) *noun.* freedom from pain, worry, or uncomfortable feelings: We were worried, but it is a *relief* to know you are safe.

re·li·gion (ri lij′ən) *noun.* **1.** a belief in God or gods. **2.** a way of living by worshipping God.

re·li·gious (re lij′əs) *adjective.* **1.** showing belief in God or a religion. **2.** having to do with religion.

re·mind (ri mīnd′) *verb.* to make or help someone remember; to tell something to someone again: He *reminded* me that we had a date. **reminded.**

re·ply (ri plī′) *verb.* to answer in words or in actions: Susan *replied* to his letter right away. **replied.**

re·ward (ri wôrd′) *noun.* **1.** something given in return for good work. **2.** money given for finding and returning something that was lost.

S

scene (sēn) *noun.* the place and time of a play or story.

a fat	oi oil	ch chin
ā ape	oo look	sh she
ä car, father	ōō tool	th thin
e ten	ou out	th then
er care	u up	zh leisure
ē even	ur fur	ŋ ring
i hit		
ir here	ə = a in ago	
ī bite, fire		e in agent
o lot		i in unity
ō go		o in collect
ô law, horn		u in focus

radio

relax

sched·ule (skej′ool) *noun.* **1.** a list of times at which things will happen; timetable. **2.** a list of things to be done with time limits given in which those things must be done.

shipwreck

schol·ar (skol′ər) *noun.* **1.** a person who learns a lot by studying. **2.** a person who goes to school or studies with a teacher. **3.** a student who enjoys study and learning.

sci·en·tist (sī′ən tist) *noun.* a person who is an expert in a particular branch of science, such as biology, agriculture, etc. **scientists.**

scold (skōld) *verb.* to tell someone what he or she is doing wrong in an angry voice: He *scolded* me for arriving late for class. **scolded.**

shortstop

seal (sēl) *noun.* a sea animal having four flippers that lives in cold waters and is covered with fur. **seals.**

sep·a·rate (sep′ə rāt) *verb.* **1.** to set apart. **2.** to put something between other things. **3.** to go away from one another. —**separated** *adjective.* set apart; divided.

se·ri·ous (sir′ē əs) *adjective.* **1.** having thoughts that are deeply felt; important. **2.** not joking or fooling around; sincere: John is *serious* about completing his project on time.

serv·ant (sur′vənt) *noun.* someone who is paid to work in another person's home as cook, butler, maid, etc.

shaft (shaft) *noun.* **1.** the long, thin part of an arrow or spear. **2.** a handle. **3.** one of the two long pieces of wood between which an animal pulls a wagon, plow, etc. **4.** a long tunnel dug into the earth, like a mine shaft. **5.** a long opening that goes through the floors of a building, such as for an elevator. **shafts.**

shim·mer (shim′ər) *verb.* to shine with a wavering kind of light: The puddle of water on the sidewalk was *shimmering* under the street light. **shimmering.**

ship·wreck (ship′rek) *noun.* the parts of a ship left after it is destroyed or lost at sea.

shiv·er (shiv′ər) *verb.* to shake as when you are very cold or afraid; to tremble. **shivered.**

short·stop (shôrt′stop) *noun.* a baseball player who fields the balls hit between second and third base.

a fat	**oi** oil	**ch** chin
ā ape	**oo** look	**sh** she
ä car, father	**ōō** tool	**th** thin
e ten	**ou** out	***th*** then
er care	**u** up	**zh** leisure
ē even	**ur** fur	**ng** ring
i hit		
ir here	ə = a *in* ago	
ī bite, fire	e *in* agent	
o lot	i *in* unity	
ō go	o *in* collect	
ô law, horn	u *in* focus	

sigh (sī) *noun.* a long, deep breathing sound made when sad, tired, or relieved. **sighs.**

sign (sīn) *noun.* a word, picture, or action that tells of something else. —*verb.* using a part of the body to show or mean something, as in nodding the head, waving the hand, etc. **signs.**

sign language *noun.* a system of hand gestures used to talk with people who are deaf.

slave (slāv) *noun.* **1.** a person owned by someone else. **2.** a person who is controlled by something else.

so·nar (sō′när) *noun.* a machine that sends sound waves through water, to locate objects; used to find submarines, measure the depth of the ocean, etc.

Sonar is an acronym. An acronym is a word which is made by putting together the first letters of a longer name or description. Sonar comes from *so*und *na*vagation *r*anging.

sort (sôrt) *noun.* **1.** a group of things that have something that is the same. **2.** type or kind: There are many *sorts* of toys in the store. **sorts.**

spar·kle (spär′k′l) *verb.* to shine as if giving off sparks or flashes of light.

sput·ter (sput′ər) *verb.* **1.** to spit out food or water from your mouth when speaking. **2.** to talk in a fast, excited way. **3.** to make hissing or popping noises. **sputtered.**

stage (stāj) *noun.* the raised platform in a theater on which actors and entertainers perform.

stall (stôl) *noun.* a space for one animal in a stable or barn.

stal·lion (stal′yən) *noun.* a full-grown male horse that can have offspring: The wild *stallion* galloped across the plains.

stub·born·ly (stub′ərn lē) *adverb.* in a very determined way; in a way that shows unwillingness to listen or to change one's mind: He acted *stubbornly* even after he knew he was wrong.

submarine

sub·ma·rine (sub′mə rēn) *noun.* a kind of ship that travels underwater and is able to stay there for a long time.

suf·fer (suf′ər) *verb.* **1.** to feel pain; be uncomfortable. **2.** to put up with problems, pain, worry, etc.

sug·gest (səg jest′) *verb.* to bring to mind as something to consider or think over.

sur·round·ings (sə roun′dingz) *plural noun.* the things that are around a person or around a place: The children did their classwork in beautiful *surroundings.*

sur·vive (sər vīv′) *verb.* to stay alive under bad conditions.

sus·pi·cious (sə spish′əs) *adjective.* **1.** thinking something is wrong without knowing for sure. **2.** questioning whether you can be sure about something.

T

Television is a new word, when compared to most of the words we use. It came into use seventy years ago, when television was first being developed. The word means "seeing at a distance."

tal·ent (tal′ənt) *noun.* a special ability that a person has from birth.

throat

tel·e·vi·sion (tel′ə vizh′ən) *noun.* **1.** a way of sending pictures from one place to another by changing them into electrical waves that travel through the air. **2.** a receiving set that picks up those waves and changes them back into pictures.

tem·per (tem′pər) *noun.* **1.** the way you feel; mood. **2.** anger: She has quite a *temper;* she yelled at everybody.

trough

thee (*th*ē) *pronoun.* you, as used long ago.

thrash (thrash) *verb.* **1.** to hit with a stick, whip, or other object. **2.** to move around wildly or without control: The fish *thrashed* around in the shallow water. **thrashed.**

throat (thrōt) *noun.* **1.** the front of the neck. **2.** the part of the neck through which air, food, and water pass from the mouth to the stomach or lungs.

thump (thump) *noun.* **1.** a blow or hit made by something heavy. **2.** the sound made by such a blow.

thy (*th*ī) *pronoun.* your, as used long ago.

ti·tled (tīt″ld) *adjective.* **1.** having a special title such as lord, knight, lady, etc. **2.** having a title or name such as the name of a book.

tour·isty (toor′ istē) *adjective.* about people who travel for pleasure. *used only in informal language.*

tre·men·dous (tri men′dəs) *adjective.* **1.** very large or huge. **2.** surprisingly wonderful, amazing, etc.

trough (trôf) *noun.* a long rectangular container often used to feed or water animals.

V

val·or (val′ər) *noun.* courage or bravery.

a fat	**oi** oil	**ch** chin
ā ape	**oo** look	**sh** she
ä car, father	**ōō** tool	**th** thin
e ten	**ou** out	***th*** then
er care	**u** up	**zh** leisure
ē even	**ur** fur	**ng** ring
i hit		
ir here	ə = a *in* ago	
ī bite, fire	e *in* agent	
o lot	i *in* unity	
ō go	o *in* collect	
ô law, horn	u *in* focus	

W

warm-blood·ed (wôrm′blud′id) *adjective.* having a body temperature that stays the same, despite the surroundings.

wasp (wosp *or* wôsp) *noun.* a flying insect, with a slender body and a narrow waist, that stings. **wasps.**

wa·ter·fall (wôt′ər fôl) *noun.* a natural stream of water that falls from a high place such as a cliff.

weap·on (wep′ən) *noun.* something used for fighting such as a club, gun, etc. **weapons.**

wea·ther vane (we*th*′ər vān′) *noun.* a device that turns in the wind to show which way the wind is blowing, often placed on a rooftop.

webbed (webd) *adjective.* having the toes joined by pieces of skin or flesh: Ducks have *webbed* feet.

week·ly (wēk′lē) *adjective.* happening or appearing once a week or every week.

wharf (hwôrf) *noun.* a long platform built from the shore out over the water so that ships can be loaded and unloaded.

wheel·ing (hwēl′ing) *verb.* turning around in a circular motion.

whin·ny (hwin′ē) *verb.* to make the low neighing sound that a horse makes. **whinnied.**

wig·gle (wig″l) *verb.* to twist or turn quickly from side to side. **wiggled.**

wasp

wor·ship (wur′ship) *noun.* **1.** a church service; prayer. **2.** great love or admiration of any kind. —*verb.* **1.** to offer prayers; attend church. **2.** to show great love or admiration.

worst (wurst) *adjective.* the most bad, harmful, etc.; least good.

wor·thy (wur′*th*ē) *adjective.* **1.** having value or being wanted. **2.** being good enough for something.

writ·er (rīt′ər) *noun.* someone who writes books, essays, poems, etc., especially as a way to earn a living; author.

weather vane

Y

yeowled (yould) *verb.* to yell or howl; give a loud howling cry.

yowl (youl) *verb.* to howl or cry out in a long, sad way.

The authors listed below have written some of the selections that appear in this book. The content of the notes was determined by a survey of what readers wanted to know about authors.

EDWARD ARDIZZONE

EDWARD ARDIZZONE

Edward Ardizzone was born in Haiphong, Indochina, in what is today the country of Vietnam. When he was five years old, he moved to England with his mother and sisters. He lived in England the rest of his life. There, Edward Ardizzone became a writer and illustrator. He once described how his children's pleas for stories led him to create his books and illustrations. They would ask, "Daddy, please, please tell us a story" or "Daddy, please, draw us a picture of two elephants having a fight." It was in this way that the stories were created. Edward Ardizzone won many awards for his books, including the Kate Greenaway Medal for *Tim All Alone.* (1900–1979)

GWENDOLYN BROOKS

GWENDOLYN BROOKS

The poet Gwendolyn Brooks was born in Topeka, Kansas. She says, "I loved poetry very early and began to put rhymes together at about seven. At the age of thirteen my poem 'Eventide' was accepted and printed in a children's magazine." When she was sixteen, she began submitting poems to a newspaper, and more than 75 of them were published. Gwendolyn Brooks won the Pulitzer Prize in poetry in 1950 for "Annie Allen." *(Born 1917)*

ANN CAMERON

ANN CAMERON

From the time Ann Cameron was in the third grade, she knew she wanted to be a writer. She says that her desire to be a writer came from her love of books. She says, "A book is something like a message in a bottle that an author throws out to sea; you never know whom it might reach, or how much it might mean to them." Ann Cameron believes that writers should write the stories they want to write: "Your story, if it's really the way you want to tell it, can never be wrong the way an arithmetic answer is wrong; and even if your mother, your father, your teacher, or your best friend doesn't understand it, it's still right for you." *(Born 1943)*

LEWIS CARROLL

LEWIS CARROLL

Lewis Carroll's real name was Charles Lutwidge Dodgson. He taught mathematics in England, but he is best known for his book *Alice's Adventures in Wonderland.* He made up the stories about Alice to tell to the children of a friend. The girls liked the stories so much they asked him to write them down. Later, he wrote another book about Alice. It is called *Through the Looking Glass.* (1832–1898)

LYDIA MARIA CHILD

LYDIA MARIA CHILD

Lydia Maria Child was born in Medford, Massachusetts. She was the youngest of six children. Her father was a baker. He made "Medford Crackers," which were very popular. He was able to give all his children a good education. Lydia Maria Child started the first U.S. magazine for children. She also wrote novels, books of games for children, and many articles against slavery. (1802–1880)

RAY CRUZ

Ray Cruz was born in New York City and still lives there. He studied at the High School of Art and Design, at Pratt Institute, and at Cooper Union. He has designed textiles and wallpapers and packaging for cosmetic firms. He has illustrated books for ten publishers. Ray Cruz says that he is now engaged in a personal project to illustrate a group of fairy tales in full color. *(Born 1933)*

RACHEL FIELD

RACHEL FIELD

Rachel Field's book *Hitty: Her First Hundred Years* won the Newbery Medal. She was the first woman to win this award. Rachel Field said she spent time writing before she did much reading. "It wasn't that I could not have read earlier. I knew the letters and all that, but it was so much more pleasant to have my mother read books to me." (1894–1942)

PAUL GALDONE

PAUL GALDONE

Paul Galdone is an author and illustrator of books for young people. He was born in Budapest, Hungary. He and his family moved to the United States in 1928. He had a difficult time in school because he did not speak English well. He liked biology class, however, because he could draw grasshoppers. "I was soon drawing them for all the other pupils." He has won awards for his books. He has twice been the runner-up for the Caldecott Medal. *(Born 1914)*

HELEN V. GRIFFITH

HELEN V. GRIFFITH

Helen V. Griffith says, "I have been writing and drawing since I could handle a pencil. When I was very young I wrote poetry, usually about animals. I have always liked animals, and a dog has had a featured role in many books I've written. I don't begin by thinking, 'I'm going to write about a dog,' but that's what happens." *(Born 1934)*

MALCOLM HALL

MALCOLM HALL

Malcolm Hall was born in Chicago, Illinois, but he grew up in Los Alamos, New Mexico. He says that the town of Los Alamos is a bit strange, because "the town itself is located on a 7000-foot mesa in the Sangre de Cristo Mountains." Both Malcolm Hall's mother and father were physicists. Malcolm Hall has written over 30 filmstrips. His book *Headlines* was a Junior Literary Guild selection. *(Born 1945)*

LEE BENNETT HOPKINS

LEE BENNETT HOPKINS

Lee Bennett Hopkins has interviewed, or talked with, many writers and illustrators. He writes about his talks with these people. He also writes poems for young people. He says, "I love doing children's books. Each one is a new challenge, a new day, a new spring for me." Lee Bennett Hopkins also puts together anthologies, or collections, of other people's poems. He goes through thousands of poems and chooses the twenty that he thinks children will enjoy most. *(Born 1938)*

JOHANNA HURWITZ

JOHANNA HURWITZ

Johanna Hurwitz is a writer and illustrator of books for young people. She is also a children's librarian. She says, "My parents met in a bookstore and there has never been a moment when books were not important in my life." Johanna Hurwitz writes many letters to friends and relatives. She thinks the letter writing she does is very good training for her book writing. Her husband is also a writer. She thinks that her two children will probably be writers, too. "After all," she says, "what do you expect? Their grandparents met in a bookstore." *(Born 1937)*

RACHEL ISADORA

RACHEL ISADORA

Rachel Isadora writes and illustrates children's books. She is also a ballet dancer. She has been dancing since she was eleven years old. Rachel Isadora is an award-winning author. One of the awards she has won is the Boston Globe–Horn Book Award for her book *Ben's Trumpet*. Rachel Isadora's husband also writes books for young people. She has illustrated some of her husband's books, too.

GENIE IVERSON

GENIE IVERSON

Genie Iverson was born in Newport News, Virginia, where her father was an officer in the Navy. She has been a reporter on a newspaper. Now she writes fables for young people as well as nonfiction. She says she writes biographies because she is interested in people and in history. *(Born 1942)*

ADA B. LITCHFIELD

ADA B. LITCHFIELD

Ada B. Litchfield grew up on Cape Cod, Massachusetts. She began writing when she was a little girl. She has published many TV scripts and books. Her TV script *Up Close and Natural* won the Ohio State Merit Award in the Natural and Physical Science Category. Ada B. Litchfield and her husband live in Stoughton, Massachusetts, with their cat Lit'l One.

PHYLLIS MCGINLEY

PHYLLIS MCGINLEY

Phyllis McGinley wrote stories and poems for children and for adults. The first children's book she wrote was *The Horse Who Lived Upstairs*. When Phyllis McGinley wrote that book, she lived in New York City. She went to Greenwich Village to see how city horses lived. She said, "I discovered one stable that cried out for story-telling. The horses all were kept on the upper floors of the building, and they surveyed the world from their second-story windows as calmly as though they were standing in country pastures. When I noticed that their watering trough was an old cast-off bathtub, I knew I had a book." She won awards for both her poems and her stories. *(1905–1978)*

EVE MERRIAM

EVE MERRIAM

Eve Merriam has written many poems for both children and adults. She has also written books, plays, and stories. "I was writing poems when I was about seven or eight. One of my first was about a birch tree that grew outside my bedroom window. It never occurred to me that someday I might like to be a writer. I just wrote. I think one is chosen to be a poet. You write poems because you must write them; because you can't live your life without writing them." Her advice to young people who want to be writers is, "Don't be discouraged." *(Born 1916)*

ABOUT THE AUTHORS

A. A. MILNE

A. A. Milne

Alan Alexander Milne wrote many stories and poems for children. Milne first began writing when he was seventeen. He said, "It was in the Christmas holidays of 1899 that I discovered the itch for writing which has never quite left me." He started out by writing poems. Later he began writing stories. Some of his stories are about a boy named Christopher Robin and a bear named Winnie-the-Pooh. Milne's only son was also named Christopher Robin. *(1882–1956)*

LILIAN MOORE

Lilian Moore

Lilian Moore was born in New York City. She writes books and poetry for young people. She has also been a schoolteacher. She taught children who had been out of school. They did not know how to read. Lilian Moore said that she was annoyed because she could not find interesting books for these children to read, so she decided to write her own books for them. She has written more than forty books since then. Some of Lilian Moore's books have been chosen as American Library Association Notable Books.

374 *About the Authors*

E. H. SHEPARD

E. H. Shepard

Ernest Howard Shepard was born in England where he lived all his life. He said that he had always intended to be an artist of some kind. Both his father and mother encouraged him in his art. He drew cartoons for the famous English magazine *Punch* for nearly fifty years. He also illustrated many books. Among the books he illustrated are *The Wind in the Willows, The Reluctant Dragon,* and *The Secret Garden.* He is probably best known for having illustrated the Christopher Robin books by A. A. Milne. He had two children. His son was killed in World War II. His daughter illustrated the Mary Poppins books. In 1972, E. H. Shepard was the recipient of the Order of the British Empire in recognition of his artistic works. *(1879–1976)*

ELIZABETH SHUB

Elizabeth Shub

Elizabeth Shub was born in Poland. She came to the United States when she was a child. She writes books for children and also translates books into English for other writers. She helped Isaac Bashevis Singer translate *Zlateh the Goat, and Other Stories* from Yiddish. One of her books is *Seeing Is Believing.*

JOHN STEPTOE

John Steptoe

John Steptoe was a painter and a writer and also taught at the Brooklyn Music School. He illustrated all of his own books as well as books for other writers. He received the Gold Medal from the Society of Illustrators for the book *Stevie.* He wrote that book when he was only sixteen years old. He said that one of the reasons he began writing books for young people was the need for "books that black children could honestly relate to." John Steptoe's new book, *Mufaro's Beautiful Daughters,* was named a Caldecott Honor Book and won the 1987 Boston Globe–Horn Book Award. *(1950–1989)*

JAMES STEVENSON

James Stevenson

James Stevenson is a writer and illustrator. Although he began his career as a cartoonist and artist, he always wanted to be a writer. He wrote magazine articles and books for adults before he began writing children's books. Now, he has written many books for young people. Several of his books have been chosen as Junior Literary Guild selections and American Library Association Notable Books. *(Born 1929)*

BRINTON TURKLE

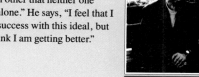
Brinton Turkle

Brinton Turkle has written and illustrated several books for children. He illustrates books for other authors, too. Brinton Turkle believes that, in a picture book, the words and the pictures should be so closely related to each other that neither one "can stand successfully alone." He says, "I feel that I have had only marginal success with this ideal, but I do keep trying and I think I am getting better." *(Born 1915)*

YOSHIKO UCHIDA

Yoshiko Uchida

Yoshiko Uchida's last name is pronounced ō chē′də. She writes books about Japan and its people and about Japanese-Americans as well. She says, "I wanted American children to become familiar with the marvelous Japanese folk tales I had heard in my childhood. I wanted them to read about Japanese children, learning to understand and respect differences in customs and culture, but realizing also that basically human beings are alike the world over, with similar joys and hopes." Some of Yoshiko Uchida's books have been selected as American Library Association Notable Books. She has also illustrated some of her own books of Japanese folk tales. *(Born 1921)*

JUDITH VIORST

JUDITH VIORST

Judith Viorst began writing poetry when she was seven years old. She says she wrote "terrible poems about dead dogs, mostly." She did not become a successful writer until she was grown and began writing about her own family. Now she is an award-winning author. Judith Viorst says, "Most of my children's books are for or about my own children." *(Born 1931)*

BERNARD WABER

BERNARD WABER

Bernard Waber is an author and illustrator. He has written several books about Lyle the Crocodile. Since he started writing the Lyle books, his house has become almost like a museum of crocodile things. He says there are stuffed toy crocodiles on "tables, sofas, stairs, floors, or whatever surface is available. A claw-footed bathtub—identical to the one shared at the Primm household—sits in our foyer together with its stuffed, Lyle-type occupant." Bernard Waber has won several awards for his books, including the Lewis Carroll Shelf Award.

About the Authors

LEONARD WEISGARD

Leonard Weisgard writes and illustrates children's books. He has won many awards for his books, including the Caldecott Medal. He says about his work, "My art studies were of value to me, but I also learned how to illustrate books by learning to dance, living, breathing, being with children, with people, being alone, reading, writing, traveling, brooding, dreaming, beachcombing, wondering, and mostly, listening to Margaret Wise Brown." He believes that an artist can find art materials in everyday things: "There is the world to choose from—clothes, bobby, or cotter pins, paper clips, metal hangers, ironing boards, baking pans, and cupcake tins. Put them all together and you have an artist's studio." *(Born 1916)*

LEONARD WEISGARD

AUTHOR INDEX

TEACHER REFERENCE FILE

BIBLIOGRAPHY

A complete listing of books referenced in this level

CUMULATIVE WORD LIST

A complete listing of all Story Critical and Support words taught
from Readiness through Level 8

SELECTION WORD LIST

Story Critical and Support words listed by category and selection

INDEX

PROGRAM REVIEWERS

ACKNOWLEDGMENTS

BIBLIOGRAPHY

Level 8
Castles of Sand

An additional bibliography that will encourage home involvement in the student's independent reading may be found in the Home Connection Letters in the Teacher Resource Kit.

UNIT 1

Benchley, Nathaniel. **George, the Drummer Boy!** Harper & Row, 1977.

Brenner, Barbara. **Wagon Wheels.** Harper & Row, 1984.

Bulla, Clyde Robert. **A Grain of Wheat.** David Godine, 1985.

Dalgliesh, Alice. **The Bears on Hemlock Mountain.** Scribner, 1952.

Farley, Walter. **The Black Stallion.** Random House, 1941.

Fritz, Jean. **And Then What Happened, Paul Revere?** Putnam, 1973.

Gleiter, Jan and Thompson, Kathleen. **Paul Revere.** Raintree Children's Books, 1987.

Goble, Paul. **The Girl Who Loved Wild Horses.** Macmillan, 1978.

Hiser, Berniece T. **Charlie and His Wheat-Straw Hat.** Dodd, Mead, 1986.

MacLachlan, Patricia. **Through Grandpa's Eyes.** Harper & Row, 1980. ≈≈

Sandin, Joan. **The Long Way to a New Land.** Harper & Row, 1981. ≈≈

Smith, E. Boyd. **The Farm Book.** Houghton Mifflin Co., 1982.

Sonberg, Lynn. **A Horse Named Paris.** Bradbury Press, 1986.

Stevenson, James. **Howard.** Greenwillow Books, 1980.

————. **Will You Please Feed Our Cat?** Greenwillow Books, 1987.

Streich, Corinne. **Grandparents' Houses.** Greenwillow Books, 1984.

Szekers, Cyndy. **Long Ago.** McGraw-Hill, 1977.

Turkle, Brinton. **Obadiah, the Bold.** Viking Press, 1965.

Weisgard, Leonard. **The Plymouth Thanksgiving.** Doubleday, 1967.

≈≈ World of Books Classroom Libraries offer a wide selection of books that may be used for independent reading with this unit.

UNIT 2

Aardema, Verna. **Rabbit Makes a Monkey of Lion.** Dial, 1989.

Anderson, Lena. **Stina.** Greenwillow Books, 1989.

Ardizzone, Edward. **Little Tim and the Brave Sea Captain.** Penguin Books, 1983.

Arnold, Caroline. **Bodies of Water: Fun, Facts and Activities.** Franklin Watts, 1985.

Aschenbrenner, Gerald. **Jack, the Seal and the Sea.** Silver Burdett Press, 1988.

Bender, Lionel. **Crocodiles and Alligators.** Gloucester Press, 1988.

De Armond, Dale. **Berry Woman's Children.** Greenwillow Books, 1985.

Freeman, Don. **Penguins, of All People.** Viking Press, 1971.

Grimm, Brothers. **The Water of Life.** Retold by Barbara Rogasky. Holiday House, 1986.

Kipling, Rudyard. **How the Rhinoceros Got His Skin.** Philomel Books, 1988.

Laurin, Anne. **Perfect Crane.** Harper & Row, 1981.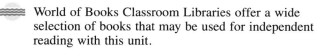

Livingston, Myra Cohn. **Sea Songs.** Holiday House, 1986.

Marzollo, Jean. **Amy Goes Fishing.** Dial, 1980.

McGovern, Ann. **Little Whale.** Scholastic Book Services, 1979.

Moore, Lilian. **I Feel the Same Way.** Atheneum, 1967.

Patent, Dorothy Hinshaw. **All About Whales.** Holiday House, 1987.

Phleger, Fred. **The Whales Go By.** Random House, 1959.

Selsam, Millicent E. **Animals of the Sea.** Scholastic Book Services, 1975.

Selsam, Millicent E. and Hunt, Joyce. **A First Look at Seashells.** Walker & Co., 1983.

Seuss, Dr. **McElligot's Pool.** Random House, 1947.

Shaw, Evelyn. **Sea Otters.** Harper & Row, 1980.

Simon, Seymour. **How to be an Ocean Scientist in Your Own Home.** Lippincott, 1988.

Steig, William. **Amos and Boris.** Puffin Books, 1971.

Stephen, R.J. **Undersea Machines.** Franklin Watts, 1986.

Uchida, Yoshiko. **The Best Bad Thing.** Macmillan, 1983.

———. **The Sea of Gold and Other Tales from Japan.** Scribner, 1965.

———. **Sumi's Special Happening.** Scribner, 1966.

Waber, Bernard. **An Anteater Named Arthur.** Houghton Mifflin, 1967.

———. **I Was All Thumbs.** Houghton Mifflin, 1975.

———. **The Snake, A Very Long Story.** Houghton Mifflin, 1978.

White, E.B. **Stuart Little.** Harper & Row, 1973.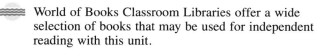

World of Books Classroom Libraries offer a wide selection of books that may be used for independent reading with this unit.

UNIT 3

Barth, Edna. **The Day Luis Was Lost.** Little, Brown, 1971.

Blair, Gwenda. **Laura Ingalls Wilder.** Putnam, 1981.

Brooks, Gwendolyn. **Bronzeville Boys and Girls.** Harper & Row, 1956.

Cameron, Ann. **More Stories Julian Tells.** Knopf, 1986.

Collins, David. **To the Point: A Story About E.B. White.** Carolrhoda Books, 1989.

Dalgliesh, Alice. **The Courage of Sarah Noble.** Scribner, 1952.

Faulkner, Georgene, and Becker, John. **Melindy's Medal.** Messner, 1945.

Flack, Marjorie and Wiese, Kurt. **The Story About Ping.** Viking Press, 1970.

Gauch, Patricia Lee. **Aaron and the Green Mountain Boys.** Coward, McCann & Geoghegan, 1972.

Hathorn, Elizabeth. **The Tram to Bondi Beach.** Kane/Miller, 1989.

Hurwitz, Johanna. **Aldo Applesauce.** Morrow, 1979.

———. **Aldo Ice Cream.** Morrow, 1981.

———. **Class Clown.** Morrow, 1987.

———. **Yellow Blue Jay.** Morrow, 1986.

Jukes, Mavis. **Like Jake and Me.** Knopf, 1987.

Lasker, Joe. **Nick Joins In.** Whitman, 1980.

Lord, Betty Bao. **In the Year of the Boar and Jackie Robinson.** Harper & Row, 1984.

MacLachlan, Patricia. **Arthur, For the Very First Time.** Harper & Row, 1980.

Martin, Charles. **Summer Business.** Greenwillow Books, 1984.

McKissack, Patricia. **Flossie and the Fox.** Dial, 1986.

Monjo, F.N. **The Drinking Gourd.** Harper & Row, 1970. ≈≈

Rowland, Florence Wightman. **Amish Boy.** Putnam, 1970.

Sabin, Francene. **Harriet Tubman.** Troll, 1985.

Schlein, Miriam. **The Girl Who Would Rather Climb Trees.** Harcourt Brace Jovanovich, 1975.

Steig, William. **Brave Irene.** Farrar, Straus & Giroux, 1986.

Stevens, Carla. **Anna, Grandpa, and the Big Storm.** Houghton Mifflin, 1982.

Wallace, Ian. **Chin Chiang and the Dragon's Dance.** Atheneum, 1984.

≈≈ World of Books Classroom Libraries offer a wide selection of books that may be used for independent reading with this unit.

UNIT 4

Aardema, Verna. **Why Mosquitos Buzz in People's Ears.** Dial, 1975.

Aesop. **Aesop's Fables.** (Kathryn Hegemen, ed.) Trillium Press, 1984.

——. **Aesop for Children.** (Milo Winter, Illus.) Macmillan, 1984.

Aliki. **Digging Up Dinosaurs.** Crowell, 1981.

Arthur, Catherine. **My Sister's Silent World.** Children's Press, 1979.

Baylor, Byrd. **Hawk, I'm Your Brother.** Scribner, 1976.

Brown, Marc. **Finger Rhymes.** Dutton, 1980.

Charlip, Remy and Ancona, George and Mary Beth. **Handtalk.** Four Winds Press, 1974.

Cole, William. **Poem Stew.** Harper & Row, 1981.

cummings, e.e. **Hist Whist and Other Poems for Children.** Liveright, 1983.

Dang Manh Kha as told to Clark, Ann Nolan. **In the Land of Small Dragon.** Viking Press, 1979.

Delton, Judy. **The Elephant in Duck's Garden.** Albert Whitman, 1985.

Fleischman, Sid. **By the Great Horn Spoon!** Little, Brown, 1963.

Galbraith, Clare K. **Victor.** Knopf, 1971.

Galdone, Paul. **Three Aesop Fox Fables.** Seabury Press, 1971.

Hall, Malcolm. **Headlines.** Coward, McCann & Geoghegan, 1973.

Hunt, Bernice Kohn. **The Whatchamacallit Book.** Putnam, 1976.

Hurwitz, Johanna. **Baseball Fever.** Morrow, 1981.

McCloskey, Robert. **Burt Dow, Deep-Water Man.** Viking Press, 1963.

Merriam, Eve. **A Word or Two with You.** Atheneum, 1981.

Michel, Anna. **The Story of Nim: The Chimp Who Learned Language.** Knopf, 1980.

Milne, A.A. **Winnie-the-Pooh.** Dutton, 1926.

Mosel, Arlene. **Tikki, Tikki, Tembo.** Scholastic Book Services, 1968.

Parish, Peggy. **Thank You, Amelia Bedelia.** Harper & Row, 1964.　≋

Patterson, Dr. Francine. **Koko's Story.** Scholastic Book Services, 1987.

Paxton, Tom. **Aesop's Fables.** Morrow, 1988.

Pomerantz, Charlotte. **If I Had a Paka: Poems in Eleven Languages.** Greenwillow Books, 1982.

Sattler, Helen Roney. **Train Whistles.** Lothrop, Lee & Shepard, 1984.

Srivastava, Jane Jonas. **Computers.** Harper & Row, 1972.

Stewig, John. **Sending Messages.** Houghton Mifflin, 1978.

Sullivan, Mary Beth and Bourke, Linda. **A Show of Hands: Say It in Sign Language.** Addison-Wesley, 1980.

Yolen, Jane. **The Seeing Stick.** Harper & Row, 1977.

≋ World of Books Classroom Libraries offer a wide selection of books that may be used for independent reading with this unit.

LEVEL 8   The cumulative vocabulary list includes all new words taught from Readiness through Level 8. The words preceded by an asterisk are introduced at this level.

A
a
*aboard
about
*absolutely
act
*actors
address
admit
adobe
adults
*adventure
adventures
advertising
*advice
afraid
after
afternoon
again
against
ago
ahead
aide
all
alone
along
*alphabet
also
although
always
am
*ambled
ambulance
Americans
amusement
*anchor
and
angry
animals
*announced
another
answer
any
anyone
anything
anywhere
apartment
appeared
apple

arctic
are
argued
armadillos
around
art
artist
as
asked
at
*attention
audience
authors
avalanche
awake
away
*awkward
ax
*axle

B
baa
*babbling
back
backward
baked
*ballet
balloon
barn
barre
baseball
basket
*beak
beanstalk
bear
beard
because
been
before
began
*beliefs
believe
bell
below
bench
beside
better
between
big

bigger
bike
bird
birthday
blew
blind
block
blow
blowing
*blubber
blue
boat
boil
book
bookmobiles
*boring
born
*borrowed
both
bought
bounced
bouquet
bowed
bowls
bow wow
boy
brave
brayed
break
breakfast
breaks
breathe
*breeches
bright
brother
brought
brown
bueno
*bugle
built
bump
bundle
*bunk
*bunt
buried
burning
bus
buses
*business

busy
but
butterfly
buttons
buy
by

C
cabbage
cabin
*cable
caboose
calf
came
can
can't
candle
cannot
cap
card catalog
carefully
carnival
carried
carrot
carrots
cart
cartoons
cartwheel
carve
carvings
cat
cave
celery
cement
certainly
chair
challenge
*chamber
characters
*charm
chase
*chattering
cheerful
*chickens
child
children
chimney
chin
chinny

chocolate
*choice
*choked
chopsticks
*chores
cider
circle
city
*clambered
clap
class
cleared
*clerk
clever
*climates
climb
clock
close
closed
closet
clothed
clothes
cluck
coach
*cobblestones
cold
collected
collection
colored
colors
comb
combs
come
comes
comfortable
coming
*communicate
company
*complain
computer
*concentrate
*congressmen
*considering
cooked
corncob
costume
could
couldn't
*council

count
country
*courage
course
courses
cousin
covered
covers
cows
crazy
cried
*crocodile
crop
crowing
*cunning
curly
curtains
cushions
*customers

D
dancing
dandelions
dandy
dangerous
*dangled
dapper
*dawn
dazed
*deaf
dear
decided
*decision
*deck
delicious
delightful
*depending
*deserve
design
*destination
*determined
did
didn't
die
different
*difficult
ding
dinner
directions
dirt
*discontented
disobey
*displeased
*distance
*distress
*dived
do
does
dog
dollars
*dolphins

done
dong
donkey
don't
door
dough
down
dragons
drank
draw
drawings
*drawn
drew
drums
duckling
ducklings
during
dye

E
*eager
early
ears
earth
East Indies
eat
*echo
*editor
*education
elegant
*elevator
else
*embarrassed
emergency
*empty
enemy
engine
*engineers
*English
enjoy
enough
enter
envelope
erase
eraser
Erl King
errands
*especially
even
ever
every
everyone
everything
everywhere
example
except
excuse
exhibits
*exit
expect
explain

extra
eyes

F
fact
fall
*fame
*familiar
family
famous
fancy
far
faraway
farm
farmer
*farmhands
fashion
fast
fastened
faster
father
*faults
*favorite
favorites
fearless
feathers
fellow
felt
*fenders
festival
*fiberglass
fiction
fiddlesticks
field
fight
figured
finally
find
fingers
finished
first
fisherman
*fishermen
fix
*flake
flew
*flippers
*flock
floor
flowers
*fluttered
fly
foil
folks
followed
food
foot
for
*forecaster
forget
forgot

fork
fortune
found
fountain
four
frames
*freight trains
friend
from
front
frost
frowned
fun
funny
fur
*future

G
gallery
*galley
*galoshes
game
garage
garden
garlic
*garments
gas station
gathered
gave
get
giants
gigantic
girl
give
glide
*glitter
*gloomily
go
*goal
goalie
goes
going
golden
gone
good
good-by
goodness
grandfather
great
greetings
grew
grinding stone
grip
groaned
ground
group
grow
guess
guests
guitar
gutter

gym

H
hair
hammer
hand
handicaps
happened
happiest
happy
hard
harmonica
has
hats
have
hawk
he
head
hear
heard
heart
heavy
held
hello
help
her
here
herself
*hesitated
higher
*hike
hill
him
himself
his
history
hobby
hokeypokey
hola
hold
hole
*honor
*hood
hooray
*hoot owl
*horn
horrible
horse
hospital
hostess
hotel
hours
house
*household
how
howdy
hugged
*hugging
Hungary

hungry
*hurricane
hurry
hurt
hurts

I
I
ice
*iceberg
ice cream
*icy
idea
*ignore
I'll
I'm
imagine
immediately
important
in
*include
information
*inning
insects
*insist
instead
*instruments
interesting
*interrupted
introduce
*introduces
inventions
*invitation
invited
is
island
islands
it
it's

J
jewels
join
joined
jokes
journal
journey
joy
jump
jumped
*jungle
just

K
*keyboard
kimono
kindergarten
*kindness
kinds
kneels
knees

knew
knife
knock
knocking
knots
know

L
ladder
*laden
*language
large
late
later
Latin
laughed
laundromat
laundry bag
law
leaps
learn
left
lemonade
lesson
let's
letter
liberty
librarians
libraries
*library
lighthouse
lights
like
liked
line
listen
*literary
little
live
lived
loggers
lonely
lonesome
look
looked
looks
loom
loop
lose
loses
lot
loud
love
lovely
lowest
*lulled
lumber
lunch
*lungs

M
*magazines
magic
magnificent
*mainland
make
*mammals
*managed
*mandolin
*mango
many
maps
*marathon
married
marry
master
matter
*mayor
me
meadows
measured
*medal
medicine
*memories
merry-go-round
*mesquite
*messenger
*meteorology
might
mightiest
migrate
migration
miller
*millet
*millions
mind
*ministers
*minnows
*mischief
*mistake
mitten
*mixture
moaned
moccasins
mohair
money
more
morning
*morsel
most
*mostly
mother
motorcar
mountain
mouse
*moustache
mouth
move
moved
*movement
moving

*mule
*muscles
museum
music
musicians
must
*mustangs
my
mystery

N
name
natural
*nature
naughty
need
*neglected
neighbor
*neighborhood
neighs
nest
never
new
news
newspaper
next
*nibble
nice
nickel
nickname
night
noise
none
noon
north
nose
not
*notes
nothing
noticed
November
now
Nutcracker
*nuzzled

O
of
off
office
*official
often
oil
oink
OK
old
on
once
only
opened
orange
ordered

organized
ostrich
other
others
ouch
our
out
*outfielders
outside
*oval
over
own
ox

P
package
painted
paper
parcels
parents
park
pas de chat
pasture
patient
*pause
paved
peace
peaches
pencil
pencils
penguins
penny
people
pepper
*perched
perfect
*performance
*performers
person
*persuade
*piano
*picnicking
pictures
piece
*Pilgrims
*pilot
pioneers
*pitcher
pizza
plan
*planet
plankton
plastered
play
player
plaza
pleasant
please
plop
*plow

T8   TEACHER REFERENCE FILE

*plugging
*plunged
pocket
*pockets
*poem
*poetry
points
police
*policeman
pollution
poor
popcorn
popped
*popular
*popularity
porcupine
*position
possible
pounds
poured
*practice
*prediction
*preparations
*prepare
president
*presses
pretended
prince
*printed
probably
problem
problema
program
promise
proud
*provided
public
*published
pueblo
pulls
*punt
puppet
puppies
puppy
purple
*purred
pushed
put

Q

quack
quarter
questions
quiet
quill

R

rabbits
race
*racketing
*radio

radish
rain
rainbow
rake
Rapunzel
*raw
read
reader
recess
*recital
recognize
record player
*recover
red
refreshment cart
*refrigerator
*relax
*relief
*religion
*religious
remember
*reminded
*replied
reptiles
rescue
restaurant
returned
*reward
ribbon
ride
riding
right
ringing
road
robber
rolled
roof
room
rooster
round
routes
rude
rulers
rules
run
running
rustle

S

sack
said
sailors
salmon
salt
sand
sandwiches
Saturday
sausage
saw
sawmill
says

scales
*scene
*schedule
*scholar
school
science
*scientists
scissors
*scolded
score
screamed
scrolls
sculptures
*seals
second
secret
see
*separated
*serious
*servant
seven
sewed
shadow
*shafts
shaking
share
sharpening
she
sheep
shelves
*shimmering
shine
*shipwreck
*shivered
shoot
*shortstop
should
shouted
show
shy
sí
side
*sigh
sighed
sighs
sight
*sign language
*signs
silk
silly
simple
sing
sister
sitting
skate
skates
skipper
sky
*slave
sleep
sleeping

slid
*slipped
slowly
small
smiles
smoothly
sneakers
snow
snowbank
snowflake
snowman
snuggles
so
soccer
soft
sold
solve
some
sometimes
*sonar
sons
soon
sorry
*sorts
soup
south
space suits
spaghetti
*sparkle
special
spider
spinach
spindle
splash
splendid
split
spoiled
sports
sprinkler
*sputtered
square
squawked
*stage
stairs
*stall
*stallion
stamps
stand
start
stationed
statue
stays
still
stir
stitches
stood
stop
stopped
stories
storm
story

storyteller
straight
strands
strange
straw
strength
stretches
string
stroked
strong
*stubbornly
student
studied
stylish
*submarine
success
suddenly
*suffer
*suggest
suitcase
sukiyaki
summer
sun
superkid
supermarket
suppose
sure
surprise
surprises
*surroundings
*survive
*suspicious
swan

T

table
tadpoles
*talent
talked
talker
tan
taste
taught
teach
tears
teasing
telephone
*television
*temper
tents
tern
terrible
thanks
that
that's
the
*thee
their
them
themselves
then

there
these
they
things
thinking
third
thirsty
this
those
thought
*thrashed
three
threw
*throat
through
throw
*thump
*thy
tickets
time
timid
tiny
tired
*titled
to
today
tofu
together
told
tomorrow
tonight
too
took
top
touch
*touristy
town
toy

travel
travelers
treasure
*tremendous
tried
tries
trimmed
trouble
*trough
truck
true
try
tune
turn
turned
turnip
turtles
twenty
twice
two

U

ugly
umbrella
under
understand
universe
unload
unruly
until
up
upon
used
utensils

V

valley
*valor

valuable
vanilla
vegetable garden
vegetables
very
view
village
visit
voice
voyages

W

wait
waiter
walk
want
wanted
warm
*warm-blooded
was
washed
*wasps
watch
water
*waterfall
waves
way
we
*weapons
weather
*weathervane
weave
weaver
web
*webbed
*weekly
weighed
went

were
Western
westward
*wharf
what
wheat
wheelchair
wheeled
*wheeling
wheels
when
where
wherever
which
*whinnied
whistles
whistling
white
who
whoever
whole
why
wick
wife
*wiggled
wilderness
will
wind
windshield
winked
winter
wipers
wise
wisely
with
woman
women
won

won't
wonder
wonderful
woodcarver
woods
wool
words
work
world
worried
*worship
*worst
*worthy
would
wove
wrapped
write
*writer
wrong
wrote

Y

yarn
yeast
yellow
*yeowled
yes
yesterday
you
you'll
young
your
yourself
*yowl

Z

zoo

*Indicates words taught at this level.

Critical Words and Support Words
Castles of Sand, Level 8

The following words are introduced in *Castles of Sand*. Critical Words are words that are essential to story comprehension. Support Words are additional words that enhance story comprehension.

Note that not all Critical Words are tested. Tested words appear in boldface.

UNIT 1: REMEMBER WHEN . . .

When I Was Nine

Critical	Support
freight trains	bugle
icy	mandolin
neighborhood	plunged
radio	racketing
television	shimmering
waterfall	touristy
weekly	tremendous

Thy Friend, Obadiah

Critical	Support
beak	breeches
distress	cobblestones
fluttered	dangled
perched	mainland
thee	raw
thy	wheeling
wharf	

Life in Pilgrim Times

Critical	Support
beliefs	ministers
difficult	provided
education	religion
English	weapons
Pilgrims	worship
religious	

Grandaddy's Place

Critical	Support
chickens	mostly
hoot owl	planet
mule	thump
purred	worst
wasps	
yowl	

The White Stallion

Critical	Support
ambled	axle
distance	clambered
mustangs	drawn
nuzzled	lulled
stallion	mesquite
whinnied	scolded

UNIT 2: A WATERY WORLD

Tim to the Rescue

Critical	Support
adventure	disobey
courage	managed
deck	mischief
galley	mixture
hurricane	neglected
medal	persuade
scholar	popular
tremendous	

The Sea of Gold

Critical	Support
aboard	deserve
anchor	echo
bunk	familiar
fishermen	glitter
prepare	kindness
reward	laden
	morsel
	sparkle

The Wonderful Underwater Machine

Critical	Support
cable	eager
engineers	fiberglass
pilot	future
scientists	iceberg
shipwreck	millions
submarine	sonar
	survive

Seals on the Land and in the Water

Critical	Support
blubber	awkward
climates	depending
flippers	dolphins
lungs	include
mammals	nature
muscles	surroundings
seals	
warm-blooded	

The Monkey and the Crocodile

Critical	Support
crocodile	chattering
cunning	choked
determined	mango
dived	replied
jungle	sputtered
shivered	thrashed

UNIT 3: ON YOUR OWN

Jason Wants a Library

Critical	Support
borrowed	embarrassed
business	favorite
council	oval
decision	serious
hesitated	suffer
library	
literary	
mayor	

The Recital

Critical	Support
concentrate	announced
keyboard	honor
notes	hugging
piano	mistake
recital	movement
relax	refrigerator
talent	stage

Lee Bennett Hopkins Interviews Johanna Hurwitz

Critical	Support
advice	ballet
goal	magazines
practice	marathon
published	memories
titled	plugging
writer	poem
	schedule

A Day When Frogs Wear Shoes

Critical	Support
boring	absolutely
customers	congressmen
fenders	especially
hike	hood
reminded	introduces
	minnows
	webbed

**Phillis Wheatley,
America's First Black Poet**

Critical	Support
choice	charm
fame	chores
poetry	popularity
popular	recover
printed	separated
	servant
	slave
	valor

Forecast

Critical	Support
considering	galoshes
editor	gloomily
flake	insist
forecaster	official
instruments	presses
meteorology	stubbornly
prediction	suspicious
	yeowled

Words in Our Hands

Critical	Support
alphabet	actors
deaf	clerk
language	invitation
performers	moustache
sign language	performance
signs	sorts
throat	wiggled

Sports Signals

Critical	Support
bunt	attention
communicate	inning
ignore	position
official	punt
outfielders	suggest
pitcher	suspicious
shortstop	

The Horse Who Lived Upstairs

Critical	Support
discontented	babbling
elevator	horn
picnicking	shafts
plow	trough
pockets	weathervane
policeman	
stall	

Mufaro's Beautiful Daughters

Critical	Support
complain	chamber
dawn	destination
displeased	garments
faults	interrupted
household	millet
messenger	preparations
temper	relief
worthy	

The Boy Who Cried Wolf

Critical	Support
exit	empty
flock	farmhands
scene	nibble
sigh	pause

INDEX

Critical thinking (continued)

problem solving, 342

researching sign language, 520

Curriculum Connections

Curriculum Connections activities extend
selection comprehension to the content areas.

Art, 35, 62, 87, 199, 229, 252, 275, 295, 350,
397, 425, 447, 503, 575, 597, 621

Careers, 253, 351, 377, 397, 551

Geography, 63, 87, 142, 446, 551

Health, 275, 527

Humanities, 229, 351, 447

Library Science, 351

Mathematics, 253, 295, 351, 397, 597

Music, 119, 143, 376, 425, 447, 621

Physical Education, 199, 377

Safety, 527

Science, 35, 63, 119, 143, 229, 252, 253, 275,
295, 425, 503, 527, 551, 575

Social Studies, 35, 62, 63, 87, 143, 199, 228,
252, 295, 350, 351, 376, 397, 446, 527, 551,
575, 597, 621

D

"Day When Frogs Wear Shoes, A," from *More
Stories Julian Tells*, 403–425

Decoding

See Consonant clusters; Digraph, vowel; Long
word decoding; Prefixes; Spelling changes;
Suffixes

Description, 24, 29, 103, 129, 220, 221, 246

Dialogue, 136, 269, 616

Digraph, vowel

ei (after *c*), 140

Dramatization

See Speaking, dramatization

Drawing conclusions, 60, 98–99

Dunn, Carlotta, 65–87

E

Edgar, Josephine, 233–253

Exaggeration, 113, 408, 417

F

Fable, 283, 290

Fantasy, 299, 300, 486, 487, 562, 622

Field, Rachel, 36–37

Figurative language, 214, 404–405, 408, 514,
516

First-person narrative, 21, 246–247, 410, 513

Folk tale, 210, 211, 229, 282, 290, 582, 592

See also Challenge activities, folk tale

"Forecast," 481–503

Forms, 114–115, 444

G

Galdone, Paul 277–295

"General Store," 36–37

Genres

See Autobiography; Biography; Fantasy; Folk

tale; Interview; Nonfiction; Play; Poetry;
Realistic fiction; Tall tale; Writing, newspaper
article

Geography, 63, 87, 142, 446, 551

Gifted and Talented

See Challenge activities; Meeting Individual
Needs, challenge

"Grandaddy's Place," 97–119

Graphic aids

forms, 114–115, 444

symbols and signs, 346–347, 373, 399, 423,
467, 526

Griffith, Helen V., 97–119

Guided Reading

Unit 1: 21–25, 47–51, 71–74, 103–109,
129–133

Unit 2: 181–187, 211–216, 239–243,
263–265, 283–287

Unit 3: 335–339, 361–365, 385–387,
409–414, 433–436

Unit 4: 487–492, 513–517, 537–540,
563–566, 583–589, 607–612

H

Hall, Malcolm, 481–503

Health, 275, 527

"Heidi," 474–479

Highlighting Literature

Highlighting Literature points out literary and
print features of each selection and may be
used as a supplement or alternative to Guided
Reading.

Unit 1: 21, 24, 47, 71, 73, 103, 105, 106, 107,
129, 132

Unit 2: 181, 182, 183, 186, 211, 214, 240, 242,
283, 286

Unit 3: 336, 338, 385, 409, 410, 411, 413, 433

Unit 4: 487, 488, 491, 513, 514, 516, 537, 583,
584, 586, 588, 607, 608, 611

Historical fiction, 46, 54, 128, 136

Homographs, 80–81, 478–479

Homophones, 392–393, 420, 443, 457, 464, 550

Hopkins, Lee Bennett, 379–397

"Horse Who Lived Upstairs, The," 557–575

"House on East 88th Street, The," 300–305

"How Doth the Little Crocodile," 296–297

Humanities, 229, 351, 447

Humor, 286, 488, 491, 497, 628

See also Writing, humor

Hurwitz, Johanna, 355–377

I

Idioms, 182, 183, 291, 338

See also Writing, idioms

Independent reading, 4, 6, 29, 55, 79, 113, 137,
146–149, 156–157, 164, 166, 191, 221,
247, 269, 291, 300–304, 310–311, 318,
320, 343, 369, 391, 419, 441, 452–454,
460–461, 470, 472, 497, 521, 545, 571,
593, 617, 622–627, 634–635

Inferences, 227, 278–279, 380–381, 394, 442,
456–457, 462–463, 596

Informal assessment

See Checkpoint

Informal Assessment Opportunity

empathizing with story characters, 53, 183, 415,
518, 567

evaluating, 27, 266, 362, 494, 608

generalizing, 131, 217, 410, 591

getting information from text, 72, 245, 367, 539

predicting, 110, 284, 340, 585

responding, 51, 188, 340, 388, 613

self-monitoring with fix-up strategies, 76, 212,
337, 565

summarizing, 23, 264, 386, 515

synthesizing across selections, 135, 289, 438,
542

visualizing, 104, 241, 434, 490

Integrated Language Arts

Language Arts activities are woven into each
lesson plan. *See* Language Arts Connections;
Listening; Oral reading; Speaking; Writing

Interest Inventory, 6, 166, 320, 472

The Interest Inventory in the Workbook helps
students choose books for independent reading
that match their own personal interests.

Interview, 136, 384, 390

See also Challenge activities, interview;
Speaking, interview

"In Which Piglet Meets a Heffalump," from
Winnie-the-Pooh, 622–628

I ◆ T Kit, 5, 27, 76, 111, 135, 165, 218, 245,
289, 319, 341, 416, 438, 471, 519, 542, 614

Iverson, Genie, 601–621

J

Jargon, 190, 544

"Jason Wants a Library," 329–351

K

Knafo, Betsey, 257–275

L

Language Arts Connections

Unit 1: 28–29, 54–55, 77–79, 112–113,
136–137

Unit 2: 190–191, 219–221, 246–247,
268–269, 290–291

Unit 3: 342–343, 368–369, 390–391,
417–419, 439–441

Unit 4: 495–497, 520–521, 543–545,
569–571, 592–593, 615–617

Learning about literature

Author's craft, 409, 411

Looking at the Setting of a Story, 400–401

Genre, 607, 608

Reading Plays, 598–599

**"Lee Bennett Hopkins Interviews Johanna
Hurwitz,"** 379–397

Library Science, 351

"Life in Pilgrim Times," 65–87

Life Skills

See Careers; Forms; Symbols and Signs

Limited English Proficiency

See Meeting Individual Needs; Achieving
English Proficiency

"Sea of Gold, The," from *The Sea of Gold and Other Tales from Japan,* 205–229

"Seals on the Land and in the Water," 257–275

"Secret Talk," 504–505

Self-selected vocabulary, 77, 112, 220, 247, 290, 418

Self-monitoring

See Comprehension monitoring; Metacognition

Semantic mapping, 18, 44, 100, 126, 208, 280, 358, 534, 560

Sensory words, 129

Sequence, 86, 124–125

Setting, 16–17, 29, 32, 138, 152, 159, 206–207, 220, 294, 326, 327, 400–401, 409, 411, 558–559

Shub, Elizabeth, 123–143

"Slower Than the Rest," 322–327

Social Studies, 35, 62, 63, 87, 143, 199, 228, 252, 295, 350, 351, 376, 397, 446, 527, 551, 575, 597, 621

Speaking

See also Rereading; Retelling a story

alliterations, 247

comparisons, 495

dialogue, 136, 269, 342

dramatization, 28, 77, 190, 269, 342, 496, 617

extemporaneously, 190

group discussion, 28, 29, 35, 54, 55, 63, 77, 78, 112, 113, 119, 136, 137, 142, 190, 191, 199, 220, 221, 228, 246, 247, 252, 268, 275, 290, 291, 295, 342, 343, 368, 369, 377, 390, 391, 397, 417, 418, 419, 439, 440, 441, 446, 447, 495, 496, 497, 503, 520, 521, 543, 544, 551, 570, 571, 592, 593, 615, 616, 617

improvisation, 77, 569, 592

interview, 112, 543

onomatopoeia, 391

oral presentations, 79, 113, 136, 190, 219, 220, 221, 229, 246, 252, 376, 397, 417, 418, 520, 521, 527, 543, 551, 592, 616, 621

poetry, 36–37, 120–121, 439

rhymes, 54

role-playing, 219, 269

story mapping, 615

Spelling changes, 141, 250

"Sports Signals," 531–551

Spyri, Johanna, 474–479

Steig, William, 168–173

Steptoe, John, 577–597

Stevenson, James, 15–35

Stoltz, Mary, 450–451

"Storm in the Night," 450–451

Story elements, 16–17, 32, 138, 152, 159, 206–207, 294, 326, 327, 400–401, 558–559

See also Writing, rewriting the story

Story mapping, 12–13, 219, 544

See also Critical thinking, mapping a story

Story structure

See Characterization; Story elements; Writing, rewriting the story

Strategic Reading

Strategic Reading activities help students monitor their own comprehension and may be used as a supplement or alternative to Guided Reading.

See Comprehension monitoring; Metacognition; Thinking strategies

Strategy for reading, 213, 215, 263, 563, 564

Making Predictions, 554–555

Understanding What You Read, 202–203

Using Headings in an Article, 254–255

Strategy for thinking

Making a Character Map, 352–353

Making a Comparison Chart, 38–39

Structural analysis

See Long word decoding; Prefixes; Spelling changes; Suffixes

Study skills

See Content-area reading; Table of contents; Test-taking

Suffixes

-able, 222–223, 248, 293, 306–307, 314, 424

-er, 56–57, 83–84, 94–95, 139, 160, 251

-ible, 222–223, 248, 293, 306–307, 314, 424

-ion, 370–371, 395, 422, 456, 466, 502

-ly, 30–31, 58, 85, 152–153, 161, 198

-ment, 344, 372, 398–399, 421, 465, 574

-ness, 192–193, 226, 231, 272, 313, 396

-or, 56–57, 83–84, 94–95, 139, 160, 251

-tion, 370–371, 395, 422, 456, 466, 502

Summarizing, 194–195, 348

Summarizing and predicting, 23, 72, 108, 131, 184, 212, 264, 284, 337, 386, 412, 435, 489, 515, 538, 564, 565, 587, 610

Syllabication

Syllabication is taught as part of the strategy for decoding long words.

See Long word decoding

Symbols and Signs, 346–347, 373, 399, 423, 467, 526

Synonyms, 34, 178

T

Tall tale

See Writing, tall tales

Testing and Management, 157, 311, 461, 635

Test-taking, 270–271, 501

Thinking strategies

See also Critical thinking; Creative thinking

inferring, 352–353, 360–365, 374

recalling/analyzing, 38–39, 46–51, 59, 75

"Thy Friend, Obadiah," 41–63

"Tim to the Rescue," 175–199

Time Out for Books, 6, 144–145, 320, 450–451, 472

Trade books, 4, 29, 55, 79, 113, 137, 144–145, 156–157, 164, 191, 221, 247, 269, 291, 310–311, 318, 343, 369, 391, 419, 441, 450–451, 460–461, 470, 497, 521, 545, 571, 593, 634–635

Turkle, Brinton, 41–63

U

Uchida, Yoshiko, 205–229

"Until I Saw the Sea," 200–201

V

Viorst, Judith, 452–455

Visualizing, 22, 104, 130, 185, 241, 285, 411, 434, 490, 539, 585, 609

Vocabulary

See Analogies; Antonyms; Classification; Homographs; Homophones; Multiple meanings; Semantic mapping; Synonyms; Word meaning

Unit 1: 18–19, 44–45, 68–69, 100–101, 126–127

Unit 2: 178–179, 208–209, 236–237, 260–261, 280–281

Unit 3: 332–333, 358–359, 382–383, 406–407, 430–431

Unit 4: 484–485, 510–511, 534–535, 560–561, 580–581, 604–605

Vowels

See Digraph, vowel

W

Waber, Bernard, 300–305

Weisgard, Leonard, 146–150

"When I Was Nine," 15–35

"White Stallion, The," 123–143

"Wonderful Underwater Machine, The," 233–253

Word lists

cumulative, T6–T10

selection, T11–T12

Word meaning, 18–19, 44–45, 68–69, 100–101, 126–127, 178–179, 208–209, 236–237, 260–261, 280–281, 332–333, 358–359, 382–383, 406–407, 430–431, 484–485, 510–511, 534–535, 560–561, 580–581, 604–605

Word play/Word study, 78, 112, 247, 290, 291, 391, 543

See also Context clues

Word referents, 532–533, 548, 552, 618, 636

"Words in Our Hands," 507–527

Working together, 156–157, 310–311, 460–461, 634–635

World of Reading Magazine

Sea Shanties, 298–299

Words and Other Codes, 528–529

Writing

See also Writing process; Writing to Learn

advice, 290, 368

announcements, 350

articles, 77, 246

character clusters, 190, 220, 593, 616

comic strips, 545

creative, 26, 28, 29, 52, 75, 77, 110, 113, 134, 136, 143, 188, 191, 217, 220, 221, 244, 246, 266, 268, 288, 290, 291, 340, 366, 369, 376, 388, 390, 415, 419, 437, 439, 441, 493, 496, 541, 544, 567, 570, 571, 590, 592, 613, 617, 621

description, 503

dialogue, 308–309, 616

expository, 35, 63, 77, 119, 143, 190, 191, 199, 217, 220, 246, 268, 527, 544, 616

feelings, 369

functional/personal, 35, 290, 368, 527

glossary entries, 543

humor, 496

idioms, 291

journal entries, 35, 79, 390, 613

letters, 191, 340, 388

PROGRAM REVIEWERS

PANEL OF LIBRARIANS

Nancy Larue
Cedar Falls, IA

Edris J. Newton
Los Angeles, CA

Linda Sheikh
Birmingham, AL

Rebecca Thomas
Stow, OH

Doris Lowry
Stockton, CA

LaVonne Sanborne
Stillwater, OK

Susanna Swade
Columbus, OH

FIELD TESTERS

Mindy Ball
Kansas City, MO

Sharron Helmholz
Saratoga, CA

Mrs. Juzang
Mobile, AL

Ruth Redding
Kansas City, MO

Maurine Willis
Wichita, KS

Kathy Cheney
Billerica, MA

Claudia Hone
Indianapolis, IN

Mrs. Lang
Mobile, AL

Donna Tutt
Columbus, OH

Karen Ciampa
Midlothian, VA

Wilma Hunt
Wichita, KS

Faye McGibboney
Columbus, OH

Joyce Walton
Garden Grove, CA

Edna Fisher
Indianapolis, IN

Carol Ichino
Carson, CA

Helen Mulley
Billerica, MA

Cindy White
N. Highlands, CA

REVIEWERS

Diana Argaranes
Hanover Park, IL

Carol Brown
Columbus, OH

Ella Dangelmaier
Reading, MA

Beth Fanning
Roselle, IL

Juanita Harrill
Appleton, WI

Cara Allen
New Brunswick, NJ

Annie Bzoch
Waldo, FL

Faye Darden
Birmingham, AL

Nancy Fischer
New Brunswick, NJ

Dr. V. J. Harris
Champaign, IL

Sandra Allen
New Brunswick, NJ

Garnetta Chain
New Brunswick, NJ

Fran Davis
New Brunswick, NJ

Teri Jo Fowler
Murfreesboro, AR

Mary Harvard
Hanover Park, IL

Mary Ann Amato
Roselle, IL

Tom Cich
Hanover Park, IL

Tina Dean
Evansville, IN

Forest Gerdes
Sunnyvale, CA

Dr. D. S. Harvey
Baltimore, MD

Dina Anderson
Santa Clara, CA

Carol Clower
Lookout Mtn, TN

Dee Delenikos
Sunnyvale, CA

Joanne Gillespie
Hanover Park, IL

Barbara Heil
San Francisco, CA

Joyce Baldwin
Evansville, IN

Suzanne Colvin
Gainesville, FL

Mrs. Diamond
De Pere, WI

Haven Glascock
Lookout Mtn., TN

Kay Herring
Lookout Mtn., TN

Robert Beathea
New Brunswick, NJ

Kathleen Conover
New Providence, NJ

Kathleen Doherty
Franklin Park, IL

Laura Goodyear
Stillwater, OK

Diane Hill
E. Bernard, TX

Candice Beattys
New Brunswick, NJ

Roosevelt Cook, Jr.
Birmingham, AL

Sr. Helen Mary Dolan
Glen Cove, NY

Clair Golazeski
New Brunswick, NJ

Marlene Hofer
Hanover Park, IL

Evelyn Blackmon
Birmingham, AL

Joanne Cory
Sunnyvale, CA

Phil Done
Sunnyvale, CA

Paula Gossett
Lookout Mtn., TN

Melinda Hoffman
New Brunswick, NJ

Deanne Bogar
New Brunswick, NJ

Katherine Costello
New Brunswick, NJ

Ann Dugger
Stillwater, OK

Marcia Graver
Roselle, IL

Stephanie Holcomb
Roselle, IL

Sue Bolton
Columbus, OH

Rachel Covington
New Brunswick, NJ

Sylvia Durden
Waldo, FL

Mary Ann Greb
Wichita, KS

Anita Holley
Stillwater, OK

Geraldine Boone
New Brunswick, NJ

Mary Jo Craft
Lookout Mtn., TN

Mary Eschelman
Columbus, OH

William Guzules
Santa Clara, CA

Dr. Jack Humphrey
Evansville, IN

Sera Bounds
Gainesville, FL

Jeanne Crawford
Lookout Mtn., TN

Anne Egan
New Brunswick, NJ

Mary Ann Hanna
Virginia Beach, VA

Camille Husby
Roselle, IL

Linda Bowles
Evansville, IN

Carla Cunningham
Waldo, FL

Theresa Ens
New Brunswick, NJ

Debbie Hardesty
Evansville, IN

Rachel Inoye
Roselle, IL

REVIEWERS (continued)

Clara Jett
Cross Lanes, WV

Caryl Jobe
Stillwater, OK

Arlene Jones
Lookout Mtn., TN

Robley Jones
Virginia Beach, VA

Brenda J. Jordan
Tampa, FL

Susan Kamprath
Santa Clara, CA

Chuck Kapes
Roselle, IL

Joan Kase
Roselle, IL

Barbara Kiefer
Eugene, OR

Jewell Kimzey
La Habra, CA

Michael Kuehne
Beloit, WI

Tim Kueper
Hanover Park, IL

Dr. P. Lattimer
New Brunswick, NJ

Marlene Lederman
New Brunswick, NJ

Mary Lee
New Brunswick, NJ

Pam Lee
Gainesville, FL

Kathleen Lennon-Pearce
Lombard, IL

Bob Leonard
Columbus, OH

Tara Linville
Stillwater, OK

Sally Long
Columbus, OH

Leslie Lucas
Virginia Beach, VA

James Lucia
Bridgewater, MA

Kay Mackan
Columbus, OH

Dr. J. P. Madison
Plattsburgh, NY

Marlene Mahan
Windsor, CA

Clarice Malone
Arlington Hts., IL

Frances Marshall
Tampa, FL

Maxine Martin
Hanover Park, IL

Jane McArdle
New Brunswick, NJ

Donna McConnell
Roselle, IL

Mary Frances McGill
Evansville, IN

Jeanette McMurdie
Sunnyvale, CA

Judee Mitchell
New Brunswick, NJ

Mary Moelling
Stillwater, OK

Florence Montague
New Brunswick, NJ

Mickey Morales
Sunnyvale, CA

Ellen Moran
New Brunswick, NJ

Marlene Moulden
Stillwater, OK

Mary Lu Mulcahy
Hanover Park, IL

Altamease Nickson
Tampa, FL

Linda Ortiz
Valinda, CA

Malissa Pate
Evansville, IN

Carol Quinney
Derry, NH

Susan Rabinovitz
New Brunswick, NJ

Virginia Rachko
Scotch Plains, NJ

Carol Ragsdale
Santa Clara, CA

Diana Reedy
Hanover Park, IL

Betsy Reeves
Sunnyvale, CA

Joe Reister
Sunnyvale, CA

Joyce Ren
El Segundo, CA

Janice Rice
Odessa, TX

Adrienne Richman
Brooklyn, NY

Jean Rickard
Evansville, IN

Elsie Riddle
Sunnyvale, CA

Frances Roberts
Tampa, FL

Elaine Robinson
Lookout Mtn., TN

Sandi Rodker
Hanover Park, IL

Dennis Russo
Jacksonville, FL

Sally Saharko
New Brunswick, NJ

Margie Sauer
Stillwater, OK

Mary Savage
New Brunswick, NJ

Betty Schmitt
Evansville, IN

Sandi Schingoethe
Roselle, IL

Jan Scorza
Hanover Park, IL

Lynne Scott
New Brunswick, NJ

Corrine Sherland
Santa Clara, CA

Rebecca B. Sipe
Anchorage, AK

Joanne Sokoloff
Brooklyn, NY

Janet Soltis
Columbus, OH

Rosie Soohoo
Davis, CA

Patricia Stevens
Windsor, CA

Helen Stewart
Oaklyn, NJ

Bruce Strassfurth
Columbus, OH

Vi Strassfurth
Columbus, OH

Beth Strege
Hanover Park, IL

Anne Strickland
Gainesville, FL

Gwen Swift
Stillwater, OK

Jackie Taylor
Waldo, FL

Richard Temperini
New Brunswick, NJ

Kristin Thompson
Wichita, KS

Lynn Thorton
Roselle, IL

Patricia Tucker
Waldo, FL

Darnell Uzzle
New Brunswick, NJ

Gloria Valadez
Dallas, TX

Sara T. Vigil
Dulce, NM

Kathie Vojtech
Roselle, IL

Barbara Walker
New Brunswick, NJ

Marvis Walker
Dallas, TX

Nancy Walters
Columbus, OH

Nancy Ward
Waldo, FL

Ruth Weatherl
Lincoln, NE

Susan Weaver
Stillwater, OK

Diana Wemert
Marietta, GA

Jerita Whaley
Stillwater, OK

Jeadenia Wilder
Chicago, IL

Gwendolyn Wilson
Evansville, IN

Jan Wilson
Waldo, FL

Merlin Wittrock
Los Angeles, CA

Jan Wood
Walla Walla, WA

Susan Wood
Reading, MA

Anne Young
Gainesville, FL

ACKNOWLEDGMENTS

Grateful acknowledgment is made to the following publishers, authors, and agents for their permission to reprint copyrighted material. Any adaptations are noted in the individual acknowledgments and are made with the full knowledge and approval of the authors or their representatives. Every effort has been made to locate all copyright proprietors; any errors or omissions in copyright notice are inadvertent and will be corrected in future printings as they are discovered.

Front Matter: Exerpt from *One Writer's Beginnings* by Eudora Welty, copyright © 1983, 1984 by Eudora Welty, published by Harvard University Press.

Pages 9–11: "Paul Bunyan Digs the St. Lawrence River" from *Paul Bunyan Swings His Axe* by Dell J. McCormick. Copyright 1936 by The Caxton Printers, Ltd., Caldwell, Idaho. Slightly adapted, reprinted and recorded by permission of the publishers.

Page 102: "Revving-Up" by Danny Prohanas from *If a Poem Bothers You,* New Day Press, Cleveland, OH. Used by permission of the publisher.

Page 102: "Lonely" by Brian Smith from *If a Poem Bothers, You,* New Day Press, Cleveland, OH. Used by permission of the publisher.

Pages 169–171: *Amos and Boris* by William Steig. Copyright © 1971 by William Steig. Reprinted and recorded by permission of Farrar, Straus & Giroux, Inc.

Page 238: ". . . to explore strange new worlds . . ." from "STAR TREK: THE NEXT GENERATION" Copyright © 1987 Paramount Pictures Corporation. All Rights Reserved. Reprinted Courtesy of Paramount Pictures Corporation.

Pages 323–325: "Slower Than the Rest" excerpt adapted, reprinted, and recorded with permission of Bradbury Press, an Affiliate of Macmillan, Inc., from *Every Living Thing* by Cynthia Rylant. Text copyright © 1985 by Cynthia Rylant.

Page 432: "Poetry" from *Eleanor Farjeon's Poems for Children*. (J. B. Lippincott). Originally published in *Sing for Your Supper* by Eleanor Farjeon. Copyright, 1938, renewed 1966 by Eleanor Farjeon. Reprinted by permission of the publisher, Harper & Row, Publishers, Inc., and of the author's agents, Harold Ober Associates Incorporated.

Page 477: Illustration by Judith Cheng from *Heidi* Golden Classic. Illustration copyright © 1986 by Judith Cheng. Used by permission of Western Publishing Company, Inc.

The following material is reprinted from our Grade 3.1 Pupil Edition by permission of the publishers, authors, and agents indicated:

Alexander and the Terrible, Horrible, No Good, Very Bad Day by Judith Viorst and illustrated by Ray Cruz. Text copyright © 1972 by Judith Viorst. Pictures copyright © 1972 by Ray Cruz. Reprinted by permission of the American publisher, Macmillan Publishing Company, of the British publisher, Angus & Robertson (UK), and of the author's agents, Lescher & Lescher, Ltd.

"The Boy Who Cried Wolf" specially adapted for Silver, Burdett & Ginn Inc. by Genie Iverson, © 1989 by Genie Iverson.

"A Day When Frogs Wear Shoes" adapted from *More Stories Julian Tells* by Ann Cameron, illustrated by Ann Strugnell. Copyright © 1986 by Ann Cameron. Illustrations copyright © 1986 by Ann Strugnell. Reprinted by permission of the American publisher, Alfred A. Knopf, Inc., and of the British publisher, Victor Gollancz Ltd.

Forecast by Malcolm Hall, illustrated by Bruce Degen. Text copyright © 1977 by Malcolm Hall, illustrations © 1977 by Bruce Degen. Adapted and reprinted by permission of Coward, McCann & Geoghegan.

"General Store" from *Taxis and Toadstools* by Rachel Field. Copyright 1926 by Rachel Field. Reprinted by permission of the American publisher, Doubleday, a division of Bantam, Doubleday, Dell Publishing Group, Inc., and of the British publisher, William Heinemann Ltd.

Grandaddy's Place written by Helen V. Griffith, illustrated by James Stevenson. Text copyright © 1987 by Helen V. Griffith. Illustrations copyright © 1987 by James Stevenson. By permission of Greenwillow Books (A Division of William Morrow).

The Horse Who Lived Upstaris by Phyllis McGinley. Reprinted by permission of Curtis Brown Ltd. Copyright © 1944 by Phyllis McGinley & Helen Stone, renewed 1972 by Phyllis McGinley and Helen Stone.

The House on East 88th Street written and illustrated by Bernard Waber. Copyright © 1962 by Bernard Waber. Reprinted by permission of Houghton Mifflin Company.

"In Which Piglet Meets a Heffalump" from *Winnie-the-Pooh* by A. A. Milne, illustrated by Ernest H. Shepard. Copyright 1926 by E.P. Dutton, renewed 1954 by A. A. Milne. Reprinted by permission of the American publishers, E.P. Dutton, a division of NAL Penguin, Inc., of the Canadian Publishers, McClelland and Stewart, Toronto, and of the British publishers, Methuen Children's Books, a division of Associated Book Publishers (U.K.) Ltd., London.

"Jason Wants a Library" by Margaret Tuley Patton, © 1989 by Silver, Burdett & Ginn Inc.

"Lee Bennett Hopkins Interviews Johanna Hurwitz," © 1989 by Silver, Burdett & Ginn Inc.

"Life in Pilgrim Times" by Carlotta Dunn, © 1989 by Silver, Burdett & Ginn Inc.

The Monkey and the Crocodile wirtten and illustrated by Paul Galdone. Copyright © 1966 by Paul Galdone. Reprinted by permission of the American publisher, Clarion Books/Ticknor & Fields, a Houghton Mifflin Company, and of the British publisher, William Heinemann Ltd.

Mr. Peaceable Paints written and illustrated by Leonard Weisgard. Reprinted by permission of Charles Scribner's Sons, Macmillan Publishing Company. Copyright © 1956 by Leonard Weisgard.

Mufaro's Beautiful Daughters written and illustrated by John Steptoe. Copyright © 1987 by John Steptoe. By permission of Lothrop, Lee & Shepard Books (A Division of William Morrow), and of Murphy and Zissu, Attorneys-at-Law, for the author's estate.

"Narcissa" from *Bronzeville Boys and Girls* by Gwendolyn Brooks. Copyright © 1956, renewed

1984 by Gwendolyn Brooks Blakely. Reprinted by permission of Harper & Row, Publishers, Inc.

"Phillis Wheatley, America's First Black Poet" by Kacey Brown, © 1989 by Silver, Burdett & Ginn Inc.

"The Recital" by Johanna Hurwitz, © 1989 by Silver, Burdett & Ginn Inc.

"Seals on the Land and in the Water" by Betsey Knafo, © 1989 by Silver, Burdett & Ginn Inc.

"The Sea of Gold" from *The Sea of Gold and Other Tales from Japan* adapted by Yoshiko Uchida, published by Charles Scribner's Sons. Text Copyright © 1965 by Yoshiko Uchida. By permission of the author.

"Secret Talk" from *A Word or Two with You* by Eve Merriam. Copyright © 1981 by Eve Merriam. All rights reserved. Reprinted with the permission of Atheneum Publishers, an imprint of Macmillan Publishing Company, and of Marian Reiner for the author.

"Sports Signals" by Gary Apple, © 1989 by Silver, Burdett & Ginn Inc.

Thy Friend, Obadiah written and illustrated by Brinton Turkle. Copyright © 1969 by Brinton Turkle. Reprinted by permission of Viking Penguin Inc.

Tim to the Rescue written and illustrated by Edward Ardizzone. © Edward Ardizzone Estate. Adapted and reprinted by permission of the British publisher, Oxford University Press, and of the Edward Ardizzone Estate in care of Laura Cecil, Literary Agent for Children's Books.

"Until I Saw the Sea" from *I Feel the Same Way* by Lilian Moore, Copyright © 1967 Lilian Moore. Reprinted with the permission of Marian Reiner for the author.

When I Was Nine written and illustrated by James Stevenson. Copyright © 1986 by James Stevenson. By permission of Greenwillow Books (A Division of William Morrow).

The White Stallion written by Elizabeth Shub and illustrated by Rachel Isadora. Text copyright © 1982 by Elizabeth Shub. Illustrations copyright © 1982 by Rachel Isadora Maiorano. By permission of Greenwillow Books (A Division of William Morrow).

"The Wonderful Underwater Machine" by Josephine Edgar, © 1989 by Silver, Burdett & Ginn Inc.

Words in Our Hands by Ada B. Litchfield. Text copyright © 1980 by Ada B. Litchfield. Adapted and reprinted by permission of Albert Whitman & Company.

Books to Enjoy

Page 99: Jacket art from *And Then What Happened, Paul Revere?* by Jean Fritz, pictures by Margot Tomes. Illustrations copyright © 1973 by Margot Tomes. Reprinted by permission of Coward, McCann & Geoghegan, Inc., a division of The Putnam Publishing Group.

Page 99: Jacket art reproduced with permission of Charles Scribner's Sons, an imprint of Macmillan Publishing Company from *The Bears on Hemlock Mountain* by Alice Dalgliesh, illustrated by Helen

Sewell. Copyright 1952 Alice Dalgliesh; copyright renewed.

Page 99: Jacket art from *The Farm Book* by E. Boyd Smith, copyright 1910 by the Fairfield County Council, Boy Scouts of America, copyright renewed 1938. Reprinted by permission of Houghton Mifflin Company.

Page 99: Jacket art from *Wagon Wheels* by Barbara Brenner, pictures by Don Bolognese. Illustrations copyright © 1978 by Don Bolognese. Reprinted by permission of Harper & Row, Publishers, Inc.

Page 181: Jacket art from *Amy Goes Fishing* by Jean Marzollo, pictures by Ann Schweninger. Pictures copyright © 1980 by Ann Schweninger. Reproduced by permission of the American publisher, Dial Books for Young Readers, and of the British publisher, The Bodley Head Ltd.

Page 181: Jacket art reproduced by permission of Walker and Company from *A First Look at Seashells* by Millicent E. Selsam and Joyce Hunt, illustrated by Harriet Springer. Illustrations copyright © 1983 by Harriet Springer. Reprinted by permission of Walker Publishing Company, Inc.

Page 181: Jacket art reproduced with permission of Four Winds Press, an Imprint of Macmillan Publishing Company from *Little Whale* by Ann McGovern, illustrated by John Hamburger. Illustration Copyright © 1979 by John Hamburger.

Page 181: Jacket art from *Sea Songs* by Myra Cohn Livingston, paintings by Leonard Everett Fisher. Illustrations copyright © 1986 by Leonard Everett Fisher. Reprinted by permission of Holiday House Inc.

Page 249: Jacket art reproduced with permission of Charles Scribner's Sons, an imprint of Macmillan Publishing Company from *The Courage of Sara Noble* by Alice Dalgliesh, illustrated by Leonard Weisgard. Copyright 1954 Alice Dalgliesh and Leonard Weisgard; copyright renewed.

Page 249: Jacket art from *Anna, Grandpa, and the Big Storm* by Carla Stevens, pictures by Margot Tomes. Illustrations copyright © 1982 by Margot Tomes. Reprinted by permission of Houghton Mifflin Company.

Page 249: Jacket art reproduced with permission of the American publisher, Margaret K. McElderry Books, an imprint of Macmillan Publishing Company, and of the Canadian publisher, Douglas & McIntyre, from *Chin Chiang and the Dragon's Dance* by Ian Wallace. Copyright © 1984 Ian Wallace.

Page 345: Jacket art from *Train Whistles: A Language in Code* by Helen Roney Sattler, illustrated by Tom Funk. Reprinted by permission of Lothrop, Lee & Shepard, a division of William Morrow & Company, Inc.

Page 345: Jacket art from *Computers* by Jane Jonas Srivastava, illustrated by James and Ruth McCrea reprinted by permission of Thomas Y. Crowell, an imprint of Harper & Row, Publishers, Inc.

Page 345: Jacket art from *The Seeing Stick* by Jane Yolen, pictures by Remy Charlip and Demetra Maraslis. Illustrations copyright © 1977 by Remy Charlip and Demetra Maraslis. Reprinted by permission of

ACKNOWLEDGMENTS

Thomas Y. Crowell, an imprint of Harper & Row, Publishers, Inc.

Page 345: Jacket art from *Finger Rhymes* collected and illustrated by Marc Brown. Copyright © 1980 by Marc Brown. Reproduced by permission of the publisher, E. P. Dutton, a division of NAL Penguin Inc.

Time Out for Books

Cover art from *The Nightingale* translated by Eva Le Gallienne, illustrated by Nancy Ekholm Burkert. Pictures copyright © 1965 by Nancy Ekholm Burkert. Reprinted by permission of the American publisher, Harper & Row, Publishers, Inc., and of illustrator's British agents, Sinnott & Associates.

Cover art from *Storm in the Night* by Mary Stolz, illustrated by Pat Cummings. Illustrations copyright © 1988 by Pat Cummings. Reprinted by permission of Harper & Row, Publishers, Inc.

Literature Links

Page 142: "Whales Are Mammals" from *Whales,* created and written by John Bonnett Wexo, copyright © 1983 John Bonnett Wexo. Published by Wildlife Education, Ltd.

Page 286: Peanuts cartoon by Charles Schulz reprinted by permission of United Feature Syndicate, Inc.

Page 311: Excerpt from "The Musicians of Bremen Town" adapted from Grimm's Fairy Tales by Walter Roberts from *Plays from Favorite Folk Tales* edited by Sylvia E. Kamerman, published by Plays, Inc.

Pupil Edition Illustration 4, (tl) Brinton Turkle, (tr) James Stevenson, (bl) James Stevenson; 5, (tr) James Stevenson, (bl) Roni Shephero, (br) Rachel Isadora; 6, (t) Scott Pollack, (c) Edward Ardizzone, (bl) Bernard Waber, (br) Linda Shute; 7, (tr) Paul Galdone, (cl) Edward Ardizzone; 8, (t) Ray Criz, (br) Troy Howell; 9, (bl) Rae Ecklund, (br) Troy Howell, 10, (tl) E.H. Shepard, (tr) Bruce Degen, (b) E.H. Shepard; 11, (bl) Ashley Wolff, (bc) Bruce Degen, (br) Lane Gregory; 14–22, James Stevenson; 24–25, Wendy Edelson; 28–36, Brinton Turkle, 56–68, James Stevenson; 70–71, Andrea Eberbach, 72–80, Rachel Isadora; 82–83, Tony Chen; 84–95, Leonard Weisgard; 84, Betsy Day; 98, Susan Jaekel; 102–114, Edward Ardizzone; 120–130, Linda Shute; 134–135, Gary Torrisi; 137, Gary Torrisi; 141, Susan Jaekel; 150–158, Paul Galdone; 159, Sharron O'Neil; 160–161, Scott Pollack; 163, Susan Banta; 164–177, Bernard Waber; 180, Sharron O'Neil; 193, Susan Lexa; 196–204, Rae Ecklund; 206, Floyd Cooper; 211, Christa Kieffer; 236–237, Pat Cummings, Troy Howell; 214–224, Ann Strugnell; 233, Susan Jaekel; 238–245, Ray Cruz; 248, Sharron O'Neil; 252–262, Bruce Degen; 252, Bob Filipowich; 263, Sharron O'Neil; 264–265, Greg Mackey; 266–275, Larry Raymond; 276–277, (b & tr) Rich Lo; 280–281, Lane Gregory; 288–294, Les Morrill; 295, Sharron O'Neil; 296–308, John Steptoe; 312–322, Ashley Wolff; 323, Sharron O'Neil; 324–341, E.H. Shephard; 344, Susan Jaekel; 347, Diane Dawson Hearn, Claudia Sargent; 348, Roberta Holmes; 351, Deirdre Griffin; 353, Roberta Holmes;

355, Diane Dawson Hearn; 356, Deirdre Griffin; 358, Roberta Holmes; 359, Claudia Sargent; 360, Diane Dawson Hearn; 361, Melinda Fabian; 362, Diane Dawson Hearn, Claudia Sargent; 363, Claudia Sargent; 364, Diane Dawson Hearn, Roberta Holmes.

Pupil Edition Photography Jen & Des Bartlett/ Bruce Coleman, Inc.; 8, Laird Roberts; 12, *Snap the Whip*, Winslow Homer (American), 50.41, The Metropolitan Museum of Art, New York; 39, The Pilgrim Society, Plymouth; 40, Bettman Archive; 41, The Pilgrim Society, Plymouth; 42, courtesy The John Hancock Mutual Life Insurance Co., Boston; 43, The Granger Collection; 100, © Susan Van Etten; 116–117, Superstock; 133, Woods Hole Oceanographic Institute, Courtesy Sygma; 135, RONA/ Bruce Coleman, Inc.; 136, Woods Hole Oceanographic Institute; 139–140, Woods Hole Oceanographic Institute; 144, Jeff Foott/Bruce Coleman, Inc.; 145, Jen & Des Bartlett/Bruce Coleman, Inc.; 146, G.L. Kooyman/Animals, Animals; 147, Jeff Foott/Tom Stack & Associates; 148, Rod Allin/Tom Stack & Associates; 162, Bettmann Archive; 182, Boy *Juggling Shell*, Hokusai (Japanese), 14.76.59.4, The Metropolitan Museum of Art, New York; 185–190, Laird Roberts; 191, Mary Anne Facelman-Miner, The White House; 192, Laird Roberts; 206, Eduardo Patino; 209, Eduardo Patino; 226, The Granger Collection; 228, Thomas Bewick, Dover Books; 229, The Granger Collection; 231, National Portrait Gallery, Smithsonian Institution; 250 *The Letter*, 1871, Mary Cassatt, American 1844–1926, gift of The William Emerson and Charles Henry Hayden Fund, 41.803, 10.84, Museum of Fine Arts, Boston; 276, Carlos Vergara; 277, (tl) North Wind Picture Archives; 278–279, Dan Helms/Duomo; 282, Steven Goldstein, Courtesy St. Louis Cardinals; 283, Focus on Sports; 348, Sera Hopkins; 349, Stephen G. Maka; 350, Stephen G. Maka; 351, Leon Poindexter; 354, Carla Palau, © Frank Siteman 1988; 355, © Frank Siteman 1988; Dante Gelmetti/Bruce Coleman, Inc.; 358, Nicholas deVore III/Bruce Coleman, Inc.; 360, © Frank Siteman 1988; 361, Mike Mazzaschi/ Stock Boston; 365, C.W. Perkins/Animals, Animals; 366, Bettmann Archive/BBC Hulton, 367, (t) *Los Angeles Times*, (b) Fernando Diaz Rivera; 368, (t & b) Bettmann Archive; 369 (t) Bettmann Archive, (c) Clarion, (b) Holiday House; 370, (t) provided by author, (b) Antique Images/Putnam; 371, (t) Viking Penguin; 373, (t) The Granger Collection; 374, (t) Bettmann Archive; 376 (b) Edward E. Davis; 377, (t) Dial Dutton, Viking Penguin, (b) McElderry Books; 378, (t) Milton Viorst, (b) H.W. Wilson Co.; 379, Western Publishing.

Teacher Edition Illustration Boston Graphics, pp. 224, 346, 377, 526, 570; Jane Caminos, pp. 439, 440, 441, 446, 447, 621; Olivia Cole, p. 199; Laura Cornell, pp. 112, 113, 119, 417, 418, 419, 425; Hilarie Crosman, p. 232; Rae Ecklund, pp. 228, 376, 377, 354, 355, 368, 369, 376, 377, 543, 544, 545, 551; Simon Galhin, p. 575; John Hancock Mutual Life Insurance Co., Boston, Courtesy of, p. 87; George Hen, p. 376; Larry Johnson, pp. 507, 508, 520, 521; Linda Knox, pp. 318, 470; Loretta Krupin-

ACKNOWLEDGMENTS

ski, pp. 28, 29, 35, 77, 78, 79; Virginia Kylberg, pp. 475, 476, 477; Don Ling, pp. 142, 346, 446, 534, 570; Yee Chi Lin, pp. 63, 190, 191; Steve McInturll, p. 4; Les Morill, pp. 556, 557, 569, 570, 571; Sal Murdocca, pp. 62, 164, 199, 252, 290, 291, 295, 592, 593, 597; Judy Nostrandt, pp. 323, 324, 325; Louis Pappas, pp. 268, 269, 275; Jan Pyk, pp. 342, 343; Doug Roy, pp. 350, 351, 390, 391, 397, 527, 575; Margaret Sanfilippo, pp. 9, 10, 11; Linda Shute, pp. 204, 205, 219, 220, 221, 229; Patrick Soper, pp. 136, 137, 142, 143; William Steig, pp. 169, 170, 171; Gary Torrisi, pp. 246, 247; Carol Vindinghoff, pp. 4, 164, 318, 470; Mel Williges, pp. 54, 55; Ashley Wolff, pp. 600, 601, 615, 616, 617.

Teacher Edition Photography The Granger Collection, pp. 64, 87; Eduardo Patino, pp. 378, 379; Laird Roberts, pp. 328, 329, 342, 343.